The American Legal System

Foundations, Processes, and Norms

Albert P. Melone

Allan Karnes

Southern Illinois University
Carbondale

Roxbury Publishing Company
Los Angeles, California

Library of Congress Cataloging-in-Publication Data

Melone, Albert P.
The american legal system: Foundations, processes, and norms /
Albert P. Melone, Allan Karnes.
    p.   cm.
Includes bibliographical references and index.
ISBN 1-891487-92-2
1. Law—United States. 2. Courts—United States. 3. Justice,
Administration of—United States. I. Karnes, Allan, 1953– II. Title.

KF386 .M45 2003
349—dc21   2002067951
                                                            CIP

THE AMERICAN LEGAL SYSTEM: FOUNDATIONS, PROCESSES, AND NORMS

Publisher: Claude Teweles
Managing Editor: Dawn VanDercreek
Production Editor: Jim Ballinger
Production Assistant: Joshua Levine
Copy Editor: Ann West
Proofreaders: Scott Oney and Anton Diether
Cover Design: Marnie Kenney
Typography: Abe Hendin <prepress@yourspeed.com>

Printed on acid-free paper in the United States of America. This book meets the standards of recycling of the Environmental Protection Agency.

ISBN 1-891487-92-2

ROXBURY PUBLISHING COMPANY
P.O. Box 491044
Los Angeles, California 90049-9044
Voice: (310) 473-3312 • Fax: (310) 473-4490
Email: roxbury@roxbury.net
Website: www.roxbury.net

Dedication

In loving memory of our mothers—

Rosaline Estelle Karnes
and
Catherine Ann Bongeorno Melone

DATE DUE	
GAYLORD	PRINTED IN U.S.A.

Acknowledgments

Writing this book was a thoroughly absorbing, challenging, and time-consuming task. But many other persons aided and abetted us in completing the task. Claude Teweles, the publisher at Roxbury, was dogged in his determination to sign the authors to a contract. He kept on top of the project in its every phrase—from the writing of the prospectus and the assessment of the various drafts to the agreement on the final title for the book. Jim Ballinger, the project manager for the book, kept abreast of the progress and evaluation of the final drafts, editing, and design of the book. Ann West of Carmel, California, copy-edited the text with an expert and meticulous eye for detail.

A long list of graduate students at Southern Illinois University Carbondale helped in a number of ways. Some tracked down materials for the original draft, others proofread numerous drafts of distinct chapters and related materials, and a few offered their own useful suggestions for change. In order of date of service, we express our appreciation to Ahmad H. Mohamed, William Bodine, Nicholas Avergin, Iwetta Pyc, and Kevin Wall of the Department of Political Science. In addition, Chris Becker, a Ph.D. assistant in the School of Accountancy, assisted preparing briefs of many of the court opinions appearing in the latter two parts of the book.

We kindly acknowledge Professor Suzanne J. Schmitz of the Southern Illinios University Carbondale School of Law for suggesting bibliographical sources on alternative dispute resolution. Later, she and her students in an Alternative Dispute Resolution class during the fall 2001 term offered useful criticisms of an early draft of what now appears in revised form as Chapter 9. We are also indebted to the excellent professional law library staff at the SIUC Law Library for their help in locating information. We are especially grateful to James E. Duggan, Adria P. Olmi, and Laurel Anne Wendt for their gracious attention to our questions.

We were granted permission to use a number of glossary items in this book that are taken from the glossary originally appearing on

iv

pages 159–182 of Albert P. Melone, *Researching Constitutional Law*, 2d ed. (Prospect Heights, IL: Waveland Press, Inc., 2000). Our special thanks to publisher Neil Rowe and to his assistant Don Rosso at Waveland Press for their kind cooperation.

We also obtained permission from the American Law Institute to reproduce and to place in the Appendix of our text several sections of the Uniform Commercial Code and the Model Penal Code.

Our department secretaries also provided useful help. Loraine Hunziker of the Department of Political Science made time to print early drafts of our manuscript and helped with the creation of the original table of contents. During the final stages of this project, Sandra Foster, Loraine's replacement, pitched in with interest and care. Rhonda Musgrave, the chairperson's secretary in the Department of Political Science, jumped in when we encountered formatting and other problems with the manuscript. Jeri Novara, Office Manager in the School of Accountancy, provided valuable assistance in printing final drafts and making numerous copies for distribution.

Many outside reviewers provided valuable criticisms of our prospectus, and of our various drafts. Some of these individuals will remain anonymous. But we are pleased to recognize the contribution of the following scholars from a variety of academic disciplines and institutions: Scott Barclay (University of Albany, SUNY), Nigel J. Cohen (The University of Texas, Pan American), Dick DeLung (Wayland Baptist University), Martin Gruber (University of Wisconsin, Oshkosh), Craig Hemmens (Boise State University), Gary L. Neumeyer (Arizona Western College), Kay Rute (Washburn University), Gregory Russell (Washington State University, Spokane), and Marco Turk (University of California, Irvine).

Finally, our spouses, Peggy and Penny, offered support in a number of ways, including reading and critiquing bits and pieces of this book, and helping from time to time with word processing tasks. We hope they will forgive us for our obvious moments of inattention. We suspect that spouses of authors are reserved a special place in heaven for their patience and understanding.

None of the persons we have named for their contributions to the completion of this project are responsible for any errors of fact, omission, or commission. In short, as we must, the authors take full responsibility for the contents of this book, including all that is worthy of praise and all that deserves criticism.

—Albert P. Melone and Allan Karnes
Carbondale, Illinois, USA

Brief Table of Contents

Part III
Law Governing Conduct, Property, and Relations Among Individuals

Part IV
Law Governing Conduct of Business

Table of Contents

Part I
The Legal System in Perspective

Part II
Contrasting Legal Processes

Part III
Law Governing Conduct, Property, and Relations Among Individuals

Part IV
Law Governing Conduct of Business

xix

Preface

All individuals living in the United States have good reason to study the legal system. Legal institutions influence us in a myriad of ways. The law affects everything from how we conduct our personal lives to how we interact in the wider political and business environments. After all, the law has teeth and it can bite. It is little wonder that for decades undergraduate students have sought course work in the American legal system. Such courses have been part of political science programs offering pre-law training, business curricula as law relates to commerce, criminal justice programs, paralegal studies, and more recently, free-standing legal studies programs.

Surveying the legal system is a daunting task because it is a complicated and many-faceted field of study. Most textbook authors settle on the justifiably proximate goal of presenting a survey of the subject matter emphasizing black-letter legal rules that students are asked to memorize. Too often, however, students obtain little understanding of the assumptions, processes, and consequences that attend such norms. To be sure, knowing the legal rules is important and a worthy near-term goal for students to attain. In writing this textbook, however, our goal was to cast an intellectually wider net. We sought to provide students with the main outlines of legal norms in American society. In addition, we wanted to give students a broad perspective on the important topic of how the law is a manifestation of social values and how the legal system is part of the much larger political, economic, social, and business environment.

Our text may be used in a wide variety of academic departments. For example, political science and criminal justice instructors may find our text particularly useful because, unlike other introduction to law texts, we nest our exposition of particular legal subfields within the broader context of American constitutional law, federalism, and the protection of civil rights and liberties. We also address how judges make decisions by providing competing explanations from both normative and empirical perspectives.

We designed this text as an alternative for professors in business administration programs who want to offer their students a broader view of the legal environment. We offer chapters on aspects of the law governing the conduct of business, such as negotiable instruments, secured transactions, employee discrimination, securities regulation, antitrust law, contracts, and federal income taxation. Unlike typical business law texts, however, our text also includes substantive chapters on criminal conduct, property, and interpersonal relations as well as providing a political context for understanding that law and government are two sides of the same coin. Many instructors who wish to provide their students with a realistic understanding of the business world realize that this goal is best served when students are made familiar with all aspects of law and government. We trust that this goal is facilitated by our treatment throughout the text of the main contours of the American system of constitutional government.

This book may also serve as an introductory text for legal studies and paralegal programs. Social scientists and humanists will find this text useful because it raises important social, economic, and political issues in both real and hypothetical situations. Moreover, these conflicts are resolved in a variety of national and state jurisdictions, not just by the U.S. Supreme Court.

In some academic disciplines, the law is treated as divisible into separate intellectual compartments. Political science, for example, concentrates on the important public law topics of constitutional and administrative law. But private law topics such as torts, contracts, and property law, for instance, are also important subjects for study because legal institutions are employed to resolve conflicts that vitally influence how private parties and businesses conduct their affairs. We believe that if students are to gain a realistic appreciation for the entire American legal system they must be familiar with the basic assumptions, processes and norms of private and public law, and civil and criminal law. Armed with this basic knowledge, they will then be well equipped to concentrate on specialized legal topics, such as criminal law, constitutional law, administrative law, a variety of business law subjects, and paralegal topics.

We divide our book into four major parts with 16 chapters. Part I introduces students to terms and concepts necessary for understanding the legal system, the legitimacy and limits of court jurisdiction and authority, the organization of the court system, and central issues surrounding the matter of judicial interpretation of case law, statutory law and constitutions, and various social science explanations of judicial decision-making.

Part II centers on legal processes, with civil suits for money damages serving as the paradigmatic example. Successive chapters compare and contrast equity processes, criminal processes, and administrative processes to civil suits for money damages. The last chapter in this part of the book delineates the various facets of alternative dispute resolution as a supplement and challenge to existing formal legal processes. Our experience teaches us that when students compare and contrast the various types of legal processes, they best understand how and why the legal system operates as it does. This is the realm of civil and criminal procedure, and it is our experience that procedure can be taught to students in ordinary language. Along the way, students are equipped with a working knowledge of the importance of different legal processes and procedural rights within our legal system.

Part III contains chapters on the substantive legal topics of torts, property, criminal law, and family law. All of these substantive law chapters include a section tracing the modern substantive law to its common law roots. We also include sections on evolving legal issues including product liability, tort reform, copyright infringement, victimless crimes, youthful offenders, artificial conception of human life, and same-sex marriages. The chapter on property highlights how the right to present and future possession of real property can be divided and assigned. We have taken this approach to better prepare students who plan to enter law school. First-year property law courses concentrate on real property, especially future interests, but students typically struggle to master this area of the law. By concentrating our coverage on real property issues, students who have had courses that employ our text should be better prepared than most.

Finally, in Part IV of the book we treat the law governing the world of business: contracts, business regulation by government, and taxation. Depending upon the goals for each course, instructors may want to assign all or some of these chapters—as they may do for any other chapters from each of the other parts of this book. Indeed, this book is designed to permit instructors to assign the various parts of the text in any order that suits their purposes without causing undue learning discontinuities. For example, instructors may want to assign Chapter 7 on criminal processes together with Chapter 13, the substantive criminal law chapter.

To illustrate general and specific substantive points as they arise, we have deliberately interspersed edited court opinions within the body of the text. We did so in the hope that students will internalize the lessons as they encounter them in the text. Within each of the edited court opinions we signify the omission of words, phrases, lines, or paragraphs by the use of ellipsis points, simply called dots. Three dots indicate an omission within a sentence or fragment of a sentence; we indicate omissions of whole sentences or more by the usual three ellipsis dots preceded by period signs. We usually deleted footnotes found in the original unedited opinions, and we did the same for many in-text references to cases and statutes. In addition, brief summaries of some landmark and significant court opinions appear within the body of the text in boxed format as we discuss them in the text. This writing strategy permits us to bring to the attention of students important cases without burdening them with excessive reading.

We trust that the edited court opinions are not so numerous that students will find the task overwhelming. We anticipate that instructors will assign at least some edited cases for briefing and class discussion. At the end of Chapter 1, we provide a model brief accompanying an edited U.S. Supreme Court opinion. By briefing court opinions found in this text, students will become familiar with and competent in the fine art of brief writing. Armed with the ability to read and brief court opinions, they will then be able to use this important learning tool in more advanced undergraduate courses, in advanced graduate courses, or as professional law students.

The court opinions as they appear in the text meet two criteria. First, the cases have historical and legal significance and they are likely to be of contemporary interest to present-day students. In short, we have included court opinions that are lively and likely to engender classroom discussion. Second, when editing court opinions we took care to limit the number of issues to the particular pedagogical objectives at hand. At the same time, we endeavored not to overly edit opinions, thereby robbing them of the clarity necessary for reader comprehension. We placed these edited court opinions interspersed within the body of the text to illustrate general and specific substantive points as they arise. However, this volume is more than a casebook. The greater part of this book contains extensive expository materials that both describe and explain the legal system.

With adequate study, all college students can master this text. We provide various learning aides within the text to help students toward that goal. At the beginning of each chapter, we have a box containing a statement of objectives. In most instances, we italicize key terms, names, and concepts as they are first encountered in each chapter. At the end of each chapter, we present lists of these same key terms, names, and concepts to help students focus on what they have just read and as a study tool for examinations. Mastering these terms will take students a long way down the path to successfully understanding the main outlines of our legal system. We also provide discussion questions at the end of each edited court opinion. At the end of each chapter, we append several discussion questions that students and instructors may find useful in mining chapter contents. We also include at the end of each chapter a brief list of selected readings for those students seeking additional information and analysis of chapter topics.

The book contains a glossary of selected legal and Latin words and terms to help students comprehend the subject. The Appendix contains a copy of the U.S. Constitution, selected sections of the Uniform Commercial Code, and relevant sections from the Model Penal Code. It also contains copies of U.S. Individual 1040 Tax Forms for 2001 and 2002.

Also included are the tax rate schedules and inflation-adjusted amounts for 2002 and 2003.

An optional **Student Study Guide** is available to accompany our text. As an instructor of courses on the U.S. legal system, Professor Bradley Best (Buena Vista University), the author of the Guide, is thoroughly familiar with the subject matter and with our pedagogical orientation. The authors of this text have prepared a variety of extensive teaching aides to facilitate instruction and student testing. Upon request, the publisher will make these aides available to all instructors that may find these materials useful in their course preparation and delivery. ✦

Table of Cases*

*Italics indicate edited opinions appearing in the text.

Part I

The Legal System in Perspective

Chapter 1

Law in Perspective

Chapter Objectives

Students are encouraged not only to learn the formal legal rules but also to discern who benefits from the law in the broader societal context. It is important to understand that legal actors possess discretion and make choices, in some part, based on their values and attitudes. Readers should become familiar with the main outlines of competing schools of jurisprudence, and they should become aware of the branches and functions of law in society. Because the power to persuade is real, students are urged to take legal reasoning seriously, for example, by learning how to read and analyze court opinions. Students are provided with guidelines for briefing court opinions, and they are urged to apply these guidelines to the edited opinions as presented throughout this book.

Human relationships are governed by informal and formal standards of conduct called norms. Law is the political mechanism by which those who are in charge of society create and enforce social, economic, and political norms. Well-meaning persons often debate whether particular norms are in the interest of the many or just a few. For the ancient Greeks, a good democracy meant that the government be responsive to the interest of the whole people. Today we refer to this as the common interest, public good, justice, and general will.

It is well understood, however, that the ancient Greek ideal of a good democracy is not easily obtained in real life. Organized political forces operate in all societies to impose their own view of the public interest on weaker interests, the dispossessed, and the powerless. In democratic polities, majorities are better situated to combat the selfish demands of special interests than they are in authoritarian or totalitarian regimes. But, even in democracies such as the United States, there is no guarantee that special interests will not get their way. Often they do. Laws are frequently the result of clashing competing interests that in the end bear little relation to the "public good."

Thus, civic realities require students, politicians, and realists of all ideological stripes to cast democratic theory and the role of law in terms related to specific contexts. Though this text asks students to read and to comprehend many court opinions in all their parts, readers are also prodded to look beyond the details of particular facts, issues, holdings, and reasoning to consider the following: who gets what, when, and how. Yes, discerning legal rules is important, but understanding the legal system itself is our fundamental goal. In sum, one needs to analyze legal issues in the broader context of political, social, and economic reality.

Consider, for example, the problem of adjudication from the lawyers' viewpoint. Attorneys try to justify or shape their clients' conduct under often ambiguous and uncertain sets of rules. Typically, they help solve problems for interest groups in society by representing them before administrative, legislative, and judicial bodies. They are asked to engage in a complex process of predicting what a court as an institution will decide given certain facts. Yet, facts are often in dispute, and what set of legal rules might be applicable to those particular facts is not always easily discernable. To make a complex problem even more problematical, the decision-making process must deal with ideas influenced by attitudes and values. Judges and juries do not always act in a dispassionate and objective manner because attitudes and values color their perception of social events. Thus, judicial reasoning is not simply an objective matter in which a mechanical formula, such as facts multiplied by rules equals decisions ($f \times r = d$), will suffice.

Then, too, judges must exercise their discretion because rules are often imprecise. What is the meaning of such words and phrases as "legal consideration," "negligence," "due process of law," "unreasonable search and seizure," and "commerce among the states"? Each concept needs interpretation, and there is no consensus about the best way to accomplish the task. Moreover, although judges are expected to be neutral toward the litigants before them, it is asking the improbable if not the impossible for them not to have attitudes toward the great issues of the day. They are, after all, products of their environments with different ideas of what is just in any given situation.

Indeed, the politics of judicial selection presupposes that attitudes and values profoundly affect case outcomes. If we were serious about recruiting judges on the basis of who knows the legal rules best, we might select them exclusively on the results of specially designed competitive examinations, ranking candidates by their test results. Instead, in many U.S. jurisdictions, political criteria are openly employed when selecting judges and justices because it is well understood that they possess considerable discretion and that their attitudes make a profound difference when deciding cases.

Nevertheless, most law and law-related courses offered at institutions of higher learning require students to carefully read and analyze the logic of judicial opinions. If judicial decision-making is not simply a matter of logic, however, why then is it important to read court opinions with a view toward understanding the legal logic inherent in the case law? The answer is that judges are constrained by institutional norms prescribing the limits of their conduct. That is, legal institutions grant legal professionals leeway, but judges do not have license to do as they please. Therefore, it is important to understand legal professionals on their own terms and in their own institutional environment. This insight permits us a realistic picture of what the legal rule is on given subjects, the rhetoric of legal reasoning, and how law changes within the U.S. legal system.

With the foregoing in mind, students are well advised to carefully study each case and to brief court opinions found in this text as the instructor may require. It is also critical that students exercise their sociological imagination—to place themselves in the shoes of decision makers—so as to comprehend the factors influencing any given judicial opinion. Carefully writing case briefs will not ensure such an outcome, but it is a valuable exercise toward this end. See the final pages of this chapter for instructions on how to brief court opinions.

Origins of Law

Ordinarily when the word *law* is used in a legal (i.e., not a scientific or a theological) context, one is referring to norms made by a sovereign to govern relations among individuals and between individuals and government in its various configurations. This is called *positive law*: rules and regulations made by executives, legislators, bureaucrats, and judges. On the other hand, it is said that *natural law* exists independent of humankind; it takes various forms as commands of the natural order in the universe. Often it is portrayed as God's law, which is known by human reason. To advocates of natural law, lawmakers ought to apply the natural law to the positive law in the implementation of justice.

In this text, your authors do not dwell on the natural law. Yet, the natural law may be a source for guidance. For example, some people claim that abortion violates God's law to protect human life and human law ought to reflect this value. Or, at the turn of the twentieth century, U.S. Supreme Court justices elevated the "liberty of contract" to a natural law, forbidding government in some cases to regulate working conditions. The justices thereby embedded *laissez-faire* economics within the constitutional system. (For example, see the summary of *Lochner v. New York* below.)

Box 1.1   **Summary of Lochner v. New York**
U.S. Supreme Court
198 U.S.45 (1905)

A New York bakery owner was convicted for violating a state statute prohibiting bakery employees from working more than 10 hours a day or more than 60 hours per week. The majority opinion of the U.S. Supreme Court found that although health and safety laws are permissible limitations on contracts, this particular law did not bear a reasonable relationship to public health or the health of bakers. Consequently, the legislation violated the liberty provision of the Due Process Clause of the Fourteenth Amendment. This and related decisions of the high court were criticized as a usurpation of legislative authority and excessively subjective, allowing justices to substitute their social philosophy for those of elected legislative officials. In dissent, Justice Oliver Wendell Holmes epitomized this criticism, writing in part:

> The Fourteenth Amendment does not enact Mr. Herbert Spencer's *Social Statics*. . . . Some of these laws embody convictions or prejudices which judges are likely to share. Some may not. But a Constitution is not intended to embody a particular economic theory, whether of paternalism and the organic relation of the citizen to the state or of *laissez faire*. It is made for people of fundamentally differing views, and the accident of our finding certain opinions natural and familiar, or novel, and even shocking, ought not to conclude our judgment upon the question whether statutes embodying them conflict with the Constitution of the United States.

Positive law makes no claims to moral superiority, however. Its authority rests either in legislation made by a duly constituted legislative or parliamentary body, administrative rules and regulations made pursuant to statutory authorization, and by judges who make law when creating new rules from preexisting rules or legal principles. Judges also make new law when there is no law to guide them, such as when no credible preexisting precedent or legislation can inform their decision in a present case.

Because a considerable number of basic legal rules have been created by judges and not by legislators, the Anglo-American legal system is often referred to as being in the *common law* tradition. In truth, the Anglo-American system is a combination of judge-made law and legislative-made law. Both types of lawmaking bodies are regarded as legitimate norm creators and interpreters. However, if legislative bodies do not approve of the law made by courts, they have the authority to rewrite the law. Ordinarily, when they do so, it effectively overrules what the judges have decided the legal rules to be.

In America, when judges and justices make rules for interpreting the meaning of the U.S. Constitution and legislators seek to overturn these court interpretations, the relationship between the legislative and judicial branches becomes less certain and interinstitutional conflict can and does occur. For example, in 1993 Congress enacted the *Religious Freedom Restoration Act* to overturn the substance of a 1990 U.S. Supreme Court decision (Employment Division, Department of Human Resources of Oregon v. Smith, 494 U.S. 872) that had used a constitutional test making it relatively easy for states to interfere with the First Amendment right to the free exercise of religion. And, in City of Boerne v. Flores, 521 U.S. 507 (1997), the U.S. Supreme Court held that Congress may not define how the Court itself exercises its own authority to determine what the Constitution means. The Court's majority used the occasion to echo John Marshall's pronouncement in Marbury v. Madison, 5 U.S. (Cranch) 137 (1803), that "it is emphatically the province and duty of the judicial department to say what the law is."

Box 1.2   Summary of City of Boerne v. Flores
U.S. Supreme Court
521 U.S. 507, 138 L.Ed.2d, 117 S.Ct. 2157 (1997)

The diocese of San Antonio, Texas, unsuccessfully sought a building permit to expand its church in the city of Boerne. City officials justified their denial by citing the historic mission style of the existing structure. Archbishop Flores then brought suit under the *Religious Freedom Restoration Act of 1991* (RFRA). The congressional enactment was passed with broad bipartisan support in an explicit attempt to reverse a prior divided Supreme Court decision [*Employment Division of the Department of Human Resources of Oregon v. Smith* (1990)]. The high court in that case employed the *rational basis test* instead of the previously accepted, but tougher, pro-civil liberties–preferred freedoms approach of *compelling state interest* when deciding free exercise of religion cases. A federal district court found in favor of the city, but the U.S. Court of Appeals reversed the lower court.

Writing for the majority, Justice Anthony Kennedy held that the RFRA provision requiring a *compelling state interest test* rather than a *rational basis test* is beyond the power of Congress under the Enforcement Clause of the Fourteenth Amendment. It is the task of the Supreme Court to say what the Constitution means, not the Congress.

In contrast to the common law system born in England, the *civil law* tradition is a system of jurisprudence based on Roman law found today in European nations and many other countries around the world.

In this family of laws, judges are said to be completely subservient to legislative institutions. Traditional adherents to this particular family of laws maintain that the only legitimate role of judges is to find and then to apply the appropriate legal rule to the case at hand. Rules are made by the legislature, usually in the form of extensive codes that systematically arrange the law into various substantive or procedural topics; for example, the criminal code, the code of civil procedure, and the tax code. The judge's task is to find and then apply an appropriate rule to particular sets of facts.

Actually, there is a growing consensus that the civil law and common law legal families have much more in common than our description suggests. In both systems, judges have opportunities to create legal rules and in both systems legislators have considerable influence over the content of the law.[1]

Most countries of Western and Eastern Europe employ the civil law system. Latin America and parts of Asia and Africa are profoundly influenced by this tradition because of the European influence of their former colonial rulers. In the United States, the state of Louisiana with its strong French ties is steeped in the civil law tradition by virtue of the application of *Code Napoleon* principles. In particular, the community property laws in California, Texas, and Louisiana are heavily influenced by the original Spanish and French settlers' ideas about family relationships, which were different from most states of the union (i.e., they were not of British origin). Washington, Nevada, New Mexico, Arizona, Idaho, and Wisconsin also adopted community property laws after they became disenchanted with the common law property system inherited from England.[2]

Schools of Jurisprudence

Jurisprudence is the philosophy or science of law. Throughout the centuries, many thoughtful persons have expressed the need to justify judicial decision-making in terms of higher principles—principles transcending petty self-interest that reflect consistent moral and ethical standards of conduct. Consequently, legal thinkers endeavor to address the question of what is law from a variety of philosophical perspectives. Although few practicing legal professionals are thoroughly consistent in their broad philosophical orientations toward the meaning of law, a number of historically important perspectives will guide students during the course of their study. These schools of thought include but are not limited to natural law jurisprudence, historical jurisprudence, utilitarianism, analytical (positivism) jurisprudence, mechanical jurisprudence, sociological jurisprudence, legal realism, and critical legal studies.

Natural Law

Natural law jurisprudence posits that humankind possesses an innate sense of right and wrong. This sense exists in the nature of the universe or in an understanding of God's will or plan that can be known through our reason. In Western thought, the ancient Greeks and Romans—for example, Plato (427–347 B.C.), Aristotle (384–322 B.C.), and Cicero (106–43 B.C.)—each articulated somewhat different views of the matter, but each contributed to the foundation of our current thinking. Aristotle in particular is responsible for the idea that humans are "political animals," meaning that our happiness and self-understanding are tied to the nature of our political community. Therefore, life outside civil society is unthinkable.

St. Thomas Aquinas (1226–1274) was a leading figure of the philosophical movement called Medieval scholasticism. This system of logic, philosophy, and theology (prominent from the tenth to the fifteenth century) synthesized the Medieval view of religious faith with the Greco-Roman emphasis upon reason as articulated especially by Aristotle. He is the author of *Summa Theologica*, a widely accepted view of natural law as a guide to human law. This work applies to specific circumstances the precepts of reason contained in natural law. St. Thomas argued that when human law departs from natural reason, it lacks the quality of law, becoming instead analogous to an act of violence.[3]

The Age of Enlightenment was an eighteenth-century European philosophical movement characterized by rationalism, skepticism, and empiricism in social and political matters. As part of the movement, natural law philosophers of the seventeenth and eighteenth centuries—including Thomas Hobbes (1588–1679), John Locke (1632–1704), and to a lesser extent Jean-Jacques Rousseau (1712–1778)—had a profound impact on the founders and early leaders of the American republic.[4] In contrast to the classical thinkers of Greek and Roman antiquity, modern Liberal-Lockean theory begins with the individual as the fundamental unit of political analysis. Aristotle's political man is rejected in favor of the view that humankind can exist independent from civil society. In the state of nature, a place without formal government, people need only consult the laws of nature to discover that they are independent and capable of reason. Natural law informs them that one ought not to deprive another of life, liberty, or possessions.

The natural state had some inherent shortcomings, however, including the lack of neutral third parties to adjudicate conflicts, based on the premise that persons should not be judges in their own case. People need a mechanism for the protection of life, liberty, and property. Therefore, civil society is formed to secure the natural rights endangered in the less than perfect state of nature. By agreement, the people consummate a contract limiting the authority of government. If the covenant is broken, then revolution is justified and a new government may be created in its place. Thomas Jefferson's Declaration of Independence is the quintessential expression of this natural law view. Consider paragraph one and part of the second paragraph of this great document, which are reproduced below (Box 1.3).

Thomas Jefferson, author of the Declaration of Independence and third President of the United States.

Natural law precepts have a profound impact on contemporary policy debates concerning the content of American law. Arguments about racial, religious, and gender discrimination, for example, often come down to an interpretation of natural law principles. The law has long recognized that the obligation parties owe one another to abide by their promises may be mitigated by equitable principles of natural justice, prohibiting the enforcement of contracts that afford unfair advantages of stronger parties over weaker parties. Today, there are serious legislative attempts to control the high cost of money damage awards to plaintiffs injured by negligent defendants. Such proposals are often countered with the argument that harmed persons have a "right" to compensation. In other words, they deserve to be made whole again or to be placed in a position they were before the tortious (wrongful) conduct of the defendant.

Box 1.3   From the *Declaration of Independence* (July 4, 1776)

When in the course of human events, it becomes necessary for one people to dissolve the political bands which have connected them with another, and to assume, among the powers of the earth the separate and equal station to which the *Laws of Nature* and of *Nature's God* entitle them, a decent respect to the opinions of mankind requires that they should declare the causes which impel them to the separation.

We hold these *truths* to be self-evident, that all men are created equal, that they are *endowed by their Creator with certain unalienable rights, that among these are life, liberty, and the pursuit of happiness.* That to secure these rights, governments are instituted among men, deriving their just powers from the consent of the governed. That whenever any form of government becomes destructive of these ends, it is the right of the people to alter or to abolish it, and to institute new government, laying its foundation on such principles, and organizing its powers in such form, as to them shall seem most likely to effect their safety and happiness. . . [emphasis added]

Though the natural law school of jurisprudence is appealing, critics point out that we cannot always agree on what the natural law really means in particular situations. For example, sincere persons of good will and equally deep religious convictions disagree about the "rightness" of capital punishment, and the abortion issue continues to divide the nation along moral lines. Although arguments are forcefully made, the discussion about punishment for homosexual conduct is likewise difficult to resolve by an agreement about what natural law commands.

Historical School

The *historical school of jurisprudence* may be viewed as an attempt to overcome the vagaries of natural law with more concrete guidance about the human origins and evolution of the law. The basic assumption is that judges find the law in the history, culture, and customs of a people. For example, modern political conservatives assert that the intentions of the framers of the U.S. Constitution can be known, and the task of jurists is to ascertain these intentions when adjudicating actual cases and controversies. Proponents of this view also mark the delivery of the 1789 U.S. Constitution as a high point in American and world history.

A competing variant of the historical perspective views history as revealing patterns of change, if not improvement, based on the experiences of a people within legal and political institutions. In this respect, it is the responsibility of jurists to view law as a series of social experiments. The law is subject to constant testing in the laboratory of the courts. This results in a body of formal norms, producing proximate solutions to difficult situations requiring conflict resolution.

The antecedents to contemporary views of historical jurisprudence in America are traceable to continental Europe and England. Friedrich Karl von Savigny (1779–1861) launched the German school, arguing that the law of a nation attains its fixed character even before recorded history. Such law is found in the *Volksgeist*, defined as the spirit of the people, otherwise known as the national character of a people. Custom is the overt manifestation of the *Volksgeist*, and the role of jurists is to let the law grow as part of the people's history, a view incompatible with universal and fixed laws of nature. Moreover, codification of the law is unnecessary, even dangerous. Hence, because we know what the law is through the *Volksgeist*, it does not have to be written down. Codification runs the risk of misinterpreting the *Volksgeist*.[5]

Among the proponents of historical jurisprudence, Sir Henry Maine (1822–1888) is probably the most cited of English legal thinkers that include Lord Chief Justice Edward Coke and Sir William Blackstone. Maine departs from Savigny in two significant ways. First, he describes stages of legal evolution whereby old ideas are discarded in favor of modern legal norms. Second, he used comparative studies to determine what ideas all legal systems have in common. Maine found two types of societies: "static" and "progressive." *Static societies* start with the personal law of the law-making ruler. The legitimate right of the ruler stems from tradition, and his commands crystallize into law through custom. As is the case for feudal cultures, in this type of society everyone has a fixed status and legal relationships are well understood by all. In *progressive societies*, relationships are not based on status. Rather, contract orders human relationships. Relationships in the family and on the job are conceptualized in terms of the freedom of contract, and the right of persons to freely bargain for goods and services is respected as a legally enforceable norm of conduct.[6]

Maine teaches that the movement in society from status to contract is accomplished in law through legal fiction, the application of equity principles, and by the passage of legislation. A legal fiction is a falsity that for legal purposes is treated as true. In feudal England, for example, adopted children had no right of inheritance. A legal fiction was created to get around this obvious injustice by treating adopted children as if they were natural blood relations. Principles of natural justice are employed within the equity jurisdiction of courts, alongside the legal rules articulated by the ordinary common law courts. Thus, while an otherwise valid contract is enforceable between parties of unequal power in courts possessing only legal jurisdiction, courts with equitable jurisdiction may intervene to nullify the ill effects of fundamentally unfair provisions. Legislation promulgated by representative bodies is perhaps the most desirable form of change, according to Maine, because it is widely viewed as the legitimate expression of the will of the people.[7] To the extent that legislation approximates the will of the majority, it is a superior form of change to that depending upon judicial inventions and interpretations of unelected or otherwise unaccountable judges.

A clear manifestation of the influence of historical jurisprudence of Europe and England in America is the *case-method* approach to legal education; credit for its creation is usually given to Christopher Columbus Langdell, although others paved the way before him. For example, in 1810, Judge Zephariah Swift of Connecticut prepared for the use of his office students a short treatise on evidence that included cases. And Elihu Root studied cases at New York University between 1865 and 1867 under the tutelage of John Norton Pomeroy. As happens today, students were expected to read cases and then to answer questions about them in class. In the preface to his 1871 textbook, Harvard Law School Dean C. C. Langdell set out the historical assumptions underlying the case method of legal education (see Box 1.4).[8]

The case method was carried from Harvard to other law schools by members of the Harvard faculty and by students trained there. By the beginning of the twentieth century, several of the leading law schools were using this approach. Casebooks in almost every division of civil,

---

Box 1.4   Preface to *Selection of Cases on the Law of Contracts* (1871) by Christopher Columbus Langdell

Law considered as a science consists of certain principles or doctrines. To have such a mastery of these as to be able to apply them with constant facility and certainty to the ever-tangled skein of human affairs, is what constitutes a true lawyer, and hence to acquire that mastery should be the business of every earnest student of law. Each of these doctrines has arrived at its present state by slow degrees; in other words, it is growth extending in many cases through centuries. Thus growth is to be traced in the main through a series of cases; and much the shortest and best, if not the only way of mastering the doctrine effectually is by studying the cases in which it is embodied. But the cases which are useful and necessary for this purpose at the present day bear an exceedingly small proportion to all that is reported. The vast majority are useless, and worse than useless, for any purpose of systematic study. Moreover, the number of fundamental legal doctrines is much less than is commonly supposed; the many different guises in which the same doctrine is constantly making its appearance, and the great extent to which legal treaties are a repetition of each other, being a cause of much misapprehension. If these doctrines could be so classified and arranged that each should be found in its proper place, and nowhere else, they would cease to be formidable from their number.

---

criminal, and constitutional law were prepared for classroom use. By 1938, the case method had been adopted by nearly all the full-time and by some of the part-time law schools.[9] Although for decades critics have attacked the case method, it remains today a central tool of legal pedagogy. Further, the everyday practice of law requires attorneys to interpret and to cite precedents to justify their clients' conduct, reinforcing in the process the assumptions underlying historical jurisprudence.

Utilitarianism

Jeremy Bentham (1748–1832), an eccentric British philosopher, was the founder of *utilitarianism*. This doctrine evaluates human law in terms of utility, or in other words, by its social consequence. Whether a law is good or bad depends upon its consequences to all individuals in society, both at present and in the future. Bentham's great contribution to law was the creation of a philosophical justification for challenging existing legal institutions and a rationale for improving them.

Based upon the ethical theory that equates good with pleasure and evil with pain, Bentham's utility principle of the greatest good for the greatest number is designed as a guide for legislators when considering proper sanctions imposed on lawbreakers. Legislators are urged to calculate, for example, the consequences of proposed penal laws that may create more harm than good. Bentham and his reform-minded follow-ers urged milder penalties, more efficient police forces, speedy trials, and the creation of legal codes that could make the law readily under-standable and accessible to citizens.[10]

Utilitarianism assumes that human beings are rational actors capa-ble of knowing and following their own self-interest in terms of maxi-mizing pleasure and avoiding the opposite. For example, criminal pen-alties need to fit the crime with a view to deterring wrongdoers and repeat offenders. Yet, we know that individuals are not always rational in their motivations or conduct, often rendering informed self-interest inoperable; indeed, individuals are not always aware of their own self-interest, let alone capable of making such calculations. Moreover, when lawmakers, including legislators and judges, are called upon to make decisions based upon the principle of the greatest good for the greatest number, the rights of minorities may be sacrificed in the weighing pro-cess.

Analytical Jurisprudence

Nineteenth- and twentieth-century leading proponents of *analytical jurisprudence* include John Austin, John Chipman Gray, Wesley New-comb Hohfeld, Hans Kelsen, and H. L. A. Hart. Although they had their disagreements, each took a positivistic view toward law as established or recognized by governmental authorities in an attempt to distinguish law from morals, ethics, or custom.[11] In this sense, analytical jurispru-dence was and remains today a response to the perceived anarchy of natural law, historical jurisprudence, and ethical theories of the just so-ciety. Natural law, they argue, is hardly a guide for law, because we can-not locate a concrete sovereign, as is also the case for international law. According to leading analytical jurists, law, to be properly so-called, must have a determinate sovereign, must operate on inferiors, must compel a habit of obedience, and must be enforceable.[12] The analytical jurists insist upon a distinction between what law ought to be and what it is in fact. Specifically, the law must be obeyed and faithfully inter-preted by jurists if it is made consistent with the law-making rules of society. Individuals may not disobey a law with which they may dis-agree on moral or policy grounds, nor, for that matter, may lay jurors seek to nullify an unjust law by ignoring the instructions given them by presiding professional judges.

Adopting, perhaps unwittingly, a positivist approach, while silently rejecting arguments about natural justice, Texas Governor George W. Bush justified going ahead with the scheduled execution of Gary Gra-ham on June 22, 2000, because the condemned African American man, a convicted murderer, had been afforded all the legal appeals permitted by the law. Execution opponents argued that because considerable doubt remained that Graham had received a fair trial, given contradictory eyewitness accounts and flawed legal representation, natural justice and fundamental principles of due process of law required the governor's intervention so that an innocent person not be wrongly put to death. Nevertheless, Bush claimed that the law allowed no discretion in such matters, and it was his legal responsibility as Governor to enforce the laws of the state of Texas.[13]

Mechanical jurisprudence is closely aligned with the principles of analytical jurisprudence, which in turn are associated with constitutional absolutism. This philosophical variation on the legal positivism theme of analytical jurisprudence views the U.S. Constitution as the highest norm within a clearly defined hierarchy of norms. For example, if an ordinary law of Congress or a state legislature contradicts constitutional norms, then the judges, who have taken an oath to uphold the Constitution as the highest law of the land, must declare the statute null and void. In short, judges are not free to apply universal principles of justice, balance competing social interests, or consider the social consequences of their decisions. The Supreme Court used its power of judicial review to strike down major legislation which had been introduced by the administration of Franklin D. Roosevelt, designed to combat the Great Depression of the 1930s. The duty of the justices is clear, as articulated by Justice Owen Roberts in the following excerpt from his famous 1936 anti-New Deal, U.S. Supreme Court opinion. Judicial decisions made in this analytical fashion are said by advocates of mechanical jurisprudence to be principled or otherwise objective and not the subjective judgments of mere unelected judges.

Box 1.5	From the Majority Opinion of Justice Owen Roberts in United States v. Butler U.S. Supreme Court 297 U.S. 1, 62–63 (1936)

There should be no misunderstanding as to the function of this court....It is sometimes said that the court assumes a power to overrule or control the action of the people's representatives. This is a misconception. The Constitution is the supreme law of the land ordained and established by the people. All legislation must conform to the principles it lays down. When an act of Congress is appropriately challenged in the courts as not conforming to the constitutional mandate, the judicial branch of the Government has only one duty—to lay the article of the Constitution which is invoked beside the statute which is challenged and to decide whether the latter squares with the former. All the court does, or can do, is to announce its considered judgment upon the question. The only power it has, if such it may be called, is the power of judgment. The court neither approves nor condemns any legislative policy.

> Its delicate and difficult office is to ascertain and declare whether the legislation is in accordance with, or is in contravention of, the provisions of the Constitution; and having done that, its duty ends.

Both the analytical and mechanical schools of jurisprudence have been widely criticized because proponents tend to confuse a normative prescription with a factual description. That is, most positivists believe that because judges and justices should behave in an objective and neutral manner, they in fact do behave in such a manner. Yet, as we all know, people do not always behave in ways that they should. In the 1990s, a movement within the positivist camp led by Professor Tom Campbell of Australia gave this approach new intellectual life. Campbell argues forcefully for the ethical view that judges should behave impartially through the subjugation of their own moral beliefs to the will of the people as revealed through legislative enactment. As a corollary, consistent with Sir Henry Maine, Campbell argues that legislation is a source of law superior to the creative acts of judges in discerning the common law. Although plainly derivative, his version of positivism is not based on the notion of a clearly discernable sovereign, as is the case for the proponents of analytical jurisprudence. Rather, Campbell argues that positivism in the postmodern world can be regarded as a way to enhance democracy and is not in conflict with democratic values. He proposes that judges must behave in ways that will better approximate the union between how they ought to behave and how they behave in fact. The clear articulation of rules by legislative authorities that are followed carefully by judges will create greater political legitimacy for the system as a whole.[14]

Sociological Jurisprudence

Adherents of *sociological jurisprudence* are especially critical of both the analytical and historical schools of thought. They reject the command notion of law favored by the analytical jurists because law is more than enforceable norms set down by an identifiable sovereign. Rather, law springs from social customs that the government attempts to enforce. In other words, the government does not make the law. Rather, it guarantees it. The real origins of the law can be found in the study of anthropology, history, psychology, and political science. Unlike the proponents of historical jurisprudence, sociological jurists tend to view legal trends not in terms of long legal epochs, such as Maine's centuries-long status-to-contract conceptualization. Rather, sociological jurists note how law reflects changing social relations in the short run, for example, how changing attitudes toward gender equality affect court interpretations of statutory and constitutional law.

Proponents of sociological jurisprudence included prominent twentieth-century luminaries Dean Roscoe Pound of the Harvard Law School and Justice Benjamin Cardozo of the U.S. Supreme Court. They viewed sociological jurisprudence as describing and explaining how the law changes, as well as explaining the law can be used to promote needed change in society. In this sense, sociological jurisprudence is both descriptive and prescriptive.[15]

Legal Realism

Legal realism emerged as a school of jurisprudence in the 1930s and remains popular in many intellectual circles. It is closely related to the sociological school but is a more radical departure from the historical assumptions implicit in the case method taught in law schools since the first half of the twentieth century. Legal realists, such as Professor Karl Llewellyn, federal judge Jerome Frank, and Supreme Court Justice William O. Douglas, were concerned less with the origins and precedents of the law than with its current impact. Realists view law as an academic discipline closely related to the social sciences, needing evidence and facts supplied by the disciplines of economics, sociology, psychology, and political science. Legal realists center much of their attention on judges and lawyers as decision makers, insisting that the law is not found or discovered in natural law, or in the customs and traditions of a people. Nor is law a matter of logic. More exactly, legal opinions exhibit the attitudes and values of legal professionals. They make the law in ways that tend to reflect their attitudes and the relative power relations of larger social interests that lurk behind litigation as well as the interpersonal relations of judges on and off multimember courts.[16]

Critical Legal Studies

The *critical legal studies (CLS)* movement began in the 1970s and remains active today. CLS has substantial similarities with the earlier legal realism movement of the first half of the twentieth century. Both the legal realists and modern proponents of critical legal studies (often referred to as "crits") seek the reform of the law school curriculum. Both reject the notion that legal decision-making is an objective enterprise, in which judges merely find the law but do not make it. Both schools of jurisprudence want to make law students and others cognizant of the many subjective factors that enter into legal processes. CLS professors, however, make an additional claim that legal realists generally did not. Although not united in their approach, CLS proponents generally view the law as a political tool in the hands of the dominant forces in society, used to enforce their view of the world upon the powerless.

For example, members of the neo-Marxist segment of CLS argue that the law is an instrument of class oppression operated by lawyers in the service of the capitalist class in American society and the world. Critical race theorists maintain that American law is not the law of all the people but is an overwhelmingly white man's enterprise that has served historically to keep African Americans in their lowly place. Some critical race theorists argue for bans on so-called racial hate speech and have attempted to devise new approaches to civil rights, including the payment of reparations to contemporary African Americans for the injustice of slavery imposed upon their African ancestors, who were imported to these shores to make white men rich from the ill-gotten proceeds of their Southern plantations. Feminist critical theorists claim that law is a product of white males. This gives the law a patriarchal character resulting in the perpetuation of the oppressive pattern of dominance and submission found in family, social, economic, and political life. Despite objections of civil libertarians, some feminist theorists have actively sought the creation and enforcement of laws against pornography, which they claim degrades women. Both African American and feminist proponents of CLS argue for greater diversity and affirmative action programs in legal institutions, including law schools, the bench and bar (judges and lawyers), and the greater economic, social, and political world.[17]

A common criticism leveled by opponents of CLS scholars is that "crits" do not believe in law, which they consider a subjective process for which there are no objective standards for ascertaining justice. CLS proponents are thus accused of practicing nihilism (i.e., the denial of any basis for the existence of knowledge or truth). Although emphasizing equality and serving as a tool in the deconstruction of central legal principles, CLS advocates are said to offer little in terms of alternative ways to understand the law that all persons regardless of class, race, or gender might agree upon. Instead, it is argued, they have busied themselves advancing their own agendas at the expense of the wider community.[18]

Nevertheless, many but not all of today's social scientists who study law-related subjects concentrate their efforts on describing and explaining law in society. They strive to offer, for example, relatively objective empirical theories about the puzzle of judicial decision-making. They spend relatively little effort in prescribing changes in particular laws, but they do explore the functions of law in society and how legal institutions and actors contribute to the overall stability of the political system and to its change. At the same time, more politically conservative scholars are rediscovering natural law and historical jurisprudence as vehicles for expressing their policy preferences and viewpoints. Still other conservatives have embraced *law and economics jurisprudence,* which favors abandoning the traditional focus on what the Constitutional framers might have intended by "rights" in favor of allowing the market system to promote economic efficiency and the maximization of wealth.[19]

Branches of Law

It is a common and useful practice to divide the law into two great categories—public and private law. *Public law* involves the relationship among government institutions, and between government and private parties in society. Constitutional law, administrative law, and criminal law are conventional subsets of this division. *Constitutions* describe the authority of public institutions as they exercise authority within their jurisdiction. In the American governmental system, the U.S. Constitution is regarded as the fundamental law that guides all ordinary legislation and executive actions. It supersedes all actions that may contradict the basic law that the people ordained and established in 1789, as amended. *Administrative law* is the branch of public law dealing with the rules and regulations promulgated by government agencies. Because of the growing complexity of society, legislative institutions delegate to administrative agencies considerable authority to deal with problems ranging from health and welfare concerns to regulation of commercial intercourse in transportation and the trading of stocks and bonds. *Criminal law* articulates offenses against society and not simply violations of another's individual rights. Murder, robbery, rape, larceny, assault, and burglary come immediately to mind as prime examples of this important branch of the public law.

Private law is a generic term referring generally to the law governing conflicts among private parties in society. Governments have an interest in adjudicating these conflicts because the enforcement of norms contributes to the overall stability of society. For example, stable business intercourse is unthinkable without the expectation that contracts are enforceable by the government acting as a neutral third party. Ownership of real and personal property is necessary if the materialistic assumptions of capitalism are to be fulfilled. Compensation for injuries resulting from the wrongful conduct of others is the hallmark of the law of torts. Most litigation in America involves private law disputes and is the bread and butter of the legal profession.

Although it is a useful distinction, one should not draw too bright a line between public and private law. The categories sometimes overlap, such as when an assault is both a criminal offense warranting criminal penalties (e.g., jail time) and tortious conduct (e.g., where an injured party may sue for the recovery of money damages). The case of O. J. Simpson is a convenient example. He was acquitted on the criminal charges of the murder of his former wife, Nicole Brown Simpson, and her friend, Ronald Goldman. Yet, O. J. Simpson lost a civil suit for wrongful death, requiring the payment of damages to family members of the deceased. Likewise, a prosecution by the attorney general for a violation of the antitrust laws may warrant both criminal and civil penalties. Private parties injured by conspiracies in the restraint of trade may sue conspirators for money damages. When various states sued tobacco companies for physical injuries to their citizens resulting from smoking, they acted on behalf of the citizens of their states to redress private wrongs that have public consequences.

Functions of Law

With basic definitions understood, we turn to the task of articulating in more formal terms the various functions performed by legal institutions in society. The famous legal anthropologist E. Adamson Hoebel spelled out four functions of law: (1) to define relationships among members of society, (2) to allocate authority within society, (3) to resolve conflict when it arises in society, and (4) to redefine relationships as societal conditions change.[20] We adopt his classification scheme with some modification and elaboration.

Defining Relationships

Societal norms prescribe power relationships among persons and institutions in society. Although many informal relationships exist that are dictated by custom and tradition, the law formalizes relationships with the full force of the state behind it. Children may be made to obey their parents. The rights and duties of parties in marriage are legally prescribed. Employer-employee relations are often defined formally, particularly with respect to working conditions and minimum wages and benefits. Pedestrians may safely cross the street on a green light because there is a legally defined relationship between themselves and drivers of automobiles.

At a higher level of abstraction, the relationship between religious institutions and government is circumscribed by the Free Exercise and Establishment Clauses of the First Amendment in the U.S. Constitution. The division of powers between the central government and the state governments in the U.S. federal system is defined broadly by the Supremacy Clause (Article VI, paragraph 2) and the Tenth Amendment. Because many provisions of the U.S. Constitution are broadly worded as statements of principles and not precise legal rules, the courts have played a central role in defining relationships among institutions, and between individuals and government itself. Given this reality, the exercise of discretion is a necessary element in fashioning judicial opinions.

Allocation of Authority in Society

The legitimate exercise of physical force distinguishes government from a band of hoodlums. There are many injustices perpetrated every day in society. But to allow individuals to decide for themselves that they have been wronged and what penalty ought to be exacted can result in chaos and, in some instances, considerable injustice. Consider the classic scene in Mario Puzo's novel, *The Godfather.* An immigrant mortician asks Don Corelone to avenge the rape of his daughter because he has not received satisfaction from the police. Although the desire for justice seems reasonable, the particular remedy sought is not. Due process, including protecting innocent parties from wrongful prosecution, to say nothing of protections against cruel and unusual punishment, is unlikely in gangland settings. It denies the government's monopoly over the use of force and acknowledges the existence of plural elites with the power over life and death. In modern America, however, criminal courts are increasingly permitting aggrieved parties to take the stand to recommend to juries and judges what penalties ought to be imposed upon the person convicted of a crime against themselves or their loved ones. These victim impact statements openly acknowledge personal revenge as a legitimate goal of law in the exercise of physical force.

When a rueful King John in 1215 was made to sign the Magna Carta, written by disgruntled barons, the principle that no person is above the law became a central feature of our legal system. Hoebel points out that in a law-governed state, the power to enforce the law is "transpersonalized." It resides in the office and not the man. The phrase "This is a nation of laws and not of men" means that no person, including a legitimate leader, is above the law. Law is for both rulers and the ruled.

When presidents, for example, abuse their authority for their own personal gain, it is regarded as anathema. Thoughtful persons of all political persuasions were appalled when it became evident that President Nixon had attempted to use the office of the presidency to punish his enemies and conspired to cover-up the burglary at the Watergate Hotel. The federal judge who presided over the lawsuit of Paula Jones against President Bill Clinton imposed a monetary fine on the president for the lies he told during a deposition about his relations with various women including Monica Lewinsky. And a bar committee recommended to the Arkansas Supreme Court that Clinton be disbarred so that he may not practice law in that state. Though he was acquitted by the U.S. Senate of the charges contained in a bill of impeachment filed by the House of Representatives, Clinton remained vulnerable to prosecution for criminal conduct after he left office. Richard Ray, the special prosecutor, and attorneys for the president finalized a negotiated settlement the day before the inauguration of the new president,

George W. Bush. In exchange for the special prosecutor's agreement not to criminally prosecute the president, Bill Clinton admitted that he knowingly made false and misleading statements to the court in the Paula Jones deposition. He also agreed to the suspension of his Arkansas law license for five years, a payment of a $25,000 fine to the Arkansas Bar Association, and not to seek reimbursement of attorney fees from the government.

Resolution of Conflict When It Arises

The peaceful settlement of conflict is an important function of the law. A basic operating principle of law is: Where there is a wrong, there must be a remedy. In other words, the law renders unnecessary an appeal to arms. Personal vendetta is likewise unnecessary if not redundant, and it is clearly dangerous to the peace and stability of the community. Moreover, legal institutions purport to provide a more or less neutral forum where objective or principled decisions are rendered without fear or favor. Fundamentally, the system works because, either tacitly or overtly, parties to disputes agree to observe the rule of civilization—to submit their dispute to a third party for resolution. This system encourages losers in legal contests to remain cooperative and law-abiding members of society even though the system has decided against them. After all, they had a fair chance to win.

Courts function to resolve conflicts, but the parties to the dispute must believe at some level that the judiciary is neither friend nor foe; at the very least, one party must not believe that the judiciary is an ally of his or her opponent. As Martin Shapiro pointed out, however, the perception that courts are objective extends not only to a feeling that they are neutral toward the parties but also that the legal norms applied to resolve conflicts do not bias the result in advance. These norms must not favor one interest over the other, and the rules are broadly understood to be the result of mutually agreed upon norms of behavior.[21]

Sometimes, however, objectivity and neutrality are lost in the legal system. For example, the riots that broke out after the not guilty verdict in the trial of the Los Angeles police officers charged with the videotaped beating of Rodney King reinforced the belief among many African Americans that the criminal justice system treats them in an unfair manner. On the other hand, the acquittal of O. J. Simpson for the murder of his former wife and her male companion was viewed by most polled white citizens as an example of jury nullification. African Americans viewed the result in the Simpson criminal trial as a vindication of their perception that members of their race are unfairly and routinely subject to criminal prosecutions.[22] Both white and African American negative perceptions threaten widespread mass support, what political scientists term "diffuse citizen support," undermining the legitimacy of the law.

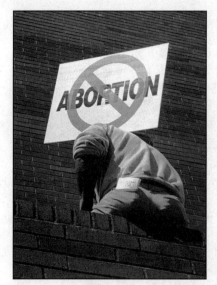

There is strong opposition to the U.S. Supreme Court decision on abortion.

Then, too, it is evident that as judicial offices become institutionalized, the interests of the third party become an element in decision-making. The interest of the regime becomes an important value, although this interest was not part of the original dispute brought by the private parties. The result can be a decision that is unsatisfactory to all parties. For example, the U.S. Supreme Court for years avoided judging the constitutionality of the Connecticut birth control statute. In two cases, the Court claimed that the parties lacked standing to sue because there had not first been an actual prosecution under the state statute. But physicians, patients, and the state clearly wanted a resolution of this dispute. Finally, they staged an arrest so that the courts could address the constitutional issue. The matter was resolved with a finding by the high court in *Griswold v. Connecticut* (1965) that the statute in question violated the plaintiff's right to privacy.

Why did members of the Supreme Court seek to avoid resolving this issue? In the name of judicial self-restraint, the Court sought not to entangle itself in the sensitive social issue of marital rights and birth control to avoid institutional attacks upon itself. To be sure, they were correct in their fear that squarely facing the constitutional issue would cause difficulties for the institution. Indeed, the decision in *Griswold v. Connecticut* (1965) is viewed by some pro-life advocates as the intellectual precursor to *Roe v. Wade* (1973), which protects a woman's right to an abortion as fundamental. Certainly, both decisions have earned the Court considerable political opposition. See Boxes 1.6 and 1.7 for greater detail.

Box 1.6   Summary of Griswold v. Connecticut
U.S. Supreme Court
381 U.S. 479, 85 S.Ct. 1678, 14 L.Ed. 2d 510 (1965)

Estelle Griswold, the executive director of the Planned Parenthood League, and others were convicted of violating a Connecticut statute for providing information and instruction to married persons on the use of birth control devices. She lost her case in the state courts, but the U.S. Supreme Court reversed the judgment against her.

Justice William O. Douglas penned the opinion of the majority, but only one other justice fully accepted Douglas's reasoning. First, Douglas explicitly avoided the subjective implications of substantive due process as illustrated by

Lochner v. New York (1905). He insisted that the right to marital privacy is established by the specific guarantees in the Bill of Rights that have penumbras, "formed by emanations from those guarantees that help them give life and substance." Five different constitutional amendments create the zone of privacy that renders the Connecticut statute null and void. They are as follow: the First Amendment guarantees the right of association protection; the Third Amendment prohibits the quartering of soldiers in any house in time of peace without the owner's consent; the Fourth Amendment protects against unreasonable search and seizure; the Fifth Amendment protects against self-incrimination; and finally, the Ninth Amendment provides that "the enumeration in the Constitution, of certain rights, shall not be construed to deny or disparage others retained by the people."

Box 1.7   **Summary of Roe v. Wade**
U.S. Supreme Court
410 U.S. 113, 93 S.Ct. 705, 35 L.Ed. 2d 147 (1973)

An unmarried pregnant woman and a physician, who had suffered past prosecutions and was presently facing additional criminal charges, challenged a Texas anti-abortion statute. A U.S. District Court held that the pregnant woman had standing to sue but the physician did not. Yet, this federal court ruled that the statute was unconstitutionally vague and overly broad.

Justice Harry Blackmun, writing for the Supreme Court, held that a woman's decision to terminate her pregnancy is a fundamental right guaranteed by the liberty provision of the Due Process Clause of the Fourteenth Amendment. However, although the privacy right is fundamental, it may be limited by a compelling state interest. During the first trimester of pregnancy the state cannot demonstrate a compelling state interest. Yet, for the stage [of pregnancy] beginning with the end of the first trimester, the state has a valid interest in promoting the health of the mother. Thereafter, it may regulate the abortion procedure in ways that are reasonably related to maternal health. But in the last trimester of pregnancy, the state may regulate and even prohibit abortion, except where it may be necessary for the preservation of the life or the health of the mother.

Redefining Relations of Individuals and Groups in Society

The law may or may not adapt as the social norms, customs, traditions, and conditions in society change. Clearly, the law by its nature is conservative. It tends to enforce the power and privileges of the dominant elites in society. The social, economic, and political values of ruling elites are enforced by lawmakers in legislative, executive, and judicial institutions. Yet, the law reflects a change in these relationships as power is redistributed within political systems—either abruptly, as in revolutionary regimes, or incrementally, as is common in more or less stable societies.

In the early nineteenth century, a husband possessed the legal right to use what physical force was reasonably necessary to compel the obedience of his wife. Courts generally avoided intervention in family matters, preferring to grant considerable discretion to husbands in the governance of their households. Without evidence of malice, cruelty, or dangerous violence, courts allowed husbands to "correct" their wives. Today, however, the physical chastisement of a wife is grounds for divorce and criminal prosecution for domestic violence. Moreover, in a growing number of communities, police no longer attempt to reconcile couples engaged in physical confrontations. Reflecting changing societal values, husbands are increasingly being carted off to jail for attacking their spouses, with few questions asked.

In the nineteenth century, labor unions were often denied the right to strike by so-called "injunction judges" because the common law viewed worker organizations as conspiracies in the restraint of trade. But in the twentieth century, as political power shifted away from business domination to a more balanced appreciation for the rights of working men and women, laws were enacted and interpreted by judges to protect the right of workers to organize and to collectively bargain with employers.

The U.S. Supreme Court's 1954 opinion in *Brown v. Board of Education,* which struck down segregation in the public schools, is an example of a judicial body helping to redefine relations of individuals and groups in society. Neither Congress nor the chief executive was ready to lead the charge for racial equality. Yet, the Court stuck out its institutional neck by proclaiming that separate but equal facilities are inherently unequal and thus in violation of the Equal Protection Clause of the Fourteenth Amendment. As this case illustrates, courts may pay a price for being ahead of the attitudes of powerful groups in society. There was considerable resistance to the Court's opinion in the South and with southern representatives in Congress. President Eisenhower did not do the cause of racial equality a favor when at one point he indicated that he did not think laws could change the hearts and minds of people. It was not until after the enactment of the Civil Rights Act of 1964, some ten years after the *Brown* decision, that substantial integration in public schools and other public accommodations took place. This result took the full cooperation of the executive branch to attack the vestiges of *de jure* (legal) segregation in America (see Box 1.8).

Then, too, when in 1999 the Supreme Court of Vermont ruled that same-sex marriages are protected by a state constitutional provision, its ruling was clearly inconsistent with prevailing social mores. It caused state legislators to fashion a new law affording gay and lesbian

---

Box 1.8   **Summary of**
Brown v. Board of Education of Topeka
U.S. Supreme Court
347 U.S. 483, 74 S.Ct. 686, 98 L.Ed. 873 (1954)

This case involved several other cases coming before the Supreme Court at the same time, where African American plaintiffs alleged that segregation of the races in public schools violated the Equal Protection Clause of the Fourteenth Amendment. In all but one of the consolidated cases, the lower courts found that the segregated schools satisfied the separate but equal rule first announced by the Supreme Court in the 1896 case of *Plessy v. Ferguson.*

Writing for a unanimous Supreme Court, Chief Justice Earl Warren directly overruled the *Plessy* doctrine. Citing social science evidence, Warren concluded that segregating children "solely because of their race generates a feeling of inferiority as to their status in the community that may affect their hearts and minds in a way unlikely ever to be undone." He also concluded, "In the field of public education the doctrine of 'separate but equal' has no place. Separate educational facilities are inherently unequal." Thus, the Equal Protection Clause of the Fourteenth Amendment prohibits *de jure* segregation of public schools.

---

couples some legal rights without approving the institution of same-sex marriages.

Law and attitude change. The nineteenth-century sociologist and philosopher William Graham Sumner argued that "stateways cannot change folkways."[23] This means that society cannot legislate social mores and patterns of behavior. The failure of prohibition laws to end the sale and consumption of alcoholic beverages is often cited as a prime example of the futility of laws that contradict existing attitudes and values. Essentially, this view holds that the fundamental role of law in society is to reinforce existing values and minimize deviance from the dominant norms of the age. Social stability is accomplished when legitimate political institutions punish unlawful conduct consistent with uniform rules.

A contrary view asserts that law is not only a means to achieve social control but also has the potential to influence and change attitudes and behaviors. That is, when norms are institutionalized by legitimate government organs, there is a good chance that many people will internalize the norms as their own. This occurs in part because the population already possesses deeply seated values suggesting they should obey law and that the new norm is part of an already existing norm in society. Thus, for example, laws outlawing racial segregation are not the result of a new value of equality imposed by some upstart political elite. Rather, the new norm may be traced to the Declaration of Independence and even further back to Judeo-Christian beliefs about God creating humans in his/her own image. Further, a reason to fight the bloody Civil War was to end slavery, and the Fourteenth Amendment was enacted to erase the badges incident to slavery.

Although, no doubt, bigotry toward African Americans endures, the dramatic changes in formal law—beginning with the 1954 Supreme Court decision in *Brown v. Board of Education* and later with the Civil Rights Acts of 1964 and the Voting Rights Act of 1965—went a long way toward changing racial attitudes. By the same token, when a law is enacted that contradicts the basic understanding of a people about its values, the new norm will not be internalized and it may even be resisted. Most Americans, for example, accept the proposition that unequal treatment of African Americans is wrongheaded. Yet, many Americans question the proposition that to make up for years of past discrimination, African Americans should be afforded preference over whites in public and private employment and in admissions to public universities.[24] In recent years, citizen-initiated campaigns have been successfully conducted in the states of California and Washington to remove affirmative action programs from the statute books; and in Florida, Governor Jeb Bush decreed an end to such programs in university admission programs.

The Method of the Common Law

Though the courts may contribute to change in society and court opinions may help to internalize new norms of conduct in the hearts and minds of a people, it is a mistake to view courts as a panacea for righting all the wrongs in society. Many Americans view the courts as a primary vehicle for change. They take their lessons from the civil rights movement and the application of the national Bill of Rights to the states by the federal courts during the 1960s as prototypical of what can be accomplished. This optimism about the ability of law courts to bring about change rests upon the natural law assumption that persons possess inalienable rights, which courts will automatically protect. But history shows that courts in America are relatively conservative institutions. The intellectual schema in which the legal profession must operate constrains their ability to behave otherwise.

The principle of *stare decisis* guides American courts to apply the rule employed in previous cases to the case at hand. That is, if the facts in the present case are the same as those in previous cases, then the previous legal rule ought to be applied to the present controversy. Simply put, this intellectual process is reasoning by example or by analogy. Whether judges are applying the common law, interpreting a statute, or giving meaning to vague constitutional provisions, they compare the facts and results in a number of controversies to justify a result in the present case.

The experimental nature of the common law is thus evident. The law learns from the application of previous results. If the rule works, then it is applied again and again. It is an inductive system that depends upon a sufficient number of observations before a general rule is enunciated.

The body of previously decided cases with similar fact patterns as the present case is known as legal *precedent*. A *rule of law* is established when a number of cases are decided in a similar way; courts declare that when certain facts are present, more or less precise legal norms apply. For example, when a person takes the life of another with premeditation and no extenuating circumstances, then the rule of first degree murder applies. If a jury finds these facts to be true, then as a matter of law they are obliged to bring in a verdict of first-degree murder.

In human experience, however, seldom do the facts in different cases exactly mirror each other. Consequently, courts must decide whether a present case is sufficiently similar to past cases to warrant the application of the same legal rule with similar legal results. This variability in life provides legal professionals with considerable room for argument and the creation of conditional rules that permeate the law. Furthermore, judges are free to interpret precedents either "strictly" or "loosely," depending upon their view of justice in the particular case. If judges want to narrowly interpret a precedent, they will strictly apply it in the present, insisting that the facts in the past and the present be as nearly alike as human experience will permit. On the other hand, if judges want to apply the previous precedent broadly, then they will apply the rule loosely. They will ignore fact pattern discrepancies between previous and present cases, choosing instead to focus on the commonalities between and among the cases under study. As Karl N. Llewellyn teaches, sometimes judges will apply both a *loose view of precedent* and a *strict view of precedent* to different aspects of the same opinion. When neither statutes nor previously decided cases serve as a guide, judges are left to their own devices. At times, they directly overrule precedent, proclaiming that the previous rule is no longer applicable.[25]

Throughout this text, readers will encounter cases in which judges must decide whether to apply precedents strictly or loosely. Sometimes, however, judges have no precedents to guide their decision-making. Hence, we see that judges possess considerable discretion. In the process, they contribute to the overall stability and orderly change in society.

The task for legal professionals is a daunting one, no matter how they apply precedent. The following case illustrates some difficult choices that judges face when exercising their discretion and the means they employ to achieve what they believe are the most desirable ends.

Board of Regents v. Southworth
U.S. Supreme Court
529 U.S. 217; 120 S. Ct. 1346; 146 L. Ed. 2d 193 (2000)

KENNEDY, J., delivered the opinion of the Court, in which REHNQUIST, C. J., and O'CONNOR, SCALIA, THOMAS, and GINSBURG, JJ., joined.

For the second time in recent years we consider constitutional questions arising from a program designed to facilitate extracurricular student speech at a public university. Respondents are a group of students at the University of Wisconsin. They brought a First Amendment challenge to a mandatory student activity fee imposed by petitioner Board of Regents of the University of Wisconsin and used in part by the University to support student organizations engaging in political or ideological speech. Respondents object to the speech and expression of some of the student organizations. Relying upon our precedents which protect members of unions and bar associations from being required to pay fees used for speech the members find objectionable, both the District Court and the Court of Appeals invalidated the University's student fee program. The University contends that its mandatory student activity fee and the speech which it supports are appropriate to further its educational mission.

We reverse. The First Amendment permits a public university to charge its students an activity fee used to fund a program to facilitate extracurricular student speech if the program is viewpoint neutral. We do not sustain, however, the student referendum mechanism of the University's program, which appears to permit the exaction of fees in violation of the viewpoint neutrality principle. As to that aspect of the program, we remand for further proceedings. . . .

We must begin by recognizing that the complaining students are being required to pay fees which are subsidies for speech they find objectionable, even offensive. The *Abood* and *Keller* cases, then, provide the beginning point for our analysis. Abood v. Detroit Bd. of Ed., 431 U.S. 209, 52 L. Ed. 2d 261, 97 S. Ct. 1782 (1977); Keller v. State Bar of Cal., 496 U.S. 1, 110 L. Ed. 2d 1, 110 S. Ct. 2228 (1990). While those precedents identify the interests of the protesting students, the means of implementing First Amendment protections adopted in those decisions are neither applicable nor workable in the context of extracurricular student speech at a university.

In *Abood*, some nonunion public school teachers challenged an agreement requiring them, as a condition of their employment, to pay a service fee equal in amount to union dues. 431 U.S. at 211-212. The objecting teachers alleged that the union's use of their fees to engage in political speech violated their freedom of association guaranteed by the First and Fourteenth Amendments. The Court agreed and held that any objecting teacher could "prevent the Union's spending a part of their required service fees to contribute to political candidates and to express political views unrelated to its duties as exclusive bargaining representative." 431 U.S. at 234. The principles outlined in *Abood* provided the foundation for our later decision in *Keller*. There we held that lawyers admitted to practice in California could be required to join a state bar association and to fund activities "germane" to the association's mission of "regulating the legal profession and improving the quality of legal services." 496 U.S. at 13-14. The lawyers could not, however, be required to fund the bar association's own political expression.

The proposition that students who attend the University cannot be required to pay subsidies for the speech of other students without some First Amendment protection follows from the *Abood* and *Keller* cases. Students enroll in public universities to seek fulfillment of their personal aspirations and of their own potential. If the University conditions the opportunity to receive a college education, an opportunity comparable in importance to joining a labor union or bar association, on an agreement to support objectionable, extracurricular expression by other students, the rights acknowledged in *Abood* and *Keller* become implicated. It infringes on the speech and beliefs of the individual to be required, by this mandatory student activity fee program, to pay subsidies for the objectionable speech of others without any recognition of the State's corresponding duty to him or her. Yet recognition must be given as well to the important and substantial purposes of the University, which seeks to facilitate a wide range of speech.

In *Abood* and *Keller* the constitutional rule took the form of limiting the required subsidy to speech germane to the purposes of the union or bar association. The standard of germane speech as applied to student speech at a university is unworkable, however, and gives insufficient pro-tection both to the objecting students and to the University program itself. Even in the context of a labor union, whose functions are, or so we might have thought, well known and understood by the law and the courts after a long history of government regulation and judicial involvement, we have encountered difficulties in deciding what is germane and what is not. The difficulty manifested itself in our decision in Lehnert v. Ferris Faculty Assn., 500 U.S. 507, 114 L. Ed. 2d 572, 111 S. Ct. 1950 (1991), where different members of the Court reached varying conclusions regarding what expressive activity was or was not germane to the mission of the association. If it is difficult to define germane speech with ease or precision where a union or bar association is the party, the standard becomes all the more unmanageable in the public university setting, particularly where the State undertakes to stimulate the whole universe of speech and ideas.

The speech the University seeks to encourage in the program before us is distinguished not by discernable limits but by its vast, unexplored bounds. To insist upon asking what speech is germane would be contrary to the very goal the University seeks to pursue. It is not for the Court to say what is or is not germane to the ideas to be pursued in an institution of higher learning.

Just as the vast extent of permitted expression makes the test of germane speech inappropriate for intervention, so too does it underscore the high potential for intrusion on the First Amendment rights of the objecting students. It is all but inevitable that the fees will result in subsidies to speech which some students find objectionable and offensive to their personal beliefs. If the standard of germane speech is inapplicable, then, it might be argued the remedy is to allow each student to list those causes which he or she will or will not support. If a university decided that its students' First Amendment interests were better protected by some type of optional or refund system it would be free to do so. We decline to impose a system of that sort as a constitutional requirement, however. The restriction could be so disruptive and expensive that the program to support extracurricular speech would be ineffective. The First Amendment does not require the University to put the program at risk.

The University may determine that its mission is well served if students have the means to engage in dynamic discussions of philosophical, religious, scientific, social, and political subjects in their extracurricular campus life outside the lecture hall. If the University reaches this conclusion, it is entitled to impose a mandatory fee to sustain an open dialogue to these ends.

The University must provide some protection to its students' First Amendment interests, however. The proper measure, and the principal standard of protection for objecting students, we conclude, is the requirement of viewpoint neutrality in the allocation of funding support. Viewpoint neutrality was the obligation to which we gave substance in Rosenberger v. Rector and Visitors of Univ. of Va., 515 U.S. 819, 132 L. Ed. 2d 700, 115 S. Ct. 2510 (1995). There the University of Virginia feared that any association with a student newspaper advancing religious viewpoints would violate the Establishment Clause. We rejected the argument, holding that the school's adherence to a rule of viewpoint neutrality in administering its student fee program would prevent "any mistaken impression that the student newspapers speak for the University." While *Rosenberger* was concerned with the rights a student has to use an extracurricular speech program already in place, today's case considers the antecedent question, acknowledged but unresolved in *Rosenberger:* whether a public university may require its students to pay a fee which creates the mechanism for the extracurricular speech in the first instance. When a university requires its students to pay fees to support the extracurricular speech of other students, all in the interest of open discussion, it may not prefer some viewpoints to others. There is symmetry then in our holding here and in *Rosenberger:* Viewpoint neutrality is the justification for requiring the student to pay the fee in the first instance and for ensuring the integrity of the program's operation once the funds have been collected. We conclude that the University of Wisconsin may sustain the extracurricular dimensions of its programs by using mandatory student fees with viewpoint neutrality as the operational principle. . . .

It remains to discuss the referendum aspect of the University's program. While the record is not well developed on the point, it appears that by majority vote of the student body a given RSO may be funded or defunded. It is unclear to us what protection, if any, there is for viewpoint neutrality in this part of the process. To the extent the referendum substitutes majority determinations for viewpoint neutrality it would undermine the constitutional protection the program requires. The whole theory of viewpoint neutrality is that minority views are treated with the same respect as are majority views. Access to a public forum, for instance, does not depend upon majoritarian consent. That principle is controlling here. A remand is necessary and appropriate to resolve this point; and the case in all events must be reexamined in light of the principles we have discussed.

The judgment of the Court of Appeals is reversed, and the case is remanded for further proceedings consistent with this opinion. In this Court the parties shall bear their own costs.

It is so ordered.

JUSTICE SOUTER, with whom JUSTICE STEVENS and JUSTICE BREYER join, concurring in the judgment.

. . . I agree that the University's scheme is permissible, but do not believe that the Court should take the occasion to impose a cast-iron viewpoint neutrality requirement to uphold it. Instead, I would hold that the First Amendment interest claimed by the student respondents . . . here is simply insufficient to merit protection by anything more than the viewpoint neutrality already accorded by the University, and I would go no further.

The parties have stipulated that the grant scheme is administered on a viewpoint neutral basis, and like the majority I take the case on that assumption. The question before us is thus properly cast not as whether viewpoint neutrality is required, but whether Southworth has a claim to relief from this specific viewpoint neutral scheme. . . .

Southworth's objection has less force than it might otherwise carry because the challenged fees support a government program that aims to broaden public discourse. As I noted in *Rosenberger v. Rector and Visitors of Univ. of Va.*, . . . the university fee at issue is a tax. The state university compels it; it is paid into state accounts; and it is disbursed under the ultimate authority of the State. Although the facts here may not fit neatly under our holdings on government speech, (and the university has expressly renounced any such claim), our cases do suggest that under the First Amendment the government may properly use its tax revenue to promote general discourse.

. . . [T]he weakness of Southworth's claim is underscored by its setting within a university, whose students are inevitably required to support the expression of personally offensive viewpoints in ways that cannot be thought constitutionally objectionable unless one is prepared to deny the University its choice over what to teach. No one disputes that some fraction of students' tuition payments may be used for course offerings that are ideologically offensive to some students, and for paying professors who say things in the university forum that are radically at odds with the politics of particular students. Least of all does anyone claim that the University is somehow required to offer a spectrum of courses to satisfy a viewpoint neutrality requirement. . . . The University need not provide junior years abroad in North Korea as well as France, instruct in the theory of plutocracy as well as democracy, or teach Nietzsche as well as St. Thomas. Since uses of tuition payments (not optional for anyone who wishes to stay in college) may fund offensive speech far more obviously than the student activity fee does, it is difficult to see how the activity fee could present a stronger argument for a refund.

In sum, I see no basis to provide relief from the scheme being administered, would go no further, and respectfully concur in the judgment.

Case Questions for Discussion

1. Should procedures be instituted at colleges and universities to ensure that student funds are not used to facilitate ideological and political speech that some students find objectionable?

2. How does the Supreme Court distinguish cases involving teachers unions and bar associations from this case? Is the Court employing a strict or a loose view of precedent and what difference does it make?

3. Under what circumstances should a judge feel free to disregard previous precedents?

4. Why does Justice Souter write a concurring opinion? How does his approach differ from that of Justice Kennedy?

Reading and Briefing Court Opinions

Board of Regents v. Southworth is the first of many abbreviated court opinions you will be asked to read, analyze, and brief. Learning to do this is an important step in understanding the legal mind. Although nearly everyone is able to master this skill, developing such an ability requires considerable effort and patience. Do not become discouraged if after briefing a few cases the task seems difficult. With practice you will become proficient. We provide below a sample brief of the case you just read. Note the various elements of the brief.

(A). The first line contains the name of the parties to the suit (i.e., *Board of Regents v. Southworth*). If you look up this case in one of the U.S. Supreme Court reporters, however, you will find the complete name of the case and not the abbreviated form we have provided. It is: BOARD OF REGENTS OF THE UNIVERSITY OF WISCONSIN SYSTEM v. SCOTT HAROLD SOUTHWORTH, ET AL. Note that the board appealing this case (i.e., in the U.S. Court of Appeals) is the university system board which is responsible for the administration of all the campuses of the University of Wisconsin system, including the Madison campus. That is, the Board of Regents is the appellant and Scott Harold Southworth and others are, therefore, the appellees. They won the case in the court immediately below the U.S. Supreme Court, a U.S. court of appeals. As it so happened, they also won the case in the court of first instance, a U.S. federal district court.

The facts as presented in the court opinion do not relate to readers the fact that Southworth and others are politically conservative students, who oppose their fees being used to support groups to which they are ideologically opposed (e.g., Amnesty International, Students of the National Organization for Women, the Campus Women's Center, the UW Greens, the Madison AIDS Support Network, the Lesbian, Gay, and Bisexual Campus Center, and others). Although the Supreme Court fails to mention this fact, and therefore it is not part of the presented fact pattern one should present in the brief, this information helps nonetheless to explain the motivation for bringing the suit in the first place. Yet, brief writers should provide only that information about the case that the court's opinion writers care to relate.

(B). The second line contains the case citation. It indicates where in the court reporter system the printed opinion for *Board of Regents v. Southworth* is found. The identical case opinion is reported in at least three places; that is, in volume 529 of the *U.S. Reports* beginning on page 217 (529 U.S. 217), in volume 120 of the *Supreme Court Reporter* beginning on page 1346 (120 S.Ct. 1346), and in volume 146 of the *United States Reports, Lawyers' Edition—Second Series* beginning on page 193 (146 L. Ed. 2d 193). The citation also indicates that this opinion was delivered in the year 2000.[26]

It is also possible to read cases online. See: <FindLaw.com>, <Lexis-Nexis.com>, and other widely used and accessible websites. At some point, one may wish to read the entire court opinion in its full unedited version. For example, to shorten *Board of Regents v. Southworth* to the most appropriate points for instruction, we deleted several pages and the original footnotes were eliminated. This common procedure used by writers and editors allows them to keep the size of textbooks within manageable word and page lengths.

(C). The statement of *Facts* should include those circumstances giving rise to the lawsuit as well as the disposition of the case in the courts below. As a general rule, try to put the facts in your own words and keep it *brief*. The brief writer should also stick to the facts articulated by the court without trying to identify the truth or falsity of its recitation. In *Board of Regents v. Southworth*, the facts are easily recited: Student activity fees were used by the University to facilitate speech on campus by funding a diverse group of ideological and political student entities that some students found offensive. The students sought to prevent the University from using student fees in this way because they felt the program violated their First Amendment rights. A federal district court and a court of appeals agreed with the objecting students, but the case was subsequently appealed to the U.S. Supreme Court. It is customary to conclude the facts section with procedural matters, such as what the courts decided below and how the case found its way to the Supreme Court. Though it is not indicated in the text, the U.S. Supreme Court in this case granted the appellant petition for a writ of certiorari ordering the Court of Appeals to send the entire record of the case to the Supreme Court. A writ is granted only if at least four members of the Supreme Court are in agreement.

(D). The *Issue* statement(s) is the next major element of a brief. This is a recitation of a legal question the opinion writer treats as necessary in order to resolve the matter before the court. In *Board of Regents v. Southworth*, the opinion writer poses more than one issue for decision, which is common. Sometimes, the brief writer may also include more than one issue in a single question.

When composing issue statements, keep two rules in mind. First, issue statements should appear in the form of questions that may be answered "yes" or "no." Second, you should phrase issues precisely and specifically with reference to concrete and not abstract legal problems. American courts do not treat hypothetical issues. They resolve real legal issues involving live disputes that affect relationships among people and their property.

(E). Place on one line the *Decision and Action*. Write "yes" or "no" to each issue question listed above in the issue statement(s). Do not attempt at this point to explain the reasons for the court's decision. The action is the court-ordered disposition of the case. In *Board of Regents v. Southworth*, the court of appeals decision is "reversed and remanded." Opinion writers are explicit about such matters, and such statements usually appear at the end of the majority's opinion.

(F). The *Reasoning of the Court* is the heart of the court's legal opinion because it contains the written justification for its disposition of the case. In *Board of Regents v. Southworth*, Justice Kennedy, writing for the majority, has a heavy burden because he contradicts two courts below that relied on the Supreme Court's previous opinions to fashion their decisions. Kennedy indicates that the precedents cited by the courts below are inappropriately applied because the facts are different in those cases. College students objecting to pay for the dissemination of views they dislike by their peers is very different from unions and bar associations forcing their members to contribute to political causes not particularly germane to collective bargaining or the regulation of attorneys in their practice of the law. Rather, Kennedy points to another precedent that is more appropriate—the University of Virginia prohibition of funding a student religious publication. Specifically, in *Rosenberger v. Rector and Visitors of the University of Virginia*, the Court employed the constitutional principle of viewpoint neutrality to strike down the University's prohibition. Sometimes, courts overrule their own previous precedents, but when they do so, justification is provided to assure the legal community and the public that they are not acting arbitrarily. However, in *Board of Regents*, the Supreme Court skillfully distinguished one case from another, fashioning an exception to a general rule based upon the particular facts in the case at hand.

Again, a brief writer should attempt to remain *brief!* Do not include all the words written by the author of the court's opinion. Indeed,

sometimes opinion writers become unnecessarily long-winded, insert-
ing arguments that are unnecessary for the conclusions they reach.
Such utterances are commonly referred to as *obiter dictum*, or simply
dicta. It is easy to confuse dicta pronouncements for reasoning when
composing written briefs. Stick to the point, though judges and justices
do not always abide by the same admonition. It is useful to insert the
opinion writer's name at the beginning of this section of the brief so
that during classroom discussion one may easily distinguish among a
number of opinion authors [e.g., (Reasoning per Kennedy)].

(G). Include a *Concurring Opinion,* if appropriate. Sometimes one
or more members of a court agree with the result of a decision but not
with the intellectual justification offered by the official opinion writer.
Therefore, they may elect to write a separate opinion, as did Justice
Souter in *Board of Regents v. Southworth*. He pens a concurring opinion
for himself and two other justices, Stevens and Breyer.

Such opinions demonstrate different intellectual routes to the same
result and reflect divisions on the court that may be useful in predicting
the results of future litigation. Souter argues that it is unnecessary to
apply a "cast-iron viewpoint neutrality requirement" to this case. He argues instead that Southworth fails to demonstrate that the University's
program is not viewpoint neutral.

(H). Also include any *dissenting opinions,* if offered. This expresses
disagreement with both the result and the reasoning of the court's opinion, although *Board of Regents v. Southworth* contains no such statements of dissent. If there had been a dissenting opinion, it is likely that
the writer would have based the opinion on the reasoning of the courts
below—to wit: the program was not germane to the University's mission, did not further a vital University policy, and imposed too great a
burden on Southworth's free speech rights.

(I). Lastly, write a *Summary of the Legal Principle* that the particular
opinion represents. It is a useful exercise to contemplate what a case
stands for, especially when preparing for student examinations. Try to
accomplish this task in a few lines. For example: University funding of
controversial speech is constitutionally permissible under the First
Amendment if it is viewpoint neutral in its application. However, the
use of student referendum procedures to decide what groups may receive financial assistance raises constitutional questions.

**Box 1.9   Sample Brief: Board of Regents v. Southworth
529 U.S. 217, 120 S.Ct. 1346, 146 L.Ed. 2d 193 (2000)**

Facts: Southworth and other students at the University of Wisconsin at
Madison brought suit challenging the University's policy of funding student
organizations engaged in political or ideological speech based upon student
activity fees that are separate from ordinary tuition fees. The selection of

groups that receive funding is administered through various student body committees and subject to oversight by the administration and the board of regents. Additionally, any group may bypass the committee system and seek funding (or defunding) by requesting a vote of the student body on a referendum requiring a majority vote. A federal district court found for Southworth and a U.S. court of appeals affirmed the district court's opinion in part and reversed and vacated the judgment in part.

Issues:

(1) Does the First Amendment permit a public university to impose activities fees upon its students to fund a program to facilitate extracurricular student speech if the program is viewpoint neutral?

(2) Is the referendum aspect of the University program, which permits a majority of the student body to vote to fund or defund a particular group's speech, potentially a violation of the viewpoint neutrality requirement of the First Amendment?

Decision and Action:

(1) Yes.

(2) Yes; Reversed and Remanded.

Reasoning (per Kennedy in which CJ Rehnquist, O'Connor, Scalia, Thomas, and Ginsburg joined):

(1) Both sides to the dispute agree that the program is viewpoint neutral. The Court's rule in *Rosenberger v. Rector and Visitors of the University of Virginia* is controlling. The program of funding diverse political and ideological groups is designed to expose Wisconsin students to a variety of viewpoints, and as long as this is its operating principle there is no violation of the First Amendment. This case is distinguishable from cases involving compulsory dues payments for political purposes of labor union and bar association members; in those cases, it is possible to distinguish speech germane to the organization from speech that is political and therefore not germane. In university life, however, all speech is in some sense germane to student education. Thus, speech in the university cannot know any bounds. Yet, First Amendment rights must be protected in the University setting, and the way to do that is by imposing the obligation of viewpoint neutrality.

(2) Subjecting participation by ideological or political groups in the University's (fee-specific) program to a majority vote in a referendum raises First Amendment questions. Because the referendum is able to substitute majority determinations for viewpoint neutrality, it may possibly undermine First Amendment protections. A remand is necessary to resolve this point, and the case must be examined in this light.

Concurring Opinion (per Justice Souter, with whom Justices Stevens and Breyer join):

There is no need to impose a "cast iron" viewpoint neutrality requirement to uphold the program that funds various political and ideological groups on campus. That is, Southworth has no claim to relief from the specific viewpoint neutral scheme of the University. First, the program does not threaten his academic freedom. Second, the government, in this case the University of Wisconsin, indirectly transmits a fraction of a student activity fee to organizations that Southworth may find offensive, but this is not the same as a govern-ment body compelling or controlling speech. The student is funding a student organization that only distributes the money to various political and ideological groups and is not itself responsible for the message conveyed by any such objectionable groups. Further, the program aims at broader public discourse and not at limiting public discussion.

Dissent: None.

Summary of Legal Principle: A public university program charging its students an activity fee used to fund a program to facilitate extracurricular student speech that is viewpoint neutral is not a violation of the First Amendment. The use of a student referendum to decide what groups get funding or are defunded may raise First Amendment issues.

Key Terms, Names, and Concepts

Administrative law	Legal positivism
Analytical (positivism) juris-prudence	Legal realism
	Liberty of contract
Aristotle	Loose view of precedent
Branches of law	Mechanical jurisprudence
Case method	Natural law jurisprudence
Civil law	Obiter dictum
Common law	Positive law
Concurring opinion	Precedent
Constitutions	Private law
Criminal law	Progressive societies
Critical legal studies	Public law
Dicta	Rule of law
Dissenting opinion	St. Thomas Aquinas
Elements of a brief	Sir Henry Maine
Friedrich Karl von Savigny	Sociological jurisprudence
Functions of law	Stare decisis
Historical jurisprudence	Static societies
Jurisprudence	Strict view of precedent
Law	Transpersonalized law
Law and economics jurispru-dence	Utilitarianism
	Volksgeist

Discussion Questions

1. What are the various views of the origins of law? Should natural law trump positive law in the making of public policy, for example, in the case of abortion?

2. Should the U.S. Congress possess the authority to prescribe to courts how provisions of the Constitution should be interpreted? In your judgment, is the Supreme Court's decision in *Boerne v. Flores* a good one?

3. What are the main differences between the common law and civil law traditions? Do you prefer the role of judges in one system over the other and why?

4. Comparing the major schools of jurisprudence discussed in this chapter, which one in your opinion is the best guide to judicial decision-making? Why?

5. Do you agree with the general criticism of the legal system offered by proponents of critical legal theory? Does it offer a viable approach to understanding the legal system?

6. If persons make and interpret the law, does the phrase "A nation of laws and not of men" make sense to you?

7. In your opinion, does the enforcement of contemporary drug laws prohibiting the distribution and consumption of drugs including marijuana effectively deter usage? Should we decriminalize the use of marijuana?

8. What are the consequences when judges apply previous precedents strictly and when they apply precedents loosely? Should judges be consistent in how they interpret precedent?

9. Why is it useful to brief court opinions? Why not simply read and mark up one's text and be done with it?

Suggested Additional Reading

Bartlett, K., and R. Kennedy. *Feminist Legal Theory.* Boulder, CO: Westview, 1991.

Baum, Lawrence. *The Puzzle of Judicial Behavior.* Ann Arbor: University of Michigan Press, 1998.

Bishin, William R., and Christopher D. Stone. *Law, Language, Ethics: An Introduction to Law and Legal Method.* Mineola, NY: Foundation Press, 1972.

Bodenheimer, Edgar. *Jurisprudence: The Philosophy and Method of the Law.* Rev. ed. Cambridge, MA: Harvard University Press, 1974.

Brkić, Jovan. *Norm and Order: An Investigation Into Logic, Semantics, and the Theory of Law and Morals.* New York: Humanities Press, 1970.

———. *Legal Reasoning: Semantic and Logical Analysis.* New York: Peter Lang, 1985.

Cardozo, Benjamin. *The Nature of the Judicial Process.* New Haven, CT: Yale University Press, 1945.

Carter, Leif H. *Reason in Law.* 5th ed. New York: Longman, 1998.

Clinton, Robert L. *God, Man and the Law.* Lawrence: University Press of Kansas, 1997.

Cohen, Morris. *Reason and Law.* New York: Free Press, 1950.

d'Entreves, A. P. *Natural Law: An Introduction to Legal Philosophy.* 2nd ed. London: Hutchinson, 1970, 1977.

Dworkin, Ronald. *Law's Empire.* Cambridge, MA: Harvard University Press, 1986.

Farber, Daniel A., and Philip P. Frickey. *Law and Public Choice: A Critical Introduction.* Chicago: University of Chicago Press, 1991.

Fine, Bob. *Democracy and the Rule of Law: Liberal Ideals and Marxist Critiques.* Wolfeboro, NH: Longwood Publishing, 1984.

Frank, Jerome. *Courts on Trial: Myth and Reality in American Justice.* Princeton, NJ: Princeton University Press, 1973.

Friedrich, Carl Joachim. *The Philosophy of Law in Historical Perspectives.* 2nd ed. Chicago: University of Chicago Press, 1963.

Fuller, Lon. *The Morality of Law.* Rev. ed. New Haven, CT: Yale University Press, 1973, 1977.

Glennon, Robert J. *The Iconoclast as Reformer: Jerome Frank's Impact on American Law.* Ithaca, NY: Cornell University, 1985.

Hall, Jerome. *Foundations of Jurisprudence.* Indianapolis: Bobbs-Merrill, 1973.

———. *Readings in Jurisprudence.* Indianapolis: Bobbs-Merrill, 1973.

Levi, Edward. *An Introduction to Legal Reasoning.* Chicago: University of Chicago Press, 1950, 1974.

Lieberman, Jethro K. *The Litigious Society.* New York: Basic Books, 1983.

Llewellyn, Karl N. *The Common Law Tradition: Deciding Appeals.* Boston: Little, Brown, 1962.

Llewellyn, Karl, and E. Adamson Hoebel. *The Cheyenne Way.* Norman: University of Oklahoma Press, 1983.

MacKinnon, Catharine. *Toward a Feminist Theory of the State.* Cambridge, MA: Harvard University Press, 1989.

Maine, Henry. *Ancient Law.* London: Oxford University Press, 1986.

Merryman, John Henry, David S. Clark, and Lawrence M. Friedman. *Law and Social Change in Mediterranean Europe and Latin America: A Handbook of Legal and Social Indicators for Comparative Study.* Dobbs Ferry, NY: Oceana Publications, 1979.

Morris, Clarence, ed. *The Great Legal Philosophers: Selected Readings in Jurisprudence.* Philadelphia: University of Pennsylvania Press, 1971.

Murphy, G. Jeffrie, and L. Jules Coleman. *The Philosophy of Law: An Introduction to Jurisprudence.* Rev. ed. Totowa, NJ: Rowman and Littlefield, 1989, 1990.

Nader, Laura, ed. *Law in Culture and Society.* Chicago: Aldine, 1969.

Neier, Aryeh. *Only Judgement: The Limits of Litigation in Social Change.* Middletown, CT: Wesleyan University, 1985.

Pound, Roscoe. *Social Control Through Law.* New Haven, CT: Yale University Press, 1968.

——. *An Introduction to the Philosophy of Law.* Rev. ed. New Haven, CT: Yale University Press, 1982.

Quinney, Richard. *Critique of Legal Order.* Boston: Little, Brown, 1974.

——. *Class, State, and Crime.* 2nd ed. New York: McKay, 1980.

Rawls, John. *A Theory of Justice.* Cambridge, MA: Belknap Press of Harvard University Press, 1973, 1980, 1986.

Savigny, Friedrick K. *Of the Vocation of Our Age for Legislation and Jurisprudence.* Translated by A. Hayward. London: Littlewood, 1900.

Scheingold, Stuart. *The Politics of Rights: Lawyers, Public Policy, and Political Change.* New Haven, CT: Yale University Press, 1974.

Schur, Edwin. *Law and Society.* New York: Random House, 1968.

Sellers, M. N. S. *The Sacred Fire of Liberty: Republicanism, Liberalism, and the Law.* New York: New York University Press, 1998.

Simon, Rita James, ed. *The Sociology of Law: Interdisciplinary Readings.* San Francisco: Chandler Publishing, 1968.

Smith, Roger M. *Liberalism and American Constitutional Law.* Cambridge, MA: Harvard University Press, 1990.

Summers, Robert. *Law: Its Nature, Functions and Limits.* Englewood Cliffs, NJ: Prentice Hall, 1972.

Tonnies, Ferdinand. *Community and Society.* Edited and translated by Charles P. Loomis. New York: Harper and Row, 1963.

Twining, William, ed. *Legal Theory and Common Law.* Oxford, UK: Basil Blackwell, 1986.

Weber, Max. *On Law in Economy and Society.* Translated with introduction by Max Rheinstein et al. Cambridge, MA: Harvard University Press, 1954.

Weinberg, Lee S., and Judith W. Weinberg, *Law and Society: An Interdisciplinary Introduction.* Washington, DC: University Press of America, 1980.

Zelermyer, William. *The Process of Legal Reasoning.* Englewood Cliffs, NJ: Prentice Hall, 1963.

Endnotes

1. Basil S. Markesinis, *Foreign Law and Comparative Methodology: A Subject and a Thesis* (Oxford, UK: Hart Publishing, 1997); Alec Stone Sweet, *Governing With Judges: Constitutional Politics in Europe* (New York: Oxford University Press, 2000), pp. 130–133.
2. Frances Olsen, "Family Law," *Encyclopedia of the American Judicial System*, Robert J. Janosik, ed. (New York: Charles Scribner's Sons, 1987), p. 312.
3. Edwin W. Patterson, *Jurisprudence: Men and Ideas of the Law* (Brooklyn, NY: Foundation Press, 1953), pp. 332–353.
4. Ibid., pp. 358–376.

5. Ibid., pp. 410–414.
6. Ibid., p. 415.
7. Ibid., pp. 415–416.
8. Albert P. Melone, "Legal Education and Judicial Decisions: Some Negative Findings," *Journal of Legal Education* 26 (1974): 570.
9. Ibid., pp. 570–571.
10. Patterson, *Jurisprudence*, pp. 439–464.
11. Ibid., pp. 67–74, 131–135, 259–273.
12. Ibid., pp. 125–126.
13. Frank Bruni with Jim Yardley, "Inmate Is Executed in Texas as 11th Hour Appeals Fail," *New York Times, National Edition* (June 23, 2000): A18.
14. Tom Campbell and Jeffrey Goldsworthy, eds., *Judicial Power, Democracy and Legal Positivism* (Brookfield, VT: Ashgate Publishing, 2000).
15. Patterson, *Jurisprudence*, pp. 509–537.
16. Ibid., pp. 537–556.
17. David O. Friedrichs, *Law in Our Lives: An Introduction* (Los Angeles: Roxbury Publishing, 2001), pp. 94–98.
18. Ibid., pp. 94–95.
19. Ibid., pp. 90–93.
20. *The Law of Primitive Man: A Study in Comparative Legal Dynamics* (New York: Atheneum, 1968), pp. 275–287.
21. *Courts: A Comparative and Political Analysis* (Chicago: University of Chicago Press, 1981), pp. 1–8.
22. George Gallup, Jr., *The Gallup Poll: Public Opinion 1997* (Wilmington, DE: Scholarly Resources, 1998), p. 207.
23. William Graham Sumner, *Folkways: A Study of the Sociological Importance of Usages, Manners, Customs, Mores, and Morals* (Boston, MA: Ginn & Co., 1913).
24. George Gallup, Jr., *The Gallup Poll*, pp. 257–258.
25. Karl Llewellyn, *The Bramble Bush* (New York: Oceana Publications, 1960), pp. 66–69.
26. For a research guide to court reports, sources of court opinions, and other tools of legal research see Albert P. Melone, *Researching Constitutional Law*, 2nd ed. (Prospect Heights, IL: Waveland, 2000), Chapter 1. ✦

Chapter 2

Legitimacy and the Limits of Authority

Chapter Objectives

Students should understand the meaning of and gain an appreciation for legalism as a dominant ideology in American culture. They should consider why public support for the interrelated concepts of judicial independence and the rule of law is crucial for the ability of courts to render decisions and to make them stick. Students should study the history of the English common law and equity courts as an example of the delicate nature of courts in political systems. They should also learn how these courts laid the groundwork for contemporary substantive and procedural law in America. Lastly, students should note how state and federal judicial institutions resolve conflicts about the power of courts to adjudicate disputes.

Legitimacy and Legalism as Ideology

Judges possess considerable power over life, liberty, property, and the allocation of boundaries of authority within the U.S. political system. Why are courts permitted to fulfill such vital functions in society? At the most simplistic level, the answer is that political authorities have given judges the power to resolve disputes in accordance with certain formal rules. However, this response begs the question.

Depending upon the political subsystem, judges and justices are either appointed, sometimes for life, or elected in partisan or nonpartisan elections that often lack genuine competition among candidates. At times, our democratic sensibilities are offended when judges, unaccountable to the people, effectively make new law and strike down or modify existing laws that are the products of popularly elected legislatures and political executives. Moreover, when disputing parties bring their cases to court, they do not ordinarily have the option of choosing the presiding judges and justices. It soon dawns on them that they have not consented to the legal norms governing the disposition of their case; they also realize that third parties called judges find, articulate, or create the norms that they have no hand in formulating. Even more offensive, the resulting decisions are often not wholly satisfactory to either party, who observe that the interests of the court or the larger political regime may assume greater importance than the determination of justice. Professor Martin Shapiro calls this the problem of *legitimacy* of courts.[1]

On the other hand, persistent efforts by public and private actors serve to ameliorate the systemic problem of legitimacy. They seek support for judicial institutions through political socialization and by overt appeals to the values implicit in the concepts of the *rule of law* and of judicial independence. Indeed, it is a matter of ideology for Americans, whose daily conversation is riddled with legalistic jargon, for whom public entertainment portrays courtroom drama, and whose political theory is immersed in such legal concepts as contracts, rights, duties, privileges, and immunities.

The belief in the rule of law, the disdain for vague generalities, the piecemeal solution to human problems, the structuring of human relations into claims and counterclaims, and the belief that rules are "there" create what Judith N. Shklar termed *legalism* as a social outlook.[2] Thus, the real strength of the political system rests neither with the violence of the state nor a ruling faction, but rather with the public acceptance of a worldview celebrating order and the rule of law as the social cement of this political system. Hence, legalism is not just another ideology; it is the dominant ideology. It teaches that justice is realized through law. Undeniably, Americans are taught that they have rights and the courts function to vindicate those basic rights.[3]

The responsiveness of U.S. citizens to legal symbols places legal professionals in the enviable position of simultaneously being "above" politics, yet in the midst of the political thicket.[4] The observations of Alexis de Tocqueville, a keen French observer of early nineteenth-century America, seems as applicable today as when he wrote his famous book, *Democracy in America* (1835).[5]

Box 2.1   From *Democracy in America* (1835), by Alexis de Tocqueville

S carcely any political question arises in the United States that is not resolved, sooner or later, into a judicial question. Hence all parties are obliged to borrow, in their daily controversies, the ideas, and even the language, peculiar to judicial proceedings. As most public men are or have been legal practitioners, they introduce the customs and technicalities of their profession into the management of public affairs. The jury extends this habit to all classes. The language of the law thus becomes, in some measure, a vulgar tongue; the spirit of the law, which is produced in the schools and courts of justice gradually penetrates beyond their walls into the bosom of society, where it descends to the lowest classes, so that at last the whole people contract the habits and tastes of judicial magistrates. The lawyers of the United States form a party which is but little feared and scarcely perceived, which has no badge peculiar to itself, which adopts itself with great flexibility to the exigencies of the time and accommodates itself without resistance to all the movements of the social body. But this party extends over the whole community and penetrates into all the classes which compose it; it acts upon the country imperceptibly, but finally fashions it to suit its own purposes. . . .

Although legalism as an ideology is evident to some degree in any organized society, Tocqueville's cultural explanation for the United States is appealing if not entirely persuasive. In other political cultures with distinct ideological divisions, however, legalism as practiced in the United States does not possess as much explanatory power.

Consider a study in the early 1970s by the Danish political scientist Mogens Pederson. He was concerned with unsatisfactory explanations of why lawyers are elected to legislatures far in excess of their numbers in the population. Pederson found that of the 21 countries he studied, excluding the United States, the total range of lawyer representation was from 2 to 33 percent; and in 11 of them, none exceeded 10 percent total lawyers. Clearly, not all Western democracies exhibit as high a rate of lawyer overrepresentation in the legislatures as the U.S. Congress, where commonly over half of its members are lawyers by profession. Pederson then tested whether the so-called explanations for this outcome applied cross-culturally; that is, he studied differences between the United States with about 56 percent lawyers in the U.S. House of Representatives and Denmark's Folketing with 4 percent lawyers. If the suggested explanations for lawyer overrepresentation were present in both political cultures, then the alleged causes could not be the explanation. He found that lawyers in both cultures enjoy relatively high status, possess similar professional skills, enjoy economic independence, and experience law and politics as convergent professions. Consequently, these four possible explanations do not meet the test of scientific scrutiny.[6]

Pederson went on to speculate that the explanation for lawyer overrepresentation in legislative settings may be found in the differences between American political parties, which tend to be nonideological and pragmatic, and Danish party organizations, which tend to be highly ideological and programmatic. In the United States, the lack of strong ideological parties permits, in fact encourages, American lawyers from both major parties to seek and be elected to public office. The lawyer is, after all, the consummate pragmatist, who is trained to take any side of an issue. The American political culture, with its seeming lack of strong ideological demands, presents an ideal environment for the high priests of system maintenance. But in Denmark, where competing ideologies of a transformative nature are historically prevalent, lawyers have been viewed as part of a conservative faction and thus were long ostracized from the political process.[7]

As powerful as the support of legalism as an ideology may be in any given culture, including the United States, the actions of courts may affect, for better or for worse, their own legitimacy. Researchers studying courts in the early and mid-1990s found that many European high courts enjoy greater public support, even higher than that enjoyed by the U.S. Supreme Court. They noted that generally when citizens are aware of courts, they tend also to support them. These researchers also found that this positive attitude is associated with being exposed to the legitimizing symbols that all courts employ. Interestingly, they concluded that public support for courts does not spontaneously arise from intellectual abstractions about the virtues entailed in the rule of law. Rather, they speculated, courts render decisions that various minorities, factions, classes, or segments in society view favorably. If over time courts rule in favor of enough minorities, public support develops incrementally and ultimately creates the deep reservoir of support necessary for them to maintain themselves against occasional attacks launched by other political actors and losing parties in litigation.[8]

Sometimes, however, judges and justices may inflict wounds upon their courts by appearing to step over the fuzzy line between law and politics. The divisions expressed among the members of the U.S. Supreme Court in the case of *Bush v. Gore* (2000) dramatically illustrate this point, as do the reactions of other legal professionals and other elites to that highly controversial decision. Nonetheless, mass public support for the U.S. Supreme Court remains relatively high. This reflects the deeply ingrained level of support (enjoyed by courts generally in this country) which is constantly being reinforced by the symbols, models, and metaphors in our public rhetoric.

Bush v. Gore and Legitimacy

The case arose as a result of the exceedingly close vote for president in Florida. By mid-evening on Election Day, November 6, 2000, it was clear that the winner of Florida's 25 electoral votes would become the new president. On the basis of exit voter interviews, the television networks first declared Vice President Albert Gore the winner in Florida. Then, later in the evening, the networks reversed themselves, declaring Bush the winner by a narrow margin. At that point, candidate Gore phoned Governor Bush, conceding the election. Later, in the wee hours of the morning, the networks reversed themselves once again, but this time they declared the election too close to call. At this point, Gore called Bush again but this time he rescinded his earlier concession. The late returns indicated that Bush held a slight lead by a few thousand votes. Almost immediately, however, there were charges of voting irregularities. Prominent among the complaints heard in the media, Jewish-American voters in West Palm Beach claimed that because of the form of the ballot (butterfly ballot), they may have cast their votes erroneously for Pat Buchanan, the candidate of the Reform Party—a person thought by many Jews to be unfriendly to the state of Israel. Even Buchanan thought it unlikely that the voters in this heavily Jewish-American and Democratic Party-oriented community really intended to vote for him. He agreed that the butterfly ballot had probably confused many elderly voters. Further, some African American and Hispanic voters claimed they were improperly turned away from the polls. In the end, however, these charges did not receive the greatest public attention or the most serious judicial scrutiny.

Will his vote count?

Because the overall difference in the total votes for each candidate was 1,784 votes (less than one half of one percent of the total votes cast in the state for president), Florida law mandated an automatic recount. The recount consisted of repeating the counting proceedings employed in the first instance, namely, running punch card ballots through automatic counting machines or recounting lever machines or optical scan ballots in those counties employing them. Reports indicated that those counties using punch cards had greater rates of undervoting than counties employing lever machines or optical scan sheets. The recount resulted in a reduced overall difference in votes between Bush and Gore. Nonetheless, Bush remained ahead in the vote tally.

In view of the closeness of the election results, the Florida Democratic Party Executive Committee requested that manual recounts be conducted in Broward, Miami-Dade, Palm Beach, and Volusia counties. Consistent with past practices and statutory law, these county-canvassing boards conducted sample manual recounts of at least one percent of the ballots cast. Several of the boards determined that the manual recounts demonstrated "error in the vote tabulation that could affect the outcome of the election."[9]

Error occurred because voters had failed to successfully punch holes through the voting cards in such a manner as to completely remove paper that remained partially attached. Adding to our popular lexicon as a nation, these dangling pieces of paper are called "chads," or "hanging chads (dangling chads)." In some instances, voters had not actually penetrated the paper with the supplied metal stylus but instead indented the punch hole space next to a candidate's name without actually removing any of the four-cornered chad. This result came to be called a "dimpled" or "pregnant" chad. Because in some unknown number of instances, the chads in their various forms of indentation or removal prevented the punched holes from being accurately read by the voting machines, these votes were never counted. Such votes are called "undervotes."

Given the evidence of undervotes, the county canvassing boards in question voted to conduct countywide manual recounts. Florida law provided, however, that all recounts must be completed within seven days of the Election Day, and the state Division of Elections issued an advisory opinion affirming the seven-day deadline. At that point, one of the counties filed suit in Leon County Court seeking declaratory and injunctive relief, and the candidates were allowed to intervene as parties to the suit. Both the Gore and Bush forces employed armies of lawyers to engage in televised battle in the trenches of the Florida courts and later to argue the matter in U.S. courts including, most decisively, the U.S. Supreme Court.

On November 14, 2000, the Leon County Court ruled that the seven-day deadline was mandatory. It also ruled, however, that the Volusia Board could amend its returns at a later date and that Republican Secretary of State Katherine Harris could exercise her discretion in determining whether to ignore the amended returns. Later on that date, the Volusia Board and the Palm Beach Board jointly filed a notice of appeal. Secretary of State Harris announced she was in receipt of the certified returns (meaning the results of the initial machine recount, not the results of manual recounts) from all the counties. She indicated that if any of the county voting officials sought any change in the results from their counties, they must file a written statement with her specifying "the facts and circumstances justifying any belief on their part that should be allowed to amend the certified returns previously filed."[10] The counties filed their written statements with Secretary Harris, but she rejected the reasons they gave and again she announced the earlier certified totals of the four counties as final.

On November 16, 2000, Vice President Gore and the Florida Democratic Party filed a motion in circuit court in Leon County seeking to compel Secretary Harris to accept amended returns from the contested counties. After conducting a hearing the court denied relief, but the plaintiffs appealed the matter to the state's First District Court of Appeal. That body certified the trial court's order to the Florida Supreme Court. On November 21, the Florida Supreme Court reversed the trial court. It stated that because of several ambiguities in the Florida Election Code, legislative intent as understood through well-accepted rules of statutory construction mandated a remedy based on the facts in this case. The next day, November 22, Governor Bush appealed the Florida Supreme Court decision to the U.S. Supreme Court, and two days later the nation's highest court accepted jurisdiction in the case. On December 1, the U.S. Supreme Court heard oral arguments of which tape recordings were made public, and within hours the electronic media aired them widely. On December 4, the Supreme Court unanimously decided to vacate the Florida Supreme Court decision, asking for a better explanation of its ruling. The Court specifically wanted the Florida Supreme Court to respond to the charge that, in its interpretation of Florida statutory and case law, it had encroached on legislative authority, violating the constitutional principle of separation of powers.

In the meantime, and consistent with usual procedures, the trial commenced on December 2 in Leon County Circuit Court with Judge N. Sanders Sauls presiding. The trial ended on December 3 after more than 22 hours of testimony before Judge Sauls, and on December 4, he rejected Gore's request for manual recounts in the four disputed counties. The Florida Supreme Court heard Vice President Gore's appeal on December 7, and on December 8, in a 4–3 decision, the Florida high court reversed Judge Sauls. From Gore's perspective, it appeared that he was now in a position to win the election because finally "all the votes would be counted."

In a stunning turn of events, on the next day, Saturday, December 9, 2000, the U.S. Supreme Court granted a request from the Bush Campaign for a stay of the Florida Supreme Court order, thereby halting any manual recounts to go forward in Florida. In fact, the Supreme Court's order came at a time when the counties were just beginning to manually recount the undercounted votes. Both sides filed written briefs on December 10, and on December 11, the U.S. Supreme Court heard oral arguments. On December 12, 2000, by a 5–4 vote, the justices declared the Florida Supreme Court-ordered recount unconstitutional.

In an unsigned, five-member per curiam opinion, the majority ruled that the Florida Supreme Court's decision violated the Equal Protection Clause of the Fourteenth Amendment because it failed to establish specific standards of counting votes to ensure its equal application throughout the state. It was possible, the majority reasoned, that a vote, disqualified in one county because of the failure of the voting machines to read chads (dimpled or otherwise), may be machine counted in another county and vice versa. Consequently, the recount procedure envisioned by the Florida courts was inconsistent with the minimum procedures necessary to protect the fundamental rights of each voter in a statewide election recount under the authority of a single state judicial officer. A significant problem with the reasoning of the majority of the U.S. Supreme Court is that in their zeal to protect the fundamental rights of citizens whose votes may not be counted, they made sure that none of the undervotes were counted. That is, the only logical way the majority could get around the problem of counting all the votes was to throw out the entire election. Yet, the Court majority conceded that it might be possible for the Florida courts to devise a uniform plan for counting all the votes in the state. But because the deadline was near for the selection of state electors to the Electoral College, there was insufficient time to fashion any such remedy.

In many academic circles, the U.S. Supreme Court's opinion was greeted with derision. Critics howled that the Supreme Court had selected the president, not the voters. Many Supreme Court observers thought that it should not have accepted jurisdiction in the first place. The process of elections is principally a state matter and the Rehnquist Supreme Court had previously ruled consistently in favor of states' rights in cases involving struggles between national and state power. Many thought that given its states' rights orientation, the Court might predictably rule that state courts may definitively rule on matters of state law and that the federal courts should defer to such judgments.

Further, members of the Rehnquist Court and its supporters claim to believe in judicial self-restraint; a political matter such as a presidential election is essentially one that ought to be decided by other institutions of government and the people themselves. In this case, if the Court had allowed the manual recounts to go forward as ordered by the Florida Supreme Court, then the political judgment concerning the rightful winner of the election would rest squarely with the voters of Florida. The spectacle of nine unelected persons deciding the election, seven of whom were appointed by Republican presidents, would have been avoided.

In fairness, however, the Supreme Court's majority was persuaded that the case presented a significant equal protection problem because, in their view, the standards set out in the Florida Supreme Court's recount order varied from county to county. Yet, they also expressed the view that although it might be possible to overcome this difficulty, calendar constraints, due to the requirement that the state select its electors in time for the meeting of the Electoral College, made such a remedy impractical. Unfortunately for Vice President Gore and his supporters, including the plurality of the nation's voters (he won the popular vote by about 350,000 votes but lost the electoral college by four votes), the U.S. Supreme Court's own actions and orders made it impossible for the design of a suitable remedy to meet the time constraints.

This lends an "I gotcha!" quality to the Court's opinion that has widely been interpreted as an exercise in sophistry. Also, the Electoral College was not scheduled to meet until December 18, six days after the Court's December 12, 2000, decision. Furthermore, the 1960 presidential election in Hawaii serves as a historical precedent for discarding the December deadlines. Hawaii appointed two slates of electors and Congress counted the one appointed on January 4, 1961, well after the December 12 and 18 statutory deadlines designed to insure that states will be able to name electors and have their votes counted in a timely fashion.

Finally, critics question the Court's sincerity about its determination to guard the Fourteenth Amendment's Equal Protection Clause. The per curiam decision explicitly states: "Our consideration is limited to the present circumstance," adding, "the problem of equal protection in election processes generally presents many complexities." Indubitably, the Supreme Court is not poised to launch a new constitutional attack on state electoral practices.

Just days before the chief justice swore in the new president, 660 professors from about half of the nation's law schools denounced the opinion in an advertisement that appeared in the *New York Times*. They complained that the justices ignored the facts and acted as political proponents for candidate Bush, not as judges. Many in and out of academia view the decision as a *coup d'état*, a power grab going against all legal precedent. Many law professors feel compelled to change their courses to reflect the legal realist perspective that judges in fact make law; they do not simply find it, as proponents of the analytical and mechanical schools of jurisprudence would have us believe.[11]

The per curiam, concurring and dissenting written opinions in *Bush v. Gore* and in-depth analyses of all parts of the opinion by pundits and scholars alike, has sparked lively debate throughout the country. One central aspect of the debate centers on the problem of legitimacy. Within the Supreme Court itself the legitimacy of the decision was plainly on the minds of the justices. There is little doubt that the Court divided along ideological lines. The most conservative members of the Court (Rehnquist, Scalia, Thomas, Kennedy, and O'Connor) voted in favor of Bush. The more moderate to liberal members of the Court (Stevens, Souter, Breyer, and Ginsburg) voted in favor of Gore. To be sure, both ideological camps were fully cognizant of the possible ill effects of this decision on the Court's deep reservoir of public support. Consider the excerpted statements of the various justices in their written opinions in this case.

Box 2.2	Excerpts From *Bush v. Gore* U.S. Supreme Court 531 U.S. 99 (2000)

From the per curiam opinion: None are more conscious of the vital limits on judicial authority than are the members of this Court, and none stand more in admiration of the Constitution's design to leave the selection of the President to the people, through their legislatures, and to the political sphere. When contending parties invoke the process of the courts, however, it becomes our unsought responsibility to resolve the federal and constitutional issues the . . . judicial system has been forced to confront.

From the concurring opinion of Chief Justice Rehnquist, with whom Justices Scalia and Thomas join: In most cases, comity and respect for federalism compel us to defer to the decisions of state courts on issues of state law. That practice reflects our understanding that the decisions of state courts are definitive pronouncements of the will of the States as sovereigns. Cf. Erie R. Co. v. Tompkins, 304 U.S. 64, (1938). Of course, in ordinary cases, the distribution of powers among the branches of a State's government raises no questions of federal constitutional law, subject to the requirement that the government be republican in character. See U.S. Const., Art. IV, § 4. But there are a few exceptional cases in which the Constitution imposes a duty or confers a power on a particular branch of a State's . . . government. This is one of them. Article II, § 1, cl. 2, provides that 'each State shall appoint, in such Manner as the Legislature thereof may direct,' electors for President and Vice President. Thus, the text of the election law itself, and not just its interpretation by the courts of the States, takes on independent significance.

From Justice Stevens' dissenting opinion, with whom Justices Ginsburg and Breyer join: The Constitution assigns to the States the primary responsibility for determining the manner of selecting the presidential electors. See Art. II, § 1, cl. 2. When questions arise about the meaning of state laws, including election laws, it is our settled practice to accept the opinions of the highest courts of the States as providing the final answers. On rare occasions, however, either federal statutes or the Federal Constitution may . . . require federal judicial intervention in state elections. This is not such an occasion. . . . What must underlie petitioners' entire federal assault on the Florida election procedures is an unstated lack of confidence in the impartiality and capacity of the state judges who would make the critical decisions if the vote count were to proceed. Otherwise, their position is wholly without merit. The endorsement of that position by the majority of this Court can only lend credence to the most cynical appraisal of the work of judges throughout the land. It is confidence in the men and women who administer the judicial system that is the true backbone of the rule of law. Time will one day heal the wound to that confidence that will be inflicted by today's decision. One thing, however, is certain. Although we may never know with complete certainty the identity of the winner of this year's Presidential election, the identity of the loser is perfectly clear. It is the Nation's confidence in the judge as an impartial guardian of the rule of law.

From Justice Ginsburg's dissenting opinion: Time is short in part because of the Court's entry of a stay on December 9, several hours after an able circuit judge in Leon County had begun to superintend the recount process. More fundamentally, the Court's reluctance . . . to let the recount go forward—despite its suggestion that 'the search for intent can be confined by specific rules designed to ensure uniform treatment,' . . . ultimately turns on its own judgment about the practical realities of implementing a recount, not the judgment of those much closer to the process.

> **From Justice Souter's dissent, joined by Justices Breyer, Stevens, and Ginsburg:** If this Court had allowed the State to follow the course indicated by the opinions of its own Supreme Court, it is entirely possible that there would ultimately have been no issue requiring our review, and political tension could have worked itself out in the Congress following the procedure provided in 3 U.S.C. § 15. The case being before us, . . . however, its resolution by the majority is another erroneous decision.

Many scholars and critics of the opinion expressed the view that the Supreme Court had probably damaged its legitimacy with the public. That is, the deep reservoir of public support for the Court, otherwise called *diffuse support*, may have been dissipated or eroded by the Court's specific opinion in *Bush v. Gore* because the decision was obviously political and motivated by partisan attachments.

No doubt many political elites and Supreme Court scholars found the decision to be flawed and badly misguided. The reasons expressed in the dissenting opinions of the justices themselves alone provide sufficient grounds for criticism. Empirical evidence supports the proposition that when opinion leaders dislike specific court decisions, their diffuse support for the institution may be adversely impacted. Because opinion leaders in Congress, for example, are in a position to adversely affect the Supreme Court through such measures as budgetary authorizations and the removal of appellate jurisdiction, their level of support may be crucial to the well-being of the judicial institution. Yet, as pointed out by astute scholarly observers, because there are many centers of political power in this country, it is possible for elites to cancel out the negative support for the Court in one institution by the support of political actors elsewhere.[12] This has probably been the case with elite reaction to the decision in *Bush v. Gore*. Though many members of Congress were upset with the Court's ruling, other elected officials in and out of Congress were highly supportive and, at least in the near term, the negative and positive views served to cancel out each other. The same can be said about support of the mass public, with some additional insights.

Political scientists who conducted surveys of the public in the immediate aftermath of *Bush v. Gore* concluded that *specific support* for the Court's ruling ran along partisan lines. Overall support for the Supreme Court as an institution increased among Republican Party identifiers and it decreased among Democratic Party supporters. Therefore, the switch in support among the party faithful cancelled the effects of each with the result that the deep level of support for the Supreme Court has remained about the same as it was before the important election decision.[13] However, one careful study found that when persons concluded that the decision was based on legal criteria, support for the court in terms of its legitimacy was enhanced.[14]

In the end, most Americans supported the actions of the Supreme Court in the presidential contest; they believe the decision was fairly made, and they believe that the Bush presidency is legitimate. African American citizens are a glaring exception to that finding. Only 22 percent, compared with 69.2 percent of whites, believe that law was the defining criterion in the outcome of the case, and only a slim majority of blacks (55.2 percent) were reported willing to regard Bush as the legitimate president, compared with about 90 percent of whites.[15] Clearly, the Supreme Court's legitimacy remains strong and enduring even in light of its direct involvement in the selection of a president of the United States who received fewer votes than his principal opponent.

Jurisdiction and Common Law Courts

It is apparent that legalism as an ideology, coupled with elite and non-elite support for judicial independence, does not just happen. It is the result of many years of historical development. In England, where the common law was born, respect for the rule of law took centuries to develop. Satisfying public needs and demands was a slow and sometimes arduous, if not dangerous, process. This took place through the adjustment and creation of boundaries of authority precipitated by the demands of a changing society. The concept and practices of *jurisdiction* lay at the center of the creation of the institutional legitimacy of courts in the Anglo-American tradition.

Jurisdiction is the power or authority of a court to adjudicate a case. Without jurisdiction, a court's judgment is null and void. The story of how the crown courts of England acquired jurisdiction is consistent with the theory that support for judicial institutions is an incremental matter of acquiring support among various publics (factions). This story is also testament to the political acumen of the crown and its judicial functionaries.

It began with the Norman Conquest of England in 1066 and entails the creation of appropriate jurisdiction for the crown's courts in competition with the older courts of the feudal landlords and church hierarchy. William the Conqueror inherited a legal system based on feudalism that began as a way for people to band together to solve common problems, such as food shortages, a lack of common currency and trade, and vulnerability to attacks by foreigners. At the center of this social structure was a class system in which all members of the community knew their place and each owed certain duties to the others. Lords and their ladies ruled the small feudal states, and they pledged their allegiance to the monarch of the realm.

The local lords were the authority figures, who maintained law and order within the local communities by providing protection to the serfs with their army of knights. Most ordinary folks in feudal states were serfs, who worked the lord's land to produce food and other necessities of life. They should not be confused with slaves, because they were not regarded as property. Nonetheless, the serfs owed their lords a certain amount of what they produced every year in return for the protection services of the lord's knights. This system of class relationships was formalized through feudal oaths of fidelity, wherein parties pledged their services in return for land or other considerations. Its fundamental unit of politics and economics was land, what today we call *real property*. Those who controlled the land controlled the wealth of the nation. As a result, local landowners and newly empowered barons—feudal tenants of the king or any higher-ranking lord—enjoyed power throughout the countryside that rivaled the king's authority.[16]

As the sovereign from 1066 to 1087, William the Conqueror granted portions of his newly conquered lands to loyal followers, and in the process Normans displaced Saxons as tenants-in-chief to the king. In turn, they swore fealty to him, promising to provide a certain number of men to serve in the king's army for a specified number of days each year and a sum of money to be deposited in the king's treasury. In addition, high-ranking churchmen were part of the feudal system because bishops and abbots also held land directly from the king and owed him a duty of prayers, counsel, and knightly service.[17] Saxons were permitted to possess land, but they held their land at the pleasure of Norman lords and barons.

In this hierarchical system, the Normans served as the king's government officials. Yet, the king's authority was not always secure. Whether the local landowners were Norman or Saxon, neither was happy to pay taxes to the crown or to yield their governing authority to a king riding to the hounds or sitting in a distant castle. If the feudal lords felt strongly that the king was abusing his privileges and failing to live up to his duty to them, then they would force the king to make concessions or cause him to be overthrown.

As a consequence of their precarious positions, monarchs had a vital interest in the centralization of government; they needed to insulate themselves from the collective might of local centers of power within the realm. Their interest included centralizing the authority of courts. The barons, together with the local hundred and shire courts of the previous Saxon era, however, controlled the local feudal courts. So the monarchs needed a way to effectively deal with these power brokers without figuratively or literally "losing their heads."

The crown found a solution in what is known as the *Eyre system* of dispute settlement. The king appointed temporary delegates who administered the crown's law by traveling the countryside as officers of the crown. In the process, they settled disputes and often satisfied pleas for justice by the less powerful in society. Professor Martin Shapiro noted that because these appointees were temporary, they were unable to establish ties with local elites. Shrewdly, therefore, the king could count on his itinerate officers to serve his interests alone. Also, from time to time, the king would travel about to render justice. When he did, he was usually accompanied by his Council. Later, the Council was given authority to hear cases when the king was abroad.[18]

Specialized Royal Courts

During his reign, Henry II (1154–1189) made a concerted effort to consolidate control over the court system, a strategic move that led to centralizing his authority over all of his subjects. Ultimately, his actions resulted in a system of royal courts and a common law applicable to England as a whole. This movement toward a common law for all of England started with the feudal assumptions and subsequent implementation of the royal claim to ownership of all the land of England.[19]

It had long been uncontested that the king's court had the authority to decide land cases involving tenants-in-chief, who held land parcels directly from the crown. Meanwhile, disputes between lesser lords were decided in the primary tenant's court. The crown interfered with the authority of the landed gentry only in matters involving important land interests, in which case a *writ of right* from the monarch was required to adjudicate a dispute. A writ of right was a formal document ordering the lord to administer justice between a plaintiff who demanded possession of the land and a defendant who was allegedly in wrongful possession of the land. The writ provided that if the lord failed in this crown-imposed duty, the monarch would adjudicate the dispute himself. Over time, a legal fiction evolved that the lords had surrendered to the king their right to hold court. Writs eventually were issued directly to the defendant, bypassing local courts altogether and bringing cases involving land to the royal courts.[20]

The generic obligation to have land (real property) disputes decided by the central authority also took the form of a *praecipe*, which instructed local sheriffs to order a person in wrongful possession of land to restore it to the complaining party. Otherwise, one must explain the failure to do so in the presence of the king's justices. This legal process caused much resentment among the feudal lords. Indeed, they won a temporary victory with Chapter 34 of the Magna Carta (1215), proclaiming, "The writ called *Praecipe* shall not for the future be issued to anyone concerning any tenement whereby a free man may lose his court." Nonetheless, this victory for the lords proved ineffective as the king's officers found ways to evade the clause.[21] In the end, whatever form the writ of right took, most litigation involving landed estates was directed by some form of writ to the royal courts.[22]

The writ of right had limited utility for wronged parties because it applied only to freeholders who had been dispossessed of their entire estates. There arose many situations, as is the case today, when property owners were not actually thrown from the land but were nonetheless prevented from the full enjoyment of their property. For example, a plaintiff's property might be flooded or otherwise devalued by a neighbor's diversion of a stream or a watermill; or, as is all too common a nuisance today, a neighbor's barking dog may prevent the landowner from getting a peaceful night's rest. Consequently, the king created a new series of writs called *possessory assizes*. They were designed to remedy defects in the writ of right, including primitive modes of proof and the ability of third parties to contest the decision of the royal court, if they acted within a year and a day.[23]

The possessory assizes proved popular with the king's subjects throughout the realm and many cases were brought to the King's Council (*Curia Regis*) for adjudication. But this method proved too heavy a burden, and in 1178 five justices were appointed from the king's attendants to hear cases. Although formally regarded as subservient to the King's Council, these justices differed from the earlier Eyre system justices of the king in that they possessed a continuing and not an ad hoc (temporary) commission. Moreover, the conclusions of their proceedings were reported in the King's Council, and in theory the Council made the formal decision.[24] But their very existence in effect marked the split from *Curia Regis* and the development of the three major common law courts: *Common Pleas, King's Bench,* and the *Exchequer of Pleas*. This development is especially significant because it is the origin of a separate and what the English call an independent judiciary that "knows neither fear nor favor."

Court of Common Pleas

Before being admitted to the Court of Common Pleas, litigants had to first purchase a writ from the office of the chancellor. The type of cases the Court of Common Pleas could hear increased only gradually because each addition to the chancellor's register of writs was an infringement on the jurisdiction of the older communal, seignorial, or ecclesiastical courts. In the century following 1178, the bench gradually freed itself of subservience to the Council. In 1234, it started to keep its own records, and in 1274 it was given a chief justice. By 1330, it acquired its final name, the Court of Common Pleas.[25]

Besides significant jurisdiction over land cases, Common Pleas soon acquired jurisdiction over what today is referred to as the law of contracts: civil disputes, such as actions for damages for nonperformance of a contractual obligation under a sealed instrument by the *writ of covenant*, and actions to enforce payment of the agreed price of goods sold and delivered by the *writ of debt*. The court could not invent these writs because only the chancellor, on authority of the Council, had the power to issue them.[26] Significantly, then, the origin of today's laws of property and contract is traceable to this great court. We discuss the main features of today's law of property and of contracts in separate chapters in Parts III and IV of this text.

Court of King's Bench

Just as the cases involving land became so numerous that a court system was demanded, the same came to pass for criminal matters. The development of King's Bench marks a second split from the King's Council. From its start, the Court of King's Bench was a criminal court and a court of review over civil cases originating in the Court of Common Pleas. Most criminal conduct, particularly instances of physical misconduct, involved culpable defendants (tortfeasors) who had inflicted harm upon damaged plaintiffs, who were seeking to be made "whole again" through the payment of money.[27] For example, a simple battery is not only a criminal offense against the sovereign but also a civil offense against a person, for whom pecuniary compensation may be appropriate. In today's world, that entails compensation to pay bills associated with the battery, such as time off from work and medical expenses.

By the time of the reign of Edward I (1272–1307), King's Bench had extended its criminal jurisdiction to the civil side of the case. When a person committed a breach of the king's peace, the Court of King's Bench took jurisdiction over the accused. But then it dropped the criminal aspect of the case and instead tried the civil suit.[28] King's Bench was responsible for aiding in the development of not only the common law of crimes but also the substantive field of law known today as torts. Both tort law and criminal law are discussed more fully in separate chapters devoted to each subject found in Part III of this text.

Exchequer of Pleas

Effective government requires the ability not only to make and enforce laws but also to raise revenues for its upkeep. The Exchequer is the British equivalent of the U.S. Treasury Department. Its name comes from the Latin word *scaccarium,* meaning "chessboard," because money due the king was placed on a table covered in a checkered cloth.[29]

As part of its function, the Exchequer had the responsibility of deciding legal questions of tax liability to the crown. In many instances, the crown's debtors claimed they could not presently pay their overdue tax bill because another who owed them a debt had failed to make payment in a timely fashion. Around 1326, the famous procedure of the *writ of quo minus* was invented, providing a win-win solution to this problem. The debtor of the crown's debtor was ordered to court to determine if in fact the debt had not been paid. If not, then the Court of Exchequer of Pleas ordered the debtor to pay the debt and in turn the crown's debtor was then in a position to pay his overdue taxes to the government. Obviously, quo minus became an ideal way to collect bad debts. As time passed, the claim of the tax debtor became entirely fictitious and the writ of quo minus became a principal way for persons to collect on bad debts. Indeed, the law of debts was created and honed in this court.[30]

We devote Chapter 16 to a discussion of tax law in the United States today.

Box 2.3   Standard Writs

The royal courts responded to the pleadings of aggrieved parties by issuing writs ordering sheriffs to bring the alleged wrongdoers before judges on prescribed days to answer complaints against them. The writs became standardized, requiring that the facts fit one of the existing writs before the court could take jurisdiction in the case. Examples of writs include the following:

   a. Assumpsit—an action for damages for the nonperformance of a contractual obligation not under seal.

   b. Covenant—an action for damages for abridging a contract under seal.

   c. Debt—an action to recover a certain specific sum of money.

   d. Detinue—an action to recover personal property from a person who had acquired it legally but retained the property without the owner's consent.

   e. Trespass—an action for damages resulting from the direct and immediate injury of a person or of property.

   f. Trespass on the Case—an action resulting in an injury to a person that was the indirect consequence of the defendant's act.

   g. Replevin—an action to recover possession of unlawfully acquired goods.

   h. Trover—an action for damages against a defendant who found a plaintiff's personal property and wrongfully converted it for his own use.

Court of Chancery-Equity

The three great common law courts (Common Pleas, King's Court, and Exchequer of Pleas) were most instrumental in creating a law common to all of England. These courts and their remedies, however, were not always adequate for the task. Although under the writ system, forms of action were stretched to cover a number of situations not originally contemplated when they were created, many forms of action brought by plaintiffs were dismissed because they did not fit the narrow requirements of particular existing writs. Recall that common law courts were created in a feudal environment. Occasionally, there were jurisdictional conflicts among these three courts and between the royal courts and church courts.[31] What is more telling about why court jurisdictions became contentious is that the economic foundations of English society began to change due to changes in trade and commerce. The movement from a feudal to a mercantile and later a manufacturing capitalist economic order meant the development of a capitalist upper class and the decline of the landed aristocracy. In this changing economic environment, legal relations were also bound to change.[32]

The institutionalization of the Court of Chancery began when appeals for remedies were made directly to the king and his Council because the existing law courts provided none. The Council then formally referred petitions to its most powerful member, the Lord Chancellor, for action. It was from the Chancellor's office that writs were first issued, which in turn started in motion the jurisdictional machinery of the common law courts. Thus, the Chancellor was in a strategic position to observe and intervene in the judicial process as he thought the situation warranted. Early in the development of the equity institution, before 1474, the Chancellor considered petitions for extraordinary remedies and would submit his recommendations to the King's Council for final action. In some cases, the Council instructed the Chancellor on how he should mete out justice. Usually, however, the Lord Chancellor made suggestions that were simply accepted by the Council.[33]

In the early years of its development, equity jurisdiction was assured because of the political status of the Lord Chancellor as a central figure in the King's Council—a status buttressed by his moral credentials as a priest. The Chancellor wielded unusual authority. Applying the penalty of imprisonment for noncompliance, he could issue the writ of subpoena ordering parties to appear before him. He did not abide by the technical rules of pleading and procedure of the common law courts. Unlike law courts, he did not employ juries as fact finders. He either personally determined disputed factual matters on the evidence or appointed a *special master in equity* to discover the facts and report findings back to him concerning the true facts in dispute. Rather than utilizing established legal norms as rules for deciding disputes and granting existing legal remedies, chancellors applied what came to be known as *equitable principles* based upon precepts of natural justice. This is an example of the practical application of the principles of the natural law school of jurisprudence, as outlined in Chapter 1 of this text. As a result of its commitment to the natural law precepts, the Court of Chancery was more likely to provide flexible and less technical judgments that seemed just and not merely legal in result.[34]

From the perspective of interinstitutional conflict, it is important to note that Chancery did not tread on the jurisdiction of the existing law courts unless petitioners could show that no adequate remedy at law was available. To this day, whenever parties seek equitable remedies, they must first formally allege the inadequacy of the law and only then will a court of equity grant jurisdiction. Nonetheless, institutional conflict and jealously developed over time—and with little wonder. At times, the Chancery court ordered the suspension of proceedings in a law court, transferring the matter to its jurisdiction. At other times, Chancery would take jurisdiction in a case already decided in a law court and try it anew in equity with the decision going the other way. For these reasons, the jurisdiction of equity courts was challenged in the seventeenth century, but a royal commission found in favor of the supremacy of Chancery versus the law courts. By the nineteenth century, however, Chancery's claim of possessing superior flexibility to that of the law courts was no longer plausible. It too had become very formal in its practices and procedures, and parliament found it necessary to reform it.[35]

Star Chamber Court

The *Star Chamber court* has by far the nastiest reputation of any of the early royal English courts. It is infamous because of its use of torture, such as the rack and the screw, to coerce confessions from enemies of the crown. Henry VII created this court in 1487 after the Chancery broke from the King's Council. It was formed by the Council to deal with powerful figures that defied the crown's regular courts and possessed jurisdiction in security matters (e.g., treason, espionage, conspiracy, forgery, and later fraud and the punishment of judicial officers). Though authorities differ, the name Star Chamber is apparently derived from the name of the room in which the court sat in the Royal Palace of Westminster. At one time, this room had gilded stars painted on the ceiling.[36]

Like its sister Chancery institution, Star Chamber employed principles of natural justice to guide deliberations and provided remedies not available from other courts. Many of the crown's opponents viewed as outrageous the unchecked power of this institution. In addition to the employment of torture to exact confessions, Star Chamber could impose fines, prison sentences, and mutilation of the guilty, but it could not impose the death penalty.[37] Abolished by Parliament in 1641, Star Chamber's jurisdiction was transferred to other courts of the realm.[38]

Impact of Royal Courts

It is important to note that the royal courts did not compel all persons to resort to them. Rather, their jurisdiction was over large fields of law, elective, and therefore not ordinarily exclusive. Consequently, the preexisting nonroyal courts could continue to exercise their proper jurisdictions, but they faced a new competitor.

How, then, did royal courts obtain legitimacy? Public support followed because the results of the system of royal courts proved functionally superior for many vital and changing interests. This situation remained substantially the same for some centuries. Although the crown was powerful, English monarchs could not acquire legal jurisdiction over all matters even if they desired it. The king's courts had to compete with other public, private, and other dispute-resolution institutions in the country. Although limited by political realities, royal jurisdiction thrived because its scope was broad and comprehensive.

American courts inherited the traditions and actions of the mother country. The substantive law of property and contracts in American courts is traceable to the Court of Common Pleas. Criminal law and the law of torts are rooted in the Court of King's Bench. The law of debts, debt collection, and taxation find their genesis in the Court of Exchequer of Pleas. Equitable remedies—including injunctive relief, declaratory judgments, and specific performance—are rooted in the decisions of the Court of Chancery. In 1848, New York was the first state to replace the English writ system with *code pleading*. The legislature mandated that pleadings were limited to complaint, answer, reply, and demurrers, or what is called today *motions to dismiss*.[39] Although the writ system has been replaced, the notion that courts are limited by the jurisdiction granted to them by a sovereign authority is a central feature of the American governmental system.

In one fashion or another, state and national constitutions and statutory laws specify the jurisdiction of courts and how jurisdiction may be created beyond what is specifically provided for in the constitutional document. If a court lacks jurisdiction to hear a case, then its proceedings are regarded as null and void. Lest their cause is not heard and justice is not done, parties in their pleadings take care to set forth the jurisdiction of the court in which they are filing. Before it can proceed, each court must determine whether it possesses jurisdiction over the subject matter or persons involved in a case. As we have seen, this essential step in a court's deliberations is clearly traceable to the common law history of England.

The power to adjudicate.

Jurisdictional Questions

Today in U.S. courts, the jurisdictional issue takes two basic forms. First, does the court possess jurisdiction over the subject matter (i.e., res)? That is, does the court have the authority to decide the issue in the controversy? For example, only federal courts have the power to hear bankruptcy cases; therefore, any state court attempting to excuse persons from their debts through a declaration of bankruptcy acts without jurisdiction. Likewise, state courts of limited jurisdiction handling juvenile delinquency matters may not try adults for criminal offenses.

Second, does the court possess jurisdiction over the person (*in personam*)? Clearly when plaintiffs file suits in particular courts, they are consenting to the authority of those courts to render judgments. Jurisdiction over the defendant, however, is another matter, especially if defendants do not reside in the *forum state* (place of litigation).

Subject matter jurisdiction is a relatively simple matter. Through the issuance of writs, the King's Council and the Lord Chancellor expanded the subject matter jurisdiction of the royal courts to include whole classes of subjects. The subject of a dispute might involve, for example, probate and wills, the enforcement of contractual obligations, negligent conduct, and criminal behavior. In modern America, subject matter jurisdiction is granted either in state and federal constitutions or more commonly by statutory enactment of state legislatures or the U.S. Congress.

Always pertinent is the query whether the constitution and laws of the sovereign body grant to the court the authority to hear particular disputes even though the court possesses both personal and subject matter jurisdiction. For example, the U.S. Supreme Court in *Ex Parte McCardle* (1869) held that Congress has constitutional authority to remove from the Court's jurisdiction the power to hear cases on appeal from lower courts. Although unsuccessful, in recent decades legislation has been introduced by conservative members of Congress to remove the Supreme Court's power to hear cases on appeal in matters relating to abortion, internal security, and school busing controversies. These legislative proposals would have required that the Court not hear any such case in its appellate jurisdiction.

Box 2.4   **Summary of Ex Parte McCardle**
U.S. Supreme Court
74 U.S. (7 Wall.) 506 (1869)

A federal military commission arrested and detained William McCardle, a Vicksburg, Mississippi, newspaper editor, for publishing libelous editorials that incited insurrection against the United States. McCardle, a civilian, sought a writ of habeas corpus, pleading that as a civilian he is not subject to trial by a military commission and therefore the Reconstruction Act (1867) was unconstitutional. A circuit court denied McCardle's petition. He then appealed directly to the U.S. Supreme Court under the Habeas Corpus Act of 1867, which directed federal courts to issue writs of habeas corpus in cases involving persons who are confined in violation of their constitutional rights. (A writ of habeas corpus directs that a person held in custody be brought before the court to determine if he or she is being lawfully detained). The Supreme Court granted review and heard the case. However, before a decision was rendered, Congress, over the veto of President Andrew Johnson, repealed the statute in question.

Writing for an 8–0 Court, Chief Justice Chase dismissed McCardle's appeal for want of jurisdiction. It did so without passing judgment on the controversial Reconstruction Act. Appellate jurisdiction is subject to congressional regulation as stated in Article III of the Constitution, argued Chase. It grants to Congress the authority to make "exceptions to the appellate jurisdiction of the Supreme Court." In brief, Congress possesses constitutional authority to enlarge or diminish the high court's appellate jurisdiction.

Compelling Court Appearances

When plaintiffs file suits with particular law courts, they are deemed to have consented to the jurisdiction of such courts. Defendants who voluntarily answer the formally filed complaints of plaintiffs also are said to have consented to such jurisdiction. Because most litigants consent by filing complaints and answering them, there is usually no issue about whether a court possesses *in personam* jurisdiction in a particular cause of action. But sometimes persons are not properly notified of a suit filed against them or they may avoid or evade proper notification and service.

American practice attempts to address the interests of both defendants and plaintiffs. First, the U.S. Supreme Court has ruled that due process of law requires that "[s]ervice of process, under longstanding tradition in our system of justice is fundamental to any procedural imposition on a named defendant."[40] The high court has observed that ". . . the core function of service is to supply notice of the pendency of a legal action, in a manner and at a time that affords the defendant a fair opportunity to answer the complaint and present defenses and objections."[41] Thus, notice and the opportunity to be heard in court is a matter of protection for named defendants.

The second reason for proper notice and service is of practical importance for plaintiffs, who bring suits against defendants so that their legal rights may be vindicated in a court of law. If legal processes were unavailable to the parties to a suit, defendants would likely avoid the jurisdiction of courts, thereby dodging their moral responsibility to resolve disputes. To ensure court appearances, the legal system has invented various ways to compel defendants into court.

A *summons* indicates that named defendants are being sued; they must appear at a specified time and place to answer the charges against them; and unless they take action to respond to the complaint, they will lose the case by default. To avoid any question that defendants are aware of the causes of action filed against them, the *personal service summons* is the common and most desirable legal process to compel persons to appear in court. Courts have interpreted the Due Process Clauses of the Fifth and Fourteenth Amendments to require that summons be served within sufficient time for defendants to mount a reasonable defense.

Because personal service is not always possible, the law often permits *substituted,* sometimes called *alternative service.* Mailing the summons and complaint to the defendant by certified mail or leaving these documents at defendants' homes with persons of suitable age and discretion are permissible forms of substituted service. State laws provide that when plaintiffs sue corporations, it is an acceptable form of service to leave the summons with a designated agent or corporate officer. Further, it is permissible to leave a summons with a state agency that charters corporations, such as a secretary of state, with the expectation that state functionaries will deliver the summons to the corporate defendants at their legally designated headquarters.

A final form of serving summons is *constructive service.* It entails repeated notice in the legal announcement section of local newspapers, for example, once a week for three weeks. Whatever the form of service, the requirements are dictated by statute in each state or federal jurisdiction.

Long-Arm Statutes and Minimum Contacts

If life were not complicated by jurisdictional boundaries, a defendant might be served a summons anywhere. In the United States, however, there are fifty states with jurisdiction limited to their own boundaries, and consequently state courts may not easily exercise jurisdiction over all persons who ought to be made to answer for their conduct. *Long-arm statutes* are the legislative tools employed by all states to reach beyond their borders. Commonly, these statutes apply to out-of-state persons or business enterprises transacting commerce within the state and who engage in tortious conduct. Married persons who have in recent years lived in the state may also be subject to long-arm statutes. When successful, these statutes require defendants to return to the state where the suit is filed, the forum state, to defend the suit. If they fail to do so, they may lose the case by default.

Long-arm statutes do not ordinarily apply to businesses having only occasional contacts with persons outside their state of residence. The U.S. Supreme Court has held that due process of law requires *minimum contacts.*[42] For example, to ship a few orders from one state to another does not constitute minimum contacts. Also, interstate travel by a corporate official who is not responsible for the culpable conduct does not constitute minimum contacts. Though courts treat these matters on a case-by-case basis, the criterion of minimum contacts requires that when a cause of action is in tort, the offending conduct must be aimed at a person within the forum state. Clearly, the minimum contacts requirement is met if a corporation is incorporated within the state where the suit is filed or is conducting business on a regular basis.

Because it is not always legally clear whether a party must make an appearance in court or lose by default, the party challenging the court's jurisdiction may seek to avoid a *general appearance* because to do so is to consent to the jurisdiction of the court. In such instances, the law permits a *special appearance*. In a special appearance, the defendant argues that the court lacks subject matter or personal jurisdiction in the case. If the court accepts the argument, then the party need not defend the case. If the jurisdictional argument is lost, the case proceeds to the disposition of other issues of law or fact. The case below involving Ben & Jerry's ice cream business illustrates the issues and the law surrounding minimum contacts and jurisdiction.

Ben & Jerry's Homemade, Inc., v. Coronet Priscilla Ice Cream Corp.
United States District Court for the District of Vermont
921 F. Supp. 1206 (1996)

William K. Sessions III, District Judge.

. . . Defendant has filed a Motion to Dismiss for lack of personal jurisdiction, pursuant to Fed. R. Civ. P. 12(b)(2). Plaintiff opposes this motion. . . .

I. Factual Background

This is a diversity action based on a breach of contract claim. Plaintiff, Ben & Jerry's Homemade, Inc., ("Ben & Jerry's Homemade") is a corporation organized under the laws of the state of Vermont and has its principal place of business in Waterbury, Vermont. Defendant, Coronet Priscilla Ice Cream Corp., ("Coronet") is a New York corporation that has its principal place of business in Hicksville, New York. Plaintiff claims that it sold ice cream to Defendant, for which Defendant has refused to pay.

The following facts are not in dispute. Coronet distributes ice cream products and frozen foods in the New York metropolitan area. It began distributing Ben & Jerry's ice cream when it acquired the Ice Cream Man, Inc., a New York corporation. At that time, Coronet purchased Ben & Jerry's ice cream from Edy's Gourmet Ice Cream, Inc., ("Edy's"), another New York corporation. In February of 1994, Ben & Jerry's of New York, Inc., ("Ben & Jerry's of New York"), replaced Edy's as the exclusive distributor of Ben & Jerry's products in the metropolitan New York area for the class of trade "less than three cash registers." Ben & Jerry's of New York is a corporation organized under the laws of the state of New York with offices in Long Island City, New York. Coronet is a sub-distributor serving the less than three cash register class of trade.

On September 22, 1994, Coronet received a shipment of $61,268.12 worth of ice cream. Coronet was given a credit of $2,268.22 so that there was an outstanding balance of $58,999.90 for the ice cream. The shipment was sent F.O.B. Waterbury, Vermont from Ben & Jerry's Homemade. Coronet initially sent a check to Ben & Jerry's of New York for $58,999.90 to pay for the ice cream. Subsequently, Coronet stopped payment on the check. Shortly thereafter, the distributorship arrangement ended. On January 19, 1995, Ben & Jerry's Homemade filed suit against Coronet for failing to pay for the ice cream.

The remaining facts are in dispute. Coronet alleges that it has never entered into a contract with Ben & Jerry's Homemade. Instead, it has dealt with Ben & Jerry's of New York, a separate legal entity. Coronet maintains that it had a distributorship agreement with Ben & Jerry's of New York, with whom it placed all orders, including the shipment in question. As a sub-distributor for Ben & Jerry's of New York, Coronet worked with its Distribution Manager, Steven Cooperman.

Coronet's contact with Ben & Jerry's Homemade purportedly has been very limited. According to Coronet, it has never made a payment for Ben & Jerry's products to Ben & Jerry's Homemade. Rather, it has sent all payments to Ben & Jerry's of New York in Long Island City, New York. Although the President of Coronet, Steven Levine, has met Jerry Greenfield, co-founder of Ben & Jerry's Homemade, in New York on occasion and has had several telephone conversations with Mr. Greenfield and Thomas D'Urso, the Manager of Treasury Operations for Ben & Jerry's Homemade, Coronet avers that it has not "reached out" to do business in Vermont or engaged in a business relationship with Ben & Jerry's Homemade. Ben & Jerry's Homemade asserts that Coronet has contracted to purchase this shipment of ice cream, a full truckload, directly from Ben & Jerry's Homemade. Al-though some sales were made by Ben & Jerry's of New York to Coronet, whenever Coronet needed a full truckload of ice cream, it purchased it from Ben & Jerry's Homemade. Mr. D'Urso asserts that the content of his telephone conversations with Mr. Levine included, among other things, a discussion of payment, shipment and credit terms. Ben & Jerry's Homemade submits a bill of lading and an invoice, both printed on letterhead of Ben & Jerry's of Vermont, as evidence of its contention that full truckloads of ice cream, including this one, were sent pursuant to an agreement between it and Coronet. The invoice indicates that payment should be remitted to Ben & Jerry's Homemade, Inc. It also notes a credit of $2,268.22. However, it shows Steven Cooperman, of Ben & Jerry's of New York, as the salesperson for the shipment. Coronet does not contest the genuineness of the bill of lading or the invoice.

II. Discussion

Personal Jurisdiction

In considering a motion to dismiss on jurisdictional grounds, the Court must take all allegations in the light most favorable to the plaintiff. Hoffritz for Cutlery, Inc. v. Amajac, Ltd., 763 F.2d 55, 57 (2d Cir. 1985). However, the plaintiff "bears the burden of demonstrating contacts with the forum state sufficient to give the court jurisdiction over the person of the defendant." Sollinger v. Nasco Intern., Inc., 655 F. Supp. 1385, 1386 (D. Vt. 1987). When there has been limited discovery and when the motion is being decided without an evidentiary hearing, as here, the plaintiff need make only a prima facie showing of jurisdiction, through its own affidavits and supporting materials. Marine Midland Bank, N.A. v. Miller, 664 F.2d 899, 904 (2d Cir. 1981). Having set forth the appropriate standard for assessing the motion to dismiss, the Court now turns to the merits.

Personal jurisdiction over a nonresident defendant in a diversity action is determined on the basis of Vermont law, which invokes a two-part analysis. . . . First, the Court must find that Vermont's long-arm statute reaches the defendant. Second, it must determine that the exercise of the state's long-arm statute does not offend due process. . . . Defendant was served pursuant to V.R.C.P. 4(e) and 12 V.S.A. § 913(b), the relevant Vermont long-arm statute. Title 12 V.S.A. § 913(b) provides:

"Upon the service [on a party outside the state], and if it appears that the contact with the state or by the party or the activity in the state by the party or the contact or activity imputable to him is sufficient to support a personal judgment against him, the same proceedings may be had for a personal judgment against him as if the process or pleading had been served on him in the state." Interpreting this section, the Vermont Supreme Court has held that an exercise of jurisdiction over an out-of-state defendant is proper if it comports with the due process clause. . . . Accordingly, the first part of the analysis merges into the second. Thus, the Court can proceed to an application of the due process clause.

The purpose of the due process clause is to ensure that a nonresident defendant is not subject to the binding judgments of a forum with which it has had no significant contacts. . . . To satisfy due process, a nonresident defendant must have established minimum contacts with the forum state

such that the defendant "should reasonably anticipate being haled into court there." World-Wide Volkswagen Corp. v. Woodson, 444 U.S. 286, 297, 62 L. Ed. 2d 490, 100 S. Ct. 559 (1980). A defendant should "reasonably anticipate" out-of-state litigation when it "purposefully avails itself of the privilege . . . of conducting activities within the forum State, thus invoking the benefits and protections of its laws." Hanson v. Denckla, 357 U.S. 235, 253, 2 L. Ed. 2d 1283, 78 S. Ct. 1228 (1958).

Arguing that its contact with Vermont has been fortuitous, attenuated and random, Defendant claims that it does not have the requisite minimum contacts with Vermont to sustain jurisdiction. Defendant does not have a Vermont office, it has no sales in Vermont, and it has never visited the state. Nonetheless, for purposes of deciding the instant matter, the Court must review the evidence in the light most favorable to the Plaintiff. Taken together, Plaintiff's claim that Defendant purchased the shipment in question from it, Mr. D'Urso's statement that he spoke with the Defendant's President about shipment, payment and credit terms, the invoice indicating that payment is to be remitted to Ben & Jerry's Homemade, and the uncontroverted evidence that Plaintiff sent the shipment F.O.B. Waterbury, Vermont, establish contacts sufficient to invoke specific jurisdiction. . . .

Intentional and affirmative action by the nonresident defendant in the forum state is the key to personal jurisdiction. . . . According to Plaintiff, Defendant has purposefully contracted for the purchase of goods manufactured, sold, and shipped in the forum state. Furthermore, the invoice indicates that payment is to be made to Ben & Jerry's Homemade and lists an account credit of $2,268.22, which Coronet presumably has with Ben & Jerry's Homemade. At this stage of the proceedings, this provides ample basis for the Court to conclude that the Defendant took intentional and affirmative action to enter into the Vermont marketplace.

Although Defendant has never traveled to Vermont, mere absence of physical presence in the state cannot defeat jurisdiction. Burger King, 471 U.S. at 476. In many commercial transactions, the parties' business relationship is conducted entirely through mail, telephone and facsimile, thus "obviating the need for physical presence within a State in which business is conducted." Id. Plaintiff and Defendant have had several telephone contacts, as well as meetings in New York, allegedly to discuss terms of the distributorship arrangement. These communications indicate the existence of a business relationship between Plaintiff and Defendant, such that the Defendant has created "continuing obligations" between itself and a Vermont resident. Id. . . .

Because a case involving the same parties and arising out of related facts is currently pending in New York state court, the Court has a concern about whether it is the most appropriate forum for resolving this dispute. Nonetheless, its concern does not rise to such a level as to defeat personal jurisdiction at this time. . . . The Court finds the Defendant to have sufficient minimum contacts with Vermont such that traditional notions of fair play and substantial justice are not violated by the exercise of jurisdiction. Defendant's Motion to Dismiss for lack of personal jurisdiction is therefore denied. . . .

III. Conclusion

It is hereby ORDERED that Defendant's Motion to Dismiss for lack of personal jurisdiction is DENIED without prejudice. . . .

Case Questions for Discussion

1. Why is a U.S. federal district court adjudicating this matter and not a Vermont or New York state court? Does the matter of legitimacy have anything to do with the answer to this question?

2. Under what theory did the defendant argue that it had not submitted to the personal jurisdiction of the court? What does Judge Sessions conclude about this point?

3. Does Vermont's long-arm statute reach the defendant, a New York company? Why or why not?

4. What does the Due Process Clause of the U.S. Constitution have to do with this case involving a contract between ice cream companies?

Key Terms, Names, and Concepts

Alexis de Tocqueville
Code pleading
Constructive service
Court of Common Pleas
Court of King's Bench
Diffuse support
Equitable principles
Exchequer of Pleas
Ex Parte McCardle
Eyre system
Feudal system
Forum state
General appearance
In personam jurisdiction
Jurisdiction
Legal forum
Legalism
Legitimacy
Long-arm statutes

Lord Chancellor
Master in equity
Minimum contacts
Personal service summons
Possessory assizes
Praecipe
Real property
Res jurisdiction
Rule of law
Special appearance
Special master in equity
Specific support
Star Chamber Court
Subject matter jurisdiction
Substituted service (or alternative service)
Summons
Writ of quo minus
Writ of right

Discussion Questions

1. May courts be truly independent in any political system that requires democratic accountability to the people?

2. Evaluate Tocqueville's description of the role of lawyers in the American political system. Why are lawyers overrepresented as an occupational group in the U.S. Congress and other elected positions?

3. Should American courts, including the U.S. Supreme Court, involve themselves in electoral politics? If so, under what circumstances? Did the Supreme Court make the right decision in *Bush v. Gore*?

4. If the monarchs of England possessed the power, why was it necessary, if at all, to gradually interfere with the jurisdiction of the lesser lords to adjudicate conflicts?

5. In light of the Supreme Court's decision in *Ex Parte McCardle*, is it constitutional for Congress to remove appellate jurisdiction from the high court to hear matters involving, for instance, state and local police interrogation of criminal suspects, cases involving abortion rights, or matters involving affirmative action?

6. If parties are compelled to adjudicate disputes in forums not of their own choosing, might this create problems about the willingness of parties to accept the outcomes of such cases?

Suggested Additional Reading

Fifoot, C. H. S. *History and Sources of the Common Law*. New York: Greenwood Press, 1970.

Friedman, Lawrence M. *American Law: An Introduction*. New York: Norton, 1984.

Gillman, Howard. *The Votes That Counted: How the Court Decided the 2000 Presidential Election*. Chicago: University of Chicago Press, 2001.

Hall, Kermit L. *The Magic Mirror: Law in American History*. New York: Oxford University Press, 1989.

——, William M. Wiecek, and Paul Finkelman. *American Legal History: Cases and Materials*. New York: Oxford University Press, 1991.

Horwitz, Morton J. *The Transformation of American Law: 1780–1860*. Cambridge, MA: Harvard University Press, 1977.

Hurst, James Willard. *The Growth of American Law: The Law Makers*. Boston: Little, Brown, 1950.

Issacharoff, Samuel, Pamela S. Karlan, and Richard H. Pildes. *When Elections Go Bad: The Law of Democracy and the Presidential Election of 2000*. New York: Foundation Press, 2001.

Nelson, William E. *Americanization of the Common Law: The Impact of Legal Change on Massachusetts Society, 1730–1830*. Cambridge, MA: Harvard University Press, 1975.

Scheingold, Stuart. *The Politics of Rights: Lawyers, Public Policy, and Political Change*. New Haven, CT: Yale University Press, 1974.

Shapiro, Martin. *Courts: A Comparative and Political Analysis*. Chicago: University of Chicago Press, 1981.

Shklar, Judith N. *Legalism*. Cambridge, MA: Harvard University Press, 1964.

Endnotes

1. Martin Shapiro, *Courts: A Comparative and Political Analysis* (Chicago: University of Chicago Press, 1981), pp. 36–37.
2. *Legalism* (Cambridge, MA: Harvard University Press, 1964), p. 1; Stuart Scheingold, *The Politics of Rights: Lawyers, Public Policy, and Political Change* (New Haven, CT: Yale University Press, 1974).
3. Albert P. Melone, "Rejection of the Lawyer-Dominance Proposition: The Need for Additional Research," *Western Political Quarterly* 33 (June 1980): 229.
4. Ibid., pp. 230–231.
5. Alexis de Tocqueville, *Democracy in America* (New York: Knopf, 1945), p. 280.

6. Mogens Pederson, "Lawyers in Politics: The Deviant Case of the Danish Folketing," in Samuel Patterson and John Wahlke, eds., *Comparative Legislative Behavior: Frontiers of Research* (New York: Wiley, 1972), pp. 25–63.

7. Ibid.

8. James L. Gibson, Gregory A. Caldeira, and Vanessa A. Baird, "On the Legitimacy of National High Courts," Paper Prepared for Delivery at the 1997 Annual Meeting of the Midwest Political Science Association, April 1997, Chicago, IL; James L. Gibson, Gregory A. Caldeira, and Vanessa A. Baird. "On the Legitimacy of National High Courts," *American Political Science Review* 92 (June 1998): 343.

9. Palm Beach County Canvassing Board v. Harris, Supreme Court of Florida, Nos. SC00-2346, SC00-2348, SC00-2349 (December 11, 2000). See also, Gore v. Harris, 772 So. 2d 1243 (2000).

10. Ibid.

11. David Abel, *"Bush v. Gore* Compels Scholars to Alter Courses at U.S. Law Schools," *Boston Globe* 2001 (February 3): A01. For an excellent analysis of *Bush v. Gore,* see Linda Greenhouse, "Election Case a Test and a Trauma for Justices," *New York Times,* 2001, February 20: 1, A18–19.

12. Gregory A. Caldeira and James L. Gibson, "The Causes of Public Support for the Supreme Court," *American Journal of Political Science* 36 (August 1992): 660.

13. Herbert M. Kritzer, "The Impact of *Bush v. Gore* on Public Perceptions and Knowledge of the Supreme Court," *Judicature* 85 (July–August 2001): 32–38; James L. Gibson, Gregory A. Caldeira, and Lester Kenyatta Spence, "The Supreme Court and the 2000 Presidential Election," <http://artsci.wustl.edu/legit/index.html>.

14. Gibson, Caldeira, and Spence, "The Supreme Court and the 2000 Presidential Election," p. 4.

15. Ibid., p. 5.

16. Shapiro, *Courts,* p. 72.

17. Clayton Roberts and David Roberts, *A History of England: Prehistory to 1714,* vol. 1 (Englewood Cliffs, NJ: Prentice Hall, 1985), pp. 75–82.

18. Shapiro, *Courts,* pp.72–73.

19. Henry J. Abraham, *The Judicial Process: An Introductory Analysis of the Courts of the United States, England, and France,* 5th ed. (New York: Oxford University Press, 1986), pp. 9–10.

20. Frederick G. Kempin, Jr., *Historical Introduction to Anglo-American Law in a Nutshell,* 3rd ed., (St. Paul, MN: West, 1990), pp. 31–32.

21. C. H. S. Fifoot, *History and Sources of the Common Law* (New York: Greenwood Press, 1970), p. 4, n. 4.

22. Ibid., p. 4.

23. Kempin, *Historical Introduction to Anglo-American Law,* p. 32.

24. Ibid., p. 33.

25. Ibid.

26. Ibid.

27. Ibid., pp. 34–35.

28. Max Radin, *Anglo-American Legal History* (St. Paul, MN: West Publishing Co., 1936), pp. 95–96; J. H. Baker, *An Introduction to English Legal History,* 3rd ed. (London: Butterworth, 1990), p. 575.

29. Kempin, *Historical Introduction to Anglo-American Law*, pp. 35–36; Radin, *Anglo-American Legal History*, p. 89.
30. Radin, *Anglo-American Legal History*, p. 89.
31. Kempin, *Historical Introduction to Anglo-American Law*, pp. 35–36.
32. Radin, *Anglo-American Legal History*, pp. 94, 98.
33. Kempin, *Historical Introduction to Anglo-American Law*, p. 37.
34. Ibid., pp. 37–38.
35. Ibid., p. 38.
36. Ibid., pp. 37–40.
37. Ibid., pp. 40–41; "Star Chamber," <www.brysons.net/miltonweb/starchamber.html> (2001).
38. "Star Chamber," <www.brysons.net/miltonweb/starchamber.html> (2001).
39. Mary Kay Kane, *Civil Procedure* (St. Paul, MN: West, 1979), pp. 79–81.
40. Murphy Bros. v. Michetti Pipe Stringing, Inc., 526 U.S. 344, 350 (1999).
41. Henderson v. United States, 517 U.S. 654, 672 (1996).
42. World-Wide Volkswagen Corp. v. Woodson, 444 U.S. 286, 297 (1980). ✦

Chapter 3

Court Organization and Jurisdiction in the Federal System

Chapter Objectives

Students should be alert to the complexity of the court system in the United States. Not only does each state define and operate its own judiciary but also the national government maintains a judicial organization. When conflicts arise between the laws and judicial opinions of the states and those of the national government, we have methods to resolve them, thanks to the constitutional framers. Further, students should be aware that the resolution of these conflicts has required considerable judicial intervention in the form of constitutional, statutory, and court-created legal rules. Courts at all levels are called upon to decide how the laws of the various states are to be interpreted and applied from one jurisdiction to another. Finally, students should understand that proponents of the expansion of fundamental rights are turning their attention to the state courts in reaction the U.S. Supreme Court's reluctance to articulate the existence of new rights. This trend is called *new judicial federalism*.

The U.S. Constitution of 1789 established a federal system of government. It divided power between the state governments and the national government located in Washington, DC. Consequently, the United States has 51 court systems with many subsystems designed to adjudicate the laws of all state and federal jurisdictions. Most private and public law disputes are handled in the state courts. Cases and controversies in law and equity that involve the constitution, laws, and treaties of the United States are tried and sometimes appealed through the federal courts system, including diversity of citizenship cases.

State Courts

At the end of the twentieth century, there were 208 general and limited jurisdiction trial court systems and subsystems in the states. Trial courts with *general jurisdiction* may hear a wide variety of criminal and civil cases, but trial courts with *limited jurisdiction* may adjudicate only narrowly defined matters, such as specialized traffic violations, divorce and child-custody cases, criminal misdemeanor and less serious felony prosecutions, juvenile matters, or cases involving relatively small amounts of money. General jurisdiction judges are selected in a wide variety of ways. Eighteen states elect trial judges on nonpartisan ballots, while 10 of the 50 states select these judges on partisan ballots where political parties are associated with the candidates. Trial judges are appointed by governors in 15 states and in three states by state legislatures. The remaining seven states employ a variety or combination of selection methods. In all states but Maine and Massachusetts, general jurisdiction trial court judges must be law school graduates.[1]

Because error resulting in an injustice may take place at trial, the legal system provides an *appellate process* in which disappointed litigants may appeal their cases from the trial courts to courts specifically designed for that purpose. These appellate courts do not retry cases *de novo*, that is, by holding new trials to ascertain both the *facts* and the applicable *law* in the cases at hand. Instead, appellate courts review the written record of the courts below and consider arguments in the form of written briefs and oral arguments. Although de novo proceedings are rare in the U.S. judicial system, about half of the states have created limited jurisdiction criminal trial courts that adjudicate criminal misdemeanors and less serious felonies to reduce the heavy volume of cases in the regular trial courts. The problem is that these limited jurisdiction courts try defendants in a less formal manner and offer fewer due process protections than is the case in courts of general jurisdiction. Defendants who are dissatisfied with the result in their initial trial may receive a de novo trial in the court of general criminal jurisdiction where all constitutional protections apply. If defendants believe that error is committed at the second trial, the normal appellate process is applicable.[2]

Appellate judges are asked to review the actions and rulings of the judges below for the existence of reversible error in procedure or interpretation of substantive law. In such instances, appellants often argue that trial judges below failed to instruct juries properly on the applicable law to be applied in cases before them, or that they either failed to admit evidence required by the criminal or civil rules of procedure or erroneously admitted evidence that is legally inadmissible. In some dramatic instances, appellate courts overrule lower court judges for failing to interpret a statute or administrative regulation properly or determine that the statute or regulation in question violates state or federal constitutions or both.

All of the states have a court of last resort, usually called a Supreme Court. For the uninitiated, the name of the court can be confusing because in some states (e.g., New York) the court of general jurisdiction is called the Supreme Court and the court of last resort is named the Court of Appeals. The U.S. Bureau of Judicial Statistics reports that in 1998, 35 states had one intermediate court of appeals, five states had two courts of appeal, and 12 jurisdictions had no such court. All states, however, have a court of last resort that ranges in size from five to nine members. A majority of state courts of last resort have seven members, including the highly populated states of California, New York, and Illinois. Twenty-one states select appellate judges through gubernatorial appointment, and state legislatures in three states appoint intermediate and final appeals court judges. Fourteen states employ nonpartisan elections, eight states use partisan elections, and four states use retention elections most often associated with merit plans to select appellate court judges.[3]

Federal Courts

Article III of the U.S. Constitution establishes one Supreme Court and what inferior courts Congress may "from time to time ordain and establish." In an attempt to promote judicial independence, the framers of the Constitution provided that federal judges shall have lifetime tenure subject to good behavior and that their compensation shall not be diminished during their continuance in office.

The *U.S. district courts* are the trial courts and consequently the workhorses of the federal judiciary. There are 94 federal judicial districts, including at least one district court located in each state of the Union, the District of Columbia, and Puerto Rico. Also, three territories of the United States—the Virgin Islands, Guam, and the Northern Mariana Islands—are served by district courts. Each tries federal cases, including bankruptcy matters.

Finally, Congress has created two special trial courts. The Court of International Trade possesses jurisdiction over international trade and customs matters. The U.S. Court of Federal Claims adjudicates most claims for money damages brought against the U.S. government. It also adjudicates contractual disputes when the U.S. government is a party to cases involving so-called unlawful takings of private property by the national government and a host of other claims involving money or property against the United States.[4]

In addition to the regular courts, a number of federal courts and other dispute settlement entities remain outside the judicial branch. These institutions, sometimes called *legislative courts* because they are not created by Congress as Article III courts, include, among others, trial and appellate military courts, the Court of Veterans Appeals, and the U.S. Tax Court. In addition, federal administrative law courts operated by executive agencies and boards apply administrative rules and procedures to resolve conflicts arising from the application of internal decisions that affect private individuals and organizations and other public bodies. Because these extra-judicial branch institutions were not created pursuant to Article III of the Constitution, the judges of these bodies do not possess life tenure.[5]

Thirteen courts hear appeals from the 94 district courts, each of which is organized under an appellate court. Each *U.S. court of appeals* hears cases not only from the federal district courts but also from decisions of federal administrative agencies. In addition to the 11 numbered circuit courts plus the District of Columbia Court of Appeals, Congress created the Court of Appeals for the Federal Circuit. It has national jurisdiction to hear specialized cases, such as those involving patent disputes and cases decided at trial by the Court of Federal Claims and the Court of International Trade.[6]

The U.S. Supreme Court sits at the top of the judicial hierarchy presently with eight associate justices and a chief justice. With few exceptions, the high court has complete discretion over its own docket. Through the *writ of certiorari*, the justices alone decide which cases

Table 3.1 United States Courts of Appeals			
Court of Appeals	**Districts Included in Circuit**	**Number of Authorized Judgeships**	**Location/Postal Address**
Federal Circuit	United States	12	Washington, DC
District of Columbia Circuit	District of Columbia	12	Washington, DC
First Circuit	Maine Massachusetts New Hampshire Rhode Island Puerto Rico	6	Boston, MA
Second Circuit	Connecticut New York Vermont	13	New York, NY
Third Circuit	Delaware New Jersey Pennsylvania U.S. Virgin Islands	14	Philadelphia, PA

Fourth Circuit	Maryland North Carolina South Carolina Virginia West Virginia	15	Richmond, VA
Fifth Circuit	Louisiana Mississippi Texas	17	New Orleans, LA
Sixth Circuit	Kentucky Michigan Tennessee Ohio	16	Cincinnati, OH
Seventh Circuit	Illinois Indiana Wisconsin	11	Chicago, IL
Eighth Circuit	Iowa Minnesota Missouri Nebraska North Dakota South Dakota	11	St. Louis, MO
Ninth Circuit	Alaska Arizona California Hawaii Idaho Montana Nevada Oregon Washington Guam N. Mariana Islands	28	San Francisco, CA
Tenth Circuit	Colorado Kansas New Mexico Oklahoma Utah Wyoming	12	Denver, CO
Eleventh Circuit	Alabama Florida Georgia	12	Atlanta, GA

Source: Adapted from Administrative Office of the United States Courts, *Understanding the Federal Courts* (1999), p. 45, <www.uscourts.gov/UFC99.pdf>.

they want to hear on appeal. Ordinarily, four justices must agree that the legal question posed by the petitioner is of sufficient importance to warrant the attention of the entire Court. This rule applies whether eight or nine justices participate.[7] Cases granted plenary review begin in federal or state courts and involve what justices regard as important questions of statutory or constitutional law.[8]

U.S. Supreme Court building in Washington, DC.

Article III of the Constitution requires that the federal courts treat cases and controversies only in law or equity. This mandates there be real litigants in actual and not contrived conflict, and that the petitioners may have been legally harmed by the defendant. In other words, formally speaking, federal courts may employ only judicial and not political power in the exercise of their jurisdiction.

In contrast, some European courts may render decisions on the constitutionality of acts of parliament even before they are applied to real-life situations. These courts sometimes render such decisions even before constitutionally suspect laws are actually made final. This procedure is called *abstract review*. However, U.S. federal courts may engage only in *concrete review* involving cases that are alive with conflict and are not otherwise moot, abstract, or hypothetical. One consequence of the American system is that our law has an *ex post facto* quality about it; that is, citizens cannot know with finality whether a legislative act or administrative rule or regulation is legally applied or constitutionally valid until it is tested in a court of law.

We already know that section 2 of Article III of the U.S. Constitution specifically grants jurisdiction to the federal courts of bona fide cases raising constitutional issues as well as interpretation of the laws and treaties of the United States. It also grants to the federal judiciary jurisdiction over all cases affecting ambassadors and other public ministers and consuls; all cases of admiralty and maritime jurisdiction; controversies to which the national government is a party; and controversies between two or more states, between a state and citizen of another state as modified by the Eleventh Amendment, between citizens of different states, between citizens of the same state claiming lands under grants of different states, and between a state or the citizens thereof and foreign states, citizens, or subjects. This same constitutional provision grants the U.S. Supreme Court the power to try in its original (trial) jurisdiction all cases affecting ambassadors, other public ministers and consuls, and those in which a state shall be a party. In all other cases in which it possesses jurisdiction, the Supreme Court

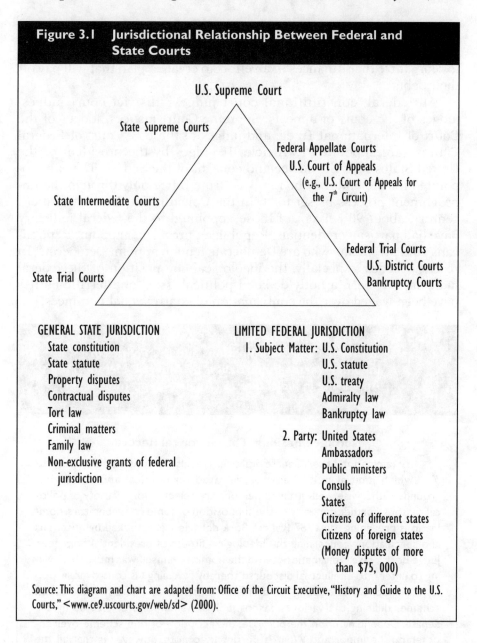

Figure 3.1 Jurisdictional Relationship Between Federal and State Courts

U.S. Supreme Court

State Supreme Courts

Federal Appellate Courts
U.S. Court of Appeals
(e.g., U.S. Court of Appeals for the 7th Circuit)

State Intermediate Courts

Federal Trial Courts
U.S. District Courts
Bankruptcy Courts

State Trial Courts

GENERAL STATE JURISDICTION
State constitution
State statute
Property disputes
Contractual disputes
Tort law
Criminal matters
Family law
Non-exclusive grants of federal jurisdiction

LIMITED FEDERAL JURISDICTION
1. Subject Matter: U.S. Constitution
U.S. statute
U.S. treaty
Admiralty law
Bankruptcy law

2. Party: United States
Ambassadors
Public ministers
Consuls
States
Citizens of different states
Citizens of foreign states
(Money disputes of more than $75, 000)

Source: This diagram and chart are adapted from: Office of the Circuit Executive, "History and Guide to the U.S. Courts," <www.ce9.uscourts.gov/web/sd> (2000).

may hear cases on appeal, both to law and fact, when Congress provides as a matter of statutory law.

The reason the constitutional framers provided a federal forum for the resolution of conflicts between citizens of different states and those of another country is to ensure fairness to the out-of-state (foreign) litigants. Congress currently limits federal *diversity jurisdiction* to cases involving more than $75,000 in total potential damages.[9] Thus, claims below that amount may be pursued only in state courts. Further, debtors seeking to relieve themselves of heavy debt burdens may use the federal courts (state courts lack jurisdiction over bankruptcy) to seek a court-supervised liquidation of their assets, or they may ask the court to reorganize their finances in an effort to create a plan that will pay off their debts.

All federal, constitutional court judges—district court judges, judges of the court of appeals, Supreme Court justices, judges of the Court of International Trade, and judges of the U.S. Court of Federal Claims—are appointed as Article III judges by the president of the United States with the advice and consent of the Senate. They are appointed for life and may be removed from office only through the impeachment process as set forth in the Constitution. In the twentieth century, about 90 percent of those appointed to the federal judiciary have had partisan credentials: Republican presidents appoint Republicans, and presidents who are Democrats tend to appoint Democrats. In recent decades, especially, the ideological composition of the federal judiciary has been a hotly debated political issue, and terrific battles have been waged over the confirmation of controversial nominees.

Box 3.1   Excerpt From: 'The Senate's Confirmation Role in Supreme Court Nominations and the Politics of Ideology Versus Impartiality,' by Albert P. Melone, First Appearing in *Judicature* 75 (August–September 1991), pp. 68–79.

Nominee Bashing: The Historical Record

An examination of past Senate practices reveals the considerable extent to which judicial nominees are evaluated on political and ideological grounds. Otherwise well-qualified persons are rejected for a variety of political reasons. Further, contrary to the supposition of some commentators, nominations preceding the 1987 Robert Bork debacle were marked by questions and speculations concerning the ideological fitness of presidential nominees. Judge Bork's case is dramatic because the nominee himself was more than willing to enter into intellectual discourse, thereby revealing his controversial policy inclinations. The existing literature contains several different classification schemes defining the various reasons judicial nominees are rejected by the Senate. Depending upon the purpose, the adoption of one scheme over another can be important. What is pertinent to note, however, is that all the schemes point out that past nominees were evaluated on political grounds unrelated to professional qualifications.

During the first decade after the adoption of the 1789 Constitution, the Senate rejected a person for reasons unrelated to professional competence. An extremely well-qualified justice of the South Carolina Supreme Court was rejected because he angered powerful Federalist politicians with his vigorous denunciation of the controversial Jay Treaty. Most Federalists viewed support for the treaty as a true indicator of party loyalty, while Republicans thought the treaty an unnecessary concession to British might. The vote to reject John

Rutledge was 14 to 10; it was a party vote with 13 Federalists voting against, and only three voting for confirmation. The remaining votes to confirm came from Anti-Federalists. The Rutledge episode is an early example of how politicians mask their real political reasons for opposing candidates by attacking nominees' personal and professional qualifications. Historians point out that Rutledge was attacked falsely as mentally unsound, and therefore unfit for Supreme Court service. The Federalist press employed this malicious tactic rather than stating the true reason for Federalist opposition. They realized that the Jay Treaty was so unpopular that to publicly attack Rutledge for his opposition to it would cause a political backlash.

There are many other examples of nominee bashing for reasons unrelated to professional competence. The Senate defeat of President James Madison's nomination of Alexander Wolcott was due in large part to the nominee's opposition to the enforcement of embargo and intercourse acts when he was U.S. Collector of Customs in Connecticut. Federalist senators and the press opposed him for this reason, although, in fairness, there were authentic questions raised about Wolcott's judicial qualifications. An otherwise well-qualified Grant appointee, Ebenezer R. Hoar, suffered rejection because as attorney general he championed the merit system in government. He also drew fire from radical Republicans because of his earlier opposition to the impeachment of President Andrew Johnson.

. . . The matter of evaluating nominees primarily on ideological grounds is better documented for the [twentieth] century than for the [nineteenth century]. There are at least two interrelated explanations. First, in the twentieth century the Senate has become more responsive to popular control. . . . By 1913 the Seventeenth Amendment had shifted the Senate's electoral base from the state legislatures that had theretofore named senators to the popular electorate. This institutional shift in accountability may have made senators more sensitive to interest group and grassroots awareness of judicial policy making. Second, it may be that judicial ideology played a more limited and ordinarily a less obvious role during the first century of the Republic than it does today. During the first 100 years of the Republic, only 17 acts of Congress were declared unconstitutional, but in the next 90 years the Court struck down 87 more, an increase of over 400 percent.

In the nineteenth century, there were fewer controversial Supreme Court opinions. Back then, the full scope of the Court's real and potential ability to affect public policy was not fully understood. However, late in that century and first third of the twentieth century, the Court's role in policy making became a matter of considerable debate. It became clear that Supreme Court justices exercise their discretion in dramatic ways including striking down popular congressional acts and state laws. The Court had become a bastion of conservative ideology. By the mid-1960s, it became equally clear that the Court had again become a policymaker; this time, however, it was a vehicle for liberal causes, and once again, many of its decisions were unpopular. In short, because the stakes are high, the judicial philosophy and ideology of potential jurists has become a subject of close scrutiny. President Wilson's appointment of Louis Brandeis is an early twentieth century example of how ideology has had a probable impact on the selection process. Wilson attempted to name the brilliant Brandeis as attorney general but met considerable opposition from the elitist Boston bar. When that appointment failed, Wilson pledged to name Brandeis to the next important vacancy. That position turned out to be Supreme Court. The Brandeis appointment was put off for months as the Senate took volumes of testimony. Much of the opposition was due to the liberal crusader's so-called radical views and his sociological jurisprudence. There is also evidence of an unhealthy dose of anti-Semitism. But many, William Howard Taft among others, were opposed to Brandeis for other reasons, including his views in support of the working classes and his alleged animosity toward big business.

Ideology was a factor in 1930 with the nominations of two otherwise well-qualified persons. Charles Evans Hughes was attacked because, among other reasons, he was regarded by liberal senators as a tool of corporate power, and conservative southerners opposed him as a city slicker who stood against states' rights. The Senate rejected John J. Parker on a close vote due in large measure to opposition generated by the American Federation of Labor and the National Association for the Advancement of Colored People. Parker was thought unfriendly to labor, and he was under attack, probably erroneously, as a racist. There would be no other Senate rejection of a presidential Supreme Court nominee for 40 years.

New Deal opposition to the high court was transparently ideological. There was an attempt to disguise the ideological source for the conflict by appealing to another motive. President Roosevelt presented his ill-fated Court-Packing plan as a way to relieve elderly justices from a heavy workload. This obvious attempt by the president to change the decision-making composition of the Court by increasing the number of justices was not lost even among the most casual observers. The plan failed to receive congressional approval not because members revered the Court and wanted to protect it from institutional attack. . . . [A]n ideologically conservative coalition existed in Congress before FDR introduced his plan. It coalesced before and functioned after the 1937 Court-Packing congressional vote. The purpose of this coalition was to put the brakes on the New Deal. Though the Court-Packing episode did not involve the confirmation of particular justices, it demonstrates that members of Congress viewed the Court in ideological terms. They did not want to give Roosevelt an opportunity to appoint to the Court a sufficient number of persons who would vote to support New Deal programs and goals. Roosevelt ultimately got his way when the Supreme Court began to uphold New Deal initiatives to save the nation's economy from ruin. The lesson is clear. Ideology has been a prominent factor in inter-branch governmental conflicts.

The Warren Court Era (1953–1969) was another period in this century when the Supreme Court came under severe attack. Decisions concerning such matters as segregation, internal security, school prayer, and criminal justice precipitated hostile reaction in and out of Congress. Many of these issues remain hotly contested . . . and so does the proper role of the Supreme Court. Warren Court opponents used the occasion of Thurgood Marshall's 1967 nomination to attack its decisions. Southern senators on the Judiciary Committee, including John McClellan, Samuel Ervin, and Strom Thurmond, questioned Marshall, a former solicitor general and then federal appeals court judge, about matters other than his professional qualifications. They also grilled him on his judicial philosophy. For example, Senator McClellan said he could not vote to confirm Marshall's nomination without an answer to his question: "Do you subscribe to the philosophy that the Fifth Amendment right to assistance of counsel requires that counsel be present at a police lineup." Marshall weathered the storm by employing the now familiar retort that a number of cases were pending before the Court and therefore he should not respond.

About a year later, in 1968, Abe Fortas became the convenient target for those opposed to the Warren Court when President Lyndon Johnson attempted unsuccessfully to promote his old friend and advisor from associate to chief justice. Senator Strom Thurmond vigorously attacked Fortas by harping on the ill effects of the Court's 1957 decision in *Mallory v. United States*. Significantly, Fortas was not on the Court at the time that this decision was handed down. Besides ideology, Fortas was charged with judicial impropriety by advising informally the president on a variety of policy matters, and also for accepting large lecture fees during the summer of 1968. Further, the nomination of Homer Thornberry as associate justice, a Texas crony of the president, to fill the empty seat upon the elevation of Fortas was another negative factor. In the end, the president was forced to withdraw the name of the liberal jurist as chief justice when a motion to invoke cloture failed by a 14-vote margin. Because the 1968 presidential election was near at hand, and since the election of a president from the other political party was thought a distinct possibility, the defeat of Fortas is an outward and visible sign of partisan and ideological politics in the modern battle over the struggle for control of the Supreme Court. Richard Nixon ran on an anti-Warren Court platform, and the selection of justices with "strict constructionist" sentiments was a part of his winning strategy.

In politics "what goes around comes around." Nixon's 1968 campaign invited intense scrutiny of judicial nominees who might exhibit any professional or personal weaknesses. As part of his "Southern Strategy" to gain grass-root support for the Republican Party in that region of the nation, Nixon sought to appoint to the Court southerners with a "strict constructionist" perspective. The code words fooled no one. This was not simply a matter of choosing for the Court persons who would exercise judicial self-restraint. Nixon wanted to reverse the liberal trend of the Warren Court. Then, as is the case today, arguments about the proper role of justices in interpreting statutes and the Constitution are really debates about judicial outcomes. Factors involving professional conduct and qualifications played important roles in the defeat of two Nixon nominees. South Carolinian Judge Clement Haynsworth was thought by organized labor and its Senate supporters to be anti-labor. Floridian Judge Harold Carswell was painted as a racist. Haynsworth was ostensibly rejected for failing to recuse himself in a few cases involving personal financial gain, and Carswell was portrayed as mediocre. But it is difficult to believe that the underlying causes for their rejections did not involve politics and concerns about the ideological direction of the Court.

Other Nixon and late Reagan appointees were subjected to ideological interrogation of one sort or another. However, the 1987 confirmation hearing on the nomination of Judge Robert Bork to the Supreme Court is the clearest case to date of the Senate concerning itself with the ideological characteristics and probable future judicial behavior of a High Court nominee. Those hearings taught Americans that questioning nominees about their judicial philosophy will not bring down the legal edifice. It is possible to probe nominees' attitudes without exacting promises or compromising judicial neutrality toward present or future litigants. In large measure, learning this lesson took place because the nominee himself wanted his views aired. Ironically, it was the ventilation of his own views that contributed directly to Judge Bork's 42 to 58 Senate vote rejection. Bork felt compelled to present his views and fully answer most questions because he felt that his many published articles on constitutional subjects could be misinterpreted, and therefore, his views may be misrepresented. He did so without invoking the oft-heard disarming refrain that discussion of constitutional matters may prejudice cases coming before the High Court. . . .

Available empirical research indicates that senatorial attitudes are affected by nominees. Controversial nominations stimulate the ideological proclivities of senators, thereby subjecting some nominees to negative votes. The extent to which ideology may adversely affect particular nominee confirmation chances depends upon the direction and intensity of that sentiment. It is little wonder, therefore, why most nominees refrain from a full disclosure of their attitudes and beliefs. . . .

The controversy surrounding the nomination of federal judicial nominees raises important questions about the nature and role of courts in the governmental system. Discussion questions raised at the end of this chapter ask students to ponder many of these issues. But for now, readers should ask themselves why Americans often employ political or ideological factors in assessing whether certain persons ought to ascend to the bench. Is it possible or advisable to separate law from politics? Further, given the importance of the U.S. courts in the federal scheme of government, should the selection of federal judges and justices be a matter of intense public scrutiny involving the representatives of the states through the U.S. Senate?

Problems of Federalism

American federalism presupposes that within each sphere of legitimate authority, state and federal courts are free to make their own rules and to interpret their own laws consistent with the constitutions, laws, and judicial opinions of each. However, there are circumstances when tensions arise between the legitimate authority of sovereign entities and where state and federal judges are brought into conflict because the laws of each jurisdiction are inconsistent. These include (1) conflicts between the constitution, laws, or treaties of the United States and a state law or judicial opinion; (2) the application of state laws as opposed to a national common law; and (3) the appropriate application of laws and rules where there are conflicts between the legal rules of two or more state or foreign jurisdictions.

National Supremacy

American federalism is a system of government wherein political power is divided between the central government and governments of the various states. Both authorities derive authority from the Constitution and, ultimately, "we the people" who, as the preamble states, "ordain and establish" it. Unlike a confederation, a federation allows both the central and state governments to act directly upon the people. It is a truism that, by virtue of the Tenth Amendment, those powers not granted to the central government are reserved to the states and to the people. Yet, because it is often unclear what powers are granted to the central authority, questions of the supremacy of national and state authority arise, resulting in legitimate conflict between the two authorities. Article VI, paragraph 2 of the Constitution, commonly referred to as the *Supremacy Clause*, is clear: "The Constitution, and the Laws of the United States which shall be made in pursuance thereof; and all treaties made, or which shall be made, under the authority of the United States, shall be the supreme law of the land; and the judges in every State shall be bound thereby, anything in the Constitution or laws of any State to the contrary notwithstanding." As interpreted by the U.S. Supreme Court, this constitutional provision promotes national supremacy and places the federal judiciary in the institutional position as the umpire and enforcer of the rules within the American federal system of government.

To understand the jurisdiction of the federal courts, we first explore the authority of the federal courts to rule on the constitutionality of federal and state laws. We then proceed to a discussion of the jurisdictional authority of federal courts over decisions of the state courts that contradict the Constitution, treaties, and laws of the United States. This analysis is followed by the presentation of the seminal Supreme Court opinion that treats conflicts between federal and state laws within the context of the loci of sovereign power, the scope of legislative authority of the national government, and national supremacy versus the rights of states.

In the well-known case of *Marbury v. Madison* (1803), the U.S. Supreme Court established the principle that Congress may not enlarge the original jurisdiction of the Supreme Court. Section 13 of the 1789

Judiciary Act was therefore declared unconstitutional and *Marbury v. Madison* became the precedent for judicial review in America.

Box 3.2	Summary of Marbury v. Madison

Summary of Marbury v. Madison
U.S. Supreme Court
5 U.S. (Cranch) 137, 2 L.Ed. 60 (1803)

D uring the waning days of his presidency, John Adams, a Federalist Party leader, named a number of judges to a variety of courts with a view of aiding and rewarding the party faithful and packing the courts with loyalists. Among others, Adams nominated William Marbury as Justice of the Peace for the District of Columbia and the Senate confirmed his nomination. However, because of the press of business, Adams' Secretary of State, John Marshall, failed to deliver the commission although he signed and sealed the document. The next president, Thomas Jefferson, the leader of the Republican Party, ordered his Secretary of State, James Madison, not to deliver the commission(s) on the theory that if the commission was undelivered, Marbury could not assume the office of Justice of the Peace. Under the provisions of Section 13 of the Judiciary Act of 1789, Marbury sought from the U.S. Supreme Court a writ of mandamus requiring Madison to deliver the commission to him.

Chief Justice John Marshall (yes, the same Secretary of State John Marshall who failed to deliver the commission in the first place) concluded for the U.S. Supreme Court that Marbury had a legal right to the commission that he demanded. Moreover, where there is a legal right there must be a remedy. Yet, the remedy sought, the issuance of the writ of mandamus to Secretary of State Madison, was not within the authority of the Supreme Court to grant because Section 13 of the 1789 Judiciary Act unconstitutionally added to its original jurisdiction as specified in Article III of the Constitution.

Chief Justice John Marshall led the U.S Supreme Court from 1801 to 1835.

Marshall based his conclusion on several interrelated points. First, the Constitution establishes a limited government. Second, the Constitution is superior to acts of Congress. Third, the judiciary must take notice of unconstitutional acts because "It is emphatically, the province and duty of the judicial department, to say what the law is." Fourth, because judges take an oath to uphold the Constitution, it would be immoral for them to give effect to an unconstitutional act. And lastly, because the phrasing of Article VI, paragraph 2 (the Supremacy Clause) mentions the constitution first before it mentions laws, and not the other way around, the framers of the Constitution must have intended that the Constitution be held superior to ordinary laws.

With the Supreme Court's pronouncement in *Marbury,* we learn that federal laws found inconsistent with the federal constitution are

---

Box 3.3	**Summary of Fletcher v. Peck**
	U.S. Supreme Court
	10 U.S. (Cranch) 87, 3 L.Ed. 162 (1810)

The state legislature of Georgia in 1795 granted a large parcel of land to speculators resulting from a bribery scheme for which many of the legislators received money bribes in return for their votes. A year later a new legislature declared the corrupt act null and void. In the meantime, however, much of the land was quickly sold to so-called innocent third parties who were left holding the proverbial bag. The matter quickly received much public attention because the various land speculators sought from Congress a financial bailout whereby they would receive compensation for their losses. Powerful political forces confronted each other and political reputations were made and lost over this issue. As part of the strategy to win approval for congressional compensation, the land speculators contrived a lawsuit to test the constitutionality of Georgia's repeal statute. Peck took possession of the land in 1800, and in his deed that he signed over to Fletcher, he indicated that all the past transactions involving the land were lawful. Fletcher sued Peck for breach of covenant because the original land grant was the result of an illegal agreement and, therefore, the land was not Peck's to sell in the first place. A circuit court entered judgment in favor of Peck and the matter was appealed to the U.S. Supreme Court.

Chief Justice John Marshall (who by the way had been similarly victimized by a land deal in Virginia) held that a land grant is an executed contract (that is, finalized), and because there is no constitutional difference between a contract that is executory and one which is executed, the original legal agreement between the Georgia state legislature and the land speculators is covered by Article I, section 10 of the Constitution (no state shall impair the obligation of contracts). Consequently, the state of Georgia was restrained from passing the repeal statute as an unconstitutional impairment of contract. Interestingly, the result of this opinion was used in the congressional debate to afford speculators the compensation they sought and eventually won.

---

null and void. In *Fletcher v. Peck* (1810), we learn that state laws inconsistent with the federal constitution are likewise unconstitutional. This opinion, written once again by Chief Justice John Marshall, is the first major decision to strike down a state law as inconsistent with the U.S. Constitution and thus is the state analogue to *Marbury v. Madison*. The decision in *Fletcher* established the principle that federal courts may exercise the power of judicial review over state laws.

In summary, the U.S. Supreme Court asserted judicial supremacy over federal statutes in *Marbury v. Madison* (1803), and in *Fletcher v. Peck* (1810) it held that it may find state law inconsistent with the federal constitution. But in *Martin v. Hunter's Lessee* (1816), the Supreme

Court exerted even greater national influence over the states by asserting its jurisdictional authority in state civil cases.

Box 3.4　　　**Summary of Martin v. Hunter's Lessee**
U.S. Supreme Court
14 U.S. (1 Wheat.) 304, 4 L. Ed. 97 (1816)

In his last will and testament, Thomas Lord Fairfax, a citizen of Virginia, bequeathed his 300,000-acre tract of land to his nephew, one Denny Martin Fairfax, a British subject living in England. However, during the War for Independence, Virginia prohibited inheritance by enemy aliens, and the state enacted a special law after Fairfax's death confiscating his property. In 1789, eight years after Fairfax's death, the state of Virginia sold some of the land to David Hunter. But Denny Martin Fairfax died and left the property in question to his heir Philip Martin. Importantly, however, in 1810 the Virginia Court of Appeals recognized Hunter's title to the land. Then, three years later, in 1813, the U.S. Supreme Court reversed the judgment of the Virginia Court of Appeals because the Jay Treaty of 1794 specifically safeguarded the property of British subjects from confiscation. But then, in response to the U.S. Supreme Court decision, the Virginia Court of Appeals declared unconstitutional section 25 of the Judiciary Act of 1789, the basis on which the U.S. Supreme Court had asserted its jurisdiction in the matter. In doing so the Virginia Court of Appeals refused to obey the U.S. Supreme Court's mandate to honor the original will of property to the Fairfax heir, Philip Martin.

The U.S. Supreme Court, faced with a direct challenge to its jurisdiction, answered two central questions. First, does the Constitution's Supremacy Clause contemplate that the scope of cases in its appellate jurisdiction includes civil cases originating in state courts? Second, does Section 25 of the Judiciary Act of 1789 authorize Supreme Court jurisdiction to review the action of the Virginia Court of Appeals? For both questions, it answered in the affirmative, reversing the Virginia Court of Appeals.

Writing for the Supreme Court, Mr. Justice Joseph Story asserted that Article III of the Constitution is the basis for the original and appellate jurisdiction of U.S. courts. He indicated it is the *cases* and not the courts that create the jurisdiction because Article III indicates those U.S. courts possess jurisdiction in all *cases and controversies* in law and in equity. In other words, the Constitution does not limit appellate jurisdiction to cases pending in the courts of the United States. The constitutional framers obviously contemplated that there may be conflicts between the Constitution, federal laws, and treaties (as in this case), and state actions. The Supremacy Clause exists to resolve such conflicts, and in this instance the conflict was resolved in favor of the Jay Treaty over the state law that authorized the confiscation of the Fairfax property. This constitutional provision plainly provides that the Constitution, treaties, and laws of the United States bind state judges.

Story then went on to rule that Section 25 of the 1789 Judiciary Act provides the judicial mechanism for implementing the principle of federal constitutional supremacy over conflicting state law. It provides for Supreme Court review of final judgments or decrees by the highest court in a state under three circumstances: First, where the validity of a federal law or treaty is questioned and the decision by the state court is against its validity; second, where a state statute is challenged as repugnant to the Constitution, treaties, or laws of the United States and the decision of the state court is in favor of the validity of the law; and third, where the construction of the federal constitution, treaty, or statute is in question and the decision of the state court is against the title, right, privilege, or exemption claimed. Therefore, Section 25 of the Judiciary Act authorizes the U.S. Supreme Court to review through a writ of error the state judicial decision in question.

Associate Justice Joseph Story's opinion in *Martin v. Hunter's Lessee* is a clear refutation of the view of states' rights advocates who believe that the national union was founded upon a compact among sovereign states that granted the central government only limited and specifically enumerated powers. This is not to suggest, however, that the U.S. courts may ride roughshod over state court decisions. To the contrary, review by the U.S. Supreme Court extends only to federal questions, meaning claims based on specific provisions of the U.S. Constitution, international treaties, or U.S. statutory provisions. In those cases where only state matters are at issue, the U.S. Supreme Court has no jurisdiction—the state decision is final and not reviewable by the federal judiciary. Indeed, in deference to state courts, the federal courts often impose the *abstention doctrine*. It holds that state supreme courts will be given a full opportunity to provide a definitive interpretation of a challenged state action that might avert the need for the federal court to make a decision based upon an interpretation of the Constitution, a treaty, or a federal law.[10] Indeed, one criticism leveled against the Rehnquist Court majority in *Bush v. Gore* is that they failed to respect the interpretations of state election law and state case law as enunciated by the Florida Supreme Court.

We now understand that the U.S. Supreme Court possesses the jurisdiction to strike down federal and state laws that are inconsistent with the U.S. Constitution, treaties, and laws of the United States. Yet, there may be circumstances when otherwise valid federal and state laws collide. *McCulloch v. Maryland* (1819) is the seminal U.S. Supreme Court opinion on the resolution of conflict between state and federal power. This opinion deserves careful study because Chief Justice Marshall emphasizes first the source of sovereign authority in the new constitutional republic. He then lectures fellow Americans about the ability of Congress to enact laws for which there is less than explicit sanction in the words of the Constitution. Finally, he definitively indicates how the Constitution settles conflicts between otherwise legitimate exercises of power by the national and state governments.

After Congress created, early in the nineteenth century, the controversial U.S. Bank, the state of Maryland levied a tax of approximately two percent on the value of all notes issued by the bank, or in the alternative a flat annual fee of $15,000, payable in advance. The state legislature set the penalty for noncompliance at $500 for each violation. The cashier of the Baltimore branch of the U.S. Bank, James McCulloch, refused to comply with the state statutes, and he was convicted in a Maryland county court. The state court of appeals affirmed his conviction.

As you read the edited opinion below, note carefully John Marshall's interpretation of the origins of national power. First, contrary to the view expressed by Maryland, the states did not create the union. Rather, the *people* "ordained and established" the Constitution. Maryland's claim that the national government usurped power from the states when it created the U.S. Bank is countered with the view that the people were free to revise the former system of confederation when, indeed, the states possessed extensive power, and national power was granted to the central authority by the states in a very limited fashion. Marshall argues that the states have no power to give to the national authority because the states did not revise the government. Rather, the people changed the confederation system, meeting as they did through their various state conventions.

Well, then, did the people grant to the national government the authority to create a national bank? Marshall admits that the federal constitution does not expressly grant to the central government the power to create a bank. Yet, he points out, the Constitution grants to Congress the power to collect taxes, to borrow money, to regulate commerce, to declare and conduct war, and to raise and support armies and navies. Paragraph (clause) eighteen of Article I, section 8, provides that Congress may make laws that are *necessary and proper* for carrying into execution the above enumerated powers. On this basis, the venerable chief justice concludes that the U.S. Bank is a constitutionally appropriate application of the Necessary and Proper Clause. Consequently, the national government possesses considerable *implied powers* through the elastic Necessary and Proper Clause. Marshall admits, nevertheless, that taxation is a legitimate function of state governments. However, in this case, because the power to tax is the power to destroy, Maryland is in the position to eliminate or curtail a legitimate function of the national government. Therefore, given the conflict between the national law and Maryland's law, the state tax scheme aimed at the U.S. Bank is null and void under the Supremacy Clause of the Constitution.

McCulloch v. Maryland
U.S. Supreme Court
17 U.S. (4 Wheat.) 316, 4 L.Ed. 579 (1819)

Mr. Chief Justice MARSHALL delivered the opinion of the Court.

The first question made in the cause is, has Congress power to incorporate a bank? . . .

In discussing this question, the counsel for the State of Maryland have deemed it of some importance, in the construction of the constitution, to consider that instrument not as emanating from the people, but as the act of sovereign and independent States. The powers of the general government, it has been said, are delegated by the States, who alone are truly sovereign; and must be exercised in subordination to the States, who alone possess supreme dominion.

It would be difficult to sustain this proposition. The Convention which framed the constitution was indeed elected by the State legislatures. But the instrument, when it came from their hands, was a mere proposal, without obligation, or pretensions to it. It was reported to the then existing Congress of the United States, with a request that it might "be submitted to a Convention of Delegates, chosen in each State by the people thereof, under the recommendation of its Legislature, for their assent and ratification." This mode of proceeding was adopted; and by the Convention, by Congress, and by the State Legislatures, the instrument was submitted to the people. They acted upon it in the only manner in which they can act safely, effectively, and wisely, on such a subject, by assembling in Convention. It is true,

they assembled in their several States—and where else should they have assembled? No political dreamer was ever wild enough to think of breaking down the lines which separate the States, and of compounding the American people into one common mass. Of consequence, when they act, they act in their States. But the measures they adopt do not, on that account, cease to be the measures of the people themselves, or become the measures of the State governments.

From these Conventions the constitution derives its whole authority. The government proceeds directly from the people; is "ordained and established" in the name of the people; and is declared to be ordained, "in order to form a more perfect union, establish justice, ensure domestic tranquility, and secure the blessings of liberty to themselves and to their posterity." The assent of the States, in their sovereign capacity, is implied in calling a Convention, and thus submitting that instrument to the people. But the people were at perfect liberty to accept or reject it; and their act was final. It required not the affirmance, and could not be negated, by the State governments. The constitution, when thus adopted, was of complete obligation, and bound the State sovereignties.

It has been said, that the people had already surrendered all their powers to the State sovereignties, and had nothing more to give. But, surely, the question whether they may resume and modify the powers granted to government does not remain to be settled in this country. Much more might the legitimacy of the general government be doubted, had it been created by the States. The powers delegated to the State sovereignties were to be exercised by themselves, not by a distinct and independent sovereignty, created by themselves. To the formation of a league, such as was the confederation, the State sovereignties were certainly competent. But when, "in order to form a more perfect union," it was deemed necessary to change this alliance into an effective government, possessing great and sovereign powers, and acting directly on the people, the necessity of referring it to the people, and of deriving its powers directly from them, was felt and acknowledged by all.

The government of the Union, then, (whatever may be the influence of this fact on the case,) is, emphatically, and truly, a government of the people. In form and in substance it emanates from them. Its powers are granted by them, and are to be exercised directly on them, and for their benefit.

This government is acknowledged by all to be one of enumerated powers. The principle, that it can exercise only the powers granted to it, would seem too apparent to have required to be enforced by all those arguments which its enlightened friends, while it was depending before the people, found it necessary to urge. That principle is now universally admitted. But the question, respecting the extent of the powers actually granted, is perpetually arising, and will probably continue to arise, as long as our system shall exist.

In discussing these questions, the conflicting powers of the general and State governments must be brought into view, and the supremacy of their respective laws, when they are in opposition, must be settled.

If any one proposition could command the universal assent of mankind, we might expect it would be this—that the government of the Union, though limited in its powers, is supreme within its sphere of action. This would seem to result necessarily from its nature. It is the government of all; its powers are delegated by all; it represents all, and acts for all. Though any one State may be willing to control its operations, no State is willing to allow others to control them. The nation, on those subjects on which it can act, must necessarily bind its component parts. But this question is not left to mere reason: the people have, in express terms, decided it, by saying, "this constitution, and the laws of the United States, which shall be made in pursuance thereof," "shall be the supreme law of the land," and by requiring that the members of the State legislatures, and the officers of the executive and judicial departments of the States, shall take the oath of fidelity to it.

The government of the United States, then, though limited in its powers, is supreme; and its laws, when made in pursuance of the constitution, form the supreme law of the land, "any thing in the constitution or laws of any State to the contrary notwithstanding."

Among the enumerated powers, we do not find that of establishing a bank or creating a corporation. But there is no phrase in the instrument which, like the articles of confederation, excludes incidental or implied powers; and which requires that every thing granted shall be expressly and minutely described. Even the 10th amendment, which was framed for the purpose of quieting the excessive jealousies which had been excited, omits the word "expressly," and declares only that the powers "not delegated to the United States, nor prohibited to the States, are reserved to the States or to the people;" thus leaving the question, whether the particular power which may become the subject of contest has been delegated to the one government, or prohibited to the other, to depend on a fair construction of the whole instrument. The men who drew and adopted this amendment had experienced the embarrassments resulting from the insertion of this word in the articles of confederation, and probably omitted it to avoid those embarrassments. A constitution, to contain an accurate detail of all the subdivisions of which its great powers will admit, and of all the means by which they may be carried into execution, would partake of a prolixity of a legal code, and could scarcely be embraced by the human mind. It would probably never be understood by the public. Its nature, therefore, requires, that only its great outlines should be marked, its important objects designated, and the minor ingredients which compose those objects be deduced from the nature of the objects themselves. That this idea was entertained by the framers of the American constitution is not only to be inferred from the nature of the instrument, but from the language. Why else were some of the limitations, found in the ninth section of the 1st article, introduced? It is also, in some degree, warranted by their having omitted to use any restrictive term which might prevent its receiving a fair and just interpretation. In considering this question,

then, we must never forget, that it is a constitution we are expounding.

Although, among the enumerated powers of government, we do not find the word "bank" or "incorporation," we find the great powers to lay and collect taxes; to borrow money; to regulate commerce; to declare and conduct a war; and to raise and support armies and navies. The sword and the purse, all the external relations, and no inconsiderable portion of the industry of the nation, are entrusted to its government. It can never be pretended that these vast powers draw after them others of inferior importance, merely because they are inferior. Such an idea can never be advanced. But it may with great reason be contended, that a government, entrusted with such ample powers, on the due execution of which the happiness and prosperity of the nation so vitally depends, must also be entrusted with ample means for their execution. The power being given, it is the interest of the nation to facilitate its execution. It can never be their interest, and cannot be presumed to have been their intention, to clog and embarrass its execution by withholding the most appropriate means. It is not denied, that the powers given to the government imply the ordinary means of execution. That, for example, of raising revenue, and applying it to national purposes, is admitted to imply the power of conveying money from place to place, as the exigencies of the nation may require, and of employing the usual means of conveyance.... The government which has a right to do an act, and has imposed on it the duty of performing that act, must, according to the dictates of reason, be allowed to select the means; and those who contend that it may not select any appropriate means, that one particular mode of effecting the object is excepted, take upon themselves the burden of establishing that exception.

But the constitution of the United States has not left the right of Congress to employ the necessary means, for the execution of the powers conferred on the government, to general reasoning. To its enumeration of powers is added that of making "all laws which shall be necessary and proper, for carrying into execution the foregoing powers, and all other powers vested by this constitution, in the government of the United States, or in any department thereof."

But the argument on which most reliance is placed, is drawn from the peculiar language of this clause. Congress is not empowered by it to make all laws, which may have relation to the powers conferred on the government, but such only as may be "necessary and proper" for carrying them into execution. The word "necessary," is considered as controlling the whole sentence, and as limiting the right to pass laws for the execution of the granted powers, to such as are indispensable, and without which the power would be nugatory. That it excludes the choice of means, and leaves to Congress, in each case, that only which is most direct and simple. . . .

Let this be done in the case under consideration. The subject is the execution of those great powers on which the welfare of a nation essentially depends. It must have been the intention of those who gave these powers, to insure, as far as human prudence could insure, their beneficial execution. This could not be done by confiding the choice of means to such narrow limits as not to leave it in the power of Congress to adopt any which might be appropriate, and which were conducive to the end. This provision is made in a constitution intended to endure for ages to come, and, consequently, to be adapted to the various crises of human affairs. To have prescribed the means by which government should, in all future time, execute its powers, would have been to change, entirely, the character of the instrument, and give it the properties of a legal code. It would have been an unwise attempt to provide, by immutable rules, for exigencies which, if foreseen at all, must have been seen dimly, and which can be best provided for as they occur. To have declared that the best means shall not be used, but those alone without which the power given would be nugatory, would have been to deprive the legislature of the capacity to avail itself of experience, to exercise its reason, and to accommodate its legislation to circumstances. If we apply this principle of construction to any of the powers of the government, we shall find it so pernicious in its operation that we shall be compelled to discard it. The powers vested in Congress may certainly be carried into execution, without prescribing an oath of office. The power to exact this security for the faithful performance of duty, is not given, nor is it indispensably necessary. The different departments may be established; taxes may be imposed and collected; armies and navies may be raised and maintained; and money may be borrowed, without requiring an oath of office. It might be argued, with as much plausibility as other incidental powers have been assailed, that the Convention was not unmindful of this subject. . . .

In ascertaining the sense in which the word "necessary" is used in this clause of the constitution, we may derive some aid from that with which it is associated. Congress shall have power "to make all laws which shall be necessary and proper to carry into execution" the powers of the government. If the word "necessary" was used in that strict and rigorous sense for which the counsel for the State of Maryland contend, it would be an extraordinary departure from the usual course of the human mind, as exhibited in composition, to add a word, the only possible effect of which is to qualify that strict and rigorous meaning; to present to the mind the idea of some choice of means of legislation not straitened and compressed within the narrow limits for which gentlemen contend.

But the argument which most conclusively demonstrates the error of the construction contended for by the counsel for the State of Maryland, is founded on the intention of the Convention, as manifested in the whole clause. . . .

1st. The clause is placed among the powers of Congress, not among the limitations on those powers. 2nd. Its terms purport to enlarge, not to diminish the powers vested in the government. It purports to be an additional power, not a restriction on those already granted. No reason has been, or can be assigned for thus concealing an intention to narrow the discretion of the national legislature under words which purport to enlarge it. The framers of the constitution wished its adoption, and well knew that it would be endangered by its strength, not by its weakness. Had they been capable of using language which would convey to the eye one idea, and, after deep reflection, im-

press on the mind another, they would rather have disguised the grant of power, than its limitation. If, then, their intention had been, by this clause, to restrain the free use of means which might otherwise have been implied, that intention would have been inserted in another place, and would have been expressed in terms resembling these. "In carrying into execution the foregoing powers, and all others," "no laws shall be passed but such as are necessary and proper." Had the intention been to make this clause restrictive, it would unquestionably have been so in form as well as in effect.

The result of the most careful and attentive consideration bestowed upon this clause is, that if it does not enlarge, it cannot be construed to restrain the powers of Congress, or to impair the right of the legislature to exercise its best judgment in the selection of measures to carry into execution the constitutional powers of the government. If no other motive for its insertion can be suggested, a sufficient one is found in the desire to remove all doubts respecting the right to legislate on that vast mass of incidental powers which must be involved in the constitution, if that instrument be not a splendid bauble.

We admit, as all must admit, that the powers of the government are limited, and that its limits are not to be transcended. But we think the sound construction of the constitution must allow to the national legislature that discretion, with respect to the means by which the powers it confers are to be carried into execution, which will enable that body to perform the high duties assigned to it, in the manner most beneficial to the people. Let the end be legitimate, let it be within the scope of the constitution, and all means which are appropriate, which are plainly adapted to that end, which are not prohibited, but consist with the letter and spirit of the constitution, are constitutional.

After the most deliberate consideration, it is the unanimous and decided opinion of this Court, that the act to incorporate the Bank of the United States is a law made in pursuance of the constitution, and is a part of the supreme law of the land.

It being the opinion of the Court, that the act incorporating the bank is constitutional; and that the power of establishing a branch in the State of Maryland might be properly exercised by the bank itself, we proceed to inquire—2. Whether the State of Maryland may, without violating the constitution, tax that branch? . . .

This great principle is, that the constitution and the laws made in pursuance thereof are supreme; that they control the constitution and laws of the respective States, and cannot be controlled by them. From this, which may be almost termed an axiom, other propositions are deduced as corollaries, on the truth or error of which, and on their application to this case, the cause has been supposed to depend. These are, 1st. that a power to create implies a power to preserve. 2nd. That a power to destroy, if wielded by a different hand, is hostile to, and incompatible with these powers to create and to preserve. 3d. That where this repugnancy exists, that authority which is supreme must control, not yield to that over which it is supreme.

That the power of taxing it by the States may be exercised so as to destroy it, is too obvious to be denied. But taxation is said to be an absolute power, which acknowledges no other limits than those expressly prescribed in the constitution, and like sovereign power of every other description, is trusted to the discretion of those who use it. But the very terms of this argument admit that the sovereignty of the State, in the article of taxation itself, is subordinate to, and may be controlled by the constitution of the United States. How far it has been controlled by that instrument must be a question of construction. In making this construction, no principle not declared, can be admissible, which would defeat the legitimate operations of a supreme government. It is of the very essence of supremacy to remove all obstacles to its action within its own sphere, and so to modify every power vested in subordinate governments, as to exempt its own operations from their own influence. This effect need not be stated in terms. It is so involved in the declaration of supremacy, so necessarily implied in it, that the expression of it could not make it more certain. We must, therefore, keep it in view while construing the constitution. . . .

If the States may tax one instrument, employed by the government in the execution of its powers, they may tax any and every other instrument. They may tax the mail; they may tax the mint; they may tax patent rights; they may tax the papers of the custom-house; they may tax judicial process; they may tax all the means employed by the government, to an excess which would defeat all the ends of government. This was not intended by the American people. They did not design to make their government dependent on the States. . . .

But if the full application of this argument could be admitted, it might bring into question. . . . The result is a conviction that the States have no power, by taxation or otherwise, to retard, impede, burden, or in any manner control, the operations of the constitutional laws enacted by Congress to carry into execution the powers vested in the general government. This is, we think, the unavoid-

able consequence of that supremacy which the constitution has declared. We are unanimously of opinion, that the law passed by the legislature of Maryland, imposing a tax on the Bank of the United States, is unconstitutional and void.

Case Questions for Discussion

1. If Maryland is not sovereign and the people are, what difference does this finding make for the outcome of the case?

2. Why is the implied powers provision, also known as the Necessary and Proper Clause, important as a determinant of national power?

3. What do you think about the validity of this statement: "The power to tax is the power to destroy"?

4. A former chief justice once stated that although the Republic might survive without the power of judicial review over congressional legislation, American federalism would be unworkable without it. Do you agree with this statement and why?

Tenth and Eleventh Amendments

Logically, it is entirely possible to arrive at the conclusion that Congress oversteps its authority when the exercise of national power may not be traced to an expressed constitutional provision or one that may not be fairly implied from the Necessary and Proper Clause. For example, as we learned in Chapter 1 of this book, if Congress does not possess the power to regulate the carrying of guns in the vicinity of schools by virtue of the commerce power found in Article 1, section 8, then under the *Tenth Amendment,* such a law infringes the power of the states [United States v. Lopez, 514 U.S. 549 (1995)]. The contemporary Supreme Court reaffirmed its reasoning in *Lopez* when it struck down the interim background check requirement of the Brady Act for the purchase of firearms in Printz v. United States, 521 U.S. 98 (1997), and again in 2000 when it struck down by a 5–4 margin the 1994 Violence Against Women Act. Congress created a right "to be free from crimes of violence motivated by gender." The law provided a right to sue in federal courts for money damages and other civil remedies to recover from such injuries. In *United States v. Morrison,* Chief Justice Rehnquist put it plainly: "We . . . reject the argument that Congress may regulate noneconomic, violent criminal conduct based solely on that conduct's aggregate effect on interstate commerce."[11]

Proponents of states' rights need not rely exclusively on the Tenth Amendment against perceived unconstitutional intrusions into the realm of state power. The so-called states' rights majority on the Rehnquist Court has also employed the largely forgotten but now resurrected *Eleventh Amendment.* Literally speaking, the terms of Article III, section 2, paragraph 1, grant jurisdiction to federal courts to adjudicate disputes between a state and a citizen of another state or a citizen of another country without the permission of the sovereign state being sued. In Chisholm v. Georgia, 2 Dallas 419

The contemporary U.S. Supreme Court. Seated, left to right: Associate Justices Antonin Scalia and John Paul Stevens, Chief Justice William H. Rehnquist, Associate Justices Sandra Day O'Connor and Anthony M. Kennedy. Standing, left to right: Associate Justices Ruth Bader Ginsburg, David H. Souter, Clarence Thomas, and Stephen G. Breyer.

(1793), the U.S. Supreme Court ordered the state of Georgia to appear before it to recover bonds due the estate of two deceased business partners whose property had been confiscated by Georgia during the Revolutionary War. Georgia refused to appear on the basis of sovereign immunity—no state may be sued without its consent. The decision had an immediate consequence. The state of Georgia refused to honor the judgment and the day following the decision a constitutional amendment was proposed in Congress. The Eleventh Amendment, which was introduced in Congress in 1794 and ratified by the states in early 1798, provides: "The judicial power of the United States shall not be construed to extend to any suit in law or equity, commenced or prosecuted against one of the United States by Citizens of another State, or by Citizens or Subjects of any Foreign State."

As early as 1821, the Supreme Court found a way to soften the attack on its jurisdiction by holding in Cohens v. Virginia, 6 Wheat. 264 (1821), that the literal language of the Eleventh Amendment does not prevent a citizen of one state from suing another state if the state *commences* a prosecution against him. This is true because, as Chief Justice John Marshall pointed out, the individual citizen did not initiate the suit. Instead, John Marshall, the judiciary's consistent champion for national power, reasoned that the individual merely continues the original case commenced or prosecuted against him by the state. Nonetheless, the matter of state immunity from suits in federal courts remains a controversial matter even today. The summary of the 1999 U.S. Supreme Court opinion in *Alden v. Maine* that follows encapsulates the point.

Box 3.5　　　　**Summary of Alden v. Maine**
U.S. Supreme Court
527 U.S. 706 (1999)

The federal statute known as the Fair Labor Standards Act (FLSA) enacted under the Constitution's Commerce Clause (Article I, section 8, clause 3), regulates employment matters affecting interstate commerce including over-time pay for state public employees. The 1938 congressional act authorizes private parties to file suit in any federal or state court of competent jurisdiction, for items including unpaid overtime compensation. It also authorizes the United States Secretary of Labor to file suit in any federal or state court to recover damages on behalf of employees denied unpaid overtime compensation and liquidated damages. A group of probation officers filed suit against their employer, the state of Maine, in the United States District Court for the District of Maine. They alleged that the state had violated the FLSA's overtime provisions, and they sought compensation and liquidated damages. While the suit was pending, the United States Supreme Court handed down its opinion in Seminole Tribe v. Florida, 517 U.S. 44 (1996). The Court held "the background principle of state sovereign immunity embodied in the Constitution's Eleventh Amendment—which expressly refers to only federal courts—prevents congressional authorization, under the commerce clause's provision concerning commerce with 'the Indian Tribes,' of private suits in federal court against non-consenting states." By virtue of this decision, the U.S. District Court dismissed the probation officers' suit and the United States Court of Appeals for the First Circuit affirmed the decision in the court below. The probation officers then filed essentially the same FLSA suit in the Superior Court of Maine. However, the state court dismissed the suit on the basis of the state's sovereign immunity and the Supreme Judicial Court of Maine affirmed on the same grounds. The U.S. Supreme Court granted certiorari.

Writing for a slim 5–4 majority, Justice Kennedy joined by Chief Justice Rehnquist, and Justices O'Connor, Scalia, and Thomas affirmed the decision of the state courts. The majority held that the sovereign immunity of the states from suit neither derives from nor is limited by the terms of the Eleventh Amendment. Instead, Kennedy argued that the Constitution's structure, its history, and the Supreme Court's authoritative interpretations make it clear that the sovereignty which the states enjoyed before the Constitution's ratification, and which they retain at the present time, does not permit the Congress under Article I of the Constitution to subject nonconsenting states to private suits for damages in the states' own courts.

Mr. Justice Souter, joined by Stevens, Ginsburg, and Breyer dissented, arguing that it was unlikely that a substantial body of thought at the time of the Constitution's framing understood sovereign immunity to be an inherent right of statehood while at the same time adopting the Constitution's Tenth Amendment. Nor is there evidence that any concept of inherent sovereign immunity was understood historically to apply when the sovereign sued was not the originator of the law. Further, the majority's view of federalism ignores the accepted authority of Congress to bind states under the FLSA and to provide for enforcement of federal rights in state courts. Lastly, the enforcement of the FLSA by the Secretary of Labor alone without a private right of seeking damages was not likely to prove adequate to assure compliance with the FLSA in the diverse circumstances of almost 5 million employees of the 50 states of the Union.

Just three years after its 1999 decision in *Alden v. Maine,* by a 5–4 decision in *Federal Maritime Commission v. South Carolina State Ports Authority* (2002), the U.S. Supreme Court extended its state immunity doctrine.[12] This decision forbade a federal administrative agency to adjudicate a private party's complaint against a state. Mr. Justice Clarence Thomas, writing for the majority, recited faithfully the states' rights mantra. He wrote: "Dual sovereignty is a defining feature of our Nation's constitutional blueprint."[13]

A private cruise line that carried passengers beyond the waters of South Carolina for the purpose of gambling was denied docking rights by the Port of Charleston, South Carolina Port Authority. The cruise line complained to the Federal Maritime Commission, an independent regulatory agency of the federal government. It argued that the port authority discriminated against it in violation of the Shipping Act of 1984, because it allowed other cruise lines engaged in gambling to dock in its ports.

All federal administrative agencies maintain a process of adjudicating complaints that assist them in making rules and resolving conflicts. Administrative law judges, sometimes called hearing examiners, function to provide relatively neutral decision-making. The explicit goal is to resolve disputes that all parties will perceive to be fair. The decisions of the agency judges may be appealed within the agency. Ultimately, agency heads may sustain, overrule, or modify the judgment below. Appeal is available beyond the agency to the regular civil courts. In this South Carolina maritime case, an administrative law judge of the Commission held a hearing on the matter. The agency judge decided that because the port authority is an arm of the state of South Carolina, it is entitled to sovereign immunity. Consequently, the complaint was dismissed. The Federal Maritime Commission reversed the decision of its administrative law judge, concluding that state sovereign immunity applies to proceedings before judicial tribunals and not to executive branch agencies. A federal Court of Appeals decided in favor of the South Carolina Port Authority.

Justice Thomas, writing for the U.S. Supreme Court, admitted that executive branch adjudications are not an exercise of the judicial power as literally understood from a reading of the Eleventh Amendment. Yet, he reasoned, administrative agency adjudications share many of the characteristics of judicial proceedings, such as the filing of complaints, answers, subpoena power, and discovery processes commonly found in civil suits. He quoted favorably from the Court of Appeals opinion, to wit: The administrative proceeding ". . . walks, talks, and squawks very much like a lawsuit."[14]

Because the framers of the Constitution and of the Eleventh Amendment could not have imagined the modern administrative state, Justice Thomas concedes there is no solid textual evidence to support the conclusion that they intended to forbid state governments from being sued by private parties before an independent regulatory agency. Yet, referring to the doctrine in *Alden v. Maine*, Thomas concludes: ". . . if the Framers thought it an impermissible affront to a State's dignity to be required to answer the complaints of private parties in federal courts, we cannot imagine that they would have found it acceptable to compel a State to do exactly the same thing before the administrative tribunal of an agency, such as the FMC [Federal Maritime Commission]."[15]

The four dissenters, led by Mr. Justice Stephen G. Breyer, made two major criticisms of the majority opinion. First, federal administrative agencies do not exercise the *judicial power of the United States*. Rather than exercising Article III power, federal agencies exercise *executive power* granted through Article II of the Constitution. The Eleventh Amendment says, "The Judicial power of the United States shall not . . . extend to any suit . . . commenced or prosecuted against one of the . . . States by Citizens of another State."[16] Second, an agency of the federal government, the Maritime Commission, was acting against the state port authority, not a private party. The order cannot be enforced by the cruise line. Only the federal government acting through the Commission or the Attorney General can take the port authority to a federal court to enforce its order. In the typical administrative proceeding, Breyer points out, private individuals file a complaint (in this case, the cruise line) with the agency (in this case, the Federal Maritime Commission). The agency adjudicates the claim by employing the services of its own administrative law judges. Then the agency reaches a decision that is either consistent or inconsistent with the judgment of the administrative law judges. The state (in this case, the South Carolina State Port Authority) may if it wishes take the matter to a federal court to obtain judicial review of any adverse agency ruling. Importantly, Breyer emphasized, its opponent in court is not a private party, but the agency itself.[17]

It is difficult to predict with certainty whether the doctrine outlined in *Federal Maritime Commission v. South Carolina State Ports Authority* will withstand future challenges and retain value as precedent. What is known is that a slim majority of justices on the contemporary Supreme Court is committed to a particular view of American federalism. It is best characterized as a states' rights or dual federalism perspective.

National Common Law

American federalism presents a serious problem for uniform decisions across the land. What is to prevent federal courts and state courts from reaching different results on the same issue of state law? Should federal courts establish a common law for the entire United States regardless of where and who the litigants might be? Given the terms of the Supremacy Clause, one might reasonably conclude that national standards ought to apply. The U.S. Supreme Court settled this thorny matter in the 1938 landmark case of *Erie R.R. Co. v. Tompkins*.

The *Erie* doctrine makes clear that except in matters governed by the U.S. Constitution or by acts of the U.S. Congress, the law to be applied in any case is the substantive law of the state. Further, the decision in *Erie* makes clear that it is not a legitimate concern of federal courts to ponder whether the law of the state is defined by its legislature in a statute or by its highest court in a judicial opinion. Importantly, there is no federal general common law. Congress has no power to declare substantive rules of common law applicable in a state whether they are local in their nature or general, or whether they impact commercial law or the law of torts. However, federal courts are free to apply federal procedural rules, such as the Federal Rules of Civil Procedure, unless they significantly affect the substantive rights of litigants.

Erie R.R. Co. v. Tompkins
U.S. Supreme Court
304 U.S. 64, 58 S. Ct. 817, 82 L.Ed. 1188 (1938)

MR. JUSTICE BRANDEIS delivered the majority opinion of the Court.

Tompkins, a citizen of Pennsylvania, was injured on a dark night by a passing freight train of the Erie Railroad Company while walking along its right of way at Hughestown in that State. He claimed that the accident occurred through negligence in the operation, or maintenance, of the train; that he was rightfully on the premises as [a] licensee because [he was] on a commonly used beaten footpath which ran for a short distance alongside the tracks; and that he was struck by something which looked like a door projecting from one of the moving cars. To enforce that claim he brought an action in the federal court for southern New York, which had jurisdiction because the company is a corporation of that State. It denied liability; and the case was tried by a jury.

The Erie insisted that its duty to Tompkins was no greater than that owed to a trespasser. It contended, among other things, that its duty to Tompkins, and hence its liability, should be determined in accordance with the Pennsylvania law; that under the law of Pennsylvania, as declared by its highest court, persons who use pathways along the railroad right of way—that is a longitudinal pathway as distinguished from a crossing—are to be deemed trespassers; and that the railroad is not liable for injuries to undiscovered trespassers resulting from its negligence, unless it be wanton or wilful. Tompkins denied that any such rule had been established by the decisions of the Pennsylvania courts; and contended that, since there was no statute of the State on the subject, the railroad's duty and liability is to be determined in federal courts as a matter of general law.

The trial judge refused to rule that the applicable law precluded recovery. The jury brought in a verdict of $30,000; and the judgment entered thereon was affirmed by the Circuit Court of Appeals, which held, that it was unnecessary to consider whether the law of Pennsylvania was as contended, because the question was one not of local, but of general law, and that "upon questions of general law the federal courts are free, in the absence of a local statute, to exercise their independent judgment as to what the law is; and it is well settled that the question of the responsibility of a railroad for injuries caused by its servants is one of general law. . . . Where the public has made open and notorious use of a railroad right of way for a long period of time and without objection, the company owes to persons on such permissive pathway a duty of care in the operation of its trains. . . . It is likewise generally recognized law that a jury may find that negligence exists toward a pedestrian using a permissive path on the railroad right of way if he is hit by some object projecting from the side of the train."

The Erie had contended that application of the Pennsylvania rule was required, among other things, by § 34

of the Federal Judiciary Act of September 24, 1789, which provides:

"The laws of the several States, except where the Constitution, treaties, or statutes of the United States otherwise require or provide, shall be regarded as rules of decision in trials at common law, in the courts of the United States, in cases where they apply."

Because of the importance of the question whether the federal court was free to disregard the alleged rule of the Pennsylvania common law, we granted certiorari.

First. Swift v. Tyson, 16 Pet. 1, 18 (1842), held that federal courts exercising jurisdiction on the ground of diversity of citizenship need not, in matters of general jurisprudence, apply the unwritten law of the State as declared by its highest court; that they are free to exercise an independent judgment as to what the common law of the State is—or should be; and that, as there stated by Mr. Justice Story: "the true interpretation of the thirty-fourth section limited its application to state laws strictly local, that is to say, to the positive statutes of the state, and the construction thereof adopted by the local tribunals, and to rights and titles to things having a permanent locality, such as the rights and titles to real estate, and other matters immovable and intraterritorial in their nature and character. It never has been supposed by us, that the section did apply, or was intended to apply, to questions of a more general nature, not at all dependent upon local statutes or local usages of a fixed and permanent operation, as, for example, to the construction of ordinary contracts or other written instruments, and especially to questions of general commercial law, where the state tribunals are called upon to perform the like functions as ourselves, that is, to ascertain upon general reasoning and legal analogies, what is the true exposition of the contract or instrument, or what is the just rule furnished by the principles of commercial law to govern the case."

The Court in applying the rule of § 34 to equity cases, in Mason v. United States, 260 U.S. 545, 559, said: "The statute, however, is merely declarative of the rule which would exist in the absence of the statute." The federal courts assumed, in the broad field of "general law," the power to declare rules of decision which Congress was confessedly without power to enact as statutes. Doubt was repeatedly expressed as to the correctness of the construction given § 34, and as to the soundness of the rule which it introduced. But it was the more recent research of a competent scholar [Charles Warren], who examined the original document, which established that the construction given to it by the Court was erroneous; and that the purpose of the section was merely to make certain that, in all matters except those in which some federal law is controlling, the federal courts exercising jurisdiction in diversity of citizenship cases would apply as their rules of decision the law of the State, unwritten as well as written.

Second. Experience in applying the doctrine of *Swift v. Tyson,* had revealed its defects, political and social; and the benefits expected to flow from the rule did not accrue. Persistence of state courts in their own opinions on questions of common law prevented uniformity and the impossibility of discovering a satisfactory line of demarcation between the province of general law and that of local law developed a new well of uncertainties.

On the other hand, the mischievous results of the doctrine had become apparent. Diversity of citizenship jurisdiction was conferred in order to prevent apprehended discrimination in state courts against those not citizens of the State. *Swift v. Tyson* introduced grave discrimination by non-citizens against citizens. It made rights enjoyed under the unwritten "general law" vary according to whether enforcement was sought in the state or in the federal court; and the privilege of selecting the court in which the right should be determined was conferred upon the non-citizen. Thus, the doctrine rendered impossible equal protection of the law. In attempting to promote uniformity of law throughout the United States, the doctrine had prevented uniformity in the administration of the law of the State. The discrimination resulting became in practice far-reaching. This resulted in part from the broad province accorded to the so-called "general law" as to which federal courts exercised an independent judgment. In addition to questions of purely commercial law, "general law" was held to include the obligations under contracts entered into and to be performed within the State, the extent to which a carrier operating within a State may stipulate for exemption from liability for his own negligence or that of his employee; the liability for torts committed within the State upon persons resident or property located there, even where the question of liability depended upon the scope of a property right conferred by the State; and the right to exemplary or punitive damages. Furthermore, state decisions construing local deeds, mineral conveyances, and even devises of real estate were disregarded.

In part the discrimination resulted from the wide range of persons held entitled to avail themselves of the federal rule by resort to the diversity of citizenship jurisdiction. Through this jurisdiction individual citizens willing to remove from their own State and become citizens of another might avail themselves of the federal rule. And, without even a change of residence, a corporate citizen of the State could avail itself of the federal rule by re-incorporating under the laws of another State, . . . The injustice and confusion incident to the doctrine of *Swift v. Tyson* have been repeatedly urged as reasons for abolishing or limiting diversity of citizenship jurisdiction. Other legislative relief has been proposed. If only a question of statutory construction were involved, we should not be prepared to abandon a doctrine so widely applied throughout nearly a century. But the unconstitutionality of the course pursued has now been made clear and compels us to do so.

Third. Except matters governed by the Federal Constitution or by Acts of Congress, the law to be applied in any case is the law of the State. And whether the law of the State shall be declared by its Legislature in a statute or by its highest court in a decision is not a matter of federal concern. There is no federal general common law. Congress has no power to declare substantive rules of common law applicable in a State whether they be local in their nature or "general," be they commercial law or a part of the law of torts. And no clause in the Constitution purports to confer such a power upon the federal courts. As stated by Mr. Justice Field when protesting in

Baltimore & Ohio R. Co. v. Baugh 149 U.S. 368, 401, against ignoring the Ohio common law of fellow servant liability:

"I am aware that what has been termed the general law of the country—which is often little less than what the judge advancing the doctrine thinks at the time should be the general law on a particular subject,—has been often advanced in judicial opinions of this court to control a conflicting law of a State. I admit that learned judges have fallen into the habit of repeating this doctrine as a convenient mode of brushing aside the law of a State in conflict with their views. And I confess that, moved and governed by the authority of the great names of those judges, I have, myself, in many instances, unhesitatingly and confidently, but I think now erroneously, repeated the same doctrine. But, notwithstanding the great names which may be cited in favor of the doctrine, and notwithstanding the frequency with which the doctrine has been reiterated, there stands, as a perpetual protest against its repetition, the Constitution of the United States, which recognizes and preserves the autonomy and independence of the States—independence in their legislative and independence in their judicial departments. Supervision over either the legislative or the judicial action of the States is in no case permissible except as to matters by the Constitution specifically authorized or delegated to the United States. Any interference with either, except as thus permitted, is an invasion of the authority of the State and, to that extent, a denial of its independence. "

The fallacy underlying the rule declared in *Swift v. Tyson* is made clear by Mr. Justice Holmes. The doctrine rests upon the assumption that there is "a transcendental body of law outside of any particular State but obligatory within it unless and until changed by statute," that federal courts have the power to use their judgment as to what the rules of common law are; and that in the federal courts "the parties are entitled to an independent judgment on matters of general law: but law in the sense in which courts speak of it today does not exist without some definite authority behind it. The common law so far as it is enforced in a State, whether called common law or not, is not the common law generally but the law of that State existing by the authority of that State without regard to what it may have been in England or anywhere else.". . . "the authority and only authority is the State, and if that be so, the voice adopted by the State as its own [whether it be of its Legislature or of its Supreme Court] should utter the last word."

Thus the doctrine of *Swift v. Tyson* is, as Mr. Justice Holmes said, "an unconstitutional assumption of powers by courts of the United States which no lapse of time or respectable array of opinion should make us hesitate to correct." In disapproving that doctrine we do not hold unconstitutional § 34 of the Federal Judiciary Act of 1789 or any other Act of Congress. We merely declare that in applying the doctrine this Court and the lower courts have invaded rights which in our opinion are reserved by the Constitution to the several States.

Fourth. The defendant contended that by the common law of Pennsylvania as declared by its highest court in Falchetti v. Pennsylvania R. R. Co., 307 Pa. 203; 160 A. 859, the only duty owed to the plaintiff was to refrain from wilful or wanton injury. The plaintiff denied that such is the Pennsylvania law. In support of their respective contentions the parties discussed and cited many decisions of the Supreme Court of the State. The Circuit Court of Appeals ruled that the question of liability is one of general law; and on that ground declined to decide the issue of state law. As we hold this was error, the judgment is reversed and the case remanded to it for further proceedings in conformity with our opinion.

Reversed.

Case Questions for Discussion

1. Given what you know about the previous decisions of the Rehnquist Court, do you think the contemporary Supreme Court would make the same decision as the 1938 Court?

2. Do you agree with the result of the *Erie* decision with respect to the holding that there shall be no federal substantive common law applicable to all of the states?

3. Upon reflection, do you think Chief Justice Rehnquist's interpretation of the *Erie* doctrine in *Bush v. Gore* (see Chapter 2) is consistent with the opinion of Justice Brandeis in *Erie v. Tompkins*?

Full Faith and Credit Clause

Because it is inappropriate to rely upon federal common law in diversity of citizenship disputes, it is obviously necessary for federal and state courts to apply the law of the states. Article IV, section 1 of the Constitution provides: "Full Faith and Credit shall be given in each State to the public Acts, Records, and judicial Proceedings of every other State. " This clause applies to judicial decisions. Thus, for example, if a person wins a judgment in Illinois against a negligent driver of an automobile and that defendant moves to Wisconsin, the plaintiff may call upon the Wisconsin courts to enforce the judgment. The same principle applies, for example, to breaches of contract or divorce proceedings. Yet, there are many occasions when it is unclear whether the laws of state A or state B should apply. For instance, if an automobile tire manufacturing company located in Ohio produced a defective tire that was the cause of a fatal accident in Kentucky, should the laws of Ohio apply or should Kentucky law, pertaining to liability, be applied by the state court hearing the case? This is a particularly important issue if the amount of damages that may be awarded a plaintiff is far greater in one state than the other.

The trend in recent years has been to interpret the Full Faith and Credit Clause as giving state courts considerable latitude in determining whether to use the laws of their own state rather than that of a sister state.[18] States have devised *conflict of laws* rules to assist courts in determining whether and under what circumstances foreign law (i.e., law not of the forum state) should be applied within its jurisdiction. In tort cases, the traditional but now outmoded approach is to apply the law of the place (*lex loci delicti*) where the wrongful conduct was committed. In recent decades, however, a majority of states have moved to a more flexible rule that is favored by the *American Law Institute*—an organization of legal specialists noted for its authoritative recommendations for revision of a wide variety of American law subjects including the *Restatement (Second) of Conflicts*. The authors of the *Restatement* recommend that state courts ask, in what jurisdiction is there a significant relationship between the parties to the suit? The *most significant relationship rule*, as it is called, takes into consideration such factors as the following: the location where the injury occurred, the place where the conduct causing the injury occurred, the residence, domicile, nationality, place of incorporation, and place of business of the parties, and the so-called place where the relationship between the parties is centered.[19] Some states use other but related rules. For cases involving contractual disputes, state courts use various but sometimes confusing rules depending upon the facts in the case at hand. Nonetheless, consistent with the underlying principle of the law of contracts, state courts will, if it can be known, honor the intent of the parties (e.g., when contracts contain a clause specifying which state law applies in the case of a breach).[20]

As the following Delaware Supreme Court opinion in *Travelers Indemnity v. Lake* illustrates, how courts employ competing views of conflict of laws is not limited to disputes originating within the United States. The description of foreign jurisdictions is broadly applied to places outside of the United States as well, in this case Quebec, Canada. Today especially, globalization of economies and politics renders conflict of laws a matter of vital interest.

Travelers Indemnity Company v. Lake
Supreme Court of Delaware
594 A.2d 38 (1991)

O PINION of Justice Moore.
      In this case we reexamine the *lex loci delicti* rule of Friday v. Smoot, 58 Del. 488, 211 A.2d 594 (1965). The appellee, Ben E. Lake, sued his uninsured motorist carrier, The Travelers Indemnity Company ("Travelers"), in the Delaware Superior Court as the result of an accident in Quebec, Canada, between Lake and an unidentified motorist. Quebec law establishes a legal limit on tort recoveries, which is considerably below the limits of Lake's coverage from Travelers. The insurance policy obligates Travelers to pay damages to Lake which he is "legally entitled to recover" from an uninsured motorist. The Superior Court ruled that Lake's suit was a contract action, and applied Delaware law. We affirm on different grounds. Thus, the limits of Lake's insurance policy, not the tort limits of Quebec, apply. We overrule *Friday v. Smoot* and adopt the prevailing "most significant relationship" test of the RESTATEMENT (SECOND) OF CONFLICTS § 145(1).

      The essential facts are not in dispute. Ben E. Lake was injured in a traffic accident while driving his employer's vehicle in Quebec, Canada. A tailgate from an unidentified truck, driving in an opposite lane, struck Lake's tractor-trailer. Lake lost control of his truck, struck a concrete barrier, and sustained serious injury. The other driver did not stop after the accident. Apparently, there were no eyewitnesses and despite his best efforts, Lake could not locate the other motorist.

      At the time of the accident, Lake had an insurance policy with Travelers covering one of his own automobiles not involved in the crash. The policy provides uninsured motorist coverage of $300,000 per occurrence.

      Lake sued Travelers in Superior Court for the uninsured motorist benefits of his policy. The parties agreed to arbitrate their dispute, but reserved the right to apply to the court to resolve certain legal issues. Travelers filed a motion . . . for a ruling confining its liability under Lake's policy to the limits Quebec law sets for bodily injury. The parties agreed that Lake could recover only $29,400 if the court applied Quebec law, whereas he could recover up to $300,000 if Delaware law applies.

Travelers argued that Quebec law determined what Lake was "legally entitled to recover" under the terms of his policy. Relying on *Friday*, Travelers reasoned that if Lake had sued the unidentified driver for negligence in Delaware, the court would have applied the *lex loci delicti* choice of law theory thereby confining his recovery to Quebec's $29,400 limit.

The Superior Court rejected Travelers' claim and refused to apply Quebec law. The court ruled that a suit challenging insurance coverage is an "action in contract." (emphasis in original). Instead of the *lex loci* rule, the court applied the RESTATEMENT (SECOND) OF CONFLICTS "most significant relationship" theory which governs conflict of law problems in contract cases. The court ultimately ruled that Delaware had the "most significant relationship" to the insurance policy and decided that Lake was thus "legally entitled" to recover under Delaware law. . . .

The present state of our law in this area is unsettled. Delaware courts apply the modern "most significant relationship" test to resolve conflicts issues arising out of the interpretation and validity of contracts. However, we also apply the *lex loci delicti* doctrine in most tort cases. . . .

The Delaware insurance statutes require insurance carriers to provide underinsured/uninsured motorist protection to all Delaware drivers in an amount up to $300,000. 18 Del. C. § 3902. . . .

Delaware courts have consistently interpreted Section 3902 as a form of supplemental coverage designed to protect Delaware motorists "from an irresponsible driver causing injury or death." Section 3902 permits a Delaware motorist to "mirror" his own liability coverage and take to the roads knowing that a certain amount of protection will always be available.

The trial court's application of contract conflict of laws principles to interpret Lake's insurance policy contravenes the mirrored benefits purpose expressed in Section 3902. The court implicitly established an unfair distinction between an uninsured policy claim involving an unknown tortfeasor and a direct tort suit against an identified defendant. For example, Lake does not deny that the court would have applied the *lex loci* rule and limited his recovery to $29,400 if he had found the other driver and sued him in Delaware for negligence. Yet Lake urges the Court to allow him to recover up to the $300,000 limit set in his uninsured motorist policy merely because he could not find the other driver.

As we have previously observed, the General Assembly enacted Section 3902 to provide only supplemental coverage to protect Delaware drivers from uninsured motorists. There is no doubt that the court would have awarded a hypothetical plaintiff $29,400 if he sued Lake in Delaware and Lake had caused the accident in Canada. Given the state of the law at the time, the trial court should have applied the tort conflict of laws rules to determine the amount of damages Lake was "legally entitled to recover" under his uninsured motorist policy. . . .

In *Friday* we confirmed the principle that Delaware courts apply the *lex loci delicti* choice of law theory in tort cases. Accordingly, *Friday* held that: "The law of the place in which a tort takes place governs the substantive rights of the parties in an action based upon the tort brought in Delaware." Lake now urges the Court to abandon the *lex loci* rule in favor of the more flexible RESTATEMENT (SECOND) OF CONFLICTS "most significant relationship" approach. Lake claims that the *lex loci* test often leads to unjust results. He also claims that the theoretical assumptions supporting the old rule are outdated. Lake points to the fact that a clear majority of the states have already abandoned *lex loci* in tort cases.

We agree that it is appropriate to reexamine the *lex loci* doctrine. The law has changed dramatically in the decades since *Friday* was decided. The so-called "litigation explosion" has congested our courts with an ever-increasing number of tort suits. Concurrently, our society has become even more mobile and transitory.

In *Friday*, the Court was confronted with the decision whether to retain the *lex loci* rule or apply the then new Restatement's (Second) approach. *Friday* retained the old rule for three basic reasons: (1) the *lex loci* rule was more predictable and certain; (2) abandoning the *lex loci* rule would encourage forum shopping; and (3) only the legislature could repeal the doctrine because it would represent "a major change" in the law. A brief review of the inherent doctrinal assumptions of the *lex loci* rule indicate that an unquestioning adherence to "predictability" is not warranted where changes in the law and national life have eroded the foundation of a legal principle.

Friday explicitly relied on both the First Restatement and a noted treatise when it retained *lex loci*. . . .

The vested rights doctrine is a common law theory first discussed in Justice Story's classic treatise COM-MENTARIES ON THE CONFLICT OF LAWS, FOREIGN AND DOMESTIC (1834). See W. COOK, THE LOGICAL AND LEGAL BASES OF THE CONFLICT OF LAWS 48 (1942). The vested rights theory is founded on respect for a state's territorial sanctity and evolves from a series of "logical" postulates. See COOK, at 49. Basically, the vested rights theory assumes: (1) that the laws of a jurisdiction have no "intrinsic force" beyond its territorial boundaries; and (2) the laws of every state bind all property and persons within its territorial jurisdiction. Id. (citing J. STORY, COMMENTARIES ON THE CONFLICT OF LAWS §§ 7-8, 17, 18 (8th ed. 1883)). Beale surmised from these two basic postulates that:

"It is impossible for a plaintiff to recover in tort unless he has been given by some law a cause of action in tort; and this cause of action can be given only by the law of the place where the tort was committed." BEALE, § 378.1 at 1288. The vested rights theory thus posits that states must uniformly respect the laws of the territory where the tort "right" first came into existence.

Most American courts, however, have completely abandoned the vested rights theory and its doctrinal cousin *lex loci*. . . . Commentators have critiqued the vested rights theory because it ignores the substantive content of a jurisdiction's legal rules and instead focuses on the territorial aspects of the "right." . . . Basically, other than respect for territorial boundaries, the vested rights theory does not adequately explain why a court must apply the law of the place where the tort occurs.

The Second Restatement of Conflicts also recognized the fundamental problem with the vested rights theory and the *lex loci* doctrine, since the last place of injury only bears "a slight relationship to the occurrence and the parties. . . ." RESTATEMENT (SECOND) OF CONFLICTS ch. 7 at 413 (1971) (Introductory Note). The Restatement also noted the increasing abandonment of the vested rights approach: "Judges are more prepared than formerly to consider the basic policies and values underlying choice of law. In reaching their decisions, the judges give greater weight to the [new Restatement's 'most significant relationship' test] than to the demands of some legal theory, as that of vested rights."

The Second Restatement also recognized that fundamental changes in American society made the *lex loci* doctrine obsolete. The vested rights theory, with its emphasis on territorial boundaries, had little relevance in the modern industrial world. The Restatement commented: "State and national boundaries are of less significance today by reason of the increased mobility of our population and of the increasing tendency of men to conduct their affairs across boundary lines."

Thus, over 31 states now have rejected the *lex loci* doctrine in tort cases. We recognize that "we do not meet our responsibilities by merely counting jurisdictions." Nonetheless, we also cannot ignore the realities of modern jurisprudence and informed scholarly debate. As we have previously stated: "The law should be an ever developing body of doctrines, precepts, and rules designed to meet the evolving needs of society. . . . While stare decisis has its place, the strength of the Common Law is its ability to grow and respond to the realities of life. Absent this, the law fails in its vital purpose." No clearer example of this evolving nature of the law is found in the area under discussion, and the treatment it has received in the Restatement.

Having briefly chronicled the fundamental weaknesses of the *lex loci* doctrine, we turn to its supposed strengths. Travelers vigorously argues that predictability and certainty is the major asset of *lex loci*. It claims that applying the law of the state where the injury occurred makes "facile the prediction of applicable tort law for claimants, insurers, lawyers and judges." A brief review of our own *lex loci* jurisprudence makes it quite clear that application of the *lex loci* doctrine is anything but facile.

First, and most significantly, this Court has already abandoned the *lex loci* doctrine for contracts cases. . . . Accordingly, as Travelers itself suggests, one way to avoid an unduly harsh application of *lex loci delicti* is to treat a tort-like case as a contract action. Travelers, however, misses the fundamental point that attempting to characterize a lawsuit with both tort and contract characteristics is no easier or more predictable than applying the alternatives to *lex loci*. Of course, the only reason why the court even has this choice is that Delaware recognizes different conflict of law principles for both torts and contracts suits. At present Delaware is one of only two jurisdictions that still recognize *lex loci* for torts, but apply the most significant relationship test on contract cases.

Second, Travelers argues that *lex loci* is more predictable. It contends that the choice of law alternatives are too vague and difficult to apply. Travelers, however, again fails to recognize that the *lex loci* doctrine is almost meaningless when considered in relation to its own broad exceptions.

Delaware courts recognize two basic exceptions to the *lex loci* rule. First, courts ignore *lex loci* when they determine that the issue in question is procedural. Second, Delaware courts refuse to apply *lex loci* when the law of the state where the accident occurred "is clearly repugnant to the settled public policy of (Delaware) the forum." A court is thus authorized, under the public policy exception of the *lex loci* rule, to abandon another state's law when its laws violate Delaware's public policy.

The public policy exception to the *lex loci* rule undercuts the certainty and predictability it was designed to promote. . . . Indeed, Lake and Travelers dedicated large sections of their briefs contesting the applicability of the public policy exception. We do not see how a court could apply *lex loci* without first considering Delaware public policy. When viewed in its most abstract form, the public policy exception is really no more than a principle which recognizes that the so-called territorial justification, inherent in the vested rights theory, is subordinate to the substantive laws of the forum state.

Finally, *Friday* refused to abandon *lex loci* because it feared that repealing the doctrine would encourage forum shopping. The Court, employing a hypothetical where two Delaware residents sued each other for negligence inflicted in another state, claimed that adopting the Restatement test would drive the Delaware residents to seek relief in a state that recognized *lex loci*. Such reasoning is not compelling in today's world.

First, when the Court decided *Friday*, only three states had adopted the new Restatement rule. Now, 31 states have rejected *lex loci*. The dan-

ger of forum shopping is obviously of reduced significance. Second, there is little we can do to prevent litigants from asserting their rights in the appropriate forum of their choice. While we discourage the use of Delaware courts as forum shopping venues, litigants generally have the right to pick their own forum as long as they satisfy all relevant jurisdictional requirements.

Finally, Travelers relies on *Friday*'s dictum that we could not rescind the *lex loci* doctrine without legislative action. The rationale being that it would represent a "major change" in the law. That notion is unpersuasive in view of the origins of the *lex loci* doctrine.

The *lex loci* doctrine was purely a judicial creation. The General Assembly has never mandated the application of *lex loci delicti* to tort cases, and we doubt that it would ever do so. Indeed, Delaware traces the origins of its *lex loci* theory to the common law and Beale's original treatises on conflicts. Additionally, at least two other jurisdictions have also recognized that *lex loci* was an artificial product of the common law vested rights theory.

. . . Thus, we overrule *Friday v. Smoot* and its automatic *lex loci delicti* choice of law standard. It is a doctrine that has lost its place in the growth of modern law.

. . . This brings us to the question of what choice of law doctrine a court should apply to decide tort cases.

Pursuant to Section 145 of the Second Restatement, the local law of the state which "has the most significant relationship to the occurrence and the parties under the principles stated in § 6" will govern the rights of litigants in a tort suit. RESTATEMENT

(SECOND) OF CONFLICTS § 145(1) (1971). Section Six of the Restatement lists the following relevant choice of law considerations:

(a) the needs of the interstate and international systems,

(b) the relevant policies of the forum,

(c) the relevant policies of other interested states and the relative interests of those states in the determination of the particular issue,

(d) the protection of justified expectations,

(e) the basic policies underlying the particular field of law,

(f) certainty, predictability and uniformity of result, and

(g) ease in the determination and application of the law to be applied.

Section 145 lists the following relevant contacts a court should consider when applying Section Six:

(a) the place where the injury occurred,

(b) the place where the conduct causing the injury occurred,

(c) the domicile residence, nationality, place of incorporation and place of business of the parties, and

(d) the place where the relationship, if any, between the parties is centered.

These contacts are to be evaluated according to their relative importance with respect to the particular issue.

Finally, Section 146 specifically directs the court to apply the law of the state where the injury occurred in a "personal injury case" unless the forum state has more "significant relationship" under the Section Six principles to the "occurrence and the parties." Id. at § 146. The commentary to Section 146 confines its definition of personal injury to either "physical harm or mental disturbance . . . resulting from physical harm or from threatened physical harm or other injury to oneself or to another."

In view of the Restatement's tests, we consider whether the substantive law of Delaware or Quebec applies here. What is Quebec's interest? The relevant Quebec statutory scheme envisions a system of no-fault insurance limiting a negligent driver's liability to a predetermined amount of damages. The Connecticut Supreme Court, in evaluating the same relevant sections of the Quebec statute, found that Quebec law "eschews investigation into the possible negligence of the defendant's conduct and limits the amount of damages the victim of the defendant's conduct may recover." As we previously noted, Lake's damages would be limited to $29,400 if Quebec law applies.

There is no compelling issue of Quebec public policy here. The parties are not residents of Quebec. The truck Lake was driving when the accident occurred was not registered in Quebec. The only connection with Quebec is that the accident occurred there.

In comparison, Delaware clearly has the "most significant relationship" to the issues presented. Lake is a resident of Delaware. Travelers obviously conducts substantial business here. The uninsured motorist coverage provision of Lake's policy arose out of Delaware law and involves issues of vital importance to all Delaware citizens. Finally, unlike Quebec, Delaware generally does not endorse a no-fault system of tort law. Delaware courts always consider fault in assessing liability in tort cases.

Adoption of the most significant relationship test does not require a court to disregard a foreign jurisdiction's law in all tort cases. The flexibil-

ity of this doctrine requires that each case be decided on its own facts. Based upon the foregoing, the judgment of the Superior Court, refusing to restrict Lake's no-fault insurance claim under Quebec law, is AFFIRMED.

Case Questions for Discussion

1. Do you agree with the Delaware Supreme Court that the substantial relationship rule makes better sense for the modern world than the lex loci doctrine?

2. Should legal rules reflect enduring principles that can stand the test of time or should they change with the needs of society?

3. Is it too cynical to suggest that the assessment of the desirability of one or the other judge-made rule depends upon whose ox is being gored?

4. When Travelers sold Lake the insurance policy in Delaware, how much did the company anticipate it might be obligated to pay under an uninsured motorist claim? Insurance companies determine the premiums they charge by employing actuarial principles to the claim they expect to pay on the policies they issue. Had this court applied Quebec law, would Travelers' profits have been unjustly high?

Same-sex marriage controversy. In contemporary America, the issue of same-sex marriages is likely to create disputes requiring judicial interpretation of the Full Faith and Credit Clause. As we discuss in Chapter 12, most states have banned same-sex marriages. In 1996, Congress passed the "Defense of Marriage Act" that grants to the states the right not to recognize same-sex marriages, and it further indicates that the federal government recognizes only heterosexual marriages for purposes of social security and government pension plans. In the year 2000, Vermont was the first state to recognize gay and lesbian civil unions. Within minutes of the effective date and time of this statute, gay and lesbian couples recited vows of fidelity.

The Vermont law entitles gay and lesbian couples to all the rights and responsibilities of heterosexual married couples. Among other things, these couples may file joint income tax returns and have the right to make medical decisions for each other. If these couples move to another state without the legal protection of their gay union or, if indeed, they move to a state that is hostile to same-sex marriages, it is likely that a serious issue will arise concerning whether that state must recognize Vermont's law under the Full Faith and Credit Clause of the U.S. Constitution.

New Judicial Federalism

Readers should be aware of a relatively new historical development concerning the ability of state courts to make policy in the area of constitutional rights. But the basic point bears repeating—although there are exceptions particularly with respect to state immunity from suits, the federal judiciary generally gets its way when there is a conflict with state courts. It is also true that the federal courts, and U.S. Supreme Court justices in particular, have used their authority to actively protect the constitutional rights of people from state abuses, including decisions of state judiciaries limiting rights. The federal judiciary, however, has not consistently taken an activist posture when using its power to interpret the U.S. Constitution to expand rights.

Recent U.S. Supreme Courts—beginning with the tenure of Chief Justice Warren Burger (1969–1986) and, more dramatically, with the contemporary Court (1986–) headed by Chief Justice William Rehnquist—have significantly slowed the march toward the expansion of rights that occurred during the Warren Court era (1953–1969). Increasingly, civil libertarians and civil rights advocates have looked to state judiciaries for leadership in the expansion of constitutional rights, including such matters as school financing through local property taxes, the right to use private shopping centers to exercise political opinions, privacy rights, mental retardation, welfare, housing, age discrimination, and government employment. Beginning in the 1970s, state supreme courts interpreted state constitutional provisions to expand rights that are not explicitly provided for in the U.S. Constitution.

In brief, some state supreme courts have assumed an activist posture, while the more conservative U.S. Supreme Court has chosen not to expand constitutional rights. In the area of Fourteenth Amendment equal protection of the laws analysis, for example, the more conservative members of the Court have managed to limit the number of claims that may be regarded as fundamental to the enjoyment of liberty and equality of all persons so that the level of judicial scrutiny is minimal. Rights advocates argue that if state high courts can be convinced to protect constitutional rights with a heightened sense of judicial scrutiny, then the ill effects of the U.S. Supreme Court's reluctance to expand rights will be less important than would otherwise be the case. Though its actual implementation is questionable, this new activism by state judiciaries has been dubbed the *new judicial federalism*.

Judicial scholars and American politicians aptly characterize the Warren era as a period of judicial activism. Court decisions concerning such controversial matters as desegregation, internal security, school prayer, reapportionment of state legislatures, and criminal justice placed the justices in the eye of a political storm. Public opinion studies indicated substantial citizen dissatisfaction with the Warren Court. At least two modern presidents, Eisenhower and Nixon, reacted negatively to several landmark decisions. The appropriate role of the federal judiciary in making policy has been a debatable subject in presidential elections, especially since 1968. Studies of the relationship between Congress and the Court concluded that the widely held academic belief that Congress treats the Supreme Court with great reverence was far from true.[21] Of particular interest to our discussion of judicial federalism are the U.S. Supreme Court opinions asserting that most of the provisions found in the Bill of Rights related to the rights of criminal defendants are applicable to the states by way of the Due Process Clause of the Fourteenth Amendment.

Overruling previous precedent, in 1961 the Warren Court in Mapp v. Ohio, 367 U.S. 643, held that illegally seized evidence is inadmissible in a state criminal proceeding. A year later, in Robinson v. California, 370 U.S. 660 (1962), the Court held that a California criminal statute punishing someone for being addicted to drugs violated the Eighth Amendment prohibition against cruel and unusual punishment. In 1963, the Supreme Court in Gideon v. Wainwright, 372 U.S. 335, held that the right to legal counsel in criminal cases, whether capital or noncapital, is obligatory upon the states. The Fifth Amendment provision against self-incrimination was made applicable to the states in 1964 in Malloy v. Hogan, 378 U.S. 1. In the following year, the confrontation-of-witnesses provision of the Sixth Amendment was likewise incorporated in Pointer v. Texas, 380 U.S. 400 (1965). In 1967, in Klopfer v. North Carolina, 386 U.S. 213, the Sixth Amendment provision of the right to a speedy trial was applied to the states, and in 1968 the right to a jury trial in criminal cases was placed as a restriction upon the states in Duncan v. Louisiana, 391 U.S. 145. Finally, in 1969, in Benton v. Maryland, 395 U.S. 784, the Court overruled the 1937 decision in Palko v. Connecticut, 302 U.S. 319. It held that the double-jeopardy provision of the Fifth Amendment applied to the states by virtue of the Fourteenth Amendment's Due Process Clause. In addition to these criminal justice decisions, the Court handled many other controversial issues (e.g., the constitutional establishment of the right to privacy, the reapportionment of state legislatures, the prohibition on school prayers, and the sometimes controversial implementation of racial desegregation orders). This controversial posture helps us to understand why, in the context of the time, the U.S. Supreme Court was viewed by many as the innovator and engine in the expansion of constitutional rights. At the same time, state courts were regarded as defenders of an old order that failed to protect the rights of all persons in society.[22]

With the arrival of the Burger Court, the expansion of civil rights and liberties began to subside. Although the Burger Court did not reverse important Warren Court decisions, the majority of the justices refused to continue the trend toward the expansion of rights. The Court nonetheless hinted that state governments might expand rights if they wished. Some state supreme courts followed suit by employing the rules and principles of their own state constitutions; for example, the California Supreme Court ruled that wide disparities in state funding of public schools violated both state and federal equal protection clauses. By 1987, it was clear to Justice William Brennan, the leader of the liberal voting bloc on the U.S. Supreme Court, that the Court could no longer be relied upon to protect and expand rights. He publicly called upon the state courts to shoulder the burden.[23]

As Professor Harry P. Stumpf cogently points out, state courts possess important tools permitting them to play an activist role in the expansion of rights. First, many state constitutions contain provisions that are not explicitly found in the U.S. Constitution. For example, there are explicitly worded provisions about the right to privacy, the protection of the environment, and equal gender treatment. As long as state courts do not denigrate federal constitutional guarantees, and if their decisions are based on separate, adequate, and independent state grounds, the U.S. Supreme Court has presumed they are valid.[24] Second, because in the U.S. federal system the states retain extensive residual powers and are not bound by enumerated delegated powers as is the national government, state judges, unlike federal judges, need not search for explicit or implied powers to justify state actions to expand rights. State judges need only convince themselves that there are no state or federal constitutional provisions forbidding the state program under scrutiny. Third, at least ten state constitutions allow for advisory court opinions, in contrast to the Article III requirement of the U.S. Constitution that there must be an actual case and controversy in law or in equity for the federal courts to exercise jurisdiction and to render decisions. *Advisory opinions* take place in the absence of an actual case or controversy where there are no bona fide litigants and live disputes. Such opinions are the result of questions of law submitted by a legislative body or a governmental official. Although they have no binding effect, advisory opinions guide public officials in the exercise of their constitutional duties. Consequently, state courts with this power are able to influence policy making more easily than their counterparts in the federal judiciary. Fourth, state judiciaries are able to interpret rights of parties without the limiting language of the Fourteenth Amendment: *no state* may make or enforce any law which shall deny any person due process of law, equal protection of the law, and the privileges and immunities of citizenship. Federal intervention in state matters is often limited by the doctrine of state action. If conduct by private parties cannot be linked to official state authority or persons who are operating under the color of state law, then the federal courts cannot enforce Fourteenth Amendments provisions. On the other hand, nothing in the language of the Fourteenth Amendment prohibits state governments and their courts from scrutinizing the private conduct of persons within their states. Lastly, unlike federal courts, state courts are not inhibited by competing views of American federalism in the creation and enforcement of rights. Since the early days of the Republic, as we have already learned, federal courts have been sensitive to competing views of American federalism, which has caused them to carefully craft opinions when invalidating state actions. Federalism presupposes respect for the powers of state government. State judiciaries are under no such restraint with respect to evaluating the conduct of state government, except when such conduct may run afoul of the U.S. Constitution or their own state constitutions. In sum, state courts are institutionally situated to play an activist role in policy making.[25] Yet, there is empirical evidence suggesting that the new judicial federalism movement has not lived up to its billing.[26]

Researchers report that most state courts of last resort have failed to use their authority to expand rights in the face of the contemporary U.S. Supreme Court's reluctance to do so. New York, California, New Jersey, and Oregon are striking examples to the contrary. Several explanations seem reasonable. State courts are subject to political pressure, and conservative political forces are well-organized in many states. These forces operate to deter judges from exercising their creativity in matters of public policy. Many judges are subject to popular election, and judicial appointments by governors and merit commissions subject them to political influences. Although political pressure may be less visible and may take different forms than it does for persons elected to legislative and executive bodies, pressure is applied nevertheless. Second, it is widely known that many contemporary state judges possess conservative political and legal views of their own.[27] Conservative ideologies coupled with a view of the judicial role that celebrates judicial self-restraint and decries judicial activism operate against the new judicial federalism. It is also true, however, that many state appellate court judges possess liberal political and legal attitudes, and that they possess an activist perspective of the judicial role.

Power and Justice

As the contemporary U.S. Supreme Court continues its pronounced tendency not to employ its creativity to expand the definition of constitutional rights, the logical place to look for leadership is within the courts of the various states of the union. Whether rights are expanded or possibly restricted depends, in some measure, upon the internal group dynamics on both the U.S. high court and state supreme courts. No doubt, outside pressures placed on the dual court systems are bound to have a major impact as well. And whether the restrictive state immunity doctrine of the Rehnquist Court will remain in place, as well as the Court's present course to restrict congressional commerce power in the name of the Tenth Amendment, depends upon the politics of judicial selection that will be necessitated by the death or resignation of the present justices.

Within the larger context of court legitimacy, as we discussed in Chapter 2, it is important to understand that the issue of federalism and the courts is a matter of political power. Whether the national government or the state governments may validly make laws, whether the national courts may require state courts to comply with national norms, and whether citizens may sue states without their consent are issues that strike at the heart of who gets what, when, and how in our federal system. Within the context of the struggle for institutional power, we should also consider whether the interests of the courts and the larger political regime assume greater importance than the determination of justice in particular cases.

Key Terms, Names, and Concepts

Abstention doctrine

Abstract review

Advice and consent

Advisory opinion

Alden v. Maine

American federalism

American Law Institute

Appellate process

Case and controversy

Concrete review

Conflict of laws

Courts of general jurisdiction

Courts of limited jurisdiction

De novo trials

Diversity jurisdiction

Eleventh Amendment

Erie doctrine

Federal Maritime Commission v. South Carolina Port Authority

Fletcher v. Peck

Full Faith and Credit Clause

General jurisdiction courts

Implied powers

John Marshall

Legislative courts

Lex loci deliciti

Limited jurisdiction courts

Marbury v. Madison

Martin v. Hunter's Lessee

McCulloch v. Maryland

Most significant relationship rule

Necessary and Proper Clause

New judicial federalism

Nominee bashing

Restatement (Second) of Conflicts

Supremacy Clause

Tenth Amendment

Trial de novo

U.S. Courts of Appeals

U.S. District Courts

Writ of certiorari

Discussion Questions

1. Should judges and justices be selected solely on the basis of their personal and professional qualifications?

2. Should the selection process of federal judges follow the system used by several states where the people elect judges and justices either on a partisan or nonpartisan ballot? Is there a better way to select members of the judiciary?

3. Should judicial terms of office be limited to a fixed number of years?

4. Are the views expressed by the Court majority in *Alden v. Maine* and in *Federal Maritime Commission v. South Carolina State Ports* consistent with the principle of sovereignty found in John Marshall's opinion in *McCulloch v. Maryland*? If not, which view is correct and why?

5. Is the "Defense of Marriage Act" constitutional?

6. Given this age of rapid communication and mass culture, does American federalism remain a sensible way to organize the U.S. governmental and legal system?

7. Should the primary responsibility for constitutional rights be a matter of the national judiciary, or should state courts play a more activist role in expanding rights?

8. In the struggle for power between federal and state courts, are the interests of the courts and the larger political regime of greater importance than the determination of justice in particular cases?

Suggested Additional Reading

Abraham, Henry J. *The Judicial Process: An Introductory Analysis of the Courts of the United States, England, and France.* 7th ed. New York: Oxford University Press, 1998.

Ball, Howard. "The Federal Court System." *Encyclopedia of the American Judicial System*, Vol. 2, R. Janosik, ed. New York: Scribner, 1987.

Carp, Robert A., and C. Y. Rowland. *Policymaking and Politics in the Federal District Courts.* Knoxville: University of Tennessee Press, 1983.

——, and Ronald Stidham. *Federal Courts.* 3rd ed. Washington, DC: Congressional Quarterly Press, 1998.

——. *Judicial Process in America.* 4th ed. Washington, DC: Congressional Quarterly Press, 1998.

Dubois, Philip J. *From Ballot to Bench: Judicial Elections and the Quest for Accountability.* Austin: University of Texas Press, 1980.

Glick, Henry. "State Court Systems." *Encyclopedia of the American Judicial System*, Vol. 2, R. Janosik, ed. New York: Scribner, 1987.

Hacker, Ronald A. "Full Faith and Credit to Judgments: Law and Reason Versus the Restatement Second." *California Law Review* 54 (March 1966): 282–291.

Lazarus, Edward. *Closed Chambers: The First Eyewitness Account of the Epic Struggles Inside the Supreme Court.* New York: Times Books, 1998.

Perry, H. W. *Deciding to Decide: Agenda-Setting in the United States Supreme Court.* Cambridge: Harvard University Press, 1991.

Provine, Doris Marie. *Case Selection in the United States Supreme Court.* Chicago: University of Chicago Press, 1980.

Rehnquist, William. *The Supreme Court: How It Was, How It Is.* Spec. ed. NewYork: William Morrow, 1992.

Slotnick, Elliot E. *Judicial Politics: Readings From Judicature.* 2nd ed. Chicago: American Judicature Society, 1999.

Stumpf, Harry P. *American Judicial Politics.* 2d ed. New York: Prentice Hall, 1997.

———, and John H. Culver. *The Politics of State Courts.* New York: Longman, 1992.

Warrick, Lyle. *Judicial Selection in the United States: A Compendium of Provisions.* 2nd ed. Chicago: American Judicature Society, 1993.

Wasby, Stephen L. *The Supreme Court in the Federal Judicial System.* 4th ed. Chicago: Nelson-Hall, 1993.

Woodward, Bob, and Scott Armstrong. *The Brethren: Inside the Supreme Court.* New York: Simon & Schuster, 1981.

Endnotes

1. David B. Rottman et al., *State Court Organization 1998* (Washington, DC: U.S. Department of Justice, Office of Justice Programs, Bureau of Justice Statistics, June 2000, NCJ 178932), p. ix. Available online at <http://www.ojp.usdoj.gov/bjs/> as of 2000.

2. David A. Harris, "Justice Rationed in the Pursuit of Efficiency: De Novo Trials in the Criminal Courts," *Connecticut Law Review* 24 (winter 1992): 382–383.

3. Rottman, *State Court Organization 1998*, p. ix.

4. Administrative Office of the U.S. Courts, *Understanding the Federal Courts—1999*, p. 5, available online at the U.S. Court's website, <www.uscourts.gov/UFC99.pdf>, as of December, 2000.

5. Ibid., p. 6.

6. Ibid., p. 5.

7. Robert L. Stern, Eugene Gressman, Stephen M. Shapiro, and Kenneth S. Geller, *Supreme Court Practice*, 7th ed. (Washington, DC: The Bureau of National Affairs, Inc., 1993), pp. 230–231.

8. Administrative Office of the U.S. Courts, *Understanding the Federal Courts—1999*, p. 6.

9. Ibid., p. 9.

10. Craig Ducat, *Constitutional Interpretation*, 6th ed. (St. Paul: West, 1996), pp. 24–25.

11. 529 U.S. 598, 617 (2000).

12. 535 U.S. (2002); No. 01-46, slip. op. (May 28, 2002).

13. Ibid., p. 6.
14. Ibid., p. 12.
15. Ibid., p. 15.
16. Ibid., Justice Breyer dissenting, p. 2.
17. Ibid., pp. 5–6.
18. 16 Am. Jur. 2d *Conflict of Laws Rules* § 21 (1998); J. W. Peltason, *Corwin & Peltason's Understanding the Constitution*, 14th ed. (Fort Worth, TX: Harcourt Brace, 1997), p. 176.
19. 16 Am.Jur.2d "Most Significant Relationship Rule" § 128 (1998).
20. 16 Am.Jur.2d "Conflict of Laws" §§ 84–123 (1998).
21. Albert P. Melone, "System Support Politics and the Congressional Court of Appeals," *North Dakota Law Review* 51 (spring 1975): 597.
22. Albert P. Melone and George Mace, *Judicial Review and American Democracy* (Ames: Iowa State University Press, 1988), pp. 16–18.
23. Harry F. Stumpf, *American Judicial Politics*, 2d ed. (Upper Saddle River, NJ: Prentice Hall, 1998), pp. 369–370.
24. Ibid., p. 370. Also see Michigan v. Long, 463 U.S. 1041 (1983).
25. Ibid., pp. 370–371.
26. Ibid., pp. 371–372.
27. Ibid., pp. 375–376. ✦

Chapter 4

Judicial Interpretation and Decision-Making

Chapter Objectives

Judges and attorneys are required to interpret and argue about the meaning of past judicial opinions, statutory law, and constitutional provisions. Yet, the most appropriate mode of interpretation for each of these functions is difficult to assess and controversial by nature. One purpose of this chapter is to introduce students to the methods employed by jurists to treat each of these functions and to alert readers to the problems inherent in performing the judicial role. For example, students should focus on how legal professionals create precedents and how they distinguish one case from another. Readers should also become familiar with competing ways of interpreting statutes. They should especially note the arguments for and against the application of the plain-meaning rule and the difficulties inherent in ascertaining the intent of legislators by consulting legislative records. In addition, students should become familiar with the problems inherent in the task of interpreting constitutions. One needs to ask how this undertaking is different from interpreting the meaning of statutes. Further, readers should understand the conceptual differences between interpretivism and noninterpretivism. In the process, they should note the variations within each of these views of constitutional interpretation. Lastly, students should review the major empirical theories of judicial decision-making. Each of these theories, either singularly or in combination, helps us to understand why judges make decisions the way they do.

Method of the Common Law

The principle of *stare decisis* is a guide for American courts holding that the rules developed in previous cases should be applied to the case at hand. If the facts in the present case before the court are similar to the facts in previous cases, then the legal rule applied in previous cases ought to be applied to the present controversy. Simply put, this intellectual process is reasoning by example or by analogy. As we first discussed in Chapter 1, when judges apply the common law they compare the facts and results in a number of previous controversies to justify a result in the present case. The experimental nature of the common law is evident. Legal actors learn from the application of previous results. If the rule works to produce acceptable results, then it is applied repeatedly. It is an inductive logical system that depends upon a sufficient number of observations before a general rule is enunciated.

The body of previously decided cases with similar fact patterns as the present case is called *legal precedent*. A *rule of law* is established when a number of cases are decided in a similar way; courts declare that when certain facts are present, more or less precise legal norms apply. For example, when a person takes the life of another with premeditation and there are no extenuating circumstances, then the rule of first-degree murder applies. If a jury finds these facts to be true, then as a matter of law they are obliged to bring in a verdict of first-degree murder.

In human experience, however, seldom do the facts in present cases exactly mirror the facts in earlier cases. Consequently, courts must decide whether the facts in the present case are sufficiently similar to past cases to warrant the application of the same legal rule with similar legal results. This fact of situational variability provides legal professionals with considerable room for argument and the creation of conditional rules that permeate the law. Furthermore, judges are free to interpret precedents either *strictly* or *loosely*, depending upon their view of justice in the particular case. If judges want to interpret narrowly a previous precedent, then they will strictly apply the previous case to the case at hand. They will insist that because the facts in the previously cited case are not identical to the present one, the previous case does not apply. This is commonly referred to as *distinguishing a precedent*. On the other hand, if judges want to apply the previous precedent broadly, they will apply the rule loosely. They will ignore or discount fact pattern discrepancies between previous and present cases, choosing instead to focus on the commonalities of cases under study. Sometimes judges will apply both a loose and a strict view of precedent to different aspects of the same opinion. In those instances when neither statutes nor previously decided cases serve as a guide, judges are left to their own devices. In rare instances, judges directly overrule precedent, proclaiming that the previous rule is no longer applicable.[1]

Judges commonly face the task of applying precedents. When they do so, they must decide if they should apply them strictly or loosely—to distinguish one case from the other. There are also instances when judges have no precedents to guide them in their decision-making. Hence, judges possess considerable discretion. It is the attorney's task to persuade judges hearing their cases that an interpretation of precedent that favors their client is preferable, and therefore the court should adopt it. Consequently, the art of argument is a particularly vital tool in the attorney's intellectual arsenal. Recall the Legal Realist argument briefly outlined in Chapter 1 of this text—ultimately the values and attitudes of judges determine how they apply or interpret precedent. Yet, whether one agrees or not with the Realist position, there is no denying the fact that words matter.

The legal order with its appellate system of review requires justification for judges' decisions. A searching examination of the factual and logical basis for judicial opinion is at the heart of advocacy and judging. The use of rhetorical skills is central to shaping the outcome of particular disputes and the future of American law. At the very least, through arguments, attorneys are in the position to stimulate judges' preexisting values and attitudes. They urge judges, however subtlely, to apply those values and attitudes to the resolution of particular contests before the court. Ideally, fair judges, regardless of their preexisting attitudes and values, are amenable to good arguments. They are willing to listen to competing arguments with an open mind. They should not permit their subjective attitudes and values toward particular litigants or controversial legal issues of the day to prejudice their balanced evaluation of the law.

Common law judges are powerful because they are free to add to or subtract from the previously established rules, based upon their interpretation of how the facts of the present case differ from the previous line of cases. Thus, common law judges are agents of change, albeit in a tentative and experimental fashion. This task raises an important question in democratic societies: Should judges make law? In civil law countries, historically speaking, the formal answer has always been no. In the United States, significant debates have revolved around the relative merits of judge-made law versus statutory law that is enacted by the elected representatives of the people in legislative bodies and placed in easily intelligible subject matter codes. Robert Rantoul, a liberal antislavery Democrat of the Jacksonian era and a distinguished attorney, eloquently summed up the hostility toward the common law tradition in his Fourth of July, 1836, "Oration at Scituate," excerpted in Box 4.1.

It is important to acknowledge that although judges contribute to the overall stability and orderly change in society, their actions raise significant questions for democratic polities. Nonetheless, the task for legal professionals is a daunting one, no matter how they apply precedent. The following modern age case of *Lake v. Wal-Mart Stores, Inc.*, illustrates some of the difficult choices that judges face when exercising their discretion and the means they employ to achieve what they believe are the most desirable ends.

Box 4.1   Excerpts From 'Oration at Scituate' by Robert Rantoul (July 4, 1836) in Kermit L. Hall, William M. Wiecek, and Paul Finkelman, *American Legal History: Cases and Materials* (New York: Oxford University Press, 1991), pp. 317–318.

Judge-made law is ex post facto law, and therefore unjust. An act is not forbidden by the statute law, but it becomes void by judicial construction. The legislature could not effect this, for the Constitution forbids it. The judiciary shall not usurp legislative power, says the Bill of Rights: yet it not only usurps, but runs riot beyond the confines of Legislative power.

Judge-made law is special legislation. The judge is human, and feels the bias which the coloring of the particular case gives. If he wishes to decide the next case differently, he has only to distinguish, and thereby make a new law. The legislature must act on general views, and prescribes at once for a whole class of cases.

No man can tell what the Common Law is; therefore it is not law: for a law is a rule of action; but a rule which is unknown can govern no man's conduct. Notwithstanding this, it has been called the perfection of human reason.

The Common Law is the perfection of human reason,—just as alcohol is the perfection of sugar. The subtle spirit of the Common Law is reason double distilled, till what was wholesome and nutritive becomes rank poison. Reason is sweet and pleasant to the unsophisticated intellect; but this sublimated perversion of reason bewilders, and perplexes, and plunges its victims into mazes of error.

The judge makes law, by extorting from precedents something which they do not contain. He extends his precedents, which were themselves the extension of others, till, by this accommodating principle, a whole system of law is built up without the authority or interference of the legislator.

Lake v. Wal-Mart Stores, Inc.
Minnesota Supreme Court
582 N.W.2d 231 (Minn. 1998)

OPINION BY: BLATZ, Chief Justice.

. . . Nineteen-year-old Elli Lake and 20-year-old Melissa Weber vacationed in Mexico in March 1995 with Weber's sister. During the vacation, Weber's sister took a photograph of Lake and Weber naked in the shower together. After their vacation, Lake and Weber brought five rolls of film to a Dilworth, Minnesota Wal-Mart store and photo lab. When they received their developed photographs along with the negatives, an enclosed written notice stated that one or more of the photographs had not been printed because of their "nature."

In July 1995, an acquaintance of Lake and Weber alluded to the photograph and questioned their sexual orientation. Again, in December

1995, another friend told Lake and Weber that a Wal-Mart employee had shown her a copy of the photograph. By February 1996, Lake was informed that one or more copies of the photograph were circulating in the community.

Lake and Weber filed a complaint against Wal-Mart Stores, Inc. and one or more as yet unidentified Wal-Mart employees on February 23, 1996, alleging the four traditional invasion of privacy torts—intrusion upon seclusion, appropriation, publication of private facts, and false light publicity. Wal-Mart denied the allegations and made a motion to dismiss the complaint under Minn. R. Civ. P. 12.02, for failure to state a claim upon which relief may be granted. The district court granted Wal-Mart's motion to dismiss, explaining that Minnesota has not recognized any of the four invasion of privacy torts. The court of appeals affirmed.

Whether Minnesota should recognize any or all of the invasion of privacy causes of action is a question of first impression in Minnesota. The Restatement (Second) of Torts outlines the four causes of action that comprise the tort generally referred to as invasion of privacy. Intrusion upon seclusion occurs when one "intentionally intrudes, physically or otherwise, upon the solitude or seclusion of another or his private affairs or concerns . . . if the intrusion would be highly offensive to a reasonable person." Appropriation protects an individual's identity and is committed when one "appropriates to his own use or benefit the name or likeness of another." Publication of private facts is an invasion of privacy when one "gives publicity to a matter concerning the private life of another . . . if the matter publicized is of a kind that (a) would be highly offensive to a reasonable person, and (b) is not of legitimate concern to the public." False light publicity occurs when one "gives publicity to a matter concerning another that places the other before the public in a false light . . . if (a) the false light in which the other was placed would be highly offensive to a reasonable person, and (b) the actor had knowledge of or acted in reckless disregard as to the falsity of the publicized matter and the false light in which the other would be placed."

This court has the power to recognize and abolish common law doctrines. The common law is not composed of firmly fixed rules. Rather, as we have long recognized, the common law is the embodiment of broad and comprehensive unwritten principles, inspired by natural reason, an innate sense of justice, adopted by common consent for the regulation and government of the affairs of men. It is the growth of ages, and an examination of many of its principles, as enunciated and discussed in the books, discloses a constant improvement and development in keeping with advancing civilization and new conditions of society. Its guiding star has always been the rule of right and wrong, and in this country its principles demonstrate that there is in fact, as well as in theory, a remedy for all wrongs.

As society changes over time, the common law must also evolve:

"It must be remembered that the common law is the result of growth, and that its development has been determined by the social needs of the community which it governs. It is the resultant of conflicting social forces, and those forces which are for the time dominant leave their impress upon the law. It is of judicial origin, and seeks to establish doctrines and rules for the determination, protection, and enforcement of legal rights. Manifestly it must change as society changes and new rights are recognized. To be an efficient instrument, and not a mere abstraction, it must gradually adapt itself to changed conditions" [Tuttle v. Buck, 119 N.W. 946, 947 (1909)].

To determine the common law, we look to other states as well as to England. The tort of invasion of privacy is rooted in a common law right to privacy first described in an 1890 law review article by Samuel Warren and Louis Brandeis, *The Right to Privacy*, 4 Harv. L. Rev. 193 (1890). The article posited that the common law has always protected an individual's person and property, with the extent and nature of that protection changing over time. The fundamental right to privacy is both reflected in those protections and grows out of them:

"Thus, in the very early times, the law gave a remedy only for physical interference with life and property, for trespass *vi et armis*. Then the 'right to life' served only to protect the subject from battery in its various forms; liberty meant freedom from actual restraint; and the right to property secured to the individual his lands and his chattels. Later, there came a recognition of a man's spiritual nature, of his feelings and his intellect. Gradually the scope of these legal rights broadened; and now the right to life has come to mean the right to enjoy life; the right to be alone; the right to liberty secures the exercise of extensive civil privileges; and term 'property' has grown to comprise every form of possession—intangible, as well as tangible" [at p. 193].

Although no English cases explicitly articulated a "right to privacy," several cases cited under theories of property, contract, and breach of confidence also included invasion of privacy as a basis for protecting personal violations. The article encour-

aged recognition of the common law right to privacy, the strength of our legal system lies in its elasticity, adaptability, capacity for growth and ability "to meet the wants of an ever changing society and to apply immediate relief for every recognized wrong" [at p. 213, n. 1].

The first jurisdiction to recognize the common law right to privacy was Georgia. In *Pavesich v. New England Life Ins. Co.* (1905), the Georgia Supreme Court determined that the "right of privacy has its foundation in the instincts of nature," and is therefore an "immutable" and "absolute" right "derived from natural law." The court emphasized that the right of privacy was not new law, as it was encompassed by the well-established right to personal liberty.

Many other jurisdictions followed Georgia in recognizing the tort of invasion of privacy citing Warren and Brandeis' article and *Pavesich*. Today, the vast majority of jurisdictions now recognize some form of the right to privacy. Only Minnesota, North Dakota, and Wyoming have not yet recognized any of the four privacy torts. Although New York and Nebraska courts have declined to recognize a common law basis for the right to privacy and instead provide statutory protection, we reject the proposition that only the legislature may establish new causes of action. The right to privacy is inherent in the English protections of individual property and contract rights and the "right to be let alone" is recognized as part of the common law across this country. Thus, it is within the province of the judiciary to establish privacy torts in this jurisdiction.

Today we join the majority of jurisdictions and recognize the tort of invasion of privacy. The right to privacy is an integral part of our humanity; one has a public persona, exposed and active, and a private persona, guarded and preserved. The heart of our liberty is choosing which parts of our lives shall become public and which parts we shall hold close.

Here Lake and Weber allege in their complaint that a photograph of their nude bodies has been publicized. One's naked body is a very private part of one's person and generally known to others only by choice. This is a type of privacy interest worthy of protection. Therefore, without consideration of the merits of Lake and Weber's claims, we recognize the torts of intrusion upon seclusion, appropriation, and publication of private facts. Accordingly, we reverse the court of appeals and the district court and hold that Lake and Weber have stated a claim upon which relief may be granted and their lawsuit may proceed.

We decline to recognize the tort of false light publicity at this time. We are concerned that claims under false light are similar to claims of defamation, and to the extent that false light is more expansive than defamation, tension between this tort and the First Amendment is increased. . . . Although there may be some untrue and hurtful publicity that should be actionable under false light, the risk of chilling speech is too great to justify protection for this small category of false publication not protected under defamation.

Thus we recognize a right to privacy present in the common law of Minnesota, including causes of action in tort for intrusion upon seclusion, appropriation, and publication of private facts, but we decline to recognize the tort of false light publicity.

This case is remanded to the district court for further proceedings consistent with this opinion.

Affirmed in part, reversed in part.

TOMLJANOVICH, Justice (dissenting).

I respectfully dissent. If the allegations against Wal-Mart are proven to be true, the conduct of the Wal-Mart employees is indeed offensive and reprehensible. As much as we deplore such conduct, not every contemptible act in our society is actionable.

I would not recognize a cause of action for intrusion upon seclusion, appropriation or publication of private facts. "Minnesota has never recognized, either by legislative or court action, a cause of action for invasion of privacy." Hendry v. Conner, 303 Minn. 317, 319, 226 N.W.2d 921, 923 (1975). As recently as 1996, we reiterated that position. See Richie v. Paramount Pictures Corp., 544 N.W.2d 21, 28 (Minn.1996).

An action for an invasion of the right to privacy is not rooted in the Constitution. "[T]he Fourth Amendment cannot be translated into a general constitutional 'right to privacy.'" Katz v. United States, 389 U.S. 347, 350, 88 S.Ct. 507, 19 L.Ed.2d 576 (1967). Those privacy rights that have their origin in the Constitution are much more fundamental rights of privacy—marriage and reproduction. See Griswold v. Connecticut, 381 U.S. 479, 485, 85 S.Ct. 1678, 14 L.Ed.2d 510 (1965) (penumbral rights of privacy and repose protect notions of privacy surrounding the marriage relationship and reproduction).

We have become a much more litigious society since 1975 when we acknowledged that we have never recognized a cause of action for invasion of privacy. We should be even more reluctant now to recognize a new tort.

In the absence of a constitutional basis, I would leave to the legislature the decision to create a new tort for invasion of privacy.

Case Questions for Discussion

1. Under what circumstances should a judge feel free to disregard previous precedents?

2. Is Justice Tomljanovich correct in his claim that *Griswold v. Connecticut* is about a different type of right to privacy than in *Lake v. Wal-Mart*? If he is correct, is his view of precedent too strict? Do you prefer a strict or loose view of precedent and why?

3. Assume that upon remand the trial court holds that Wal-Mart violated Lake and Weber's privacy rights with respect to appropriation but not seclusion or publication of private facts. Does the state of Minnesota have one or three invasion of privacy causes of action?

4. What did the court in *Lake v. Wal-Mart Stores* do? Did it follow precedent? Did it overrule precedent?

5. Is a state supreme court applying common law when it looks to decisions of other state courts for guidance?

Statutory Interpretation

Proponents of democratic government, such as Robert Rantoul, maintain that legislation enacted by elected officials represents the will of the people. Consequently, in this sense, statutory law, preferably in codified form, is superior to judge-made common law. When interpreting statutes, the argument goes, judges should give full effect to the intent of the people by faithfully applying the law equally to all persons. Often, however, statutes are vague, and how they should apply in particular circumstances is unclear. Indeed, an ordinary and everyday function of courts is to apply statutes to facts before the court in a way that conforms to reason and at the same time produces just results.

American politics is replete with examples of conflicts between legislative bodies and judiciaries concerning the proper application of statutes to real disputes. In contemporary America, for example, affirmative action statutes, welfare laws, disability legislation, and religious freedom issues pose vexing controversies between the legislative and judicial branches of the national government. There are several good reasons why this happens.

First, statutory language is often ambiguous. Because words cannot speak for themselves, legal professionals try to ascertain the intent of legislators by reading their minds; in other words, they read between the lines to give precise meaning to vague language. Second, there is no agreement among jurists about the best way to interpret statutes. Some argue, for example, that judges should read statutory text strictly, regardless of the consequences, while others counsel a search for what legislators had in mind when they enacted the statute in the first place. Third, sometimes legislators knowingly enact laws with language that is deliberately vague, expecting that the courts will have to resolve the ambiguity when live disputes arise requiring interpretation. Because the legislative body lacks consensus about such controversial matters, but believing that some legislation is better than none, legislative leaders implicitly consign the details of the law for jurists to work out in the course of the judicial process. Fourth, if legislators disapprove of the results of the court interpretation of their work product, they may reverse judicial decisions by enacting new law. There are many instances of congressional reversals of court decisions, although it is not clear just how many. Fifth and lastly, knowing how difficult a task statutory interpretation is for judicial actors, legislators attempt to build a record in the legislative histories of statutes to guide judges to conclusions consistent with their own viewpoints. Thus, it is common for members of Congress with particular viewpoints to insert in various legislative documents, including the *Congressional Record*, their own interpretation of what a statute really means. At the same time, members with differing policy viewpoints insert their own contradictory interpretations in hopes of providing historical ammunition in support of their own particular policy preferences. Critics of the use of *legislative intent* deride judges who, they claim, pick and choose from the various sources of legislative history to impose their own interpretation of law consistent with personal ideological orientations.[2]

Associate Justice Antonin Scalia, articulate contemporary critic of the search for legislative intent.

Associate Justice Antonin Scalia, of the contemporary U.S. Supreme Court, is the most visible modern critic of the search for intent outside of the actual words found in statutes. He argues that because legislative records are notoriously ambiguous, the use of such documents as committee reports or congressional debates permits judges to find what meaning they think best in the same fashion that common law judges interpret precedents to create new law. For Scalia, the problem is obvious. In this age of legislation, there exists a real danger that judges usurp legislative authority that does not belong to the judicial branch in a constitutional system featuring separation of powers. Scalia abhors the modern practice of referring to committee reports on legislation. First, because members of Congress do not vote on the reports that are usually written by legislative staff and not by elected members. Second, there are good reasons to believe that often these reports are not read by members of the committees that produce them or by other members of Congress who vote for or against legislation. In sum, Mr. Scalia argues that the only object of statutory interpretation is the ascertainment of the meaning of the written words, requiring jurists to focus solely on the plain words of the statute and forsaking excursions into legislative histories of any kind.[3]

Scalia argues further that not only are committee reports unreliable as a way to discover the intent of legislators, but also, as required by Article I, section 7 of the Constitution, judges must disregard such legislative historical materials completely. He maintains that the only enactments of Congress are the words found in the statutes, not committee reports or speeches made on the floor of Congress.[4] Although Scalia's attack on current practices has produced a loud chorus of disagreement, most commentators now agree that we should not view legislative history as authoritative in the same way statutory text is treated. That is, the statutory text possesses the force of law, while legislative history is, at best, evidence of what the law really means. Yet, most agree that when faced with ambiguous statutes, such as when there exist seemingly contradictory provisions, jurists should endeavor to carry out the purposes for which the legislation was drafted.[5]

The *plain-meaning rule* is the most straightforward approach to statutory interpretation. As articulated in *Caminetti v. United States* below, it dictates that when the statutory language is "plain and admits of no more than one meaning the duty of interpretation does not arise and the rules which are to aid doubtful meanings need no discussion." Yet, as this case illustrates, the application of the plain-meaning rule may result in decisions that are at odds with what members of Congress probably intended when the law was enacted.

Caminetti and others were convicted under the 1910 Mann Act, the "White-Slave Traffic Act," for taking their mistresses across state lines with the intent of engaging in immoral acts. The statute provides in its relevant part: "Any person who shall knowingly transport or cause to be transported, or aid or assist in obtaining transportation for, or in transporting, in interstate or

Did Congress intend to prohibit this behavior?

foreign commerce or in any territory or in the District of Columbia, any woman or girl for the purpose of prostitution or debauchery, or for any other immoral purpose, or with the intent and purpose to induce, entice or compel such woman or girl to become a prostitute, or to give herself up to debauchery, or to engage in any other immoral practice . . . shall be deemed guilty of a felony." In easy cases, where there may be little difference between what legislators actually wrote in the form of a statute and what they might have really intended, the plain-meaning rule seems harmless enough. Most jurists would agree with the proposition that the plain meaning of the words should be applied with little or no debate. However, in the more difficult cases, such as this one, plain meaning raises serious questions of fundamental fairness and democratic government. The majority and dissenting opinions below illustrate problems inherent in the plain-meaning rule.

Caminetti v. United States
U.S. Supreme Court
242 U.S. 470, 37 S.Ct. 192, 61 L.Ed. 442 (1917)

MR. JUSTICE DAY delivered the opinion of the Court.

. . . The indictment was in four counts, the first of which charged him [Caminetti] with transporting and causing to be transported and aiding and assisting in obtaining transportation for a certain woman from Sacramento, California, to Reno, Nevada, in interstate commerce for the purpose of debauchery, and for an immoral purpose, to wit, that the aforesaid woman should be and become his mistress and concubine. A verdict of not guilty was returned as to the other three counts of this indictment. As to the first count defendant was found guilty and sentenced to imprisonment for eighteen months and to pay a fine of $1,500.00. Upon writ of error to the United States Circuit Court of Appeals for the Ninth Circuit, that judgment was affirmed.

It is contended that the act of Congress is intended to reach only "commercialized vice," or the traffic in women for gain, and that the conduct for which the several petitioners were indicted and convicted, however reprehensible in morals, is not within the purview of the statute when properly construed in the light of its history and the purposes intended to be accomplished by its enactment. In none of the cases was it charged or proved that the transportation was for gain or for the purpose of furnishing women for prostitution for hire, and it is insisted that, such being the case, the acts charged and proved, upon which conviction was had, do not come within the statute.

It is elementary that the meaning of a statute must, in the first instance, be sought in the language in which the act is framed, and if that is plain, and if the law is within the constitutional authority of the law-making body which passed it, the sole function of the courts is to enforce it according to its terms.

Where the language is plain and admits of no more than one meaning the duty of interpretation does not arise and the rules which are to aid doubtful meanings need no discussion. There is no ambiguity in the terms of this act. It is specifically made an offense to knowingly transport or cause to be transported, etc., in interstate commerce, any woman or girl for the purpose of prostitution or debauchery, or for "any other immoral purpose," or with the intent and purpose to induce any such woman or girl to become a prostitute or to give herself up to debauchery, or to engage in any other immoral practice.

Statutory words are uniformly presumed, unless the contrary appears, to be used in their ordinary and usual sense, and with the meaning commonly attributed to them. To cause a woman or girl to be transported for the purposes of debauchery, and for an immoral purpose, to wit, becoming a concubine or mistress . . . or to transport an unmarried woman, under 18 years of age, with the intent to induce her to engage in prostitution, debauchery and other immoral practices . . . would seem by the very statement of the facts to embrace transportation for purposes denounced by the act, and therefore fairly within its meaning.

While such immoral purpose would be more culpable in morals and attributed to baser motives if accompanied with the expectation of pecuniary gain, such considerations do not prevent the lesser offense against morals of furnishing transportation in order that a woman may be debauched, or become a mistress or a concubine from being the execution of purposes within the meaning of this law. To say the contrary would shock the common understanding of what constitutes an immoral purpose when those terms are applied, as here, to sexual relations. . . .

But it is contended that though the words are so plain that they cannot be misapprehended when given their usual and ordinary interpretation, and although the sections in which they appear do not in terms limit the offense defined and punished to acts of "commercialized vice," or the furnishing or procuring of transportation of women for debauchery, prostitution or immoral practices for hire, such limited purpose is to be attributed to Congress and engrafted upon the act in view of the language of § 8 and the report which accompanied the law upon its introduction into and subsequent passage by the House of Representatives.

In this connection, it may be observed that while the title of an act cannot overcome the meaning of plain and unambiguous words used in its body . . . the title of this act embraces the regulation of interstate commerce "by prohibiting the transportation therein for immoral purposes of women and girls, and for other purposes." It is true that § 8 of the act provides that it shall be known and referred to as the "White-Slave Traffic Act," and the report accompanying the introduction of the same into the House of Representatives set forth the fact that a material portion of the legislation suggested was to meet conditions which had arisen in the past few years, and that the legislation was needed to put a stop to a villainous interstate and international traffic in women and girls. Still, the name given to an act by way of designation or description, or the report which accompanies it, cannot change the plain import of its words. If the words are plain, they give meaning to the act, and it is neither the duty nor the privilege of the courts to enter speculative fields in search of a different meaning.

Reports to Congress accompanying the introduction of proposed laws may aid the courts in reaching the true meaning of the legislature in cases of doubtful interpretation. . . . But, as we have already said, and it has been so often affirmed as to become a recognized rule, when words are free from doubt they must be taken as the final expression of the legislative intent, and are not to be added to or subtracted from by considerations drawn from titles or designating names or reports accompanying their introduction, or from any extraneous source. In other words, the language being plain, and not leading to absurd or wholly impracticable consequences, it is the sole evidence of the ultimate legislative intent. . . .

The judgment in each of the cases is affirmed. Mr. Justice McReynolds took no part in the consideration or decision of these cases.

DISSENT: MR. Justice McKenna, with whom concurred the Chief Justice and Mr. Justice Clarke, dissenting.

Undoubtedly in the investigation of the meaning of a statute we resort first to its words, and when clear they are decisive. The principle has attractive and seemingly disposing simplicity, but that it is not easy of application or, at least, encounters other principles, many cases demonstrate. The words of a statute may be uncertain in their signification or in their application. If they be ambiguous, the problem they present is to be resolved by their definition; the subject-matter and the lexicons become our guides. But here, even, we are not exempt from putting ourselves in the place of the legislators. If the words be clear in meaning but the objects to which they are addressed be uncertain, the problem then is to determine the uncertainty. And for this a realization of conditions that provoked the statute must inform our judgment. Let us apply these observations to the present case.

The transportation which is made unlawful is of a woman or girl "to become a prostitute or to give herself up to debauchery, or to engage in any other immoral practice." Our present concern is with the words "any other immoral practice," which, it is asserted, have a special office. The words are clear enough as general descriptions; they fail in particular designation; they are class words, not specifications. Are they controlled by those which precede them? If not, they are broader in generalization and include those that precede them, making them unnecessary and confusing. To what conclusion would this lead us? "Immoral" is a very comprehensive word. It means a dereliction of morals. In such sense it covers every form of vice, every form of conduct that is contrary to good order. It will hardly be contended that in this sweeping sense it is used in the statute. But if not used in such sense, to what is it limited and by what limited? If it be admitted that it is limited at all, that ends the imperative effect assigned to it in the opinion of the court. But not insisting quite on that, we ask again, By what is it limited? By its context, necessarily, and the purpose of the statute.

For the context I must refer to the statute; of the purpose of the statute Congress itself has given us illumination. It devotes a section to the declaration that the "Act shall be known and referred to as the 'White-Slave Traffic Act.'" And its prominence gives it prevalence in the construction of the statute. It cannot be pushed aside or subordinated by indefinite words in other sentences, limited even there by the context. It is a peremptory rule of construction that all parts of a statute must be taken into account in ascertaining its meaning, and it cannot be said that § 8 has no object. Even if it gives only a title to the act it has especial weight. But it gives more than a title; it makes distinctive the purpose of the statute. The designation "White-slave traffic" has the sufficiency of an axiom. If apprehended, there is no uncertainty as to the conduct it describes. It is commercialized vice, immoralities having a mercenary purpose, and this is confirmed by other circumstances.

The author of the bill was Mr. Mann, and in reporting it from the House Committee on Interstate and Foreign Commerce he declared for the Committee that it was not the purpose of the bill to interfere with or usurp in any way the police power of the States, and further that it was not the intention of the bill to regulate prostitution or the places where prostitution or immorality was practiced, which were said to be matters wholly within the power of the States and over which the federal government had no jurisdiction. And further explaining the bill, it was said that the sections of the act had been "so drawn that they are limited to cases in which there is the act of transportation in interstate commerce of women for purposes of prostitution." And again:

"The White-Slave Trade." A material portion of the legislation suggested and proposed is necessary to meet conditions which have arisen within the past few years. The legislation is needed to put a stop to a villainous interstate and international traffic in women and girls. The legislation is not needed or intended as an aid to the States in the exercise of their police powers in the suppression or regulation of immorality in general. It does not attempt to regulate the practice of voluntary prostitution, but aims solely to prevent panderers and procurers from compelling thousands of women and girls against their will and desire to enter and continue in a life of prostitution." House Report No. 47, 61st Cong., 2d sess., pp. 9, 10.

In other words, it is vice as a business at which the law is directed, using interstate commerce as a facility to procure or distribute its victims.

Case Questions for Discussion

1. Given what you know about human behavior (and the behavior of some public officials), do you think Congress could have intended to criminalize all sexual conduct of an illicit nature that crossed state lines?

2. What does the report accompanying the legislation teach us about the purpose of the "White-Slave Traffic Act"?

3. Under what circumstances do the dissenters in this case prescribe that a search for intent apart from the plain meaning of statutes should take place?

4. In this case, which view of statutory interpretation, the majority or dissenting, do you think would produce the best result?

Other Statutory Canons

The plain-meaning rule is the most widely discussed canon of statutory construction. But in fact many more canons employed by courts are designed to assist jurists in discerning statutory meaning. William Eskridge, Jr., and Philip Frickey studied the canons employed by the U.S. Supreme Court during its 1986 through 1993 terms. They found that the Court noted 118 different canons of construction arrayed in three broad categories: textual canons, extrinsic source canons, and substantive policy canons.[6] Though laypersons need not be conversant in the many canons, it is nevertheless helpful for them to be aware of the conceptual framework in which statutory interpretation takes place.

Textual canons address the meaning of written words. This entails the examination of grammar and syntax, linguistic inferences, and textual integrity. Examples of the twenty textual canons include the following: "*expressio unius*: expression of one thing suggests the exclusion of others"; " 'May' is usually precatory, while 'shall' is usually mandatory"; and "Each statutory provision should be read by reference to the whole act. Statutory interpretation is a 'holistic endeavor.' "[7]

Extrinsic source canons address how legislatures and executive agencies view the meaning of statutes through usage in the case of administrative agencies and how legislatures treat specific statutes with subsequent amendments. Extrinsic source canons look to the legislative history of statutes when necessary and exhibit a general deference to Congress about its desire to create and maintain continuity in law. Of the 18 extrinsic source canons, three are as follows: "Rule of continuity: assume that Congress does not create discontinuities in legal rights and obligations without some clear statement"; "Interpret provision consistent with subsequent statutory amendments, but do not consider subsequent legislative discussions"; and the "Super-strong presumption of correctness for statutory precedents."[8]

Substantive policy canons is the largest subset of canons outlined by Eskridge and Frickey. These canons emphasize the U.S. Supreme Court's determination to allow the regular policy-making bodies in the American constitutional system of separation of powers, federalism, and due process of law to make policy choices, not the judiciary. In addition to the constitution-based substantive policy canons, the Court has also articulated statute-based canons. Just as in constitutionally based substantive policy canons, the Supreme Court emphasizes the importance of giving full effect to the will of lawmakers by adhering to the policy goals inherent in legislation. Also within the substantive policy canons category are common law-based canons. These canons follow the principle that when statutes are unclear and the common law speaks to the possible meaning of such statutes, the Court will apply the common law consistent with the assumption, when not contradicted, that legislators wish to enact laws consistent with legal traditions. Eskridge and Frickey found eighty substantive policy canons. Three of them are as follows: "Avoid interpretations that would render a statute unconstitutional. Inapplicable if statute would survive constitutional attack, or if statutory text is clear"; "Presumption of finality of state convictions for purposes of habeas review"; and the "Rule against state taxation of Indian tribes and reservation activities."[9]

Though the words "statutory canons" imply a logically grounded formal system of legal reasoning, experts observe that American courts do not consistently apply statutory canons. Similar to the matter of applying precedent to case law, judges exercise their discretion concerning when and if to employ one or more of the sometimes contradictory canons to a dispute before them. In the end, whether one particular canon or another is applied to a case at hand is a matter of judicial discretion. Such judgments are rooted in the experiences, values, and attitudes of jurists charged with the duty of interpretation. Attorneys for opposing sides must be conversant in the canons so that they may be in the position to offer convincing arguments to judges. If nothing else, however, the canons are useful checklists to assist the parties and the judges about the array of possibilities to resolve doubtful meanings.[10]

Constitutional Interpretation

The problem of interpreting the meaning of constitutional provisions is similar to statutory interpretation. In both instances, judges are asked to interpret the meaning of words on a printed page. Yet, there is a profound difference stemming from the nature of constitutions as distinguished from ordinary laws. It helps to place the matter in proper relief by first considering the following question: Is a constitution a statement of general principles, or is it a fundamental document containing a bundle of specific rules similar to codified statutes?

The answer is that constitutions contain both statements of specific rules and broader principles. For example, the U.S. Constitution requires that members of the House of Representatives be at least 25 years of age and that their terms of office shall be two years. These provisions require little imagination or insight into the thinking of the framers of the Constitution. But there are many provisions of the U.S. Constitution that contain principles that are not easily interpreted by examining the text. For example, the Constitution speaks of "commerce among the states," "due process of law," "executive power," "unreasonable search and seizure," and "privileges and immunities of citizenship." These are but a few examples of statements of principles that require interpretation, usually in light of disputes that rise to the level of a Supreme Court case.

If the Constitution is viewed as a statement of mostly principles or, at least, if the difficult cases involve principles and not rules, then legal professionals and citizens may see fit to interpret it to accommodate the needs of the day. Proponents of this view speak of a "living constitution," but opponents of this view regard this characterization as a license for judges and justices to substitute their judgments for that of the original framers. Although there are historical differences, in an earlier age, rule-oriented proponents were called *strict constructionists*. Today they are often called *interpretivists*. Those who view the Constitution as a set of principles were earlier called *broad constructionists*, but today they are labeled *noninterpretivists*.

Interpretivism

Interpretivism is the view that binds judges to the strict text of the Constitution or the intention of the constitutional framers. It is a type of literalism or fundamentalism that insists that the Constitution means just what it says. Justice Owen Roberts put it succinctly in his famous 1936 opinion in United States v. Butler, 297 U.S. 1. Writing in simple mechanistic terms he advises:

> There should be no misunderstanding as to the function of this court. . . . It is sometimes said that the court assumes a power to overrule or control the action of the people's representatives. This is a misconception. The Constitution is the supreme law of the land ordained and established by the people. All legislation must conform to the principles it lays down. When an act of Congress is appropriately challenged in the courts as not conforming to the constitutional mandate, the judicial branch of the Government has only one duty—to lay the article of the Constitution which is invoked beside the statute which is challenged and to decide whether the latter squares with the former. All the court does, or can do, is to announce its considered judgment upon the question. The only power it has, if such it may be called, is the power of judgment. This court neither approves nor condemns any legislative policy. Its delicate and difficult office is to ascertain and declare whether the legislation is in accordance with, or in contravention of, the provisions of the Constitution; and having done that, its duty ends.[11]

Textualism is the most extreme expression of interpretivism. It insists that interpreters of the Constitution consider only the literal text of the basic document. Justice Hugo Black was a principal proponent of this view because he believed it would curb the appetite of judges to go outside the Constitution and to impose their own preferences on the body politic. He abhorred appeals to "natural law," "due process of law," "fairness," "decency," or "fundamental values" as vague prescriptions that convert judges from interpreters into framers of the Constitution.[12]

When a textual approach does not yield a clear answer to the meaning of the text, proponents of interpretivism counsel *originalism,* that is, inquiries into the intentions of those who wrote and ratified the Constitution. This view assumes that we can know with some precision the original intent of the constitutional framers. Nonetheless, as is also the case with statutory interpretation, the record containing the intent of the framers is not always, one might even say not usually, easily known. President Reagan's Attorney General Edwin Meese, and Judge Robert Bork, insisted that contemporary jurists should confine themselves to the rules and principles found in the written Constitution as originally intended by its framers.[13] Indeed, Judge Bork's 1987 nomination to the Supreme Court went down to defeat due in large measure to his interpretivist view of constitutional interpretation.

Noninterpretivism

During this same period in the 1980s when Edwin Meese and Robert Bork were championing interpretivism, Justice William J. Brennan, Jr., was the torchbearer for political liberals who vigorously defended *noninterpretivism.* He argued that along with the constitutional text and the intention of the framers and ratifiers, other sources are relevant in constitutional interpretation. He maintained that

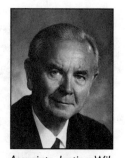

> ... the ultimate question must be, what do the words of the text mean in our time. For the genius of the Constitution rests not in any static meaning it might have had in a world that is dead and gone, but in the adaptability of its great principles to cope with current problems and current needs. What the constitutional fundamentals meant to the wisdom of other times cannot be their measure to the vision of our time. Similarly, what those fundamentals mean for us, our descendants will learn, cannot be the measure to the vision of their time.[14]

Associate Justice William J. Brennan, Jr., articulate spokesman for noninterpretivism. Served on the Supreme Court from 1956 to 1990, and was leader of the liberal bloc.

The softest variation on the noninterpretivist viewpoint is *conceptualism,* sometimes called *moderate originalism.* This approach commits judges to ascertain the underlying purposes of the various constitutional provisions and to apply them in developing contemporary governing principles.[15] Another form of noninterpretivism, *fundamental law,* argues that beyond the written Constitution there is a great reservoir of binding principles that judges can employ to supplement the constitutional text to give the U.S. Constitution meaning in contemporary settings. For example, natural rights that originate from natural law are the source for the right to privacy, various parental rights, and even the right to die.[16] Some noninterpretivists believe that behind the

Constitution lie the basic aspirations of the American people, *symbolism*, and that jurists should consider such beliefs when they interpret the basic document.[17]

Consequence of the Debate

The debate over the proper mode of constitutional interpretation is not a matter of idle academic speculation. Indeed, as a candidate for the presidency in 2000, George W. Bush emphasized his desire to appoint persons to the federal judiciary who are committed to a strict-constructionist (interpretivist) view. No doubt, outcomes of constitutional cases depend in large part on how jurists view the matter. The right to privacy debate is an example with which readers are already familiar. Other problems concern whether schoolchildren are entitled to equal per pupil expenditures of state funds, whether illegitimate children are entitled to the same treatment as legitimate offspring, whether women are entitled to equal pay, whether mental patients are entitled to due process of law, and whether welfare benefits may be limited to new residents of states. These are a few of the modern issues in American jurisprudence, the resolution of which depends in great part on how jurists interpret the Constitution. The following recent case of *Saenz v. Roe* illustrates the point. The Supreme Court found unconstitutional a California statute that limited the amount of welfare payments to a family that had resided in the state for less than 12 months to the amount payable by the family's prior state residence. Employing a noninterpretivist line of reasoning, the majority resuscitated from its historical grave the Privileges and Immunities Clause of the Fourteenth Amendment. The dissenting opinion of Associate Justice Clarence Thomas is a good example of interpretivism with a heavy emphasis upon originalism.

Saenz v. Roe
U.S. Supreme Court
526 U.S. 489, 119 S.Ct. 1518, 143 L.Ed. 2d 689 (1999)

OPINION BY: Justice Stevens.

In 1992, California enacted a statute limiting the maximum welfare benefits available to newly arrived residents. The scheme limits the amount payable to a family that has resided in the State for less than 12 months to the amount payable by the State of the family's prior residence. . . .

Because in 1992 a state program either had to conform to federal specifications or receive a waiver from the Secretary of Health and Human Services in order to qualify for federal reimbursement, §11450.03 required approval by the Secretary to take effect. In October 1992, the Secretary issued a waiver purporting to grant such approval.

On December 21, 1992, three California residents who were eligible for AFDC benefits filed an action in the Eastern District of California challenging the constitutionality of the durational residency requirement in §11450.03. Each plaintiff alleged that she had recently moved to California to live with relatives in order to escape abusive family circumstances. One returned to California after living in Louisiana for seven years, the second had been living in Oklahoma for six weeks and the third came from Colorado. Each alleged that her monthly AFDC grant for the ensuing 12 months would be substantially lower under §11450.03 than if the statute were not in effect. Thus, the former residents of Louisiana and Oklahoma would receive $190 and $341 respectively for a family of three even though the full California grant was $641; the former resident of Colorado, who had just one child, was limited to $280 a month as opposed to the full California grant of $504 for a family of two.

The District Court issued a temporary restraining order and, after a hearing, preliminarily enjoined implementation of the statute. District Judge Levi found that the statute "produces substantial disparities in benefit levels and makes no accommodation for the different costs of living that exist in different states." Relying primarily on our decisions in Shapiro v. Thompson, 394 U.S. 618 (1969), and Zobel v. Williams, 457 U.S. 55 (1982), he concluded that the statute placed "a penalty on the decision of new residents to migrate to the State and be treated on an equal basis with existing residents," Green v. Anderson, 811 F. Supp. 516, 521 (ED Cal. 1993). In his view, if the purpose of the measure was to deter migra-

tion by poor people into the State, it would be unconstitutional for that reason. And even if the purpose was only to conserve limited funds, the State had failed to explain why the entire burden of the saving should be imposed on new residents. The Court of Appeals summarily affirmed for the reasons stated by the District Judge. Green v. Anderson, 26 F.3d 95 (CA9 1994). . . . [California sought review by the U.S. Supreme Court].

The word "travel" is not found in the text of the Constitution. Yet the "constitutional right to travel from one State to another" is firmly embedded in our jurisprudence. United States v. Guest, 383 U.S. 745, 757 (1966). Indeed, as Justice Stewart reminded us in Shapiro v. Thompson, 394 U.S. 618 (1969), the right is so important that it is "assertable against private interference as well as governmental action . . . a virtually unconditional personal right, guaranteed by the Constitution to us all." Id., at 643 (concurring opinion). In Shapiro, we reviewed the constitutionality of three statutory provisions that denied welfare assistance to residents of Connecticut, the District of Columbia, and Pennsylvania, who had resided within those respective jurisdictions less than one year immediately preceding their applications for assistance. Without pausing to identify the specific source of the right, we began by noting that the Court had long "recognized that the nature of our Federal Union and our constitutional concepts of personal liberty unite to require that all citizens be free to travel throughout the length and breadth of our land uninhibited by statutes, rules, or regulations which unreasonably burden or restrict this movement." We squarely held that it was "constitutionally impermissible" for a State to enact durational residency requirements for the purpose of inhibiting the migration by needy persons into the State. We further held that a classification that had the effect of imposing a penalty on the exercise of the right to travel violated the Equal Protection Clause "unless shown to be necessary to promote a compelling governmental interest," and that no such showing had been made.

In this case California argues that §11450.03 was not enacted for the impermissible purpose of inhibiting migration by needy persons and that, unlike the legislation reviewed in Shapiro, it does not penalize the right to travel because new arrivals are not ineligible for benefits during their first year of residence. California submits that, instead of being subjected to the strictest scrutiny, the statute should be upheld if it is supported by a rational basis and that the State's legitimate interest in saving over $10 million a year satisfies that test. Although the United States did not elect to participate in the proceedings in the District Court or the Court of Appeals, it has participated as amicus curiae in this Court. It has advanced the novel argument that the enactment of PRWORA allows the States to adopt a "specialized choice-of-law-type provision" that "should be subject to an intermediate level of constitutional review," merely requiring that durational residency requirements be "substantially related to an important governmental objective." The debate about the appropriate standard of review, together with the potential relevance of the federal statute, persuades us that it will be useful to focus on the source of the constitutional right on which respondents rely.

The "right to travel" discussed in our cases embraces at least three different components. It protects the right of a citizen of one State to enter and to leave another State, the right to be treated as a welcome visitor rather than an unfriendly alien when temporarily present in the second State, and, for those travelers who elect to become permanent residents, the right to be treated like other citizens of that State.

It was the right to go from one place to another, including the right to cross state borders while en route, that was vindicated in Edwards v. California, 314 U.S. 160 (1941), which invalidated a state law that impeded the free interstate passage of the indigent. We reaffirmed that right in United States v. Guest, 383 U.S. 745 (1966), which afforded protection to the " 'right to travel freely to and from the State of Georgia and to use highway facilities and other instrumentalities of interstate commerce within the State of Georgia.'" Id., at 757.

Given that §11450.03 imposed no obstacle to respondents' entry into California, we think the State is correct when it argues that the statute does not directly impair the exercise of the right to free interstate movement. For the purposes of this case, therefore, we need not identify the source of that particular right in the text of the Constitution. The right of "free ingress and regress to and from" neighboring States, which was expressly mentioned in the text of the Articles of Confederation, may simply have been "conceived from the beginning to be a necessary concomitant of the stronger Union the Constitution created."

The second component of the right to travel is, however, expressly protected by the text of the Constitution. The first sentence of Article IV, §2 provides: "The Citizens of each State shall be entitled to all Privileges and Immunities of Citizens in the several States." Thus, by virtue of a person's state citizenship, a citizen of one State who travels in other States, intending to return home at the end of his journey, is entitled to enjoy the "Privileges and Immunities of Citizens in the several States" that he visits. This provision removes "from the citizens of each State the disabilities of alienage in the other States." Paul v. Virginia, 8 Wall. 168, 180 (1869) ("[W]ithout some provision . . . removing from citizens of each State the disabilities of alienage in the other States, and giving them equality of privilege with citizens of those States, the Republic would have constituted little more than a league of States; it would not have constituted the Union which now exists"). It provides important protections for nonresidents who enter a State whether to obtain employment, Hicklin v. Orbeck, 437 U.S. 518 (1978), to procure medical services, Doe v. Bolton, 410 U.S. 179, 200 (1973), or even to engage in commercial shrimp fishing, Toomer v. Witsell, 334 U.S. 385 (1948). Those protections are not "absolute," but the Clause "does bar discrimination against citizens of other States where there is no substantial reason for the discrimination beyond the mere fact that they are citizens of other States." Id., at 396. There may be a substantial reason for requiring the nonresident to pay more than the resident for a hunting license, see Baldwin v. Fish and Game Comm'n of Mont., 436 U.S. 371, 390-391 (1978), or to enroll in the state university, see Vlandis v. Kline, 412 U.S. 441, 445 (1973), but our cases

have not identified any acceptable reason for qualifying the protection afforded by the Clause for "the 'citizen of State A who ventures into State B' to settle there and establish a home." Zobel, 457 U.S., at 74 (O'Connor, J., concurring in judgment). Permissible justifications for discrimination between residents and nonresidents are simply inapplicable to a nonresident's exercise of the right to move into another State and become a resident of that State.

What is at issue in this case, then, is this third aspect of the right to travel—the right of the newly arrived citizen to the same privileges and immunities enjoyed by other citizens of the same State. That right is protected not only by the new arrival's status as a state citizen, but also by her status as a citizen of the United States. That additional source of protection is plainly identified in the opening words of the Fourteenth Amendment: "All persons born or naturalized in the United States, and subject to the jurisdiction thereof, are citizens of the United States and of the State wherein they reside. No State shall make or enforce any law which shall abridge the privileges or immunities of citizens of the United States. . . ." Despite fundamentally differing views concerning the coverage of the Privileges or Immunities Clause of the Fourteenth Amendment, most notably expressed in the majority and dissenting opinions in the Slaughter-House Cases, 16 Wall. 36 (1873), it has always been common ground that this Clause protects the third component of the right to travel. Writing for the majority in the Slaughter-House Cases, Justice Miller explained that one of the privileges conferred by this Clause "is that a citizen of the United States can, of his own volition, become a citizen of any State of the Union by a bona fide residence therein, with the same rights as other citizens of that State." Justice Bradley, in dissent, used even stronger language to make the same point: "The states have not now, if they ever had, any power to restrict their citizenship to any classes or persons. A citizen of the United States has a perfect constitutional right to go to and reside in any State he chooses, and to claim citizenship therein, and an equality of rights with every other citizen; and the whole power of the nation is pledged to sustain him in that right. He is not bound to cringe to any superior, or to pray for any act of grace, as a means of enjoying all the rights and privileges enjoyed by other citizens." That newly arrived citizens "have two political capacities, one state and one federal," adds special force to their claim that they have the same rights as others who share their citizenship. Neither mere rationality nor some intermediate standard of review should be used to judge the constitutionality of a state rule that discriminates against some of its citizens because they have been domiciled in the State for less than a year. The appropriate standard may be more categorical than that articulated in Shapiro but it is surely no less strict.

Because this case involves discrimination against citizens who have completed their interstate travel, the State's argument that its welfare scheme affects the right to travel only "incidentally" is beside the point. Were we concerned solely with actual deterrence to migration, we might be persuaded that a partial withholding of benefits constitutes a lesser incursion on the right to travel than an outright denial of all benefits.

See Dunn v. Blumstein, 405 U.S. 330, 339 (1972). But since the right to travel embraces the citizen's right to be treated equally in her new State of residence, the discriminatory classification is itself a penalty.

It is undisputed that respondents and the members of the class that they represent are citizens of California and that their need for welfare benefits is unrelated to the length of time that they have resided in California. We thus have no occasion to consider what weight might be given to a citizen's length of residence if the bona fides of her claim to state citizenship were questioned. Moreover, because whatever benefits they receive will be consumed while they remain in California, there is no danger that recognition of their claim will encourage citizens of other States to establish residency for just long enough to acquire some readily portable benefit, such as a divorce or a college education, that will be enjoyed after they return to their original domicile. See, e.g., Sosna v. Iowa, 419 U.S. 393 (1975); Vlandis v. Kline, 412 U.S. 441 (1973).

The classifications challenged in this case—and there are many—are defined entirely by (a) the period of residency in California and (b) the location of the prior residences of the disfavored class members. The favored class of beneficiaries includes all eligible California citizens who have resided there for at least one year, plus those new arrivals who last resided in another country or in a State that provides benefits at least as generous as California's. Thus, within the broad category of citizens who resided in California for less than a year, there are many who are treated like lifetime residents. And within the broad sub-category of new arrivals who are treated less favorably, there are many smaller classes whose benefit levels are determined by the law of the States from whence they came. To justify §11450.03, California must therefore explain not only why it is sound fiscal policy to discriminate against those who have been citizens for less than a year, but also why it is permissible to apply such a variety of rules within that class.

These classifications may not be justified by a purpose to deter welfare applicants from migrating to California for three reasons. First, although it is reasonable to assume that some persons may be motivated to move for the purpose of obtaining higher benefits, the empirical evidence reviewed by the District Judge, which takes into account the high cost of living in California, indicates that the number of such persons is quite small—surely not large enough to justify a burden on those who had no such motive. Second, California has represented to the Court that the legislation was not enacted for any such reason. Third, even if it were, as we squarely held in Shapiro v. Thompson, 394 U.S. 618 (1969), such a purpose would be unequivocally impermissible.

Disavowing any desire to fence out the indigent, California has instead advanced an entirely fiscal justification for its multitiered scheme. The enforcement of §11450.03 will save the State approximately $10.9 million a year. The question is not whether such saving is a legitimate purpose but whether the State may accomplish that end by the discriminatory means it has chosen. An even-handed, across-the-board reduction of about 72 cents per month for every beneficiary would produce the same result. But our negative answer to the question does not rest on the weakness of the State's purported fiscal justification. It rests on the fact that the Citizenship Clause of the Fourteenth Amendment expressly equates citizenship with residence: "That Clause does not provide for, and does not allow for, degrees of citizenship based on length of residence." Zobel, 457 U.S., at 69. It is equally clear that the Clause does not tolerate a hierarchy of 45 subclasses of similarly situated citizens based on the location of their prior residence. Thus §11450.03 is doubly vulnerable: Neither the duration of respondents' California residence, nor the identity of their prior States of residence, has any relevance to their need for benefits. Nor do those factors bear any relationship to the State's interest in making an equitable allocation of the funds to be distributed among its needy citizens. As in Shapiro, we reject any contributory rationale for the denial of benefits to new residents: "But we need not rest on the particular facts of these cases. Appellants' reasoning would logically permit the State to bar new residents from schools, parks, and libraries or deprive them of police and fire protection. Indeed it would permit the State to apportion all benefits and services according to the past tax contributions of its citizens." 394 U.S., at 632-633. See also Zobel, 457 U.S., at 64. In short, the State's legitimate interest in saving money provides no justification for its decision to discriminate among equally eligible citizens.

The question that remains is whether congressional approval of durational residency requirements in the 1996 amendment to the Social Security Act somehow resuscitates the constitutionality of §11450.03.

That question is readily answered, for we have consistently held that Congress may not authorize the States to violate the Fourteenth Amendment. Moreover, the protection afforded to the citizen by the Citizenship Clause of that Amendment is a limitation on the powers of the National Government as well as the States. . . .

Citizens of the United States, whether rich or poor, have the right to choose to be citizens "of the State wherein they reside." U.S. Const., Amdt. 14, § 1. The States, however, do not have any right to select their citizens. The Fourteenth Amendment, like the Constitution itself, was, as Justice Cardozo put it, "framed upon the theory that the peoples of the several states must sink or swim together, and that in the long run prosperity and salvation are in union and not division." Baldwin v. G. A. F. Seelig, Inc., 294 U.S. 511, 523 (1935).

The judgment of the Court of Appeals is affirmed. It is so ordered.

Chief Justice Rehnquist, with whom Justice Thomas joins, dissenting (opinion not included here).

JUSTICE THOMAS, with whom the Chief Justice joins, dissenting.

I join The Chief Justice's dissent. I write separately to address the majority's conclusion that California has violated "the right of the newly arrived citizen to the same privileges and immunities enjoyed by other citizens of the same State." In my view, the majority attributes a meaning to the Privileges or Immunities Clause that likely was unintended when the Fourteenth Amendment was enacted and ratified. The Privileges or Immunities Clause of the Fourteenth Amendment provides that "[n]o State shall make or enforce any law which shall abridge the privileges or immunities of citizens of the United States." U.S. Const., Amdt. 14, § 1. Unlike the Equal Protection and Due Process Clauses, which have assumed near-talismanic status in modern constitutional law, the Court all but read the Privileges or Immunities Clause out of the Constitution in the Slaughter-House Cases, 16 Wall. 36 (1873). There, the Court held that the State of Louisiana had not abridged the Privileges or Immunities Clause by granting a partial monopoly of the slaughtering business to one company. The Court reasoned that the Privileges or Immunities Clause was not intended "as a protection to the citizen of a State against the legislative power of his own State." Rather the "privileges or immunities of citizens" guaranteed by the Fourteenth Amendment were limited to those "belonging to a citizen of the United States as such." The Court declined to specify the privileges or immunities that fell into this latter category, but it made clear that few did. . . .

Unlike the majority, I would look to history to ascertain the original meaning of the Clause. At least in American law, the phrase (or its close approximation) appears to stem from the 1606 Charter of Virginia, which provided that "all and every the Persons being our Subjects, which shall dwell and inhabit within every or any of the said several Colonies . . . shall HAVE and enjoy all Liberties, Franchises, and Immunities . . . as if they had been abiding and born, within this our Realme of England." Federal and State Constitutions, Colonial Charters and Other Organic Laws 3788 (F. Thorpe ed. 1909). Other colonial charters contained similar guarantees. Years later, as tensions between England and the American Colonies increased, the colonists adopted resolutions reasserting their entitlement to the privileges or immunities of English citizenship.

The colonists' repeated assertions that they maintained the rights, privileges and immunities of persons "born within the realm of England" and "natural born" persons suggests that, at the time of the founding, the terms "privileges" and "immunities" (and their counterparts) were understood to refer to those fundamental rights and liberties specifically enjoyed by English citizens, and more broadly, by all persons. Presumably members of the Second Continental Congress so understood these terms when they employed them in the Articles of Confederation, which guaranteed that "the free inhabitants of each of these States, paupers, vagabonds and fugitives from justice excepted, shall be entitled to all privileges and immunities of free citizens in the several States." Art. IV. The Constitution, which superceded the Articles of Confederation, similarly guarantees that "[t]he Citizens of each State shall be entitled to all Privileges and Immunities of Citizens in the several States." Art. IV, §2, cl. 1.

Justice Bushrod Washington's landmark opinion in Corfield v. Coryell, 6 Fed. Cas. 546 (No. 3, 230) (CCED Pa. 1825), reflects this historical understanding. In Corfield, a citizen of Pennsylvania challenged a New Jersey law that prohibited any person who was not an "actual inhabitant and resident" of New Jersey from harvesting oysters from New Jersey waters. Id., at 550. Justice Washington, sitting as Circuit Justice, rejected the argument that the New Jersey law violated Article IV's Privileges and Immunities Clause. He reasoned, "we cannot accede to the proposition . . . that, under this provision of the constitution, the citizens of the several states are permitted to participate in all the rights which belong exclusively to the citizens of any other particular state, merely upon the ground that they are enjoyed by those citizens." Instead, Washington concluded: "We feel no hesitation in confining these expressions to those privileges and immunities which are, in their nature, fundamental; which belong, of right, to the citizens of all free governments; and which have, at all times, been enjoyed by the citizens of the several states which compose this Union, from the time of their becoming free, independent, and sovereign. What these fundamental principles are, it would perhaps be more tedious than difficult to enumerate. They may, however, be all comprehended under the following general heads: Protection by the government; the enjoyment of life and liberty, with the right to acquire and possess property of every kind, and to pursue and obtain happiness and safety; subject nevertheless to such restraints as the government may justly prescribe for the general good of the whole. The right of a citizen of one state to pass through, or to reside in any other state, for purposes of trade, agriculture, professional pursuits, or otherwise; to claim the benefit of the writ of habeas corpus; to institute and maintain actions of any kind in the courts of the state . . . and an exemption from higher taxes or impositions than are paid by the other citizens of the state . . . the elective franchise, as regulated and established by the laws or constitution of the state in which it is to be exercised. These, and many others which might be mentioned, are, strictly speaking, privileges and immunities." Washington rejected the proposition that the Privileges and Immunities

Clause guaranteed equal access to all public benefits (such as the right to harvest oysters in public waters) that a State chooses to make available. Instead, he endorsed the colonial-era conception of the terms "privileges" and "immunities," concluding that Article IV encompassed only fundamental rights that belong to all citizens of the United States.

Justice Washington's opinion in Corfield indisputably influenced the Members of Congress who enacted the Fourteenth Amendment. When Congress gathered to debate the Fourteenth Amendment, members frequently, if not as a matter of course, appealed to Corfield, arguing that the Amendment was necessary to guarantee the fundamental rights that Justice Washington identified in his opinion. See Harrison, Reconstructing the Privileges or Immunities Clause, 101 Yale L. J. 1385, 1418 (1992) (referring to a Member's "obligatory quotation from Corfield"). For just one example, in a speech introducing the Amendment to the Senate, Senator Howard explained the Privileges or Immunities Clause by quoting at length from Corfield. Cong. Globe, 39th Cong., 1st Sess., 2765 (1866). Furthermore, it appears that no Member of Congress refuted the notion that Washington's analysis in Corfield undergirded the meaning of the Privileges or Immunities Clause.

That Members of the 39th Congress appear to have endorsed the wisdom of Justice Washington's opinion does not, standing alone, provide dispositive insight into their understanding of the Fourteenth Amendment's Privileges or Immunities Clause. Nevertheless, their repeated references to the Corfield decision, combined with what appears to be

the historical understanding of the Clause's operative terms, supports the inference that, at the time the Fourteenth Amendment was adopted, people understood that "privileges or immunities of citizens" were fundamental rights, rather than every public benefit established by positive law. Accordingly, the majority's conclusion—that a State violates the Privileges or Immunities Clause when it "discriminates" against citizens who have been domiciled in the State for less than a year in the distribution of welfare benefit appears contrary to the original understanding and is dubious at best.

As The Chief Justice points out, it comes as quite a surprise that the majority relies on the Privileges or Immunities Clause at all in this case. That is because, as I have explained The Slaughter-House Cases sapped the Clause of any meaning. Although the majority appears to breathe new life into the Clause today, it fails to address its historical underpinnings or its place in our constitutional jurisprudence. Because I believe that the demise of the Privileges or Immunities Clause has contributed in no small part to the current disarray of our Fourteenth Amendment jurisprudence, I would be open to reevaluating its meaning in an appropriate case. Before invoking the Clause, however, we should endeavor to understand what the framers of the Fourteenth Amendment thought that it meant. We should also consider whether the Clause should displace, rather than augment, portions of our equal protection and substantive due process jurisprudence. The majority's failure to consider these important questions raises the specter that the Privileges or Immunities Clause will become yet another convenient tool for inventing new rights, limited solely by the "predilections of those who happen at the time to be Members of this Court." Moore v. East Cleveland, 431 U.S. 494, 502 (1977).

I respectfully dissent.

Case Questions for Discussion

1. In what sense does the Court majority in this case reason like common law judges?

2. Why does the majority insist that California's law must be subjected to the highest level of judicial scrutiny? Does it make any difference in the outcome of this case?

3. How compelling is Justice Thomas's argument about the history of the Privileges and Immunities Clause?

4. Should all rights be deemed fundamental and therefore receive the greatest constitutional protection? Alternatively, are some rights less fundamental, such as the payment of welfare benefits in this case?

5. Might the outcome have been different if California's statute limited benefits to one half the normal benefit for those recipients who had resided in the state for less than one year? What if California had required a one-year residency for citizenship and limited benefits to citizens?

6. Do you agree that jurists should always interpret the U.S. Constitution from a historical perspective? One way to phrase the matter is, if the framers did not anticipate the issue in question, should jurists afford constitutional protection? Is there a better way to frame the question?

Empirical Theories of Decision-Making

How judges *should* behave may not be consistent with how they *actually* behave. Logically, these are two different questions. The former is a normative question and the latter is an empirical matter. There is little question that judges must exercise discretion in the fulfillment of their duty to adjudicate disputes. They interpret and apply case precedents, statutes, and constitutional provisions to resolve matters that come before them. Yet, because they are constrained by institutional and professional norms, judges are not free to do as they please. They are obliged to exercise their judgment, and in the process, they make value choices. Commentators commonly say, therefore, that judges possess leeway, not license.

Social scientists, and political scientists in particular, along with some legal scholars, have devoted considerable intellectual energy to the task of describing and explaining judicial behavior. They have explored a number of empirical approaches in an attempt to understand why judges make decisions the way they do. Scholars often view these approaches as competing scientific paradigms, arguing that one approach is more explanatory than another and that serious attention should be paid to it and not to the others. The authors of your text are not committed to a single approach. Rather, we think various approaches aid in understanding how and why judges make their decisions the way they do. The approaches we describe have received the greatest attention in recent decades. These approaches are judicial attitude, judicial role, social background, small group theory and strategic interaction, and neo-institutionalism.

Judicial Attitude Approach

Proponents of the *judicial attitude approach* assert the belief that policy preferences (attitudes) are "the primary determinant of choices by judges in their voting patterns."[18] They maintain that once we know the attitude of judges or justices, there is little need to explore other variables to predict their behavior. How then do scholars define and count judicial attitudes?

Consistent with principles of social psychology, Professor Harold Spaeth defines an attitude as a "relatively enduring set of interrelated beliefs that describe, evaluate, and advocate action with respect to some object or situation."[19] This definition has two important parts. First, attitudes are relatively stable, meaning that they do not easily change because they are acquired in the case of jurists through a lifetime of experience and learning. Second, attitudes must be stimulated either by objects in the social environment or by social or political situations that all people encounter. In the judicial decision-making environment, judges react to the litigant(s) (the object) and the conduct (situation) that gave rise to the case before them. If in their voting behavior judges on collegial courts cast their collective votes in a consistently "liberal" or "conservative" way, then it is said that such patterns reveal an underlying attitudinal dimension.

For cases involving criminal justice matters, most researchers, for example, code a vote for the criminal defendant as a liberal vote and a vote for the government as a conservative vote. In freedom of speech cases, a vote to allow speech is coded as a liberal vote and a vote to prohibit or inhibit speech is regarded as a conservative vote. In labor management cases, a vote for a labor union is coded as a liberal vote and a vote for management is coded as a conservative vote. In brief, for most fact situations, there are a number of coding rules that researchers usually apply in a simple manner. Once the votes are coded, there are a number of ways to perform the empirical analysis. Techniques range from simple Guttman scaling to more mathematically sophisticated factor analysis.[20]

Though the judicial attitude approach appears scientifically impressive, it is not beyond criticism. First, the methodology infers attitudes from behavior. That is, by knowing how judges or justices vote in a set of nonunanimous cases, researchers claim that their attitudes are known. It would be better to first establish jurists' attitudes independently of judicial voting and then determine if there is a correlation between their attitudes and votes. But because most jurists are unwilling to complete attitude questionnaires, the most obvious fix for the problem is not usually possible.

Judicial attitude proponents attempt to overcome the criticism by citing one significant research finding, however. Researchers read and coded editorial comments in leading newspapers about the nomination of persons to the U.S. Supreme Court, but before their actual service on the Court. When a sufficient number of editorial writings consistently labeled nominees as liberal, moderate, or conservative, researchers coded each as possessing such attitudes. The researchers correlated how the justices subsequently voted on the Supreme Court with their ideological proclivities (attitudes) as established by the content analysis of the previous editorial newspaper statements. The researchers found a high correlation between the justices' "attitudes" and their "votes," leading them to conclude that judicial votes alone are sufficiently similar to attitudes to justify treating them as one and the same.[21] The following figure presents the basic relationship:

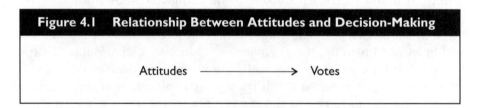

Figure 4.1   Relationship Between Attitudes and Decision-Making

Attitudes ⟶ Votes

A second major criticism of the attitude approach is that summarizing all the possible reasons why justices may vote one way or another in a given case tends to bury the judges' rationale in a single symbol or number. There are a number of possible reasons why judges vote the way they do. Yet, the desire to test for voting consistency tends to blind analysts to the possible existence of multidimensional reasons for voting patterns. Possible reasons may include institutional factors such as leadership and various small group dynamics within the court, external political factors including court reaction to public opinion, congressional support or attacks, litigation mobilization by interest groups, and problems of compliance. One aspect of this problem that we discuss in the next section is the attitude toward precedent, or what scholars call the *judicial role*. In other words, the one-dimensional nature of attitudinal analysis creates artifacts of judicial decisions that cannot be used to disconfirm multidimensional decision-making hypotheses.[22]

Judicial Role Approach

As students, teachers, significant others, and offspring, we wear different social hats that require us to conduct ourselves appropriately for each role expectation. Judges also play roles that carry with them certain expectations of behavior. For example, judges should avoid the appearance of conflicts of interests, they should be impartial toward litigants, and they should acknowledge the importance of precedent in our common law system. Judges and justices, however, do not always share role expectations. One prominent question discussed earlier in this text is whether jurists should assume an activist's posture in the service of expanding rights, or should they exercise judicial self-restraint in the preservation of the status quo. The problem of determining the appropriate judicial role was the subject of much commentary during recent senatorial confirmation hearings and elsewhere. However, as we know from our previous discussion in this chapter, it is not limited to constitutional interpretation and the exercise of judicial review alone. Judicial attitudes toward precedent and statutory interpretation are also central concerns.

Scholars who study judicial role generally conceive of it as a separate, intervening independent variable between judicial attitudes and actual judicial votes. In other words, they view judicial role as mediating the raw influences of ideology in the decision-making process.

Scholars have conducted most of their empirical judicial role research on state courts. Usually, researchers have greater access to state judges than is typically the case in the federal courts, where they usually must rely on statements found in the written judicial opinions of judges and justices, and other public pronouncements. Yet, the combined research efforts in state and federal courts offer intellectual grist for the theoretical mill.

Researchers have used several different conceptions of the judicial role. Some have classified the state supreme court judge as lawmaker, law interpreter, and pragmatist. Others have classified legal roles in terms of innovator, realist, and pragmatist.[23] The work by Theodore L. Becker is particularly interesting given the discussion at the beginning of this chapter about the various uses of precedent.

Becker was interested in identifying and isolating what he regarded as the judicial factor within the broader conception of judicial role. He wanted to know what makes judges different from legislators and political executives. His hypothesis was that the restraint on personal values (attitudes) in favor of references to and deference toward precedent, and the rule of law more generally, distinguishes the judicial role from roles played by other political actors. He operationalized his hypothesis by first comparing responses of law students with undergraduate political science students in their judgments about hypothetical cases Becker had asked them to decide. The respondents were given the facts of the case and the applicable precedents. Becker found that despite their value orientations to the contrary, law students had a much greater propensity than did the undergraduates to decide in favor of precedent. This finding reinforces the common observation that law students undergo an intense process of socialization that serves to internalize legal norms at the expense of maintaining their preexisting attitudes. He also interviewed Hawaiian judges, and he came to the same conclusion that respect for precedent constrains jurists in the exercise of their function. Then, based on a scaled interview schedule, Becker compared the responses of a small sample of judges in Hawaii, Hong Kong, and the Philippines. The responses from the Hawaiian and Hong Kong judges displayed more reliance on precedent than on common sense or views of justice in particular cases. This, however, was not as prevalent a norm for Philippine judges. Yet, the responses from all three cultures indicated that precedent, when clearly and directly relevant, was a major determinant in judicial decision making.[24]

Nevertheless, as James Gibson pointed out, what is the meaning of the statement that a judge is strongly oriented toward precedent? We know that judges are adept at using precedent to justify any policy result—remember that judges may apply precedents either loosely or strictly and still maintain that they are faithfully following precedent. The real question is to what extent do judges feel it is permissible to achieve the policy goals they desire? Analyzing the responses to questionnaires administered to Iowa and California judges, Gibson found considerable consensus among judges that a good judge adheres closely to precedent. However, consensus broke down when the judges were asked about the appropriate use of their discretion. Gibson concluded that there are at least two groups of judges: result-oriented and process-oriented judges. For our purposes, the result-oriented judges may be labeled lawmakers or activists, and process-oriented judges may be labeled restraintists. Moreover, he found, role orientations interact with judicial attitudes to influence judicial votes.[25]

One of the most interesting studies focusing on the interaction between judicial attitudes and role orientations is of Florida court of appeals judges. Researchers distributed questionnaires asking them to (1) respond to questions that reveal their ideology (attitudes) and (2) respond to a series of questions depicting competing views of judicial role. After coding the judges' responses and labeling them as liberal versus conservative and activists versus restraintists, the researchers then examined how the judges actually voted in criminal appeals over a two-year time period. Using these data, they computed reversal rates for the judges who responded to their questionnaires. Interestingly, they found, with respect to their propensity to reverse criminal convictions, that judges who were labeled "liberal/restraintists" based on their questionnaire responses were statistically indistinguishable from their "conservative/restraintists" colleagues. This means that liberal/restraintists were just as likely as conservative/restraintists to reverse criminal convictions. But "liberal/activists" had a much greater tendency to reverse lower courts than did "conservative/activists."[26] If we venture to extrapolate this finding to other court settings, the question of why judicial nominee confirmation controversies and judicial election debates are important becomes manifestly evident. If potential judges have liberal attitudes but at the same time possess restraintists' conceptions of the judicial role, then the results of their actual decisions may exhibit little difference from conservative jurists regardless of their role perceptions.

The picture that emerges thus far from our analysis of judicial decision-making looks something like the representation in Figure 4.2. But the true picture is probably more complicated, as readers are about to learn.

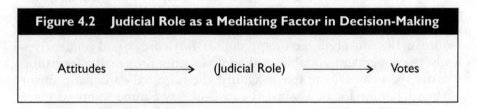

Figure 4.2 Judicial Role as a Mediating Factor in Decision-Making

Attitudes ⟶ (Judicial Role) ⟶ Votes

Social Background Approach

One does not need to be a professional social scientist to observe that our social backgrounds have an impact on attitudes and behavior. Social scientists have well documented that families, peer groups, churches, schools, clubs, and workplaces are socializing agents. We understand that certain advantages come with having wealthy parents that less wealthy offspring do not share. We know that those brought up in families with strong religious beliefs and with strong partisan views toward politics tend to behave differently than persons without such attributes. In short, although there are individual deviations, we observe that persons with similar backgrounds tend to display similar attitudes and behavior traits.

In the early part of the twentieth century, there were a few empirical studies of the social backgrounds of judges. However, it was not until John R. Schmidhauser published his pioneering study in 1959 that the social backgrounds of judges and justices received serious consideration by political scientists. Among other things, he found that most of the justices of the U.S. Supreme Court from its beginning in the late eighteenth century up until the late 1950s were white, Anglo-Saxon, and Protestant.[27] It is little wonder that from a historical per-

spective, the Supreme Court has been a relatively conservative institution. However, Schmidhauser and other social background scholars
recognized a methodological flaw in their analysis. Namely, they were
only inferring behavior, not demonstrating a correspondence between
background and behavior.

They then set out to establish the link between background and behavior by testing *bivariate relationships* between a host of background
variables and decision-making propensities. Researchers accomplish
this task by examining the relationship between two variables, looking
for differences among categories of the independent variable. For each
independent and dependent variable, researchers create cross-classifi-
cation or contingency tables to test the hypothesis of a relationship between the two variables. Conducted mostly in the 1960s, these studies
had universes that were not limited to the U.S. Supreme Court. Scholars also studied U.S. appellate courts, state appellate courts, and later
U.S. district courts. The independent variables studied included such
factors as political party affiliations, appointing president, prior judicial experience, region of country, religion, father's occupation, ethnic
background, age, prior government experience, prior business experience, size of home town, education (undergraduate and law school),
tenure on the court (elected or appointed), birth order, and gender. Typically, the dependent variable studied was voting propensity; for example, did the justices vote for or against the criminal defendant, for or
against labor, or for or against the civil liberty claim? Many of these
studies demonstrated a strong association between background and
behavior.

By the mid-1960s, however, the social background approach came
under attack. Don Bowen, in his 1965 Yale Ph.D. dissertation, conducted research on 373 state and federal judges sitting in 1960. Predictably, he found associations at the bivariate level. But when he subjected
the numbers to multiple regression analysis, he found that all the independent background variables included in his study (party, region, religion, prestige of schools attended, age, and tenure) explained only
somewhere between 20 and 30 percent of the total variation, depending
upon the issue area under study. Unlike simple bivariate analysis, multiple regression permits researchers to assess the influence of several
independent variables simultaneously. This is termed *multivariate analysis*. Translated from mathematics into simpler terms, this means that
if we were to explain 100 percent of all variation on the dependent variable, about 70 to 80 percent would go unexplained by the combination
of the independent variables included in Bowen's multiple regression
equations.[28]

Bowen's study of judicial voting in a single year (1960) led some serious scholars to conclude that studying social background characteristics possessed insufficient explanatory power and therefore little promise as an approach to understanding judicial decision-making.[29] Yet, in

fairness, given the state of knowledge available at the time, explaining 20 to 40 percent of the variance was not too shabby a finding. Moreover, social background theorists never said that background variables alone would explain judicial behaviors—there are many other factors to consider in explaining decision-making. Additionally, future multiple regression studies found considerably more variation explained by the background variables than did Bowen's early study.[30] Most important, a significant flaw in Bowen's methodology was in time uncovered by additional research.

A 1981 study by Neal Tate examined voting patterns of U.S. Supreme Court justices in nonunanimous civil rights/liberties and economic cases from 1946 through 1977. Employing multiple regression models, Tate found that 87 percent of the variance is explained by background variables in the justices' voting in civil rights/liberties decisions, and 72 percent of the variance is explained in economic decisions.[31] Robert Carp and C. Y. Rowland studied decisions by federal district court judges. They looked at 27,772 decisions of these judges in 20 different issue areas from 1933 to 1977. They found that case outcomes are affected by political partisanship, appointing president, region, and the urban-rural character of the judicial district.[32] S. Sidney Ulmer looked at Supreme Court justices' support for the government in government versus underdog cases, including support for the government in criminal cases between 1903 and 1968. Ulmer employed three independent variables: father as state government officer, justice as firstborn child, and political party of the justice. It is significant that, for the period from 1903 to 1935, the three independent variables explained only about 18 percent of the variation. But between the years 1936 and 1968, the independent variables explained 72 percent of the variation. Across the entire 66-year period (1903–1968), he explained almost 36 percent of the variation.[33]

The conclusion is obvious. The social background model is not time-neutral. Much depends upon the issues that come before the Court in any given time period. Bowen examined decisions in only one year, and other researchers examined either a single year or just a few years during the 1950s or early 1960s. Perhaps, issues facing the bench during this particular period did not excite the type of passions that divided judges and justices by their social background characteristics. Clearly, when scholars take a longer view, a different picture emerges. Divisive issues are more likely to be a factor in judicial decision-making, and background characteristics appear to make a difference on how justices vote.

Although scholars differ on the relationship among the variables, Figure 4.3 is a convenient but not the only way to view the interactive effect of background factors, attitudes, judicial role, and judicial decisions.

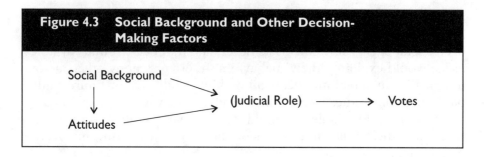

Figure 4.3 Social Background and Other Decision-Making Factors

Small Group and Strategic Interactions

Most trial courts in the United States are presided over by a single judge. But the collegial court system is common in appellate tribunals, including intermediate appellate state courts and supreme courts, the regional U.S. Courts of Appeal, most of the specialized federal courts, and the U.S. Supreme Court. In addition, on occasion, federal district courts use three-judge panels. Because these judges make decisions in a group setting rather than by single individuals, it is reasonable to suppose that group processes are related to decision-making. Studies about small groups generally confirm the everyday observation that there are strong pressures to conform to majority wishes and to abide by both formal and informal group norms. We also observe that the amount and quality of communication among the members of small groups affect individual decision-making.[34] Walter F. Murphy, the author of the seminal work on the subject, has emphasized that collegial courts bring judges together in face-to-face interaction with an obligation to resolve disputes. Consequently, studying the group dynamics of courts is a necessary condition for understanding judicial decision-making.[35]

Judicial biographies and the private and public papers of retired jurists provide information indicating that the appellate courts, particularly the U.S. Supreme Court, operate much like any other small group. Over time, systems of interactions develop whereby bargaining, negotiation, and strategic behavior on the part of individual justices influence judicial outcomes. We know, for example, that the extraordinary leadership skills of particular chief justices, such as John Marshall and Earl Warren, directed the U.S. Supreme Court toward important institutional and policy goals.

Through the cunning application of his leadership skills, John Marshall established judicial review. He successfully discouraged his colleagues from writing their own opinions in each case (*seriatim* opinion writing). Instead, the Supreme Court adopted what is ostensibly the current practice; the justices write single institutional opinions for the Court, preferably written by the chief himself. The creation of this institutional norm helped the Supreme Court develop the reputation as a prestigious co-equal branch of government. Earl Warren is justly famous for leading an otherwise divided Supreme Court to a unanimous opinion in the landmark desegregation case, *Brown v. Board of Education* (1954). He convinced his colleagues that if a constitutional revolution was to take place, the Court must speak with one voice. He then performed the difficult task of penning an opinion on which they could all agree. Warren also exhibited extraordinary task and social leadership skills in the expansion of civil rights and liberties in the late 1950s and 1960s. He provided the Court with able intellectual and organizational leadership, while at the same time creating a sense of goodwill among members of the Court. In the process, Warren was able to head off dysfunctional interpersonal friction that is often present when strong personalities are in intimate contact and the stakes are high. Although chief justices often possess either task or social leadership skills, few have displayed both skills simultaneously.[36]

Studies of voting coalitions on appellate courts establish that blocs of judges or justices regularly vote together in many issue areas that result in nonunanimous opinions. The existence of blocs is evidence of coalitional behavior. Such observations aid researchers in describing patterns of interagreement and predicting outcomes in future cases. This type of analysis also has the practical political consequence of placing death and retirement in political perspective. For instance, if a member of the five-justice conservative bloc retires from the contemporary Supreme Court led by Chief Justice William Rehnquist, and he or she is replaced by a liberal or moderate justice, then the Court may change direction, at least with respect to the particular issues around which the conservative bloc exists.

There is a major difficulty with bloc analysis, however. Computing the percentage of times that pairs of justices have voted together does not demonstrate why they voted together. Bloc analysis confirms only the existence of a bloc. Justices may agree because of similar judicial attitudes, strong leadership, bargaining, and other influences on and off the Court. In this sense, bloc analysis is only descriptive. It does not possess explanatory power—a major goal of social science.[37] Nevertheless, bloc analysis and other quantitative methods have been useful in studying the integration of new members on the Supreme Court (freshman effect hypotheses), patterns of opinion assignment, and leadership patterns.[38]

Strategic interaction. A recent development in small group theory is the application of rational choice theory to Supreme Court decision-making. It assumes that although justices want to vote their sincere beliefs, they must also calculate how they can convince other justices to vote with them. For this reason, rational actors will vote in a politically sophisticated way. That is, justices are willing to tone down their preferred and sincere beliefs in order to win a sufficient number of the other justices' votes to achieve their policy goals. In other words, they are willing to negotiate agreements with their colleagues that do not truly represent what they ideally believe is the best possible decision in a case.

Consider the following hypothetical example. An ideologically conservative justice may be opposed to the expansion of gender rights. But because his colleagues wish to use the occasion of a given case to expand these rights, he negotiates with his more moderate and liberal colleagues. In exchange for his vote, he gets them to agree to include wording in the majority opinion that minimizes the precedential value of the opinion by the explicit statement that the principle of the case should not be interpreted to extend beyond the particularly extraordinary facts of the case at hand. The moderate and liberal justices get a decision in favor of gender rights, but the conservative justice is able to limit the reach of the opinion.

The intellectual origins of the strategic interaction approach is traceable to the 1964 work of Walter F. Murphy mentioned earlier. Instead of basing their conclusions on mostly anecdotal evidence, Lee Epstein and Jack Knight, and others writing in the late 1990s and the early years of the new century, employed data that are more systematic. They gained access to the conference notes, case files, and docket books of justices William J. Brennan, William O. Douglas, Thurgood Marshall, and Lewis F. Powell for all cases in the Supreme Court's 1983 term and landmark cases handed down during the Burger Court years (1969–1985 terms).[39] Asserting improvement over the explanatory power of the judicial attitude advocates, strategic theorists claim that they can ". . . best explain the choices of justices as strategic behavior and not merely as responses to ideology values."[40] Rational choice advocates claim that justices act intentionally and optimally toward obtaining specific policy objectives. Particularly in garnering the votes necessary for majority decisions and minimizing concurring and dissenting opinions, justices behave strategically in making their voting choices through bargaining and negotiation about the content of judicial opinions. In the strategic environment, justices consider the institutional context in which they operate—both the formal and informal norms and conventions within the judiciary, as well as how other institutions of government are liable to react to particular decisions.[41]

There are criticisms of the strategic interactions approach. However, most scholars, even critics, think the approach is promising. Justices may act strategically in conference but during the last stage of action, the final vote, they are not constrained in their choices. Therefore, they are free to vote their sincere policy preferences. Moreover, justices, like the rest of us, do not always behave as rational actors hoping to achieve short-run objectives. Many voters in the 2000 presidential election, for instance, voted for third party candidates Ralph Nader and Pat Buchanan, but not because they believed either had much of a chance to become president of the United States. Rather, many voted for the political mavericks to express displeasure with the major party presidential candidates and to make a statement about the programs and policies of the two major parties. Likewise, there is evidence that some justices do not think they have any opportunity to convince, compromise, or negotiate with their colleagues. They obtain considerable self-satisfaction by expressing their sincere beliefs. They also write concurring and dissenting opinions so that the general public and particularly attentive interest groups may know that their points of view are being represented on the U.S. Supreme Court. One should also consider the paucity of available data. It may be that justices act more strategically during some historical periods than others. But the data needed to test such a hypothesis are either difficult or impossible to obtain. We do not have systematic access to the internal discussions of Supreme Court justices or judges of other courts over the life of these institutions. Further, although strategic interaction researchers are able to document cases of such behavior, what are we to make of those cases where no evidence can be used to support the hypothesis? In brief, the search for the definitive scientific paradigm must go on.[42] Figure 4.4 is one way to conceptualize how small group processes are interrelated with other independent variables to influence judicial votes.

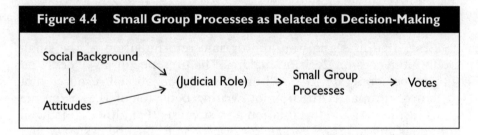

Figure 4.4   Small Group Processes as Related to Decision-Making

Social Background → (Judicial Role) → Small Group Processes → Votes

Attitudes →

Neo-institutionalism

The emphasis on psychological and sociological variables in judicial decision-making research tends to ignore the institutional settings in which judges make their judgments. Courts are relatively autonomous organizations with lives of their own. These institutions produce their own expectations, which influence decision-making independent of the deep economic, social, and psychological structures and social backgrounds of judicial actors.

Rogers Smith, in a 1988 article, made a clarion call for integrating models of judicial behavior. He asserted that scholars should focus on the ". . . interrelationships between human institutions and structures and the decisions and actions of political actors" because, as he explained, institutions shape the interests, resources, and ultimately the conduct of all political actors, including judges.[43] In other words, the judicial institution itself is an independent variable that will contribute to explanation.

Scholars advocating the neo-institutional approach to understanding judicial decision-making focus their attention on the institutional rules, norms, and behavioral expectations of courts in shaping decisional outcomes. One promising strain of this focus is explaining dissent behavior among judges of state supreme courts. Researchers have found that institutional factors inhibit or promote the expression of judges' personal preferences, leading in some cases to greater consensus and in other instances, to dissent behavior.[44]

Bradley Best's book-length treatment of the decline of the consensus norm on the U.S. Supreme Court employs a neo-institutional approach. He found that justices write more concurring and dissenting opinions than they did in the past because in part they have greater institutional support. Over the years, the number of law clerks and support staff available to the individual justices increased substantially. Increasing numbers of clerks and support personnel assigned to the Supreme Court between 1935 and 1995 parallels a growth in the number of concurring, dissenting, and separate opinions written by Court members. As a practical matter, in the past, workloads required that the justices conserve their energy. Today, with additional clerks and other support staff, the justices are less restrained in writing concurring and dissenting opinions than they were in the past. Increased institutional support naturally alters the justices' ability to engage in time-consuming opinion writing.[45]

Best's finding signals an appropriate reformulation of the small group influences on decision-making. The presence of law clerks and support personnel may be an important organizational resource that structures ultimately the opinion-writing behavior of U.S. Supreme Court justices. This reformulation also suggests that although judicial attitude is an important explanatory variable, it must be nested within a larger conceptual framework that accounts for the impact of institutional factors in decision-making. Although various scholars may disagree about the proper juxtaposition of each of the independent variables in relationship to the dependent variable, we provide Figure 4.5 to help clarify matters.

Figure 4.5   Institutional Norms as Among Decision-Making Factors

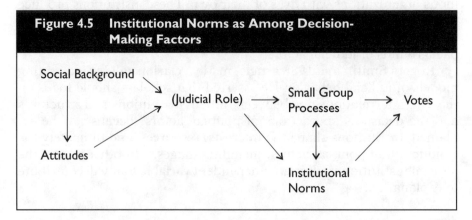

Empirical Theories in Perspective

Although some scholars express strong support for particular empirical theories of judicial decision-making, the authors of your text believe that decision-making is multicausal and a complex process. We might have mentioned in detail several other factors that judges consider when making decisions. Public opinion and the willingness of the public to accept their decision are important matters going to the heart of the legitimacy of judicial institutions that jurists sometimes consider. The reaction of other political institutions and elites to court opinions is another factor that scholars have studied. Moreover, the influence of outside forces on the decision-making process itself, such as the filing of *amicus curiae* briefs by interested third parties, may possess explanatory power.

Whatever empirical approach one finds most convincing, it is necessary to understand that institutions, interests, ideas, and individuals all play a part in the decision-making calculus. The actual portions attributable to each are matters for empirical investigation. Further, good arguments matter to lawyers and judges alike. Fair-minded judges are willing to consider the arguments presented to them in a spirit of intellectual honesty.

The remainder of this text is devoted to a description of how various legal processes operate within the American legal system and legal norms in the major fields of law as we know it today.

Key Terms, Names, and Concepts

Antonin Scalia

Bivariate relationship

Broad constructionists

Canons of statutory interpretation

Conceptualism (moderate originalism)

Constitutional interpretation

Distinguishing a precedent

Edwin Meese

Extrinsic source canons

Fundamental law

Interpretivism

Judicial attitude approach

Judicial role approach

Legal precedent

Legislative intent

Loose view of precedent

Multivariate analysis

Neo-institutionalism

Noninterpretivism

Originalism

Plain-meaning rule

Privileges and Immunities Clause

Robert Bork

Rule of law

Small group approach

Social background approach

Stare decisis

Strategic interactions

Strict constructionists

Strict view of precedent

Substantive policy canons

Symbolism and noninterpretivism

Textual canons   Theodore L. Becker
Textualism   William Brennan

Discussion Questions

1. Do judges make law when they apply precedent to new or novel situations? If true, does this practice represent a usurpation of legislative authority when it occurs?

2. How does the method of the common law accommodate change in society?

3. Should the law reflect changing social attitudes in society, and should the U.S. Constitution be interpreted as a "living document" subject to the changing needs of society?

4. Where should judges search for legislative intent? Should they rely on the words of the author(s) of bills, legislative reports, congressional debates, or what?

5. Where do you come down on the interpretivist/noninterpretivist debate? Should judges and justices always adhere to one or the other viewpoint?

6. Try to construct a model of judicial decision-making. What variables should go into such a model? How, if at all, does each of the independent variables interact with the others?

Suggested Additional Reading

Agresto, John. *The Supreme Court and Constitutional Democracy*. Ithaca, NY: Cornell University Press, 1986.

Antieau, Chester J. *Adjudicating Constitutional Issues*. Dobbs Ferry, NY: Oceana Publications, 1985.

Barnum, David G. *The Supreme Court and American Democracy*. New York: St. Martin's, 1993.

Berger, Raoul. *Government by Judiciary: The Transformation of the Fourteenth Amendment*. Cambridge, MA: Harvard University Press, 1977.

Bobbitt, Philip. *Constitutional Fate: Theory of the Constitution*. New York: Oxford University, 1984.

Brenner, Saul, and Harold J. Spaeth. *Stare Decisis: The Alteration of Precedent on the Supreme Court*. New York: Cambridge University Press, 1995.

Cannon, Mark, and David O'Brien, eds. *Views From the Bench: The Judiciary and Constitutional Politics*. Chatham, NJ: Chatham House, 1985.

Carter, Lief H. *Contemporary Constitutional Lawmaking: The Supreme Court and the Art of Politics*. Elmsford, NY: Pergamon, 1985.

Choper, Jesse H. *Judicial Review and the National Political Process: A Functional Reconsideration of the Role of the Supreme Court.* Chicago: University of Chicago Press, 1983.

Clinton, Robert L. *From Precedent to Myth: Marbury v. Madison and the History of Judicial Review in America.* Lawrence: University Press of Kansas, 1989.

Dimond, Paul A. *The Supreme Court and Judicial Choice: The Role of Provisional Review in Democracy.* Ann Arbor: University of Michigan Press, 1989.

Ducat, Craig R. *Modes of Constitutional Interpretation.* St. Paul, MN: West, 1978.

Ely, John Hart. *Democracy and Distrust: A Theory of Judicial Review.* Cambridge, MA: Harvard University Press, 1980.

Epp, Charles R. *The Rights Revolution: Lawyers, Activists, and the Supreme Courts in Comparative Perspective.* Chicago: University of Chicago Press, 1998.

Gabin, Sanford Byron. *Judicial Review and the Reasonable Doubt Test.* Port Washington, NY: Kennikat Press, 1980.

Greenawalt, Kent. *Legislation Statutory Interpretation: 20 Questions.* New York: Foundation Press, 1999.

Hall, Kermit L., William M. Wiecek, and Paul Finkelman. *American Legal History: Cases and Materials.* New York: Oxford University Press, 1991.

Halpern, Stephen C., and Charles M. Lamb. *Supreme Court Activism and Restraint.* Lexington, MA: Lexington Books, 1983.

Higgins, Thomas J. *Judicial Review Unmasked.* Norwell, MA: Christopher Publications, 1981.

Horowitz, Donald L. *The Courts and Social Policy.* Washington, DC: Brookings Institution, 1977.

Lazarus, Edward. *Closed Chambers: The First Eyewitness Account of the Epic Struggles Inside the Supreme Court.* New York: Times Books, 1998.

Levi, Edward. *An Introduction to Legal Reasoning.* Chicago: University of Chicago Press, 1950, 1974.

Llewellyn, Karl. *The Common Law Tradition: Deciding Appeals.* Boston: Little, Brown, 1962.

McCann, Michael W., and Gerald L. Houseman, eds. *Judging the Constitution: Critical Essays on Judicial Lawmaking.* Glenview, IL: Scott, Foresman and Company, 1989.

McDowell, Gary L. *Taking the Constitution Seriously: Essays on the Constitution and the Constitutional Law.* Dubuque, IA: Kendall/Hunt, 1981.

——. *Equity and the Constitution: The Supreme Court, Equitable Relief, and Public Policy.* Chicago: University of Chicago Press, 1982.

Melone, Albert P., and George Mace. *Judicial Review and American Democracy.* Ames: Iowa State University Press, 1988.

Mendelson, Wallace. *Supreme Court Statecraft: The Rule of Law and Men.* Ames: Iowa State University Press, 1985.

Miller, Arthur Selwyn. *Toward Judicial Activism: The Political Role of the Supreme Court.* Westport, CT: Greenwood Press, 1982.

——. *Politics, Democracy, and the Supreme Court: Essays on the Frontier of Constitutional Theory.* Westport, CT: Greenwood Press, 1985.

Murphy, Walter F., C. Herman Pritchett, and Lee Epstein. *Courts, Judges, and Politics.* 5th ed. Boston: McGraw-Hill, 2002.

Neely, Richard. *How Courts Govern America.* New Haven, CT: Yale University, 1981.

O'Brien, David M. *Storm Center: The Supreme Court in American Politics.* 5th ed. New York: Norton, 1999.

Perry, Michael J. *The Constitution, the Court, and Human Rights: An Inquiry Into the Legitimacy of Constitutional Policy-Making by the Judiciary.* New Haven, CT: Yale University Press, 1984.

Rehnquist, William. *The Supreme Court: How It Was, How It Is.* Spec. ed. New York: William Morrow, 1992.

Segal, Jeffrey A., and Howard J. Spaeth. *The Supreme Court and the Attitudinal Model Revisited.* Cambridge, UK: Cambridge University Press, 2002.

Tribe, Laurence. *God Save This Honorable Court.* New York: Random House, 1986.

——. *Constitutional Choices.* Cambridge, MA: Harvard University Press, 1985.

Wolfe, Christopher. *The Rise of Modern Judicial Review: From Constitutional Interpretation to Judge-Made Law.* Rev. ed. New York: Basic Books, 1994.

Woodward, Bob, and Scott Armstrong. *The Brethren: Inside the Supreme Court.* New York: Simon & Schuster, 1981.

Endnotes

1. Karl N. Llewellyn, *The Bramble Bush* (New York: Oceana Publications, 1960), pp. 66–69.
2. R. Shep Melnick, *Between the Lines: Interpreting Welfare Rights* (Washington, DC: The Brookings Institution, 1994), pp. 6–7.
3. Antonin Scalia, *A Matter of Interpretation: Federal Courts and the Law* (Princeton, NJ: Princeton University Press, 1997), pp. 3–47.
4. See Scalia's concurring opinion in Bank One Chicago v. Midwest Bank & Trust Co., 516 U.S. 264, 279; see also William N. Eskridge, Jr., Philip P. Frickey, and Elizabeth Garrett, *Legislation and Statutory Interpretation* (New York: Foundation Press, 2000), pp. 227–230.
5. Eskridge, Frickey, and Garrett, *Legislation and Statutory Interpretation,* p. 230.
6. William Eskridge, Jr., and Philip Frickey, "The Supreme Court, 1993 Term—Foreword: Law as Equilibrium," *Harvard Law Review* 108 (1994): 26, 97–108.
7. Ibid., p. 97.
8. Ibid., pp. 99, 100–101.
9. Ibid., pp. 101, 103, 105.
10. This view is well expressed by Eskridge, Frickey and Garrett, *Legislation and Statutory Interpretation,* pp. 369–374.
11. 297 U.S. at 62–63.

12. Louis Fisher, "Methods of Constitutional Interpretation: The Limits of Original Intent," *Cumberland Law Review* 18 (winter 1988): 45.
13. Federalist Society, *The Great Debate: Interpreting Our Written Constitution* (Washington, DC: Federalist Society, 1986), pp. 1–10, 31–41, 43–52.
14. Ibid., p. 17.
15. Erwin Chemerinsky, "The Price of Asking the Wrong Question: An Essay on Constitutional Scholarship and Judicial Review," *Texas Law Review* 62 (April 1984): 1234.
16. Thomas C. Grey, "Do We Have an Unwritten Constitution?" *Stanford Law Review* 27 (February 1975): 712.
17. Michael J. Perry, "The Authority of Text, Tradition, and Reason: A Theory of Constitutional Interpretation," *Southern California Law Review* 58 (January 1985): 551–602.
18. Jeffrey A. Segal and Harold J. Spaeth, *The Supreme Court and the Attitudinal Model* (New York: Cambridge University Press, 1993), pp. 33–73.
19. Harold J. Spaeth, *Supreme Court Policy Making: Explanation and Prediction* (San Francisco: W. H. Freeman, 1979), pp. 119–120.
20. Albert P. Melone, *Researching Constitutional Law*, 2nd ed. (Prospect Heights, IL: Waveland Press, 2000), pp. 67–75.
21. Jeffrey A. Segal and Albert D. Cover, "Ideological Values and the Votes of U.S. Supreme Court Justices," *American Political Science Review* 83 (1989): 557–565.
22. Theodore L. Becker, *Comparative Judicial Politics: The Political Functions of Courts* (Chicago: Rand McNally, 1970), pp. 27–34.
23. Sheldon Goldman and Austin Sarat, *American Court Systems: Readings in Judicial Process and Behavior* (San Francisco: W. H. Freeman, 1978), pp. 468–469.
24. Theodore L. Becker, *Comparative Judicial Politics*, pp. 45–63.
25. James L. Gibson, "Judges' Role Orientations, Attitudes, and Decisions: An Interactive Model," *American Political Science Review* 72 (1978): 911–924; James L. Gibson, "The Role Concept in Judicial Research," *Law and Policy Quarterly* 3 (1981): 291–311.
26. John M. Scheb II, Thomas D. Ungs, and Allison L. Hayes, "Judicial Role Orientations, Attitudes, and Decision Making: A Research Note," *Western Political Quarterly* 42 (1989): 427–435.
27. John R. Schmidhauser, "The Justices of the Supreme Court: A Collective Portrait," *Midwest Journal of Political Science* 3 (1959): 1–57.
28. D. R. Bowen, "The Explanation of Judicial Voting Behavior From Sociological Characteristics of Judges" (unpublished Ph.D. dissertation, Yale University, 1965), p. 201.
29. See, Walter F. Murphy and Joseph Tanenhaus, *The Study of Public Law* (New York: Random House, 1972), pp. 107–108.
30. Stuart S. Nagel, "Multiple Correlation of Judicial Backgrounds and Decisions," *Florida State University Law Review* 2 (spring 1974): 258–280.
31. Neal C. Tate, "Personal Attribute Models of the Voting Behavior of U.S. Supreme Court Justices: Liberalism in Civil Liberties and Economic Decisions, 1946–1978," *American Political Science Review* 75 (1981): 51–82.
32. Robert A. Carp and C.Y. Rowland, *Policymaking and Politics in the Federal District Courts* (Knoxville: University of Tennessee Press, 1983).

33. S. Sidney Ulmer, "Social Background as an Indicator to the Votes of Supreme Court Justices in Criminal Cases, 1947–1956," *American Journal of Political Science* 17 (1973): 622–630; S. Sidney Ulmer, "Are Social Background Models Time-Bound?" *American Political Science Review* 80 (1986): 957–967.

34. Sheldon Goldman and Austin Sarat, *American Court Systems: Readings in Judicial Process and Behavior* (San Francisco: W. H. Freeman, 1978), pp. 490–491.

35. Walter F. Murphy, *Elements of Judicial Strategy* (Chicago: University of Chicago Press, 1964).

36. Goldman and Sarat, *American Court Systems*, pp. 506–522.

37. Melone, *Researching Constitutional Law*, 2nd ed., pp. 75–79.

38. John D. Sprague, *Voting Patterns of the United States Supreme Court: Cases in Federalism* (Indianapolis: Bobbs-Merrill, 1968); Elliot E. Slotnick, "Judicial Career Patterns and Majority Opinion Assignment on the Supreme Court," *Journal of Politics* 41 (1979): 640–648; S. Sidney Ulmer, "Toward a Theory of Sub-Group Formation in the United States Supreme Court," *Journal of Politics* 27 (1963): 133–152; Kenneth L. Grambihler and Albert P. Melone, "Initial Behavior of Newly Appointed Supreme Court Justices," *Illinois Political Science Review* 4 (fall 1998): 63–71; and Albert P. Melone, "Revisiting the Freshman Effect Hypothesis: The First Two Years of Justice Anthony Kennedy," *Judicature* 74 (June/July 1990): 6–13.

39. Lee Epstein and Jack Knight, *The Choices Justices Make* (Washington, DC: Congressional Quarterly, 1998): xiv–xv.

40. Ibid., p. 10.

41. Ibid., pp.10–18. Also see Lee Epstein and Jack Knight, "Field Essay: Toward a Strategic Revolution in Judicial Politics: A Look Back, A Look Ahead," *Political Research Quarterly* 53 (September 2000): 625–661.

42. For a general discussion and criticism of strategic behavior applied to judicial decision-making, see Lawrence Baum, *The Puzzle of Judicial Behavior* (Ann Arbor: University of Michigan Press, 2000), pp. 89–124.

43. Rogers M. Smith, "Political Jurisprudence, the 'New Institutionalism,' and the Future of Public Law," *American Political Science Review* 82 (1988): 91.

44. Melinda Gann Hall and Paul Brace, "Order in the Courts: A Neo-Institutional Approach to Judicial Consensus," *Western Political Quarterly* 42 (1989): 391–407; Paul Brace and Melinda Gann Hall, "Neo-institutionalism and Dissent in State Supreme Courts," *The Journal of Politics* 52 (1990): 44–70; and Melinda Gann Hall and Paul Brace, "Toward an Integrated Model of Judicial Voting Behavior," *American Politics Quarterly* 20 (1992): 147–168.

45. Bradley J. Best, *Law Clerks, Support Personnel, and the Decline of Consensual Norms on the United States Supreme Court, 1935–1995* (New York: LFB Scholarly Publishing, 2002), pp. 133–141, 219–223, and 227–232. ✦

Part II

Contrasting Legal Processes

Chapter 5

Civil Suits for Money Damages

Chapter Objectives

In Part II of this book, the authors focus on the major legal processes found in the U.S. legal system. This section begins with an examination of the paradigmatic case of civil suits for money damages. Students should first firmly implant in their minds the details of the various phases of legal processes. They will then be in a position to compare and contrast these processes with those presented in the remaining chapters in this part of the book: equity suits, criminal prosecutions, administrative processes, and alternative dispute resolution. Early in this chapter, we introduce readers to the sociology of the legal profession for the purpose of alerting them to how social stratification influences the ways lawyers practice in the private and public realms. Students will also learn about the various types of damage awards available in civil suits for money damages. This will prepare them to compare and contrast these types of verdicts with final dispositions available when other legal processes are used.

Disputes between and among private parties commonly involve injuries and damages to persons and property. A suit for money damages may arise, for example, when an automobile driver negligently causes an accident resulting in the need for repairs to another's car or compensation for hospital bills and time away from work. A hostile neighbor commits a battery when, in the course of an argument over a barking dog, he strikes another, resulting in a broken nose. In these types of cases, a civil suit for money damages to recover compensation for the losses resulting from the injuries is in order. A false newspaper story about a citizen that damages her ability to do business in the community may represent facts that permit the citizen to sue for libel and accordingly to recover for damages. Failure to live up to the terms of a contract may result in a civil suit for money damages. These are just a few examples of the myriad of other instances in our daily lives that may result in civil litigation. In short, conflicts arise that result in pecuniary losses of one sort or another, and suing the wrongful party is deemed appropriate conduct under the terms of our legal order. The aspiration of the legal system is to make the wronged party "whole again."

Legal Profession

How do wronged parties proceed? In the automobile accident example, the parties commonly contact their insurance companies and leave it up to their insurers to settle the liability question and what amounts should be paid in compensation. In a good number of instances, however, it is not that simple. Insurers may deny liability and refuse compensation. Culpable parties may not have insurance in the first place or if they are insured they are not covered for the full amount of the damages. Worse yet, they may be *judgment proof,* meaning that they have few if any assets sufficient to pay damages. Parties may attempt to negotiate a settlement by themselves without invoking outside help. Failing this, however, they may feel the need to enlist legal counsel. Although most persons possess a sense of right and wrong, particularly when their self-interest is involved, they are usually unfamiliar with the procedural and substantive niceties of the law. They seek legal advice so that they may exercise all their options. They rationally calculate that the intervention of a lawyer will encourage the other side to settle the matter before it escalates to a court battle, thereby driving costs higher than is otherwise necessary.

Throughout most of U.S. history, the choice of a lawyer was the result of seeking recommendations from family, friends, or business associates. Indeed, this remains a principal means of engaging a lawyer. Beginning in the 1970s, when the United States Supreme Court struck down statutory restrictions on the use of public advertisement by lawyers,[1] news print and electronic media have been used by attorneys to aggressively solicit business. Particularly for young lawyers and legal firms without long-established reputations, mass directed advertisements are a way to bring potential clients to their offices. Older, more established firms tend to eschew such tactics; they rely instead on what they regard as the more dignified ways of offering their services to the public, including referrals from satisfied clients and a good reputation in the legal and wider community. Then, too, one should know that the legal profession, as is the case for other vocations such as medicine and academia, is a highly stratified professional community.

Stratified Bar

Substantial and persistent differences in type of practice, clientele represented, firm recruitment practices, and bar participation divide lawyers into differentiated informal status groups. Private law office practice includes individual (solo) practice, shared office space practice of two or more lawyers who are not in partnership, law firm partners, and those lawyers in the employ of law firms called associates. As can be seen in Table 5.1, almost three fourths of all lawyers practice their profession in one of these ways with others working as full-time counsel for businesses, foundations and other organizations, and government attorneys serving in one capacity or another.

Large-firm lawyers earn the highest average incomes, they represent the wealthiest and highest social-status clients, and they have the greatest contact with the higher echelons of government. They compose the elite of the legal profession. Conversely, individual practitioners and small-firm lawyers generally have the lowest incomes, they tend to represent less affluent and low-status clients, and they tend to confine their courtroom appearances to courts of original jurisdiction. High-status lawyers tend to practice in large metropolitan areas, they are predominately white, male, and Protestant, and they tend to have attended the more prestigious, private and public colleges and law schools.[2] Although in recent decades the barriers against women and members of ethnic and racial minorities joining the high-status firms have been eroded, as of yet, they are not fully erased. Therefore, finding one's way to a particular lawyer may be a function of social and economic status consistent with the patterns of professional bar stratification in particular communities.

Hiring a Lawyer

Because it is not about a contractual relationship, the initial discussion between a party seeking legal advice and an attorney is usually regarded as *exploratory*. One or more attorneys listen carefully to the potential client's recitation of events surrounding the dispute in question. Depending on what they hear, the attorney(s) may offer a quick judgment on the advisability of proceeding further. On the other hand, they may ask to conduct their own independent investigation, after which all will meet once again to determine a course of action. It is the responsibility of the attorney to explain the available options, including the likelihood of success for each.

Depending upon the nature of the legal dispute, *attorney fees* may take a number of different forms. A *flat fee* is often charged for common and routine matters, such as real estate title searches, wills and trusts, many criminal law defenses, family law disputes involving divorce and child custody, and bankruptcy. The flat rate may be $1,000 for a divorce or, for example, $5,000 for a criminal case. The *hourly fee* arrangement

Table 5.1 Style of Legal Practice (1995)		
Practice	**Numbers Engaged**	**Percentage of All Lawyers**
All Lawyers	N = 860,040	100.0%
Private Practice	N = 636,585	74.0 (N = 636,585)
Sole Practitioner	N = 297,702 (46.8%)	34.6
2 to 10 Lawyer Firms	N = 144,132 (22.6%)	16.8
11 to 50 Lawyer Firms	N = 89,225 (14.0%)	10.4
51 or More Lawyer Firms	N = 105,526 (16.6%)	12.3
Legal Aid/Public Defender	N = 8,499	1.0
Private Industry and Association	N = 76,842	9.0
Federal/State/Local Government	N = 65,628	7.6
Federal/State/Local Judiciary	N = 21,627	2.5
Education	N = 8,186	1.0
Retired/Inactive	N = 42,673	5.0

Source: Composite of tables found in Report of the New York State Bar Association, Special Committee on the Law Governing Firm Structure and Operation, *Preserving the Core Values of the American Legal Profession: The Place of Multidisciplinary Practice in the Law Governing Lawyers* (Albany, NY: New York Bar Association, 2000), pp. 34, 36.

is a charge for the time expended on a dispute. For example, an attorney may charge $150 an hour for researching a case, preparing petitions, preparing witnesses, discovery procedures, time spent at the actual trial, and possible appeals. Such charges vary from city to city and some law firms, depending upon their reputations, are able to charge more per hour than less highly regarded firms or solo practitioners. The flat fee is the most common form of attorney compensation. It is common in all fields of legal specialization.

Individuals and business entities that regularly need legal services may choose to have an attorney or legal firm on *retainer*. In a retainer relationship, the client pays an annual fee and is entitled to a number of hours of legal work by the retained attorney or firm. For example, a business might retain a local law firm for $10,000 annually. For that fee, the law firm agrees to perform up to 100 hours of legal work, typically involving routine matters such as dealing with late-paying customers, making timely legal filings with regulatory agencies, handling ordinary lawsuits, and drafting contracts.

Conducting research on legal questions can be a time-consuming process.

When plaintiffs agree to a *contingency fee* arrangement, they understand that in the event they win their suit in court or arrive at an out-of-court settlement, their attorneys will share a percentage of the award. Thirty-three to 40 percent is the amount for court victories and 20 to 33 percent is the usual charge for out-of-court settlements, although the actual percentage varies from firm to firm and city to city. The meaning of the word *contingency* is clear when it is understood that if the plaintiff client loses, the attorney receives nothing.[3] Trial lawyers representing plaintiffs in cases where large money awards are anticipated, such as medical malpractice cases, generally prefer contingency arrangements, but they are taking a huge risk if they lose, particularly if the litigation is costly and time-consuming. Costs include the charges courts assess to cover the processing of paperwork, and jury fees on a daily basis. Expert witness fees, costs of medical examinations when needed, costs associated with the discovery of evidence, and payment to private investigators are also examples of litigation costs. Depending upon the lawyer-client contract, clients are technically responsible for costs associated with litigation when the plaintiff loses. Yet, in many instances, attorneys do not ask their clients to pay. When clients win their causes of action, however, costs are typically deducted from the gross award. Whether costs are deducted from the award before or after the computation of the attorney's fee may dramatically affect how much attorneys and their clients actually receive for their trouble. Clients may fire their attorneys at any time, but their lawyers are entitled to recover for the value of the services rendered.[4] At times, as the following California case of *Kroff v. Larson* suggests, the value placed on the services is unclear.

After the plaintiff attorney is retained, potential defendants are informed that, unless an out-of-court settlement can be reached, they will be sued. The potential defendant will usually hire an attorney for a fixed sum or a per hour amount. In the case of a business corporation, litigation may be handled by in-house legal counsel and/or retained law firms specializing in trial work with appropriate substantive legal subject expertise. It is the function of the defense team to minimize costs to the client, both in the present instance and in future cases that may be spawned by the case at hand. After the attorneys for both sides are in place, one or more *settlement conferences* may take place. The goal of these meetings is to negotiate the terms of a settlement short of a trial. In the United States, the number of settlement conferences resulting in agreements is unknown, but this is thought to be very great. At times, however, plaintiffs do not want to enable their opponents to destroy valuable evidence and therefore eschew early settlement conferences in the belief that it is best not to alert them fully to the case that is yet to unfold. In any event, the parties cannot always agree to a reasonable settlement. It is at this point that plaintiff lawyers file a formal complaint with the clerk of the court with jurisdiction in the case.

Kroff v. Larson
Court of Appeal of California, Sixth Appellate District
167 Cal. App.3d 857 (1985)

Opinion by Panelli, P. J., with Agliano and Brauer, J. J., concurring.

This is an appeal from a judgment of dismissal entered on plaintiff's (appellant) first amended complaint following the sustaining of defendants' (respondents) demurrer. On this appeal we are asked to determine whether an attorney hired to prosecute a bodily injury action, pursuant to a contingent fee agreement, may, after being substituted out of the case, recover costs advanced on behalf of the client, while the bodily injury suit is still pending. We determine he may not and affirm the judgment of dismissal.

Facts

Appellant, an attorney, was employed by respondents, pursuant to a "Legal Services Contract—Contingent Fee Case" to represent them in a bodily . . . injury action. The agreement provided for a percentage attorney fee and the reimbursement of costs advanced by the attorney, contingent on recovery by the clients. Appellant proceeded to represent the respondents and filed a lawsuit on their behalf. Before any recovery was obtained, respondents discharged appellant and retained another attorney to represent them. Appellant wrote respondents seeking reimbursement for costs advanced in the amount of $702.48. When respondents failed to pay appellant for the costs advanced, he filed a law suit to collect attorney fees and costs.

Appellant's complaint alleged that he was discharged by respondents without cause. The complaint also sought to recover attorney fees and costs advanced. Respondents filed a general demurrer contending that the action was premature since the contingency (recovery by the client) had not yet occurred. The demurrer was sustained on this ground, without leave to amend. A judgment of dismissal was entered and this appeal follows.

On this appeal, appellant challenges the judgment rendered below only as to the causes of action which sought reimbursement of costs advanced by him on behalf of the respondents.

Discussion

In California it is clear that a client has an absolute right at any time to discharge an attorney, with or without cause. (Fracasse v. Brent

(1972), 100 Cal.Rptr. 385, 494 P.2d 9). An attorney discharged by a client without cause has a *quantum meruit* cause of action for the reasonable value of services rendered to the date of discharge. Such cause of action, however, does not accrue until the occurrence of the stated contingency, i.e., recovery by the client either by settlement or judgment.

In this case it is appellant's contention that *Fracasse* is not controlling since our high court considered the issue of attorneys fees due under a contingent fee contract and did not address the issue of costs. Appellant argues that the reasoning of the court has no applicability to the issue of whether costs advanced by the attorney may be recovered before the contingency occurs. We do not read *Fracasse* so narrowly.

As appellant correctly suggests, in *Fracasse,* one of the concerns of our high court was the impossibility of ascertaining an attorney fee which is dependent on the "result obtained," until the "amount involved" has been determined by a resolution of the client's claim. Accordingly, appellant argues that, where, as here, the amount of costs advanced is known and precise, "Fracasse" is not controlling. We disagree. The speculativeness of the fee was only one factor considered by the court. As it stated, "[second], and perhaps more significantly, we believe it would be improper to burden the client with an absolute obligation to pay his former attorney regardless of the outcome of the litigation." (6 Cal. 3d at p. 792.) The court clearly was concerned that a client not be burdened with any financial obligation to his former attorney before the *occurrence* of the stated contingency. We believe this concern is reasonable

and justifiable. We believe this is especially true here, in view of the express provisions contained in the contingent fee agreement under review.

The agreement signed by the parties to this appeal provided in part, "[costs] advanced will be reimbursed to attorney *out of the gross recovery* on behalf of client." (Italics added.) The agreement also provided for a "lien for reimbursement of costs advanced . . . on *any recovery* made for client. . . ." (Italics added.) It is clear to us that the parties expressly contemplated that costs be paid from a *recovery* by the client, whether it be by settlement or judgment. Recovery was therefore the contingency which had to occur before the client was obligated to reimburse the attorney for costs.

Our conclusion, moreover, is buttressed by two cases decided after *Fracasse.* In Bandy v. Mt. Diablo Unified Sch. Dist. (1976) 56 Cal.App.3d 230, a discharged attorney attempted to file a lien against his client's pending personal injury suit. The contingent fee contract entered into by the attorney and client gave the attorney a lien for attorney fees and costs on any recovery by the client. The trial court granted the attorney's motion for a lien and the client appealed. The appellate court reversed, stating, "[under] the holding and reasoning of *Fracasse* the orders of the court below determining the amount of reasonable attorney fees *and costs* in each action was improper and premature *as the contingency stated in the contract had not occurred.*" (Id., at p. 234; italics added; see also Mason v. Levy & Van Bourg (1978) 77 Cal.App.3d 60, 66 [any action based on a contingent fee contract accrues only when the stated contingency occurs].)

Based on the foregoing authority, the obligation to reimburse the attorney for costs advanced, matures, if at all, only upon the occurrence of the agreed contingency, i.e. recovery by the client. Accordingly, appellant was premature with his lawsuit and the trial court correctly sustained respondents' demurrer. . . .

Case Questions for Discussion

1. Should the original counsel in cases such as this one receive a portion of the damage award in the event of a court victory? Why?

2. Did the author of this opinion take a strict or a loose view of precedent, and what difference might it make in the final outcome of the case?

3. If the respondent should lose the case, is the appellant attorney entitled to recovery for services rendered? Why?

Pleadings, Answers, and Replies[5]

The plaintiff's *complaint* informs the defendant formally why she is being sued, by whom, and in what court she is being sued, and also provides a statement of facts that forms the basis for recovery. A *summons* is issued at the same time and typically accompanies the formal complaint. The complaint is the initial *pleading* containing allegations of fact. No attempt is made at this phase of litigation to prove the facts. The complaint only alleges that because certain facts are true, the plaintiff is entitled to recover damages and/or other relief. Reflecting the historically important jurisdictional question, the plaintiff's complaint also indicates that the court in which the initial pleading is filed may exercise jurisdiction in the particular case.

The law acknowledges the distinct possibility that a potential defendant may attempt to ignore a complaint rather than to face the time, costs, and emotional aggravation of a formal lawsuit. Consequently, depending upon the court in which the complaint is filed, state or federal law dictates the amounts of time defendants have to respond. In the federal courts, it is 20 days and in state jurisdictions, the number may be 10, 15, 30, or perhaps 60 days depending upon the law and local court rules. The law provides, however, that courts may permit *answers* to be filed after the expiration of the statutory period. If defendants fail to answer complaints, they could lose by default.[6]

The defendant's answer contains admissions or *denials of specific facts* as alleged in the plaintiff's complaint. We place the emphasis upon the words *specific facts* because plaintiffs must prove at trial whatever facts defendants deny in their answers. Consequently, if a defendant admits all the facts as alleged in the plaintiff's complaint, there is no need for a trial. Alternatively, the defendant may deny all of the plaintiff's allegations. This is called a *general denial.* The more likely form of answer contains the admission of some facts and the denial of others. For example, "Yes, I was driving the automobile at 2:00 A.M. on November 9, 2000, in Carbondale, Illinois, and yes, the automobile struck the plaintiff's vehicle, but I was not driving at an excessive speed nor was I under the influence of alcohol." This type of answer is called a *denial of specific allegations.* Rules of procedure in both federal and state courts require *good faith* in pleading—meaning honesty of intention.[7] General denials are typically out of order because, in the usual course of events, some facts alleged in complaints are true. For example: "Yes, I was driving the automobile at 2:00 A.M., on November 9, 2000, in Carbondale, Illinois."

The assertion of *new facts* by the defendant is a third form of answer. The defendant admits that certain facts as alleged by the plaintiff are true but that the complaint left out pertinent facts that are exculpatory. Consider, for example, the defendant in our hypothetical negligence automobile accident case. She may first deny her own negligence, claiming not to have been driving at an excessive speed or under the influence of alcohol, but then she adds the new fact that "the plaintiff ran a red light, thereby causing the accident along with the resulting injuries." When the defendant alleges new facts, the plaintiff must then *reply.* She does so by either admitting or denying the defendant's claims; for example, "No, I did not run the red light as alleged by the defendant" or "Yes, I ran the red light." The defendant may also file a *counterclaim,* creating a separate cause of action by seeking relief against the plaintiff. This suit arises out of the same set of facts that the plaintiff raised in the original suit, but in this case the litigant roles are reversed. Finally, besides denials and counterclaims, the defendant's answer should contain defenses to each of the plaintiff's claims in the complaint.[8]

Careful readers already know there are disputes about whether a specific fact pattern falls within a recognized legal concept. In *Lake v. Wal-Mart Stores, Inc.,* found in Chapter 4 of this text, Wal-Mart made a motion to dismiss Elli Lake's complaint because Minnesota had not recognized the invasion of privacy tort upon which the young woman's complaint was founded. A district and appellate court agreed with Wal-Mart, only to be overruled in the final analysis by the Minnesota Supreme Court.

In this case, Wal-Mart did not file an answer to Lake's complaint. Instead, it filed a motion to dismiss the action based on the plaintiff's failure to state a claim upon which relief may be granted. In the past and in some state jurisdictions today, as illustrated by the *Kroff v. Larson* case reproduced earlier in this chapter, this type of motion is called a *demurrer,* but under the contemporary Federal Rules of Civil Procedure and in many state jurisdictions, it is simply called a *motion to dismiss.*[9] When defendants file motions to dismiss, judges ask themselves a *so what* question: So what that Wal-Mart employees responsible for processing film revealed to persons in the community that a photograph was taken of 19-year-old Elli Lake and 20-year-old Melissa Weber naked in the shower together? Will Lake and Weber be able to win their case if these facts are found to be true? Is there a legal rule permitting plaintiffs to recover for damages resulting from the invasion of their privacy? If the court answers affirmatively, then the case can proceed; if not, the case is dismissed.

Besides the instance of no law on the subject of the suit, there is the situation of significant facts that are not in dispute. Parties usually file a *motion for a summary judgment* after investigating facts that were earlier thought to be in dispute; if it turns out that the plaintiff and the defendant are in substantial agreement about the facts in the case, the judge is asked to make a judgment based upon the applicable legal rules. In such cases, the matter need not go to trial because the facts are not in dispute, and the judge appropriately pronounces the legal rule according to the established facts.

In contrast to a *motion to dismiss,* a motion for a summary judgment often involves an assertion by the moving party that the material facts cannot be proved in court. In our hypothetical automobile accident case, for example, the defendant might claim that as a matter of fact she was hospitalized or in jail at the time of the accident and therefore cannot be held responsible for driving the automobile that injured the plaintiff. Motions for summary judgment may also ask the court to ascertain what material facts are without substantial controversy. The moving party asks the judge to direct that all further proceedings in the action be consistent with such findings.[10]

When the pleading phase of litigation is complete, the case is now joined or, as it is sometimes said, the case is *at issue.* Given the complaint, the answer, and the reply, when appropriate, the contentions of each party become known and the boundary lines for the dispute are drawn. The result of the pleading phase is therefore the knowledge of what facts are in dispute. Without the consent of the presiding judge, these pleadings may not be amended. The law insists on boundaries so that conflicts may not be expanded beyond the original disputes, which would frustrate the dispute settlement function of the law, thereby making the legal system itself part of the problem. Though the procedure is intended to provide litigants with a level and unbiased playing field, legal institutions and officials do have a life of their own, as we have seen. Hence, the interests of disputants and of the legal institutions and actors that are designed to serve them are not always the same.

Figure 5.1   Civil Suits for Money Damages

Plaintiff

Phase	Plaintiff
2. Exploratory Discussion	retain counsel
3. Settlement Conference Between Attorneys	retain counsel
4. Pleading Phase	complaint, reply
(motion)	motion for a summary judgment
5. Discovery Phase	depositions, interrogatories, production of documents, physical and mental exams, request for admissions
6. Pretrial Conference	
7. Trial Phase	jury selection, opening statement, presentation of evidence, rebuttal evidence, motion for directed verdict, jury summation, rebuttal, jury instructions, jury verdict, post trial motions
8. Appeal Phase	appellant petition (losing side in court below), file written brief, oral argument, opinion of court

1. Dispute Arises

Defendant

Phase	Defendant
4. Pleading Phase	answer, counterclaim, motion to dismiss
(motion)	motion for a summary judgment
5. Discovery Phase	depositions, interrogatories, production of documents, physical and mental exams, request for admissions
7. Trial Phase	jury selection, opening statement, motion for nonsuit, presentation of evidence, answer to plaintiff's rebuttal evidence, motion for directed verdict, jury summation, jury instructions, jury verdict, post trial motions
8. Appeal Phase	appellee (respondent), file written brief responding to appellate brief, oral argument, opinion of court

Discovery

As a second phase in the legal process, *discovery* is designed as a means of uncovering what evidence is available to test the facts in the case. Discovery is a means to get at the true facts in a case without resorting to surprise or trickery. Hollywood scripts that have Perry Mason-type characters presenting evidence in court at the very last minute to the surprise of everyone, and in the process making the other side look like bungling idiots, are not permitted in modern American jurisprudence. The *Federal Rules of Civil Procedure*, adopted in 1938 and subsequently adopted in most of its parts by most state jurisdictions, requires a full disclosure of facts prior to trial. For the most part, this measure has taken the surprise out of litigation. Moreover, because all the parties are aware of the facts before trials actually commence, modern discovery practices encourage pretrial settlements. Based on the knowledge of what evidence is available to prove the facts, parties may reasonably conclude that they are likely to lose their cases, or at least that there is sufficient doubt about the outcome of the case to use pretrial settlement as a rational strategy.[11]

The tools of discovery used by lawyers to determine what evidence is available to prove the facts are depositions, interrogatories, production of documents, physical and mental examinations, and requests for admissions.

A *deposition* is the out-of-court testimony of a witness or party to a suit taken under oath. Depositions are sometimes called mini-trials because the person deposed is asked to answer questions in the same manner as is the practice in courtrooms. Persons to be deposed appear usually at a law office in the presence of attorneys for the parties to the suit and a court stenographer. They give sworn testimony in response to attorney questions concerning what they know about the facts in the case. Although there are some limitations on the questions that may be asked, including matters of privileged information, the rules of evidence (discussed in this chapter) that apply in the formal courtroom are generally relaxed during the taking of a deposition. This is permissible because lay jurors are not present during depositions. However, attorneys may object to certain "inappropriate" questions and may direct their client not to answer. Such questions are noted and brought before the presiding judge for a later ruling on whether the question is appropriate and therefore must be answered. Because each side to the dispute may cross-examine witnesses, all parties to the case must be notified and given a fair opportunity to be present. If witnesses or parties refuse to appear for a deposition, the court will issue a subpoena to compel the testimony. All of the deposed testimony is transcribed, signed, and sworn to under oath.[12]

In sum, attorneys use depositions to ascertain what facts gave rise to the suit. Depositions serve as a primary guide for assessing the likely outcome of a trial if a prior settlement cannot be reached. Depositions aid attorneys in their effort to become familiar with the quality and credibility of the witnesses and the parties, helping them to assess the likely outcome of their cases. Although the pretrial function of gathering evidence is important, depositions play another role in the next stage of litigation. They may be used during trial to impeach the creditability of witnesses when their in-court testimony differs from their depositions. Also, at trial a deposition may be used in place of an actual appearance when a witness dies or a witness is sick or in prison at the time of trial. Specified before trial, these so-called *paper witnesses* may also be used when witnesses live considerable distances from the courthouse. In federal trials, if witnesses live more than 100 miles from the federal courthouse, they may be deposed. States have similar exceptions based on geographical considerations.[13]

The use of depositions can be costly and include attorneys' fees, witness fees, stenographers' fees, and transcription expenses. However, a little-used variation on the usual deposition is designed to cut costs. Unlike the ordinary deposition, with the *deposition upon written questions,* all the questions in this alternative process are known in advance of the actual testimony. The party requesting this variation communicates a list of questions to opposing counsel, who in turn submits a series of cross-examination questions. In turn, the requesting party may submit re-direct questions, followed if necessary by re-cross examination questions submitted by opposing counsel. The *deponent,* the person being deposed, appears before a court reporter and responds to the set of prepared questions, and all the answers are transcribed, signed, and sworn under oath. In this way, counsel for both sides are not billing clients for appearances at an actual formal deposition. A major disadvantage to this procedure is that it eliminates a certain degree of spontaneity that is ordinarily present in the deposition process.[14] It also makes it impossible to read the body language and other gestures normally associated with live testimony.

Interrogatories are written questions for which written answers are prepared and signed under oath. They differ from depositions upon written questions because they may be directed only to the parties to the suit and not to witnesses. Interrogatories may be used to ferret out basic information about the parties, such as age and job history, as well as more personal matters (e.g., financial well-being and even information about marital infidelity).

Interrogatories are most often used to discover organizational knowledge, such as corporate records, including when a manufacturer first knew that its product was defective by virtue of internal tests or written consumer complaints. Interrogatories permit lawyers to obtain descriptions of evidence in the possession of the other side. They are not normally entered as evidence at trial because the rules of evidence forbid the use of hearsay and require the use of only the best evidence available. Attorneys often conceive of interrogatories as a kind of start-up device whereby the information obtained can then be used to frame depositions.[15]

Production of documents is a third form of discovery. At the request of one of the parties to the suit, the opposing party must provide for inspection and copying of any document, writing, computer file, graph, chart, map, photo, and so on, that may be in his or her possession or control. In most instances, the document exchange process takes place with little difficulty—the lawyers exchange documents, copying such materials as medical records with little conflict or intervention on the part of the court. Lawyers may also request the original copy if they think it is vital. Sometimes, however, requests for documents are drafted carelessly, and as a result the request imposes a huge burden on the responding party to gather the documents. In response, parties have been known to open warehouses where records are kept and invite the requesting party to look for the materials themselves. In the same spirit, they may also dump so much information on requesting parties that the costs of sifting through the records may be prohibitively high. Further, parties have been known to "shuffle" documents before producing them; they do not present the requested materials in neatly organized categories, thereby rendering the discovery task burdensome. In some jurisdictions, such tactics are specifically prohibited.[16]

Physical and mental examinations are a fourth discovery tool. In cases involving physical and mental harm, it may be necessary to compel the complaining party to submit to an examination by a medical doctor hired by the defendant. The chief purpose of this request is to balance the testimony of plaintiff's expert witnesses. In many cases, the defendant attorney will use information obtained in this way to dispute the findings of plaintiff's doctors. The task then falls upon the jury to evaluate the evidence offered by competing expert testimony. Nonetheless, because physical and mental examinations may create uncertainty in the minds of jurors or confirm plaintiff's allegations, information obtained in this way may encourage pretrial settlements.[17]

The last and the most minor of the five discovery tools is a process called *requests for admissions*. At trial, a party wishing to introduce a document or a set of facts into evidence must go through an extensive ritual for establishing the authenticity of each, unless the other side stipulates that they are indeed genuine. Thus, as part of discovery practices, parties ask the other side to admit or deny certain specific facts. If no reply is forthcoming, then, for purposes of the suit, the matter is considered admitted. In our hypothetical automobile accident case, for example, the defendant may be asked to admit she owned and possessed the automobile she was driving at the time of the mishap. Thus, requests for admissions help to facilitate the legal process that otherwise would be even more cumbersome without this tool.[18] Careful attorneys make use of this relatively minor tool if for no other reason than to back their opponents into an evidentiary corner. Strategic use of requests for admissions may require adversaries to admit or deny facts early in the litigation that later during trial they wish they had not.

Pretrial Conference

Following discovery, but before a case goes to trial, attorneys meet with the judge assigned to the case to discuss the outstanding issues that remain for adjudication. Presumably, through the pleading and discovery phases of litigation, some conflicts about facts and legal issues have been resolved to the satisfaction of the parties. Sitting informally with the judge, the parties attempt to narrow the scope of the trial and to reduce remaining obstacles. The function of the judge is to identify areas of agreement between the parties and to suggest ways to facilitate the administration of justice, while at the same time becoming familiar with the facts and issues likely to arise at trial. At the conclusion of the conference, the judge enters a *pretrial order*. This order contains a list of witnesses and evidence that each party agrees upon and all of the parties' stipulations and admissions. The pretrial order supplants the pleadings and represents the new boundary lines for the dispute at trial. Because the parties rely on the pretrial order when preparing their cases for trial, judges are reluctant to allow attorneys to introduce new evidence unless grave injustices would otherwise occur.[19]

There is little doubt that overburdened judges have an institutional interest independent of the parties to the suit; they seek to process efficiently the cases pending before the court as well as reining in those attorneys who are "overzealous" in their representation of their client's cause. But judges are sometimes accused of being overbearing in their zeal to clear their court dockets. Although attorneys must represent the best interests of their clients, at times they may feel coerced by judges into accepting settlements or procedures that are inconsistent with that responsibility. Some critics suggest that a way of getting around this problem is to have different judges sit for pretrial conferences and for actual trials. In this way, attorneys need not fear consequences at trial for their decisions to stand up to disagreeable judges. Consequently, at pretrial conferences, judges could use their good offices only to persuade

The judge is a central player in pretrial conferences.

and not to coerce attorneys. The problem with this suggestion is that the incentive for pretrial judges to become fully familiar with the cases before them would be diminished—rendering pretrial conferences less effective than otherwise might be the case.[20]

Trial Phase of Litigation

Discovery procedures and the pretrial conference reveal which factual and/or legal issues remain in dispute. Understanding the trial phase of a civil action for money damages entails knowledge of how the adversary system works, meaning the proper roles of the attorneys, the judge, and the jury. This also requires knowledge about how a case is presented and conducted, such as the rules of evidence governing what facts are presented to the jury.

In the United States, the parties through their attorneys are responsible for finding and presenting their side of the case. The term *adversary process* is a good description for what goes on. Like a sporting event, one side opposes another, and through the clash of forces what passes for truth and justice, or at least a result, is the final score or outcome in the case. That is, one side wins and the other side loses.

Each side of the contest is responsible for planning and executing its courtroom strategy and tactics, and the conclusion of the struggle is based upon what the parties have presented as evidence in the form of witnesses, documents, and exhibits. Similar to athletic events, when one team evidences a particular weakness in its abilities, and if it does not want to use a particular witness (player), the coach (attorney) may make the choice not to expose that weakness to attack. Further, if it is not advantageous to execute a line of reasoning or questioning (a particular play), the coach may avoid it altogether. The underlying assumption of the adversary system is that each side knows and will pursue its own self-interest, resulting in justice or what passes for it. This system also assumes that each side of the controversy is equally equipped to prepare and execute its case and that the rules are fairly applied to all. Yet, similar to unequally matched athletic teams, not all parties in a legal dispute are equally endowed with competent and talented legal counsel, backed by the financial resources necessary to attain optimal results.

Americans rarely question the assumptions of the adversary system because, to a large extent, they are fundamentally consistent with liberal capitalist democratic ideology. First, Adam Smith, in his oft-quoted eighteenth-century justification for capitalism, *The Wealth of Nations*, argued that if individuals each pursue their own economic self-interest, "as if by an invisible hand the common good will be realized." Americans are taught from their earliest years that through the exercise of their free will, they are responsible for their own lives, and that their own decisions and energy dictate their individual economic standing in the community. Social Darwinism is an extreme variation on that theme. It goes so far as to proclaim that if we fail as economic actors, we have no one else to blame but ourselves. In this dog-eat-dog worldview, government should not interfere with the natural law of survival of the fittest, lest the human species cease to adapt itself to the environment and in the process fail to rid the unfit from the economic marketplace. Further, the ideology of *laissez-faire* economics proposes that government intervention in the economy should be restricted to minimum functions, such as the enforcement of contracts, other fundamental legal obligations, and the bare requirements of law enforcement.

Likewise, the major premise of our political theory is that the state (civil society) exists to protect individual rights (i.e., life, liberty, and property) against the claims of those who may possess the physical power but not the moral or legal right to impose their will on others. Community interests in a well-ordered society are always weighed against the interests of individuals. It is little wonder—given the American preoccupation with individualism, self-reliance, and materialism—that the adversary system is easily accepted as the best way for finding the truth, although competing worldviews provide alternative ways to organize justice systems.

If attorneys are the active players in the litigation process, then judges play the passive referee role. It is not the function of judges to involve themselves in the planning, strategy, or presentation of cases. Rather, judges require the parties to conduct themselves according to the legal rules, but they generally apply the rules only when one or the other party objects to what the other side is doing. Indeed, if one side does not object when a rule violation takes place, in all but the most grievous circumstances, the judge is not obligated to correct the situation. In this sense, the judge is a passive participant, whose intervention in the game is carefully measured. Yet, the judge's role is vital to the outcome of many cases, because rulings from the bench may seriously affect the introduction of evidence and the framing of legal instructions that go to the jury as it deliberates case outcomes. Further, judges are ever mindful that extreme conduct on their part may result in an appeal and the scrutiny of their conduct by a higher authority, possibly resulting in a slap on the proverbial judicial wrist.

Juries in civil actions for money damages, as in other types of cases, are assigned the task of ascertaining facts and rendering verdicts based upon the legal rules as instructed by judges. Ostensibly, jurors are in the courtroom to listen, to observe, and to draw conclusions on what they hear and see. Although there are ongoing experiments to the contrary, jurors are not permitted to direct questions to attorneys, witnesses, or parties. Many courts permit jurors to take notes, however. But they are forbidden to discuss the case among themselves before all the evidence is presented and they retire to the jury room for private deliberations. Some jurists, including the late chief justice of the U.S. Supreme Court Warren Burger, argue that certain cases, such as protracted antitrust cases, are too complicated for lay jurors and that, instead, panels of judges with particular expertise in the substantive subject area of the suit should perform the fact-finding function. Most judges, however, do not seem to share this viewpoint; rather, they prefer to stick with the centuries-long commitment to the common sense verdicts of lay jurors.[21] Further, though more evident in criminal than in civil proceedings, political wisdom places a group of lay citizens between officials of the government, in the form of judicial officials, and disputing parties. It serves as a break on the influence of dominant elites in society and the tendency of the powerful to gang up on the weak and dispossessed.

Today, the role of juries in civil suits for money damages is controversial because juries have a reputation for awarding excessive damages. Plaintiff trial lawyers generally defend the use of juries, but defendant lawyers representing large corporations and insurance companies deride their use, calling for limitations on the amount of awards juries may render. Republicans in Congress have introduced legislation and have campaigned for damage caps. Some states have enacted limits, particularly on punitive awards, although the Alabama Supreme Court in Moore v. Mobile Infirmary Association, 592 So. 2d 156 (Ala. 1991) declared a cap on noneconomic losses a violation of that state's constitution. It is little wonder why Democratic Party candidates for various offices have received financial campaign support from trial lawyers and Republicans have received considerably less support from this segment of the bar. Moreover, those interest groups that benefit from the posture of the defendant bar (e.g., insurance companies, large corporations, and medical lobbies) have lobbied and contributed financially to campaigns to limit jury awards, but labor and consumer groups have been supportive of jury discretion in awarding damages.

Jury Selection

Although parties may waive their right, the Seventh Amendment of the U.S. Constitution guarantees the right to a jury trial in civil suits in federal courts. State constitutions generally provide for jury trials in state cases. The Sixth Amendment guarantees jury trials in federal criminal cases, and the U.S. Supreme Court has interpreted the Fourteenth Amendment as obliging state governments to do the same in state criminal trials.

For reasons not clearly understood, the traditional trial (*petit*) jury is composed of 12 persons. The number 12 is a prominent one in Western history; the Twelve Tribes of Israel, the Twelve Tablets of Rome, the Twelve Apostles, and a dozen eggs come immediately to mind. In the

1970s, nevertheless, state courts began the movement to reduce the size of juries from 12 to some lesser number. The U.S. Supreme Court ruled that although 12 is the traditional number in criminal trials, there is no logical reason why due process of law requires a dozen jurors. Federal district courts have converted to juries of fewer than 12, but not fewer than six, in civil cases. A majority of states now authorize such smaller juries in some or all civil trials. Moreover, it is no longer universally necessary for criminal juries to reach unanimous verdicts, though only a few states permit it. Most states and the federal courts permit simple majority verdicts in civil cases.[22]

Theoretically, every person who is called for jury service has a duty to serve. In the past, certain occupational groups have been exempted from service, including mothers with small children, ministers, teachers, and government officials. But such exemptions sometimes produced jury pools that did not reflect the character of the community. In the 1970s, a movement starting in California swept aside all exemptions and has since spread to virtually every state in the union. In fact, then California Governor Jerry Brown, a chief sponsor of this legislation, was among the very first public officials called to jury service.

Over the centuries, jurors have been selected in a number of ways. Methods range from commandeering them off the street in front of the courthouse, to selecting from lists of property owners, to having key men in the community recommend others to serve on juries. Today, the most common technique is random selection from lists of eligible voters. Whatever the method, it must be random, and potential jurors must be selected from a fair cross-section of the community. Systematic bias resulting from racial discrimination is deemed a violation of the U.S. Constitution.[23]

Although techniques vary, court clerks working from voting lists, for example, first mail questionnaires to potential jurors soliciting information about their backgrounds, including their occupations and whether they have ever been arrested for a crime. Subsequently, those persons meeting the initial eligibility hurdles receive a formal summons notifying them that they should appear at the courthouse on a certain date and time; and if they cannot, they must offer a justifiable reason to the clerk. Such reasons may include plans to be away from the community, hospitalization, care of others, and so on. If the clerk grants an exemption, it is only temporary. Usually, a later time is stipulated when the potential juror may be called for duty. A warning accompanies the clerk's letter to potential jurors saying that if they do not appear, they may be held in contempt of court.

A large panel of potential jurors is always called to the courthouse where roll is taken at a predetermined time. Before the selection for actual trials begins, the clerk or presiding judge will instruct potential jurors on their responsibilities and inform them about compensation that may be due them for travel, time away from work, and other expenses. Many jurisdictions now use videotape messages in addition to live presentations. Commonly, potential jurors are expected to appear at the courthouse for one- or two-week periods when trials are being conducted. If they are not selected during that period, they may be called for possible service at some later date.

When a particular case is assigned to a courtroom for trial, a smaller group of prospective jurors is sent to that room. Their names are selected at random from computer programs or some other random method; for example, their names are written on slips of paper, dropped in a box, and shuffled. The clerk of the court then draws out a sufficient number of names to make up a panel; and, as the names are called, the individuals take their places in the jury box. The potential jury members must next swear under oath to give true answers to all questions asked of them in the qualifying examination. This question and answer session is called the *voir dire* (vwor deer) examination. It is French for "to speak the truth." Questioning of the prospective jurors is primarily the task of the lawyers, but sometimes with some questions supplied by the attorneys, judges alone conduct the examinations. At other times, both the judge and the attorneys examine the potential jurors.

Questions are asked to discover whether the potential jurors can fairly render justice in the case. They are often asked, for example, whether they have prior knowledge of the case before them, do they know the litigants or attorneys, have they had personal experience similar to one or both of the litigants, do they know key witnesses, and do they have an opinion of them. If, after questioning a prospective juror, an attorney feels that the party is not qualified to serve on the jury, she can *challenge* the juror *for cause*. In such instances, the judge either agrees or disagrees with the for cause challenge. Sometimes judges will dismiss a prospective jury without attorneys uttering a single word: for example, when a potential juror is related to one of the litigants or has clearly made up his or her mind on how he or she will vote before the trial commences. The number of for cause challenges is unlimited. There are celebrated cases with a huge number of such challenges.

Because judges are charged with the responsibility for the administration of justice, however, they have an interest in retaining control over the process. Sometimes they are reluctant to grant the challenges when it is less than clear that prospective jurors are not qualified to serve. It is important to note that each side may excuse a certain number of jurors without offering any justification at all. These are called *peremptory challenges*. Statute or court rule limits these challenges to a certain number, ranging from two to six for misdemeanors, or 15 to 20 for capital murder. For civil cases in Illinois, for example, it is set at five and in the federal district courts the number of peremptory challenges in civil cases is three.[24] It is common for attorneys not to use all their peremptory challenges because they fear that once they use their last one, the next person called may be much worse than the previously excused juror. The voir dire examination process continues until the full jury is empanelled.

Because the adversary process assumes that each side is responsible for making its own decisions affecting the outcome of litigation, the conflict between the value of justice and the importance of winning is quite evident in jury selection. Justice demands that a fair, impartial, and objective set of jurors be selected to serve on each and every jury. But given the emphasis on winning implicit in the adversary system, each side tries to select juries that are most likely to be sympathetic with their client. Effective trial attorneys have always had a good idea of the background and attitudes of jurors most likely to decide in their favor. In recent decades, the attorney's subjective talent to select the "best jurors" has been supplemented by modern social science techniques. Since the celebrated 1973 trial of Father Philip Berrigan, who was accused of plotting to raid draft board offices during the Vietnam War and other alleged criminal misdeeds, including a plot to kidnap Dr. Henry A. Kissenger, jury consulting has become a big business. In the Berrigan case, a group of antiwar social scientists came together to advise Berrigan's attorneys that the ideal juror was a "female Democrat with no religious preference and a white collar or skilled blue collar job."[25]

Opening Statements

As we know from our own personal experiences, first impressions—whether they are favorable or unfavorable—are often long lasting, because they may stimulate preexisting attitudes that could have a significant impact on how we regard the future representations of others. With jury selection complete, the attorneys prepare jurors for the task of considering the evidence about to be presented to them. Attorneys for each side make their *opening statements*, giving the jury an overall picture of the case from their respective viewpoints. They sketch in outline form what they expect to prove and how they will go about that task. Because opening statements are not properly regarded as evidence, these utterances may sound to the untutored ear as mere formality. Yet, opening statements are vitally important because they create first impressions in the minds of jurors. Opening statements allow attorneys to present their theory of the case and to establish a degree of credibility with jurors. When the facts are later related to the jury in the course of the trial, and those facts comport with the attorney's opening statement, jury confidence in that attorney is confirmed and enhanced. Conversely, if the facts presented at trial are different than the attorney's opening statement, jury confidence in the attorney is diminished or even destroyed.

The plaintiff attorney makes her opening statement first. Defense attorneys may opt to make their statements immediately after the plaintiff attorney finishes her opening statement, or they may choose to wait until the plaintiff finishes the presentation of her entire case with accompanying evidence, witnesses, exhibits, and so on. If defense attorneys elect to wait, they make their opening statements prior to presenting their entire case to the jury.[26]

Parties and the Burden of Proof

Burden of proof refers to the concept that one of the parties in a lawsuit must demonstrate that the weight of the evidence is on its side. The general rule is that the burden of proof is on the moving side. Because in a civil suit for money damages, the plaintiff brings the suit against the defendant for recovery of damages, the plaintiff must shoulder the burden. As such, the plaintiff in most instances has the right both to open and to close the case. This means that the plaintiff speaks first to the jury in presenting and attempting to prove the case against the defendant. Sometimes, however, this pattern does not take place. When defendants admit every allegation in their answers but go on to allege "new facts" that are subsequently denied in the plaintiff's reply, the burden of proof is shifted to the defendant to prove the new facts.[27] In the usual course of proceedings, however, if the plaintiff is to win the case, then he or she must carry the burden—a tie goes to the defendant.

Attorneys present evidence by direct examination of their witnesses, who are placed under oath, and by producing documents or other exhibits. This process is governed by the rules of evidence. Facts must be tested for their truthfulness and reliability. Consequently, the legal process provides opportunity for the other side to *cross-examine* witnesses about matters for which they have offered testimony. It is commonly said that good attorneys ask questions only for which they already know the answer. Otherwise, counsel may inadvertently help the other side make its case by soliciting unexpected answers that support the opponent's case.

After cross-examination, the party calling the witness has an additional opportunity to ask more questions. This practice is termed *re-direct examination*. But this is not the end. The attorney for the opposing party may *re-cross examine* the witness, and the other party may then *re-re-direct*, and this can go on until they run out of ques-

Examination of a witness.

tions to ask. They eventually run out of questions, because the examination in each instance is limited to what the witnesses testified in the previous sequence of questions and answers. Consequently, cross-examination is limited to those matters raised in the direct examination. The re-direct is limited to answers given in cross-examination. The re-cross examination is limited to answers that result from matters or issues raised during the re-direct, and so on. In brief, as the question-and-answer sequence continues, the testimony of witnesses becomes narrower until ultimately there is no question left to ask. If it were otherwise, trials might last indefinitely.[28]

Rules of Evidence

The rules of evidence have evolved over centuries by trial and error. Because evidentiary rules are designed to keep juries from hearing evidence that might result in unfair verdicts, the attorneys are required by law to stay within them. Appeals to irrational prejudices within the community, and subjective judgments that do not reflect the truth or falsity of what really happened, are patently unfair. However, it must be remembered that in the adversary system, each side is responsible for objecting to the introduction of incompetent or prejudicial evidence. Consider a few of the most basic limitations on the conduct of trials.

Ordinary witnesses cannot usually give their opinion in court. They may testify only about matters for which they have direct knowledge. On the other hand, *expert opinion* is permitted because experts possess special knowledge about a pertinent matter in the trial. For example, a physician specializing in certain types of injuries, such as spinal injuries, may well be regarded as an expert in a case involving damages in which the defendant is complaining of back pain resulting from an automobile accident. A chemist in an environmental pollution case may be used as an *expert witness* to describe the relationship between certain toxic substances and incidents of cancer in the population. Sometimes, rather exotic and unexpected expert witnesses might be called to testify, such as ex-prostitutes in *White-Slave Traffic Act* cases, or reformed moonshiners in prohibition cases. It is common for each party to present competing expert opinion. During cross-examination, each side attempts either to discredit or discount the expert opinion offered by opposing counsel. Often, however, in the last analysis, jurors are left to their own wits about which, if any, expert witness to believe.[29]

Attorneys may not ask their witnesses *leading questions*, which put in the mouth of the witness the answer the attorney wants to hear. The question solicits, in other words, an echo and not the spontaneous answer that best serves the truth. We hasten to add, however, that because discovery procedures have taken place well in advance of trial, the attorneys know how most witnesses will probably respond to given sets of questions. A question that can be answered yes or no may also be a leading question, as is a question asking if a statement just made by the attorney is true or false. And while leading questions posed to one's own witness are impermissible, such queries are allowed in cross-examination. This seemingly double standard is justified because cross-examination is conceived as the great "truth-finder." Leading questions can trip up a witness, exposing inaccurate or untruthful statements.[30]

Hearsay evidence is inadmissible because such information is not based upon the witness's personal knowledge of the events in question. The law treats such information as rumor—grapevine information about which the witness does not have direct knowledge but rather is information provided by another. The hearsay evidence rule is founded on a principle that is lodged in the American Constitution; namely, defendants have a right to confront witnesses brought against them. If a witness testifies about an understanding of events told by some other person, it is not possible to cross-examine that individual unless that person is in court and is the source of the information in the first place. With most rumors, it is difficult and often impossible to track down the source of the information because the story often changes when retold by successive individuals. Finally, because the third party that allegedly gave the witness the information is not under oath, the law views such testimony as highly suspect. Yet, because such dubious information may be the best available, there are a good number of exceptions to the hearsay evidence rule. These include family histories, pedigree of animals where there are no records, local customs or land boundaries where there are no recorded deeds and recorded surveys, reputation as to character, and notations made by unknown persons on business records.[31]

Attorneys are required under the *best evidence rule* to produce written documents or exhibits when they claim such physical evidence exists. It is improper to claim that such documents or writings exist without providing them to the judge and jury for firsthand inspection. For example, a so-called contract may not be a contract at all, but only a vaguely worded letter expressing preferences without promises and offers of legal consideration. Also, reporting to the jury the substance of a medical report orally is not the same as the jury actually reading and studying the report for the purpose of ascertaining the full extent of physical harm caused in an automobile accident.[32]

In our popular culture, we often hear actor-attorneys objecting to evidence that is "irrelevant and immaterial!" When evidence is submitted that has nothing to do with the matters in contention, the law treats it as *irrelevant*. For example, a relevancy objection is in order if a party is suing a defendant for negligently driving her automobile into his, and he introduces evidence that the defendant driver is known to be a child molester. The aberrant conduct has nothing to do with driving an automobile in a negligent fashion. Obviously, if the plaintiff is permitted to introduce the irrelevant matter of child molestation, the jury may decide against the defendant based upon the widespread disgust for such conduct, and not on whether the defendant is culpable for driving negligently.

It is difficult to disconnect the matter of immaterial evidence from irrelevant evidence. Nevertheless, there is a significant difference. *Immaterial* evidence is information not essential to the legal cause of action being litigated; at the same time, however, it may be information relevant to discovering what happened in the case. For example, in our hypothetical automobile accident case, the defendant driver of the automobile may claim that her children, located in the back seat of the vehicle, distracted her by fighting with one another. This misbehavior motivated her to turn her head to speak to the children in the back seat, and in the process she took her eyes off the road, resulting in injury to the plaintiff. The fact that the children were misbehaving is relevant to knowing what happened, but it is an immaterial fact because drivers have a legal duty to drive with care, regardless of any distractions caused by unruly children riding in the back seat of the car.[33]

The *privileged communication rule* reflects a basic imperative in our culture. It postulates that certain relationships among persons in society must be protected from the glare of public disclosure. The value to society of confidential communications between physicians and their patients, attorneys and clients, clergy and penitents, and husbands and wives is superior to the value of finding the truth in legal suits. Our culture is willing to make this trade-off despite the obvious downside. Consequently, those persons whom the law recognizes to be in confidential relationships may not be compelled or allowed to testify concerning their private communications.[34] Some journalists have argued unsuccessfully that the First Amendment protection of freedom of the press affords them an absolute right not to reveal confidential sources for their information published in news stories. Some journalists have also been held in contempt of court and sent to jail for what they believe should be a constitutionally protected form of privileged or confidential information. Nevertheless, some jurisdictions have held that the First Amendment provides a degree of privilege to newspapers and reporters, requiring a balancing of interests approach on a case-by-case basis.

It is beyond the scope of this book to discuss all the rules of evidence. Indeed, there are many more, such as the prohibition against providing information about whether defendants are covered by insurance policies. Permitting into evidence this information may cause members of the jury to base their verdict upon the fact that the defendant indeed has "deep pockets" (i.e., in many cases, an insurance company can afford to pay and the defendant will not have to personally pay for damages done to the plaintiff).[35]

It is important to remember that the adversary system presupposes that each side through proper objection will ask the judge to enforce the rules of evidence when it is in its interest to do so. Legal norms require that each side make its objections known at the time when the evidence is thought to be improperly introduced. This establishes the record and constitutes the basis for appeals to higher courts if the losing side decides that an appeal is warranted after the conclusion of the trial. Successful attorneys know the rules of evidence and are aggressive in entering motions based on the rules. Inexperienced attorneys may lose otherwise good cases when they are unable to get their evidence into the record pursuant to the rules of evidence. Regardless of their experience, however, attorneys battle over the admissibility of evidence because the rules are not always clear, requiring interpretation by judges, as the following opinion in *Daubert* illustrates.

Daubert v. Merrell Dow Pharmaceuticals, Inc.
Supreme Court of the United States
509 U.S. 579, 113 S. Ct. 2786, 125 L. Ed. 2d 469 (1993)

OPINION: JUSTICE BLACKMUN:
In this case we are called upon to determine the standard for admitting expert scientific testimony in a federal trial.

I.

Petitioners Jason Daubert and Eric Schuller are minor children born with serious birth defects. They and their parents sued respondent in California state court, alleging that the birth defects had been caused by the mothers' ingestion of Bendectin, a prescription anti-nausea drug marketed by respondent. Respondent removed the suits to federal court on diversity grounds.

After extensive discovery, respondent moved for summary judgment, contending that Bendectin does not cause birth defects in humans and that petitioners would be unable to come forward with any admissible evidence that it does. In support of its motion, respondent submitted an affidavit of Steven H. Lamm, physician and epidemiologist, who is a well-credentialed expert on the risks from exposure to various chemical substances. Doctor Lamm stated that he had reviewed all the literature on Bendectin and human birth defects—more than 30 published studies involving over 130,000 patients. No study had found Bendectin to be a human teratogen (i.e., a substance capable of causing malformations in fetuses). On the basis of this review, Doctor Lamm concluded that maternal use of Bendectin during the first trimester of pregnancy has not been shown to be a risk factor for human birth defects.

Petitioners did not (and do not) contest this characterization of the published record regarding Bendectin. Instead, they responded to respondent's motion with the testimony of eight experts of their own, each of whom also possessed impressive credentials. These experts had concluded that Bendectin can cause birth defects. Their conclusions were based upon "in vitro" (test tube) and "in vivo" (live) animal studies that found a link between Bendectin and malformations; pharmacological studies of the chemical structure of Bendectin that purported to show similarities between the structure of the drug and that of other substances known to cause birth defects; and the "reanalysis" of previously published epidemiological (human statistical) studies.

The District Court granted respondent's motion for summary judgment. The court stated that scientific evidence is admissible only if the principle upon which it is based is " 'sufficiently established to have general acceptance in the field to which it belongs.' " 727 F. Supp. 570, 572 (SD Cal. 1989), quoting United States v. Kilgus, 571 F.2d 508, 510 (9th Cir. 1978). The court concluded that petitioners' evidence did not meet this standard. Given the vast body of epidemiological data concerning Bendectin, the court held, expert opinion which is not based on epidemiological evidence is not admissible to establish causation. 727 F. Supp. at 575. Thus, the animal-cell studies, live-animal studies, and chemical-structure analyses on which petitioners had relied could not raise by themselves a reasonably disputable jury issue regarding causation. Ibid. Petitioners' epidemiological analyses, based as they were on recalculations of data in previously published studies that had found no causal link between the drug and birth defects, were ruled to be inadmissible because they had not been published or subjected to peer review.

The United States Court of Appeals for the Ninth Circuit affirmed.

951 F.2d 1128 (1991). Citing Frye v. United States, 54 App. D.C. 46, 47, 293 F. 1013, 1014 (1923), the court stated that expert opinion based on a scientific technique is inadmissible unless the technique is "generally accepted" as reliable in the relevant scientific community. 951 F.2d at 1129-1130. The court declared that expert opinion based on a methodology that diverges "significantly from the procedures accepted by recognized authorities in the field . . . cannot be shown to be 'generally accepted as a reliable technique.' " Id., at 1130, quoting United States v. Solomon, 753 F.2d 1522, 1526 (9th Cir. 1985).

The court emphasized that other Courts of Appeals considering the risks of Bendectin had refused to admit reanalyses of epidemiological studies that had been neither published nor subjected to peer review. 951 F.2d at 1130-1131. Those courts had found unpublished reanalyses "particularly problematic in light of the massive weight of the original published studies supporting [respondent's] position, all of which had undergone full scrutiny from the scientific community." Id., at 1130. Contending that reanalysis is generally accepted by the scientific community only when it is subjected to verification and scrutiny by others in the field, the Court of Appeals rejected petitioners' reanalyses as "unpublished, not subjected to the normal peer review process and generated solely for use in litigation." Id., at 1131. The court concluded that petitioners' evidence provided an insufficient foundation to allow admission of expert testimony that Bendectin caused their injuries and, accordingly, that petitioners could not satisfy their burden of proving causation at trial.

We granted certiorari, . . . in light of sharp divisions among the courts regarding the proper standard for the admission of expert testimony. . . .

II.

In the 70 years since its formulation in the *Frye* case, the "general acceptance" test has been the dominant standard for determining the admissibility of novel scientific evidence at trial. . . . Although under increasing attack of late, the rule continues to be followed by a majority of courts, including the Ninth Circuit.

The *Frye* test has its origin in a short and citation-free 1923 decision concerning the admissibility of evidence derived from a systolic blood pressure deception test, a crude precursor to the polygraph machine. In what has become a famous (perhaps infamous) passage, the then Court of Appeals for the District of Columbia described the device and its operation and declared:

Just when a scientific principle or discovery crosses the line between the experimental and demonstrable stages is difficult to define. Somewhere in this twilight zone the evidential force of the principle must be recognized, and while courts will go a long way in admitting expert testimony deduced from a well-recognized scientific principle or discovery, "the thing from which the deduction is made must be sufficiently established to have gained general acceptance in the particular field in which it belongs." 54 App. D.C. at 47, 293 F. at 1014 (emphasis added).

Because the deception test had "not yet gained such standing and scientific recognition among physiological and psychological authorities as would justify the courts in admitting expert testimony deduced from the discovery, development, and experi-

ments thus far made," evidence of its results was ruled inadmissible. Ibid.

The merits of the *Frye* test have been much debated, and scholarship on its proper scope and application is legion. Petitioners' primary attack, however, is not on the content but on the continuing authority of the rule. They contend that the *Frye* test was superseded by the adoption of the Federal Rules of Evidence. We agree.

We interpret the legislatively enacted Federal Rules of Evidence as we would any statute (1988). . . . Rule 402 provides the baseline: "All relevant evidence is admissible, except as otherwise provided by the Constitution of the United States, by Act of Congress, by these rules, or by other rules prescribed by the Supreme Court pursuant to statutory authority. Evidence which is not relevant is not admissible."

"Relevant evidence" is defined as that which has "any tendency to make the existence of any fact that is of consequence to the determination of the action more probable or less probable than it would be without the evidence." Rule 401. The Rules' basic standard of relevance thus is a liberal one.

Frye, of course, predated the Rules by half a century. In United States v. Abel, 469 U.S. 45, 83 L. Ed. 2d 450, 105 S. Ct. 465 (1984), we considered the pertinence of background common law in interpreting the Rules of Evidence. We noted that the Rules occupy the field, id., at 49, but, quoting Professor Cleary, the Reporter explained that the common law nevertheless could serve as an aid to their application:

"In principle, under the Federal Rules no common law of evidence remains." All relevant evidence is admissible, except as otherwise provided. . . . . "In reality, of course, the body of common law knowledge continues to exist, though in the somewhat altered form of a source of guidance in the exercise of delegated powers." Id., at 51–52.

We found the common law precept at issue in the *Abel* case entirely consistent with Rule 402's general requirement of admissibility, and considered it unlikely that the drafters had intended to change the rule. Id., at 50–51. In Bourjaily v. United States, 483 U.S. 171, 97 L. Ed. 2d 144, 107 S. Ct. 2775 (1987), on the other hand, the Court was unable to find a particular common law doctrine in the Rules, and so held it superseded.

Here there is a specific Rule that speaks to the contested issue. Rule 702, governing expert testimony, provides:

If scientific, technical, or other specialized knowledge will assist the trier of fact to understand the evidence or to determine a fact in issue, a witness qualified as an expert by knowledge, skill, experience, training, or education, may testify thereto in the form of an opinion or otherwise.

Nothing in the text of this Rule establishes "general acceptance" as an absolute prerequisite to admissibility. Nor does respondent present any clear indication that Rule 702 or the Rules as a whole were intended to incorporate a "general acceptance" standard. The drafting history makes no mention of *Frye,* and a rigid "general acceptance" requirement would be at odds with the "liberal thrust" of the Federal Rules and their "general approach of relaxing the traditional barriers to 'opinion' testimony." Beech Aircraft Corp. v. Rainey, 488 U.S. at 169 (citing Rules 701 to 705). . . . Given the Rules' permissive backdrop and their inclusion of a spe-

cific rule on expert testimony that does not mention "general acceptance," the assertion that the Rules somehow assimilated *Frye* is unconvincing. *Frye* made "general acceptance" the exclusive test for admitting expert scientific testimony. That austere standard, absent from, and incompatible with, the Federal Rules of Evidence, should not be applied in federal trials.

That the *Frye* test was displaced by the Rules of Evidence does not mean, however, that the Rules themselves place no limits on the admissibility of purportedly scientific evidence. Nor is the trial judge disabled from screening such evidence. To the contrary, under the Rules the trial judge must ensure that any and all scientific testimony or evidence admitted is not only relevant, but reliable.

The primary locus of this obligation is Rule 702, which clearly contemplates some degree of regulation of the subjects and theories about which an expert may testify. "If scientific, *technical, or other specialized* knowledge will assist the *trier of fact* to understand the evidence or to determine a fact in issue" an expert "may testify *thereto*." (Emphasis added.) The subject of an expert's testimony must be "scientific . . . knowledge." The adjective "scientific" implies a grounding in the methods and procedures of science. Similarly, the word "knowledge" connotes more than subjective belief or unsupported speculation. The term "applies to any body of known facts or to any body of ideas inferred from such facts or accepted as truths on good grounds" (*Webster's Third New International Dictionary* 1986: 1252). Of course, it would be unreasonable to conclude that the subject of scientific testimony must be "known" to a certainty; arguably, there are no certainties in science.... But, in order to qualify as "scientific knowledge," an inference or assertion must be derived by the scientific method. Proposed testimony must be supported by appropriate validation—i.e., "good grounds," based on what is known. In short, the requirement that an expert's testimony pertain to "scientific knowledge" establishes a standard of evidentiary reliability.

Rule 702 further requires that the evidence or testimony "assist the trier of fact to understand the evidence or to determine a fact in issue." This condition goes primarily to relevance. "Expert testimony which does not relate to any issue in the case is not relevant and, ergo, non-helpful." 3 Weinstein & Berger p. 702[02], pp. 702–18. See also United States v. Downing, 753 F.2d 1224, 1242 (3rd Cir.1985) ("An additional consideration under Rule 702—and another aspect of relevancy—is whether expert testimony proffered in the case is sufficiently tied to the facts of the case that it will aid the jury in resolving a factual dispute"). . . . The study of the phases of the moon, for example, may provide valid scientific "knowledge" about whether a certain night was dark, and if darkness is a fact in issue, the knowledge will assist the trier of fact. However (absent creditable grounds supporting such a link), evidence that the moon was full on a certain night will not assist the trier of fact in determining whether an individual was unusually likely to have behaved irrationally on that night. Rule 702's "helpfulness" standard requires a valid scientific connection to the pertinent inquiry as a precondition to admissibility.

That these requirements are embodied in Rule 702 is not surprising. Unlike an ordinary witness, see Rule 701, an expert is permitted wide latitude to offer opinions, including those that are not based on firsthand knowledge or observation. . . .

Faced with a proffer of expert scientific testimony, then, the trial judge must determine at the outset, pursuant to Rule 104(a), whether the expert is proposing to testify to (1) scientific knowledge that (2) will assist the trier of fact to understand or determine a fact in issue. This entails a preliminary assessment of whether the reasoning or methodology underlying the testimony is scientifically valid and of whether that reasoning or methodology properly can be applied to the facts in issue. We are confident that federal judges possess the capacity to undertake this review. Many factors will bear on the inquiry, and we do not presume to set out a definitive checklist or test. But some general observations are appropriate.

Ordinarily, a key question to be answered in determining whether a theory or technique is scientific knowledge that will assist the trier of fact will be whether it can be (and has been) tested. . . .

Another pertinent consideration is whether the theory or technique has been subjected to peer review and publication. Publication (which is but one element of peer review) is not a *sine qua non* of admissibility; it does not necessarily correlate with reliability. . . . Some propositions, moreover, are too particular, too new, or of too limited interest to be published. But submission to the scrutiny of the scientific community is a component of "good science," in part because it increases the likelihood that substantive flaws in methodology will be detected. . . . The fact of publication (or lack thereof) in a peer reviewed journal thus will be a relevant, though not dispositive, consideration in assessing the scientific validity of a particular technique or methodology on which an opinion is premised.

Additionally, in the case of a particular scientific technique, the court ordinarily should consider the known or potential rate of error. . . .

Finally, "general acceptance" can yet have a bearing on the inquiry. A "reliability assessment does not require, although it does permit, explicit identification of a relevant scientific community and an express determination of a particular degree of acceptance within that community." United States v. Downing, 753 F.2d at 1238. . . . Widespread acceptance can be an important factor in ruling particular evidence admissible, and "a known technique which has been able to attract only minimal support within the community," Downing, 753 F.2d at 1238, may properly be viewed with skepticism.

The inquiry envisioned by Rule 702 is, we emphasize, a flexible one. Its overarching subject is the scientific validity—and thus the evidentiary relevance and reliability—of the principles that underlie a proposed submission. The focus, of course, must be solely on principles and methodology, not on the conclusions that they generate.

Throughout, a judge assessing a proffer of expert scientific testimony under Rule 702 should also be mindful of other applicable rules. Rule 703 provides that expert opinions based on otherwise inadmissible hearsay are to be admitted only if the facts or data are "of a type reasonably relied upon by experts in the particular field

in forming opinions or inferences upon the subject." Rule 706 allows the court at its discretion to procure the assistance of an expert of its own choosing. Finally, Rule 403 permits the exclusion of relevant evidence "if its probative value is substantially outweighed by the danger of unfair prejudice, confusion of the issues, or misleading the jury. . . ." Judge Weinstein has explained: "Expert evidence can be both powerful and quite misleading because of the difficulty in evaluating it. Because of this risk, the judge in weighing possible prejudice against probative force under Rule 403 of the present rules exercises more control over experts than over lay witnesses." Weinstein, 138 F.R.D. at 632.

We conclude by briefly addressing what appear to be two underlying concerns of the parties and *amici* in this case. Respondent expresses apprehension that abandonment of "general acceptance" as the exclusive requirement for admission will result in a "free-for-all" in which befuddled juries are confounded by absurd and irrational pseudoscientific assertions. In this regard respondent seems to us to be overly pessimistic about the capabilities of the jury and of the adversary system generally. Vigorous cross-examination, presentation of contrary evidence, and careful instruction on the burden of proof are the traditional and appropriate means of attacking shaky but admissible evidence. . . . Additionally, in the event the trial court concludes that the scintilla of evidence presented supporting a position is insufficient to allow a reasonable juror to conclude that the position more likely than not is true, the court remains free to direct a judgment, Fed. Rule Civ. Proc. 50(a), and likewise to grant summary judgment, Fed. Rule Civ. Proc. 56. . . . These conventional devices, rather than wholesale exclusion under an uncompromising "general acceptance" test, are the appropriate safeguards where the basis of scientific testimony meets the standards of Rule 702.

Petitioners and, to a greater extent, their *amici* exhibit a different concern. They suggest that recognition of a screening role for the judge that allows for the exclusion of "invalid" evidence will sanction a stifling and repressive scientific orthodoxy and will be inimical to the search for truth. . . . It is true that open debate is an essential part of both legal and scientific analyses. Yet there are important differences between the quest for truth in the courtroom and the quest for truth in the laboratory. Scientific conclusions are subject to perpetual revision. Law, on the other hand, must resolve disputes finally and quickly. The scientific project is advanced by broad and wide-ranging consideration of a multitude of hypotheses, for those that are incorrect will eventually be shown to be so, and that in itself is an advance. Conjectures that are probably wrong are of little use, however, in the project of reaching a quick, final, and binding legal judgment—often of great consequence—about a particular set of events in the past. We recognize that, in practice, a gatekeeping role for the judge, no matter how flexible, inevitably on occasion will prevent the jury from learning of authentic insights and innovations. That, nevertheless, is the balance that is struck by Rules of Evidence designed not for the exhaustive search for cosmic understanding but for the particularized resolution of legal disputes.

To summarize: "General acceptance" is not a necessary precondition to the admissibility of scientific evidence under the Federal Rules of Evidence, but the Rules of Evidence—especially Rule 702—do assign to the trial judge the task of ensuring that an expert's testimony both rests on a reliable foundation and is relevant to the task at hand. Pertinent evidence based on scientifically valid principles will satisfy those demands.

The inquiries of the District Court and the Court of Appeals focused almost exclusively on "general acceptance," as gauged by publication and the decisions of other courts. Accordingly, the judgment of the Court of Appeals is vacated, and the case is remanded for further proceedings consistent with this opinion.

It is so ordered.

Chief Justice Rehnquist and Justice Stevens filed an opinion concurring in part and dissenting in part.

Case Questions for Discussion

1. Why should statutory law trump case law?

2. How is scientific knowledge different from knowledge gained in the courtroom? Why is the distinction worth noting?

3. How might the vigorous cross-examination of the petitioners' expert witnesses in this case serve to guard against the introduction of unreliable knowledge?

Motion for a Nonsuit

After plaintiff attorneys finish presenting evidence in support of their client's claims for damages, they typically utter the words "I rest my case." This means they have presented what evidence they wish to be included in their case, and now it is time for defense attorneys to cast doubt on those claims by the presentation of their own version of the facts. Sometimes, however, defense attorneys do not proceed directly to their case. Rather, they file what is often referred to as a *motion for a nonsuit* or alternatively, depending upon the jurisdiction, it is simply called a *motion for directed verdict.* This motion asks the judge to dismiss the suit at this point in the trial proceedings because the plaintiff was unable to prove adequately the essential allegations necessary for prevailing in the suit. As a matter of law, the judge will grant such a motion only if a reasonable person could not find in favor of the plaintiff after viewing the evidence in the light most favorable to the plaintiff. In other words, without listening to the defendant's case at all, the plaintiff's presentation of evidence fails to prove the essential elements in the case so that a reasonable person could not decide in the plaintiff's favor. For instance, let us say that as the plaintiff you are suing a defendant for driving his or her automobile into yours in a negligent manner. But when you finish the presentation of your case, you fail to prove that the defendant was driving the car at the time of the accident. Consequently, you have no chance of winning the case and the judge would be justified in granting the defendant's motion for a nonsuit. In essence, a motion for a nonsuit resembles the demurrer (motion to dismiss) in the pleading stage of litigation. In each instance, the defendant says "so what is the fuss all about?" The demurrer says "so what?" to the plaintiff's *complaint,* claiming that the facts alleged, even if true, will not allow that side to win. The defendant's motion for a nonsuit says "so what?" to the *evidence* presented in court, asserting that the plaintiff's evidence is insufficient to win the case. If the judge grants the motion, the lawsuit is over.[36]

Defendant's Presentation

In most cases, judges deny defense motions for a nonsuit. Though not impossible, it is improbable that a case might proceed to trial if the plaintiff's evidence is so insufficient that such a motion will be granted. In most cases, motions for directed verdicts are the result of the inability of attorneys to offer their evidence under the rules of evidence. Therefore, counsel must be prepared to present and to rebut evidence in support of the plaintiff's claim. Defense attorneys may choose not to place any evidence before the jury, relying entirely upon their ability to discredit the plaintiff's witnesses and other evidence during cross-examination. Assuming, however, they lack complete confidence in the case outcome premised on such a strategy, defense attorneys proceed in the same way as plaintiff attorneys—with evidence introduced through witnesses and the presentation of documents and other exhibits. Logically, the plaintiff has the right to cross-examine, and the defense to redirect, and so on in the same question and answer pattern as exists for the plaintiff's presentation.[37]

Plaintiff's Rebuttal and Defendant's Answer

The plaintiff may seek to rebut unfavorable evidence presented by the defense by calling additional witnesses or presenting documents or exhibits that may cast doubt on the defendant's claims. After the defense has presented all her evidence, counsel for the plaintiff may bring in *rebuttal evidence*, which is limited in scope to issues raised by the defense. The defendant, however, has a right to counter the rebuttal evidence by answering such claims. Indeed, each side may present additional evidence to counter the rebuttal evidence of the other. The law permits each side to contribute more evidence in this rebuttal-answer pattern, until finally one or the other side exhausts the available evidence. Then both parties *rest their cases.*[38]

Request for a Directed Verdict

At this point in the trial, the case is almost ready for closing arguments and for the jury to render a verdict. However, the presiding judge may prevent the case from going further by deciding to grant a motion by either side for a *directed verdict*. The judge takes the extraordinary step of taking the matter out of the hands of the jury by concluding that a reasonable person could not differ that the moving party should win. If the judge grants the motion for a directed verdict, the trial is over. If, however, the motion for a directed verdict is denied, then the trial continues. Parties routinely make such motions, but judges rarely honor them.[39] As is true for *motions to dismiss* that are entered earlier in the legal process, motions for a directed verdict are not irrational acts of desperate attorneys. They serve to create a record for appellate review and as one additional tactic to achieve eventual victory.

Jury Summations

When all the evidence has been presented, and after the directed verdict motions are concluded, counsels make their closing arguments, otherwise called *jury summations*. Counsel for the plain-

Attorney summing up his case before jury.

tiff makes the first summation, which is then followed by the defense's closing argument. Attorneys for the plaintiff may set aside part of the time reserved to them for the purpose of rebutting, if need be, the defense's closing arguments. During the course of the trial, by virtue of the introduction of evidence, the attorneys create a formal record. The rules covering summation require that each attorney *stay within that record*. Though the facts may very well be in dispute, the attorneys are obliged to argue that the jury should render a verdict in their favor because the evidence as properly introduced at trial mandates such a result.[40]

Judge's Instructions to the Jury

The judge instructs jurors on matters of law before they retire to a designated jury room to consider their verdict. Because the applicable law is often a subject of dispute between the parties to the suit, counsel for each side may submit to the judge preferred sets of instructions. The judge will often hear arguments, but in the end it is the judge's call. Yet, because of the possibility of reversible error, such decisions are subject to appellate review.

Usually the judge provides jury instructions orally and in writing, making it plain to the jurors that they are required to base their verdict upon the law as she describes and explains it and upon their understanding of the true facts in the case. Juries do not have the authority to create new law or to discard the facts consistent with their own values or views of justice. When juries engage in such behavior, they are said to engage in *jury nullification*.

The judge instructs the jury that if they find certain facts to be true, then as a matter of law they are obliged to bring in a certain verdict. In civil suits for money damages, this can be a rather complicated matter. For instance, in negligence cases the judge will instruct the jury about the standard of care that the plaintiff owes the defendant and then the jury must determine whether the defendant's conduct falls below that standard resulting in a compensatory harm. Jury members must evaluate the evidence to determine if by a *preponderance of the evidence* the defendant is in fact culpable under the law.

The test for culpability is not proof beyond a reasonable doubt as is the case in criminal matters. The sports metaphor may be helpful for clarifying this distinction: A basketball team makes a winning basket at the game-ending buzzer. In the bottom of the ninth inning with the score tied at one run each, the home team scores the winning run. During sudden death overtime, a football team kicks a winning field goal. In each example, no one, with the possible exception of the most devoted fan, will claim that the winning team is the better team *beyond a reasonable doubt*. Rather, because one team out-scored the other, objective observers conclude that by a *preponderance of the evidence* one team is better on that given day. In brief, the *standard of proof* is considerably lower in civil suits for money damages than in criminal prosecutions. Further, because jurors award damages, they must be convinced that a certain dollar amount is fair, given the circumstances of the case.

Jury Deliberation and Verdict

Upon receiving their instructions from the presiding judge, jurors are then escorted by a bailiff to a jury room where they are left to make their collective decision. They are isolated from outside contact and generally eat their meals together. Sometimes they are not allowed to go home to sleep at night, although in civil suits while trials are in progress, judges permit jurors to go home at night but with strict instructions not to discuss the matter with anyone and to avoid contact with media news stories concerning the events surrounding the trial. Typically, as jurors begin their deliberations, a *jury foreman* is elected from among their ranks to lead them in discussion, to conduct votes, and to act as their spokesperson. Discussions are often intense, requiring jurors to draw upon their knowledge of how society works, human psychology, and a lifetime of experiences that permit them to ferret out what might be the true facts in a given case. At times this process requires considerable imagination, wherein jurors put themselves in the proverbial shoes of litigants and witnesses to judge the merits of the evidence and arguments presented to them in court.

The jury system is often criticized today because of what is perceived by some as outrageously large awards for damages. Some states have imposed limitations, particularly on punitive damages, and especially in the 1990s, the Republican Party in Congress sought to impose limitations on damages in the federal courts. If a jury cannot agree upon a verdict after deliberating for a reasonable period of time, the judge will declare a mistrial and a new trial is ordered. But in comparison to criminal cases, mistrials are relatively infrequent in civil suits for money damages where the stakes are thought to be much lower. In civil suits, mere money and property are at stake; but in criminal prosecutions, life itself and one's liberty are in jeopardy. Over three fifths of the states permit less than unanimous decisions, with three-fourths or five-sixth voting margins.[41] If a verdict is reached, the jury is brought back into the courtroom where the verdict is delivered. In many states, the jury foreman reads the verdict. To guard against the possible occurrence of jury members being subjected to coercion by other members of that body, and depending upon local court rules and customs, the judge may poll the jury by asking each member if the verdict is correct.

Remedies in Civil Suits for Money Damages

The assumption underlying recovery for damages is that injured parties should be compensated for the losses inflicted by defendants. In other words, this puts the plaintiff in the position she was in before the harm caused by the defendant. Depending upon the circumstances of each case, jurors may award different types of damages. Damages come in four different forms: nominal damages, compensatory damages, exemplary damages, and liquidated damages. The amount of damages is a matter of fact determination that is within the province of juries to decide. Damage awards vary considerably because each case is different, requiring juries to make unique judgments.

Nominal Damages

Nominal damages are awarded when the jury determines that the plaintiff was wronged by the conduct of the defendant but that the damages inflicted are slight. Juries will sometimes award nominal damages in the amount of $1.00 to make the point about which party to the dispute is right, such as when a defendant defames the plaintiff, but the degree of probable harm is so little that compensatory or exemplary damages are unwarranted. In essence, a small or trivial amount is awarded, signaling the jury's agreement that the defendant committed a technical violation of the plaintiff's legal rights. By the way, plaintiffs in defamation suits are sometimes satisfied with such a result because all they want is the vindication of their good names and reputations.[42] Also, in some instances, a finding of nominal damages supports a much greater financial payoff for the plaintiff in the form of exemplary or punitive damages.

Compensatory Damages

In most civil suits for money damages, plaintiffs seek *compensatory damages,* defined as compensation for losses due to past and future harm created by the conduct of defendants. A monetary figure is placed upon ascertainable losses resulting from temporary and permanent pain and suffering, disabilities, injury to one's good name and reputation, and mental anguish. The theory of compensatory damages holds that those damages that are arguable or speculative, indirect, or remote are not recoverable. Thus, the burden of proof is upon the plaintiff, who must demonstrate that the compensation sought is directly attributable to the conduct of the defendant.

It must be emphasized that the underlying purpose of compensatory damages is not to enable the plaintiff to make a profit or get rich based on her or his injury. The *doctrine of avoidable harm,* for example, requires that a person hurt in an automobile accident seek medical care as soon as practical to avoid having her injuries become further aggravated due to neglect. A person who stands in the street knowing she is likely to be run down is responsible for getting out of the way under this same doctrine.[43] Also, the *benefit rule* dictates that though the defendant's culpable acts may be the basis for compensation, if at the same time the plaintiff benefits in some part from the defendant's conduct, then the plaintiff's claim should be reduced by the amount of the benefit conferred. Assume, for example, that while you are away from campus during spring break your college roommate borrows without your permission your poorly running 1985 automobile. Through reckless conduct, he causes a dent in the front bumper. Before you arrive back on campus, your sorry roommate voluntarily takes the car for a much-needed tune-up, causing a benefit to be conferred upon you. That benefit may be reduced from the damage award to the plaintiff. The benefit rule applies to both tort and contract cases.[44]

There are two types of compensatory damages. The first is *general damages*. These damages are assumed to exist and do not need to be pleaded in the plaintiff's complaint. For example, if one ends up in a hospital due to an automobile accident, pain and suffering are assumed and it is granted that, at least during the convalescence period, the plaintiff missed out on the various enjoyments of life. On the other hand, *special damages* are awarded for the unique circumstances of the case that might include actual medical bills, loss of earnings due to hospitalization, and even the inability to work in the future. As such, *special damages* must be specifically listed in the pleadings and proved at trial.[45]

Exemplary Damages

Exemplary damages, alternately called *punitive damages*, are designed to punish defendants for their conduct and to make them an example to others. Awarded in tort cases, but not contract cases unless tortious conduct is present, exemplary damages are above and beyond compensatory damages. Consequently, a defendant may be awarded both compensatory and punitive damages for the same conduct. Juries are known to grant greater punitive awards than compensatory damages as a way of making a statement about their outrage and indignation over the defendant's conduct. Corporations that knowingly manufacture products that are likely to cause bodily harm and injuries are likely candidates for punitive damages.[46]

Liquidated Damages

In the event of a breach of contract, parties may agree in advance to compensate the other for losses resulting from any such breach. The amount stipulated in the contract is called *liquidated damages*. These damages are only appropriate when the actual damages resulting from the breach of contract are difficult to ascertain or uncertain. Moreover, the sum stipulated in the contract is enforceable at law only when it is reasonably proportionate to the loss actually sustained by the plaintiff.[47]

Comparing Compensatory and Exemplary (Punitive) Damages

Today, the most controversial issue surrounding damages is the matter of punitive damages. There is a general perception that the country is awash with civil suits demanding both compensatory and punitive damages for actions that are often trivial. Yet, courts have imposed standards that plaintiffs must satisfy if they are to prevail in such suits. In the following section, we have excerpted a portion of an April 2001 U.S. Court of Appeals opinion that illustrates the elements necessary for the award of both compensatory and punitive damages.

In this case, two African American women, Ms. Hampton and her niece Demetrai Cooper, were stopped while shopping with children by Tom Wilson, a security officer at a Dillard's department store in Overland Park, Kansas. Wilson stated that one of the women, Ms. Cooper, was observed in a dressing room at a different location in the store, placing an item under her coat. He then requested that the Dillard's bag carried by Ms. Hampton be emptied for inspection. However, the customer receipt matched the bag's contents and therefore there was no evidence of shoplifting. At the time of the incident, the women became emotionally distressed and subsequently suffered emotional harm. They sued Dillard's, claiming that the department store was guilty of a pattern of arresting and detaining African American shoppers at a much greater rate than white shoppers. The case was complicated by § 1981 of the Civil Rights Act that pertains to the interference with contractual rights, because at the time of the incident, the African American women were in the process of redeeming a coupon for perfume at the cosmetic counter of the store. A U.S. district court ruled against Dillard's motion for a summary judgment and awarded compensatory and punitive damages to Ms. Hampton, but dismissed Ms. Cooper's claims.

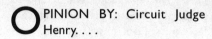

Hampton v. Dillard's Department Stores, Inc.
United States Court of Appeals for the Tenth Circuit
347 F.3d 1091 (2001)

OPINION BY: Circuit Judge Henry. . . .

Damages
a. Compensatory Damages

Dillard's contends that the compensatory damage award of $56,000 is not supported by the evidence and must be set aside. When a party complains there was insufficient evidence to support a damage award, we must determine whether the damage award is supported by substantial evidence. . . . We view the evidence in the light most favorable to the prevailing party. . . .

Dillard's states that any emotional damages Ms. Hampton suffered resulted from Mr. Wilson's belief that her niece was shoplifting and not from any alleged § 1981 interference with her contract. In addition, Dillard's contends that Ms. Hampton's emotional distress, if any, is unsupported by the record.

Ms. Hampton counters that the damages from the accusation and interference with the contract were substantial: She felt humiliated and disgraced by the accusations. Clearly the accusation, though directed at her niece, implicated her as part of the entourage in the dressing room. In addition, Ms. Hampton claims that she, too, was accused of stealing. She contends that her emotional damages were immediately evident, as she was visibly upset after the incident, as well as lasting, as she is now unable to shop with her children for fear of future ridicule and humiliation. Ms. Hampton also claimed her daughter had repeated nightmares regarding the incident.

We note first that any economic damage that resulted from the store's intentional interference with the redemption of the fragrance sample was negligible. Our review of compensatory damages is limited to Ms. Hampton's testimony regarding her emotional suffering. Ms. Hampton testified as to her emotional distress and that of her daughter. See Migis v. Pearle Vision, Inc., 135 F.3d 1041, 1047 (5th Cir. 1998) (noting that, in a § 1981(a) discrimination case, victim's "testimony of anxiety, sleeplessness, stress, marital hardship and loss of self-esteem was sufficiently detailed to preclude us from holding that the district court abused its discretion in its award of compensatory damages"). Ms. Hampton's testimony here was similarly detailed. As the district court noted:

> In this case plaintiff gave eloquent and emotionally moving testimony that Wilson disgraced and humiliated her, in front of her children, that she was too emotionally distraught to drive, and that she had to call her husband for a ride home. Immediately after the incident she was crying and she was so upset that she could not write out a customer comment card, and a Dillard's employee filled it out for her. She testified that "I don't feel that my life will ever be the same." The jury was entitled to credit this testimony and to compensate plaintiff accordingly.

We conclude that the award of compensatory damages was well within the district court's discretion.

b. Punitive Damages

Dillard's also seeks to reduce or eliminate the $1.1 million *punitive damage* award. Dillard's argues that there was insufficient evidence for the jury to conclude that the defendant discriminated against plaintiff willfully or maliciously, which is required for an award of *punitive damages* under § 1981. . . . It also asks us to conclude as a matter of law that the punitive damage award is excessive.

(1) Award of Damages

"In the Tenth Circuit, the standard for punitive damages for discrimination in violation of federal civil rights is that the discrimination must have been 'malicious, willful, and in gross disregard of plaintiff's rights.'" Jackson v. Pool Mortgage Co., 868 F.2d 1178, 1181 (10th Cir. 1989) (quoting Gaddis, 733 F.2d at 1380). " 'The allowance of such damages inherently involves an evaluation of the nature of the conduct in question, the wisdom of some form of pecuniary punishment, and the advisability of a deterrent. Therefore, the infliction of such damages, and the amount thereof when inflicted, are of necessity within the discretion of the trier of fact.'" Gaddis, 733 F.2d at 1390. . . .

Based on the testimony presented, the jury could reasonably find that Dillard's took part in the intentional discriminatory conduct. See id. at 1379 (holding that trial court's finding of intentional discrimination was correct and noting that "where the evidence supports a conclusion either way the choice between two permissible views of the weight of the evidence is not clearly erroneous"). . . . The jury found Ms. Hampton's witnesses credible. The jury also weighed testimony regarding the store's training policies, its incident reports, its close observation of African-American customers who were engaging in objectively innocent behavior, and its arrest reports. The jury's findings as a whole are sufficient to establish that the discrimination by Dillard's, acting through Mr. Wilson, was malicious, willful, and in gross disregard of Ms. Hampton's rights. We will not disturb the decision to award punitives.

(2) Amount of Damages

Dillard's also argues that the severity of the punitive damage award violates its constitutional right to due process. "One must receive fair notice both that certain conduct will subject him to punishment, and the possible severity of the punishment that may be imposed." Deters, 202 F.3d at 1272 (affirming punitive damage award for sexual harassment claims pursued under Title VII). The Supreme Court has outlined three guideposts to determine whether a defendant has received fair notice. See BMW of N. Am. v. Gore, 517 U.S. 559, 574-75, 134 L. Ed. 2d 809, 116 S. Ct. 1589 (1996). "First, and most important, is the reprehensibility of the defendant's conduct." Deters, 202 F.3d at 1272. Next is the ratio of the punitive damage award to the compensatory damage award. See id. at 1272. Third is the measure of the punitive damage award in relation to awards for comparable misconduct. See id. We also must keep in mind the deterrent goal of punitive damages in conjunction with the impact the size of the award will have on a defendant and with the wealth and size of the defendant as relevant factors. See id.

The availability of punitive damages under § 1981 is well established. See Johnson v. Railway Express Agency, Inc., 421 U.S. 454, 459–60, 44 L. Ed. 2d 295, 95 S. Ct. 1716 (1975) ("Section 1981 affords a federal remedy against discrimination in private employment on the basis of race. An individual who establishes a cause of action under § 1981 is entitled to both equitable and legal relief, including compensatory and, under certain circumstances, punitive damages"). Applying the three factors reprehensibility, ratio, and comparability—to this case, we are unpersuaded by the store's arguments. Dillard's had ample notice it was subject to punitive damages for conduct that was malicious, willful, and in gross disregard of plaintiff's rights.

a. Reprehensibility

Dillard's argues that it is authorized to engage in reasonable loss prevention activity and that, during the five-minute episode, Ms. Hampton was "free to leave" at any time. . . . Dillard's suggests that the reprehensibility of its conduct is further minimized because Ms. Hampton "had shopped at Dillard's hundreds of times, but was stopped only this once." Finally, Dillard's purports its surveillance tactics involved no verbal or physical abuse, and thus are inappropriate for punitive damages.

As discussed above, the jury was presented with evidence about the coding and close surveillance of African-American shoppers. The jury must have agreed with Ms. Hampton that the store's surveillance tactics are particularly reprehensible.

b. Ratio

Dillard's next contends that the punitive damages ratio of approximately 20 to 1 is impermissibly excessive and unconstitutionally disproportionate. Dillard's relies primarily on the BMW Court's admonitions regarding economic damage cases, where a ratio of 10:1 was cited with approval. See BMW, 517 U.S. at 581 (citing TXO Prod. Corp. v. Alliance Resources Corp., 509 U.S. 443, 460-462, 125 L. Ed. 2d 366, 113 S. Ct. 2711 (1993)). Ms. Hampton counters that in cases where "the injury is hard to detect and the monetary value of noneconomic harm . . . is difficult to determine," a higher ratio of punitive damages to compensatory damages is justified. Bielicki v. Terminix Int'l Co., 225 F.3d 1159, 1166 (10th Cir. 2000) (quoting BMW, 517 U.S. at 583).

As stated above, the economic injury suffered here was nominal, but the actual injury is more difficult to quantify. "Both the Supreme Court and this court acknowledge that low awards of compensatory damages may support a higher ratio if a particularly egregious act has resulted in a small amount of economic damages.

Additionally, . . . where the injury is primarily personal, a greater ratio than 10:1 may be appropriate." Deters, 202 F.3d at 1273 (citations omitted). Looking at the harm that might result from the store's conduct in relation to the harm that actually occurred, see BMW, 517 U.S. at 581, and eschewing mathematical formulae, see id. at 582, we hold that the punitive damage award in this case is justified. See United States v. Big D Enters., Inc., 184 F.3d 924, 934 (8th Cir. 1999) (upholding maximum punitive damages award in Fair Housing Act case and stating that "the punitive damage award in this case . . . reinforces the nation's commitment to protecting and preserving the civil rights of all"); see also Deters, 202 F.3d at 1273 (stating that "we are not persuaded that the ratio between compensatory damages of $5,000 and punitive damages of $295,000 as adjusted under Title VII . . . is unconstitutionally disproportionate").

c. Sanctions for Comparable Misconduct

The third prong of inquiry further supports our holding. Section 1981 does not have a statutory cap that limits punitive damages as does Title VII. See 42 U.S.C. § 1981a (b) (1). As stated above, few § 1981 claims involve retail transactions, and fewer reach trial. We thus consider whether the award would "shock the judicial conscience, and constitute a denial of justice." Deters, 202 F.3d at 1273. . . . Dillard's does not argue that the award would "result in its financial ruin" or that the award is a disproportionally large percentage of its net worth. Luciano v. Olsten Corp., 110 F.3d 210, 221 (2d Cir. 1997). . . . Because the reprehensibility of the store's conduct as found by the jury was particularly offensive, and the resulting punitive damage award was therefore reasonable, we conclude that the district court did not err in refusing to reduce the punitive damage award. . . .

For the reasons stated above we AFFIRM the district court's denial of Dillard's motion for judgment as a matter of law and motion for a new trial; we AFFIRM the district court's award of compensatory and punitive damages; we AFFIRM the district court's grant of summary judgment dismissing Ms. Cooper's claims; and we AFFIRM the district court's award of attorney's fees to Ms. Hampton.

Dissent by Judge Anderson excluded.

Case Questions for Discussion

1. Do you think jury members can ascertain the extent, if any, of the infliction of emotional harm? Are they qualified to assess a dollar amount to the harm?

2. Should laws be enacted limiting the amounts that may be assessed for punitive damages awards?

3. What are the criteria set out by the U.S. Supreme Court for determining whether defendants have received fair notice that certain conduct will subject them to punishment? How does the appellate court in this case apply the criteria to the actions of the Dillard's department store?

Post-Trial Motions

Because error may occur at any time during trial and juries may err in their judgments, the case is not necessarily over when a jury renders its verdict. One of the parties to the suit may ask the judge that tried the case to grant a new trial or to grant some other reasonable remedy. For instance, losing parties may ask the judge to grant a new trial because *the verdict goes against the weight of the evidence.* In such a case, before granting a new trial, the judge must agree that the evidence simply cannot support the jury's verdict. Perhaps the judge may approve the verdict but grant instead what is known as a *remittitur.* It gives the plaintiff the option of taking less in damages or going through a new trial. At times, when judges view the damage awards as excessive, they order a partial new trial, not to determine culpability but only to ascertain appropriate damages. Moreover, the judge's rulings during the course of the trial may serve as a basis for a new trial or an appeal to a higher court. These rulings made during the trial, and objections timely noted, may serve as the basis for asking the trial judge to reconsider her ruling. But this requires the unlikely agreement of that judge that she made a mistake and that the error in question warrants a new trial. Consequently, such questions involving reversible error are usually left to appellate courts for final determination.[48]

Appeal Phase of Litigation

If a losing party is unable to convince the judge with post-trial motions that a serious error was made during trial, it is then appropriate to seek a reversal by petitioning an appeals court for relief. Although there are some differences between civil and criminal procedures, an appeal to an intermediate court of appeals is usually a matter of right in the state and federal courts. Appeals from intermediate appellate courts to the highest court are almost always by permission, although there are exceptions for a small number of cases that the legislature regards as particularly important—such as administrative law matters involving the government as a party, and capital criminal cases. In the case of the U.S. Supreme Court, where almost all appeals are within its complete discretion through the writ of certiorari, Congress has authorized direct appeal from orders granting or denying interlocutory or permanent injunctions by three-judge courts.[49]

What are the most common grounds for appeal to a higher court? Admitting evidence or refusing to admit evidence that should have been excluded and improper jury instructions top the list. As we have previously indicated, trial court lawyers create the basis for appeals by objecting in trial at the time supposed errors occur. In essence, duly noted objections make the record. Ordinarily, if attorneys fail to object in a timely fashion, then appellate courts will not treat issues raised later as a valid basis for appeal.

For the purpose of review, appellate courts treat failure to object as a waiver to a later claim of judicial error. The philosophy behind this general rule is motivated by organizational and bureaucratic concerns. First, there is a desire to give trial courts opportunities to correct their own errors and therefore to make appeals to higher courts unnecessary. In well-operated hierarchical organizations, superiors wisely encourage their inferiors to correct their own mistakes. This makes for a less divisive bureaucratic organization and demonstrates respect for the difficult tasks of those conducting the daily business of the complex organization—in our case, the trial court judges. Second, there is a recognition that some crafty attorneys might deliberately fail to object to judicial errors at the time they are committed. Instead, some attorneys may bring up the occurrence of possible errors at a later time if they should lose at trial. That is, lawyers may hold back from making timely objections as a litigation tactic. In the process, they unnecessarily use the resources of the judicial system. Third, because possible judicial errors are duly noted in the record at the time they are made, this requirement helps appellate courts develop and clarify the record. In other words, the appellate court need not carefully search the record to locate possible errors. Each is clearly noted so that appellate judges may quickly and efficiently focus on the issues before them.[50]

Appellants are typically required to file notice of appeal, not with the appellate court but with the trial court that rendered the judgment. The appeal must indicate which party is making the appeal and what parts of the judgment are to be appealed. Appellants are required in most instances to pay a fee along with the formal appeal. In many instances, they must also post a bond for costs associated with the appeal, often guaranteeing payment of the respondent's costs on appeal in case the judgment of the trial court is upheld. Appeals must be filed within prescribed time limits. In the case of the federal courts, notice of appeal must be filed within 30 days of the entry of judgment by the trial court or follow other prescribed circumstances in civil actions between private parties.[51]

The entire record of the trial court is then usually reduced to writing. This can be a very expensive process because the court reporter, who it is hoped took down every word faithfully during the trial, must then transcribe his notes. Besides the written record of the trial, all pleadings, the court verdict, and its judgment must be delivered to the appellate court for its study. However, some courts permit appellants to prepare a narrative summary of the record, subject to objections by appellees and certification by the trial court.[52]

Written arguments in the form of *legal briefs* are prepared by both sides. Not to be confused with writing a brief of a court opinion, legal briefs provided by counsel are typically elaborate arguments why the appellate court should find that the lower court did or did not make one or more reversible errors. Briefs contain references to appropriate case precedents and to statutory and constitutional law when appropriate. They also can appeal to good public policy, which may or may not be anchored in law. Consistent with the principle of the adversary system, each side is responsible for his or her own case. Although brief writers often try to create the impression that their arguments are objective scholarly commentaries on the law, there is no mistake that briefs are exercises in legal rhetoric. The goal of brief writing is to convince appellate court judges that they should decide in favor of the brief writer's client. The presumption is that opposing brief writers will present good arguments to the contrary and that appellate judges will base their final decisions on the merits of each argument. Usually, the appellant files the first brief, and the appellee (respondent) then answers. The appellant then may file a reply. Some jurisdictions permit the parties to support their briefs with joint appendixes containing pertinent excerpts from the lower court record.[53]

Oral arguments characteristically follow the filing and reading of the briefs before the appellate court judges. Today, only a few jurisdictions permit oral arguments as a matter of right. Before the mid-nineteenth century, oral argument was the principal form of advocacy before the U.S. Supreme Court. In 1849, the Court mandated that attorneys could not be heard before it unless they first filed a formal written brief.[54] In recent years, appellate courts in both federal and state court systems have sought to reduce their workloads by limiting oral argument in favor of a summary disposition based on the written briefs and records alone.[55]

Appellate courts grant counsels a limited amount of time to make their oral arguments. The time may be as little as fifteen minutes, but usually no more than one-half hour and in some cases one hour for each side. Attorneys are expected to present their cases in an extemporaneous manner, meaning spoken with some preparation but not written out or memorized. Appellate judges or justices often interrupt the attorneys, asking them to elaborate upon or justify their arguments. Characteristically, judges use the occasion to educate themselves and to alert fellow judges about the strengths or weaknesses of the arguments as they are presented. At times, judges behave in ways supportive of particular arguments; they seek to reveal strengths in arguments with which they may fully agree. Occasionally, members of appellate courts disagree from the bench during oral arguments, thereby alerting an attentive public to potential divisions within the appeals court itself. Though chief judges attempt to carefully keep the attorneys within prescribed time limits for their arguments, from time to time advocates are granted additional minutes to make their case. The appellant makes the first oral argument, followed by the appellee, and then the appellant may be allowed to rebut the appellee. Rebuttal time is permitted if the appellant counsel has asked at the beginning of the oral argument to reserve part of her total time for that possibility.

Sometime after oral arguments are completed, the judges or justices of the appellate court retire to their chambers to take a vote of first impression. The rules for speaking and voting in conference vary from one appellate court to another. Usually, the chief judge, or chief justice in the case of the U.S. Supreme Court, speaks first. Then the other justices speak in order of seniority. They discuss the merits of the case and how an opinion might be fashioned. Typically, the presiding judge or justice, if he is in the majority, will assign the opinion-writing task either to himself or some other member of the court likely to write an opinion that other court members can agree upon. If the chief is in the minority, the senior-most member in order of seniority of the court in the majority will make the opinion assignment. Most courts, such as the U.S. Supreme Court, are presumed to share the norm that opinion assignments should be made on a relatively equal basis so that all of the justices will carry their fair share of the opinion-writing burden.[56]

The opinions that are written often reflect those compromises necessary to obtain and keep a majority and, ideally, all the court members united behind a single opinion. As may be surmised from a reading of Chapter 4, this process may involve strategic interactions among court members. The jurist assigned the task of writing the court's opinion then usually circulates a preliminary draft of the opinion to the other court members for their review and comments. Based upon the comments received in reply, the opinion writer may then revise the original draft with the idea of maintaining or expanding a winning coalition in favor of the opinion. Those judges or justices who disagree with the court's judgment may write a dissenting opinion of their own or they may join other justices in a dissenting opinion. If they agree with the result of the decision but disagree with the reasons of the majority or plurality, they may write a concurring opinion.

The opinion is then announced in writing, sometimes first orally from the bench. The losing party may then request a rehearing, if it is believed that the court may be convinced that it erred through some mistaken understanding of the facts in the case, the applicable law, or both. Assuming that such a petition fails, and most do, the appellate court decision is then sent to the trial court for enforcement.[57]

Res Judicata

An important function of the legal system is to put an end to disputes and to allow people to get on with their lives. To allow people to bring up the same matter over again even after they have had a full opportunity to have their case litigated and reviewed by appellate courts is to keep the wounds of social conflict festering with the potential of further infecting and damaging relationships for a long time to come. For this reason, once all appeals to higher courts have been exhausted, the judgment in the case is final. This is the legal principle called *res judicata:* literally, the thing has been decided; the case is closed. The parties may not bring additional suits involving the same questions of law and fact. Note that this does not mean that the same parties may not sue each other once again if the legal issues are different from the original case.[58] To be sure, continuing legal feuds between warring parties are widely known in American folklore, as in the Hatfields and the McCoys. In the U.S. federal system, the Full Faith and Credit Clause (Art. IV, sec. 1) of the Constitution dictates that a judgment that is res judicata in one state is res judicata in every other state.[59] Nonetheless, the courts have held that a res judicata judgment may be attacked, if the court that adjudicated the case did not possess appropriate jurisdiction over the person or subject matter. Exceptions to res judicata are also made for judgments involving collusion of witnesses or jurors and for cases tainted by fraud or perjury. Also, res judicata does not apply if the legal issue in question was not fully litigated in the previous case—meaning the issue was minor in the previous case and the parties did not present evidence concerning the matter.[60]

Enforcing Judgments

Suppose a party wins a judgment involving the payment of money for damages caused by the defendant. What happens if the defendant refuses to honor the judgment? In most instances and accompanied by little fanfare, the parties negotiate payment agreements. But when payments are not forthcoming, the *judgment creditor* needs a legal mechanism for enforcing the judgment against the *judgment debtor*. A *writ of execution* issued by the court with appropriate jurisdiction is the logical first step. It is a routine court order directing an appropriate officer (usually a county sheriff) to seize and to sell as much of the judgment debtor's property as may be necessary to pay the judgment. The sheriff conducts a public sale of the debtor's property and delivers the proceeds to the judgment creditor. In the event that the public sale yields more cash than is necessary to cover the judgment, the debtor is given the remainder. Automobiles or other personal property items are commonly sold and sometimes wages are subject to *garnishment*, whereby employers are ordered to withhold from an employee's paycheck a certain amount over time, and to deliver that amount to the judgment creditor for payment of an outstanding judgment. Consistent with the principle underlying the abolition of debtor prisons, the current legal system avoids rendering defendants destitute. State statutes typically permit judgment debtors to keep their clothes, the tools of their trade or profession, living quarters, and part of their current income from employment.[61]

Judgment debtors sometimes file for bankruptcy. Once completed, this allows them to forever eliminate the judgment against them, although depending upon personal circumstances it may be a heavy price to pay. Many people do not believe that selling off one's property and ruining one's creditworthiness for a substantial period of time is a suitable strategy. Nonetheless, bankruptcy rates have steadily increased over the last several decades, indicating that the financial and social stigma associated with bankruptcy may not be as dire as once thought.

A plaintiff who wins a judgment may not necessarily be left without anything if a defendant files for bankruptcy or otherwise is unable or unwilling to pay. Depending upon personal financial circumstances, it may be sensible for the judgment creditor to wait and collect the judgment later, when the judgment debtor acquires property by work, inheritance, or other means.[62] Meanwhile, judgments continue to grow because interest accrues until the judgment is fully paid. The plaintiff may simply keep the judgment locked in a file cabinet until the right moment arrives. State and federal statutes provide that judgments are collectible for considerable lengths of time, such as ten years, and the law permits renewal for additional periods of time. It may also be a rational act, again, depending upon one's financial situation, to treat the inability to collect a judgment as a bad debt for income tax purposes.[63]

Key Terms, Names, and Concepts

Adversary process
Answer
At issue
Attorney fees
Benefit rule
Best evidence rule
Burden of proof
Compensatory damages
Complaint
Contingency fee
Counterclaim
Cross-examination
Denial of specific allegations
Denial of specific facts
Deponent
Deposition
Depositions upon written
  questions
Direct examination
Directed verdict
Discovery
Doctrine of avoidable harm
Exemplary damages
Expert opinion
Expert witness
Exploratory discussion
Federal rules of civil
  procedure
Flat fee
For cause challenge
Garnishment
General damages
General denial
Good faith pleading
Hearsay evidence rule
Hourly fee
Immaterial evidence

Interrogatories
Irrelevant evidence
Judgment
Judgment creditor
Judgment debtor
Judgment proof
Jury foreman
Jury nullification
Jury summations
Leading questions
Legal briefs
Liquidated damages
Motion for a nonsuit
Motion for a summary
  judgment
Motion for directed verdict
Motion to dismiss
New facts
Nominal damages
Opening statements
Oral arguments
Paper witnesses
Peremptory challenge
Petit jury
Physical and mental
  examinations
Pleadings
Preponderance of
  the evidence
Pretrial conference
Pretrial order
Privileged communication
Production of documents
Punitive damages
Rebuttal evidence
Re-cross examination
Re-direct examination

Re-re-direct
Remittitur
Reply
Res judicata
Rest case
Retainer
Request for admissions
Settlement conference
Special damages

Standard of proof
Stratified bar
Summary judgment
Summons
Verdict against the weight of
    the evidence
Voir dire examination
Writ of execution

Discussion Questions

1. What is the "best" style of legal practice and why? In other words, is it better to be a solo practitioner working for oneself, or is it better to be member of a law firm, a legal aid/public defender, working exclusively for a private sector business firm, employed in government, or something else?

2. Make a list of the pros and cons of contingency fee arrangements for compensating attorneys. Is it good public policy to compensate plaintiff attorneys on a contingency fee basis?

3. After studying the adversary process with respect to civil suits for money damages, do you think that it is the best way of finding the truth? What are the pros and cons of what critics have called the "fight theory of justice"? What might be an alternative way of conceptualizing the process?

4. Notice that civil suits for money damages presume that the payment of money as compensation for injury will make the plaintiff "whole again." Do you think such a system makes the plaintiff whole again? Is there a better way to approach the matter of personal injury?

5. What interest is served with the general rule that attorneys must make timely objections when they believe that judicial errors are made? Does your answer to this question bear on the issue of the legitimacy of courts?

Suggested Additional Reading

Anderson, Michelle, and Robert MacCoun. "Goal Conflict in Juror Assessments of Compensatory and Punitive Damages." *Law and Human Behavior* 23(3) (1999): 313–330.

Easton, Stephen D. " 'Yer Outta Here!' A Framework for Analyzing the Potential Exclusion of Expert Testimony Under the Federal Rules of Evidence." *University of Richmond Law Review* 32 (January 1998): 1–62.

Epstein, Lee, and Jack Knight. *The Choices Justices Make.* Washington, DC: Congressional Quarterly Press, 1998.

Franklin, Marc A. *The Biography of a Legal Dispute: An Introduction to American Civil Procedure.* Mineola, NY: Foundation Press, 1968.

Harr, Jonathan. *A Civil Action.* New York: Vintage Books, 1996.

Hazard, Geoffrey C., and Michele Taruffo. *American Civil Procedure: An Introduction.* New Haven, CT: Yale University Press, 1993.

Jackson, T. Warren. "The Judicial Blame Game; Despite What Critics Say, Judges Have the Right to Undo Verdicts." *Los Angeles Daily Journal* (December 3, 1996): 6.

Kritzer, Herbert M. "Public Perceptions of Civil Jury Verdicts." *Judicature* 85 (September-October 2001): 79–82.

Levine, James P. *Juries and Politics.* Pacific Grove, CA: Brooks/Cole, 1992.

O'Brien, David M. *Storm Center: The Supreme Court in American Politics.* 5th ed. New York: Norton, 1999.

Salman, Robert R. "No Hermits for the Jury." *National Law Journal* 15 (May 1995): A21.

Spence, Gary. "Poverty Not Protected Criterion for Jury Selection." *New York Law Journal* 29 (September 1998): 1.

Sunnstein, Cass R. *Punitive Damages: How Juries Decide.* Chicago: University of Chicago Press, 2002.

Vargas, Jorge A. "Enforcement of Judgments in Mexico: The 1988 Rules of the Federal Code of Civil Procedure." *Northwestern Journal of International Law & Business* 14 (winter 1994): 376–412.

Wasby, Stephen L. *The Supreme Court in the Federal Judicial System,* 4th ed. Chicago: Nelson-Hall, 1993.

Endnotes

1. Bates v. State Bar of Arizona, 433 U.S. 350, 97 S.Ct. 2691, 53 L. Ed.2d 810 (1977).
2. Frances Kahn Zemans, "The Legal Profession and Legal Ethics," in *Encyclopedia of the American Judicial System*, vol. 2, edited by Robert J. Janosik (New York: Scribner, 1987), pp. 627–643.
3. Ibid., pp. 635–636.
4. 7A Corpus Juris Secundum, *Attorney & Client* § 221 (1980); for additional information about the hiring and firing of attorneys, see Donald L. Carper et al., *Understanding the Law*, 2nd ed. (St. Paul, MN: West, 1995), pp. 162–168.
5. This and succeeding sections dealing with the trial phase of litigation is a modified treatment of the model provided by William T. Schantz in his fine text, *The American Legal Environment: Individuals, Their Business, and Their Government* (St. Paul, MN: West, 1976), pp. 166–182. Both federal and state codes of civil procedure are arranged in a similar fashion.
6. 35A Corpus Juris Secundum, *Federal Civil Procedure* § 302 (1960).
7. *Federal Rules of Civil Procedure*, Rule 8(b).
8. Gene R. Shreve and Peter Raven-Hansen, *Understanding Civil Procedure* (Newark, NJ: LexisNexis, 2002), pp. 238–242.

9. Ibid., Rule 41.

10. Ibid., Rule 56(d).

11. 35A Corpus Juris Secundum, *Federal Civil Procedure* § 527 (1960); see also, Lief Carter et al., *New Perspectives on American Law: An Introduction to Law in Politics and Society* (Durham, NC: Carolina Academic Press, 1997), pp. 36–37.

12. 35A Corpus Juris Secundum, *Federal Civil Procedure* §§ 526–542 (1960).

13. *Federal Rules of Civil Procedure*, Rule 32(a); Mary Kay Kane, *Civil Procedure* (St. Paul, MN: West, 1978), p. 116.

14. Ibid., pp. 117–118.

15. Ibid., pp. 118–119.

16. Wayne D. Brazil and Gregory S. Weber, "Discovery," in *Encyclopedia of the American Judicial System*, edited by Robert J. Janosik (New York: Scribner, 1987), vol. 2, pp. 815–816.

17. Mary Kay Kane, *Civil Procedure*, pp. 121–122.

18. Ibid., pp. 122–124.

19. Ibid., pp. 135–136.

20. Ibid., pp. 132–136.

21. Jon Van Dyke, "Trial Juries and Grand Juries," in *Encyclopedia of the American Judicial System*, edited by Robert J. Janosik (New York: Scribner, 1987), vol. 2, p. 748.

22. See Rule 48 of the *Federal Rules of Civil Procedure*.

23. Henry J. Abraham, *The Judicial Process: An Introductory Analysis of the Courts of the United States, England, and France*, 7th ed. (New York: Oxford University Press, 1998), p. 119.

24. 50A Corpus Juris Secundum, "Juries," § 425 (1997); Peremptory Challenges—Alternative Jurors, 735 Smith-Hurd Illinois Compiled Statutes Annotated §§ 5/2-1106 (1992).

25. Henry J. Abraham, *The Judicial Process*, p. 128.

26. William T. Schantz, *The American Legal Environment*, p. 173.

27. Ibid., pp. 173–174.

28. Ibid.

29. 97 Corpus Juris Secundum, *Witnesses* §§ 52, 119, 459, 492 (1957); 31A Corpus Juris Secundum, *Evidence* §§ 509–759 (1996).

30. William T. Schantz, *The American Legal Environment*, p. 178.

31. 31A Corpus Juris Secundum, *Evidence* §§ 259, 261, 263 (1996); see also *Federal Rules of Evidence*, Rule 803.

32. 32A Corpus Juris Secundum, *Evidence* § 1055 (1996).

33. Ibid., §§ 197–208.

34. 97 Corpus Juris Secundum, *Witnesses* §§ 252–264 (1957).

35. *Federal Rules of Evidence*, Rule 411.

36. William T. Schantz, *The American Legal Environment*, p. 175.

37. Ibid., p. 176.

38. Ibid.

39. Mary Kay Kane, *Civil Procedure*, pp. 169–170.

40. William T. Schantz, *The American Legal Environment*, p. 176.

41. Jon Van Dyke, "Trial Juries and Grand Juries," p. 747.

42. 25 Corpus Juris Secundum, *Damages* § 2 (1966).

43. Ibid., *Damages*, § 32.

44. 22 American Jurisprudence, 2d *Damages* § 32 (1988).

45. Ibid., *Damages* §§ 36–39.

46. 25 Corpus Juris Secundum, *Damages* § 117 (1966).
47. Ibid., *Damages* § 101.
48. Mary Kay Kane, *Civil Procedure*, pp. 181–184.
49. Gene R. Shreve and Peter Raven-Hansen, *Understanding Civil Procedure*, 3rd ed., pp. 460–461.
50. Ibid., p. 465.
51. Ibid., p. 462.
52. Ibid.
53. Ibid.
54. Albert P. Melone, *Researching Constitutional Law*, 2nd ed. (Prospect Heights, IL: Waveland, 2000), p. 6.
55. Gene R. Shreve and Peter Raven-Hansen, *Understanding Civil Procedure*, 3rd ed., p. 462.
56. See, for example, Harold Spaeth, "Distributive Justice: Majority Opinion Assignments in the Burger Court," *Judicature* 67 (1984): 301–302.
57. For a good summary of the U.S. Supreme Court at work, see Henry J. Abraham, *The Judicial Process*, 7th ed., pp. 206–254.
58. Mary Kay Kane, *Civil Procedure*, pp. 189–195.
59. J. W. Peltason, *Understanding the Constitution*, 14th ed. (Fort Worth, TX: Harcourt Brace, 1997), pp. 175–176.
60. 50 Corpus Juris Secundum, *Judgment* §§ 719-721 (1997).
61. Mary Kay Kane, *Civil Procedure*, pp. 184–189.
62. William T. Schantz, *The American Legal Environment*, p. 182.
63. Iowa Southern Utilities Co. v. United States, 348 F.2d 492 (1965). ✦

Chapter 6

Equity Processes

Chapter Objectives

Readers should focus attention on how equity processes differ from the paradigmatic example of civil suits for money damages discussed in Chapter 5. Beginning with noting equitable remedies and then by comparing and contrasting the pleading, discovery, and trial phases of litigation, students should consider not only the similarities and differences between the two legal processes but also why those differences exist at all. They should focus on the exercise of equitable jurisdiction, when legal remedies are inadequate but remedies are available in equity. Note the differences between the roles of judges and juries in civil suits for money damages and in equity, the differences between judgments and equitable decrees, and the application of *res judicata*.

In the previous chapter, we outlined civil processes associated with the recovery of money damages. Yet, monetary relief is not always sufficient. Many disputes are not amenable to resolution by virtue of the payment of money damages because plaintiffs will sometimes seek remedies that require something other than money to make them "whole again." These solutions are beyond the jurisdiction of courts possessing only remedies at law.

Readers will recall that in Chapter 2 we outlined the development of equity courts in English history, pointing to the fact that the Chancery Court became a competitor to the traditional law courts of Common Pleas, King's Bench, and Exchequer of Pleas. Chancery was the institutional vehicle for filling in the gaps left by the lack of jurisdiction of the common law courts because the latter were captives of their own rules; they did not always provide justice in particular disputes consistent with natural law principles. The Chancery Court had to proceed carefully because every new equity ruling that interfered with the jurisdiction of the law courts was a source of either potential or real conflict. Consequently, the processes and procedures used when courts employ their equity jurisdiction are considerably different from those utilized in civil suits for money damages. It is important that students compare the equity remedies, procedures, phases, and rules in this chapter with their counterparts from the previous chapter. Once the differences between civil suits for money damages and equity suits are firmly understood, we then recommend that students move on to the following chapter concerning criminal processes. By comparing and contrasting the differences among the three processes, students will gain a solid grasp of legal processes.

Equitable Remedies

Figure 6.1 diagrams the types of remedies available in the exercise of a court's equity jurisdiction. *Injunctive relief* is the appropriate remedy if one wishes to stop another party from engaging in annoying or otherwise harmful conduct. A *prohibitory injunction* is the appropriate equitable remedy when, for example, a plaintiff home dweller asks a court to enjoin a neighbor from dumping garbage upon his property or from emitting loud sounds from the dwelling at all hours of the night and day. A *mandatory injunction* directs a person to perform a specific activity, such as ordering the offensive neighbor to haul his noxious refuse to a landfill for appropriate disposal or lowering the volume on his boom box. Although in our two hypothetical examples suing the neighbor for money damages is actionable in the law of torts as legal nuisances, such suits may not necessarily achieve the objective of compelling neighbors to cease and desist in their wrongful conduct. Requesting and receiving injunctive relief from a court is an appropriate remedy for each example.

Time is also a factor in the type of injunctions that courts issue. First, there are *preliminary*, sometimes called *interlocutory* or *temporary* injunctions. A court grants this type of injunction before a full hearing on the merits of the case is adjudicated. It is designed to preserve the existing rights of the parties upon a showing that irreparable harm will or is likely to occur if the order is not issued. Preliminary injunctions last only until the court has an opportunity to consider the merits of the issue at trial. The court order in *Doe v. Anderson*, reproduced

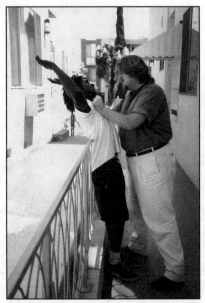

Troublesome neighbors fall within the court's equity jurisdiction.

Figure 6.1   Equitable Remedies

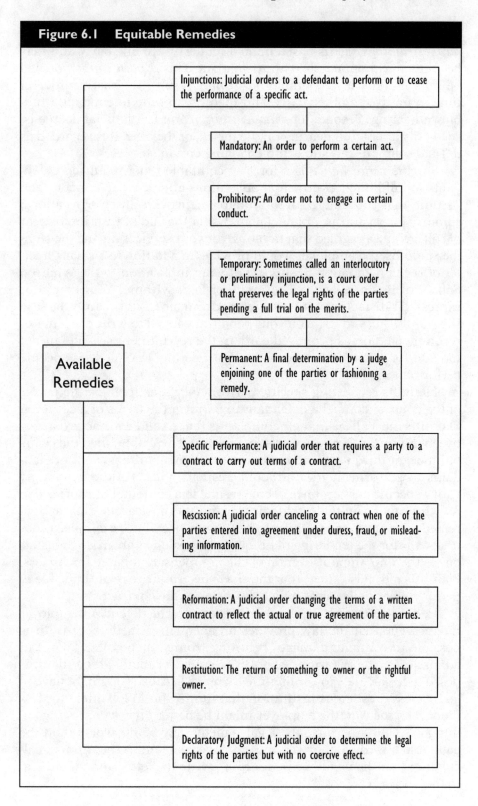

Injunctions: Judicial orders to a defendant to perform or to cease the performance of a specific act.

Mandatory: An order to perform a certain act.

Prohibitory: An order not to engage in certain conduct.

Temporary: Sometimes called an interlocutory or preliminary injunction, is a court order that preserves the legal rights of the parties pending a full trial on the merits.

Permanent: A final determination by a judge enjoining one of the parties or fashioning a remedy.

Available Remedies

Specific Performance: A judicial order that requires a party to a contract to carry out terms of a contract.

Rescission: A judicial order canceling a contract when one of the parties entered into agreement under duress, fraud, or misleading information.

Reformation: A judicial order changing the terms of a written contract to reflect the actual or true agreement of the parties.

Restitution: The return of something to owner or the rightful owner.

Declaratory Judgment: A judicial order to determine the legal rights of the parties but with no coercive effect.

at the end of this chapter, illustrates this form of injunction. A *temporary restraining order* is based upon a request from one party and may be granted without notice to the defendant. This *ex parte injunction* will be granted only if irreparable harm may result, there is insufficient time to notify the other party, and there is no time to conduct a full-blown hearing. Second, a *permanent injunction* is a judicial decree issued only after a full hearing on the merits of the case; it is regarded as a "final solution" but subject to changing circumstances.[1]

Specific performance is a form of equitable relief requiring defendants to fulfill their contractual obligations after a breach of contract. Assume that you entered into an agreement with an employer for a summer internship as a financial analyst at the end of your junior year of college. It was agreed that in return for your services during the summer months, the employer would provide, in addition to a salary, a letter of recommendation in support of your application to the Wharton School of Business at the University of Pennsylvania. Your employer expressed satisfaction with your job performance, but because she says she was too busy to write on your behalf, she failed to write the letter of recommendation as promised early in the recruitment season but not too late for you to gain admission. Your equitable remedy is specific performance.

Plaintiffs requesting specific performance seek to enlist the power of the court to compel a defendant to perform the terms of a contract. Plaintiffs must allege in their complaints that a valid contract exists between the parties. Specific performance is not available when the rights of innocent third parties intervene or it is beyond the power of defendants to perform their contractual responsibility. Failure to comply with a specific performance decree results in a contempt of court order. As with other equitable remedies, plaintiffs must argue that a legal remedy is inappropriate under the circumstance. If, for example, a contract calls for the tendering of unique goods, such as an artistic masterpiece, then no amount of money can compensate a party for its loss. Plaintiffs must also allege that they have been and are ready and able to perform their obligations under the terms of the contract.

In our letter of recommendation example, the defendant employer might argue that the law provides an adequate remedy because it is possible to compute damages resulting from your possible failure of admission to the Wharton School. The employer might argue that it is possible to calculate lower lifetime earnings because you might have to go to a less prestigious institution that may result in job offers for less money. By the way, the employer might be better off not contesting equity jurisdiction because the legal remedy may be far worse than the equitable remedy. Better yet, the employer may make the rational calculation that she would be better off to write the letter and put an end to the matter.

Defenses to a claim for specific performance include inability to perform, laches, unclean hands, fraud, mistake, undue influence, or duress (see Equitable Maxims in this chapter). The Statute of Frauds and the Uniform Commercial Code discussed in Chapter 14 of this text provide additional defenses mitigating specific performance.[2]

When seeking specific performance, plaintiffs must show more than a mere preponderance of evidence, as is often the case in both equity matters and civil suits for money damages. This is especially true when there is a controversy over the existence of an oral contract. In some cases, judges use the words *clear and convincing evidence,* or evidence that is *strong and conclusive.* This degree of proof does not mean proof that is undisputed or an absolute certainty. Reasonable certainty is a sufficient degree of proof, and there is no question that it is less than that required in criminal processes—proof beyond a reasonable doubt.[3]

Reformation and *rescission* are available remedies in equity when a written expression in a contract or other agreement does not truly express the original intent of the parties; in some instances, the court cancels the agreement altogether. For example, you thought you had entered into a written agreement with a friend to sell your automobile to him for $4,000 at $400 per month for the next 10 months. In committing the agreement to writing, however, you mistakenly wrote the selling price as $40 a month for the next 10 months and your now ex-friend refuses to recognize the writing error. He insists upon paying you only $400 for a car that is obviously worth much more. A court exercising its equity jurisdiction will most likely *reform* the agreement to reflect the true intent of the parties.

Rescission is available for more dramatic and less innocent incidents of unfairness when, for example, a party to a contract consents to an agreement under various forms of duress, fraud, undue influence, or otherwise innocent misrepresentation. It is conceivable, for example, that your friend "makes you an offer you cannot refuse." He pledges to protect you from a gang of which he is a member if you sell him the vehicle for $400. Upon your petition, a court in exercising its equity jurisdiction should rescind the agreement because you made it under duress.

Reformation is applicable to a narrower range of circumstances than rescission. In reformation, it must be demonstrated that both parties actually agreed to the terms of a contract that is different from its written expression. They made a mistake in writing the agreement that failed to capture their true thinking. In business, this might be the actual quantity of goods to be produced or the price to be paid for the product in question. An equity court may not create a new agreement by virtue of adding provisions that were never agreed to in the first place. Moreover, the standard of proof required for reformation is not preponderance of the evidence. Instead, it requires that the proof must be clear and convincing.[4] Again, in the equity context, the clear and convincing evidence rule means more than a preponderance of the evidence, as in civil suits for money damages, but less than proof beyond a reasonable doubt required in criminal cases.

Restitution is the appropriate equitable remedy when a person is unjustly enriched at the expense of another. For example, without your permission, a college roommate takes possession of your laptop computer to use at the library and refuses to give it back to you until her term paper project is complete. You want the return of your specific computer because you have created files located in the memory containing important course materials that are not easily replaceable and that are needed in the near future to fulfill course requirements. Restoration *in specie* may be achieved by asking the court for restitution, in this case through returning your computer. Let us say that your roommate no longer has your laptop that was worth $1,000 when you allowed her to borrow it. But subsequently she sold it to a foolish classmate for $1,500. You would be entitled to sue your roommate for $1,500 because in equity she is not entitled to "unjust enrichment"; this equitable remedy is called *restitution by substitution*. Incidentally, in this hypothetical fact situation you would have a cause of action in the law of torts and you may sue your roommate for her conversion of your property as her own. But the damages in tort would be limited to compensation of your loss (which may include the computer and the value of the files located on it), and therefore the more rational approach may be to seek the equitable remedy instead.

Sometimes a party seeks a declaration of the legal rights of the parties to a dispute without seeking an enforcement order. This is called a *declaratory judgment* and is distinguished from a hypothetical case because an actual case or controversy with real parties is in dispute. In this respect, declaratory judgments are different from advisory opinions. Further, unlike an injunction, a declaratory judgment does not coerce any party to do or not to do something. Rather, it defines the respective rights

During a strike, workers often look to the court to protect their rights.

of the parties under a contract, will, statute, or some other document. It declares whether further relief is possible that the present or other courts are authorized to render if properly requested by the parties.

Today, the federal government and about three-quarters of the states permit such actions.[5]

Pleadings, Answers, and Replies

For the most part, in equity, the pleading phase is identical to the practices for civil suits for money damages. The *complaint*, the *answer*, and, where appropriate, the *reply*, are the same with one very important exception. The complaint must state the facts upon which the plaintiff seeks equitable relief as well as the names of the parties to the suit. In their complaint, plaintiffs must allege the insufficiency of law, arguing that equity provides the most suitable remedy. In turn, the defendant may answer the complaint by alleging the sufficiency of law and consequently that the extraordinary measures sought (equity) are unnecessary. Rather than filing a formal answer, the defendant may alternatively file a motion to dismiss (a demurrer) on the same ground, alleging the sufficiency of law to provide a remedy.[6] Although modern American courts possess both law and equity jurisdiction, an important distinction lies between the two. If a court tries a case in its equity jurisdiction, many of the rules and procedures that apply in civil suits for money damages do not apply or are applied in different ways. It is also possible for a court to try part of a case in its equity jurisdiction and other parts of the case in its legal jurisdiction. Typically, when plaintiffs seek to try legal and equitable actions separately, they must plead them in separate counts and specifically make a notation in the pleadings to that effect. The case of *Johnson v. North American Life & Casualty Company* which follows illustrates the importance of the pleadings when asking courts for equitable relief.[7] It shows how a cause of action might be dismissed when equitable relief is not clearly expressed in the complaint.

Johnson v. North American Life & Casualty Co.
Appellate Court of Illinois, Fifth District, Second Division
100 Ill. App. 2d 212, 241 N.E.2d 332 (1968)

OPINION BY: JUDGE MORAN
Plaintiff and her decedent husband, Richard Johnson were married and plaintiff was named the beneficiary of a life insurance policy issued by defendant. Plaintiff deposited significant sums of money into a joint account, both adopted each other's children, and plaintiff cared for decedent when he became seriously ill. Decedent changed the beneficiary under his life insurance policy to his natural children. Plaintiff sought a determination that she was equitably entitled to the insurance proceeds, because decedent was obligated to her. The complaint concludes with a prayer that the court decree that

plaintiff is equitably entitled to the proceeds of the insurance policy. The policy in question, attached to the complaint by amendment contains a provision giving the insured the right to change beneficiaries successively. Plaintiff appeals from an order of the Circuit Court of Franklin County dismissing her complaint for failure to state a cause of action in a cause initiated in chancery against the beneficiaries named in a life insurance policy by plaintiff's deceased husband and against the insurer, to establish the equitable interest of the plaintiff in the proceeds of the policy.

Plaintiff-Appellant contends that the complaint shows the existence of a contract, express or implied, which obligated the insured to leave plaintiff as beneficiary and she thereby became vested with an equitable interest in the policy.

There is little doubt that equities may arise in favor of the beneficiary named in a life insurance policy which will deny the insured the right to change the beneficiary even though such right is reserved to the insured, as, for example, where the insured, for a valuable consideration, estops himself from changing his designation of the beneficiary. "The rule in this state is, that while the assured may, in the absence of intervening equities, change at will the beneficiary named in his insurance policy, equitable rights may be acquired in a beneficiary certificate of insurance which a court of equity will recognize and enforce." Columbian Circle v. Mudra, 132 N.E. 213. In the *Mudra* case, supra, the Supreme Court affirmed the chancellor's determination that the insured was estopped from removing the plaintiff as beneficiary under a life insurance policy without

plaintiff's consent where the evidence disclosed that the insured delivered the insurance policy to the plaintiff and, at his request, plaintiff paid the premiums thereafter.

Numerous other cases have recognized equitable relief where an agreement can be proven between the insured and the designated beneficiary whereby for a valuable consideration the beneficiary acquires a vested equitable interest in the insurance proceeds.

The question here, however, is whether plaintiff has pleaded sufficient allegations to invoke equitable relief under the accepted theories of recovery. "A motion to dismiss admits all facts well pleaded as well as all reasonable inferences therefrom favorable to the plaintiff." Bishop v. Ellsworth, 234 N.E.2d 49, 52. If, on the basis of the alleged facts and all reasonable inferences drawn therefrom, standing alone and uncontested, there exists any possibility of recovery, the order of dismissal must be vacated. . . .

Having brought this action in equity, plaintiff's complaint must show that no adequate remedy at law exists. . . . Contrary to defendants' contentions, we believe that the complaint does show the absence of an adequate legal remedy. The object of plaintiff's complaint, as recited in her prayer for relief, is not to obtain a mere money decree, but to reach a particular fund, namely, insurance proceeds, in which plaintiff alleges she has a vested interest. Under these circumstances courts of chancery have jurisdiction since the plaintiff is effectively requesting enforcement of a trust in her favor, not unlike those cases where equity has intervened to enforce alleged equitable assignments of particular funds. . . .

Furthermore, while defendants suggest that plaintiff may have a legal remedy directly against her deceased husband's estate, the fact that a remedy at law is available does not oust an equity court of jurisdiction. The question to be determined is whether the remedy at law compares favorably with the remedy afforded by the equity court. Plaintiff alleges that at his death, Richard M. Johnson was insolvent. Taking this allegation as true, it is a reasonable inference that any judgment at law procured by plaintiff against her husband's estate would not be efficacious. Such a consideration is significant in exercising equitable jurisdiction. . . .

Pleadings should be designed to advise the court and the adverse party of the issues and what is relied upon as the cause of action, so that the court may declare the law and the adverse party may be prepared on trial to meet the issues. . . . The pleader need not state the legal conclusion to be drawn from the facts, where specific facts are set out in a pleading, "as the law would infer them from the direct statement of facts," Leitch v. Sanitary Dist. of Chicago, 369 Ill. 469, 473, 17 N.E.2d 34. While the instant complaint may initially appear confusing because of the absence of express statements charging the inadequacy of available legal remedy and the existence of contractual offer and acceptance, yet facts are alleged from which these conclusions may be inferred.

Under the alleged facts, while plaintiff has not established his claim with certainty, it is possible that evidence could be introduced upon which the trier of fact could conclude that plaintiff is entitled to recovery. It is sufficient that the complaint set forth facts establishing the mere possibility of recovery. . . . The collective force of the allegations in the present complaint suggests that an implied in fact agreement may have existed between plaintiff and Richard M. Johnson whereby for a valuable consideration, the insured promised not to remove plaintiff as beneficiary under his life insurance policy, that plaintiff thereby acquired a vested equitable interest in the policy proceeds, and that the purported change of beneficiary in December, 1966, was a fraud on plaintiff's equitable rights.

For the foregoing reasons the order of dismissal of plaintiff's complaint for failure to state a cause of action is reversed and the cause is remanded for further proceedings not inconsistent with this opinion.

Reversed and remanded.

Case Questions for Discussion

1. In a suit requesting equitable remedies, must the complaint always clearly allege the inadequacy of law?

2. What are the competing legal and equitable principles concerning the right of a person to change beneficiaries named in his or her insurance policy?

3. Did a remedy at law exist for the plaintiff against her deceased husband's estate? If so, does this stop the plaintiff from pursuing equitable relief? Why or why not?

4. What factual matters did the court say might be inferred about the plaintiff's claim that she had provided "valuable consideration" for an implied promise by her husband to retain her as the exclusive beneficiary under his insurance policy?

Discovery

With respect to discovery, there are no differences between equity and civil suits for money damages. In the exercise of equity jurisdiction, courts allow and enforce discovery rules, including those applicable to depositions, production of documents, physical and mental examinations, and requests for admissions.[8] Review Chapter 5 for a discussion of each of these discovery tools.

Pretrial Conferences

Although pretrial conferences may be scheduled for cases involving equity disputes, they are typically less frequent or necessary than in civil suits for money damages. This is true because at trial there is normally no jury and, therefore, less need to carefully consider what evidence may be offered at trial and made part of the record. Nonetheless, pretrial conferences are useful for all participants. Judges have an opportunity to acquaint themselves with the facts in the case, and together opposing counsel and the court can narrow the scope of the upcoming case and can determine whether to proceed to the actual trial.

Trial Phase of Litigation

As with civil suits for money damages, legal counsels in equity cases make their opening statements to the court. Unlike civil suits for money damages, these remarks are directed to the judge because in the typical case there is no jury. In most equity suits, the judge decides both questions of fact and of law, and it is left to the judge to fashion appropriate remedies. Because there is no jury, less attention is paid to the details of the rules of evidence. This relaxation in the rules is justified because the legal training of judges allows them to distinguish, for example, hearsay or otherwise irrelevant and immaterial evidence from admissible evidence.[9]

This is not to suggest that the rules of evidence are not followed. Legal counsel may make timely objections to improperly admitted evidence, such as the admission of confidential communications. What is evident, however, is that in equity suits there are typically fewer objections and the atmosphere during the trial is less formal than is otherwise the case. When law and equity matters are joined in a single suit,

the parties may agree to have all matters decided by the judge. Upon a
timely and proper demand, however, law issues involving the determination of facts and judgment awards may be matters for jury determination, and equitable matters remain within the judge's province.[10] In
Illinois, state law allows the unusual step of permitting trial judges to
submit factual matters involving equity to a jury when the court is adjudicating both legal and equitable issues together. But even in Illinois,
law and equity questions involving matters of fact are normally reserved to juries and judges, respectively.

The judge hears the evidence presented in the form of witnesses,
documents, and exhibits, but sometimes the judge will appoint a person to gather information and to suggest recommendations for a final
disposition in a case. This person is called a *special master in equity*.
Cases involving complicated accounting matters and judicial sales of
property are typical of situations when judges employ these ad hoc
court officers. In the case of the 2000 presidential election, the Gore
forces asked a Florida court to assign the task of counting votes in
counties to a special master when the task was not accomplished to
their satisfaction. Courts often appoint special masters to consider and
to suggest redistricting of legislative districts when equal protection issues are difficult to resolve. Special masters do not have the authority
to adjudicate matters with finality, though their factual assessments
typically carry great weight with appointing judges.

Equitable Maxims

Because law and equity are founded upon different legal premises
and traditions, judges sitting in equity jurisdiction apply "rules of conscience," otherwise known as *equitable maxims*. They employ these
maxims in an effort to do what is just, right, or best under the circumstance. Although legal rules dictate one outcome, equitable maxims
may dictate an opposite result. We present a partial list, including descriptions of commonly used equitable maxims available to judges to
assist them in exercising their sound judicial discretion. Our list is followed by an Illinois Appellate Court opinion, *Finke v. Woodard*; it illustrates the difference between law and equity that results from the
application of these maxims.

1. *Equity will not suffer a right to be without a remedy.*[11] We know
that a principal reason courts with equity jurisdiction were created in
the first place was the inability of the common law courts of England to
provide justice in the many instances when these courts lacked jurisdiction to adjudicate certain disputes. In fact, the notion that whenever
there is a legal right there must be a remedy was recognized by John
Marshall in his famous U.S. Supreme Court opinion in *Marbury v. Madison* (1803).[12] Today this maxim is firmly implanted in our legal consciousness, as made certain, for example, in the Illinois State Constitu-

tion, Article I, section 12. It reads: "Every person shall find a certain remedy in the laws for all injuries and wrongs which he receives to his person, privacy, property, or reputation. He shall obtain justice by law, freely, completely and promptly."

2. *Equity Looks to Substance Rather Than Form.*[13] The intent of the parties to an agreement is more important than the form in which the agreement was framed. The technicalities of a written agreement may result in a grave injustice if the parties meant something quite different. This maxim allows judges to regard the intent of the parties as more important than how the words might be interpreted literally. Our previous hypothetical example of the reformation of a written contractual agreement of the seller of an automobile who mistakenly wrote the monthly sum of $40 instead of $400 is an example of equity looking at substance over form.

3. *Equity Regards That as Done Which Ought to Be Done.*[14] Under this equitable maxim, a court of equity may require, for example, a defendant lessee of an apartment who refuses to vacate the premises at the end of the lease to surrender possession of the premises.

4. *Equality Is Equity.*[15] This maxim dictates that the burden imposed is equally borne by all persons upon whom it is imposed. For example, if the parties are partners in a business venture, then the costs of doing business should be proportionate to their share in the business. Today, this doctrine is also found in law, but its origins are traced to equity.

5. *He Who Comes Into Equity Must Come With Clean Hands.*[16] The purpose of this maxim is to prevent equity courts from aiding litigants in accomplishing unlawful and unethical conduct. Chancery was originally a court of conscience, and such an institution should not be used to accomplish acts of parties who themselves behave improperly. For example, if you sue your neighbor for burning rubbish in his backyard but at the same time you do the same on your premises, both literally and legally you lack the requisite clean hands.

6. *He Who Seeks Equity Must Do Equity.*[17] This maxim is connected to the clean hands doctrine. It holds that persons who seek equity must be prepared to perform their responsibility in the same spirit in which they are asking the defendant to perform. For example, if a plaintiff asks the court to order the defendant to specifically perform on some aspect of a contractual obligation, the plaintiff must also be ready and willing to perform his or her end of the bargain.

7. *Equity Aids the Vigilant, Not Those Who Sleep on Their Rights.*[18] This maxim, also known as the *doctrine of laches,* requires that once a party is aware of the harmful conduct of another, he has a responsibility to bring the matter to the attention of a court in a reasonably swift manner. If your neighbor burns rubbish in his backyard, preventing you from the full enjoyment of your property and thereby creating a legal nuisance, and if you want him to cease and desist, you cannot wait

years before you sue in equity because your delay reflects a willingness to live with the nuisance created by your neighbor. You may have a cause of action for the recovery of money damages, but your delay will seriously compromise an action for an equitable remedy. Moreover, a defendant relying on the *doctrine of laches* must not only show unreasonable delay on the part of the plaintiff, but also that the defendant was prejudiced by that delay. For instance, if you watched your neighbor construct, over a period of time and at great expense, an incinerator before you sued to enjoin his burning of refuse, your delay may very well have prejudiced him. The case of *Finke v. Woodard* illustrates the issues surrounding the doctrine of laches and the equitable remedy of rescission.

Finke v. Woodard
Illinois Appellate Court, Fourth District
122 Ill.App.3rd 911, 462 N.E.2d 13, 78 Ill.Dec. 297 (1984)

OPINION BY: JUDGE TRAPP:
This action was brought by plaintiffs, Gary and Teresa Finke, to recover damages and an order of rescission as a result of defects in a new home built and sold by defendant Elmer Woodard. Among the issues to be considered in this appeal are whether plaintiffs' suit is barred by section 13-214 of the Code of Civil Procedure (Ill.Rev.Stat.1981, ch. 110, par. 13-214) or laches, whether plaintiffs are entitled to rescind the sale, and the appropriate measure of restitution following a rescission of the sale. We affirm the award of rescission, but reverse and remand this cause for appropriate findings on the proper amount of restitution to which plaintiffs are entitled.

At trial, plaintiffs testified that on April 23, 1977, they executed a purchase agreement with defendant for the sale of a new house under construction by him in Heather Hills subdivision near Champaign. Plaintiffs paid $52,050 for the house, moved in on June 16, 1977, and continued to occupy it at the time of trial. Plaintiffs

testified that they began to experience problems with the home upon taking possession, leading them to file this lawsuit in which they sought recovery on theories of implied warranty of habitability, negligence, gross negligence, and fraud. The plaintiffs testified to a number of complaints within the home: the water conditioner was installed backwards causing filtering chemicals to be discharged; the dishwasher was improperly installed allowing water from the garbage disposal to drain into the dishwasher; a septic system malfunctioned forming a pool of effluent in the backyard; the interior walls of the house were weak and separated from the ceiling; nails continuously popped out in various locations in the house; doors would not close, a crack developed in the concrete floor of an outside storage shed, and a portion of the bathroom plumbing broke loose from its connection causing water damage to the floor and tile. The jury found for plaintiffs on theories of warranty, negligence, and gross negligence and returned a not guilty verdict on the fraud count. The jury also awarded plaintiffs both rescission of the sales contract and deed and damages.

Defendant's first argument on appeal is that plaintiffs' suit is barred by section 13-214 (a) of the Code of Civil Procedure, which provides:

Actions based upon tort, contract or otherwise against any person for an act or omission of such person in the design, planning, supervision, observation or management of construction, or construction of an improvement to real property shall be commenced within 2 years from the time the person bringing an action, or his or her privity, knew or should reasonably have known of such act or omission.

Plaintiffs' home was completed by June 16, 1977, and the original complaint was filed on July 7, 1981, well beyond the two years in which plaintiffs knew or reasonably should have known of the acts or omissions of the defendant as provided in that section. If this were the only circumstance to consider, then defendant's argument would be well taken, but defendant fails to point out that the statute was amended after plaintiffs' suit was filed.

Effective November 29, 1979, Public Act 81-1169 added paragraph 22.3 of the former Limitations Act, the current section 13-214 of the Code of Civil Procedure. (1979 Ill.Laws 4480; Ill.Rev.Stat.1981, ch. 83, par. 22.3.) At that time, Public Act 81-1169 provided in subsection (e) that "[t]he limitations of this section [current section 13-214] shall apply to acts or omissions which occur on or after the effective date of this amendatory Act of 1979." On July 7, 1981, plaintiffs filed their suit when the statute contained that section. On September 16, 1981, Public Act

82-539 deleted subparagraph (e) (1981 Ill.Laws 2709) and on July 1, 1981, Public Act 82-280 incorporated chapter 83 into chapter 110 of the new Code of Civil Procedure erroneously including old subparagraph (e) (1981 Ill.Laws 1591). Finally, on July 13, 1982, the Revisory Act of 1982, Public Act 82-783, deleted subparagraph (e). 1982 Ill.Laws 397.

Thus, at the time plaintiffs filed their suit, former paragraph 22.3 of the Limitations Act had a prospective application, applying to acts or omissions occurring after November 29, 1979. The acts or omissions at issue here, the improper construction of the home, occurred on or before 1977 and were outside of the plain language of that section. When plaintiffs filed suit, the only applicable limitation period was paragraph 15 of the Limitations Act which provided a period of five years for all civil actions not otherwise provided for. To retroactively apply the deletion of subparagraph (e) as defendant urges, would result in the barring of plaintiffs' action, a result which is clearly not permitted. As noted by the supreme court in *Hupp v. Gray* (1978), an amendment which shortens a limitations period may not operate to divest a litigant of a cause of action if his suit has already been filed. We conclude that plaintiffs' suit was not barred by section 13-214 of the Code of Civil Procedure.

Although plaintiffs' suit was brought within the five-year limitations period, defendant next argues that the equitable remedy of rescission is not available because plaintiffs failed to timely assert this claim earlier. Plaintiffs' original complaint, filed on July 7, 1981, sought damages for the various defects and on July 30, 1982, plaintiffs were granted leave to amend their complaint to seek a claim of rescission without objection by the defendant. The motion for leave to amend as well as testimony at trial indicates that the addition of this claim resulted from an opinion of plaintiffs' expert that the problems plaintiffs were experiencing were not isolated defects but were interrelated complaints pointing out latent structural defects in the walls.

In Pyle v. Ferrell (1958), 147 N.E.2d 341, the supreme court upheld a defense of laches in bar of plaintiff's suit to quiet title to a mineral estate which was brought more than 18 years after plaintiff learned of his interest. The Pyle court noted that laches is defined as such delay in enforcing one's rights as would work to the disadvantage of another. The doctrine is founded not merely upon the amount of time involved but is properly invoked where there has been some change of condition or circumstances of the property or the parties, making relief inequitable. Whether the delay is sufficient to constitute laches depends upon the circumstance of the case and requires an examination of when the party became aware of the reasons which would support the equitable remedy. In Pinelli v. Alpine Development Corp. (1979), 388 N.E.2d 943, for example, the court upheld an order rescinding a stock sale agreement on the basis of fraud five years after the transaction, even though the claim for rescission was not made until after the close of evidence at trial. The court there noted that the plaintiff had not become aware of the defendant's fraud or misrepresentation until the close of the evidence.

An examination of when plaintiffs became aware of the availability of the equitable remedy also requires

some consideration of when a breach of contract will support an award of rescission. . . .

We conclude that the trial court correctly rejected defendant's claim of laches. The plaintiffs testified that the cracks in the walls became progressively worse each year; they apparently did not realize the magnitude of the problems until the house was examined by a structural engineer in 1981 and 1982. The septic system was noticed to be deficient in 1978, and when plaintiffs informed defendant he attributed the problem to excessive groundwater and suggested that plaintiffs reduce the amount of laundry for a few weeks. On April 13, 1981, plaintiffs received a complaint regarding the septic system from the Illinois Department of Public Health notifying them that they had to take immediate action to correct a sewage eruption on their property. This evidence suggests that plaintiffs were not aware of the substantial problems until shortly before they amended their complaint to seek rescission and we find no evidence of any prejudicial change in circumstance to warrant application of laches to bar plaintiffs' equitable remedy.

The evidence also suggests that the breach of the implied warranty of habitability was substantial and justified rescissionary relief. Plaintiffs' witness, John Frauenhoffer, a structural engineer, investigated the cause of the defects in the walls and he stated that they had not been secured and properly framed and that the ongoing movement of the walls would cause a softening of the structure. He stated that it was highly possible that a wall would fall out of the structure making the home uninhabitable. Defendant did not present evidence refuting that plaintiffs experienced problems with the septic system, the water softener, the cracked floor in the storage shed, the wall/ceiling separation and the nail popping. Defendant's subcontractor and defendant both testified that the wall/ceiling separation could be cured by covering it up with moulding and they both stated that the home was built in a commercially reasonable manner. An architect also testified for defendants that the house was more than commercially acceptable.

Plaintiffs presented evidence that the septic system installed by defendant's subcontractor was inappropriate for the size of plaintiffs' land and the type of soil. Plaintiffs performed percolation tests at the direction of the Illinois Department of Health which indicated that a seepage system septic system could not be used on their lot. Defendant's subcontractor who installed the system performed similar tests with substantially different results and he stated that the system was installed in a proper manner.

Upon this conflicting evidence, we will not disturb the award. We agree that not every breach of an implied warranty of habitability is sufficient for an award of rescission, but the proof here shows a substantial breach of defendant's contractual duty to construct a house reasonably fit for its intended use. "The rule that a contract once executed may not be rescinded by either of the parties is based upon the rule of pari delicto."

Defendant also claims that the trial court erred in submitting to the jury the issue of whether plaintiffs were entitled to rescind the sales agreement. Defendant suggests that the question of rescission was for the court and not the jury. We agree that

there is no right to a jury trial on equitable issues [Lazarus v. Village of Northbrook (1964), 199 N.E.2d 797], but it was not beyond the court's power to submit this equitable question to the jury. Section 2-1111 of the Civil Practice Law provides that the court may in its discretion direct an issue or issues to be tried by a jury, whenever it is judged necessary in an action seeking equitable relief. Section 2-614 of the Civil Practice Law provides that legal and equitable issues may be tried together, but such a procedure is limited to cases where no jury is employed. Defendant has never made this argument in either the trial court or this court, however, and we decline to consider that section here.

Plaintiffs were entitled to seek both remedies, legal and equitable, even though they were inconsistent, unless it could be said that they had elected one remedy or the other. This doctrine of election of remedies, does not prevent a party from seeking relief on inconsistent remedies unless a party has formerly manifested an intent to seek one remedy and the defendant makes a substantial change of position in reliance upon that intention or a possibility of double recovery exists. As we have indicated in our discussion of laches, we find no change of position to create an estoppel here and find no abuse of discretion in submitting both the legal and equitable claim to the jury.

Defendant next charges that the jury instructions on rescission and elements of damage were improper because the damage instruction included improper elements of recovery and the rescission instruction did not adequately define the issues for the jury. . . .

The purpose of a rescissionary award is to disaffirm the transaction of the parties and restore them to the status quo as it existed prior to the execution of the contract. Where rescission is awarded then, the proper measure of recovery is restitution of the consideration and other benefits received by the parties under the contract. We find it inconsistent to both disaffirm the transaction and yet at the same time award plaintiffs the fair market value of the home as it would have existed without defects. The proper measure of recovery should have been simply a return of the consideration and other benefits received by the parties under the contract. . . . We conclude that the jury instruction on damages was erroneous in including those items referred to above. All plaintiffs should have received as their measure of restitution was the return of the purchase price and the costs they incurred in correcting the defective problems with the house and septic system.

We have predicated our analysis of the rescission remedy upon the count seeking this relief for a breach of the implied warranty of habitability as this is the only theory which supports the award. . . . Thus, since we affirm the rescission award but find reversible error in the damage instructions, we remand this cause to the trial court to make findings on the appropriate amount of money re-quired to return the parties to the status quo ante, including plaintiffs' purchase price, and the amounts of money plaintiffs spent in correcting the defects in the home and septic system. . . .

Finally, we note the parties have argued extensively in their briefs as to whether the proper measure of damages in this case should have been the diminution in fair market value as a result of the breach or the cost of repairing the defects. The cost of repair measure of damages was included in the jury instruction as an alternative measure in the event the jury did not recommend rescission. Since the jury recommended rescission, the trial court accepted their verdict, and we have affirmed this remedy, those questions as to what the proper measure of damages should be is moot. The only remaining question is the appropriate amount of restitution to which plaintiffs are entitled to return them to the status quo ante.

For the foregoing reasons, the judgment of the circuit court of Champaign County is affirmed in part, reversed in part and remanded for a hearing on the proper amount of restitution required.

Affirmed in part; reversed in part and remanded for proceedings consistent with this opinion.

MILLS, P. J., and WEBBER, J., concur.

Case Questions for Discussion

1. Does the two-year statute of limitations apply in this case? Why or why not?

2. What is the rule used by the court in determining when a delay in bringing a suit constitutes laches?

3. May a court sitting in its equity jurisdiction ever direct an issue to be tried by a jury?

4. What is the difference between a statute of limitations and laches? To prevail in the suit, must a plaintiff meet both the requirements of the statute of limitations and laches?

Judicial Decrees

In a civil suit for money damages, the court issues a judgment; that is, the decision of the jury is in the form of a judgment with a verdict for or against the plaintiff. Instead of a judgment, the judge in an equity suit issues a *decree*.[19] The distinction is important. Because money damages are not involved, a decree requires a party to do something or refrain from doing something. If a party disobeys a decree, the presiding judge has the power to hold the offending party in contempt of court. The judge may fine or confine the offending party to jail.[20]

The legal battle that took place in Florida in the days following the disputed 2000 presidential election is a good example of the distinction between law and equitable remedies. During the protracted conflict over the counting of presidential ballots, the Supreme Court of Florida on November 17, 2000, issued a decree commanding:

> In order to maintain the status quo, the Court, on its own motion, enjoins the Respondent, Secretary of State and Respondent, the Elections Canvassing Commission from certifying the results of the November 7, 2000, presidential election, until further order of this Court. It is NOT the intent of this Order to stop the counting and conveying to the Secretary of State the results of absentee ballots or any other ballots.[21]

The court gave the Secretary the authority to certify the results on November 26, 2000.[22] If the Florida high court found that the Secretary of State, Katherine Harris, had violated this order, she may have been held in contempt of court, and she may have been fined or imprisoned; in any event, the certification of the election before November 26, 2000, would have been nullified and without legal sanction.

This Florida case illustrates an additional distinction worth noting between equity and law suits for money damages. The Florida Supreme Court's order was temporary, otherwise known as an interlocutory or preliminary injunction. When the court issued its November 17, 2000, order to Secretary of State Harris, it had not heard full arguments on the merits of the case. The plaintiffs (lawyers acting on behalf of Vice President Gore and several Florida county officials) convinced the justices of the Florida high court that irreparable harm would be done if Harris was not enjoined from certifying the results of the election on the following day, November 18, 2000, as she had indicated she would. The irreparable harm was the election of a candidate who may not have received the greatest number of votes in the Florida presidential election. The decree required the submission of briefs by both sides and oral arguments before the court by legal counsel the following Monday, November 20, 2000. The court then issued its final judgment requiring the Secretary of State not to certify the election results before November 26, 2000, at 5:00 P.M., although at her discretion she may have waited until the following morning. This recent and dramatic event in U.S. political history illustrates the fact that judges possess the power to grant immediate relief even before a hearing on the merits of the case.

Courts decide how far police or security can go in searching for contraband at recreational events.

Moreover, injunctions and decrees of all sorts are always under the complete control of the court. The court may dissolve or modify temporary or even permanent injunctions or orders at any time, depending upon changing circumstances. Consequently, unlike civil suits for money damages, the principle of *res judicata* does not apply to equitable decrees or injunctions. As we will learn in Chapter 12 on family law, this aspect of equity practice is applied widely to child custody cases, in which because the situation of parents may change, it is possible for one or both parents to ask the court to change the original decision of the court with respect to that issue. Although the divorce decree may not be changed, child custody or other matters, including child support and alimony payments, may be altered well after the court renders its original decision.

The following order of a federal district court judge illustrates the legal dexterity available to judges in the fashioning of an equitable remedy. Notice how Judge Benson weighs the constitutional rights of the plaintiff in the enjoyment of his Fourth Amendment rights against the right of the community to provide for the health and safety of those attending rock concerts in the city's civic auditorium. For a good reason, we are not revealing the true name of the plaintiff in this case.

Doe v. Anderson
U.S. District Court for the District of North Dakota
Southeastern Division
No. A77-3041 (August 26, 1977)

PAUL BENSON, CHIEF JUDGE:

The above entitled matter came before this court at 1:30 P.M. on August 24, 1977, on Plaintiff's motion for a preliminary injunction, to enjoin Defendants, their successors, their agents or employees from authorizing or conducting searches of persons attending "rock" concerts at the Fargo Civic Auditorium, Fargo, North Dakota.

The court finds there is a substantial likelihood that Plaintiff will prevail on his claim for equitable relief, based on his allegations that the warrantless searches conducted by members of the Fargo Police Department under the authority and control of Defendants have violated, and if allowed to continue, will violate, Plaintiff's rights, privileges and immunities under the Fourth and Fourteenth Amendments to the United States Constitution. Searches conducted outside the judicial process, without prior approval by a judge or a magistrate, are per se unreasonable under the Fourth Amendment, subject only to "a few specifically and well-delineated exceptions." Coolidge v. New Hampshire, 403 U.S. 443, 454-55 (1971). These exceptions are " 'zealously and carefully drawn,' and there must be 'a showing by those who seek exemption . . . that the exigencies of the situation made that course imperative.' " Id. Based on the present record in the case at bar, there appear to be no clear and definitive standards established for the searches conducted by the police officers at the Fargo Civic Auditorium.

Patrons entering the auditorium are informed by posted signs and loudspeaker announcements that alcoholic beverages and narcotic drugs are not allowed in the auditorium. They are further informed that upon entering the auditorium "you may be searched." Counsel for Defendants argue that in practice the search is a limited search which does not extend beyond a search of handbags, packages and clothing in which contraband, particularly alcoholic beverages, could be concealed. They contend such searches are consensual or administrative searches and are thereby excepted from the mandate of Coolidge v. New Hampshire, 403 U.S. 443, 454, 55 (1971).

Any exceptions must, however, be zealously and carefully drawn, and it is the opinion of this court that on the basis of the record now before the court these searches do not meet that test. No zealously or carefully drawn standards limiting and prescribing the search procedures exist. There are no written standards or procedures in effect other than the posted signs. All of the patrons entering the auditorium are not searched, and the decision as to who is going to be searched, when and where in the auditorium a patron will be searched, and the extent of the search of an individual patron is left to the discretion of the law enforcement officers on duty at the auditorium, or their superiors. While the public safety purpose behind the search procedures appears to be legitimate, there is a substantial likelihood that Plaintiff will prove at trial that searches now conducted under existing procedures cannot withstand constitutional challenge. See Collier v. Miller, 414 F. Supp. 1357 (S.D. Tex. 1976).

The court further finds that if a preliminary injunction is not granted, Plaintiff will incur irreparable harm. The court finds an absence of substantial harm to Defendants if the injunction is granted.

The court further finds there has been no showing of serious harm to the public interest if the injunction is granted. Although Defendants assert that damage may result to the public if the search procedure is halted, it appears the risk is not so great that it could not be controlled by other methods of police protection which may be constitutionally valid.

IT IS ORDERED that Defendants, their successors, their agents or employees and those in active concert or participation with them are preliminarily enjoined and restrained from conducting systematic and continuous random, warrantless searches of persons attending events at the Fargo Civic Auditorium. Nothing herein affects the authority of law enforcement officials to conduct warrantless searches at the auditorium based on probable cause.

This Order becomes effective upon Plaintiff filing a cash security bond in the sum of Five Hundred Dollars ($500.00) conditioned for the payment of such costs and damages as may be incurred or suffered by any party who is found to have been wrongfully enjoined and restrained.

IT IS FURTHER ORDERED that the within action is certified to be a class action.

Dated this 25th day of August, 1977.

Postscript: After the trial on the permanent injunction, Judge Benson fashioned an equitable decree that gave a little to both sides in the dispute. He ordered that the random searches cease but with the following provision. The City should establish a check-in system that permits patrons to deposit bulky items of clothing and handbags or packages before they enter the auditorium, without having those items searched. However, persons who insist on carrying such items into the auditorium may be subject to a police search. Moreover, the judge left open the option of changing his decree if circumstances warranted. Either party could ask the judge to change his order.

Case Questions for Discussion

1. What is the test employed by the court when issuing preliminary injunctions?

2. Is the protection against searches and seizures an absolute right? What interests does the court use in weighing the rights of the parties?

3. Should it be permissible for judges to fashion equitable remedies, or should they strictly apply the law?

Key Terms, Names, and Concepts

Clear and convincing evidence

Declaratory judgment

Decree

Doctrine of laches

Equitable maxims

Equity aids the vigilant

Equity is equality

Equity looks to substance rather than form

Equity regards that as done which ought to be done

Equity will not suffer a right to be without a remedy

Ex parte injunction

He who comes into equity must come with clean hands

He who seeks equity must do equity

Injunction

Injunctive relief

Interlocutory injunction

Mandatory injunction

Permanent injunction

Preliminary injunction

Prohibitory injunction

Reformation

Rescission

Restitution

Restitution by substitution

Special master in equity

Specific performance

Strong and conclusive evidence

Temporary injunction

Temporary restraining order

Discussion Questions

1. Why are there major differences between the remedies available in civil suits for money damages and equity?

2. Given the underlying assumptions of equity and law, why are there significant differences between the two when litigating disputes?

3. If factual matters are properly before juries in civil suits for money damages, does it make sense in this age for judges to possess such authority in equity suits?

4. What is the justification, if any, for why *res judicata* applies in civil suits for money damages but not uniformly in equity?

Suggested Additional Reading

Bryson, W. Hamilton. "Equity and Equitable Remedies." *Encyclopedia of the American Judicial System,* Robert J. Janosik, ed. New York: Scribner, 1987, Vol. 2, pp. 545–533.

Burby, William. *Law Refresher: Equity.* 3rd ed. St. Paul, MN: West, 1961.

Farber, Daniel A. "Equitable Discretion, Legal Duties, and Environmental Injunctions." *University of Pittsburgh Law Review* 45 (spring 1984): 513–545.

Fregeau, Jason David. "Statutes and Judicial Discretion: Against the Law . . . sort of." *Boston College Environmental Affairs Law Review* 18 (spring 1991): 501–542.

Hoffer, Peter Charles. *The Law's Conscience: Equitable Constitutionalism in America.* Chapel Hill: University of North Carolina Press, 1990.

McClintock, Henry L. *McClintock on Equity.* 2nd ed. St. Paul, MN: West, 1948.

McDowell, Gary L. *Equity and the Constitution.* Chicago: University of Chicago Press, 1982.

Shreve, Gene R., and Peter Raven-Hansen. *Understanding Civil Procedure.* 3rd ed. Newark, NJ: LexisNexis, 2002.

Waddell, Sarah. "Equitable Resolution of Contaminated Land Disputes (Australia)." *Environmental and Planning Law Journal* 13 (October 1996): 348–363.

Zelermyer, William. *The Legal System in Operation: A Case Study From the Procedural Beginning to the Judicial Conclusion.* St. Paul, MN: West, 1977.

Endnotes

1. Jonathan T. Howe et al., "Injunctions," in *Chancery and Special Remedies* (Springfield: Illinois Institute for Continuing Legal Education, 1992/1994), §§ 2.1–2.9.
2. 71 American Jurisprudence, 2d, *Specific Performance, Degree of Proof* § 208 (1973).
3. Michael A. Braun et al., "Specific Performance," in *Chancery and Special Remedies* (Springfield: Illinois Institute for Continuing Legal Education, 1992/1994), §§ 3.1–3.34.
4. Diane I. Jennings and Kathryn C. Wyatt, "Rescission and Reformation," in *Chancery and Special Remedies* (Springfield: Illinois Institute for Continuing Legal Education, 1992/1994), §§ 4.2–4.3.
5. Henry J. Abraham, *The Judicial Process: An Introductory Analysis of the Courts of the United States, England, and France,* 7th ed. (New York: Oxford University Press, 1998), p. 393.
6. William T. Schantz, *The American Legal Environment: Individuals, Their Business, and Their Government* (St. Paul, MN: West, 1976), p. 287.
7. See, for example, the Illinois practice, in Robert D. Ericsson and John B. Murnigan, "Guideposts in Chancery: The Maxims of Equity" in *Chancery and Special Remedies* (Springfield: Illinois Institute for Continuing Legal Education, 1992/1994), § 1.3.
8. William T. Schantz, *The American Legal Environment,* p. 287.
9. Ibid.
10. Robert D. Ericsson and John B. Murnigan, "Guideposts in Chancery," § 1.5.
11. Ibid., § 1.7.

12. For a description of events surrounding this famous opinion and the related subject of judicial review, see Albert P. Melone and George Mace, *Judicial Review and American Democracy* (Ames: Iowa State University Press, 1988), pp. 37–48.
13. Robert D. Ericsson and John B. Murnigan, "Guideposts in Chancery," § 1.8.
14. Ibid., § 1.9.
15. Ibid., § 1.10.
16. Ibid., § 1.16.
17. Ibid., § 1.17.
18. Ibid., § 1.15.
19. William T. Schantz, *The American Legal Environment*, p. 288.
20. Geoffrey C. Hazard, Jr., and Michele Taruffo, *American Civil Procedure: An Introduction* (New Haven, CT: Yale University Press, 1993), pp. 159, 202–203.
21. Decree without published opinion.
22. Gore v. Harris, No. SC00-2431 (Fla. Dec. 8, 2000). Also cited as 772 So.2d 1243 (2000). ✦

Chapter 7

Criminal Processes

Chapter Objectives

Readers should obtain from this chapter an understanding of how offenses against the people are prosecuted by government using criminal processes. Students are admonished to pay special attention to the basic assumptions of the criminal justice system, including the notion of presumed innocence and the heavy burden of proof required to convict persons and in the process to deprive them of their life, liberty, or property. While studying the various phases of the criminal process, including juvenile justice, students should become cognizant of the various similarities and contrasts with processes that are utilized in civil suits for money damages and in equity.

As it did for the preceding two chapters on civil suits for money damages and equity processes, the discussion here examines various phases of the legal process (pleading, discovery, trial, and appellate). Students should focus on how criminal processes differ significantly from civil and equity matters. These differences stem from what is at stake. Although money and other material pleasures are important, in the case of the criminal law, the government may take away a person's life, liberty, and property. In other words, the state can fine, imprison, or execute those who transgress the norms of society.

Moreover, in the name of all the people, the collective power of the state is used to enforce societal norms. This is quite different from situations making persons whole again, resulting from the wrongdoing of private parties or from processes affording equitable remedies consistent with principles of natural justice. In the criminal law, the offense is against all the people, and in their collective name, the power of government is pervasive, exclusive, and punitive.

251

Values and the Criminal Justice System

Because the stakes are relatively high, the criminal justice system goes to great lengths to protect persons from wrongful arrest and conviction. Authoritarian governments exhibit less concern for civil liberties because in nondemocratic political cultures, order is valued more than individual rights. In democratic societies, however, individual liberty and life are highly respected values. This view stems from the political theory that humans are entitled to "life, liberty, and the pursuit of happiness," and that the goal of civil society is to protect and honor those basic natural rights. Indeed, when government becomes intolerably abusive of our fundamental rights, then, as in the words of the Declaration of Independence, "it is the right of the people to alter or abolish it." This bias in favor of individual rights is manifest in constitutional protections found both in the body of the basic document and in the Bill of Rights.

A consequence of the American focus upon individual rights is that we deliberately make it hard to convict persons of crimes. More precisely, the law makes it difficult to convict guilty parties of crimes because there is a fear that innocent persons may be wrongly convicted when authorities are overzealous in the performance of their duties. Consequently, in our desire to protect the innocent from the harsh realities of punishment, we are willing to make mistakes that result in occasionally freeing the guilty. While Americans are anxious to rid the streets of crime and to punish wrongdoers, we are at the same time deeply disturbed to learn that innocent persons have been sent to prison and, in some cases, executed in the name of all the people.

Evidence of this American concern for justice was made dramatically clear when, in March 2000, George Ryan, the Republican governor of Illinois, declared a moratorium on executions in his state. Ryan's decision came after 13 men on death row were cleared of charges by new evidence. In one highly publicized case, Anthony Porter, an African American with an IQ of 51, was released two days before his scheduled execution at an Illinois penitentiary as a result of evidence uncovered by Northwestern University journalism students. The students in a 1998 class project uncovered evidence that led to the videotaped confession by the real killer. Within three months of that revelation, two more Illinois death-row inmates were exonerated, one the result of discrediting an informant's testimony and the other resulting from DNA evidence. Subsequently, the *Chicago Tribune* newspaper published a study revealing that more than one third of all 285 Illinois capital convictions since 1977 were reversed on appeal because of fundamental error.[1] And a study of all capital cases in the United States from 1973 to 1995 found that 75 percent of the persons whose death sentences were set aside were later given lesser sentences after retrials or plea bargains, and 7 percent were found not guilty on retrial.[2] Just a few days before leaving office in 2003, Governor Ryan pardoned four death row inmates and he commuted the death sentences of another 164 men and three women to either life without parole or a few number of years. In a dramatic speech delivered at the Northwestern University Law School, Governor Ryan said:

> The facts I have seen in reviewing each and every one of these cases raised questions not only about the innocence of people on death row, but about the fairness of the death penalty system as a whole. . . . Our capital system is haunted by the demon of error, error in determining guilt and error in determining who among the guilty deserve to die.[3]

At the same time, no one doubts that many guilty persons go free because of their personal cunning, police blundering, or the application of controversial judge-created legal rules. In any event, the American criminal justice process weighs the value of life and liberty against the value of order and crime control. It clearly comes down on the side of liberty. At least, this is the theory. There are many state and federal penitentiary residents who would gladly attest to the contrary view, as well as members of the criminal defense bar who deal with this issue on a daily basis.

Given the assumptions that support the foundations of the criminal justice system, Americans have designed criminal procedures to insure the integrity of the criminal trial to protect the innocent from wrongful conviction. For this reason, the burden of proof is on the government to prove its case beyond a reasonable doubt. The police must use methods of obtaining evidence that are consistent with rules designed to protect individual rights. And finally, state and federal judges are in the position to carefully scrutinize the actual procedural treatment of defendants from the time of their arrest through appeal.

Pleading Phase: Commencing Prosecution

Before the government formally charges a person with a crime, there is an investigation, an arrest, and a booking. At the initial court appearance, the accused person is brought before a judicial officer. The prosecution gives formal notice of the charges against the accused, and he or she is apprised of legal rights. If the charge is a misdemeanor, the arrestee may be arraigned at that time and be required by law to enter a plea. However, if the charge is a felony, the arrested person is not required to enter a plea at this time. Instead, the arrestee is held over for a preliminary examination on the felony charge, at which time he or she is required to enter a plea. At times, the preliminary examination is bypassed, and the matter is brought directly to a grand jury for a true bill of indictment.

A criminal charge takes one of three forms: complaint, information, or indictment. Whatever the form of the accusation, all criminal charges must be in writing and a copy of the written accusation must be handed personally to the accused by an officer of the court in which the charge is filed. Depending upon the jurisdiction, the court officer might be a federal marshal, a county sheriff, or a local constable. The *personal service* requirement for a criminal charge distinguishes it from civil suits for money damages and suits seeking equitable relief, where service may be by publication, mail, or personal. The requirement reflects again the seriousness with which society regards criminal conduct when compared with civil matters. More important, it also reflects a collective desire to remove accused persons from the community because of the danger posed by allowing them to circulate freely.

Complaint

As a charge, a *criminal complaint* is little more than one person's statement taken under oath and subject to penalties for perjury, which accuses another of a criminal act. A victim of a crime or an eyewitness may "swear out" a complaint, as may a police officer who has witnessed a crime in progress. Complaints are usually employed at the level of petty crimes and misdemeanors because, when used by the lay public, they may be used for personal reasons of animus, including a desire to punish a personal enemy, even though a crime may not have been committed.

Criminal complaints are often used, however, by prosecutors as evidence that may justify asking a grand jury to consider an indictment or the filing of a criminal information with a court possessing appropriate jurisdiction. A sworn complaint by a police officer who witnessed a crime is more compelling than one sworn by members of the lay public because it clearly signifies that the officer believes probable cause exists that the accused committed a crime. Because complaining police officers possess knowledge of the law and take oaths of office to uphold the law, there is sufficient reason to treat their complaints with greater credibility than for most other members of the public.[4] Further, prosecutors can count on police officers to testify at trial. Many lay complainants refuse or are reluctant to testify after their initial anger subsides.

Information

Sometimes called a glorified complaint, a *criminal information* is a document signed by a prosecutor that recites the details of the alleged crime and is filed with a court possessing appropriate jurisdiction in the matter. The word *information* is a good descriptor because the prosecutor swears upon "information and belief" given to him or her by other persons. The prosecutor's knowledge is secondhand because he

Figure 7.1   Criminal Prosecutions

Prosecution

	1. Alleged Criminal Conduct	2. Prosecution Commencement	3. Criminal Charge	4. Discovery	5. Trial	6. Appeal
Prosecution	investigation booking arraignment or preliminary exam	complaint information indictment plea bargain		evidentiary disclosures	jury selection opening statement to jury (first) evidence introduced rebuttal evidence closing arguments (first) rebuttal arguments jury instructions jury verdict sentencing	may not appeal guilty verdict may appeal a decision of appeals court to higher court
Accused Defendant		constitutional warnings initial appearance and plea bail	notice of charges plea bargain	requests for evidence self-incrimination privilege disclosure of defenses at hearing or trial list of defense witnesses and evidence to be introduced at trial	jury selection opening statement acquittal and mistrial motions defense evidence rebuttal evidence closing arguments jury instructions jury verdict sentencing	right to appeal writ of habeas corpus

Accused Defendant

or she does not have personal knowledge of the crime. Therefore, the prosecutor is unable to swear by virtue of personal knowledge that the accused performed what is believed to be a criminal act.[5]

Thoughtful persons may wonder, given the secondhand knowledge of the facts of the case, whether a complaint is a better charging device than an information. The answer is, not necessarily. Prosecutors are in a position to screen charges coming from private parties and the police. In this sense, the information may better protect the innocent from frivolous and unfounded charges or cases with insufficient evidence to warrant proceeding further. Depending upon the jurisdiction, the information may be used both in misdemeanor and in felony cases. In those states that use a grand jury system, an indictment is commonly required in felony offenses and the information is employed only for misdemeanor cases.

Grand Jury Indictment

A third way to charge a person with a crime is through grand jury *indictment.* It is important to note first that the function of a grand jury differs from a petit (small) jury, otherwise known as a trial jury. Grand juries rule on whether there is sufficient evidence to warrant a trial. These bodies, composed of lay citizens, do not determine the guilt or innocence of persons, as do trial juries. Consequently, grand juries do not return verdicts. After it hears a presentation of evidence by a prosecutor, the grand jury returns either an indictment, also known as a *true bill,* or an *ignoramus,* also known as a *no bill.*

The Fifth Amendment of the U.S. Constitution guarantees grand jury indictment in federal cases, but it is not obligatory on the states by virtue of the Due Process Clause of the Fourteenth Amendment. Twenty states, however, currently employ grand juries as part of the criminal justice system, but some states employ grand juries only to investigate crime and corruption among public officials.[6] The intercession of lay persons, who are not associated in a professional capacity with the police, prosecutors, or the judiciary, is intended to insulate persons from prosecution by overzealous officials. Besides serving as a buffer against officialdom, grand juries function to protect the reputations of persons who might be suspected by government officials of wrongdoing when there is insufficient evidence to warrant prosecution. It is for this reason that grand jury deliberations are secretive.

No one has a right to appear before a grand jury. Persons are either requested or ordered to make appearances. Persons appearing before grand juries have no right to know the nature of the grand jury proceedings or the alleged crime under investigation.[7] Although persons under investigation for a crime are entitled to know the names of witnesses who have appeared before the grand jury, they are not entitled to cross-examine witnesses. Only a few states permit defense attorneys to be present at grand jury deliberations, and even judges may not be present. It is permissible for persons testifying before grand juries to consult with their lawyers, but usually only outside the physical presence of the grand jury quarters.[8]

The justification for not allowing attorneys and judges in grand jury proceedings, but requiring them at trial, is that at grand jury proceedings no one is being tried in the sense of actually being accused of a crime. Yet, it is widely known that prosecutors have considerable influence over grand jury proceedings; indeed, prosecutors usually get their way.[9] For this reason, many persons argue that grand juries are functionally useless as protectors of rights of the innocent; they are little more than a formality. Further, judges hearing an information, as the argument goes, can perform just as well and even better than laypersons, who usually lack legal training.

Federal grand juries are composed of 23 members, who are chosen randomly usually from lists of registered voters and are questioned by a federal district court judge and federal prosecutors to determine their qualifications to serve.[10] The appropriate judge selects a foreman and a deputy foreman. State grand juries range in size from five to 23 members, depending upon the jurisdiction. Grand juries are empanelled for much longer periods of time than trial juries. Federal grand juries sit from three to 18 months. Typically, they meet a few days each week or less, depending upon the request of the prosecuting attorney.[11]

Arrest and Arraignment

Arrest.

Criminal suspects must be advised of their constitutional rights consistent with the U.S. Supreme Court's ruling in Miranda v. Arizona, 384 U.S. 436 (1966). In the event that a person has not been arrested, the indictment or information serves as the basis for an arrest warrant that is issued by a judge upon the request of prosecuting authorities. Police subsequently take the person charged in the warrant into custody. Except for minor offenses, an *arraignment* takes place in the presence of the accused. Affording the accused an opportunity to enter a plea, this brief court appearance takes place only after notice of a scheduled time and place. The accused persons are first informed of their constitutional rights; the indictment or information is then read to them. Defendants sometimes ask for a change of venue. They may also move to have the charges dismissed if they believe the facts stated in the accusatory instrument do not constitute a crime in the jurisdiction of the arraignment. The defendant is then asked to plead guilty, nolo contendere, or not guilty.[12]

Box 7.1   Miranda Warnings Based Upon the Supreme Court Opinion in Miranda v. Arizona, 384 U.S. 436 (1966)

This case was part of a group of state and federal cases dealing with the admissibility of statements or confessions made by defendants during custodial interrogations. The Court pondered the question of what procedures are necessary to assure rights contained in the Fifth, Sixth, and Fourteenth Amendments.

Writing for a divided Court, Chief Justice Earl Warren emphasized that the holding in the case is not an innovation in American jurisprudence. Rather, the opinion is based upon long-standing principles of criminal justice. Warren noted that absent a clear, intelligent waiver of constitutional rights, a criminal suspect "must be warned prior to any questioning that he has a right to remain silent, that anything he says may be held against him in a court of law, that he has a right to the presence of an attorney, and that if he cannot afford an attorney one will be appointed for him prior to any questioning if he so desires." Further, the suspect has a right to refrain from answering any questions, even after answering prior questions, until such time that the suspect has had an opportunity to consult with legal counsel and consents to further questioning.

The warnings that are typically read to a person at the time of arrest and during arraignment are as follows:

1. You have a right to remain silent.
2. Anything you say can be used against you in a court of law.
3. You have a right to the presence of an attorney.
4. If you cannot afford an attorney, one will be appointed for you prior to questioning.
5. You have the right to terminate this interview at any time.

Postscript: The U.S. Supreme Court reaffirmed its controversial decision in *Miranda v. Arizona* 34 years later in Dickerson v. United States, 530 U.S. 428 (2000).

If the defendant pleads *guilty,* no trial is necessary and only sentencing remains. Yet, the matter is not as simple as it may seem. The guilty plea may be reversed on appeal if the record does not show that it was made voluntarily and that the accused understood its consequences, including the waiving of important constitutional rights, such as the right to a jury trial, the right against self-incrimination, and the right to confrontation of witnesses. Moreover, not all guilty pleas are directly responsive to the charge that the prosecutor originally brought against the accused. *Plea-bargaining,* in which the defendant pleads guilty to a lesser offense as an attractive alternative to going to trial for a crime with potentially harsher penalties, has become a common practice in most jurisdictions.

Prosecutors employ plea-bargaining as a way to reduce the size of their workload and court dockets, and at the same time to impose criminal penalties on wrongdoers. Often defendants gladly enter such pleas rather than face the uncertainties of a trial. Yet, the role of plea-bargaining has been severely criticized by civil libertarians, who seek to protect the rights of the criminally accused, and by those who advocate the imposition of maximum penalties to punish lawbreakers and to deter future crime. There is a legitimate suspicion that some defendants are coerced to enter into unfavorable pleas, and for this reason federal procedure permits the withdrawal of guilty pleas resulting from plea-bargains before sentencing.[13] In some extreme instances, courts are allowed to accept the withdrawal of guilty pleas even after sentencing. Some states follow the federal practice, but others do not permit the withdrawal of any voluntary pleas.[14]

Arraignment of person charged with a crime.

In certain jurisdictions, defendants may enter a plea that does not admit guilt but nonetheless does not contest the prosecutors' accusation. This form of criminal plea is called *nolo contendere.* Although a nolo plea resembles a guilty plea, it admits only that there is sufficient evidence to convict and, therefore, the defendant will not contest the charge. Significantly, nolo pleas afford defendants protection in civil suits stemming from the same behavior as the criminal conduct, because admissions by way of nolo contendere may not be used as evidence of culpability in civil suits for money damages.[15] However, nolo contendere pleas are not acceptable in capital offenses and some courts will not accept such pleas when imprisonment is mandatory. In some states, nolo contendere pleas are acceptable only in misdemeanor cases.[16] In a highly visible case, Vice President Spiro Agnew in 1973 pleaded nolo contendere to federal charges of income tax evasion. When Agnew was Baltimore county executive and governor of Maryland, he allegedly received bribes from engineers seeking government contracts. As part of a plea bargain, he pleaded no contest to a single criminal charge that he had failed to report $29,500 of income received in 1967, and he was fined $10,000 and placed on probation for three years. Just hours before the imposition of his sentence, Agnew resigned as Vice President of the United States. Though the Internal Revenue Department reserved the right to pursue a civil suit against Agnew for failure to pay back taxes in this and other cases, the nolo contendere plea could not be introduced in subsequent proceedings as evidence that he actually committed any offense because there had been no admission of culpability that could be used in a subsequent civil case.[17]

If the defendant pleads *not guilty*, the prosecution must prove at trial every specific charge in the indictment or information. Upon the entry of the not guilty plea, the court schedules a trial to take place on a certain date. Depending upon the court docket, the trial is usually scheduled within a few months, although this may be the exception rather than the rule. Between the not guilty plea and the start of trial, the defense may file written motions dealing with a wide variety of legal matters, such as the suppression of evidence or a change of venue.

Bail

Before trial, either after arrest or at the arraignment itself, the accused may be released from jail in return for a promise to appear in court as needed. *Bail* may also be granted after conviction pending an appeal. The promise is secured by the payment of money or property. If the defendant does not return to court, the security is forfeited. Most defendants are entitled to bail, with the exception of those accused of a capital offense and those who present a risk of flight if they are released from custody. In most ordinary misdemeanor cases, courts operate under a fixed bail schedule that specifies the precise amounts for each offense. In serious misdemeanor or felony cases, however, the defendant must appear before a court for the setting of bond, at which time the circumstances of each case are carefully scrutinized by the court. The presiding judicial officer takes into consideration the recommendations of both the prosecution and defense counsel.[18]

When the court sets bail, the task of the criminally accused is to figure out how to pay it. Obviously, if the accused has the cash, the easiest way to handle the matter is to pay it in full. Often, however, this is not the case and the defendant, friends, or relatives may post a *property bond*, which is title to property. A third method of raising bond money is to employ the services of a *bail bondsman*, who posts the amount of bail with the court, guaranteeing the appearance of the accused.[19] Bail bondsmen are in business to make a profit. The fee is usually around 10 percent of the bond's face value. Some states have attempted to reduce defendants' reliance upon bail bondsmen by enacting laws permitting the payment of a small percentage of the bond to the court, bypassing bondsmen altogether. Finally, judges may release the accused on their own personal recognizance or the recognizance of another person.[20]

This approach is taken only if the judge believes the accused person is unlikely to flee the jurisdiction.

In a judicial system that assumes a person is innocent until proven guilty, it makes no sense to punish a person through incarceration while awaiting trial without more justification. Although the danger of fleeing the reach of the law is a serious reason for not granting bail, there is increasing discussion about the need to protect society from dangerous persons who might commit additional crimes while out on bail. Unless carefully employed, however, pretrial *preventive detention* schemes may render it difficult for accused persons to plan and mount adequate defenses on their own behalf.

Discovery in Criminal Cases

Due process of law requires that prosecutors comply with defendant attorney requests for evidence that is favorable to their clients. Some courts require complete disclosure of all evidence favorable to the accused, even if requests for specific evidence are not made. On the other hand, defendants need not disclose evidence in their possession because they possess a constitutional *privilege against self-incrimination*. That is, accused persons may not be compelled to testify against themselves—to aid the state in proving the charges against them. Therefore, discovery in criminal processes is very different than in civil law and equity processes.

Court rules spell out the details of disclosure to the accused and to the prosecution. Illinois Practice Rules, for example, are quite explicit. The prosecution must disclose the following: the names and last known addresses of persons whom the state intends to call as witnesses, written or recorded statements pertinent to the case, transcripts of portions of grand jury minutes containing testimony of the accused and relevant testimony of persons the prosecution intends to call as witnesses, reports of expert witnesses including results of scientific evidence, and mental and physical examinations. Moreover, the state is required to inform defense counsel of any electronic surveillance of conversations to which the accused was a party or of the premises of the accused. The rules also permit the defendant's counsel to petition the court for any information not covered by the rule as long as the information in question can be shown to be material to the preparation of the defense.[21]

The most notorious violation in recent years of the federal disclosure rules occurred in connection with the prosecution and conviction of Timothy McVeigh for the April 19, 1995, bombing of the Oklahoma City Federal Building that resulted in the deaths of 168 persons and injury to hundreds more. It was learned just days before McVeigh's scheduled execution in May 2001 that the Federal Bureau of Investiga-

tion had failed to turn over to the defense approximately 4,000 documents in time for his 1997 trial, required of the government under the
Federal Rules of Criminal Procedure. The explanation given was mis-
management of feeble computer systems and inadequate attention to
the basic collection and retrieval of investigative materials.

There are, however, some matters that the prosecution need not
disclose. The *work product* of the prosecution—defined as legal research or memoranda that contain opinions, theories, or conclusions
of the prosecution—is not subject to disclosure. Nor is the identity of
informants required when it is a prosecution secret and a case in which
the constitutional rights of the defendant are not abridged. The same
holds for any person who may be at substantial risk of physical harm,
intimidation, bribery, economic reprisals, or unnecessary annoyance
or embarrassment resulting from the disclosure. The same principle
applies to matters of national security, but once again, the information
may not be disclosed only when it does not infringe the constitutional
rights of the accused.[22]

Although it is true that the protection against self-incrimination affords criminal defendants rights in discovery not enjoyed by the prosecution, persons accused of crimes must nonetheless make disclosures
that do not infringe upon their rights. Under Illinois court rules, for example, persons accused of crimes may be required by a judicial officer
to appear in a line-up and speak for witness identification purposes.
Further, they may be fingerprinted, be forced to pose for photographs,
and asked to try on articles of clothing. The law also permits the prosecution to require defendants to make themselves available for the taking of specimens of materials under their fingernails; the taking of sam-
ples of blood, hair, and urine; providing a sample of handwriting; and
submitting to reasonable physical or medical inspection of their bodies. Subject to constitutional limitations, the prosecution has a right to
examine physical, mental, or other scientific evidence of expert witnesses if defense counsel intends to use it at a hearing or trial.

In all situations, defendants have a right to reasonable notice and
the assistance of legal counsel. Additionally, defense counsels are under
an affirmative duty to inform prosecutors of any defenses they may intend to employ at a hearing or trial. Defense attorneys must also provide the names and last known addresses of persons they intend to call
as witnesses, together with any books, papers, documents, or other materials they intend to introduce as evidence or for the impeachment of
witnesses at a hearing or trial. If a defendant intends to offer an alibi,
counsel is required to provide specific information about the place
where the defendant was at the time of the alleged crime. In the event
that witnesses may not be present at the hearing or trial, a deposition
may be taken if it is relevant for the preservation of testimony.[23]

Trial Phase of Criminal Processes

The most obvious difference between criminal and civil processes is that in the criminal law, the standard of proof necessary to convict defendants is guilt *beyond a reasonable doubt*. Although the reasonable doubt test does not mean 100 percent certainty, it does mean that triers of fact are firmly convinced that the defendant is guilty of the crime as charged. They cannot be absolutely sure because in life few if any issues are absolutely sure. Besides a guilty plea, there is no more absolute certainty than the reasonable doubt test. Clearly, the standard of proof in criminal cases is considerably greater than plaintiffs must shoulder in civil cases or in equity disputes when a preponderance of the evidence or weight of the evidence (clear and convincing) tests are the legal requirements.

Various provisions of the U.S. Bill of Rights guarantee basic rights designed to insure a fair trial for those who are accused of crimes in federal prosecutions. The U.S. Supreme Court has made these rights applicable to the states through interpretations of the Due Process Clause of the Fourteenth Amendment. Furthermore, many state constitutions and laws also guarantee these identical rights. The most basic of these rights are the right to an attorney, the right to a fair and impartial trial, the right to a trial by jury, the right to a speedy and public trial, the right against self-incrimination, and the right to confront witnesses.

Right to Counsel

If an accused cannot afford the services of a private attorney, the court must appoint one. This right applies to capital and noncapital felony cases and to all misdemeanor cases in which a person may be imprisoned. Defendants, however, have a constitutional right to defend themselves without the services of an attorney.

The basic constitutional principle underlying the right to counsel was spelled out in Gideon v. Wainwright, 372 U.S. 335 (1963). Clarence Gideon was convicted of a felony for breaking into a pool hall with the intent to commit a crime. At his Florida trial, Gideon, an indigent, requested that the court appoint him legal counsel. Under Florida law, however, he was not entitled to appointed counsel. The trial judge indicated that under Florida law, indigents are entitled to appointed counsel only in capital cases. Subsequently, Gideon represented himself to no avail, and while serving a five-year prison sentence he petitioned the Florida Supreme Court for relief. He then successfully asked the U.S. Supreme Court for a new trial. Overruling precedent, the nation's high court ruled that Gideon was not afforded the fundamental Sixth Amendment right to effective legal counsel and that the right is obligatory on the states through the Due Process Clause of the Fourteenth

Amendment. The holding in this case rests upon the empirical observation that the adversarial system generally, and the criminal justice system in particular, presupposes that each side in a legal contest must be able to mount a credible presentation in support of its positions. Without the aid of trained legal counsel to defend the accused, the awesome power of government may be used to place otherwise innocent persons in prison.

There is no uniform rule for determining indigency. Judges employ wide discretion and they look at such things as unemployment and the lack of housing or other possessions, such as an automobile. In some cases, judges find persons indigent if they cannot post bail. More than half of all defendants charged with felonies are indigent.[24]

Since the Supreme Court's 1963 decision in *Gideon v. Wainwright*, programs to assist indigents have grown dramatically. Local *public defender* programs operate in 32 states and 15 states operate statewide programs. More common in highly populated venues, these programs provide full-time or part-time attorneys for indigent representation. In the alternative, *assigned counsel programs* are systems where private attorneys are appointed to represent indigent defendants as needed. In some assigned counsel programs, judges appoint attorneys as needed on an ad hoc basis, and in others there is a coordinated system with an administrator overseeing the program. Finally, in smaller counties around the country, governments contract with individual attorneys, law firms, or bar associations to represent indigents. These *contract systems* are also used in some counties to ease the burden on public defenders. Also, with the goal of avoiding possible conflicting defenses, some county governments use contract lawyers when the public defender's office represents a codefendant.[25]

Criminal bar. Among attorneys, criminal practice is widely regarded as extremely arduous with few rewards. Especially in the large urban centers, criminal lawyers in private practice are often solo practitioners or function in small firms requiring them to work long hours interviewing clients, conducting investigations, making court appearances, and filing appropriate motions with courts. Although there are celebrated exceptions in which clients are wealthy, as in the O. J. Simpson trial, criminal defendants are typically poor with few if any resources of their own. When they are forced to track down information, attorneys sometimes find themselves in dangerous neighborhoods dealing with unsavory characters. To meet their expenses, criminal attorneys in private practice hope to generate other business from their clients and their friends and relatives, including tort cases that may yield substantial contingency fees, divorce actions, and relatively quick and easy bankruptcy filings. Thus, even though criminal law practice is highly romanticized in our public entertainment, one study found that most interviewed criminal lawyers indicate they harbor serious doubts and regrets about choosing the criminal law as an area of specialization.[26] At the same time, many criminal defense attorneys enjoy the "action," and they also view themselves as the last bastion against the oppressive use of government power.

Right to a Fair and Impartial Trial

Ideally, jury members should approach their task with an open mind and with a willingness to treat defendants as innocent until proven guilty. Yet, as human beings, jurors have certain attitudes and values. If stimulated, these may cause them to base their judgment upon considerations not litigated at the trial, or otherwise to base their consideration of guilt or innocence on matters that inhibit their ability to make decisions free from prejudice. Especially in the modern age of the 24-hour news cycle, media attention to high-profile cases may prevent a fair trial within communities where crimes are committed. Because the Fifth and Fourteenth Amendments require a fair and impartial trial, judges are required to take action when achieving this goal is in serious question.

A judge may order a *change of venue* that moves the trial to a place within the same jurisdiction, where it is less likely that potential jurors have already made up their minds or had their judgments impaired by excessive publicity. Alternatively, a judge may order a *continuance*, which postpones the trial until a later date after the most intense publicity falls from public view. Before and during trial, the presiding judge may issue a *gag order*. This prohibits the police, the prosecution, the defense, the witnesses, and members of the jury from speaking to others about the case before or during the proceedings. It is constitutionally impermissible to stop the press from publishing stories about investigations or trials. Yet, in cooperation with the criminal justice system, some media organizations choose not to release information that the public need not know about defendants and the details of cases while trials are pending. The case of *Sheppard v. Maxwell* provided the occasion for a landmark U.S. Supreme Court opinion, pitting one constitutional right against another—fair trial and freedom of the press. This celebrated case was the inspiration for the long-running television drama, and later a feature motion picture starring Harrison Ford, called *The Fugitive*.

Sheppard v. Maxwell
United States Supreme Court
384 U.S. 333, 86 S.Ct. 1507, 16 L.Ed.2d 600 (1966)

OPINION BY: JUSTICE CLARK. This federal habeas corpus application involves the question whether Sheppard was deprived of a fair trial in his state conviction for the second-degree murder of his wife because of the trial judge's failure to protect Sheppard sufficiently from the massive, pervasive and prejudicial publicity that attended his prosecution. . . . We granted certiorari. We have concluded that Sheppard did not receive a fair trial consistent with the Due Process Clause of the Fourteenth Amendment and, therefore, reverse the judgment.

Marilyn Sheppard, petitioner's pregnant wife, was bludgeoned to death in the upstairs bedroom of their home in Bay Village, Ohio, a suburb of Cleveland. On the day of the tragedy, July 4, 1954, Sheppard pieced together for several local officials the following story: He and his wife had entertained neighborhood friends . . . on the previous evening at their home. After dinner they watched television in the living room. Sheppard became drowsy and dozed off to sleep on a couch. Later, Marilyn partially awoke him saying that she was going to bed. The next thing he remembered was hearing his wife cry out in the early morning hours. He hurried upstairs and in the dim light from the hall saw a "form" standing next to his wife's bed. As he struggled with the "form" he was struck on the back of the neck and rendered unconscious. On regaining his senses he found himself on the floor next to his wife's bed. He rose, looked at her, took her pulse and "felt that she was gone." He then went to his son's room and found him unmolested. Hearing a noise he hurried downstairs. He saw a "form" running out the door and pursued it to the lake shore. He grappled with it on the beach and again lost consciousness. Upon his recovery he was lying face down with the lower portion of his body in the water. He returned to his home, checked the pulse on his wife's

neck, and "determined or thought that she was gone." He then went downstairs and called a neighbor, Mayor Houk of Bay Village. . . . The local police were the first to arrive. They in turn notified the Coroner and Cleveland police. . . . When the Coroner, the Cleveland police and other officials arrived, the house and surrounding area were thoroughly searched, the rooms of the house were photographed, and many persons . . . were interrogated. The Sheppard home and premises were taken into "protective custody" and remained so until after the trial. . . .

From the outset officials focused suspicion on Sheppard. After a search of the house and premises on the morning of the tragedy, Dr. Gerber, the Coroner, is reported—and it is undenied—to have told his men, "Well, it is evident the doctor did this, so let's go get the confession out of him." He proceeded to interrogate and examine Sheppard while the latter was under sedation in his hospital room. . . .

On July 9, Sheppard, at the request of the Coroner, re-enacted the tragedy at his home before the Coroner, police officers, and a group of newsmen, who apparently were invited by the Coroner. The home was locked so that Sheppard was obliged to wait outside until the Coroner arrived. Sheppard's performance was reported in detail by the news media along with photographs. The newspapers also played up Sheppard's refusal to take a lie detector test and "the protective ring" thrown up by his family. . . .

On the 20th, the "editorial artillery" opened fire with a front-page charge that somebody is "getting away with murder." The editorial attributed the ineptness of the investigation to "friendships, relationships, hired lawyers, a husband who ought to have been subjected instantly to the same third-degree to which any other person under similar circumstances is subjected. . . ." The following day, July 21, another page-one editorial was headed: "Why No Inquest? Do It Now, Dr. Gerber." The Coroner called an inquest the same day and subpoenaed Sheppard. It was staged the next day in a school gymnasium; the Coroner presided with the County Prosecutor as his advisor and two detectives as bailiffs. In the front of the room was a long table occupied by reporters, television and radio personnel, and broadcasting equipment. The hearing was broadcast with live microphones placed at the Coroner's seat and the witness stand. A swarm of reporters and photographers attended. Sheppard was brought into the room by police who searched him in full view of several hundred spectators. Sheppard's counsels were present during the three-day inquest but were not permitted to participate. When Sheppard's chief counsel attempted to place some documents in the record, he was forcibly ejected from the room by the Coroner, who received cheers, hugs, and kisses from ladies in the audience. Sheppard was questioned for five and one-half hours about his actions on the night of the murder, his married life, and a love affair with Susan Hayes. At the end of the hearing the Coroner announced that he "could" order Sheppard held for the grand jury, but did not do so.

Throughout this period the newspapers emphasized evidence that tended to incriminate Sheppard and pointed out discrepancies in his statements to authorities. At the same time, Sheppard made many public statements to the press and wrote feature articles asserting his innocence. . . .

A front-page editorial on July 30 asked: "Why Isn't Sam Sheppard in Jail?" It was later titled "Quit Stalling—Bring Him In." After calling Sheppard "the most unusual murder suspect ever seen around these parts" the article said that "except for some superficial questioning during Coroner Sam Gerber's inquest he has been scot-free of any official grilling. . . ." It asserted that he was "surrounded by an iron curtain of protection [and] concealment."

That night at 10 o'clock Sheppard was arrested at his father's home on a charge of murder. He was taken to the Bay Village City Hall where hundreds of people, newscasters, photographers and reporters were awaiting his arrival. He was immediately arraigned—having been denied a temporary delay to secure the presence of counsel—and bound over to the grand jury.

The publicity then grew in intensity until his indictment on August 17. Typical of the coverage during this period is a front-page interview entitled: "DR. SAM: 'I Wish There Was Something I Could Get Off My Chest—But There Isn't.'" Unfavorable publicity included items such as a cartoon of the body of a sphinx with Sheppard's head and the legend below: "'I Will Do Everything in My Power to Help Solve This Terrible Murder.'—Dr. Sam Sheppard." Headlines announced, *inter alia,* that: "Doctor Evidence Is Ready for Jury," "Corrigan Tactics Stall Quizzing," "Sheppard 'Gay Set' Is Revealed by Houk," "Blood Is Found in Garage," "New Murder Evidence Is Found, Police Claim," "Dr. Sam Faces Quiz At Jail On Marilyn's Fear Of Him." On

August 18, an article appeared under the headline "Dr. Sam Writes His Own Story." And reproduced across the entire front page was a portion of the typed statement signed by Sheppard: "I am not guilty of the murder of my wife, Marilyn. How could I, who have been trained to help people and devoted my life to saving life, commit such a terrible and revolting crime?" We do not detail the coverage further. There are five volumes filled with similar clippings from each of the three Cleveland newspapers covering the period from the murder until Sheppard's conviction in December 1954. The record includes no excerpts from newscasts on radio and television but since space was reserved in the courtroom for these media we assume that their coverage was equally large.

With this background the case came on for trial two weeks before the November general election at which the chief prosecutor was a candidate for common pleas judge and the trial judge, Judge Blythin, was a candidate to succeed himself. Twenty-five days before the case was set, 75 veniremen were called as prospective jurors. All three Cleveland newspapers published the names and addresses of the veniremen. As a consequence, anonymous letters and telephone calls, as well as calls from friends, regarding the impending prosecution were received by all of the prospective jurors. The selection of the jury began on October 18, 1954.

The courtroom in which the trial was held measured 26 by 48 feet. A long temporary table was set up inside the bar, in back of the single counsel table. It ran the width of the courtroom, parallel to the bar railing, with one end less than three feet

from the jury box. Approximately 20 representatives of newspapers and wire services were assigned seats at this table by the court. Behind the bar railing there were four rows of benches. These seats were likewise assigned by the court for the entire trial. The first row was occupied by representatives of television and radio stations, and the second and third rows by reporters from out-of-town newspapers and magazines. One side of the last row, which accommodated 14 people, was assigned to Sheppard's family and the other to Marilyn's. The public was permitted to fill vacancies in this row on special passes only. Representatives of the news media also used all the rooms on the courtroom floor, including the room where cases were ordinarily called and assigned for trial. Private telephone lines and telegraphic equipment were installed in these rooms so that reports from the trial could be speeded to the papers. Station WSRS was permitted to set up broadcasting facilities on the third floor of the courthouse next door to the jury room, where the jury rested during recesses in the trial and deliberated. Newscasts were made from this room throughout the trial, and while the jury reached its verdict.

On the sidewalk and steps in front of the courthouse, television and newsreel cameras were occasionally used to take motion pictures of the participants in the trial, including the jury and the judge. Indeed, one television broadcast carried a staged interview of the judge as he entered the courthouse. In the corridors outside the courtroom there was a host of photographers and television personnel with flash cameras, portable lights and motion picture cameras. This group photographed the prospective jurors during selection of the jury. After the trial opened, the witnesses, counsel, and jurors were photographed and televised whenever they entered or left the courtroom. Sheppard was brought to the courtroom about 10 minutes before each session began; he was surrounded by reporters and extensively photographed for the newspapers and television. A rule of court prohibited picture-taking in the courtroom during the actual sessions of the court, but no restraints were put on photographers during recesses, which were taken once each morning and afternoon, with a longer period for lunch.

We now reach the conduct of the trial. While the intense publicity continued unabated, it is sufficient to relate only the more flagrant episodes:

1. On October 9, 1954, nine days before the case went to trial, an editorial in one of the newspapers criticized defense counsel's random poll of people on the streets as to their opinion of Sheppard's guilt or innocence in an effort to use the resulting statistics to show the necessity for change of venue. The article said the survey "smacks of mass jury tampering," called on defense counsel to drop it, and stated that the bar association should do something about it. It characterized the poll as "non-judicial, non-legal, and nonsense." The article was called to the attention of the court but no action was taken.

2. On the second day of *voir dire* examination a debate was staged and broadcast live over WHK radio. The participants, newspaper reporters, accused Sheppard's counsel of throwing roadblocks in the way of the prosecution and asserted that Sheppard conceded his guilt by hiring a prominent criminal lawyer. Sheppard's counsel objected to this broadcast and requested a continuance, but the judge denied the motion. When counsel asked the court to give some protection from such events, the judge replied that "WHK doesn't have much coverage," and that "after all, we are not trying this case by radio or in newspapers or any other means. We confine ourselves seriously to it in this courtroom and do the very best we can."

3. While the jury was being selected, a two-inch headline asked: "But Who Will Speak for Marilyn?" The front-page story spoke of the "perfect face" of the accused. "Study that face as long as you want. Never will you get from it a hint of what might be the answer. . . ." The two brothers of the accused were described as "Prosperous, poised. His two sisters-in law. Smart, chic, well-groomed. His elderly father. Courtly, reserved. A perfect type for the patriarch of a staunch clan." The author then noted Marilyn Sheppard was "still off stage," and that she was an only child whose mother died when she was very young and whose father had no interest in the case. But the author—through quotes from Detective Chief James McArthur—assured readers that the prosecution's exhibits would speak for Marilyn. "Her story," McArthur stated, "will come into this courtroom through our witnesses." . . .

4. As has been mentioned, the jury viewed the scene of the murder on the first day of the trial. Hundreds of reporters, cameramen and onlookers were there, and one representative of the news media was permitted to accompany the jury while it inspected the Sheppard home. The time of the jury's visit was revealed so

far in advance that one of the news-papers was able to rent a helicopter and fly over the house taking pictures of the jurors on their tour.

5. On November 19, a Cleveland police officer gave testimony that tended to contradict details in the written statement Sheppard made to the Cleveland police. Two days later, in a broadcast heard over Station WHK in Cleveland, Robert Considine likened Sheppard to a perjurer and compared the episode to Alger Hiss' confrontation with Whittaker Chambers. Though defense counsel asked the judge to question the jury to ascertain how many heard the broadcast, the court refused to do so. The judge also overruled the motion for continuance based on the same ground, saying:

"Well, I don't know, we can't stop people, in any event, listening to it. It is a matter of free speech, and the court can't control everybody. . . . We are not going to harass the jury every morning. . . . It is getting to the point where if we do it every morning, we are suspecting the jury. I have confidence in this jury. . . ."

6. On November 24, a story appeared under an eight-column headline: "Sam Called A 'Jekyll-Hyde' By Marilyn, Cousin To Testify." It related that Marilyn had recently told friends that Sheppard was a "Dr. Jekyll and Mr. Hyde" character. No such testimony was ever produced at the trial. The story went on to announce: "The prosecution has a 'bombshell witness' on tap who will testify to Dr. Sam's display of fiery temper—countering the defense claim that the defendant is a gentle physician with an even disposition." Defense counsel made motions for change of venue, continuance and mistrial, but they were denied. No action was taken by the court.

7. When the trial was in its seventh week, Walter Winchell broadcast over WXEL television and WJW radio that Carole Beasley, who was under arrest in New York City for robbery, had stated that, as Sheppard's mistress, she had borne him a child. The defense asked that the jury be queried on the broadcast. Two jurors admitted in open court that they had heard it. The judge asked each: "Would that have any effect upon your judgment? " Both replied, "No." This was accepted by the judge as sufficient; he merely asked the jury to "pay no attention whatever to that type of scavenging. . . . Let's confine ourselves to this courtroom, if you please."

8. On December 9, while Sheppard was on the witness stand he testified that he had been mistreated by Cleveland detectives after his arrest. Although he was not at the trial, Captain Kerr of the Homicide Bureau issued a press statement denying Sheppard's allegations which appeared under the headline: "'Bare-faced Liar,' Kerr Says of Sam." Captain Kerr never appeared as a witness at the trial.

9. After the case was submitted to the jury, it was sequestered for its deliberations, which took five days and four nights. After the verdict, defense counsel ascertained that the jurors had been allowed to make telephone calls to their homes every day while they were sequestered at the hotel. Although the telephones had been removed from the jurors' rooms, the jurors were permitted to use the phones in the bailiffs' rooms. The calls were placed by the jurors themselves; no record was kept of the jurors who made calls, the tele-

phone numbers or the parties called. The bailiffs sat in the room where they could hear only the jurors' end of the conversation. The court had not instructed the bailiffs to prevent such calls. By a subsequent motion, defense counsel urged that this ground alone warranted a new trial, but the motion was overruled and no evidence was taken on the question.

The principle that justice cannot survive behind walls of silence has long been reflected in the "Anglo-American distrust for secret trials." . . . A responsible press has always been regarded as the handmaiden of effective judicial administration, especially in the criminal field. Its function in this regard is documented by an impressive record of service over several centuries. The press does not simply publish information about trials but guards against the miscarriage of justice by subjecting the police, prosecutors, and judicial processes to extensive public scrutiny and criticism. This Court has, therefore, been unwilling to place any direct limitations on the freedom traditionally exercised by the news media for "what transpires in the court room is public property." . . . And where there was "no threat or menace to the integrity of the trial," . . . we have consistently required that the press have a free hand, even though we sometimes deplored its sensationalism.

But the Court has also pointed out that "legal trials are not like elections, to be won through the use of the meeting-hall, the radio, and the newspaper." . . . "Freedom of discussion should be given the widest range compatible with the essential requirement of the fair and orderly administration of justice." . . . But it must not be allowed to divert the trial from the "very purpose of a court system . . . to adjudicate controversies, both criminal and civil, in the calmness and solemnity of the courtroom according to legal procedures.". . . Among these "legal procedures" is the requirement that the jury's verdict be based on evidence received in open court, not from outside sources. . . .

From the cases coming here we note that unfair and prejudicial news comment on pending trials has become increasingly prevalent. Due process requires that the accused receive a trial by an impartial jury free from outside influences. Given the pervasiveness of modern communications and the difficulty of effacing prejudicial publicity from the minds of the jurors, the trial courts must take strong measures to ensure that the balance is never weighed against the accused. And appellate tribunals have the duty to make an independent evaluation of the circumstances. Of course, there is nothing that proscribes the press from reporting events that transpire in the courtroom. But where there is a reasonable likelihood that prejudicial news prior to trial will prevent a fair trial, the judge should continue the case until the threat abates, or transfer it to another county not so permeated with publicity. In addition, sequestration of the jury was something the judge should have raised *sua sponte* with counsel. If publicity during the proceedings threatens the fairness of the trial, a new trial should be ordered. But we must remember that reversals are but palliatives; the cure lies in those remedial measures that will prevent the prejudice at its inception. The courts must take such steps by rule and regulation that will protect their processes from prejudicial outside interferences. Neither prosecutors, counsel for defense, the accused, witnesses, court staff nor enforcement officers coming under the jurisdiction of the court should be permitted to frustrate its function. Collaboration between counsel and the press as to information affecting the fairness of a criminal trial is not only subject to regulation, but is highly censurable and worthy of disciplinary measures. Since the state trial judge did not fulfill his duty to protect Sheppard from the inherently prejudicial publicity which saturated the community and to control disruptive influences in the courtroom, we must reverse the denial of the habeas petition. The case is remanded to the District Court with instructions to issue the writ and order that Sheppard be released from custody unless the State puts him to its charges again within a reasonable time.

It is so ordered.

MR. JUSTICE BLACK dissents.

Case Questions for Discussion

1. Does the Court in *Sheppard v. Maxwell* treat either the freedom of the press or the right to a fair trial as absolutes? How must a court interpret competing constitutional rights?

2. Do the media owe a special duty to the public to report all events surrounding criminal matters, including pretrial activity?

3. Do you favor cameras in the courtroom and why?

4. Had O. J. Simpson been convicted, do you think he may have had a *Sheppard* issue at the appellate level?

Right to a Jury Trial

Two specific constitutional provisions guarantee a right to trial by jury in criminal cases. Article III, section 2, clause 3 provides for the trials of federal crimes except in cases of impeachment, and the Sixth Amendment provides for a jury trial in the states and districts where crimes are committed. The Due Process Clause of the Fourteenth Amendment makes this Sixth Amendment guarantee applicable to the states. Yet, the U.S. Supreme Court in Baldwin v. New York, 399 U.S. 66 (1970), held that the right to a jury trial extends only when there is a "serious charge" as opposed to a "petty offense." This is true even if the actual sentence is six months or less in prison. In contradistinction to a petty offense, if the maximum penalty that may result from a prosecution is more than six months in jail, then by definition it is a serious offense. Sometimes defendants are persuaded that they are likely to receive better treatment at the hands of a judge. They may *waive* their right to a jury trial, if the waiver is given freely and intelligently.[27] With the consent of presiding judges, prosecutors at times bargain with defendants to waive incarceration as a penalty in exchange for a jury waiver. They do so because jury trials expend considerable prosecutorial effort, time, and resources, and because juries are less predictable than judges, who are usually well-known to prosecutors.

Right to a Speedy and Public Trial

Without speedy trials, persons might languish in jail for months and years while their families, fortunes, and reputations fall into ruin. From a law enforcement perspective, moreover, those persons released on bond, and who are awaiting trial for extended periods of time, are in a position to commit additional crimes and even to flee from the court's jurisdiction. Although the U.S. Supreme Court has failed to prescribe actual time limits, the Sixth and Fourteenth Amendments require that in all criminal prosecutions, the accused shall enjoy the right to a speedy trial. This constitutional guarantee is not interpreted to outlaw simple delay, but rather it applies to delays that are unnecessary and unwarranted.

Many states have enacted statutes that require trials within a specified number of days after arraignment. In 1974, Congress enacted the Speedy Trial Act, 18 U.S.C. §§ 3161–74, requiring that criminal trials commence sixty days after arraignment. However, this and similar acts in the states have contributed to a backlog of civil cases. Because the courts have a duty to provide for speedy criminal trials and because there has been a huge increase in criminal cases, due in large part to the growth in recent decades of drug-related prosecutions, suits for money damages and other judicial remedies can in some instances take years to come to trial.[28] In some jurisdictions, however, this problem has been remedied, in part, by placing civil and criminal cases on separate dockets and systems, and the use of alternative dispute resolution techniques.

History teaches that trials conducted in secret present problems of fairness and justice. The best disinfectant for despotism is a government whose operations are open for public inspection. The Sixth and Fourteenth Amendments guarantee trials that are open to the public. Yet, in some instances, courtroom spectators may be excluded from trial. When the presence of certain spectators may intimidate witnesses and prevent them from testifying easily, judges have been known to exclude them from the courtroom. In cases involving sexual abuse of children, spectators have been barred from the courtroom, particularly when children are on the witness stand. Assuming proper decorum, close friends and relatives of the accused are ordinarily allowed in the courtroom.[29] The Bush Administration regulations sanctioning secret military trials of suspected terrorists has been met with opposition from some quarters as a denial of the prohibition against secret trials. It surely raises the question of whether fundamental American principles apply in times of "emergency."

Modern mass media now make it possible for the public to observe trials. The press has long advocated such access, but some jurists are opposed to "cameras in the courtroom" because they fear that attorneys and witnesses will play to the cameras and turn trials into circuses. Yet, America's growing experience with televised court proceedings argues well for expanding coverage. The trial of O. J. Simpson served to educate the country on many aspects of the criminal justice system, and the people of the nation and the world were captivated by the television coverage of the Florida trial and appellate courts in the vote-counting cases growing out of the November 2000 presidential election.

Privilege Against Self-Incrimination

Readers know from our discussion about discovery proceedings that accused persons are protected from revealing incriminating information about themselves, although there are exceptions relating to physical as opposed to communicative self-incrimination. The stock phrase is that the defendant "may stand mute, clothed in the presumption of innocence." Both defendants and witnesses enjoy the right against self-incrimination. If at any time during the direct or cross-examination they are asked questions that would implicate them in a crime, they have a right to invoke this Fifth Amendment protection. However, when defendants take the stand in their own behalf, the privilege is waived and they are subject to cross-examination. To the extent of their direct testimony, they must respond to all pertinent questions on cross-examination about their alleged crimes. In civil matters, the privilege against self-incrimination applies only when criminal culpability may be implicated in a question asked during direct or cross-examination. Ordinarily, criminal liability does not pertain in civil suits for money damages or in equity, and parties and witnesses are expected to be forthcoming during examination by legal counsels.

Confrontation of Witnesses

Defendants, through their attorneys, may cross-examine witnesses against them. They also have the right to be physically present in the courtroom when witnesses are testifying against them. Defendants may be removed from the courtroom, however, if they behave in a disrespectful or disorderly manner. Judges are also known to go to great lengths to maintain order in their courtrooms. U.S. District Court Judge Julius J. Hoffman ordered Bobby Seale, a leader of the Black Panther Party, to be gagged and tied to a chair during the famous Chicago Eight Trial growing out of demonstrations at the 1968 Democratic Party Convention held in Chicago. During the course of the proceedings, Seale and Judge Hoffman became embroiled in bitter conflict when Seale accused Hoffman of racism in denying his motion for a postponement until counsel of his choice might be present. Seale's rhetoric escalated, calling the judge not only a racist but also a fascist and a pig. Finally, Judge Hoffman ordered Seale bound and gagged. The vivid image of this black defendant subjected to what attorney William Kunstler called "medieval torture" reverberates throughout the African American and progressive communities even today.[30]

The U.S. Supreme Court held in Coy v. Iowa, 487 U.S. 1012 (1988), that screening of the defendant from the view of a youthful witness in a sex abuse trial violated the defendant's constitutional right to confront the witnesses against him. A few years later, however, in *Maryland v. Craig*, the high court carved out an exception to the general rule when it permitted a child to offer testimony in another room while the judge, jury, and defendant remained in the main courtroom viewing the testimony over closed-circuit television.

Maryland v. Craig
U.S. Supreme Court
497 U.S. 836, 110 S.Ct. 3157, 111 L.Ed.2d 666 (1990)

OPINION BY: JUSTICE O'CONNOR.

This case requires us to decide whether the Confrontation Clause of the Sixth Amendment categorically prohibits a child witness in a child abuse case from testifying against a defendant at trial, outside the defendant's physical presence, by one-way closed circuit television. . . .

We have never held . . . that the Confrontation Clause guarantees criminal defendants the *absolute* right to a face-to-face meeting with witnesses against them at trial. Indeed, in *Coy v. Iowa* we expressly "left for another day . . . the question whether any exceptions exist" to the "irreducible literal meaning of the Clause: 'a right to *meet face to face* all those who appear and give evidence *at trial*.'" 487 U.S. at 1021. . . . The procedure challenged in *Coy* involved the placement of a screen that prevented two child witnesses in a child abuse case from seeing the defendant as

they testified against him at trial. . . . In holding that the use of this procedure violated the defendant's right to confront witnesses against him, we suggested that any exception to the right "would surely be allowed only when necessary to further an important public policy"—i.e., only upon a showing of something more than the generalized, "legislatively imposed presumption of trauma" underlying the statute at issue in that case. . . . We concluded that "since there had been no individualized findings that these particular witnesses needed special protection, the judgment [in the case before us] could not be sustained by any conceivable exception." Id., at 1021. Because the trial court in this case made individualized findings that each of the child witnesses needed special protection, this case requires us to decide the question reserved in *Coy*.

The central concern of the Confrontation Clause is to ensure the reliability of the evidence against a criminal defendant by subjecting it to rigorous testing in the context of an adversary proceeding before the trier of fact. The word "confront," after all, also means a clashing of forces or ideas, thus carrying with it the notion of adversariness. . . .

[T]he right guaranteed by the Confrontation Clause includes not only a "personal examination,". . . but also "(1) insures that the witness will give his statements under oath—thus impressing him with the seriousness of the matter and guarding against the lie by the possibility of a penalty for perjury; (2) forces the witness to submit to cross-examination, the 'greatest legal engine ever invented for the discovery of truth'; [and] (3) permits the jury to decide the defendant's fate to observe the demeanor of the witness in making his statement, thus aiding the jury in assessing his credibility." . . .

. . . [This Court] never insisted on an actual face-to-face encounter at trial in *every* instance in which testimony is admitted against a defendant. Instead, we have repeatedly held that the Clause permits, where necessary, the admission of certain hearsay statements against a defendant despite the defendant's inability to confront the declarant at trial. . . . We have accordingly stated that a literal reading of the Confrontation Clause would "abrogate virtually every hearsay exception, a result long rejected as unintended and too extreme." Roberts, 448 U.S. at 63. Thus, in certain narrow circumstances, "competing interests, if 'closely examined,' may warrant dispensing with confrontation at trial." Id., at 64. We have recently held, for example, that hearsay statements of non-testifying co-conspirators may be admitted against a defendant despite the lack of any face-to-face encounter with the accused. . . . Given our hearsay cases, the word "confronted," as used in the Confrontation Clause, cannot simply mean face-to-face confrontation, for the Clause would then, contrary to our cases, prohibit the admission of any accusatory hearsay statement made by an absent declarant—a declarant who is undoubtedly as much a "witness against" a defendant as one who actually testifies at trial.

In sum, our precedents establish that "the Confrontation Clause reflects a *preference* for face-to-face confrontation at trial," Roberts, supra, at 63, a preference that "must occasionally give way to considerations of public policy and the necessities of the case,". . . "We have attempted to harmonize the goal of the Clause—placing limits on the kind of evidence that may be received against a defendant—with a societal interest in accurate fact finding, which may require consideration of out-of-court statements.". . .

Maryland's statutory procedure, when invoked, prevents a child witness from seeing the defendant as he or she testifies against the defendant at trial. We find it significant, however, that Maryland's procedure preserves all of the other elements of the confrontation right: The child witness must be competent to testify and must testify under oath; the defendant retains full opportunity for contemporaneous cross-examination; and the judge, jury, and defendant are able to view (albeit by video monitor) the demeanor (and body) of the witness as he or she testifies. Although we are mindful of the many subtle effects face-to-face confrontation may have on an adversary criminal proceeding, the presence of these other elements of confrontation—oath, cross-examination, and observation of the witness' demeanor—adequately ensures that the testimony is both reliable and subject to rigorous adversarial testing in a manner functionally equivalent to that accorded live, in-person testimony. These safeguards of reliability and adversariness render the use of such a procedure a far cry from the undisputed prohibition of the Confrontation Clause: trial by *ex parte* affidavit or inquisition. . . . Rather, we think these elements of effective confrontation not only permit a defendant to "confound and undo the false accuser, or reveal the child coached by a malevolent adult," Coy, supra, 487 U.S. at 1020, but may well aid a defendant in eliciting favorable testimony from the child witness. Indeed, to the extent the child witness' testimony may be said to be technically given out of court (though we do not so hold), these assurances of reliability and adversariness are far greater than those required for admission of hearsay testimony under the Confrontation Clause. . . . We are therefore confident that use of the one-way closed circuit television procedure, where necessary to further an important state interest, does not impinge upon the truth-seeking or symbolic purposes of the Confrontation Clause.

The critical inquiry in this case, therefore, is whether use of the procedure is necessary to further an important state interest. The State contends that it has a substantial interest in protecting children who are allegedly victims of child abuse from the trauma of testifying against the alleged perpetrator and that its statutory procedure for receiving testimony from such witnesses is necessary to further that interest.

. . . Given the State's traditional and " 'transcendent interest in protecting the welfare of children,'" (Ginsberg, 390 U.S. at 640), and buttressed by the growing body of academic literature documenting the psychological trauma suffered by child abuse victims who must testify in court, . . . we will not second-guess the considered judgment of the Maryland Legislature regarding the importance of its interest in protecting child abuse victims from the emotional trauma of testifying. Accordingly, we hold that, if the State makes an adequate showing of necessity, the state interest in protecting child witnesses from the trauma of testifying in a child abuse case is sufficiently important to justify the use of a special procedure that permits a child witness in such cases to testify at trial against a defendant in the absence of face-to-face confrontation with the defendant.

The requisite finding of necessity must of course be a case-specific one: The trial court must hear evidence and determine whether use of the one-way closed circuit television procedure is necessary to protect the welfare of the particular child witness who seeks to testify. . . . The trial court must also find that the child witness would be traumatized, not by the courtroom generally, but by the presence of the defendant. . . . Denial of face-to-face confrontation is not needed to further the state interest in protecting the child witness from trauma unless it is the presence of the defendant that causes the trauma. In other words, if the state interest were merely the interest in protecting child witnesses from courtroom trauma generally, denial of face-to-face confrontation would be unnecessary because the child could be permitted to testify in less intimidating surroundings, albeit with the defendant present. Finally, the trial court must find that the emotional distress suffered by the child witness in the presence of the defendant is more than *de minimis*, i. e., more than "mere nervousness or excitement or some reluctance to testify," at 524, 530 A.2d at 289; . . . We need not decide the minimum showing of emotional trauma required for use of the special procedure, however, because the Maryland statute, which requires a determination that the child witness will suffer "serious emotional distress such that the child cannot reasonably communicate," . . . clearly suffices to meet constitutional standards. . . .

In sum, we conclude that where necessary to protect a child witness from trauma that would be caused by testifying in the physical presence of the defendant, at least where such trauma would impair the child's ability to communicate, the Confrontation Clause does not prohibit use of a procedure that, despite the absence of face-to-face confrontation, ensures the reliability of the evidence by subjecting it to rigorous adversarial testing and thereby preserves the essence of effective confrontation. Because there is no dispute that the child witnesses in this case testified under oath, were subject to full cross-examination, and were able to be observed by the judge, jury, and defendant as they testified, we conclude that, to the extent that a proper finding of necessity has been made, the admission of such testimony would be consonant with the Confrontation Clause.

. . . We therefore vacate the judgment of the Court of Appeals of Maryland and remand the case for further proceedings not inconsistent with this opinion.

It is so ordered.

DISSENT: JUSTICE SCALIA, with whom JUSTICE BRENNAN, JUSTICE MARSHALL, and JUSTICE STEVENS join.

Seldom has this Court failed so conspicuously to sustain a categorical guarantee of the Constitution against the tide of prevailing current opinion. The Sixth Amendment provides, with unmistakable clarity, that "in all criminal prosecutions, the accused shall enjoy the right . . . to be confronted with the witnesses against him." The purpose of enshrining this protection in the Constitution was to assure that none of the many policy interests from time to time pursued by statutory law could overcome a defendant's right to face his or her accusers in court. . . .

The Court characterizes the State's interest which "outweigh[s]" the explicit text of the Constitution as an "interest in the physical and psychological well-being of child abuse victims,". . . an "interest in protecting" such victims "from the emotional trauma of testifying.". . . That is not so. A child who meets the Maryland statute's requirement of suffering such "serious emotional distress" from confrontation that he "cannot reasonably communicate" would seem entirely safe. Why would a prosecutor want to call a witness who cannot reasonably communicate? And if he did, it would be the State's own fault. Protection of the child's interest—as far as the Confrontation Clause is concerned—is entirely within Maryland's control. The State's interest here is in fact no more and no less than what the State's interest always is when it seeks to get a class of evidence admitted in criminal proceedings: more convictions of guilty defendants. That is not an unworthy interest, but it should not be dressed up as a humanitarian one. . . .

The Court today has applied "interest-balancing" analysis where the text of the Constitution simply does not permit it. We are not free to conduct a cost-benefit analysis of clear and explicit constitutional guarantees, and then to adjust their meaning to comport with our findings. The Court has convincingly proved that the Maryland procedure serves a valid interest, and gives the defendant virtually everything the Confrontation Clause guarantees (everything, that is, except confrontation). I am persuaded, therefore, that the Maryland procedure is virtually constitutional. Since it is not, however, actually constitutional I would affirm the judgment of the Maryland Court of Appeals reversing the judgment of conviction.

Case Questions for Discussion

1. Are the risks of child trauma sufficient to override the constitutional guarantee to confront witnesses?

2. How might *interpretivists* evaluate the statement that the Supreme Court's precedents express a "preference" for face-to-face confrontation at trial?

3. Is Mr. Justice Scalia correct in his argument that the Court should not balance the interests in this case?

4. What arguments are in favor of strictly adhering to the confrontation requirements of the Sixth Amendment?

Jury Selection

Court officials follow the same procedures for the selection of jury members in criminal cases as they do for selecting jurors in civil suits for money damages, as discussed in Chapter 5 of this text. The voir dire procedure is designed to ensure that those selected to serve on the jury are relatively objective in that they have not already formed an opinion in the case or they are not otherwise biased in favor or against the defendant. Challenges for cause are unlimited, as is the case for civil suits. But unlike trials involving money damages, states generally permit, for serious crimes, a greater number of peremptory challenges. Misdemeanor cases might involve approximately a half-dozen permissible peremptory challenges, but felony cases might include twice that number, and capital crimes, given the gravity of the matter, statutory law, or court rules, permit many more. Recall that peremptory challenges do not require giving the court any reason for dismissing possible jurors.[31] Yet, the U.S. Supreme Court, in Swain v. Alabama, 380 U.S. 202 (1965), held that challenges based on race are constitutionally impermissible and form a basis for reversible error.

Case Presentation to the Jury

Consistent with the practice found in civil suits for money damages, the party with the burden of proof in criminal cases presents its case first. Because the government has the burden to prove its case beyond a reasonable doubt, prosecutors open by outlining the case against the accused without drawing conclusions about the evidence that the jury is about to hear. Defense counsel then opts to either make her opening statement immediately after the prosecutor's opening statement or wait until after the government has completed the presentation of its case to the jury. Witnesses are directly examined by the prosecution, subject to cross-examination by defense counsel, and, as is the case for civil suits for money damages, witnesses may be redirected by the prosecution and subsequently re-crossed by the defense and so on until each side has exhausted the question-answer examination sequence.

If after the prosecution finishes its presentation of the entire case to the jury the defense believes that the government has failed to make a *prima facie* case, namely, meet its burden of proof, then the defense makes for a *motion of acquittal.* When considering a motion to acquit, the judge must ask the following: If the court hears no other evidence, including the evidence that may be presented by the defense, is it possible for the prosecution to win? For example, if the prosecution fails to place the defendant at the scene of the robbery, it is beyond reason to expect the jury to find for the government. The prosecution has failed to present, on the face of it (prima facie), sufficient evidence to convict the defendant. It is rare for judges to grant these motions because the prosecution is characteristically careful to present evidence on all elements of the offense. Successful motions are usually the result of an inability to admit evidence on an element of the offense, such as a piece of physical evidence excluded as a result of an illegal search and seizure.

Defense attorneys then present what evidence they wish the jury to consider. Of course, because the burden of proof is upon the prosecution, it is theoretically possible for the defense not to present any evidence. Counsel would simply point out that the prosecution has failed to prove its case beyond a reasonable doubt. Although the burden of proof never shifts to the defense, except for affirmative defenses, it is usually advisable to present evidence that might exonerate the defendant, including, in our robbery example, the alibi defense that sworn witnesses observed the defendant at a different location at the time the criminal act allegedly took place. A common tactic is to point the finger at someone else to create a reasonable doubt in the minds of the jurors.

Sometimes, given the lack of other credible evidence that may clearly exonerate the defendant, counsel will put his or her client on the stand to answer questions, hoping that the jury will believe the defendant. This is a risky tactic because once defendants take the stand voluntarily on their own behalf, they lose the privilege against self-incrimination and are subjected to the prosecutor's grilling cross-examination.[32]

Following the completion of the defendant's presentation of the case, defense counsel may immediately request a *motion for a directed verdict of acquittal.* The motion asks the judge to remove the case from further jury consideration, deciding instead that the prosecution has failed to introduce sufficient evidence for the jury to bring in a guilty verdict. Defense counsel may also enter a *motion for a mistrial,* arguing that serious errors were made during the course of the trial—such as the admission of privileged information or prejudicial evidence that may taint the jury's judgment. If the motion for a mistrial is granted, the prosecution may choose to retry the defendant at a later date. A decision to retry the defendant does not constitute double jeopardy in violation of the Fifth or Fourteenth Amendments because a judge or jury never determined a defendant's guilt or innocence—that matter remains in legal limbo. Following the presentation of the defendant's case, either side may present rebuttal evidence. Such evidence seeks to present the jury with additional information that might contradict the opponent's evidence as presented in their respective cases.[33]

Final Arguments

Because the government has the burden of proof, prosecutors make their closing arguments first, followed by the closing arguments of defense counsel. Most jurisdictions permit the prosecution the option of rebutting the arguments of the defense. Both sides are required to stay within the record as developed in the trial on the basis of legally included evidence. Reference to evidence that might have been rejected by the court as impermissible may not be argued in the final arguments. Improper remarks by either side may form the basis for a mistrial or an appeal.[34]

Jury Instructions and Deliberations

As is the practice for civil suits for money damages, in criminal trials, the presiding judge instructs the jury on all matters of law. Judges admonish jurors to apply the law as defined by the court to the particular facts in the case. As fact finders, jurors draw upon their collective experiences to evaluate the evidence presented at trial, including whether the requisite criminal intent (*mens rea*) was or was not present. In all criminal cases, judges advise jurors to carefully consider whether the prosecution has met the required burden of proof. Many states permit judges to comment on the evidence, but other jurisdictions specifically prohibit judicial commentary. Although judges possess the sole authority over the content of jury instructions, it is common for both sides to submit to the judge proposed instructions. Subsequently, the prosecutor, defense counsel, and the judge meet informally to discuss what those instructions should be. Whatever the outcome of such conferences, the judge's instructions to the jury may be in error and therefore subject to review and reversal by appellate courts.[35] An appeal can be based on judicial error if a judge wrongly refuses to include a defense demand for inclusion of a specific instruction favorable to the defendant.

If it becomes known that jurors did not apply the judge's instructions properly, then the judge may reverse the jury's guilty verdict and order a new trial. This occurred in the trial of three Los Angeles police officers involved in the notorious "Rampart Scandal." The officers were convicted in November 2000 of conspiracy and other charges involving the framing of gang members, in which it had been reported that officers beat, robbed, framed, and shot innocent people in the Rampart district of Los Angeles. The trial judge, in reversing the convictions, said that jurors had failed to follow her instructions, to wit: Were the policemen struck by a vehicle driven by a gang member? Rather, jurors indicated to the media after the trial that they focused on whether the injuries to the police officers rose to the level of "great bodily harm."[36]

The time needed to reach agreement among members of the jury depends upon many factors, including the vagaries of small group dynamics, the complexity of the facts, and whether the jurors clearly understand the legal rules as enunciated by the judge in her instructions. Jurors are not relieved of their responsibility to render a verdict unless the judge is satisfied that no agreement is possible. If this is the case, the judge declares a mistrial based on a *hung jury. Jury sequestration* means that members may not go home at night until they render a verdict. The judge sequesters a jury when there is a legitimate fear that the jury may be influenced to render a particular judgment by media, family, or friends. Although this is a valid consideration, most jury members take a dim view of being deprived of the comforts of home and of being separated from their families and friends. In any event, sequestration is the exception and not the rule. Judges tend to employ it in the most celebrated cases, such as the O. J. Simpson trial.[37]

Sentencing the Convicted

All jurisdictions require that the sentencing of convicted parties must take place within specified time parameters. In most cases, judges impose sentences for a period of imprisonment, the imposition of a monetary fine, or both. But in capital punishment cases, both the verdict and the sentencing decisions in many jurisdiction are made in a bifurcated trial—after the jury deliberates on the guilt or innocence of the defendant, it then deliberates again, this time on the sole question of the appropriate sentence. In all types of criminal felony cases, during the sentencing stage, courts permit government and defense attorneys to present evidence on what each believes to be an appropriate punishment under the circumstances. In most cases, judges impose sentences after a few weeks. During the interim, after the verdict is handed down but before sentencing, probation or social service officers prepare a report. These reports commonly contain an evaluation of the convicted person's criminal record, social and family background, and probation recommendations. Convicted persons have a right to be represented by legal counsel during sentencing proceedings, and most jurisdictions allow defendants to make a statement on their own behalf.[38]

Judge announces the sentence.

During the last few decades, state legislatures and the U.S. Congress have enacted guidelines that in many cases considerably reduce the discretion exercised by judges in sentencing those convicted of crimes. Many federal judges in particular complain that mandatory sentencing laws require that they impose harsh penalties, although it seems to them that too often the punishment does not fit the crime. Some states have enacted what is euphemistically called "three strikes and you're out" legislation, otherwise known as "habitual offender" laws. These laws require placing repeat offenders in prison for long periods of time and are based on the principle that when repeat offenders are in prison, their ability to commit crimes is incapacitated. Lawmakers also assume that these mandatory sentencing statutes will deter other persons from committing crime. Critics retort that it is unfair to impose a life sentence on a person for stealing a bicycle, for example, or committing similarly mild crimes simply because it is the third conviction. In short, the punishment does not fit the crime.[39]

Appealing Convictions

Upon conviction, but before a formal appeal, defendants have a right to ask presiding judges for a new trial. The formal motion is based either upon some error committed at the trial or upon the discovery of new evidence exonerating the defendant. In the first instance, the judge would have to agree that he or she made an error, for example, in admitting inadmissible evidence or some other equally serious error. Obviously, in most cases, it is unlikely that a judge will agree to such requests. Consequently, parties usually seek the reversal of the trial court decision through the appellate process.

Defendants have a right to appeal. State jurisdictions usually permit at least one appeal and any additional appeal is within the discretionary authority of courts of last resort. Prosecutors, however, may not appeal a verdict of acquittal because to win an appeal requires a new trial and any new trial would violate the Double Jeopardy provision of the Fifth Amendment and the Due Process Clause of the Fourteenth Amendment. Yet, this does not mean that prosecutors may never appeal the release of defendants. If a defendant wins an appeal of a conviction in an intermediate court of appeals, then the prosecution may appeal the appellate court's reversal, hoping to reinstate the original conviction. Because the prosecution is not asking for a retrial, but only for a reinstatement of the original conviction, there is no double jeopardy problem.

Res Judicata Exception

The civil law principle that once a case is tried and all appeals are finally exhausted, a case involving the same dispute between the same parties may not be revisited, is inapplicable to the criminal law.[40] It is possible, however, to try exonerated defendants again, based on the same facts, but for violations of other laws. When, for instance, Los Angeles police officers involved in the videotaped and widely televised beating of Rodney King were acquitted of state criminal charges, federal authorities then successfully prosecuted them under federal law for violating King's civil rights. There was no violation of the Double Jeopardy provision of the Fifth Amendment because the federal government prosecuted the police officers for a different crime, and the federal government is a "separate sovereign" from the state.

It is a matter of consensus that it is a grave injustice to keep a person in custody for a crime that he or she has not committed. If new evidence is uncovered that exonerates convicted persons, then justice requires that their convictions should be overturned. Where a mistake is uncovered, the typical remedy is through a *writ of habeas corpus*, which asks for the release of the prisoner. However, a court decision to issue the writ may be appealed to a higher court. The words *habeas corpus* mean "he who has the body," and the writ demands that prison officials produce the prisoner to a judge to determine whether that person is lawfully detained. When there is an allegation that a person is held in a federal or state facility in violation of a U.S. constitutional right, then the federal district courts have appropriate jurisdiction to conduct habeas corpus proceedings. The U.S. Supreme Court in *Stone v. Powell* imposed a limitation on this jurisdiction in cases involving Fourth Amendment search and seizure claims. For the purpose of understanding the justification of each, readers should carefully note the history of the writ of habeas corpus and the interpretation of the controversial exclusionary rule.

Stone v. Powell
United States Supreme Court
428 U.S. 465, 96 S. Ct. 3037, 49 L. Ed. 2d 1067 (1976)

OPINION BY: JUSTICE POWELL. Respondents in these cases were convicted of criminal offenses in state courts, and their convictions were affirmed on appeal. The prosecution in each case relied upon evidence obtained by searches and seizures alleged by respondents to have been unlawful. Each respondent subsequently sought relief in a Federal District Court by filing a petition for a writ of federal habeas corpus under 28 U.S.C. § 2254. The question presented is whether a federal court should consider, in ruling on a petition for habeas corpus relief filed by a state prisoner, a claim that evidence obtained by an unconstitutional search or seizure was introduced at his trial, when he has previously been afforded an opportunity for full and fair litigation of his claim in the state courts. The issue is of considerable importance to the administration of criminal justice. . . .

. . . Lloyd Powell was convicted of murder in June 1968 after trial in a California state court. At about midnight on February 17, 1968, he and three companions entered the Bonanza Liquor Store in San Bernardino, California, where Powell became involved in an altercation with Gerald Parsons, the store manager, over the theft of a bottle of wine. In the scuf-

fling that followed Powell shot and killed Parsons' wife. Ten hours later an officer of the Henderson, Nevada, Police Department arrested Powell for violation of the Henderson vagrancy ordinance, and in the search incident to the arrest discovered a .38-caliber revolver with six expended cartridges in the cylinder.

Powell was extradited to California and convicted of second-degree murder in the Superior Court of San Bernardino County. Parsons and Powell's accomplices at the liquor store testified against him. A criminologist testified that the revolver found on Powell was the gun that killed Parsons' wife. The trial court rejected Powell's contention that testimony by the Henderson police officer as to the search and the discovery of the revolver should have been excluded because the vagrancy ordinance was unconstitutional. In October 1969, the conviction was affirmed by a California District Court of Appeal. Although the issue was duly presented, that court found it unnecessary to pass upon the legality of the arrest and search because it concluded that the error, if any, in admitting the testimony of the Henderson officer was harmless beyond a reasonable doubt under Chapman v. California, 386 U.S. 18 (1967). The Supreme Court of California denied Powell's petition for habeas corpus relief.

In August 1971 Powell filed an amended petition for a writ of federal habeas corpus under 28 U.S.C. § 2254 in the United States District Court for the Northern District of California, contending that the testimony concerning the .38-caliber revolver should have been excluded as the fruit of an illegal search. He argued that his arrest had been unlawful because the Henderson vagrancy ordinance was unconstitutionally vague, and that the arresting officer lacked probable cause to believe that he was violating it. The District Court concluded that the arresting officer had probable cause and held that even if the vagrancy ordinance was unconstitutional, the deterrent purpose of the exclusionary rule does not require that it be applied to bar admission of the fruits of a search incident to an otherwise valid arrest. In the alternative, that court agreed with the California District Court of Appeal that the admission of the evidence concerning Powell's arrest, if error, was harmless beyond a reasonable doubt.

In December 1974, the Court of Appeals for the Ninth Circuit reversed. The court concluded that the vagrancy ordinance was unconstitutionally vague, that Powell's arrest was therefore illegal, and that although exclusion of the evidence would serve no deterrent purpose with regard to police officers who were enforcing statutes in good faith, exclusion would serve the public interest by deterring legislators from enacting unconstitutional statutes. After an independent review of the evidence the court concluded that the admission of the evidence was not harmless error since it supported the testimony of Parsons and Powell's accomplices. . . .

The authority of federal courts to issue the writ of habeas corpus *ad subjiciendum* was included in the first grant of federal-court jurisdiction, made by the Judiciary Act of 1789, c. 20, § 4, 1 Stat. 81, with the limitation that the writ extend only to prisoners held in custody by the United States. The original statutory authorization did not define the substantive reach of the writ. It merely stated that the courts of the United States "shall have power to issue writs of . . . *habeas corpus*. . . ." Ibid. The courts defined the scope of the writ in accordance with the common law and limited it to an inquiry as to the jurisdiction of the sentencing tribunal. . . .

In 1867 the writ was extended to state prisoners. Act of Feb. 5, 1867, c. 28, § 1, 14 Stat. 385. Under the 1867 Act federal courts were authorized to give relief in "all cases where any person may be restrained of his or her liberty in violation of the constitution, or of any treaty or law of the United States. . . ." But the limitation of federal habeas corpus jurisdiction to consideration of the jurisdiction of the sentencing court persisted. . . . And, although the concept of "jurisdiction" was subjected to considerable strain as the substantive scope of the writ was expanded, this expansion was limited to only a few classes of cases until Frank v. Mangum, 237 U.S. 309, in 1915.

In *Frank,* the prisoner had claimed in the state courts that the proceedings which resulted in his conviction for murder had been dominated by a mob. After the State Supreme Court rejected his contentions, Frank unsuccessfully sought habeas corpus relief in the Federal District Court. This Court affirmed the denial of relief because Frank's federal claims had been considered by a competent and unbiased state tribunal. The Court recognized, however, that if a habeas corpus court found that the State had failed to provide adequate "corrective process" for the full and fair litigation of federal claims, whether or not "jurisdictional," the court could inquire into the merits to determine whether a detention was lawful. . . .

In the landmark decision in Brown v. Allen, 344 U.S. 443, 482-487 (1953), the scope of the writ was expanded still further. In that case and its companion case, . . . state prisoners applied for federal habeas corpus relief claiming that the trial courts had erred in failing to quash their indictments due to alleged discrimination in the selection of grand jurors and in ruling certain confessions admissible. In *Brown,* the highest court of the State had rejected these claims on direct appeal, . . . and this Court had denied certiorari. Despite the apparent adequacy of the state corrective process, the Court reviewed the denial of the writ of habeas corpus and held that Brown was entitled to a full reconsideration of these constitutional claims, including, if appropriate, a hearing in the Federal District Court. In *Daniels,* however, the State Supreme Court on direct review had refused to consider the appeal because the papers were filed out of time. This Court held that since the state-court judgment rested on a reasonable application of the State's legitimate procedural rules, a ground that would have barred direct review of his federal claims by this Court, the District Court lacked authority to grant habeas corpus relief.

This final barrier to broad collateral re-examination of state criminal convictions in federal habeas corpus proceedings was removed in Fay v. Noia, 372 U.S. 391 (1963). Noia and two codefendants had been convicted of felony murder. The sole evidence against each defendant was a signed confession. Noia's codefendants, but not Noia himself, appealed their convictions. Although their appeals were unsuccessful, in subsequent state proceedings they were able to establish that their confessions had been coerced and their convictions therefore procured in violation of the Constitution. In a subsequent federal habeas corpus proceeding, it was stipulated that Noia's confession also had been coerced, but the District Court followed *Daniels* in holding that Noia's failure to appeal barred habeas corpus review. . . . The Court of Appeals reversed, ordering that Noia's conviction be set aside and that he be released from custody or that a new trial be granted. This Court affirmed the grant of the writ, narrowly restricting the circumstances in which a federal court may refuse to consider the merits of federal constitutional claims.

During the period in which the substantive scope of the writ was expanded, the Court did not consider whether exceptions to full review might exist with respect to particular categories of constitutional claims. Prior to the Court's decision in Kaufman v. United States, 394 U.S. 217 (1969), however, a substantial majority of the Federal Courts of Appeals had concluded that collateral review of search-and-seizure claims was inappropriate on motions filed by federal prisoners under 28 U.S.C. § 2255, the modern postconviction procedure available to federal prisoners in lieu of habeas corpus. The primary rationale advanced in support of those decisions was that Fourth Amendment violations are different in kind from denials of Fifth or Sixth Amendment rights in that claims of illegal search and seizure do not "impugn the integrity of the fact-finding process or challenge evidence as inherently unreliable; rather, the exclusion of illegally seized evidence is simply a prophylactic device intended generally to deter Fourth Amendment violations by law enforcement officers." 394 U.S., at 224. . . .

The discussion in *Kaufman* of the scope of federal habeas corpus rests on the view that the effectuation of the Fourth Amendment, as applied to the States through the Fourteenth Amendment, requires the granting of habeas corpus relief when a prisoner has been convicted in state court on the basis of evidence obtained in an illegal search or seizure since those Amendments were held in Mapp v. Ohio, 367 U.S. 643 (1961), to require exclusion of such evidence at trial and reversal of conviction upon direct review. Until these cases we have not had occasion fully to consider the validity of this view. . . . Upon examination, we conclude, in light of the nature and purpose of the Fourth Amendment exclusionary rule, that this view is unjustified. We hold, therefore, that where the State has provided an opportunity for full and fair litigation of a Fourth Amendment claim, the Constitution does not require that a state prisoner be granted federal habeas corpus relief on the ground that evidence obtained in an unconstitutional search or seizure was introduced at his trial.

The Fourth Amendment assures the "right of the people to be secure in their persons, houses, papers, and effects, against unreasonable searches and seizures." The Amendment was primarily a reaction to the evils associated with the use of the general warrant in England and the writs of assistance in the Colonies, . . . and was intended to protect the "sanctity of a man's home and the privacies of life," Boyd v. United States, 116 U.S. 616, 630 (1886), from searches under unchecked general authority.

The exclusionary rule was a judicially created means of effectuating the rights secured by the Fourth Amendment. Prior to the Court's decisions in Weeks v. United States, 232 U.S. 383 (1914), and Gouled v. United States, 255 U.S. 298 (1921), there existed no barrier to the introduction in criminal trials of evidence obtained in violation of the Amendment. . . . In *Weeks* the Court held that the defendant could petition before trial for the return of property secured through an illegal search or seizure conducted by federal authorities. In *Gouled* the Court held broadly that such evidence could not be introduced in a federal prosecution. . . . Thirty-five years after *Weeks* the Court held in Wolf v. Colorado, 338 U.S. 25 (1949), that the right to be free from arbitrary intrusion by the police that is protected by the Fourth Amendment is "implicit in 'the concept of ordered liberty' and as such enforceable against the States through the [Fourteenth Amendment] Due Process Clause." Id., at 27-28. The Court concluded, however, that the *Weeks* exclusionary rule would not be imposed upon the States as "an essential ingredient of [that] right." 338 U.S., at 29. The full force of *Wolf* was eroded in subsequent decisions, . . . and a little more than a decade later the exclusionary rule was held applicable to the States in Mapp v. Ohio, 367 U.S. 643 (1961).

Decisions prior to *Mapp* advanced two principal reasons for application of the rule in federal trials. The Court in . . . the context of its special supervisory role over the lower federal courts, referred to the "imperative of judicial integrity," suggesting that exclusion of illegally seized evidence prevents contamination of the judicial process. . . . But even in that context a more pragmatic ground was emphasized: "The rule is calculated to prevent, not to repair. Its purpose is to deter—to compel respect for the constitutional guaranty in the only effectively available way—by removing the incentive to disregard it." . . . The *Mapp* majority justified the application of the rule to the States on several grounds, but relied principally upon the belief that exclusion would deter future unlawful police conduct.

Although our decisions often have alluded to the "imperative of judicial integrity" e.g., United States v. Peltier, 422 U.S. 531, 536-539 (1975), they demonstrate the limited role of this justification in the determination whether to apply the rule in a particular context. Logically extended this justification would require that courts exclude unconstitutionally seized evidence despite lack of objection by the defendant, or even over his assent. . . . It also would require abandonment of the standing limitations on who may object to the introduction of unconstitutionally seized evidence, . . . and retreat from the proposition that judicial proceedings need not abate when the defendant's person is unconstitutionally seized, . . . Similarly, the interest in promoting judicial integrity does not prevent the use of illegally seized evidence in grand jury proceedings. . . . Nor does it require that the trial court exclude such evidence from use for impeachment of a defendant, even though its introduction is certain to result in conviction in some cases. . . . While courts, of course, must ever be concerned with preserving the integrity of the judicial process, this concern has limited force as a justification for the exclusion of highly probative evidence. The force of this justification becomes minimal where federal habeas corpus relief is sought by a prisoner who previously has been afforded the opportunity for full and fair consideration of his search-and-seizure claim at trial and on direct review.

The same pragmatic analysis of the exclusionary rule's usefulness in a particular context was evident earlier . . . where the Court permitted the Government to use unlawfully seized evidence to impeach the credibility of a defendant who had testified broadly in his own defense. The Court held, in effect, that the interests safeguarded by the exclusionary rule in that context were outweighed by the need to prevent perjury and to assure the integrity of the trial process. The judgment . . . revealed most clearly that the policies behind the exclusionary rule are not absolute. Rather, they must be evaluated in light of competing policies. In that case, the public interest in determination of truth at trial was deemed to outweigh the incremental contribution that might have been made to the protection of Fourth Amendment values by application of the rule. The balancing process at work in these cases also finds expression in the standing requirement. Standing to invoke the exclusionary rule has been found to exist only when the Government attempts to use illegally obtained evidence to incriminate the victim of the illegal search. . . . The standing requirement is premised on the view that the "additional benefits of extending the . . . rule" to defendants other than the victim of the search or seizure are outweighed by the "further encroachment upon the public interest in prosecuting those accused of crime and having them acquitted or convicted on the basis of all the evidence which exposes the truth." Alderman v. United States, supra, at 174-175.

We turn now to the specific question presented by these cases. Respondents allege violations of Fourth Amendment rights guaranteed them through the Fourteenth Amendment. The question is whether state prisoners—who have been afforded the opportunity for full and fair consideration of their reliance upon the exclusionary rule with respect to seized evidence by the state courts at trial and on direct review—may invoke their claim again on federal habeas corpus review. The answer is to be found by weighing the utility of the exclusionary rule against the costs of extending it to collateral review of Fourth Amendment claims.

The costs of applying the exclusionary rule even at trial and on direct review are well known: the focus of the trial, and the attention of the participants therein, are diverted from the ultimate question of guilt or innocence that should be the central concern in a criminal proceeding. Moreover, the physical evidence sought to be excluded is typically reliable and often the most probative information bearing on the guilt or innocence of the defendant. . . . Application of the rule thus deflects the truth-finding process and often frees the guilty. The disparity in particular cases between the error committed by the police officer and the windfall afforded a guilty defendant by application of the rule is contrary to the idea of proportionality that is essential to the concept of justice. Thus, although the rule is thought to deter unlawful police activity in part through the nurturing of respect for Fourth Amendment values, if applied indiscriminately it may well have the opposite effect of generating disrespect for the law and administration of justice. These long-recognized costs of the rule persist when a criminal conviction is sought to be overturned on collateral review on the ground that a search-and-seizure claim was erroneously rejected by two or more tiers of state courts.

Evidence obtained by police officers in violation of the Fourth Amendment is excluded at trial in the hope that the frequency of future violations will decrease. Despite the absence of supportive empirical evidence, we have assumed that the immediate effect of exclusion will be to discourage law enforcement officials from violating the Fourth Amendment by removing the incentive to disregard it. More importantly, over the long term, this demonstration that our society attaches serious consequences to violation of constitutional rights is thought to encourage those who formulate law enforcement policies, and the officers who implement them, to incorporate Fourth Amendment ideals into their value system.

We adhere to the view that these considerations support the implementation of the exclusionary rule at trial and its enforcement on direct appeal of state-court convictions. But the additional contribution, if any, of the consideration of search-and-seizure claims of state prisoners on collateral review is small in relation to the costs. To be sure, each case in which such claim is considered may add marginally to an awareness of the values protected by the Fourth Amendment. There is no reason to believe, however, that the overall educative effect of the exclusionary rule would be appreciably diminished if search-and-seizure claims could not be raised in federal habeas corpus review of state convictions. Nor is there reason to assume that any specific disincentive already created by the risk of exclusion of evidence at trial or the reversal of convictions on direct review would be enhanced if there were the further risk that a conviction obtained in state court and affirmed on direct review might be overturned in collateral proceedings often occurring years after the incarceration of the defendant. The view that the deterrence of Fourth Amendment violations would be furthered rests on the dubious assumption that law enforcement authorities would fear that federal habeas review might reveal flaws in a search or seizure that went unde-

tected at trial and on appeal. Even if one rationally could assume that some additional incremental deterrent effect would be present in isolated cases, the resulting advance of the legitimate goal of furthering Fourth Amendment rights would be outweighed by the acknowledged costs to other values vital to a rational system of criminal justice.

In sum, we conclude that where the State has provided an opportunity for full and fair litigation of a Fourth Amendment claim, a state prisoner may not be granted federal habeas corpus relief on the ground that evidence obtained in an unconstitutional search or seizure was introduced at his trial. In this context the contribution of the exclusionary rule, if any, to the effectuation of the Fourth Amendment is minimal and the substantial societal costs of application of the rule persist with special force.

Accordingly, the judgments of the Courts of Appeals are *Reversed.*

Chief Justice Burger wrote a concurring opinion.

Justice Brennan, with whom Justice Marshall concurs, dissented.

Case Questions for Discussion

1. Describe the history of the authority of the federal courts to issue writs of *habeas corpus*. Do the words of the Constitution require the application of the exclusionary rule?

2. Are violations of the Fourth Amendment different from denials of Fifth or Sixth Amendment rights?

3. Given the Supreme Court's holding in *Stone v. Powell*, should any illegally obtained evidence be excluded at trial?

4. What are the costs and benefits of the exclusionary rule, and how should the two be weighed, if at all?

Juvenile Justice

Juvenile justice in the United States is a special part of the broader criminal justice system. Juvenile courts operate under a set of specialized rules designed to provide special protections for young criminal offenders. In some states, juvenile courts function independently from the regular courts, established either by constitutional mandate or by ordinary legislation. Most often, however, juvenile courts are administrative branches of the regular courts of original jurisdiction that ordinarily handle criminal and other matters. Although organizational forums for juvenile matters vary a great deal from state to state, jurisdiction and procedures are similar everywhere in the United States.

For the first century of this country's history, youthful offenders were treated not much differently than adult criminal defendants. There was a widespread belief, however, that children between the ages of 7 and 12 could not be held responsible for their offenses against society because they lacked the requisite reason necessary to be held responsible for their conduct. Yet, teenagers were treated as adults, finding themselves ensnarled in the criminal justice system with all the harshness that goes with its processes and punishments.[41]

At the turn of the twentieth century, American cities were impacted by the infusion of large numbers of immigrant groups. Moreover, population shifts from rural regions of the country to urban centers took place because of the likelihood of greater employment opportunities. The poverty and social upheaval experienced by many of the transplants were associated with a variety of social problems and antisocial behavior. Many youthful offenders were processed through the criminal justice system, and they were often incarcerated in the same facilities as were seasoned adult criminals.

Juvenile proceeding.

This situation appalled a group of mostly middle-class reform-minded women. Chicago was the site of the most significant reform movement, where reformers insisted that youthful offenders should be treated differently from adult criminals. They believed that young people are not born evil, but rather because of environmental factors they failed to learn good citizenship traits. Rather than punishing juveniles, we should treat and rehabilitate them, thus saving them from a downward spiral into a life of crime. The goal with both the juvenile delinquent and the semidelinquent is not to punish, but to help children realize their potential as law-abiding members of society. In 1899, Cook County, Illinois, established the first juvenile court system in the United States. Within 20 years, juvenile courts were established in most jurisdictions of this country.[42]

Juvenile courts deal with criminal conduct of youthful offenders. Criminal conduct when committed by the young is called *delinquency.* These courts also deal with *truancy* (absence from school without excuse), *incorrigibility* (defying correction or control), and *neglect* (without appropriate adult supervision). In most jurisdictions, juvenile courts have original jurisdiction over children in delinquency matters up through 17 years of age. In some states the age limit is 16, and in just a few states, the upper limit is 15 years of age. Many states have upper age limits as high as 20 years of age for behavior not considered criminal if committed by an adult (status offenses), abuse, neglect, or dependency matters.[43] Characteristically, juvenile courts do not hear traffic matters.

Children found in violation of the criminal law may be sent to reform school, sometimes called state industrial schools. Those children found in need of supervision because they are disorderly may be subjected to special supervision by the court. Professionally trained probation officers are given the responsibility by the juvenile court to supervise, treat, or rehabilitate the noncriminal juvenile in a nonprison setting. Community treatment, involving vocational guidance training, educational tutoring, and special recreation groups, is available in some locations. Given the purpose of the juvenile court system, judges inquire into the social and psychological needs of the children that come before them.

The downside of this approach is that procedural requirements of the criminal law can be ignored, working to the disadvantage of children. Consequently, the U.S. Supreme Court has found it necessary to intervene to protect the constitutional rights of youths. The way the Supreme Court has responded to due process issues is an interesting story. By describing the case law, we can gain an appreciation for the many problems attendant to the juvenile justice system.

Due Process Rights

There are three ways a juvenile may be tried as an adult. First, a prosecutor may decide to file the case in a criminal court when criminal and juvenile courts possess concurrent jurisdiction. Second, the legislature may require that certain serious offenses be tried by the regular criminal courts—despite the fact that a juvenile is the alleged perpetrator of the offense. And third, a juvenile judge may waive jurisdiction and transfer the case to a criminal court.[44] It is this last circumstance that gave rise to the first modern case to confront the general issue of due process rights for juvenile defendants.

In Kent v. United States, 383 U.S. 541 (1966), a 16-year-old boy had his case transferred from juvenile court in Washington, DC, to the regular criminal court. The judge waived jurisdiction without a hearing on the matter, although the boy's attorney objected. The juvenile court judge responded that he had fully investigated the matter himself and therefore a formal hearing was unnecessary. By the way, the boy was convicted in criminal court of six counts of housebreaking and robbery. He was sentenced to 30 to 90 years in prison. The U.S. Supreme Court rejected the judge's explanation. It held that only after a full hearing in which the defendant is entitled to legal counsel, access to the juvenile's social records, and a statement by the court giving the reasons for its actions may a juvenile court transfer jurisdiction to a criminal court.[45]

Though the decision in *Kent v. United States* imposed an important due process requirement, the U.S. Supreme Court's opinion in In Re Gault, 387 U.S. 1 (1967), went much further. It guaranteed to juveniles many of the same constitutional rights afforded adult criminal defendants. Gerald Gault, 15 years old, and a friend were arrested by police on the complaint of a neighbor, Mrs. Cook. She said that they made lewd remarks to her over the telephone. Gault's parents were not notified by the police of the arrest; in fact, they later learned of their son's predicament secondhand. Nor did the Gaults receive a copy of a petition filed by the police for a court hearing. Gerald was not advised of his right to remain silent and to be represented by counsel. In addition, Mrs. Cook did not appear at any time in court as a witness, nor was there any record made of the proceedings. The juvenile court judge subsequently declared Gault a juvenile delinquent and committed him to a state industrial school for a maximum of six years (until he reached 21 years of age). Because Arizona law did not permit appeals in juvenile cases, Mr. and Mrs. Gault filed a petition in a state court for a writ of habeas corpus. They challenged the constitutionality of Arizona's Juvenile Code on numerous due process grounds. They argued that juveniles should be afforded the same due process constitutional protections as adults. A state superior court dismissed the writ. The Arizona Supreme Court affirmed, and Gault's parents appealed to the U.S. Supreme Court.

The issue in the case, though long-winded, may be summed up as follows. Was the Juvenile Code of Arizona invalid on its face as applied in this case, contrary to the Due Process Clause of the Fourteenth Amendment, because the juvenile court possessed virtually unlimited discretion, in which the following basic rights were denied: (1) notice of the charges, (2) right to counsel, (3) right to confrontation and cross-examination, (4) privilege against self-incrimination, (5) right to a transcript of the proceedings, and (6) right to appellate review? The Supreme Court answered yes, in part. The judgment was reversed and remanded with directions.

Justice Abe Fortas' opinion in *In Re Gault* is particularly interesting because after laying out the historical and sociological assumptions that are at the foundation of the existence of the juvenile justice system, he explained how certain legal assumptions had made such a system possible and why it is necessary to alter those assumptions to comport with due process principles. Fortas pointed out that the law avoided coming to grips with the inherent constitutional difficulties by treating juvenile offenses not as "criminal" matters, but rather as "civil" in nature. Because juvenile matters were conceptualized in civil law terms, the requirements that restrict the state when it seeks to deprive a person of his liberty were thought not applicable.

This fundamental legal assumption was made operational by insisting that juvenile proceedings are not adversarial. Instead, the state proceeded as *parens patriae* (the state as parent) in fulfillment of its duty to protect the child. This made it possible for the state to deny the child procedural rights available to his or her elders because a child, unlike an adult, has a right "not to liberty but to custody." Most parents desire, if only a fantasy, that their child may be made to atone to them, to attend school, and generally to be guided by their wisdom borne of experience. If parents default in effectively performing their custodial functions, that is, if the child is "delinquent," the state may intervene. Consequently, the state does not deprive the child of any rights because, in essence, the child has none. The state simply provides the "custody" to which the child is properly entitled. Mr. Fortas then pointed out that this system for juveniles was unknown to our law in any comparable context. Obviously, it suffered from many debatable assumptions. Indeed, he cited Dean Pound, who argued: "The powers of the Star Chamber were trifle in comparison with those of our juvenile courts."[46]

As a practical matter, Fortas argued that the absence of procedural rules based upon constitutional principle has not always produced fair, efficient, and effective procedures. Departures from established principles of due process have frequently resulted not in enlightened procedure, but in arbitrariness. Moreover, the evidence was impressive that the juvenile courts did not do a good job at rehabilitating the young people who come under their protection and guidance. He cited one District of Columbia study that found 56 percent of those in the Receiving Home were repeat offenders. In brief, the idea of a fatherly judge talking over the child's problem was in too many cases fictitious. Unfortunately, it gave the judge the opportunity to behave in an arbitrary manner.

Yet, Fortas was not prepared to scrap the juvenile justice system altogether. He qualified the Court's holding by stipulating that due process does not mean that juvenile defendants must be referred to as criminals and not as delinquents. In keeping with this perspective, the application of due process requirements should not interfere with statutory requirements that juvenile proceedings shall not, for example, operate as a civil disability or disqualify persons for civil service appointments. Emphatically, however, Mr. Fortas stated that the "... condition of being a boy does not justify a kangaroo court."[47]

The Court's 7–2 majority opinion in *In Re Gault* then spelled out four due process of law requirements applicable to juvenile proceedings. These are (1) adequate and timely notice of charges, (2) right to counsel, (3) privilege against self-incrimination, and (4) that without a valid confession, a determination of delinquency and an order to a state institution cannot be sustained in the absence of sworn testimony subjected to the opportunity for cross-examination. The court did not explicitly rule on the failure to provide a transcript or on the right to appellate review.

Beginning in the 1970s, the U.S. Supreme Court in a number of divided opinions further elaborated on due process requirements. The case of In Re Winship, 397 U.S. 358 (1970), involved a 12-year-old charged with stealing. The child had been convicted under a New York statute allowing a guilty judgment to be based on "a preponderance of the evidence" test. The U.S. Supreme Court insisted that "proof beyond a reasonable doubt" is among the essential due process protections designed to afford fair treatment when a juvenile is charged with an act that would constitute a crime if committed by an adult. But in McKeiver v. Pennsylvania, 403 U.S. 528 (1971), the Court held that juvenile offenders are not constitutionally entitled to jury trials. In Breed v. Jones, 421 U.S. 519 (1975), the Supreme Court extended the constitutional protection against double jeopardy to juvenile offenders. In Fare v. Michael C., 442 U.S. 707 (1979), a state court ruled that a juvenile's request to have his probation officer present at custodial interrogation, like an accused's request for an attorney, is per se an invocation of his Fifth Amendment rights, requiring that all interrogation cease. Significantly, the juvenile in this particular instance did not ask to consult an attorney. Rather, he asked to see his probation officer. In a 5–4 decision, the Supreme Court held that the lower court had erred. Michael C. did not ask to see an attorney, and he did not expressly assert his right to remain silent. Additionally, courts must consider the totality of the circumstances surrounding the interrogation, and not just a specific omission or commission. Consequently, we know that although juveniles are entitled to consult with their attorneys, they do not have a right to consult with their probation officers without considering the totality of the circumstances.

In the late 1970s, the norm that youthful offenders should not be subjected to public exposure that could affect their reputations and future life chances was compromised. The prohibition was modified in two U.S. Supreme Court opinions that resulted from court-ordered press silence surrounding juvenile proceedings. In Oklahoma Publishing Co. v. District in and for Oklahoma City, 480 U.S. 308 (1977), the nation's high court overruled an order prohibiting the press from reporting the name and photograph of a juvenile offender that was legally obtained elsewhere. The Supreme Court found the prohibition a violation of the free press provision of the First Amendment. A few years later in Smith v. Daily Mail Publishing Company, 443 U.S. 97 (1979), the U.S. Supreme Court affirmed its Oklahoma decision. It permitted the press to report otherwise lawfully obtained information to the public, as long as it was achieved without consulting juvenile court proceedings.

The U.S. Supreme Court has held that courts are free to detain juveniles in jails pending trial under certain circumstances. In Schall v. Martin, 476 U.S. 253 (1984), a New York law authorized pretrial detention of an accused juvenile when a judge found there was a "serious risk" that the juvenile may, before the return date set for his hearing, commit an act that, if committed by an adult, would constitute a crime. The U.S. Supreme Court addressed the issue of whether the New York law violated fundamental fairness guaranteed by the Due Process Clause of the Fourteenth Amendment. It upheld the statute. The 6–3 majority found that the legitimate interest of protecting both the juvenile and society from the hazards of pretrial crime justified pretrial detention. They were satisfied that the various procedural protections afforded such juvenile detainees (e.g., notice, a hearing, a statement of facts and reasons, and a formal probable-cause hearing shortly afterward) comported with the Due Process Clause of the Fourteenth Amendment. These protections provide sufficient shields against unnecessary and erroneous deprivations of an accused juvenile's liberty.

In 1988 and 1989, the U.S. high court rendered two opinions concerning the application of the death penalty to youthful defendants: Thompson v. Oklahoma, 487 U.S. 815 (1988), and Stanford v. Kentucky consolidated with Wilkins v. Missouri, 492 U.S. 361 (1989). In Oklahoma, Kentucky, and Missouri, laws permitted the imposition of the death penalty, after juvenile courts conducted hearings to transfer juveniles to the regular criminal courts for trial as adults. In these cases, one involving a 15-year-old, one a 17-year-old, and the other a 16-year-old, the Supreme Court held that there was no violation of the Cruel and Unusual Punishment provision of the Eighth Amendment as applied to the states by way of the Due Process Clause of the Fourteenth Amendment. In one of the 5–4 majority opinions, Mr. Justice Scalia stated that at least 281 offenders under 18 years of age and 126 under 17 years of age have been executed in this country. Moreover, of the 37 states that permitted capital punishment, 15 declined to impose it on 16-year-olds and 12 states on 17-year-olds. Scalia argued that these data do not establish the degree of national agreement the Supreme Court had previously thought sufficient to label a punishment "cruel and unusual."

From a constitutional interpretation perspective, Scalia's reasoning raises at least one very interesting problem. For a penalty to be cruel and unusual there must be contemporaneous agreement that it is. This means that a constitutional right is premised on national agreement. Yet, constitutions are justified as limitations on majority rule in the service of other democratic ideals, including the preservation of life. Interpretivists such as Scalia must believe the two terms, "cruel" and "unusual," constitute separate tests that must be linked by the conjunctive word "and." In other words, although some might argue that capital punishment is per se cruel, the fact that many states employ it against juveniles means that it is not unusual. Indeed, as of the year 2000, 38 states authorized the use of the death penalty and 23 of these states permitted the execution of offenders who commit capital crimes before their eighteenth birthdays. Between 1973 and 2000, 17 men were executed for crimes for which they were convicted as juveniles, and 74 others during this same period sat on death row awaiting execution.[48]

A matter of contemporary interest is the way alien juveniles are treated by the juvenile justice system. In part, the U.S. Supreme Court addressed this concern with its decision in Reno v. Flores, 507 U.S. 292 (1993). This case dealt with a regulation of the Immigration and Nationalization Service (INS) allowing release of alien juveniles detained pending deportation hearings only to parents, other close relatives, or guardians. The problem with this regulation is that many alien children arrive in the United States without parents, close relatives, or guardians, and therefore they must remain in the custody of a government-operated or government-selected child care institution, where other responsible adults are able and willing to care for them, pending a formal INS hearing and disposition. The Court held that the INS regulation does not facially violate the alien juvenile's "fundamental rights" under the Fifth Amendment. The INS need not release a juvenile to some "other responsible adult" if it determines it is not in the best interest of the juvenile and the government's goal of assuring that the juvenile appears at a designation hearing on his or her deportation.

Recent Trends in Juvenile Justice

The Supreme Court's decision not to extend the doctrine of fundamental rights to alien juveniles comes as no surprise. The conservative bloc on the contemporary Supreme Court is resistant to the idea of expanding fundamental rights protections to a wider variety of groups than currently enjoy this special constitutional protection. As we discussed in Chapter 4, they are hesitant to employ strict or heightened judicial scrutiny in favor of the ordinary rational basis test when confronting charges of unconstitutional discrimination against groups or classifications of persons in society.

Contemporary public attitudes and legislative actions concerning juveniles make it even more likely that young criminal offenders will receive no special treatment because of their status. During the 1990s, public fear and outrage about juvenile violence prompted a get-tough policy toward youthful criminal offenders. In almost every state, the jurisdiction of juvenile courts was substantially depleted and transferred to the regular criminal courts. Once subject to the protective environment of juvenile courts, youths accused of serious crimes, older juveniles, and repeat offenders are now exposed to the greater discretion of publicly pressured prosecutors. The principle of confidentiality of records that is central to the idea that youth should be treated in a special way has given way to procedures of open and public trials with considerable, although not unlimited, press access. And the idea that children should be saved from a downward spiral into a life of crime with an emphasis on rehabilitation has been de-emphasized in favor of retribution and prison time. In short, the treatment model of the juvenile justice system is giving way to a harsher crime control model that includes the imposition of long prison sentences and the death penalty.[49]

Key Terms, Names, and Concepts

Arraignment	Indictment
Assigned counsel programs	Jury sequestration
Bail	Juvenile delinquency
Bail bondsman	Miranda warnings
Change of venue	Mistrial motion
Confrontation of witnesses	Motion for directed verdict
Continuance	Motion of acquittal
Contract systems	Neglect
Criminal complaint	No bill
Criminal information	Nolo contendere
Cruel and unusual punishment	Not guilty
Exclusionary rule	Parens patriae
Gag order	Personal service
Grand jury	Plea-bargain
Guilty plea	Preventive detention
Habitual offender laws	Prima facie evidence
Hung jury	Proof beyond a reasonable doubt
Ignoramus	Property bond
Incorrigibility	Public defender

Public trial	True bill
Right to counsel	Verdict of acquittal
Self-incrimination privilege	Waiver of right
Serious criminal offense	Work product nondisclosure
Speedy trial	Writ of habeas corpus
Truancy	

Discussion Questions

1. What are the arguments for and against the proposition, "It is better to release a guilty person than to convict an innocent one"? Where do you come down on this issue and why?

2. Although most jurisdictions require unanimous jury verdicts to convict or acquit criminal defendants, do you think it is a good idea to accept less than unanimous verdicts? For example, a two-thirds vote of the jury? Why not a simple majority? Do you think the size of the jury makes any difference with respect to the burden of proof?

3. Should state governments be free to interpret the U.S. Constitution with respect to the rights of the criminally accused consistent with the experience of each? In other words, should the U.S. Bill of Rights be applicable to all states when it comes to the criminal law?

4. In periods of national emergency, such as the War on Terrorism following the events of September 11, 2001, do you think it is justifiable to permit government to discard or alter existing criminal justice processes in the name of protecting the United States from violent attack?

5. Is the recent trend toward treating juvenile offenders similarly to adult criminal defendants justified?

6. You are now familiar with the similarities and contrasts between and among civil suits for money damages, equity suits, and criminal prosecutions. Which if any of these processes would you recommend for change in the public interest?

Suggested Additional Reading

Abraham, Henry J., and Barbara A. Perry. *Freedom and the Court: Civil Rights & Liberties in the United States*. 7th ed. New York: Oxford University Press, 1998.

Amar, Akhil Reed. *The Constitution and Criminal Procedure: First Principles*. New Haven, CT: Yale University Press, 1997.

Becker, Theodore L., ed. *Political Trials.* Indianapolis and New York: Bobbs-Merrill, 1971.

Fairchild, Erika, and Anthony Champagne, eds. *The Politics of Crime and Criminal Justice.* Beverly Hills, CA: Sage, 1985.

Fletcher, George P. *A Crime of Self-Defense: Bernhard Goetz and the Law on Trial.* New York: Free Press, 1988.

Hastie, Reid, Steven Penrod, and Nancy Pennington. *Inside the Jury.* Cambridge, MA: Harvard University Press, 1983.

Heumann, Milton. *Plea Bargaining.* Chicago: University of Chicago Press, 1978.

Israel, Jerold H., Yale Kamisar, and Wayne R. LaFave. *Criminal Procedure and the Constitution—Leading Supreme Court Cases and Introductory Text.* 2001 Edition. Eagan, MN: West Group, 2001.

Janikowski, Richard. *Criminal Procedure: A Process Approach.* Los Angeles: Roxbury Publishing, 2003.

Lewis, Anthony. *Gideon's Trumpet.* New York: Vintage Books, 1964.

McDonald, William R., ed. *The Defense Counsel.* Beverly Hills, CA: Sage, 1983.

McInnis, Thomas N. *The Christian Burial Case: An Introduction to Criminal and Judicial Procedure.* Westport, CT: Praeger, 2000.

McIntyre, Lisa J. *The Public Defender: The Practice of Law in the Shadows of Repute.* Chicago: University of Chicago Press, 1987.

Melone, Albert P. "The Politics of Criminal Code Revision: Lessons for Reform." *Capital University Law Review* 15 (Winter 1986): 191–204.

Nagel, Stuart S., Erika Fairchild, and Anthony Champagne, eds. *The Political Science of Criminal Justice.* Springfield, IL: Charles C. Thomas, 1983.

Schubert, Frank. *Criminal Law: The Basics.* Los Angeles, CA: Roxbury, 2003.

Wice, Paul. *Judges and Lawyers: The Human Side of Justice.* New York: HarperCollins, 1991.

Wolfe, Linda. *Wasted: The Preppie Murder Case.* New York: Simon & Schuster, 1989.

Endnotes

1. Bruce Shapiro, "A Talk With Governor George Ryan," *The Nation* (January 8/15, 2001): 17.
2. Fox Butterfield, "Death Sentences Being Overturned in 2 of 3 Appeals," *New York Times (National Edition)* (June 12, 2000): 1, A21.
3. Jodi Wilgoren, "Illinois Expected to Free 4 Inmates," *New York Times (National Edition)* (January 10, 2003): A1, A19; Jodi Wilgoren, "Two Days Left in Term, Governor Clears Out Death Row in Illinois," *New York Times (National Edition)* (January 12, 2003): 1, 22.
4. 22 Corpus Juris Secundum, *Criminal Law,* §§ 324–333 (1989).
5. *West's Encyclopedia of American Law,* "Prosecutor" (1998), p. 205.

6. Henry J. Abraham, *The Judicial Process: An Introductory Analysis of the Courts of the United States, England, and France*, 7th ed. (New York: Oxford University Press, 1998), p. 113.

7. Ibid., pp. 113–114.

8. 38 American Jurisprudence 2d, "Grand Jury," § 36 (1999).

9. Henry J. Abraham, *The Judicial Process*, p. 114.

10. 38 American Jurisprudence 2d, "Grand Jury," § 16 (1999).

11. Henry J. Abraham, *The Judicial Process*, p. 114; 38 American Jurisprudence 2d, "Grand Jury," § 8 (1999).

12. 21 American Jurisprudence 2d, "Criminal Law," §§ 600–614 (1998).

13. Ibid., §§ 683–725. The most widely cited study on the plea-bargain practice is, Milton Heumann, *Plea Bargaining: The Experiences of Prosecutors, Judges, and Defense Attorneys* (Chicago: University of Chicago Press, 1981).

14. Rolando V. del Carmen, *Criminal Procedure: Law and Practice*, 3rd ed. (Belmont, CA: Wadsworth, 1995), p. 41.

15. 21 American Jurisprudence 2d, "Criminal Law," § 737 (1998).

16. Ibid., § 730.

17. "Agnew, Spiro Theodore," Microsoft® Encarta® Online Encyclopedia (2000); Ben A. Franklin, "Agnew Plea Ends 65 Days of Insisting on Innocence," *New York Times* (October 11, 1973): 31.

18. 8A American Jurisprudence 2d, "Bail and Recognizance," §§ 1–25 (1997).

19. Ibid., §§ 51–64.

20. Rolando V. del Carmen, *Criminal Procedure*, pp. 31–32.

21. Illinois Supreme Court Rules, S.Ct. Rule 412.

22. Ibid.

23. Ibid., S.Ct. Rules 413, 414.

24. Rolando V. del Carmen, *Criminal Procedure*, p. 370.

25. Ibid., pp. 370–371.

26. Paul Wice, *Criminal Lawyers: An Endangered Species* (Beverly Hills, CA: Sage, 1978), pp. 212–221.

27. 21A American Jurisprudence 2d, "Criminal Law," § 1079 (1998).

28. Ibid., §§ 1030-1040. For data on the criminal justice system, see Patricia G. Barnes, *Desk Reference on American Criminal Justice*, (Washington, DC: CQ Press, 2000).

29. William T. Schantz, *The American Legal Environment: Individuals, Their Business, and Their Government* (St. Paul, MN: West, 1976), p. 300.

30. David J. Danelski, "The Chicago Conspiracy Trial" in *Political Trials*, edited by Theodore L. Becker (Indianapolis and New York: Bobbs-Merrill, 1971), p. 157.

31. 21A American Jurisprudence 2d, "Criminal Law," §§ 1085–1091 (1998).

32. Rolando V. del Carmen, *Criminal Procedure*, p. 43.

33. Ibid., p. 44.

34. Ibid., pp. 44–45.

35. Ibid., p. 45.

36. "Los Angeles Judge Dismisses Police Convictions," *The New York Times, National Edition* (December 24, 2000): Y17.

37. Rolando V. del Carmen, *Criminal Procedure*, pp. 45–46.

38. Ibid., pp. 412–413.

39. Don M. Gottfredson, *Exploring Criminal Justice: An Introduction* (Los Angeles: Roxbury Publishing, 1999), pp. 194, 252, 426–428.

40. William T. Schantz, *The American Legal Environment*, p. 302.

41. Don M. Gottfredson, *Exploring Criminal Justice: An Introduction*, p. 378.

42. Ibid. Also see majority opinion of Justice Abe Fortas in the case of In Re Gault, 387 U.S. 1 (1967).

43. Don M. Gottredson, *Exploring Criminal Justice: An Introduction*, pp. 380, 384.

44. Ibid., pp. 384–385.

45. Ibid., p. 382.

46. 387 U.S. 1 at 19.

47. 387 U.S. 1 at 28.

48. Lynn Cothern, *Juveniles and the Death Penalty* (Washington, DC: U.S. Department of Justice, Office of Juvenile Justice and Delinquency Prevention (November 2000), p. 1.

49. Office of Juvenile Justice and Delinquency Prevention, *Juveniles Facing Criminal Sanctions: Three States That Changed the Rules* (Washington, DC: U.S. Department of Justice, April 2000), p. 1. ✦

Chapter 8

Administrative Processes

Chapter Objectives

Students should gain an understanding of how administrative law operates at all levels of government and its profound impact on how Americans go about their daily existence. Readers should become acquainted with how government agencies come into existence, how agencies make rules and regulations, and how executive agencies interact with the other branches of government. Whenever feasible, students should identify similarities and differences of administrative law processes and other legal processes already studied in the previous chapters of this part of the book.

In today's complex world, government bureaucracies play an important role in the application and creation of legal rules governing our daily lives. Legislators create administrative agencies to carry out general policies and empower bureaucrats to implement the collective will of the people through the creation of rules and regulations consistent with statutory mandates. Legislatures grant administrative agencies powers because it is difficult, if not impossible, for legislators without expert knowledge and experience to promulgate rules and regulations to treat intricate problems in policy arenas of a highly specialized nature. Regulation of air and water pollution, for example, requires the exercise of judgment involving specific scientific information that is beyond the education and expertise of most elected officials. Inspection of meat and poultry is carried out by trained personnel of the U.S. Department of Agriculture, the function of which is vital to the health and well-being of millions of people in the United States and abroad. The Nuclear Regulatory Agency is responsible for safety standards and inspections at the nation's many nuclear power plants, and the Federal Energy Regulatory Commission monitors and regulates the supply and wholesale price of a substantial portion of electric power in this country.

There are dozens of federal government administrative agencies that make and enforce rules and regulations designed to serve the public interest. They regulate matters ranging from advertisement, trade practices, the money supply, the sale of securities, and unemployment insurance to minimum wage laws. Until recently, federal agencies were deeply involved in setting rates and schedules for railroads, buses, and airlines. They remain responsible for insuring public safety in the operation of these conveyances. State and local governments also employ hundreds of administrative agencies that are responsible for a variety of regulatory functions, such as building inspections, enforcement of minimum requirements for practicing trades and professions, automobile licensing, and the promulgation and enforcement of regulations pertaining to liquor retail establishments. Moreover, public agencies dispose of many more formal disputes than do federal and state civil courts. In addition, state and federal agencies informally make millions of decisions every year without formal hearings. About 122,000 federal bureaucrats adopt approximately 5,000 federal rules annually, compared with 435 members of the House of Representatives and 100 senators who pass less than 200 public laws each year.[1] Whether agency decisions are formal or informal, each rule and regulation legally binds individual citizens. And, unless administrative decisions are appealed to the courts or are overturned in the political process, bureaucratic judgments are binding.

Within the national and state governments, there are basically three types of executive branch organizations. Reflecting their unique histories, however, each of these governments organizes its administrative agencies somewhat differently. Because the federal government is the most prominent, we briefly review its pattern of organization.

The largest administrative units of the executive branch are called *departments*. They possess broad responsibility, with members of the president's cabinet serving as secretaries or heads of the departments of State, Treasury, Justice, Defense, Health and Human Services, Homeland Security, Interior, Agriculture, Commerce, Labor, Education, Energy, Transportation, Urban Development, and Veteran Affairs. Each of these departments contains sub-units, and they are called *agencies, bureaus, offices*, or *services*.

Not part of any cabinet department and controlled by the president to a lesser degree are *independent regulatory agencies*. The Central Intelligence Agency (CIA) reports directly to the president, but most others were created by Congress to operate as independent regulatory agencies. Examples include the Federal Trade Commission, the Federal Reserve System, and the Nuclear Regulatory Commission. The nation's chief executive appoints members of the regulatory commissions for fixed terms, but each body operates without formal presidential control.

Congress has also created a small number of *government corporations* that perform functions that private enterprise might also provide. The postal service was once a cabinet-level department, but today it is a government corporation that provides mail service for both profitable and unprofitable routes. In recent years especially, the postal service has encountered stiff competition from private businesses, including *Federal Express* and *United Parcel Service*. Amtrak train service exists because the private railroads essentially got out of the rail passenger business in favor of the more profitable freight service beginning in the late 1950s. The Tennessee Valley Authority (TVA) provides electric power to a vast area of Appalachia and beyond, because in the 1930s, without it, homes and businesses in this economically depressed region of the country would have been without this important utility, and economic development would have been retarded without it. Today, private utility companies argue for the curtailment of TVA functions in favor of the competitive marketplace.

Creating Administrative Agencies

Administrative agencies are created by legislatures through what is termed *enabling legislation*. That is, legislatures through the passage of legislation bring administrative agencies into existence. Enabling statutes set out broad operational standards governing how agencies must conduct their work. Because enabling legislation lays out broad standards of operational conduct, agencies are charged with *rule-making* responsibility: the details of how they will fulfill their assigned tasks, including descriptions of safeguards for the rights of persons who come in contact with them.

Authorization statutes are legislative grants of power to existing agencies requiring them to undertake new programs or duties.[2] In the case of the U.S. government, most of these rules are prescribed by the Administrative Procedure Act, 5 U.S.C. § 550 et seq. (2000), first enacted in 1946. Section 552 of the Act requires that each agency describe its central and field organization, the locations of its offices, and the methods whereby the public may attain information, make submittals or requests, or obtain decisions. The law requires that agencies make public how they function and how they formally and informally make decisions. Ultimately, this process produces a set of rules describing the agency's purpose, organization, and its practices and procedures.

Once the agency is in place, it is ready to make specific rules interpreting existing law. These rules are validly made on a daily basis. These include such matters as occupational safety regulations in factories, allowable levels of noxious emissions from automobiles and other pollutants, protection of environmentally sensitive habitat for wildlife, compensation for time spent on the job, interpretation of the tax code, and other regulations that affect our daily lives in a myriad of ways.

Rule-Making

Section 553 of the Administrative Procedure Act requires that proposed rules, regulations, or standards contemplated by agency officials be publicly announced. The public must be informed of the time, date, and place of the hearing on the proposed rule or standard, and all interested parties must be afforded many opportunities to comment before any standard or rule is adopted.

Congress creates federal administrative agencies.

Many states have adopted similar procedures.

In the case of the U.S. government, proposed rules are published in the *Federal Register*. Beginning in 1936, this daily publication is the original site of all federal administrative rules and regulations, including notice of proposed regulations and rules, dates of administrative hearings, and decisions of administrative bodies. Attentive interest groups, including business organizations subject to federal regulation, keep abreast of the *Federal Register* and are keen to comment on proposed agency rules that may affect how the agency and their own organization may interface. Upon receiving comments from interested persons or organizations, agency employees then review the comments and revise the rules for republication. Typically, the proposed rules do not become final for a period of 30 days to permit additional time for comment or protest.

Because the *Federal Register* is arranged chronologically and not by subject matter, persons or organizations interested in the rules and regulations of particular agencies or subject matters should consult the *Code of Federal Regulations* (C.F.R.). Similar in organization to the United States Code (U.S.C.), this publication appears under 50 separate titles and is revised each year.[3]

During the 1990s, there was a serious effort to simplify the rule-making process of the federal government, and a number of agencies devised new rules for rule-making under the general rubric of the "Rule-Making Process for Administrative Simplification." The Department of Health and Human Services (HHS) has been a leader in the simplification movement, but while the goal is simplification, the process is far from simple. It is a purposeful process, however, designed to achieve consensus within HHS and across other departments of the federal government.

In 1998, for example, implementation teams within HHS drafted notices of proposed new rules involving: Administrative and Financial Transaction Standards and Code Sets; National Provider Identifier for Health Care Providers; Identifier for Health Plans; Identifier for Employers; and Security Standards to Protect Health Care Information. Prior to the publication of a proposed new rule in the *Federal Register,* it must be reviewed and approved within the Federal government in a three-stage process. First, the proposed new rule must be approved by the HHS Data Council's Committee on Health Data Standards. The Committee, whose members are from many federal agencies, monitors the entire administrative simplification implementation process for the HHS Secretary. The Committee must approve the content of the new rule before it goes to the next review step. Next, because new rules may impact a variety of agencies within HHS, agency heads acting as formal advisors to the HHS Secretary must agree on the content of the rules before it may go to the next review step. Finally, the Office of Management and Budget (OMB) reviews proposed rules from a government-wide perspective to determine how each might affect federal departments other than HHS. OMB also reviews each proposed rule for its effects on the federal budget, intergovernmental relations, and small business. It also considers whether the proposed rule complies with other executive orders. Only then is the proposed new rule made public through publication in the *Federal Register,* followed by a public comment period, public inspection of comments, analysis of comments, and the publication of the final rule (see Box 8.1 for the HHS statement of these steps).[4]

Box 8.1   Health and Human Services (HHS) Statement of Rule-Promulgation Rules*

1. **Publication of Proposed Rule.** A Notice of Proposed Rule-Making (NPRM) is published in the *Federal Register* and on the Administrative Simplification (AS) [website].

2. **Comment Period.** Each NPRM is followed by a period set aside for public comment. Comments will be accepted through this website and by postal mail for 60 days following publication. The purpose of the comment period is to provide an opportunity for the public and interested and affected parties to influence the outcome by raising issues and questions that can be addressed before the regulation is finalized.

3. **Public Inspection of Comments.** Comments received are made available for public inspection. Traditionally, comments submitted by mail are

available for public viewing in a room at HHS Headquarters in Washington, DC. Comments will be available for public viewing at this website after the comment period has ended.

4. **Analysis of Comments.** Comments are analyzed and summarized, and responses are prepared by the Implementation Teams responsible for the content.

5. **Publication of Final Rule.** The Final Rule is published in the *Federal Register* and on the AS Home Page. The Final Rule includes a summary of the comments and responses to the comments, including any changes that were made to the proposed regulation as a result of the comments.

*<http://aspe.os.dhhs.gov/admnsimp/8steps.htm> [7-2-1999].

Constitutional Limitations

Though our administrative system may seem a rational way to treat complex societal problems, nonetheless there is a fundamental problem. It is exceedingly difficult for either the executive or the legislative branch to control administrative agencies. History teaches us that in human affairs it is advisable to hold institutions accountable. In our constitutional system, the people have granted Congress the power to make law and the executive branch the power to execute it. Article I, section 1 of the Constitution is explicit in this regard: "All legislative Powers herein granted shall be *vested* in a Congress of the United States, which shall consist of a Senate and a House of Representatives" [emphasis added]. And Article II *vests* all executive power in the president of the United States.

Many thoughtful Americans believe that Congress has alienated its legislative power. It has passed enabling legislation and authorizing statutes providing administrative agencies with substantial authority to create rules on their own. Compounding the matter, presidents are relatively impotent to control the bureaucracies for which they possess ostensible constitutional authority as the nation's "chief executive." Congress has sought to ameliorate the problem by establishing and maintaining oversight functions that monitor bureaucratic activity. Legislative oversight permits members of Congress to develop subject matter expertise and close relationships with agency officials, personnel, and affected interest groups regulated by the government agencies. Further, because of its appropriations power, Congress is in a position to constrain the president's role in the performance of his chief executive function. Congress has also attempted to control unwanted bureaucratic decisions through the *legislative veto*: a device included in some twentieth-century legislation that allows the rejection of an administrative or executive action by either the House of Representatives or the Senate, or of both, without the consent of the president. The U.S.

Supreme Court, however, declared in Immigration & Naturalization Service v. Chadha, 462 U.S. 919 (1983), that a one-house veto of a deportation order violated the Constitution's Presentment Clause (Art. I, sec. 7, cl. 3). Chief Justice Warren Burger ruled that the one-house veto amounts to an amendment to a law, although under the Constitution, all laws and amendments must be the product of the vote of two houses of Congress and must be presented to the president for his signature.

Congressional Delegation of Law-Making Power

Three early twentieth-century U.S. Supreme Court landmark opinions illustrate the problem of congressional delegation of legislative authority: Hampton & Co. v. United States, 276 U.S. 394 (1928), Panama Refining Co. v. Ryan, 293 U.S. 388 (1935), and Schechter Poultry Corp. v. United States, 295 U.S. 495 (1935).

The *Hampton* opinion focused on Title III, Section 315(a), of the *Tariff Act of 1922.* This statutory provision granted the president authority to increase or decrease import duties imposed on foreign goods with the goal of equalizing the differences in production costs of articles manufactured in the United States and in other lands. After a hearing held in 1924 before the United States Tariff Commission, the President issued an order raising the four cents per pound duty on barium dioxide to six cents. This action adversely affected the business fortunes of J.W. Hampton & Company, and the company challenged the constitutionality of Section 315(a) as an invalid delegation of legislative power. The company lost in the lower federal courts. It then appealed to the U.S. Supreme Court.

At issue was whether the law granting the president discretionary authority to increase or decrease duties was an unconstitutional delegation of the power of Congress to lay and collect taxes, duties, imposts, and excises. Writing for the Supreme Court, William Howard Taft, the former president and now Chief Justice, held that it was not. Taft, who was an articulate advocate of a restricted view of presidential power, conceded nevertheless that in the modern world there is a need to act quickly and conveniently, and that Congress may delegate to the executive branch the power to make rules to confront particular situations. Clearly, Taft understood that Congress granted to the president the authority to make law, despite the fact that the constitutional framers vested all lawmaking power in the Congress of the United States. This admission was a major concession to the demands of modernity. Through constitutional interpretation, the Chief Justice created an important exception to the plain meaning of the words of Article I. He ruled that when Congress delegates its authority to the executive, it must lay down by legislative act *an intelligible principle* to which the person or body is directed to obey the rules. In other words, Congress may grant to the president lawmaking power, but that power must be guided by clear legislative principles.

Contrast the *Hampton* opinion with the Supreme Court's opinion in *Panama Refining Company v. Ryan* (1935). In an attempt to deal with the economic calamity of the Great Depression in the 1930s, Congress and President Franklin D. Roosevelt enacted a number of laws to do something that might turn the economy around. One attempt was the creation of the *National Industrial Recovery Act*. Among its provisions, Section 9 (c) of this law created so-called "codes of fair competition" that granted the president authority to prohibit the transportation of petroleum products in interstate and foreign commerce that were produced or withdrawn from storage in excess of the amounts permitted by state officials. Ironically, this provision, while contrary to the ideology of market capitalism, was intended to control the supply of petroleum and therefore save the industry from excessive internal competition.

Writing for the majority of the Supreme Court, Chief Justice Charles Evans Hughes declared Section 9 (c) an unconstitutional delegation of legislative authority. He found the law declared no policy, established no standards, and laid down no rules to guide the president in defining the circumstances and conditions in which the transportation of petroleum should be allowed or prohibited. In short, the president became the lawmaker, because the entire discretion in the matter rested with him and members of his executive team.

The most famous New Deal era delegation case is *Schechter Poultry Corp. v. United States* (1935), popularly known as the *Sick Chicken* case. This opinion is particularly noteworthy from a political perspective because the Supreme Court left no question that the *National Industrial Recovery Act* was unconstitutional and, in the process, it rebuffed the Roosevelt administration's attempt to rescue the economy from the Great Depression.

As with the *Panama Refining* case, this dispute with the Schechter brothers involved the establishment of a code of fair competition, but in this instance the code was aimed at the poultry business. It involved wages, hours, employment practices, general working conditions, and methods of competition, including the selling of diseased poultry in interstate commerce. The Schechter brothers owned slaughterhouses in New York City that received live chickens from outside the state. They slaughtered the poultry and then sold the products to local retail butchers. They were convicted in U.S. District Court for violating the Live Poultry Code on a number of counts, including filing false sales and price reports and selling diseased chickens. The U.S. Court of Appeals for the Second Circuit affirmed the conviction in part and both the defendants and the government successfully sought a writ of certiorari from the U.S. Supreme Court.

Chief Justice Hughes struck down the *National Industrial Recovery Act* because, in this instance, the congressional act did not adequately define the subject to which the codes are to be addressed. At least in the *Panama Refining* case, Hughes pointed out, the subject of the statutory prohibition was defined (the transportation of petroleum). In the *Sick Chicken* regulation, the congressional enactment provided no indication that the poultry industry may be regulated. Further, the National Industrial Recovery Act did not define "fair competition." It granted to the president unfettered discretion to make whatever laws he deemed advisable, but Congress supplied no standards for any trade, industry, or activity. In brief, Congress did not prescribe rules of conduct. Instead, it authorized the making of codes to prescribe conduct, and this represented an unconstitutional delegation of legislative power.

Along with other negative Court opinions during this same period, the decision showed that the U.S. Supreme Court had become a major opponent of the New Deal. President Roosevelt met this attack with an attack of his own—the ill-fated "Court Packing Plan." Roosevelt proposed to increase the number of Supreme Court justices from the current nine to a maximum of fifteen. One new seat would be created for each justice who, upon reaching the age of 70 years, declined to retire. The president justified his proposal in humanitarian terms—as a way to relieve the workload of aging Supreme Court justices, but it was widely viewed as a transparent attempt to stack the Court with persons favorable to the New Deal.[5]

Since the New Deal era, members of Congress have made an effort to prescribe standards for the delegation of legislative power to the president. Many authorities believe, however, that there are few limitations on the power of Congress to delegate legislative authority. Yet, for all its obstructionism, the conservative Supreme Court of the first third of the twentieth century contributed importantly to circumscribing unlimited presidential power. It insisted that when Congress delegates its law-making power to the executive, it must lay down intelligible principles that the executive must follow, guided by clear legislative mandates.

Presidential Powers and Constraints

Although the complex problems of the modern world tend to move effective power away from legislative chambers, it does not mean necessarily that the nation's chief executives are the beneficiaries. Administrative agencies have a life of their own that makes it difficult for presidents or governors of the various states of the union to control them with precision. There is, however, an important distinction between the executive power in foreign affairs and domestic matters.

The *sole organ theory* of presidential power is attributable to U.S. Supreme Court Justice George Sutherland in his famous opinion in United States v. Curtiss-Wright Export Corp., 299 U.S. 304 (1936). He emphasized that the power of the national government when dealing with foreign affairs is vastly different from that concerning domestic matters. He made this problematic argument:

Official residence of the Chief Executive and Commander-in-Chief.

> The broad statement that the federal government can exercise no powers except those specifically enumerated in the Constitution, and such implied powers as are necessary and proper to carry into effect the enumerated powers, is categorically true only in respect to our internal affairs.[6]

This statement is questionable because it denies the fundamental supposition that the Constitution limits power and that power may be granted only by the people. Sutherland then went on to write:

> In this vast external realm with its important, complicated, delicate and manifold problems, the President alone has the power to speak or listen as a representative of the nation. He makes treaties with the advice and consent of the Senate; but he alone negotiates. In the field of negotiation the Senate cannot intrude; and Congress itself is powerless to invade it.[7]

One year later in United States v. Belmont, 301 U.S. 324 (1937), the high court approved pacts between the president and the heads of other governments called *executive agreements*. The Supreme Court held that the president's constitutional authority as commander-in-chief, and in his capacity as the nation's chief spokesperson in international affairs, does not require senatorial approval of executive agreements, as is the case for formal treaties. Significantly, in the name of the sole organ theory presidents have taken the country into undeclared wars without formal congressional approval. Congress, however, has attempted to limit presidential power in foreign affairs with the passage of the 1972 Case-Zablocki Act, 1 U.S.C. § 112b (2000), which requires presidents to notify Congress of each promulgated executive agreement. The 1973 War Powers Resolution, 87 Stat. 555, limits the ability of presidents to conduct undeclared wars. Despite these laws, however, all modern presidents, re-

The President is in a strong position to initiate war.

gardless of their political party, have resisted congressional attempts to limit their powers with respect to external affairs.

As we have already learned from our discussion of legislative delegation of law-making power, presidential power, though substantial, is limited. Except for the pardoning power, the chief executive's power is constitutionally limited to carrying out the laws made by Congress. At times, however, presidents do not comply with laws, either by failing to enforce statutes believed unwise or unenforceable or by refusing to spend funds appropriated by Congress. When presidents impound funds, they are often challenged in court; and though Congress has attempted to control such practices through the passage in 1974 of the Budget and Impoundment Control Act, 2 U.S.C. §§ 665, 1401-1407 (2000), recent presidents nonetheless impound about $12 billion each year.[8]

Bureaucratic intransigence. Though legislators and chief executives struggle to obtain hegemony, each is faced with the seemingly intractable problem of controlling the bureaucracy. All modern presidents have complained that it is difficult to move government agencies to reflect their wills. Agency rules, regulations, and procedures tend to insulate bureaucrats from political control. Although presidents appoint the heads of many agencies and Congress controls agency appropriations, the routine ways of conducting agency business and the difficulty in removing entrenched civil servants function to impede and defeat proposals for rapid change. Elected officials and political appointees come and go. Advantage goes to those possessing expertise and first-hand familiarity with administrative matters. Insisting on the rule of law is an important barrier to otherwise unrestrained bureaucratic power. The following case involves the rule-making authority of the Environmental Protection Agency. It illustrates that the courts represent a formidable barrier to the unrestrained law-making authority of administrative agencies.

**Flue-Cured Tobacco Cooperative Stabilization Corp.
v. United States Environmental Protection Agency
United States District Court
for the Middle District of North Carolina
4 F. Supp. 2d 435 (1998)**

Opinion by Judge Osteen.

This case is before the court on the parties' cross motions for partial summary judgment on Counts I-III of the Complaint. These counts raise Administrative Procedure Act (APA) challenges to EPA's report, Respiratory Health Effects of Passive Smoking: Lung Cancer and Other Disorders, EPA/600/6-90/006F, December 1992 (ETS Risk Assessment). EPA claims its authority to conduct the ETS Risk Assessment derives from the Radon Gas and Indoor Air Quality Research Act of 1986, Pub. L. No. 99-499, 100 Stat. 1758-60 (1986) (Radon Research Act) (codified at 42 U.S.C. § 7401 (1994)). In the ETS Risk Assessment, EPA evaluated the respiratory health effects of breathing secondhand smoke (environmental tobacco smoke or ETS) and classified ETS as a Group A carcinogen, a designation meaning there is sufficient evidence to conclude ETS causes cancer in humans. Disputing the Assessment, Plaintiffs argue: EPA exceeded its authority under and violated the restrictions within the Radon Research Act; EPA did not comply with the Radon Research Act's procedural requirements; EPA violated administrative law procedure by making a conclusion regarding ETS before it concluded its risk assessment, and EPA's ETS Risk Assessment was not the result of reasoned decision making. EPA denies the same and argues the administrative record . . . demonstrates reasoned decision making. . . .

The Radon Research Act

The Radon Research Act was enacted by Congress as Title IV of the Superfund Amendments and Reauthorization Act of 1986 (SARA) and codified with the Clean Air Act at 42 U.S.C. § 7401. The Act was based on Congress' finding: "exposure to naturally occurring radon and indoor air pollutants poses public health risk[s]," id. § 402(2); "Federal radon and indoor air pollutant research programs are fragmented and underfunded," id. § 402(3); and an "information base concerning exposure to radon and indoor air pollutants should be developed. . . ." Id. § 402(4). The act provides

(a) Design of Program.—[The EPA] shall establish a research program with respect to radon gas and indoor air quality. Such program shall be designed to—
(1) gather data and information on all aspects of indoor air quality in order to contribute to the understanding of health problems associated with the existence of air pollutants in the indoor environment;
(2) coordinate Federal, State, local, and private research and development efforts relating to the improvement of indoor air quality; and
(3) assess appropriate Federal Government actions to mitigate the environmental and health risks associated with indoor air quality problems.
(b) Program requirements.— The research program required under this section shall include—

(1) research and development concerning the identification, characterization, and monitoring of the sources and levels of indoor air pollution. . . .
(2) research relating to the effects of indoor air pollution and radon on human health. . . .
(6) the dissemination of information to assure the public availability of the findings of the activities under this section. . . .

Congress also required a narrow construction of the authority delegated under the Radon Research Act. Nothing in the act "shall be construed to authorize the [EPA] to carry out any regulatory program or any activity other than research, development, and related reporting, information dissemination, and coordination activities specified in [the Radon Research Act]." . . .

The Act requires EPA to establish two advisory groups to assist EPA in carrying out its statutory obligations under the Radon Research Act. One of the advisory groups is to be a committee comprised of representatives of federal agencies concerned with various aspects of indoor air quality, and the other group is to be "an advisory group comprised of individuals representing the States, the scientific community, industry, and public interest organizations. . . ." The Act requires EPA to submit its research plan to the EPA Science Advisory Board which, in turn, would submit comments to Congress. . . .

Standard of Review

Administrative agencies have no power to act beyond authority conferred by Congress. . . . Title 5 U.S.C. § 706(2)(C) requires the court to "hold unlawful and set aside agency action . . . found to be . . . in excess of statutory jurisdiction, authority, or limitations, or short of statutory right. " The initial inquiry for judicial review of agency action is "whether Congress has directly spoken to the precise question at issue. If the intent of Congress is clear, that is the end of the matter; for the court, as well as the agency, must give effect to the unambiguously expressed intent of Congress." Chevron, U.S.A., Inc. v. Natural Resources Defense Council, Inc., 467 U.S. 837, 842-43 (1984). "The task of resolving the dispute over the meaning of [the statute] begins where all such inquiries must begin: with the language of the statute itself." United States v. Ron Pair Enter., Inc., 489 U.S. 235, 241 (1989). "The judiciary . . . is the final authority on issues of statutory construction and will reject administrative interpretations which are contrary to the clear congressional intent. " Adams v. Dole, 927 F.2d 771, 774 (4th Cir. 1991).

"If the statute is silent or ambiguous with respect to the specific issue, the question for the court is whether the agency's answer is based on a permissible construction of the statute." Chevron, 467 U.S. at 843 . . . Courts do not always abide by this *Chevron* deference. Although the circuits appear divided, the majority of post-*Chevron* cases hold no deference is accorded to an agency's view of a statute where the statute does not confer rule making authority on the agency. . . . Another factor in determining an agency's discretion in statutory interpretation is the specificity of interpretation. Courts determine the general meaning of legislation, whereas agencies are often better equipped to determine interstitial meanings. . . .

EPA's Procedural Requirements Under the Radon Research Act

. . . Plaintiffs argue EPA failed to establish and consult the advisory group mandated by the Radon Research Act, therefore, EPA's conduct under the Act was unlawful and must be vacated. EPA responds by arguing it satisfied its procedural requirements by consulting the EPA Science Advisory Board (SAB). EPA states it formed an advisory group within SAB which included representatives of all the statutorily identified constituencies. EPA further argues that even if it did not satisfy the Radon Research Act's procedural requirements: (1) the Act speaks in general terms and committee formation was not a prerequisite to research activity under the Act, and (2) Plaintiffs were not prejudiced because EPA utilized public participation and peer review procedures in developing the ETS Risk Assessment. In reply, Plaintiffs analyze SAB and the members of the board which reviewed the ETS Risk Assessment. . . .

In reviewing the parties' arguments, the court has given the benefit of many doubts to EPA by allowing the Agency to adopt third party statements, such as IAQC [Indoor Air Quality/Total Human Exposure Committee] reviews, as Agency reasoning. EPA, the decision maker, not IAQC, the independent advisor, has the duty to demonstrate reasoned decision making on the record. . . . The Administrator will still have the responsibility for making the decisions required of him by law. If EPA's appendages speak on behalf of the Administrator, the opposing conclusions reached between IAQC and the EPA Risk Criteria Office would demonstrate schizophrenia. Even allowing EPA the benefit of now adopting IAQC reasoning, the record does not provide answers to Plaintiffs' questions.

EPA determined it was biologically plausible that ETS [Environmental Tobacco Smoke] causes lung cancer. In doing so, EPA recognized problems with its theory, namely the dissimilarities between MS [Mainstream Smoke] and ETS. In other areas of the Assessment, EPA relied on these dissimilarities in justifying its methodology. EPA did not explain much of the criteria and assertions upon which EPA's theory relies. EPA claimed selected epidemiologic studies would affirm its plausibility theory. The studies EPA selected did not include a significant number of studies and data which demonstrated no association between ETS and cancer. EPA did not explain its criteria for study selection, thus leaving itself open to allegations of "cherry picking."

Using its normal methodology and its selected studies, EPA did not demonstrate a statistically significant association between ETS and lung cancer. This should have caused EPA to reevaluate the inference options used in establishing its plausibility theory. A risk assessment is supposed to entail the best judgment possible based upon the available evidence. . . . Instead, EPA changed its methodology to find a statistically significant association. EPA claimed, but did not explain how, its theory justified changing the Agency's methodology. With the changed methodology and selected studies, EPA established evidence of a weak statistically significant association between ETS and lung cancer.

Conclusion

In 1988, EPA initiated drafting policy-based recommendations about controlling ETS exposure because

EPA believed ETS is a Group A carcinogen. . . . Rather than reach a conclusion after collecting information, researching, and making findings, EPA categorized ETS as a "known cause of cancer" in 1989. . . . EPA's Administrator admitted that EPA "managed to confuse and anger all parties to the smoking ETS debate. . . ." The Administrator also conceded, "Beginning the development of an Agency risk assessment after the commencement of work on the draft policy guide gave the appearance of . . . policy leading science. . . ."

In conducting the Assessment, EPA deemed it biologically plausible that ETS was a carcinogen. EPA's theory was premised on the similarities between MS, SS [diluted Sidestream Smoke], and ETS. In other chapters, the Agency used MS and ETS dissimilarities to justify methodology. Recognizing problems, EPA attempted to confirm the theory with epidemiologic studies. After choosing a portion of the studies, EPA did not find a statistically significant association. EPA then claimed the bioplausibility theory, denominated the *a priori* hypothesis, justified a more lenient methodology. With a new methodology, EPA demonstrated from the selected studies a very low relative risk for lung cancer based on ETS exposure. Based on its original theory and the weak evidence of association, EPA concluded the evidence showed a causal relationship between cancer and ETS. The administrative record contains glaring deficiencies.

The Radon Research Act authorizes information collection, research, industry inclusion, and dissemination of findings. Whether these actions authorize risk assessments is a matter of general and interstitial statutory construction. So long as information collection on all relevant aspects of indoor air quality, research, and dissemination are the lodestars, the general language of the Radon Research Act authorizes risk assessments as they are defined by NRC [National Resource Council] and explained in EPA's Risk Assessment Guidelines.

It is clear that Congress intended EPA to disseminate findings from the information researched and gathered. In this case, EPA publicly committed to a conclusion before research had begun; excluded industry by violating the Act's procedural requirements; adjusted established procedure and scientific norms to validate the Agency's public conclusion, and aggressively utilized the Act's authority to disseminate findings to establish a de facto regulatory scheme intended to restrict Plaintiffs' products and to influence public opinion. In conducting the ETS Risk Assessment, EPA disregarded information and made findings on selective information; did not disseminate significant epidemiologic information; deviated from its Risk Assessment Guidelines; failed to disclose important findings and reasoning; and left significant questions without answers. EPA's conduct left substantial holes in the administrative record. While so doing, EPA produced limited evidence, then claimed the weight of the Agency's research evidence demonstrated ETS causes cancer.

Gathering all relevant information, researching, and disseminating findings were subordinate to EPA's demonstrating ETS a Group A carcinogen. EPA's conduct transgressed the general meaning of the Radon Research Act's operative language. Further, to the extent EPA's conduct in this matter entailed interstitial construction of the Act, the court affords no deference to EPA. Congress did not delegate rule making or regulatory authority to EPA under the Act. EPA's conduct of the ETS Risk Assessment frustrated the clear Congressional policy underlying the Radon Research Act. . . . ([P]urpose of the Act is to provide clear, objective information about indoor air quality).

EPA also failed the Act's procedural requirements. In the Radon Research Act, Congress granted EPA limited research authority along with an obligation to seek advice from a representative committee during such research. Congress intended industry representatives to be at the table and their voices heard during the research process. EPA's authority under the act is contingent upon the Agency hearing and responding to the represented constituents' con-

cerns. The record evidence is overwhelming that IAQC was not the representative body required under the Act. Had EPA reconciled industry objections voiced from a representative body during the research process, the ETS Risk Assessment would very possibly not have been conducted in the same manner nor reached the same conclusions.

Because EPA exceeded its authority under the Radon Research Act and also failed the Act's procedural requirements, the court will direct the entry of judgment in favor of Plaintiffs' motion for summary judgment and vacate Chapters 1–6 of and the Appendices to EPA's Respiratory Health Effects of Passive Smoking: Lung Cancer and Other Disorders, EPA/600/6-90/006F (December 1992). . . .

An order and judgment in accordance with this memorandum opinion will be filed contemporaneously herewith.

Smoker and second-hand risks.

Case Questions for Discussion

1. What is the standard of review for the courts in discerning whether administrative agencies are acting within the authority granted by Congress?

2. How closely should legislative bodies and the courts monitor the way that laws are implemented by administrative agencies?

3. Why did Congress include advisory industry groups as part of the *Radon Research Act*? Should such representatives be part of the decision-making process?

4. Given the complexity of determining health risks, do you think the judge acted properly when he concluded that Congress did not authorize the EPA to make a rule concerning the relationship between ETS and lung cancer? Is it best to leave such matters to the experts?

Information and Investigation

If government agencies are to fulfill their rule-making and other functions, they must have access to factual information. Agencies enjoy considerable latitude when obtaining information necessary for carrying out their functions. Legislators empower agencies to subpoena records, reports, and other printed or electronically generated materials that are reasonably pertinent to matters at issue. Physical inspection of property with a warrant issued by a judge, and often without one, permits agencies to inspect places of businesses that may present a health and safety hazard to the public, such as restaurants, bars, hotels, and manufacturers that use hazardous chemicals or other dangerous materials. Even private homes may be subject to a search by welfare agencies if, for example, there is sufficient reason to believe that children are subjected to an unhealthy or abusive home environment, or if a crime has been or is about to be committed therein. Administrative agencies may compel testimony by requiring the presentation of company records and by requiring that certain records be kept. Likewise, as in other legal processes, individuals and bodies in conflict with agencies must be able to procure information in defense of their own interests, including a limited right of subpoena, a similar but less pronounced version of the type employed in a regular civil trial. And in a democratic society that values individual rights, protecting the privacy of persons coming in contact with bureaucracy is warranted and widely prized. The Internal Revenue Service, for example, may not release personal or corporate income tax return information to the public. Nor, for that matter, may academic transcripts be revealed to others without student permission.[9]

The 1966 U.S. Freedom of Information Act (FOIA), 5 U.S.C. § 552 (2000), and state sunshine laws require government agencies to function in the open. The federal law requires federal agencies to publish their acts, functions, final orders, rules, and staff manuals. State sunshine laws require that most meetings of public bodies be open to the public.[10] These laws are based on the assumption that the best disinfectant to be applied to a factually or potentially corrupt or abusive government is direct exposure to the hot sunlight of public scrutiny. The U.S. Freedom of Information Act requires the government to release information in its possession to a requesting party, unless such information is exempted under the act, including trade secrets, evidentiary privileged information, or information that compromises privacy rights. The 1974 Privacy Act, 5 U.S.C. § 552a (2000), permits individuals to access files that government agencies may have on them. One can obtain this information by filing a freedom of information request. Finally, the 1976 open meetings provision of the Administrative Procedure Act, 5 U.S.C. § 552b (2000), requires agencies that conduct public business to notify the public of any meetings. There are, of course, exemptions, as is the case with all these laws.[11]

The constitutional principle of *executive privilege* is an exception to the norm of government openness. It is the doctrine that executive officials, including the president, possess a constitutional right to refuse to appear and give testimony before Congress or the courts. The application of this principle permits presidents to refuse to reveal communications between themselves and their subordinates founded upon the separation of powers principle. The controversial nature of this hotly debated topic limits the extent to which chief executives have chosen to employ this doctrine.[12]

The Minnesota case that follows illustrates the serious issues that arise when government agencies seek to secure documents and interrogatories from businesses. In this particular case, the corporation and its owner were suspected of cheating customers in its mail-order trade. Most issues are resolved in favor of the state, but only after an interesting discussion of statutory and constitutional rights.

In re Kohn v. Minnesota
Supreme Court of Minnesota
336 N.W.2d 292 (1983)

Opinion by Justice Simonett:
The district court granted the motion of the Minnesota Attorney General on behalf of the state to compel respondents in a civil investigative proceeding to produce business documents and to answer interrogatories, and it denied respondents' motion for a protective order. Granting discretionary review of the trial court's order, we affirm in part, reverse in part, and remand for further proceedings.

Minn. Stat. § 8.31 (1982) instructs the Attorney General to investigate violations of the business and trade laws of this state and authorizes discovery without commencement of a civil action. Pursuant to this authority, the Attorney General seeks to investigate the affairs of respondents Gary Kohn and three Minnesota corporations, Racing Unlimited, Inc., Sports Accessories International, and Minnesota Auto Specialties. Kohn and the three corporations are here as appellants seeking appellate review.

Gary Kohn owns, is an officer of, and operates several Minnesota corporations, including the three involved here, all of which are engaged in the mail order sale of merchandise. Racing Unlimited, Inc. and Minnesota Auto Specialties sell auto parts and accessories, and share product line, building, and records. Sports Accessories International markets auto-related novelty items such as T-shirts and decals. The companies advertise and do business on a national scale. The businesses, as measured by the number of orders placed, have grown significantly over the last 3 years.

The state and also the Minnesota Better Business Bureau have received numerous complaints from customers claiming that they received neither the ordered merchandise nor a refund of the cash deposit which must accompany each order, usually a sum in the range of $60 to $120. As of July 1982, the Attorney General's office had received 29 complaints against the three corporations, of which 15 remained unresolved. The Attorney General also reviewed the Minnesota Better Business Bureau files which revealed 103 complaints against the three companies, 62 remaining unresolved. In addition, the state has received requests for assistance from attorney general's offices in 12 states and from Better Business Bureaus in three of those states and nine others. In a motion to expedite this appeal, the Attorney General claims it continues to receive complaints.

On June 29, 1982, the state issued a Civil Investigative Demand (here referred to as the Demand or a C.I.D.) addressed to Gary Kohn consisting of a demand for the production of six kinds of documents and a set of 27 interrogatories. The demand for documents included copies of advertisements, manufacturers' agreements and monthly bank statements. The interrogatories dealt with advertising practices, customer orders and source of products. The Demand indicated that it was issued pursuant to Minn. Stat. § 8.31 (1982) to determine whether Kohn and the three companies had violated Minn. Stat. §§ 325D.44 (deceptive trade practices), 325F.67 (false statement in advertising), or 325F.69 (consumer fraud) (1982). Kohn's counsel countered with a letter to the Attorney General denying the legality of the Civil Investigative Demand, but offering to discuss the resolution of specific complaints. The state promptly responded by initiating this proceeding, filing with the district court a motion for an order compelling compliance with the C.I.D. Kohn then filed a cross-motion for the issuance of a protective order. Both parties filed supporting affidavits. The affidavits of the Attorney General's office summarized the extent and general nature of the complaints, stated that the Better Business Bureau had been unsuccessful in resolving many of the complaints and that, as to complaints handled directly by the Attorney General, some were resolved but only after repeated requests, typically requiring at least three letters to Kohn.

On September 8, 1982, the trial court granted the state's motion to compel and denied Kohn's motion to protect. On appeal, Kohn claims that the Attorney General did not make a sufficient showing of the statutory grounds for compelling compliance with a Civil Investigative Demand, and that the Demand was an unreasonable search and seizure under the fourth amendment, compelled self-incrimination contrary to the fifth amendment, and was discriminatory law enforcement in violation of the equal protection clause of the fourteenth amendment.

1. We first discuss appellant Kohn's claim that the Attorney General failed to make the sufficient factual showing required by the statute for issuance and enforcement of a Civil Investigative Demand. Minn. Stat. § 8.31, subd. 2 (1982), provides in part:

"When the attorney general, *from information in his possession, has reasonable ground to believe* that any person has violated, or is about to violate, any of the laws of this state referred to in subdivision 1 [the state consumer protection laws], he shall have power to investigate those violations, or suspected violations." [Emphasis added]

The subdivision goes on to authorize the Attorney General to obtain discovery by various means such as written interrogatories, demand for production of documents and depositions. Subdivision 2a then deals with failure to comply:

"If any person fails or refuses to answer interrogatories, to produce materials, or to be examined under oath, as required by the provisions of subdivision 2, the attorney general may give notice that he will apply to a district court, and the court, *on a showing by the attorney general of cause therefor,* may issue such order as may be required to compel compliance with the discovery procedures authorized by this section." [Emphasis added]

Appellants argue that the trial court erred in finding, on the affidavits submitted, that the Attorney General had reasonable grounds to believe that Kohn had violated or was about to violate the law. Kohn points out that his affidavit shows that, for the 3-year period involved, his companies received 47,655 orders and only 111 complaints, or complaints for only 0.2% of orders received, and that of the complaints received, a large number have been resolved. Further, Kohn argues that the Attorney General has not made any independent investigation to determine the merits of any individual consumer complaint. For these reasons, Kohn asserts that the Attorney General has failed to show a reasonable ground for believing there has been or will be a violation of the law.

Appellants' argument misconceives the nature of these proceedings. The Attorney General is currently conducting only an investigation. No complaint has been filed and the parties are not at the trial stage. The purpose of the state's investigation is not to prove pending charges, for the state has made none, but to ascertain if there is any substance to the customer complaints so that charges should or should not be brought. . . . This precomplaint procedure was created because other methods of obtaining information had proved unsatisfactory. The voluntary cooperation of the party being investigated was not always forthcoming. Nor did it seem fair for the state to file a bare-bones complaint, as it could do, and then undertake discovery in an adversary setting to ascertain if it had a case. Experience has indicated that the precomplaint investigative procedure, somewhat akin to a state's visitorial powers over corporations, is often the best and fairest manner in which to proceed.

Thus, to obtain discovery, our statute requires only that the Attorney General has reasonable grounds to believe there is or may be a violation of state law. It is enough to show, on the basis of information the Attorney General already has, that it is reasonable for the investigation to continue.

Kohn argues that the Attorney General has made an inadequate showing for a Civil Investigative Demand because the consumer complaints were not first investigated or substantiated. But the purpose of the discovery is to ascertain if there is any substance to the consumer complaints from the party who is perhaps in the best position to know, namely, the party against whom the complaint is made.

The fact that Kohn files an affidavit controverting the allegations of the state does not necessarily establish a lack of reasonable grounds for the Attorney General to believe that there have been violations. This is not to say that a respondent may not dispute the state's showing of reasonable grounds and that there may not be instances where a C.I.D. should not issue. . . .We simply hold that at this administrative investigatory stage the trial court is not required to weigh evidence and resolve factual disputes in the same manner as at a trial. Though the factual showing be disputed, even so, if it affords a reasonable ground for believing the investigation should continue, it will suffice. To require the state to substantiate its case before it may be allowed to investigate it would put the cart before the horse.

Next, appellant Kohn argues that there was no "reasonable ground to believe" that he had violated or was about to violate the law because the consumer complaints constituted a small fraction of his total business. We do not find this argument persuasive. The presence of over 100 complaints is not *de minimis,* nor does it follow, as appellants suggest, that all the customers who did not file complaints were necessarily content. Moreover, of the number of complaints that were filed, a high percentage were alleged to have been handled in a dilatory manner.

We affirm the trial court's finding that the Attorney General, at the time he issued the Civil Investigative Demand, had, in his possession, information which afforded him reasonable grounds to believe the law had been or was about to be violated.

II. Appellant Kohn next argues that the state's demand for production of business documents constitutes a "constructive search" of the business premises and violates the fourth amendment prohibition against unreasonable search and seizure. The trial court found no merit to this argument and neither do we.

A demand for documents may be so unbounded or so over-inclusive or vague as to constitute a "constructive search." See generally Oklahoma Press Publishing Co. v. Walling, 327 U.S. 186, 202-05 (1946). The permissible breadth, however, is considerable. In *Oklahoma Press* the United States Supreme Court likened the administrator seeking information to a grand jury. The administrator's investigation is "essentially the same as the grand jury's and is governed by the same limitations. These are that he shall not act arbitrarily or in excess of his statutory authority, but this does not mean that his inquiry must be 'limited by forecasts of the probable result of the investigation.' " 327 U.S. at 216. The fourth amendment "at the most guards against abuse only by way of too much indefiniteness or breadth in the things required to be 'particularly described,' if also the inquiry is one the demanding agency is authorized by law to make and the materials specified are relevant." Id. at 208.

Oklahoma Press was extended and summarized in United States v. Morton Salt Co., 338 U.S. 632 (1950). While acknowledging the possible burdensomeness of a federal agency's demand for information, the court upheld the request, stating:

"Of course a governmental investigation into corporate matters may be of such a sweeping nature and so unrelated to the matter properly under inquiry as to exceed the investigatory power. But it is sufficient if the inquiry is within the authority of the agency, the demand is not too indefinite and the information sought is reasonably relevant." Id. at 652.... To this we might add that an investigation that is undertaken for an improper purpose, such as harassment, would violate due process. ...

Oklahoma Press and *Morton Salt* are dispositive here. Kohn concedes that the Attorney General is acting within his statutory powers. The Civil Investigative Demand asks specific questions and requests sufficiently described documents. Kohn claims that delays in filling orders are due to lack of items in stock and that time must be allowed for customers' checks to clear and to verify orders. The information requested by the state is reasonably relevant to these claims. Here, as in civil discovery, relevance should be given a liberal interpretation, with the recognition that

relevancy limits would be more circumscribed at any subsequent trial. We hold, therefore, that the state's request here for business documents does not violate the fourth amendment prohibition against an unreasonable search and seizure.

III. Appellant Kohn's argument for Fifth Amendment protection presents a somewhat greater problem. Since a subsequent criminal fraud action is possible against Kohn, the privilege against self-incrimination is implicated insofar as he personally is required to answer questions. It is essential, however, that we distinguish Kohn personally from his corporations and that we distinguish between the demand to produce documents and the demand to answer interrogatories.

First of all, it is well established that corporations, partnerships and other business entities cannot claim the privilege against self-incrimination. State v. Alexander, 281 N.W.2d 349, 353 (Minn. 1979). This is true even when the corporation is merely an alter ego of the owner. Hair Industry, Ltd. v. United States, 340 F.2d 510 (2d Cir.), cert. denied 381 U.S. 950 (1965). Further, a long line of cases has established that "an individual cannot rely upon the privilege to avoid producing the records of a collective entity which are in his possession in a representative capacity, even if these records might incriminate him personally." Bellis v. United States, 417 U.S. 85, 88 (1974).

Here the documents requested are corporate documents. The appellant corporations have no privilege not to produce them. Neither does Kohn, since, if he is holding them, clearly he is doing so as a representative of the corporations. Kohn seeks to escape this conclusion by arguing that the Civil Investigative Demand is addressed to him, individually, and therefore in his personal rather than representative capacity. There is no merit to the argument. Here the Demand asks for business records, not Kohn's personal papers. "The papers and effects which the privilege protects must be the private property of the person claiming the privilege, or at least in his possession in a purely personal capacity." United States v. White, 322 U.S. 694 (1944). The Attorney General's Demand is not to be read myopically; when the title of the proceedings, the definitional section and the information requested are read together as a whole, it is plain that Kohn was served as an agent of his corporations to obtain records of those corporations. We hold that neither Kohn nor his corporations may assert any privilege against self-incrimination against production of the requested documents and that Kohn, as the corporate agent, must produce the documents.

This brings us to the 27 interrogatories served by the Attorney General. Here again, since the corporations have no privilege against self-incrimination, the corporations must answer the interrogatories. A corporation, however, acts only through individuals who are its agents. When the agent answers interrogatories for the corporation, he or she is being compelled to give testimony. Since the Fifth Amendment prohibits testimonial self-incrimination, agents may assert the privilege on their own behalf. The United States Supreme Court resolved this paradox in United States v. Kordel, 397 U.S. 1 (1970), holding that the corporate agent may invoke the privilege, but, in that case, the corporation must appoint an agent who can, without fear of self-incrimination, furnish the requested information insofar as it is available to the corporation. 397 U.S. at 8. The Court in *Kordel* deferred resolution of the situation where no one can answer for the corporation without fear of self-incrimination, and neither is there any reason for us to reach that issue at this time.

We hold, therefore, that Kohn cannot be compelled to give testimony that may incriminate him by answering the state's interrogatories. In the current posture of this case, we can do no more than make this general holding, and we remand to the trial court for further proceedings as to how the interrogatories might be answered. It seems to us the state has several options: . . .

IV. Kohn's final claim, that he is the victim of discriminatory enforcement contrary to the equal protection clause, is without merit. Even assuming the selective prosecution defense is available at this time, when Kohn is not being prosecuted but only investigated, Kohn has not made any showing of discrimination. Indeed, it appears the Attorney General's office has other mail-order auto parts operations under investigation. Nor is there any merit to his claim that he is being punished for his failure to cooperate with the Minnesota Better Business Bureau. Nor does the mere assertion in Kohn's affidavit that compliance with the C.I.D. would impose "an undue burden" establish that any such burden exists to the extent that a protective order might issue.

Affirmed in part, reversed in part, and remanded for further proceedings.

Case Questions for Discussion

1. Is it good public policy to permit administrative agencies to compel the production of documents and other information about businesses for purposes of investigation?

2. What Minnesota statute authorizes the attorney general to demand documents and other information from businesses? Why is such a law necessary? What legal mechanism did the attorney general employ to compel Kohn to comply with his demands?

3. Should corporations have the same constitutional rights as individuals?

Agency Hearings and Judicial Review

Administrative agencies are sometimes asked to review their own actions. Individuals, business groups, and other interest groups that come into contact with agencies, and are adversely affected by particular decisions, have a right to ask for a formal hearing to review such decisions. Typically, before any hearing is held, there must be an effort to informally resolve the matter. Given a failure to reach an acceptable solution, a party may request that the agency conduct a hearing. These hearings are presided over by *hearing examiners,* often called *administrative law judges,* and the results of these proceedings may be reviewed internally by agency officials. Only when all internal remedies are exhausted may a disappointed party take his or her case to the regular courts.

As the following case of *Jackson Mobilphone Co. v. Tennessee Public Service Commission* illustrates, an administrative law judge first rules on the matter, subject to final review by the agency itself, and then the civil courts are employed as a final appeal. Both the administrative judge assigned to the initial case and the commission itself must abide by procedural rules designed to insure fair play.

Agencies are subject to their own review procedures.

Prior to the scheduled hearing, the case is assigned to an examiner, who, similar to a judge, usually sits alone as the presiding officer. Examiners are empowered to administer oaths, to issue subpoenas for documents and witnesses, and to regulate and conduct the hearing itself. In the case of the U.S. government, Section 556 of the Administrative Procedure Act, 5 U.S.C. (2000), also permits examiners to suggest to parties the availability of one or more alternative means to resolve disputes and to encourage the use of such methods, including holding conferences to negotiate settlements. Administrative hearings are relatively informal when compared to civil or criminal trials. Hearing examiners consider a range of information and argument that is not normally permissible in civil and criminal trials, and both sides are usually permitted to be accompanied by an attorney if they wish, although in many situations attorneys are unnecessary. Written arguments, and sometimes formal briefs, are often filed after the oral arguments are presented before the examiner assigned to the case. The examiner then studies all the materials, after which he or she prepares a decision both as to matters of fact and law. Parties are entitled to present their own cases or defenses. They may submit rebuttal evidence, with the proponent of a rule or order having the burden of proof. The transcript of testimony and exhibits is the official record on which decisions are made.[13]

Written decisions of hearing examiners are delivered to all the parties to the dispute and if one or more of the parties are dissatisfied with the outcome, they may submit additional arguments to agency heads. Depending upon the agency, the parties may be permitted to present oral arguments to agency heads that make the final decision in the matter. Sometimes, agency heads will consult with hearing examiners when they make their final judgments.[14]

The resolution of conflicts within agencies is valued because agency officials are well equipped by virtue of their subject-specific knowledge and experience to understand the complex factual and administrative issues. Further, if disputes can be resolved informally first, and, if not, then more formally with the aid of a hearing examiner, there is no need to involve ordinary civil courts. Once an agency decision is final and there is no further review available within the agency itself, then, depending upon statutory requirements, the courts may be asked to review the decision in a trial court, or the matter may go directly to an appellate court.[15]

It bears repeating that before a court will exercise jurisdiction in an administrative case, the parties must have exhausted all their remedies within the agencies in which the case arose. The concept of *exhaustion of administrative remedies,* though reasonable, often leads private parties seeking a favorable decision to their own personal exhaustion. In other words, they become worn down by the psychological, time, and financial burdens that usually come with confronting a powerful government agency. Citizens will sometimes seek to circumvent this debilitating process by asking their legislative representatives to intervene on their behalf. To be sure, elected representatives regularly provide "casework service" for their constituents. They contact bureaucracies to resolve, for example, granny's social security payment problem, an immigration or naturalization matter for a friend or relative, a veteran's benefit for retired military personnel in their legislative district, or a dispute between a farmer and the U.S. Department of Agriculture about farm subsidy payments.

Judges in the civil courts are generally loath to second-guess administrators about the meaning and interpretation of the case facts before them. They tend to defer to the judgment of administrators about such matters. Those who seek to challenge administrative decisions generally have the burden of proof, and the standard of proof required to overcome the presumption in favor of agency decisions is the *substantial evidence rule*. This rule requires evidence that is less than a preponderance of evidence but more than a *scintilla of evidence*—the least particle of evidence in a case. Bureaucrats behave arbitrarily and capriciously when they base their decisions on evidence that does not furnish a reasonably sound factual basis. This does not mean that for a court to overrule an agency decision it must necessarily disagree with the agency's judgment about the best resolution of the dispute. Rather, civil court judges inquire whether there is a rational basis for the decision, not whether they agree with the policy result in the case. In other words, judges of the civil courts are not free, in principle, to substitute their ideas of what is in the public interest. They leave those policy decisions to the administrative experts. If, however, there is no rational basis for the agency decision, then that decision violates elementary due process principles. Moreover, civil court judges are duty bound to protect the due process rights of persons. As the following Tennessee case illustrates, jurisdiction of the ordinary courts will also be invoked to require administrative officials to abide by basic statutory and constitutional protections.

Jackson Mobilphone Co.
v. Tennessee Public Service Commission
Court of Appeals of Tennessee, Middle Section, at Nashville
876 S.W.2d 106 (1993)

Opinion by Judge William C. Koch, Jr. for three-judge court.

This appeal involves one of three related proceedings before the Public Service Commission dealing with Tennessee's growing electronic paging business. Jackson Mobilphone Co. and Multipage, Inc. sought authority to operate as radio common carriers in the three-county Memphis market area. The commission reversed its administrative judge's initial order awarding the authority to Jackson Mobilphone and granted the authority to Multipage. Jackson Mobilphone has appealed directly to this court, asserting that the commission had no rational basis for its decision. We have determined that the commission's decision is arbitrary and is not supported by substantial and material evidence. Accordingly, we vacate the order granting Multipage the authority to serve the Memphis market area and remand the case to the commission for further proceedings.

1. The Public Service Commission has regulated radio common carriers in Tennessee for at least thirty years. The General Assembly specifically defined the commission's authority over radio common carriers in 1972 when it enacted the State Radio Common Carrier Act (SRCCA) that is now codified at Tenn. Code Ann. §§ 65-30-101-112 (1993). The General Assembly's declaration of public policy states that the public's interest in adequate, economical, and efficient radio common carrier services would be best served by a regulatory scheme that eliminated "unfair or destructive competitive practices."

The commission initially authorized only one radio common carrier to operate in each market area. In 1975 it granted authority to a second radio common carrier to operate in the Nashville market area; however, the Tennessee Supreme Court overruled the commission's decision and held that the SRCCA created a preference for existing radio common carriers as long as they were rendering adequate service. Nashville Mobilphone Co. v. Atkins, 536 S.W.2d 335, 340 (Tenn. 1976). The Court's construction of the SRCCA effectively erected an insurmountable barrier to other radio common carriers entering the market for the next fifteen years. . . .

The commission's decision to open the Chattanooga, Nashville, and Memphis market areas caused a flurry of applications from companies desiring to enter these lucrative radio telecommunications markets. Between 1989 and March 1991, nine

companies applied for authorization to provide radio common carrier services in one or more of the Chattanooga, Nashville, or Memphis market areas. Jackson Mobilphone, a radio common carrier already serving areas of West Tennessee contiguous to Memphis, was one of the applicants seeking authorization to serve the Memphis market area. . . .

By late 1991, the commission had received radio common carrier applications from ten companies who desired to provide paging service in one or more of the Chattanooga, Nashville, or Memphis market areas. Four of these applicants eventually withdrew, and of the six remaining applicants, four sought authority for the Memphis market area. By the time of the hearing before the administrative law judge, only Jackson Mobilphone and Multipage were still seeking approval to operate in the Memphis market area.

The administrative law judge assigned to conduct all the radio common carrier hearings heard evidence in February and March, 1992 concerning the Chattanooga, Nashville, and Memphis market areas. The commission's staff recommended that Jackson Mobilphone should receive the authority in the Memphis market area, and on June 19, 1992, the administrative law judge filed a detailed initial decision awarding the Memphis market area to Jackson Mobilphone. Multipage filed exceptions to the initial order. On September 15, 1992, the commission affirmed the administrative law judge's decisions concerning the Nashville and Chattanooga market areas but awarded the authority for the Memphis market area to Multipage. The commission based its decision on the same evidentiary record that its administrative law judge had relied upon to reach the opposite conclusion. . . .

II. This court reviews the commission's adjudicatory decisions using the same standards of review applicable to the decisions of other administrative agencies. Thus, in accordance with Tenn. Code Ann. § 4-5-322(h) (1991), we review the commission's "findings, inferences, conclusions or decisions" to determine whether they are:

(1) In violation of constitutional or statutory provisions;

(2) In excess of the statutory authority of the agency;

(3) Made upon unlawful procedure;

(4) Arbitrary or capricious or characterized by abuse of discretion or clearly unwarranted exercise of discretion; or

(5) Unsupported by evidence which is both substantial and material in light of the entire record.

Jackson Mobilphone bases its challenge to the commission's decision to award Multipage the Memphis market on Tenn. Code Ann. § 4-5-322(h) (4) and Tenn. Code Ann. § 4-5-322(h) (5).

The standards of review in Tenn. Code Ann. § 4-5-322(h) (4) and Tenn. Code Ann. § 4-5-322(h) (5) are narrower than the standard of review normally applicable to other civil cases. They are also related but are not synonymous. Agency decisions not supported by substantial and material evidence are arbitrary and capricious. . . . However, agency decisions with adequate evidentiary support may still be arbitrary and capricious if caused by a clear error in judgment. . . .

A reviewing court should not apply Tenn. Code Ann. § 4-5-322(h)

(4)'s "arbitrary and capricious" standard of review mechanically. In its broadest sense, the standard requires the court to determine whether the administrative agency has made a clear error in judgment. . . . An arbitrary decision is one that is not based on any course of reasoning or exercise of judgment, or one that disregards the facts or circumstances of the case without some basis that would lead a reasonable person to reach the same conclusion.

Likewise, a reviewing court should not apply Tenn. Code Ann. § 4-5-322(h) (5)'s "substantial and material evidence" test mechanically. Instead, the court should review the record carefully to determine whether the administrative agency's decision is supported by "such relevant evidence as a rational mind might accept to support a rational conclusion." The court need not reweigh the evidence . . . and the agency's decision need not be supported by a preponderance of the evidence. . . . The evidence will be sufficient if it furnishes a reasonably sound factual basis for the decision being reviewed. . . .

III. Contested case proceedings involving certificates of authority for radio common carriers must be consistent not only with the SRCCA and the commission's enabling statutes but also with the Uniform Administrative Procedures Act (UAPA). While the commission may conduct contested case proceedings itself, it may also appoint a hearing officer to hear all or any part of a particular case. Tenn. Code Ann. § 4-5-301(a) (2) (1991); Tenn. Code Ann. § 65-2-111(1993).

An administrative judge who hears a contested case without the commission present must prepare a proposed or initial order containing findings of fact, conclusions of law, and the policy reasons for the decision. Tenn. Code Ann. §§ 4-5-314(c), 65-2-111. Parties dissatisfied with the proposed or initial order may file exceptions requesting the commission to review the administrative judge's order and to enter its own final order. Tenn. Code Ann. §§ 4-5-315(a), 65-2-111.

The commission is not simply acting as an error-correcting body when it reviews a proposed or initial order. It must personally review the relevant portions of the administrative record, and then it must reach its own decision. Tenn. Code Ann. §§ 4-5-315(f), 65-2-111. When the commission agrees with the administrative judge's proposed decision, it may simply adopt the initial order as its own. When, however, the commission disagrees with the administrative judge's proposed decision, it must file its own final order that identifies its disagreements with the initial order and includes its own findings of fact, conclusions of law, and policy reasons for its decision. Tenn. Code Ann. §§ 4-5-315(i), 65-2-112.

The portions of the commission's September 15, 1992 order awarding Multipage the certificate of authority to provide radio common carrier service in the Memphis market area are deficient for three reasons. First, the commission misconstrued several of its administrative judge's findings and conclusions concerning Multipage. Second, the commission's order emphasizes the commission's disagreements with the administrative judge's decision without evaluating all the factors that must be considered in awarding a radio common carrier certificate of authority. Third, several of the commission's conclusions concerning

Multipage's ability to provide paging services efficiently are not supported by substantial and material evidence.

IV. Radio common carrier licensing decisions require a comparative analysis when two or more applicants are competing for authority to serve the same market area. The purpose of the analysis is to determine which of the competing applicants will best promote the SRCCA's policy objectives. The SRCCA directs the commission to weigh each application in light of these objectives. Thus, our role is not to substitute our judgment for the commission's but rather to determine whether the commission's findings are based on substantial and material evidence and whether the commission's decision rests on sound reasoning consistent with the SRCCA.

A. The SRCCA contains seven factors intended to focus the commission's attention on the needs of the public, the qualifications of the applicants, and the radio common carrier industry's competitive environment. Tenn. Code Ann. § 65-30-102 and Tenn. Code Ann. § 65-30-105(e) focus on the need for the service by directing the commission to consider "public need," to promote "adequate, economical, and efficient radio common carrier service to the citizens and residents of this state," and to maintain "harmony between radio common carriers and their subscribers."

In addition to public need, Tenn. Code Ann. § 65-30-105(e) focuses on the applicants' qualifications by directing the commission to consider each applicant's "suitablity," "financial responsibility," and "ability . . . to perform efficiently." Likewise, Tenn. Code Ann. §§ 65-3-102 and 65-30-105(f)(2) focus on competition within the radio common carrier industry by requiring the commission to consider whether its decisions promote "meaningful competition within any service area" while at the same time discouraging "unjust discrimination, undue preferences or advantages, or unfair or destructive competitive practices."

While the commission's licensing decisions must take all the SRCCA's factors into consideration, nothing in the SRCCA prevents the commission from considering other factors that might be relevant in a particular proceeding. In fact, Tenn. Code Ann. § 65-30-105 (e) specifically empowers the commission to take "other things" into consideration.

B. The proof concerning the history and background of the two competing applicants and their principals is straightforward and undisputed. The disagreements concern the applicants' service plans, their respective ability to provide adequate, economical, and efficient radio common carrier service to the public, and the effect of the commission's decision on competition within the radio common carrier industry.

Jackson Mobilphone is a corporation headquartered in Jackson that has provided radio common carrier service to counties in West Tennessee for over twenty years. By the time of the administrative hearing, it served approximately 1,700 subscribers in all West Tennessee counties in the 901 area code except the three-county Memphis market area. Its total assets amounted to $296,154.11, and its total stockholder's equity was $114,403.08. It operates eleven transmitter sites with a twelfth under construction, and it employs seven persons.

Fred Birmingham, Jackson Mobilphone's president, has worked for the carrier since 1986. His family purchased the business in 1988, and he became president in 1989. He has significant, current training and expertise in the radio common carrier business. Within two years after becoming president, Mr. Birmingham expanded the carrier's service area, improved its service, and restored the business to profitability.

Jackson Mobilphone's strategy is to concentrate on the West Tennessee market. It has no plans to expand into Middle or East Tennessee, and its goal is to provide area-wide service in all West Tennessee counties. It plans to hire six additional employees and to build at least one new transmitting tower if the commission permits it to expand into the Memphis market area. Jackson Mobilphone also anticipates that it will begin serving its Memphis subscribers quickly and for a low start-up cost by using its existing facilities and staff. It also estimates that its expansion into the Memphis market will become profitable within three years and that its available funds are sufficient to defray its operating expenses until that time.

Two brothers, Alvin and Frank Escue, incorporated Multipage in 1991 to take advantage of the new business opportunities created by the 1991 amendments to the SRCCA. Both Escues possessed great personal wealth and were familiar with the page business through their ownership of paging businesses in Alabama, Kentucky, South Carolina, and Tennessee. Their relationship with the paging business is somewhat dated since they sold most of their paging holdings a number of years ago except for Frank Escue's interest in a small, private carrier in South Carolina.

Multipage existed only on paper at the time of the administrative hearing. It had never received authority to provide radio common carrier service in any Tennessee market, and it had no employees, no transmitter or other equipment, and no assets except for $1,000 of paid-in capital. The Escue brothers were not only seeking authority to serve the Memphis market area but were also seeking authority to operate in the Nashville, Chattanooga, and Knoxville market areas. They planned to construct five transmitters to serve the Memphis market but had no plans to serve the less populated counties in West Tennessee. They also planned to contract for their sales and technical needs instead of using their own employees.

C. We now turn to the manner in which the commission weighed the SRCCA's decision-making factors. For the sake of clarity, we will review the commission's conclusions with regard to each factor in light of the evidence in the administrative record and the administrative judge's initial order.

Public Need

The public's need for adequate, economical, and efficient paging services is a seminal issue in any SRCCA licensing proceeding. It is a multi-dimensional matter broad enough to include consideration not only of the number of carriers in a particular market but also the nature and quality of the services to be provided. While the General Assembly's enactment of Tenn. Code Ann. § 65-30-105(f)(2) in 1991 addressed the number of radio common carriers to be permitted in each market area . . . . it

did not foreclose the consideration of the other facets of the public need factor. . . .

The commission never directly addressed the public need question in its opinion. Without explanation, it affirmed the administrative judge's decision concerning the Chattanooga market area but reversed his decision concerning the Memphis market area. The administrative record contains substantial and material evidence concerning the subscribers' need for area-wide service and the added costs for these services if subscribers must contract with two carriers to obtain it. The commission should have addressed these public need questions and should have articulated its reasons for treating West Tennessee subscribers differently than the subscribers in Chattanooga and its surrounding counties. Tenn. Code Ann. § 65-30-102 prohibits unjust discrimination and undue preferences, and thus the commission should not have arbitrarily failed to consider the needs of all West Tennessee subscribers when it was making its Memphis market area licensing decision.

The Applicants' Suitability

The commission also misconstrued its administrative judge's conclusions with regard to the applicants' comparative suitability. The administrative judge found that the principals of both Jackson Mobilphone and Multipage had adequate education and experience to serve the Memphis market area. Yet, the commission stated that the administrative judge "correctly found that the principals of Multipage, Inc. have more experience in the paging business."

The administrative record does not contain substantial and material evidence that the Escue brothers' experience is superior to Fred Birmingham's. Mr. Birmingham directly manages Jackson Mobilphone's day-to-day business affairs and has a background in computers and ten years of experience in the telephone and paging industry. Under his leadership during the past four years, Jackson Mobilphone improved the quality of its service, expanded its service area, and became profitable and financially sound.

The Escue family has a long history of owning communications and paging businesses, but the extent of Alvin and Frank Escue's operating knowledge and experience is less clear. Alvin Escue has owned paging businesses since the late 1960's, but these businesses were actually operated first by a deceased brother and then by other managers who are not involved with Multipage's present application. Frank Escue has experience operating paging businesses in Kentucky and South Carolina but apparently no experience in Tennessee, and the extent of his planned involvement with Multipage's Tennessee operations is unclear.

Multipage's application indicates that it intends to hire a manager for its Tennessee operations. The person the Escues plan to hire has experience managing paging businesses outside of Tennessee. Nothing in the nature, duration, or quality of his experience, however, provides a basis for concluding that he is a better manager than Mr. Birmingham or that Multipage under his leadership will be a more suitable carrier than Jackson Mobilphone under Mr. Birmingham's leadership.

The commission's conclusion that Multipage was more suitable than Jackson Mobilphone influenced its decision to award the Memphis market area to Multipage. The record, however, does not contain substantial and material evidence supporting Multipage's superior suitability. Accordingly, we find that the commission acted arbitrarily when it based its decision on this ground.

The Applicants' Financial Responsiblity

The commission also determined that Multipage was more financially responsible than Jackson Mobilphone because its shareholders were wealthier than Jackson Mobilphone's. The Escue family is undoubtedly wealthier than the Birmingham family. It does not necessarily follow, however, that the personal assets of either family will be used to benefit the corporate applicants. . . .

Both the Escue and Birmingham families expressed their intent to make additional investments in their companies in order to serve the Memphis market area. However, the administrative record contains no legally enforceable agreements between Multipage and the Escues or between Jackson Mobilphone and the Birminghams that contractually bind either the Escues or the Birminghams to make specific additional investments in their businesses should they receive authority to serve the Memphis market area. Thus, we find that the commission improperly weighed both parties' legally unenforceable promises to use their personal funds to finance their companies' expansion into the Memphis market area. If anything, the Birmingham family is more likely to infuse additional capital into Jackson Mobilphone in order to preserve the large financial investment they have already made.

Contrary to Commissioner Cochran's concern that Jackson Mobilphone was a "small, struggling carrier," the administrative record contains substantial and material evidence that Jackson Mobilphone is financially sound. The commission's manager of revenue requirements and special studies concluded that "each applicant is fully capable of providing the services they are planning to provide" despite his concerns about the "thin capitalization of each applicant." The administrative record contains no proof contrary to this conclusion.

The administrative record likewise does not support the administrative judge's and the commission's conclusion that Multipage's revenue and cost projections were more conservative than Jackson Mobilphone's. In fact, Jackson Mobilphone's projections appear to be more sound than Multipage's for the following reasons. First, Jackson Mobilphone's projections are extrapolations from an ongoing business while Multipage's are purely theoretical. Second, Multipage appears to have underestimated its start up costs when its projections are compared to all other carriers seeking to serve the Memphis market area. Third, the reliability of Multipage's revenue projections is undermined by discrepancies in its presentation concerning the number of pagers it expected to sell and the rates it intended to charge. The commission's manager of revenue requirements and special studies concluded that he could not determine how many pagers Multipage expected to sell because of the conflicts between Alvin Escue's testimony, Multipage's five-year projections, and Multipage's proposed rates.

In summary, we find that the conclusion that Multipage's projections are more conservative than Jackson Mobilphone's is not supported by substantial and material evidence. The commission, therefore, acted arbitrarily when it based its decision to award the Memphis market area to Multipage on this factor.

The Applicant's Ability to Perform Efficiently

Both Jackson Mobilphone and Multipage intend to offer the same basic types of paging services and to charge essentially the same rates for local service in the Memphis market area. The administrative record supports the conclusion of the manager of revenue requirements and special studies that both applicants would be able to provide the services they are planning to provide. Thus, the issue concerns which of the two competing applicants will be able to provide the services more efficiently.

As the administrative judge found, Jackson Mobilphone will be able to provide paging services in the Memphis market area quickly because it is an existing carrier with transmitters already covering portions of the Memphis market area. It will also be able to use its existing sales and technical staff. Multipage, on the other hand, must begin operations from scratch and will necessarily encounter more delay since it must find and lease transmitter sites, hire a sales and technical staff, and sell pagers before it can begin operating.

The commission discounted the administrative judge's conclusion concerning Jackson Mobilphone's ability to begin providing service in the Memphis market area more quickly than Multipage. It determined that the administrative judge has placed too much weight on this consideration because Multipage could lose its authority to serve the Memphis market area if it failed to meet the SRCCA's timetable for obtaining FCC approval and beginning operations.

The prospect that Multipage might lose its authority to serve the Memphis market if it did not begin operating within twelve months has little direct relationship to the comparative efficiency of the two applicants or to fulfilling the SRCCA's mandate of making radio common carrier service easily available to all Tennessee residents. If anything, Multipage's failure to begin operating would only inconvenience customers in the Memphis market area because it would deprive them of the benefit of a second radio common carrier competing for their business.

The cost of providing service is also another aspect of efficiency. Jackson Mobilphone has already incurred most of the capital costs needed to enter the Memphis market area. It has already constructed all but one or two of the transmitters it will need to serve the new market area. On the other hand, Multipage's costs to enter the Memphis market area will be much higher because it must build at least twice as many transmitters as Jackson Mobilphone.

Jackson Mobilphone's and Multipage's proposed local rates are similar. However, Jackson Mobilphone's current rate structure is based partially on the capital expenses it has already incurred in setting up its wide area network in rural West Tennessee. Entering the Memphis market area would enable Jackson Mobilphone to use some of these existing resources in a more lucrative market area and thus increase the return on its existing investment. Accordingly, Jackson Mobilphone anticipates that it should eventually be able to offer paging services at lower rates because of increased revenues from the Memphis market area where its costs are lower.

The commission's failure to make specific findings concerning the applicants' comparative efficiency undermines its decision. The administrative record contains substantial and material evidence that Jackson Mobilphone will perform more efficiently in the Memphis market area than will Multipage. The commission arbitrarily failed to consider and weigh this evidence.

The Effect on Competition in the Paging Business

The administrative record contains extensive testimony concerning the impact that the commission's decision would have not only on the applicants themselves but also on the paging industry as a whole. The commission, however, did not directly address the competitive consequences of its decision in the final order, and its oversight is inconsistent with the SRCCA.

The administrative judge directly addressed the proof in the record concerning the competitive impact of the decision and made several pertinent findings. First, he found that Jackson Mobilphone was the only applicant planning to compete with MCCA to provide area-wide radio common carrier service in all of West Tennessee. Second, he found that Jackson Mobilphone was presently operating at a competitive disadvantage because it was facing increased competition in the Jackson market area from carriers who were not serving the other less profitable parts of rural West Tennessee. Third, he found that denying access to the Memphis market area would undermine Jackson Mobilphone's ability to compete in West Tennessee and to provide radio common carrier services to areas in rural West Tennessee that were not being served by any other carrier.

The administrative record contains substantial and material evidence supporting the administrative judge's conclusions about Jackson Mobilphone's competitive position. Preserving Jackson Mobilphone as a viable competitor is consistent with the SRCCA's purposes. The commission should have addressed these is-

sues directly, and its arbitrary failure to do so further undermines the validity of its decision.

V. We find that the commission's decision to award Multipage the certificate of authority to operate as a radio common carrier in the Memphis market area was arbitrary and was not supported by substantial and material evidence. Accordingly, we vacate the portion of the commission's order concerning the Memphis market area and remand the matter to the commission for further proceedings consistent with this opinion. We also tax the costs of this appeal to Multipage, Inc. for which execution, if necessary, may issue.

Case Questions for Discussion

1. Why does Tennessee law require commission members to write a justification for their decision when they disagree with the decision of an administrative law judge?

2. How does a court know when an administrative decision is arbitrary or capricious?

3. Review the various degrees of proof employed in legal processes. How does the substantial evidence rule differ from the rule employed in civil suits for money damages, equity matters, and in criminal cases?

Key Terms, Names, and Concepts

Administrative law judges
Administrative Procedure Act
Authorization statute
Code of Federal Regulations
Delegation of legislative power
Enabling legislation
Executive agreements
Executive privilege
Exhaustion of administrative remedies
Federal Register

Freedom of Information Act
Government corporation
Hearing examiners
Independent regulatory agency
Intelligible principle
Legislative veto
Open Meetings Act
Power of investigation
1974 Privacy Act
Rule-making

     Scintilla of evidence   Substantial evidence rule
     Sole organ theory

Discussion Questions

1. Why is it advisable for administrative agencies to make rules and regulations? If rules and regulations are the functional equivalents of laws, then is such rule-making a violation of Article 1, section 1 of the U.S. Constitution?

2. Why do the law courts generally require that all administrative procedures must be exhausted before persons may use the regular law courts to resolve conflicts with administrative agencies?

3. Should the law courts give deference to the decisions of administrative agencies? If yes, why? If no, why not?

4. Consider the various standards of proof available in various legal processes, beginning with Chapter 5 and concluding with this one. Order the following standards of proof from the *least* to the *most* demanding: preponderance of the evidence, scintilla of evidence, proof beyond a reasonable doubt, clear and convincing evidence, and substantial evidence rule. Associate each standard of proof with the following: civil suits for money damages, equity suits, criminal prosecutions, and administrative processes. What is the justification for applying particular and differing standards of proof to each legal process?

5. How extensive should the investigatory power of administrative agencies be? When the nation is facing an emergency, such as the "War on Terrorism," should extraordinary powers be employed even though constitutional protections of the rights of individuals may be sacrificed in the process?

Suggested Additional Reading

Aberbach, Joel D. *Keeping a Watchful Eye: The Politics of Congressional Oversight.* Washington, DC: Brookings Institution, 1990.

Ball, Howard. *Cancer Factories: American's Tragic Quest for Uranium Self-Sufficiency.* Westport, CT: Greenwood Press, 1993.

———. *Controlling Regulatory Sprawl.* Westport, CT: Greenwood Press, 1984.

Berger, Raoul. "Administrative Arbitrariness and Judicial Review." *Columbia Law Review* 65 (January 1965): 55–95.

Bryer, Stephen. *Regulation and Its Reform.* Cambridge, MA: Harvard University Press, 1982.

Cann, Steven. *Administrative Law.* 3rd ed. Thousand Oaks, CA: Sage Publications, 2001.

Davis, Kenneth Culp. *Discretionary Justice: A Preliminary Inquiry.* Urbana: University of Illinois Press, 1971 [1969].

Frankfurter, Felix. "The Task of Administrative Law." *University of Pennsylvania Law Review* 75 (March 1927): 614–621.

Goldberg, Arthur, J. "A Defense of the Bureaucracy in Corporate Regulation and Some Personal Suggestions for Corporate Reform." *George Washington Law Review* 48 (May 1980): 514–520.

Goodnow, Frank. *Comparative Administrative Law.* New York: Putman, 1893.

Goodsell, Charles. *The Case for Bureaucracy.* 3rd ed. Chatham, NJ: Chatham House, 1994.

Horowitz, Donald L. *The Courts and Social Policy.* Washington, DC: Brookings Institution, 1997.

Jacobini, H. B. *Introduction to Comparative Administrative Law.* New York: Oceana Publications, 1991.

Kerwin, Cornelius M. *Rulemaking: How Government Agencies Write Law and Make Policy.* 2nd ed. Washington, DC: Congressional Quarterly Press, 1999.

Lowi, Theodore. *The End of Liberalism.* New York: Norton, 1969.

Markham, Jerry W. "Sunshine on the Administrative Process: Wherein Lies the Shade." *Administrative Law Review* 28 (summer, 1976): 463–482.

Nader, Ralph, Peter Petkas, and Kate Blackwell. *Whistle Blowing.* New York: Grossman, 1972.

Ogul, Morris. *Congress Oversees the Bureaucracy.* Pittsburgh, PA: University of Pittsburgh Press, 1976.

O'Leary, Rosemary. *Environmental Change: Federal Courts and the EPA.* Philadelphia, PA: Philadelphia University Press, 1993.

Osborne, David, and Ted Gaebler. *Reinventing Government.* New York: Penguin, 1992.

Perry, James, ed. *The Handbook of Public Administration.* 2nd ed. San Francisco: Jossey-Bass, 1996.

Rossenbaum, Walter A. *Environmental Politics and Policy.* 4th ed. Washington, DC: Congressional Quarterly Press, 1998.

Shapiro, Martin. *Who Guards the Guardians: Judicial Control of Administration.* Athens: University of Georgia Press, 1994.

——. *The Supreme Court and Administrative Agencies.* New York: Free Press, 1968.

Wald, Martin, and Jeffrey D. Kahn. "Privacy Rights of Public Employees." *The Labor Lawyer* 6 (spring, 1990): 301–318.

Endnotes

1. Steven Cann, *Administrative Law,* 2nd ed. (Thousand Oaks, CA: Sage, 1998), p. 19.
2. Phillip J. Cooper, *Public Law and Public Administration,* 3rd ed. (Itasca, IL: Peacock Publishers, 2000), p. 133.

3. Albert P. Melone, *Researching Constitutional Law*, 2nd ed. (Prospect Heights, IL: Waveland Press, 2000), p. 18.
4. See U.S. Department of Health and Human Services, *Administrative Simplification Rule-Making Process*, <http://aspe.os.dhhs.gov/admnsimp/8steps.htm>, as of January, 2003.
5. Joan Biskupic and Elder Witt, *The Supreme Court and the Powers of American Government* (Washington, DC: Congressional Quarterly, 1997), pp. 228–230.
6. 299 U.S. 304 at 315–316 (1936).
7. 299 U.S. 304 at 319 (1936).
8. Steven Cann, *Administrative Law*, 2nd ed., pp. 24–25.
9. H.B. Jacobini, Albert P. Melone, and Carl Kalvelage, *Research Essentials of Administrative Law* (Pacific Palisades, CA: Palisades Publishers, 1983), p. 4.
10. Ibid.; Steven Cann, *Administrative Law*, p. 163.
11. Steven Cann, *Administrative Law*, pp. 163–164. For a useful citizen guide to both the Privacy Act and the Freedom of Information Act, see First Report by Subcommittee on Information, Justice, Transportation, and Agriculture, House Report 103–104, 103rd Congress, 1st Session Union Calendar No. 53, The House Committee on Government Operations, *A Citizen's Guide on Using the Freedom of Information Act and the Privacy Act of 1974 to Request Government Records*, 1993 Edition. Provisions are posted on the Web at various sites.
12. H. Jacobini, Albert P. Melone, and Carl Kalvelage, *Research Essentials of Administrative Law*, p. 4.
13. William T. Schantz, *The American Legal Environment: Individuals, Their Business, and Their Government* (St. Paul, MN: West, 1976), p. 308.
14. Ibid.
15. Ibid. See 5 U.S.C. §§ 701–706 (2000). ✦

Chapter 9

Alternative Dispute Resolution

Chapter Objectives

Readers are asked to consider alternative dispute resolution (ADR) as a theoretical solution to the problem of the legitimacy of courts and as a practical solution to overcrowded court dockets brought about by the proliferation of litigation. We array various forms of widely employed arbitration and mediation techniques along a continuum of the most coercive to the least coercive forms of each. For each ADR form, students should be able to identify similarities and differences among them. Students should also be able to compare and contrast ADR assumptions and processes with the legal processes previously studied in Chapters 5 through 8.

Although the United States is among the most litigious societies in the world, thoughtful Americans are ambivalent about the use of formal legal processes to solve their disputes. Both theoretical and practical difficulties are associated with using formal legal institutions to settle disputes. Traditional litigation is often costly, cumbersome, time consuming, and destructive of ongoing relationships. *Alternative dispute resolution* (ADR) mechanisms and tools are rapidly supplementing, and in some cases replacing, formal legal processes; they are viewed as preferable methods of resolving disputes between and among private parties, labor and management, family members, and a variety of public bodies. In this chapter, we examine arbitration, mediation, and hybrid forms of each as useful solutions to the problems inherent in modern litigation.

In Chapter 2 of this book, we first raised the problem of the *legitimacy of courts*. As Martin Shapiro points out, the legitimacy of the court system rests upon the practical wisdom that two parties in conflict can submit their dispute to a neutral third party for resolution. The basic assumption of this system is that parties in dispute eschew violence and various forms of raw power; instead, they value formal legal rules based in reason. They are content to submit their dispute to judges in the belief that third-party neutrals will treat each fairly by employing mutually agreed to and widely held legal principles and rules to resolve their conflict. The judge, moreover, will not favor one party over the other because of personal, family, or professional reasons or due to bias or prejudice.

The legitimacy of this triadic relationship, however, is seriously threatened by the substitution of office and law for the ideal condition of mutual consent. In the first place, one of the parties may adopt the view, whether deserved or not, that the judge is really an ally of her opponent. Likewise, this view may be supplemented by the understanding that the legal rules applied by the third party favor her opponent.[1] This initial suspicion may become firmly implanted if it becomes evident that similarly situated parties tend to suffer the same negative fate at the hands of the law. For example, support for the legal system among members of racial minority groups is placed in serious jeopardy when they observe that persons of color are more likely to be stopped and arrested by the police and subsequently convicted of crimes than is the case for members of the white majority. The practice of racial or ethnic profiling, as it is known, is also evident to American citizens of Middle Eastern and Arab descent in the wake of the World Trade Center tragedy on September 11, 2001.

It is commonly observed that the process of taking their disputes to courts and employing legal professionals as their champions may cause litigants to become embittered toward each other. Most often the lawyers have a vested interest in winning, and this means that during the course of litigation, the parties may become even further alienated, exacerbating already damaged personal feelings. This result is particularly dysfunctional when the disputing parties have an ongoing relationship. Family members, business partners, employers and employees, teachers and students, landlords and tenants, construction contractors and their clients, and buyers and sellers, for example, may find it difficult to continue their relationship during and after a lawsuit. The cost and duration of litigation that can last for years exacerbates the matter even further, begging for a more satisfactory way to resolve conflicts.

ADR comes in a variety of forms, but each falls somewhere between doing nothing to settle a dispute and full-blown litigation. All ADR forms are less formal than ordinary legal processes, and each permits the parties to take a more active role in the process of solving their own problems. Though courts and administrative agencies are now employing ADR techniques, most of these methods were developed in the private sector.[2] As illustrated in Figure 9.1, court-based litigation is the most coercive and least consensual, while arbitration is less so. Mediation is the least coercive and most consensual mode of dispute resolution.

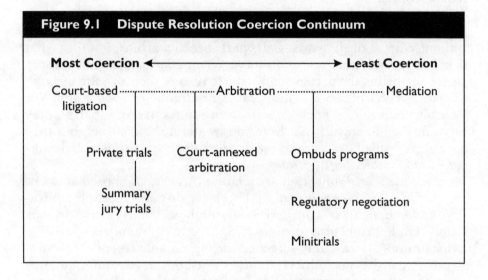

Figure 9.1   Dispute Resolution Coercion Continuum

Most Coercion ◄──────────────► Least Coercion

Court-based ··························· Arbitration ···················· Mediation
litigation

Private trials   Court-annexed   Ombuds programs
                  arbitration

Summary
jury trials   Regulatory negotiation

Minitrials

Arbitration

Of the three forms of dispute resolution modes arrayed along the coercion continuum in Figure 9.1, arbitration is most closely related to litigation. *Arbitration* is defined as the referral of a dispute to an impartial person or persons chosen by the parties to the dispute who agree in advance to abide by the arbitrator's decision issued after a full hearing on the matter.[3] The decision of the arbitrator is final. The process avoids most of the formalities, delays, and expenses of ordinary litigation.

English and early American law was hostile toward arbitration and many judges refused to enforce arbitration contracts because the process threatened the jurisdiction of courts. By the 1920s, however, state and federal legislators began to counter negative judicial attitudes with statutes promoting arbitration. In 1920, New York was the first state to enact a statute giving parties the right to assign future disputes and to settle existing ones through arbitration. The New York statute provided the model for the *Uniform Arbitration Act of 1955*, adopted by the National Conference of Commissioners on Uniform State Laws in 1955, amended in 1956, and approved by the House of Delegates of the American Bar Association in 1955 and 1956. Since then, a majority of the states have enacted it in one form or another.[4] In 1925, Congress enacted the Federal Arbitration Act, 9 U.S.C. § 1 et seq. (2000), that favors the arbitration of commercial transactions. In 1947, with the passage of the Labor Management Relations Act, 29 U.S.C. 173(d), Congress extended the policy to collective bargaining agreements, and in 1960, the U.S. Supreme Court in United Steelworkers v. Enterprise Wheel & Car Corp., 363 U.S. 593, ruled that arbitration awards are enforceable in federal courts.[5]

Parties to modern contracts often agree in advance to submit all disputes involving the performance of contractual obligations to arbitration. When a dispute arises, the party seeking arbitration files what is known as a *demand for arbitration*. When contracts do not contain such a provision, the parties may agree to resolve their dispute through the process of arbitration. This is called *arbitration by submission*. Not all arbitration rulings are compulsory. In some situations, parties may be compelled to engage in arbitration by statute or contract, but they are not compelled to accept the arbitrator's decision; this is called *mandatory but nonbinding arbitration*.[6]

The American Arbitration Association (AAA) is composed of about 17,000 experts, who are organized to resolve disputes through arbitration and other out-of-court ADR techniques. The Association was founded in 1926 and now operates in 38 countries. Members who serve as arbitrators are carefully screened for their management skills, substantive expertise, and ethics. Members must possess a minimum of 10 years of business experience at senior levels, or they must have a legal practice and training in the field of arbitration. They are bound by a Code of Ethics prepared by a joint committee of the American Arbitration Association and the American Bar Association.[7] The AAA has created specialty panels and programs to resolve specific types of disputes and case types that include the following: the Large Complex Case Panel, the Mass Torts Panel, the National Energy Panel, and the [AAA] President's Panel of Mediators. The qualifications of persons to serve on these panels of neutrals vary with the function of each and may exceed the minimum qualifications outlined above.[8] Although the AAA is the oldest provider of arbitration and related ADR services, other private provider organizations engage in the same or similar activities; among the best known are Judicial Arbitration and Mediation Services (JAMS), Endispute, ADR Associates, and National Arbitration Forum.

In addition to providing neutral arbitrators, the AAA provides customized in-house training on the art and practice of settling disputes for individual corporations, law firms, insurance companies, and labor/management relations firms. In recent years, the AAA has worked with major corporations—including the Boeing Company, Coca-Cola Enterprises, General Electric, Lockheed Martin, Merrill Lynch, and United Parcel Service—to develop internal training curricula and courses specifically designed for the special needs of each enterprise. These programs provide training to managers who may have a special need to understand how arbitration works when the organization comes into conflict with other parties.[9]

Phases of Arbitration

When a dispute is submitted for arbitration, the parties first choose an arbitrator who usually possesses expertise in the substantive field of the dispute. If an arbitration panel is to have three members, the parties each chose one arbitrator, and the named arbitrators then have the responsibility of choosing the third arbitrator—often called the *neutral arbitrator.* Each party carefully reviews the credentials of each potential arbitrator. The rules of the American Arbitration Association require that arbitrators disclose any potential situation in their backgrounds or associations that may affect their ability to be impartial, such as business, family, or social relationships with any of the parties.[10] After disclosure, if both parties agree that someone should be removed, a new arbitrator is selected. If the parties disagree, the AAA requires that it rule conclusively on the matter. In the event an arbitrator fails to make a full disclosure that is later discovered by one or both of the parties, a court may vacate any judgment rendered by that arbitrator.[11]

After the arbitrator or arbitration team is selected, the hearing commences with each side presenting opening statements. As is the case for ordinary civil or criminal cases, both parties or their attorneys briefly indicate what they intend to prove and what remedy they seek. The party seeking a remedy then submits evidence in support of her case by presenting documents, exhibits, and testimony through witnesses. Depending upon statutory authorization, arbitrators may possess subpoena power and the authority to order discovery, but in many instances they do not. Consequently, arbitration as a dispute resolution technique does not uniformly provide parties with the same powerful ability to discover facts as is available in ordinary litigation. Nonetheless, similar to court procedures, the respondent is entitled to cross-examine any witnesses presented by the other side. The claimant then rests her case, followed by the respondent placing on the record her case accompanied by witnesses, documents, and exhibits. Consistent with ordinary trial procedure, the claimant is provided an opportunity to cross-examine witnesses. Finally, each side presents final arguments, summarizing the evidence in a way that is personally most beneficial for it. Unlike a regular civil or criminal trial and resembling more closely equity trials, in arbitration proceedings, the rules of evidence are relaxed and considerable evidence is typically admitted as long as it is not irrelevant, immaterial, or otherwise prejudicial. The arbitrator then closes the proceedings. Sometimes, posthearing closing briefs are filed and then, usually within a short period of time, a final binding decision is rendered.

In most instances, the arbitrators' decisions are enforceable in a court of law.[12] Section 9 of the Federal Arbitration Act, 9 U.S.C. § 1 et seq. (2000), provides that if the parties in their agreement to arbitrate agreed that a judgment of the court shall be entered upon the award made pursuant to the arbitration and that the court is specified in the agreement, then, at any time within one year after the award is made, any party to the arbitration may apply to the court confirming the award, unless the award is vacated, modified, or corrected. Section 10 of the Act enumerates the circumstances in which a court may vacate or otherwise modify an award, including such reasons as that the award was procured by corruption, fraud, or undue means; there is evidence of partiality or corruption in the arbitrators; or there is evidence of material miscalculation of figures or a mistake in the description of persons, things, or property referred to in the award. Section 12 of the Federal Arbitration Act, 9 U.S.C. § 1 et seq. (2000), provides that notice of a motion to vacate, modify, or correct an award must be served upon the adverse party within three months after the award is filed or delivered.

It is in the best interest of the parties to select arbitrators cautiously. After all, when arbitration is chosen over litigation, the carefully considered rules of civil procedure and rules of evidence developed over a considerable period of time are less important than the good sense of the arbitrators making the actual judgment in the case at hand. If not otherwise specified in contracts or other agreements, the standards of proof, as well as the standard of decision that arbitrators employ to resolve conflicts, are up to the parties. If the parties do not specify which standard of proof is to be used—for example, a substantial evidence rule or a preponderance of the evidence test, or when the arbitrator should use an existing legal standard or what might be customary in the industry or trade, or whether some equitable principle should apply—then arbitrators decide these vital matters themselves.

The great advantage of arbitration over litigation is its relatively low cost and the swift resolution of disputes. The parties pay a filing fee, an administration fee, and the arbitrator's fee. Given the long delays encountered due to today's extensive court calendars, when it could take months and even years to adjudicate a matter, it makes good sense for commercial as well as other private interests to be able to resolve disputes more quickly. Even so, arbitration is not as conducive to full discovery as is ordinary litigation; consequently, parties may hide information that otherwise would be discovered in a civil court proceeding. Another negative impact is that many arbitration contracts limit the right of the parties to appeal the arbitrator's decision to a law court, in addition to the fact that federal and state law limits judicial review.

Voluntary arbitration is most commonly used to resolve commercial and labor disputes. It is also proving useful in construction consumer disputes, copyright, trademark, and patent infringement disputes, and matters involving insurance.[13] The following case illustrates how arbitration is being imposed on credit-card holders and how the courts are reluctant to interfere with a policy designed to side-step their jurisdiction in favor a less litigious process to resolve disputes.

Pick v. Discover Financial Services, Inc.
U. S. District Court for the District of Delaware
2001 U.S. Dist. LEXIS 15777

Opinion by Judge Robinson.

I. Introduction

Plaintiff Michael C. Pick filed this action on behalf of himself and a putative class of Discover cardholders on November 7, 2000 against defendant Discover Financial Services, Inc. Plaintiff alleges violation of the Truth in Lending Act, 15 U.S.C. §1601, et seq., consumer fraud and breach of contract arising out of defendant's amendment to the terms of the Discover Cardmember Agreement. Currently before the court are defendant's motions to compel arbitration and to stay the proceedings pending completion of the arbitration. For the following reasons, the court shall grant defendant's motion to compel arbitration and dismiss the action, and deny defendant's motion to stay as moot.

II. Background

In March 1999, plaintiff applied for a Discover Platinum Card (the "Card") issued by defendant. Plaintiff's application was approved, and defendant mailed plaintiff the Card with a "Pricing Schedule" stating that the Fixed Annual Percentage Rate ("Fixed APR") for purchases was 12.99%. Defendant also included a copy of the Discover Cardmember Agreement (the "Agreement") which provided the following terms:

CHANGE OF TERMS: We may change any term or part of this Agreement, including any finance charge rate, fee or method of computing any balance upon which the finance charge rate is assessed, or add any new term or part to this Agreement by sending you a written notice at least 15 days before the change is to become effective. We may apply any such change to the outstanding balance of your Account on the effective date of the change and to new charges made after that date. If you do not agree to the change, you must notify us in writing within 15 days after the mailing of the notice of change at the address provided in the notice of change, in which case your Account will be closed and you must pay us the balance that you owe us under the existing terms of the unchanged Agreement. Otherwise, you will have agreed to the changes in the notice. Use of your Account after the effective date of the change will be deemed acceptance of the new terms as of such effective date, even if you previously notified us that you did not agree to the change.

Pursuant to the above provision, each time defendant changed the Agreement, defendant sent a written "Notice of Amendment" to its cardholders that documented the details of the new terms and conditions. Effective for billing periods beginning after September 1, 1999, defendant changed the method of calculating periodic finance charges and the payment due date, and added an arbitration section to the Agreement. The "Terms Level 11" Notice of Amendment, mailed to existing Discover cardholders with their monthly bills from July 1999 to August 1999, stated:

This notice informs you of changes to your current Discover Platinum Cardmember Agreement. Please note the effective date of the changes shown below and retain this notice for your records. WE ARE ADDING A NEW ARBITRATION SECTION WHICH PROVIDES THAT IN THE EVENT YOU OR WE ELECT TO RESOLVE ANY CLAIM OR DISPUTE BETWEEN US BY ARBITRATION, NEITHER YOU NOR WE SHALL HAVE THE RIGHT TO LITIGATE THAT CLAIM IN COURT OR TO HAVE A JURY TRIAL ON THAT CLAIM. THIS ARBITRATION SECTION WILL NOT APPLY TO LAWSUITS FILED BEFORE THE EFFECTIVE DATE. We are also changing the way we calculate Periodic Finance Charges. These changes do not apply if your Account is closed at the time you receive this notice.

The "Arbitration Section" provided:

ARBITRATION OF DISPUTES. In the event of any past, present or future claim or dispute (whether based upon contract, tort, statute, common law or equity) between you and us arising from or relating to your Account, any prior account you have had with us, your application, the relationships which result from your Account or the enforceability or scope of this arbitration provision, of the Agreement or of any prior agreement, you or we may elect to resolve the claim or dispute by binding arbitration.

IF EITHER YOU OR WE ELECT ARBITRATION, NEITHER YOU NOR WE SHALL HAVE THE RIGHT TO LITIGATE THAT CLAIM IN COURT OR TO HAVE A JURY TRIAL ON THAT CLAIM. PRE-HEARING DISCOVERY RIGHTS AND POST-HEARING APPEAL RIGHTS WILL BE LIMITED. NEITHER YOU NOR WE SHALL BE ENTITLED TO JOIN OR CONSOLIDATE CLAIMS IN ARBITRATION BY OR AGAINST OTHER CARDMEMBERS WITH RESPECT TO OTHER ACCOUNTS, OR ARBITRATE ANY CLAIMS AS A REPRESENTATIVE OR MEMBER OF A CLASS OR IN A PRIVATE ATTORNEY GENERAL CAPACITY. Even if all parties have opted to litigate a claim in court, you or we may elect arbitration with respect to any claim made by a new party or any new claims later asserted in that lawsuit, and nothing undertaken therein shall constitute a waiver of any rights under this arbitration provision. . . .

Your Account involves interstate commerce, and this provision shall be governed by the Federal Arbitration Act (FAA). The arbitration shall be conducted, at the option of whoever files the arbitration claim, by either JAMS/Endispute (JAMS) or the National Arbitration Forum (NAF) in accordance with their procedures in effect when the claim is filed. . . . At your written request, we will advance any arbitration filing, administrative and hearing fees which you would be required to pay to pursue a claim or dispute as a result of our electing to arbitrate that claim or dispute. The arbitrator will decide who will ultimately be responsible for paying those fees. In no event will you be required to reimburse us for any arbitration filing, administrative, or hearing fees in an amount greater than what your and our combined court costs would have been if the claim had been resolved in a state court with jurisdiction.

Any arbitration hearing will take place in the federal judicial district where you reside. . . .

Effective Date. If you do not agree to the changes, you must notify us in writing by September 15, 1999, at the following address: Discover Card, P.O. Box 15355, Wilmington, DE 19850-5355. If you notify us, we will close your Account and you will pay us the balance that you owe us under the current terms of the Agreement. If you do not notify us, the changes set forth in this notice will be effective and will apply to your Account for billing periods beginning after September 1, 1999. Use of your Account on or after October 1, 1999, means that you accept the new terms, even if you previously notified us that you did not agree to the changes.

Plaintiff did not notify defendant by September 15, 1999 that he disagreed with the Notice of Amendment, and continued to use his Card after October 1, 1999.

Plaintiff allegedly first noticed a change in terms upon receipt of his July 20, 2000 statement, which stated a Fixed APR for purchases of 15.49%. Plaintiff did not pay that balance in full. Plaintiff then realized that the Fixed APR for purchases on his June 20, 2000 statement was 14.99%, although he timely paid that balance in full. On August 26, 2000, plaintiff sent defendant a letter requesting copies of the written notifications that he should have received prior to the increases in rates. . . . On October 30, 2000, in response to plaintiff's letter, defendant sent plaintiff a copy of the amended Agreement.

III. Discussion

The Federal Arbitration Act (FAA) provides that written agreements to arbitrate disputes "shall be valid, irrevocable, and enforceable." 9 U.S.C.§ 2. The FAA mandates that district courts shall direct parties to proceed to arbitration on issues for which arbitration has been agreed, and to stay proceedings while the arbitration is pending. See 9 U.S.C. §§ 3, 4; Dean Witter Reynolds Inc. v. Byrd, 470 U.S. 213(1985); Harris v. Green Tree Financial Corp., 183 F.3d 173, 179-80 (3d Cir. 1999) ("If . . . a court deems a controverted arbitration clause a valid and enforceable agreement, it must refer questions regarding the enforceability of the terms of the underlying contract to an arbitrator, pursuant to section four of the FAA."); Great W. Mortgage Corp. v. Peacock, 110 F.3d 222, 228 (3d Cir. 1997) ("In conducting this inquiry the district court decides only whether there was an agreement to arbitrate, and if so, whether the agreement is valid."). The FAA requires the court to look to the principles of contract law to determine if arbitration clauses are valid and enforceable. See 9 U.S.C. § 2. In construing the scope of an arbitration clause, courts generally operate under a pronounced "presumption of arbitrability." Battaglia v. McKendry, 233 F.3d 720, 725 (3d Cir. 2000). . . .

A. Delaware Consumer Fraud Act Claim Is Subject to Arbitration.

Plaintiff argues that his claim under the Delaware Consumer Fraud Act is not subject to arbitration because it alleges fraudulent inducement and false advertising by defendant. Under the Supremacy Clause, the federal substantive law created by Section 2 of the FAA preempts state law. See Southland Corp. v. Keating, 465 U.S. 1, 10, (1984). Moreover, the Supreme Court has stated that allegations of fraudulent inducement and false advertising, because they pertain to the entire contract and not just the arbitration clause, are properly addressed by an arbitrator. See Prima Paint Corp. v. Flood & Conklin Mfg. Co., 388 U.S. 395, 403-04, (1967) ("If the claim is fraud in the inducement of the arbitration clause itself—an issue which goes to the 'making' of the agreement to arbitrate—the federal court may proceed to adjudicate it. But the statutory language [of the FAA] does not permit the federal court to consider claims of fraud in the inducement of the contract generally."). Thus, the court concludes that plaintiff's Delaware Consumer Fraud Act claim is subject to arbitration. . . .

B. Plaintiff Received Adequate Notice of Arbitration Section.

To amend credit card agreements regarding changing interest rates, banks are required under Delaware law to follow certain procedures. See 5 Del. C. § 952(b) (1)-(2). These procedures provide for a notice to the cardholder of the proposed amendment, and opting out by sending notice to the bank of the rejection of the amendment. See id. Defendant claims that it sent notice a Terms 11 Notice of Amendment to plaintiff in his July 20, 1999 monthly statement, in accordance with Delaware law and defendant's business practice of ensuring complete delivery to all of its cardholders. Although plaintiff claims that he never received the Notice of Amendment, defendant's mailing procedures and plaintiff's payment of his July 20, 1999 bill are sufficient evidence to satisfy defendant's burden of demonstrating adequate notice to plaintiff. . . . Thus, the court finds that defendant adequately notified plaintiff of the Arbitration Section.

C. Arbitration Section Is Valid and Enforceable.

Plaintiff also claims that even if he received adequate notice of the Arbitration Section, it is nevertheless invalid and unenforceable because it provides him no real choice to reject the Agreement, is the product of unequal bargaining power, lacks mutuality of remedy and prevents aggregation of class-wide claims.

Delaware law expressly permits banks to amend credit card agreements to add arbitration clauses.

Unless the agreement governing a revolving credit plan otherwise provides, a bank may at any time and from time to time amend such agreement in any respect, whether or not the amendment or the subject of the amendment was originally contemplated or addressed by the parties or is integral to the relationship between the parties. Without limiting the foregoing, such amendment may change terms by the addition of new terms or by the deletion or modification of existing terms, whether relating to . . . arbitration or other alternative dispute resolution mechanisms. 5 Del. C. § 952(a). Furthermore, Delaware provides for an opt-out procedure that allows credit cardholders to reject any change in terms simply by providing written notice to the bank before the change goes into effect: Any amendment that increases the rate or rates of periodic interest . . . may become effective as to a particular borrower if the borrower does not, within 15 days of the earlier of the mailing or delivery of the written notice of the amendment . . . furnish written notice to the bank that the borrower does not agree to accept such amendment. . . .

Any borrower who furnished timely notice electing not to accept an amendment in accordance with the procedures [above] . . . shall be permitted to pay the outstanding unpaid indebtedness in such borrower's account under the plan . . . [and] the bank may convert the borrower's account to a closed end credit account. 5 Del. C. § 952(b)(2), (b)(5).

Courts have routinely upheld Delaware's statutory scheme of permitting banks to unilaterally amend agreements with opt-out availability. . . .

Furthermore, more than a disparity in bargaining power is needed to show that an arbitration clause is unconscionable or unenforceable. . . .

Thus, the court concludes that the Arbitration Section is not invalid because it lacks meaningful choice and is created with unequal bargaining power.

Moreover, mutuality is not a requirement of a valid arbitration clause, provided that the underlying contract is supported by consideration. . . . The court finds that the Agreement, pursuant to which plaintiff received the benefits of the Card and defendant gained plaintiff's subscription, is supported by adequate consideration. Therefore, no mutuality is necessary to ensure validity of the Arbitration Section.

Finally, it is generally accepted that arbitration clauses are not unconscionable because they preclude class actions. See Gilmer, 500 U.S. at 32 (ADEA claims); Johnson v. West Suburban Bank, 225 F.3d 366, 377 (3d Cir. 2000), cert. denied, 148 L. Ed. 2d 957, 121 S. Ct. 1081, 69 U.S.L.W. 3552 (U.S. Feb. 20, 2001) (No. 00-846) (Truth in Lending Act claims). Thus, plaintiff's argument that the Arbitration Section is invalid because it deprives him of the right to class-action relief is unavailing.

D. The Action Should Be Dismissed.

The FAA provides that courts shall enter a stay pending arbitration when issues brought before the courts are subject to arbitration clauses. See 9 U.S.C. § 3. Courts have interpreted the provision, however, to permit dismissal if all issues raised in an action are arbitrable and must be submitted to arbitration. . . . Since plaintiff's claims must be submitted to arbitration, the court concludes that this action should be dismissed. The court will not retain jurisdiction pending the completion of arbitration.

IV. Conclusion

For the reasons stated, defendant's motion to compel arbitration is granted and the action is dismissed. Defendant's motion to stay proceedings pending completion of arbitration is denied as moot.

. . . IT IS ORDERED that defendant's motion to compel arbitration is granted and the action is dismissed. Plaintiff's motion to stay is denied as moot.

Case Questions for Discussion

1. Why does federal law trump state law? What is the constitutional basis for this conclusion?

2. What are the possible reasons why a financial institution might want to require arbitration rather than to employ the courts to resolve disputes with their customers?

3. How many people do you know who read the fine print that accompanies agreements with credit card companies? Should they be so required?

4. Should credit card companies be prohibited from soliciting on college campuses?

Mediation

Mediation lies at the polar opposite of litigation and is substantially less coercive than both court-based litigation and arbitration. A mediator assists parties to settle their dispute by mutual agreement.[14] Further, unlike court-based litigation or arbitration, disputing parties may agree upon the norms to be employed in settling their dispute. In other words, the parties need not look to the case law or statute books for a solution to their mutual problem, although, if that is their desire, they may do so. They are free to create their own rules and to agree upon a mutually acceptable resolution of their dispute.

Mediation is said to be superior to other forms of dispute resolution because the parties consent to all aspects of the decision. And because the parties have agreed to the result, there is a greater likelihood that the decision will be honored. Unlike litigation, and to a lesser extent arbitration, mediation does not view dispute resolution as a zero-sum game wherein one party loses at the expense of the other. Rather, it is anticipated that both parties will get something of value from the process. In this sense, mediation is a "win-win" proposition for all concerned. Ideally, then, mediation involves mutuality in all senses. The parties agree upon the mediation itself, the norms for settling their dispute, and the ultimate settlement. It is for this reason that Martin Shapiro regards mediation as superior to other forms of dispute resolution—because the parties are most likely to regard the process as legitimate.[15]

Mediation is an alternative to arbitration.

Empirical studies support Shapiro's conclusion. One study of small claims disputes in Maine, for example, concludes that mediation is more likely to produce greater compliance by the parties than civil litigation. Interestingly, researchers found that consensual settlements do not require explicit justification as is the case for formal judicial opinions. It is enough that the parties believe the decision is "fair" or "the best that I can expect." Judicial decisions are subject to exacting scrutiny, wherein rationales are evaluated on more or less objective criteria of what constitutes a well-reasoned judgment consistent with general rules. In mediated agreements, on the other hand, it is acceptable that decisions are founded upon idiosyncratic value preferences that are not easily articulated and may even be internally inconsistent. Moreover, the parties mediating a conflict are afforded an opportunity to confront the other with normative arguments to lever their position with appeals, asking the other side to "do the right thing"—to compel the other party to recognize the unfairness of its conduct giving rise to the conflict. Taking the form "we can save time and money," this process also reminds mediating parties of the practical reasons for settling their dispute without resort to courts. Mediators make note of values expressed by the parties during face-to-face sessions, pointing out the values that were mutually expressed and form the basis for a consensual agreement. Finally, evidence suggests that agreements reached through mediation tend to generate greater commitment to compliance than solutions imposed by legal authorities because the parties make personal commitments to each other. They comply because they have given their personal word to do so, not because a functionary of government requires it of them.[16]

Conciliation, Facilitation, and Mediation

Conciliation and facilitation processes are often mistaken for mediation. *Conciliation* usually involves a third party bringing together competing parties or carrying messages between them. For instance, when in 1992 Norwegian diplomats secretly brought together representatives of Israel and the Palestine Liberation Organization, they did not mediate the conflict. Instead, they convened the parties, acting as an expeditor for important negotiations outside the glare of public scrutiny and interest group influences at home and abroad.[17]

In *facilitation*, an individual moderates a large meeting. The facilitator's task is to permit all those who wish to speak to have an opportunity to do so, and at the same time to keep participants focused on the subject. Facilitators do not volunteer their own opinions or attempt to achieve a consensus that all the parties can agree upon. This being said, however, as dispute resolution processes, conciliation and facilitation are often used as synonyms for mediation.[18]

Mediation is particularly useful in resolving disputes among parties that are locked into ongoing relationships. Disputes among family members, neighbors, workers and employers, college roommates, probate disputants, construction contractors, and mutually dependent businesses are appropriate examples of parties who need and generally want to maintain a relationship in the future. Neighbors cannot easily move out of the neighborhood. Children cannot normally move out of their parents' home. Workers must go to work every day with a minimum of conflict between and among them and with their employers. Roommates ordinarily must remain together in the same room or apartment until their leases have expired. Family members want to remain on speaking terms with their relatives during and after distributing the property of a deceased relative. Subcontractors want to continue to do business with other contractors on future jobs. And businesses that supply goods or services to other companies want to maintain a good working relationship for the sake of future profits. In the mediation environment, disputing parties are encouraged to resolve their conflict by retreating in some fashion from their original position. Failure to do so may mean that they will have to turn to the courts for a resolution or to remain in a permanent state of antagonism, with the potential for violence looming in the background.

In the United States for the past two to three decades, hundreds of mediation programs have been established around the country.[19] These programs are often called neighborhood justice centers or resolution centers. Other programs are closely linked to local courts that refer disputes to these centers. The same private provider organizations that furnish arbitration services also provide mediation services. The American Arbitration Association (AAA), the United States Arbitration and Mediation, Inc. (USA&M), and the Judicial Arbitration and Mediation Services (JAMS) are prominent among the organizations in this field. When it becomes clear to the parties that if they do not settle their dispute through mediation their case may be returned to a court for a final disposition, the value of voluntary agreement becomes evident to them and settlement is more likely.

In some instances, criminal cases are mediated with an agreement by the perpetrator of a criminal act to make restitution and to offer expressions of sorrow and apology; and perhaps, the perpetrator may be rehabilitated by the experience. Although through mediation they may be compensated for the harm, some victims may be left with the feeling that the perpetrator is not being adequately punished for his or her actions.[20] Notwithstanding this drawback, there is considerable interest in mediation in the criminal process.

The Victim-Offender Reconciliation Program (VORP) was originally started in Canada in the 1970s. It has since been transplanted to many jurisdictions in the United States and other countries. The central activity of VORP is to bring together victims and offenders in face-to-face meetings facilitated by trained mediators. Victims may share their sense of pain, humiliation, and fear with their offenders, and in turn, offenders are afforded an opportunity to explain their antisocial conduct and to offer expressions of regret directly to their victims. In most instances, a restitution contract is negotiated between the victim and the offender that may take the form of personal service to the victim and to the community. Financial reimbursement or other forms of restitution agreeable to the parties may also be part of the restitution package.

VORP is reported to aid in humanizing the criminal justice system through face-to-face interaction between victim and offender. It is also believed that the process increases the offender's personal accountability for his or her own actions. The benefits for society are severalfold.

First, this process provides an alternative to the costly and often dysfunctional system of incarceration in the nation's prison system. Second, it enhances community understanding of the causes of crime and the problems with the criminal justice system. And third, where victims and offenders are previously connected by family, personal, or business relationships, mediation makes it more likely that victims and offenders may resume their association than if offenders are sent to prison.[21] Of course, VORP cannot work in the case of so-called victimless crimes because there is no party other than the prosecution to mediate an outcome, and plea bargaining is already widely available in the regular criminal justice system. Then, too, defense attorneys are naturally reluctant to participate in any process in which they are forced to plead without prior knowledge of what the opposing party wants in return.

Phases of Mediation

Private providers, court-based programs, and community-based mediation centers, among others, provide the public with trained mediators. They may or may not be attorneys, although a good number of law schools now provide formal classes for law students in the art of alternative dispute resolution that includes mediation.[22] Assigned mediators should explain to the parties who they are, as well as discuss their backgrounds, to reduce suspicion about their ability to behave in a neutral and impartial manner. Sometimes, two persons serve as mediators.

As the parties enter the room where the session is held, each mediator shakes hands with both parties and then invites each to sit at a table or in a circle, where all the participants face each other. The seating can be a significant detail because it is important that each party is regarded as equal as possible under the circumstances. The mediators are not in a physically hierarchical position to the parties, like judges sitting on an elevated bench looking down. In short, the room is a common meeting place with a minimum of formality, pomp, and circumstance. The mediators then explain to the parties why they are there. They indicate that any agreement must be acceptable to all the parties to the dispute. The steps in the mediation process are then outlined by the mediators, who explain that, unlike in a court of law, the process is entirely private and confidential. At the end of this introductory phase, the mediators answer any questions the parties may have about the process.[23]

Although there is currently no mediation law guaranteeing that communications involving mediators are privileged, such as communications by lawyers and clients or physicians and patients, there is a movement to do just that. The May 4, 2001, "Draft of the Uniform Mediation Act of the National Conference of Commissioners of Uniform State Laws" recommends the creation of a mediator privilege. Meanwhile, formal mediation agreements, such as those executed by the Judicial Arbitration and Mediation Services (JAMS), explicitly provide that

> All offers, promises, conduct and statements, whether oral or written, made in the course of the mediation by any of the parties, their agents, employees, experts and attorneys, and by the mediator and JAMS employees, who are the parties' joint agents and mediators for purposes of these compromise negotiations, are confidential.

The agreements further stipulate that such information is "privileged and inadmissible for any purpose, including impeachment, under Rule 408 of the *Federal Rules of Evidence* and any applicable federal or state statute, rule or common law provisions."[24]

The second phase of the process takes place in the presence of both parties. Mediators ask each party to describe the nature of the conflict, along with the background that preceded the dispute. Mediators avoid putting words in the mouths of the parties, although this is difficult to achieve. At the same time, they are attentive while not appearing overly sympathetic. At this phase, mediator questions are limited to the facts in dispute. They seek to acquire an accurate representation of the facts from the perspectives of the parties. Mediators ordinarily take notes, attempting to identify points of agreement and disagreement between the parties. With this done, mediators then decide whether to continue the mediation as a joint conference of the parties or to choose to caucus.[25]

If they choose to use *private caucuses*, mediators then meet with the parties privately. Mediators carefully assure each of the parties that what they say during private sessions will be revealed to the other party only if it grants permission. At this point in the process, mediators attempt to identify the true feelings of each party; they understand that if all such matters are known, the likelihood of finding a permanent solution will be greater. Mediators seek to identify areas of agreement among the parties and to probe whether compromise might be possible. There may be a temptation to split the difference between the parties, but good mediators realize that compromise solutions can be unsatisfactory to both parties. Consequently, mediators must walk a thin line of identifying areas of agreement and compromise without imposing an unsatisfying solution upon the parties. Private caucuses may be repeated as many times as necessary.[26]

Upon completion of the private caucuses, mediators call for a second session with all the parties present. The mediators then indicate areas of agreement, but although it is a difficult task, they should try to get the parties themselves to suggest a solution using their own words. Again, an underlying assumption of mediation is that if both parties voluntarily agree to a solution, then there is a strong probability that the agreement will be honored.[27] For later reference, mediators often place the details of the agreement in writing and provide copies to each party with the understanding that the mediated agreement is normally enforceable by a court of law if it meets the elements of a legal contract.[28]

Ombuds Programs

Scandinavians developed the position of *ombudsman*. His (ombudsman) or her (ombuds) function is to investigate citizen complaints about government agencies and to offer mediated solutions. In the United States, the ombuds' function has spread to nongovernmental corporations, newspapers, universities, and a variety of government and private agencies and institutions. However, unlike their Scandinavian counterparts, most U.S. ombudspersons work directly for the institutions they are asked to monitor. They usually report directly to the chief executive officer (CEO) in charge. Thus, by getting around the chain of command, the ombudsperson is insulated from the undue influence of those whom he or she might need to advise and correct. Ideally, ombudspersons should help parties settle their disputes without resort to formal legal proceedings. They aid complainants (or grievants, as they are often called) to prepare written grievances against fellow workers or superiors, in the case of a workplace, and to settle disputes with the least amount of disturbance to the everyday workings of the institution. Operating as intermediaries whenever possible, ombudspersons offer their recommendations for a settlement only after a resolution of the conflict fails to materialize. Consequently, they do not fit the ideal model of mediators as persons who aid disputants solve their problems for themselves.[29] That is, organizational interests in finding solutions to problems may dictate deviation from the ideal type.

Michael Barrera, current National Ombudsman for the U.S. Small Business Administration.

Many universities and colleges employ full- or part-time ombudspersons. Some deal with student complaints, and others deal with staff and faculty concerns. Students seek the advice and intervention of ombudspersons when they feel they are in too weak a position to command the attention and respect of administrators or faculty members. Faculty members, dealing with a rule-bound or in some cases dictatorial bureaucracy, use the ombudspersons office to help them negotiate successfully the hazards of university politics. In many universities and colleges, judicial review boards, composed of distinguished members of the faculty, render decisions when disputes are not successfully negotiated by ombudspersons. In some instances, such as a collective bargaining agreement between administration and faculty, arbitration panels may be established when all else fails.

Regulatory Negotiation

A variation on the mediation model, *regulatory negotiation* is an open recognition by legislators and other governmental actors that interest groups affected by the regulations and rules of an administrative agency should participate in the making of public policies that affect them directly. Given this model, the government agency in question reportedly acts as a mediator among conflicting interests in society to create agreements among plural groups within policy arenas; working together, government agencies and competing interest groups forge rules and regulations impacting government policy. Opposing stakeholders composed of manufacturers, unions, and consumers, for example, come together under agency auspices to negotiate government rules covering such topics as workplace safety, environmental protection, and consumer protection.[30]

The basic assumption underlying regulatory negotiation is that the common good of society may be realized through the clash of competing interests. This approach represents the explicit acceptance of the *pluralist model of democracy*, which views government policy making not as the act of political majorities, but rather the result of organized groups pressing their conflicting demands on government. A problem with the pluralist approach, however, is that not all interests are equal, because some groups possess greater political power than others. Moreover, large numbers of Americans are often not adequately represented by well-organized and effective power-brokering groups.

Admittedly, the problem of equality of conflicting parties is apparent in many instances in which mediation is employed, such as between employers and employees, or teachers and students. Yet, a government official, whose source of power stems from the consent of the governed, is constitutionally responsible for discerning and pursuing the interests of the entire political community. That is, the public interest is not necessarily served when interest groups within specific policy arenas achieve agreement about particular agency rules and regulations. This is particularly true in those policy arenas where not all affected interests are adequately represented. In such cases, it is the task of government officials to represent the best interests of the entire community. As a practical matter, moreover, regulatory negotiation, with its attention to satisfying conflicting group demands, is liable to produce weaker rules than otherwise might be the case when administrative agencies make rules and regulations employing the standards established by the enabling statutes that brought them into existence.

The Negotiated Rule-Making Act of 1990, 5 U.S.C. §§ 500, 581-590 (2000), attempts to treat the inherent problems associated with implementing the pluralist model of democracy. It requires agency heads to ascertain whether the negotiated ruling is in the public interest. The act mandates that agency heads consider the following: the need for such a rule, that a limited number of identifiable interests are significantly affected by such a rule, that it is possible to convene a reasonably balanced representation of interest groups concerned with the issue in question, that these groups may reasonably achieve consensus within a fixed time period, that the creation of a new rule may not be unduly postponed by the process of negotiating a rule, that the agency has adequate resources to expend in the process, and the extent to which the agency is prepared to base its new rule on the version accepted by the negotiated rule-making committee. If an agency wants to use negotiated rule making, it must publish in the *Federal Register* a notice announcing that decision, and it must describe the issues and rules that are to be created. It must also explain how interested parties may become members of the rule-negotiating committee. With varying levels of success, negotiated rule making under the 1990 Act has been used, for example, by the Federal Communications Commission, the Department of Labor, the Federal Trade Commission, and the Environmental Protection Agency.[31]

Court-Centered ADR

The litigation explosion in the United States has prompted judges, legislators, and private parties to consider ADR methods to ease overcrowded court dockets. Their eminently practical goal is to bring an end to festering legal disputes in a timely fashion. As illustrated in Figure 9.1, private trials and summary jury trials are the most coercive and most nearly similar to ordinary court-based litigation. As an ADR technique, *court-annexed arbitration* exerts somewhat less coercion upon disputing parties, and the minitrial is the least coercive court-based ADR technique. Though these court-centered ADR techniques vary in their reliance on the use of coercion to encourage the parties to settle their disputes short of actual trial, each tool shares the common premise that it is best for the parties and for the efficient functioning of judicial institutions to avoid full-blown trials.

Private Trials

The slow course of the wheels of justice in this country has prompted almost every state to enact statutes permitting *reference procedures*—disputing parties "rent-a-judge" (sometimes called a *referee*) to adjudicate their dispute. Rather than wait for the court calendar to work its way through the numerous cases pending trial, litigants who have already filed their pleadings may request the court's permission to hire their own judge to try the case. This gives the parties an opportunity to choose a person whom they both feel will be fair, someone who may be particularly knowledgeable about the subject under litigation and the procedural rules of the jurisdiction. Indeed, a growing number of firms sell their services to parties seeking to rent-a-judge, usually a retired jurist who works for the private provider firm. The court first grants the petition for reference procedures, and then the case is transferred to the hired judge, whom the parties pay. The hired judge hears the case and issues a decision on the basis of the evidence and existing legal precedents.[32] In some states, the referee's decision has the same force and effect as a trial court judgment.[33] Typically, the referee's decision is transmitted to the original judge, who then converts it into an enforceable court order.[34]

The major benefits of reference procedures are speed and a definite date to commence proceedings, which are made possible by bypassing the existing court structure. Parties can resolve their disputes in a timely fashion, permitting them to settle matters and to get on with their affairs. In contrast to public judging, private judging allows commercial organizations with high profiles to avoid media attention that may reflect badly on their products or business practices. Further, when parties are able to select their own judge, they have a greater tendency to accept the result as legitimate.

Unlike traditional arbitration, reference procedures give litigants the right to seek review of the referee's decision.[35] In California, these decisions may be appealed through regular court processes. A major criticism of the rent-a-judge approach is that it permits parties with sufficient personal wealth to opt out of the regular public court system while preserving their right to appeal to that same system. In essence, the rent-a-judge system creates a two-tier system of justice.[36]

Summary Jury Trials

One way to encourage litigants to negotiate a settlement short of a trial is to conduct a mock jury trial, otherwise known as a *summary jury trial.* Attorneys present an abbreviated version of their case before a group of prospective jurors, who in turn render an advisory verdict. Usually, jurors are not told that they are participating in a mock trial. After they deliberate and return a verdict, jurors are asked to answer attorney questions about the strength and weaknesses of their respective cases. The attorneys are permitted to ask the advisory jury members about their thinking, including the reasons for their decision. Jurors are free not to participate in the question-and-answer session. Summary jury trials are often successful in getting parties to negotiate settlements before the advent of full-blown trials. However, because it is relatively expensive for courts to conduct summary jury trials, they are generally reserved for disputes that will otherwise take weeks or months to try.[37]

Though the results of summary jury trials are not usually binding, the process serves to alert parties to the probable outcome of their dispute in the event of a full-blown trial. This information is then factored into the parties' decision-making calculus of whether to proceed further. If settlement proves impossible or inadvisable, parties are free to resume their case before a new judge and jury.[38] Some lawyers resist summary jury trials, arguing that it is costly to their clients and that a settlement in the particular case cannot be reached short of an actual trial and verdict.[39] They are also concerned about alerting opponents to valuable evidence and tactics in advance of trial. Presumably, however, the philosophy and procedures of discovery now in place throughout the United States should minimize such concerns. Despite any reservations, because a primary bar in many cases to pretrial settlement is the uncertainty about how a jury might assign liability and damages, summary jury trials are proving to be a useful predictor tool for counsel. For example, there may be considerable uncertainty about the degree of care a farmhand should exercise when working around agricultural equipment. The question is what degree of care might a "reasonable person" exercise when around dangerous farm machinery? Legal rules are not specific enough to answer such a question without the use of a jury to consider a particular fact situation. Nor does the existence of precedents provide for a comfortable and reliable determination of damage awards when farm workers are injured while using dangerous machinery. Thus, having parties spend anywhere from one-half to a full day to participate in a no-risk method to ascertain how jurors perceive the merits of the case without needing a large investment of time or money seems an appropriate method for dealing with uncertainty.[40] Though summary jury trials seem reasonable as a way to avoid the pitfalls of a full-blown trial, lawyers sometimes privately conduct mock trials on their own. In this way, they are able to discover possible problems in their cases without divulging tactics and information to opponents during a summary jury trial.

Born of the contemporary desire to expedite dispute resolution, summary jury trials are obviously not rooted in common law tradition. Nor is there explicit constitutional authorization for this ADR procedure. Yet, the Federal Rules of Civil Procedure and similar state rules of procedure form the basis for authorizing summary jury trials. First, the rules grant to courts the power to control and manage their own dockets. Rule 1 of the Federal Rules of Civil Procedure provides that the rules "shall be construed to secure the just, speedy, and inexpensive determination of every action." With respect to pretrial activities, Rule 16(a)(1) and (5) state:

> In any action, the court may in its discretion direct the attorneys for the parties and any unrepresented parties to appear before it for a conference or conferences before trial for such purposes as

(1) expediting the disposition of the action . . . and (5) facilitating the settlement of the case.

Furthermore, Rules 16(c)(7) and (11) explicitly provide for conferences to discuss the possibility of pretrial settlements or the use of extrajudicial procedures to resolve disputes and any other matters that may aid in the final disposition of cases.

Although the U.S. Court of Appeals for the Seventh Circuit declared in 1987 that a federal district court order mandating a summary jury trial was not within the federal rules,[41] Congress settled the issue with finality when it enacted the Civil Justice Reform Act of 1990. 28 U.S.C. § 473(a)(6)(B) provides that U.S. district courts may adopt plans that include: "authorization to refer appropriate cases to alternate dispute resolution programs that . . . (B) the Court may make available, including . . . summary jury trials." Subsequently, district courts promulgated local rules providing for both voluntary and mandatory summary jury trials.[42] Although specific rules vary with particular courts, we present a list of the rules used by Judge James L. Foreman when conducting summary jury trials in the U.S. District Court for the Southern District of Illinois.[43]

Summary jury trials have been used in a number of substantive areas of the law, including products liability; personal injury; contracts; age, gender, and race discrimination; and antitrust matters. The amount of the judgment award that can be asked by a plaintiff is not a limiting factor.[44]

Box 9.1   List of Rules for Summary Jury Trials in the U.S. District Court for the Southern District of Illinois*

1. Summary trials are conducted before six-member juries. Counsel are permitted two challenges each by way of a brief *voir dire* examination conducted by the judge. There are no alternate jurors.

2. Legal counsel are expected to submit proposed jury instructions in abbreviated form.

3. Attendance of clients or client representatives during summary jury trial is mandatory unless excused by the court for good cause.

4. All evidence is presented through attorneys for the parties. Only evidence that would be admissible at trial upon the merits may be presented. Attorneys may summarize and comment upon the evidence. In other words, they mingle representations of fact with argument, but they must observe responsibility and restraint. Counsel may present only factual representations supportable by reference to discovery materials, including depositions, stipulations, signed statements of witnesses, or other documents, or by a professional representation saying

that counsel personally spoke with the witness and is repeating what the witness stated.

5. Prior to trial, counsel are to confer with regard to physical exhibits, including documents and reports, and reach such agreement as is possible about the use of such exhibits.

6. Objections are not encouraged, but will be received if, in the course of a presentation, counsel goes beyond the limits of propriety in presenting statements as to evidence or argument thereon.

7. After counsels' presentations, the jury is given an abbreviated charge on the applicable law.

8. The jury is encouraged to return a unanimous verdict. Barring unanimity, the jury is to submit a special verdict consisting of an anonymous statement of each juror's findings on liability and/or damages.

9. Unless specifically ordered by the court, the proceedings are not recorded. Counsel may, if desired, arrange for a court reporter.

10. Although the proceedings are nonbinding, counsel may stipulate that a consensus verdict of the jury will be deemed a final determination on the merits, and the judgment may be entered thereon by the court. They may also stipulate to any other use of the verdict that will aid in the resolution of the case.

*Revised 9/16/1992.

Court-Annexed Arbitration

Court-annexed arbitration is the diversion of certain civil cases from the regular courts to a court-supervised arbitration processes. In this system, either the court appoints one or more arbitrators, or the parties appoint the arbitrators. These persons are responsible for applying the law of the jurisdiction to the case at hand. However, inconsistent with the strict arbitration model, if the jurisdiction permits, parties who disagree with the decision of the arbitrator may request a trial *de novo*— meaning the entire matter is tried anew by a civil court with appropriate jurisdiction. If, on the other hand, the parties feel they can live with the result, the arbitration ruling is converted into a court order by the judge overseeing the case.[45] Often decisions resulting from arbitration prompt the parties to negotiate further and consequently settle their dispute prior to trial.[46]

Though court-annexed arbitration is similar to the traditional arbitration model, it differs in important respects. First, because it operates under court supervision, it is neither private nor consensual. Second, although a litigant may appeal the arbitrator's award, some systems require that they must pay court costs and/or the arbitrator's fees if they do not improve their position as a result of the trial *de novo*. These fee systems may serve as a disincentive to exercising a litigant's right to a trial. Furthermore, there have been Seventh Amendment challenges to court-annexed arbitration as a denial of the constitutional right to a jury trial. Leading court opinions, however, have upheld court-ordered compulsory arbitration, finding that the desirability of a speedy, less expensive, and efficient trial system outweighs the right to a jury trial.[47] Anecdotal evidence indicates that court-annexed arbitration can shorten docket backlogs considerably. One informed participant in the process told us that for Cook and Lake Counties in Illinois, arbitrators in recent years were able to shorten court docket backlogs from one to nine years.

Minitrial

Though similar to summary jury trials, the *minitrial* employs a paid neutral advisor instead of a jury to determine the merits and probable outcome of the case presented by the parties' attorneys. Most often, testimony is in the form of depositions, but live witnesses are sometimes called. The attorneys for each side present their case in an expedited manner with no record made of the proceedings. The rules of evidence are relaxed because advisors, who are either experienced attorneys or retired judges, are capable (by virtue of their professional training and experience) of discerning the difference between competent and incompetent or prejudicial evidence. Consistent with the goal of dispensing with the conflict as quickly as possible but prudently, closing arguments are conducted within an agreed time limit. When the minitrial is complete, the paid neutral advisor and the parties meet to discuss the advisability of a settlement. The advisor may at first function as a mediator, taking no position on the merits of a particular settlement. If, however, an impasse is reached during negotiations, upon the request of the parties, the advisor may arbitrate the dispute.[48]

Minitrials are not adjudications in any real sense. Rather, they are, as ADR expert Linda Singer puts it, "information exchanges."[49] In essence, minitrials allow business executives on both sides of a controversy to hear the arguments of the other party and in the process come to a negotiated settlement. When large corporations are embroiled in a conflict and that dispute is consuming considerable time and expense, leading executives from both sides sit down to hear competing attorneys present their best case. After the presentation of evidence and arguments, including rebuttals, the executives meet privately to settle the case without the aid of their lawyers. The neutral advisor's major function at this stage is to preserve order during the presentations of the attorneys. If after their initial meetings the executives fail to reach an agreement by themselves, they may ask the advisor to give them an opinion in writing about the merits of the competing sides' arguments. Equipped with the written opinion, executives then meet once again in an attempt to reach a settlement. Another variation on the settlement scenario is to ask the advisor to issue a binding decision that both sides agree in advance to honor.[50]

Besides the obvious advantage of saving time and money, there are a number of reasons why corporate managers are attracted to this form of alternative dispute resolution. First, there is the perception that lawyers sometimes get in the way of a settlement. Because attorneys often invest considerable time and ego in preparing their cases, managers occasionally believe that they can turn particular disputes into something of a holy crusade; and this attitude becomes an impediment to settlement itself. Because they want to please their clients, lawyers are also suspected of painting a rosier picture than the facts of the case may warrant. Although this dim view of lawyers does not necessarily comport with reality, managers may nonetheless want to find out first-hand the status of their dispute; they need not rely completely on their lawyers' sometimes distorted view of the matter brought about by their emotional commitment to particular results. Second, minitrials afford corporate executives an opportunity to interact directly with their opposition's managerial counterparts, and in the process, their opponents are humanized. This interaction may encourage an innovative solution that otherwise may not be in the offing. Also, when corporate executives invest themselves in the process, there is an expectation that it will bring about a solution. And, finally, when the neutral advisor's opinion is requested, it may be used by persons or factions within each competing organization to bolster their own positions about how the particular dispute should be settled.[51]

Minitrials are effective in complex civil litigation, in which mixed questions of law and fact portend uncertain outcomes in the ordinary law courts. This method of dispute settlement has been successfully employed in cases involving construction disputes, contract enforcement, antitrust matters, patent infringements, products liability, and government contracts. One possible downside of the minitrial approach to dispute settlement is that it may be emotionally unsatisfying if the parties are seeking public vindication for their positions.[52]

As rational as it may seem, it is hard to conceive, at the time of this writing in the summer of 2001, for example, that Ford Motor Company and Bridgestone Tire Company, the manufacturer of Firestone tires implicated in fatal accidents of the Ford Explorer, would agree to settle their dispute by minitrial. Far too many public charges and countercharges have been made for the two giant corporations to agree to settle their dispute by way of an "information exchange." Another negative aspect concerning the use of minitrials is obvious. If one of the parties is not serious about settlement, the minitrial can become just another waste of time and money.[53]

Trends

There is little question that the movement toward alternative dispute resolution is here to stay. The American Arbitration Association (AAA) reported that its caseload reached an all-time high in the year 2000. In that year, 198,491 cases were filed, up almost 42 percent over the 1999 record high. In addition, the AAA reported that it processed 4,188 cases in mediation in 2000, a 17 percent increase over 1999.[54] These numbers do not include the hundreds of other providers of ADR services. At the same time, citizens continue to petition the ordinary courts for redress of their grievances, and the number of lawyers continues to grow.

The ideal mix between litigation, arbitration, and mediation is difficult to assess. Much depends upon how different groups of people within society decide to rely upon each. It is our prediction, however, that all dispute resolution techniques will continue to expand as the population grows and conflicts among individuals and groups in society increase.

Key Terms, Names, and Concepts

American Arbitration Association (AAA)

Alternative dispute resolution (ADR)

Arbitration

Arbitration by submission

Civil Justice Reform Act of 1990

Conciliation

Court-annexed arbitration

Demand for arbitration

Facilitation

Federal Arbitration Act

Information exchanges

Labor Management Relations Act

Legitimacy of courts

Mandatory but non-binding arbitration

Mediation

Minitrial

Negotiated Rule-Making Act of 1990

Neutral arbitrator

Ombudsperson

Private caucus mediation

Private trials

Pluralist model of democracy

Referee

Reference procedures

Regulatory negotiation

Summary jury trial

Discussion Questions

1. List and discuss both the theoretical and practical reasons why alternative dispute resolution techniques might be preferable to litigation.

2. Make a list of situations in college life in which mediation may seem appropriate.

3. How do you feel about the use of mediation in matters involving criminal conduct? What are the arguments pro and con?

4. Given what you know about the training and approach of lawyers, do you think attorneys and judges make ideal arbitrators and mediators?

Suggested Additional Reading

Bingham, Gail. *Resolving Environmental Disputes: A Decade of Experience.* Washington, DC: Conservation Foundation, 1986.

Brazil, Wayne D. *Effective Approaches to Settlement: A Handbook for Lawyers and Judges.* Clifton, NJ: Prentice Hall Law and Business, 1988.

Cuomo, Mario. *Forest Hills Diary: The Crisis of Community Low-Income Housing.* New York: Random House, 1974.

Green, Eric D. "Corporate Alternative Dispute Resolution." *Ohio State Journal on Dispute Resolution* 1 (1986): 203–297.

Harrington, Christine B. *Shadow Justice: The Ideology and Institutionalization of Alternatives to Court.* Westport, CT: Greenwood Press, 1985.

Haynes, John. *Divorce Mediation: A Practical Guide for Therapists and Counselors.* New York: Springer, 1981.

Lax, David A., and James K. Sebenius. *The Manager as Negotiator: Bargaining for Cooperative and Competitive Gain.* New York: Free Press, 1986.

Lovenheim, Peter. *Mediate, Don't Litigate: How to Resolve Disputes Quickly, Privately, and Inexpensively Without Going to Court.* New York: McGraw-Hill Publishing Company, 1989.

McGillis, Daniel. *Consumer Dispute Resolution: A Survey of Programs.* Washington, DC: National Institute for Justice, 1986.

Palmer, Michael, and Simon Roberts. *Dispute Processes: ADR and the Primary Forms of Decision Making.* London: Butterworths, 1998.

Plapinger, Elizabeth, and Donna Stienstra. *ADR and Settlement in the Federal District Courts: A Sourcebook for Judges and Lawyers.* Washington, DC: Federal Judicial Center and CPR Institute for Dispute Resolution, 1996.

Provine, D. Marie. *Settlement Strategies for Federal District Judges.* Washington, DC: Federal Judicial Center, 1986.

Rogers, Nancy H., and Richard A. Salem. *A Student's Guide to Mediation.* New York: Bender, 1987.

Tomasic, Roman, and Malcolm M. Feeley, eds. *Neighborhood Justice: Assessment of an Emerging Idea.* New York: Longman, 1982.

United Nations. *Handbook on the Peaceful Settlement of Disputes Between States.* New York: United Nations, 1992.

Ury, William. *Getting Past No: Negotiating With Difficult People.* New York: Bantam Books, 1991.

Endnotes

1. Martin Shapiro, *Courts: A Comparative and Political Analysis* (Chicago: University of Chicago Press, 1981), pp. 1–60.
2. Linda Singer, *Settling Disputes: Conflict Resolution in Business, Families, and the Legal System*, 2nd ed. (Boulder, CO: Westview, 1994), p. 5.
3. Margaret C. Jasper, *The Law of Alternative Dispute Resolution*, 2nd ed. (Dobbs Ferry, NY: Oceana Publications, Inc., 2000), p. 165.
4. 'Lectric Law Library's Stacks, "The Uniform Arbitration Act," available at: <http://www.lectlaw.com/files/adr06.htm>, as of 2000.
5. Jacqueline M. Nolan-Haley, *Alternative Dispute Resolution in a Nutshell* (St. Paul, MN: West, 1992), pp. 120–123.
6. Jasper, *The Law of Alternative Dispute Resolution*, pp. 10–11.
7. Ibid., pp. 4–5.
8. American Arbitration Association, "Speciality Panels and Programs," available online at, <http://www.adr.org> (2000), as of 2000.
9. American Arbitration Association, "Education and Training," available at: <http:// www. adr.org> (1999), as of 2000.
10. American Arbitration Association, "The Code of Ethics for Arbitrators in Commercial Disputes," available at: <http://www.adr.org> (1999), as of 2000.
11. Jasper, *The Law of Alternative Dispute Resolution*, p. 15.
12. Ibid., pp. 10–11.
13. Ibid., pp. 9–10.
14. Ibid., p. 168.
15. Shapiro, *Courts*, pp. 9–10.
16. John S. Murray, Alan Scott Rau, and Edward F. Sherman, *Processes of Dispute Resolution: The Role of Lawyers*, 2nd ed. (Westbury, NY: Foundation Press, 1996), pp. 319–322.
17. Singer, *Settling Disputes*, pp. 11–12.
18. Ibid., p. 24.
19. Ibid., p. 115.
20. Ethan Katsh and Janet Rifkin, "Student Guide to Mediation," in *Out of Court: A Simulation of Mediation* (Springfield, MA: Legal Studies Simulations, 1982), p. 3.
21. Robert B. Coates, "Victim-Offender Reconciliation Programs in North America: An Assessment," in Burt Galaway and Joe Hudson, eds., *Criminal Justice, Restitution, and Reconciliation* (Monsey, NY: Criminal Justice Press, 1990), pp. 126–127.
22. Singer, *Settling Disputes*, pp. 169–173.
23. Ethan Katsh and Janet Rifkin, "Out of Court Mediator's Manual," in *Out of Court: A Simulation of Mediation* (Springfield, MA: Legal Studies Simulations, 1982), pp. 3–4.
24. Rule 408, *Compromise and Offers of Compromise of the Federal Rules of Evidence* states: "Evidence of (1) furnishing or offering or promising to furnish, or (2) accepting or offering or promising to accept, a valuable consideration in compromising or attempting to compromise a claim which was disputed as to either validity or amount, is not admissible to prove liability for or invalidity of the claim or its amount. Evidence of conduct or statements made in compromise negotiations is likewise not admissible. This rule does not require the exclusion of any evidence otherwise discoverable merely because it is presented in the course of

compromise negotiations. This rule also does not require exclusion when the evidence is offered for another purpose, such as proving bias or prejudice of a witness, negativing a contention of undue delay, or proving an effort to obstruct a criminal investigation or prosecution."

25. Katsh and Rifkin, *Student Guide to Mediation,* pp. 5–6.
26. Ibid., pp. 7–9.
27. For a good discussion of the various strategies mediators use, see: Leonard L. Riskin, "Mediator Orientations, Strategies, and Techniques," in Murray, *Processes of Dispute Resolution: The Role of Lawyers,* pp. 362–366.
28. Katsh and Rifkin, "Student Guide to Mediation," pp.10–11; see also, American Arbitration Association, "Roster of Neutrals-Mediation: Questions and Answers," available at: <http://www.adr.org/roster/mediators/start.html>, as of January, 2003.
29. Singer, *Settling Disputes,* pp. 25–26.
30. Ibid., p. 24.
31. Ibid., pp. 148–149.
32. Jasper, *The Law of Alternative Dispute Resolution,* p. 6.
33. Nolan-Haley, *Alternative Dispute Resolution in a Nutshell,* p. 199.
34. Jasper, *The Law of Alternative Dispute Resolution,* p. 6.
35. Nolan-Haley, *Alternative Dispute Resolution in a Nutshell,* pp. 199–200.
36. Singer, *Settling Disputes,* p. 29.
37. Ibid., pp. 64–65.
38. Nolan-Haley, *Alternative Dispute Resolution in a Nutshell,* pp. 128–129.
39. Singer, *Settling Disputes,* p. 5.
40. "Procedures Followed for Summary Jury Trials in Judge James L. Foreman's Court," U.S. District Court for the Southern District of Illinois, p. 2. Available through the Clerk of the U.S. District Court, Southern District of Illinois (revised September 16, 1992).
41. Standell v. Jackson County, 838 F. 2d 884 (7th Cir. 1987).
42. "Procedures Followed for Summary Jury Trials in Judge James L. Foreman's Court," p. 4.
43. Ibid., pp. 4–8.
44. Ibid., p. 6.
45. Jasper, *The Law of Alternative Dispute Resolution,* p. 13.
46. Singer, *Settling Disputes,* p. 27.
47. Nolan-Haley, *Alternative Dispute Resolution in a Nutshell,* p. 128.
48. Jasper, *The Law of Alternative Dispute Resolution,* p. 7.
49. Singer, *Settling Disputes,* p. 59.
50. Ibid., pp. 59–62.
51. Ibid., pp. 63–64.
52. Nolan-Haley, *Alternative Dispute Resolution in a Nutshell,* p. 195.
53. Ibid.
54. American Arbitration Association, "2000 Annual Report," available at: <http://www.adr.org/upload/LIVESITE/About/annual_reports/annual_report_2000.pdf>, available as of January, 2003. ✦

Part III

Law Governing Conduct, Property, and Relations Among Individuals

Torts

Tort case awards often appear in the media as examples of the out-of-control U.S. legal system. The plaintiff bar is usually portrayed as a group of legal vultures who entice ordinary citizens into litigation with contingency fees. Most people recall the woman who got millions by suing McDonald's after spilling coffee in a car and burning herself. Most people also remember hearing about the mugger in the New York City subway who was shot by police and later collected millions in a lawsuit against the city. Public reaction is generally negative to these types of stories, because they seem to contradict common sense. Most people have had a painful, but otherwise injury-free experience with a spilled hot beverage. Likewise, most people want the police to stop

375

muggings and other dangerous crimes. Rewarding the criminal seems ludicrous.

In reality, both of the above cases were reasonable. McDonald's maintained the temperature of its coffee between 180 and 190 degrees for taste purposes. Most other establishments serve coffee about forty degrees cooler. McDonald's knew that food items served above 140 degrees pose a burn danger and that coffee at the higher temperatures can cause serious burns in two to seven seconds. In fact, the com-

Torts is the area of law that accident victims may look to for compensation.

pany had 700 reports of coffee burns in a 10-year period. The woman in question suffered third-degree burns over six percent of her body, and she required skin grafts. In effect, the courts said to McDonald's that it is unreasonable for a company to serve coffee at a temperature that is likely to cause serious burns, given the propensity of people to spill drinks.

In the subway mugger case, the public did not know that the mugger was unarmed, and he was shot twice in the back when fleeing after the commission of the crime. The shooting was a clear violation of the U.S. Supreme Court's ruling in *Tennessee v. Garner,* which allows police to shoot at a fleeing criminal only if they have probable cause to believe there is a threat of "serious physical harm" to an officer or bystander. In addition, the police attempted to conceal the fact that the mugger had been shot in the back while fleeing. The message from the courts to the police: Even suspected criminals are owed a duty of care. Police are expected and required to act in accordance with the law.[1]

What Is Tort Law?

Legal commentators have struggled to define *tort law.* Consider the following attempts by well-known tort specialists:

- Prosser: "A tort is a civil wrong, other than breach of contract, for which a court will provide a remedy in the form of an action for damages."

- Kionka: "A civil wrong, wherein one person's conduct causes a compensable injury to the person, property, or recognized interest of another, in violation of a duty imposed by law."

- Sir John Salmond: ". . . there is no such thing as a law of Tort, but only a law of particular unconnected torts—that is, a set of pigeon holes, each bearing a name, into which the act or omission of the defendant must be fitted before the law will take cognizance of it and afford a remedy."

- Dobbs: "A tort is conduct that amounts to a legal wrong and that causes harm from which courts will impose civil liability. . . . The essence of tort is the defendant's potential for civil liability to the victim for harmful wrongdoing and correspondingly the victim's potential for compensation or other relief."[2]

The definitional troubles stem from the wide variety of actions that fall under the tort umbrella (everything from simple trespassing, personal injury, medical malpractice, and products liability to invasion of privacy) and the common law nature of torts. For example, not all torts involve wrongdoing. It is possible for the defendant in a tort action to have exercised every caution in his or her actions, but to be held legally responsible for damages caused by his or her actions, under a strict liability theory. For instance, one who keeps tigers is responsible for harm they cause even if the owner takes all precautions to prevent any injury to others.[3] It is also possible for a defendant to have caused no injury other than a technical violation of an interest of the plaintiff, such as an entry on another's property that causes no damage, but that conduct will entitle the plaintiff to nominal damages (usually $1 or some other token amount).[4]

For our purposes, we will adopt the following working definition of tort law: *A tort action is one not based in contracts or criminal law, whereby the plaintiff seeks damages or equitable relief in lieu of damages for actual or technical injuries to his person, property, or legally protected interests, caused by the acts or omissions of the defendant.*

Evolution of Modern American Tort Law

What is today the group of civil actions collectively referred to as torts had its origination in the English courts of the thirteenth and fourteenth centuries. There were two basic forms: trespass and trespass on the case. *Trespass* required some actual contact with the plaintiff's interest, such as physically entering the plaintiff's land or striking the plaintiff. Fault was not at issue. If the defendant accidentally struck the plaintiff, he was liable for any injuries. The plaintiff did not need to show the defendant was careless. Actual damages were not required either. The mere fact that the plaintiff had entered the defendant's land without permission was enough to support a successful action. *Trespass on the case* evolved to address indirect injuries. If the defendant had left a bucket of water on plaintiff's doorstep and plaintiff tripped on it coming out of his house, trespass, as a cause of action, would not be available to plaintiff because defendant did not trip the plaintiff directly. Instead, trespass on the case was the proper action. In addition to indirect injuries, trespass on the case required some wrongful action. The plaintiff had to show that the defendant was negligent or had acted purposefully. In our example, the plaintiff would have to show that the defendant had negligently or purposefully set the bucket of water where he knew the plaintiff would trip on it. The plaintiff had to show the defendant's actions had caused actual damages as well. A technical violation of a protected interest was not sufficient to support a cause of action under trespass on the case.

With respect to the law of torts, all U.S. states except Louisiana accepted the common law of England. Because the American courts generally did not require formal writs like the English courts, the distinction between trespass and trespass on the case fell into disuse, and trespass was the form of action for all tort-like actions. In 1850, strict liability for direct injuries was abandoned in the Massachusetts case of Brown v. Kendall, 60 Mass. (6 Cush.) 292. In that case, the defendant attempted to break up a dogfight with a stick. He accidentally struck the plaintiff when he raised the stick over his head. The court refused to impose liability on the defendant because he had not purposefully or negligently caused the plaintiff's injury. It was merely an unfortunate accident. After *Brown v. Kendall,* a general principal of American tort liability was recognized: Some wrongdoing (negligent or intentional act) by the defendant must be the cause of the plaintiff's injuries.

The balance of this chapter examines some of the more common tort subdivisions: intentional torts, negligence actions, and product liability actions. We also present a short review of the tort reform movement. Although the four subject areas above provide a full plate for intellectual digestion, they are by no means an exhaustive treatment of actions included under the wide tort umbrella.

Intentional Torts

Intentional torts are most directly related to the old English trespass action. The common element is the state of mind of the actor. The actor must intend to take the action, whereas in negligence-based actions, the actor almost never intends to take the action causing the harm. Although there are other intentional torts, we will limit our discussion to battery, assault, false imprisonment, infliction of mental distress, trespass to land, and interference with chattels.

Battery

A *battery* occurs when an actor intentionally causes a *harmful* or *offensive* contact with another's person. Intentional harmful contact is the easy case. If defendant sees plaintiff talking to his girlfriend and angrily punches him in the nose and breaks it, defendant is liable to plaintiff for the cost of his medical expenses and other resulting damages. Offensive contact is a more difficult case. Offensive does not necessarily mean repugnant. The principle underlying liability for intentional offensive contact is that people should be free to restrict contact with their bodies. An offensive touching occurs when one makes contact with another in a manner for which he or she has no permission. This issue can be quite tricky. For instance, a man and woman, who are otherwise strangers, are at a New Year's Eve party and he kisses her at midnight. This probably is not a battery, because she probably gave an *implied consent* (i.e., being at the party and not leaving the area when the New Year turned, given the custom of giving New Year's kisses). In the absence of an express prohibition of contact, an implied consent of touching that does not offend a reasonable sense of personal dignity can be inferred. However, had the woman fallen asleep at the New Year's party before midnight, it is more likely that a battery occurred if the man kissed her at midnight, because her consent may not have been implied. Casual touching in a crowded airplane, when boarding and deplaning, most likely carries an implied consent. Express prohibitions of contact are usually respected, but they must be reasonable in the normal course of social interaction. A passenger on a crowded airplane could not reasonably prohibit any casual contact with other passengers if she wanted to board and deplane when other passengers did. Some express prohibitions must be respected, however, even if most members of society would find them unreasonable.[5] Consider whether Cohen's express prohibition was reasonable in the following case.

Cohen v. Smith
Appellate Court of Illinois, Fifth District
269 Ill. App. 3d 1087, 648 N.E.2d 329 (1995)

JUSTICE CHAPMAN delivered the opinion of the court: Patricia Cohen was admitted to St. Joseph Memorial Hospital ("Hospital") to deliver her baby. After an examination, Cohen was informed that it would be necessary for her to have a cesarean section. Cohen and her husband allegedly informed her physician, who in turn advised the Hospital staff, that the couple's religious beliefs prohibited Cohen from being seen unclothed by a male. Cohen's doctor assured her husband that their religious convictions would be respected.

During Cohen's cesarean section, Roger Smith, a male nurse on staff at the Hospital, allegedly observed and touched Cohen's naked body. Cohen and her husband filed suit against Nurse Smith and the Hospital. The trial court allowed defendants' motions to dismiss. We reverse. . . .

The Restatement (Second) of Torts provides that an actor commits a battery if: "(a) he acts intending to cause a harmful or offensive contact with the person of the other or a third person, or an imminent apprehension of such a contact, and (b) a harmful contact with the person of the other directly or indirectly results."

Liability for battery emphasizes the plaintiff's lack of consent to the touching. "Offensive contact" is said to occur when the contact "offends a reasonable sense of personal dignity."

Historically, battery was first and foremost a systematic substitution for private retribution. Protecting personal integrity has always been viewed as an important basis for battery. Consequently, the defendant is liable not only for contacts which do actual physical harm, but also for those relatively trivial ones which are merely offensive. This application of battery to remedy offensive and insulting conduct is deeply ingrained in our legal history. As early as 1784, a Pennsylvania defendant was prosecuted for striking the cane of a French ambassador. The court furthered the distinction between harmful offensive batteries and nonharmful offensive batteries: "As to the assault, this is, perhaps, one of that kind, in which the insult is more to be considered than the actual damage; for, though no great bodily pain is suffered by a blow on the palm of the hand, or the skirt of the coat, yet these are clearly within the definition of assault and battery, and among gentlemen too often induce dueling and terminate in murder."

Causing actual physical harm is not an element of battery. "A plaintiff is entitled to demand that the defendant refrain from the offensive touching, although the contact results in no visible injury. . . ."

The only reason there is some hesitancy over the issue of whether a battery occurred in this case is because the contact took place in a hospital between a medical professional and a patient. If Patricia Cohen had been struck in the nose by Nurse Smith on a public street, everyone would agree that a battery occurred, and under those limited facts, there would be no defense to the battery. In contrast, medical professionals are allowed to touch patients during the course of medical treatment because patients consent, either explicitly or implicitly, to the touching. The violation of a plaintiff's right to bodily and personal integrity by an unconsented to touching is the essence of a claim for battery.

The plaintiffs had no grievance over how the medical procedure was performed or the medical consequences of the cesarean section. Rather, the plaintiffs' complaint addressed their fundamental right to refuse treatment that conflicts with their religious views. The plaintiffs' complaint against Nurse Smith alleges that Smith touched Cohen's naked body after being informed of her moral and religious beliefs against such touching by a male. Similarly, the plaintiffs' complaint against the Hospital alleges that the doctor performing the surgery told Nurse Smith that the operation was to be performed without any male seeing Cohen naked. According to the complaint, despite being informed of Cohen's religious beliefs, Nurse Smith, an agent and employee of the Hospital, intentionally saw and touched Cohen's naked body.

The allegation that both Nurse Smith and the Hospital were informed in advance of plaintiffs' religious beliefs is important in this case, because the religious convictions of plaintiffs might not be those of most people who enter the hospital to give birth. As a matter of fact, plaintiffs' counsel candidly conceded that there would be no cause of action for battery if Patricia Cohen had been placed in Nurse Smith's and the Hospital's care in an emergency situation in which Patricia had been unable to inform the Hospital or its agents of her beliefs. . . . The fact that the plaintiffs hold deeply ingrained religious beliefs which are not shared by the majority of society does not mean that those beliefs deserve less protection than more mainstream religious beliefs. The plaintiffs were not trying to force their religion on other people; they were only insisting that their beliefs be respected by the Hospital and the Hospital staff. . . .

Although most people in modern society have come to accept the necessity of being seen unclothed and being touched by members of the opposite sex during medical treatment, the plaintiffs had not accepted these procedures and, according to their complaint, had informed defendants of their convictions. . . .

Case Questions for Discussion

1. Is this a case of harmful touching?
2. What is the justification for making offensive touching an actionable tort?
3. Do you think Mr. and Mrs. Cohen's request was reasonable? Does it need to be reasonable?
4. What if only male nurses and doctors had been available at the hospital when Mrs. Cohen was having her baby? Would that have altered the outcome of the case?

Assault

As we have already explained, one who intentionally touches another in a harmful or offensive manner is subject to liability for a battery. Instead of actually making contact with another, what happens if the actor only threatens to batter another? Does the law have an interest in making it actionable to threaten others? The intentional tort of *assault* recognizes the interest of being free from apprehension of a harmful or offensive contact. The law has an interest in keeping the peace. By recognizing assault as an actionable offense, the threatened person has the option of seeking legal redress instead of employing self-defense or retribution. As a result, general peace in society is promoted.

An actor is liable to another for assault if he or she acts in such a way to put another person in *imminent apprehension* of harmful or offensive contact. The one who is threatened need not feel frightened. "Apprehension" merely means the one who is threatened believes the act *may* result in imminent contact. For example, Gambler lost $10,000 on the Tyson-Hollyfield boxing match when Tyson was disqualified for biting Hollyfield's ear. Several months later, Gambler, after drinking for several hours, sees Tyson on the street and after threatening Tyson, takes a swing at him. Tyson is sober and amused at the threat and deftly avoids the punch. Gambler is nonetheless liable to Tyson for assault.

Although Tyson was not afraid, Gambler's actions put him in imminent apprehension of a harmful or offensive contact. Only Tyson's ability to slip the punch avoided the contact. To be actionable, the apprehension must be of imminent contact or, in other words, without a significant delay in the contact. Pointing an uncocked pistol at another is actionable since the pistol can be cocked quickly. However, if one threatens to shoot another and leaves to go get a pistol, because there is a significant delay, the threatened contact is not imminent enough to support liability. Words alone will not support the action. Words coupled with acts or circumstances, which make the apprehension of imminent contact reasonable, are required.[6] If you were Mr. Cullison in the following case, would the words and circumstances put you in imminent apprehension of harmful contact?

Cullison v. Medley
Supreme Court of Indiana
570 N.E.2d 27 (1991)

OPINION BY KRAHULIK: According to Cullison's deposition testimony, on February 2, 1986, he encountered Sandy, the 16-year-old daughter of Ernest, in a Linton, Indiana, grocery store parking lot. They exchanged pleasantries and Cullison invited her to have a Coke with him and to come to his home to talk further. A few hours later, someone knocked on the door of his mobile home. Cullison got out of bed and answered the door. He testified that he saw a person standing in the darkness who said that she wanted to talk to him. Cullison answered that he would have to get dressed because he had been in bed. Cullison went back to his bedroom, dressed, and returned to the darkened living room of his trailer. When he entered the living room and turned the lights on, he was confronted by Sandy Medley, as well as by father Ernest, brother Ron, mother Doris, and brother-in-law Terry Simmons. Ernest was on crutches due to knee surgery and had a revolver in a holster strapped to his thigh. Cullison testified that Sandy called him a pervert and told him he was sick, mother Doris berated him while keeping her hand in her pocket, convincing Cullison that she also was carrying a pistol. Ron and Terry said nothing to Cullison, but their presence in his trailer home further intimidated him. Primarily, however, Cullison's attention was riveted to the gun carried by Ernest. Cullison testified that, while Ernest never withdrew the gun from his holster, he grabbed for the gun a few times and shook the gun at plaintiff while threatening to jump astraddle of Cullison if he did not leave Sandy alone. Cullison testified that Ernest kept grabbing at it with his hand, like he was going to take it out, and took it to mean he was going to shoot me when Ernest threatened to jump astraddle of Cullison. Although no one actually touched Cullison, his testimony was that he feared he was about to be shot throughout the episode because Ernest kept moving his hand toward the gun as if to draw the revolver from the holster while threatening Cullison to leave Sandy alone.

As the Medleys were leaving, Cullison suffered chest pains and feared that he was having a heart attack. Approximately two months later, Cullison testified that Ernest glared at him in a menacing manner while again armed with a handgun at a restaurant in Linton. On one of these occasions, Ernest stood next to the booth where Cullison was seated while wearing a pistol and a holster approximately one foot from Cullison's face. Shortly after the incident at his home, Cullison learned that Ernest had previously shot a man. This added greatly to his fear and apprehension of Ernest on the later occasions when Ernest glared at him and stood next to the booth at which he was seated while armed with a handgun in a holster. In count two of his complaint, Cullison alleged an assault. The Court of Appeals decided that, because Ernest never removed his gun from the holster, his threat that he was going to jump astraddle of Cullison constituted conditional language, which did not express any present intent to harm Cullison, and, therefore, was not an assault. Further, the Court of Appeals decided that even if it were to find an assault, summary judgment was still appropriate because Cullison alleged only emotional distress and made no showing that the Medleys' actions were malicious, callous, or willful or that the alleged injuries he suffered were a foreseeable result of the Medleys' conduct. We disagree.

It is axiomatic that assault, unlike battery, is effectuated when one acts intending to cause a harmful or offensive contact with the person of the other or an imminent apprehension of such contact. It is the right to be free from the apprehension of a battery, which is protected by the tort action, which we call an assault. As this Court held approximately 90 years ago in Kline v. Kline (1901), 158 Ind. 602, 64 N.E. 9, an assault constitutes "a touching of the mind, if not of the body." Because it is a touching of the mind, as opposed to the body, the damages, which are recoverable for an assault, are damages for mental trauma and distress. "Any act of such a nature as to excite an apprehension of a battery may constitute an assault. It is an assault to shake a fist under another's nose, to aim or strike at him with a weapon, or to hold it in a threatening position, to rise or advance to strike another, to surround him with a display of force."

Additionally, the apprehension must be one, which would normally be aroused in the mind of a reasonable person. Id. Finally, the tort is complete with the invasion of the plaintiff's mental peace. The facts alleged and testified to by Cullison could, if believed, entitle him to recover for an assault against the Medleys. A jury could reasonably conclude that the Medleys intended to frighten Cullison by surrounding him in his trailer and threatening him with bodily harm while one of them was armed with a revolver, even if that revolver was not removed from its holster. Cullison testified that Ernest kept grabbing at the pistol as if he were going to take it out, and that Cullison thought Ernest was going to shoot him. It is for the jury to determine whether Cullison's apprehension of being shot or otherwise injured was one, which would normally be aroused in the mind of a reasonable person. It was error for the trial court to enter summary judgment on the count two allegation of assault.

[Editor's note: The court reversed the entry of summary judgment on the assault count, vacated the Court of Appeals decision, and remanded the case back to the trial court.]

Case Questions for Discussion

1. If Ernest did not have the gun when the Medleys confronted Cullison in his trailer, would they still have been liable for an assault?

2. Would Ernest's actions in the restaurant have constituted an assault if the confrontation in the trailer had not been an assault?

3. Was it reasonable for the Medleys to be concerned about Cullison and Sandy's relationship? If yes, was it unreasonable for them to come to his trailer that night? What if they had visited the trailer the next morning? Would that conduct have been more reasonable?

False Imprisonment

Individuals have an interest in not being confined against their will that courts enforce through actions for *false imprisonment*. Although the name of the action implies imprisonment, it is not necessary for an individual to be detained in a prison or a jail (although an unlawful detainment in a jail or prison would certainly support a false imprisonment action). To establish a case of false imprisonment, the plaintiff must show that the defendant intentionally confined or caused the plaintiff's confinement, and that plaintiff was aware of the confinement. The requisite intent is the intent to confine. If the defendant was lawfully confining the plaintiff or acting under a privilege, the defendant must raise it as a defense.

A plaintiff must show that he or she was confined or not permitted to go beyond boundaries established by the defendant. The required boundaries need not be four walls, and the exact limits of the boundary can be unspecified. The plaintiff must not have been aware of a reasonable means of escape. The plaintiff is not required to use an unsafe or offensive means of escape. For instance, a plaintiff would not be expected to jump out of a moving car.[7] The confinement need only be for an appreciable amount of time, however short that may be. Confinement can be physical, such as locking plaintiff in a room, blocking plaintiff's means of escape, or otherwise physically restraining the plaintiff's movement. Confinement can also be accomplished through duress or threat, or by submission to legal authority. A lawful confinement can turn into false imprisonment if the defendant fails to release plaintiff, or to allow plaintiff to seek bail, or to bring plaintiff before a magistrate in a timely manner.[8]

Some false imprisonment cases are easy. If Alex and five of his compatriots surrounded Barb in the park and refused to allow her to leave until she pays $20, a false imprisonment occurred. Alex and his compatriots intended to restrict Barb's movement, she had no reasonable means of escape, it lasted for an appreciable amount of time, and she was aware of the confinement. A much tougher case occurs when the defendant acted in what he believed to be a reasonable and lawful manner, such as a store employee detaining a suspected shoplifter or a deprogrammer trying to break the hold of a cult on an individual. The following case examines a deprogramming situation.

Taylor v. Gilmartin
United States Court of Appeals for the Tenth Circuit
686 F.2d 1346 (1982)

OPINION BY DOYLE: . . . The essence of the case is an attempted religious deprogramming effort together with the means which were employed to accomplish the objective. The charges revolve around the particular circumstances which led up to the deprogramming, the actual techniques which were employed in an effort to persuade the subject to abandon the religion which he had adopted.

All of this commenced when Taylor took up residence in the monastery of the Holy Protection of the Blessed Virgin Mary, a local religious organization, in Oklahoma City, Oklahoma. Appellant had reached the age of 21 when the deprogramming effort occurred. Taylor's parents were opposed to his joining the religion and in July of 1976 they took the action which led to this cause. They employed an organization called the Freedom of Thought Foundation, a corporation which carries on the business of deprogramming religious zealots. Deprogramming is a process of attempting a psychological shock treatment on members of non-mainstream religious sects in an effort to sever their involvement with a religious cult lifestyle.

As part of the program, appellant's father, through Freedom of Thought, applied to the Oklahoma County District Court to be appointed as "temporary" guardian of the appellant. Appellees Howard and Trauscht, lawyers for Dr. Taylor, the father of appellant, visited Judge John A. Benson, an Oklahoma state district judge who was temporarily assigned in Oklahoma City, and conferred with him ex parte. They asked him to hear the case. Benson contacted the Probate Judge who would ordinarily hear such a matter and obtained permission to hear it. Only after that was the petition for a guardianship filed. Judge Benson ordered the temporary guardian of plaintiff's person be appointed in order to determine whether plaintiff was under the influence of a religious cult. Judge Benson said that he wanted the plaintiff taken into custody "so that (plaintiff) could be given notice of a [permanent] guardianship hearing." Plaintiff was at the monastery when the deputies came for him. He offered no resistance. The hearing occurred before Judge Benson as soon as Taylor was brought in to court. Although Judge Benson found him to be normal, he formally entered an order appointing Taylor's father as Temporary Guardian of the Person. The reason for the Judge's action was ". . . the right of [Plaintiff's] father and . . . family to know [Plaintiff] decided . . . to spend the rest of [his] life away from them secluded in a monastery . . . probably overrides any individual right [Plaintiff] might possibly have on a temporary basis . . . to be free from . . . custody. . . ."

On the basis of the order heretofore cited plaintiff was taken that same day, that is July 15, 1976, from Oklahoma City, Oklahoma to Akron, Ohio. . . . Taylor was held for approximately one week in Akron where he was kept at a motel and under constant guard. There followed the deprogramming. . . . He was deprived of sleep and was told that he would be subject to shock treatment. He suffered severe gastritis, diarrhea and abdominal cramping and when he complained, the deprogramming seemed to intensify. They threw cold water on him, shined a light in his eyes, tore his clothing off, cut his hair and beard and they told him they

called friends and religious leaders from a list plaintiff had given them of people who would vouch for him, and they stated that the friends reported his religion was not legitimate. The deprogrammers indicated the pressure would cease if plaintiff would renounce his religion. On July 23rd or 24th, 1976, plaintiff was taken from Akron to Phoenix, Arizona, where apparently his mother was staying. He was held, still under guard, for the rehabilitation phase of the deprogramming. However, he escaped July 31, 1976 and returned to Oklahoma City and to the seminary. He has been there ever since. Subsequently, Taylor instituted this present suit in the United States District Court for the Eastern District of Oklahoma against not only the deprogrammers, but also his parents and his brother. However, the Taylor family members were dismissed by an agreement prior to trial. The deprogrammers remain.

The Invalidity of the Guardianship Order: . . . (I)t is plain that the hearing in Judge Benson's court was not styled as a mental health hearing to determine whether Taylor should be committed to the state mental hospital or to a private facility, as required by statute.

Apparently the judge fashioned this order to suit something that was not even provided for in any statute. Appellees' petition to Judge Benson, as mentioned above, invoked only the language of 58 O.S. § 851. Section 55 requires a petitioner to seek an order directing the hospitalization of one who is asserted to be mentally ill. Commitment was not a subject even mentioned at the temporary hearing. Section 55 requires that upon receiving the petition the court appoint a sanity commission under § 54, Title 43A. This commission is to be composed of two qualified examiners and one licensed actively practicing attorney and is to certify its findings on the mental health of the person under examination. Judge Benson, of course, appointed no sanity commission. The judge considered the guardianship order to be for the purpose of determining whether Taylor had been brainwashed in the monastery, not whether he was mentally ill and should be hospitalized, an objective which, of course, is not provided for in any Oklahoma statute. Due to the fact that no statutory jurisdiction gave rise to this temporary guardianship order and due also to the fact that there was no proper notice, even were we to assume authority for the proceeding, the order is void. . . .

The Validity of the False Imprisonment Claim: The trial court directed a verdict for the appellees on the false imprisonment claim and the reason for that was the trial court's determination that Judge Benson's temporary guardianship order was proper; that any imprisonment could not be false in view of the lawfulness of the order. We must disagree with the action taken by the trial court.

The argument of the appellees is that the false imprisonment claim is a collateral attack on the temporary guardianship order. Where a judgment appointing a guardian appears to be regular on its face, so it is argued, there is jurisdiction for such an order and it cannot be attacked collaterally. Concededly, though, where the order is void on its face, a collateral attack is permissible. In the case before us the facts are such as to support the conclusion that there is a lack of jurisdiction and voidness in Judge Benson's order. There remains, however, the question whether the order purporting to create a temporary guardian shields the deprogrammers from legal action.

It is, of course, fundamental that an action for false imprisonment arising from a commitment or guardianship order is not cognizable where there has been regular and legal process observed, where the order is regularly issued with authority to issue the order and lawfully executed. In the decision of the Oklahoma court in Yahola v. Whipple, 189 Okla. 583, 118 P.2d 395, 397, the court said: A person who causes the arrest of another in a civil proceeding must answer in damages even though the arrest was in pursuance of an order of court, when the court issuing the order has exceeded its jurisdiction, or had no authority to do so. . . . Judgment in favor of all other defendants . . . is reversed. The case shall be remanded for further proceedings, a new trial to a jury, in accordance with the foregoing.

Case Questions for Discussion

1. Were Taylor's parents justified in seeking to deprogram their son?
2. What was the deprogrammers' intent when Taylor was taken into their care?
3. What should the parents and deprogrammers have done? What did they do wrong?

> 4. Who do you think was behind this action, Taylor or the religious cult?
>
> 5. Could the facts of this case support a battery as well? Could the facts support an assault?

Intentional Infliction of Emotional Distress

Although courts have been valuing and compensating defendants for emotional or mental damages for some time, the American legal system has long been suspicious of claims for emotional distress without some evidence of an accompanying physical injury. Even now, under the authoritative *Restatement (Second) of Torts*, an action for the *intentional infliction of emotional distress* requires (1) intentional or reckless action by the defendant, (2) conduct that is extreme and outrageous, (3) conduct that causes the plaintiff's mental distress, and (4) emotional distress that is severe. The defendant must know or should know that the conduct in question would cause the plaintiff's injuries. The defendant's conduct must be something more than insulting, threatening, and annoying. Even actions that may be considered tortious, or criminal, or sufficient in malice to support punitive damage awards, may not rise to the level of outrageous conduct required under this action. For example, if Al sees Betty walking down the street and calls her dirty names and questions her sexual orientation in front of others, Al's actions are certainly insulting to Betty and could cause her to suffer severe mental distress. Most members of the community would consider Al's actions out of bounds, but his behavior probably does not rise to the level of outrageous. To be "outrageous," the actions of the defendant must be so extreme that virtually all members of the community would be outraged. For example, Alice is new in town and attends a party at Bill's home. Bill has a swimming pool and several other guests are swimming on a hot evening. Alice did not bring her suit, but Bill loans her one, knowing it is made of a fabric that will dissolve in water. Once Alice gets wet, the suit dissolves, and she is naked in front of the other guests. Alice is extremely embarrassed and humiliated. This is the type of conduct that is generally considered outrageous enough to support an action for intentional infliction of emotional distress. In addition to showing that the defendant's action caused the emotional distress, the plaintiff must show that it caused more than embarrassment or short-term despondency.

The relationship between the plaintiff and defendant can affect the degree of outrageous behavior required by the defendant to support the action. Those in a position of dominance over another may be held liable for acts that an equal would not. For instance, it may be actionable if a school principal threatens to expel a student if the student's mother does not submit to his sexual advances. In effect, the principal's act is considered an extreme abuse of his position. If that abuse is likely to cause the plaintiff extreme mental distress, it should be actionable.[9]

The following Connecticut case is a good illustration of the type of outrageous behavior and the type of severe mental distress required in a successful cause of action for intentional infliction of emotional distress.

Blair v. LaFrance
Superior Court of Connecticut, Judicial District of Waterbury
2000 Conn. Super. LEXIS 2558 (2000)

OPINION BY ROGERS: . . . The defendant is the uncle of the plaintiff. . . . The plaintiff was sexually molested by the defendant when she was eight years old. He came into the room that she was sleeping in at her uncle's house and inserted his fingers and tongue in her vagina. When the defendant got up and left the room, plaintiff ran into her cousin's room and hid under his bed. Plaintiff did not tell anyone about this incident at the time of its occurrence. When plaintiff was twelve, she was again molested by the defendant while she was sleeping in her own bed in her own home. She immediately told her mother about the incident. Her mother did not confront the defendant and did nothing to protect her daughter. When plaintiff was fourteen, the defendant attempted to molest her during a family camping trip. On this occasion plaintiff screamed at the defendant and grabbed a knife to protect herself. She then ran and hid until other individuals came back to the camping site. . . .

Plaintiff met her husband, Hollis, in 1992 and married him in 1993. They had a child on July 4, 1996. When plaintiff was initially involved with Hollis she did not tell him about the abuse. However, her behavior before having to go to family events

with her aunts and the defendant was troubling to Hollis. She would yell at him for no reason and be extremely short tempered. She would also avoid her uncle at family gatherings. Plaintiff finally told Hollis about the molestation after a family summer party at which the defendant was present. . . .

Based on the tests that Dr. Grant-Hall administered to plaintiff during the first evaluation, she testified that plaintiff was significantly depressed and in need of antidepressant medication. Plaintiff also scored very high on the Traumatic Stress Inventory, which is a test, developed to assess sexual and physical abuse survivors. She had a high degree of anger. She scored in the significant range for having intrusive traumatic experiences. She scored in the significant range for distress and paranoia and was extremely distrustful of people. Her anxiety and fear level were high. Plaintiff had overwhelming rage and pain and was found to be obsessive compulsive. Finally, her suicide potential was found to be moderately high. As a result of these test results, Dr. Grant-Hall referred plaintiff to a psychiatrist for counseling and antidepressant medication. Plaintiff also has a history of recurring nightmares, sleeps in sweat pants and a sweatshirt and always sleeps away from the door and against the wall. Plaintiff describes herself as having extremely low self-esteem. She thinks that she is ugly and fat. She has a history of being bulimic. She also testified that she hates herself for what she let her uncle do. . . .

In order to prevail on a claim for intentional infliction of emotional distress, plaintiff must establish by a preponderance of the evidence, the following four elements: (1) that the actor intended to inflict emotional distress or that he knew or should have known that emotional distress was the likely result of his conduct; (2) that the conduct was extreme and outrageous; (3) that the defendant's conduct was the cause of the plaintiffs distress; and (4) that the emotional distress sustained by the plaintiff was severe. Liability for intentional infliction of emotional distress requires conduct exceeding all bounds usually tolerated by decent society, of a nature which is especially calculated to cause, and does cause, mental distress of a very serious kind. . . .

By sexually molesting the plaintiff when she was eight and twelve years old, defendant engaged in conduct exceeding all bounds usually tolerated by a decent society. He knew or should have known that this conduct would result in mental distress of a very serious kind to the plaintiff. Based on the testimony of the plaintiff and Dr. Grant-Hall, plaintiff has also proven that the conduct of the defendant was the cause of the plaintiff's distress and the distress suffered was severe.

Case Questions for Discussion

1. If defendant had attempted to have sexual relations with his niece only after she was the age of consent and she had declined his advances, could she have recovered for intentional infliction of emotional distress if she suffered from the same mental problems?

2. If plaintiff brought suit against her mother for having failed to protect her, would she have been successful?

3. Why do you think plaintiff decided to proceed in a tort action, instead of pursuing criminal charges of child molestation against her uncle?

Intentional Intrusions on Land (Trespass to Land)

To this point, the intentional torts we have discussed protect the integrity of an individual's body. In this section and the next, we discuss intentional torts that protect the integrity of an individual's property.

The theory of *intentional intrusion on land* holds an actor liable to another if he intentionally enters land in possession of another or causes a third person or thing to enter the land. Actors are also liable if they intentionally remain on the land or fail to remove a thing from the land when they should. The intention required is the intent to enter, not the intent to wrongfully occupy the property of another. One need not be the owner of the land to be in possession of it. A renter has the right of present possession of leased property. Likewise, those who occupy land with the intent to own it through adverse possession are in possession of the land, although they are not entitled to possession against the true owner. Suppose Absent properly owns Blackacre, although she lives in another state. Present enters upon Blackacre and declares publicly that he is going to openly occupy Blackacre, although he knows it is owned by Absent. Camper enters Blackacre, puts up a tent and stays the night. Camper is himself a trespasser against Present, although Present is not entitled to possession of Blackacre and is himself a trespasser against Absent.

An entry can be a momentary invasion of the land in question by a person or a thing. The entry can be on, below, or above the surface. Consider the following examples:

(1) Alvin on his way home crosses the corner of Barb's property. Alvin has entered Barb's property and is a trespasser.

(2) Cindy is hunting ducks in a boat on a public lake and shoots at a duck. The pellets cross Bob's land 10 feet above the ground and fall in another portion of the lake. Cindy is a trespasser.

(3) Denise constructs a building on the border of her and Bart's property. The roof hangs over Bart's property. Denise is a trespasser.

Failing to leave when requested or failing to remove things from land also supports a cause of action in trespass. For example, Tyrone with Julio's permission drives his off-road vehicle onto Julio's land for the purpose of going mudding. Tyrone gets his vehicle stuck on one of the trails Julio maintains for off-road mudding. Julio tells Tyrone he must have the vehicle removed by the next weekend so that others may use the trail. Tyrone does not remove the vehicle by the next weekend. Tyrone is a trespasser, because his permission or license to have his vehicle on Julio's land expired.[10]

Before the advent of modern aviation, an owner of land was considered to own the surface and everything below and above the surface. Once airplanes flying over property became commonplace, it was clear there was a need to balance the public's interest in being able to fly in open airspace against landowners' right to enjoy the possession of their property. In 1946, the U.S. Supreme Court held that the air above minimum altitudes of flight is a public highway. Landowners, according to the Court, still have exclusive control of the immediate reaches of enveloping atmosphere, and invasions of that space are the same as invasions of the surface.[11]

Trespass to Chattel and Conversion

Actors commit a *trespass to a chattel* (an article of personal property as opposed to real property) if they intentionally *dispossess* the chattel from one who is in possession or if the trespass involves *intermeddling* with a chattel in the possession of another. The intent required is the intent to use or dispossess the chattel. It is not necessary for actors to know that their use of the chattel is a violation of the possessor's rightful possession. A dispossession occurs when actors intentionally take possession of the chattel from another without consent through fraud, barring access of the possessor to the chattel, destroying or damaging the chattel, or taking the chattel into the custody of the law. An intermeddling with a chattel is intentionally bringing about physical contact with a chattel in the possession of another. For example, Alicia grabs onto the back bumper of Zack's car and is pulled along for a hundred yards on a snowy day. Alicia has intermeddled with Zack's car. If actors dispossess a chattel, they are liable to the possessor, even if the damages are only nominal. On the other hand, if the trespass to the chattel is intermeddling, there is liability to the possessor only if the intermeddling causes a decline in the condition, value, or quality of the chattel, or if the possessor is deprived of the use of the chattel for a substantial period of time. In our bumper example, although Alicia intentionally intermeddled with Zack's car, Alicia is not liable, even on a nominal basis. If, however, the bumper is damaged during Alicia's thrill ride, she is liable to Zack for the cost of repair and for the rental value of the automobile during the period it is in the repair shop.

The basic damage rule under trespass to chattels is the cost of repair or the rental value of the property for the period the possessor of the chattel was dispossessed. Title to the chattel remains with the plaintiff. Under the theory of *conversion,* on the other hand, the plaintiff sues for the full value of the chattel, and title to the chattel is transferred to the defendant. In other words, the plaintiff forces the defendant to buy the chattel. Because conversion is a more dramatic remedy, the action usually requires a serious interference with the interest of the plaintiff in the chattel. An actor can commit conversion by intentionally dispossessing, destroying, materially altering, materially using, disposing, misdelivering, or refusing to surrender a chattel. The required intent is the intent to exercise dominion and control over the chattel. The use required must be material. If your neighbor mows his lawn with your mower once without permission, it probably would not be conversion, because his use was immaterial. However, it would probably be conversion if he used your mower for the whole mowing season, without your permission. Likewise, if he asked permission to use your mower while his was in the shop being repaired and he kept and used the mower all season, it would probably constitute conversion.[12]

As illustrated in the following case, the trespass to chattels action has proven useful to victims of computer hacking and Spam (electronic junk mail) mailers.

CompuServe, Inc. v. Cyber Promotions, Inc.
United States District Court for the Southern District of Ohio
962 F. Supp. 1015 (1997)

Plaintiff's motion for a preliminary injunction GRANTED.

OPINION BY GRAHAM: This case presents novel issues regarding the commercial use of the Internet, specifically the right of an online computer service to prevent a commercial enterprise from sending unsolicited electronic mail advertising to its subscribers.

Plaintiff CompuServe Incorporated (CompuServe) is one of the major national commercial online computer services. It operates a computer communication service through a proprietary nationwide computer network. In addition to allowing access to the extensive content available within its own proprietary network, CompuServe also provides its subscribers with a link to the much larger resources of the Internet. This allows its subscribers to send and receive electronic messages, known as e-mail, by the Internet. Defendants Cyber Promotions, Inc. and its president Sanford Wallace are in the business of sending unsolicited e-mail advertisements on behalf of themselves and their clients to hundreds of thousands of Internet users, many of who are CompuServe subscribers. CompuServe has notified defendants that they are prohibited from using its computer equipment to process and store the unsolicited e-mail and has requested that they terminate the practice. In-

stead, defendants have sent an increasing volume of e-mail solicitations to CompuServe subscribers. CompuServe has attempted to employ technological means to block the flow of defendants' e-mail transmission to its computer equipment, but to no avail. This matter is before the Court on the application of CompuServe for a preliminary injunction which would extend the duration of the temporary restraining order issued by this Court on October 24, 1996 and which would in addition prevent defendants from sending unsolicited advertisements to CompuServe subscribers.

For the reasons which follow, this Court holds that where defendants engaged in a course of conduct of transmitting a substantial volume of electronic data in the form of unsolicited e-mail to plaintiff's proprietary computer equipment, where defendants continued such practice after repeated demands to cease and desist, and where defendants deliberately evaded plaintiff's affirmative efforts to protect its computer equipment from such use, plaintiff has a viable claim for trespass to personal property and is entitled to injunctive relief to protect its property. . . .

Over the past several months, CompuServe has received many complaints from subscribers threatening to discontinue their subscription unless CompuServe prohibits electronic mass mailers from using its equipment to send unsolicited advertisements. CompuServe asserts that the volume of messages generated by such mass mailings places a significant burden on its equipment, which has finite processing, and storage capacity. CompuServe receives no payment from the mass mailers for processing their unsolicited advertising. However, CompuServe's subscribers pay for their access to CompuServe's services in increments of time and thus the process of accessing, reviewing and discarding unsolicited e-mail costs them money, which is one of the reasons for their complaints. CompuServe has notified defendants that they are prohibited from using its proprietary computer equipment to process and store unsolicited e-mail and has requested them to cease and desist from sending unsolicited e-mail to its subscribers. Nonetheless, defendants have sent an increasing volume of e-mail solicitations to CompuServe subscribers. . . .

CompuServe predicates this aspect of its motion for a preliminary injunction on the common law theory of trespass to personal property or to chattels, asserting that defendants' continued transmission of electronic messages to its computer equipment constitutes an actionable tort. Trespass to chattels has evolved from its original common law application, concerning primarily the asportation of another's tangible property, to include the unauthorized use of personal property. Its chief importance now, is that there may be recovery . . . for interferences with the possession of chattels, which are not sufficiently important to be classed as conversion, and so to compel the defendant to pay the full value of the thing with which he has inter-

fered. Trespass to chattels survives today, in other words, largely as a little brother of conversion. The scope of an action for conversion recognized in Ohio may embrace the facts in the instant case. . . . The Restatement § 217(b) states that a trespass to chattel may be committed by intentionally using or intermeddling with the chattel in possession of another. Restatement § 217, Comment e defines physical intermeddling as follows: intentionally bringing about a physical contact with the chattel. The actor may commit a trespass by an act, which brings him into an intended physical contact with a chattel in the possession of another.

Electronic signals generated and sent by computer have been held to be sufficiently physically tangible to support a trespass cause of action. State v. McGraw, 480 N.E.2d 552, 554 (Ind. 1985) (Indiana Supreme Court recognizing in dicta that a hacker's unauthorized access to a computer was more in the nature of a trespass than criminal conversion). . . . It is undisputed that plaintiff has a possessory interest in its computer systems. Further, defendants' contact with plaintiff's computers is clearly intentional. Although electronic messages may travel through the Internet over various routes, the messages are affirmatively directed to their destination.

Defendants, citing Restatement (Second) of Torts § 221, which defines dispossession, assert that not every interference with the personal property of another is actionable and that physical dispossession or substantial interference with the chattel is required. Defendants then argue that they did not, in this case, physically dispossess plaintiff of its equipment or substantially interfere with it.

However, the Restatement (Second) of Torts § 218 defines the circumstances under which a trespass to chattels may be actionable. One who commits a trespass to a chattel is subject to liability to the possessor of the chattel if, but only if, (a) he dispossesses the other of the chattel, or (b) the chattel is impaired as to its condition, quality, or value, or (c) the possessor is deprived of the use of the chattel for a substantial time, or (d) bodily harm is caused to the possessor, or harm is caused to some person or thing in which the possessor has a legally protected interest. . . . In the present case, any value CompuServe realizes from its computer equipment is wholly derived from the extent to which that equipment can serve its subscriber base. Michael Mangino, a software developer for CompuServe who monitors its mail processing computer equipment, states by affidavit that handling the enormous volume of mass mailings that CompuServe receives places a tremendous burden on its equipment. . . .

Next, plaintiff asserts that it has suffered injury aside from the physical impact of defendants' messages on its equipment. Restatement § 218(d) also indicates that recovery may be had for a trespass that causes harm to something in which the possessor has a legally protected interest. Plaintiff asserts that defendants' messages are largely unwanted by its subscribers, who pay incrementally to access their e-mail, read it, and discard it. Also, the receipt of a bundle of unsolicited messages at once can require the subscriber to sift through, at his expense, all of the messages in order to find the ones he wanted or expected to receive. These inconveniences decrease the utility of CompuServe's e-mail service and are the foremost subject in recent complaints from CompuServe subscribers. Patrick Hole, a customer service manager for plaintiff, states by affidavit that in November 1996 CompuServe received approximately 9,970 e-mail complaints from subscribers about junk e-mail, a figure up from approximately two hundred complaints the previous year. Many subscribers have terminated their accounts specifically because of the unwanted receipt of bulk e-mail messages. Defendants' intrusions into CompuServe's computer systems, insofar as they harm plaintiff's business reputation and goodwill with its customers, are actionable under Restatement § 218(d). . . .

Case Questions for Discussion

1. Does CompuServe recover damages from defendants as a result of this action?

2. If defendants continue to send bulk e-mail solicitations to CompuServe subscribers, will they owe CompuServe anything?

3. If damages were awarded, how would CompuServe compute them? What damage has CompuServe suffered? Was this a dispossession or an intermeddling with CompuServe's chattels?

4. When Judge Graham spoke of *dicta* by the Indiana Supreme Court, what did he mean?

Defenses and Privileges

Not all intentional invasions of bodily and property interests are actionable. For example, a parent can confine a child to his room or apply reasonable force for the purpose of discipline. One may strike another in *self-defense,* as long as the force used was a reasonable response to the threat of harm. Police may confine someone who is under arrest. One involved in a boxing match *consents* to being hit by the other boxer. Police may enter one's land to affect a search warrant or to arrest an individual. *Private and public necessity* also provides protection for actors who invade or destroy another's property to avoid serious threats to the individual or the public. Assume that Willard, seeing an approaching tornado, breaks his neighbor's window and takes shelter in the basement. Under the *privilege of private necessity,* Willard is liable for the actual damage done, but he is not a trespasser. If, however, Willard breaks the window to allow a bus full of tourists to enter the basement of his neighbor to seek shelter from the tornado, he would not be liable for the damage to the window, as a result of the *public necessity privilege.* The rationale is that if Willard is acting to protect himself, he should compensate the owner for any damage done. But in the case of public necessity, it would be an undue burden to require one who is acting to protect the public to pay for necessary damages.[13]

Negligence

Under the intentional torts discussed above, actors intended to invade the protected interest. Under *negligence* theory, actors do not desire the result of their actions or inactions. However, if the actor's action or inaction results in an injury to another, the injured party may hold the actor legally responsible. It is commonly said that everyone has a general duty of reasonable care to protect others from injury. A wide range of injuries may be redressable under negligence actions, including those resulting from traffic accidents, slips and falls, medical and other professional malpractice, and a myriad of other unintended misfortunes.

The *Restatement (Second) of Torts* lists four necessary elements in a successful cause of action for negligence: (1) The interest invaded must have been one that is protected against unintentional invasions, (2) the conduct of the actor was negligent, (3) the actor's conduct was the legal cause of the damage, and (4) the damaged party's conduct did not disable his ability to bring the action.[14] We now turn to an examination of each of these elements.

The Interest Invaded

The first element merely requires that the actor have a *duty of reasonable care* not to harm the interests of other parties. Does the actor have an obligation to act in accordance with a standard of conduct for the protection of others against unreasonable risk? Professor Kionka prefers to argue that all actors have a general duty of care, unless there is a rule limiting the care required, such as the lack of liability for negligent conduct toward a trespasser.[15]

Negligent Conduct

What constitutes *negligent conduct?* It is a question of fact. The trier of fact (in most cases the jury) must determine what a *reasonable person* under like circumstances would have done. If the trier of fact decides a reasonable person would not have acted differently, then the actor's conduct did not create an unreasonable risk and no negligence occurred. Who or what is the reasonable person? It is a hypothetical person, not one of the jurors or lawyers or, for that matter, the judge. By using a hypothetical person, the standard is an objective community-based standard and is the same for all persons. It is what is expected by the community of all persons of normal capabilities. The reasonable person is not perfect; he or she can make mistakes. The reasonable person is also referred to as the *reasonably prudent person,* which indicates that the reasonable person is alert for and attempts to avoid unreasonable risks.[16]

Negligent conduct is not necessarily conduct that is morally wrong or careless. An actor can actively try to reduce or eliminate unreasonable risk and still be negligent.[17] For example, after a big snow, Picabo sees a snowdrift on her street immediately around a blind curve. Fearful of a motorist coming around the curve and hitting the drift, she shovels the snow from the street into the gutter. That night, the temperature rises and it rains very hard. The snow Picabo shoveled into the gutter acts as a dam as the rain runs off and floods the road. Bob drives his car around the blind curve, runs into the water, and loses control, hitting a tree, damaging his car, and suffering a broken arm. Picabo, although actively trying to reduce the risk she perceived from the snowdrift, negligently created another unreasonable risk by piling the snow in the gutter and blocking the water runoff.

The reasonable person standard is altered if the actor is a minor or has certain disabilities, special skills, or talent. It would be unfair to hold a deaf person responsible for heeding the audio warning signals heavy equipment emit when traveling in reverse. The standard of care for a deaf actor is what is expected of a reasonable deaf person. Deaf people might be expected to be more vigilant, however, by looking in all directions if they have knowledge of heavy equipment working in the area they are walking through. Likewise, children are not held to the same standard as adults. If the actor is a child, the standard for the child's conduct is that of a reasonable person of similar age, intelligence, and experience. A 13-year-old child is expected to act as would a reasonable 13-year-old. Very young children (under age 4 or 5) are probably incapable of negligence in all but very special circumstances. The standard of conduct for people with mental illness or other mental deficiencies traditionally is not altered to account for their impairment. Surgeons, attorneys, engineers, and others who hold themselves out to the public as possessing special skills, knowledge, or talents are held to a more demanding standard.[18] Assume that Casey, an engineer, uses low-strength steel to construct a bridge across a creek. The bridge fails when a truck carrying a heavy load of rock attempts to cross it. How should Casey's conduct be tested? If we use the reasonable person standard, Casey's conduct might not be negligent because the reasonable person might not have knowledge sufficient to know what strength of steel is needed to build a bridge. The proper standard to be used in our hypothetical case is that of a reasonable engineer. A reasonable engineer would be expected to know the load-carrying requirements of a bridge and the materials needed to support those load requirements.

The law expects that the reasonable person possesses knowledge common in the community. The plaintiff need not show that the defendant actually knew her conduct created an unreasonable risk. It is enough to show that a reasonably prudent person in the community should have known. An actor's ignorance of common community knowledge will not excuse her action creating an unreasonable risk. For example, Ann, raised in a northern city, is ignorant of the dangers of alligators and snakes in the Florida everglades. She leads a group of children into the swamps, without outfitting the children with protective boots or other protection against snakebite, to study the tropical plants growing there. One of the children is bitten. Ann's conduct is negligent, because a reasonable person from the community would know snakebite is a risk associated with walks in the swamp. Ann should have known of the risk and anticipated that the children could be injured when walking in the swamp.

Legal Cause of the Damage

Causation questions raise two pertinent issues. Although courts often refer to both issues as *proximate cause* issues, two distinct issues must be addressed. First, it must be shown that the defendant's negligence conduct was the *factual cause* of the damage. This issue is generally factual in nature. What did the defendant's negligent conduct cause? Second, it must be shown that the defendant's negligent conduct was the *proximate* or *legal cause* of the damage. This is a legal policy issue. Was the injured party protected from the defendant's negligent conduct? Should the law hold the defendant responsible for the plaintiff's injury? Was the injury to the plaintiff foreseeable by the defendant?[19]

A couple of examples illustrate the different questions being raised. Suppose Anson is standing near Bill and is tossing his knife into the air and catching it. On one of the tosses, he fails to catch the knife and it lands on and cuts Bill's foot. There is no question that Anson's negligent conduct (tossing a knife into the air close to Bill) was the *factual cause* of Bill's injury. Anson's conduct will also be the *legal or proximate cause* of Bill's injury. Anson should have known that tossing the knife into the air near Bill could cause an injury to Bill. Because the injury was foreseeable, the law should hold Anson responsible for Bill's injury. Suppose, however, that instead of sticking into Bill's foot, the knife lands on Bill's dog. Upon being struck by the knife, the dog begins running wildly and knocks Candy (a stranger who is standing 20 yards away) into a busy street, where a car driven by Deb hits Candy. Was Anson's negligent conduct the *factual cause* of Candy's injury? The answer is yes. There is no doubt that Anson's negligent conduct (tossing the knife into the air) set off the chain of events that led to Candy's injury. Anson's conduct was also the cause in fact of the dog's injury and also the cause of any damage done to Deb's car.

Some other issues may come up, such as was Bill negligent by allowing his dog to stand next to Anson when he was tossing the knife? Was Candy standing too close to the street, and was Deb negligent in operating her automobile? These issues are discussed below. The more difficult issue, however, is whether Anson's negligent conduct was the legal or proximate cause of Candy's injury. Was Candy's injury foreseeable? Should Anson have recognized that tossing the knife into the air could cause Candy to be struck by a moving car? Should the law, as a matter of policy, hold Anson legally responsible for Candy's injury? We first discuss factual cause issues, then legal or proximate cause issues.

Factual cause. As we have discussed, issues of factual cause are many times quite simple. Anson dropped the knife on Bill's foot and it injured Bill. Anson's negligent conduct is the factual cause of Bill's injury. Courts have traditionally used a *but for* test when determining factual cause.[20] But for Anson's negligent conduct in tossing the knife, Bill would not have suffered the injury. The but for test works well in simple cause-and-effect situations. It can produce unjust results in some situations, however.

Suppose both Anson and Nancy are tossing knives into the air. Both knives are dropped and, at the same time, they fall and stick into Bill's foot. The but for test may now excuse Anson and Cindy from liability for Bill's injury. If not for Anson's negligent conduct, would Bill have suffered injury? In this situation, the answer would be yes. Bill would have suffered an injury without Anson's negligent conduct, because he would have been injured by Nancy's knife. The same is true of Nancy's conduct. However, it would be unjust to excuse both Anson and Nancy for causing Bill's injury. The Restatement (Second) of Torts § 432 suggests the *substantial factor* test should be used in these situations instead of the but for test. The question becomes, was Anson's conduct a substantial factor in Bill's injury? Was Nancy's conduct a substantial factor in Bill's injury? The answer is yes on both counts, and as a result, both Anson and Nancy are liable for Bill's injury.

Other factual causation issues can arise involving multiple actors. When is Anson's negligent conduct excusable as a result of Bill's conduct? The Restatement (Second) of Torts § 440 excuses the original actor's negligent conduct if there is a *superseding* cause of the defendant's injury. A superseding cause is a negligent act that is a substantial cause of the plaintiff's injury that occurred after the original negligent act (an *intervening force*). Only in a few situations will an intervening force excuse the original actor's negligent conduct. One of those situations is when a third person discovers the danger created by the original negligent act, and that person has some special duty to act but fails to do so.

For example, Home Dairy delivers milk to the local elementary school that is consumed on a daily basis by the schoolchildren. After delivering the milk to the school, the dairy manager discovers that some of the milk may have been tainted and, if consumed, could cause serious illness. The dairy manager notifies the school principal and tells her not to allow anyone to consume the milk. The principal gets another phone call and loses track of time. She fails to prevent the milk from being consumed and several children fall ill. The principal's failure to act is the superseding cause of the injury to the children, because she had a special duty to protect the children under her care. Her failure to act upon her special duty should excuse Home Dairy's negligent conduct. Intentional or criminal acts of a third person subsequent to the original negligent conduct also excuse the original actor.

Another factual cause problem can arise when a plaintiff is injured, but cannot prove the defendant's negligent act was the cause of his injury. In certain situations, courts allow an inference to be drawn by the jury that the defendant negligently caused the plaintiff's injury. *Res ipsa loquitur* (the thing speaks for itself) is similar to a circumstantial evidence rule. It allows the jury to find that the defendant was responsible for the plaintiff's injury without physical evidence or testimony proving the defendant's negligent conduct. Contrary to common belief, circumstantial evidence is not necessarily unreliable. If you get up in the morning and there is fresh snow on the ground, you are certain it snowed while you slept, although you did not see it snowing.

Res ipsa loquitur is the operable rule when (1) the event ordinarily does not occur in the absence of negligence, (2) other possible causes have been eliminated, and (3) the instrument causing the injury was in the exclusive control of the defendant.[21] The seminal case for the res ipsa loquitur rule [Byrne v. Boadle, 159 Eng. Rep. 299 (1863)] involved a barrel from defendant's premises falling on the plaintiff as he walked by. The plaintiff was unable to prove why the barrel fell, but nonetheless he was allowed to recover for his injury.

Consider the following examples. Tamika is walking in front of the Broadway Hotel when a brick that fell out of a window facing strikes her. Tamika should be able to use the res ipsa loquitur doctrine to support her claim that the Broadway Hotel is culpable. Bricks do not ordinarily fall off buildings unless there has been a lack of reasonable maintenance. As far as Tamika knows, no other action caused the brick to fall (this knowledge may be in the hotel's possession). The building and bricks were in the exclusive control of the hotel. Assume that instead of being hit by a brick, Tamika was hit by a chair that came out of a second floor window as she walked in front of the hotel. Res ipsa should not be available to her. The second and third elements are not present. Although the furniture in the hotel is under the hotel's control, it is also under the control of the hotel's guests. Broadway Hotel could have taken all reasonable steps to insure guests do not throw things out windows, but short of posting guards in rooms (an unreasonable measure) the hotel cannot insure that no furniture will be thrown out of windows.[22]

Rashad is a passenger on the defendant's commercial charter flight. Two hours into the flight, radio contact is lost. The plane, crew, and Rashad are never found. No black box or wreckage is available to provide an explanation of what went wrong. If Rashad's heirs sue and use the res ipsa rule, should the defendant be able to show a lack of negligence on its part with testimony that it followed FAA regulations on maintenance and inspection of its planes? In this type of situation, the answer is no. By simply offering evidence of general care, the defendant has not helped explain why this accident occurred. Rashad was killed. He was a passenger in a plane under the defendant's exclusive control, and these types of accidents do not normally occur without negligence.[23]

Proximate or legal cause. Once the factual cause of an injury is established, the next question to be answered is whether the defendant's negligent conduct was the legal or proximate cause of the injury. It is really a policy issue. Should the law hold this defendant responsible for the harm suffered by this plaintiff as a result of the defendant's negligent conduct? The question may be framed as follows: Was the injury one that the defendant could foresee as a result of his negligent conduct? In most cases, the issue is simple to resolve.

When Justin negligently drives his car, injury to other motorists and their property clearly is at risk. However, how would you resolve the following fact situation? Justin is helping Barb onto a moving train. In the process, Justin negligently jostles Barb causing her to drop the package she is carrying, that, unbeknown to Justin, contains fireworks. The fireworks explode and cause a scale to topple over and injure Curtis, who is waiting for a train one hundred feet away. Should Justin be liable for Curtis's injury? There is no question that Justin set off the chain of events causing Curtis's injury. Did Justin foresee the risk of

Curtis being injured when he negligently helped Barb onto a moving train? In the most famous American proximate cause case, *Palsgraf v. Long Island Railroad Co.* (1928), the New York Court of Appeals held that Curtis was not one of the people Justin put at risk through his negligent act.[24] The case also has a much cited dissenting opinion that reasoned since the explosion set off by Justin's negligent act was the direct cause of Curtis's injuries, recovery for his injuries should not be denied merely because the chain of events was somewhat unusual.

The *Palsgraf* case is indicative of many proximate cause cases, in that good, easy solutions are hard to come by. The foreseeability of the type of harm risked and the class of people or property put at risk by the defendant's negligent conduct are key. The more remote the type of harm suffered, and the people or property injured, the more likely it is that no proximate cause will be found.

Palsgraf occurred in a setting much like this.

The Damaged Party's Conduct

Plaintiffs are required to exercise due care for their own protection. Even after showing that the defendant's negligent conduct was a legal cause of their injury, plaintiffs may be denied a damage award under the concept of *contributory negligence*. Under a contributory negligence regime, if the plaintiff is found to be negligent (exercising less care for his own protection than a reasonably prudent person would) and that negligence is at least one of the legal causes of the injury, the plaintiff may not recover from the defendant. Contributory negligence, once the prevailing law in the United States, is an all-or-nothing rule that can produce harsh results.[25]

For example, Josh is walking on the sidewalk, reading a book. Ruth, in violation of a municipal ordinance, is riding a bicycle on the same sidewalk from the opposite direction. As they near each other, Ruth goes to her left to pass Josh. At the same time, Josh, not seeing Ruth approach, veers to his right. They collide, and Josh is injured. Josh proves Ruth was negligent because she was riding the bicycle on the sidewalk, and was a legal cause of his injury. Ruth alleges Josh was negligent in that he was reading a book as he walked on the sidewalk. Had Josh not been reading the book, he would have seen Ruth approach on the bicycle, and the collision would have been avoided. Under a contributory negligence regime, if Ruth is able to show Josh was at least 1 percent responsible for the injury, Josh can recover nothing from Ruth, although she was 99 percent responsible for the injury.

Because of the harsh results contributory negligence can produce, today the rule survives in only four states (Alabama, Maryland, North Carolina, and Virginia). It has been replaced by *comparative negligence,* under which the plaintiff's negligence is compared with the defendant's. If the plaintiff is 20 percent negligent and defendant is 80 percent negligent and the damages are $100,000, then the defendant's damage award is reduced to $80,000.

There are two main forms of comparative negligence. Under the *pure form,* a plaintiff can be as much as 99 percent responsible and still be awarded damages. Under the *modified form,* there is a cutoff point beyond which a plaintiff can no longer be awarded damages. The cutoff point is generally either 50 percent (the defendant must be more responsible than the plaintiff) or 51 percent (the defendant must be at least as responsible as the plaintiff). In effect, the modified form still retains some aspect of contributory negligence. Instead of any amount of negligence by the plaintiff cutting off damage recovery, the modified form of comparative negligence sets a higher threshold for denying a negligent plaintiff recovery of damages.[26]

A plaintiff can also be denied a recovery of damages if it is shown she assumed the risk of being injured. *Assumption of risk* can be express or implied. An *express assumption of risk* is a deliberate waiver of the right to seek compensation if injured. For example, Alice goes skydiving. Before being allowed to skydive, the skydive operator requires Alice to sign a release stating that she assumes all risk of injury while skydiving. If Alice is injured during her skydive, she will not be able to sue the skydive operator for her injuries, unless the operator is found to have intentionally or through gross negligence caused her injuries.

Implied assumptions of risk can be found if the plaintiff knew of the dangers and voluntarily consented to the risk. Suppose Alice has been going to the local college basketball games for several years. Her seat is in the first row behind one of the baskets. She likes being close to the action. It is not uncommon for players to fall into the first few rows of seats behind the baskets as they drive to the basket. In fact, Alice has witnessed players fall into the spectators near her seat on numerous occasions. On the night in question, two players become tangled on a fast break and fall on Alice, breaking her arm. She will not be able to sue the university, the players, or the coaches. She knew of the risk of players coming into the stands, and she voluntarily consented to it by continuing to purchase tickets and sit in a seat where players are likely to fall. In some comparative negligence states, however, assumption of risk may be a factor in determining the extent of the plaintiff's negligence, while not totally barring the claim.[27]

Product Liability

Product liability is an area of tort law that has exploded since the early part of the twentieth century. For a long time, it was very difficult to recover damages from a manufacturer or distributor of a product that caused an injury to the consumer, unless the consumer bought the product directly from the party responsible for the defect. The concept of *privity* (party to a contract) insulated defendants who were up the supply chain.[28] Assume that Julio purchased a new car from a local car dealer. The dealer purchased the car from the manufacturer. The car was equipped with an air bag that was supposed to inflate only after an accident. Two weeks after purchasing the car, Julio was driving on an interstate highway and the bag inflated with no impact, causing Julio to lose control of the car and crash. Julio was injured and the car was damaged. Under the historical rule, Julio would not be able to recover from the automobile manufacturer because there was a lack of contractual privity between Julio and the manufacturer. If Julio could make any recovery, it would only be against the local car dealer, because Julio had privity of contract with the car dealer.

The privity rules were seriously eroded in a series of cases beginning with the 1916 opinion in *McPherson v. Buick Motor Company*.[29] Despite a lack of privity between plaintiff and defendant, the New York Court of Appeals found Buick responsible for negligently failing to detect a defective wooden wheel on a new 1909 Buick Runabout. The spokes on the wheel collapsed shortly after the plaintiff bought it from a dealer, and the plaintiff was injured. Privity was further eroded in 1932, when the Supreme Court of Washington held in *Baxter v. Ford Motor Company*[30] that privity was not a requirement after the defendant had made an express warranty (advertising and representations that new Ford Model A's had shatterproof glass). The plaintiff had bought the car from a dealer and was injured when the glass shattered after a pebble had hit the windshield. In 1960, the Supreme Court of New Jersey ruled in *Henningsen v. Bloomfield Motors, Inc.* that when a manufacturer puts a good into the stream of commerce and promotes its sale to the public, an implied warranty of reasonable fitness is made to the ultimate consumer, despite a lack of privity between the consumer and the manufacturer.[31]

After the *Bloomfield Motors* case, privity between the plaintiff and the defendant in a product liability case under a warranty theory was no longer a requirement. The plaintiff need not prove negligence, but rather that the defendant breached a warranty. The Uniform Commercial Code (UCC) (and a prior version called the Uniform Sales Act) has three principal warranty sections consumers can rely on. The UCC is a model statute, covering topics such as the sale of goods, credit, and banking transactions. It has been adopted in all states except Louisiana and is responsible for much of the comparability from state to state for

most common business transactions. The warranty sections are reproduced in Box 10.1.

**Box 10.1   Principal Warranty Sections
Uniform Commercial Code**

§ 2-313. EXPRESS WARRANTIES BY AFFIRMATION, PROMISE, DESCRIPTION.

(1) Express warranties by the seller are created as follows:

   (a) Any affirmation of fact or promise made by the seller to the buyer which relates to the goods and becomes part of the basis of the bargain creates an express warranty that the goods shall conform to the affirmation or promise.

   (b) Any description of the goods which is made part of the basis of the bargain creates an express warranty that the goods shall conform to the description.

(2) It is not necessary to the creation of an express warranty that the seller use formal words such as "warrant" or "guarantee" or that he have a specific intention to make a warranty, but an affirmation merely of the value of the goods or a statement purporting to be merely the seller's opinion or commendation of the goods does not create a warranty.

§ 2-314. IMPLIED WARRANTY: MERCHANTABILITY; USAGE OF TRADE.

(1) Unless excluded or modified a warranty that the goods shall be merchantable is implied in a contract for their sale if the seller is a merchant with respect to goods of that kind. Under this section the serving for value of food or drink to be consumed either on the premises or elsewhere is a sale.

(2) Goods to be merchantable must be at least such as

   (a) pass without objection in the trade under the contract description; and

   (b) in the case of fungible goods, are of fair average quality within the description; and

   (c) are fit for the ordinary purposes for which such goods are used; and

   (d) run, within the variations permitted by the agreement, of even kind, quality and quantity within each unit and among all units involved; and

   (e) are adequately contained, packaged, and labeled as the agreement may require; and

   (f) conform to the promise or affirmations of fact made on the container or label if any.

(3) Unless excluded or modified other implied warranties may arise from course of dealing or usage of trade.

---

§ 2-315. IMPLIED WARRANTY: FITNESS FOR PARTICULAR PURPOSE.

Where the seller at the time of contracting has reason to know any particular purpose for which the goods are required and that the buyer is relying on the seller's skill or judgment to select or furnish suitable goods, there is unless excluded or modified under the next section an implied warranty that the goods shall be fit for such purpose.

Liability under a breach of warranty is *strict*. The contractual nature of claims under breach of warranty actions can nonetheless produce problems for plaintiffs. Notice of breach requirements and disclaimers of warranties may defeat some claims.[32] For example, the Supreme Court of California in *Greenman v. Yuba Power Products, Inc.*,[33] was faced with a claim by a manufacturer that it did not receive timely notice of a breach. Mr. Greenman received a power tool manufactured by Yuba for Christmas. He was using it as a lathe, when the piece of wood he was turning flew out of the power tool and struck him in the head, causing severe injury. At trial, it was shown the setscrews that held part of the tool together were inadequate, given the normal vibrations operation of the power tool produced. Had alternative fastening methods been employed, the injury would have been prevented. Justice Traynor, writing for the majority, held that it is unnecessary to establish an express or implied warranty case when a manufacturer places an article on the market knowing it will be used without inspection, and where that article proves to have a defect that causes injury. The manufacturer should be strictly liable in tort. Traynor reasoned that the courts should (1) abandon the requirement of a contract between the parties, (2) recognize liability is not imposed by contract but by law, and (3) refuse to allow manufacturers to define the scope of their liability for defective products.

Two years later, (1965) Section 402A was added to the Restatement (Second) of Torts, adopting the *Greenman v. Yuba* strict liability in torts theory for product liability cases.[34] The pendulum was now swinging toward the consumer. Section 402A is presented in Box 10.2.

**Box 10.2   Restatement (Second) of Torts
Product Liability—Strict Liability**

§ 402A. SPECIAL LIABILITY OF SELLER OF PRODUCT FOR PHYSICAL HARM TO USER OR CONSUMER.

(1) One who sells any product in a defective condition unreasonably dangerous to the user or consumer or to his property is subject to liability for physi-

cal harm thereby caused to the ultimate user or consumer, or to his property, if

    (a) the seller is engaged in the business of selling such a product, and

    (b) it is expected to and does reach the user or consumer without substantial change in the condition in which it is sold.

(2) The rule stated in Subsection (1) applies although

    (a) the seller has exercised all possible care in the preparation and sale of his product, and

    (b) the user or consumer has not bought the product from or entered into any contractual relation with the seller.

Subsequently, most states adopted the theory of strict liability found in § 402A of the *Second Restatement*. Legal policy had swung all the way to the consumer side.[35] Proponents advanced several theories to support holding manufacturers liable for injuries caused by their products, even if they exercised due care. First, it is unfair to subject individual consumers to all the risk and cost of injury from a manufacturer's product. Second, the manufacturer is in the best position to spread the cost of injury among all its customers. And finally, holding manufacturers liable for defects promotes safer products. Critics argued, on the other hand, that strict liability would force small companies into bankruptcy. They also argued that instead of safer products, manufacturers would be hesitant to introduce new products, because they may fear the product could prove dangerous in a situation or manner of which the manufacturer was unaware.[36]

The *Second Restatement's* § 402A requires injured plaintiffs to show the product had a defect that made it unreasonably dangerous. Generally, there are three types of defects: manufacturing defects, design defects, and warning defects. *Manufacturing defects* occur when the product produced does not comply with its design. Examples include defective products that are not detected by the quality control procedures employed by the manufacturer, such as glass shards in canned food, step ladders with invisible cracks in one of the wooden steps making them unsafe for 150-pound persons, and automobiles with defective brakes, steering mechanisms, or seat belts. A consumer injured by one of these defects should prevail in court by showing that the product was in a defective condition unreasonably dangerous to the plaintiff. A new car with defective brakes meets both requirements. There is no question that a car with brakes that do not work is in a defective condition, and there is no question that defective brakes on a car create an unreasonable danger.

After plaintiffs show the product was defective, they must also show that the defect existed at the time the product left the manufacturer and that the defect caused the injury.[37] Sometimes, it is difficult to show the defect existed at the time the product left the manufacturer.

The product may have been destroyed in the accident, or it may be difficult to prove a defect with physical evidence.

For example, in the case of a brake failure on a new automobile, testimony that the plaintiff applied the brakes, but they did not work, would be compelling evidence, especially if substantiated by testimony of bystanders and other witnesses. This evidence would also establish causation. The defendant, of course, could try to rebut the evidence by showing that someone may have altered the brakes (a mechanic had worked on the brakes or the brake line had been cut). Absent such a showing by the defendant, a kind of res ipsa loquitur could operate to show the defect was present at the time the car left the manufacturer, if the car was sufficiently new (well under the minimum number of miles for normal brake wear). Expert testimony may also establish the defect. A master mechanic, who examined the brake system after the accident and who testified that the seal on the master cylinder was defective, and that such a defective seal would cause the hydraulic system to loose pressure causing a brake failure, would also serve to show the defect and causation.[38] The manufacturer is strictly liable once the plaintiff has shown the three elements of manufacturing defects. No showing of due care by the manufacturer, such as performing detailed inspections and a strong quality control program, may excuse the manufacturer.

Products with *design defects* are manufactured as the defendant intended. Plaintiffs who are injured by a product with no manufacturing defect must also meet the § 402A test; that is, the product must have been in a defective condition unreasonably dangerous to the user or consumer. A clear example is a new lawnmower sold without a guard over the discharge chute. If a consumer bought such a mower and her son was injured when the mower threw a rock out the discharge chute, she would allege the product had a design fault that made the product unreasonably dangerous.

Assuming the injury occurred while using the mower to mow the grass (its intended use), plaintiffs would commonly rely on two theories to advance their claim. First, the plaintiff may claim the materials that were used to produce the product were deficient, causing it to break or fail. Under the second theory, the plaintiff may claim the design was defective in that a safety feature could have been added to the product that would have avoided the injury. In our lawnmower example, the safety device proposition is the appropriate legal theory. The cost of the added safety device must be balanced against the magnitude of the harm it could have prevented. The cost of the safety device must also be compared with the cost of the original product. A safety device costing $300 on a $100 lawnmower may be too much. Defendants have some defenses available to them. For example, they could show that their mower was state-of-the-art when it was sold (i.e., all mowers were manufactured without guards). Nonetheless, a jury could still find that

Trucks with fuel tanks that explode upon contact would be a design defect regardless of the test used.

risk was so obvious and the cost of providing the guard was small, when compared to the gravity of the harm created by manufacturing a mower without the guard. Such a finding would be similar to finding that all mowers are defective.[39]

Courts in design defect cases have devised and used several tests to determine whether the product was defective. The following passage in Box 10.3, from a Michigan Supreme Court case, describes the four most commonly used tests.

Box 10.3　　**Excerpt From Prentis v. Yale Manufacturing Co.**
Supreme Court of Michigan
421 Mich. 670, 686 365 N.W. 2d 176, 184 (1985)

The approaches for determination of the meaning of "defect" in design cases fall into four general categories. The first, usually associated with Dean Wade, employs a negligence risk-utility analysis, but focuses upon whether the manufacturer would be judged negligent if it had known of the product's dangerous condition at the time it was marketed. The second, associated with Dean Keeton, compares the risk and utility of the product at the time of trial. The third focuses on consumer expectations about the product. The fourth combines the risk-utility and consumer-expectation tests. While courts have included many other individual variations in their formulations, the overwhelming consensus among courts deciding defective design cases is in the use of some form of risk-utility analysis, either as an exclusive or alternative ground of liability. Risk-utility analysis in this context always involves assessment of the decisions made by manufacturers with respect to the design of their products.

The *consumer-expectation* test evolved out of comment (g) to § 402A of the *Restatement (Second) of Torts*. It states: "The product is, at the time it leaves the seller's hands, in a condition not contemplated by the ultimate consumer, which will be unreasonably dangerous to him." The comment and test were an adaptation of a test that had been applied by courts to tainted food products, and the test did not always lend itself well to other products. As the Connecticut Supreme Court explains in Box 10.4, the test often subjected plaintiffs to a heavy burden by requiring proof that the product was unreasonably dangerous to the consumer.

Box 10.4   Excerpt From Potter v. Chicago Pneumatic Tool Co.
Supreme Court of Connecticut
241 Conn. 199, 212, 694 A.2d 1319, 1329 (1997)

[Under the] consumer expectation test, a manufacturer is strictly liable for any condition not contemplated by the ultimate consumer that will be unreasonably dangerous to the consumer. Some courts, however, have refused to adopt the unreasonably dangerous definition, determining that it injects a concept of foreseeability into strict tort liability, which is inappropriate in such cases because the manufacturer's liability is not based upon negligence. Cronin v. J.B.E. Olson Corp., 8 Cal. 3d 121, 133, 501 P.2d 1153, 104 Cal. Rptr. 43 (1972). We think that a requirement that a plaintiff also prove that the defect made the product unreasonably dangerous places upon him a significantly increased burden and represents a step backward.

Many jurisdictions have adopted some form of the *risk-utility* test, a negligence type of analysis that balances the risks associated with the product against the utility of the product. Factors associated with the test include the usefulness of the product, likelihood and gravity of the possible harm, the manufacturer's ability to eliminate the risk, and whether the user is aware of and can avoid the harm.[40] There are two main variations of the test. Under the conventional test, the manufacturer's product should be judged at the time the product was manufactured. The modified version of the risk-utility test judges the product at the time of trial. The modified version, in effect, holds the manufacturer responsible for information and knowledge discovered after the product was sold.[41] It has been justified on the theory that the manufacturer is able to spread the cost of injury among all the users of the product.

A New Era—The Restatement (Third) of Torts, Product Liability

In 1997, the American Law Institute issued the *Restatement (Third) of Torts, Product Liability.*[42] Under the Third Restatement, the risk-utility test is the only test for design defects and instruction and warning defects.[43] In effect, negligence is again required in design defect cases, and the pendulum is beginning to swing away from the consumer. The Third Restatement, however, does not modify the test for manufacturing defects. It is still a strict liability test. The defendant is not able to avoid liability by showing reasonable care. It is likely the new Restatement (see Section 2 in Box 10.5) will have much influence over product liability cases for some time.

Box 10.5   Section 2
Restatement (Third) of Torts
Product Liability

Topic I
Liability Rules Applicable to Products Generally
§ 2 Categories of Product Defect

A product is defective when, at the time of sale or distribution, it contains a manufacturing defect, is defective in design, or is defective because of inadequate instructions or warnings. A product:

(a) contains a manufacturing defect when the product departs from its intended design even though all possible care was exercised in the preparation and marketing of the product;

(b) is defective in design when the foreseeable risks of harm posed by the product could have been reduced or avoided by the adoption of a reasonable alternative design by the seller or other distributor, or a predecessor in the commercial chain of distribution, and the omission of the alternative design renders the product not reasonably safe;

(c) is defective because of inadequate instructions or warnings when the foreseeable risks of harm posed by the product could have been reduced or avoided by the provision of reasonable instructions or warnings by the seller or other distributor, or a predecessor in the commercial chain of distribution, and the omission of the instructions or warnings renders the product not reasonably safe.

Section 2(a) sets out the strict liability rule for manufacturing defects. The section is in accord with the law in a majority of jurisdictions. The reporters (legal scholars and experts, who participated in the project) defend retention of strict liability for manufacturing defects based on the conscious decisions that manufacturers make concerning their quality control procedures. Unless a quality control system is set up to not allow any defective products to go undetected, it is inevitable that defective products will get into the hands of consumers. Some of those products will cause injury to innocent consumers who are unable to avoid the injury.

Section 2(b) sets out the risk-utility balancing test for design defects. The test includes a showing of a reasonable alternative design. Would an alternative design, at a reasonable cost, have reduced the foreseeable risk of harm associated with the product? If yes, was it unreasonable (negligent) for the defendant to have omitted the reasonable alternative design when the product was produced? Assume that Manufacturer sells User a small backhoe. While using the backhoe to clear a parking lot after a snowstorm, User is injured when the backhoe rolls over on her as she is attempting to push snow up on a pile she had previously cleared. At trial, User's expert witness testifies that User's injury could have been prevented if Manufacturer had equipped the backhoe with a roll cage. A suitable roll cage would add roughly $500 to the cost of a new $15,000 small backhoe. The question for the jury is: Was Manufacturer negligent for failing to equip the bulldozer with a roll cage?

The burden is on the plaintiff to show that a reasonable alternative design was available. In some cases, a prototype of the alternative design may be necessary. Prototypes are usually required when there is some question whether the alternative design would be practicable or make the product less desirable or useful. In other cases, expert testimony concerning the alternative design may be sufficient. In our backhoe example, a mechanical engineer testifying that roll cages could have been installed on small bulldozers that would prevent rollover injuries would probably be sufficient to carry the plaintiff's burden of showing a reasonable alternative design.

In some cases, the alternative design is obvious and easily understood without expert testimony. For example, a doll was sold with eyes made of buttons that came off and became lodged in a toddler's throat. The plaintiff should be able to establish a "prima facie" case by claiming the injury could have been avoided if the eyes had been drawn on the doll or attached in such a manner that they were not removable. In rare cases, a court could decide the product in question has so little social utility compared with the risk of serious injury that no alternative design proof is necessary; toy guns marketed to young children that shoot hard rubber bullets at high speed or exploding cigars are obvious examples.

Once the plaintiff has met the burden of showing an alternative design, the trier of fact must consider several factors to determine whether the alternative design is reasonable, and whether the omission of the alternative design rendered the product unreasonably unsafe, including the probability and gravity of the foreseeable harm. Another factor is what consumers expect of the product, considered in light of how the product was portrayed and marketed by the defendant. Also relevant are the cost of the alternative design, its effect on the utility of the product, its effect on maintenance requirements, and whether consumers would be less likely to purchase the product if it were equipped with the alternative design.

Defendants can offer evidence that when the product was produced, no other manufacturer offered the product with the alternative design and, as a result, may argue that the product was as safe as all other similar products. This so-called *state-of-the-art defense* makes it difficult for the plaintiff to show that not incorporating the alternative design rendered the product unreasonably dangerous. Yet, this defense is a question of fact that in most cases the jury must resolve.

Another defense available to a defendant is that the product has an *open and obvious danger*. Products like swimming pools are a good example. It is common knowledge that young children and people who cannot swim may drown in swimming pools. As a result, the manufacturer is not liable for failing to design a pool that is equipped with a mechanical device that raises everything off the bottom once every few minutes. The fact that a product has an open and obvious danger does not automatically insulate a defendant from liability, however. The open and obvious danger is a factor to be considered when deciding if the product was unreasonably unsafe. Disposable cigarette lighters could be a closer call. Everyone knows disposable lighters are dangerous, especially in the hands of children. It is still possible to purchase lighters with no mechanism designed to prevent young children from operating the lighter. It is also probably foreseeable that disposable lighters are often misplaced by the purchaser, making it likely that young children will come upon them. If a young child finds a disposable lighter that is not childproof and is burned, should the fact that the danger is open and obvious insulate the manufacturer? Should the use of alternative designs by other manufacturers (or even this manufacturer) be a factor?

Instructions and warnings are addressed in section 2(c), as has been shown above. The adequacy of instructions and warnings are subject to the same risk-utility test as are design defects. In effect, the instructions and warnings are part of the design of the product. Instructions and warnings serve two purposes. First, they alert users and consumers to the risks associated with the product and how to reduce those risks while using the product. For example, a Weed Eater® (grass trimmer) might carry the following warning: "Normal operation of this product may cause grass, weeds, dirt, pebbles, sticks, and other objects to fly up and strike the user at high speed, causing injury. When using, operator should always wear appropriate safety goggles, shoes, long pants, and gloves." Warnings and instructions also alert potential buyers or users to risks unknown to the common consumer associated with the product.

The second purpose allows potential buyers and users of the product to make an informed decision whether to purchase or use the product. For example, an adhesive that is flammable should clearly warn the potential buyer or user that the product and its fumes are flammable and may ignite, causing injury. An informed potential buyer or user may choose to look for another product that is not flammable. Sellers down the distribution chain have an obligation to warn and instruct customers on the safe use of the product, if the manufacturer's warnings and instructions are inadequate.

The adequacy of instructions and warnings is difficult to judge. Many factors must be considered, including the detail of the warning and instructions, the educational level, and the experience level of the user. A balance between too much detail (due to the danger of consumers and users not paying attention to the most important warnings) and too little detail must be struck. When striking the balance, the manufacturer should consider the foreseeable consumers and users of the product. Products for children, for example, should include warnings that are concise and bold. A product intended for more sophisticated users should have more detailed warnings. The mere existence of a warning does not relieve a manufacturer of liability for a design defect. A warning on a bottle of bleach to keep out of the reach of children would probably not insulate a manufacturer from liability for an injury to a small child who drank some bleach if a childproof cap could have prevented the injury. There need not be warnings for unreasonable abuses and risks, but care must be taken to warn of reasonably foreseeable misuses of a product. Manufacturers of ladders must take heed of the fact that some people have been know to use the platform provided to hold paint cans and other tools as a step. Failure to post a warning such as, "Do not step here—This is not a step," would be unreasonable and probably subject the manufacturer to liability for damages to a user who fell and was injured after stepping on the flimsy platform.

Nor are warnings or instructions required for obvious and generally known risks. If manufacturers were required to warn of obvious risks, consumers might become immune to warnings and not pay attention to warnings of nonobvious risks. For instance, a warning in the automobile owner's manual such as, "Collisions with other automobiles or other objects may cause injury," is unnecessary. Likewise, a warning that injuries in motor vehicle accidents may be more severe if seat belts are not worn would also be unnecessary. In both cases, it is common knowledge that injuries can be suffered in auto accidents and that seat belts can avoid many such injuries.

Products or components of products that cause allergic reactions usually require warnings, especially if the risk of severe harm is great. Suppose a manufacturer produces and sells a lipstick in a unique shade of red that gets its color from a derivative of poppies. Also suppose that the manufacturer knows (or should know) that a small percentage of the general population may develop painful blisters after being exposed to poppy derivatives. The manufacturer would be under a duty to warn consumers that the product contains a poppy derivative and that a small percentage of people can have severe allergic reactions to poppy derivatives. The warning should include a statement that before using the product, consumers should test the product on a part of the body other than the lips. If the manufacturer did not know of the possible allergic reaction, it would be under a duty to test before distributing for sale.

If the product or ingredient in the product is a well-known allergen, such as aspirin, it may not be necessary to warn of the specific allergic reaction. The manufacturer must, however, warn that the product contains the known allergen. Suppose a manufacturer produces and sells an over-the-counter cough syrup that contains aspirin. It is commonly known that many people can become severely ill, and that children can develop Reye's syndrome, after ingesting aspirin. It is probably unnecessary for the manufacturer to warn of the dangers of ingesting aspirin. Merely warning that the cough syrup contains aspirin should be warning enough to consumers and users.

Consider the following warning case concerning car batteries. The court held that the warning was sufficient.

Hudgens v. Interstate Battery
Court of Appeal of Louisiana, Third Circuit
393 So. 2d 940 (1981)

OPINION BY DOMENGEAUX:
. . . On Friday, February 17, 1978, at about 6 P.M., plaintiff was at his home in Lena, Louisiana, and was preparing to return his employer's truck to his employer's place of business in Alexandria, Louisiana. His wife was to follow him in her son's car in order to provide plaintiff with a ride home after the truck was returned. The car, however, would not start. Plaintiff raised the car's hood and peered at the engine. It was dark, though, so Mrs. Hudgens offered to get a flashlight from the house. Plaintiff refused this offer and lit a match for light instead. He jiggled the battery cables, thinking they might be loose, but they were not. He then extinguished the flame since the fire had nearly consumed the length of the match. . . .

According to plaintiff, who was the only witness, he then lit a second match and was poised directly over the radiator, about two feet from the battery (which was to his left), when a small explosion highlighted by a flash of light occurred, splashing battery acid in his face, causing the eye and facial injuries complained of herein. . . . After the incident plaintiff discovered that one of the two battery caps was missing, although he testified he remembered seeing both caps on the battery prior to the explosion. He also discovered that a small hole in a bottom corner of the battery had allowed electrolyte to escape from one cell of the battery. This explained why Mrs. Hudgens could not start the car.

Before the manufacturer of the battery, Globe Union, Inc., will be held liable, plaintiff must establish (1) that the battery was defective (that is, unreasonably dangerous in normal use), (2) that the battery was in normal use when the explosion occurred, and (3) that the defect caused the injury. Plaintiff's action is defeated because he failed to prove that the battery was defective.

Plaintiff argues in brief that the battery was defective because . . . the battery contained an insufficient warning label. . . . Was the warning label adequate?

We turn now to a consideration of whether the warning printed on the battery cap was sufficient. We hold that it was. . . . [A] battery is an electrochemical device which stores and releases electrical current through chemical processes. A natural and unavoidable result of these processes is the generation of explosive hydrogen and oxygen gases. In its reasons for judgment, the trial court acknowledged this fact. . . . [T]he battery industry has, for many years, been aware of the explosive potential of batteries. Therefore, warnings are placed on all wet cell automotive batteries such as the one in this case. The warning label on the battery involved herein, printed in white against a bright green background, reads: DANGER—EXPLOSIVE GASES. BATTERIES PRODUCE EXPLOSIVE GASES. KEEP SPARKS, FLAME, CIGARETTES AWAY. VENTILATE WHEN CHARGING OR USING IN ENCLOSED SPACE. ALWAYS SHIELD EYES WHEN WORKING NEAR BATTERIES.

We believe the above warning complies with the Consumer Products Safety Commission's labeling requirements. The warning label on the battery herein is virtually identical to examples of acceptable warnings found in the record. Chappuis v. Sears Roebuck and Company, 358 So.2d 926 (La.1978), is cited by plaintiff to support his claim that the battery contained an inadequate warning.

The case involved a hammer whose face was already chipped when used by plaintiff. While in use by plaintiff the face chipped again, striking plaintiff in the eye. All the experts agreed that a hammer whose face is chipped should be discarded because it will likely chip again. However, the warning "discard this hammer if it becomes chipped" was not on the warning label. The Court held the manufacturers liable because the absence of such a warning was unreasonable. The Court reasoned: ". . . There may be many tools or other products which become dangerous for normal use in certain conditions. But when the danger is known to the manufacturer and cannot justifiably be expected to be within the knowledge of users generally, the manufacturer must take reasonable steps to warn the user. It would have been reasonable, in this case, for the manufacturer to add to the warning label the words discard this hammer if it becomes chipped. This record makes it difficult to understand why the warning was not made."

In the instant case, the label on the battery cap warned users to keep flames away. If plaintiff had obeyed the warning this unfortunate accident would not have occurred. We find this set of facts clearly distinguishable from the facts in *Chappuis*, wherein the user of a chipped hammer was not warned by the label that such a use was dangerous. . . .

Case Questions for Discussion

1. Why did Hudgens lose?
2. Did you know lighting a match near a battery could cause an explosion?
3. Would the result in the *Hudgens* case be different if the plaintiff was not familiar with batteries and had not read the warning or one like it on other batteries?

Tort Reform

No description of American tort law would be complete without a discussion of the *tort reform movement*. Since the 1970s, business interests, including the insurance industry and the medical industry, have agitated for reform of the tort system. Personal injury lawyers have been caricatured as ambulance chasers only out for themselves. Recently, plaintiff lawyers in the tobacco cases have been singled out for seeking exorbitant fees. Other complaints include fictitious claims, excessive punitive and compensatory damage awards, joint and several liability, and high insurance premiums. The reform advocates also point to the financial ruin that some companies have faced as a result of defective products. For example, A H Robbins sought bankruptcy reorganization in the late 1980s as a result of the onslaught of litigation over its Dalcon Shield, an intrauterine birth control device that was found to cause injury. In the late 1990s, Dow Corning, a manufacturer of silicon breast implants, sought the same relief, as did Owens Corning, a manufacturer of asbestos, in 2000. To be sure, a manufacturer of a product that proves to be dangerous and causes injury to many users can face financial ruin.

The tort reformers have been relatively successful. Since 1986, 35 states have enacted reforms of *joint and several liability*. Joint and several liability is a common law rule that allows a defendant to collect all of a judgment from a single defendant, although more than one defendant may have been found liable. If a plaintiff successfully sues several parties, and one of those parties has financial resources sufficient to satisfy the judgment and the other defendants do not, it is likely that the financially well off defendant will be the only party to pay. The paying defendant has the right to sue the other defendants for contribution (or to be reimbursed for the other defendants' portion of the damage award). If the other defendants are uninsured, have low limits on their insurance, or are otherwise financially unable to pay, reimbursement is unlikely. The typical reform proposal calls for *allocation of damages*. For example, if there are three defendants and it has been determined that defendant A is 30 percent liable, B is 45 percent liable, and C is 25 percent liable, and the damage award is $100,000, A would be liable for $30,000, B for $45,000, and C for $25,000. Absent any reform, under the principal of joint and several liability, all three would be liable for the full $100,000.

Thirty-two states have addressed punitive damages. Other reforms include damage caps on pain and suffering associated with personal injury and the reform of state product liability laws.[44] Despite these reforms, a recent study shows that median damage awards in product liability lawsuits have more than tripled (from $500,300 to more than $1.8 million) from 1993 to 1999. At the same time, the number of cases dropped about 50 percent between 1997 and 1999. Some commentators speculate that only *high dollar* cases are being filed by attorneys due to the efforts of the tort reform movement.[45]

Critics of tort reform insist that the reformers are simply trying to guard their treasure at the expense of innocent consumers, who are injured as a result of negligent and reckless behavior by business interests. It is clear, nevertheless, that tort reform in some manner will take hold. Both major political parties have at various times embraced the movement. Ralph Nader attacked both George W. Bush and Al Gore/Bill Clinton during the 2000 presidential election for allegedly selling out to the tort reformers.[46]

Some members of the judiciary have viewed tort reform legislation as an intrusion into an area reserved for the judiciary. For example, consider the words of Judge Hernden in *Best v. Taylor Machine Works*. The Circuit Court of the Third Judicial Circuit in Illinois held that the 1995 Tort Reform legislation in Illinois was unconstitutional.

> [I]t is abundantly clear that there isn't a rational basis for this legislation. Its effect is to turn our courts into a limited and hostile environment for injured citizens to pursue their inalienable right to complete compensation and to have an impartial panel of fellow citizens make that decision. The public policy of this state is that disputes between citizens are best decided by a jury of other citizens without interference of an overreaching government. The Illinois Constitution restricts the legislature from manipulating public policy in the manner demonstrated by this Act.

The third circuit court was later affirmed by the Illinois Supreme Court in 1997, Best v. Taylor Machine Works, 179 Ill. 2d 367, 689 N.E.2d 1057 (1997). Other tort reform enactments have been struck down in Indiana, Oregon, Florida, and Ohio.[47]

In Alabama, the courts and the legislature have been in a decade-old battle concerning damage cap reforms. A 1987, $400,000 cap on noneconomic losses (like punitive damages, pain and suffering, and mental anguish) was declared unconstitutional in Moore v. Mobile Infirmary Ass'n, 592 So.2d 156 (Ala. 199). The Supreme Court of Alabama held that the damage cap legislation infringed upon the right of Alabama citizens to a jury trial. The struggle among the proreformers, the antireformers, and the courts in Alabama is typical of the controversy in many states.[48]

Key Terms, Names, and Concepts

Allocation of damages	Battery
Assault	But for test
Assumption of risk	Comparative negligence

Consumer-expectation test
Contributory negligence
Conversion
Design defects
Dispossess
Duty of reasonable care
Factual cause
False imprisonment
Imminent apprehension
Implied consent
Intentional infliction of emotional distress
Intentional intrusion on land (Trespass to land)
Intentional torts
Intervening force
Intermeddling
Joint and several liability
Manufacturing defects
Negligence
Open and obvious danger
Private necessity privelege

Privity
Product liability
Proximate cause
Public necessity privilege
Reasonable person
Res ipsa loquitur
Restatement (Second) of Torts
Restatement (Third) of Torts: Product Liability
Risk-utility test
Self-defense
State-of-the-art defense
Strict liability
Substantial factor test
Superseding cause
Tort law
Tort reform movement
Trespass
Trespass on the case
Trespass to chattel
Warning defect

Discussion Questions

1. The Village of Compton, a bedroom suburb of a large city, grew so quickly that its sewer system was inadequate. One holiday weekend, when nearly all of the residents were at home, the sewer system became overloaded. The village sewer commissioner ordered the sewer system closed down to allow it to clear. During the time it was closed, Mrs. Cheer was doing her laundry. Because the sewer system was closed, all of the wastewater that was being released down the drains in Mrs. Cheer's house backed up into her basement. Mrs. Cheer did not realize what was going on until she went into the basement, where she discovered two inches of water and many of her possessions damaged by the wastewater. Does Mrs. Cheer have any action available to her against the village?

2. John, a 30-year-old who enjoys sports, underwent surgery to have his left knee ligaments repaired. He awoke after the surgery to discover his right knee had been operated on instead of his left knee. Does he have a tort action available other than medical malpractice?

3. Assume that instead of the right knee being operated on as in Question 2, the surgeon operated on the left knee. During the operation, however, John's windpipe became clogged, and he was unable to breathe. The surgeon performed a tracheotomy, opening a passage for air to enter John's lungs. John recovered, but now has an unsightly scar. Does he have any action other than medical malpractice available to him?

4. Sue is shopping at the city market. She is looking at some vegetables when a crate of tomatoes that falls off a stack strikes her and injures her shoulder. No one seems to know who put up the stack of crated tomatoes, nor if anyone jostled them. No one saw what happened. What can Sue do?

5. Alice went to a major league baseball game and sat down near the first base line. She was buying a beer when a foul ball left the field of play and struck her, giving her a severe concussion. May she sue the baseball stadium operator? Instead of being in her seat when the ball struck her, assume that Alice was at the beer stand behind the seats in the stadium concourse. May she hold the stadium operator liable?

6. John's patio deck grew some mold over the past two years. He was able to kill and remove the mold with chlorine bleach, but a residual stain remained. He was able to remove the stains with ammonia. He decided it would be quicker to combine the two products, but when he did, the resulting gas injured him. Can he recover from the manufacturers of the two products?

7. Do you believe damage caps and other tort reforms unduly restrict citizens' rights? Why or why not?

8. On the subject of tort reform, are business interests too powerful, or are personal injury and class action lawyers out of control?

9. Do you think courts overstep their bounds when they declare tort reform legislation unconstitutional?

10. Would you be willing to trade lower potential damage awards, if you were injured, for lower insurance rates and lower product costs under tort reform initiatives?

11. Do you think lower costs to businesses as a result of tort reform would be passed on to the consumer?

Suggested Additional Reading

Costello, Nancy. "Note: Allocating Fault to the Empty Chair: Tort Reform or Deform?" *University of Detroit Mercy Law Review* 76 (winter 1999): 571–605.

Epstein, Richard. *Introduction to Torts*. New York: Aspen Publishers, 1999.

Henderson, James, Richard Pearson, and John Siliciano. *The Torts Process.* 5th ed. New York: Aspen Publishers, 1999.

Keeton, W. Page, Dan Dobbs, Robert Keeton, David Owen, and William Prosser. *Prosser and Keeton on the Law of Torts*. 5th ed. St. Paul, MN: West, 1984.

Levmore, Saul. *Foundations of Tort Law*. New York: Oxford University Press, 1994.

Meiners, Roger, and Bruce Yandle, eds. *The Economic Consequences of Liability Rules: In Defense of Common Law Liability*. New York: Quorum Books, 1991.

Peck, Robert, Richard Marshall, and Kenneth Kranz. "Tort Reform 1999: A Building Without a Foundation." *Florida State University Law Review* 27 (winter 2000), pp. 397–445.

Rubin, Paul. *Tort Reform by Contract*. Washington, DC: AEI Press, 1993.

Schwartz, Victor, Kathyrn Kelly, and David Partlett. *Cases and Material on Torts*. 10th ed. New York: Foundation Press, 2000.

Endnotes

1. For these and other cases that have received negative publicity, see *The Other Side of the Story*, by the Association of Trial Lawyers of America, at <http://www.atlanet.org/cjfacts/other/othrmenu.html>. Tennessee v. Garner, 471 U.S. 1 (1984).
2. William L. Prosser, *Law of Torts*, 4th ed. (St. Paul, MN: West, 1971) § 1; Edward J. Kionka, *Torts in a Nutshell*, 3rd ed. (St. Paul, MN, West, 1999) § 1-1; Salmond, *Law of Torts*, 7th ed. (1928) § 2, quoted in Prosser, § 1 above at note 6; and Dan B. Dobbs, *The Law of Torts* (St. Paul, MN: West, 2000), § 1.
3. Irvine v. Rare Feline Breeding Center, Inc., 685 N.E.2d 120 (Ind. App. 1997).
4. Restatement (Second) of Torts § 158 (1965).
5. Ibid., §§ 13-20 and Dobbs, *The Law of Torts*, § 30.
6. Restatement (Second) of Torts, §§ 21-33 (1965).
7. Noguci v. Nakamura, 2 Haw. App. 655, 638 P.2d 1383 (1982).
8. Restatement (Second) of Torts, §§ 35, 38, and 42, Dobbs, *The Law of Torts*, §§ 36-38, and Kionka, *Torts in a Nutshell*, § 6-4.
9. Restatement (Second) of Torts, § 46 (1965), and Dobbs, *The Law of Torts*, §§ 303-307.
10. Restatement (Second) of Torts, §§ 158-164 & 196-197 (1965), and Dobbs, *The Law of Torts*, §§ 50-58.
11. United States v. Causby, 328 U.S. 256 (1946).
12. Restatement (Second) of Torts, §§ 216-228 (1965), Dobbs, *The Law of Torts*, §§ 59-67, and Kionka, *Torts in a Nutshell*, §§ 6-7.
13. Restatement (Second) of Torts, §§ 49-53, 147-151, and 196-197 (1965), Dobbs, *The Law of Torts*, §§ 94-97 and 107-108, and Kionka, *Torts in a Nutshell*, §§ 7-1 through 7-7.
14. Restatement (Second) of Torts, § 281 (1965).
15. Kionka, *Torts in a Nutshell*, §§ 4-1 & 4-5.

16. Restatement (Second) of Torts, § 283 (1965).
17. Kionka, *Torts in a Nutshell*, §§ 4-1.
18. Restatement (Second) of Torts, §§ 283A, 283B, 283C, 299 & 299A (1965).
19. Kionka, *Torts in a Nutshell*, §§ 4-4 and Dobbs, *The Law of Torts*, § 167.
20. Dobbs, *The Law of Torts*, § 168.
21. Restatement (Second) of Torts, § 328D (1965).
22. Larson v. St. Francis Hotel, 83 Cal. App. 2d 210, 188 P.2d 513 (1947).
23. Cox v. Northwest Airlines, 379 F.2d 893 (7th Cir. 1967).
24. 248 N.Y. 339, 162 N.E. 99 (1928).
25. Kionka, *Torts in a Nutshell*, §§ 5-1.
26. Dobbs, *The Law of Torts*, § 201.
27. Ibid., § 211.
28. Ibid., § 353.
29. 217 N.Y. 382, 111 N.E. 1050 (1916).
30. 168 Wash. 456, 12 P.2d 409 (1932).
31. Henningsen v. Bloomfield Motors, Inc., 32 N.J. 358, 161 A.2d 69 (1960). (Steering mechanism failed on a new Chrysler.)
32. Kionka, *Torts in a Nutshell*, §§ 8-9.
33. 59 Cal. 2d. 57, 377 P.2d 897 (1963).
34. Kionka, *Torts in a Nutshell*, §§ 8-9.
35. As a general rule, all members of the distribution chain (manufacturer, assembler, wholesaler, and retailer) are proper defendants in a product liability case. Although a downstream member of the distribution chain may have acted with due care and an upstream member created the defect, the defendant may collect from the downstream member, who then may look to the upstream member for indemnification.
36. Dobbs, *The Law of Torts*, § 353.
37. Friedman v. General Motors, 43 Ohio St.2d 209, 331 N.E.2d 702 (S.Ct. 1975).
38. Dobbs, *The Law of Torts*, § 362.
39. Ibid., §§ 356-362.
40. Ibid., § 357, discussing Wade's factors for the risk-utility test.
41. Prentis v. Yale Manufacturing Co., 421 Mich. 670, 365 N.W.2d 176 (1985).
42. The discussion in this section is based on the extensive comments and reporters' notes to § 2 Restatement (Third) Torts, Product Liability, American Law Institute, (1997).
43. At the time of the issuance of the *Restatement (Third) of Torts,* only six states continued to use the consumer expectation test for design defects—Alaska, Arkansas, Hawaii, Nebraska, Oklahoma, and Wisconsin.
44. "2000 Tort Reform Record," compiled by the American Tort Reform Association, available online at <http://www.atra.org/record/>, available as of January 15, 2001.
45. Greg Winter, "Jury Awards Soar as Lawsuits Decline on Defective Goods," *New York Times* (30 January 2001): A1.
46. "Tort Reform, In Great Detail,"—an issue paper put out by the Nader Campaign, available online at <http://www.votenader.com/issues/tort_full.html>, available as of January 15, 2001.
47. See the American Trail Lawyers Association home page at <http://www.atlanet.org/homepage/jud0909.htm>, available as of January 15,

2001. The ATLA played an active role in the decisions and advocates constitutional challenges to tort reform legislation.
48. For an excellent and balanced discussion of the issues, see "Comment: Damage Caps in Alabama's Civil Justice System: An Uncivil War Within the State," *Cumberland Law Review* 29 (1998/1999): 201. ✦

Chapter 11

Property

Chapter Objectives

Combined with the material found in Chapter 2, this chapter will help students understand how American property law is directly descended from the English feudal system. Students should be able to identify how real estate is owned after a grant of present and future interests. The tension between those who want to determine the future ownership of their property and those who want to insure the free alienability of land should be appreciated. Students need to be able to identify different methods of joint property ownership and be able to explain the advantages and disadvantages of each type. Readers will also be able to identify each of the three major classifications of property: real property, fixtures, and personal property. Finally, students must understand how technological advances have quickly stretched the limits of the copyright laws.

The concept of private property is one of the cornerstones of a capitalistic society. The ability to acquire, control, and dispose of property must be protected by government if individuals and business entities are to compete in a market-driven economy. The law of property is concerned with the bundle of rights and responsibilities that accompanies ownership of a tangible or intangible object. Property is concerned with a right or interest in something rather than the thing itself and is the right to possess, use, and dispose of that something in such a manner as is not inconsistent with the law.[1] Assume you bought a new pair of jeans yesterday. If asked what you own, your reply is likely to be "a pair of new jeans." In a technical legal sense, however, what you own is the right to use the jeans as you see fit, the ability to allow others to use them, the ability to give the jeans to someone else or to sell them, and the ability to destroy them if you wish. This chapter is an examination of the rights and responsibilities surrounding the ownership of tangible and intangible objects.

There are three classes of property: real property, fixtures, and personal property. *Real property* is concerned with the rights and obligations surrounding land. Real property can be divided into the right of present possession (freeholds) and the right of future possession (*future*

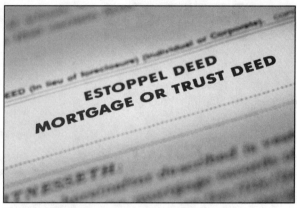

The orderly transfer of private property is one of the basic tenets of our legal system.

interests). *Fixtures* are affixed to real estate, such as heating and air conditioning systems, built-in appliances, and the like. *Personal property* is that which is not land or related to land. It is generally movable and without title. Personal property can be either tangible (it can be seen, held, or felt) or intangible (not of a physical nature, including stock in a corporation, a bank account, or a protected interest in an idea such as a copyrighted song or a patented product or process).

In this chapter, we focus mainly on real property, as do most first-year law school property classes. The following section briefly looks at the roots of American property law. Later, we present shorter sections on fixtures and personal property. Finally, we introduce readers to an area of intellectual property law (copyrights) that is adapting to technological change.

Roots of American Property Law

Like other areas of American law, the law of property is traced to the common law of England. Under the feudal system, land was the measure of wealth and the method of providing the Crown with an army and revenue. As we discussed in Chapter 2, after the Norman Conquest (1066), William redistributed English lands to his supporters (lords) in exchange for *military tenure* (an agreement to supply a certain number of knights when the king needed them). The lords in turn often granted military tenures to their knights (in effect, they subcontracted their duty out). Over time, the military tenures were supplemented with *serjeanty tenures*, which called for the tenant to provide a service instead of knights in exchange for the use of the land. Free and common *socage tenures* evolved, which called for agricultural services or money in exchange for use of the land. Eventually socage tenures replaced military and serjeanty tenures. *Unfree tenures* bound the *villeins* (or serfs) to labor for their lord in exchange for a hut and use of a small

strip of common land. Although bound to the lord, a villein was otherwise a free man. In the mid-1300s, the Black Death created a labor
shortage, and the lords were forced to substitute monetary rents for the
labor service. Eventually, the unfree tenures became *copyhold tenures,*
which could be transferred by the holders if they paid a *fine* to the lord,
although copyhold tenures did not become freehold estates in England
until the 1920s.

In Colonial America, land was held in tenure to the king. After the
revolution, most states replaced the king with the state as the sovereign. Some of the states abolished tenure and deemed all land to be
held *allodially* (free of any lord—i.e., a freehold estate). In any case,
today all land in the United States emanates from the sovereign (the
state) or dates back to a grant from the Crown.[2]

Interests in Real Property

Interests in real property are measured in terms of time and possession. One may have the right of possession presently or may gain the
right of possession at some point in the future. This section first examines those interests having the right of present possession. Then the
right of future possession (future interests) will be discussed.

Present Possessory Interests in Real Property

A *present possessory interest in real property* is one that entitles the
holder to exclusive possession of the land. These interests may be held
by one person or jointly by two or more persons (or entities). The following sections describe various interests in real property. Methods of
joint ownership will be discussed in a later part of this chapter.

Fee simple absolute. The largest interest in real property one can
own is the *fee simple,* often called *fee simple absolute.* The owner of a fee
simple interest in real estate owns all of the present interests and all of
the future interests in the property. Theoretically, the owner and the
owner's heirs may hold land owned in fee simple forever. Because the
common law preferred life estates, creating a fee simple interest required specific terminology in the granting document. "Oliver to Alex
and his heirs" would create a fee simple absolute in Alex, provided Oliver had a fee simple absolute interest at the time of the grant. Anything
else would be construed to create a life tenancy in Alex, even "to Alex in
fee simple."

Today, most states have statutes providing that grantees take whatever interest in the land their grantor had, unless the grant specifically
grants less than the full interest. As a result, a grant from "Oliver to
Alex" or "Oliver to Alex in fee simple" would create a fee simple absolute in Alex as long as Oliver had a fee simple interest at the time of the
grant. The owner of a fee simple interest in real property may use,

abuse, have exclusive possession of, take the fruits of, and dispose of the interest in the real property. The interest will last as long as the owner has heirs to inherit the real property.[3]

Variations of fee simple absolute. Variations of fee simple absolute still exist in some forms. *Fee simple determinable with possibility of reverter* is one. Under this type of interest, the grantor specifies that the real property interest is a fee simple interest, but only as long as the property is used in a specific manner. Assume Oliver has a fee simple absolute interest in Whiteacre. If Oliver makes the following conveyance, "Oliver conveys Whiteacre to Alexia and her heirs so long as Whiteacre is used as a game preserve," Oliver has created a fee simple determinable with possibility of reverter. Alexia would have a fee simple absolute in Whiteacre as long as it is used as a game preserve. However, Oliver would have a *possibility of reverter.* Should Alexia or her heirs allow Whiteacre to be used in a manner other than as a game preserve, Alexia's estate would end and Oliver would once again have a fee simple absolute interest. No action on the part of Oliver is necessary.[4]

A *fee simple subject to a condition subsequent* is similar to a fee simple determinable. A typical grant is as follows: "Oliver to Alexia and her heirs, but if mobile homes are rented on the premises, then Oliver has the right to reenter and repossess the land." Unlike a fee simple determinable above, if the condition occurs (Alexia bringing in and renting mobile homes), Alexia's interest does not automatically terminate. Oliver must reenter and bring an action to terminate Alexia's estate. If it seems to you that the grant just described is like private zoning or a covenant, you are correct. Since the occurrence of the condition and re-entry by a grantor causes the termination or forfeiture of a grantee's interest in the land, courts may insist upon clear language and evidence of the grantor's intent before termination of a grantee's estate.[5]

Consider the Illinois Supreme Court's language in *Sanitary District of Chicago v. The Chicago Title & Trust Co.*

> In case of doubt as to whether a provision in a deed is a condition or a covenant it will be construed to be a covenant to prevent the destruction of the estate, but here the express stipulation for the forfeiture of the estate and its immediate vesting in the grantor removes all doubt as to the intention of the parties to create a condition subsequent.[6]

Another variation on the fee simple estate is the *fee tail*. Fee tails were common in England after 1285 with the adoption of the *Statute of De Donis*. Fee tails were designed to control the alienation of property by the grantor. "Ozzie to Alvin and the heirs of his body," or similar words, allowed the grantor to limit the grant of land to the lineal descendants of Alvin or to Ozzie's heirs. Generally, the grant above was construed as giving Alvin a life estate in the property with remainders going to Alvin's bodily heirs. Once those heirs' interests became possessory (after Alvin's death), they had only life estates with remainders to their heirs. Should the Alvin line die out, the property would revert back to Ozzie or his heirs. By 1834 in England, the fee tail tenant (Alvin in our grant above) could convey a fee simple interest in the property to a third party and defeat the remainder in his heirs and the reversionary interest of Ozzie. Today, 33 American states do not allow for the creation of fee tails (construed as a fee simple or a fee simple with limitations) because they inhibit the free alienability of property. In contrast, Arkansas, Colorado, Florida, Georgia, Illinois, Missouri, and Vermont give the grantee a life estate with a contingent remainder in the grantee's lineal heirs. Once the grantee dies, the heirs may convey a fee simple to a third person. Massachusetts, Rhode Island (deeds), Maine, and Delaware give the grantee a fee tail, but allow the grantee to convey a fee simple. Connecticut, Ohio, and Rhode Island (wills) give the grantee a fee tail for life, but allow the first lineal descendent to convey a fee simple. Iowa, Oregon, and South Carolina give the grantee a fee simple conditional (upon the existence of lineal heirs at death). Iowa, however, allows the grantee to convey a fee simple upon the birth of a lineal ancestor.[7]

Life estates and non-freehold estates. A more limited present possessory interest is the *life estate.* The holder of a life estate has the right of exclusive possession, to use the property, to enjoy the fruits of the property, and to dispose of his or her interest. The holder may not waste or injure the property.[8] A typical grant is as follows: "Olivia to Alex for life." It creates a life estate in Alex with a reversion to Olivia. "Olivia to Alex for life then to Bob and his heirs" creates a life interest in Alex with a fee simple remainder to Bob. "Olivia to Alex for the life of Bob, then to Carmen and her heirs" creates a life estate in Alex that is measured by the life of Bob (*life estate pur autre vie*) with a fee simple remainder in Carmen. Bob has no interest.

At common law, life estates were common due to *dower* and *curtesy.* Dower gave a surviving wife a life interest in one third of all lands her husband owned in fee simple or fee tail during the marriage (even that property the husband had sold or otherwise conveyed that the wife did not join in the conveyance). curtesy gave a surviving husband a life estate in all lands owned by his wife in fee simple or fee tail as long as a child of the married couple was born alive.[9] Imagine the confusion these common law interests could create. Assume Husband, a married man, owns 1,000 acres of agricultural land in fee simple. Husband sells the 1,000 acres to Bob. Twenty years later, Husband dies and is survived by Wendy, his wife. Wendy could enter and possess one third of the 1,000 acres owned by Bob for the rest of her life. She would have a life estate by dower. After Wendy's death, Bob would own the 1,000 acres in fee simple. Gratefully, curtesy has been abolished in all American jurisdictions.

Dower rights, in some form, survive in Arkansas, the District of Columbia, Iowa, Kentucky, Michigan, Massachusetts, and Ohio. For example, Kentucky grants a life estate in one third of the property the deceased spouse owned in fee simple during the marriage and a one-half fee simple interest in all property owned at death. Whereas common dower applied only to surviving wives, modern American dower accrues to surviving wives and husbands.[10] Obviously, a legal practitioner in a jurisdiction that still recognizes dower must be sure to include both spouses in a conveyance even if legal title to the property is in the name of only one spouse.

Waste is an issue that pits a life estate holder against the holder of the reversion or remainder.[11] The life tenant has the right to use the property, but not to waste it. What is the legal rule when the life tenant mines gold that she discovers on the property? At common law, no waste was permissible, even *ameliorative* waste, defined as a change in the property that added to its value. In the United States today, ameliorative waste is generally permitted, reflecting the need to change the use of land as market conditions warrant.[12] For example, assume there is a life tenant on a 20-acre parcel of farmland with frontage on the main road near a new sports arena. Assume that the life tenant grades and paves two acres of the frontage and allows arena patrons to park their cars for five dollars. The life tenant is able to produce more income using the two acres as a parking lot than was possible by farming the plot. Would the life tenant's actions be waste, and would the remainderman (the person who will take the land after the life tenant), be able to bring an action for damages to his interest in the 20-acre parcel of farmland? Under the English common law, the answer is yes, because the nature of the property was changed. The paved area can no longer be used for agricultural purposes. Under the American view of ameliorative waste, the answer is probably no. As long as the life tenant's actions do not decrease the value of the property or diminish the property's ability to produce income, no actionable waste occurs.[13]

Cutting trees and extracting minerals, however, from the land are two activities that may subject a life tenant to a waste action. Under the English common law, the cutting of mature trees by the holder of less than a full fee estate was regarded as waste. Exceptions were made for the cutting of sufficient trees for fires and repairs, but only if dead or downed trees were not available. Likewise, one could thin out immature trees to promote better growth of larger trees.

American courts did not apply the rigid English common law rules. On the American frontier, trees needed to be cut to allow farming. As long as the life tenant used good husbandry principles when cutting trees, he would not be subject to a waste action. If, however, the life tenant cut the trees only to sell the timber, he would be committing waste. Mining minerals or extracting oil or gas from the land is generally viewed as waste by American courts. If a life tenant discovers gold or other minerals and begins mining, the income from the mining is considered the remainderman's. Nevertheless, the life tenant may take any interest earned from investing the principal amounts. The *open mine exception* allows a life tenant to operate a mine that was in existence when his life estate began without committing waste.[14]

The acts described above are all examples of affirmative waste, in that the waste occurs as a result of actions by the life tenants. Life tenants may commit permissive waste as well, or waste that occurs as a result of the life tenant failing to act. Not paying property taxes, not paying interest due on an existing mortgage, and failing to make repairs to prevent further injury to the property may constitute permissive waste. The life tenant's duty is limited to the income from the property (or the imputed rental value if the property is occupied by the life tenant). Life tenants are not responsible for normal wear and tear, but they are expected to keep the property in the condition it was in when their life estates began.[15]

Non-freehold estates (leaseholds) are similar to life estates in that they entitle the holder to the exclusive possession of the property for a limited amount of time. Life estates end when the measuring life ends. A non-freehold estate ends on a date certain or upon the happening of an event. "Olive to Albert for 10 years, beginning January 1, 2002, and ending December 31, 2012," creates an estate for years in Albert with a reversion in Olive. Importantly, an estate for years may be for less than a year. For example, if the grant above were "Olive to Albert for one month beginning January 1, 2002, and ending January 31, 2002," it would create an estate for years in Albert with a reversion in Olive. The period of time is not important in determining an estate for years. What is important is that the estate begins and ends on dates certain.

"Olive to Albert, month-to-month, beginning January 1, 2002" creates a *periodic tenancy* in Albert with a reversion in Olive. Note that estates for years end on a date certain, whereas a periodic tenancy begins on a date certain but automatically renews for the stated period unless a termination notice is given. A notice to terminate must be given before the new period begins. In our example above, an effective notice must be given before the first day of a month. The notice would be effective the last day of the following month. A six-month termination is usually sufficient when the periodic tenancy is year-to-year or longer.[16]

At common law, estates for years and periodic tenancies were considered conveyances of real property interests. *Landlord-Tenant* statutes now apply contract principles to residential leases. Typical statutes provide a warranty of habitability, eviction procedures for non-payment of rent, a covenant for quiet enjoyment of the property, and landlord remedies if the tenant abandons the property.[17]

Methods of Joint or Concurrent Ownership

There are eight methods or ways that property can be owned by more than one person or entity: tenancies in coparcenary, tenancy in common, joint tenancy, tenancy by the entirety, community property, tenancy in partnership, the cooperative, and time-sharing.[18] In this section, we will discuss the three most common methods of concurrent ownership: tenancy in common, joint tenancy, and tenancy by the entirety.

Tenancy in common. A grant from "Oliver to Alice and Ralph in fee simple absolute, each taking a one-half interest therein," creates a tenancy in common in fee simple absolute in Alice and Ralph. Oliver gave away all he had, so he has no interest. A tenancy in common has one unity, possession. Each co-tenant may occupy all of the property. If Alice and Ralph each own an undivided one-half interest in an acre of land, neither may put up a fence across the middle of the land to keep the other co-tenant on their half. Again, each of the co-tenants may occupy all of the land. Co-tenants may own different portions. For example, Alice could own an undivided two-thirds interest and Ralph could own an undivided one-third interest. Alice could have a life interest and Ralph could have fee simple absolute. During their lifetimes, each co-tenant may dispose of or encumber their interest as they see fit. If a co-tenant has an inheritable interest, he or she may devise their interest or it will pass to their heirs upon their death.[19] For instance, assume Alice and Ralph each own an undivided one-half interest in an acre of land as tenants in common. If Alice dies intestate (without a will) and has two heirs, Alice$_1$ and Alice$_2$, the ownership of the one acre would now be Alice$_1$, an undivided one-fourth interest, Alice$_2$, an undivided one-fourth interest, and Ralph, an undivided one-half interest as tenants in common. As discussed in the following section, had Alice and Ralph held the acre of land as joint tenants, Ralph would be the sole owner of the one acre of land. Alice's interest would have vanished upon her death.

Joint tenancy. The principal characteristic of a *joint tenancy* is the *right of survivorship*. For example, if Alice and Ralph own an acre of land in joint tenancy and Alice dies, her interest disappears. Ralph becomes the sole owner of the acre of land in fee simple. Alice's heirs would have no interest in the land, nor may Alice devise (transfer by will) her interest. If Alice and Ralph die simultaneously, most states, under the *Uniform Simultaneous Death Act*, treat Alice and Ralph's interests as *tenancies in common* and allow the land to descend to the heirs of Alice and Ralph. The early common law favored joint tenancies over tenancies in common, so a grant from "Oliver to Alice and Ralph" would be construed as a joint tenancy.[20]

Joint tenancies have four unities: *time, title, interest,* and *possession.* Joint tenants must have their interest created at the same time (time), their interests must be created in the same document (title), their interests must be of the same share (interest), and each may possess all of the property (possession).[21] The common law preference for joint tenancies has been supplanted in the United States with a presumption for a tenancy in common. Some states have even abolished the joint tenancy or the right of survivorship.[22] Illinois' *Joint Tenancy Act*[23] is typical.

**Box 11.1   Excerpt from Illinois Joint Tenancy Act
765 ILCS 1005/1 (2001)**

No estate in joint tenancy in any lands, tenements or hereditaments, or in any parts thereof or interest therein, shall be held or claimed under any grant, legacy or conveyance whatsoever heretofore or hereafter made, other than to executors and trustees, unless the premises therein mentioned shall expressly be thereby declared to pass not in tenancy in common, but in joint tenancy . . . wherein the premises therein mentioned were or shall be expressly declared to pass not in tenancy in common, but in joint tenancy, are hereby declared to have created an estate in joint tenancy with the accompanying right of survivorship. . . .

Under the presumption created in statutes like the Illinois Joint Tenancy Act, the grant from "Oliver to Alice and Ralph," previously described, which would have been construed as a joint tenancy at common law, will on the other hand be construed as a tenancy in common in most U.S. jurisdictions today.

A joint tenant has the right to sever the joint tenancy. Permission of the other joint tenant or tenants is unnecessary. A joint tenant conveying her interest to another or to herself will accomplish severance. The taking of a joint tenant's interest in satisfaction of a debt also severs the joint tenancy. An agreement between the joint tenants for one of them to exclusively possess a portion of the premises may or may not sever the joint tenancy. When a joint tenancy is severed, the resulting co-owners hold the property in tenancy in common as between themselves. In effect, one joint tenant may defeat another's expectation of survivorship rights. If there are more than two joint tenants and only one severs, the severing party (or his grantee) is a tenant in common in relation to the other joint tenants, but the nonsevering joint tenants remain joint tenants in relation to each other.[24]

Tenancy by the entirety. A *tenancy by the entirety* is a joint tenancy with one additional unity—the marriage of the tenants. Married couples are considered one person with respect to the property owned in tenancy by the entirety.[25] At common law, tenancy by the entirety was the sole method of a husband and wife co-owning property. Because a woman's property rights were subordinate to her husband's, the one person in the marriage unity was the husband. Married women's property acts in most states abolished or made the status of tenancy by the entirety uncertain, despite a common law presumption of tenancy by the entirety of property conveyed to a husband and wife. Today, 16 states have either abolished or refuse to recognize tenancies by the entirety. In four other states, tenancy by the entirety is referenced only in statutes based on uniform acts, rendering its existence uncertain.[26]

In states that recognize tenancy by the entirety, some still follow the common law rule that any conveyance to a husband and wife creates a tenancy by the entirety. Others follow the presumption that absent the clear intent to create something other than a tenancy in common, all conveyances to more than one person are tenancies in common. To be sure, the conveyance should make clear that a tenancy by the entirety is being created.[27] Like a joint tenancy, upon the death of one spouse, that spouse's interest in the property held in tenancy by the entirety disappears and the surviving spouse holds the property in fee simple. Generally, if the unity of marriage is broken (through divorce or annulment), the tenancy by the entirety becomes a tenancy in common. Because a tenancy by the entirety assumes the married couple is one, one spouse may not convey his or her separate interest like a joint tenant may, although in some jurisdictions, the individual spouses may convey or encumber their contingent survivorship rights. A few states still embrace the common law rule that prevents a creditor of one spouse from selling the property to satisfy a debt or judgment.[28] The following Illinois Supreme Court case illustrates how a tenancy by the entirety may be used to frustrate the collection efforts of a creditor.

Premier Property Management, Inc. v. Chavez
Supreme Court of Illinois
191 Ill. 2d 101, 728 N.E.2d 476 (2000)

OPINION BY: BILANDIC: . . . Premier and Jose Chavez had a business relationship. In May of 1995, Premier filed a separate lawsuit against Jose Chavez and El Torero, Inc. At that time, Jose Chavez held title to his residence in his name alone.

On or around June 1, 1996, Jose Chavez conveyed his interest in the residence from himself, as sole owner, to himself and his wife, as tenants by the entirety. This conveyance was recorded on July 19, 1996. In late 1996, a judgment was entered in the sepa-

rate lawsuit in favor of Premier and against Jose Chavez and El Torero, Inc., for the amount of $190,566.30.

On May 27, 1997, Premier filed the instant action to set aside the conveyance. Premier contended that the conveyance should be set aside as fraudulent pursuant to the terms of the Uniform Fraudulent Transfer Act.

Defendants filed a motion to dismiss Premier's complaint under section 2-619 of the Code of Civil Procedure. Defendants argued that the tenancy by the entirety provision of the Code of Civil Procedure protects their marital residence from being sold to pay a judgment entered against only one of the tenants. According to defendants, the tenancy by the entirety provision offers this protection regardless of whether the conveyance was made with fraudulent intent. In support, defendants relied on a decision of the Second District of the Appellate Court, E.J. McKernan Co. v. Gregory, 268 Ill. App. 3d 383, 205 Ill. Dec. 763, 643 N.E.2d 1370 (1994), appeal dismissed with prejudice, No. 78487 (May 23, 1995).

Premier filed a response to defendants' motion to dismiss. Premier maintained that a conveyance of property to tenancy by the entirety may be set aside where made with fraudulent intent. In support, Premier relied on In re Marriage of Del Giudice, 287 Ill. App. 3d 215, 222 Ill. Dec. 640, 678 N.E.2d 47 (1997), a decision of the First District of the Appellate Court. Premier also argued to the circuit court that it was required to follow *Del Giudice,* the decision in its district, because a conflict existed between *Del Giudice* and *McKernan.*

The circuit court determined that *Del Giudice* and *McKernan* are reconcilable on their facts. The circuit court then applied *McKernan* to the instant case, reasoning that *McKernan* is more factually analogous. Consequently, the circuit court granted defendants' motion to dismiss Premier's complaint with prejudice.

Premier appealed. The appellate court ruled that *Del Giudice* and *McKernan* are in direct conflict. The appellate court further ruled that the circuit court was bound to follow Del Giudice, the decision in its district. The appellate court therefore reversed the dismissal of Premier's

complaint and remanded the cause for additional proceedings. In doing so, the appellate court noted that the General Assembly had recently amended the tenancy by the entirety provision relied upon by defendants. We allowed defendants' petition for leave to appeal.

ANALYSIS: Tenancy by the entirety is an estate in real property provided for by the Joint Tenancy Act. . . . Only spouses may hold property in this estate. In addition, the estate is limited to homestead property. . . .

1. Tenancy by the Entirety Provision: According to the tenancy by the entirety provision of the Code of Civil Procedure, holding property in tenancy by the entirety protects spouses in that the property cannot be sold to satisfy the debt of only one spouse. . . . At issue here is the extent of that protection when a creditor attempts to avoid a transfer of property to tenancy by the entirety, claiming that it was made with fraudulent intent.

When Jose Chavez conveyed his property to tenancy by the entirety on or around June 1, 1996, the tenancy by the entirety provision stated in pertinent part: "Any real property, or any beneficial interest in a land trust, held in tenancy by the entirety shall not be liable to be sold upon judgment entered on or after October 1, 1990 against only one of the tenants.". . .

Premier asserts that Jose Chavez's conveyance was fraudulent and may be set aside under the Fraudulent Transfer Act. The Fraudulent Transfer Act provides in relevant part that a creditor may avoid a transfer "if the debtor made the transfer . . . with actual intent to hinder, delay, or defraud any creditor of the debtor. . . ." Our appellate court has reached conflicting conclusions as to whether the Fraudulent Transfer Act may be used against a debtor who is relying on the protection furnished by the tenancy by the entirety provision.

In *McKernan*, a husband and wife held their home in joint tenancy. A creditor obtained a judgment against the husband and initiated proceedings for a sale of the home. The husband and wife then transferred title to the home to tenancy by the entirety. The husband moved to restrain the sale based on the protection provided by the tenancy by the entirety provision. The creditor asserted that the transfer of title was fraudulent under the Fraudulent Transfer Act. . . .

The appellate court in *McKernan* held that the Fraudulent Transfer Act can never be applied to property held in tenancy by the entirety. According to the appellate court, the Fraudulent Transfer Act allows creditors to avoid transfers made with actual intent to defraud. Intent, however, "is irrelevant in a tenancy by the entirety conveyance because it simply cannot be fraudulent to engage in conduct that is specifically and unambiguously sanctioned by statute. . . ."

The appellate court in *Del Giudice* declined to follow *McKernan*. In *Del Giudice*, a husband and wife held their home in joint tenancy. A creditor obtained a judgment against the husband and initiated proceedings for a sale of the home. The husband and wife then transferred title to the home to tenancy by the entirety. The husband moved to restrain the sale based on the protection provided by the tenancy by the entirety provision. The creditor asserted that the transfer of title was fraudulent under the Fraudulent Transfer Act. . . .

The appellate court held that, pursuant to the terms of the Fraudu-lent Transfer Act, a creditor can avoid a transfer of property to tenancy by the entirety if that transfer was made with actual intent to defraud the creditor. The appellate court acknowledged that the statutes concerning tenancy by the entirety allow married couples to effect such transfers, and that the General Assembly intended tenancy by the entirety to shield a marital homestead from the creditors of one spouse. Nonetheless, the court found no indication in those statutes or their legislative history that the General Assembly intended to include fraudulent conduct within the scope of afforded protection. According to the *Del Giudice* court, because the Fraudulent Transfer Act may be used to invalidate an otherwise lawful transaction made with fraudulent intent, that Act may be used to invalidate an otherwise lawful transfer of property to tenancy by the entirety if made with fraudulent intent. . . .

After *Del Giudice* was filed, the General Assembly amended the tenancy by the entirety provision. With that amendment, the tenancy by the entirety provision states in pertinent part: "Any real property, or any beneficial interest in a land trust, held in tenancy by the entirety shall not be liable to be sold upon judgment entered on or after October 1, 1990 against only one of the tenants, except if the property was transferred into tenancy by the entirety with the sole intent to avoid the payment of debts existing at the time of the transfer beyond the transferor's ability to pay those debts as they become due. . . ." The General Assembly also added language explaining that this amendment "is intended as a clarification of existing law and not as a new enactment.". . .

Having determined that the amended tenancy by the entirety provision applies here, we now address the primary issue before this court: whether the Fraudulent Transfer Act's actual intent standard may be used to set aside a transfer of property to tenancy by the entirety. We hold that the answer is no, for the following reasons.

As amended, the tenancy by the entirety provision expressly includes its own standard to be used when a creditor challenges a transfer to that estate. Under the standard provided, property held in tenancy by the entirety cannot be sold to satisfy the debt of only one spouse, unless the property was transferred into tenancy by the entirety "with the sole intent to avoid the payment of debts existing at the time of the transfer beyond the transferor's ability to pay those debts as they become due...." This standard governs when a creditor challenges a transfer of property to tenancy by the entirety. . . .

This sole intent standard stands in contrast to the actual intent standard of the Fraudulent Transfer Act. Under the Fraudulent Transfer Act, a creditor may avoid a transfer if the debtor made the transfer with actual intent to hinder, delay, or defraud any creditor of the debtor. . . . Section 5(b) of that Act lists 11 factors that may be considered in determining the debtor's actual intent in making the transfer. . . . If a sufficient number of the factors are present, the requisite actual intent may be found.

The sole intent standard of the amended tenancy by the entirety provision is substantially different from the actual intent standard of the Fraudulent Transfer Act. The sole intent standard provides greater protection from creditors for transfers of property to tenancy by the entirety. Under the sole intent standard, if property is transferred to tenancy by the entirety to place it beyond the reach of the creditors of one spouse and to accomplish some other legitimate purpose, the transfer is not avoidable. Such a transfer, however, would be avoidable under the actual intent standard, which only requires any actual intent to defraud a creditor. The General Assembly, by adopting the sole intent standard, has made it clear that it intends to provide spouses holding homestead property in tenancy by the entirety with greater protection from the creditors of one spouse than that provided by the Fraudulent Transfer Act. Accordingly, the Fraudulent Transfer Act's actual intent standard is not to be used to avoid transfers of property made to tenancy by the entirety. . . .

Given that *Del Giudice* applied the actual intent standard of the Fraudulent Transfer Act, *Del Giudice* is not consistent with the sole intent standard of the amended tenancy by the entirety provision, nor is *McKernan,* which held that intent is never relevant. Hence, *Del Giudice* and *McKernan* are no longer correct statements of the law and should be disregarded. . . .

In the present case, Premier's complaint to set aside Jose Chavez's conveyance relied upon the Fraudulent Transfer Act and, ultimately, *Del Giudice*. Defendants' motion to dismiss Premier's complaint relied upon *McKernan*. Applying *McKernan,* the circuit court granted defendants' motion to dismiss with prejudice. We hold, however, that the amended tenancy by the entirety provision governs this case, to the exclusion of the actual intent standard of the Fraudulent Transfer Act, *Del Giudice* and *McKernan*. In light of this holding, Premier must be given the opportunity to amend its complaint to reflect the amendment to the tenancy by the entirety provision. This cause is therefore remanded to the circuit court of Cook County. The circuit court is directed to enter an order dismissing Premier's complaint without prejudice and to afford Premier the opportunity to file an amended complaint. . . .

Case Questions for Discussion

1. What are the competing public policy issues involved in this case? Which public policy has the Illinois legislature decided is most important?
2. Do you agree with the legislature's choice?
3. Can you think of any negative consequences that could result from the public policy choice made by the legislature?
4. How should prudent spouses hold their real property in Illinois?
5. Upon remand, what will Premier need to show to prevail?
6. Upon remand, what will Chavez need to show to prevail?

Future Interests

In the previous sections, we have examined the means of holding a present possessory interest in property. The future right to possess property has also been long recognized by the law. This area of property law is commonly referred to as the law of *future interests*. Future interests are legal means of orchestrating who will own property in the future. The concept of the *free alienability of property* is in conflict with controlling property "from the grave." As a result, rules evolved restricting the ability of owners to decide who will own their property long after they are dead. In the following sections we examine some of the more common future interests and the rules restricting their use.

Remainders. Interests in property that are preceded by a life estate or a fee tail are called *remainders*. "Omar to Alice for life, then to Bob and his heirs" creates a life estate in Alice and a remainder in Bob. Assuming Bob is a live person, Bob's remainder is *indefeasibly vested*, because Bob is alive and the interest will become possessory immediately upon the death of Alice. If Bob predeceases Alice, then Bob's heirs will take the property upon Alice's death.[29]

Vested remainders can also be subject to *divestment*. For example, "Omar to Alice for life, then to Brenda and her heirs, but if Cindy marries $Omar_1$, then to Cindy and her heirs." Alice has a life estate. Brenda has a *vested remainder subject to complete divestment*. If Cindy marries $Omar_1$ before Alice dies, Brenda's vested remainder is defeated. Brenda will take nothing. On the other hand, if Alice dies before Cindy marries

Omar₁ (or if Cindy never marries Omar₁), then Brenda's interest becomes possessory upon Alice's death. A *partial divestment* is also possible. "Omar to Alice for life, then to the children of Brenda" is an example. Again, Alice has a life estate. Assuming Brenda is alive and Brenda has at least one child, Brenda₁, that child has *a vested remainder subject to open.* If Brenda has additional children before Alice dies, Brenda₁'s interest will be diminished since the additional children will join in her remainder. Once Alice dies, Brenda dies, or Brenda is no longer able to have children, the class closes and the interests become vested and are not subject to further partial divestment.[30]

Contingent remainders are remainders that are subject to a condition precedent, such as the birth of a child, the identification of an unknown person, or one person surviving another. "Omar to Alice for life, then if Brenda survives Alice, to Brenda and her heirs" is an example. Alice has a life estate, Brenda has a contingent remainder, and Omar retains a reversionary interest. Brenda's interest is contingent upon her surviving Alice. If Alice survives Brenda, the property will revert back to Omar and his heirs upon Alice's death. A contingent remainder is similar to vested remainders subject to complete divestment, except the condition in the latter is a condition subsequent.

As a general rule, if the condition follows the *words of purchase* (the words identifying the person or persons the interest is being given to, or to whom it is sold), it is a *condition subsequent*. If the condition precedes the words of purchase, it is a *condition precedent*. For example, "Omar to Alice for life, then if Brenda is married, to Brenda and her heirs" is a condition precedent, and the grant creates a contingent remainder in Brenda, because the condition (if Brenda is married) precedes the words of purchase (to Brenda and her heirs). However, if the grant were "Omar to Alice for life then to Brenda and her heirs, but if Brenda is not married, then to Charles and his heirs" creates a vested remainder subject to complete divestment in Brenda. Note that the condition (Brenda's marriage) follows the words of purchase (Brenda and her heirs).

At common law, under the Rule of Destructibility, contingent remainders were destroyed if the condition had not occurred by the time the life tenant died. In our example, if Brenda had not married by the time of Alice's death, the property reverted to Omar and Brenda's interest would never come into possession, even if she later married. Today, under the general rule, to be explained below, if Brenda does marry after Alice's death, her interest will become possessory as an executory interest.[31]

Reversions. What is left of a grantor's interest when she conveys less than she has is called a *reversion*. "Olivia to Al for life" gives Al a life interest and Olivia retains a reversion. After Al's death, the interest will revert back to Olivia. Other forms of reversions include the *possibility of reverter* and *powers of termination*. Possibilities of reverter are retained when the grantor owning a fee simple absolute interest conveys a fee simple determinable.

For example, as discussed above in the sections on variations of fee simple, if "Oliver conveys Whiteacre to Alexia and her heirs so long as Whiteacre is used as a game preserve," Oliver retains a possibility of reverter. If Alexia or her heirs use Whiteacre in a manner other than a game preserve, Alexia's interest ends (without any action by Oliver) and Whiteacre reverts back to Oliver or Oliver's heirs in fee simple absolute. *Powers of termination* or *right of reentry for condition broken* are retained when a fee simple absolute owner conveys a fee simple subject to a condition subsequent. Again, as discussed in the section on variations on fee simple absolute, "Oliver to Alexia and her heirs, but if mobile homes are rented on the premises, then Oliver has the right to reenter and repossess the land," leaves Oliver with a power of termination or a right of reentry for condition broken. Unlike a possibility of reverter, if the condition is broken, Oliver must reenter the premises (or more likely today, Oliver must bring an action to terminate Alexia's interest for the broken condition subsequent) and take possession to end Alexia's interest.[32]

Executory interests. Future interests that come into present possession by divesting another present possessory interest are called *executory interests*. A *springing executory interest* divests a reversionary interest that has come into present possession, usually due to a gap in time between the end of a life interest and the present possession of a remainder interest. For example, "Omar to Alice for life, then if Brenda is age 21, to Brenda and her heirs." Alice has a life estate and Brenda has a contingent remainder. If Alice dies when Brenda is 20 years old, Brenda has not met the condition precedent, and the property reverts to Omar. At common law, before the Rule of Destructibility was abolished and the enactment of the Statute of Uses, Brenda's interest was gone. Today, however, at Alice's death, the property reverts to Omar, and Brenda has a springing executory interest. Once Brenda reaches the age of 21, her springing executory interest terminates Omar's reversion and Brenda will own the property in fee simple.[33]

A *shifting executory interest* terminates the present possession of another transferee or a vested interest of another transferee. "Omar to Alice and her heirs, but if Alice has no children by the age of 30, then to Bob and his heirs." Bob's interest is a shifting executory interest. It will come into present possession only if Alice reaches the age of 30 and she has not had any children. In order for Bob to gain present possession, his executory interest must terminate Alice's interest.[34]

Common law rules limiting future interests. Historically, the law of future interests has been a battle between property owners, who want to control the ownership of their property long into the future (from the grave), and those who believe property should be freely alienable. Many rules that tend to convert future interests into interests that may be transferred have evolved over time. In this section, we briefly discuss three of the most common rules.

In the motion picture *Body Heat,* one of those rules, the *Rule Against Perpetuities* (RAP), played a prominent role. The devious Kathleen Turner character stole letterhead from the William Hurt character (an attorney) and forged a new will for her husband. It contained a RAP violation, but because Hurt's character had been grossly negligent in another matter before the movie takes place, it seems reasonable that he had made another big error. In this new faked will, Turner was to inherit only half of her husband's property. When the probate court finds the error and voids the will, Turner inherits all of her husband's property under the intestate statute. Hurt is in no position to dispute that he wrote the voided will, because he is Turner's lover and the co-murderer of her husband.[35]

A lack of understanding of the RAP is common, even among attorneys. Violated many times in practice, it is a trap for the unwary lawyer. A statement of the RAP is simple: "No interest is good unless it must vest, if at all, not later than 21 years after some life in being at the creation of the interest."[36] The purpose of the RAP is simple enough: Owners of property are limited in how far into the future they may control the ownership of property. The following example illustrates how the RAP works: "Omar to Alice for life, then to Alice's children who reach age 25." Omar has attempted to give Alice a life estate and Alice's children vested remainders subject to open. The grant to the children would fail because Alice could have additional children who would take more than 21 years to reach age 25. Had the grant been to the live children of Alice who reach age 21, it would have survived the RAP. The RAP does not apply to present possessory interests, reversions, vested remainders in individuals, charitable trusts, and resulting trusts.

Because the RAP is arbitrary and often works to frustrate the intentions of the grantor, three approaches have been used to mitigate its effect. First, the *Wait and See Doctrine* does not invalidate the grant until it becomes apparent that it will fail under the RAP. Applying the previous illustration, suppose that at the date of the grant Alice had two children, age 7 and 10 at the time of the conveyance. Alice dies with no additional children. Under the Wait and See Doctrine, the conveyance to Alice's two live children would be good because they both would reach

The Rule Against Perpetuities *prevents real property being controlled from the grave.*

age 25 within 21 years. Under the *Cy Pres Doctrine,* those grants that violate the RAP are modified to conform. In our example, "then to the children of Alice who reach age 25" would be modified to, "then to the children of Alice who reach age 21." Finally, the Uniform Commissioners on State Laws have proposed an absolute vesting time limit of 90 years.[37]

The *Rule in Shelly's Case* (RSC) merges a life estate with a remainder to the life tenant's heirs. For instance, under the RSC, "Omar to Alice for life, then to Alice's heirs" would give a fee simple absolute to Alice. The RSC promotes the free alienability of property, because Alice may, having a fee simple absolute under the RSC, sell or otherwise dispose of the property. The RSC was once almost universal in this country, but most states have now statutorily abolished it.[38]

The *Doctrine of Worthier Title* (DWT) invalidates an *inter vivos* (during life) conveyance of a remainder or other interest to the grantor's heirs and creates a reversion in the grantor. For example, "Omar to Alice for life, then to Omar's heirs" would be subject to the DWT. The remainder to Omar's heirs would be invalid, and a reversion would be reserved in Omar. This grant would in effect be identical to "Omar to Alice for life." The DWT is generally applicable in most jurisdictions today for conveyances of real property.[39]

Fixtures

"Fixtures are in the twilight zone between things real and things personal."[40] The determination of whether a particular item is a *fixture* has been problematic for American courts. Several definitions of fixtures have been offered. "A fixture is an article which though originally a chattel is by reason of its annexation regarded as part of the land, partaking of the character of realty and ordinarily belonging to the owner of the land."[41] "A fixture may be defined as an item of property which was a chattel but which has been so affixed to realty for a combined functional use that it has become a part and parcel of the realty."[42] "A fixture is a chattel brought in and upon and annexed to real property which retains its separate identity and becomes realty but which under certain circumstances may become personality again."[43]

No definition has proven useful in all situations. The determination of whether a particular item is a fixture or personal property usually determines who has superior rights (ownership or security) in the property. Assume that last school year you rented an apartment. During the year you bought and installed a television bracket in the bedroom so you could comfortably watch television in bed. At the end of your lease, as you were moving out, your landlord tells you not to take down the TV bracket. She says, "It has been attached to my real property and as such is now a fixture and belongs to me." Is she right? She could be, although because you were a tenant, it was probably not your intent to convert your personal property into a fixture and increase the value of the landlord's property.

Selling real estate presents another issue. When an owner sells real estate, what goes with the property? Fixtures do, but personal property of the owner does not. When a lender finances a real estate purchase with a mortgage, what property is encumbered? Fixtures are secured. Personal property of the landowner is not. Generally, items like sprinkler systems and heating and cooling units are considered fixtures. Those items of personal property that are temporarily installed, such as refrigerators and window air conditioners, are usually not considered fixtures.

Those who finance the purchase of personal property must look to the *Uniform Commercial Code* for guidance on how to secure their loans. Article 9 has creditor filing procedures for three different types of property: goods that retain their personal property nature, goods that are integrated into real estate (building materials) and become part of the real estate, and fixtures that are goods that become part of the real property but retain their chattel character in relation to security interests.[44] To be effective, the creditor must use the correct filing procedure.

The English common law looked to whether the item was attached to the real property in such a manner that removal would cause material injury to the real property. Early American cases generally followed the English common law. In 1853, the Ohio Supreme Court articulated a three-part test that has been adopted by a majority of U.S. jurisdictions. The test asks the following: (1) was there actual annexation to the realty, (2) was there appropriation to the use or purpose of the realty, and (3) what was the intention of the party making the annexation? Although each part of the test was originally intended to be an equal factor, the intent factor is dominant today.[45]

The following bankruptcy court case applying Alabama law illustrates the modern use of the three-part test.

In the Matter of: Albright
U.S. Bankruptcy Court for the Northern District of Alabama,
Northern Division
214 B.R. 408 (1997)

OPINION BY: JACK CADDELL: . . . On October 17, 1996, the Albrights executed a note with the bank in the amount of $129,000.00. As security for the note, the debtors executed a mortgage in favor of the bank on the real property described in the mortgage, as well as, a security interest in after-acquired property. Subsequently, the Albrights purchased two heat pumps to replace the existing heating and air-conditioning system in their home. The Tennessee Valley Authority (TVA) financed the heat pumps and a third party co-signed the loan for same. On or about November 8, 1996, TVA filed a financing statement maintaining a purchase money security interest in the heat pumps.

On March 23, 1997, the Albrights filed a voluntary petition for relief under chapter 13 of title 11 of the Bankruptcy Code. On schedules B and C of their petition, debtors listed an "air conditioner unit" as exempt personal property in the amount of $7,500.00 pursuant to section 6-10-6 of the Alabama Code. The debtors seek to remove the subject property from the real estate as exempt personal property.

In determining whether the heat pumps become part of the real estate so as to fall under the after acquired property provisions of the mortgage, "improvements," it is necessary to determine whether they are fixtures or personal property. To do so, the Court must look to applicable state law. . . . The Alabama Code defines fixtures as goods that have "become so related to a particular real estate that an interest in them arises under real estate law. . . ." Alabama courts have held that a fixture is "an article which was once a chattel, but which, by being physically annexed or affixed to the realty, has become accessory to it and part and parcel of it. . . ." In the oft quoted case of Langston v. State, 96 Ala. 44, 11 So. 334 (Ala. 1891), the Alabama Supreme Court established the criteria for determining whether an item is to become part and parcel of the real estate to which it is attached as follows: (1) Actual annexation to the realty or to

something appurtenant thereto; (2) appropriateness to the use of purposes of that part of the realty with which it is connected; (3) the intention of the party making the annexation of making permanent attachment to the freehold. . . .

For the reasons set forth below, the Court finds that the movant has satisfied these requirements in the case at bar.

With regard to the first element, actual annexation, the Albrights allege that the financing company required debtors to install the heat pumps so as to allow same to be removed without damage to the realty. It is not essential, however, to the element of actual annexation that a fixture's annexation to the freehold be made absolutely permanent. . . . Indeed, the Alabama Supreme Court has held that the general rule for purposes of determining whether a good is a fixture is that "whatever is attached to the realty, though but slightly, is prima facie part thereof." Silverman v. Mazer Lumber & Supply Co., 252 Ala. 657, 42 So. 2d 452, 453 (1949).

Although the parties were unable to cite any Alabama cases concerning the attachment of heat pumps to realty, the case of Household Fin. Corp. v. BancOhio, 62 Ohio App. 3d 691, 577 N.E.2d 405 (Ohio Ct. App. 1989) is instructive on the issue. In that case an Ohio appellate court determined that a heat pump was a fixture where the heat pump was located outside the house and bolted to a concrete slab with wires and tubes going into the house. The court noted that the element of annexation is satisfied by slight physical attachment. . . . Although the heat pumps in the present case could undoubtedly be removed from the house, the Court finds the same to be sufficiently, even if slightly, attached to the realty to satisfy the element of actual annexation.

To satisfy the second element of a fixture, the heat pumps must be appropriate to the purpose of the use of the realty to which they are attached. In the *Household Finance* case, the court discussed the function and purpose of heat pumps for purposes of determining the second test as follows: [The heat pump is] indispensable for the comfortable enjoyment of a dwelling house in this climate. When installed, it certainly became an integral and necessary part of the whole premises. . . . Similarly, the Court finds that the heat pumps in the case at bar are clearly integral to the function and the purpose of the subject house.

With regard to the final element of a fixture, intent can be inferred from the nature of the article annexed, the relation of the party making the annexation, the structure and mode of annexation, and the purposes and uses for which the annexation has been made. . . . The intention of the party making the annexation is the controlling factor in determining the character of the article annexed. Intent to affix property to the realty is presumed where a debtor voluntarily annexes same to the realty. . . .

In the case at bar, the Court finds that the heat pumps satisfy the third element of a fixture. The heat pumps are connected to the house and constitute the heat and air-conditioning source for same. Removal of the heat pumps would necessitate the replacement of the heat source to make the house habitable. The Albrights enjoyed the benefit of the original heating and air-conditioning system securing the bank's mortgage. Although the Albrights were under no obligation to replace the system when worn out by their use, they chose to purchase replacement heat pumps to benefit their home. These actions evidence an intent on the part of the Albrights to permanently affix the heat pumps to their residence such that the same became a part of the realty.

Therefore, the Court finds that the Albrights cannot remove the heat pumps from the house because debtors' mortgage contains an after-acquired property clause granting the bank a security interest in all "improvements now or hereafter erected on the property, . . . deemed to be and remain a part of the property conveyed by this Mortgage.". . .

Case Questions for Discussion

1. Do you agree with the ultimate outcome in this case?

2. Do you think the decision would have been different if the property in question was an in-ground swimming pool? What about an above-ground swimming pool?

3. If the Albrights had replaced the dining room light fixture with an expensive chandelier, would they have been able to exempt it? How about a large mirror mounted on a large piece of plywood and affixed to a wall? See Strain v. Green, 25 Wash. 2d 692, 172 P.2d 216 (1946).

Personal Property

Personal property includes all objects and rights capable of being owned that are not real property or fixtures. Personal property may be *tangible* or *intangible*. Tangible personal property is that which can be seen or felt, such as clothing, automobiles, animals, and other objects. Intangible property is property that cannot be seen or felt, like bank accounts, stock in a corporation, bonds, debts, ideas, copyrighted materials, patents, and trade secrets. Intangible personal property is often evidenced by a document, but the document (e.g., passbook, stock certificate, bond) only represents the property. The document is not the property itself.

The *Uniform Commercial Code* provides statutory authority for most personal property transactions, including sales (Article 2), security interests in personal property (Article 9), and negotiable instruments (Article 3). This section concentrates on issues that arise when there is no evidence of title for personal property. Assume you bought this book at the local bookstore. You are the true owner of the book. How do you prove your ownership? You may have retained your sales receipt, or perhaps you have marked the book in some unique manner, but there is no title to the book, as there is with real estate or an automobile. Problems can arise if someone else comes into possession of your book (perhaps they found it, stole it, or were entrusted with it) and sells it to a third person. Whose interests (the true owner or the innocent third person) does the law choose to protect?

Finders of Property

Finders of personal property lawfully acquire possession of property that is *lost, mislaid,* or *abandoned*. A finder may also come into lawful possession of treasure trove. At common law, property was lost when the true owner involuntarily terminated his or her possession and did not know the property's location. Property was mislaid if the owner placed it somewhere and then forgot to reclaim it or forgot where she had placed it.[46] For example, this morning before class you discover your book is not in your backpack. It must have fallen out sometime yesterday while you were walking across campus. Your book is lost. You did not voluntarily terminate possession of the book and you do not know where it is. However, if you laid the book on a table in the local bar and left it there, the book is mislaid. At common law, the distinction between lost and mislaid property had legal ramifications if the lost or mislaid property was found. If the found property was lost property, the finder had superior title to the property against all but the true owner. In our lost book example, if another student finds your book on a campus sidewalk, she would have the right to possess the book against all but you. The common law rule that the one with prior possession had superior title to all but the true owner was modified for mislaid property, since the true owner was more likely to be reunited with the property if its location does not change. If the property was mislaid and it was found in a public place (like a shop or an inn), then the owner of the public place had the superior right of possession.[47] Again, back to our example—if another student finds your book in the local bar where you left it, at common law the owner of the bar has a superior right to possession than does the student. Of course, as the true owner, the bar owner's right of possession is inferior to your right of possession.

Abandoned property is property for which true owners intentionally relinquished their ownership rights. Assume you threw your book into the trash bin outside of your apartment building, knowing the trash bin is emptied the next morning. The finder of abandoned property at common law was treated in a similar manner to the finder of lost property.[48] Most states today have discarded distinctions between lost, misplaced, or abandoned property. Lost property statutes typically require the finder of property to deposit the property with the local law enforcement agency. After a period of time (and publication in some cases), the rights of the true owner are terminated and the finder is vested with ownership.[49]

Treasure trove at common law was intentionally secreted gold or silver that was usually buried. Eventually, the term came to include all secreted valuables. It belonged to the king, no matter who found it. In the United States, however, the general rule is that treasure trove is treated like lost property.[50]

Bailments, Thieves, and Innocent Third Parties

Bailments are created when one person delivers personal property to another for a specific purpose. A bailment can be for the sole benefit of the *bailor* (the person delivering the property), for the sole benefit of the *bailee* (the party accepting the property), or for the benefit of both. Bailments for the sole benefit of the bailee or the bailor are *gratuitous bailments*.[51] If you hand your book to a classmate and ask her to watch your book while you buy a drink, a gratuitous bailment for the sole benefit of the bailor has been created. On the other hand, if you loan your classmate your book overnight so she can read the assigned material, a gratuitous bailment for the sole benefit of the bailee has been created. When the bailment is for the sole benefit of the bailor, the bailee is responsible only for gross negligence. The bailee is liable for even slight negligence if the bailment is for the sole benefit of the bailee. In some jurisdictions, all bailments are subject to normal negligence rules.[52] In the example of your classmate watching your book, if someone steals it while she is talking with the instructor, she is most likely not liable for the loss. Although she may have been negligent, she was probably not grossly negligent. However, had she thrown the book out into the hall and it was stolen, she would probably be liable for the loss. Revisiting the example of a bailment for the sole benefit of the bailee, if your class-mate loses your book while she is borrowing it, she will likely be liable for the loss, unless she can show she was not even slightly negligent.

In the case of *nongratuitous bailments*, the bailee must redeliver the goods under bailment on demand of the bailor. The bailee is liable for damages or loss if he or she is negligent in his or her care of the goods. However, if the bailee misdelivers the goods or refuses to deliver the goods upon demand, he or she is strictly liable for the conversion of the goods (a forced sale).[53] Assume you take your book to the bookbinder to have it repaired. A nongratuitous bailment has been created (it is for the benefit of both parties). If you return on the day the book was to have been repaired and the bookbinder explains that he had spilled grape juice on the book, he would be liable if it can be shown that he was negligent (drinking grape juice over a book would likely be negli-gent). If, however, the bookbinder says that he gave the book to some-one who looks just like you, he would be liable in conversion for the value of the book, even if he used reasonable care.

Commercial establishments often attempt to limit bailee liability by *adhesion contract*, such as the parking ticket that limits a parking ga-rage's liability for stolen vehicles, damage to vehicles, or items stolen from automobiles parked in the garage. As a general proposition, the use of adhesion contracts to limit bailee liability is not commonly al-lowed. Justice DeBruler of the Indiana Supreme Court provides a good summary of the law in his dissent in *Carr v. Hoosier Photo Supplies, Inc.*[54]

> As a general rule, professional bailees escape or diminish liability for their own negligence by posting signs or handing out receipts. . . . [P]rinted forms of similar import which commonly appear on packages, signs, chits, tickets, tokens or receipts with which we are all bombarded daily. No one does, or can reasonably be expected to take the time to carefully read the front, back, and sides of such things.

It must be noted, however, that bailees and bailors are free to form their own bailment contract. If a bailee can show that the bailor was aware of the terms of the adhesion contract and accepted those terms (by de-livering the property after becoming aware of the terms), the liability limitations will be upheld. The plaintiff in *Carr v. Hoosier Photo Sup-plies, Inc.* was a lawyer and acknowledged that he knew of the liability limitation when he delivered the rolls of film for developing. He was held to the terms of the adhesion contract.

Many commercial bailments are regulated by statute. Personal property leases are governed by Article 2A of the *Uniform Commercial Code* (UCC), and consumer personal property leases are treated under the *Federal Consumer Leasing Act.* Article 7 of the UCC controls commercial warehousing. Most jurisdictions also specify the liability of innkeepers and safe deposit box lessors for the personal property of their customers.[55]

Bailees may, in certain situations, transfer a better title to property to an innocent third party than the bailee had. Under both the common law and § 2-403 of the UCC, if a bailor entrusts goods to a bailee under circumstances in which a reasonable person could believe the bailee was the owner of the property, and the bailee sells those goods to a *bona fide purchaser,* defined as a buyer who is acting in good faith and without knowledge of a contrary ownership claim, the bailor may not proceed against the bona fide purchaser.[56] A typical situation might involve a jewelry store. Assume your watch quits working. You take it to the local jewelry store for repair. The jeweler sells the brand of watch you are having repaired. He tells you to pick up the watch in a week, gives you a claim ticket, and you leave the premises. During the week, the jeweler repairs the watch. He puts it in the display case and sells it to a customer who had no knowledge that the watch did not belong to the jeweler. Although your actions were not wrongful, you would have no action against the customer who bought your watch. The legal rule amounts to a balancing of your rights as the rightful owner against the rights of the innocent bona fide purchaser. In this situation, the scale tips in favor of the innocent bona fide purchaser. Of course, you still have a cause of action against the jeweler.

Even a thief has the right to possession of property that is superior to all except the true owner (or law enforcement personnel or others acting on behalf of the true owner). Assume that someone stole your book. The thief has the right to stop another person from taking the book from him. Unlike the case of certain bailments, a bona fide purchaser of stolen property does not acquire title that is superior to that of the true owner. Although the possession of stolen property by bona fide purchasers is lawful, it becomes unlawful if they refuse a demand for the property by the true owner.[57]

Digital Barbarians at the Gate: Copyrighted Property Under Siege

The 1990s to early 2000s has been a time of tremendous growth in Internet use and the digitalization of products distributed by the entertainment industry, especially audio, video, and photographic products. The digitalization of copyrighted entertainment industry products has led to mass "pirating," defined as using or acquiring the product without paying. There are two types of copyright infringement: direct and secondary. *Direct copyright infringement* is the copying and unauthorized use of copyrighted material by the individual or entity being sued.

No intent is required, just a showing of copying and unauthorized use. *Secondary copyright infringement* is applicable when the party being charged did not personally take part in the infringing activity, but still may have some responsibility for the activity.

There are two subcategories of secondary copyright infringement: vicarious and contributory infringement. Liability for *vicarious copyright infringement* requires that the defendant had the right and ability to control the infringer's activities and the defendant received a direct financial benefit from the infringer's activities. *Contributory copyright infringement* requires a showing that the defendant had knowledge of the infringing activity and induced, caused, or materially contributed to the infringement activity.[58]

Before we look at the court case generating the most publicity (*Napster*), we present a brief review of the entertainment industry's methods of distributing its product, and how it has reacted to technology that threatened its business models. A sketch of the statutory scheme that existed at the time of the *Napster* controversy follows.

Entertainment Industry Reaction to Technology Advances

Once upon a time, audio recordings were distributed on phonographic records. Consumers bought the "albums" and played them on turntables.[59] When audio tape recorders became available to the general public, consumers were able to record copyrighted audio products onto a tape and play (or share) the resulting recorded material. Because of the technology, however, the unauthorized taped recordings were inferior in quality rendering their commercial appeal minimal, because the analog recordings produced a persistent background hiss. The recording industry turned next to digital recordings on compact disks (CDs). Again, due to the inferior quality of analog audio tape recorders, commercial pirating activity was minimal.

Significantly, all that changed when digital audio tape recorders (DATs) became available to the public. For the first time, members of the general public could produce high-quality copies of copyright protected materials. An agreement between the music industry and DAT manufacturers led to a fee paid by the DAT manufacturers into a fund for royalty payments to artists and others holding copyrights. As we discuss in the following section, the agreement was codified as part of the *Audio Home Recording Act of 1992*. Nonetheless, because mass production of DAT tapes remained time-consuming, mass sharing proved unlikely. However, it did not take long for a new technology to upset the apple cart. MP3 technology allowed a consumer to "rip" the digital data from a CD into a compressed file and store it on a computer hard drive. The audio quality was virtually the same as found on the CD. Since the audio recording was now on a computer hard disk, sharing or selling the ripped files became widespread.

The film industry traditionally distributed its product on film to theaters that exhibited the films for the public. The film industry charged the theater owners, who in turn, charged the public. Unauthorized copying of film was expensive and unusual. Television networks and independent television channels also broadcast copyrighted video products. Television broadcasters paid copyright holders a fee for broadcasting rights. The broadcasters then sold advertising and broadcast the copyrighted material to be viewed by consumers at home or other locations. When videotape recorders (VCRs) became available to the public, consumers were able to record and own a copy of any copyrighted material broadcast over television. The film industry was troubled, and as a result moved against Sony Corporation (the manufacturer of Betamax recorders) for copyright infringement. In *Sony Corp. of America v. Universal City Studios,*[60] the U.S. Supreme Court held that Sony was not vicariously liable for copyright infringement by selling its videotape recorders.

The decision applied two important copyright law doctrines. First, the *Fair Use Doctrine.* Generally, under the Fair Use Doctrine, a third party may copy or use a copyrighted work without the consent of the owner if it is done in a fair or reasonable manner. There are four factors a court should consider: (1) the purpose and character of the use, including whether the use is commercial or for nonprofit educational purposes; (2) the nature of the copyrighted work; (3) the amount and substantiality of the portion used in relation to the copyrighted work as a whole; and (4) the effect of the use upon the potential market for or value of the copyrighted work.[61] The *Sony* Court determined that consumers' taping free broadcasts of copyrighted programming was a fair use of the material because they were simply time shifting when they viewed the program.[62] The second important copyright doctrine that influenced the *Sony* Court is the *Staple Article of Commerce Doctrine.* The Court reasoned that

> the sale of copying equipment, like the sale of other articles of commerce, does not constitute contributory infringement of a copyright if the product is widely used for legitimate, unobjectionable purposes, or even if merely capable of substantial noninfringing uses.[63]

The film industry altered its business model in reaction to videotape technology. Movies and other video products became widely available for sale or rental via videotape once the product was no longer in first run at theaters or on television. In effect, an additional and lucrative market was established that added significant revenues.

In the mid-1990s, video products began to be distributed on digital video disks (DVDs). The DVDs are encrypted with the Content Scrambling System (CSS). Manufacturers of DVD players are given a license to use a descrambling system that allows the playing of encrypted

DVDs. In 1999, a young Norwegian developed DeCSS, a program that descrambles encrypted DVDs and copies the DVD files to a computer hard drive. Those files may be played on nonauthorized computers and the files can be shared or sold. The DeCSS program was posted on the Internet, and other websites copied and posted it as well. One of those websites, <2600.com>, owned by the publisher of the *Hackers Quarterly,* refused to take down the DeCSS program after receiving a cease and desist letter from the Motion Picture Association of America (MPAA). The MPAA brought suit against the website owner, seeking an injunction to mandate that the DeCSS program be taken down. In *Universal Studios, Inc. v. Reimerdes,*[64] the website owner was found to be in violation of the Digital Millennium Copyright Act of 1998 (discussed below).

The vicarious liability of Internet Service Providers (ISPs) and Bulletin Board Service (BBS) owners for the copyright infringement activity of their subscribers has also been at issue. As a general rule, the more knowledge and control of the items their subscribers place on the service, the more likely it is the owner or operator of the service will be held liable for his or her subscribers' copyright infringements. Two cases illustrate the general rule. The first, *Religious Technology Center v. Netcom,*[65] involved a vocal critic of the Church of Scientology, who subscribed to a BBS and posted portions of L. Ron Hubbard's copyrighted works on the BBS. Netcom's sole involvement was providing the BBS access to the Internet. Netcom was asked by the copyright holder to keep the critic off the Internet. Netcom refused. The court compared Netcom's role to that of an owner of a public photocopier. All the ISP did was build and maintain a computer system that allowed its subscribers access to the Internet. To support a charge of vicarious copyright infringement, the holder would need to show that Netcom had the right and ability to control the infringer's actions and that Netcom received a direct financial benefit from the infringement. Although there was some question whether Netcom had the right and ability to control the infringer's actions, the court determined that Netcom did not receive a direct financial benefit. Netcom charged a flat monthly fee and there was no evidence that the infringer's postings on the BBS increased the number of Netcom subscribers. The claim of vicarious copyright infringement was dismissed.[66]

In *Playboy Enterprises, Inc. v. Hardenburgh,*[67] the level of the defendant's policing activities contributed to his eventual direct and contributory copyright infringement liability. Hardenburgh was the owner of a BBS that allowed paid subscribers to download a set number of photos per month from the collection Hardenburgh maintained on the BBS. To increase the number of photos on the BBS and possibly increase the number of subscribers, Hardenburgh gave subscribers credits if they uploaded pictures not already on the BBS. Uploaded pictures were maintained in a separate file until an employee inspected them to determine if they were copyrighted. Only after the inspection were they made available to subscribers. This procedure was obviously ineffective or a ruse, for substantial numbers of pictures copyrighted by Playboy were on the BBS available to the public. The court determined that Hardenburgh's solicitation of photo uploads and prescreening activity took him out of the passive role a BBS owner or ISP owner might occupy. Rather, he was directly involved in infringement activities. The court found Hardenburgh's activities constituted contributory infringement as well. He had at least constructive knowledge of the infringement activity, and he induced, caused, or encouraged the infringement activity of his subscribers.[68]

Federal Copyright Statutes

The *Copyright Act of 1976*, as amended in 1992 and 1998, is the foundation for a statutory scheme protecting original works of authorship fixed in any tangible medium of expression, now known or later developed.[69] A copyright holder may exclusively do or authorize the following:

(1) to reproduce the copyrighted work in copies or phonorecords;

(2) to prepare derivative works based upon the copyrighted work;

(3) to distribute copies or phonorecords of the copyrighted work to the public by sale or other transfer of ownership or by rental, lease, or lending;

(4) in the case of literary, musical, dramatic, and choreographic works; pantomimes; and motion pictures and other audiovisual works, to perform the copyrighted work publicly; and

(5) in the case of literary, musical, dramatic, and choreographic works; pantomimes; and pictorial, graphic, or sculptural works, including the individual images of a motion picture or other audiovisual work, to display the copyrighted work publicly.[70]

The use of copyrighted material under one of the fair use exceptions or uses not specifically enumerated is not protected.[71]

In reaction to the introduction of DAT recorders, Congress enacted the *Audio Home Recording Act of 1992*. As discussed above, manufacturers of digital recording devices pay fees into a fund, out of which royalties are paid to copyright holders. At the same time, the Act protects consumers from copyright infringement liability for the private noncommercial taping of copyrighted audio or video products.[72]

The 1998 amendments encompassed two pieces of legislation. Title I of the *Digital Millennium Copyright Act* implements two treaties [the World Intellectual Copyright Organization (WIPO) Copyright Treaty and the WIPO Performances and Phonograms Treaty]. Title I prohibits circumventing the technological protection (encryption) that controls access to a digital copyrighted work. It also prohibits the creation or making available the means of circumventing the protection technology or manufacturing, importing, offering to the public, providing, or otherwise trafficking in any technology that allows the circumvention of protection technology for any digitized copyrighted work. To apply, the prohibited technology must be designed primarily for circumvention, have limited commercial noncircumvention uses, and be marketed primarily for circumvention. Exceptions exist for reverse engineering, encryption research, privacy protection, some analog devices, government activities, and use by educational institutions and law enforcement.[73] This is the statutory provision that the defendant in *Universal Studios, Inc. v. Reimerdes* was found to have violated by making the DeCSS program available to the public on his website.

Title II of the Digital Millennium Copyright Act consists of the *Online Copyright Infringement Liability Limitation Act.*[74] It adds section 512 to title 17 of the U.S. Code. Section 512 provides ISPs four safe harbors from liability for copyright infringement. The first two safe harbors apply to infringing data that go through the ISP's system. First, the ISP is not liable for infringing material that is transmitted, routed, or using its connections in a transitory manner. Second, an ISP is not liable for infringing material that is temporarily cached. To qualify for treatment under the first two safe harbors, the ISP must be only a passive data conduit. The third safe harbor protects an ISP from liability for infringing material residing on its system at the direction of others. The ISP must have no actual knowledge of, or knowledge of facts and circumstances of, the infringing activity. No financial benefit may accrue to the ISP from storing the infringing material. Once the ISP possesses knowledge of a user's infringing activity, the ISP must act expeditiously to remove or disable access to the infringing material. The fourth and final safe harbor protects ISPs from liability for resident links, search engines, and other references to other Internet locations that may contain infringing material. Again, the ISP must have no actual knowledge of, or knowledge of facts and circumstances about, the infringing activity and receive no financial benefit from it. Once knowledge of the infringing activity is acquired, expeditious removal or disabling is required. To be eligible for any of the safe harbors of section 512, the ISP must have and use a policy that provides for the termination of repeat copyright infringers, and it must register an agent with the copyright office to receive notice of infringing materials or activity. The ISP must also have a policy of noninterference with standard copyright protection measures.[75]

The foregoing sections have set the technological, judicial, and statutory stages for the *Napster* case. What follows are portions of the U.S. Court of Appeals for the Ninth Circuit's 2001 decision.

A&M Records, Inc. v. Napster, Inc.
U.S. Court of Appeals for the Ninth Circuit
239 F.3d 1004 (2001)

OPINION BY: BEEZER: Circuit Judge: Plaintiffs are engaged in the commercial recording, distribution and sale of copyrighted musical compositions and sound recordings. The complaint alleges that Napster, Inc. (Napster) is a contributory and vicarious copyright infringer. On July 26, 2000, the district court granted plaintiffs' motion for a preliminary injunction. The injunction was slightly modified by written opinion on August 10, 2000. A&M Records, Inc. v. Napster, Inc., 114 F. Supp. 2d 896 (N.D. Cal. 2000). The district court preliminarily enjoined Napster "engaging in, or facilitating others in copying, downloading, uploading, transmitting, or distributing plaintiffs' copyrighted musical compositions and sound recordings, protected by either federal or state law, without express permission of the rights owner.". . .

We entered a temporary stay of the preliminary injunction pending resolution of this appeal. We affirm in part, reverse in part and remand. . . .

In 1987, the Moving Picture Experts Group set a standard file format for the storage of audio recordings in a digital format called MPEG-3, abbreviated as MP3. Digital MP3 files are created through a process colloquially called "ripping." Ripping software allows a computer owner to copy an audio compact disk (audio CD) directly onto a computer's hard drive by compressing the audio information on the CD into the MP3 format. The MP3's compressed format allows for rapid transmission of digital audio files from one computer to another by electronic mail or any other file transfer protocol.

Napster facilitates the transmission of MP3 files between and among its users. Through a process commonly called "peer-to-peer" file sharing, Napster allows its users to: (1) make MP3 music files stored on individual computer hard drives available for copying by other Napster users; (2) search for MP3 music files stored on other users' computers; and (3) transfer exact copies of the contents of other users' MP3 files from one computer to another via the Internet. These functions are made possible by Napster's MusicShare software, available free of charge from Napster's Internet site, and Napster's network servers and server-side software. Napster provides technical support for the indexing and searching of MP3 files, as well as for its other functions, including a chat room, where users can meet to discuss music, and a directory where participating artists can provide information about their music. . . .

Plaintiffs claim Napster users are engaged in the wholesale reproduction and distribution of copyrighted works, all constituting direct infringement. The district court agreed. We note that the district court's conclusion that plaintiffs have presented a prima facie case of direct infringement by Napster users is not presently appealed by Napster. We only need briefly address the threshold requirements.

A. Infringement

Plaintiffs must satisfy two requirements to present a prima facie case of direct infringement: (1) they must show ownership of the allegedly infringed material and (2) they must demonstrate that the alleged infringers violate at least one exclusive right granted to copyright holders under 17 U.S.C. § 106. . . . Plaintiffs have sufficiently demonstrated ownership. The record supports the district court's determination that as much as eighty-seven percent of the files available on Napster may be copyrighted and more than seventy percent may be owned or administered by plaintiffs. . . .

The district court further determined that plaintiffs' exclusive rights under § 106 were violated: here the evidence establishes that a majority of Napster users use the service to download and upload copyrighted music. . . . And by doing that, it constitutes—the uses constitute direct infringement of plaintiffs' musical compositions, recordings. We agree that plaintiffs have shown that Napster users infringe at least two of the copyright holders' exclusive rights: the rights of reproduction, and distribution. Napster users who upload file names to the search index for others to copy violate plaintiffs' distribution rights. Napster users who download files containing copyrighted music violate plaintiffs' reproduction rights. . . .

B. Fair Use

Napster contends that its users do not directly infringe plaintiffs' copyrights because the users are engaged in fair use of the material. . . . The fair use of a copyrighted work . . . is not an infringement of copyright. Napster identifies three specific alleged fair uses: sampling, where users make temporary copies of a work before purchasing; space-shifting, where users access a sound recording through the Napster system that they already own in audio CD format; and permissive distribution of recordings by both new and established artists.

The district court considered factors listed in 17 U.S.C. § 107, which guide a court's fair use determination. These factors are: (1) the purpose and character of the use; (2) the nature of the copyrighted work; (3) the amount and substantiality of the portion used in relation to the work as a whole; and (4) the effect of the use upon the potential market for the work or the value of the work. The district court concluded that Napster users are not fair users. We agree. . . .

1. Purpose and Character of the Use

This factor focuses on whether the new work merely replaces the object of the original creation or instead adds a further purpose or different character. In other words, this factor asks whether and to what extent the new work is transformative. . . . The district court first concluded that downloading MP3 files does not transform the copyrighted work. . . . This conclusion is supportable. Courts have been reluctant to find fair use when an original work is merely retransmitted in a different medium. . . .

This purpose and character element also requires the district court to determine whether the allegedly infringing use is commercial or noncommercial. . . . A commercial use weighs against a finding of fair use but is not conclusive on the issue. The district court determined that Napster users engage in commercial use of the copyrighted materials largely because (1) a host user sending a file cannot be said to engage in a personal use when distributing that file to an anonymous requester and (2) Napster users get for free something they would ordinarily have to buy. . . . The district court's findings are not clearly erroneous. . . .

2. The Nature of the Use

Works that are creative in nature are closer to the core of intended copyright protection than are more fact-based works. . . . The district court determined that plaintiffs' copyrighted musical compositions and sound recordings are creative in nature . . . which cuts against a finding of fair use under the second factor. . . . We find no error in the district court's conclusion.

3. The Portion Used

While wholesale copying does not preclude fair use per se, copying an entire work militates against a finding of fair use. . . . The district court determined that Napster users engage in wholesale copying of copyrighted work because file transfer necessarily involves copying the entirety of the copyrighted work. We agree. We note, however, that under certain circumstances, a court will conclude that a use is fair even when the protected work is copied in its entirety. . . .

4. Effect of Use on Market

Fair use, when properly applied, is limited to copying by others that does not materially impair the marketability of the work which is copied. . . . The importance of this [fourth] factor will vary, not only with the amount of harm, but also with the relative strength of the showing on the other factors. . . . The proof required to demonstrate present or future market harm varies with the purpose and character of the use:

. . . If the intended use is for commercial gain, that likelihood [of market harm] may be presumed. But if it is for a noncommercial purpose, the likelihood must be demonstrated.

Addressing this factor, the district court concluded that Napster harms the market in at least two ways: it reduces audio CD sales among college students and it raises barriers to plaintiffs' entry into the market for the digital downloading of music. . . . The district court relied on evidence plaintiffs submitted to show that Napster use harms the market for their copyrighted musical compositions and sound recordings. . . . Notably, plaintiffs' expert, Dr. E. Deborah Jay, conducted a survey (the Jay Report) using a random sample of college and university students to track their reasons for using Napster and the impact Napster had on their music purchases. The court recognized that the Jay Report focused on just one segment of the Napster user population and found evidence of lost sales attributable to college use to be probative of irreparable harm for purposes of the preliminary injunction motion. . . .

Plaintiffs also offered a study conducted by Michael Fine, Chief Executive Officer of Soundscan, (the

Fine Report) to determine the effect of online sharing of MP3 files in order to show irreparable harm. Fine found that online file sharing had resulted in a loss of album sales within college markets. . . .

Plaintiffs' expert Dr. David J. Teece studied several issues (Teece Report), including whether plaintiffs had suffered or were likely to suffer harm in their existing and planned businesses due to Napster use. . . . We, therefore, conclude that the district court made sound findings related to Napster's deleterious effect on the present and future digital download market. Moreover, lack of harm to an established market cannot deprive the copyright holder of the right to develop alternative markets for the works. . . . Here . . . the record supports the district court's finding that the record company plaintiffs have already expended considerable funds and effort to commence Internet sales and licensing for digital downloads. . . . Having digital downloads available for free on the Napster system necessarily harms the copyright holders' attempts to charge for the same downloads. . . .

We first address plaintiffs' claim that Napster is liable for contributory copyright infringement. Traditionally, one who, with knowledge of the infringing activity, induces, causes or materially contributes to the infringing conduct of another, may be held liable as a contributory infringer. . . . The district court determined that plaintiffs in all likelihood would establish Napster's liability as a contributory infringer. The district court did not err; Napster, by its conduct, knowingly encourages and assists the infringement of plaintiffs' copyrights.

A. Knowledge

Contributory liability requires that the secondary infringer know or have reason to know of direct infringement. . . . The district court found that Napster had both actual and constructive knowledge that its users exchanged copyrighted music. The district court also concluded that the law does not require knowledge of specific acts of infringement and rejected Napster's contention that because the company cannot distinguish infringing from noninfringing files, it does not know of the direct infringement. . . .

It is apparent from the record that Napster has knowledge, both actual and constructive, of direct infringement. Napster claims that it is nevertheless protected from contributory liability by the teaching of Sony Corp. v. Universal City Studios, Inc., 464 U.S. 417 (1984). We disagree. We observe that Napster's actual, specific knowledge of direct infringement renders Sony's holding of limited assistance to Napster. . . .

We are bound to follow *Sony*, and will not impute the requisite level of knowledge to Napster merely because peer-to-peer file sharing technology may be used to infringe plaintiffs' copyrights. . . . We depart from the reasoning of the district court that Napster failed to demonstrate that its system is capable of commercially significant noninfringing uses. . . . The district court improperly confined the use analysis to current uses, ignoring the system's capabilities. . . . Consequently, the district court placed undue weight on the proportion of current infringing use as compared to current and future noninfringing use. . . . Nonetheless, whether we might arrive at a different result is not the issue here. . . . The instant appeal occurs at an early point in the proceedings and the fully developed factual record may be materially different from that initially before the district court. Regardless of the number of Napster's infringing versus noninfringing uses, the evidentiary record here supported the district court's finding that plaintiffs would likely prevail in establishing that Napster knew or had reason to know of its users' infringement of plaintiffs' copyrights. . . .

We agree that if a computer system operator learns of specific infringing material available on his system and fails to purge such material from the system, the operator knows of and contributes to direct infringement. . . . Conversely, absent any specific information which identifies infringing activity, a computer system operator cannot be liable for contributory infringement merely because the structure of the system allows for the exchange of copyrighted material. . . . To enjoin simply because a computer network allows for infringing use would, in our opinion, violate *Sony* and potentially restrict activity unrelated to infringing use.

We nevertheless conclude that sufficient knowledge exists to impose contributory liability when linked to demonstrated infringing use of the Napster system. . . . The record supports the district court's finding that Napster has actual knowledge that specific infringing material is available using its system, that it could block access to the system by suppliers of the infringing material, and that it failed to remove the material. . . .

B. Material Contribution

Under the facts as found by the district court, Napster materially contributes to the infringing activity. [T]he district court concluded that without the support services defendant provides, Napster users could not find and download the music they want with the ease of which defendant boasts. . . . We agree that Napster provides the site and facilities for direct infringement. . . .

We affirm the district court's conclusion that plaintiffs have demonstrated a likelihood of success on the merits of the contributory copyright infringement claim. . . .

We turn to the question whether Napster engages in vicarious copyright infringement. . . . In the context of copyright law, vicarious liability extends beyond an employer/employee relationship to cases in which a defendant has the right and ability to supervise the infringing activity and also has a direct financial interest in such activities. . . .

A. Financial Benefit

The district court determined that plaintiffs had demonstrated they would likely succeed in establishing that Napster has a direct financial interest in the infringing activity. We agree. Financial benefit exists where the availability of infringing material acts as a draw for customers. . . . Ample evidence supports the district court's finding that Napster's future revenue is directly dependent upon increases in user-base. More users register with the Napster system as the quality and quantity of available music increases. . . .

B. Supervision

The district court determined that Napster has the right and ability to supervise its users' conduct. . . .

The ability to block infringers' access to a particular environment for any reason whatsoever is evidence of the right and ability to supervise. . . . Here, plaintiffs have demonstrated that Napster retains the right to control access to its system. Napster has an express reservation of rights policy, stating on its website that it expressly reserves the right to refuse service and terminate accounts in [its] discretion, including, but not limited to, if Napster believes that user conduct violates applicable law . . . or for any reason in Napster's sole discretion, with or without cause.

To escape imposition of vicarious liability, the reserved right to police must be exercised to its fullest extent. Turning a blind eye to detectable acts of infringement for the sake of profit gives rise to liability. . . . The district court correctly determined that Napster had the right and ability to police its system and failed to exercise that right to prevent the exchange of copyrighted material. The district court, however, failed to recognize that the boundaries of the premises that Napster controls and patrols are limited. . . . Put differently, Napster's reserved right and ability to police is cabined by the system's current architecture. As shown by the record, the Napster system does not read the content of indexed files, other than to check that they are in the proper MP3 format.

Napster, however, has the ability to locate infringing material listed on its search indices, and the right to terminate users' access to the system. The file name indices, therefore, are within the premises that Napster has the ability to police. We recognize that the files are user-named and may not match copyrighted material exactly (for example, the artist or song could be spelled wrong). For Napster

to function effectively, however, file names must reasonably or roughly correspond to the material contained in the files, otherwise no user could ever locate any desired music. As a practical matter, Napster, its users and the record company plaintiffs have equal access to infringing material by employing Napster's search function.

Our review of the record requires us to accept the district court's conclusion that plaintiffs have demonstrated a likelihood of success on the merits of the vicarious copyright infringement claim. Napster's failure to police the system's premises, combined with a showing that Napster financially benefits from the continuing availability of infringing files on its system, leads to the imposition of vicarious liability.

We next address whether Napster has asserted defenses which would preclude the entry of a preliminary injunction.

Napster alleges that two statutes insulate it from liability. First, Napster asserts that its users engage in actions protected by § 1008 of the Audio Home Recording Act of 1992. Second, Napster argues that its liability for contributory and vicarious infringement is limited by the Digital Millennium Copyright Act. . . . We address the application of each statute in turn.

A. Audio Home Recording Act

The statute states in part: No action may be brought under this title alleging infringement of copyright based on the manufacture, importation, or distribution of a digital audio recording device, a digital audio recording medium, an analog recording device, or an analog recording medium, or based on the noncommercial use by a consumer of such a device or medium for making digital musical recordings or analog musical recordings. . . . Napster contends that MP3 file exchange is the type of noncommercial use protected from infringement actions by the statute. Napster asserts it cannot be secondarily liable for users' nonactionable exchange of copyrighted musical recordings. . . .

We agree with the district court that the Audio Home Recording Act does not cover the downloading of MP3 files to computer hard drives. First, under the plain meaning of the Act's definition of digital audio recording devices, computers (and their hard drives) are not digital audio recording devices because their primary purpose is not to make digital audio copied recordings. . . .

B. Digital Millennium Copyright Act

Napster also interposes a statutory limitation on liability by asserting the protections of the safe harbor from copyright infringement suits for Internet service providers contained in the Digital Millennium Copyright Act. . . . The district court did not give this statutory limitation any weight favoring a denial of temporary injunctive relief. The court concluded that Napster has failed to persuade this court that subsection 512(d) shelters contributory infringers.

We need not accept a blanket conclusion that § 512 of the Digital Millennium Copyright Act will never protect secondary infringers. . . . The limitations in subsections (a) through (d) protect qualifying service providers from liability for all monetary relief for direct, vicarious, and contributory infringement. . . .

We do not agree that Napster's potential liability for contributory and vicarious infringement renders the Digital Millennium Copyright Act inapplicable per se. We instead recognize that this issue will be more fully developed at trial. At this stage of the litigation, plaintiffs raise serious questions regarding Napster's ability to obtain shelter under § 512, and plaintiffs also demonstrate that the balance of hardships tips in their favor. . . . Plaintiffs have raised and continue to raise significant questions under this statute, including: (1) whether Napster is an Internet service provider as defined by U.S.C. § 512(d); (2) whether copyright owners must give a service provider official notice of infringing activity in order for it to have knowledge or awareness of infringing activity on its system; and (3) whether Napster complies with § 512(i), which requires a service provider to timely establish a detailed copyright compliance policy. . . .

Napster contends that even if the district court's preliminary determinations that it is liable for facilitating copyright infringement are correct, the district court improperly rejected valid affirmative defenses of waiver, implied license and copyright misuse. . . .

A. Waiver

Napster argues that the district court erred in not finding that plaintiffs knowingly provided consumers with technology designed to copy and distribute MP3 files over the Internet and, thus, waived any legal authority to exercise exclusive control over creation and distribution of MP3 files. The district court, however, was not convinced that the record companies created the monster that is now devouring their intellectual property rights. . . . We find no error in the district court's finding that in hastening the proliferation of MP3 files, plaintiffs did nothing more than seek partners for their commercial downloading ventures and develop music players for files they planned to sell over the Internet.

B. Implied License

Napster also argues that plaintiffs granted the company an implied license by encouraging MP3 file exchange over the Internet. Courts have found implied licenses only in narrow circumstances where one party created a work at the other's request and handed it over, intending that [the other] copy and distribute it. . . . The district court observed that no evidence exists to support this defense: indeed, the RIAA gave defendant express notice that it objected to the availability of its members' copyrighted music on Napster.

C. Misuse

The defense of copyright misuse forbids a copyright holder from securing an exclusive right or limited monopoly not granted by the Copyright Office. . . . Napster alleges that online distribution is not within the copyright monopoly. According to Napster, plaintiffs have colluded to use their copyrights to extend their control to online distributions.

We find no error in the district court's preliminary rejection of this affirmative defense. The misuse defense prevents copyright holders from leveraging their limited monopoly to allow them control of areas outside the monopoly. . . . There is no evidence here that plaintiffs seek to control areas outside of their grant of monopoly. Rather, plaintiffs seek to control reproduction and distribution of their copyrighted works, exclusive rights of copyright holders. . . . That the copyrighted works are transmitted in another medium—MP3 format rather than audio CD—has no bearing on our analysis. . . .

The preliminary injunction which we stayed is overbroad because it places on Napster the entire burden of ensuring that no copying, downloading, uploading, transmitting, or distributing of plaintiffs' works occur on the system. As stated, we place the burden on plaintiffs to provide notice to Napster of copyrighted works and files containing such works available on the Napster system before Napster has the duty to disable access to the offending content. Napster, however, also bears the burden of policing the system within the limits of the system. Here, we recognize that this is not an exact science in that the files are user named. In crafting the injunction on remand, the district court should recognize that Napster's system does not currently appear to allow Napster access to users' MP3 files. . . .

Affirmed in part, reversed in part and remanded.

[Editor's note:[76]]

Case Questions for Discussion

1. Do you think Napster planned to make its site a profit-generating business?

2. Do you think Napster should be insulated from secondary copyright infringement liability as an ISP? Why or why not? How is Napster like an ISP? How is Napster different from an ISP?

3. What do you think was Napster's best argument?

4. If Napster had been successful in this case, how would artists and the music industry be compensated? Had Napster prevailed, would it have been the demise of the music industry?

5. If AOL users are exchanging copyright protected MP3 files via e-mail, would AOL be subject to an injunction like Napster was? If yes, why? If no, why not?

6. Do you think that if Congress had known a computer could be used to make digital audio recordings, they would have included computers as a digital audio recording device under the Audio Home Recording Act? If yes, do you think the Court of Appeals should have judicially recognized computers as a covered digital audio recording device?

Key Terms, Names, and Concepts

Abandoned property

Audio Home Recording Act of 1992

Bailment

Bona fide purchaser

Condition precedent

Condition subsequent

Contingent remainder

Contributory copyright infringement

Copyhold tenures

Curtesy

Cy Pres Doctrine

Direct copyright infringement

Doctrine of Worthier Title

Dower

Executory interest

Fair Use Doctrine

Fee simple

Fee imple determinable with possibility of reverter

Fee simple subject to a condition subsequent

Fee tail

Fixture

Free alienability of property

Freeholds

Future interests

Gratuitous bailment

Joint tenancy

Life estate

Life estate pur autre vie

Lost property

Military tenure

Mislaid property

Non-freehold estate

Nongratuitous bailment

Possibility of reverter

Periodic tenancy

Personal property

Powers of termination

Present possessory interest in real property

Real property

Remainder

Reversion

Right of reentry for condition
broken

Right of survivorship

Rule against perpetuities

Rule in Shelly's Case

Secondary copyright in-
fringement

Serjeanty tenure

Shifting executory interest

Socage tenure

Staple Article of Commerce
Doctrine

Springing executory interest

Tenancy by the entirety

Tenancy in common

Treasure trove

Unfree tenures

Unity

Vested remainder

Vested remainder subject to
complete divestment

Vested remainder subject
to open

Villein

Vicarious copyright in-
fringement

Wait and See Doctrine

Waste

Words of purchase

Discussion Questions

1. What are the three classes of property? Describe each class.

2. What is the largest interest in land one can own? What rights does it give the owner? Write a typical grant conveying such an interest.

3. "Omar to Ann for life, then to Bob and his heirs." What interests do Omar, Ann, and Bob have as a result of the grant? "Omar to Ann for life." What interests do Omar and Ann have as a result of the grant? "Omar to Ann for the life of Bob, then to Candy and her heirs." What are the interests of Omar, Ann, Bob, and Candy as a result of the grant?

4. "Omar to Alice and Bob." At common law, what interest would this grant create? How about in current practice in most states? Describe the rights that Alice and Bob have in each situation.

5. "Omar to Allan for life, then to the children of Allan who have reached the age of 20." What interests do each of the parties have as a result of the grant? Assume that Allan dies when his one child, Jane, is 15 years old. Who has what after Allan's death? What happens after Jane reaches age 20?

6. Alice employs Bob to plow and plant her field. As Bob is plowing, he hits something hard and discovers it is a steel box. He pries it open and to his surprise it is filled with 100-year-old gold coins. Just about that time, Alice stops by to check on Bob's progress and sees the gold coins. She demands that Bob give the coins to

her since they were found on her land. Bob refuses. Alice sues Bob for the gold coins. Who wins?

7. Andrew takes his mountain bike to the bike shop to have some routine maintenance done. He is to call for it in one week. Blake, an employee of the bike shop, does the maintenance and parks it in the showroom, where new and used bikes are displayed for sale. Two days later, Sue enters the shop, sees Andrew's bike, and asks Jeff, another employee of the bike shop, how much they want for Andrew's bike. There is no price on the bike, but there is a similar model and Jeff sells Andrew's bike to Sue for the same price as the shop was asking for the similar model. Later that day, Andrew sees Sue riding the bike, follows her, and is able to determine it is his bike (he had installed an unusual water bottle). He demands that Sue return his bike. She refuses. He sues her for the bike. Who wins?

8. What would be the result in question 7, if Jeff had charged Sue only half the price of the similar bike?

9. What would be the result if Jeff had stolen the bike from Andrew and sold it to Sue out of the bike shop for full price?

10. When Napster was open for business, did you download any music? Did you feel you were *stealing* it? If it were open today, knowing what you know, would you download music? Would you feel you were stealing it?

11. If Napster were allowed to continue to operate, do you believe the music industry, as we know it, could survive? Do you think artists and others who create original works should be afforded the exclusive right to their product?

12. Assume that all the major music companies join together and begin offering music downloads in the MP3 format for a fee. Would you pay to download music? How much would you pay in comparison to the cost of a CD by the same artist?

Suggested Additional Reading

Burke, Barlow, Ann M. Burkhart, and R. H. Helmholz. *Fundamentals of Property Law.* Charlotsville, VA: Lexis Law Publishing, 1999.

Burke, D. Barlow, Jr. *Personal Property in a Nutshell.* St. Paul, MN: West, 1983.

Brown, Ralph S., and Robert C. Denicola. *Copyright, Unfair Competition, and Other Topics Bearing on the Protection of Literary, Musical, and Artistic Works.* 7th ed. Westbrook, NY: Foundation Press, 1998.

Hill, David S. *Landlord and Tenant Law in a Nutshell.* 3rd ed. St. Paul, MN: West, 1995.

Rabin, Edward H., and Roberta Rosenthall Kwall. *Fundamentals of Modern Real Property Law*. 4th ed. Westbrook, NY: Foundation Press, 2000.

Sapherstein, Michael B. "Intelligent Agents and Copyright: Internet Technology Outpaces the Law . . . Again." *Boston College Intellectual Property & Technology Forum*. 102801 (October 28, 1997), available at: <http://www.bc.edu/itpf>, as of June 6, 2001.

Endnotes

1. State v. Ensley, 240 Ind. 472, 164 N.E.2d 342 (1960).
2. Cornelius J. Moynihan, *Introduction to the Law of Real Property* (St. Paul, MN: West, 1982), pp. 2–27.
3. Ralph E. Boyer, Herbert Hovenkamp, and Sheldon F. Kurtz, *The Law of Property: An Introductory Survey*, 4th ed. (St. Paul, MN: West, 1991) § 5[I][1].
4. Ibid., § 5[I][2]. "Until the property no longer is used as XXX" will also create a fee simple determinable.
5. Ibid., § 5[I][3].
6. 278 Ill. 529, 116 N.E. 161 (1917).
7. Boyer, *Introduction to the Law of Real Property*, § 5[I][5].
8. Ibid., § 5[I][6].
9. Ibid., §§ 5[I][7 & 8].
10. Michael Allen Wolf, ed., *Powell on Real Property* (original author the late Richard R. Powell) (New York: Matthew Bender and Co., 2001), § 15.08.
11. The discussion of waste applies generally to those who hold real property as periodic tenants as well.
12. Wolf, *Powell on Real Property*, § 56.05.
13. The leading U.S. case on ameliorative waste is Melms v. Pabst Brewing Co., 104 Wis. 7, 79 N.W. 738 (1899).
14. Wolf, *Powell on Real Property*, § 56.05.
15. *Ibid.*
16. Boyer, *Introduction to the Law of Real Property*, §§ 5[II][1 & 2].
17. Ibid., §§ 9.1–9.12. See also, the Residential Landlord and Tenant Act, drafted in final form by the National Conference of Commissioners on Uniform State Laws in 1972 at <http://www.lectlaw.com/files/lat03.htm>, as of June 6, 2001. It has been adopted in whole or in part by the following states: Alaska, Arizona, Connecticut, Florida, Hawaii, Iowa, Kansas, Kentucky, Michigan, Mississippi, Montana, Nebraska, New Mexico, Oklahoma, Oregon, Rhode Island, South Carolina, Tennessee, Virginia, and Washington. Uniform Law Commissioners' web site at <http://www.nccusl.org/nccusl/uniformact_factsheets/uniformacts-fs-urlta.asp>, as of June 6, 2001.
18. Wolf, *Powell on Real Property*, § 49.01. In general, all eight of the methods of concurrent ownership are still used in the United States today, except tenancies in coparcenary. A tenancy in coparcenary was created when an ancestor died with surviving daughters, but no son. The daughters would take equal shares in coparcenary. Today in states that still follow the common law, the daughters generally take as tenants in common. Boyer, *Introduction to the Law of Real Property*, § 5[III][4].
19. Boyer, *Introduction to the Law of Real Property*, § 5[III][3].

20. Wolf, *Powell on Real Property*, §§ 51.01, 51.03, & 51.06. Delaware, Louisiana, Maryland, Michigan, and Wyoming are the only states that have not adopted the Uniform Simultaneous Death Act.
21. Boyer, *Introduction to the Law of Real Property*, § 5[III][1]. Alabama, Georgia, Michigan, Minnesota, Missouri, Utah, Washington, and Wisconsin no longer require all four unities to create a joint tenancy. Usually, the unities of time and title are the ones relaxed. This allows A, an owner of land, to create a joint tenancy in A and B without the artificial use of a strawman (a conveyance from A to the strawman, who then conveys to A and B as joint tenants). Wolf, *Powell on Real Property*, § 51.01.
22. Jurisdictions with statutes creating presumption in favor of tenancies in common are Alabama, Arizona, Arkansas, California, Colorado, Connecticut, Delaware, District of Columbia, Florida, Georgia, Hawaii, Idaho, Illinois, Indiana, Iowa, Kansas, Maine, Maryland, Massachusetts, Michigan, Minnesota, Mississippi, Missouri, Montana, Nebraska, Nevada, New Hampshire, New Jersey, New Mexico, New York, North Carolina, North Dakota, Ohio, Pennsylvania, Rhode Island, South Carolina, South Dakota, Texas, Utah, Vermont, Washington, West Virginia, Wisconsin, and Wyoming. Alaska, Kentucky, Louisiana, Oregon, Tennessee, and Virginia have abolished either joint tenancies or the right of survivorship. Wolf, *Powell on Real Property*, § 50.02.
23. 765 ILCS 1005/1 (2001).
24. Wolf, *Powell on Real Property*, § 51.04.
25. Boyer, *Introduction to the Law of Real Property*, § 5[III][2].
26. Wolf, *Powell on Real Property*, § 52.01. The sixteen states that do not recognize tenancy by the entirety are California, Connecticut, Louisiana, Maine, Minnesota, Montana, Nevada, New Hampshire, New Mexico, North Dakota, Ohio, South Carolina, South Dakota, Washington, West Virginia, and Wisconsin, at note 98. The four states with uncertainty are Idaho, Kansas, Texas, and Utah, at note 99.
27. Wolf, *Powell of Real Property*, § 52.02.
28. Ibid., §§ 52.03 & 52.05.
29. Boyer, *Introduction to the Law of Real Property*, § 5[IV][4].
30. Ibid., §§ 5[IV][5 & 6].
31. Ibid., § 5[IV][7].
32. Ibid., §§ 5[IV][1–3].
33. Ibid., § 5[IV][8].
34. Ibid., § 5[IV][9].
35. Intestate statutes exist in all 50 states. They apply when someone dies without a will (or there is a will that does not completely dispose of all the decedent's property). Typically under intestate statutes, surviving children and spouses get a stated share of the property owned at death by the decedent. If there are no surviving spouses or children, then other relatives are awarded the property. In the rare case that there are no surviving relatives, the property goes to the state.
36. Boyer, *Introduction to the Law of Real Property*, § 8.4.
37. Ibid., §§ 8.4 & 8.5.
38. Ibid., § 8.1.
39. Ibid., § 8.2.
40. Frost v. Schinkel, 121 Neb. 784, 238 N.W. 659 (1931).
41. Warrington v. Hignutt, 42 Del. 274, 31 A.2d 480 (Del.Super.1943).

42. Holland Furnace Co. v. Trumbull S. & L. Co. 135 Ohio St. 48, 19 N.E.2d 273 (1939).

43. Flyge v. Flynn, 63 Nev. 201, 166 P.2d 539 (1946).

44. Alphonse M. Squillante, "The Law of Fixtures: Common Law and the Uniform Commercial Code," *Hofstra Law Review* 15 (winter 1987): 192.

45. Ibid., p. 195, discussing Teaff v. Hewitt, 1 Ohio St. 511 (1853).

46. 1 Am. Jur. 2d *Abandoned, Lost and Unclaimed Property,* § 4 (2000).

47. Boyer, *Introduction to the Law of Real Property,* §§ 1.3 & 1.4.

48. 1 Am. Jur. 2d *Abandoned, Lost, and Unclaimed Property,* §§ 11, 12, & 15 (2000).

49. Boyer, *Introduction to the Law of Real Property,* § 1.3.

50. Ibid.

51. 8A Am. Jur. 2d *Bailments,* §§ 1 & 7 (2000).

52. Boyer, *Introduction to the Law of Real Property,* § 2.3.

53. Ibid., §§ 2.3 & 2.4.

54. 441 N.E.2d 450 (Ind. 1982).

55. 8A Am. Jur. 2d *Bailments,* § 6.

56. Boyer, *Introduction to the Law of Real Property,* § 2.6.

57. 63C Am. Jur. 2d *Extinguishment or Loss: Alienation and Transfer* § 34 (2000). However, UCC 2-304(1)(d) gives good title to a bona fide purchaser from one who enticed delivery of the goods by the true owner by trickery or other actions that would be larceny under the criminal law. *See, for example,* Arena Auto Auction v. Schmerler Ford Inc., 60 Ill. App. 3d 484, 377 N.E. 2d 43 (1978). The distinction is that the true owner delivers the goods to the larcener and, as a result, clothes the larcener with a perception of ownership, while a thief dispossesses the true owner.

58. Mark E. Harrington, "On-Line Copyright Infringement Liability for Internet Service Providers: Context, Cases, and Recently Enacted Legislation," *Boston College Intellectual Property and Technology Forum,* (June 4, 1999): 060499, available at: <http://www.bc.edu/iptf>, as of June 26, 2001.

59. The discussion in this section, unless otherwise cited, is based on Sarah H. McWane, "Comment: Hollywood vs. Silicon Valley: DeCSS Down, Napster to Go?" *CommLaw Conspectus* 9 (2001): 87, and Harrington, "On-Line Copyright Infringement."

60. 464 U.S. 417 (1984).

61. The four factors were codified at 17 U.S.C. § 107 as part of the Copyright Act of 1976, McWane, "Comment."

62. 464 U.S. at 448.

63. 464 U.S. at 442.

64. 111 F. Supp. 2d 294 (S.D.N.Y. 2000).

65. 907 F. Supp. 1361 (N.D. Cal. 1995).

66. Harrington, "On-Line Copyright Infringement," at notes 82–105.

67. 982 F. Supp. 503 (N.D. Ohio 1997).

68. Harrington, "On-Line Copyright Infringement," at notes 118–141.

69. Codified at 17 U.S.C. §§ 101–1101 (1994 and Supp. V 1999), McWane, "Comment," at notes 83–85.

70. 17 U.S.C. § 106 (1994 and Supp. V 1999), discussed in Blackmun's dissenting opinion in Sony Corp. of America v. Universal City Studios, 464 U.S. 417, at 462 (1984).

71. Blackmun's dissenting opinion in Sony Corp. of America v. Universal City Studios, 464 U.S. 417, at 464 (1984).

72. Codified at 17 U.S.C. §§ 1001–1010, McWane, "Comment," at notes 60–66.

73. Codified at 17 U.S.C. §§ 1201–1205 (Supp. IV 1998), McWane, "Comment," at notes 124–130.

74. 17 U.S.C. 512 (Supp. IV 1998).

75. McWane, "Comment," at notes 131–153, and Melville B. Nimmer and David Nimmer, *Nimmer on Copyright* (New York: Mathew Bender, 2000), § 12B.01.

76. The following message was on the Napster site as of December 15, 2001. "If you've tried to search for music on Napster since July, you've noticed that file sharing is disabled. The decision to turn it off was a tough but necessary call. We want you to know that the decision was ours—not the court's, and not the recording industry's. While our file identification technology was highly accurate, we decided that we wanted it to be even better. We also wanted to focus on building a reliable new system that would protect and pay rights holders. File sharing will remain offline until we launch our new membership service in early 2002." <http://www.napster.com/lowdown.html>. ✦

Chapter 12

Family Law

Chapter Objectives

Students will gain an understanding of how the institution of marriage has evolved in this country and how family law continues to change. Readers should understand the processes available for ending marriages. One needs to comprehend how and why the property of divorcing couples is divided and how courts determine alimony or maintenance awards. Students must become familiar with child custody and child support matters. Finally, readers will be introduced to how nontraditional families challenge the premises of family law and how reproductive science is pushing the boundaries of family law.

Thirty years ago, family law was concerned primarily with divorce, support for spouses and children, child custody issues, visitation by noncustodial parents, and the division of property. The traditional family law issues will be examined, including marriage, ending marriages, children born out of wedlock, and children of divorced parents. Although those issues remain important today, society and science have complicated this area of the law. The 2000 census reported a large increase (71 percent) since 1990 in the number of couples living together without the benefit of marriage, compared with only a 7 percent increase in the number of married couples over the past decade.[1] Besides the movement for same-sex marriage by gay rights groups (and the recognition of civil unions by the state of Vermont), other politically contentious issues surround the adoption process and the availability of court-ordered child visitation for those other than parents. These new viewpoints are testing the wisdom of judges and legislators. Further, the sometimes startling advancement in reproductive science finds the law playing catch-up. Who, for example, should control the use of frozen embryos? Who are the parents of a child born with the use of donated sperm or a surrogate mother? What issues may arise as a result of human cloning?

Marriage

Marriage as an institution is quite old, even if it was not always similar to marriage today. For example, *polygamy* (multiple spouses) was common in many cultures. Marriage was a way of assuring the perpetuation of the species and or culture. It was also a method of granting property rights. The Augustan marriage laws of A.D. 9 penalized women who had not given birth by the age of 20. The legal age to marry was 12. Roman law provided for two types of marriage. The first type, *in manu* marriage, transferred the power of life and death over the woman from the father to the husband. It gradually gave way to the second type, *free marriage,* in which the woman remained under the control of her father, but could seek emancipation. Upon her father's death, the woman became a person who could conduct her own affairs. Marriage also had religious roots. St. Paul deemed it a sacrament. The church viewed marriage as a way to prevent sin, provide companionship, and promote procreation. Christian religious ceremonies appeared in the fourth century. Often, our ancestors had no say in whom they married. Marriages were often arranged on the basis of title or property. Dower and bride fees were also common.[2]

Today, marriage laws in the United States are a matter of state law. They are derived from the English common law courts, which assumed jurisdiction from the ecclesiastical courts.[3] There is no national marriage law, but rather 50 independent and sometimes widely different state statutes. Although the National Conference of Commissioners on Uniform State Laws has drafted and proposed

Should a couple be able to alter the state marriage contract?

uniform acts—including the *Uniform Marriage and Divorce Act* (UMDA), the *Uniform Parentage Act* (UPA), and others—only the *Reciprocal Enforcement of Support Act* has gained widespread adoption by the states.[4] The U.S. Supreme Court has, however, provided some national unity by limiting the ability of the states to regulate marriage through the Fourteenth Amendment's Equal Protection and Due Process Clauses.[5]

Illinois has a typical marriage and divorce statute. It has process provisions, such as obtaining a license, performing the ceremony, registering the marriage certificate, and so on. The statute also has provisions setting minimum age limits (18 or 16 with parental or judicial consent) and prohibiting the marriage of certain people (related persons down to first cousins, those who are already married to another, and persons of the same sex).[6]

Who May Marry?

The prohibition of marriage between certain parties has been the source of constitutional attacks on the power of the states to regulate marriage. The 1967 landmark U.S. Supreme Court opinion in *Loving v. Virginia*[7] centered on a white man and a black woman who were residents of Virginia, but were married in Washington, DC. At the time, Virginia and 16 other states prohibited interracial marriages. Upon their return to Virginia, the Lovings were indicted and sentenced to one year in jail for violating the statute. The Supreme Court held that the right to marry is a basic civil right and that Virginia's *miscegenation* statute violated the Equal Protection and the Due Process Clauses of the Fourteenth Amendment. There have been other successful constitutional challenges of state statutes restricting the ability of persons to marry, including a statute that would not allow a Wisconsin resident under a child support order to marry without court permission. Under the Wisconsin statute, permission would be granted only upon a showing that the person was not behind on child support payments, and that the child was not or was not likely to become a ward of the state.[8] In yet another U.S. Supreme Court case, a Missouri Division of Corrections regulation was struck down that prohibited the marriage of inmates without the permission of the superintendent of the prison. Permission was to be granted only when there were compelling reasons to do so.[9] However, constitutional challenges have failed against polygamy statutes, prohibitions on same-sex marriages, and minimum age requirements.[10] Prohibitions against same-sex marriages have been struck down in Hawaii, Vermont, and Alaska, however, based on *state* constitutional provisions. The Hawaii case appears below.

Baehr v. Lewin
Supreme Court of Hawaii
74 Haw. 530, 852 P.2d 44 (1993)

OPINION BY: LEVINSON:

The plaintiffs-appellants Ninia Baehr (Baehr), Genora Dancel (Dancel), Tammy Rodrigues (Rodri-gues), Antoinette Pregil (Pregil), Pat Lagon (Lagon), and Joseph Melilio (Melilio) (collectively the plaintiffs) appeal the circuit court's order (and judgment entered pursuant thereto) granting the motion of the defendant-appellee John C. Lewin (Lewin), in his official capacity as Director of the Department of Health (DOH), State of Hawaii, for judgment on the pleadings, resulting in the dismissal of the plaintiffs' action with prejudice for failure to state a claim against Lewin upon which relief can be granted. Because, for purposes of Lewin's motion, it is our duty to view the factual allegations of the plaintiffs' complaint in a light most favorable to them (i.e., because we must deem such allegations as true) and because it does not appear beyond doubt that the plaintiffs cannot prove any set of facts in support of their claim that would entitle them to the relief they seek, we hold that the circuit court erroneously dismissed the plaintiffs' complaint. Accordingly, we vacate the circuit court's order and judgment and remand this matter to the circuit court for further proceedings consistent with this opinion.

I. BACKGROUND

On May 1, 1991, the plaintiffs filed a complaint for injunctive and declaratory relief in the Circuit Court of the First Circuit, State of Hawaii, seeking, inter alia: (1) a declaration that Hawaii Revised Statutes (HRS) § 572-1 (1985) the section of the Hawaii Marriage Law enumerating the [r]equisites of [a] valid marriage contract is unconstitutional insofar as it is construed and applied by the DOH to justify refusing to issue a marriage license on the sole basis that the applicant couple is of the same sex; and (2) preliminary and permanent injunctions prohibiting the future withholding of marriage licenses on that sole basis.

In addition to the necessary jurisdictional and venue related averments, the plaintiffs' complaint alleges the following facts: (1) on or about December 17, 1990, Baehr/Dancel, Rodrigues/Pregil, and Lagon/Melilio (collectively the applicant couples) filed applications for marriage licenses with the DOH, pursuant to HRS § 572-6 (Supp. 1992); (2) the DOH denied the applicant couples' marriage license applications solely on the ground that the applicant couples were of the same sex; (3) the applicant couples have complied with all marriage contract requirements and provisions under HRS ch. 572, except that each applicant couple is of the same sex; (4) the applicant couples are otherwise eligible to secure marriage licenses from the DOH, absent the statutory prohibition or construction of HRS § 572-1 excluding couples of the same sex from securing marriage licenses; and (5) in denying the applicant couples' marriage license applications, the DOH was acting in its official capacity and under color of state law.

Based on the foregoing factual allegations, the plaintiffs' complaint avers that: (1) the DOH's interpretation and application of HRS § 572-1 to deny same-sex couples access to marriage licenses violates the plaintiffs' right to privacy, as guaranteed by article I, section 6 of the Hawaii constitution, as well as to the equal protection of the laws and due process of law, as guaranteed by article I, section 5 of the Hawaii Constitution;* (2) the plaintiffs have no plain, adequate, or complete remedy at law to redress their alleged injuries; and (3) the plaintiffs are presently suffering and will continue to suffer irreparable injury from the DOH's acts, policies, and practices in the absence of declaratory and injunctive relief. . . .

In his memorandum, Lewin urged that the plaintiffs' complaint failed to state a claim upon which relief could be granted for the following reasons: (1) the state's marriage laws contemplate marriage as a union between a man and a woman; (2) because the only legally recognized right to marry is the right to enter a heterosexual marriage, [the] plaintiffs do not have a cognizable right, fundamental or otherwise, to enter into state-licensed homosexual marriages; (3) the state's marriage laws do not burden, penalize, infringe, or interfere in any way with the [plaintiffs'] private relationships; (4) the state is under no obligation to take affirmative steps to provide homosexual unions with its official approval; (5) the state's marriage laws protect and foster and may help to perpetuate the basic family unit, regarded as vital to society, that provides status and a nurturing environment to children born to married persons and, in addition, constitute a statement of the moral values of the community in a manner that is not burdensome to [the] plaintiffs; (6) assuming the plaintiffs are homosexuals (a fact not pleaded in the plaintiffs' complaint), they are neither a suspect nor a quasi-suspect class and do not require heightened judicial solicitude; and (7) even if heightened judicial solicitude is warranted, the state's marriage laws are so removed from penalizing, burdening, harming, or otherwise interfering with [the] plaintiffs and their relationships and perform such a critical function in society that they must be sustained. . . .

II. JUDGMENT ON THE PLEADINGS WAS ERRONEOUSLY GRANTED.

. . . Notwithstanding the absence of any evidentiary record before it, the circuit court's October 1, 1991 order granting Lewin's motion for judgment on the pleadings contained a variety of findings of fact. For example, the circuit court "found" that: (1) HRS § 572-1 does not infringe upon a person's individuality or lifestyle decisions, and none of the plaintiffs has provided testimony to the contrary; (2) HRS § 572-1 does not . . . restrict [or] burden . . . the exercise of the right to engage in a homosexual lifestyle; (3) Hawaii has exhibited a history of tolerance for all peoples and their cultures; (4) the plaintiffs have failed to show that they have been ostracized or oppressed in Hawaii and have opted instead to rely on a general statement of historic problems encountered by homosexuals which may not be relevant to Hawaii; (5) homosexuals in Hawaii have not been relegated to a position of political powerlessness. . . . [T]here is no evidence that homosexuals and the homosexual legislative agenda have failed to gain legislative support in Hawaii; (6) the [p]laintiffs have failed to show that homosexuals constitute a suspect class for equal protection analysis under [a]rticle I, [s]ection 5 of the Hawaii State Constitution; (7) the issue of whether homosexuality constitutes an immutable trait has generated much dispute in the relevant scientific community; and (8) HRS § 572-1 is obviously designed to promote the general welfare interests of the community by sanctioning traditional man-woman family units and procreation. . . .

We conclude that the circuit court's order runs aground on the shoals of the Hawaii Constitution's equal protection clause and that, on the record before us, unresolved factual questions preclude entry of judgment, as a matter of law, in favor of Lewin and against the plaintiffs. Before we address the plaintiffs' equal protection claim, however, it is necessary as a threshold matter to consider their allegations regarding the right to privacy (and, derivatively, due process of law) within the context of the record in its present embryonic form. . . .

It is now well established that a right to personal privacy, or a guarantee of certain areas or zones of privacy, is implicit in the United States Constitution. . . . And article I, section 6 of the Hawaii Constitution expressly states that "[t]he right of the people to privacy is recognized and shall not be infringed without the showing of a compelling state interest. . . ." The framers of the Hawaii Constitution declared that the "privacy concept" embodied in article I, section 6 is to be treated as a fundamental right[.] . . .

Accordingly, there is no doubt that, at a minimum, article I, section 6 of the Hawaii Constitution encompasses all of the fundamental rights expressly recognized as being subsumed within the privacy protections of the United States Constitution. In this connection, the United States Supreme Court has declared that the right to marry is part of the fundamental right of privacy implicit in the Fourteenth Amendment's Due Process Clause. . . . The issue in the present case is, therefore, whether the right to marry protected by article I, section 6 of the Hawaii Constitution extends to same-sex couples. Because article I, section 6 was expressly derived from the general right to privacy under the United States Constitution and because there are no Hawaii cases that have delineated the fundamental right to marry, this court, . . . looks to federal cases for guidance. . . .

The United States Supreme Court has set forth its most detailed discussion of the fundamental right to marry in Zablocki v. Redhail, 434 U.S. 374 (1978), which involved a Wisconsin statute that prohibited any resident of the state with minor children not in his custody and which he is under obligation to support from obtaining a marriage license until the resident demonstrated to a court that he was in compliance with his child support obligations. . . . The *Zablocki* court held that the statute burdened the fundamental right to marry; applying the "strict scrutiny" standard to the statute, the court invalidated it as violative of the fourteenth amendment to the United States Constitution. In so doing, the *Zablocki* court delineated its view of the evolution of the federally recognized fundamental right of marriage as follows: Long ago, in Maynard v. Hill, 125 U.S. 190 (1888), the Court characterized marriage as the most important relation and as the foundation of the family and of society, without which there would be neither civilization nor progress. . . . In Meyer v. Nebraska, 262 U.S. 390 (1923), the Court recognized that the right to marry, establish a home and bring up children is a central part of the liberty protected by the Due Process Clause, and in Skinner v. Oklahoma ex rel. Williamson, 316 U.S. 535 (1942), marriage was described as fundamental to the very existence and survival of the race. . . .

The foregoing case law demonstrates that the federal construct of the fundamental right to marry subsumed within the right to privacy implicitly protected by the United States Constitution presently contemplates unions between men and women. (Once again, this is hardly surprising inasmuch as such unions are the only state-sanctioned marriages currently acknowledged in this country). . . .

Applying the foregoing standards to the present case, we do not believe that a right to same-sex marriage is so rooted in the traditions and collective conscience of our people that failure to recognize it would violate the fundamental principles of liberty and justice that lie at the base of all our civil and political institutions. Neither do we believe that a right to same-sex marriage is implicit in the concept of ordered liberty, such that neither liberty nor justice would exist if it were sacrificed. Accordingly, we hold that the applicant couples do not have a fundamental constitutional right to same-sex marriage arising out of the right to privacy or otherwise. . . .

In addition to the alleged violation of their constitutional rights to privacy and due process of law, the applicant couples contend that they have been denied the equal protection of the laws as guaranteed by article I, section 5 of the Hawaii Constitution. On appeal, the plaintiffs urge and, on the state of the bare record before us, we agree that the circuit court erred when it concluded, as a matter of law, that: (1) homosexuals do not constitute a "suspect class" for purposes of equal protection analysis under article I, section 5 of the Hawaii Constitution; (2) the classification created by HRS § 572-1 is not subject to "strict scrutiny," but must satisfy only the "rational relationship" test; and (3) HRS § 572-1 satisfies the rational relationship test because the legislature obviously designed [it] to promote the general welfare interests of the community by sanctioning traditional man-woman family units and procreation. . . .

The power to regulate marriage is a sovereign function reserved exclusively to the respective states. . . . So zealously has this court guarded the state's role as the exclusive progenitor of the marital partnership that it declared, over seventy years ago, that common law marriages i.e., marital unions existing in the absence of a state-issued license and not performed by a person or society possessing governmental authority to solemnize marriages would no longer be recognized in the Territory of Hawaii. . . .

The applicant couples correctly contend that the DOH's refusal to allow them to marry on the basis that they are members of the same sex deprives them of access to a multiplicity of rights and benefits that are contingent upon that status. Although it is unnecessary in this opinion to engage in an encyclopedic recitation of all of them, a number of the most salient marital rights and benefits are worthy of note. They include: (1) a variety of state income tax advantages, including deductions, credits, rates, exemptions, and estimates . . . ; (2) public assistance from and exemptions relating to the Department of Human Services . . . ; (3) control, division, acquisition, and disposition of community property . . . ; (4) rights relating to dower, curtesy, and inheritance . . . ; (5) rights to notice, protection, benefits, and inheritance under the Uniform Probate Code; (6) award of child custody and support payments in divorce proceedings . . . ; (7) the right to spousal support . . . ; (8) the right to enter into premarital agreements. . . ; (9) the right to change of name . . . ; (10) the right to file a nonsupport action . . . ; (11) post-divorce rights relating to support and property division . . . ; (12) the benefit of the spousal privilege and confidential marital communications . . . ; (13) the benefit of the exemption of real property from attachment or execution . . . ; and (14) the right to bring a wrongful death action. . . . For present purposes, it is not disputed that the applicant couples would be entitled to all of these marital rights and benefits, but for the fact that they are denied access to the state-conferred legal status of marriage.

HRS § 572-1, on its face, discriminates based on sex against the applicant couples in the exercise of the civil right of marriage, thereby implicating the equal protection clause of article I, section 5 of the Hawaii Constitution. . . . The equal protection clauses of the United States and Hawaii Constitutions are not mirror images of one another. The fourteenth amendment to the United States Constitution somewhat concisely provides, in relevant part, that a state may not deny to any person within its jurisdiction the equal protection of the laws. Hawaii's counterpart is more elaborate. Article I, section 5 of the Hawaii Constitution provides in relevant part that [n]o person shall . . . be denied the equal protection of the laws, nor be denied the enjoyment of the person's civil rights or be discriminated against in the exercise thereof because of race, religion, sex, or ancestry. (Emphasis added.) Thus,

by its plain language, the Hawaii Constitution prohibits state-sanctioned discrimination against any person in the exercise of his or her civil rights on the basis of sex. . . .

Whenever a denial of equal protection of the laws is alleged, as a rule our initial inquiry has been whether the legislation in question should be subjected to strict scrutiny or to a rational basis test. . . . This court has applied strict scrutiny analysis to laws classifying on the basis of suspect categories or impinging upon fundamental rights expressly or impliedly granted by the [c]onstitution, in which case the laws are presumed to be unconstitutional unless the state shows compelling state interests which justify such classifications, . . . and that the laws are narrowly drawn to avoid unnecessary abridgments of constitutional rights. . . .

By contrast, [w]here suspect classifications or fundamental rights are not at issue, this court has traditionally employed the rational basis test. Under the rational basis test, we inquire as to whether a statute rationally furthers a legitimate state interest. Our inquiry seeks only to determine whether any reasonable justification can be found for the legislative enactment. . . .

As we have indicated, HRS § 572-1, on its face and as applied, regulates access to the marital status and its concomitant rights and benefits on the basis of the applicants' sex. As such, HRS § 572-1 establishes a sex-based classification.

Our decision in Holdman v. Olim, 59 Haw. 346, 581 P.2d 1164 (1978) is key to the present case in several respects. First, we clearly and unequivocally established, for purposes of equal protection analysis under the Hawaii Constitution, that sex-based classifications are subject, as a per se matter, to some form of heightened scrutiny, be it strict or intermediate, rather than mere rational basis analysis. Second, we assumed, arguendo, that such sex-based classifications were subject to strict scrutiny. Third, we reaffirmed the long-standing principle that this court is free to accord greater protections to Hawaii's citizens under the state constitution than are recognized under the United States Constitution. And fourth, we looked to the then current case law of the United States Supreme Court for guidance.

. . . [I]t is time to resolve once and for all the question left dangling in *Holdman.* Accordingly, we hold that sex is a "suspect category" for purposes of equal protection analysis under article I, section 5 of the Hawaii Constitution and that HRS § 572-1 is subject to the "strict scrutiny" test. It therefore follows, and we so hold, that (1) HRS § 572-1 is presumed to be unconstitutional (2) un-less Lewin, as an agent of the State of Hawaii, can show that (a) the statute's sex-based classification is justified by compelling state interests and (b) the statute is narrowly drawn to avoid unnecessary abridgments of the applicant couples' constitutional rights.

III. CONCLUSION

Because, for the reasons stated in this opinion, the circuit court erroneously granted Lewin's motion for judgment on the pleadings and dismissed the plaintiffs' complaint, we vacate the circuit court's order and judgment and remand this matter for further proceedings consistent with this opinion. On remand, in accordance with the strict scrutiny standard, the burden will rest on Lewin to overcome the presumption that HRS § 572-1 is unconstitutional by demonstrating that it furthers compelling state interests and is narrowly drawn to avoid unnecessary abridgments of constitutional rights. . . .

*Article I, section 6 of the Hawaii Constitution provides: The right of the people to privacy is recognized and shall not be infringed without the showing of a compelling state interest. The legislature shall take affirmative steps to implement this right. Article I, section 5 of the Hawaii Constitution provides: No person shall be deprived of life, liberty or property without due process of law, nor be denied the equal protection of the laws, nor be denied the enjoyment of the person's civil rights or be discriminated against in the exercise thereof because of race, religion, sex or ancestry.

Bans on same-sex marriages are being challenged by gay and lesbian groups.

Postscript. Upon remand, Lewin was unable to make the required showing, and the state was enjoined from denying marriage licenses to same-sex couples.[11] An Alaskan court made a similar ruling regarding a prohibition of same-sex marriages.[12] In reaction, both Hawaii and Alaska amended their constitutions to permit bans on same-sex marriages.[13] Vermont's Supreme Court found that a prohibition against same-sex marriages violated the *Common Ben-*

efits Clause of the state constitution. It suggested that the legislature craft a civil union statute to afford same-sex couples rights similar to married couples. Vermont's legislature passed legislation authorizing civil unions for same-sex couples that became law in July 2000. Vermont's law treats same-sex couples who enter into civil unions as spouses with most of the rights and benefits usually afforded married persons within the state.[14] Outside of Vermont, the civil union statute's reach may be limited, however. For instance, the federal *Defense of Marriage Act* defines marriage for any federal purpose as a legal union between "one man and one woman." For example, neither member of a same-sex couple who entered into a civil union in Vermont would be able to qualify as a surviving spouse under the social security system. The Defense of Marriage Act also provides that no state, territory, possession, or tribe must recognize a same-sex marriage sanctioned in another state, territory, possession, or tribe.[15] State legislatures are also erecting barriers to same-sex marriage recognition. Illinois' provision is typical: "A marriage between two individuals of the same sex is contrary to the public policy of this State. All marriages . . . that were valid at the time of the contract . . . are valid in this State, except where contrary to the public policy of this State."[16] In April of 2001, the Netherlands began allowing same-sex couples to marry. However, licenses are available only to Dutch citizens or residents who reside with a Dutch citizen.[17]

Case Questions for Discussion

1. Hawaii's Supreme Court discusses the proper mode of constitutional interpretation when dealing with sex as a suspect classification. What is the definitional difference between a strict scrutiny test and a rational basis test? Which test does the Court employ? What difference, if any, does it make in the outcome of the case?

2. Had the Equal Rights Amendment to the U.S. Constitution been ratified, which would have prohibited discrimination based on sex, would state statutes limiting marriage to unions between men and women have been able to survive an equal protection challenge?

3. Why is it important to the gay and lesbian community to win legal recognition of their relationships?

4. Ellen and Ann, a lesbian couple who entered into a civil union in Vermont, moved to Illinois after Ellen took a position with an Illinois company in Chicago. If that employer provides health insurance and life insurance coverage for employee spouses, is it also required to provide coverage to Ann?

5. Suppose that Ellen and Ann, instead of moving to Chicago, took a vacation in a state where lesbian sex acts were criminal. Would they be subject to prosecution in that state, although they were legally united in Vermont?

6. Do you think there should be some national unity on the issue of same-sex marriages or civil unions?

Common Law Marriage

It is possible in 11 states to marry without the government's official sanction. Although requirements vary from state to state, in general, a *common law marriage* may be established by cohabiting with the intent to be married and holding oneself out to be married. In other words, the couple must act and deal with the community and government as married couples ordinarily do, such as filing joint tax returns, commingling funds, and referring to each other as spouses. Once established, a common law marriage is like any other marriage and is recognized as valid even by states that do not allow for the creation of common law marriages. Spouses inherit property from each other and have all the other rights and responsibilities of married persons.[18] The main difference between common law marriages and state-sanctioned marriages is that common law spouses may be forced to "prove up" (offer evidence in court to establish the elements of a common law marriage) the marriage when attempting to exercise a spousal right, such as inheritance. Consider the following Idaho case. That state abolished common law marriages entered into after January 1, 1996.

In Re Estate of Wagner
Supreme Court of Idaho
126 Idaho 848, 893 P.2d 211 (1995)

OPINION BY: SILAK:

. . . In approximately September 1992, the decedent, Bryan Rudolph Wagner (Wagner), and respondent, Elizabeth Becker (Becker), and her 10-year-old daughter from a previous marriage, Crystal Lee Becker, began living together in Becker's house in Lewiston, Idaho. In November 1992, Wagner proposed marriage to Becker and she accepted. Becker claims that she and Wagner consented to a common law marriage at the time he asked her to marry him in November 1992, and that they had an oral contract of marriage from that time on. A ceremonial marriage was planned for April 1993 in Reno, Nevada. Becker testified that even though they were common law married in November 1992, the cou-

ple wanted a ceremonial marriage for religious purposes.

Becker's Idaho driver's license expired in December 1992. She testified that she did not renew it under the name of Wagner because she did not know how to legally change it due to the common law marriage. In January 1993, Wagner and Becker purchased wedding rings on layaway. The rings were paid off in early March 1993, and Becker immediately began wearing her ring. In February 1993, Becker changed the name on her checking account at First Security Bank to Wagner. Although Becker received a letter from the bank informing her that in order for her to change the name on her account she was required to provide new signature cards and a copy of a marriage license, the checks were printed with the change. Becker wrote checks on this account, but not until after Wagner died. Wagner and Becker did not have a joint checking or savings account at any time.

Becker also ordered and received a First Security Cash Card in the name of Liz Wagner, and a Sprint Foncard in the name of Liz A. Wagner. The cash card was ordered at the same time she changed the name on her checking account, and the Sprint card was changed in early March 1993. Becker testified that she and Wagner each contributed funds for groceries and each paid certain of the household bills. She also testified that they saved cash in a coffee can for the purchase of the wedding rings and the planned trip to Reno, Nevada in April 1993.

On March 19, 1993, Wagner died intestate. Thereafter, Becker filed an application for informal appointment as personal representative claiming that her interest in Wagner's estate was that of spouse at common law. Pursuant to her application, the magistrate, acting as registrar, appointed Becker personal representative of the decedent. At the same time, he issued letters of administration to Becker. In April 1993, Appellant Terry Lynn Hall (Hall), the mother of the decedent, filed a petition for removal of personal representative, claiming that Becker either mistakenly or intentionally misrepresented in her petition for appointment that she was the common law wife of Wagner.

After a hearing on Hall's petition, the magistrate issued an opinion and order ruling that a common law marriage did not exist between Wagner and Becker. Hall's petition was therefore granted and letters of administration were issued to her. On appeal, the district court reversed the magis-

trate's ruling, finding that a common law marriage existed between Wagner and Becker. Becker was thus reappointed personal representative of Wagner's estate. Hall appealed to this Court. . . .

A nonceremonial marriage may be proven by a preponderance of the evidence in Idaho. Once a common law claimant proves the elements of a common law marriage by a preponderance of the evidence, this Court has held that a presumption of validity of the marriage arises and the burden of production shifts to the opposing party to show by clear and positive proof that the asserted marriage is invalid. . . .

In deciding whether a common law marriage exists, we must first look to the pertinent statutory provisions. They are:

I.C. § 32-301. How solemnized—Marriage must be solemnized, authenticated and recorded as provided in this chapter, but noncompliance with its provisions does not invalidate any lawful marriage.

I.C. § 32-201. What constitutes marriage—Marriage is a personal relation arising out of a civil contract, to which the consent of parties capable of making it is necessary. Consent alone will not constitute marriage; it must be followed by a solemnization, or by a mutual assumption of marital rights, duties or obligations.

I.C. § 32-203. Proof of consent and consummation—Consent to and subsequent consummation of marriage may be manifested in any form, and may be proved under the same general rules of evidence as facts in other cases.

These statutes set forth two general requirements for a finding that a common law marriage exists: 1) consent by the parties to enter into a contact of marriage, given at the time of contracting; and 2) the mutual assumption of marital rights, duties and obligations. . . .

Although not separately designated elements of the doctrine under the statutory framework, proof of cohabitation of the parties and holding oneself out as being married are two of the best methods for proving that there was consent to the contract in the absence of a writing to that effect. With respect to the consent element, we have held that it need not be manifest by any identifiable conduct nor are there any magic words which must be spoken. Rather, consent may be express or implied from the parties' conduct. Evidence of conduct by and between the parties consistent with the existence of a common law marriage thus may be probative of consent. For example, when competent parties have held themselves out to be husband and wife and have gained the general reputation in the community as being such, or where they acknowledge they are husband and wife, a court may draw the inference that there was mutual consent between the parties to assume a marital relationship. . . .

With respect to the present case then, Becker was required to make a prima facie showing of consent to marriage along with an assumption of marital rights, duties and obligations. This showing could have been made by evidence that she and Wagner assumed marital rights, duties, and obligations, cohabited, and held themselves out as being married. If she made such a showing, a presumption of the validity of the marriage would arise, shifting the burden to Hall to rebut the presumption by clear and positive proof of its invalidity. . . .

In the present case, the magistrate found that Wagner and Becker began cohabiting in approximately September 1992. We hold that his finding is clearly supported by the record, and that the parties cohabited from September 1992 until Wagner's death in March 1993.

With respect to the element of the assumption of marital rights, duties and obligations, Hall argues that the magistrate correctly found that Becker had failed to offer sufficient proof of such assumption. We agree.

Becker claims that she and Wagner became common law husband and wife in November 1992 when Wagner proposed to her. However, for the year ending December 31, 1992, she filed a separate Head of Household income tax return. Wagner filed a Single tax return rather than a Married return even though, the magistrate found, he had recently had severe tax liability problems and the filing of a Married return would have affected both his and Becker's tax consequences for 1992. Additionally, between the date of the alleged marriage in November 1992, and Wagner's death in March 1993, Becker did not change her employment records. Although she did change the name on her checking account, ATM card and her Sprint Foncard from Becker to Wagner, these changes were not made until February and March 1993, and are more indicative of preparation for her upcoming April wedding.

Wagner and Becker did not commingle their funds. Although allegedly married in November 1992, they held no joint financial accounts at the time of Wagner's death, and neither deposited funds into the other's accounts. While the evidence shows that there was some commingling in the form of cash being set aside by both of them in a coffee can to pay for wedding rings and a trip to Reno, Nevada, for the wedding ceremony, such commingling is too minimal to warrant a finding of assumption of the rights, duties and obligations of marriage. Further, the finding that Becker and Wagner were each responsible for certain household debts is evidence of noncommingling of funds. Thus, we hold that Becker failed to make an adequate showing that she and Wagner assumed the rights, duties and obligations of marriage.

With respect to the element of holding themselves out in the community as being married, the magistrate found the evidence to be conflicting. According to the record, there were a few occasions in which Wagner may have referred to Becker in such a way that the listener could believe they were married. However, the instances in which both Wagner and Becker could have addressed the other as husband and wife, but did not do so, far outweigh the other. Indeed, Becker testifies that she never introduced Wagner as her husband and he never introduced her as his wife. In fact, there was evidence that Wagner introduced Becker as his "fiancée" at a Christmas party in December 1992. We hold that the magistrate's findings are supported by substantial and competent evidence, even though conflicting. The magistrate is in the best position to judge the demeanor and credibility of the witnesses.

We do not place too much weight on the magistrate's finding that Becker and Wagner were not married because Becker did not change the name on her driver's license in December 1992 when she had an opportunity to do so due at its expiration. In our current times, many women for many reasons choose to retain their maiden names after they are married. This may not be the case here, however, since Becker did change her name on two accounts prior to the planned April 1993 wedding. In any event, we hold that the evidence on the element of Becker and Wagner holding themselves out as being married is conflicting, and therefore defer to the findings of the trial court. . . .

Accordingly, the order of the district court is vacated, and the order of the magistrate is reinstated. . . .

Case Questions for Discussion

1. Do you think Becker and Wagner intended to be married under common law once they began cohabiting? Why might intent make a difference?

2. Why would Becker claim they were married if they were not?

3. What is the degree of proof required in this case? What is required to rebut that proof? Would the outcome be the same if the court had employed a different degree of proof?

4. Had Wagner introduced Becker as his wife instead of his fianceé, do you think the case would have gone the other way?

5. Should commingling of funds be necessary to establish a common law marriage? Is it unusual for married couples to keep separate bank accounts and split up who pays what bill?

6. Make a legal argument that common law marriage should not be recognized in any state.

7. Make a legal argument that common law marriage should be recognized in all states.

Antenuptial (Premarital) Agreements

It was once the general rule that a couple could not alter the marriage contract: namely, the rights and responsibilities of parties to a marriage. It was considered against public policy because altered agreements might facilitate or promote the procurement of a divorce.[19] In 1970, the Florida Supreme Court in *Posner v. Posner* recognized the validity of an *antenuptial agreement* that contemplated divorce, and it suggested such contracts could actually be conducive to marital tranquillity.[20] *Posner* began a trend of national recognition so swift that 18 years later a California appellate court judge noted that all states except Iowa, New Mexico, South Dakota, Vermont, Michigan, Mississippi, Washington, and Wyoming permit premarital waivers of spousal support.[21] In 1983, the National Conference of Commissioners on Uniform State Laws proposed the *Uniform Premarital Agreement Act* (UPAA). As of April of 2001, 25 states and the District of Columbia have adopted the UPAA in whole or in part. It was pending in three other states in 2001.[22] Box 12.1 contains sections 3 and 6 of the UPAA.

Box 12.1   Uniform Premarital Agreement Act

SECTION 3. CONTENT.

(a) Parties to a premarital agreement may contract with respect to:

  (1) the rights and obligations of each of the parties in any of the property of either or both of them whenever and wherever acquired or located;

  (2) the right to buy, sell, use, transfer, exchange, abandon, lease, consume, expend, assign, create a security interest in, mortgage, encumber, dispose of, or otherwise manage and control property;

  (3) the disposition of property upon separation, marital dissolution, death, or the occurrence or nonoccurrence of any other event;

  (4) the modification or elimination of spousal support;

  (5) the making of a will, trust, or other arrangement to carry out the provisions of the agreement;

  (6) the ownership rights in and disposition of the death benefit from a life insurance policy;

  (7) the choice of law governing the construction of the agreement; and

  (8) any other matter, including their personal rights and obligations, not in violation of public policy or a statute imposing a criminal penalty.

(b) The right of a child to support may not be adversely affected by a premarital agreement.

SECTION 6. ENFORCEMENT.

(a) A premarital agreement is not enforceable if the party against whom enforcement is sought proves that:

(1) that party did not execute the agreement voluntarily; or

(2) the agreement was unconscionable when it was executed and, before execution of the agreement, that party:

(i) was not provided a fair and reasonable disclosure of the property or financial obligations of the other party;

(ii) did not voluntarily and expressly waive, in writing, any right to disclosure of the property or financial obligations of the other party beyond the disclosure provided; and

(iii) did not have, or reasonably could not have had, an adequate knowledge of the property or financial obligations of the other party.

(b) If a provision of a premarital agreement modifies or eliminates spousal support and that modification or elimination causes one party to the agreement to be eligible for support under a program of public assistance at the time of separation or marital dissolution, a court, notwithstanding the terms of the agreement, may require the other party to provide support to the extent necessary to avoid that eligibility.

(c) An issue of unconscionability of a premarital agreement shall be decided by the court as a matter of law.

Section 6 of the Uniform Act requires full disclosure and voluntary execution of the agreement. *Unconscionable* agreements may be voided and agreements that leave one of the spouses in a position that makes him or her eligible for public assistance may be reformed. Indiana and Connecticut moved the time of examination of the agreement to the time of the divorce rather than the time of execution.[23] Courts have been reluctant to find an agreement unconscionable, absent a finding of nondisclosure. For example, the Indiana Supreme Court defined unconscionable as a gross disparity when it enforced an antenuptial that denied support or property rights to either party to the marriage. By enforcing the agreement, the court set aside a $225-per-month support award to the wife, who was unable to work due to health problems. The husband's income was $1,247 per month, but the wife had possession of the marital home she could sell for approximately $65,000.[24] New Jersey considers antenuptials to be unconscionable when a spouse is left a public ward, or when a spouse is left with a standard of living far below that which was enjoyed by that spouse before and during the marriage.

An agreement is not unconscionable just because it provides a substantially different standard of living from what a court would grant absent the agreement. As long as the agreement allows the spouse to return to a reasonably comfortable standard of living enjoyed before the marriage, it should be enforced.[25] Under the New Jersey standard, an agreement leaving a wheelchair-bound wife with multiple sclerosis virtually penniless was found unconscionable, while a talk show hostess who owned a life interest in a trust with assets in excess of $2,000,000 per year was bound by a prenuptial agreement that gave her only a small or inadequate share of her husband's substantial property holdings.[26] The Texas Court of Appeals looked to commercial or contract law and held that unconscionable under the terms of the UPAA means more than just unfair. To be unconscionable, the terms of the agreement must be grossly unfair or one-sided.[27]

Ending a Marriage

Divorce and annulment end marriages. Annulments declare that no valid marriage took place due to some impediment that existed at the time of the wedding. Generally, divorces end valid marriages for reasons that occur after the wedding, although some states allow an annulment ground to serve as a divorce ground as well.

Annulment

Annulment laws have not undergone significant change since the time of the ecclesiastical courts of England, which treated a marriage as indissoluble. A party could, however, seek an annulment if some *canonical disability* existed at the time of the marriage.[28] Consent obtained by fraud going to the essence of the marriage is a ground for annulment, including concealment of pregnancy or venereal disease at time of wedding, misrepresentation as to religion, and concealment of intent not to assume marital duties. False pretensions of pregnancy, love and affection, chastity, parenthood, or condition in life have been found not to constitute sufficient fraud to support an annulment. However, incurable impotency by either party at the time of the marriage is a valid ground for annulment. Other grounds include being underage, lacking mental capacity to give consent, bigamy, and giving consent under duress so great that the party under duress was unable to escape or resist.[29]

Divorce

Modern *divorce* law is a blend of ecclesiastical law, statutory law, and equity principles and processes. Many of the processes we have discussed in previous chapters concerning civil suits for money damages and equity processes apply to marital law, but with some significant differences. First, the defendant in a divorce action may be served by publication only if the plaintiff seeks to dissolve the marriage. If the plaintiff seeks alimony, child support, or division of marital property, then most states require personal service. Second, federal courts do not have the power to grant divorces. Under the Tenth Amendment to the U.S. Constitution, this matter is part of the residual powers reserved to the states. Nonetheless, federal courts possess the power to enforce alimony and property settlement decrees in diversity of citizenship cases involving a minimum of $75,000. Third, the privilege of confidential communications between spouses does not apply in divorce cases between contesting spouses. Finally, the legal concept of *res judicata* does not apply to alimony or child custody matters because conditions may change. Either party may return to court at any time, requesting the court to change its decree.[30]

Although divorce was available more freely in colonial courts than in England, the number of divorces before 1700 in New England is estimated at less than 200. Between the end of the Revolutionary War and the mid-1800s, divorce was made more available, especially in the north and west. In some southern states, divorce necessitated an act of the legislature. South Carolina did not authorize divorce until 1949. By the mid-1960s, all states allowed divorce under fault grounds (adultery, cruelty, and neglect, for example). By 1985, all states allowed no fault divorce.[31]

No fault divorce. There are two basic types of *no fault divorce* laws. First is a group that allows a divorce after the parties have lived apart for a specified period of time. The second type of no fault divorce is predicated on a marriage that is irretrievably broken. The duration of time required under the living apart statutes ranges from six months[32] to five years.[33] In addition, some states require the time apart be pursuant to an agreement or a legal separation. New York is the only state that requires a period of time living apart pursuant to an agreement and does not provide any other no fault provision.[34]

The second type of no fault divorce statute uses terms such as irreconcilable differences, irretrievably broken, incompatibility, and insupportability. All are based on the same theme; namely, the marriage is not working, and reconciliation or repair of the marriage is unlikely. As a rule, both parties agree to no fault divorces. When a no fault divorce action is contested or sought unilaterally, some states make it more difficult for the party asking for the divorce.[35] Thirty-one states simply added a no fault provision to the fault-based grounds for divorce. In the 19 states listed in Box 12.2, no fault is the only basis for divorce.

Fault-based divorce. The theory behind *fault-based divorce* is that one of the parties has not complied with marital obligations or duties and, as a result, the injured party should be granted a divorce. The statutory language varies widely between jurisdictions, but the most popular grounds include adultery, abandonment or desertion, mental illness, criminal conviction, substance abuse, and cruelty. Some juris-

---

Box 12.2   States in Which No Fault Is the Only Basis for Divorce[36]

Arizona, California, Colorado, Delaware, Florida, Hawaii, Iowa, Kentucky, Michigan, Minnesota, Missouri, Montana, Nebraska, Nevada, North Carolina, Oregon, Washington, Wisconsin, and Wyoming.

---

dictions have more specific grounds, but they usually are subsumed within one of the grounds we have listed.

Adultery is a common fault-based ground for divorce. Some states have expanded their definition of adultery to include gay and lesbian activity and other acts that fall short of intercourse, but generally it is intercourse between a married person and a person of the opposite sex.[37] *Desertion or abandonment* is usually found when one of the spouses physically vacates the marital abode for a continuous period of time (usually one year or less) with the intention of not returning or continuing the marital relationship.[38] Desertion or abandonment can also be found constructively in some states for refusing to provide support, or unjustly refusing to engage in sexual relations. Locking the other spouse out of the home, or acting in such a way to force the other spouse to leave the abode, may also support desertion or abandonment claims.[39]

Domestic violence is often a cause of divorce.

Although people stricken with *mental illness* or mental incapacity are not at fault, since the 1920s it has been included as a ground for divorce under many fault-based divorce statutes. Generally, the affected spouse must be mentally ill for an extended period of time, be declared incurable, or both.[40] *Criminal conviction* serves as a ground for divorce in many states. Jurisdictions vary on whether a conviction alone is sufficient (minority view) or whether the convicted spouse must spend time in prison as well. The crime involved generally must be a felony.[41] Like mental illness, *alcohol abuse* was not common as a divorce ground until the early 1900s. Drug abuse began to be incorporated into divorce grounds at the end of the twentieth century. The abuse generally must be habitual, and some states require a minimum time period of abuse.[42]

Before no fault laws, *cruelty* in some form was the most common ground for divorce. Its popularity was probably due to the nebulous nature of the acts that may constitute cruelty. Although it generally requires more than a showing of a temper tantrum, repeated acts that tend to affect one spouse's mental and physical well-being, such as apprehension of physical harm, accusations of infidelity, or ridicule, are usually sufficient. A showing of cruelty is easier to prove up than grounds such as adultery, drunkenness, or abandonment that require a showing of specific facts.[43] Cruelty is a ground, under various wordings, in virtually every state that retains fault-based divorce.[44] A few states provide for divorce based on a ground of indignities or neglect, which are less stringent versions of cruelty and based on mental abuse.[45]

Fault-based divorce grounds may be defended in most states retaining fault-based grounds. The most common defenses are recrimination, condonation and reconciliation, collusion and connivance, and mental illness. A comprehensive discussion of defenses is beyond the scope of this chapter. *Recrimination* warrants discussion, however, because its use may prevent the dissolution of the worst marriages. For instance, if a wife sues for divorce alleging adultery and her husband does not offer a defense, but he instead raises recrimination as an affirmative defense and proves the wife had an adulterous affair as well, no divorce should be granted. It is based on the *clean hands* doctrine of equity, discussed in Chapter 6; it requires the moving party in equity to be without fault.[46]

Division of Property

Historically, the great majority of states adhered to separate property laws (the common law states). In general, they operated under the *title theory* and divided property upon divorce based on which spouse had title to the property. Property owned at the time of the marriage and property acquired during the marriage by the efforts of one spouse was usually awarded to that spouse. Before women began working outside the home in great numbers, their share of property upon divorce was often meager, since the husband's earnings usually paid for property acquired during the marriage. A spouse could acquire an interest in the other spouse's property through gift (both actual and presumptive), but the general rule was that the property should be distributed to the one who acquired it, or to the one who was the title owner of the property.

The situation in the *community property* states (Arizona, California, Idaho, Nevada, New Mexico, Louisiana, Texas, Washington, and Wisconsin) was different. In community property states, marriage was (and is) viewed as a *partnership*. Both spouses had a vested one-half interest in all property acquired and income earned during the marriage. Property held before the marriage and property acquired by gift or inheritance by one spouse was considered *separate property.* As a result, when property was divided upon divorce, the division was more even. All of the separate property states now have adopted some form of *equitable* division or distribution of property that incorporates much of the community property theory of marital partnership.[47]

Box 12.3   Dual Property Theory States

Alabama, Arizona, Arkansas, California, Colorado, Delaware, District of Columbia, Florida, Georgia, Idaho, Illinois, Kentucky, Louisiana, Maine, Maryland, Minnesota, Missouri, Nebraska, Nevada, New Jersey, New York, North Carolina, Ohio, Oklahoma, Pennsylvania, Rhode Island, South Carolina, Tennessee, Texas, Virginia, Washington, West Virginia, Wisconsin, and Utah.

Over half of the U.S. states now operate under a *dual property* theory. In dual property states, property is either marital (or community) or nonmarital (separate). *Marital property* is that property acquired during the marriage by the labor, efforts, or industry of each of the spouses. Separate or *nonmarital property* is property acquired by one of the spouses before the marriage or by gift or inheritance or in exchange for other nonmarital property during the marriage. Only marital property is subject to equitable division upon divorce.[48]

Other states follow an *all property* theory that permits a court to equitably divide all property owned by either spouse at the time of divorce.[49]

Box 12.4   All Property Theory States

Alaska, Connecticut, Hawaii, Indiana, Iowa, Kansas, Massachusetts, Michigan, Montana, New Hampshire, North Dakota, Oregon, South Dakota, Vermont, and Wyoming.

Equitable distribution has different meanings in different states. Courts in some states have wide discretion to distribute the assets in a manner that will recognize the contributions of both spouses to the marriage, both economic and noneconomic (such as the contribution of services by a homemaker). A few states have a rebuttable presumption that each spouse should be awarded one half the marital property.[50]

When determining how to equitably distribute marital property, most states list factors that courts should consider. The most commonly used factors include the economic circumstances of the parties at the time of the divorce (especially amount and sources of income), the contributions of each party to the acquisition of the assets, the length of the marriage, the parties' age and health, the desirability of awarding the marital home to the spouse with custody of any children, the determination that the property division will replace or supplement spousal maintenance, the parties' station in life and standard of living, the parties' income and property at the time of the marriage, and the parties' conduct (especially concerning disposition or dissipation of assets).[51]

It is also commonly settled that when a state employs more than one factor, no one factor should be dominant. In Texas, no spousal support award is allowed after the granting of a final divorce. As a result, the equitable division of property should include the future economic needs of both spouses. In other states, whether a court has granted a spousal support award is a factor in the equitable division of property.[52] This approach is consistent with one of the goals of equitable property division—providing a means of support for an economically dependent spouse that is not contingent on periodic alimony being paid on a timely basis and does not require further contact between the former spouses.[53]

The economic condition of the spouses at the time of the divorce and the contribution each spouse made to the acquisition of assets are important factors. If one spouse has a substantial income, and the other has little or no employment experience or earning potential, courts usually consider the disparity in future earning capacity when making an equitable distribution of marital property. The noneconomic contributions made by a spouse (such as homemaking and the care of children) do not directly contribute to the acquisition of assets, but the majority of jurisdictions consider these noneconomic contributions when distributing the marital property. If one spouse contributed to the other's education or increase in earning power, that will usually be considered as well, especially when that spouse's career or education was interrupted. When the marriage is of short duration, economic contributions by one spouse to the acquisition of marital assets are generally more important.[54]

For example, shortly after John and Mary's wedding, the couple purchased a $100,000 home using $35,000 of Mary's savings as a down payment. They financed the balance with a 20-year mortgage. Two years later, they are divorced. Since Mary contributed nearly all of the assets used to acquire the home, it is likely she will be awarded the home in an equitable distribution. A long-term marriage tends to negate economic contributions made by the spouses, especially if they were made early in the marriage. If instead of divorcing after two years,

John and Mary divorced after 20 years, it is more likely that each spouse would be credited with half the value of the home.

Two types of fault may be a factor in some states, marital fault and economic fault. *Marital fault* (behavior by one spouse leading to the breakup of the marriage) may be considered in a minority of the states.[55] The consideration of *economic fault* is more commonplace, especially the *dissipation of assets*. Dissipation occurs when one spouse uses marital assets for his or her sole benefit at a time when the marriage is in jeopardy, such as clearing out bank accounts or selling assets or simply going on spending sprees. Dissipation can also be found when one of the spouses fails to maintain property in his or her care, allowing it to lose value.[56]

The equitable division of property varies by jurisdiction. The discussion thus far has been limited to factors used in most states. Individual states may or may not consider factors discussed above. A complete discussion is beyond the scope of this chapter, as is the next subject, spousal support or alimony. One more issue deserves some attention, however. Is a professional license property that is subject to equitable division?

In a typical fact pattern, a couple meets in college and they marry. One of the spouses is admitted to medical school, law school, or some other postgraduate study program that will lead to a highly compensated career. The other spouse works to support the one in the postgraduate program. Shortly after graduation, the supported spouse files for divorce. Because the high earning years are just beginning, the couple has few marital assets, and in fact, may be in quite a bit of debt. Only a minority of states have held a professional license or advanced degree to be property subject to equitable division. The following New York case of *O'Brien v. O'Brien* is the leading case to do so. Valuation problems are often cited as reasons for not recognizing the degree or license as marital property. Courts usually are able to find some other method of compensating the supporting spouse, such as alimony or considering the disparity in earning capacity when making the equitable distribution of other property.[57]

O'Brien v. O'Brien
Court of Appeals of New York
66 N.Y.2d 576, 489 N.E.2d 712 (1985)

OPINION BY: SIMONS: In this divorce action, the parties' only asset of any consequence is the husband's newly acquired license to practice medicine. The principal issue presented is whether that license, acquired during their marriage, is marital property subject to equitable distribution under Domestic Relations Law § 236 (B) (5). Supreme Court held that it was and accordingly made a distributive award in defendant's favor. . . . [Editor's note: Mrs. O'Brien was the defendant in this action]. On appeal to the Appellate Division, a majority of that court held that plaintiff's medical license is not marital property and that defendant was not entitled to an award for the expert witness fees. It modified the judgment and remitted the case to Supreme Court for further proceedings, specifically for a determination of maintenance and a rehabilitative award. The matter is before us by leave of the Appellate Division.

We now hold that plaintiff's medical license constitutes "marital property" within the meaning of Domestic Relations Law § 236 (B) (1) (c) and that it is therefore subject to equitable distribution pursuant to subdivision 5 of that part. . . .

Plaintiff and defendant married on April 3, 1971. At the time both were employed as teachers at the same private school. Defendant had a bachelor's degree and a temporary teaching certificate but required 18 months of postgraduate classes at an approximate cost of $3,000, excluding living expenses, to obtain permanent certification in New York. She claimed, and the trial court found, that she had relinquished the opportunity to obtain permanent certification while plaintiff pursued his education. At the time of the marriage, plaintiff had completed only three and one-half years of college but shortly afterward he returned to school at night to earn his bachelor's degree and to complete sufficient premedical courses to enter medical school. In September 1973 the parties moved to Guadalajara, Mexico, where plaintiff became a full-time medical student. While he pursued his studies defendant held several teaching and tutorial positions and contributed her earnings to their joint expenses. The parties returned to New York in December 1976 so that plaintiff could complete the last two semesters of medical school and internship training here. After they returned, defendant resumed her former teaching position and she remained in it at the time this action was commenced. Plaintiff was licensed to practice medicine in October 1980. He commenced this action for divorce two months later. At the time of trial, he was a resident in general surgery.

During the marriage both parties contributed to paying the living and educational expenses and they received additional help from both of their families. They disagreed on the amounts of their respective contributions but it is undisputed that in addition to performing household work and managing the family finances defendant was gainfully employed throughout the marriage, that she contributed all of her earnings to their living and educational expenses and that her financial contributions exceeded those of plaintiff. The trial court found that she had contributed 76 percent of the parties' income exclusive of a $10,000 student loan obtained by defendant. . . .

Defendant presented expert testimony that the present value of plaintiff's medical license was $472,000. . . . The court, after considering the life-style that plaintiff would enjoy from the enhanced earning potential his medical license would bring and defendant's contributions and efforts toward attainment of it, made a distributive award to her of

$188,800, representing 40 percent of the value of the license, and ordered it paid in 11 annual installments of various amounts beginning November 1, 1982 and ending November 1, 1992. . . .

A divided Appellate Division, relying on its prior decision in Conner v Conner, 97 A.D.2d 88 and the decision of the Fourth Department in Lesman v Lesman 88 A.D.2d 153, concluded that a professional license acquired during marriage is not marital property subject to distribution. . . .

The Equitable Distribution Law contemplates only two classes of property: marital property and separate property. The former, which is subject to equitable distribution, is defined broadly as all property acquired by either or both spouses during the marriage and before the execution of a separation agreement or the commencement of a matrimonial action, regardless of the form in which title is held Plaintiff does not contend that his license is excluded from distribution because it is separate property; rather, he claims that it is not property at all but represents a personal attainment in acquiring knowledge. He rests his argument on decisions in similar cases from other jurisdictions and on his view that a license does not satisfy common law concepts of property.

Neither contention is controlling because decisions in other States rely principally on their own statutes, and the legislative history underlying them, and because the New York Legislature deliberately went beyond traditional property concepts when it formulated the Equitable Distribution Law. . . . Instead, our statute recognizes that spouses have an equitable claim to things of value arising out of the marital relationship and classifies them as subject to distribution by focusing on the marital status of the parties at the time of acquisition. Those things acquired during marriage and subject to distribution have been classified as "marital property" although, as one commentator has observed, they hardly fall within the traditional property concepts because there is no common law property interest remotely resembling marital property. . . . Having classified the property subject to distribution, the Legislature did not attempt to go further and define it but left it to the courts to determine what interests come within the terms of section 236 (B) (1) (c).

We made such a determination in Majauskas v Majauskas 61 N.Y.2d 481 holding there that vested but unmatured pension rights are marital property subject to equitable distribution. Because pension benefits are not specifically identified as marital property in the statute, we looked to the express reference to pension rights contained in section 236 (B) (5) (d) (4), which deals with equitable distribution of marital property, to other provisions of the equitable distribution statute and to the legislative intent behind its enactment to determine whether pension rights are marital property or separate property. A similar analysis is appropriate here and leads to the conclusion that marital property encompasses a license to practice medicine to the extent that the license is acquired during marriage.

Section 236 provides that in making an equitable distribution of marital property, the court shall consider: any equitable claim to, interest in, or direct or indirect contribution made to the acquisition of such marital property by the party not having title, including joint efforts or expenditures and contributions and services as a spouse, parent, wage earner and homemaker, and to the career or career potential of the other party [and] . . . the impossibility or difficulty of evaluating any component asset or any interest in a business, corporation or profession. Where equitable distribution of marital property is appropriate but "the distribution of an interest in a business, corporation or profession would be contrary to law" the court shall make a distributive award in lieu of an actual distribution of the property. . . .

The words mean exactly what they say: that an interest in a profession or professional career potential is marital property which may be represented by direct or indirect contributions of the nontitle holding spouse, including financial contributions and nonfinancial contributions made by caring for the home and family.

The history which preceded enactment of the statute confirms this interpretation. Reform of section 236 was advocated because experience had proven that application of the traditional common law title theory of property had caused inequities upon dissolution of a marriage. The Legislature replaced the existing system with equitable distribution of marital property, an entirely new theory which considered all the circumstances of the case and of the respective parties to the marriage. . . . Equitable distribution was based on the premise that a marriage is, among other things, an economic partnership to which both parties contribute as spouse, parent, wage earner or homemaker. . . .

The determination that a professional license is marital property is also consistent with the conceptual base upon which the statute rests. As this case demonstrates, few undertakings during a marriage better qualify as the type of joint effort that the statute's economic partnership theory is intended to address than contributions toward one spouse's acquisition of a professional license. In this case, nearly all of the parties' nine-year marriage was devoted to the acquisition of plaintiff's medical license and defendant played a major role in that project. She worked continuously during the marriage and contributed all of her earnings to their joint effort, she sacrificed her own educational and career opportunities, and she traveled with plaintiff to Mexico for three and one-half years while he attended medical school there. The Legislature has decided, by its explicit reference in the statute to the contributions of one spouse to the other's profession or career that these contributions represent investments in the economic partnership of the marriage and that the product of the parties' joint efforts, the professional license, should be considered marital property. . . .

Accordingly, in view of our holding that plaintiff's license to practice medicine is marital property, the order of the Appellate Division should be modified, with costs to defendant, by reinstating the judgment and the case remitted to the Appellate Division for determination of the facts, including the exercise of that court's discretion and, as so modified, affirmed. . . .

Case Questions for Discussion

1. A professional license is like a patent or a copyright, except patents or copyrights can be sold or licensed. Should this difference preclude the finding that a professional license is marital property subject to distribution?

2. The court speaks of the underlying theory of the marriage as a partnership. Do you think marriages should be looked upon as partnerships?

3. If the professional license were not marital property, would Dr. O'Brien have been unjustly enriched during the marriage?

4. Do you agree that Mrs. O'Brien contributed to the attainment of the medical license?

Spousal Support, Maintenance, or Alimony

Alimony was once considered a continuation of the duty of spousal support after marriage ended. It has its roots in the limited divorces permitted under English and early American family law. Although the couple no longer lived together, the husband still owed the wife (the laws were gender oriented) a duty of support. By the 1970s and with the advent of no fault divorce, alimony came to be based more on need and consistent with the goal of putting both spouses on a self-sufficient basis. Today, alimony is most commonly referred to as *maintenance* or spousal support. Section 308 of the Uniform Marriage and Divorce Act (UMDA) allows the granting of a maintenance award only if the spouse seeking support lacks sufficient property to provide for his or her reasonable needs and is unable to support himself or herself through appropriate employment, or is the custodian of a child whose circumstances or condition renders it inappropriate for the custodial parent to seek employment outside of the home. Once the initial threshold is met, the court considers the following factors when determining the award: (1) assets owned, including marital property awarded; (2) child support orders awarded a custodial parent; (3) time necessary to acquire education or training to find adequate employment; (4) the standard of living during the marriage; (5) the duration of the marriage; (6) the age and condition of the spouse seeking support; and (7) the ability of the paying spouse to provide for personal needs as well as to make support payments.[58]

Although the UMDA is not widely adopted, its theory of viewing alimony as a tool to allow a spouse to become self-sufficient has been influential. The *rehabilitative* theory of alimony provides financial support to the recipient spouse for a relatively short period of time to allow her or him to acquire training or education to become self-sufficient.[59] Fault is irrelevant in the majority of states, while in others it may be a bar to an alimony award.[60] States differ about determining the standard of living the spouse seeking support should be able to provide for herself or himself. Some require only that an ex-spouse be able to fulfill his or her basic needs, whereas others look to the standard of living enjoyed during the marriage. In general, courts possess discretion on the issue. Judges take into account such factors as duration of the marriage and whether the spouse seeking support sacrificed to raise children.[61]

In 1997, the American Law Institute issued *Principles of the Law of Family Dissolution* (ALIPLFD). It embraces the concept of temporary (rehabilitative) spousal support payments. It recommends that each state adopt a formula to determine the length of spousal support payments (e.g., half the number of months the marriage lasted). Permanent support payments should be awarded only when the age of the payee spouse and the length of the marriage are in excess of minimums to be determined by the states (e.g., 55 years old and 25 years of marriage).[62]

Individual states differ on how they approach the matter of spousal support. Some, for example, may be more likely to consider fault and may make permanent alimony awards. It is essential to research the individual statutes and the case law in the state under question. A good starting point is on the web at <http://www.Divorceinfo.com>.[63]

Children

Children are often at issue when a marriage is ending. Custody, visitation, and support are serious matters that often give rise to extended litigation. Children born out of wedlock, adoption, and artificial conception issues are also important matters we discuss in the final section of the chapter.

Dependent Children of Divorcing Parents

Although divorcing couples may battle over economic assets, the most emotionally charged issue is often *child custody*. When both parents want custody, all states charge the court with making a decision in the *best interest of the child*. Although the actual statutory language differs from state to state (e.g., welfare of the child, or happiness and welfare of the child), the standard is the same—the best interest of the child.

Under the Uniform Marriage and Divorce Act, courts should consider all relevant factors, including the five in Box 12.5, when determining child custody in accordance with the best interests of the child.

When considering the factors, the court should not consider conduct of a proposed custodian that does not affect his or her relationship

---

Box 12.5   UMDA Child Custody Factors § 402

1. The wishes of the child's parent or parents as to his custody.
2. The wishes of the child as to his custodian.
3. The interaction and interrelationship of the child with his parent or parents, his siblings, and any other person who may significantly affect the child's best interest.
4. The child's adjustment to his home, school, and community.
5. The mental and physical health of all individuals involved.

---

to the child.[64] The 27 jurisdictions listed in Box 12.6 have enacted factors patterned after the UMDA provision.

Box 12.6   UMDA Patterned Child Custody Factors Jurisdictions[65]

Alaska, Arizona, Colorado, Delaware, District of Columbia, Florida, Idaho, Illinois, Indiana, Iowa, Kansas, Kentucky, Louisiana, Maine, Michigan, Minnesota, Missouri, Montana, Jew Jersey, North Dakota, Ohio, Oregon, Texas, Vermont, Virginia, Washington, and Wisconsin.

Popular additional factors include the desirability of not making the child move; moral fitness; allegations of child abuse or domestic violence; which parent is more capable of giving the child love, affection, guidance, and education; and which parent is more likely to cooperate with the noncustodial parent on visitation and decision-making. States with no or few statutory factors have judicially created factors that are much like the statutory ones.[66]

Historically, mothers routinely were awarded custody of children, especially young children, under the *tender years doctrine*. However, in recent decades, the tender years doctrine came under attack, and many states legislatively or judicially repealed the preference for the mother. West Virginia countered with the *primary caretaker preference,* which created a presumption for custody to the spouse that performed the task of primary caretaker. The ALIPLFD (American Law Institute's Principals of the Law of Family Dissolution) endorses the primary caretaker presumption.[67] Outside of West Virginia, however, the primary caretaker preference is used as a factor instead of a presumption. But if both parents are equally fit when considering other factors, the primary caretaker usually has an advantage.[68] Fathers have had success gaining custody by showing they were the primary caretaker.[69] The child's (if old enough) preference is given weight by most courts, but it is not controlling, especially if the parent the child prefers to live with is unfit or is likely to provide inadequate supervision. States differ about how old a child must be, but usually children older than 12 are considered mature enough to have a reasoned preference.[70]

Custody battles can become especially nasty when one parent alleges the other is morally unfit. As a general rule, courts consider a parent's behavior, but only to determine if the activity in question is likely to affect the child's emotional, moral, or physical well-being. Heterosexual affairs will not ordinarily affect the outcome, unless it can be shown the parent involved exposes the child to immoral actions or fails to protect or to properly supervise the child. Gay and lesbian conduct by a parent is usually given more weight, especially if the parent is indiscreet or attempts to influence the child's sexual preference. Substance abuse may be a highly weighted factor if the abuse is likely to affect the child's welfare. If it can be shown that a parent is chronically impaired, courts often conclude it is in the child's best interest to live with the nonimpaired parent. Likewise, courts weigh heavily evidence of child abuse or criminal activity by one of the parents.[71]

Joint custody is authorized by statute in a majority of states. Some of the states listed in Box 12.7 have created presumptions in favor of joint custody, which must be overcome before awarding custody to one parent.[72]

Box 12.7   States With Statutory Joint Custody[73]

Alabama, Arizona, California, Colorado, Connecticut, Delaware, Florida, Hawaii, Idaho, Illinois, Indiana, Iowa, Kansas, Kentucky, Louisiana, Maine, Maryland, Massachusetts, Michigan, Minnesota, Mississippi, Missouri, Montana, Nebraska, Nevada, New Hampshire, New Jersey, New Mexico, North Carolina, Ohio, Oklahoma, Oregon, Pennsylvania, South Dakota, Tennessee, Texas, Utah, Vermont, Virginia, Washington, and Wisconsin.

Even where not authorized by statute, courts have the discretion to award joint custody, by employing the best interest of the child standard. There are two types of joint custody. Under *joint legal custody,* both parents retain decision-making authority regarding the child's health, education, and welfare. With *joint physical custody,* both parents possess the same joint decision-making authority as in joint legal custody. In addition, the parents also enjoy a near equal sharing of where the child resides. Joint physical custody arrangements are less common because they require the child to move back and forth between two residences. They also require more financial costs, because both parents need to maintain households for the child. Generally, if a joint custody decree is issued, but one of the parents is designated the primary physical custodian, the arrangement is one of joint legal custody.[74]

Children can suffer when divorcing parents cannot find some common ground on custody and visitation.

In almost all cases, the parent without physical custody of the child is granted visitation. It is very difficult to deny a parent the ability to visit with a child. To deny visitation, it must be shown that the child would be subject to physical or emotional harm. Even in situations where the noncustodial parent has been shown to be of some emotional or physical danger to the child, courts usually opt to limit visitation (such as supervision by a third party or in a public place) rather than to deny it altogether. Under § 407 of the Uniform Marriage and Divorce Act, termination of visitation is allowable only if the child's mental, moral, physical, or emotional health would be seriously endangered.[75] Visitation by the noncustodial parent can often be a point of contention between former spouses. It is far better for the child if former spouses cooperate with one another. Children should know both of their parents and not be the center of a continuing dispute. Financially and emotionally, it is usually to no one's benefit to continually litigate visitation.

Frustrated parents sometimes kidnap their own children and move them to a secreted location. Most jurisdictions and the federal government have enacted legislation aimed at stopping the practice. The federal *Parental Kidnapping Prevention Act* provides that sister states must give full faith and credit to custody orders if the original rendering state had jurisdiction. This prevents a noncustodial parent from secretly relocating with the child to another state, and then petitioning the courts there for a modification of the custody order after residency is established. In addition, if the original state has made parental child-napping a felony, the federal Fugitive Felon Act applies. The United States is a party to the Hague Convention on the Civil Aspects of International Child Abduction along with over thirty other countries. It provides a mechanism for returning children who have been child-napped by a parent over international borders.[76]

Since the 1970s, grandparents and other nonparents have gained legal standing to seek visitation. All jurisdictions allow grandparents to seek visitation. Most require that certain circumstances exist before a grandparent may seek visitation rights. The statutes vary widely on the required circumstances, but the two most common are as follows: (1) the parents are divorced, or (2) the grandparent's child is dead. Courts typically possess broad discretion when considering whether to grant grandparent visitation, and judges do so by employing the best interest standard. Among the considerations are whether the grandparent and child had an ongoing love relationship, whether it would be traumatic for the child to lose contact with the grandparent, and the child's wishes.[77]

These statutes may be in jeopardy, however. The Supreme Court of Illinois recently invalidated the state's grandparent visitation statute. It held the statute violated a parent's fundamental liberty interest in making decisions concerning a child's care, custody, and control without due process of law.[78] Persons other than grandparents, such as stepparents, siblings, and others, have increasing access to visitation. Although not universal like grandparent visitation standing, more states are allowing this class of individuals access to visitation. Typically, visitation will be allowed only when a preexisting important relationship exists between the child and the person seeking visitation. Again, the best interest standard is used.[79]

The setting of and the collection of child support obligations have been nagging problems in the United States. "Deadbeat dads" (and "deadbeat moms") who fail to pay child support and yet live well, while their children sink into poverty, are common. Politicians have railed against the problem, and the states and the federal government have been cooperating in locating and extracting back support obligations.

Prior to the 1980s, child support orders were discretionary in most states and varied widely. In 1984, the federal Child Support Enforcement Amendments required all states to adopt nonbinding child support guidelines. In 1988, Congress required the states to make the guidelines a rebuttable presumption.[80] As the states adopted guidelines for child support under the federal mandate, three general types evolved. First, there are *flat percentage schemes*. These guidelines typically assign a flat percentage of the noncustodial parent's net or gross income for each child. For example, Wisconsin sets 17 percent of the noncustodial parent's gross income for one child, 25 percent for two, 29 percent for three, and 31 percent for four. Some states make adjustments for certain expenses, while others do little or no adjusting.[81]

Under the second type, the *income shares model*, a support obligation is computed on the gross or net income of both parents. A basic support obligation (after adjustments for self-support) is added to actual work-related expenditures for child care and extraordinary medical expenses. The total support obligation is then allocated to the parents based on their share of the total income.[82] For example, assume that the basic support obligation is $600 per month, plus a work-related child care expense of $300 per month for a total support obligation of $900 per month. Also assume that the custodial parent's income is $2,000 per month, and the noncustodial parent's income is $4,000 per month. The $900 per month total support obligation would be allocated one third to the custodial parent ($900 x $2,000/$6,000 = $300) and two thirds to the noncustodial parent ($900 x $4,000/$6,000 = $600). The custodial parent retains his or her share of the obligation to spend on the child, and the noncustodial parent would make child support payments of $600 per month.

The *Delaware Melson formula* is the third type of guideline. It adds another step to the income shares model. Once the total support obligation is computed (the $900 from the example above), children are allowed to share in any additional income of the parents. The policy goal is to permit the child or children to enjoy the parents' standard of living.[83]

Other Issues Involving Children

Children born out of wedlock, adoption, and artificial conception methods all raise issues involving children. We now turn to a discussion of each topic.

Children Born out of Wedlock

In the common law tradition, illegitimate children had no parents (mother or father) and, as a result, had no bloodline through which they could inherit property. The legal policy was founded on the assumption that the nonrecognition of "bastards" would strengthen the stability of families and promote social order. In reality, it unjustly punished the innocent children of illicit liaisons. This legal fiction soon disappeared as it applied to the mother because it was impossible for the mother to deny she was the parent. But with respect to the father, it remained ingrained in the law.[84]

Today, as long as parentage is established, illegitimate children enjoy near equality with their legitimate siblings. Actions to establish paternity are civil in nature and require only a preponderance of the evidence. Where once it was difficult to prove paternity, modern science has provided the courts with a considerable degree of certainty. Typically, once paternity is established, the father must provide support. As illustrated in the *Baby Jessica* and *Baby Richard* cases, an unmarried father has custodial rights that are afforded due process protection. Both of the much publicized and criticized cases involved illegitimate children given up for adoption by their mothers without the consent or knowledge of the biological fathers. Both fathers asserted their parental rights as soon as they became aware that they had fathered children. Although the children were with the adoptive parents for at least two years, the adoptions were voided and the fathers gained custody of their children.[85]

Adoption

Adoption severs the rights of the natural parents and creates parental rights and responsibilities in the adoptive parents. Likewise, an adopted child has no legal relationship with the natural parents and full legal status as a child in relation to the adoptive parents. As adoption was not recognized under common law, all adoptions are governed by statute. Children may be adopted if their natural parents are dead, have abandoned them, are unknown, or consent to the adoption. Some states even provide for the adoption of adults.

Adoptions usually occur in one of two ways in the United States. First, agency placements are made through a public agency or a private agency licensed by the state. Agency placements involve investigation of the adoptive parent's lifestyle and finances. Typically, agency placements take many months or years. Advantages include privacy (the birth parents are unaware of who adopted their child) and minimal costs. Private placements involve the direct placement of the adopted child by the natural parents, usually just the birth mother, or a representative of the natural parents. These placements are commonly expensive and can involve many risks unassociated with agency adoptions, such as the natural parents changing their mind, wanting to be paid for the child, or later seeking contact with the child. Many of the common adoption horror stories one sees in the news media involve private placement adoptions. Foreign adoptions have become more common as the demand for healthy babies far outstrips the supply.[86] The laws of the country where the child resides govern foreign adoptions.[87] Often the adopting parents must endure a lengthy stay in the country of the child and negotiate with the foreign country's bureaucracy. Black markets plague private placements and foreign adoptions.

Many legal and social issues surround adoption. May gay and lesbian couples adopt? At least two states, New Hampshire and Florida, say no.[88] May race play a role in deciding whether a child should be placed with prospective parents? The National Association of Black Social Workers has called interracial adoptions "cultural and racial genocide."[89] A federal statute makes it a violation of Title VI (Title VI applies to organizations or persons receiving federal funds) of the Civil Rights Act of 1964 for a person or government to deny or delay a child's adoption due to the race, color, or national origin of the child or the person seeking the adoption.[90] Should adopted children have access to their natural parents at some point in their lives? Many adoptees call for the unsealing of their original birth certificates to be able to contact birth mothers and fathers, especially for the purpose of gaining knowledge of medical histories. Some advocate the release of all nonidentifying information. Four states—Alaska, Kansas, Tennessee, and Oregon—allow adoptees access to their original birth certificates.[91] Most states have some type of provision allowing adoptees and birth parents to register their consent to meet.[92]

Science and Family Law

Reproductive science has advanced so quickly that the law has been playing catch-up. Couples who have been unable to conceive children naturally have embraced the new technology. So have nontraditional family units. Single people and gay and lesbian couples have turned to reproductive science to have children. Quite often the issues arising out of the new reproductive methods have not been anticipated by legislatures, and the courts have had to deal with them on a case-by-case basis. In this section we briefly explore the issues surrounding artificial insemination, in vitro fertilization, and surrogacy. Cloning, when it eventually occurs, will present a fresh slate of issues, for cloned children will truly have only one parent.

Artificial insemination increases the chance of a woman getting pregnant because this technology bypasses the cervical barrier. It is also used when a man is infertile. When a husband's sperm is used, no real issues arise. The wife and the husband are genetically related to the child in the same manner as a child born naturally. If artificial insemination is being used because a husband is unable to produce viable sperm, donor sperm is used. In that case, the wife is genetically related, but the husband is not. At least 30 states have enacted statutes that recognize the husband as the legal father if he consents to his wife being artificially inseminated with donor sperm and a child is born. At least 15 states statutorily sever the parental rights of sperm donors who deliver their sperm to a licensed physician,[93] which is adequate as long as artificial insemination is used by married couples.

However, if an unmarried couple, a single woman, or a lesbian couple use artificial insemination and donated sperm to produce a child, there is no legal father under these statutes. The biological father is the sperm donor, but whether he should be responsible for the child and also have the right to visit or seek custody can be very murky, especially because of the enhanced recognition given to fathers of children born out of wedlock. In *McIntyre v. Crouch*,[94] Oregon's Court of Appeals held that a statute barring a sperm donor from initiating an action to have his parentage of a child established violated his due process rights. The sperm donor was known to the woman, and he alleged there was an agreement whereby he would be the father of the child.

With *in vitro fertilization*, a woman's eggs are removed and fertilized with sperm outside of the woman's body. The fertilized egg is then inserted in the woman's womb, where it is gestated. These children are commonly called "test tube babies." As long as a wife's eggs are inseminated with her husband's sperm and the wife carries the baby to birth, there is no need to change existing legal policy. Complications arise, however, when donated eggs or sperm are used, and when unmarried women or lesbian couples employ in vitro fertilization. Further complications can arise when a single man or a gay couple provide the sperm and have a surrogate mother carry the baby to term.[95] In parentage disputes, two states, California and New York, use an *intent test* to determine parentage. The parties intending to create and raise a child through artificial means are deemed the natural parents of the child, despite the child's genetics.[96] Ohio, on the other hand, looks strictly at genetics to determine parentage.[97]

Because in vitro fertilization creates preembryos outside the woman's body, the issue of who controls the disposition of these preembryos has proven troublesome. The Tennessee Supreme Court held that frozen preembryos were neither persons nor property, and absent an agreement, either ex-spouse could choose to have them destroyed.[98] Based on a contract analysis, the New York Court of Appeals decided that the disposition of frozen preembryos created by a married couple before they were divorced should be controlled by a disposition contract they had agreed to prior to the divorce.[99] In a dispute between a fertility clinic and a married couple who had frozen preembryos created for them, a federal district court determined the preembryos were property. Because the clinic entered into a bailment with the couple, the clinic must follow the couple's wishes concerning the disposition of the preembryos.[100] A California fertility clinic's actions provide one of the most bizarre situations. The clinic implanted preembryos preserved for previous patients into the wombs of current patients without informing any of the parties. Some of the resulting children were several years old before the genetic parents or the birth parents became aware of what had happened.[101]

In *surrogacy,* a woman agrees to be impregnated (generally either through artificial insemination or in vitro fertilization) and to carry a child to term, then surrender the child to another person or couple. The child born by the surrogate may or may not carry the surrogate's genetics. Likewise the child may or may not carry the genetics of the couple or person for whom the child is being carried. Usually the surrogate is paid for her services. She contractually agrees to surrender the baby and any parental rights to it once it is born. The most famous surrogacy case is *In re Baby M.* In that case, the surrogate was impregnated by artificial insemination with the sperm of the husband of a married couple who were unable to have a child normally. The surrogate and the couple had entered into a contract that paid the surrogate $10,000 in exchange for her service and her promise to relinquish her rights to the child. Upon the birth of the child, the surrogate backed out of the agreement, and she refused to give up the child. The New Jersey Supreme Court held that the contract was unenforceable because it was the equivalent of "baby selling." As a result, the surrogate was the legal mother and the husband of the couple was the legal father. The court decided custody under the best interest standard and awarded custody to the father.[102]

Surrogacy statutes are common. Some states allow unpaid agreements, others declare all surrogate contracts void, and others declare compensated surrogate contracts void but do not mention unpaid agreements. A few states do not specifically prohibit or validate surrogacy agreements, but these states do exempt them from laws prohibiting payments in connection with adoptions.[103] Three states, New Hampshire, Nevada, and Virginia, allow commercial surrogate contracts.[104]

Other countries have either enacted comprehensive statutory schemes or commissioned groups to study the issues and to recommend comprehensive legislation on the subject of technologically assisted conception and birth. To date, the Uniform Parentage Act and the Uniform Status of Children of Assisted Conception Act have been proposed in the United States. Only a minority of jurisdictions has adopted either of the two acts. Neither of the acts adequately deals with all of the legal issues that arise as more and more people take advantage of the rapidly advancing science of reproduction.[105]

Key Terms, Names, and Concepts

Abandonment

Adoption

Adultery

Alcohol abuse

Alimony

All property theory

Annulment

Antenuptial (premarital)
   agreements

Artificial insemination

Best interest of the child

Canonical disability

Child custody

Child support

Civil unions

Common law marriage

Community property

Criminal convictions

Cruelty

Defense of Marriage Act

Delaware Melson Formula

Dissipation of assets

Divorce

Dual property theory

Economic fault

Equitable division of
   property

Fault-based divorce

Flat percentage schemes

In manu marriage

In vitro fertilization

Income shares model

Intent test

Joint legal custody

Joint physical custody

Maintenance

Marital property

Mental illness

Miscegenation statutes

No fault divorce

Nonmarital property

Parental Kidnapping Prevention Act

Partnership theory of
　marriage
Polygamy
Principles of the Law of
　Family Dissolution
Primary caretaker preference
Reciprocal Enforcement of
　Support Act
Recrimination
Rehabilitative theory
　of alimony

Surrogate mother
Tender years doctrine
Title theory
Unconscionable
Uniform Marriage and Divorce Act
Uniform Parentage Act
Uniform Premarital Agreement Act

Discussion Questions

1. Anna (an African American woman), Bill, and Chuck (both white men) present themselves at the county clerk's office and request a marriage license. The clerk refuses, saying that the state's marriage statute allows only one man and one woman to be married. Would Anna, Bill, and Chuck be successful in a *Loving v. Virginia* or *Baehr v. Lewin* type action, requesting the court to order the clerk to issue them a marriage license?

2. Jason and Lisa were childhood sweethearts in Pennsylvania. He was the star quarterback, and she was the prettiest cheerleader. As soon as they graduated from high school, they began living together. Lisa began using Jason's last name, they bought property together as man and wife, they used joint bank accounts and credit cards, and they told all of their friends and relatives they had eloped. In fact, they never formally married. After nine years of cohabitation, while Jason was a backup for the Philadelphia Eagles, he signed a huge free agent contract with the New York Giants and moved to New York. Lisa remained behind after they agreed Jason would commute. One morning, Lisa opened the morning paper and read that Jason had married a beautiful young actress. After reaching Jason by phone, Lisa was told she could keep the money in the joint checking account and their Pennsylvania home, but he was moving on. Lisa visits your law office and asks whether she has any right to the millions Jason will be paid over the next five years by the Giants. How do you advise her?

3. Ann and Bob were married in a ceremony at their church after getting a proper marriage license. At the time of their marriage, Ann told Bob she was a virgin. About a month after the marriage, Ann told Bob she was pregnant. Bob soon discovered Ann

was pregnant with another man's child conceived two months before the wedding. May Bob have the marriage annulled?

4. Defend the proposition that divorce should be granted only if one of the parties is at fault. Defend the proposition that divorce should be freely available without fault.

5. The rehabilitative theory of alimony, endorsed by the Uniform Marriage and Divorce Act, views alimony as a tool to be used to prepare a former spouse to support him- or herself. Do you agree with that theory?

6. Should commercial surrogacy contracts be enforceable? Do you believe that it is baby selling?

7. Assume that Mr. and Mrs. Ames are both infertile, but wish to have a child. They find an egg donor and a sperm donor, and they have an in vitro fertilization procedure done at a local fertility clinic. One of the resulting preembryos is implanted in Mrs. Baines, who has agreed to voluntarily carry the baby to term. Mr. Baines does not know of the agreement until after the procedure has been completed. The other four preembryos are frozen and held by the clinic.

    a. How many legal parents could the resulting child have?

    b. Who should be the parents under the *intent test* of California and New York? What might be the result under the *genetic test* of Ohio?

    c. Whom do you think should be the legal parents?

    d. Mr. and Mrs. Baines give up the child as agreed, but decide they want to have a child like the one they gave up. Should Mr. and Mrs. Ames be able to stop the clinic from implanting one of the frozen preembryos into Mrs. Baines, despite sharing no genetics with the preembryos? If yes, under what theory of law?

8. Mr. and Mrs. Cahill have been unable to have a child. They visit a fertility clinic and have an in vitro fertilization procedure performed using their own eggs and sperm. Five preembryos are created, and one is implanted in Mrs. Cahill. She has a child nine months later. The other four preembryos are frozen. Mr. and Mrs. Dobs are both infertile. They visit the same fertility clinic and ask to have an in vitro fertilization procedure with donor eggs and sperm. The clinic agrees, but implants one of the preembryos created for Mr. and Mrs. Cahill into Mrs. Dobs. She has a child nine months later. One year later, the Cahills become aware of what happened. Who should be the legal parents of the child born by Mrs. Dobs?

9. Mr. and Mrs. Els are both infertile. They visit a fertility clinic and arrange for an in vitro fertilization procedure using donor eggs and sperm. Mrs. Els becomes pregnant, but before the child is born, Mr. Els files for divorce and disclaims the child being carried by Mrs. Els. Should Mr. Els be able to disavow the unborn child?

10. Would your answer to Question 9 be different if instead of the child being carried by Mrs. Els, it is carried by a surrogate?

Suggested Additional Reading

Cucci, Nichole, L. "Constitutional Implications of In Vitro Fertilization." *St. John's Law Review* 72 (spring 1998): 417–449.

Eiseman, Connie E. "The Maryland Survey: 1997–1998: Recent Decisions: The Maryland Court of Appeals." *Maryland Law Review* 58 (1999): 920–959.

Faust, Susan M. "Comment: Baby Girl or Baby Boy? Now You Can Choose: A Look at New Biology and No Law." *Albany Law Journal of Science and Technology* 10 (2000): 281–303.

Johnson, Greg. "Vermont Civil Unions: The New Language of Marriage." *Vermont Law Review* 25 (fall 2000): 15–59.

Lal, Meena. "The Role of the Federal Government in Assisted Reproductive Technologies." *Santa Clara Computer & High Technology Law Journal* 13 (May 1997): 519–543.

Lenoir, Noelle. "French, European, and International Legislation on Bioethics." *Suffolk University Law Review* 27 (winter 1993): 1249–1270.

Malo, Peter E. "Deciding Custody of Frozen Embryos: Many Eggs Are Frozen but Who Is Chosen?" *DePaul Journal of Health Care Law* 3 (winter 2000): 307–334. "Recent Legislation: Domestic Relations-Same Sex Couples-Vermont Creates System of Civil Unions. Act Relating to Civil Unions." *Harvard Law Review* 114 (February 2001): 1421–1426.

Reiss, Claudine, R. "The Fear of Opening Pandora's Box: The Need to Restore Birth Parents' Privacy Rights in the Adoption Process." *Southwestern University Law Review* 28 (1998): 133–156.

Silbaugh, Katherine, B. "Marriage Contracts and the Family Economy." *Northwestern University Law Review* 93 (Fall 1998): 65–143.

Sites, Billy. "Court-Ordered Grandparent Visitation: The Best Interest of the Child or Child Abuse." Available online at the website of the *Coalition for the Restoration of Parental Rights*, at <http://www.parentsrights.org/>, as of May 10, 2001.

Endnotes

1. Associated Press (Washington), "Census: Big Increase in Unmarried Couples," available online at <http://www.cnn.com/2001/US/05/15/census2000.ap/>, as of May 22, 2001.
2. Laura Reynolds, "Marriage in the Middle Ages II," available online as of 04/03/2001 at <http://marriage.about.com/people/marriage/library/weekly/aa070198.htm>. See also, "History of Marriage, Concept Basically the Same?" at the same site.
3. Arnold H. Rutkin, ed., *Family Law and Practice*, (New York: Matthew Bender and Company, 2000), § 5.01.
4. Harry D. Krause, *Family Law in a Nutshell*, 3rd ed. (St. Paul, MN: West, 1995), § 1.2.
5. Ibid., § 1.4.
6. 750 ICLS 5/201 through 219 (1998 State Bar Edition).
7. 388 U.S. 1 (1967).
8. Zablocki v. Redhail, 434 U.S. 374 (1978).
9. Turner v. Safley, 482 U.S. 78 (1987).
10. Judith Areen, *Family Law, Cases and Materials*, 4th ed. (New York: Foundation Press, 1999), pp. 14–27 and 46–60. Reynolds v. United States, 98 U.S. 145 (1879) (polygamy), Jones v. Hallahan, 501 S.W.2d 588 (Court of Appeals of Kentucky, 1973) (same-sex marriages), and Moe v. Dinkins, 533 F. Supp. 623 (S.D.N.Y. 1981), *aff'd* 669 F.2d 67 (2nd Cir. 1982) (minimum age requirements).
11. Baehr v. Miike, 1996 WL 694234 (Haw. Cir. Ct., 1st Cir., 1996), reprinted in Areen, *Family Law, Cases and Materials*, p. 28.
12. Brause v. Alaska, 1998 WL 88743 (Alaska Super. 1998).
13. Areen, *Family Law, Cases and Materials*, p. 42.
14. An Act Relating to Civil Unions, No. 91, 2000 Vt. Adv. Legis. Serv. 68 (LEXIS) (to be codified in scattered sections of Vt. Stat. Ann. tits. 4, 8, 14, 15, 18, 32, 33).
15. Pub. L. No. 104-99, 110 Stat. 2419 (1996), codified at 1 U.S.C. § 7 & 28 U.S.C. § 1738C (2000).
16. 750 ICLS 5/213.1 & 213 (1998 State Bar Edition).
17. Anthony Deutsch, "Dutch Law Allows Same-Sex Marriages," *Associated Press*, Amsterdam, March 31, 2001, available online at <http://www.s-t.com/daily/09-00/09-13-00/a02wn013.html, as of January 12, 2002.
18. Rebecca Berlin, "Is Common Law Marriage an Alternative to the Real Thing?" available online as of April 16, 2001, on AllLaw.com site at <http://www.alllaw.com/articles/family/divorce/article61.asp>. The eleven states are Alabama, Colorado, Iowa, Kansas, Montana, Oklahoma, Pennsylvania, Rhode Island, South Carolina, Texas, and Utah.
19. Crouch v. Crouch, 53 Tenn. App. 594, 385 S.W. 2d 237 (Tenn. App. 1964).
20. 233 So. 2d 381 (S.Ct. Fla. 1970).
21. Pendleton v. Fireman, 72 Cal. Rptr.2d 840 (Ct. App. 1998), *a'ffd*, 24 Cal. 4th 39, 5 P.3d 839 (S. Ct. Cal. 2000).
22. Arizona, Arkansas, California, Connecticut, Delaware, District of Columbia, Hawaii, Idaho, Illinois, Indiana, Iowa, Kansas, Maine, Montana, Nebraska, Nevada, New Mexico, North Carolina, North Da-

kota, Oregon, Rhode Island, South Dakota, Texas, Utah, Virginia, and Wisconsin. Bills are pending in Mississippi, Rhode Island, and West Virginia. Commissioners on Uniform State Laws web page at <http://www.nccusl.org/uniformact_factsheets/uniformacts-fs-upaa.html, available as of April 17, 2001.

23. Charlotte K. Goldberg, "If It Ain't Broke, Don't Fix It: Premarital Agreements and Spousal Support Waivers in California," *Loyola of Los Angeles Law Review* 33 (summer 2000): 1245, at note 106.

24. Rider v. Rider, 669 N.E.2d 166 (Ind. 1996) discussed in Goldberg, "If It Ain't Broke."

25. Marschall v. Marschall, 477 A.2d 833 (N.J. Super. Ct. Ch. Div. 1984), discussed in Goldberg, "If It Ain't Broke."

26. Jacobitti v Jacobitti, 623 A.2d 794 (N.J. Super. Ct. App. Div. 1993) and DeLorean v. DeLorean, 511 A.2d 1257 (N.J. Super. Ct. Ch. Div. 1986), discussed in Goldberg, "If It Ain't Broke."

27. Marsh v. Marsh, 949 S.W.2d 734 (Tx. Ct. App. 1997), discussed in Goldberg, "If It Ain't Broke."

28. Rutkin, *Family Law and Practice*, § 5.01.

29. Ibid., § 5.02.

30. William T. Schantz, *The American Legal Environment: Individuals, Their Business, and Their Government* (St. Paul, MN: West, 1976), pp. 288–290.

31. Rutkin, *Family Law and Practice*, § 4.01.

32. Six months in Connecticut, District of Columbia, Illinois, Louisiana, Minnesota, Montana, and Vermont. Rutkin, *Family Law and Practice*, § 4.02 at note 25.

33. Idaho, Rutkin, *Family Law and Practice*, § 4.02 at note 30.

34. Mississippi and New York require an agreement. Hawaii, Louisiana, and Utah require a legal separation. New York and Tennessee allow the living apart to be pursuant to an agreement or a legal separation. Rutkin, *Family Law and Practice*, § 4.02 at notes 32–34.

35. Illinois allows a period of living apart of six months for parties agreeing to a divorce, but requires two years for those who cannot agree on the divorce. Rutkin, *Family Law and Practice*, § 4.02.

36. Washington, DC, is also no fault only. Rutkin, *Family Law and Practice*, § 4.02, at notes 36–39.

37. South Carolina judicially recognized homosexual activity as adultery in RGM v. DEM, 410 S.E.2d 564 (1991). See, 78 A.L.R. 2d 807 (Annotation: Homosexuality as a Ground for Divorce) for a discussion of other jurisdictions. Sexual activity other than intercourse is adultery in Louisiana, Bonura v. Bonura, 505 So.2d 143, *aff'd*, 506 So.2d 113 (1987). New York has done so legislatively, N.Y.D.R.L. § 170(4). Rutkin, *Family Law and Practice*, § 4.03, at notes 39–41.

38. Alabama, Alaska, Arkansas, Connecticut, Georgia, Idaho, Illinois, Maryland, Massachusetts, Mississippi, New Hampshire, New Jersey, New Mexico, New York, North Dakota, Ohio, Oklahoma, Pennsylvania, South Dakota, Tennessee, Texas, Utah, Virginia, and West Virginia have periods of one year or less. Maine (three years), Rhode Island (five years with court discretion to accept shorter period), and Vermont (seven years) have longer periods. Rutkin, *Family Law and Practice*, § 4.03, at notes 25 & 26.

39. Refusal to engage in sexual relations—Mississippi, New Jersey, New York, and South Dakota; Failure to support—Wisconsin; eviction—South Carolina and Delaware. Rutkin, *Family Law and Practice*, § 4.03, at notes 28–34.

40. California, Florida, Nevada, North Carolina, and Wyoming retain mental illness as the only fault-based or traditional ground for divorce in otherwise no fault statutes. Alabama, Alaska, Arkansas, Connecticut, Delaware, Georgia, Idaho, Indiana, Kansas, Maine, Maryland, Mississippi, New Jersey, North Dakota, Oklahoma, Pennsylvania, Texas, Utah, Vermont, West Virginia, and Wisconsin include mental illness or incompetence as one of their traditional or fault-based grounds for divorce. Rutkin, *Family Law and Practice*, § 4.03, at notes 13 & 14.

41. Alabama, Connecticut, Georgia, Louisiana, Maryland, Massachusetts, Mississippi, New Hampshire, New Jersey, New York, Ohio, Oklahoma, Pennsylvania, Rhode Island, Tennessee, Texas, Vermont, and Virginia require conviction and incarceration. Alaska, Idaho, Illinois, Indiana, North Dakota, Utah, and West Virginia require conviction alone. Rutkin, *Family Law and Practice*, § 4.03, at notes 55 & 56.

42. Habitual drunkenness or intemperance—Alaska, Arkansas, Connecticut, Idaho, New Hampshire, North Dakota, Ohio, Oklahoma, South Dakota, and Utah. Habitual drunkenness or drug abuse—Illinois, Maine, South Carolina (gross and confirmed habits), and Tennessee. Habitual drunkenness and use of specified drugs—Alabama, Georgia, Massachusetts, Mississippi, New Jersey, Rhode Island, and West Virginia. Rutkin, *Family Law and Practice*, § 4.03, at notes 59–61.

43. Rutkin, *Family Law and Practice*, § 4.03.

44. Alabama, Alaska, Arkansas, Connecticut, Georgia, Idaho, Illinois, Maine, Massachusetts, Mississippi, New Hampshire, New Jersey, New Mexico, New York, North Dakota, Ohio, Oklahoma, Pennsylvania, Rhode Island, South Carolina, South Dakota, Texas, Utah, Vermont, Virginia, and West Virginia. Rutkin, *Family Law and Practice*, § 4.03, at note 47.

45. Alaska, Arkansas, North Dakota, Pennsylvania, and South Dakota. Rutkin, *Family Law and Practice*, § 4.03, at note 51.

46. Rutkin, *Family Law and Practice*, § 4.04.

47. Krause, *Family Law in a Nutshell*, §§ 26.1–26.3.

48. Rutkin, *Family Law and Practice*, § 37.01, at note 45.

49. Ibid., § 37.01, at note 50.

50. Alaska, Arkansas, North Carolina, West Virginia, and Wisconsin. Rutkin, *Family Law and Practice*, § 37.01, at note 27.

51. Rutkin, *Family Law and Practice*, § 37.06.

52. Ibid., § 37.01.

53. Ibid.

54. Ibid., § 37.06.

55. Connecticut, Maryland, Massachusetts, Missouri, New Hampshire, South Carolina, and Virginia by statute. Michigan, Rhode Island, and Texas judicially. Rutkin, *Family Law and Practice*, § 37.06, at notes 117–119.

56. Rutkin, *Family Law and Practice*, § 37.06.

57. Ibid., § 37.10.

58. Krause, *Family Law in a Nutshell*, §§ 25.1–25.5.

59. Rutkin, *Family Law and Practice*, § 35.02[2a].

60. Ibid., § 35.02[2b].
61. Ibid., § 35.02[2c].
62. Areen, *Family Law, Cases and Materials,* p. 781.
63. Available online at <http://www.divorceinfo.com/alimony.htm>, as of April 30, 2001.
64. § 402 of UMDA.
65. Rutkin, *Family Law and Practice,* § 32.06, at note 16.
66. Ibid., § 32.06.
67. Krause, *Family Law in a Nutshell,* § 18.3.
68. Rutkin, *Family Law and Practice,* § 32.06.
69. Schmaltz v. Schmaltz, 586 N.W.2d 852 (N.D. 1998), In re Marriage of Milburn, 98 Or. App. 668 (1989), Smith v. Smith, 727 So. 2d 113 (Ala. Civ. App. 1998), and Pearson v. Pearson, 726 A.2d 71 (Vt. 1999). Rutkin, *Family Law and Practice,* § 32.06, at note 67.
70. Rutkin, *Family Law and Practice,* § 32.06[e].
71. Ibid., § 32.06[f].
72. California, Connecticut, Florida, Idaho, Louisiana, Montana, Nevada, New Hampshire, New Mexico, and Utah. Rutkin, *Family Law and Practice,* § 32.08, at note 44.
73. Ibid., § 32.08, at note 40.
74. Rutkin, *Family Law and Practice,* § 32.08[2][b].
75. Krause, *Family Law in a Nutshell,* § 18.15.
76. Ibid., §§ 18.21 & 18.22.
77. Rutkin, *Family Law and Practice,* § 32.09[7].
78. Wickham v. Bryne, 199 Ill.2d 309, 769 N.E.2d 1 (2002).
79. Rutkin, *Family Law and Practice,* § 32.09[7].
80. Pub. L. No. 98-378, codified at 42 U.S.C. § 667(b). Amended in 1998 by Pub. L. No. 100-485.
81. Alaska, Illinois, Massachusetts, Minnesota, New York, Texas, and Wisconsin are examples. Rutkin, *Family Law and Practice,* § 33.06, at notes 1–8.
82. Colorado, Michigan, Missouri, Montana, Nebraska, New Jersey, and Vermont are examples of Income Shares Model states. Rutkin, *Family Law and Practice,* § 33.06, at notes 10–17.
83. Delaware, Hawaii, and Iowa are examples. Rutkin, *Family Law and Practice,* § 33.06, at notes 18–23.
84. Krause, *Family Law in a Nutshell,* § 11.7.
85. Krause, *Family Law in a Nutshell,* Chapter 11. In the Interest of B.G.C. (Jessica), 496 N.W.2d 239 (Iowa 1993), In re Petition of Doe v. Kirchner (Richard), 159 Ill. 2d 347, 638 N.E.2d 181 (1994), *cert denied,* 513 U.S. 994, 115 S.Ct. 1195 (1994).
86. Marsha Garrison, "Law Making for Baby Making: An Interpretive Approach to the Determination of Legal Parentage," *Harvard Law Review* 113 (February 2000): 835. It is estimated that 1,000,000 couples attempt to adopt the 33,000 white babies available for adoption each year. Independent placements account for 30 percent and international adoptions make up one fifth to one sixth of all nonrelative adoptions, at notes 258–260.
87. "Adoption," excerpted from *West's Encyclopedia of American Law,* available online at West Legal Directory home page at www.wld.com and at <http://adoption.about.com/parenting/adoption/gi/dynamic/

offsite.htm?site=http%3A%2F%2Fwww.wld.com%2Fch2000%2Fweal%2Fwadopt1.asp>, as of May 15, 2001.

88. Areen, *Family Law, Cases and Materials*, p. 1443, note 1.
89. Krause, *Family Law in a Nutshell*, § 12.5.
90. 42 USCS §1996b (2001) and Areen, *Family Law, Cases and Materials*, p. 1443 note 2.
91. Brett S. Silverman, "The Winds of Change in Adoption Laws: Should Adoptees Have Access to Adoption Records," *Family Court Review* 39 (Jan. 2001): 85.
92. Garrison, "Law Making for Baby Making," at note 261.
93. Ibid., at notes 35–37. These statutes are based on the Uniform Parentage Act.
94. 98 Ore. App. 462, 780 P.2d 239 (Ct. App 1989), *reh denied*, 308 Or. 593, 784 P.2d 1100, (1989), *cert denied*, 495 U.S. 905, 110 S. Ct. 1924 (1990).
95. Florida and Texas create presumptions that a married woman who bears a child created with a donated egg or preembryo is the mother, provided the husband and wife have consented to the procedure. Garrison, "Law Making for Baby Making," at note 62.
96. Johnson v. Calvert, 851 P.2d 776 (Cal. 1993) *cert. denied*, 510 U.S. 874 (1993), McDonald v. McDonald, 608 N.Y.S.2d 477 (N.Y.App. Div. 1994) and In re Marriage of Buzzanca, 72 Cal. Rptr.2d 280 (Cal. Ct. App. 1998), discussed in Alice M. Noble-Allgire, "Switched at Fertility Clinic: Determining Maternal Rights When a Child Is Born From Stolen or Misdelivered Genetic Material," *Missouri Law Review* 64 (summer 1999): 517.
97. Belsito v. Clark, 644 N.E.2d 760 (Ohio Ct. C.P. 1994), discussed in Noble-Allgire, "Switched at Fertility Clinic," at note 168.
98. Davis v. Davis, 842 S.W.2d 588, 597, 604 (Tenn. 1992), and Garrison, "Law Making for Baby Making," at note 63.
99. Kass v. Kass, 696 N.E.2d 174, 182 (N.Y. 1998), Garrison, "Law Making for Baby Making," at note 63, and Vincent F. Stemple, "Procreative Rights in Assisted Reproductive Technology: Why the Angst?" *Albany Law Review* 62 (1999): 1187.
100. York v. Jones, 717 F. Supp. 421 (E.D. Va. 1989), discussed in Noble-Allgire, "Switched at Fertility Clinic," at note 185.
101. Noble-Allgire, "Switched at Fertility Clinic."
102. 537 A.2d 1227 (N.J. 1988), discussed in Garrison, "Law Making for Baby Making," at note 71.
103. Unpaid valid—Florida, Nevada, and Virginia. All void—Arizona, District of Columbia, Indiana, Michigan, New York, North Dakota, and Utah. Paid void—Kentucky, Louisiana, Nebraska, and Washington. Silent but exempted from laws prohibiting payments in connection with adoptions—Alaska, Iowa, and West Virginia. Noble-Allgire, "Switched at Fertility Clinic," at notes 100–103.
104. Garrison, "Law Making for Baby Making," at note 77.
105. Ibid., at note 79. ✦

Chapter 13

Criminal Law

Chapter Objectives

Students should gain an understanding of how modern American criminal law evolved from the English common law. Students need to be able to identify and explain the limitations on the different sources of police power held by the federal government and the individual states. Readers must be able to explain why an act (actus reus) and a specified state of mind (mens rea) are required for almost all criminal conduct. Students will also acquire a general knowledge of the elements of the major crimes against persons and crimes against property. Students should achieve an appreciation of the issues surrounding select areas of criminal law, such as victimless crimes, attempt, and conspiracy. Finally, students will learn the basic tenets of select defenses available to those accused of a crime.

When an individual causes injury to another's property or person through negligent conduct, that individual may be subject to a civil suit for damages. The injured party must initiate the action and hope to recover through the tort system, as we discussed in Chapter 10. More serious sanctions result from an actor's conduct that is criminal. The entity holding police power—usually the government, but at various times in some nations religious organizations—deems some conduct so wrongful that it is considered injurious to society as a whole and subjects the actor to punishment for his or her actions. The government brings criminal charges against offending parties, who must appear in court for a determination of guilt or innocence. All the power and resources of the government are available to prosecute those who violate the criminal laws. Chapter 7 of this text examines how criminal charges are brought, prosecuted, and defended. This chapter examines the substantive criminal law.

We outline the roots of American criminal law, the sources of police power, the requirement of an act, and the state of mind necessary for a successful criminal prosecution. Sections follow on crimes against persons and crimes against property. We conclude this chapter with briefer discussions of victimless crimes, attempt, conspiracy, and defenses. The list of suggested additional readings at the end of the chapter contains some excellent publications on other areas of criminal law that are beyond the scope of this chapter but may interest students contemplating careers in areas of criminal law. These areas include "RICO" prosecutions, mandatory sentencing laws, "three strikes, you're out" legislation, and accomplice liability.

Criminal Law Roots

Like other areas of substantive law, common law crimes and defenses in the majority of American states came from mother England. Under the English common law system, common law judges could decide that an actor's conduct was criminal, although it did not fall within a recognized misdemeanor or felony. By the seventeenth century, common law judges had created the felonies of murder, manslaughter, burglary, robbery, larceny, rape, sodomy, and mayhem. Common law misdemeanors at that time included assault, battery, false imprisonment, perjury, and intimidation of jurors. Between 1660 and 1860, the crimes of blasphemy, conspiracy, sedition, forgery, attempt, and solicitation were created.[1]

When the 13 colonies gained their independence, they retained the English common law with its statutory modifications as it applied in America. In the nineteenth century, a few states enacted comprehensive criminal codes that stated no crimes existed unless defined in the relevant statutes. The 1962 issuance of the *Model Penal Code* (MPC) by the American Law Institute spurred further overhauls of state criminal statutes.[2] Because the MPC is a model code and not a uniform code, however, the overhauls of state criminal laws that it spurred have differed widely. Section 1.05(1) of the MPC attempts to eliminate the common law from American criminal law. It reads: "No conduct constitutes an offense unless it is a crime or violation under this Code or another statute of this state." But not all of the state codifications eliminated common law crimes and defenses. Other states statutorily en-

Criminal laws are designed to protect people and property from those who refuse to act in accordance with the law.

acted crimes but did not define the elements of each crime, forcing courts to look to common law definitions.[3] As a result, criminal law today, though mainly statute-based, retains elements of the English common law.

Sources of Police Power

Under the Tenth Amendment to the U.S. Constitution, powers not granted to the federal government by the constitution are reserved to the states, or to the people. The only specific grants of *police power* to the federal government are found in Article I, § 8 (for the District of Columbia), and Article IV, § 3 (for federal territories). The federal courts have interpreted the federal territory grant of police power to include federal enclaves within states, such as parks, forts, military bases, post offices, federal office buildings, and courthouses. This is the federal police power that was used to prosecute Timothy McVeigh, who bombed the federal building in Oklahoma City. The Supreme Court has also recognized the federal government's power to regulate the conduct of U.S. nationals abroad. For crimes occurring within the territorial jurisdiction of the states, the federal government has limited direct police power and indirect police power. Section 8 of Article I specifically grants the federal government the power to punish counterfeiting and offenses against the law of nations. Section 3 of Article III grants the power to punish treasonous conduct. Of wider scope is the indirect police power, found in the Necessary and Proper Clause of Article I, § 8, clause 18. It grants the federal government the power to make laws that are necessary and proper to carry out other powers expressly granted to it, such as regulating interstate commerce.[4]

States have the power to regulate conduct (police power) inherent in their status as sovereign entities. They are limited only by constitutional and jurisdictional limitations.[5] For example, a state is unable to make it a crime to criticize the governor. Such a law would restrict freedom of speech, protected in federal and state constitutions. Likewise, Alabama, or any state other than Colorado, may not make it a crime for a citizen of Colorado to assault another citizen of Colorado within the state of Colorado. Alabama simply lacks the jurisdiction to regulate the conduct of citizens of Colorado in Colorado.

In many situations, both the federal government and a state government criminalize the same actions. Recall the Los Angeles police officers who were caught on videotape beating Rodney King. California prosecuted the officers, but they were acquitted, sparking riots in Los Angeles. The federal government then tried and convicted the officers for violating Rodney King's civil rights. Both criminal prosecutions were based on the same actions. It seems on its face that the successive prosecutions for the same act would violate the constitutional protection against double jeopardy. In fact, it does not. The Supreme Court has held that prosecutions by different sovereigns (state and federal) do not constitute double jeopardy.[6]

The Requirements of an Act and a State of Mind

Generally, a crime has two elements. First, the actor must take a physical action that is proscribed. This element is called the *actus reus*. Second, the actor must possess the required criminal intent or state of mind, referred to as *mens rea*. The required state of mind of the actor committing the prohibited act may range from a specific intent to commit the crime in question to negligence.[7] Generally, the act and the required state of mind must be concurrent.[8] One cannot be convicted of thinking he would like to kill another without some positive act to carry out the bad intent. Likewise, an act without a bad state of mind is generally not enough to subject one to criminal sanction. For example, if you mistakenly took your classmate's book home after class, thinking it is your own, you are not guilty of theft, because you did not intend to steal your classmate's book. If, however, once you realize it is not your book, and you decide to keep it, then you have the requisite intent to constitute a crime.

An exception to the mens rea requirement is a narrow class of crimes called *strict liability* offenses. Generally, these offenses deal with regulating public safety and welfare and carry only fines as punishment.[9] For instance, a city might have an ordinance that requires all property owners to remove snow and ice from their sidewalks within twenty-four hours of a snowstorm, or be subject to a $25 fine. If a property owner was unaware it had snowed overnight and failed to remove the snow from his sidewalk, he may still be fined by the city, despite the fact that he had no intent to violate the ordinance. The interest of keeping the sidewalks safe outweighs the requirement of making the city prove that the property owner had intended not to remove the snow within the required time limit.

The actus reus must generally be a *voluntary physical act*. A physical act means some bodily action, not an internal act like thinking. The external physical act may be as slight as an indication to another to proceed, or uttering a few words. Involuntary movements like a reflex, a convulsion, or acts taken while unconscious or asleep are generally not considered acts that may subject the actor to criminal liability.[10] Assume that a man who is unaware he has a brain tumor falls unconscious while driving his automobile. His automobile hits another vehicle head on, and a passenger in the other vehicle is killed. He is not guilty of vehicular homicide.[11]

The actus reus may also take the form of failing to act (an *omission*) if the actor has knowledge or should have knowledge of facts or circumstances requiring him or her to act. For example, one is required to file an income tax return. Failure to do so provides the act necessary for the crime of failure to file.[12] The requirement (duty) to act may arise from a relationship, a statute, a voluntary assumption of care, or the creation of a peril.[13]

Making it criminal or punishing individuals for having a bad reputation or associating with others who have a bad reputation is a deprivation of liberty without due process of law.[14] For example, convicting people as vagabonds because they have reputations as habitual criminals or because they associate with others who have reputations as habitual criminals, is a due process of law violation. Likewise, a statute making it criminal to associate with a prostitute is also an unconstitutional restriction of personal liberty (of course, if an act of prostitution actually takes place, then the situation is different).[15]

Although it has not been universally held, under the better view, criminalizing a person's status (*status crimes*) is a violation of the Eighth Amendment's prohibition against Cruel and Unusual Punishments.[16] (That was the case with a California statute that made it a crime to be addicted to narcotics.[17]) Vagrancy statutes have generated much litigation with divergent decisions. It is common for municipalities to have vagrancy statutes, because they tend to cut down on the number of "undesirables." In general, however, if the statute criminalizes who someone is, rather than what they do, the statute raises serious due process issues.[18]

Vagrancy statutes often now contain a prohibited act. The act must be clearly defined, as the following 1992 Nevada case illustrates. The vagrancy statute in question is similar to many others, in that it was designed to keep "undesirables" away from important commercial centers—in this case, gaming and hotel industry properties in Las Vegas.

Nevada v. Richard
Supreme Court of Nevada
108 Nev. 626, 836 P.2d 622 (1992)

OPINION BY: PER CURIAM
    The respondents, four homeless persons and four advocates for the rights of the homeless, brought suit in the United States District Court, District of Nevada, challenging the constitutionality of certain state and municipal loitering laws, including NRS 207.030(1)(i)* and Las Vegas Municipal Code sections 10.74.010 and 10.74.020.** The respondents claimed that the law and ordinance are facially void because they are unconstitutionally vague and overbroad. Subsequently . . . the United States District Court certified the issue of the constitutionality of the state statute and municipal codes to this court. After reviewing the laws in question, we conclude that the challenged provisions of both the Nevada statute and the Las Vegas Municipal Code are unconstitutionally vague.

Initially, we note that criminal statutes are designed to punish persons because they have committed specific prohibited acts. Traditional vagrancy laws, however, have sought to punish persons based on their status as vagrants, and not merely for culpable acts. . . . As a remnant of these traditional status-based laws, the Nevada vagrancy statute retains language that ostensibly punishes persons because they are vagrants. Specifically, subsection (1) of NRS 207.030 lists certain acts and character traits which define a person as a vagrant; subsection (2) states that "[e]very vagrant shall be punished." Vagrants may not be punished for being vagrants; only persons who commit culpable acts are liable for criminal sanctions.

Aside from its language prescribing punishment for being a vagrant, NRS 207.030 is unenforceable because it is unconstitutionally vague, as are Las Vegas Municipal Code sections 10.74.010 and 10.74.020. A vague law is one which fails to provide persons of ordinary intelligence with fair notice of what conduct is prohibited and also fails to provide law enforcement officials with adequate guidelines to prevent discriminatory enforcement. In this case, the Nevada laws criminalize "loitering" on private property when an individual has no "lawful business with the owner or occupant thereof." We conclude that this language is inadequate to inform the public of what conduct is prohibited. References to loitering and lawful business fail to provide sufficient notice of when stepping onto private property will subject an individual to arrest. Under these laws, an individual must necessarily guess as to when an innocent stroll becomes a criminal loitering.

Because they lack articulable standards, these laws fail to provide law enforcement officials with proper guidelines to avoid arbitrary and discriminatory enforcement. . . . We conclude that the challenged provisions of the Nevada vagrancy statute and the Las Vegas Municipal Codes are vague and therefore unconstitutional under the due process clauses of the federal and state constitutions.

*NRS 207.030, entitled VAGRANTS, provides in part: 1. Every person who: (i) Loiters, prowls or wanders upon the private property of another, without visible or lawful business with the owner or occupant thereof . . . is a vagrant. 2. Every vagrant shall be punished: . . . for a misdemeanor.

**LVMC § 10.74.010 provides: It is unlawful for any person to loiter or prowl upon the private property of another without lawful business with the owner or occupant thereof. LVMC § 10.74.020 provides: Among the circumstances which may be considered in determining whether or not a person who loiters or prowls upon the private property of another has lawful business with the owner or occupant thereof is the fact that such a person takes flight upon the appearance of a police officer or endeavors to conceal himself or any object.

Case Questions for Discussion

1. Before this statute was struck down, if a police officer observed two men, one dressed nicely and the other shabbily dressed, standing in front of a

large casino, to which man do you think the officer would attempt to apply the statute?

2. Do you agree that the law was too vague?

3. Do you think governments should be able to *control* who stands in the street?

4. What did the statutes make illegal? By whom?

A Chicago ordinance allowed police to order suspected gang members to move along.

A similar situation involved gang members in Chicago who congregated in public places and intimidated other citizens or conducted illegal activities. The City of Chicago adopted an ordinance that allowed the police to order suspected gang members and their associates to "move along." Failure to comply with the police command was punishable with up to six months of imprisonment. The U.S. Supreme Court held that the ordinance violated the Due Process Clause of the Fourteenth Amendment, because it was vague. A majority of the Court agreed that the ordinance gave the police too much unbridled discretion. The statute defined loitering as "remaining in one place with no apparent purpose." As a result, the police had great discretion about who had no apparent purpose for congregating in a place and who was a suspected gang member.[19]

Crimes Against Persons

One of the principal purposes of criminal law is to protect citizens from harm by others. Taking a life, causing the physical harm of another, taking another captive, and various sexual offenses all have their roots in the common law. In the following sections, we will discuss four common law crimes against persons in the context of the Model Penal Code. These crimes are murder, rape, assault, and battery. The specifics of individual state statutes vary, but in general, the overall offenses are quite similar.

Common Law Murder and Modern Variations

At common law, *murder* was divided into four categories: intent to kill murder, intent to do serious bodily harm murder, depraved heart murder, and felony murder. Many states retain these categories, although they may be subsumed or combined within the statutory classifications of homicide.[20] After we discuss one of the essential elements of all homicide crimes, we will then explore each of the categories more fully.

Live human being. One of the basic elements in murder or homicide is that a live human being must have been killed. It is impossible to kill a dead person, but it does not lessen the crime if a person kills another who is already mortally ill or injured. Whether the human being in question *was alive* can be a source of controversy. For example, if a relative "pulls the plug" on a brain-dead loved one, was the loved one alive or dead when the plug was pulled? Likewise, if one intentionally injures a woman who is pregnant causing her to miscarry, was the fetus alive?

Brain death is the near universally accepted medical determination of an unrecoverable fatal injury or condition.[21] If the law does not recognize the medical definition of death, various questions can arise. For example, if one with intent to kill causes a serious injury to another resulting in brain death, is that person liable for murder if the injured person is put on life support and survives for two years? At common law, if an injury did not cause death within one year and a day, there was a presumption that the original injury was not the cause of death—even if the person never recovered. If instead of surviving for two years, assume the attending physician withdrew life support of the brain-dead patient six months after the injury. Did the doctor's action cause the death of the patient, or should the original actor be subject to a murder charge? The following Indiana case addresses the question of when death occurs.

Swafford v. State
Supreme Court of Indiana
421 N.E.2d 596 (1981)

OPINION BY HUNTER: The defendant, Gary L. Swafford, was convicted of murder by a jury. . . . He was sentenced to the Indiana Department of Corrections for a period of thirty-two years. He presents the following issue for our review . . . Whether the trial court erred in instructing the jury on "brain death." . . .

The record reveals that on the evening of September 8, 1979, defendant and the decedent, William Robinson, met at the Omni Tavern in Bloomington, Indiana. After consuming a few drinks together at the Omni, the two men went to Robinson's apartment. There, Robinson made several homosexual advances toward the defendant, who eventually became angry, produced a handgun, and shot Robinson in the back of the head. Robinson, who remained conscious, summoned an ambulance and was taken to Bloomington Hospital. There, an examination revealed that the bullet had penetrated the right cerebellum and was located near the center of the brain, close by the brain stem. Based on the nature of the wound and location of the bullet, doctors determined that Robinson should be taken to Methodist Hospital in Indianapolis, where expert neurosurgical care and facilities were available.

Neurological surgeons at Methodist Hospital, concerned over the extremely close proximity of the bullet to Robinson's brain stem, elected to defer an operation to extricate the bullet pending any deterioration of Robinson's condition. During the evening hours of September 9, Robinson's condition took a dramatic turn for the worse; his heartbeat and respiration stopped, his pupils fixed and dilated, and he turned blue. Resuscitative efforts of the Methodist Hospital emergency team, including the use of mechanical support systems, resulted in the restoration of Robinson's heartbeat and respiration. Neurosurgeons then opened the skull in an attempt to relieve pressure building on the brain, which had caused the stoppage of respiration and heartbeat. . . . The following day, neurosurgeons made a preliminary diagnosis that Robinson's brain had died. He no longer responded to painful external stimuli, such as pinching, and his spontaneous movements had ceased. On September 10 and 11, two studies of blood flow within Robinson's brain were conducted and revealed no arterial flow of blood to the brain. Based on the blood flow studies, the lack of spontaneous movement, the nonresponsiveness to external stimuli, and the examination of the brain, neurosurgeons con-

cluded that Robinson had suffered an irreversible cessation of all brain functions.

After consulting with family members, neurological surgeon Dr. Julius Goodman formally declared Robinson dead at approximately 7:00 PM on September 11, 1979. The immediate cause of death listed on the certificate of death was brain death; the cause thereof was attributed to the gunshot wound. At the time Robinson was formally declared dead and the certificate issued, his heartbeat and respiration—sustained by the mechanical ventilator—continued. There is no evidence in the record regarding the withdrawal of the mechanical support system or the termination of decedent Robinson's heartbeat and respiration. The record does reveal, however, that an autopsy was conducted on Robinson's body on September 12. . . .

Defendant has . . . challenged the trial court's instruction* to the jury that brain death satisfies the element of murder requiring proof of the death of the victim. . . .

We observe at the outset that our research, as well as that of the parties involved, reveals that Indiana has never adopted a legal definition of "death," either by statute or judicial decree. Defendant maintains, however, that the definition of death contained in the Fourth Edition of Black's Law Dictionary controls our disposition. . . . We disagree. Black's definition of death reads: "The cessation of life; the ceasing to exist; defined by physicians as a total stoppage of the circulation of the blood, and a cessation of the animal and vital functions consequent thereon, such as respiration, pulsation, etc."

No source is credited for the definition. If it had derived from common law or statutes of England made prior to the fourth year of the reign of James the First (1607), defendant's position would warrant consideration; those laws have by statute been incorporated into the body of law which governs this state. . . .

The fact that death has not been legally defined in Indiana merely reflects the fact that, until recent medical history, no reason existed for the traditional medical definition of death detailed in Black's Fourth Edition to engender legal controversy. . . . In tandem with the development of the mechanical capacity to sustain heartbeat and respiration, the concept of brain death has gained virtually universal acceptance in the medical profession. . . .

This evolution in medicine has spawned concomitant developments in law. See, e.g., In the Matter of Quinlan, (1976) 70 N.J. 10, 355 A. 2d 647, cert. den. 429 U.S. 922, 50 L. Ed. 2d 289, 97 S. Ct. 319. Twenty-eight states, either by statute or judicial fiat, have adopted brain death definitions to supplement the traditional medical standards by which death is determined. And, significantly, months prior to the shooting which precipitated this action, the Fifth Edition of Black's Law Dictionary—bearing for the first time in that tome's history a definition of brain death—was published. . . .

Here, defendant concedes that recognition of brain death is a general consensus of the medical community, but argues that this Court should defer to the legislature to determine whether it should be recognized in law. Defendant's contention that the issue is purely a legislative matter rests on the claim that the medical profession is far from unanimous as to the most reliable criteria for the determination of brain death; consequently, legislative study and discussion should precede legal recognition of brain death, he argues.

Defendant's argument begs the question. Our sole concern here is whether, for purposes of the law of homicide, the irreversible cessation of total brain functions should be recognized as a standard by which death may be determined. If so, the manner and means by which an assessment of brain condition should be made would remain a purely medical question.

We do note that we find little of the disagreement alluded to by defendant with respect to the criteria by which the medical community presently determines brain death. . . .

The determination of what condition constitutes death, however, can no longer be regarded exclusively as a medical question. . . . We recognize the authority of the legislature to define by statute—and for all legal purposes—the standards by which death is to be determined in Indiana. Indeed, in the face of advancing medical technology, we encourage them to so act, as have the legislatures of twenty-five other states. Here, as was the case with our brethren in Massachusetts, Colorado, and Washington, we have no statute to guide us in the resolution of the question put to us. . . . Like those jurisdictions, we are unable to ignore the advances made in medical science and technology during the last two decades. Among the members of today's medical community the irreversible cessation of total brain functions is commonly accepted as tantamount to death as traditionally defined, for it is acknowledged as fact that only through artificial means will heartbeat and respiration continue thereafter. On that basis, we hold that for purposes of the law of homicide proof of the death of the victim may be established by proof of the irreversible cessation of the victim's total brain functions. The trial court did not err in so instructing the jury.

*The instruction reads: "If you find beyond a reasonable doubt that William Robinson had suffered brain death before he was removed from the respirator, then the state has satisfied the essential element of the crime of murder requiring proof beyond a reasonable doubt of the death of the victim. Brain death occurs when, in the opinion of a licensed physician, based on accepted medical standards, there has been a total and irreversible cessation of spontaneous brain functions and further attempts at resuscitation or continued supportive maintenance would not be successful in restoring such functions."

Case Questions for Discussion

1. If the defendant was able to convince the court that his definition of death should have been used, could he have been convicted of murder? Why or why not?

2. Could the doctor who withdrew life support have been charged with murder under the defendant's definition of death?

3. Do you think the court was wise in its redefinition of death for homicide cases in Indiana?

4. Should the legislature have acted first?

At common law, the general rule was that a fetus was not a live human being until it was born alive. For example, if a pregnant woman was shot, causing injury to the fetus and the ultimate miscarriage or premature delivery of a dead fetus, no homicide charge could be brought against the woman's assailant unless the fetus was born alive. Live birth usually required that only a breath be taken, although some states required at least the establishment of independent circulation by the child after the umbilical cord was severed. Some states have adopted *feticide statutes,* which establish a separate homicide for destroying a fetus whether or not it was born alive. Without a statute like the one in Box 13.1 from Illinois, violent attacks against a pregnant woman causing the death of the fetus before a live birth do not subject the attacker to criminal liability for the death of the unborn child.[22]

In a Minnesota case, a defendant was convicted of killing a 27- or 28-day-old embryo when he shot and killed the mother. Minnesota's feticide statute did not require that the defendant knew or should have known the woman was pregnant. The Minnesota Supreme Court was clear in what the statute required. "Criminal liability here requires only that the genetically human embryo be a living organism that is growing into a human being. Death occurs when the embryo is no longer living, when it ceases to have the properties of life."[23]

Box 13.1   720 ILCS 5/9-1.2
Intentional Homicide of an Unborn Child

(a) A person commits the offense of intentional homicide of an unborn child if, in performing acts which cause the death of an unborn child, he without lawful justification:

   (1) either intended to cause the death of or do great bodily harm to the pregnant woman or her unborn child or knew that such acts would cause death or great bodily harm to the pregnant woman or her unborn child; or

   (2) he knew that his acts created a strong probability of death or great bodily harm to the pregnant woman or her unborn child; and

   (3) he knew that the woman was pregnant.

(b) For purposes of this Section, (1) unborn child shall mean any individual of the human species from fertilization until birth, and (2) person shall not include the pregnant woman whose unborn child is killed.

Intent to kill murder. To sustain a prosecution for *intent to kill murder*, there must exist the aim to kill, and the defendant's conduct must be the legal cause of the victim's death with no justification or excuse for the killing. Intent generally is inferred from the defendant's actions. For example, Joe points a gun at Jane and fires. The shot kills Jane. Since Joe used a deadly weapon, it can be inferred that Joe intended to kill Jane. Likewise, if Alice puts ground glass into a piece of candy and gives it to Bob, who eats it and dies, it can be inferred that Alice intended to kill Bob.[24]

At times, *premeditation* is required, but the better rule is that intent to kill alone is sufficient. Some jurisdictions that divide intent to kill murder into degrees require premeditation for first-degree murder, and just the intent to kill for second-degree murder.[25] Premeditation can be a difficult concept to apply. How long does a defendant need to think about killing someone for it to constitute premeditation? Judicial decisions range from just a few seconds (each additional stab of a knife) to some evidence of planning or motive.[26]

The Model Penal Code does not require premeditation and does not divide murder into degrees. All unlawful killings are criminal homicide with the most serious type being murder. Persons are subject to a murder charge if they purposefully, knowingly, or with recklessness manifesting extreme indifference for human life take the life of another. The requisite recklessness can be shown if the killing took place while the defendant or an accomplice was committing, attempting to commit, or fleeing from the commission of robbery, rape, deviant sexual intercourse by force, arson, burglary, kidnapping, or felonious escape.[27]

Massachusetts is a jurisdiction that requires premeditation and divides murder into degrees. Compare the statute in Box 13.2 to the MPC murder scheme.

Box 13.2   Massachusetts Annotated Laws Chapter 265, § 1, Murder Defined

Murder committed with deliberately premeditated malice aforethought, or with extreme atrocity or cruelty, or in the commission or attempted commission of a crime punishable with death or imprisonment for life, is murder in the first degree. Murder which does not appear to be in the first degree is murder in the second degree.

Intent to do serious bodily harm murder. At common law, acts taken with less than the intent to kill could be punished as murder, if the intent of the actor was to do serious bodily harm. For example, Ann swings a baseball bat and hits Bill in the head when Bill ducks. If Ann intended to break Bill's arm, Ann could be prosecuted for murder because she intended to seriously injure Bill. Again, proof of intent may be inferred from the acts of the defendant. In our example, it can be inferred that Ann intended to cause Bill serious injury, because hitting someone with a baseball bat is likely to cause a serious injury. Generally, assaulting someone with any deadly weapon can furnish the act from which intent may be inferred.[28]

In most jurisdictions that recognize intent to cause serious bodily harm as sufficient intent for murder, it is usually applicable only for the less serious degrees of murder, like second-degree murder or manslaughter.[29] Under the Model Penal Code, intent to injure is not specifically included as an intent justifying a murder prosecution. Depending on the defendant's acts, one intending to do serious bodily harm who kills another will usually be liable for manslaughter as a homicide committed in a reckless manner. In some cases, the defendant's acts may be shown to be so reckless that they exhibit extreme indifference to the value of human life. In that case, murder is the appropriate charge.[30]

Depraved heart murder. The Model Penal Code's "reckless conduct that exhibits extreme indifference to the value of human life" is more like common law *depraved heart murder* than intent to do serious bodily harm murder. Under depraved heart murder at common law, the necessary intent for murder was provided by the defendant's outrageous actions. For example, Andy, knowing a crowd of people is below him, throws bricks off a building into the crowd. Although Andy may have had no intent to kill anyone (he may have just wanted to see the crowd scatter in fear), his act is so outrageous that if someone is killed he should be accountable for murder.[31] Many jurisdictions have followed the MPC formulation, but a significant minority of states do not recognize depraved heart murder.

A difficulty with depraved heart murder is the question of what acts in what context show the necessary outrageousness. It is usually a combination of the act and the situation. Shooting into what is thought to be an abandoned house is probably not sufficient, but shooting into an obviously occupied house (the same act but a different situation) probably is sufficient. At times, the social utility of the act comes into play. For those acts with little or no social utility, the degree of risk can be lower than for those acts with social utility. If one drives wildly through a crowded intersection for thrills, the complete lack of social utility makes it easier for a depraved heart risk to be found than if the same act of driving wildly through a crowded intersection was done to rush a gravely wounded child to a hospital.[32]

Felony murder. At common law, if an actor caused someone's death while committing or attempting to commit a felony, the perpetrator of the felony could be prosecuted for murder, even though the felony committed was not inherently dangerous.[33] Consider the following example. Alicia notices that the storekeeper left $1,000 cash on the counter of his store when he went into the back room. Alicia grabs the cash and runs toward the door. As Alicia pushes open the front door, she slams it into a young woman, who was about to enter the store. The force of the door swinging open catches the young woman in the head and kills her. Alicia would be subject to a charge of felony murder at early common law. The intent to kill would have been found in the intent to commit the felony.

Today, felony murder has generally been limited to the commission of inherently or foreseeably dangerous felonies. Many states now list felonies that will suffice statutorily. These types of statutes have been interpreted in two ways. California, for example, enumerates a list of felonies that are sufficiently heinous to subject a perpetrator to first-degree murder. The statute then adds that all other types of murder not listed in the statute are second degree. California courts have taken the position that the statutory enactment of first-degree felony murder did not eliminate second-degree felony murder, but second-degree felony murder requires the commission of inherently dangerous felonies not listed under first-degree felony murder.[34]

Arizona courts have taken the opposite view under a similar statute. These courts have held that by specifically enumerating the felonies sufficient for first-degree murder, with no similar listing for second-degree murder, the legislature did not intend to incorporate common law felony murder into second-degree murder.[35] Another variation among jurisdictions deals with whether courts should consider the elements of the felony in question or whether the court may examine how this defendant or defendants actually acted or planned to act during the commission of the felony. In those jurisdictions that look at the acts, it is easier to find felony murder.[36] The Model Penal Code takes a different view. Committing, attempting to commit, or flight from rape, robbery, deviant sexual intercourse by force, arson, burglary, kidnapping, and felonious escape furnish a presumption of recklessness sufficient for its version of depraved heart murder.[37] To date, only New Hampshire has modeled a statute after the MPC for felony murder.[38]

Other homicide crimes. Most states and the Model Penal Code have created categories of homicide that are less blameworthy than murder. Under the MPC, *manslaughter* is a criminal homicide that is committed recklessly or under the influence of an extreme mental or emotional disturbance for which there is an excuse. This higher degree of manslaughter is often referred to as *voluntary manslaughter*. The MPC also has a negligent homicide category, often referred to as *involuntary manslaughter*. Voluntary manslaughter is usually the proper charge for heat of passion killings (generally the defendant must show provocation and lack of a cooling-off period) and for killings in which the actor was acting in self-defense, but took actions that were out of proportion to the danger posed. Involuntary manslaughter usually is the charge when the actor acted recklessly or negligently.[39] Vehicular homicide crimes are generally classified as involuntary manslaughter.

Rape

Rape at common law was "when a man hath carnall [sic] knowledge of a woman by force and against her will."[40] Notice that under the common law, only a man was capable of rape and only a woman was capable of being raped. In brief, rape at common law was male-female sexual intercourse without the consent of the woman. It was not considered an act of violence, merely sex without consent. In addition, one could not rape one's wife. To convict one accused of rape, it was necessary to show that the victim resisted and called out. Acquiescence under duress without a struggle was generally not considered resistance.

The common law version of rape was carried over to American jurisdictions and prevailed until the 1970s and 1980s. Problems arose over the question of consent. Without evidence of a struggle, the contest often came down to the victim's word versus that of the accused. Often, the actions of the victim before the attack became relevant. Did she dress provocatively? Did she drink and dance? Did her actions convince the accused she wanted to engage in sexual relations? Whether women enjoyed forcible sex was often brought into the cases as well. Did the victim say no, but really want to be taken?[41]

Under the Model Penal Code, most of the common law elements of rape are retained. "A *man* who has sexual intercourse with a *female not his wife* is guilty of rape if [emphasis added]" he compels her to submit by force or threat of death, serious injury, extreme pain, or kidnapping of herself or another, or if he impairs her judgment by giving her drugs or other intoxicants without her knowledge, or if the female is unconscious or less than 10 years old. The MPC also provides a lesser degree of rape called *gross sexual imposition*. The threat of force required is only that which would prevent resistance by a woman of ordinary resolution. A final category of rape under the MPC is intercourse (including anal sex) between two human beings (gender neutral) without consent. It is called *deviant sexual intercourse by force or imposition*. An even less severe crime (misdemeanor) occurs if a person (gender neutral) has sexual contact with another who is not that person's spouse, and if the actor knows the contact is offensive to the other person, and if there are present a number of other conditions indicating lack of consent. Sexual contact is defined as the touching of the sexual or other intimate parts of the body with the purpose of arousing or gratifying sexual desire.[42]

Most jurisdictions have made statutory changes to their rape laws. Most of the changes have been evidentiary in nature, for example, shield laws that deny the defense the ability to show the victim has a history of promiscuous conduct. Most jurisdictions retain the marital exclusion as long as the spouses are living together,[43] but most state statutes are now gender neutral.[44] How much force or threat of force is necessary can vary from state to state, but the general rule is that nonconsensual sex that the victim does not resist (e.g., the victim said no, but did not resist when the defendant did not stop) is a lesser included offense.[45] The question of whether a defendant is guilty of rape when he or she fraudulently induces another to have sex is problematic, as illustrated by the following Montana case.

State v. Thompson
Supreme Court of Montana
243 Mont. 28, 792 P.2d 1103 (1990)

OPINION BY SHEEHY: . . . The defendant, Gerald Roy Thompson, the principal and boys basketball coach at Hobson High School, was accused of two counts of sexual intercourse without consent, and one count of sexual assault. . . . This appeal only concerns the two counts of sexual intercourse without consent. The information, filed with the District Court, alleged the defendant committed the crime of sexual intercourse without consent, and stated the following: Count I: On or between September, 1986 and January, 1987 in Judith Basin County, Montana the defendant knowingly had sexual intercourse without consent with a person of the opposite sex; namely Jane Doe, by threatening Jane Doe that she would not graduate from high school and forced Jane Doe to engage in an act of oral sexual intercourse. . . . [Editor's note: Count II alleges the same facts, except the dates are from February through June 1987].

The State contended that fear of the power of Thompson and his authority to keep her from graduating forced Jane Doe into silence until after she graduated from high school in June of 1987. On November 25, 1988, Jane Doe filed a letter with the Hobson School Board describing the activities against her by Thompson. After investigations by both the school board and the Judith Basin County prosecutor's office, the prosecutor filed an information on May 25, 1989. . . .

Defendant filed a number of motions, requesting, among other things, a motion to dismiss Counts I and II of the information for lack of probable cause in the supporting affidavit. The District Court granted Thompson's motion, due to the fact the State failed to meet the element of "without consent" under §45-5-501, MCA.

We agree with the District Court that the facts in the information, in regards to Counts I and II, fail to state offenses. The code of criminal procedures requires that an affidavit be filed for application for leave to file an information. . . . The affidavit must include sufficient facts to convince a judge that there is probable cause to believe the named defendant may have committed the crime described in the information. If there is no probable cause, the District Court lacks jurisdiction to try the offense. . . . This Court has held that a showing of mere probability that defendant committed the crime charged is sufficient for establishing probable cause to file a criminal charge. . . .

The allegations in the affidavit, however, do not indicate a probability that Thompson committed the crime of sexual intercourse without consent. Thompson was charged with two counts of alleged sexual intercourse without consent under §45-5-503, MCA. Section 45-5-503, MCA, states the following: "A person who knowingly has sexual intercourse without consent with a person of the opposite sex commits the offense of sexual intercourse without consent." The phrase "without consent" the key element of the crime has a very specific definition in Montana's criminal code. This phrase is defined in § 45-5-501, MCA, which states in pertinent part: "As used in 45-5-503 and 45-5-505, the term without consent means: "(i) the victim is compelled to submit by force or by threat of imminent death, bodily injury, or kidnapping to be inflicted on anyone. . . ."

Thompson challenged the probable cause affidavit in the District Court, contending it failed to state any fact or circumstance showing that Jane Doe's submission to an alleged act of sexual intercourse was obtained by force or by any of the threats listed in sec. 45-5-501, MCA. In contrast, the State argues that Thompson's actions constitute sexual intercourse through force or threats. The District Court, in its opinion and order, agreed with Thompson's contentions, and found that the facts in the affidavit supporting the information failed to show the element of without consent. In reaching this conclusion, the District Court first considered whether or not there were facts or circumstances in the probable cause affidavit to indicate that submission to the alleged act of sexual intercourse without consent was obtained "by force." In order to determine whether Thompson forced Jane Doe to submit to the sexual act, the District Court had to define the phrase "by force" since there is no definition contained in the Montana Criminal Code.

The District Court in its order defined force as follows: "The word force is used in its ordinary and normal connotation: physical compulsion, the use or immediate threat of bodily harm, injury." Next, the District Court examined the information and probable cause affidavit to determine if there were any facts or circumstances constituting force. The District Court found that force was not alleged in the information nor in the affidavit in support of it.

In contrast, the State argues the District Court's definition of force is too limited. The State, relying on Raines v. State (1989), 191 Ga. App. 743, 382 S.E.2d 738, 739, argues that intimidation and fear may constitute force. The State also contends that Thompson, in his position of authority as the principal, intimidated Jane Doe into the alleged acts. Furthermore, the State argues the fear and apprehension of Jane Doe show Thompson used force against her. We agree with the State that Thompson intimidated Jane Doe; however, we cannot stretch the definition of force to include intimidation, fear, or apprehension. Rather, we adopt the District Court's definition of force.

Other jurisdictions, such as California, have expanded the definition of force, beyond its physical connotation. People v. Cicero (1984), 157 Cal.App.3d 465, 204 Cal.Rptr. 582.

The California Supreme Court adopted the following reasoning to expand the word force: ". . . the fundamental wrong at which the law of rape is aimed is not the application of physical force that causes physical harm. Rather, the law of rape primarily guards the integrity of a woman's will and the privacy of her sexuality from an act of intercourse undertaken without her consent. Because the fundamental wrong is the violation of a woman's will and sexuality, the law of rape does not require that force cause physical harm. Rather, in this scenario, force plays merely a supporting evidentiary role, as necessary only to ensure an act of intercourse has been undertaken against a victim's will." The California Supreme Court's definition of the word force is too broad under Montana's definition of the crime. Until the legislature adopts a definition for the word force, we must adopt the ordinary and normal definition of the word force as set forth by the District Court. . . .

This case is one of considerable difficulty for us, as indeed it must have been for the District Court judge. The alleged facts, if true, show disgusting acts of taking advantage of a young person by an adult who occupied a position of authority over the young person. If we could rewrite the statutes to define the alleged acts here as sexual intercourse without consent, we would willingly do so. The business of courts, however, is to interpret statutes, not to rewrite them, nor to insert words not put there by the legislature. With a good deal of reluctance, and with strong condemnation of the alleged acts, we affirm the District Court.

Case Questions for Discussion

1. Do you think Jane Doe was justified in believing her high school principal might not let her graduate if she did not submit?

2. Given the defendant's position of authority over Jane Doe, was his threat more "forceful" than other coercive acts?

3. Do you think California's position is better than Montana's? Why or why not?

Battery and Assault

At common law, *battery* was defined as the intentional injuring of another or the intentional touching of another in an offensive manner. If Abe intentionally punched Bart on the chin, he committed battery. Likewise, if Jane grabbed Bart's groin area without permission, she committed battery. Three elements were necessary at common law for a criminal battery prosecution. First, the defendant must have committed the act (hit, touched, or caused contact with another's body). Second, the defendant must have had the intent to injure or touch offensively. Criminal negligence (a more reckless or knowledgeable form of negligence than tort type negligence) was sufficient. Finally, the result of the defendant's conduct must have been harmful or offensive. Generally, at common law even a momentary painful blow was sufficient.[46]

Assault, at common law, was defined as an attempted battery. A more modern trend also allowed a defendant to be charged with assault for intentionally frightening another (putting them in apprehension of imminent bodily injury). Ann points a gun at Bob and acts as if she will shoot him. Bob has no idea that Ann has no intention of shooting him, but rather is just trying to scare him. As long as a reasonable person put in Bob's position would believe he is in danger of being shot, Ann could be charged with assault.[47]

The Model Penal Code and many state codes do not have common law assault provisions, only criminal battery. Under many state codes, common law assault is relegated to attempt statutes or threatening or menacing statutes. Interestingly, the common law crime of battery is now referred to by the MPC and most modern criminal codes as assault. Under the MPC, only intent to injure assault (battery) is recognized. Offensive touching is covered by the sexual assault provision.[48]

Aggravated assault (battery) statutes raise the crime to felony status, when the assault is committed against an identified class afforded extra protection by the legislature. Generally, those afforded extra protection by the legislature include police and other public safety officials. It is not uncommon, however, for a state to include teachers, court officials, state officials, school bus drivers, the young, the elderly, and pregnant women. Aggravated assault or battery statutes are also applicable when the actor commits the assault with a deadly or dangerous weapon.[49] The MPC provides that assault (battery) is aggravated only by the manner in which the assault (battery) is carried out. Using a deadly weapon or committing the assault (battery) with extreme indifference to human life are the only two aggravating elements.[50]

Crimes Against Property

Just as the law protects one's person, it also protects one's property. If a defendant takes another's property with the intent of permanently depriving the owner of its use, the criminal law provides sanctions. Likewise, if a defendant intentionally harms or destroys another's property, criminal sanctions apply. A brief discussion on the common law development of the root of all property crimes (larceny) is followed with discussions of robbery, burglary, theft, receiving stolen property, and extortion or blackmail.

Common Law Larceny

At early common law, *larceny* was the only theft type of crime, and it was punishable by death. As a result, the crime of larceny was construed strictly. It required the intent to steal another's personal property. In addition, the property must have been taken in a trespassory manner or, in other words, taken from the owner's possession and transported away (moved at least a substantial amount). Although larceny at common law protected personal property, the crime also was viewed as a way to keep the peace, because an in-person theft of property was likely to ignite an altercation. Common law judges expanded the crime to include other types of theft, such as the defendant lying to the owner in order to take possession of the property and then absconding with the property.[51]

Larceny by trick could be found when the common law judges deemed the owner of the property to be in *constructive possession* of the property, although the thief had actually converted it. For example, Albert tells Bill he is going to the market and he will take Bill's apples with him, sell them, and return with Bill's money. Bill loads up a wagon of apples, which he entrusts to Albert. In fact, Albert does take the apples to market and sells them, but he does not return with Bill's money. Instead of returning, Albert takes Bill's money and flees the area. Under a strict construction of larceny, there was no trespassory taking, because Bill voluntarily delivered the apples to Albert. Under the concept of *constructive possession,* Bill was still considered in possession of his property when Albert took off (converted or took the property from its owner). When Albert took off, the necessary trespatory taking occurred. Albert would be guilty of larceny by trick. As the economy of England became more mercantile, Parliament eventually added different types of theft crimes like embezzlement and acquiring title by false pretenses.[52]

At common law, the lines between larceny, embezzlement, and false pretenses were often gray. For example, an employer gives an employee a number of checks to cash at the bank and return with the cash. The employee goes to the bank, cashes the checks, but takes off for Borneo with the cash instead of returning it to the employer. Because the employer gave the checks to the employee, and the employee first took possession of the checks from the owner, the crime may be larceny. Because, however, the employee fled with cash taken from a bank employee, the crime also appears to be embezzlement. This type of problem often plagued American prosecutors in jurisdictions that embraced the common law property crimes. The Model Penal Code has attacked this problem by consolidating several property crimes into one larger crime called *theft*. Theft under the MPC encompasses larceny, false pretenses, embezzlement, receiving stolen property, and blackmail or extortion.[53]

Robbery

Robbery is theft by force or intimidation. It requires the defendant to take the property in question from the victim in person. As such, it is a crime against property and persons. Under the Model Penal Code, theft is robbery if the defendant inflicts serious bodily injury on another, threatens another or puts another in fear of serious bodily injury, or commits or threatens to commit any felony of the first or second degree.[54] Many state statutes generally follow the MPC scheme except that they include one other factor, "the use of force upon another," which does not require injury or threat of injury.[55]

Questions arise about how much force is necessary for the higher penalties associated with robbery, as opposed to other theft from persons crimes. For example, a thief reaches out and peacefully lifts a woman's purse off her arm. Was the energy expended by the thief enough force to justify a robbery charge? The majority view is no.

> [S]imple snatching or sudden taking of property from the person of another does not of itself involve sufficient force to constitute robbery, though the act may be robbery where a struggle ensues, the victim is injured in the taking or the property is so attached to the victim's person or clothing as to create resistance to the taking.[56]

Burglary

Burglary is another property crime that is enhanced due to the danger it creates to people. At common law, burglary was the breaking and entering of a dwelling house at night with the intent to commit a felony inside.[57] Under the Model Penal Code, persons may be charged with burglary if they enter a building or occupied structure, or separately secured or occupied portion thereof, with the purpose of committing a crime. If the premises are open to the public, the actor is licensed to enter the structure, or if the structure is abandoned, it is not burglary. It is a second degree felony if the actor enters a dwelling structure at night, is armed with explosives or a deadly weapon, or if he or she injures or attempts to injure another person. Absent the conditions above, it is a third degree felony.[58]

A peculiar aspect of burglary is that the intended crime does not have to be completed for burglary to have been committed. For example, if the actor breaks a window and enters a home intending to steal a television set, but is discovered before he is able to steal anything, he is still guilty of burglary. Also, the penalties for burglary are often more severe than the intended crime. For example, it may be worse for the criminal to break into a car and steal a radio than to steal the whole car.[59]

State statutes vary widely. Consistent with the MPC, some laws require no breaking, just an entry, although courts often require some "unauthorized" entry, even under statutes patterned after the MPC. Other statutes break the crime into various degrees, depending on when entry was made or what structure was entered. For those states that require breaking, a question often arises whether enlarging or entering an existing break constitutes breaking. In general, the answer is yes. In fact, the modern trend is to deem it a breaking if the entry by the intruder was unlawful or unprivileged. Opening an unlocked door usually will suffice.[60]

Theft

As we have already discussed, under the Model Penal Code several property crimes are consolidated under the general heading of *theft*. The MPC and state codes differentiate between felony theft and misdemeanor theft by the value of the property or services taken. Under the MPC, the dividing line is $500.[61] Persons who unlawfully take or exercise control over movable property with the intent to deprive the owner of the property are guilty of theft. For example, if Alley gets on your bicycle and rides off on it intending to sell it for money, it is theft. But if Alley wanted only to borrow the bike and intended to return the bike, it would not be theft. Likewise, if one unlawfully transfers the ownership of, or an interest in, unmovable property with the purpose of securing a benefit for him- or herself or another, he or she is guilty of theft.[62]

One can also steal services. *Theft of services* is purposely obtaining services the actor knows are available only for compensation.[63] Examples include the unauthorized receipt of cable television or premium cable channels, staying in hotel rooms, and riding in taxicabs without paying.

Receiving Stolen Property

Often a key player in theft, robbery, or burglary crimes is called "the fence"—someone who can turn stolen goods into cash. Under the Model Penal Code, one who purposely receives, retains, or disposes of property knowing it has been stolen or believing it has probably been stolen is guilty of theft.[64] The requisite knowledge is often a problem in the prosecution of this crime. In some cases, it is easy. For instance, if Alvin is found to possess property that was stolen from several residences over a six-month period and he has no proof of purchase, the inference is strong that Alvin knew the property was stolen. However, if Alvin has only one item of stolen property and he paid market value for the property, there may be no inference of knowledge. In fact, Alvin may have had no idea the property was stolen when he acquired it. Generally, if one pays little for an item of considerable value, knowledge that the property was stolen may be inferred.[65]

The MPC limits a presumption of knowledge to dealers (those in the business of buying or selling goods, including pawnbrokers) who are found to be in possession of stolen property from two or more persons, who have received stolen property in another transaction within a year, or who pay far below the property's reasonable value.[66] Evidence of whether a nondealer had knowledge or believed the property was stolen would be admissible, however. Receiving stolen property is an *accessory after the fact* crime. If the defendant is guilty of stealing the property in question, he cannot be guilty of receiving the stolen property as well.[67]

Extortion or Blackmail

At common law, *extortion* was limited to public officials extracting money from citizens under color of the official's office when no fee, or a smaller fee, was due. Such public extortion or corruption remains today a crime in all states and under the U.S. Criminal Code. In addition, statutory extortion or blackmail exists in all jurisdictions. The statutes vary widely, but in general, the crime entails acquiring money or property from another by threatening to harm the person or some other person, or to expose some activity of the threatened person that would cause them embarrassment, ridicule, or harm. Abe would be guilty of extortion or blackmail if he threatens to snatch Bonnie's son from school unless Bonnie pays Abe $1,000. Likewise, if Bonnie was having an extramarital affair or using illegal drugs and Abe threatens to expose Bonnie's actions unless she pays Abe $1,000, Abe would also be guilty of extortion or blackmail.[68] Under the Model Penal Code, seven categories describe threatened actions, ranging from physical harm, accusing another of a crime, exposing any secret tending to subject the threatened person to hatred, contempt, or ridicule, to inflicting any other harm that would not benefit the actor. The MPC, like some state statutes, requires defendants to have actually obtained property as a result of their threats for conviction.[69]

Victimless Crimes

All jurisdictions criminalize drug use and most criminalize prostitution, gambling, and various forms of sexual activity. Whereas crimes against property and persons are designed to protect the victim of the crime, laws criminalizing prostitution, consensual sex between persons of the same sex, certain sexual acts, gambling, and drug use are essentially *victimless crimes* in the traditional sense of that term. Advocates for enforcing victimless crimes argue that the prohibited acts harm society in general. For example, if Chuck and Bryan are allowed to openly gamble, use drugs, and engage in illegal sexual activities, they are less likely to hold gainful employment, support their families, and contribute to the moral development of children.

Some argue victimless crimes like prostitution and drug use should be legalized and regulated.

Critics argue that government should not try to control what people do in the privacy of their homes, and that victimless crime enforcement tends to erode respect for the law itself. As part of the "War on Drugs" initiated by President Reagan, for example, mandatory minimum sentences for certain drug offenses have led to a fourfold increase in the federal prison population from 1978 to 1998. During that same period, the percentage of federal prisoners incarcerated for drug-related crimes has gone from 25 to 59 percent. In 1997, the average sentence for federal drug crimes was 82 months, compared with 34 months for manslaughter and 38 months for assault.[70]

Attempt Crimes

It makes sense to punish those who attempt to commit a crime. If Abel, intending to kill Carrie, shoots and misses, he has the same mens rea as if he had hit and killed Carrie. Although Abel's aim may be bad, he is still a danger to society (and Carrie). He should be punished. Generally, the punishment for *attempt crimes* is less than that of the underlying substantive crime, but depending on the jurisdiction and the specific underlying crime, the punishment may be the same.[71]

Generically, attempt has two elements—the intent to commit a crime and an act in furtherance of that intent beyond mere preparation.[72] In our example, Abel had the intent to kill Carrie (intent to commit murder) and took an act (shot at Carrie) in furtherance of that intent, which was beyond mere preparation. There can be no prosecution for attempt if the defendant is convicted of the substantive crime, but proving the substantive crime when the defendant is charged only with attempt does not preclude conviction on attempt. A defendant may be charged and convicted of both attempt and conspiracy to commit a crime without running afoul of double jeopardy protections.[73]

It is also generally not possible to convict one of attempting to commit a crime if the necessary state of mind for the substantive crime is not specific intent. If Alex, intending to rob Bill, inadvertently kills Bill by running him over while fleeing the scene of the robbery, Alex can be convicted of felony murder. This is true despite the fact that his specific intent was only to rob Bill. However, if Bill is only hurt and not killed when struck by Alex's automobile, Alex cannot be convicted of attempted murder because he did not have the specific intent of killing Bill.[74]

An interesting issue that often arises during attempt prosecutions is whether the actor may be convicted of attempt if what he or she intended to do was impossible. The case of *United States v. Hair* illustrates this problem.

United States v. Hair
U.S. District Court for the District of Columbia
356 F. Supp. 339 (1973)

FLANNERY, District Judge. This matter is before the court upon the defendant's motion to suppress evidence. It appears from the evidence that Officer James E. Blackburn of the Metropolitan Police Department was advised by a previously reliable informer that the defendant had expressed an interest in buying a stolen television set. The informer also advised Officer Blackburn that he had sold stolen merchandise to the defendant on more than five occasions within the past year and on at least two occasions within the past month. . . . The police checked the criminal arrest record of the defendant and ascertained that over a 20-year period, he had been arrested for a variety of criminal offenses including larceny and receiving stolen property. The informer reported also that within the past 72 hours he had overheard conversations between the defendant and certain other individuals in which the defendant indicated that he wanted to buy certain property including television sets and that within the past 48 hours the informer had seen other property on the premises which the informer believed to be stolen. Officer Blackburn then secured a new color television which he gave to the informer with instructions to sell it to the defendant and to advise the defendant that it was a stolen set. The informer proceeded to follow the Officer's directions and sold the television set to the defendant at his grocery store, advising him that it had been stolen.

The police then applied for a search warrant for the defendant's grocery store known as the 24-hour Store, located at 1642 Vermont Avenue, N.W., and in an affidavit accompanying the application for the search warrant related the background information which the informer had furnished to them concerning the defendant's illegal activities, and relating that the informer within the past 48 hours had sold the color television set to the defendant and had represented to the defendant that the set had been illegally purchased. A Judge of the Superior Court for the District of Columbia then issued a search warrant for the premises of 1642 Vermont Avenue, N.W., on the grounds that the affidavit established probable cause to believe that "certain electronic equipment, including a television set, which is attempted stolen property in violation of D.C. Code 2205" was located within the premises. Thereafter, the police executed the search warrant and seized a substantial amount of stolen property in addition to the aforesaid color television set. . . .

The core question in this case is whether the defendant committed a crime when he received the color television set from the informer with intent to defraud, believing the property to be stolen, when, in fact, the property had not been stolen. The defendant . . . asserts the defense of impossibility, maintaining that the act of attempted or actual receipt of property which was not, in fact, stolen is not a crime in the District of Columbia.

There is no statutory or case law in the District of Columbia dealing with this question, but the subject has been discussed in other jurisdictions. In People v. Jaffe, 185 N.Y. 497, 78 N.E. 169 (1906), the Court of Appeals for New York, held that where the property was not stolen, there can be no attempted receipt of stolen property. In *Jaffe* a clerk stole goods from his employer under an agreement to sell them to the accused, but before delivery of the goods, the theft was discovered and the goods were recovered. Later, the employer redelivered the goods to the clerk to sell to the accused who purchased them for about half of their value believing them to be stolen. The court held that the goods had lost their character as stolen goods at the time the defendant had purchased them and that his criminal intent was insufficient to sustain a conviction for an attempt to receive stolen property knowing it to have been stolen. In People v. Rollino, 37 Misc. 2d 14, 233 N.Y.S. 2d 580 (1962), the Supreme Court of New York followed the holding in the *Jaffe* case and found that an unsuccessful attempt to do that which is not a crime, when effectuated, cannot be held to be an attempt to commit the crime specified. Since the completed act did not and could not, as a matter of law, constitute larceny, the court held that it was legally impossible for the defendant to be guilty of attempted larceny. . . .

The California courts have held that there may be the crime of attempt to receive stolen property even though the property is not stolen. See, e.g., People v. Parker, 217 Cal. App. 2d 422, (1963); People v. Meyers,

213 Cal. App. 2d 518, (1963); People v. Rojas, 55 Cal. 2d 252, 358 P. 2d 921 (1961) and People v. Siu, 126 Cal. App. 2d 41, 271 P. 2d 575 (1954). In *Parker* the defendant was charged with attempted receipt of stolen confidential phone directories from the Pacific Telephone & Telegraph Company. Defendant argued that since the directories were delivered by the company's special agent to the district attorney's investigator who delivered them to the defendant, the directories were not stolen and consequently there could be no attempted receipt of stolen property. The court relied on *People v. Siu,* supra, and held that where a person formulates the intent to commit a crime and then proceeds to do something more which in the usual course of natural events will result in the commission of the crime, the attempt to commit that crime is complete even though the intended crime itself could not have been completed due to some extrinsic fact unknown to the person who intended it.

In *Rojas* and *Faustina,* supra, stolen goods were recovered by police, unknown to the defendants, whereupon the police delivered them to defendants who received them believing them to be stolen. Both cases rejected *Jaffe,* distinguishing between what a person actually does and what he intends to do. . . . The court in *Meyers,* supra, echoed the findings in *Rojas* and *Faustina,* holding that a person will not be guilty of an attempt to commit a crime only when the results intended by the person, if they happened as he envisioned, would still not be a crime.

Other jurisdictions adhere to the California position that a person be charged with attempt to commit a crime even though the crime itself

cannot be fully consummated due to an extrinsic fact unbeknown to that person. See, e.g., State v. Moretti, 52 N.J. 182, 244 A. 2d 499 (1968) and People v. Huff, 339 Ill. 328, 171 N.E. 261 (1930). (Both cases held that a man could be convicted of attempted abortion even though the woman, an undercover officer, was not pregnant—pregnancy being a required element for the substantive crime of abortion).

Added to the lack of uniformity among other jurisdictions on this issue is the morass of commentary surrounding the defense of impossibility in attempt crimes. Many courts compartmentalize fact patterns into the category of "factual impossibility" and "legal impossibility. . . ." This court agrees with the position taken by the court in *Moretti,* supra, that the defense is "so fraught with intricacies and artificial distinctions that [it] has little value as an analytical method for reaching substantial justice." However, this court respectfully disagrees with the *Moretti* court's position that the place to remedy the problem is in the courts. Rather, this court believes that the issue must be resolved through legislation. The American Law Institute has proposed a statute to cure a situation like the one presented in this case. Its Model Penal Code § 5.01 (proposed official draft, May 4, 1962) provides: "(1) Definition of attempt. A person is guilty of an attempt to commit a crime if, acting with the kind of culpability otherwise required for commission of the crime, he: (a) purposely engages in conduct which would constitute the crime if the attendant circumstances were as he believes them to be; or (b) when causing a particular result is an element of the crime, does or omits to do anything with the purpose of causing or with the belief that it will cause such result, without further conduct on his part; or (c) purposely does or omits to do anything which, under the circumstances as he believes them to be, is a substantial step in a course of conduct planned to culminate in his commission of the crime."

The Institute justifies the necessity for § 5.01 in its tentative Draft No. 10 of the Model Penal Code: It should suffice, therefore, to indicate at this stage what we deem to be the major results of the draft. They are: "(a) to extend the criminality of attempts by sweeping aside the defense of impossibility (including the distinction between so-called factual and legal impossibility) and by drawing the line between attempt and non-criminal preparation further away from the final act; the crime becomes essentially one of criminal purpose implemented by an overt act strongly corroborative of such purpose."

However, until the statutes are revised, this court is persuaded that the rationale of *Jaffe* and *Rollino* is the more logical and should be followed. Because the television set received by the defendant was not stolen, this court, after careful review of the authorities, finds that no crime was committed since an unsuccessful attempt to do that which is not a crime cannot be held to be an attempt to commit the crime specified. The court further finds that the affidavits supporting the two warrants involved herein did not establish probable cause to believe that the defendant had committed the crime of attempted receipt of stolen property, and that the remaining averments in the warrants were insufficient to establish probable cause to believe that the defendant was secreting stolen property in premises 1642 Vermont Avenue, N.W. Therefore, for the reasons stated above, it is this 28th day of March, 1973, Ordered that defendant's motion to suppress evidence be and hereby is granted.

Case Questions for Discussion

1. Was the defendant in the case any less blameworthy than he would have been had the television set actually been stolen?

2. What problem does *United States v. Hair* create for sting operations in Washington, DC?

3. A husband puts a gun to his wife's head and pulls the trigger twice. He did not know the gun was unloaded. As a result, it did not fire. Under the New York and District of Columbia positions, what is the result? What is the result under the California position and the Model Penal Code?

Conspiracy

Criminal *conspiracy* punishes an agreement between two or more people to commit an unlawful act or to perform a legal act in an illegal manner. The actus reus is the agreement itself and the mens rea is the intent to perform the unlawful act. A criminal conspiracy is often regarded as more dangerous to society than a criminal working alone; by combining their efforts, two or more persons bent on crime may increase the chances of their criminal efforts being successful.[75] Conspiracy laws have been dubbed the "prosecutor's darling," because it is often easier to bring and prosecute a conspiracy case than to wait for the commission of the substantive crime or to prosecute the conspirators for the actual commission of the substantive crime. Because those involved in criminal conspiracies generally act secretly, courts in conspiracy prosecutions are also more likely to admit and consider circumstantial evidence and inferences.[76]

Under the common law, conspiracy required no *overt act* in addition to the agreement. The general federal criminal conspiracy statute (18 U.S.C.A. § 371) requires an overt act in furtherance of the plan, as do most state statutes. The Model Penal Code [§ 5.03(5)] does not require an overt act for conspiracy prosecutions of first- or second-degree felonies. The function of the overt act requirement, when present, is to show the conspiracy is at work and not merely a thought in the minds of the conspirators. The act need not in itself be illegal, but merely in furtherance of the object of the conspiracy.[77]

For example, Al, Bill, and Cindy conspire to rob a bank. Al's role is to block the view of a surveillance camera mounted on a pole outside the bank. To do so, he parks his box van in a legal parking place at the front of the bank the night before the planned robbery. If the robbery does not take place, Al, Bill, and Cindy could be prosecuted for conspiracy to rob a bank if it can be shown there was an agreement to rob the bank in question. The overt act, if required, would be Al parking the van. Although parking the van in a legal parking place is not illegal in itself, it was parked in furtherance of the criminal agreement and shows the conspiracy was at work.

For one to be convicted of conspiracy, it must be proven that the defendant knew of the agreement and participated in it. It does not matter that the defendant did not know all the members of the conspiracy, nor that he or she was aware of all of the illegal activities the conspiracy entailed. All that is required is that he or she agreed to participate in illegal activities and that he or she participated in some manner.[78] For example, Al, Bill, and Cindy agree to rob a bank. Cindy then contacts Deb (an explosives expert) and asks her to provide an explosive charge that would be sufficient to blow open a bank vault. Deb agrees and provides the charge for Cindy. The government should be able to convict Deb of conspiracy to rob a bank. Deb agreed to provide Cindy with an explosive charge that Deb knew Cindy was going to use to blow open a bank vault. Although Deb did not know Al or Bill, which bank was to be robbed, or when, she is nevertheless guilty of conspiracy to rob a bank.

Conspiracy, by its nature, requires two or more conspirators. Under the federal statute, for example, if Al and Bill agree to rob a bank, but Al is an undercover policeman, Bill cannot be convicted of conspiracy. However, if Al, Bill, and Cindy agree to rob a bank and Al is an undercover policeman, Bill and Cindy could be convicted of conspiracy. This is called the bilateral approach to conspiracy.[79]

The MPC takes a unilateral approach. Section 5.03(1) defines conspiracy in terms of a person; it allows conspiracy convictions of a single person. Under the MPC unilateral approach, Bill could be convicted of conspiracy if he agreed with Al (an undercover policeman) to rob a bank. Many state statutes follow the MPC approach, but not all state courts have interpreted unilateral approach conspiracy statutes as allowing conviction of a single person for agreeing with another (not a co-conspirator). For example, the Washington state statute, based on the MPC model, has been interpreted as requiring mutual agreement.[80]

A conspirator may withdraw, but he or she must do so before any overt act in furtherance of the conspiracy is taken. To withdraw, the actor must take affirmative acts inconsistent with the objective of the conspiracy and communicate those acts in a manner in which they will reasonably reach the co-conspirators.[81] Unlike attempt crimes, a defendant may be charged and convicted of both the substantive crime and conspiracy to commit the crime.[82]

Defenses

Defendants charged with a crime have some defenses available to them. Most defenses relate to the required mens rea. Bob is about to shoot Tom, but just in time Tom pulls out his own gun and shoots Bob before Bob can fire. Tom can claim self-defense. Tom's intent was to stop Bob from killing him, rather than to kill Bob. Other common defenses are insanity, necessity, duress, entrapment, and infancy. We now turn to brief discussions of each of these defenses.

Insanity

A person with an extreme mental illness may in fact lack the criminal intent required for a criminal conviction. One suffering from paranoid schizophrenia may hear voices or have hallucinations and delusions. A common delusion is that one is working for the CIA. If someone who is so afflicted shoots a passerby thinking the passerby is about to capture and torture her until she reveals national secrets, should that person be subject to criminal penalties? It is often a difficult question. David Berkowitz, the serial killer known as "Son of Sam," claimed his neighbor's dog was telling him to kill his victims. Berkowitz pled guilty to the murders and later recanted his story,[83] but had he really been convinced he was doing his duty as instructed by his neighbor's dog, should he have been subject to criminal sanctions? Surely his actions were horrible, but should he be personally responsible? This issue has troubled the courts and the public for hundreds of years. The evolution of the insanity defense is interesting.

The majority of jurisdictions follow the *M'Naghten* rule, which came out of an 1843 English case, M'Naghten's Case, 8 Eng. Rep. 718. Under this rule, defendants must prove that at the time of their criminal act, they were laboring under a defect of reason from a disease of the mind as not to know the nature and quality of the act, or they did not know the act as wrong. Stated another way, the question is: Was the defendant's mental state such that he or she did not know the difference between right and wrong?[84] Consider our example involving the paranoid schizophrenic who believes he is in the CIA and shoots a passerby thinking he is protecting national secrets. He probably knows the nature and quality of his act (shooting the one he believes is after him is likely to kill him), but he probably did not know the act was wrong (in fact, he probably believed he was doing the right thing).

Some of the jurisdictions that follow the *M'Naghten* rule supplement it with the *irresistible impulse* test. Simply stated, the test is: Persons should not be held criminally responsible if they have a mental disease that keeps them from controlling their conduct. The test is badly named because it covers not only sudden actions, but also planned actions that the defendant is unable to control as a result of a mental defect or disease.[85]

The authors of the Model Penal Code considered a version of the *Durham* rule that was followed in the District of Columbia for 20 years, before they adopted a modernized version of the *M'Naghten* rule and the irresistible impulse test. Under *Durham*, a defendant was not responsible for his unlawful act if it was a product of mental disease or mental defect. The MPC does not hold persons responsible for criminal conduct if, as a result of mental disease or defect, they lack substantial capacity either to appreciate the criminality of their conduct or to conform their conduct to the requirements of the law. The mental illness or defect in question cannot include any abnormality manifested only by repeated criminal or antisocial conduct.[86]

Despite the various tests and many judicial interpretations of the different rules concerning the insanity defense, the question whether someone should be responsible for his or her acts regardless of one's mental state remains today a controversial matter. After John Hinckley, an obviously troubled man, was found not guilty by reason of insanity for shooting President Ronald Reagan and Press Secretary James Brady, the public was outraged.[87] Several jurisdictions have now added a separate *guilty but mentally ill* option for the finder of fact faced with an insanity defense. Persons found guilty but mentally ill are sentenced for the crime as if they had been found guilty of the crime as charged. Before beginning their sentence, defendants are examined by psychiatrists and transferred to a mental hospital if found in need of treatment. If they regain their mental health before the end of the sentence, they are incarcerated for the remainder of the sentence. If the sentence ends before they regain their mental health, they are released unless the state or some other party brings civil commitment proceedings.[88]

A lawyer considering an insanity defense for a client needs to consider another issue. Many times, a defendant may be worse off being judged insane than if he or she were convicted of the crime as accused. Often, under state mental health laws, as long as one is determined to be a danger to others or oneself, he or she may be held in a mental hospital—in some cases confinement could be for life. If instead, the defendant is convicted of the crime, the defendant would be released at the end of the sentence.

Necessity and Duress

At times, individuals are faced with a choice of following the law and allowing harm to be done, or purposefully breaking the law but avoiding the threatened harm. The defenses of *necessity* and *duress* excuse the criminal acts when the harm threatened is worse than the harm done by the criminal act. Historically, necessity applies to naturally occurring harms like storms and floods, and duress applies to human-induced threats. For example, the necessity defense is probably available in a homicide case to a dam operator who opened a floodgate knowing he would flood a single house to avoid the dam breaking, thereby flooding a whole town. Duress should be available to the husband who is told to shoot another man or his captor will kill his son and wife. Arguably, in both situations, the harm done is less than the harm threatened. The Model Penal Code abandons the historical divergence in the two defenses. Instead, it adopts a *choice of evils* defense that encompasses necessity and duress.[89]

Entrapment

Entrapment is a defense available to those who have been unduly induced to commit a crime by the government. For example, Alexia, a government undercover agent, offers to sell illegal drugs to Bob. Bob buys the drugs and then Alexia arrests Bob for possession of illegal drugs. Bob may be able to assert the entrapment defense. The defense is not available if a private person induces another to commit a crime.

There are two approaches to entrapment: subjective and objective. Under the predominate *subjective approach* (also called the *Sherman-Sorrels* approach), two inquiries are made. First, did the government induce the criminal activity? If yes, then the pertinent question becomes: Was this defendant predisposed to commit the crime? If predisposition was present on the part of the defendant, then entrapment is not a defense. The focus under the subjective approach is on the defendant's conduct prior to the crime. If the defendant was engaged in the type of criminal activity for which he is accused, then entrapment is not an available defense.[90]

Under the minority *objective approach*, however, only the activity of the inducers (the government) is relevant. The question is: Did the government use methods of persuasion creating a substantial risk so that individuals, other than the one the inducements were aimed at, would be induced to commit the crime? The effective difference between the two approaches is that one who is predisposed to commit a crime may be able to employ entrapment as a defense if the government's activities were overreaching under the objective approach. On the other hand, one with no predisposition may not be able to use the defense if the government's inducement activities were not flagrant.[91]

Infancy

At common law, actors under the age of 7 were irrebuttably presumed to lack capacity to commit a crime because they lacked the ability to form the mens rea necessary for the crime. For those between 7 and 14 years of age, there was a rebuttable presumption of incapacity. A showing of malice on the part of the actor could rebut the presumption. Those over age 14 were presumed to have the capacity to form the necessary mens rea for the crime.[92]

As first discussed in Chapter 7, all states have created juvenile court systems. Generally, states grant jurisdiction for transgressions of criminal law by persons under a certain age to the juvenile court system. Some grants of jurisdiction are exclusive, with specified exceptions, and others are concurrent with the criminal courts. There are three types of waivers of juvenile court jurisdiction for juvenile defenders: judicial, prosecutorial, and legislative. Judicial waivers are granted by juvenile court judges when they, applying specific criteria, determine that the offender should be subject to criminal court jurisdiction. The waivers may be ordered only after a hearing and a statement of reasoning by the juvenile court judge. Prosecutorial waivers are applicable when both the criminal and juvenile courts have jurisdiction. The prosecution has sole discretion in deciding which defendants to waive into criminal court. Finally, under legislative waivers, the legislature by statute determines that juveniles over a certain age who have committed certain crimes shall be tried in criminal court.[93]

The decision to try a juvenile as an adult is a serious matter. If tried in criminal court as an adult, a juvenile offender would be subject to the same punishment as an adult and could be sentenced to prison if convicted. The juvenile system is focused on rehabilitation, whereas the prison system in the United States today leans toward retribution. Public outrage over youth crime, especially violent crimes, has fueled a race by jurisdiction to make transfer to criminal court easier. Florida is one of 15 states employing the prosecutorial waiver system, which has been in place there since 1981. In 1995, Florida prosecutors sent 7,000 juveniles to criminal court compared with 9,700 juveniles sent to criminal courts by judges in the balance of the country. Critics of the Florida approach argue that children sent to prison end up committing more crimes than youthful offenders who enter the rehabilitation-based juvenile system. As a result, Florida's high violent crime rate by juvenile offenders has not responded to the "get tough" policies.[94] Florida officials seem to be reconsidering the policy. As of July 1, 2001, youthful offenders, like 14-year-old Nathaniel Brazil, who was sentenced to 28 years for murdering a school teacher, will serve their sentence in a youth facility, instead of prison, until they reach adulthood.[95]

Key Terms, Names, and Concepts

Accessory after the fact

Actus reus

Assault

Attempt crimes

Battery

Brain death

Burglary

Choice of evils defense

Conspiracy

Depraved heart murder

Deviant sexual intercourse by force or imposition

Duress defense

Durham rule

Entrapment defense

Extortion or blackmail

Felony murder

Feticide statute

Gross sexual imposition

Guilty but mentally ill

Infancy defense

Insanity defense

Intent to do serious bodily harm murder

Intent to kill murder

Involuntary manslaughter

Irresistible impulse test

Larceny

Larceny by trick

Manslaughter

Mens rea

M'Naghten rule

Model Penal Code

Necessity defense

Objective approach to entrapment

Omission

Overt act requirement

Police power

Premeditation

Rape

Receiving stolen property

Robbery

Sherman-Sorrels (subjective approach to entrapment)

Status crime

Strict liability offense

Theft

Theft of services

Victimless crimes

Voluntary manslaughter

Voluntary physical act

Discussion Questions

1. The defendant testifies that when he awoke, he was standing next to his bed with a bloody hammer in his hand. On the bed in front of him was his wife, dying of blows to the head from the hammer. Defendant's expert witness testifies that defendant is a sleepwalker, and that it is possible for sleepwalkers to perform motor acts while in an unconscious state. If believed by the jury, should it find defendant guilty of murder? Why or why not?

2. Defendant receives a package in the mail from her brother, who has a history of drug abuse and has been under surveillance by the police. The package contains a smaller box and a letter from her brother asking defendant to put the box away and he will retrieve it later that month. Defendant does as the letter instructs. Later that night, the police arrive with a search warrant and find the box. It contains an ounce of cocaine. Defendant is charged with possession of cocaine. Is defendant guilty? Why or why not?

3. As part of her annual physical examination, Jane had blood drawn and sent to a lab for analysis. A couple of days later, Jane received a phone call from defendant, who was posing as a medical specialist. Defendant told Jane she had contracted a dangerous and rare form of a blood-born disease. Defendant told her there were two options for treatment, the first being an expensive ($10,000) and painful surgical procedure. The other option was for Jane to have sexual intercourse with a man who had been injected with a special serum. The second option was less expensive ($500) and required no rehabilitation. Jane reluctantly agreed to the second option. Defendant arranged to meet Jane at a hotel, they had sexual intercourse as agreed, and Jane paid defendant $500. Jane later finds out defendant had tricked her into having sexual intercourse. Defendant is charged with rape. Is he guilty? Why or why not?

4. Defendant approaches Julie and Alisha, who are walking down the street. He pulls out a gun, points it at Julie, and demands their purses. Alisha pulls out her own gun and fires it at defendant. She misses the defendant, but the bullet strikes and kills Joshua, a passerby who is 100 feet behind defendant. Defendant is arrested and charged with murder. Is he guilty? Why or why not?

5. Defendant was a prisoner at a state prison farm. Other prisoners wanted him to engage in homosexual acts, but he refused. He was threatened and later beaten by other prisoners. He reported the assault to prison authorities, but the prisoners he named as his assaulters were not disciplined, and defendant was not

placed in protective custody. Later, those prisoners that defendant reported to authorities became aware that defendant had reported them and threatened they would kill defendant at the first opportunity. Defendant walked out of the work farm and was not captured until three days later. He was charged with escape. Does defendant have any defenses? Explain.

6. John is a cancer patient who struggles with nausea following chemo- and radiation therapy. His weight is down from 175 to 95 pounds, and he is becoming weak and vulnerable to other illnesses. John just found out that he will need to undergo an additional two months of chemotherapy. Defendant, John's sister, buys some marijuana and gives it to John. After smoking it, John finds that he is no longer nauseous and is able to eat. As a result, John actually gains a few pounds. Defendant makes another trip to buy marijuana and is arrested soon after purchasing an ounce of the drug. She is charged with possession. Can defendant use the necessity defense? Why or why not?

7. Explain what a defendant must show to successfully use the insanity defense under the *M'Naghten* rule. Explain what a defendant must show to successfully use the insanity defense under the irresistible impulse test. Do you agree or disagree with states that have adopted guilty but mentally ill verdicts?

8. Which approach to testing for entrapment do you think is preferable, the majority subjective approach (*Sherman-Sorrels* test) or the minority objective test? Why?

9. Do you think prostitution should be legal? What about marijuana use? What about gambling? How can states justify jailing bookies, when states operate a lottery of their own?

10. If a 14-year-old commits a serious crime, should that teenager be sentenced to prison? Should the convicted teen be put in a juvenile center? Explain your answers. Would your answers change if the actor were 11 years old when he or she committed the crime?

Suggested Additional Reading

Adams, Teresa, E. "Note: Tacking on Money Laundering Charges to White Collar Crimes: What Did Congress Intend, and What Are the Courts Doing?" *Georgia State Law Review* 17 (winter 2000): 531–573.

Agthe, Dale R. "Validity and Construction of Statute Defining Homicide by Conduct Manifesting 'Depraved Indifference.' " 25 *American Law Reports* 4th (2001), p. 311.

Blum, George L. "Validity, Construction, and Effect of Hate Crimes Statutes, Ethnic Intimidation Statutes, or the Like." 22 *American Law Reports* 5th (2001), p. 261.

Bradley, Craig, M. "Symposium: RICO Thirty Years Later: A Comparative Perspective: Now v. Scheidler Round Two." *Syracuse Journal of International Law and Commerce* 27 (summer 2000): 233–242.

Bryden, David P. "Redefining Rape." *Buffalo Criminal Law Review* 3 (2000): 317–512.

Cole, Susannah Rawl. "Criminal Law: II. Sewing up the Loophole in Accessory After the Fact Crimes." *South Carolina Law Review* 50 (summer 1999): 901–915.

Estrich, Susan. *Real Rape*. Cambridge, MA: Harvard University Press, 1987.

Ghent, Jeffery F. "Impossibility of Consummation of Substantive Crime as Defense in Criminal Prosecution for Conspiracy or Attempt to Commit Crime." 37 *American Law Reports* 3rd (2000), p. 375.

Harrington, W. A. "Criminal Conspiracy Between Spouses." 74 *American Law Reports* 3rd (2001), p. 838.

Jacoby, Joseph E. and Francis T. Cullen. "The Structure of Punishment Norms: Applying the Rossi-Berk Model." *Journal of Criminal Law & Criminology* 89 (fall 1998): 245–312.

McCord, David. "State Death Sentencing for Felony Murder Accomplices Under the Enmund and Tison Standards." *Arizona State Law Journal* 32 (fall 2000): 843–896.

Slocum, Brian. "RICO and the Legislative Approach to Federal Criminal Lawmaking." *Loyola University Chicago Law Journal* 31 (summer 2000): 639–692.

Vitiello, Michael. "Three Strikes: Can We Return to Rationality?" *Journal of Criminal Law & Criminology* 87 (winter 1997): 395–463.

Endnotes

1. Wayne R. LaFave, *Criminal Law*, 3d ed. (St. Paul, MN: West, 2000), § 2.1.
2. Ibid., at § 1.1(b). From 1962 to 1983, 34 revised criminal codes were enacted. Sanford H. Kadish, "Fifty Years of Criminal Law: An Opinionated Review," *California Law Review* 87 (July 1999): 943, 948.
3. LaFave, *Criminal Law*, § 2.1.
4. Ibid., § 2.8. United States v. Cassidy, 571 F.2d 534 (10th Cir. 1978) (enclaves), and Balckmer v. United States, 284 U.S. 421 (1932) (U.S. nationals abroad).
5. LaFave, *Criminal Law*, § 2.9.
6. Ibid., § 2.8(d). Bartcus v. Illinois, 359 U.S. 121 (1959), and Abbate v. United States, 359 U.S. 187 (1959). In *Bartcus*, the defendant had been acquitted in federal court on a bank robbery charge, then later convicted in state court of bank robbery for the same robbery. In *Abbate*, the defendant was convicted first in state court and later in federal court of conspiracy to destroy another's property (state) and conspir-

acy to destroy a communications facility (federal) for trying to blow up a telephone company's property.

7. 21 Am. Jur. 2d *Criminal Law*, §§ 4 & 126 (2000).

8. LaFave, *Criminal Law*, § 3.1.

9. 21 Am. Jur. 2d *Criminal Law*, § 145 (2000).

10. LaFave, *Criminal Law*, §§ 3.2(b) & (c).

11. State v. Hinkle, 200 W.Va. 280, 489 S.E.2d 257 (S. Ct. App. 1996).

12. 21 Am. Jur. 2d *Criminal Law*, § 32 (2000).

13. LaFave, *Criminal Law*, § 3.3.

14. 21 Am. Jur. 2d *Criminal Law*, § 30 (2000).

15. People v. Belcastro, 356 Ill. 144, 190 N.E. 301 (1934) (vagabond) and City of Watertown v. Christnacht, 39 S.D. 290 194 N.W. 62 (1917) (prostitute).

16. 21 Am. Jur. 2d *Criminal Law*, § 31 (2000).

17. Robinson v. California, 370 U.S. 660 (1962).

18. I.J. Schiffres, "Validity of Vagrancy Statutes and Ordinances," 25 A. L. R. 3rd (2001), p. 792.

19. City of Chicago v. Morales, 527 U.S. 41 (1999), as discussed in Erik Luna, "Criminal Law: Constitutional Roadmaps," *Journal of Criminal Law and Criminology* 90 (summer 2000): 1125.

20. LaFave, *Criminal Law*, § 7.1.

21. Ibid., § 7.1(d).

22. Ibid. See, Keeler v. Superior Ct. of Amador County, 2 Cal. 3d 619, 470 P.2d 617 (1970), State v. Dickinson, 23 Ohio App.2d 259, 263 N.E.2d 253 (1970) and People v. Greer, 79 Ill. 2d 103, 402 N.E.2d 203 (1980).

23. State v. Merrill, 450 N.W.2d 318, 324 (Minn. S. Ct. 1990).

24. LaFave, *Criminal Law*, § 7.2.

25. Ibid.

26. Arnold H. Loewy, *Criminal Law in a Nutshell*, 3d ed. (St. Paul, MN: West, 2000), § 2.02. See People v. Anderson, 70 Cal.2d 15, 447 P.2d 942 (1968) (some plan or motive) and State v. Ollens, 107 Wash.2d 848, 733 P.2d 1984 (1987) (repeated stabs).

27. Model Penal Code §§ 210.1 and 210.2.

28. LaFave, *Criminal Law*, § 7.3.

29. Loewy, *Criminal Law in a Nutshell*, § 2.03.

30. Model Penal Code §§ 210.2 and 210.3.

31. Loewy, *Criminal Law in a Nutshell*, § 2.08.

32. LaFave, *Criminal Law*, § 7.4.

33. Loewy, *Criminal Law in a Nutshell*, § 2.09.

34. Erwin S. Barbre, "What Felonies Are Inherently or Foreseeably Dangerous to Human Life for Purposes of Felony-Murder Doctrine," 50 A. L. R. 3rd (2001), p. 397. Massachusetts also takes this view, Commonwealth v. Matchett, 386 Mass. 492, 436 N.E.2d 400 (1982).

35. State v. Dixon, 109 Ariz. 441, 511 P.2d 623 (1973), discussed in LaFave, *Criminal Law*, 7.5(b).

36. Barbre, "What Felonies Are Inherently or Foreseeably Dangerous to Human Life for Purposes of Felony-Murder Doctrine."

37. Model Penal Code § 210.2.

38. LaFave, *Criminal Law*, § 7.5(h).

39. Loewy, *Criminal Law in a Nutshell*, § 2.01.

40. Christina M. Tchen, "Rape Reform and a Statutory Consent Defense," *Journal of Criminal Law and Criminology* 74 (winter 1983): 1518, 1521, quoting Lord Edwin Coke's 1628 definition.
41. Ibid., at 1522–1528.
42. Model Penal Code §§ 213.0–213.4.
43. Michael G Walsh, "Criminal Responsibility of Husband for Rape, or Assault to Commit Rape on Wife," 24 A. L. R. 4th (2001), p. 105.
44. Joseph G. Cook and Paul Marcus, *Criminal Law*, 4th ed. (New York, NY: Mathew Bender & Co., 1998), p. 346. See also, People v. Liberta, 64 N.Y.2d 152, 474 N.E.2d 567 (1984), a New York Court of Appeals case holding a statute criminalizing only males raping females (nongender-neutral) was a violation of the Equal Protection Clause.
45. Loewy, *Criminal Law in a Nutshell*, § 4.02.
46. LaFave, *Criminal Law*, §§ 7.14–7.16.
47. Ibid.
48. Model Penal Code §§ 211.1. (Assault) & 213.4 (Sexual Assault).
49. LaFave, *Criminal Law*, § 7.15(d).
50. Model Penal Code §§ 211.1(2)(a) & (b).
51. LaFave, *Criminal Law*, §§ 8.1–8.2.
52. Ibid.
53. Model Penal Code § 223 (Theft and Related Offenses.)
54. Model Penal Code § 222.1.
55. For example, see N.J.S.A. 2C:15-1 (New Jersey) and New York State Consolidated Laws Title JA § 160.
56. People v. Patton, 76 Ill. 2d 45, 49, 389 N.E.2d 1174, 1175 (1979), quoted in State v. Stein, 124 N.J. 209, 590 A.2d 665 (1991), discussed in Cook, *Criminal Law*, at § 5.02.
57. Cook, *Criminal Law*, at § 5.03.
58. Model Penal Code § 221.1.
59. Loewy, *Criminal Law in a Nutshell*, § 14.06A.
60. LaFave, *Criminal Law*, § 8.13.
61. Model Penal Code § 223.1(2). Even if the value is less than $500, if the property stolen is a firearm, airplane, motor vehicle, or motor boat, it is still a felony. If the value of the property is less than $50, it is a petty misdemeanor.
62. Model Penal Code § 223.2.
63. Model Penal Code § 223.7.
64. Model Penal Code § 223.6(1).
65. LaFave, *Criminal Law*, § 8.10(d). See also, United States v. Werner, 160 F.2d 438 (2nd Cir. 1947) and State v. Chester, 707 So. 2d 973 (La. 1997).
66. Model Penal Code § 223.6(2).
67. Loewy, *Criminal Law in a Nutshell*, § 7.07.
68. LaFave, *Criminal Law*, § 8.12.
69. Model Penal Code § 223.4.
70. Stephanie Barry, "War on Drugs has Many P.O.W.s," *In-depth With the Union News*, 2 May 1998, available online at <http://www.masslive.com/indepth/war/050299war.html>, and Peter McWilliams, *Ain't Nobody's Business if You Do: The Absurdity of Consensual Crimes in Our Free Country*, (Prelude Press, 1996), available online at <http://www.mcwilliams.com/books/aint/101.htm>, as of August 14, 2001.
71. Loewy, *Criminal Law in a Nutshell*, § 14.01.
72. LaFave, *Criminal Law*, § 6.2.

73. Ibid., § 6.3(c), and E. H. Schopler, "Conviction or Acquittal of Attempt to Commit Particular Crimes as Bar to Prosecution for Conspiracy to Commit Same Crime, or Vice Versa," 53 A. L. R. 2d (2001), p. 622.
74. LaFave, *Criminal Law*, § 6.2(c).
75. Loewy, *Criminal Law in a Nutshell*, § 16.01.
76. Mia V. Carpiniello and Abigail Roberts, "Federal Criminal Conspiracy," *American Criminal Law Review* 37 (spring 2000): 496.
77. LaFave, *Criminal Law*, § 6.5(c).
78. Carpiniello, "Federal Criminal Conspiracy," pp. 504–505.
79. Ibid., p. 499.
80. LaFave, *Criminal Law*, § 6.4 (c). *See also*, State v. Pacheco, 125 Wash.2d 150, 882 P.2d 183, (1994), rejecting unilateral approach and Miller v. State, 955 P.2d 892 (Wyo. 1998), embracing the unilateral approach.
81. Carpiniello, "Federal Criminal Conspiracy," p. 512.
82. Ibid., p. 523.
83. J. P. Essene, "Son of Sam! Exposes His Connection to Satanic Church of Sacrifice!" (Nov. 15, 1997), *Underground News and Reviews From the Underground*, <http://www.theeunderground.com/Features/features131 sonofsam.shtml>, available as of August 23, 2001.
84. LaFave, *Criminal Law*, § 4.2.
85. Ibid.
86. Ibid., § 4.3. See also, Durham v. United States, 214 F.2d 862 (D.C.Cir. 1954) and MPC § 4.01.
87. "Man Who Shot Reagan Wins Mental Hospital Release," *CNN.com*, (Jan. 15, 1999), <http://www.cnn.com/US/9901/15/hinckley.leave/>, available as of August 23, 2001.
88. LaFave, *Criminal Law*, § 4.5(h).
89. Ibid., § 5.4, and MPC § 3.02.
90. LaFave, *Criminal Law*, § 5.2. The subjective approach is the result of two Supreme Court cases, Sherman v. United States, 356 U.S. 369 (1958), and Sorrels v. United States, 287 U.S. 435 (1932). The objective theory came out of concurring opinions written by Justices Roberts and Frankfurter in the same two cases. The MPC adopted the objective theory in section 2.13.
91. Ibid.
92. LaFave, *Criminal Law*, § 4.11.
93. Ibid.
94. Justice Policy Institute, "Fact Sheet: Florida's Experience With Trying Juveniles as Adults," <http://www.cjcj.org/florida/factsheet.html>, available as of August 25, 2001.
95. Warren Richey, "Has Florida's Justice for Juveniles Gone Too Far?" *The Christian Science Monitor*, July 25, 2001, <http://www.csmonitor.com:5000/2001/0725/p2s1-usju.html>, available as of August 25, 2001. ✦

Part IV

Law Governing Conduct of Business

Chapter 14

Contracts

Chapter Objectives

The overall objective of this chapter is to help students gain a basic understanding of what a contract is and what rights and responsibilities are created in each party when a contract is formed. Readers need to be able to understand and explain the basic elements of contract formation, including capacity, offer, acceptance, and consideration. Students should also be able to determine when an oral contract is enforceable and when Statute of Fraud provisions require written contracts. Readers will gain an understanding of the basic methods and rules that courts employ to interpret and construe contracts. Students should also achieve a basic understanding of express, implied, and constructive conditions and be able to explain how these conditions are effected when performance is due under a contract. Finally, students must understand how the rights and responsibilities of the parties to a contract may change once the contract has been breached.

Everyday life could be chaotic if courts did not enforce contractual rights. Imagine, if after working a month for an employer, that the employer decided not to pay you; or if after paying your rent, the landlord decided to rent the premises to someone else, and they moved into the apartment for which you had already paid. If courts could not be called upon to force a party to a contract to perform, or to at least compensate the other party, all of us would have many more things to worry about. Knowledge that contracts are legally enforceable motivates parties to make contracts to perform their promises. It is usually in their best interest to do so. However, not all promises are enforceable. A promise generally does not rise to the level of a contract unless both parties give valuable consideration, such as another promise, money, or forbearance. Think of all the promises typical college students make to their parents. "I promise to study hard every night. I promise not to go out until all of my homework is finished. I promise not to drink until I am 21 years old. I promise not to try controlled substances. I promise not to have sex until I am married." If parents could bring breach of contract actions for their children's broken promises, some students would be in court all the time.

Simply stated, a contract is a promise or set of promises that courts will enforce. A universal definition of *contract*, however, has proven troublesome. The difficulty lies in the wide range of situations in which contracts are formed, the many ways in which contracts may be formed, and the many different perspectives from which contracts are viewed. Professor Williston's definition, "a promise or set of promises for the breach of which the law gives a remedy, or the performance of which the law in some way recognizes as a duty," has been the most influential. Williston's definition was used in both the first and second Restatements of Contracts issued by the prestigious American Law Institute.[1]

Contracts may be complicated formal documents that are negotiated by professionals or informal oral agreements between friends.

The law of contracts is diverse, with many subspecialties, such as consumer transactions, labor law, sales, international transactions, construction contracts, and more. In this chapter, we provide a brief overview of American contract law. First, we offer a short discussion of the evolution of contract law in the United States to give readers a historical perspective. Then we describe the basic elements of contract formation. We subsequently turn to sections on oral and written contracts, how contracts are interpreted, when performance is due, and what remedies are available when contracts are breached.

Historical Evolution of Modern American Contract Law

The beginnings of what today is the law of contracts in the United States can be traced to the Romans. Under Roman law, there was not a general scheme for enforcement of promises, but instead, specific types or forms of promises that could be enforced. A *stipulation* (*stipulatio*) was a promise one made to another in a formal ceremony. A stipulated promise required no consideration from the other party.

Under a *real contract,* a party became bound to return something after it was delivered to them. *Consensual contracts* allowed both parties to promise to do something, but only if the agreements covered sales, partnerships, employment, and mandate. Finally, by the sixth century, *innominate contracts* were being enforced. Innominate contracts were not limited to specific types of transactions and required promises on the part of both parties (thus, the phrase *quid pro quo*). Until one of the parties had performed, either party could cancel and render the innominate contract unenforceable.[2]

The early English common law courts, specifically the Court of Common Pleas as discussed in Chapter 2, allowed the contract-like actions of covenant and debt. Both were limited in usefulness, however. *Covenant* required a written document bearing the wax seal of the parties. *Debt* was limited to those actions in which the party in breach had received what it was promised. The action was cast as if the plaintiff had loaned the defendant something and was asking for it to be repaid. A form of trespass on the case, *assumpsit,* was a tort-like action. It allowed recovery for promises badly performed (misfeasance). An extension of the action allowed recovery when one party failed to perform, if the party in compliance suffered damages because it had relied on the other party's promise. By the late sixteenth century, the action had evolved to allow for recovery for breaches of promises without reliance. Finally, by the early seventeenth century, a form of assumpsit, *general assumpsit,* was recognized as an alternative to debt when a party to a contract sued to recover amounts due it under a contract. This was important, because under the debt action, the defendant could take advantage of the *wager of law,* which allowed defendants to swear they did not owe the amount and to bring in a number of oath-helpers to testify that the defendants were telling the truth. Assumpsit actions were tried before juries.[3]

When the United States inherited the British common law, the law of contracts was almost entirely judge-made law. That distinction remains today. Although legislatures and Congress have from time to time adopted statutes that regulate specific types of contracts, general contract law is still based on common law. Two important influences on the law of contracts have been the Restatements on Contracts and the Uniform Commercial Code. *The Restatement, Second, Contracts* (hereinafter Restatement, Second), published in 1981 by the American Law Institute, is a general statement of the law of contracts and is based on existing case law. Courts often look to the Restatement, Second, for guidance, now that it has replaced the original Restatement, Contracts, published in 1932. The Uniform Commercial Code (UCC) is a set of model statutes designed to be adopted by the states to promote uniformity in commerce. It has been adopted by all states (with minor differences) except Louisiana. The UCC has nine articles, but only articles 1 and 2 influence general contract law. Because the UCC's main thrust is contractual relations among merchants, we will not focus on its provisions in this chapter.

Basic Elements of Contract Formation

How are contracts formed? The parties must have capacity, there must be an offer, the offer must be accepted, and there must be consideration.

Capacity

All natural persons have the legal *capacity* to bind themselves under a contract, unless they are under a guardianship, are an infant, are mentally ill or possess a mental defect, or are intoxicated.[4] Typically, contracts entered into by persons who are incapacitated are voidable, but not void. As a result, a person without capacity may hold the other party to the contract, but may disaffirm the contract if sued for breach. An *infant* is a person who has not yet reached the age of majority in his or her state of residence. Traditionally, infants have been able to contract for necessities on a quasi-contractual theory. Some states statutorily hold infants liable on contracts, such as withdrawals of bank deposits and payment of life insurance premiums. Once the infant reaches the age of majority, contracts entered into as an infant must be disaffirmed to avoid liability.[5]

Transactions entered into by persons with mental illness or disabilities result in voidable contracts if the person is unable to reasonably "understand" the consequences of the transaction. Contracts are also voidable if the person is unable to "act" reasonably, in relation to the transaction, and if the other party had a reason to know of the condition. Intoxicated persons may void contracts if the other party had reason to know the intoxicated person was unable to reasonably understand the nature of the transaction or was unable to act reasonably in relation to the transaction.[6]

It is more difficult to disaffirm a contract on the basis of intoxication than mental illness. Likewise, it is more difficult to disaffirm a contract on the basis of mental illness or defect than because of infancy. In the case of intoxication, a voluntary affliction, the critical factor is the conduct of the other party. If the other party has no

Contracts entered into by persons with mental illnesses or disabilities may be voidable.

reason to know of the intoxicated party's condition, and the contract is reasonable, the courts will usually refuse to void the agreement.[7] Traditionally, for persons with mental illness or defect, a *cognitive* test has been employed. Under the cognitive test, the sole inquiry is: At the time of the transaction, did the afflicted person have the capacity to understand the transaction? Whether the other party had knowledge of the affliction is irrelevant. A *volitional* test is at times employed when the afflicted person has the capacity to understand the transaction but is unable to control his or her actions, such as manic-depressives in the manic stage. The critical question becomes: Could the person control him- or herself? The Restatement, Second, endorses both tests, but under the volitional test, it adds the requirement that the other party must have reason to know of the afflicted person's inability to control his or her acts.[8]

Infants have an almost unrestricted ability to disavow their contracts. Absent a statutory exception, the law favors protection of infants over the interests of those entering into contracts with them. Even infants who lie about their age usually can avoid the consequences of transactions they enter into. In some jurisdictions, infants who lie about their age may be liable for tortuous misrepresentation damages, however.[9] Because of the importance of children and teenagers to many consumer-oriented products and services, some commentators have advocated making it harder for infants to disavow contracts, if the other party acted reasonably.[10] Lack of contractual capacity can make common transactions difficult for minors. Seventeen-year-olds, who have graduated high school and are working full time, may need a parent or some other adult to join them as a party in a contract to purchase an automobile or other common purchases. Adults can also contractually bind infants in a manner that the infant may later be unable to disavow. Consider the following case. The Court of Appeals of New York is the state's highest court.

Shields v. Gross
Court of Appeals of New York
58 N.Y.2d 338, 448 N.E.2d 108 (1983)

O PINION BY: SIMONS: The issue on this appeal is whether an infant model may disaffirm a prior unrestricted consent executed on her behalf by her parent and maintain an action pursuant to section 51 of the Civil Rights Law against her photographer for republication of photographs of her. We hold that she may not.

Plaintiff is now a well-known actress. For many years prior to these events she had been a child model and in 1975, when she was 10 years of age, she obtained several modeling jobs with defendant through her agent, the Ford Model Agency. One of the jobs, a series of photographs to be financed by Playboy Press, required plaintiff to pose nude in a bathtub. It was intended that these photos would be used in a publication entitled "Portfolio 8" (later renamed "Sugar and Spice"). Before the photographic sessions, plaintiff's mother and legal guardian, Teri Shields, executed two consents in favor of defendant. After the pictures were taken, they were used not only in "Sugar and Spice" but also, to the knowledge of plaintiff and her mother, in other publications and in a display of larger-than-life photo enlargements in the windows of a store on Fifth Avenue in New York City. Indeed, plaintiff subsequently used the photos in a book that she published about herself and to do so her mother obtained an authorization from defendant to use them. Over the years defendant has also photographed plaintiff for Penthouse Magazine, New York Magazine and for advertising by the Courtauldts and Avon companies.

In 1980 plaintiff learned that several of the 1975 photographs had appeared in a French magazine called "Photo" and, disturbed by that publication and by information that defendant intended others, she attempted to buy the negatives. In 1981, she commenced this action in tort and contract seeking compensatory and punitive damages and an injunction permanently enjoining defendant from any further use of the photographs. . . .

Historically, New York common law did not recognize a cause of action for invasion of privacy. . . . In 1909, however, the Legislature enacted sections 50 and 51 of the Civil Rights Law. Section 50 is penal and makes it a misdemeanor to use a living person's name, portrait or picture for advertising purposes without prior "written consent." Section 51 is remedial and creates a related civil cause of action on behalf of the injured party permitting relief by injunction or damages. . . . Section 51 of the statute states that the prior "written consent" which will bar the civil action is to be as "above provided," referring to section 50, and section 50, in turn, provides that: "A person, firm or corporation that uses for advertising purposes, or for the purposes of trade, the name, portrait or picture of any living person without having first obtained the written consent of such person, or if a minor of his or her parent or guardian, is guilty of a misdemeanor" [emphasis added].

Thus, whereas in Roberson v. Rochester Folding Box Co., 171 N.Y. 538, the infant plaintiff had no cause of action against the advertiser under the common law for using her pictures, the new statute gives a cause of action to those similarly situated unless they have executed a consent or release in writing to the advertiser before use of the photographs. The statute acts to restrict an advertiser's prior unrestrained common law right to use another's photograph until written consent is obtained. Once written consent is obtained, however, the photograph may be published as permitted by its terms. . . .

Concededly, at common law an infant could disaffirm his written consent . . . or, for that matter, a consent executed by another on his or her behalf. . . . Notwithstanding these rules, it is clear that the Legislature may abrogate an infant's common law right to disaffirm . . . or, conversely, it may confer upon infants the right to make binding contracts. . . . Where a statute expressly permits a certain class of agreements to be made by infants, that settles the question and makes the agreement valid and enforceable. That is precisely what happened here. The Legislature, by adopting section 51, created a new cause of action and it provided in the statute itself the method for obtaining an infant's consent to avoid liability. Construing the statute strictly, as we must since it is in derogation of the common law, . . . the parent's consent is binding on the infant and no words prohibiting disaffirmance are necessary to effectuate the legislative intent. Inasmuch as the consents in this case complied with the statutory requirements, they were valid and may not be disaffirmed. . . .

It should be noted that plaintiff did not contend that the photographs were obscene or pornographic. The trial court specifically found that the photographs were not pornographic and it enjoined use of them in pornographic publications. Thus, there is no need to discuss the unenforceability of certain contracts which violate public policy . . . or to equate an infant's common law right to disaffirm with that principle, as the dissent apparently does.

Finally, it is claimed that the application of the statute as we interpret it may result in unanticipated and untoward consequences. If that be so, there is an obvious remedy. A parent who wishes to limit the publicity and exposure of her child need only limit the use authorized in the consent, for a defendant's immunity from a claim for invasion of privacy is no broader than the consent executed to him. . . . The order of the Appellate Division should be modified by striking the further injunction against use of the photographs for uses of advertising and trade, and as so modified, the order should be affirmed.

DISSENT BY: JASEN: Since I believe that the interests of society and this State in protecting its children must be placed above any concern for trade or commercialism, I am compelled to dissent. The State has the right and indeed the obligation to afford extraordinary protection to minors.

At the outset, it should be made clear that this case does not involve the undoing of a written consent given by a mother to invade her infant daughter's privacy so as to affect prior benefits derived by a person relying on the validity of the consent pursuant to sections 50 and 51 of the Civil Rights Law. Rather, what is involved is the right of an infant, now 17 years of age, to disaffirm her mother's consent with respect to future use of a nude photograph taken of her at age 10.

The majority holds, as a matter of law, not only in this case but as to all present and future consents executed by parents on behalf of children pursuant to sections 50 and 51 of the Civil Rights Law, that once a parent consents to the invasion of privacy of a child, the child is forever bound by that consent and may never disaffirm the continued invasion of his or her privacy, even where the continued invasion of the child's privacy may cause the child enormous embarrassment, distress and humiliation.

I find this difficult to accept as a rational rule of law, particularly so when one considers that it has long been the rule in this State that a minor enjoys an almost absolute right to disaffirm a contract entered into either by the minor or by the minor's parent on behalf of the minor . . . and the statute in question does not in any manner abrogate this salutary right.

This right has been upheld despite the fact that the minor held himself out to be an adult . . . or that a parent also attempted to contractually bind the minor. Significantly, whether or not the minor can restore the other contracting party to the position he was in prior to entering the contract is pertinent only to the extent that the minor, by disaffirming the contract, cannot put himself into a better position than he was in before entering the contract. . . . In the past, this court has noted that those who contract with minors do so at their own peril.

Understandably, such a broad right has evolved as a result of the State's policy to provide children with as much protection as possible against being taken advantage of or exploited by adults. The right to rescind is a legal right established for the protection of the infant. . . . This right is founded in the legal concept that an infant is incapable of contracting because he does not understand the scope of his rights and he cannot appreciate the consequences and ramifications of his decisions. Furthermore, it is feared that as an infant he may well be under the complete influence of an adult or may be unable

to act in any manner which would allow him to defend his rights and interests. . . . Allowing a minor the right to disaffirm a contract is merely one way the common law developed to resolve those inequities and afford children the protection they require to compensate for their immaturity.

Can there be any question that the State has a compelling interest in protecting children? . . . Recognizing this compelling interest in children, the State has assumed the role of *parens patriae,* undertaking with that role the responsibility of protecting children from their own inexperience. Acting in that capacity, the State has put the interests of minors above that of adults, organizations or businesses. . . . The broad right given a minor to disaffirm a contract is, of course, an obvious example of the State's attempt to afford an infant protection against exploitation by adults. . . . Thus, I am persuaded that, in this case, 17-year-old Brooke Shields should be afforded the right to disaffirm her mother's consent to use a photograph of her in the nude, taken when she was 10 years old, unless it can be said, as the majority holds, that the Legislature intended to abrogate that right when it enacted sections 50 and 51 of the Civil Rights Law. . . .

Case Questions for Discussion

1. Which opinion, the majority or the dissent, is most convincing?

2. If Brooke Shields had signed the consent herself, would she have been able to disaffirm?

3. Without Sections 50 and 51 of the Civil Rights Act, would the court have allowed Brooke to disaffirm?

4. How aware was Miss Shields of what she was doing when she was 10 years old?

5. Should a parent ever be able to bind a 10-year-old child to any contract?

6. Would it make sense to allow all children affected by the Civil Rights Act waivers, as suggested by Judge Jasen, to disaffirm, upon reaching the age of majority, the future publication of photographs?

Offers

A contract has been described as a "meeting of the minds." The description is a good one. Both parties agree on the terms and agree to bind themselves to each other. When courts get involved in determining if a contract has in fact been formed, however, a meeting of the minds may not be necessary. There are two theories, or approaches, to determining if a contract has been formed. The *subjective* theory looks for an actual "meeting of the minds." Did the parties think they agreed to the same terms? The *objective* theory is dominant today, although subjective elements still arise. Under the objective theory, a meeting of the minds is not always necessary. What the parties thought they assented to and their intent are not relevant. The objective theory focuses on what a party says and does, viewed from the perspective of a reasonable person, such as the other party. In other words, would a reasonable party believe a contract was formed?[11]

The Restatement, Second, defines an *offer* as "a manifestation of willingness to enter into a bargain, so made as to justify another person in understanding that his assent to the bargain is invited and will conclude it."[12] Put more simply, an offer is a communication to the other party that if they accept the stated terms, a contract will be formed. For instance, if you say to your classmate, "If you give me $30, I will give you this book," you have made an offer. Your classmate can form a contract with you by agreeing to give you $30, or by simply giving you $30. If, however, in a moment of frustration, you say, "I will give you this book if you give me $1," you have not made an offer. A reasonable person in your classmate's position would know that the book is worth much more than $1 and that your statement was not made seriously.

An offer can be oral, written, or merely a type of conduct. No magic words are required. To be effective, however, an offer must be received by the *offeree*. Under the objective theory, whether an offer has been made is a question of fact to be determined by examining all the facts and circumstances, including past dealings. In general, the more specifics contained in a statement, the more likely it will be found to be an offer. Courts are reluctant to find an offer without specifics, because it subjects the maker to legal liability. The fact that the statement contains the word "offer" is to be considered, but it is not controlling. Phrases such as "this offer is not binding until approved by the home office," or "this offer is subject to approval by legal counsel," usually indicate that the statement was not an offer. Statements made in advertisements, circulars, and other communications to the general public are usually considered offers to make an offer. Holding these types of communications to the general public to be offers could subject the advertiser to nearly unlimited liability, if the public's response to the advertisement is much higher than anticipated. Advertisements are more likely to be considered offers if they limit the author's liability in some manner, such as "first come, first served," "as long as they last," or "the first ten shoppers."[13]

Accepting Offers

An acceptance is a promise or performance making the offer a contract.[14] It is said that an offer creates a power of acceptance in the *offeree*. Once an offer is accepted, the *offeror* no longer has the power to revoke or change the offer. Whether an offer has been accepted is generally determined under the objective theory.[15] Would a reasonable offeror believe the offer was accepted? This is especially true when the contract in question is *bilateral* (a promise for a promise). Once the offeree makes the requested promise, the contract is formed. If the contract is *unilateral* (promise for performance) under the traditional view, the question is more troublesome. Assume Alicia offers to pay Bill $10 if Bill tears up his textbook. Bill tears up his textbook. Is there a contract? Subjective intent in this type of a situation is important. Perhaps Bill tore up the textbook because he was mad at the professor or because he did badly on the midterm examination. Perhaps Bill would have torn up his textbook without the $10 offer. Under the traditional view, as long as the finder of fact (a jury or a judge) believes the testimony by Bill that his motive included collection of the $10 offered by Alice, even if he had other motives, he will prevail. The traditional method's reliance on subjective intent creates evidentiary problems. In most cases, only the offeree possesses any evidence concerning the offeree's intent. In our example, only Bill knows why he tore up the book, and he has a vested interest in testifying that at least one of his motives was to collect the $10 offered by Alice. The Restatement, Second, § 53(3), expresses the modern view that absent some sign the offeree did not intend to accept, acceptance is presumed.[16] Back to our example, as long as there is no evidence indicating that Bill was not tearing up his book to collect the $10, he will prevail against Alice.

As a general rule, only the party to whom the offer was made may accept. Lacking a provision in the offer, it is not transferable. The rule applies even when the offeree has sold the business to which the offer relates, has died, or has lost the capacity to contract. If one who is not the offeree attempts to accept the offer, it will usually be considered a new offer to the original offeror.[17] Assume Ashraf offers to sell his textbook to Belinda, if Belinda promises to pay him $40 at the end of the semester. Carlos, who overheard the offer, tells Ashraf, "I promise to pay

you $40 for your textbook at the end of the semester." Is there a con-
tract between Ashraf and Carlos? The answer is no. Carlos cannot accept Ashraf's offer, because it was directed to Belinda. Belinda is the
offeree, not Carlos. Carlos's promise to pay $40 to Ashraf at the end of
the semester for the textbook is an offer to Ashraf. Ashraf can accept
Carlos's offer, but unless he has two textbooks, or he revokes his offer to
Belinda, Ashraf will still be bound to sell the textbook at the end of the
semester to Belinda, if she accepts the original offer.

The offeror is commonly referred to as the "master of the offer."
This means the offeror sets the terms for acceptance. If the offer asks
for performance as the means of acceptance, an offeree generally may
not accept by offering a promise to perform.[18] If the Sheriff offers
$1,000 to the first person who provides evidence leading to the convic-
tion of the person responsible for vandalizing his patrol car, the local
private detective may not accept the offer by promising to provide the
evidence. The Sheriff's offer may be accepted only by providing the
evidence (performing).

When an offer invites acceptance by a promise (to form a bilateral
contract), there are three general requirements for valid acceptances.
First, the offeree must unambiguously commit to the offer. Assume
Imelda offers to sell Darva *all* of her size 10 shoes, if Darva promises to
pay her $10 per pair. Darva replies that she promises to pay Imelda $10
per pair, for up to *50 pairs* of size 10 shoes. Darva has not accepted
Imelda's offer, because Imelda offered to sell *all* of her size 10 shoes.
Darva's purported acceptance is in reality a counter offer. Her acceptance was not in accord with the original offer. Second, the acceptance
must not be conditioned upon some further act or decision of either
party. If Darva replies to Imelda that she promises to pay her $10 for all
of her size 10 shoes, *as long as they fit*, it is not an acceptance of Imelda's
offer. The offer was for *all* of the size 10 shoes. When Darva replied that
she would take all the size 10 shoes that fit, her purported acceptance
was conditional upon Darva's decision that the shoes fit. Third, the
offer must be accepted on its exact terms. If Imelda's original offer indicated that the shoes would be available for pickup at her house in Hawaii, Darva could not accept by agreeing to promise to pay $10 per pair
for all the size 10 shoes if they were shipped to Darva's home in California, at Darva's expense. Because Darva would not be accepting the original offer on its exact terms, she would be making Imelda a counter
offer. Imelda may accept or decline.[19]

The offeror, as the "master of the offer," also has the ability to specify the means of acceptance. If the offer asks for a signed reply in writing, only a signed writing will be a binding acceptance. If no specifica-
tion of the manner of acceptance is indicated, however, any reasonable
form of acceptance is satisfactory.[20]

Consideration

Each party to a contract must give *consideration* for the other party's promise or performance. As we have discussed in the introduction to this chapter, a promise given for no consideration is usually not enforceable. Two types of promises not supported by consideration are donative promises and gratuitous promises. A *donative* promise is a promise to give someone a gift. Assume your university's foundation contacts you and asks for a donation. You promise to send them $100 after you graduate. If you fail to do so, they may send you reminders of your pledge, but they may not successfully sue you for breach of promise. Because no consideration was given by the foundation in exchange for your promise, there was no enforceable contract. A *gratuitous promise* is also made without consideration. However, a gratuitous promise is for something other than a gift. Assume Zeb enters into a contract with Jake, the local grain elevator owner, to sell Jake 20,000 bushels of Zeb's corn crop for $3.00 per bushel. The crop is to be harvested in the next week. Before the crop can be harvested, a disastrous storm hits the Corn Belt, destroying 50 percent of all the corn in several states and Zeb's entire corn crop. The market price for corn goes to $4.50 per bushel. Because Zeb lost his crop, Jake realizes that Zeb will need to buy 20,000 bushels of corn on the open market at $4.50 per bushel to fulfill his promise to sell Jake 20,000 bushels of corn at $3.00 per bushel. Jake feels sorry for Zeb and does not want him to lose $1.50 per bushel on their contract. Jake contacts Zeb and agrees to pay $4.50 per bushel for the grain Zeb must sell him. Jake's promise to pay $4.50 per bushel for the corn is a gratuitous promise. It is not a gift, but it is unsupported by consideration. It is probably not enforceable.[21]

Three elements are necessary for a promise to be supported by consideration. All three elements must be present. First, the one to whom the promise is made must suffer some *legal detriment*. To suffer some legal detriment means to do something, or promise to do something one is not legally bound to do, or refrain from doing something one may legally do.[22] Assume you promise to pay someone money. Your promise is to your legal detriment, because you are under no obligation to pay anyone money. Now, assume you promise your father you will not to go to Florida over spring break. This promise of yours is to your detriment, because you have a legal right to travel to Florida. Second, the detriment suffered by the promisee must induce the promise.[23] In other words, agreeing to suffer the legal detriment induced the other party to make a promise to do something or to not do something. In our example about not going to Florida over spring break, your agreement to not go induced the other party (your father) to promise you something in return, perhaps to pay you $200. Without the legal detriment, the promise would not have been made. And finally, the promise must induce the legal detriment.[24] In our example, you must have been induced not to go to Florida by what your father promised you. Your father promised to pay you $200 if you do not go to Florida over spring break. Your father's promise must be the reason you agreed not to go to Florida. (For these purposes, we will ignore any problems one may encounter enforcing contracts between parents and children.) The analysis must work from both parties' perspective. Consideration must be present on both sides. Generally, the courts will not consider the adequacy of the consideration, except as evidence of overbearing, fraud, or duress.[25]

The consideration must be bargained for on both sides. Past consideration will not support an agreement made in the present.[26] Let us return to our Florida and spring break example. Assume you decided on your own to forgo spring break in Florida. Instead, you decided to stay on campus to study. Your father, upon hearing of your decision to study over spring break, declares he is so proud of your maturity that he is going to pay you $200. There is no contract. Your grades, or your work ethic, induced you not to go to Florida. Your father's promise to pay you $200 was not induced by your promise to stay on campus. His motive was to reward you, not to induce you. His promise was gratuitous.

Determining whether agreements are supported by consideration on both sides, making them enforceable contracts, is an extensive area of contract law, including doctrines such as promissory estoppel, stipulations, illusory promises, and alternative and conjunctive promises. Further discussion is beyond the scope of this chapter. What is important to understand is that both parties must do or promise to do something they were not obligated to do, or refrain from doing something they were entitled to do. And both parties must promise or do so, at least in part, because of the other party's promise or act. As you read the following case, attempt to find consideration on both sides of the agreement.

Whitten v. Greeley-Shaw
Supreme Judicial Court of Maine
520 A.2d 1307 (1987)

OPINION BY: NICHOLS:
On appeal the Defendant, Shirley C. Greeley-Shaw, contends that the Superior Court (Cumberland County) committed error when it entered judgment . . .when the court refused to recognize a certain writing entered into by the parties as a valid contract, that writing being the

basis of the Defendant's counterclaim. We reject . . . Defendant's claim of error and deny the appeal. . . .

Emerging as a counterclaim to the Plaintiff's foreclosure action [*Author's note: In an omitted portion of the opinion, the Defendant contended the mortgage was a gift.*] is the Defendant's request that the court enforce the terms of a written "agreement" entered into by the parties. The parties had engaged in an intermittent extra-marital affair from 1972 until March 1980. At the time of this writing the Plaintiff, a Massachusetts contractor, had traveled to his Bermuda home to vacation with friends, and expected to soon be joined there by his wife. . . .

The precise facts surrounding the creation of the agreement are in dispute. However, it is the testimony of the Defendant that she wanted to have "something in writing" because of all the past promises to her that she said the Plaintiff had broken. She testified that the Plaintiff told her, "You figure out what you want and I will sign it." She added that she unilaterally drew up the "agreement" while in Bermuda, and the Plaintiff signed it without objection. There was an original and a copy, and only he signed the original.

On his part the Plaintiff testified that he had agreed to visit with the Defendant, who had come to his Bermuda home uninvited, because "She demanded I see her or she would come up and raise hell with my friends" and embarrass him in front of his wife.

Basically, the "agreement" is a one-page typewritten document, prepared by the Defendant, that begins "I, George D. Whitten . . . agree to the following conditions made by Mrs. Shirley C. Shaw . . ." and then goes on to list four "conditions" required of the Plaintiff. The "conditions" require the Plaintiff to make payments to the Defendant of $500.00 per month for an indeterminate period, make any major repairs to the Harpswell home, pay for any medical needs, take one trip with the Defendant and supply her with one piece of jewelry per

year, and visit and phone the Defendant at various stated intervals. The only "condition" that approaches the recital of a promise or duty of the Defendant is the statement "Under no circumstances will there be any calls made to my homes or offices without prior permission from me."

The Plaintiff contends that, inter alia, this writing is unenforceable because of a lack of consideration. The Defendant argues that the writing is enforceable because there is the necessary objective manifestation of assent on each side, supported by the "stated" consideration of the Defendant not to call the Plaintiff without his prior permission, that, she asserts, constituted her "promise."

The Superior Court found that no legally enforceable contract had been created. We agree. Every contract requires "consideration" to support it, and any promise not supported by consideration is unenforceable. . . . The Defendant asks this Court to recognize the "agreement" as an enforceable bilateral contract, where the necessary consideration is the parties' promise of performance. . . . Generally, the Defendant's promise to forbear from engaging in an activity that she had the legal right to engage in, can provide her necessary consideration for the Plaintiff's return promises. . . . However, the Plaintiff's allegation of lack of consideration draws attention to the bargaining process; although the Defendant's promise to forbear could constitute consideration, it cannot if it was not sought after by the Plaintiff, and motivated by his request that the Defendant not disturb him. . . . Of this there was no evidence whatsoever. This clause, the only one that operates in the Plaintiff's favor, was only included in the contract by the Defendant, because, she asserts, she felt the Plaintiff should get something in exchange for his promises. Clearly, this clause was not "bargained for" by the Plaintiff, and not given in ex- change for his promises, and as such cannot constitute the consideration necessary to support a contract. . . . Judgment affirmed.

Case Questions for Discussion

1. Why did Plaintiff agree to sign the agreement? Do you think he bargained for anything? What? Her silence? Her leaving Bermuda and not "raising hell" with his friends or embarrassing him in front of his wife?

2. Had she agreed to keep silent about their affair in the agreement, do you think the court would have found that the agreement was enforceable?

3. Do you think the agreement, as written, should have been enforceable?

4. Can you think of any policy reasons not to enforce the agreement, even if the court had found consideration on both sides?

Oral and Written Contracts, and the Statute of Frauds

People enter into and perform oral contracts all the time. Assume a millionaire says to Darva, "I promise to pay you $1,000,000, if you promise to marry me." Darva replies that she accepts the offer and promises to marry the millionaire if he pays her $1,000,000. The millionaire pays Darva $1,000,000. If Darva marries the millionaire, both promises were performed, and the oral contract has not posed a problem. If, however, either of the two parties does not perform, the fact that there was no written contract could prove to be troublesome. The parties may not have the same recollection of the terms of the agreement. An even more troubling prospect is the possibility that one or both parties may lie about the terms or even deny the existence of the agreement.

In the late seventeenth century, the English adopted the original *Statute of Frauds* to prevent perjury and other frauds that were common in the English courts. The Statute of Frauds required that certain types of contracts be in writing to be enforceable.

A contract for the sale of an interest in land must be in writing under the Statute of Frauds.

The Statute of Frauds provisions have been adopted in most American jurisdictions. Oddly, the trend in the United States has been to extend writing requirements, usually in the name of consumer protection, while in England and internationally, the trend has been to abandon writing requirements.[27]

Written contracts offer advantages over oral contracts. A writing provides the best evidence of what was agreed to, and the parties are able to refer to the writing when their memory fades. Further, parties are usually more cautious about what they agree to in writing.

The typical Statute of Frauds in most jurisdictions requires writings for the enforcement of the following types of contracts:

1. A contract of an executor or administrator to answer for a duty of his decedent (the executor administrator provision);

2. A contract to answer for the duty of another (the suretyship provision);

3. A contract made upon consideration of marriage (the marriage provision);

4. A contract for the sale of an interest in land (the land contract provision); and

5. A contract that is not to be performed within one year from the making thereof (the one-year provision).[28]

Provisions in the Uniform Commercial Code require writings for the following types of transactions:

1. A contract for the sale of goods for the price of $500 or more (UCC § 2-201) and

2. A contract for the sale of personal property not otherwise covered, for amounts in excess of $5,000 (UCC § 1-206).

Many states also require writings for the enforcement of agreements to pay commissions to real estate brokers, for promises to make a testamentary disposition, for promises to pay debts discharged in bankruptcy, and for promises to pay a debt contracted for while an infant.[29]

The Land Contract and One-Year Provisions

Because application of the Statute of Frauds may lead to injustice in some situations, many courts have narrowly construed the statute's provisions.[30] At times, fact patterns that intuitively seem within the statute have been not held subject to the writing requirement. In this section, we provide a closer look at two of the original Statute of Frauds provisions as they are presently applied.

The *land contract provision* applies to promises to transfer or buy any interest in land. Once the promise to transfer the interest has been performed, a promise to pay the price, even if originally within the statute, does not require a writing. As a result, an oral promise to pay the price is enforceable. Assume Alice orally agrees to sell Blackacre to Bob for $10,000. At this point, neither party may enforce the oral contract, because the agreement is not in writing. If Alice prepares and delivers a deed to Blackacre as promised, and Bob refuses to pay, Alice may now enforce the oral contract. The promise to pay is now considered outside the statute's scope. Although leases are interests in land, most states exempt one-year leases of property from the statute. Leases longer than one year must be in writing to be enforceable.[31]

Under the *one-year provision,* if any promise within the contract *cannot* be fully performed within a year from when the contract was made, all promises within the contract are within the statute until one party completes performance. The provision has been narrowly construed. The key is to determine if there is any way the promise may be fully performed within a year.[32] For example, if Michael Jordan agreed to a lifetime contract with the Chicago Bulls for $10,000,000 per year when he came out of college, the contract would not be within the Statute of Frauds. Although Jordan may live until he is 90 years old, and the contract may cover nearly 70 years, he could also die within a year of the contract date, and his performance would be complete within a year. If there is any possibility that a promise can be performed within a year of the contract date, however slight that possibility might be, the contract is not within the statute. Hindsight does not apply. Likewise, the fact that Michael Jordan is still alive does not move the lifetime contract within the statute.

Assume that Farmer, who grows sweet corn on 100 acres in Iowa, agrees to sell the next five crops of sweet corn which he grows on his Iowa acreage to the Del Monte Corporation. The agreement is within the Statute of Frauds. It is *impossible* for Farmer to grow and harvest five crops of sweet corn in Iowa within a year.

Although the one-year time period begins with the date of the contract, a *subsequent restatement of the terms* restarts the clock. Assume Jill College finds work as a lifeguard during her X0 summer break. After working all summer, on August 15 of X0, as Jill is preparing to return to school, her employer says, "Next summer, if you agree to work until Labor Day, I promise to pay you a bonus of $1,500." Jill orally accepts and agrees to work until Labor Day during the summer of X1 in exchange for a bonus of $1,500. The contract is within the statute. It is impossible for Jill to work until Labor Day of X1, within one year of August 15, X0 (a period of slightly less than 13 months). When Jill reports for work the following summer on June 1, X1, she says to her employer, "As I remember, if I promise to work until Labor Day this summer, you promise to pay me a bonus of $1,500." Her employer replies, "That is right." Jill must have taken this college law course, for now the contract is outside the statute. Upon the subsequent restatement of the terms, on June 1, X1, the clock restarted. Jill may complete performance within one year (a little over three months). She may now enforce the contract against her employer, although there is no writing.[33]

Acceptable Writings and Effect of Statute of Frauds Violations

To be certain what constitutes an acceptable writing, the applicable state statute should be examined. In general, an acceptable writing is one that allows identification of the parties, the subject matter of the agreement, the essential terms and conditions of all the promises comprising the agreement, and to whom and by whom the promises are made. The standard to be used is with *reasonable certainty*. Outside evidence may be used in the identification process. Parties do not need to be specifically named in the writing, if the parties can be identified with reasonable certainty from the writing or with the aid of outside evidence.[34] Generally, the party to be charged (the one being sued to enforce the contract) must have signed or authenticated the writing. *Authentication* means an indication that the party agrees with and accepts the writing. Electronic records are beginning to gain acceptance as writings, and electronic affirmations are beginning to be accepted as signatures.[35]

If it is determined that an oral contract is one that must be in writing under the Statute of Frauds, the contract is unenforceable. At times this can create an unjust result. A defendant in a contract action usually raises the Statute of Frauds as an affirmative defense. To avoid injustice, courts have employed various means to put parties back into the position they were before the oral contract, such as restitution of conferred benefits and the employment of promissory estoppel. In rare cases, in which other methods are not available and one party reasonably relied on the other's promise to his or her detriment, courts may actually enforce the oral contract to the extent necessary to avoid injustice.[36]

Contract Interpretation

In a narrow sense, contract *interpretation* is the process courts use to determine the meaning given by the parties to contractual terms. Contract *construction*, on the other hand, is the process used to determine the legal effect of those terms. The distinction between the two processes can be summed up as follows. When courts engage in interpretation, they are trying to determine what the parties promised. When engaged in construction, courts are trying to determine what the law requires of the parties as a result of their promises. Interpretation looks at the terms, whereas construction looks at the contract as a whole. The distinction between the two processes is technical and, in a sense, academic. Courts often ignore it. A court that engages in construction might describe its action as interpretation, and vice versa.[37] We will follow the courts in the subsequent discussion and use the term interpretation to include both processes.

The Problem of Language and the Plain-Meaning Rule

When parties to a contract dispute what the rights and duties are under the contract, courts are often called upon to settle the dispute. Often the contract in question contains vague or conflicting terms, or it was drafted in a haphazard manner. Even the carefully crafted contract is likely to contain vague words, due to the nature of language. For instance, if you promise to sell your professor 15 blue ink pens for $1 each, and your professor promises to pay, you and your professor have a simple contract that seems very clear. Even this simple contract, however, has vague terms. What if you deliver ballpoint pens and your professor responds that she wanted felt tips? Who is right, and who is wrong? What about the word *blue*? Does it mean light blue, dark blue, or royal blue? If you thought your promise was to supply 15 royal blue ballpoint pens, and your professor thought she was promising to pay for 15 dark blue felt-tip pens, was there ever a meeting of the minds? Did you in fact form a contract? This is the type of messy situation courts are usually required to untangle—making sense of ambiguous contractual terms.

Although most contracts are entered into and performed with no need for judicial involvement, those with disputes about what was promised, and whether the promises are being kept, can be a burden on the courts. Over the years, rules have evolved to limit the amount of evidence, called *extrinsic* or outside evidence, that may be introduced to show what the parties intended a term or provision to mean. One such rule is the *plain-meaning rule*, first discussed in Chapter 4 of this text as it applies to statutory interpretation. Here we analyze the plain-meaning rule as it applies to contractual interpretation. First, we discuss how these rules of limitation on extrinsic evidence in contract interpretation cases are applied. Often, it depends on whether the objective or subjective theory of contracts, as discussed above in the sections on contract formation, is being employed.[38]

Under the objective theory, a standard of reasonableness is applied to determine the meaning to be given a term, or word. The subjectivists, on the other hand, seek the meaning given to the term, or word, by both parties. The subjective theory almost always requires more extensive testimony and other extrinsic evidence, because its goal is to determine what the parties thought when the contract was formed. The objective theory requires little more than determining what a reasonable person would have thought, given the facts and circumstances. Neither theory works well in all cases. The objective approach may produce a meaning that neither party agreed to, but the subjective approach may find that no contract exists. As a result, courts usually follow a mixed approach. If one party knows the other has attached a different meaning to a term, the party with the knowledge will usually be held to the meaning attached by the other.[39]

In our example about the ink pens, if your professor knew you regularly sold only royal blue ballpoint ink pens, and you told her you would have to check on how many pens you had left before you agreed, she would know you were promising to sell her 15 royal blue ballpoint pens, and she should be held to that meaning. A similar result is reached when neither party had actual knowledge of the meaning attached to the term by the other party, but one of the parties had reason to know the other was attaching a different meaning to the term. For example, had your professor held up a dark blue felt-tip pen when she agreed to buy 15 ink pens, you should have known she was agreeing to buy fifteen dark blue felt-tip pens, instead of 15 royal blue ballpoint pens. The professor should prevail. In both of these examples, the objective theory is being employed. If neither party knew, or had reason to know, the other was attaching a materially different meaning to a term, the subjective theory should prevail, and a court should return a finding that no contract was formed.

Let us return to our example. Assume the professor has arthritis and is unable to use ballpoint pens. She assumed you knew of her problem, since she has trouble grasping small items and always uses felt-tip pens in class. You, however, had never really noticed the professor's arthritis or that she always used felt-tip pens. You, on the other hand, assumed that the professor had, in the past, seen you selling ballpoint pens to other students before and after class. As a result, you thought she was promising to buy the ballpoint pens. In fact, the professor had not noticed you conducting business with your fellow students. Given these facts, a court should find that no contract existed. There was no mutual assent. Neither party knew, or should have known, that the other party was attaching a different meaning to the term "ink pens." The subjective theory should prevail.[40]

When interpreting a contract, if the language is vague or capable of different meanings, courts are free to examine any type of evidence.[41] If it is alleged the language is not vague, however, the plain-meaning rule may limit the amount of extrinsic evidence, especially evidence of prior negotiations which may be helpful in explaining what the parties meant by the term or words in question. Although the rule has many critics, it survives today in most jurisdictions.

Typically, the rule is applied in two stages. First, the court must determine whether the terms or words in question are clear or vague. Courts generally determine whether the terms are clear or vague, in light of all the surrounding circumstances or in the context in which the contract was formed. For instance, assume the term in question is *gas*. The buyer contends that she meant natural gas, and the seller contends he meant gasoline. Evidence that the buyer is a natural gas distributor and does not sell gasoline should be admissible. Evidence of prior negotiations has been more problematic. Under the old restrictive view, evidence of prior negotiations was not allowed. Today, a more liberal view that recognizes the inherent vagueness of language has taken hold. Moreover, evidence of prior negotiations is allowed in most jurisdictions for the sole purpose of determining whether the contractual language is vague. No evidence of additional or contradictory terms may be offered at this stage. If the court determines the terms are clear, then no other evidence is admissible, and the clear or plain meaning of the terms is applied. If the terms are ambiguous, then all evidence, including prior negotiations, may be introduced and considered to determine what meaning should be given to the contractual terms in question.[42]

Rules of Interpretation

Courts often make use of rules that aid them when interpreting vague or conflicting contractual terms. Commentators argue that because there are so many rules, courts may choose the rule they wish to apply to support a decision the court has already made. Although this may be true, some of the rules make sense and are usually applied, unless there is compelling extrinsic evidence to the contrary. For instance, if the contract includes a list of items to be sold, transferred, or somehow included within the terms of the contract, and if there is no additional general inclusion term, courts will usually conclude that only those items listed are covered under the contract. The rule goes by the Latin term *expressio unius est exclusio alterius* (the inclusion of one thing is the exclusion of another).[43] Assume you promise to sell your materials from this class, including the textbook, class notes, and outline to an underclassman. The rule should exclude from the sale any copies of old tests you have in your possession.

A related rule, *ejusdem generis* (of the same kind) includes items of the same type as those listed but excludes items unlike those listed. Let us return to our example. Assume you promise to sell all materials needed for this class, including textbook, class notes, outline, and other materials relevant to this course to an underclassman. Under ejusdem generis, the old tests probably would be included, because they are relevant to this course. The bar examination materials given to you by your older sibling, however, would probably not be included, because they are not relevant to this "particular" course. To some degree, they would be relevant to all law courses but not to this course in particular. The old tests, on the other hand, would be especially relevant to this particular course, like the textbook, class notes, and outline.[44]

Other rules relate more to how language is used. For example, a rule called *the specific controls the general* is used by courts to make sense of conflicting terms: it dictates that a term that is more specific will usually take precedence over (or be treated as an exception to) a more general term. Another rule, based on how people generally use the language, states that *if a word is used repeatedly in a contract, it is assumed it has the same meaning throughout*. Absent compelling evidence to the contrary, the rule makes sense. Another example is the assumption that *the parties intended every part of the agreement to mean something*. Again, let us return to our example about the class materials. You promise to sell all materials needed for this class, including textbook, class notes, outline, and other materials relevant to this course to an underclassman. An additional term in the contract states that the seller has bar examination materials in his possession. A court should conclude that the bar examination materials are included in the transaction. To decide otherwise would render the term unnecessary.[45]

Other rules are based to a greater extent on principles of fairness, or the public interest. *Interpretation contra proferentem* (against the profferer) may be applied when a term could be interpreted to the benefit of one party at the expense of the other party, or vice versa. Under the rule, the meaning that disfavors the author of the term should be given to the term in question. The rule is most often applied when the contract is a form contract that was supplied by a party experienced in the type of transaction covered by the contract, and especially in the case of adhesion contracts.[46] Obviously, this is only an illustrative discussion of rules of interpretation. There are many more rules of interpretation.

The Parol Evidence Rule

Although not formally a rule of interpretation, the *parol evidence rule* can exclude evidence of additional terms not embodied in the written contract. The origins of the rule are similar to the Statute of Frauds—the rule is intended to protect the sanctity of written contracts against perjury or bad memories. The rule also has roots in the rationale that subsequent final agreements take precedence over earlier tentative agreements. Although the term parol evidence means oral evidence or testimony, the rule operates to exclude all extrinsic evidence.[47]

The following example illustrates how the rule comes into play. You sign a contract agreeing to buy a neighbor's automobile for $5,000. She delivers the car, and you pay as promised. Two weeks later, the transmission goes out, and the mechanic tells you it will cost $2,000 to repair. You sue your neighbor on the contract and allege she promised to pay 75 percent of all repairs required within 30 days of the transaction. Your neighbor objects to any evidence of any promise of warranty, under the parol evidence rule. She argues that if she had promised to warrant the auto for 30 days, it would have been in the written contract. Under the rationale behind the parol evidence rule, although the two of you may have discussed a warranty, the final agreement must not have included a warranty, because there was no warranty in the written contract.

When the parol evidence rule is at issue, the first question is whether there is an *integrated agreement*. An integration is a final expression of the agreement. If the writing is found to be a total integration, no extrinsic evidence of additional or conflicting terms is allowed. If the writing is found to be a *partial integration*, extrinsic evidence of additional terms is admissible, but no extrinsic evidence concerning conflicting terms is admissible. The rule is controversial, and there are several methods of applying it. The strictest method is the *four corners rule*. Under the four corners rule, the court looks only to the written document to determine if it appears complete on its face. If it does, the contract is considered totally integrated. Because the four corners rule often produces unjust results, the *collateral contract concept* evolved to allow evidence of an additional contract, if the additional contract was supported by separate consideration. Two views of the collateral contract concept developed. The liberal approach allows evidence of a separate oral contract about any matter not addressed in the written contract, as long as it is not contradictory to the written contract (in effect, there are no complete integrations). The narrower approach allows evidence of separate oral agreements, but only if the separate oral contract addresses matters that are distinct from the written agreement.[48]

Two eminent commentators, Professors Williston and Corbin, formulated rules to provide clear guidance for courts faced with parol evidence issues. Under Williston's approach, if the writing contains a *merger clause* (a statement in the contract that the writing is the complete agreement between the parties) it is a total integration, and no extrinsic evidence of additional or contradictory terms is allowed. With no merger clause, the determination of whether the writing is integrated is made on its face. Evidence of additional consistent terms is allowed, if the writing appears incomplete on its face. If the writing appears complete, it is considered a total integration, and no evidence of additional or inconsistent terms is allowed. An exception is made if the additional terms are of the type that parties would usually choose to address in a separate agreement—a reasonableness test, or an objective approach. In effect, if the exception applies, the writing is only a partial integration. The exception has proven difficult to apply. Corbin's approach rejects Williston's reasonableness test, and it allows the consideration of all evidence to determine whether the parties intended to merge all prior agreements into the written agreement—a subjective approach. Williston's approach is the majority view, but the Restatement, Second, has adopted a modified version of Corbin's approach.[49]

To illustrate the difference between Williston's and Corbin's approaches to this issue, let us return to our example about buying your neighbor's car for $5,000. Assume that when negotiating the purchase of the car with your neighbor, you asked for a 75 percent of all repair costs warranty for 30 days. She agreed to furnish the warranty but asked to keep it out of the sales contract. She explained that her husband wanted her to sell the car as is. She said the warranty would be "just between you and me," and it would be best for her if it remained an oral agreement. You agreed. As a result, the written contract was silent as to warranties, or the condition of the car. Under Williston's approach, the additional term (the warranty) is not a type of term parties would usually address in a separate agreement, and no evidence of the warranty would be admitted. Corbin, however, would allow testimony showing why you and your neighbor decided to keep the warranty term out of the written contract. A court using Corbin's approach would probably hold that the warranty was a consistent additional term.

The following case is an illustration of how careless wording can come back to haunt parties to contracts, under the rules of interpretation discussed above.

Grove v. Charbonneau Buick-Pontiac, Inc.
Supreme Court of North Dakota
240 N.W.2d 853 (1976)

OPINION BY: SAND: This is an appeal from the decision of the Stark County District Court awarding to Lloyd B. Grove damages equivalent to the value of the automobile which was offered by Charbonneau Buick-Pontiac, Inc. as a prize in a golf contest.

The Dickinson Elks Club conducted its annual Labor Day Golf Tournament on September 1 and 2, 1974. Posters were placed at various locations in the area announcing the tournament and the prizes to be awarded to the flight winners and runners-up. Included in the posters was an offer by Charbonneau of a 1974 automobile "to the first entry who shoots a hole-in-one on Hole No. 8." This offer was also placed on a sign on the automobile at the tournament. Grove testified that he learned of the tournament from a poster placed at the Williston golf course. He then registered for the tournament and paid his entry fee.

The Dickinson golf course at which the tournament was played has only 9 holes, but there are 18 separately located and marked tee areas so that by going around the 9-hole course twice the course can be played as an 18-hole golf course. The first nine tees are marked with blue markers and tee numbers. The second nine tees are marked with red markers and tee numbers. Because of this layout of the course, the tee area marked "8" and the tee area marked "17" are both played to the eighth hole. The tee area marked "17" lies to one side of tee area "8" and is approximately 60 yards farther from the hole.

Grove scored his hole-in-one in hole No. 8 on the first day of the tournament while playing from the 17th tee in an 18-hole match. He had played from the 8th tee previously on the same match and had scored a 3 on the hole.

Grove claimed he had satisfied the requirements of the offer and was entitled to the prize. Charbonneau refused to award the prize, claiming that Grove had not scored his hole-in-one on the 8th hole, as required, but had scored it on the 17th hole.

The trial court found that Grove had performed all of the conditions set out in the offer by Charbonneau so that there was a completed contract which Charbonneau had unlawfully breached by failing to donate the car. The court awarded damages to Grove of $5,800.00, plus interest.

Charbonneau claims the evidence was insufficient to support the trial court's finding that Grove had properly accepted and performed in accordance with the offer made by Charbonneau so as to impose a contractual duty upon Charbonneau to deliver the automobile or in the alternative be liable for damages. He also claims the trial court applied the wrong rule of law and that the findings of fact are clearly erroneous. . . .

The offer under consideration was as follows: "As an added addition to this year's Labor Day Tournament, Charbonneau Buick-Pontiac will donate a 1974 Pontiac Catalina 4-door sedan with factory air to the first entry who shoots a hole-in-one on Hole No. 8. . . ." The problem arises from the fact that the golf course used for the tournament was a 9-hole course upon which 18 holes were played by going around the course twice. If the course would have been an 18-hole course we do not believe a question would have

arisen because each hole would have had its own designation from 1 through 18, but because a 9-hole course was converted to an 18-hole course each hole had an actual number and a hypothetical number.

Under this setting we are required to construe and interpret the language of the offer. The North Dakota Legislature has enacted statutes designed to help in the interpretation of contracts and obligations.

Section 9-07-09, NDCC, states: "The words of a contract are to be understood in their ordinary and popular sense rather than according to their strict legal meaning, unless used by the parties in a technical sense, or unless a special meaning is given to them by usage, in which case the latter must be followed."

The record before us does not disclose that any of the phrases or words used in the offer have a special meaning because of usage. If there is a special meaning to be ascribed to a phrase or word, it has not been brought to our attention.

If the language in the offer has a special meaning to the ordinary golfer, the record does not disclose this. The record before us contains no evidence in this respect. . . . Section 9-07-10, NDCC, states: "Technical words are to be interpreted as usually understood by persons in the profession or business to which they relate, unless clearly used in a different sense."

None of the words used in the offer stand out as being technical words. The argument was made by Charbonneau that the offer provided for a hole-in-one on hole No. 8, not in hole No. 8. However, this in itself is not controlling.

This court stated in Overboe v. Overboe, 160 N.W.2d 650 (N.D.

1968), that when a word is used in an agreement between two parties, and the courts are called upon to interpret the agreement, such word is to be given its ordinary, popular meaning. The words are given the common prevailing meaning as generally understood among people.

Grove contends that the words of the offer, when used in their ordinary sense, mean that any time in the process of an official play in the tournament a ball is hit into the eighth hole in one stroke, from either tee No. 8 or tee No. 17, the conditions of the offer are satisfied. Charbonneau, however, contends that the language of the offer has a technical meaning under the rules of golf and that there cannot be a hole-in-one on hole No. 8 unless the ball, with a single stroke, is hit from tee area No. 8 and lands in hole No. 8. Charbonneau also contends that the offer implies that The Rules of Golf apply and that an announcement was made to that effect to the players (golfers) before play began.

We have examined the rules, but have not found any, nor has any rule been called to our attention, which applies or covers the dispute under consideration. . . . The principal or sole dispute, in reality, between Grove and Charbonneau relates to the interpretation or construction of the words and phrases used in the offer. There is no significant dispute as to what happened on the golf course.

If the language of a contract leaves an uncertainty as to its meaning, the Legislature has provided for another test to be applied by the court in Section 9-07-19, NDCC, which states: "In cases of uncertainty not removed by the preceding rules, the language of a contract should be interpreted most strongly against the party who caused the uncertainty to exist. The promisor is presumed to be such party, except in a contract between a public officer or body, as such, and a private party, and in such case it is presumed that all uncertainty was caused by the private party.". . .

Where a contract contains ambiguous terms which are in dispute it is the duty of the court to construe them. . . . The ambiguous terms of a contract will be interpreted most strongly against the party who caused the ambiguity. . . . We believe the rule on ambiguous contracts applies to this case, and therefore any language of this contract which is not clear and definite or in which an uncertainty exists as to its meaning must be interpreted most strongly against Charbonneau. . . .

The crucial or pivotal point in this case rests upon the meaning of the language "a hole-in-one on Hole No. 8," where the 9-hole golf course was converted to or used as an 18-hole course without adding any additional holes. Does this language, "on Hole No. 8," refer to the actual, physical designation of the hole, which is generally identified with the number on the flagstick, or does it refer to the hypothetical number given to the hole because of the sequence in which it is played? If it is the latter, the 8th hole could also become the 17th hole in the second round of an 18-hole game of golf where the course is played around twice to make an 18-hole course out of a 9-hole course. The term could also mean the 8th hole in sequence of play regardless of the actual physical identification of the hole; as an example, if a player were to start his game with or on hole No. 2 (actually so marked) the

8th hole in sequence would be the 9th hole (actually so marked). The 8th hole under this concept would change depending upon the actual numerical designation of the hole from which the player started.

Charbonneau claims that the hole-in-one was actually accomplished on hole No. 17 because the course was a 9-hole golf course which was converted into an 18-hole course by going around the course twice. However, Charbonneau's own testimony in this respect is not in support of his contention but rather tends to suggest a basis for the ambiguity.

Q. [Anseth] In reality there is no such thing as hole number 17 at the Dickinson Golf Course.

A. [Charbonneau] There is. Oh, I am sorry, no.

Q. [Anseth] Is there, in reality, a hole on green—what is called a green number 8 that says hole number 17 on it?

A. [Charbonneau] No; there isn't.

Q. What would the marker of the hole say on green 8?

A. On green 8?

Q. Yes.

A. It would remain as the flag would say, yes.

Q. Hole number 8?

A. There is only one flag, and that's 8.

Q. It would be 8 on the flag?

A. Right.

In this instance, Grove and his group of players started with (from) tee No. 4 or hole No. 4. "On Hole No. 8" would then correspond to either hole No.11 or No. 2, depending upon the particular sequence in which the holes were played, if the term "on Hole No. 8" refers to and means the hole played in sequence, as

distinguished from the actual numerical designation of the hole.

Grove, on the other hand, argues that "hole-in-one on Hole No. 8" simply means a hole-in-one on the actual numerical designated hole No. 8 from any legitimate tee, in this instance from either No. 8 or No. 17, each having hole No. 8 as the final destination for the ball.

In an effort to learn more about the term "on hole No." or if it has a meaning peculiar to golfers, we resorted to an article by John P. May, entitled "Hole-in-One Roundup" found in Golf Digest for March, 1976. . . . [T]he following interesting description of consecutive holes-in-one (apparently on a 9-hole course converted and used as an 18-hole course) was found: ". . . finished an 18-hole round on the nine-hole . . . Golf Club course in Frampton, Quebec, Aug. 24 by holing tee shots on the 220-yard eighth and the 155-yard ninth (the 17th and 18th holes of the day for him)."

We presume this article used golfer's language, but whether it did or not is not significant. However, we note specifically that in describing where the consecutive holes-in-one occurred the actual numerical designation for each hole instead of the hypothetical number was used, such as "on the eighth and the ninth" with the hypothetical numbers, 17th and 18th, in parenthesis. While our conclusion does not rest upon this article, we are satisfied that it clearly demonstrates the need for greater clarity and specificity where a 9-hole course is converted or used for an 18-hole course, instead of a regular course with 18 holes.

The offer does not contain any qualifications, restrictions, or limitations as to what is meant by the phrase "on hole No. 8." Neither does the award or offer make any statement restricting or qualifying that the hole-in-one on hole No. 8 may be accomplished only from tee No. 8. If Charbonneau had in mind to impose limitations, restrictions, or qualifications he could have made this in the offer so that a person with ordinary intelligence would have been fully apprised of the offer in every respect.

The distance from tee No. 17 to hole No. 8 was greater than the distance from tee No. 8 to hole No. 8. Thus an argument cannot be made that a player had an advantage playing from tee No. 17 to hole No. 8, as compared to playing from tee No. 8 to hole No. 8. Actually, it would be a disadvantage.

The record does not disclose that either Grove or any other party made inquiries of Charbonneau or that Charbonneau made any explanation as to what was intended by the offer, particularly on the phrase "on hole No. 8," prior to the event here in question. We are thus limited to the actual words themselves. . . .

Charbonneau argues that if "on Hole No. 8" were construed to mean the hole having an actual No. 8 as distinguished from a hypothetical number, the flight of players doing an 18-hole course would have a double chance. This argument falls short of a legal basis for construing the offer and is, therefore, rejected.

It has become quite obvious that the answer or solution to the overriding question which initially may have seemed relatively simple and easy, even suspiciously so, is now actually, upon closer examination and after further analysis, considerably more challenging, demanding, and difficult.

This court in In re Estate of Johnson, 214 N.W.2d 112 (N.D. 1973), in substance said that when good arguments can be made for either of two contrary positions as to the meaning of a term in a document an ambiguity exists. It also stated that the question whether or not an ambiguity exists is a question of law for the court. The contending parties have made good arguments, if not convincing arguments, for their positions.

Taking into account all of the foregoing considerations, we are satisfied that the language in question, "hole-in-one on Hole No. 8," in the offer, under this setting is ambiguous. Having concluded as a matter of law that the offer in this setting is ambiguous, the rule of law providing that the ambiguous terms will be construed and interpreted most strongly against the party who caused the ambiguity applies. . . . We are not suggesting that Charbonneau intended to trifle with the public, but if we do not apply the rule of law on ambiguous contracts, as set out earlier herein, to this situation we would permit promoters to trifle with the public, which we do not believe the law should permit, and in fact, does not permit. . . .

Both of the constructions and interpretations of the language in the offer as contended by the parties are reasonable and each has some strong convincing points, but that does not constitute legal grounds for not applying the rule of law as to how ambiguities in a contract are to be resolved in a situation or setting we have here.

By interpreting and construing the ambiguous provisions of the offer most strongly against the party who caused them as set out in § 9-07-19, NDCC, and as announced in case law developed on this subject, we construe it to mean that an entrant in the golf tournament who had paid the fee and who during regular tournament play drives the ball in one stroke into hole No. 8 from either the 8th or 17th tee has made a hole-in-one on hole No. 8, and has met the conditions of the offer and is entitled to the award or the equivalent in money damages.

The judgment of the district court is affirmed.

Case Questions for Discussion

1. Do you think Charbonneau intended its offer to include a hole in one on the 8th green from the 17th tee?

2. Do you think Grove thought the offer by Charbonneau included a hole in one on the 8th green from the 17th tee, before he hit the shot in question?

3. How should the offer have been stated to make Charbonneau's interpretation of the contract clear?

4. Assume the following facts. A country club has an annual tournament and has a hole-in-one contest on the 15th hole, a par 3. The club promises to award $5,000 to the first participant who makes a hole in one on the 15th hole. The club purchases hole-in-one insurance. The insurance contract specifies that the yardage for the hole should be no less than 170 yards. The club professional sets up the men's (white) tees at 175 yards for the tournament. Four women enter the tournament. The tournament rules state that men shall play from the white tees, and women shall play from the red tees. The red tees on hole 15 are 145 yards from the hole. Kari, one of the female participants, following the tournament rules, makes a hole in one from the red tees on the 15th hole. The insurance company refuses to pay the $5,000 prize. Does Kari collect the prize money? See Harms v. Northland Ford Dealers, 1999 S.D. 143, 602 N.W.2d 58 (1999).

5. Do you think *interpretation contra proferentem* produced a just result in this case? If not, why does the law interpret ambiguous language in a manner that disfavors the author of the language, although it may produce harsh results?

Contract Performance, Conditions, and Breach

To this point, we have viewed contracts as a set of promises the parties make to each other. Of course, in the case of a unilateral contract, such as the one in the case above, there is only one promise. In fact, most contracts are made up of promises and conditions. One party's performance may not be due until the other has satisfied a condition. Conditions may be express, implied, or constructive. An *express condition* is found in the contract itself. Assume you promise to pay a premium of $10 per month for an extended warranty on a used car. The dealer promises to provide any repairs needed to the engine and transmission, but only if the dealer has changed the oil and filter, at least every 3,000 miles, for the life of the warranty. The agreement contains a promise on both sides, but the dealer's promise does not come due unless he has changed the oil at least every 3,000 miles. It is an express condition. If you have a breakdown after 4,000 miles, and have not had the oil changed by the dealer, the dealer owes no performance on the promise. Many times, courts will attempt to construe an express condition as an additional promise, especially if one of the parties is facing forfeiture. In our example, a court could interpret the oil change condition as an additional promise in the contract. If that were the case, the dealer would be required to perform, but you would be responsible for any damage the dealer could prove was attributable to your failure to have the oil changed as specified. It could be that all the damage is traceable to your failure to perform. However, if you could show that you had the oil changed every 3,000 miles by another reputable auto mechanic shop, or that the breakdown would have occurred anyway, it is possible that your responsibility for the damages would be zero, or close to zero.[50]

Implied and constructive conditions are not found in the contract itself, but are supplied by the court. An *implied condition* is one that, although not stated in the contract as such, is implied in the contract.[51] Assume your professor promises to pay you $100, and you promise to make a set of curtains that match the bedspread in her bedroom. After a period of time has elapsed, your professor claims you are in breach of the contract, because you have not made the curtains. You respond that she has not allowed you to see the bedspread. A court should find an implied condition to your performance. In order for you to perform, you must know what the bedspread looks like. Your performance is not due until your professor allows you to see what the bedspread looks like, so you can make the curtains to match.

A *constructive condition* is unlike express and implied conditions, in that it does not necessarily reflect the intent of the parties but is supplied by the court to do justice or bring order to a transaction. Assume you promise to dig a trench in your neighbor's back yard that is two feet deep, 25 feet long, and three feet wide. He promises to pay you $250. The express agreement has two promises, and no conditions. Can you demand that your neighbor pay the $250 before you dig? Without a provision in the agreement calling for advance payment, the answer is no. A court would probably find a constructive condition that the promise requiring time to perform (to dig the trench) is a condition to the promise that can be performed at once (to pay $250). If the promises are such that they may be performed at the same time, courts will usually find that there are concurrent conditions on each promise. Assume you and your neighbor agree to trade lawnmowers. You promise to give her your lawnmower, and she promises to give you her lawnmower. Nothing in the agreement spells out who must perform first. If neither party attempts to perform, neither party should be able to bring a breach action. Each party's performance is constructively conditioned on the other party's performance. Your neighbor's performance becomes due once you perform, or attempt to perform, and vice versa.[52]

Breach

Once a party is in *breach*, several remedies are available. The general rule is that the nonbreaching party should get the benefit of the bargain, commonly referred to as *expectation damages*.[53] Assume you promised to sell your professor 100 pencils, and she promised to pay you 20 cents per pencil. Shortly after forming the contract, there is a worldwide pencil shortage. You once paid 15 cents for each pencil, but now your supplier is charging 25 cents per pencil. You refuse to deliver the pencils as promised. Your professor should be able to get the benefit of her bargain. To acquire the 100 pencils she needs, she is forced to pay 28 cents apiece. You should be liable to your professor for eight cents per pencil, or the difference between what she had to pay and the contract price. Obviously, you would be better off, in this situation, to furnish the pencils under the contract at a loss of five cents per pencil. The nonbreaching party must minimize the damages. There is a duty to seek the lowest replacement price available. This is called a *duty of mitigation*. If it can be shown she could have bought pencils for 25 cents apiece, her damages will be based on the lower price.[54]

In the alternative, the nonbreaching party may ask for *reliance damages*, or amounts expended preparing to perform, before the breach took place. Assume you promise to paint your neighbor's house with a specially mixed shade of blue paint. She promises to pay you $500, if you supply the paint. You go to the paint store, have the paint mixed, and pay $100 for it. Your trip to the paint store takes two hours. Your neighbor then informs you she will not pay and no longer wants you to paint her house. Your reliance damages would be the $100 you paid for the paint (assuming it cannot be returned), plus the cost of your time for two hours (which you must prove). Reliance damages are limited to the amount of expectation damages. If your neighbor can show that your profit on the contract would have been less than the reliance damages, you may recover only the lost profit.[55]

Unjust enrichment, or *restitution*, although not formally a contract remedy, may be relied on by a plaintiff who acted upon the mistaken assumption that there was a contract, or upon a contract that was void or rescinded by the other party. The basic assumption underlying unjust enrichment is that a defendant should be required to disgorge benefits received as a result of dealings between the parties. The action is sometimes referred to as a *quasi contract action* or *quantum meruit*. Assume you promised to paint your neighbor's fence, and you believed she promised to pay you $200. In reality, she promised to think about it and let you know. She can produce a witness that will attest to her version of the facts. The next day, after your neighbor leaves for the day, you begin to paint the fence. When your neighbor arrives home that evening, you have painted 75 percent of the fence. She asks what you are doing, and you respond, "Painting the fence, as I promised." She replies that she did not agree to have you paint the fence, and that she had decided that day to wait until the next spring to have it painted. You have conferred a benefit on your neighbor and may not be able to recover under breach of contract, because there may have been no contract. It would be unjust to allow your neighbor to keep the benefit conferred upon her. She has been unjustly enriched. A suit in restitution may allow you to recover the benefit conferred. Recovery in restitution is measured by the value of the benefit conferred, not the benefit of the bargain, as a contract action would require.[56]

Special, or *consequential,* damages may also be recoverable in a contract action. To be liable for special damages, the breaching party must know that the nonbreaching party would suffer the special damages, if a breach occurred. Assume that on April 25, you promise to paint your neighbor's house by May 6, and in return she promises to pay you $300. She tells you that her lease requires her to have the house painted by May 6, or she will forfeit her entire $1,000 damage deposit. The next day, she leaves on a business trip and does not return until May 7. While she is gone, you win a 10-day trip to the Kentucky Derby and leave town without painting the house. Upon finding you did not paint the house, she contracts with another painter for $350. He does the job, but it is too late to avoid losing the $1,000 damage deposit under the terms of the lease. In a breach of contract action, your neighbor should be able to recover $50 in expectation damages ($350–$300), plus the $1,000 she lost on her lease, as special damages. Had you not known of the lease provision, your neighbor probably would not be able to recover the special damages.[57]

Liquidated damages, or damages spelled out in the contract (also referred to as *stipulated damages*), are typically recoverable if they reflect an attempt by the parties to estimate actual damages, and if the actual damages would be difficult to compute if a breach occurs. For example, you promise to build a Christmas tree display rack outside the grocery store by the first day of December. The grocery store promises to pay you $400. In a stipulated damages provision, you agree to pay $100 for each day your performance is late. Although the grocery store has never sold Christmas trees before, it estimates that beginning with the first day of December, it will sell enough trees to generate profits of $100 per day. Given these facts, the stipulated damages should be recoverable if you fail to deliver the Christmas tree rack by the first day of December. The provision appears to be an estimate of actual damages.

Because the store has no history selling Christmas trees, it also appears it would be difficult to compute actual damages if a breach occurred. If the provision for stipulated damages acts as a penalty, however, most courts will not enforce stipulated damage clauses.[58]

All of the remedies discussed above provide money damages. Courts of law do not force a party to a contract to perform as promised. Courts of equity will, in a few situations, order *specific performance,* or require the party in breach to perform as promised. Specific performance is granted only when the remedy at law is inadequate. Examples include contracts for the sale of unique property or contracts that are somehow unique. Real estate is always considered unique. No parcel of land is exactly like another. Other examples include one-of-a-kind items with special value, such as paintings or historical documents. Of course, because the action for specific performance occurs in an equity court, the plaintiff must have clean hands.[59]

Key Terms, Names, and Concepts

Acceptance

Assumpsit

Authentication

Bilateral contract

Breach of contract

Capacity

Cognitive test

Collateral contract concept

Consensual contract

Consequential damages

Consideration

Constructive condition

Contract

Contract construction

Contract interpretation

Covenant

Debt

Donative promises

Duty of mitigation

Ejusdem generis

Expectation damages

Express condition

Expressio unius est exclusio alterius

Extrinsic evidence

Four corners rule

General assumpsit

Gratuitous promises

Implied condition

Infancy

Innominate contract

Integrated agreement

Interpretation contra proferentem

Land contract provision

Legal detriment

Liquidated damages

Master of the offer

Mental illness or defect

Merger clause

Objective theory

Offer

Offeree

Offeror

One-year provision

Parol evidence rule

Partial integration

Plain-meaning rule

Quantum meruit

Quasi contract action

Real contract
Reliance damages
Restatement, Second,
  Contracts
Restitution
Special damages
Specific performance
Statute of Frauds

Stipulated damages
Stipulation
Subjective theory
The specific controls
  the general
Unilateral contract
Unjust enrichment
Volitional test

Discussion Questions

1. Mrs. Smith, a schoolteacher, is a member of a retirement plan and has elected a lower monthly benefit in order to provide a benefit to her husband if she dies first. At age 60, she suffers a "nervous breakdown" and takes a leave of absence. Soon after Mrs. Smith's leave of absence begins, she is diagnosed with terminal colon cancer. When the leave of absence expires, Mrs. Smith applies for retirement, revokes her previous election, and elects a larger annuity with no death benefit. Two months after the changed election, Mrs. Smith dies. Mr. Smith had no knowledge of the change in election until after Mrs. Smith's death. What, if anything, can Mr. Smith do? Explain your answer.

2. Although they are of meager means, Bill and his wife plan on celebrating their fifth wedding anniversary with a good meal and an expensive bottle of wine. Bill visits the local package store and looks over their selection. He finds an expensive cabernet but debates whether he can afford the $75 price. Finally, he decides that his wife is worth it. Just as he is placing the bottle in the cart, Bill loses his grip, and the bottle falls to the floor and breaks. The storeowner demands that Bill pay for the bottle of wine. Does the storeowner have an action in contract against Bill for the price of the wine? Explain your answer.

3. Jill has a history of being unable to control her drinking and substance abuse. Over the past two years, she has lost her job and most of her friends. She owns a home but has not been able to pay the mortgage for nine months. The mortgage holder is about to begin foreclosure proceedings. The house is worth about $25,000 on the market, and the mortgage has a balance of $10,000. Joe hears of Jill's problem and inquires about buying the house. Jill tells him she wants to get her "equity" out of the house and have enough money to put a down payment on a mobile home. Joe tells Jill that would be fine with him, and that he will draw up a contract and a deed. He tells her to meet him at his attorney's office in one week. On the appointed day, Jill and

Joe meet with Joe's attorney. Under the contract drawn up by Joe's attorney, Joe is to pay Jill $1,500 cash and pay off the $10,000 mortgage. Jill, obviously intoxicated, signs the contract, signs the deed, and accepts the $1,500 of cash. The next morning, Jill reads the contract and realizes she has not received as much money as she wanted for the house. She calls Joe and tells him the deal is off. Can Jill cancel or void the contract? Why or why not?

4. Lance suffers major injuries when one of the metal treads on a snowmobile he is riding fails and strikes him in the head. Lance bought the snowmobile from an American subsidiary of a Canadian corporation. The Canadian parent company bought worldwide liability insurance from a Canadian insurance company. The insurance policy limits coverage per incident to "500,000 dollars." Lance sues the American subsidiary for damages and agrees to settle for the policy limits. The insurance company pays Lance 500,000 in Canadian dollars, which converts to 300,000 U.S. dollars. Lance sues for an additional $200,000 U.S., contending the term "dollars" is ambiguous, because the policy contract does not specify whether the policy limits are in U.S. or Canadian dollars. Because the term is ambiguous, Lance contends, the court should construe the term against the author (the insurance company). Does Lance have a valid claim? Why or why not?

5. Carlos and Nancy, a married couple, own a home as joint tenants in Chicago with a market value of $100,000. Nancy accepts a job offer in Denver. She is to report for the new job in one month. Carlos and Nancy list the Chicago home with a real estate broker for $100,000. Three weeks later, Carlos and Nancy receive a written offer to buy the house from Dom for $90,000. Although Dom's offer is for less money than they could get if they waited for other offers, Carlos and Nancy decide to accept the offer because they are eager to put a down payment on a new home in Denver. The next day, Carlos goes to the realtor's office and signs the contract to sell the Chicago home. Nancy is to stop by and sign the contract on her way home from work that evening. That afternoon, however, a fire breaks out at the Chicago home, and it is completely destroyed. Carlos and Nancy have a replacement value fire insurance policy on the home that will pay them $100,000. Nancy refuses to sign the contract, preferring to collect the $100,000 of insurance proceeds. Dom, however, demands that Carlos and Nancy accept the $90,000 he promised to pay, deliver the deed to the property, and pay the $100,000 of insurance proceeds. Was there a contract to sell the Chicago

home? Who is entitled to the $100,000 of insurance proceeds? Explain your answer.

6. Tamra has health insurance through a group policy offered by her husband's men's club. The policy excludes coverage for medical expenses for illnesses "caused wholly or partly by a disease of organs of the body not common to both sexes." Tamra becomes ill and is diagnosed with a fibroid tumor of the uterus. The insurance company refuses her claim, citing the exclusionary language in the policy. Is the insurance company's denial of coverage valid? Why or why not?

7. Perry and Tonya enter into the following agreement. Tonya promises to clean Perry's apartment twice each week for a period of 52 weeks, and Perry promises to pay Tonya $100 each week for the 52-week period. Tonya and Perry perform as promised for two months. Perry approaches Tonya when she is cleaning in the third month of the contract and says that because she is doing such a good job, he is going to pay her $150 per week for the rest of the 52-week period. Three weeks later, Perry pays Tonya only $100 for the week. May Tonya collect the other $50 from Perry? Why or why not?

8. You did very well in your first year in college. Your father, after seeing your grades, says: "In consideration of your great performance at college over the past year, I will pay you $500." He does not pay you, however. May you force your father to pay you $500? Does it make a difference in your answer if your father says: "In consideration of your great performance over the past year in college, and in consideration of your promise to work hard next year in college, I will pay you $500"?

9. Randy is a collector of classic sports cars. He notices that Betty has been driving a 1960 roadster that Randy would like to add to his collection. On May 1, Randy writes Betty a letter asking, "Will you sell me your 1960 roadster, for the sum of $10,000?" One week later, Randy receives a letter from Betty in which she states: "I am in receipt of your letter of May 1, in which you inquire about my 1960 roadster. Because I recently replaced the convertible top and installed a new engine and transmission in my 1960 roadster, it would not be possible for me to sell it for less than $15,000." Upon receipt of the letter from Betty, Randy wires her $15,000 and sends her a letter stating: "I accept your offer to sell your 1960 roadster for $15,000. I have wired the funds payable to your bank account. I will come to your home next weekend to pick up the roadster. Please be prepared to sign over the title at that time." Must Betty sell the 1960 roadster to Randy? Explain your answer.

Suggested Additional Reading

Barnes, David W., and Lynn A. Stout. *Economics of Contract Law.* St. Paul, MN: West, 1992.

Burton, Steven J. *Principles of Contract Law.* St. Paul, MN: West, 1992.

Danzig, Richard. *The Capability Problem in Contract Law: Further Readings on Well-Known Cases.* Westbury, NY: Foundation Press, 1978.

Eggleston, Karen, Eric A. Posner, and Richard Zeckhauser. "The Design and Interpretation of Contracts: Why Complexity Matters." *Northwestern University Law Review* 95 (fall 2000): 91–132.

Farnsworth, E. Allan, and William F. Young. *Cases and Materials on Contracts.* 5th ed. Westbury, NY: Foundation Press, 1995.

Gillette, Clayton P. "XML and the Legal Foundations for Electronic Commerce: Interpretation and Standardization in Electronic Sales Contracts." *Southern Methodist University Law Review* 53 (fall 2000): 1431–1445.

Kidd, Donnie L., Jr., and William H. Daughtrey, Jr. "Adapting Contract Law to Accommodate Electronic Contracts: Overview and Suggestions." *Rutgers Computer and Technology Law Journal* 26 (2000): 215–276.

Kniffen, Margaret N. "A New Trend in Contract Interpretation: The Search for Reality as Opposed to Virtual Reality." *Oregon Law Review* 74 (summer 1995): 643–664.

Perillo, Joseph M. "The Origins of the Objective Theory of Contract Formation and Interpretation." *Fordham Law Review* 69 (November 2000): 427–477.

Posner, Eric A. "Essay: The Parol Evidence Rule, the Plain Meaning Rule, and the Principles of Contractual Interpretation." *University of Pennsylvania Law Review* 146 (January 1998): 533–577.

Prince, Harry G. "Contract Interpretation in California: Plain Meaning, Parol Evidence, and Use of the 'Just Result Principle.' " *Loyola of Los Angeles Law Review* 31 (January 1998): 557–651.

Smedinghoff, Thomas J., and Ruth Hill Bro. "Moving With Change: Electronic Signature Legislation as a Vehicle for Advancing E-Commerce." *John Marshall Journal of Computer and Information Law* Vol. XVII, No. 3 (spring 1999): 723–768.

Endnotes

1. Samuel Williston, *Contracts,* 4th ed. (Lord, 1990), § 1.1, Restatement, Contracts (1932), § 1.1, and Restatement, Second, Contracts (1981), § 1.1, as cited in John D. Calamari and Joseph M. Perillo, *The Law of Contracts,* 4th ed. (St. Paul, MN: West, 1998), § 1.1.
2. E. Allan Farnsworth, *Contracts* (Boston: Little, Brown, 1982), § 1.4.
3. Ibid., § 1.5.
4. Restatement, Second, Contracts (1981), § 12.
5. Ibid., § 14, and Comments (b) & (c).
6. Ibid., § 15.
7. Ibid., § 15, Comment (a).

8. E. Allan Farnsworth, *Farnsworth on Contracts*, 2nd ed. (New York: Aspen Publishers, Inc. 1998), § 4.6.

9. Calamari, *The Law of Contracts*, § 8.7(b).

10. Larry A. Dimatteo, "Deconstructing the Myth of the 'Infancy Law Doctrine': From Incapacity to Accountability," *Ohio Northern Law Review* 21 (1995): 481, as cited in Farnsworth, *Farnsworth on Contracts*, § 4.6, at footnote 12. See also, the Reporters Notes to Comment (c), of § 14 of the Restatement, Second, Contracts, where Dean Prosser, the leading scholar of tort law in the United States for much of the twentieth century, is quoted as follows: "The effect of the decisions refusing to recognize tort liability for misrepresentations [of age by minors] is to create a privileged class of liars who are a great trouble to the business world."

11. Calamari, *The Law of Contracts*, § 2.2.

12. Restatement, Second, Contracts (1981), § 24.

13. Farnsworth, *Farnsworth on Contracts*, § 3.10.

14. Ibid., § 3.3.

15. Calamari, *The Law of Contracts*, §§ 2.11 & 2.12.

16. Ibid., § 2.13.

17. Farnsworth, *Farnsworth on Contracts*, § 3.11.

18. Ibid., § 3.12.

19. Ibid., § 3.13.

20. Restatement, Second, Contracts (1981), § 30.

21. Calamari, *The Law of Contracts*, § 4.1. Some remnants of contracts under seal (formal sealed documents that, in effect, provided a nonrebuttable presumption of consideration) still exist in some jurisdictions. In a few situations, a sealed donative or gratuitous promise may be enforceable, see Calamari, *The Law of Contracts*, Chapter 9. Promissory estoppel may also be used to enforce a gratuitous promise the promisee relied on, see Calamari, *The Law of Contracts*, Chapter 6.

22. Ibid., § 4.2.

23. Ibid.

24. Ibid.

25. Ibid., § 4.4.

26. Ibid., § 4.3.

27. Claude D. Rohwer and Anthony M. Skrocki, *Contracts in a Nutshell*, 5th ed. (St. Paul, MN: West, 2000), § 3.1.

28. Restatement, Second, Contracts (1981), § 110.

29. Restatement, Second, Contracts (1981), Statutory Note to Chapter 5. The note provides a comprehensive listing of state Statute of Fraud provisions and other writing requirement statutes.

30. Calamari, *The Law of Contracts*, § 19.1.

31. Restatement, Second, Contracts (1981), § 125.

32. Calamari, *The Law of Contracts*, § 19.18.

33. Restatement, Second, Contracts (1981), § 130.

34. Calamari, *The Law of Contracts*, § 19.29.

35. A draft of the National Conference of Commissioners on Uniform State Laws' *Uniform Computer Information Transaction Act* (last Revisions or Amendments completed year 2000) has the following definition of signature, "Any signature under other law is an authentication under this Act. In addition, authentication includes qualifying use of any identifier, such as a personal identification number (PIN) or a typed or other-

wise signed name. It can include actions or sounds such as encryption, voice and biological identification, and other technologically enabled acts if done with proper intent." Likewise, a November, 2000, draft of a revision of Article Two of the *Uniform Commercial Code* contains the following definition: Section 2-102(a)—In this article, unless the context otherwise requires: (1) "Authenticate" means: (i) to sign, or (ii) to execute or adopt a record with the intent to sign, and to attach to or logically associate with the record an electronic sound, symbol, or process. Both uniform acts accept electronic records as writings, providing certain conditions are met. The proposed acts and revisions can be found at <http://www.law.upenn.edu/bll/ulc_frame.html>, available as of January 27, 2002.

36. Restatement, Second, Contracts (1981), § 139. See also, Restatement, Second Contracts (1981) § 90.

37. Farnsworth, *Farnsworth on Contracts*, § 7.7.

38. Ibid.

39. Ibid., § 7.8.

40. Ibid., § 7.9. The Restatement, Second, Contracts (1981), §§ 201(2) and 20 are in accord. One of the most famous contract interpretation cases is Raffles v. Wichelhaus, 159 Eng. Rep. 375 (Ex. 1864), an English case that involved the purchase of cotton to be shipped on a ship named *Peerless* when it sailed from Bombay. Amazingly, two ships named *Peerless* were to sail from Bombay, one in October and one in December. The buyer expected shipment on the October *Peerless,* while the seller meant the December *Peerless.* Neither the buyer nor the seller knew or had reason to know of the other ship. The courts held for the seller in a breach action brought by the buyer. In effect, there was no breach because there was no agreement.

41. Rohwer, *Contracts in a Nutshell,* § 4.8.

42. Farnsworth, *Farnsworth on Contracts,* § 7.12. The Restatement, Second, Contracts (1981), § 212, Comment b offers support for the liberal view.

43. Ibid., § 7.11.

44. Ibid.

45. Ibid.

46. Ibid.

47. Calamari, *The Law of Contracts,* § 3.2.

48. Ibid., § 3.4.

49. Ibid.

50. Rohwer, *Contracts in a Nutshell,* § 8.1.3. See also, Restatement, Second, Contracts (1981), § 224.

51. Ibid., § 8.1.3.

52. Ibid.

53. Ibid., § 9.1.

54. Ibid., § 9.2.3.

55. Ibid., § 9.3.

56. Ibid., §§ 10.1, 10.1.5, & 10.2.

57. Ibid., § 9.2.1.

58. Ibid., § 9.5.

59. Ibid., § 9.6. ✦

Chapter 15

Government Regulation of Business

Chapter Objectives

Students should understand and be able to explain the sources of federal and state power to regulate businesses and business activities. Readers will also gain an understanding of negotiable instruments, including differences between order paper and bearer paper, indorsements, and holders in due course. Students need to be able to explain the meaning of a secured transaction, when and how a security interest attaches, and how to perfect a security interest. Readers should understand the three primary federal employment discrimination statutes and be able to explain violations under each statute. Students will gain an understanding of how a security is registered, and what issuers of securities traded on a national exchange must do to maintain their registered security status. Readers must gain a basic understanding of federal antitrust statutes and be able to describe the methods courts employ to analyze alleged antitrust violations. Finally, students need to be able to describe the various types of business activities that may constitute antitrust violations.

It is nearly impossible for an individual living in the United States to go through a day without interacting in some manner with a business entity. A utility company sells us electricity for our homes. Agriculture and grocery companies process, package, distribute, and sell the food we eat. Oil companies refine, distribute, and sell gasoline for our vehicles, and telecommunications companies sell us access to communication media. These examples are a small sampling of the day-to-day contact each of us has with business concerns. Life would be very hard without such daily contact. In fact, to avoid contact with business entities, one would need to gather food in the wild, forgo television and radio, start a fire by rubbing sticks together, and either sleep on the ground on animal skins or in a cabin made with self-harvested lumber and secured with self-made spikes or mud.

The regulation of business is extensive. Almost every action taken by a business, whether large or small, is subject to a statute or a regulation.[1] Just starting a business, depending on the size of the venture, the form of business being contemplated, and how it is financed, requires filings with state and/or federal government agencies. The extensive regulation of business is usually justified as a means of protecting consumers or workers. Other types of regulations, however, facilitate the conduct of business itself. This chapter examines the major, but not all, statutory and regulatory schemes that affect everyone in one way or another. Our initial task is to briefly sketch the evolution and sources of regulatory power over business in the United States.

Business entities chase the almighty dollar, but government has the power to regulate how they do business.

Historical Perspective of Governmental Regulation of Business

The regulation of business predates the United States. Mercantilism, the economic system followed by most western European countries from roughly 1600 through 1800, required state control or regulation of business entities and practices. Under mercantilism, each country attempted to be self-sufficient and maximize its holdings of precious metals. A favorable balance of trade with other nations was necessary to minimize the outflow of precious metals. To achieve this goal, governments heavily regulated businesses, individuals, and business practices. Elizabethan laws of the latter half of the sixteenth century gave English justices of the peace the power to fix prices, regulate hours, and compel all individuals to work at a useful trade. The nation's interest was also advanced by industrial or commercial innovation. Often, monopolies were granted to companies or individuals to insure the maximization of profits.[2] For example, Charles II granted a charter for the Hudson Bay Company to his cousin and 17 other English gentlemen. The charter gave the Hudson Bay Company a monopoly over trade in the region watered by streams flowing into Hudson Bay.[3]

Governmental licensing of brokers dates back to 1285 in the city of London. The first disclosure laws arose from the rubble created by the "Bubble Mania" that swept parts of Europe in the early 1700s. "Bubble Mania" in France and England saw a spectacular run-up in the price of two companies granted monopolies over trade in the South Sea areas of the New World. Before the bubble burst, shares in the Mississippi Company (the French company) and the South Sea Company (the British company) were sold to the public at inflated prices. In addition, the run-up of the share prices spawned at least 200 other joint stock company offerings in Britain, as well as widespread speculation and fraud. When the bubble burst, it caused financial panic and many investors, both large and small, were ruined. As a result, the *Bubble Act of 1720* prohibited false or irregular charters and the taking of investment in such enterprises. It created penalties for brokers selling unlawful shares and gave injured merchants and traders the right to sue for treble damages if their legitimate ventures were damaged by illegitimate business activities.[4]

Federal Power to Regulate Business

Many of the leading business, commercial, banking, and agricultural interests in post-Revolutionary America argued successfully for a new constitution to replace the Articles of Confederation. This would permit the national government to pay off debts incurred during the War of Independence from England and to create the institutional and constitutional requirements for a strong and vibrant national economy. Under the Articles of Confederation (1781–1789), the national government had to requisition the states for money to operate the national bureaucracy, but the states proved reluctant to aid the national government in fulfilling this and other responsibilities. Moreover, the national government was unable to prevent states from imposing trade barriers against goods imported from sister states, foreign nations, and the Native American populations. Discriminatory practices made it difficult for the new republic to develop a truly national economy with all the benefits that flow from free trade. The state practice of issuing currency and the growing propensity of state legislatures to enact laws that impaired the obligation of contracts also required remedial action. The latter problem was met through the adoption of a constitutional provision that prohibits states from impairing the obligation of contracts.

Taxing and Spending Power

A major source of power for the national government is the power to tax and to spend. Article 1, section 8, paragraph 1, of the Constitution grants to Congress the ". . . power to lay and collect taxes, duties, imposts and excises, to pay the Debts and provide for the Common Defense and general Welfare of the United States." This grant of authority, augmented by the Sixteenth Amendment, permits Congress to raise and spend billions of dollars each year that have a direct impact on American business. Federal subsidies to farmers are well-known to the public. But other businesses and individuals receive aid in the form of loans; financial bailouts; the creation of infrastructures in the form of highways, airports, and seaports; unemployment programs; and transfer payments to the poor, the aged, and the disabled. Because none of these programs are mentioned specifically in the Constitution, they must be inferred from the taxing and spending power of Article 1. Otherwise, they would be prohibited as invasions of the reserved power of the states under the Tenth Amendment.

Congress has used its taxing and spending power to induce state and local governments to comply with national policy through "categorical grants." These grants require that state governments comply with certain regulations if they want to take advantage of the federal largess. For example, if states want to obtain federal highway dollars to aid in the construction of roadways within their borders, they must agree to enact laws prohibiting persons under the age of 21 from purchasing alcoholic beverages. Laws exist mandating how states must train their National Guard units and how college and university student grades may be posted. There is also a requirement that institutions receiving federal funds for student loans must have a method of keeping class attendance records.[5] A high priority of the early George W. Bush administration was to tie the receipt of federal funding by local school districts to a requirement that those school districts regularly test each student to measure the success of the school in meeting national learning objectives.

Congress not only has the power to spend for the purpose of regulation, it may also use its taxing power to regulate. Congress can make certain business enterprises unprofitable by imposing burdensome taxes on them. The manufacture and sale of dangerous matches is an example.[6] Clearly, the imposition of high federal taxes on tobacco and alcoholic beverages is designed not only to raise revenue for the national government, but also to discourage consumption of these products. Congress has also enacted elaborate tax laws that require gamblers, arms peddlers, and narcotic pushers to report their incomes and in the process place them in jeopardy of prosecution. On occasion, however, the courts have declared these laws in violation of the self-incrimination provision of the Fifth Amendment.[7]

Commerce Clause

Article 1, section 8, paragraph 3, of the U.S. Constitution grants to Congress plenary power to regulate commerce with foreign nations, among the several states, and with the Indian Tribes. The word "commerce" has been judicially interpreted to entail the traffic in transportation, navigation, and the buying and selling of goods and services of all kinds, including the regulation of business and employment practices that are related to interstate activity.

The U.S. Supreme Court's interpretation of the Commerce Clause has profoundly affected the boundaries of authority between the federal and state governments. Although the Court's historical interpretation of this clause has reflected competing views of the relationship between the federal and state governments, the basic principle of constitutional law is settled. The congressional power to regulate interstate commerce is *plenary*. Because the power is complete, when Congress validly enacts laws pursuant to the Commerce Clause, it does not invade the reserved power of the states as guaranteed by the Tenth Amendment. Although the definition of interstate commerce is a matter of controversy, the Court has granted to Congress plenary authority over all matters involving commercial intercourse. It has authorized Congress to regulate many aspects of American business and the economy and to enact laws protecting the civil rights of citizens in all the states.

Gibbons v. Ogden, 22 U.S. (9 Wheat.) 1 (1824), is the seminal case defining commerce. Chief Justice Marshall held that commerce is intercourse between nations and parts of nations in all its branches, and that Congress has plenary power to prescribe rules to carry out that intercourse. Navigation is part of commerce, and the power of Congress to regulate such activity cannot stop at the state boundaries because the power to regulate "among the states" means intermingling with traffic in the interior of states. Nonetheless, Marshall ruled that commerce that is completely within a state is reserved for state regulation.

In Cooley v. Board of Wardens of the Port of Philadelphia, 53 U.S. (12 How.) 299 (1852), the Court held that if Congress manifests a clear intention to leave the matter of commerce regulation to the states, then individual states may regulate interstate commerce. In later decisions, the high court found that states may regulate commerce in the absence of congressional regulation, if that regulation is wholly local and does not create uniform national standards. The rule in *Cooley* was subsequently supplemented with a balancing of interests test designed to ascertain whether the litigated state regulation creates an "undue burden on interstate commerce." For instance, the Supreme Court found that a width and weight limitation on trucks driving through South Carolina was a reasonable safety limitation when balanced against the national interest in the free flow of interstate commerce.[8] Interest balancing, however, does not automatically result in upholding the state regulation, as was the case when Arizona attempted to limit the length of freight trains traveling through that state.[9]

How far within the confines of state boundaries may federal legislation penetrate to regulate commerce? In one instance, the Interstate Commerce Commission ordered an end to the discriminatory practices of a railway company in charging lower rates for intrastate shipments among east Texas locations than for interstate shipments over similar distances. In what is popularly referred to as the *Shreveport Rate* case, the Supreme Court held that although the rate fixing was completely intrastate, Congress may regulate intrastate carriers in all matters that have a "close and substantial relation" to interstate commerce.[10] Subsequently, in Stafford v. Wallace, 258 U.S. 495 (1922), the Court ruled that Congress could authorize the Secretary of Agriculture to regulate business conducted in stockyards even when the cattle were not in transit. Chief Justice William Howard Taft wrote: "[T]he stockyards are but a throat through which the current flows, and the transactions which occur therein are only incident to this current from the West to the East, and from one state to another."[11]

Even though matters affecting transportation were found to be firmly within the regulatory power of Congress, the Supreme Court limited the power of Congress under the Commerce Clause during this era by creating a sharp distinction between commerce and manufacturing. In United States v. E.C. Knight Co., 156 U.S. 1 (1895), the Supreme Court held that the Sherman Antitrust Act of 1890 was not applicable to monopolies in manufacturing or production because they have only an incidental or indirect relationship to commerce. Consequently, as applied in this case, the Sherman Act represented an intrusion into the reserve power of the states under the Tenth Amendment. After *E.C. Knight*, the Supreme Court was firmly in support of big business interests and used similar reasoning to strike down congressional attempts to regulate child labor, codes of fair competition, wages and hours of workers in mining, and even agricultural subsidies, although not as a violation of the Commerce Clause. These and other Supreme Court decisions were viewed by proponents of President Franklin Roosevelt's New Deal as a serious threat to economic recovery.[12] As a result, the Supreme Court was subjected to considerable pressure that no doubt led to the alteration in the Court's Commerce Clause interpretation.

By the late 1930s, the Supreme Court began to change its anti-federal government and probusiness interpretations. The most dramatic transition took place when the Court discarded its direct-indirect decision rule with the 5–4 decision in NLRB v. Jones and Laughlin Steel Corp., 301 U.S. 1 (1937). The Court ruled that the Wagner Act, which established the right of organized labor to bargain collectively, was a valid regulation of commerce. It found that although labor-management relations are intrastate in character when they are considered separately, these relationships have a "close and substantial relation"[13] to interstate commerce as part of the "flow of commerce."[14]

In subsequent decisions pertaining to maximum hours and minimum wage laws, United States v. Darby, 312 U.S. 100 (1941), and the regulation of farm acreage allotments, Wickard v. Filburn, 317 U.S. 111 (1942), the Supreme Court upheld the power of Congress to regulate commerce. Virtually any amount of economic activity in one place affects activity elsewhere; consequently, there seemed to be no limit to the power of the federal government. By the 1960s, there was little question that Congress possessed considerable authority. However, beginning in the 1970s and, as we will discuss, culminating in the late 1990s, the U.S. Supreme Court returned to a states' rights posture that diminished the authority of Congress to enact laws that purport to regulate the economy.

Reflecting the expansive status of the Commerce Clause, the Court opted to base its interpretation of the 1964 Civil Rights Act on that clause alone, not on the more obvious Equal Protection Clause and its enforcement provision found in the Fourteenth Amendment. The Supreme Court ruled that discrimination in public accommodations included such matters as hotels as they relate to interstate travel, Heart of Atlanta Motel v. United States, 379 U.S. 241 (1964); service at a restaurant because foodstuffs were shipped via interstate carriers, Katzenbach v. McClung, 379 U.S. 294 (1964); and even a resort business located many miles from an interstate highway because the private resort leased equipment from an out-of-state supplier, Daniel v. Paul, 395 U.S. 298 (1969). We present below an edited version of the *McClung* opinion, commonly referred to as the *Ollie's Barbecue* case. It is a good example of what many feel is the "stretching" of the Commerce Clause into a general police power. Congressional commerce power extends to local activity in both the state of origin and the state of destination, when the activity in question has a substantial and harmful effect upon interstate commerce.

Reflecting a more ideological conservative perspective favoring states' rights, today's Supreme Court, headed by Chief Justice William Rehnquist, has struck down a number of federal laws purporting to regulate interstate commerce. Because of its actions, we must conclude that the Commerce Clause is no longer a "blank check" authorizing Congress to enact laws that impact the exercise of state power.

In the landmark case of United States v. Lopez, 514 U.S. 549 (1995), the 5–4 conservative majority of the Rehnquist Court struck down the Gun Free School Zones Act of 1990. The Court held that the federal law violated the reserved power of the states, because the statute was a criminal statute that had little to do with "commerce" or any type of economic activity. The Court outlined the circumstances when Congress may regulate commercial activity: First, it may regulate the channels of interstate commerce; second, it may regulate and protect the instrumentalities of interstate commerce, even though the threat may come only from intrastate activities; and third, it may regulate those activities that substantially affect interstate commerce. Finding that the first two circumstances do not fit the law in question, Rehnquist dismissed the last category by rejecting the view of the Justice Department and the four-member Court minority—that a violent atmosphere in schools adversely affects the learning environment, which in turn ultimately and substantially affects the economy. If the federal law against the carrying of weapons near and on school grounds was constitutionally permissible, then Chief Justice Rehnquist could find no reason why Congress may not enact laws prescribing curriculum for local elementary and secondary schools.

Building on the *Lopez* precedent, the Supreme Court in Printz v. United States, 521 U.S. 98 (1997), ruled unconstitutional a section of the Brady Handgun Act of 1993. The offending provision required local law enforcement officials to run background checks on prospective gun purchasers, pending the creation of a computerized national criminal check system. Likewise, in United States v. Morrison, 529 U.S. 598 (2000), the Court found unconstitutional a federal civil remedy for victims of gender-motivated violence provided in the Violence Against Women Act of 1994.

Federal preemption and commerce regulation. Commerce Clause litigation sometimes involves the so-called *federal preemption doctrine:* if a state law conflicts with a federal law, then the national law supersedes it. Courts must ask whether Congress intended to take over a field by its extensive regulation, such as nuclear power.[15] Because Congress in 1871 declared that there would be no more treaties with Native Americans, the Commerce Clause is also the primary constitutional tool that Congress possesses when legislating in the field of Indian affairs. Lastly, the U.S. Supreme Court has consistently held that the congressional regulation of commerce with foreign nations is quite extensive, especially in light of state attempts to tax foreign products. This is particularly appropriate because it is important for the nation to speak with one voice in matters of foreign affairs.[16]

Katzenbach v. McClung
Supreme Court of the United States
379 U.S. 294 (1964)

O PINION BY: CLARK: This case was argued with No. 515, Heart of Atlanta Motel v. United States, decided this date, ante, p. 241, in which we upheld the constitutional validity of Title II of the Civil Rights Act of 1964 against an attack by hotels, motels, and like establishments.

This complaint for injunctive relief against appellants attacks the constitutionality of the Act as applied to a restaurant. The case was heard by a three-judge United States District Court and an injunction was issued restraining appellants from enforcing the Act against the restaurant. On direct appeal, . . . we noted probable jurisdiction. . . . We now reverse the judgment. . . .

Ollie's Barbecue is a family-owned restaurant in Birmingham, Alabama, specializing in barbecued meats and homemade pies, with a seating capacity of 220 customers. It is located on a state highway 11 blocks from an interstate one and a somewhat greater distance from railroad and bus stations. The restaurant caters to a family and white-collar trade with a take-out service for Negroes.

It employs 36 persons, two-thirds of whom are Negroes. In the 12 months preceding the passage of the Act, the restaurant purchased locally approximately $150,000 worth of food, $69,683 or 46 percent of which was meat that it bought from a local supplier who had procured it from outside the State. The District Court expressly found that a substantial portion of the food served in the restaurant had moved in interstate commerce. The restaurant has refused to serve Negroes in its dining accommodations since its original opening in 1927, and since July 2, 1964, it has been operating in violation of the Act. The court below concluded that if it were required to serve Negroes it would lose a substantial amount of business.

On the merits, the District Court held that the Act could not be applied under the Fourteenth Amendment because it was conceded that the State of Alabama was not involved in the refusal of the restaurant to serve Negroes. It was also admitted that the Thirteenth Amendment was authority neither for validating nor for invalidating the Act. As to the Commerce Clause, the court found that it was "an express grant of power to Congress to regulate interstate commerce, which consists of the movement of persons, goods or information from one state to another" and it found that the clause was also a grant of power "to regulate intrastate activities, but only to the extent that action on its part is necessary or appropriate to the effective execution of its expressly granted power to regulate interstate commerce." There must be, it said, a close and substantial relation between local activities and interstate commerce which requires control of the former in the protection of the latter. The court concluded, however, that the Congress, rather than finding facts sufficient to meet this rule, had legislated a conclusive presumption that a restaurant affects interstate commerce if it serves or offers to serve interstate travelers or if a substantial portion of the food which it serves has moved in commerce.

This, the court held, it could not do because there was no demonstrable connection between food purchased in interstate commerce and sold in a restaurant and the conclusion of Congress that discrimination in the restaurant would affect that commerce. . . .

Section 201 (a) of Title II commands that all persons shall be entitled to the full and equal enjoyment of the goods and services of any place of public accommodation without discrimination or segregation on the ground of race, color, religion, or national origin; and § 201 (b) defines establishments as places of public accommodation if their operations affect commerce or segregation by them is supported by state action. Sections 201 (b) (2) and (c) place any restaurant . . . principally engaged in selling food for consumption on the premises under the Act if . . . it serves or offers to serve interstate travelers or a substantial portion of the food which it serves . . . has moved in commerce.

Ollie's Barbecue admits that it is covered by these provisions of the Act. The Government makes no contention that the discrimination at the restaurant was supported by the State of Alabama. There is no claim that interstate travelers frequented the restaurant. The sole question, therefore, narrows down to whether Title II, as applied to a restaurant annually receiving about $70,000 worth of food which has moved in commerce, is a valid exercise of the power of Congress. The Government has contended that Congress had ample basis upon which to find that racial discrimination at restaurants which receive from out of state a substantial portion of the food served does, in fact, impose commercial burdens of national magnitude upon interstate commerce. The appellees' major argument is directed to this premise. They urge that no such basis existed. It is to that question that we now turn.

As we noted in Heart of Atlanta Motel both Houses of Congress conducted prolonged hearings on the Act. And, as we said there, while no formal findings were made, which of course are not necessary, it is well that we make mention of the testimony at these hearings the better to understand the problem before Congress and determine whether the Act is a reasonable and appropriate means toward its solution. The record is replete with testimony of the burdens placed on interstate commerce by racial discrimination in restaurants. A comparison of per capita spending by Negroes in restaurants, theaters, and like establishments indicated less spending, after discounting income differences, in areas where discrimination is widely practiced. . . . This diminutive spending springing from a refusal to serve Negroes and their total loss as customers has, regardless of the absence of direct evidence, a close connection to interstate commerce. The fewer customers a restaurant enjoys the less food it sells and consequently the less it buys. . . .

We believe that this testimony afforded ample basis for the conclusion that established restaurants in such areas sold less interstate goods because of the discrimination, that interstate travel was obstructed directly by it, that business in general suffered and that many new businesses refrained from establishing there as a result of it. Hence the District Court was in error in concluding that there was no connection between discrimination and the movement of interstate commerce. The court's conclusion that such a connection is outside common experience flies in the face of stubborn fact.

It goes without saying that, viewed in isolation, the volume of food purchased by Ollie's Barbecue from sources supplied from out of state was insignificant when compared with the total foodstuffs moving in commerce. But, as our late Brother Jackson said for the Court in Wickard v. Filburn, 317 U.S. 111 (1942): "That appellee's own contribution to the demand for wheat may be trivial by itself is not enough to remove him from the scope of federal regulation where, as here, his contribution, taken together with that of many others similarly situated, is far from trivial.". . .

Article I, § 8, cl. 3, confers upon Congress the power "to regulate

Commerce . . . among the several States" and Clause 18 of the same Article grants it the power "to make all Laws which shall be necessary and proper for carrying into Execution the foregoing Powers. . . ." This grant, as we have pointed out in *Heart of Atlanta Motel* extends to those activities intrastate which so affect interstate commerce, or the exertion of the power of Congress over it, as to make regulation of them appropriate means to the attainment of a legitimate end, the effective execution of the granted power to regulate interstate commerce. . . . Much is said about a restaurant business being local but even if appellee's activity be local and though it may not be regarded as commerce, it may still, whatever its nature, be reached by Congress if it exerts a substantial economic effect on interstate commerce. . . . The activities that are beyond the reach of Congress are those which are completely within a particular State, which do not affect other States, and with which it is not neces-sary to interfere, for the purpose of executing some of the general powers of the government. . . .

Congress has determined for itself that refusals of service to Negroes have imposed burdens both upon the interstate flow of food and upon the movement of products generally. Of course, the mere fact that Congress has said when particular activity shall be deemed to affect commerce does not preclude further examination by this Court. But where we find that the legislators, in light of the facts and testimony before them, have a rational basis for finding a chosen regulatory scheme necessary to the protection of commerce, our investigation is at an end. . . .

The Civil Rights Act of 1964, as here applied, we find to be plainly appropriate in the resolution of what the Congress found to be a national commercial problem of the first magnitude. We find it in no violation of any express limitations of the Constitution and we therefore declare it valid.

Case Questions for Discussion

1. Why do you think Congress passed the Civil Rights Act of 1964? Do you think it was to regulate commerce, or to create sanctions against those who discriminate?

2. Do you think that interstate commerce was affected by the discriminatory practices of restaurants and hotels?

3. Do you think Congress should have the power to deal with matters such as discrimination? States have the power to deal with these types of matters. Why not just leave it to the states?

Contracts Clause

The general police power retained by the states (for health, safety, and welfare) is sufficiently broad to enable states to regulate business as well as many other aspects of ordinary life. There are restrictions on the states' power, however. Under the *Contracts Clause* of the U.S. Constitution, Article 1, section 10, the states may not pass laws that change any contractual obligations existing at the time the law was enacted. Although the Contracts Clause was once an effective curb on state power, today it will usually be found to be subordinate to the states' ability to regulate business through their general police powers.[17] If a state law is found to be merely a technical impairment of private contracts, the courts will uphold it, unless it is found to be unnecessary and unreasonable in light of a legitimate state interest.[18] For example, a state could probably pass a law requiring that all employers allow workers time off to attend parent-teacher conferences. Although existing employment contracts would, in effect, be altered to include the parent-teacher benefit, the law would likely survive a Contracts Clause challenge as a necessary and reasonable impairment in light of the legitimate state interest in educating children.

Negotiable Instruments

Effective commerce requires methods of payment other than cash. If all payments for goods or services could be made only in cash, imagine how difficult (and somewhat dangerous) it would be to pay monthly bills. Take $110.55 to the power company, take $37.03 to the water company, take $330.00 to the landlord, and take $256.50 to the bank that loaned you money to purchase a car. Instead of just sitting down and writing out several checks and putting them in the mail, you must make several trips to merchants and others on bill-paying day. Businesses, who often buy huge quantities of expensive items, would be even more inconvenienced. When it buys semiconductor chips, Dell Computer might need to find a way to deliver millions of dollars in cash to Intel. Merchants in medieval England faced similar problems, but instead of scrip, their *tender* was gold or silver. They developed *bills of exchange,* which ordered the holder of the maker's gold or silver to deliver the specified portion of the maker's precious metal to the bearer of the bill.[19]

Fortunately, cash substitutes (*commercial paper*) are available for everyday use. Articles 3 and 4 of the Uniform Commercial Code (UCC) regulate the use of commercial paper. Because the UCC has been adopted by nearly all states, the law from state to state is fairly uniform. Article 3 deals with negotiable instruments. In this section, we describe the most commonly used negotiable instruments and the legal requirements for negotiability. We also discuss the use of negotiable instruments and their legal effect.

Requirements of Negotiability

The most common forms of *negotiable instruments* are *checks, drafts,* and *notes.* Under the UCC, a negotiable instrument must be in writing, and it must be signed by the *maker* (the one undertaking to pay) or the *drawer* (the one giving an order to pay). The signing may be by signature or stamp. Ordinarily, a negotiable instrument is created by filling in the blanks on a preprinted form (e.g., a blank check), but it is not necessary. A perfectly fine negotiable instrument could be created with a pen and a piece of scrap paper.[20]

By the way it is written, the negotiable instrument must signify an unconditional promise to pay or an order to pay a fixed amount of money.[21] For instance, if you write a $100 check to your classmate Joe Brown, it must unequivocally order your bank to pay $100 to Joe Brown. Likewise, if you give Joe Brown a $100 note, it must state you will pay Joe Brown $100 on demand or on a certain date. Merely stating you owe Joe Brown $100 does not create a negotiable instrument, but only acknowledges the debt.[22] The fixed amount of money refers to the principal of a note. If a note includes interest, it must state a rate, or a formula for the rate if a variable interest rate is being charged. If the rate cannot be ascertained, then one would apply the judgment rate (the rate courts charge losing parties until they pay a judgment) that is in effect when the interest first accrues.[23]

The instrument must be payable on demand or at a specified time in the future. *Payable on demand* means the holder of the instrument may demand payment immediately. Instruments are payable on demand if they so state or if no date for payment is indicated. The purpose of the rule is to be able to determine with certainty when payment is due. An instrument that is payable upon the occurrence of a contingency is not negotiable.[24] Assume that your father gives you a check for $10,000, payable when you graduate from college. The check is not a negotiable instrument, because you may or may not graduate from college. That is, the check's payment is subject to a contingent event.

The instrument must be payable to *bearer* or to the order of a specified party. An instrument is considered payable to bearer if it is written to "bearer," or to "cash." For all negotiable instruments other than checks, use of the words "to the order of" or "to bearer" is mandatory for negotiability. The use of these specific words indicates the maker of the instrument intended the instrument to be negotiable. A check written to "Joe Brown" is an exception to the rule. When Article 3 of the UCC was revised in 1990, the drafters did not want check writers to be able to defeat negotiability by striking out the preprinted words on blank checks to the detriment of the payee.[25]

Effects of Negotiability

An instrument meeting the requirements for the negotiability that we have discussed may move through the economy as a money substitute. For example, if your mother writes a check to the order of you

(Jane Poorstudent) for $100, you may use it, if properly indorsed, to pay any $100 debt you may have.

Negotiable instruments are either order paper (made to the order of a specific person or entity) or bearer paper (to bearer or to cash). The check your mother wrote to the order of Jane Poorstudent for $100 is *order paper*. Order paper may be negotiated by transferring it to another person or entity after indorsement. Transfer alone may negotiate *bearer paper*. No indorsement is necessary. To negotiate the $100 check your mother wrote to you, you must indorse it and then transfer possession of the check to another person or entity.[26]

You may indorse the check in three ways. If you simply sign your name on the back of the check and give it to your landlord for your share of the rent, you have executed a *blank indorsement*. By blank indorsing the check, you transformed order paper to bearer paper. If instead of just signing your name when indorsing the check, you write, "Pay to the order of James Landlord, Jane Poorstudent," you have *specially indorsed* the instrument. The check remains order paper, and your landlord must indorse the check before negotiating it. You may also *restrictively indorse* the check. "For deposit only into account XXX, Jane Poorstudent" obligates the next holder of the check (typically your bank) to deposit the funds as directed. In all three of the indorsement scenarios, the indorser (you, Jane Poorstudent) is obligated on the instrument (liable to the transferee), if the check is not honored by your mother's bank. You may negate any liability by offering a *qualified indorsement*, such as "Jane Poorstudent, without recourse."[27]

Holders in Due Course

Once a negotiable instrument is negotiated (transferred for bearer paper or transferred and indorsed for order paper), the party to whom it was transferred is now the *holder* of the instrument. If that transferee is considered a *holder in due course*, the instrument is taken free of *personal defenses*. Personal defenses are claims to the instrument itself, and claims in recoupment of a third party or the maker.[28] Return to our example of the $100 check from your mother that you indorsed to your landlord to pay your rent. Further, assume that your mother (the maker) gives you the check to pay you for watering her plants while she is away. When she returns home, she finds you have not watered and, consequently, all her plants have died. She goes to the bank and stops payment. If your landlord is a holder in due course, once he accepts the check as payment, he is free from any liability to your mother.[29] A holder in due course of commercial paper is like a good faith purchaser of land or personal property. A good faith purchaser of real property is protected by the recording system against claims by third parties to the property. Although no recording system exists to protect a holder in due course of commercial paper, he or she is protected from ownership claims to the commercial paper itself, as well as against defenses to payment by third parties.[30] Holders in due course, however, are not insulated from *real defenses*. Real defenses include the following: forgery, fraud in the execution (e.g., the signer of a note thinking he was signing a receipt), material alteration of the instrument (e.g., changing the amount), discharge in bankruptcy (a holder in due course cannot expect payment of a note she purchased after the note was discharged in a bankruptcy proceeding), illegality if by statute the transaction is declared void, adjudicated mental incapacity, and extreme duress.[31]

To be a holder in due course, a person must be a holder. When the holder takes the instrument, it must not bear apparent evidence of forgery or alteration, or otherwise appear so irregular or incomplete that it appears to be less than authentic. The holder must also have paid value for the instrument, taken it in good faith, and taken it without notice of overdueness, dishonor, or an unauthorized signature or alteration. In addition, the holder must have taken the instrument without knowledge of any defense or claim in recoupment by any party.[32] One who accepts an instrument that is obviously altered or incomplete should not later be able to claim the holder in due course status. The condition of the instrument gives the transferee notice of a claim or defense.[33] Assume that your mother did not sign the $100 check she gave to you for watering her plants, but your landlord accepted it anyway as payment for the rent. Your landlord could not later claim holder in due course status after your mother's bank refused to honor the check. In effect, he lacks good faith. The landlord should have known something was wrong.

The holder gives value for the instrument when he or she exchanges something for the instrument, including security interests, other negotiable instruments, and irrevocable obligations to third parties. If the consideration given for the instrument is a promise to perform, value is considered to have been given only to the extent the promise has been performed.[34] Assume you enter into a contract with a cabinetmaker to build a workstation for your computer for $1,000. The cabinetmaker is in high demand and requires a 10 percent down payment. You indorse the $100 check from your mother and transfer it to the cabinetmaker for the down payment. He later discovers your mother stopped payment on the check. As long as he has not begun performing on the contract, he is not considered a holder in due course, because he did not give value (only a promise to perform). To take an instrument in good faith, the transferee must act with honesty in fact and observe reasonable commercial standards of fair dealing.[35] In general, good faith in accepting a negotiable instrument requires honesty, rather than a duty to act carefully.[36] Assume you accepted an instrument from a transferor for value and that you acted honestly. The fact that a careful person might have run a credit check before accepting the instrument should not endanger your status as a holder in due course under the good faith requirement. However, if the instrument you accepted from the transferor was a note payable to your transferor for $1,000, and she sold it to you for $50, you would probably not meet the good faith requirement. The situation is similar to one who purchases a Rolex watch for $100 from a street merchant. The gross disparity in value and price should put the purchaser on notice that either the watch is stolen or it is not a real Rolex. Something must be amiss if the transferor is willing to sell a note with a face value of $1,000 for $50.

For one to take a negotiable instrument without notice of overdueness, dishonor, an unauthorized signature, or alteration, the transferee must not have notice as defined in the UCC. Pursuant to UCC § 1-201(24), a person has notice when he has actual knowledge of a fact, he has received a notice or notification of the fact, or he has a reason to know of a fact from all the facts and circumstances known to him at the time of the transaction. That notice can be inferred from the instrument itself in some cases. For instance, if a check is more than 90 days old, an overdue notice may be inferred. Likewise, if a note is past due on its face, notice of overdueness may be inferred. Overdueness of a demand note may be inferred if an unreasonable amount of time has passed since its issuance. For example, if 10 years have passed since the issuance of a $1,000 demand note, it is likely the note is overdue. Notice of dishonor, unauthorized signature, alteration, ownership claims, defenses, and claims in recoupment are tested under the UCC § 1-201(24) definition, as well. Default, however, requires the transferee to have actual notice.[37]

Secured Transactions

A lender is more willing to advance a borrower funds if the borrower provides *collateral*. Collateral is an interest in, or a lien against, property owned by the borrower that the lender can look to for payment upon default by the borrower. Article 9 of the UCC governs *secured transactions* for personal property. In this section, we describe some of the common secured transactions entered into by most of us in everyday life.

Real property mortgages and vehicle loans are common forms of secured transactions. Real estate mortgages are not covered by the UCC, but a short description may be helpful. In most cases when people buy real estate, they must borrow a good deal of the purchase price. Under a conventional real estate loan, the lender advances up to 80 percent of the property's purchase price. The borrower then repays the borrowed funds over a long period of time, usually between 15 and 30 years. To protect the lender's investment, the borrower (*mortgagor*) gives the lender (*mortgagee*) a mortgage. At common law, when the mortgagor gave a mortgage to the mortgagee, he or she actually transferred title to the lender. After repayment of the loan, the lender transferred title to the property back to the borrower. In most jurisdictions today, title to the property remains with the borrower, but the mortgage is *recorded* as a *lien* against the real property. As a rule, real property, especially single-family homes, is widely regarded as good collateral. Real property does not move, and typically it retains its value or appreciates. State recording and mortgage statutes protect the interests of the lender and the borrower.

Personal property as collateral poses challenges that real property does not. First, most personal property can be moved. If a lender wants to sell the collateral to satisfy the loan, at times the collateral cannot be found. Second, most personal property, especially consumer goods such as automobiles and household appliances, depreciates in value. Under Article 9 of the UCC, a borrower with ownership rights in personal property may offer a lender a security interest in that personal property as collateral for a loan. To create a *security interest* in the lender, or in other words, for the lender to become a *secured creditor*, three elements must be present. First, the secured creditor must have possession of the property by agreement of the parties, or the borrower (*debtor*) must sign a *written security agreement* that describes the property to be secured. Second, the secured creditor must give value (usually the loan). Finally, the debtor (the borrower or the person offering the property as collateral—it can be someone other than the borrower) must have an interest in the property to be used as collateral. As long as the three elements are satisfied, the creditor's rights attach to the collateral giving the creditor an enforceable security interest.[38]

Once the security interest attaches, the secured party needs to perfect his or her interest in the collateral. *Perfection* is a means of protecting the secured creditor's interest in the collateral against claims by third parties. Assume you borrow $500 from a lender and offer a high-definition television with a value of $750 as collateral. Also assume that all three elements required for the security interest to attach have been satisfied. At this point, the lender has a security interest in the high-definition television. Assume that a month after you borrow the $500, another creditor gets a judgment for nonpayment of a $400 debt and attaches the only asset you own, the high-definition television. The television is worth only $750. If it is sold, who gets what? If the lender perfected his security interest, he will get all $500 you owe him. If not, he will not be paid in full.

Perfection can be accomplished in one of four ways. First, for debts secured by pledges of stock, negotiable instruments, and certificates of deposit, possession of the pledged security perfects the security interest.[39] For other collateral, such as farm products, inventory, business equipment, and documents of title (such as bills of lading, warehouse receipts, and chattel paper), perfection can be accomplished either by possession or by filing a *UCC financing statement*.[40] A UCC financing statement is a document that is filed with the county clerk, county recording office, or the state's secretary of state. It is a notice requirement. By filing a UCC financing statement with the proper public offi-

Figure 15.1   North Dakota UCC Financing Statement

UNIFORM COMMERCIAL CODE FINANCING STATEMENT STANDARD UCC-1/CNS-1
NORTH DAKOTA SECRETARY OF STATE/COUNTY RECORDERS
SFN 14009 (09-27-01)

PLEASE TYPE. Please read instructions on back before completing.

A. File In
☐ UCC Index   ☐ Farm Products Central Notice (CNS)

B. Customer Billing Number   C. Submitted By Facsimile   D. Transmitting Utility
                               FAX # ☐   ☐

E. Debtor's Exact Full Legal Name - do not abbreviate or combine names
If individual Last Name First   Individual ☐   Organization ☐   SSN or TIN

1. _____   _____

ADDRESS: _____

ADD'L INFO RE ORGANIZATION DEBTOR | TYPE OF ORGANIZATION | JURISDICTION OF ORGANIZATION | ORGANIZATIONAL ID #, if any
Individual ☐   Organization ☐ | | | ☐ NONE

2. _____   _____

ADDRESS: _____

Reserved for Filing Officer Use

ADD'L INFO RE ORGANIZATION DEBTOR | TYPE OF ORGANIZATION | JURISDICTION OF ORGANIZATION | ORGANIZATIONAL ID #, if any
 | | | ☐ NONE

F. SECURED PARTY NAME AND ADDRESS (from which security info is obtainable)   G. ASSIGNEE NAME AND ADDRESS (if any)

SSN/TIN: Telephone #   SSN/TIN: Telephone #

H. Check If Covered: I. This financing statement covers the following collateral: (If filing in Farm Products Central Notice, include a reasonable description of the property, including the county in which the property is located.)

☐ PROCEEDS

☐ PRODUCTS

━━━━━━━━━━ **FARM PRODUCTS CENTRAL NOTICE CNS-1** ━━━━━━━━━━

This FARM PRODUCT Central Notice filing is presented to the filing officer pursuant to NDCC 41-09-40. **Signature of Debtor and Secured Party required.**

J. COUNTY CODE	FARM PRODUCT CODE	DESCRIPTION (if applicable)	CROP YEAR (if applicable)	QUANTITY (if applicable)	COUNTY CODE	FARM PRODUCT CODE	DESCRIPTION (if applicable)	CROP YEAR (if applicable)	QUANTITY (if applicable)
1. —	—	—	—	2. —	—	—	—
3. —	—	—	—	4. —	—	—	—
5. —	—	—	—	6. —	—	—	—

K. Debtor Signature _____

By _____   By _____   By _____
Name & Title   Name & Title   Name & Title

Secured Party Signature _____   By _____
                                                       Name & Title

RETURN ACKNOWLEDGEMENT COPY TO: (name and address)

Please do not type outside of bracketed area

Available online at <http://www.state.nd.us/sec/pdf/14009.pdf>, as of December 31, 2002.

cial, all others are notified of the creditor's interest in the collateral. The financing statement must have the debtor's and creditor's name and address, be signed by the debtor, and have a description of the collateral.[41] The only method of perfecting a creditor's security interest in intangible property, such as accounts receivable, copyrights, trademarks, and goodwill, is by filing a UCC financing statement.[42]

Purchase money security interests in consumer goods are perfected by attachment. *Consumer goods* are items of personal property used in the household by the purchaser or the purchaser's family. A purchase money security interest attaches when a merchant sells consumer goods on credit, or a lender advances the funds to the consumer to purchase the consumer goods.[43] Motor vehicles, boats, trailers, motorcycles, and other vehicles that are titled under a state statute are not perfected under the purchase money security interest rule described above, even if the proceeds are used to purchase the titled vehicle. To perfect a security interest in a titled vehicle or trailer, the creditor must have the security interest entered on the vehicle's title.[44]

Employment Discrimination

The common law doctrine of *employment at will* evolved by the end of the nineteenth century in the United States. Under the doctrine, employment was at the will of the employer. Employers could choose to hire and fire as they saw fit. The doctrine grew out of a contract approach to the employment relationship that reflected the theory of economic individualism, which was popular during the Industrial Revolution. Any governmental regulation of the employment relationship was considered an unwarranted restriction on the freedom of contract. Employment at will remains today as the prevalent common law rule in most jurisdictions.[45] A few common law exceptions[46] have been carved out by the courts, but absent the discrimination statutes we discuss below, the general rule is that private sector employers may terminate their employees at will, unless employees are protected under a collectively bargained contract.[47]

The Federal Discrimination Statutes

There are three primary federal statutes that prohibit employment discrimination. The three statutes are *Title VII of the Civil Rights Act of 1964* (Title VII),[48] the *Age Discrimination in Employment Act of 1967* (ADEA),[49] and the *Americans With Disabilities Act of 1990* (ADA).[50] Taken together, the three statutes prohibit employment discrimination based on race, color, sex, national origin, religion, age, and disability. Be aware that there are many other statutes, at both the federal and state levels, that regulate aspects of employment and at times overlap the three primary federal discrimination statutes.[51]

Title VII. Title VII applies to employers, employment agencies, labor organizations, and state and local government agencies with 15 or more employees. It prohibits discrimination against employees in hiring or discharge, or regarding compensation, terms, conditions, or privileges of employment based on race, color, sex, national origin, or religion.[52]

Three types of employer behavior are actionable under Title VII. The first is *disparate treatment*, which is blatant discrimination against one of the protected groups. An employer refusing to hire or promote African Americans, women, or Muslims would be actionable as disparate treatment. A discriminatory motive must be proven for disparate treatment actions. The second type of actionable employer behavior is to employ policies that result in a *disparate impact*. This occurs when an employer uses a policy, test, rule, or selection criteria, which, although appearing to be neutral, has an adverse impact on a protected group. For instance, a requirement that all employees be at least six feet tall would probably exclude a disportionate percentage of women and Asians. The third type of prohibited employer behavior applies only to religion. The employer may not refuse to *reasonably accommodate* an employee's religious beliefs.[53]

There are exceptions or defenses available to employers. The *bona fide occupational qualification defense* can excuse disparate treatment violations. An employer could legitimately exclude men from consideration for a job as a women's locker room attendant. Race can never be a bona fide occupational qualification.[54] To prevail on the bona fide occupational qualification defense, the employer must show that all or substantially all of the excluded class cannot perform essential job functions. It is not enough to show that a substantially larger percentage of the excluded class may not perform the essential job functions. For instance, if a job requires physical strength, an employer may not exclude all females under the bona fide occupational qualification defense simply because substantially more females than males would not possess the physical strength necessary to perform the essential job function. A test of physical strength can be used to identify which applicants have the necessary strength.[55] The *business necessity defense* may be raised by an employer in a disparate impact action. An employer may legitimately require that successful applicants be college graduates, despite the discriminatory effects of the requirement, if the employer can prove a connection between job performance and a college education. Employers who make promotions and distribute job benefits based on a *fair seniority system*, such as one based on years of service, have a good defense against an action seeking the promotion of minorities ahead of nonminorities to correct past discriminatory practices as long as the employer has no present intent to discriminate.[56]

To gain access to the courts under Title VII, one must exhaust available administrative remedies. If there is a state or local antidiscrimination agency, a claim must be filed in a timely manner. The state or local agency has 60 days to resolve the complaint. After the 60-day period has expired, one must then file a claim with the *Equal Employment Opportunity Commission* (EEOC). The EEOC has 180 days to investigate the complaint. It can choose to dismiss the claim, to try and eliminate the problem, or to initiate court proceedings. If the EEOC initiates legal proceedings against the employer, the claimant may intervene. If the EEOC does not initiate proceedings, the claimant may obtain a *right to sue letter* 180 days after the claim is filed.[57]

Once in court, a plaintiff in a disparate treatment action can make out a prima facie case by proving the following elements: (1) the plaintiff is a member of a protected class; (2) the plaintiff applied and was qualified for a position; (3) the plaintiff was rejected by the employer; and (4) the employer continued to seek applicants for the position or filled the position with a person who is not a member of the protected class. Once the prima facie case is proven, the burden of proof shifts to the employer. To meet the burden of proof, the employer must then show a legitimate reason for not hiring the plaintiff. If the employer is able to show a legitimate reason, the burden shifts back to the plaintiff. The plaintiff can prevail by proving that the employer's legitimate reason was actually just a cover for a discriminatory intent.[58]

To prove a prima facie case, a plaintiff in a disparate impact action must only show there is a connection between the policy or selection practice in question and the discriminatory effect. Because a discriminatory intent is not required in a disparate impact action, the employer must be able to show the practice in question was a *business necessity* to avoid liability.[59]

Discrimination based on gender includes discrimination due to pregnancy and sexual harassment. Discrimination based on pregnancy is established only if similar restrictions are not imposed on employees in similar situations who are not pregnant. For example, it is not discriminatory to expect pregnant employees to perform at the same levels as employees who are not pregnant. It is, however, discriminatory to deny pregnant employees temporary leaves of absence, if other employees with disabling conditions are allowed to take temporary leaves of absence. Even employers with no leave policy must allow pregnant employees to take unpaid leaves of absence, if the refusal to do so would have an adverse impact on women.[60]

Two types of sexual harassment are actionable under Title VII: quid pro quo harassment and hostile environment harassment. *Quid pro quo* harassment occurs when promotions, raises, or other job benefits are offered in return for sexual favors. *Hostile environment* harassment occurs when an employee is exposed to sexual conduct or comments that the employee finds offensive. Two tests of "offensive" conduct or comments must be met. An objective test requires that the conduct or comments be offensive to a reasonable person. A subjective test requires the conduct or comments to be offensive to this plaintiff.[61] In quid pro quo actions, an employer held strictly liable for the actions of its managers and supervisors. Whether the employer had, or should have had, knowledge of the harassment is not relevant. In hostile environment actions, courts will usually hold employers liable only if they had knowledge, or should have had knowledge, of the harassment and failed to take remedial action.[62]

Sexual harassment in the workplace is actionable under Title VII of the Civil Rights Act of 1964.

Before 1998, it was unclear whether Title VII protected employees from same-sex sexual harassment. The Supreme Court resolved the issue in the following case.

Oncale v. Sundowner Offshore Services, Inc.
Supreme Court of the United States
523 U.S. 75 (1998)

OPINION BY: SCALIA: This case presents the question whether workplace harassment can violate Title VII's prohibition against "discrimination . . . because of . . . sex," 42 U.S.C. § 2000e-2(a)(1), when the harasser and the harassed employee are of the same sex.

The District Court having granted summary judgment for respondent, we must assume the facts to be as alleged by petitioner Joseph Oncale. The precise details are irrelevant to the legal point we must decide, and in the interest of both brevity and dignity we shall describe them only generally. In late October 1991, Oncale was working for respondent Sundowner Offshore Services on a Chevron U.S.A., Inc., oil platform in the Gulf of Mexico. He was employed as a roustabout on an eight-man crew which included respondents John Lyons, Danny Pippen, and Brandon Johnson. Lyons, the crane operator, and Pippen, the driller, had supervisory authority. On several occasions, Oncale was forcibly subjected to sex-related, humiliating actions against him by Lyons, Pippen and Johnson in the presence of the rest of the crew. Pippen and Lyons also physically assaulted Oncale in a sexual manner, and Lyons threatened him with rape.

Oncale's complaints to supervisory personnel produced no remedial action; in fact, the company's Safety Compliance Clerk, Valent Hohen, told Oncale that Lyons and Pippen "picked [on] him all the time too," and called him a name suggesting homosexuality. Oncale eventually quit—asking that his pink slip reflect that he "voluntarily left due to sexual harassment and verbal abuse." When asked at his deposition why he left Sundowner, Oncale stated "I felt that if I didn't leave my job, that I would be raped or forced to have sex."

Oncale filed a complaint against Sundowner in the United States District Court for the Eastern District of Louisiana, alleging that he was discriminated against in his employment because of his sex. Relying on the Fifth Circuit's decision in Garcia v. Elf Atochem North America, 28 F.3d 446, 451–452 (5th Cir. 1994), the district court held that "Mr. Oncale, a male, has no cause of action under Title VII for harassment by male co-workers." On appeal, a panel of the Fifth Circuit concluded that Garcia was binding Circuit precedent, and affirmed. . . . We granted certiorari. . . .

Title VII of the Civil Rights Act of 1964 provides, in relevant part, that "it shall be an unlawful employment practice for an employer . . . to discriminate against any individual with respect to his compensation, terms, conditions, or privileges of employment, because of such individual's race, color, religion, sex, or national origin. . . ." We have held that this not only covers terms and conditions in the narrow contractual sense, but evinces a congressional intent to strike at the entire spectrum of disparate treatment of men and women in employment. . . . When the workplace is permeated with discriminatory intimidation, ridicule, and insult

that is sufficiently severe or pervasive to alter the conditions of the victim's employment and create an abusive working environment, Title VII is violated. Harris v. Forklift Systems, Inc., 510 U.S. 17, 21, 126 L. Ed. 2d 295, 114 S. Ct. 367 (1993).

Title VII's prohibition of discrimination "because of . . . sex" protects men as well as women, and in the related context of racial discrimination in the workplace we have rejected any conclusive presumption that an employer will not discriminate against members of his own race. . . . In Johnson v. Transportation Agency, Santa Clara Cty., 480 U.S. 616, 94 L. Ed. 2d 615, 107 S. Ct. 1442 (1987), a male employee claimed that his employer discriminated against him because of his sex when it preferred a female employee for promotion. Although we ultimately rejected the claim on other grounds, we did not consider it significant that the supervisor who made that decision was also a man. . . . If our precedents leave any doubt on the question, we hold today that nothing in Title VII necessarily bars a claim of discrimination "because of . . . sex" merely because the plaintiff and the defendant (or the person charged with acting on behalf of the defendant) are of the same sex. . . .

Because we conclude that sex discrimination consisting of same-sex sexual harassment is actionable under Title VII, the judgment of the Court of Appeals for the Fifth Circuit is reversed, and the case is remanded for further proceedings consistent with this opinion.

Case Questions for Discussion

1. If Oncale had been a woman, would there be any question whether the harassment would have been actionable under Title VII?

2. Do you think Oncale was too sensitive? Should he have been able to "shrug off" his coworkers' sexual slurs?

3. Should men or women be required to alter the way they interact with fellow employees if a member of the opposite sex begins working with them?

4. Jan, a lesbian, worked as an attorney with a large law firm. Other women at the law firm, including her supervisor, Susan, suspected she was a lesbian. On several occasions, she overheard the other women calling her a "dyke" and other derogatory terms. Jan also felt that her supervisor held her sexual preference against her, resulting in poor performance ratings. Finally, Susan fired Jan. Susan cited Jan's inability to perform her duties in a satisfactory manner. Jan feels that she was fired because of her sexual preference. Does Jan have a cause of action under Title VII? See Ianetta v. Putnam Investments, Inc., 183 F. Supp. 2d 415 (D. Mass. 2002).

Although Title VII expressly states that the law requires no preferential treatment for any group based on prior imbalances, courts have allowed narrowly tailored *affirmative action plans* despite their adverse effect on members of majority groups.[63] Private employers may adopt affirmative action plans only when there is a conspicuous imbalance in a traditionally segregated job category. The imbalance must be a comparison of the minorities who hold jobs in the job classification with the minorities in the community who are qualified to do the job. The plan must be reasonable and remedial with the goal of achieving a balance with the community. A plan is unreasonable if it calls for the hiring of unqualified minorities over qualified nonminorities. It is also unreasonable for the plan to call for the layoff of nonminorities for the purpose of hiring minorities. In addition, it is also unreasonable to favor minorities during times of layoff to achieve balance. The plan must be temporary in nature, and it must terminate once the goal of balance is achieved. Affirmative action plans of public employers must survive a strict scrutiny standard.[64]

The Age Discrimination in Employment Act of 1967 (ADEA). The *ADEA* prohibits discrimination in the employment of persons who are at least 40 years old. At one time, there was an upper age limit of 70, but in 1987 Congress removed the upper limit.[65] Like Title VII, the ADEA regulates all aspects of the work environment: hirings, promotions, assignments, discharges, wages, and working conditions. The Equal Employment Opportunity Commission (EEOC) is responsible for enforcement of ADEA provisions. The ADEA was modeled on Title VII of the Civil Rights Act of 1964; therefore, much of the analysis is similar.[66] Our discussion centers on the differences between Title VII and the ADEA.

The ADEA covers all employers, labor unions, employment agencies, and state or local governmental agencies with at least 20 employees. The coverage is somewhat less comprehensive than Title VII, which only requires 15 or more employees.[67] Although the statute forbids discrimination because of "age," protection is afforded only to those employees who are at least 40 years old. Assume that an employer places an advertisement inviting applications from prospective employees between the ages of 25 and 35. The advertisement is a blatant violation of the ADEA. Assume that the same employer places an advertisement inviting applications from prospective employees who are at least 40 years old. In this scenario, the advertisement is not discriminatory under the ADEA, despite its obvious discriminatory nature. Because the employer is discriminating against an unprotected class of prospective employees, ADEA affords no protection.

Title VII, on the other hand, has been interpreted to protect against this type of reverse discrimination. For instance, whites have standing to bring race discrimination claims, and males have standing to bring sex discrimination claims.[68] It is not necessary, however, that the age discrimination occur between an employee in the protected class and an employee outside of the protected class. Assume an employer replaces a 59-year-old employee with a 25-year-old employee. This is a clear example of prohibited age discrimination because the employee suffering the discrimination is within the protected class and the employee who benefited is outside the protected class. It is also prohibited age discrimination, however, if the employer replaces the 59-year-old employee with a 42-year-old employee. The employee who suffered the discrimination is within the protected class. It is irrelevant that the employee who benefited is in the protected class as well, as long as the replacement employee was significantly younger than the employee who was replaced.[69] It is not clear, however, how far *in-class discrimination* can be extended. The U.S. Supreme Court, in *O'Connor v. Consolidated Coin Caterers Corp.* (1996), implied that a 44-year-old worker being replaced by a 42-year-old employee would not provide the necessary inference of discrimination required to establish a prima facie case of age discrimination.[70]

Disparate treatment and disparate impact actions may be brought under the ADEA. Employers may raise the bona fide occupational qualification defense in the same manner as under Title VII. Disparate impact actions, under the ADEA, are subject to the *factor other than age* defense, which is not available under Title VII. If an employer can prove that the adverse impact on older workers was created by a reasonable factor other than age, the resulting discriminatory effect does not violate the ADEA. Laying off the highest paid workers first to generate the largest cost savings is not actionable, although it may adversely affect the protected group of older workers. Paying higher wages to the newest employees for the purpose of attracting them to the business is not a violation of the law, although the policy may result in older workers being paid less than younger employees.[71]

The ADEA, unlike Title VII, also allows employers to follow the terms of a bona fide employee benefit plan, even if the plan adversely affects older employees, as long as the plan is not a subterfuge to evade the purposes of the Act. As such, if benefits are reduced because of age-related factors, as is the case with life insurance benefits under standard mortality tables, it is not a violation of the ADEA. The EEOC does not permit employers to require older employees to pay more for their benefits as they age, even if the cost of the benefits justifies such a charge. Employers may offer voluntary increased payments to allow older employees to maintain their benefits, however.[72]

The Americans With Disabilities Act of 1990 (ADA). Title I of the *ADA* forbids covered employers from discriminating against *qualified disabled individuals* because of their disability. The ADA covers the same employers as Title VII does. The procedural aspects of the ADA, and the employment situations in which discrimination is prohibited, also mirror Title VII provisions. To qualify as an individual with a disability, the individual must have a disability but be able to perform the essential work functions with or without a *reasonable accommodation.* Employers are required to make a reasonable accommodation only to assist *qualified individuals* with a disability. If accommodating the disabled person is an undue hardship on the employer, then no action on the part of the employer is required.[73]

To proceed under the ADA, complaining individuals must prove that they have a disability. An ADA disability includes physical or mental impairments that substantially limit one or more of an individual's major life activities. This determination is generally made on a case-by-case basis and may be difficult for a plaintiff to prove.[74] Whether an impairment is considered a disability under the ADA depends on the effect the impairment has on the life of the afflicted individual. The impairment must substantially limit one or more major life activities, such as eating, breathing, speaking, hearing, seeing, learning, working, performing manual tasks, walking, sitting, standing, lifting, reaching, and having sexual relations.[75]

Actions brought by two individuals with the same impairment may have dissimilar results under the ADA. Assume that John has cancer. If John's cancer has not affected his ability to perform all major life activities, or affected his ability only in a nonsignificant manner, he would not be considered disabled under the ADA. On the other hand, if Jill has cancer and is unable to walk very far, lift heavy objects, or even stand very long without becoming fatigued, she would probably be considered disabled under the ADA.

The EEOC has not identified any specific disabling physical impairments, but it has identified four disabling mental impairments: mental retardation, organic brain syndromes, emotional or mental illness, and specific learning disabilities.[76] Individuals with an enumerated disabling mental impairment are nonetheless required to show that the impairment limits one or more major life activities. In addition to actual physical or mental impairments, those with a record of having an impairment and those who are regarded as having an impairment are also protected.[77] This provision of the act extends the ban on discrimination to those individuals an employer believes to be disabled, whether they are or not.

Another relevant issue is whether one's disabling impairment should be measured with or without mitigating appliances or medication. The U.S. Supreme Court, in *Sutton v. United Airlines* (1999), held that two sisters, whose uncorrected vision was 20/200, or worse, should be evaluated with corrective lenses that improved their vision to 20/20. The *Sutton* court, however, indicated that side effects of available mitigating measures should be considered, and that the effectiveness of available mitigating measures may not be sufficient in all cases.[78]

Once plaintiffs have established that they are "disabled," they still face another hurdle. To be considered qualified individuals under the ADA, they must be qualified to perform the essential job functions, with or without reasonable accommodation. Those who cannot perform the essential job functions have no claim. An employer may set performance standards, minimum educational levels, experience requirements, and minimum skill levels, as long as those requirements are applied to all employees or applicants.[79] Assume an employer is advertising for a data processor. The primary duty of the position is inputting data from daily receipts into the employer's accounting information system. The employer requires that data processors be able to input 60 transactions per hour. Jim, who has disabling carpel tunnel syndrome, is unable to input more than 30 transactions per hour. Assume there is no reasonable accommodation that the employer could provide to allow Jim to meet the performance standard. In this case, Jim would not be a qualified individual under the ADA because he cannot perform the essential function of the job. An inability to perform a nonessential function of the job does not disqualify the individual. The determination of whether a function is essential is done on a case-by-case basis. Some of the factors considered include the following: the amount of time spent performing the function, the number of employees performing the function, whether the function is the reason the position exists, and how much of a disruption it would cause the employer if the function were assigned to someone else. For instance, a postal worker, who could not lift large sacks of mail, was found to be a qualified individual because the essential function of his job was sorting mail. Although lifting the large sacks of mail was a part of the job, it was a nonessential function. On the other hand, a building inspector who could not climb in exposed places was found not to be a qualified individual because climbing was an essential function of the job, although a majority of the inspection work did not require climbing.[80]

If the individual cannot perform an essential function of the job without accommodation, the issue becomes: Is there a reasonable accommodation the employer can make to allow the individual to perform the essential job function? A reasonable accommodation is one designed to remove barriers to equal access for the disabled person. The employer is not required to insure that the employee is successful. The barriers to be removed can be both physical and nonphysical. Examples of reasonable accommodations include wheelchair ramps, flexible working schedules, adjustments in the manner the work is to be performed, extra or alternative training methods, and alternative communication methods. In most situations, the employer is not required to anticipate the need for a reasonable accommodation. The disabled person should let the employer know what accommodations are needed.[81] Employers are not required to make an accommodation if it would cause an *undue burden*. But the employer has the burden of proving that an accommodation would cause an undue burden. Again, the determination is on a case-by-case basis.

The ADA standard for reasonable accommodation is more rigid than the *de minimus* cost standard used to measure accommodation of religious beliefs under Title VII.[82] Some of the factors to be considered are the nature and the cost of the accommodation, the size and resources of the employer, the type and operations of the employer, and any impact the accommodation would have on the employer's operations. Generally, modifications of work schedules are not considered undue burdens, unless the employer's operations require that all employees be present during certain times. The removal of physical barriers is not usually considered an undue burden. Hiring an assistant to help a blind or deaf person may be an unreasonable burden if the employer operates a business that has limited resources.[83]

Security Regulation

The United States is host to the largest accumulation of investment capital in the world. Stakes in publicly held companies change hands daily. Individual investors, mutual fund managers, corporate treasurers, money managers, trust fund managers, private and public endowment managers, and retirement fund managers all buy and sell on a daily basis stocks, bonds, notes, limited partnerships, and other investment vehicles. Decisions to buy or sell are based on the investor's need for cash, whether they think the business operations underlying the securities will generate profits, and whether they believe the price of the securities will be going up or down. Capital markets that operate in the United States and other financial centers around the world, simply could not function without reliable information. American capital markets vividly demonstrated how important reliable information is to investors in late 2001 and early 2002 when first Enron, a giant energy trading company, and then Global Crossing, a telecommunications giant, declared bankruptcy amid charges of management, accounting, and stock analyst misrepresentations. Suddenly, nervous investors worried that Enron and Global Crossing were not the only widely held companies that had reported more profits than they really had, or had much more exposure to debt than they had reported.[84] Those fears grew by the middle of 2002 as more listed companies announced restated earnings, including household names like Xerox, Adelphia Communications, and WorldCom. Merrill Lynch admitted that some of its stock analysts had overrated the securities of companies the financial services firm was trying to attract to its investment banking business. Even Martha Stewart, America's favorite homemaker, was alleged to be involved in an insider trading scheme. The Arthur Andersen Accounting firm (Enron's auditor) was convicted of obstruction of justice and its future was in doubt. At the time this book was going to press, Congress was considering criminal sanctions for corporate executives who were responsible for material financial reporting irregularities, and politicians were calling for more oversight for the accounting profession and more personal responsibility for corporate executives. The Securities and Exchange Commission (SEC), meanwhile, was ordering CEOs to swear that their recent financial reports were accurate. The securities markets in the United States continued to sag as each new revelation became public.

Before the great market crash of 1929, at the beginning of the Great Depression, security regulation was limited to state *blue-sky laws* that regulated sales of securities within the state. Called blue-sky laws because some of the promoters were said to be selling the blue sky itself, the original statute was passed in Kansas in 1911 after an energetic Kansas banking commissioner convinced the legislature that citizens, especially newly affluent farmers, were being swindled. The statute required those wanting to sell investments in Kansas to apply for a permit. Operating without a permit subjected the operator to fines and penalties. Once the Kansas statute was enacted, several other farm states enacted similar statutes, but states with big banks and investment houses resisted or adopted less stringent laws.[85] As a result, by the time of the 1929 stock market crash, state security regulation was at best a patchwork of uneven and poorly designed laws. Today, all 50 states have security registration laws, and 40 states have modeled their statutes on the Uniform Securities Act.[86]

Shortly after Franklin Roosevelt became President, the Securities Act of 1933 (*33 Act*)[87] became law. The 33 Act regulates the initial offering of securities by a company. The Securities Exchange Act of 1934 (*34 Act*)[88] created the SEC and regulates exchanges, brokers, dealers, and the companies that are traded on the exchanges.[89] While the 33 Act regulates the initial offering of a security, the 34 Act regulates subsequent

transfers of securities. The SEC has broad legislative (rule-making), executive (administering security laws and investigating violations), and
judicial (conducting administrative law hearings) powers. Both the 33
and 34 Acts have civil and criminal sanctions. The SEC may fine viola-
tors and issue cease and desist orders. This independent regulatory
agency also may petition the federal courts for injunctive and ancillary
relief, such as the disgorgement of profits. Criminal sanctions (prison
terms of up to five years under the 33 Act and 10 years under the 34 Act)
are prosecuted by the U.S. Justice Department.[90]

33 Act Offerings

The 33 Act is a disclosure law. The purpose of the registration process is to provide potential investors with sufficient reliable information to make an informed decision about purchasing a security.[91] The
SEC makes no effort to evaluate the worthiness of the security being
registered. In fact, as long as the information provided in the filings is
accurate, a worthless security could be registered and sold. Under the
33 Act, a registration statement must be filed with the SEC, and a prospectus must be furnished to all investors.[92]

There are three critical periods during the registration process. The
first is the *pre-filing period*. This is the time when the *issuer*, the company that will issue the securities, is preparing for the required filing.
Typically, during this period, the issuer, its accountants, and its attorneys are preparing the *registration statement*. The registration statement is a detailed document containing historical and current financial
information and other data prepared by the issuer. Negotiations with
underwriters are also conducted during this period. During the pre-filing period, the issuer and others associated with the anticipated filing
may publish only a notice stating that a prospective offering by the issuer will be made. Any other publicity will usually be construed as an
offer of an unregistered security.[93]

Once the registration statement has been filed, the *waiting period*
begins. The SEC has 20 days to act on a registration statement. During
the waiting period, offers to sell the securities may be made in person
and by telephone. In addition, offers may be made through a preliminary *prospectus*. A prospectus is the primary written offer to sell securities. It contains much of the same information as the registration statement and is the potential investors' means of evaluating the securities
to be sold. A *tombstone ad* may also be run during the waiting period.
Tombstone ads typically appear in financial publications (such as the
Wall Street Journal) and describe the security to be sold, the under-
writer, the price at which it will be sold, and other information. The
tombstone ad must state that it is not an offer to sell because no securities may be sold during the waiting period.[94]

Finally, after the SEC declares the registration of the securities effective, the *post-effective period* begins. During the post-effective period, the securities may be offered and sold, as long as all investors receive a final prospectus.[95]

Willful misrepresentation in the registration statement, the prospectus, or both carries criminal sanctions. Civil liability arises when the registration statement or the prospectus contains a material error, misrepresentation, or omission. Although the plaintiff does not need to prove negligence or reliance to prevail, the defendant may defend by showing due diligence (a reasonable investigation was conducted and there was no reason to believe that the representations in the filings or prospectus were false or misleading).[96]

34 Act Filings and Regulations

Issuers of securities must register their securities under the 34 Act in these cases: (1) if they have assets of more than $10,000,000, they have more than 500 holders of the securities, and the securities are traded in interstate commerce; or (2) if the securities are traded on a national exchange. A *34 Act registration statement* calls for much of the same information that must be included in a 33 Act filing. Issuers of 34 Act registered securities must file a Form 10-K once per year, a 10-Q each quarter, and an 8-K each month the issuer has a material event. A 10-K must include audited financial statements and other information, including management's discussion of the company's financial condition. A 10-Q contains much less information, and the summarized financial information is unaudited. An 8-K is required when the company revalues its assets, such as writing off a material receivable, or when it makes a major acquisition or disposition of assets, such as buying another company. An 8-K must also be filed if there is a change in the control of the company, such as someone purchasing enough shares (on the open market or from a major shareholder) to exercise control of the company.[97]

The 34 Act also regulates *insider trading*. The prohibition of insider trading is designed to protect common investors from being manipulated by those with access to information. Assume that the vice-president of a biotech firm learns that the company's researchers discovered a way to alter a human cell's genetics in a manner that will destroy cancer cells in the body. Obviously, this discovery will generate substantial revenues and profits for the company. The next day, before any announcement about the discovery is made, the vice-president goes into the market and buys 10,000 of the company's shares at $10, the current market price. Two weeks later, the company announces the discovery, and the shares go to $85 in two days. The vice-president sells the 10,000 shares she bought and gains $750,000. Because she had access to information not available to the general public, the vice-president will not be allowed to keep the profits and may be subject to criminal penalties and civil liability.

Under the 34 Act, there are two types of prohibited insider trading. First, under Section 16 of the Act, *corporate insiders* are prohibited from profiting from *short swing sales*. A short swing sale is the purchase and sale, or sale and purchase, of the company's securities within a six-month period.[98] A corporate insider is (1) one who owns at least 10 percent of a company's securities registered under the 34 Act, or (2) an officer or director of a company with a registered security under the 34 Act.[99] The Section 16 prohibition on short swing profits is a strict liability provision. Corporate insiders are prohibited from profiting from a short swing sale, whether or not they possess material information unavailable to the public.[100] Assume that the CEO of a company registered under the 34 Act buys 10,000 shares in her company for $50 per share on January 2, 20X0. In May of 20X0, the CEO purchases a new home, and sells the 10,000 shares of her company for $55 per share to pay the down payment on the new home. Although the CEO may have done nothing wrong, and she may have had legitimate investment and cash flow reasons for buying and selling the shares, under the short swing rule she must disgorge the profits of $5 per share. Had she waited until June 3, 20X0, to sell the shares, the short swing rule would not have applied to her transactions.

Insider trading can also be prosecuted under the general antifraud provisions of Section 10(b) and Rule 10(b)-5. One need not be an insider to fall prey to a 10(b)-5 prosecution. People can be prosecuted for insider trading under Rule 10(b)-5 if they are in possession of material information not available to the public and if they are considered a *tippee*. A tippee is one who receives information from an insider or one who misappropriates the information from his or her principal.[101] Return to our example about the genetic discovery. Assume that the vice-president, instead of buying company stock herself, tells her friend of the discovery. Her friend buys the company's stock before the discovery is announced and makes a large profit. The friend could be prosecuted under Rule 10(b)-5 as a tippee. The theory behind tippee liability is that insiders should not be able to profit indirectly when they are prohibited from profiting directly. Now, assume one of the scientists in our genetic discovery example purchased the company's stock, before news of the discovery was announced, and made a large profit. The scientist could be prosecuted under Rule 10(b)-5 as a tippee. The scientist misappropriated the information about the genetic discovery from his or her principal, the company. The following case is a recent example of the federal courts applying the misappropriation theory to punish those who profit from information before it is available on the street.

United States v. Falcone
United States Court of Appeals for the Second Circuit
257 F.3d 226 (2001)

OPINION BY: SOTOMAYOR:
Defendant Joseph Falcone appeals from a judgment of the United States District Court for the Eastern District of New York (Platt, J.) convicting him after a jury trial of thirteen counts of securities fraud, in violation of section 10(b) of the Securities Exchange Act of 1934, 15 U.S.C. § 78j(b) (section 10(b)), and one count of conspiracy to commit securities fraud, in violation of 18 U.S.C. § 371, based on the "misappropriation theory" of insider trading. . . .

Defendant's conviction arose from his participation in a scheme in which an employee of Hudson News, a magazine wholesaler, faxed a stockbroker acquaintance of defendant's, Larry Smath, pre-release confidential copies of a column in *Business Week* magazine "Inside Wall Street" that discussed companies and their stocks. *Business Week* is a weekly financial publication owned by McGraw-Hill, Inc. Smath himself used the information to trade securities and also passed the information along to defendant, who likewise traded in the securities discussed in the column.

Evidence was introduced at trial indicating that the value of stocks discussed favorably in the column tended to increase after the magazine was released to the public and that, because of this impact, *Business Week* imposed a strict confidentiality policy prior to that release on all those involved in the magazine's production and distribution. This policy applied to Hudson News and was implemented through a broader company policy, applicable to all the magazines Hudson News distributed, prohibiting employees from taking copies of the magazines or portions thereof out of the company's delivery department. . . .

On appeal, defendant argues that under the misappropriation theory as defined in United States v. O'Hagan, 521 U.S. 642 (1997), it is not sufficient for the purposes of section 10(b) liability that a misappropriation ultimately results in securities trading. Instead, he argues, the misappropriation in breach of a duty must itself have a certain nexus with securities trading that is lacking in the scenario at issue in United States v. Libera, 989 F.2d 596 (2nd Cir. 1993), and the instant case. Defendant further argues that even assuming *Libera* applies here, there was insufficient evidence to convict him of securities fraud or conspiracy to commit securities fraud. Although the first contention merits some discussion, we ultimately reject both arguments.

Section 10(b) of the Securities Exchange Act of 1934 is violated when: (1) any manipulative or deceptive device is used, (2) in connection with the purchase or sale of any security. 15 U.S.C. § 78j(b). Pursuant to this section, the Securities and Exchange Commission has adopted Rule 10b-5, which provides in relevant part that: It shall be unlawful for any person, directly or indirectly, by the use of any means or instrumentality of interstate commerce, or of the mails or of any facility of any national securities exchange, I. To employ any device, scheme, or artifice to defraud, [or] . . . (c) To engage in any act, practice, or course of business which operates or would operate as a fraud or deceit upon any person, in connection with the purchase or sale of any security. 17 C.F.R. § 240.10b-5.

Under traditional insider trading theory, section 10(b) is violated when a corporate insider, such as an officer of the corporation, trades in the securities of his corporation on the basis of material, nonpublic information. . . . Such trading constitutes deception under section 10(b) because a relationship of trust and confidence [exists] between the shareholders of a corporation and those insiders who have obtained confidential information by reason of their position with that corporation, and this relationship gives rise to "a duty to disclose [or to abstain from trading] because of the necessity of preventing a corporate insider from . . . taking unfair advantage of . . . uninformed . . . stockholders."

In Dirks v. SEC, 463 U.S. 646, (1983), the Supreme Court held that under the traditional theory, it is equally a section 10(b) violation if, under certain circumstances, the corporate officer does not actually trade but instead "tips" a corporate outsider (e.g., a friend or a family member) with the information for the purpose of having the outsider trade. In deciding *Dirks,* the first issue for the Supreme Court was what duty of disclosure, if any, a corporate outsider was subject to, such that his or her trading in violation of that duty would constitute deception under section 10(b). The Court emphasized that there was no general duty of disclosure between all those who invest in the stock market, . . . and that, unlike corporate officers, corporate outsiders have no relationship with

the corporation's shareholders from which any duty to disclose could arise. . . . While the Court ultimately determined that tippees could nevertheless still be in violation of section 10(b), it held that the circumstances under which that could occur were limited: [A] tippee assumes a fiduciary duty to the shareholders of a corporation not to trade on material nonpublic information only when the insider has breached his fiduciary duty to the shareholders by disclosing the information to the tippee and the tippee knows or should know that there has been a breach.

The second issue for the Court in *Dirks* was to determine when an insider's duty was breached where the insider had not himself or herself traded based on material nonpublic information but had simply given outsiders such information. In *Dirks,* the corporate insider had given the defendant, an officer of a securities broker-dealer, information that a massive fraud was occurring at the corporation, in an attempt to expose that fraud. . . . The defendant informed others of what he had been told and certain investors sold their securities in the corporation. The question was whether the insider's actions constituted a breach of the insider's fiduciary duty to shareholders because, notwithstanding the insider's benign motives, trading in the corporation's securities without disclosure had still resulted from his provision of information to the defendant. The Court held that no such breach had occurred. . . .

To constitute a violation of section 10(b), according to *Dirks,* the test is whether the insider personally will benefit, directly or indirectly, from his disclosure. Absent some personal gain, there has been no breach of duty to stockholders. And absent a breach by the insider, there is no derivative breach. Thus, the tippee could not be held liable for a federal securities fraud violation simply because he or she in fact traded in securities or helped others to trade in securities based on the material nonpublic information. Rather, the key factor was the tipper's intent in providing the information.

The Second Circuit was the first to recognize a different theory of insider trading: the misappropriation theory. . . . Under the misappropriation theory, a person violates Rule 10b-5 when he misappropriates material nonpublic information in breach of a fiduciary duty or similar relationship of trust and confidence and uses that information in a securities transaction. In contrast to [the traditional theory], the misappropriation theory does not require that the buyer or seller of securities be defrauded. Focusing on the language "fraud or deceit upon any person" (emphasis added), we have held that the predicate act of fraud may be perpetrated on the source of the nonpublic information, even though the source may be unaffiliated with the buyer or seller of securities.

Under this theory, this Court upheld the securities fraud convictions of a newspaper reporter, a former newspaper clerk, and a stockbroker who traded securities based on misappropriated information similar to the type of information at issue in this case: the timing and content of the Wall Street Journal's confidential schedule of columns of acknowledged influence in the securities market. United States v. Carpenter, 791 F.2d 1024, 1027 (2nd Cir. 1986). . . .

The main issue in *Libera* was whether, in order to find the tippees

liable under Section 10(b) pursuant to the misappropriation theory, the tipper must have known that his breach of a fiduciary obligation would lead to the tippee's trading on the misappropriated information. Under the traditional theory of insider trading, tippee liability was in fact premised on the intent of the tipper to provide the tippee with information that the tippee could use to make money in securities trading. . . . *Libera* held, however, that tippee liability under the misappropriation theory did not require this type of knowledge by the tipper, and that the tipper's knowledge that he or she was breaching a duty to the owner of confidential information suffices to establish the tipper's expectation that the breach will lead to some kind of a misuse of the information. . . . To allow a tippee to escape liability solely because the government cannot prove to a jury's satisfaction that the tipper knew exactly what misuse would result from the tipper's wrongdoing would not fulfill the purpose of the misappropriation theory, which is to protect property rights in information. Thus, *Libera* held that the only required elements for tippee liability were: (i) a breach by the tipper of a duty owed to the owner of the nonpublic information; and (ii) the tippee's knowledge that the tipper had breached the duty. . . .

As defined by the Supreme Court in *O'Hagan,* the misappropriation theory holds that a section 10(b) violation occurs when an individual misappropriates confidential information for securities trading purposes, in breach of a duty owed to the source of the information. Under *O'Hagan,* the "deception" requirement of section 10(b) is satisfied by the misappropriator's feigning fidelity to the source of [the confidential] information. According to the Court, company's confidential information . . . qualifies as property to which the company has a right of exclusive use and the undisclosed misappropriation of such information, in violation of a fiduciary duty . . . constitutes fraud akin to embezzlement—the fraudulent appropriation to one's own use of the money or goods entrusted to one's care by another. . . . Because the lawyer O'Hagan had breached the fiduciary duty he owed both to his law firm and to the firm's client to keep their information confidential and not appropriate such information to his own use, he had engaged in deception within the meaning of section 10(b).

The Court held that section 10(b)'s requirement that the deception be in connection with the purchase or sale of any security was satisfied because the fiduciary's fraud is consummated, not when the fiduciary gains the confidential information, but when, without disclosure to his principal, he uses the information to purchase or sell securities. The securities transaction and the breach of duty thus coincide. That is, O'Hagan legitimately possessed the information given his fiduciary relationship with the source of the information, and the misappropriation occurred only when he used that information to trade securities. . . .

While, as the district court in the instant case pointed out, the coincidence of a securities transaction and breach of duty—identified in *O'Hagan* as contributing to the satisfaction of the in connection with requirement—is not present where, as here, the misappropriator tips the information to an outsider but does not trade or have others trade on his or her behalf, the Supreme Court in *O'Hagan* did not purport to set forth the sole combination of factors necessary to establish the requisite connection in all contexts. Accordingly, this Circuit after *O'Hagan* has applied the misappropriation theory to schemes involving nontrading tippers, albeit without discussion of the in connection with requirement. . . . Application of *Libera* to the instant case is therefore not undermined by the lack of a trading tipper here, notwithstanding the intervening decision in *O'Hagan*. . . .

To support a conviction of the tippee defendant, the government was simply required to prove a breach by Salvage, the tipper, of a duty owed to the owner of the misappropriated information, and defendant's knowledge that the tipper had breached the duty. . . . Defendant argues that this case differs factually from *Libera* because no fiduciary duty existed here and, even if it did, he did not know that the information he was receiving from Salvage had been obtained in violation of that duty. We disagree.

Defendant claims that while the confidentiality of the "Inside Wall Street" column may have been clearly communicated to *Business Week*'s printer, . . . such confidentiality was not made sufficiently clear here to those further down the distribution chain—such as Hudson News. Thus, he claims, there was no fiduciary duty to be breached. . . . Sufficient evidence was introduced at trial, however, from which a reasonable jury could find that these elements were present here. The evidence indicated that periodically *Business Week* would ask Curtis, the distributor, to issue a policy statement to the wholesalers requesting that *Business Week* not be distributed before 5:00 p.m. on Thursday afternoon. Curtis understood and communicated to Hudson News that this policy was needed because there was highly confidential information in the "Inside Wall Street" column that *Business Week* had agreed not to make known to the general public before 5 p.m. on Thursday. . . .

Defendant also claims that he did not know the source of the information he received from Smath. How-

ever, as the district court noted, Smath testified that in fact he told defendant the details of the scheme. In addition, Smath testified that defendant paid him $200 for each column, substantially in excess of the magazine's sale price. The jury could therefore believe Smath rather than defendant in finding that defendant knew he was obtaining stolen information. For the reasons set forth above, we affirm defendant's convictions.

Case Questions for Discussion

1. How was Falcone able to profit from the information he received?
2. Was Falcone an insider? If not an insider, what was he?
3. Were Falcone and Smath connected with any of the companies they traded stock in?
4. Under *Dirks,* as long as the tipper (the insider) did not benefit personally from the material inside information, the tippee could not be held liable under Section 10(b). Do you think the Dirks approach is a good one? Why or why not?
5. In the instant case, who was the tipper? Did he trade on the material nonpublic information? Does that make a difference according to this court? Should it?
6. Suppose you found a copy of the faxed "Inside Wall Street" column the day before it went on sale. You read it and decide to buy some of the securities discussed favorably in the column. Would you be subject to a Section 10(b) prosecution?

Antitrust Law

As you may recall from history courses, the 1870s and 1880s were the time of the robber barons and the great trusts, including the oil, sugar, and rubber trusts. The business leaders of the time found they could control their markets by joining with their competitors in a trust arrangement. Typically, several large companies within an industry would transfer shares of their corporation into a trust. Because the trustees of one of these trusts controlled the vast majority of the means of production within a given industry, they were able to control prices and production levels. The trusts were also able to intimidate suppliers and companies in the product distribution channels. For instance, assume there is a steel trust in operation today. The steel trust controls 80 percent of all shares of U.S. Steel, Inland Steel, and Bethlehem Steel. One of the raw materials used in producing steel is coal. The steel trust routinely buys its coal from members of the Coal Association. The steel trust accounts for 40 percent of the Coal Association members' coal sales. Coal Association members also sell coal to two small independent steel manufacturers, who compete with the steel trust. By threatening to buy their coal from other coal producers, the steel trust could pressure the Coal Association members to refuse to sell coal to the independent steel producers. If the Coal Association members agree to the steel trust's demand, the independent steel producers may no longer be able to produce steel at a competitive price.

Congress responded in 1890 with the *Sherman Act*. The Sherman Act prohibited two kinds of anticompetitive business practices. First, it outlawed contracts, combinations, and conspiracies in restraint of trade or commerce. Second, it prohibited monopolies and attempts to monopolize.[102] The Sherman Act is a short piece of legislation, but it is still the backbone of federal antitrust legislation. Portions of Sections 1 and 2 are presented in Box 15.1.

Box 15.1   Portions of §§ 1 & 2 of Sherman Act of 1890, 15 USC §§ 1 & 2

Section 1—Every contract, combination in the form of trust or otherwise, or conspiracy, in restraint of trade or commerce among the several States, or with foreign nations, is declared to be illegal.

Section 2—Every person who shall monopolize, or attempt to monopolize, or combine or conspire with any other person or persons, to monopolize any part of the trade or commerce among the several States, or with foreign nations shall be guilty of a felony. . . .

Congress strengthened the antitrust prohibitions of the Sherman Act with the *Clayton* and the *Federal Trade Commission Acts of 1914*, and the *Robinson-Patman Act of 1936*. The Clayton Act added four types of conduct or activities that are illegal if they substantially lessen competition or tend to create monopoly power. The four types of conduct singled out in the Clayton Act are price discrimination, exclusionary practices, mergers, and interlocking directorates. The Federal Trade Commission Act established the *Federal Trade Commission,* which shares the responsibility of administering the federal antitrust laws with the Antitrust Division of the Department of Justice. It also added a catchall provision that prohibits all unfair methods of competition, and all unfair or deceptive acts or practices in, or affecting, commerce.[103] The Robinson-Patman Act prohibits predatory pricing practices for goods that are to be resold.[104] The antitrust laws provide criminal penalties for some violations and civil penalties for others, and they allow individuals or business entities who are injured as a result of illegal business practices to sue for triple damages. In addition, courts may use their injunctive powers to force those in violation to take corrective actions.[105]

Analysis of Allegations of Antitrust Violations

The courts use two approaches to analyze alleged antitrust violations: the *rule of reason* and the *per se treatment*. In some cases, an abbreviated version of the rule of reason may be employed. It is referred to as *quick look*.[106] Quick look analysis is used for activities that tend to have a negative effect on competition but do not rise to the level of a per se illegality. It is a middle ground that applies an abbreviated rule of reason analysis.[107] The rule of reason dates from a 1911 Supreme Court decision.[108] In 1997, Justice O'Connor described the first two tests in *State Oil Co. v. Kahn*.

Box 15.2   Excerpt From State Oil Co. v. Kahn
Supreme Court of the United States
522 U.S. 3, 10 (1997)

Although the Sherman Act, by its terms, prohibits every agreement "in restraint of trade," this Court has long recognized that Congress intended to outlaw only unreasonable restraints. As a consequence, most antitrust claims are analyzed under a "rule of reason," according to which the finder of fact must decide whether the questioned practice imposes an unreasonable restraint on competition, taking into account a variety of factors, including specific information about the relevant business, its condition before and after the restraint was imposed, and the restraint's history, nature, and effect. Some types of restraints, however, have such predictable and pernicious anticompetitive effect, and such limited potential for procompetitive benefit, that they are deemed unlawful per se. Per se treatment is appropriate "once experience with a particular kind of restraint enables the Court to predict with confidence that the rule of reason will condemn it."

Specific Activities

In this section, we discuss examples of business activities that often subject the businesses or individuals that engage in them to antitrust prosecutions.

Horizontal concerted efforts. *Horizontal concerted efforts* are agreements among competitors to control prices or to somehow share the market. If competitors agree to fix prices, it is a per se antitrust violation. The price-fixing need not be a specific agreement. If there have been contacts between competitors, and after the contacts the prices they charge move in unison, then an inference of an agreement could be found. The prohibition goes beyond an agreement on prices alone. Agreements on policies concerning terms of sale or discount policy, for example, may be considered agreements on prices, if those agreements affect the prices customers ultimately pay. Assume that automobile manufacturers agreed not to offer rebates or low-interest financing on new car sales for a one-year period. This agreement, although not specifically about price, would be considered horizontal price-fixing because not offering rebates or low-rate financing affects the ultimate price consumers must pay for new automobiles. The size of the business involved or the reasons for the agreement do not matter. Assume that there are two independently owned pharmacies in Collegetown. Both pharmacies mark up prescriptions they sell to between 50 and 75 percent. In other words, if they pay their suppliers $10 for 30 tablets of a prescription antacid, they charge their customers between $15 and $17.50. Then, Wal-Mart with a pharmacy is built on the edge of town. Assume that Wal-Mart marks up prescription drugs to an average of 40 percent. If the two independent pharmacy owners meet and agree to reduce their markups to 33 percent, they would be guilty of horizontal price-fixing. It does not matter that they are small, or that their intention was to meet competition from a competitor that is much larger and more powerful.[109]

Agreements among competitors to allocate the market or customers among themselves is a per se violation as well.[110] For instance, if the two independent pharmacy owners in our example agreed that one of them would fill all the prescriptions written by all the pediatricians in town and the other would fill all the prescriptions written by all other doctors in town, they would be guilty of horizontal allocation of the market.

Vertical actions that may restrain trade. Horizontal agreements are between competitors that are at the same level in the distribution chain. *Vertical actions* or agreements are between individuals or businesses on different levels of the distribution chain, such as sellers and producers. Because different levels of trade are involved in vertical restraints, courts tend to give them more deference. Vertical price-fixing has historically been treated by courts as a per se violation.[111] Assume that a golf shirt manufacturer begins producing a new high-quality shirt that the manufacturer wants to market to upscale consumers. To protect the reputation it plans to create in an advertising campaign, the manufacturer will sell the shirt only to retailers who agree not to sell the shirt for less than $85. The manufacturer and the retailers who comply would be guilty of per se illegal vertical price-fixing. Had the agreement established a maximum price for the shirt, the Supreme Court in a 1997 case decided that the per se analysis should be abandoned in favor of a rule of reason analysis. The Court raised the possibility that although a vertical maximum price agreement may reduce *intrabrand competition* (competition among retailers selling the shirt in our example), it might stimulate *interbrand competition* (the shirt in our example might be more competitive with other manufacturers' shirts).[112]

It is important to prove an agreement in a vertical price-fixing case. Manufacturers or wholesalers may "suggest" a retail price that downstream sellers may adhere to or not as they please.[113] Under the *Colgate doctrine*, manufacturers are also free to announce their retail price and refuse to deal with those who do not comply.[114]

Vertical restraints on distribution are sometimes legal and sometimes not. A manufacturer may validly assign exclusive territories to its dealers. For example, Ford Motors will sell new Fords only to the Ford dealers it has franchised. Part of that franchise agreement grants the franchisee an exclusive territory. If, however, Ford prohibited its franchisees to sell new Fords to customers who lived outside the franchisee's exclusive territory, it is likely that the agreement would be an antitrust violation. In theory, by limiting a Ford dealer's ability to sell outside of its exclusive territory, the agreement would dampen competition among Ford dealers and have an adverse effect on the public's ability to bargain for the best price. These types of agreements were once illegal per se, but since the Supreme Court's 1977 decision in *Continental T.V., Inc. v. GTE Sylvania, Inc.*, the rule of reason analysis must be applied. Prior to *GTE Sylvania*, analysis focused on the effect the agreement had on intrabrand competition. Now, as long as the party imposing the restriction does not have a large market share, the focus is on interbrand competition (new Fords versus other manufacturers' new cars).[115]

Tying agreements also expose parties to antitrust prosecutions. Tying agreements link the purchase of one good or service to the purchase of another good or service. Assume that Sony brings out a new video game that is a big hit. Retailers all over the country try to buy as many copies of the new game as possible. Sony, however, will sell the "hit" game only to retailers who agree to purchase two other Sony video games that are not popular. The Supreme Court laid out a four-part test for determining the illegality of a tying agreement in *U.S. Steel Corp. v. Fortner Enterprises, Inc.*: The agreement must involve two or more separate items; the tying product (the hit game) cannot be purchased unless the tied product(s) are purchased; the seller has sufficient market power in the tying product to restrain trade; and more than a substantial amount of commerce is affected by the seller's tying agreement.[116]

Monopolies

Section 2 of the Sherman Act prohibits *monopolization*, attempts to monopolize, or conspiracies to monopolize a line of commerce. As such, it is not unlawful to be a monopoly. The courts have interpreted Section 2 violations to require that the defendant be in possession of monopoly power, and that the defendant willfully acquired or maintained that power.

We offer only a brief sketch of antitrust structural offenses. The first step in an antitrust monopoly case is determining whether the defendant has monopoly power. Critical to that determination is the *relevant market*. For example, what is the relevant market for a steel manufacturer? If it is determined that the relevant market includes only steel, then it is more likely that a steel manufacturer has monopoly power than if the relevant market were determined to be all manufactured metals, including alloys and aluminum. As a general rule, the narrower the relevant market is defined, the more likely it is that a given defendant will possess monopoly power. Monopoly power is the power to control prices and exclude competitors. Generally, that power will be found if the defendant controls more than 50 percent of the relevant market. However, the individual circumstances of the relevant market must also be considered.[117]

Once it is determined a defendant has monopoly power, it must then be proven the defendant willfully acquired that power or willfully maintained that power. Although willfulness must be proven, an evil intent is not required. As a result, it is not unlawful to acquire monopoly power by offering the public a great product or because the defendant is a superior marketer of its product. It must be proved that the defendant took actions that were designed to acquire or maintain its market position. Examples include acquiring competitors, exclusive dealing agreements, and selling products below cost with the expectation of recouping losses after eliminating competition.[118]

Section 7 of the Clayton Act prohibits acquisitions that will likely result in a substantial lessening of competition or a tendency toward monopoly power in a relevant market. Horizontal mergers or acquisitions (two competitors) are more likely to be challenged than are vertical mergers and acquisitions (supplier and customer).[119]

The Debate Behind the Law

The antitrust laws are administered by two federal agencies, the Department of Justice and the Federal Trade Commission.[120] The federal courts interpret the antitrust laws and apply them to the facts of the cases that come before them. If those institutions are populated with officials and judges who do not agree with the theoretical underpinnings of the law, enforcement and interpretation of the law can significantly undermine the law's effectiveness. One of the basic tenets underlying the antitrust laws is that the concentration of economic power is not in the best interest of individual citizens. Once power is concentrated, those in possession of that power will inevitably increase prices to consumers and will exclude competitors. This basic idea was the prevalent view of economic and legal scholars from the 1930s through the 1960s, collectively referred to as the *Harvard School*. The Harvard School advocated that effective enforcement of the antitrust laws called for the government to stringently control predatory pricing policies.[121]

A competing economic theory, called the *Chicago School*, arose after John McGee's study of the 1911 Standard Oil breakup. McGee concluded there was no evidence that Standard Oil had employed illegal predatory pricing. Chicago School theory rejects the premise that concentration of economic power is, by definition, bad for the economy and society. In fact, the Chicago School argues that enforcement of the antitrust laws actually harms American competitiveness. Chicago School theorists argue that the concentration of economic power allows economies of scale and economic efficiency. They also argue that there is almost never a predatory pricing policy because, once competitors are eliminated or reduced, if the holders of economic power charge too much for a good or service, competitors will enter the market. In other words, Chicago School proponents would have us trust market forces to cure all evils. Chicago School theorists also argue that per se analysis of antitrust violations should be eliminated and that economic theory, unsupported by facts, should be employed in rule of reason analysis. During the Reagan administration (1980–1988), the president appointed many adherents of the Chicago School to the federal bench. Reagan's assistant attorney general for antitrust, William Baxter, a Chicago School devotee, dismissed the antitrust investigation of IBM in 1982.[122]

Chicago School theory won major victories in the U.S. Supreme Court, including Continental T.V., Inc. v. GTE Sylvania, Inc., 435 U.S. 35 (1977), and Matsushita Electric Industrial Co. v. Zenith Radio Corp., 475 U.S. 574 (1986). Some thought the Chicago School was doomed after the Supreme Court's decision in Eastman Kodak Co. v. Image Technical Services, 504 U.S. 451 (1992), wherein the Court rejected many of the Chicago School arguments that it embraced in *GTE Sylvania* and *Matsushita*.[123] Subsequent to *Eastman Kodak*, however, Chicago School theory arguments prevailed in Brooke Group LTD. v. Brown and Williamson Tobacco Corp., 509 U.S. 209 (1993), and State Oil Co. v. Kahn, 522 U.S. 3 (1997). The tug and pull between competing theories is likely to continue for some time in the future.

Other Examples of Governmental Regulation of Business

Other areas of government regulation or oversight of business operations are widespread and extensive. For example, in addition to its antitrust role, the Federal Trade Commission has an extensive consumer protection role. Under its consumer protection responsibilities, it administers the truth in lending laws, regulates product labeling (other than food and drugs), telemarketers, credit reporting, and many other business activities that affect consumers. The Food and Drug Administration regulates what must appear on food and drug labels, and it controls what drugs may be offered for sale in the United States.[124] The list of suggested additional readings found at the end of this chapter contains some sources of information on other significant governmental regulatory activities in connection with business.

Any student of the relationship between government and business must recognize that governmental regulation of business does not operate in a vacuum. Business organizations are legitimate participants in the political process. They hire lobbyists and make political contributions to protect their interests. Political appointees head most governmental regulatory agencies. The Microsoft antitrust action is an example of governmental regulatory policy being affected by the political process. Microsoft was aggressively pursued and prosecuted as a monopoly by the Democratic administration of Bill Clinton. After being found a monopoly, however, a settlement that left the company largely as it was before the prosecution was quickly agreed upon after the Republican administration of George W. Bush came into power. As is the case for legal policy in general, one's perspective often turns on whose ox is being gored.

Key Terms, Names, and Concepts

34 Act Registration Statement	Clayton Act of 1914
Affirmative action plan	Colgate Doctrine
Age Discrimination in Employment Act of 1967	Collateral
	Commerce Clause
Americans With Disabilities Act of 1990	Commercial paper
	Consumer goods
Bearer	Contracts Clause
Bearer paper	Corporate insiders
Bona fide occupational qualification defense	Debtor
	Disparate impact
Blank indorsement	Disparate treatment
Blue-Sky Laws	Draft
Bubble Act of 1720	Drawer
Business necessity defense	Employment at will
Check	Equal Employment Opportunity Commission
Chicago School	

Factor other than age defense

Fair seniority system

Federal preemption doctrine

Federal Trade Commission

Federal Trade Commission
Act of 1914

Harvard School

Holder

Holder in due course

Horizontal concerted efforts

Horizontal price fixing

Hostile environment
harassment

In-class discrimination

Insider trading

Interbrand competition

Intrabrand competition

Issuer of securities

Lien

Maker

Monopolization

Mortgagee

Mortgagor

Negotiable instruments

Note

Order paper

Payable on demand

Perfection

Personal defenses

Post-effective period

Plenary power

Pre-filing period

Prospectus

Purchase money security interests

Qualified disabled individual

Qualified indorsement

Quid pro quo harassment

Quick look

Reasonable accommodation

Real defenses

Registration statement

Relevant market

Restrictive indorsement

Right to sue letter

Robinson-Patman Act of 1936

Rule of reason

Secured creditor

Secured transactions

Securities Act of 1933

Securities Exchange Act
of 1934

Security interest

Sherman Antitrust Act
of 1890

Short swing sales

Special indorsement

Tippee

Title VII of the Civil Rights
Act of 1964

Tombstone ad

Tying agreements

UCC financing statement

Undue hardship

Vertical actions that may restrain trade

Vertical price-fixing

Waiting period

Written security agreement

Discussion Questions

1. John bought a bond with writing on it that says, *pay bearer* $1,000. John is unable to locate the bond, but he isn't worried because he has not indorsed the bond. Should he worry? Why or why not?

2. Jill has a $1,000 check from her mother that Jill is to use to pay her tuition. The check says, *Pay to the order of Jill Smith, $1,000.* Before leaving for classes, Jill indorses the check by signing her name on the back of the check, and she puts it in her backpack. After classes, Jill cannot find the check in her backpack. It must have fallen out sometime during the day when she was getting her books out of the backpack. Although Jill is angry at herself for losing the check, she is not worried. She figures she can just have her mother write her a substitute check. Should Jill be worried? Explain your answer.

3. Bill Badpay buys a new high-definition television from "Buy It Here, Pay Here," a local electronics dealer that self-finances most of electronic equipment it sells. The price of the television is $1,500, but Bill agrees to pay "Buy It Here, Pay Here" $100 per month for 24 months, because he wants to pay for the television over time. Two months later, Bill is short on cash. He applies for a $1,000 loan at "Bad Risk Credit." The loan officer agrees to loan Bill $1,000 if he can offer collateral worth at least $1,200. Bill offers the high-definition television that he bought two months ago. The loan officer agrees, and a UCC financing statement and note are prepared, listing the television as collateral on the loan. Bill signs the two documents and receives the $1,000. The next day, "Bad Risk Credit" files the UCC financing statement with the county clerk. If Bill pays neither of his two debts as he promised, between "Buy It Here, Pay Here" and "Bad Risk Credits," who may sell the television to satisfy the amount owed to them by Bill? Explain your answer.

4. John, a white 32-year-old man, worked for a railroad as a mechanic for eight years. John and his supervisor did not like each other. In fact, they argued several times about John missing work without cause. Finally, after six unexcused absences, John was terminated. Two years later, the railroad needed to hire several experienced mechanics. John applied for one of the positions. John's former supervisor conducted the interviews. John was not hired, but two other mechanics who were previously terminated by the railroad for drunkenness were rehired, and the seniority and vacation benefits they had accumulated during their previous employment with the railroad were restored. John feels he is being discriminated against by his former supervisor. As evidence, he notes that the company was rehiring "drunks," but had not rehired him. May John file a complaint under Title VII of the Civil Rights Act of 1964 for employment discrimination? Explain your answer.

5. Ann is a schoolteacher in Pennsylvania. She recently married a devout Muslim and converted to Islam. As part of her religious

beliefs, Ann is required to cover her head and body at all times in public. The public school at which she teaches refuses to allow her to teach while she is wearing religious "garb," pursuant to a state statute that prohibits any teacher in a public school to teach while wearing any "dress, mark, emblem, or insignia indicating the fact that such teacher is a member or adherent of any religious order, sect, or denomination." Ann sues the school district under Title VII of the Civil Rights Act of 1964. She alleges that the school district is discriminating against her based on religion, or in the alternative, that the school district refuses to reasonably accommodate her religious beliefs. Will she be successful? Explain your answer.

6. Tabitha tossed a Molotov cocktail into her estranged boyfriend's house that he owned and occupied as a personal residence. The house burned to the ground. She was convicted under a federal statute that made it a federal crime to "maliciously damage or destroy . . .by means of fire or an explosive, any building . . .used in interstate or foreign commerce or in any activity affecting interstate or foreign commerce." Tabitha appeals her conviction on the basis the federal government lacks the power to criminalize her actions under the cited statute. Will she win? Why or why not?

7. Sigmund is a psychiatrist. One of his patients, Ms. Rich, is the wife of a highly sought after corporate manager, who has a history of taking over failing companies and "turning them around" in a short period of time. During one of Dr. Sigmund's sessions with Ms. Rich, she complained that her husband had not often been at home because he was negotiating with Big Company to become its CEO. Big Company had fallen on hard times, and its stock, once priced at $75 per share, was selling for around $5 per share. After the session, Sigmund told his broker what Ms. Rich had told him. The broker suggested Sigmund buy 10,000 shares of Big Company for $5 per share. Sigmund bought the stock. Ten days later, Big Company announced Mr. Rich had agreed to become its CEO. The stock went to $8 per share on the announcement. Sigmund sold all 10,000 shares for $8 per share, netting a profit of $30,000. May Sigmund be prosecuted for insider trading under Section 10(b) of the Securities and Exchange Act of 1934? Explain your answer.

8. Three gasoline distributors have traditionally sold approximately 60 percent of all the gasoline sold on the wholesale market in Big Metro, an area where five million people reside. They distribute and sell their gasoline to affiliated retail gas stations. In the past year, however, a new distributor began operating in the area, and it has been successful in substantially increasing

the supply of gasoline available to independent gas station owners not affiliated with one of the other three distributors. The independent station owners have been able to sell gasoline to the public at lower prices than they had before. The retail gas station owners affiliated with the three established distributors are unhappy with their distributors because they have had to lower the prices at which they sell gasoline to the public, and this has resulted in lower profits. In reaction, the three established distributors offer to buy all the gasoline the independent distributor has available. The three established distributors plan to store the gasoline until their supply is diminished. The independent distributor agrees. May the independent gas station owners pursue an antitrust action? Explain your answer.

9. You may recall that in 2000 a federal court found that Microsoft was a monopoly. An initial recommendation of the federal judge was that the company be broken apart along functional lines. The proposal would have resulted in two or three companies being formed out of what is one company. After the election of George W. Bush as President, Microsoft was able to come to an agreement with the Department of Justice that left the company intact. Do you think Microsoft should have been broken up, or do you think the economy and the software industry is better off with Microsoft left intact? Give reasons for your answer, comparing the perspectives of the Harvard and Chicago schools of thought.

Suggested Additional Reading

Anbarci, Melanie A. "The Laidlaw Decision: Shield or Sword?" *Hastings West-Northwest Journal of Environmental Law and Policy* 7 (winter 2001): 143–153.

Bagenstos, Samuel R. "The Americans With Disabilities Act as Risk Regulation." *Colombia Law Review* 101 (October, 2001): 1479–1513.

Bailey, Henry J., III, and Richard B. Hagedorn. *Secured Transactions in a Nutshell.* 4th ed. St. Paul, MN: West, 2000.

Baxter, Maurice G. *The Steamboat Monopoly: Gibbons v. Ogden, 1824.* New York: Alfred A. Knopf, 1972.

Belton, Robert. *Remedies in Employment Discrimination Law.* New York: Aspen Publishing, 1999.

Benson, Jr., Paul R. *The Supreme Court and the Commerce Clause, 1937–1970.* New York: Dunellen, 1970.

Campbell-Mohn, Celia, Jan G. Laitos, and John S. Applegate. *The Regulation of Toxic Substances and Hazardous Wastes.* St. Paul, MN: West, 2000.

Cooper, Mark. "Perspectives on Antitrust Law: Antitrust as Consumer Protection in the New Economy: Lessons from the Microsoft Case." *Hastings Law Journal* 52 (April, 2001): 813–899.

Cortner, Richard C. *The Jones and Laughlin Case.* New York: Alfred A. Knopf, 1970.

Crandall, Thomas D., and Michael J. Herbert. *Secured Transactions: Problems, Materials, and Cases.* St. Paul, MN: West, 1999.

Dhooge, Lucien J. "The Revenge of the Trail Smelter: Environmental Regulation as Expropriation Pursuant to the North American Free Trade Agreement." *American Business Law Journal* 38 (spring 2001): 475–556.

Frankfurter, Felix. *The Commerce Power Under Marshall, Taney, and Waite.* Chapel Hill: University of North Carolina, 1937.

Gifford, Daniel J., and Leo J. Raskin. *Federal Antitrust Law: Cases and Materials.* Cincinnati, OH: Andersen Publishing, Inc., 1998.

Hazen, Thomas Lee. *Hornbook on Securities Regulation.* 3rd ed. St. Paul, MN: West, 1996.

Kessler, David. *A Question of Intent: A Great Battle With a Deadly Industry.* New York: Public Affairs, 2001.

Lauricella, A. "The Real 'Contract With America': The Original Intent of the Tenth Amendment and the Commerce Clause." *Albany Law Review* 60 (1997): 1377–1408.

Melone, Albert P. "Mendelson v. Wright: Understanding the Contract Clause." *Western Political Quarterly* 41 (December, 1988): 791–799.

——. "The Contract Clause and Supreme Court Decisonmaking: A Bicentennial Retrospective." *Midsouth Political Science Journal* 9 (1988): 41–63.

Merrill, Thomas W. "Toward a Principled Interpretation of the Commerce Clause." *Harvard Journal of Law and Public Policy* 22 (1998): 31–43.

Pierce, Richard J. *Economic Regulation: Cases and Materials.* Cincinnati, OH: Andersen Publishing, 1994.

Polse, Jennifer L. "III. Constitutional Law A. First Amendment 1. Indecent Speech a) Cable Television: United States v. Playboy Entertainment Group, Inc." *Berkeley Technology Law Journal* 16 (winter 2001): 347–365.

Rai, Arte K. "Fostering Cumulative Innovation in the Biopharmaceutical Industry: The Role of Patents and Antitrust." *Berkeley Technology Law Journal* 16 (spring 2001): 813–853.

Shelanski, Howard A., and J. Gregory Sidak. "Antitrust Divestiture in Network Industries." *Columbia Law Review* 101 (October, 2001): 1479–1513.

Endnotes

1. Kenneth W. Clarkson, et al., *West's Business Law,* 7th ed. (St. Paul, MN: West, 1998), p. 27.

2. Gerhard Rempel, "Course Lecture Notes on Mercantilism, Western New England College," available online at <http://mars.acnet.wnec.edu/~grempel/courses/wc2/lectures/mercantilism.html>, as of September 25, 2001.

3. *Microsoft Encarta Online Encyclopedia 2001*, "Hudson's Bay Company," available at <http://encarta.msn.com>, as of September 25, 2001.

4. Lois Loss and Joel Seligman, *Securities Regulation*, 3rd ed. (New York: Aspen Publishers, 1999), § 1-A.

5. J. W. Peltason, *Corwin & Peltason's Understanding the Constitution*, 14th ed. (Forth Worth, TX: Harcourt Brace, 1997), p. 84.

6. Ibid., p. 85.

7. Ibid.

8. South Carolina State Highway Dept. v. Barnwell Brothers, Inc., 303 U.S. 177 (1938).

9. Southern Pacific Co. v. Arizona, 325 U.S. 761 (1945).

10. Houston E. & W. Texas Ry. v. United States, 234 U.S. 342 (1914).

11. 258 U.S. at 516.

12. Albert P. Melone, "Commerce, Regulation of," *Encyclopedia of the Supreme Court*, Thomas T. Lewis and Richard L. Wilson, eds., (Pasadena, CA: Salem Press, 2001), p. 200.

13. 301 U.S. at 37.

14. Ibid., pp. 37–38.

15. See, Pacific Gas & Electric Co. v. State Energy Resources Conservation & Development Commission, 461 U.S. 190 (1983).

16. Melone, "Commerce, Regulation of," p. 202.

17. Jane P. Mallor, et al., *Business Law and the Regulatory Environment: Concepts and Cases*, 10th ed. (New York: Irwin/McGraw-Hill, 1998), p. 49.

18. Albert P. Melone, "Contracts Clause," *Encyclopedia of the Supreme Court*, Thomas T. Lewis and Richard L. Wilson, eds., (Pasadena, CA: Salem Press, 2001), pp. 238–239.

19. Clarkson, *West's Business Law*, p. 436.

20. Mallor, *Business Law and the Regulatory Environment: Concepts and Cases*, pp. 618–619, and UCC §§ 1–201 and 3–103.

21. Ibid., p. 620, & UCC § 3–104.

22. UCC § 3–103(9).

23. Mallor, *Business Law and the Regulatory Environment: Concepts and Cases*, p. 621, and UCC § 3–112.

24. Ibid., p. 622, and UCC §§ 3–104(a)(2), 108, and 113.

25. Ibid., pp. 622–623. To qualify for the exception, the check must meet all other requirements of negotiability plus the definition of a check in UCC § 3–104(c).

26. Ibid., pp. 633–635.

27. Ibid.

28. Ibid., p. 637.

29. Example based on Official Comment 23 to UCC § 3–302 (1990 Version).

30. *Negotiable Instruments Under the Uniform Commercial Code on the LEXIS Service* (Mathew Bender, 2001), § 11.01. (Hereinafter referred to as NIUCC).

31. Clarkson, *West's Business Law*, pp. 466–468.

32. NIUCC § 1C.40.

33. Official Comment 1 to UCC § 3–302 (1990 Version), cited in NIUCC § 1C.41.
34. NIUCC § 1C.43 and UCC § 3–303(a).
35. UCC § 3–103(a)(4).
36. NIUCC § 1C.44.
37. NIUCC § 1C.45.
38. UCC § 9–203 and Clarkson, *West's Business Law*, p. 521.
39. Clarkson, *West's Business Law*, p. 527, and UCC §§ 9–304 & 9–305.
40. Ibid., pp. 527–528, and UCC §§ 9–302, 304, & 305.
41. Ibid., pp. 524–526, and UCC § 9–401.
42. Ibid., p. 527, and UCC § 9–302.
43. Ibid., p. 528, and UCC § 9–302.
44. Ibid., p. 529, and UCC § 9–302.
45. Lex K. Larson, *Unjust Dismissal* (Newark, NJ: Mathew Bender, 2001), § 1.01.
46. The principal common law exception to the employment at will doctrine is the public policy exception. Under the public policy exception, an at will employee may not be terminated if the purpose of the termination is to frustrate a clear public policy. For example, an employee may not be terminated for refusing to perform an illegal act or for exercising a statutory right, such as filing a workmen's compensation claim. See, Mack A. Player, *Federal Law of Employment Discrimination in a Nutshell*, 4th ed. (St. Paul, MN: West, 1999), § I–1.03.
47. Larson, *Unjust Dismissal*, § 1.01. Most public sector employees and employees represented by labor unions have some protection against termination without cause.
48. 42 U.S.C. §§ 2000e–2000e-17.
49. 29 U.S.C. §§ 621–634.
50. 42 U.S.C. §§ 12102–12118.
51. For example, §§ 1983 and 1985 of the Reconstruction Statutes provide enforcement vehicles for the violation of employee's constitutional rights. The Federal Equal Pay Act of 1963 requires employees of both sexes to be paid on an equal basis for equal work. In addition, most states statutorily prohibit discrimination in employment. Lex K. Larson, *Larson on Employment Discrimination* (Newark, NJ: Mathew Bender, 2001), § 1.02.
52. Larson, *Unjust Dismissal*, § 11.02.
53. Larson, *Larson on Employment Discrimination*, § 1.09.
54. Clarkson, *West's Business Law*, p. 653.
55. Player, *Employment Discrimination in a Nutshell*, § IV-8.01.
56. Clarkson, *West's Business Law*, p. 653.
57. Larson, *Larson on Employment Discrimination*, § 3.07.
58. Clarkson, *West's Business Law*, p. 643.
59. Ibid., pp. 643–644.
60. Player, *Employment Discrimination in a Nutshell*, § VI-15.02.
61. Harris v. Forklift Systems, Inc., 510 U.S. 17 (1993), as discussed in Clarkson, *West's Business Law*, p. 646.
62. Clarkson, *West's Business Law*, pp. 645–647.
63. Johnson v. Transportation Agency, Santa Clara County, 480 U.S. 616 (1987).
64. Player, *Employment Discrimination in a Nutshell*, § IV-8.02.

65. There are some remnants of the upper-age limit remaining. Employees may still be subject to a mandatory retirement provision if they are nonfederal employees holding positions as executives or high-level policy makers, or if they have held the position for at least two years and are eligible to receive a pension benefit of at least $44,000. Also exempt are state and local firefighters and law enforcement officers, and federal law enforcement officers, firefighters, and air traffic controllers. Larson, *Larson on Employment Discrimination*, § 134.01.

66. Player, *Employment Discrimination in a Nutshell*, § VI-18.01.

67. Ibid.

68. Larson, *Larson on Employment Discrimination*, § 123.02.

69. O'Connor v. Consolidated Coin Caterers Corp., 517 U.S. 308 (1996).

70. Ibid.

71. Player, *Employment Discrimination in a Nutshell*, § VI-18.05. Davidson v. Board of Governors, State Colleges and Universities, 920 F.2d 441 (7th Cir. 1990).

72. Ibid., § VI-18.08.

73. Mallor, *Business Law and the Regulatory Environment: Concepts and Cases*, pp. 1119–1120.

74. Clarkson, *West's Business Law*, p. 650.

75. Johnathon R. Mook, *Americans With Disabilities Act: Employee Rights and Employer Obligations* (Newark NJ: Mathew Bender, 2001), § 3.02. Some of the life activities are identified in EEOC regulations (29 C.F.R. 1630.2), while others have been identified by the courts. The list is fluid.

76. Ibid.

77. Mallor, *Business Law and the Regulatory Environment: Concepts and Cases*, pp. 1119–1120.

78. 527 U.S. 471 (1999). The Court's directive to consider side effects, and the effectiveness of available mitigating measures, has led to some disabilities being measured without an available mitigating measure. For example, in Finical v. Collections Unlimited, 65 F. Supp. 2d 1032 (D. Ariz. 1999), the court assessed the plaintiff's deafness without a hearing aid that plaintiff did not wear because of annoying background noises. Mook, *Americans With Disabilities Act*, § 3.02.

79. Player, *Employment Discrimination in a Nutshell*, § VI-17.03.

80. Ibid. Gilbert v. Frank, 949 F. 2d 637(2nd Cir. 1991), and Chiari v. League City, 920 F. 2d 311 (5th Cir. 1991).

81. Mook, *Americans With Disabilities Act*, § 5.05, and Clarkson, *West's Business Law*, p. 650.

82. Mook, *Americans with Disabilities Act*, § 7.01.

83. Player, *Employment Discrimination in a Nutshell*, § VI-17.04.

84. Daniel McGinn, "The Ripple Effect," *Newsweek*, Feb. 18, 2002, pp. 29–32, and Jane Bryant Quinn, "How to Find Honest Stocks," *Newsweek* Feb. 18, 2002: 33.

85. Jonathan R. Macey and Geoffrey P. Miller, "Origin of the Blue Sky Laws," *Texas Law Review* 70 (Dec. 1991): 347–363.

86. Legal Information Institute, *Uniform Business and Financial Law Locater*, available online at <http://www.law.cornell.edu/uniform/vol7.htm>, as of November 26, 2001. The Uniform Securities Act was originally adopted by the National Conference of Commissioners on

Uniform State Laws in 1956. The original Uniform Act was replaced in 1985 with a new Uniform Act, which was amended in 1988.

87. 15 USC § 77.

88. 15 USC § 78.

89. Clarkson, *West's Business Law*, pp. 766–767 and 772.

90. Mallor, *Business Law and the Regulatory Environment: Concepts and Cases*, p. 919.

91. U.S. Securities and Exchange Commission, "The Laws That Govern the Securities Industry," available online at <http://www.sec.gov/about/laws.html>, as of November 27, 2001.

92. O. Lee Reed, et al., *The Legal and Regulatory Environment of Business*, 12th ed. (New York: McGraw-Hill Irwin, 2002), pp. 364–365.

93. Mallor, *Business Law and the Regulatory Environment: Concepts and Cases*, pp. 924–926.

94. Ibid.

95. Ibid.

96. Reed, *The Legal and Regulatory Environment of Business*, p. 365.

97. Mallor, *Business Law and the Regulatory Environment: Concepts and Cases*, pp. 939–940.

98. A. A. Sommer Jr., ed., *Federal Securities Exchange Act of 1934*, 2 vols. (Newark, NJ: Mathew Bender, 2001), 2: § 8.01.

99. Ibid., § 8.02.

100. Ibid., § 8.01.

101. Reed, *The Legal and Regulatory Environment of Business*, pp. 367–369.

102. Ibid., p. 376.

103. Clarkson, *West's Business Law*, pp. 847–851.

104. Reed, *The Legal and Regulatory Environment of Business*, p. 407.

105. Richard M. Steuer, "Executive Summary of the Antitrust Laws," (Copyright owned by Kaye, Scholer, Fierman, Hays & Handler, LLP: 1999), available on *FindLaw.com for Legal Professionals*, at <http://profs.lp.findlaw.com/antitrust/antitrust_1.html>, as of Feb. 18, 2002.

106. Reed, *The Legal and Regulatory Environment of Business*, p. 381, and California Dental Association v. Federal Trade Commission, 526 U.S. 756, 770–771 (1999).

107. Reed, *The Legal and Regulatory Environment of Business*, p. 382.

108. Standard Oil Co. v. United States, 221 U.S. 1 (1911).

109. Steuer, "Executive Summary of the Antitrust Laws."

110. Ibid.

111. Ibid.

112. State Oil Co. v. Kahn, 522 U.S. 3 (1997).

113. Steuer, "Executive Summary of the Antitrust Laws."

114. Reed, *The Legal and Regulatory Environment of Business*, p. 392.

115. Mallor, *Business Law and the Regulatory Environment: Concepts and Cases*, pp. 1051–1052, and 443 U.S. 26 (1977).

116. 429 U.S. 610 (1977), as discussed in Mallor, *Business Law and the Regulatory Environment: Concepts and Cases*, p. 1055.

117. Steuer, "Executive Summary of the Antitrust Laws."

118. Ibid.

119. Ibid.

120. Most states also have antitrust statutes. In addition, states' attorneys general may sue under the federal antitrust laws.

121. Graham Lea, "What the Heck Is . . . the Chicago School?" posted on *The Register,* Nov, 1999, available at <http://www.theregister.co.uk/content/archive/7986.html>, as of Feb. 20, 2002.

122. Ibid.

123. Ronald S. Katz and Janet Arnold, *"Eastman Kodak Co. v. ITS:* The Downfall of the Chicago School," available at <http://www.coudert.com/practice/kodakits.html>, available as of Feb. 20, 2002. Originally published in *The Computer Lawyer* (July 1992).

124. See the Palidan Legal Resources, *Federal Legal Resources* page at <http://www.palidan.com/federal.html> for entry into the pages of most Federal Departments and Agencies with responsibilities for regulating business and business relationships with various groups of consumers and citizens. Available as of November 30, 2001. ✦

Chapter 16

Taxation

Chapter Objectives

Students will be introduced to the statutory and regulatory schemes underlying the government's administration of the federal income tax. Students will gain an understanding of how federal income tax disputes move through the administrative and judicial systems. Students should gain a basic understanding of tax concepts, such as gross income, gross income exclusions, trade or business expenses, adjustments to gross income, itemized deductions, standard deductions, taxable income, tax credits, and tax rates. Readers must also understand how the choice of business entity could materially affect the amount of income tax a business and its owners must pay. Students need to understand how the federal income tax is used to influence taxpayer behavior and to stimulate or slow the economy. Finally, students will be familiar with how business, social, and other types of special interest groups influence tax policy.

Taxation is an area of law that touches Americans in everyday life, but it is also one of the most misunderstood and feared. Most people realize that their wages or earnings from a business are subject to taxation, because they see the amount of federal and state income tax withheld from their paychecks, or they are advised that they must make estimated income tax payments by their accountant. Whether people realize it or not, almost every trip to a convenience store, gas station, discount store, airline ticket counter, hotel, or sporting event is a taxable event as well. Just owning a piece of real estate (part of the American dream) subjects the owner to taxation by cities, counties, townships, school districts, park districts, fire districts, airports, and a myriad of other local taxing bodies. Even the final event in life, death, is a taxable event. A complete examination of taxation at the federal level alone is worthy of a master's degree or special law degree. In this chapter, we provide a basic understanding of federal income taxation. Be aware, however, that this brief look at the federal income taxation scheme will not make you a tax expert. You should gain enough knowledge to understand the complexity and pervasiveness of the federal income taxation system, and why a good tax advisor is a necessity for most gainfully employed Americans.

First, we discuss how the federal income tax is administered. Then, we explain the individual income tax. Finally, we briefly examine other business entities subject to the federal income tax, and pass-through entities. A word of caution for the reader: although this is not meant to be an accounting textbook, some numbers are necessary for illustrating how the tax system works. But we promise to keep the math simple.

Most Americans struggle with their federal tax return on an annual basis.

Federal Tax Authority

Unlike torts, property, and other areas of law that were initially inherited from the common law of England, the federal income tax has no common law heritage. It is an area of the law based entirely on federal statutes. All authority for the federal government to extract part of an American's income as a tax must be found in a federal statute, or it does not exist.[1] Federal tax law is found in Title 26 of the U.S. Code. Title 26 is commonly referred to as the Internal Revenue Code (IRC). Although an official citation to § 61 of the Internal Revenue Code is 26 U.S.C. § 61, it is generally referred to as IRC § 61.

The U.S. Constitution empowers the federal government to levy a tax on incomes. At one point in our history, the Constitution did not provide this power. Article 1, section 8, clause 1 of the Constitution does grant Congress the power to lay and collect taxes, duties, imposts, and excises. Section 2, clause 3, and section 9, clause 4, qualify that power, however, requiring that all *direct taxes* must be apportioned among the states and that all duties, imposts, and excises must be uniform among the states. The uniform qualification simply means that if the federal government lays an excise tax on a product, such as whiskey, the rate of the excise tax must be the same in all states. It would be unconstitutional for the excise tax to be $1 per gallon in New York and

$2 per gallon in all other states. The apportionment qualification proved to be a problem for an early version of the federal income tax.

A *direct tax* is a tax, such as a property tax or an income tax, that is collected from the one upon whom the tax is imposed. An *indirect tax,* such as a sales tax, is generally collected from a person or entity other than the one who pays it. Because an income tax is a direct tax, to pass constitutional muster before the ratification of the *Sixteenth Amendment,* it needed to be designed in a way that the revenue collected under the tax in a given state was in the same proportion to the total tax collected nationwide as that state's share of the nation's population.[2] For example, if 5 percent of the population lives in Florida, 5 percent of the total revenue collected under an income tax must come from Florida taxpayers. Such a taxation scheme would be nearly impossible to design and implement. In Pollock v. Farmer's Loan and Trust Company, 157 U.S. 429 (1895), the U.S. Supreme Court held that a tax on income from rental property was unconstitutional as a direct tax that was not apportioned. In reaction to the Court's decision in *Pollock,* the Sixteenth Amendment was adopted in 1913.

Box 16.1   The Sixteenth Amendment to the U.S. Constitution

The Congress shall have the power to lay and collect taxes on incomes, from whatever source derived, without apportionment among the several states, and without regard to any census or enumeration.

Administration of Tax Law

Congress must pass all laws relating to the imposition or collection of any federal tax. It is unusual for a year to go by with no amendments to the IRC. The Senate Finance Committee and the House Ways and Means Committee are the two principal congressional committees responsible for the income and other tax laws. Usually when the two houses of Congress pass a tax measure, they will differ in some respects. A joint committee on taxation is convened to work out the differences, and the revised bill is sent back to the individual houses of Congress for final passage. In most cases, all three committees issue committee reports that explain the reasoning behind the new provisions. They often contain examples that illustrate how the new provision should be implemented. These committee reports provide an invaluable aid to the serious tax student, practitioner, or attorney. The president must sign the new tax measure before it becomes law, unless there are enough votes in Congress to override a veto.

The executive branch, through the Treasury Department, administers the tax code. Treasury issues regulations that inform the public how IRC sections will be interpreted and applied by the Treasury and the *Internal Revenue Service* (IRS). All regulations that interpret income tax provisions begin with a 1, followed by a period. A typical *Treasury Regulation* appears as follows: *Treas. Reg. § 1.61-4*. The 1 indicates that the regulation concerns the income tax, the 61 indicates that the regulation is about IRC § 61, and the 4 indicates that the regulation is the fourth regulation issued under IRC § 61.

The IRS is under the jurisdiction of the Treasury Department. It is responsible for collecting taxes imposed by Congress. Auditing tax returns is part of the IRS's responsibility. An audit can result in *no proposed adjustment* (the IRS agrees the return was proper), a *proposed adjustment in tax due*, or a *proposed tax refund adjustment*. If the taxpayer agrees, the additional tax is paid or refunded, and the matter is settled. If not, administrative hearings are available. If the taxpayer and the IRS cannot agree on a resolution after the administrative process, then the matter may be litigated. As shown in Table 16.1, a taxpayer may choose one of four trial courts in which to litigate a federal tax matter. First, there is a special federal court that hears only tax cases, the *U.S. Tax Court*. The Tax Court has several judges that ride circuit, or in other words, they visit your district to hear cases locally. The *Small Claims Division of the U.S. Tax Court* may only hear matters involving $50,000 or less. The small claims division is less formal than other courts, so litigation costs are minimized, but there is no appeal available. The U.S. Tax Court can hear matters involving any sum. A big advantage of the U.S. Tax Court for taxpayers is that the amount in dispute does not have to be paid before litigation. Appeals from the Tax Court go to the U.S. Circuit Court of Appeals in which the taxpayer resides.

Taxpayers who pay the amount demanded by the IRS may choose to sue the government for money due them in either the U.S. District Court in the district where the taxpayer resides, or in the U.S. Court of

Table 16.1 Trial and Appellate Courts for Federal Tax Cases			
Trial Court	**Amount in Dispute & Must Taxpayer Remit Before Trial**	**Location of Trial Court**	**Location of U.S. Court of Appeals**
U.S. Tax Court-Small Claims Division	$50,000 or Less & No	In Home District	No Appeal
U.S. Tax Court	Any Amount & No	In Home District	Home Circuit
U.S. District Court	Any Amount & Yes	In Home District	Home Circuit
U.S. Court of Federal Claims	Any Amount & Yes	Washington, DC	Federal Circuit

Federal Claims in Washington, DC. Both have advantages. First, a jury trial is available in the U.S. District Courts. Jury trials are not available in the U.S. Tax Court or the U.S. Court of Federal Claims. The chief advantage of the U.S. Court of Federal Claims is the availability of appellate review by the Federal Circuit of the U.S. Court of Appeals. Federal trial courts are bound to follow the rulings of the Circuit Court to which appeals of their rulings are made. Although the U.S. Supreme Court is the court of final appeal in all tax cases arising out of the U.S. Courts of Appeals, the circuits are often split on issues. Astute forum shopping by the taxpayer may increase the chance of a successful outcome. Assume a professional football player living in Chicago did not report the value of a Superbowl ring given to him by his team after a championship season. The IRS maintains that the ring is a form of compensation, and the Seventh Circuit agrees. Although the Federal Circuit has not specifically ruled on Superbowl rings, it has held that a valuable painting given to a baseball player after pitching a perfect game was more in the nature of a trophy and not compensation. The football player is best advised to sue in the Federal Claims Court if the extra travel and other costs balance favorably against the amount of tax due.

Uses of the Federal Tax System

Although the federal income tax was originally designed to raise revenue for just the operation of the federal government, Congress and the executive branch soon realized this tax could help accomplish other governmental objectives. Economic policy is one. When federal income tax rates are reduced, taxpayers have more disposable income. As a result, they are encouraged to spend and save more. The increased spending tends to help the economy grow. Increased savings provide more capital for new business ventures or the expansion of existing businesses. Conversely, when the federal government increases tax rates, taxpayers have less money to spend or save. Lower spending tends to slow economic growth and may in fact trigger a recession. Consumers may react by spending money they previously saved and causing capital to shrink, which can result in higher capital costs and a slowdown in business expansion. Tax cuts and increases are blunt fiscal policy tools. Tax legislation often takes many months to get through Congress and become law. By the time a tax cut or increase becomes effective, the economy may have already changed directions on its own. Another problem with using the federal tax system as an economic tool is that once a new rate scheme is in place, it is politically difficult to reverse, especially tax cuts. An economically unneeded tax cut could cause the economy to expand too quickly, resulting in inflationary pressures. Inflationary pressures will usually prompt the Federal Reserve Bank to increase interest rates. Those higher interest rates tend to slow spending and business expansion. An unneeded tax increase could slow an economic recovery or cause the national economy to slip back into recession.

Federal tax law is also used to encourage taxpayers to make decisions in accordance with governmental policies. For example, taxpayers may make tax-free contributions to pension plans. This encourages taxpayers to save for their retirement and decrease the chance they will become economically dependent on the government once they become too old to work. Special tax breaks are offered to those involved in finding and developing oil and gas reserves, to businesses that hire economically depressed employees, and to businesses that increase spending on research and development. All of these tax incentives encourage business activities that are consistent with government policies. The tax code is also used to discourage business practices that are in disfavor. Examples include special penalty taxes on the receipt of *greenmail* and *golden parachute* payments,[3] and the nondeductibility of salary to corporate officers in excess of $1,000,000.

The tax system is also used to encourage activities deemed beneficial to society in general. To encourage taxpayers to support charitable organizations, the charitable contribution deduction is available. To help families provide care for children and disabled family members, a credit is provided. To make home ownership more affordable, a deduction for interest paid on home mortgages is available. To help individuals attend institutions of higher education, the hope scholarship and lifetime learning credits allow taxpayers to recoup some of the costs. And under the most overt social policy provision, the earned income credit, lower-income workers are provided a refundable credit that amounts to a "no strings attached" welfare payment to those working taxpayers who do not earn enough income to provide an adequate standard of living for themselves and their families.

Political Nature of Tax Legislation

Nothing brings out the lobbyists like major tax legislation working its way through the halls of Congress. Nearly every industry, major business, and special interest group has great interest in influencing the final legislation. A seemingly innocuous provision, hidden among hundred of pages of tax legislation, could prove to be a windfall for the industry or business it is intended to benefit. At times, provisions are added to tax legislation that are written so narrowly that only one company will be eligible for the benefit. Birnbaum and Murray's *Showdown at Gucci Gulch* is a fascinating account of the intense and often over-the-top big-money lobbying that took place during the consideration of the sweeping Tax Reform Act of 1986. Martha Brant reported another assault by the K Street lobbyists as newly elected George W. Bush's tax plan was being wheeled out to Congress in late winter 2001.

Box 16.2   An Excerpt From Martha Brant's 'Hot Time in Gucci Gulch'

The corporate tax lobbyists were all smiles and backslaps as they poured into the upscale Watergate Hotel a week ago Friday to meet with Larry Lindsey, the president's chief economic adviser. They were eyeing George Bush's tax proposal as if it were a medium-rare porterhouse. . . . Gucci Gulch, the Capitol corridors where well-shod lobbyists ply their trade, is always busy this time of year. But the Bush tax-cut package has the K Street crowd on overdrive. Lobbyist Charles Walker—a veteran of the Reagan tax battles—has come out of semiretirement to lead the charge for capital-gains tax cuts. And there are whole new categories of commerce eager for favors. The software industry thinks its products should be considered a depreciable asset. Amana and Whirlpool want extra credits for producing energy-efficient appliances.[4]

Arguments about the way tax rates are designed have spawned political camps. Those in favor of *flat tax rates,* such as Steve Forbes, advocate one tax rate for all income groups, with minimal deductions. They often advocate their plans by pointing out how simple it would be for everyone to file their return. A flat tax, however, is a *regressive tax*—one that taxes the income of those with lower incomes at higher rates than those with larger incomes. For example, assume there is a flat tax of 10 percent for all taxpayers and there are no deductions. Jill has an income of $30,000. As a result, Jill would pay $3,000 in income tax. Richie has an income of $200,000 and would pay a tax of $20,000. On its face it seems fair, but if we look at it in a slightly different manner, we might reach a different conclusion. Both Jill and Richie must have shelter, food, and clothing. They must get to work, pay for medical care, and pay for other necessities. Jill will pay much of her $30,000 of income just meeting her basic needs. Richie, on the other hand, will have a much larger portion of his income left after meeting his basic needs. Assume for our purposes that Jill must spend $20,000 to pay for her needs, and Richie (allowing him more luxury) spends $100,000. Their income

Nothing brings out lobbyists like tax legislation.

tax must be paid out of their remaining, or disposable, income. Jill pays a tax rate of 30 percent on her disposable income ($3,000/$10,000), while Richies's rate on his disposable income is only 20 percent ($20,000/$100,000). One of the major components of George W. Bush's tax plan in 2001 was an across the board cut in rates, which tended to make the *progressive* U.S. tax rates flatter. The following is a typical media report of the political bickering that Bush's tax cut spawned.

Box 16.3   An Excerpt From Fineman and Thomas's 'Snip, Snip, Snip'

A s tax plans go, Bush's is simple enough. It calls for reducing the five-bracket personal-income-tax structure to four: 10 percent, 15 percent, 25 percent and 33 percent. (The top rate now is 39.6 percent.). . . Drawing bottom lines is a partisan exercise. Bush says that the plan would save the average family of four some $1,600 in annual payments—enough, say, to pay for a semester's tuition at a community college. The proposal also is targeted to ease taxes on those just above the poverty line. But by Democratic reckoning, 43 percent of benefits (including the estate-tax repeal) flows to the wealthiest one percent of Americans. . . . [T]he congressional leadership is trotting out the old-time populism. Their favorite props are drawn from a Sen. Tom Daschle sound bite: a shiny new Lexus and homely muffler—said to approximate the differing value of tax cuts for a millionaire and a typical working person.[5]

Of course, the Democratic Party leader in the Senate, Tom Daschle, and other politicians aligned with him were correct. Across-the-board tax rate reductions provide large tax cuts to the very wealthy, because they have more dollars of income being taxed at lower rates. Daschle and his allied were doomed to fail, however. The tax cut opponents, casting themselves in the role of the fiscally responsible, charged that the Republicans were spending the surplus on the rich. The Republicans countered, however, that all they wanted to do was let taxpayers "keep their own money" and that the surplus did not belong to the government, it belonged to the people who earned it. The fight was over when the Republicans decided that the first stage of the tax rate reductions should be retroactive, and that all taxpayers who had paid tax in the year 2000 would get a tax rebate check that, in most cases, was $300 per taxpayer. In the face of an impending recession and pressure from taxpayers who wanted the rebate, the tax cut opponents yielded, after extracting some compromises. President Bush signed the Economic Growth and Tax Relief Reconciliation Act of 2001,[6] hereinafter referred to as EGTRRA, into law on June 7, 2001.

EGTRRA has some curious features. First, many of the tax reductions take place over a ten-year period, and many do not start for several years. The most curious feature, however, has to do with the temporary nature of the legislation. All provisions expire after December 31, 2010.[7] For example, the repeal of the estate tax is phased in over the next ten years. After December 31, 2010, however, the estate tax is back. The political nature of tax policy is so pervasive that Republican House leaders announced their intention to make the tax cuts permanent on the same day EGTRRA was signed into law by President Bush.[8] By the beginning of 2002, the House of Representatives had passed the Republican version of an economic stimulus package that would make many of the tax cuts from EGTRRA permanent. In addition, the plan would repeal the corporate alternative minimum tax retroactive to 1986. The repeal of the corporate alternative minimum tax would create refunds of approximately 25 billion dollars to U.S. corporations. Little action could be expected in the Democratic-controlled Senate, as each party was positioning itself for the 2002 election.[9]

The most regressive type of tax is one based on spending. National *consumption taxes* have been proposed in Congress.[10] A consumption tax is like a sales tax. Tax is imposed only when the taxpayer buys, or consumes, a good or service. Advocates of consumption taxes argue these measures will increase personal saving and investment, because individuals will avoid unnecessary spending to avoid paying the consumption tax. They also argue that a consumption tax allows taxpayers to control how much tax they pay. If they cut down on spending, they also cut down on their tax burden. Those arguments work, however, only for taxpayers who are able to spend less. Taxpayers who earn a modest income commonly spend nearly every dollar they make just to get by. Choosing to spend less is usually not an option. On the other hand, those who earn large incomes often do not spend all of their income. A consumption tax would allow them to avoid taxation by saving and investing more of their income. The end result of a consumption tax would be to subject the poor and lower-middle class to a tax on all, or nearly all, of their income, while the wealthy and upper-middle class would be taxed on only a part of their income. Most states have sales taxes, which are consumption taxes. Many states attempt to mitigate some of the regressive nature of these taxes by excluding purchases of food, medicines, and other basic necessities from the tax base.

People tend to gravitate to a tax regime based on how it will affect their pocketbook. If they will pay less tax under a regressive tax regime, they will tend to support it and allow the tax burden to fall on someone else. Progressive tax schemes are designed to approximate the tax burden with the ability to pay. Typically, progressive tax schemes have increasing tax rates for higher incomes. The U.S. Individual Tax system is a form of a progressive tax system, because high-income taxpayers pay higher rates on their marginal income (last dollar of income) than do lower-income tax payers. Yet, the U.S. system has become less progressive over the last four decades. As recently as the 1960s and 1970s, the top tax rate was 70 percent. As of December 31, 2001, the top U.S. rate was 39.1 percent. Progressive tax rates must be carefully balanced, however, for they can impede growth or cause a *wealth flight*. If a taxpayer can keep only thirty cents of each additional dollar earned, after paying tax, there is not much incentive to invest or to seek out additional sources of income. It is also possible that high-income taxpayers and capital sources may seek more tax-friendly sites to reside in, or for investment.[11]

Income Taxation of Individuals: The Tax Formula

All individuals earning gross income are subject to the personal income tax. The basic computation is shown in Table 16.2. The computation is relatively simple. We discuss each of the components of the tax computation in the following sections.

Table 16.2　Basic Tax Computation*		
Gross Income		XXXXXXXX
Less:	Adjustments for Adjusted Gross Income	(XXXXXX)
	Adjusted Gross Income	XXXXXXXX
Less: Greater of	(A) Itemized Deductions	
	OR	
	(B) Standard Deduction	(XXXX)
Less:	Personal & Dependency Exemptions	(XXXX)
Taxable Income		XXXXXX
Tax Before Credits		XXXXX
Less:	Tax Credits	(XXXX)
Tax Due		**XXXXXX**

*See Appendix III for 2002 and 2003 Tax Rate Schedules. Also included in Appendix III are 2002 and 2003 inflation-adjusted amounts for the standard deduction, personal and dependency exemptions, and relevant phase-out ranges.

Gross Income

IRC § 61 defines *gross income*. Congress chose ambiguous and open language and tracked the language of the Sixteenth Amendment. Gross income is defined as income. Without greater specificity, however, such a definition can be problematic. For example, an economist might include unrealized gains and losses in income, while an accountant would not.

Box 16.4   IRC Section 61 Gross Income Defined

(a) General definition—Except as otherwise provided in this subtitle, gross income means all income from whatever source derived, including (but not limited to) the following items:

(1) Compensation for services, including fees, commissions, fringe benefits, and similar items;

(2) Gross income derived from business;

(3) Gains derived from dealings in property;

(4) Interest;

(5) Rents;

(6) Royalties;

(7) Dividends;

(8) Alimony and separate maintenance payments;

(9) Annuities;

(10) Income from life insurance and endowment contracts;

(11) Pensions;

(12) Income from discharge of indebtedness;

(13) Distributive share of partnership gross income;

(14) Income in respect of a decedent; and

(15) Income from an interest in an estate or trust.

In 1955, in *Commissioner v. Glenshaw Glass Co.,* the Supreme Court provided some guidance when it laid out a three-part test for determining whether an item should be included as gross income, absent a statutory exclusion. The three part test is:

1. An undeniable accession of wealth;

2. Clear realization; and

3. Complete dominion.[12]

Under the first test, *undeniable accession of wealth,* an item will be included in gross income if the taxpayer's net wealth has increased. Net wealth is defined as assets less liabilities. For example, assume your net wealth is $8,000 (assets of $10,000 [a $10,000 car] less liabilities of $2000 [$2,000 car loan] = $8,000). You paint your neighbor's house, and she pays you $1,000. Your net wealth has increased by $1,000 to $9,000 (assets $11,000 less liabilities $2,000 = $9,000). Although you expended time and labor, they are not considered financial assets, and you incurred no additional liabilities. The only change is that now, in addition to your $10,000 car, you have $1,000 in cash, which is an additional asset. Now assume that instead of painting your neighbor's house, she simply loaned you $1,000 so you could pay your tuition. Now you fail the first test, because there is no increase in your net wealth. Your assets increased to $11,000, but your liabilities are now $3,000, and your net wealth remains $8,000.

The second test requires *realization*. Realization requires that the taxpayer receive, or has access to, the income. It also requires that any gain or loss be reduced to possession or not be subject to additional fluctuations in fair market value. Assume you work for the university and are paid the first day of each month. Assume you are owed $600 for the hours you worked in December. Did you realize the income you earned in December, as of the last day of December? The answer is no, because you did not receive the income or have access to it until January 1. The realization of the income you earned in December is deferred until January 1. Note that a few individuals, and most businesses of any size, use the accrual basis of accounting for federal income tax purposes. Under the accrual method, income is recognized when it is earned, not when it is reduced to cash. Now assume that your rich aunt gave you $1,000 when you graduated from high school. Following her advice, you invested the $1,000 by buying 1,000 shares of a dot.com company for $1 per share. Today, the stock you bought is selling for $20 per share. Do you have gross income? Your net wealth has increased by $19,000, so you pass the first test. The $19 per share gain on the shares you bought is called an unrealized gain, and as a result it will not be considered gross income until the stock is sold or otherwise disposed of. This makes a lot of sense. The gain at this point is a paper gain. Given the fortunes of the stock market, the gain could be reversed tomorrow. Therefore, until the stock is sold or otherwise disposed of, any gain or loss is temporary and should not be included in the tax base.

The third test, *complete dominion*, requires that the taxpayer receive the income with "no strings attached." The income item must be the exclusive property of the taxpayer and not subject to reversion. Recall your rich aunt, from our previous example above. Assume that she runs a large political consulting business, and she has a large contract that she will be starting the following summer. Just before the start of the fall semester of your senior year, she says to you:

> I need you to be ready to work on the big campaign I am launching next summer. The contract requires all consultants to have college

degrees. I will pay you $5,000 if you graduate by the end of the spring semester and come to work for me. I will pay the $5,000 now to help you pay the expenses of your senior year. If you do not graduate on time, or fail to come to work for me next summer, you must pay back the $5,000.

You accept her offer, and she pays you $5,000. When you received the $5,000, did you have gross income? The first two tests are passed. Your net wealth went up, and you have taken receipt of the $5,000. The third test is not passed, however. It is not certain the $5,000 is your money. There is a contingent liability attached to the money. If you fail to graduate or do not go to work for your aunt, you will owe her $5,000.

In general, due to the inclusive wording of IRC § 61, if an item of potential gross income passes the three *Glenshaw Glass* tests, it will be included in gross income, unless Congress has specifically excluded it in some other IRC section.

Gross income exclusions. For a variety of reasons, Congress has chosen not to subject certain types of income to taxation. Principal exclusions include life insurance proceeds, gifts and inheritances, scholarships, employer provided medical insurance, medical insurance benefits to the extent of medical costs, gain from the sale of a principal residence, other employee fringe benefits, social security benefits for taxpayers with limited incomes, and interest from municipal obligations.[13]

Life insurance proceeds paid as a result of the death of the insured are excludable under IRC § 101. The provision makes sense. The purpose of life insurance is to provide for those who depend upon the deceased for support, to pay final expenses, to pay educational expenses for surviving children, or to provide a method of financing the continuation of a business. Subjecting the proceeds to taxation could frustrate the good intentions of the deceased and may subject the survivors to an impoverished existence. The exclusion does not apply to proceeds paid to the beneficiary, as a result of valuable consideration paid for the insurance contract. In other words, a taxpayer cannot buy life insurance contracts from individual policyholders and then exclude the proceeds when the insured dies. A special provision allows terminally ill individuals to exclude life insurance proceeds paid before death, pursuant to a terminal illness payout clause, or pursuant to a sale of the contract to a viatical settlement company (a company that purchases life insurance contracts from the insured).[14]

Section 102 excludes the value of property (including money) acquired by "gift, bequest, devise, or inheritance" [*gifts and inheritances*]. On the one hand, this exclusion is somewhat baffling. What rationale can explain this potential windfall? What did the beneficiary of the largess do to not only acquire assets without laboring, risking capital, or giving other consideration, but to also receive them tax-free? There is another federal taxation scheme that taxes large gratuitous asset transfers (the unified transfer tax—commonly referred to as the gift and estate tax), but not all such transfers are taxable. On the other hand, the exclusion takes multitudes of common asset transfers out of the taxation computation. Imagine if all taxpayers had to declare the value of their Christmas, birthday, anniversary, graduation, wedding, and other gifts on their tax returns. It would be a bureaucratic nightmare. Due to the difficulty of differentiating, for tax purposes, between compensation and true gifts, after 1986 Congress denied gift treatment for all transfers from employers to employees.[15] Outside of the employer-employee relationship, however, because gifts and inheritances are tax free, a common tax strategy is to cast an asset transfer that might actually be in exchange for a service, another asset, or a promise as a gift. Differentiation is at times difficult. The Supreme Court in *Commissioner v. Duberstein* set out a test: "A gift . . . proceeds from a detached and disinterested generosity . . . out of affection, respect, admiration, charity or like impulses."[16] The determination of gift or income is a question for the trier of fact. Whether a transfer is a gift must be determined by reading the donor's mind. Did they intend to make a gratuitous transfer, or did the grantor expect something in return?

In the *Woody* and *Olk* cases that follow, the taxpayers claimed that the items they received were gifts and did not report them as income.

Woody v. United States
United States Court of Appeals for the Ninth Circuit
368 F.2d 668 (1966)

OPINION BY: JERTBERG: . . . Taxpayer Ronald Woody, appellant herein, and wife, both residents of Oregon, filed a joint income tax return for the year 1960. In that return, Woody reported as non-taxable gifts the strike benefits totaling $5,286.00 which he had received during 1960. The Commissioner determined that these benefits were properly taxable as income and asserted a deficiency of $736.84. Appellant paid the disputed tax with interest on July 30, 1963, and November 1, 1963. A timely claim for refund of the tax was filed on November 1, 1963, and rejected on February 18, 1964. The present action was filed in the

Federal District Court for the District of Oregon on November 24, 1964.

At all times relevant to this case, appellant was a member of Stereotypers and Electrotypers' International Union, Local No. 48, hereinafter referred to as Local 48. Appellant was a journeyman stereotyper employed by the Journal Publishing Company of Portland, Oregon, publishers of a newspaper known as the Journal. In 1959, there arose a labor dispute between the Union and the two daily Portland, Oregon newspapers, the Journal and the Oregonian. When negotiations broke down, the members of Local 48 voted to go out on strike. The strike was duly authorized by the Local Union and the International Union on November 3, 1959. Appellant voted in favor of the strike. The strike commenced on November 10, 1959, and affected about 600 employees of the two newspapers.

During the strike benefits were paid to the strikers through Local 48. Article XII, Sec. 14 of the Constitution of the International Union required the International's Executive Board to pay to the Local Union during the first eight weeks of an authorized strike an amount totaling $70 per week for each journeyman on strike and $47.50 per week for each apprentice on strike. After the initial eight-week period, such payments could be continued or terminated at the discretion of the Board. The Board made the required payments, which extended into the early part of 1960, and thereafter, the payments were continued as an exercise of the Board's discretion. Two other sources contributed to the strike fund from which Local 48 paid its strike benefits. The Pacific Slope Conference Mutual Aid Pact, otherwise known as the Pacific Slope Conference, a regional grouping of local unions in the Western States, organized primarily to provide a pool of funds for strikes and other emergencies, contributed a maximum of $15 per week for each striking journeyman, and $7.50 per week for each striking apprentice. In addition, contributions from other unions and individuals totaled a maximum of $15 per journeyman and $30 per apprentice. Thus, the total strike benefits from the three sources were $100 per week for each journeyman and $85 per week for each apprentice.

The pre-strike annual gross earnings of a journeyman were $6,569.20. The same pre-strike earnings for an apprentice were a minimum of $3,284.60 and a maximum of $5,912.28, depending on the number of years served. Recipients of the strike benefits totaled as many as 56 during 1960. But the number decreased as the strike wore on. In June 1962, the International Union and the Pacific Slope Conference terminated their contributions indefinitely. Local 48 continued its payments until 1963, when the International and Pacific Conference resumed theirs. But by November 1964, all strike benefit payments from any source had ceased.

To be eligible for these benefits, appellant had to do no more than be and remain on strike. He was required only to be a union member in good standing and to sign in daily at Strike Headquarters. He was not required to picket or solicit cancellation of subscriptions to the struck newspapers, although he did do this on a voluntary basis. If a striking union member secured other employment, his strike benefit pay was reduced one-fifth for each day he was otherwise employed, and anyone doing four days' work in any single week received no strike benefits for that week. . . .

Trial was had before a judge and jury. At the close of the evidence, the case was submitted to the jury on special interrogatories, three in number, each dealing with the payments received through Local 48 from one of the three sources: the International, the Conference, and other unions and individuals. The interrogatories were as follows:

I. Were the $70.00 per week payments contributed to plaintiffs, through Local No. 48, by the International Union, gifts, as that word has been defined to you?

II. Were the $15.00 per week payments contributed to plaintiffs, through Local No. 48, by Pacific Slope Conference, gifts, as that word has been defined to you?

III. Were the $15.00 per week payments contributed to plaintiffs, through Local No. 48, by other contributing unions and individuals, gifts, as that word has been defined to you?

The jury replied in the negative to the first two interrogatories and answered "No Verdict" on the third. On the basis of these replies, the District Judge dismissed appellant's refund claim pertaining to the sources in the first two interrogatories. As to the claim based on the third source, a mistrial was declared and the claim dismissed, without prejudice to appellant's right to file a motion to reinstate the claim. On this appeal, the appellant is not questioning the trial court's disposition of such claim.

The question of whether a monetary payment is a gift and therefore nontaxable for income tax purposes is basically an issue of fact. But the question here remains basically one of fact for determination on a case-by-case basis. Commissioner v. Duberstein, 363 U.S. 278 (1960). In *Duberstein,* the Court made quite plain, after a full airing of the difficulties involved, that this issue was to be committed to the trier of fact. . . .

Accordingly, this court is confined to the normal strictures of appellate review of the fact-finder's determinations. Where a jury has tried the matter upon correct instructions, the only inquiry is whether it cannot be said that reasonable men could reach differing conclusions on the issue. . . .

These principles were applied by the Court in a case handed down the same day as *Duberstein,* involving strike benefits paid by a union to a striking nonmember. In that case, the jury had determined that the benefits, in the form of redeemable food vouchers and payment of the non-member's room rent, were gifts. United States v. Kaiser, 363 U.S. 299 (1960). The Court carefully limited its review to a determination of whether the jury's verdict had reasonable support in the record. . . .

On our review of the record in this case, we are of the opinion that there is sufficient evidence to support the jury's negative answers to the interrogatories. Perhaps the strongest, though of course not conclusive, support is the fact that the union made no inquiry into the personal financial situations and needs of its individual striking members. As appellant points out, the union's officers may well have been aware of financial hardship in appellant's case. But this awareness was not determinative of the amount appellant received as strike benefits. One of the "Admitted Facts" in the Pretrial Order makes this clear: The amount of the strike benefit depended on the classification of the particular member as a journeyman, probationary journeyman or apprentice. The amount of the strike benefit was not affected by his marital status, number of dependents or financial condition. There was no obligation to submit a questionnaire relating to actual need of the recipient. Analogies to or distinctions from the factual situation in *Kaiser* are not helpful. The facts of that case were not determinative of the issue before the Supreme Court, contrary to appellant's suggestion. That Court had decisively rejected the invitation to find gift or income as a matter of law on the facts of that case. The Court in *Kaiser* was reviewing the evidence only to determine whether it was sufficient to support the outcome, not whether it compelled the outcome. Therefore, we are not bound by the facts in *Kaiser* except insofar as the issue raised by the facts in both cases confines our review to the sufficiency of the evidence.

Whether job classification was the sole criteria for determining the amount of the benefit is beyond the scope of our inquiry. We cannot know the grounds on which the jury ultimately based its findings. It is enough for an appellate court that a reasonable basis exists in the record for the finding. The same may be said of the dispute in this case over the motives of the donors of the strike benefits. The evidence provided reasonable grounds for several motives. But it is not for us to say that one motive is more reasonably supported than another, so long as the "non-gift" motivation inferred by the jury has reasonable support. "It was for the triers of the facts to seek among competing aims or motives the ones that dominated conduct. Perhaps, if such a function had been ours, we would have drawn the inference favoring a gift. That is not enough. If there was opportunity for opposing inferences, the judgment of the Board [i. e. Tax Court, acting as fact-finder in this case] controls." Bogardus v. Commissioner, 302 U.S. 34 (1937) (dissenting opinion).

The jury could reasonably infer that these payments were not gifts because the amount was not determined according to personal financial need; rather, it depended upon the type of job and the number of years of service. . . .

The second instruction to which appellant objects is as follows: If you find that the payments were made as a form of compensation in order to enable and encourage the plaintiff Mr. Woody and others on strike to continue the strike, then you cannot find that the payments were gifts. This instruction also focuses on the intention of the donor. It properly injects the element from *Kaiser* of whether the payments were "a recompense for striking. . . ." Moreover, it is in conformity with a recent decision of the Tax Court, in which the judge, sitting as a trier of fact, stated: ". . . we are convinced that the motivating force behind the payments here involved proceeded from the anticipation of economic benefit both to the local guild and to the petitioner. Through the force and power of a strike the local guild intended to benefit its members by securing additional job security. Strike benefits were paid to members of the local guild, including petitioner, to enable them to continue with the strike so that the aims of the [American Newspaper Guild] could be accomplished. In our opinion, this does not amount to a gift." John N. Hagar, 43 T.C. 468, 485 (1965).

The third instruction to which appellant objects is as follows: The fact that either the union or its members might regard the payments as gifts is not in and of itself determinative. The expectations or the hopes of Mr. Woody, the union or its members as to the income tax consequences or treatment of the payments have nothing to do with whether the payments were gifts.

This instruction was fully in accord with the law. While the intent of the donor, rather than the donee, is the important factor, the label which the donor attaches to his payment is not conclusive. The Court makes this clear in *Duberstein*: "Moreover, the *Bogardus* case itself makes it plain that the donor's characterization of his action is not determinative—that there must be an objective inquiry as to whether what is called a gift amounts to it in reality. . . . It scarcely needs adding that the parties' expectations or hopes as to the tax treatment of their conduct in themselves have nothing to do with the matter." The instruction on this matter was proper. The judgment of the District Court must be and is affirmed.

Case Questions for Discussion

1. If Woody had been a nonunion member who was out of work as a result of the strike, would payment of strike benefits by the union have been a gift?

2. Assume that Woody was given food and had his electric bill paid by the union because he was destitute. Would that have been a gift? Would the case be stronger if Woody had been the only union member to receive such benefits?

3. If the jury had decided that the payments were gifts, would the appellate court have reversed upon a government appeal?

Olk v. United States
United States Court of Appeals for the Ninth Circuit
536 F.2d 876 (1976)

OPINION BY: SNEED: This is a suit to obtain a refund of federal income taxes. The issue is whether monies, called "tokes" in the relevant trade, received by the taxpayer, a craps dealer employed by Las Vegas casinos, constitute taxable income or gifts within the meaning of section 102(a), INT. REV. CODE of 1954. The taxpayer insists tokes are non-taxable gifts. If he is right, he is entitled to the refund for which this suit was brought. The trial court in a trial without a jury held that tokes were gifts. The Government appealed and we reverse and hold that tokes are taxable income.

There is no dispute about the basic facts which explain the setting in which tokes are paid and received. The district court's finding with respect to such facts which we accept are, in part, as follows: In 1971 plaintiff was employed as a craps dealer in two Las Vegas gambling casinos, the Horseshoe Club and the Sahara Hotel. The basic services performed by plaintiff and other dealers were described at trial. There are four persons involved in the operation of the game, a boxman and three dealers. One of the three dealers, the stickman, calls the roll of the dice and then collects them for the next shooter.

The other two dealers collect losing bets and pay off winning bets under the supervision of the boxman. The boxman is the casino employee charged with direct supervision of the dealers and the play at one particular table. He in turn is supervised by the pit boss who is responsible for several tables. The dealers also make change, advise the boxman when a player would like a drink and answer basic questions about the game for the players.

Dealers are forbidden to fraternize or engage in unnecessary conversation with the casino patrons, and must remain in separate areas while on their breaks. Dealers must treat all patrons equally, and any attempt to provide special service to a patron is grounds for termination. At times, players will give money to the dealers or place bets for them. The witnesses testified that most casinos do not allow boxmen to receive money from patrons because of their supervisory positions, although some do permit this. The pit bosses are not permitted to receive anything from patrons because they are in a position in which they can insure that a patron receives some special service or treatment.

The money or tokes are combined by the four dealers and split equally at the end of each shift so that a dealer will get his share of the tokes received even while he is taking his break. Uncontradicted testimony indicated that a dealer would be terminated if he kept a toke rather than placed it in the common fund. Casino management either required the dealers to pool and divide tokes or encouraged them to do so. Although the practice is tolerated by management, it is not encouraged since tokes represent money that players are not

wagering and thus cannot be won by the casino. Plaintiff received about $10 per day as his share of tokes at the Horseshoe Club and an average of $20 per day in tokes at the Sahara.

Additional findings of fact by the district court are that the taxpayer worked as a stickman and dealer and at all times was under the supervision of the boxman who in turn was supervised by the pit boss. Also the district court found that patrons sometimes give money to dealers, other players or mere spectators at the game, but that between 90–95 percent of the patrons give nothing to a dealer. No obligation on the part of the patron exists to give to a dealer and dealers perform no service for patrons which a patron would normally find compensable. Another finding is that there exists no direct relation between services performed for management by a dealer and benefit or detriment to the patron.

There then follows two final findings of fact, which taken together constitute the heart of the controversy before us. These are as follows: 17. The tokes are given to dealers as a result of impulsive generosity or superstition on the part of players, and not as a form of compensation for services. 18. Tokes are the result of detached and disinterested generosity on the part of a small number of patrons.

These two findings bear the unmistakable imprint of Commissioner v. Duberstein, 363 U.S. 278 (1959), particularly that portion of the opinion which reads as follows: The course of decision here makes it plain that the statute does not use the term "gift" in the common law sense, but in a more colloquial sense. This Court has indicated that a voluntary executed transfer of his property by one to another, without any consideration or compensation therefor, though a common law gift, is not necessarily a gift within the meaning of the statute. For the Court has shown that the mere absence of a legal or moral obligation to make such a payment does not establish that it is a gift. . . . And, importantly, if the payment proceeds primarily from the constraining force of any moral or legal duty, or from the incentive of anticipated benefit of an economic nature, . . . it is not a gift. And, conversely, where the payment is in return for services rendered, it is irrelevant that the donor derives no economic benefit from it. What controls is the intention with which payment, however voluntary, has been made. . . .

The position of the taxpayer is simple. The above findings conform to the meaning of gifts as used in section 102 of the Code. *Duberstein* further teaches, the taxpayer asserts, that whether a receipt qualified as a non-taxable gift is basically one of fact and appellate review of such findings is restricted to determining whether they are clearly erroneous. Because none of the recited findings are clearly erroneous, concludes the taxpayer, the judgment of the trial court must be affirmed.

We could not escape this logic were we prepared to accept as a finding of fact the trial court's finding number 18. We reject the trial court's characterization. The conclusion that tokes are the result of detached and disinterested generosity on the part of those patrons who engage in the practice of toking is a conclusion of law, not a finding of fact. Finding number 17, on the other hand, which establishes that tokes are given as the result of impulsive gener-

osity or superstition on the part of the players is a finding of fact to which we are bound unless it is clearly erroneous which it is not.

The distinction is between a finding of the dominant reason that explains the player's action in making the transfer and the determination that such dominant reason requires treatment of the receipt as a gift. Finding number 17 is addressed to the former while number 18 the latter. A finding regarding the basic facts, i.e., the circumstances and setting within which tokes are paid, and the dominant reason for such payments are findings of fact, our review of which is restricted by the clearly erroneous standard. Whether the dominant reason justifies exclusion from gross income under section 102 as interpreted by *Duberstein* is a matter of law. Finding number 18 is a determination that the dominant reason for the player's action, as found in number 17, justifies exclusion. This constitutes an application of the statute to the facts. Whether the application is proper is, of course, a question of law.

Freed of the restraint of the "clearly erroneous" standard, we are convinced that finding number 18 and all derivative conclusions of law are wrong. Impulsive generosity or superstition on the part of the players, we accept as the dominant motive. In the context of gambling in casinos open to the public such a motive is quite understandable. However, our understanding also requires us to acknowledge that payments so motivated are not acts of detached or disinterested generosity. Quite the opposite is true. Tribute to the gods of fortune which it is hoped will be returned bounteously soon can only be described as an involved and intensely interested act.

Moreover, in applying the statute to the findings of fact, we are not permitted to ignore those findings which strongly suggest that tokes in the hands of the ultimate recipients are viewed as a receipt indistinguishable, except for erroneously anticipated tax differences, from wages. The regularity of the flow, the equal division of the receipts, and the daily amount received indicate that a dealer acting reasonably would come to regard such receipts as a form of compensation for his services. The manner in which a dealer may regard tokes is, of course, not the touchstone for determining whether the receipt is excludable from gross income. It is, however, a reasonable and relevant inference well grounded in the findings of fact.

Our view of the law is consistent with the trend of authorities in the area of commercial gratuities as well as with the only decision squarely in point, Lawrence E. Bevers, 26 T.C. 1218 (1956), and this Circuit's view of tips as revealed in Roberts v. Commissioner, 176 F.2d 221 (9th Cir. 1949). Generalizations are treacherous but not without utility. One such is that receipts by taxpayers engaged in rendering services contributed by those with whom the taxpayers have some personal or functional contact in the course of the performance of the services are taxable income when in conformity with the practices of the area and easily valued. Tokes, like tips, meet these conditions. That is enough. The taxpayer is not entitled to the refund he seeks. REVERSED.

Case Questions for Discussion

1. The Ninth Circuit Court in *Woody* made it clear that an appellate court, reviewing a question of fact determined by a jury, should reverse that jury's decision only when no reasonable jury could have decided as it did. Did the Ninth Circuit Court find that the judge's decision (that tokes were gifts) was "unreasonable" when it reversed the trial court in *Olk*?

2. The court found that players giving tokes expect to receive good luck in exchange. Do you think this "expectation of luck" should be regarded as consideration?

3. When a father gives a car to his son or daughter on his or her 18th birthday, it is no doubt out of love and affection. Do you think the donor father also expects respect and hopes that when the time comes, he can expect support and care from his son or daughter? Could this be regarded as consideration based on the reasoning in *Olk*?

4. Make an argument that tips received by a waitress are gifts.

For many taxpayers, their most significant personal asset is the family home. Taxpayers, who live in a home for a number of years, often can sell the property for much more than its original cost, resulting in a large gain. Fortunately, an exclusion of up to $250,000 ($500,000 for married joint filers) of *gain on the sale or exchange of a principal residence* is available for sales or exchanges occurring after May 7, 1997. The taxpayers must have owned and occupied the residence as a principal residence for two of the last five years. The exclusion can be used every two years.[17] Losses experienced on the sale or exchange of a personal residence, however, are nondeductible personal losses.

There are limited gross income exclusions available to students. IRC § 117 excludes from gross income the value of *qualified scholarships* received. A qualified scholarship includes amounts paid to, or on the behalf of, a student only for tuition, fees, books, supplies, and equipment required for courses at an educational institution. Students receiving scholarships that pay room and board, or that confer any other benefit that would be considered gross income, must include those amounts in gross income. The Economic Growth and Tax Relief Reconciliation Act of 2001 (EGTRRA) amended IRC § 117 to exclude amounts received under the national Health Service Corps Scholarship Program and the Armed Forces Scholarship Program as a scholarship, although the recipients must perform services in return for the scholarship.[18] IRC § 108(f) excludes from gross income student loans canceled as a result of the taxpayer working for a period of time in a certain profession or in a specified location. A physician working in an underserved region after graduating from medical school is one example.

Deductions

As we have discussed, there is a presumption that all income items are included in gross income, unless the income item is specifically excluded in the Internal Revenue Code (IRC). The opposite presumption operates when considering whether a cost or expenditure is a deduction for federal income tax purposes. Unless Congress has expressly granted a deduction in the IRC, it is presumed that no deduction is available. Deductions are often referred to as a matter of *legislative grace*.[19] Recall how IRC § 61 functions as the catchall provision for gross income. IRC § 162 serves a similar role in the area of deductions. It authorizes a host of deductions related to carrying on a trade or business. A portion of IRC § 162 appears in Box 16.5.

The most problematic phrases in the statute have been *ordinary and necessary* and *carrying on a trade or business*. In *Welch v. Helvering*,[20] the U.S. Supreme Court made it clear that deductions under IRC § 162 must survive separate tests under the statutory language. Simply being "necessary" does not mean an expenditure is also "ordinary." In *Welch*, the taxpayer was a grain buyer for a company that went bankrupt. The company did not pay a group of farmers for the grain they had sold to the company through Welch, the company's agent. After his former company's demise, Welch found employment with the Kellogg Com-

---

Box 16.5   IRC § 162 Trade or Business Expenses

(a) In general. There shall be allowed as a deduction all the ordinary and necessary expenses paid or incurred during the taxable year in carrying on any trade or business, including

  (1) a reasonable allowance for salaries or other compensation for personal services actually rendered;

  (2) traveling expenses (including amounts expended for meals and lodging other than amounts which are lavish or extravagant under the circumstances) while away from home in the pursuit of a trade or business; and

  (3) rentals or other payments required to be made as a condition to the continued use or possession, for purposes of the trade or business, of property to which the taxpayer has not taken or is not taking title or in which he has no equity. . . .

---

pany as a grain buyer servicing the same geographical area. He personally paid the debts owed to the farmers by his former company to entice them to once again sell grain through him. Welch attempted to deduct the payments as trade or business expenses under IRC § 162. The Supreme Court held that payment of the debts was necessary, because it was likely that the farmers would not have sold grain through Welch again, if they had they not been paid for the grain they had previously sold through him. The Court, however, determined that it was "extraordinary" for a business person to pay someone else's debts. As a result, because Welch's payments were necessary but not ordinary, he was denied a deduction.

The requirement that a deductible expense must be incurred in "carrying on a trade or business" has led to costs that a taxpayer had paid while he was deciding whether to purchase a business being denied, because they were incurred "before the taxpayer was in a trade or business."[21] The same principal usually denies newly graduated college students a deduction for their job-hunting expenses, because they are not yet in a "trade or business." Also, expenditures made in support of activities to make a profit that failed to rise to the level of a trade or business, such as investing in the stock market and owning rental property, have been held nondeductible under IRC § 162.[22]

Adjustments to gross income. *Adjusted gross income* (AGI) is part of the tax computation unique to individual taxpayers. IRC § 62 defines adjusted gross income as gross income less certain deductions. Section 62 does not authorize deductions. It merely designates at what point in the individual income tax formula the deductions should be taken. A *deduction for AGI*, often referred to as an "above-the-line deduction" or an *adjustment to gross income,* is usually more valuable to taxpayers than an itemized deduction. It does not need to be compared to the standard deduction, it can make other deductions that are dependent on AGI larger, and it can reduce the amount of state income tax the tax-payer must pay. Common deductions for AGI include trade and business deductions, losses from the sale or exchange of property held for the production of income (such as losses on the sale of stock), expenses incurred to produce rental or royalty income, retirement savings contributions (IRAs and pension, profit sharing, and annuity plans of self-employed individuals), interest paid on qualified student loans, moving expenses, penalties for premature withdrawals of certificates of deposit, qualified higher education expenses, and alimony payments.[23]

Since 1998, IRC § 221 has provided a limited above-the-line deduction for *interest paid on qualified student loans.* For 2001, up to $2,500 of interest per year for the first 60 months the loan is payable may be deducted. The deduction begins to be phased out once AGI is over $40,000 ($60,000 for married joint filers). No deduction is allowed for taxpayers with AGI over $55,000 ($75,000 for married joint filers). EGTRRA liberalized the deduction. For interest paid after December 31, 2001, the 60-month time limit is dropped. Interest paid on qualified student loans will be deductible for the entire repayment period. In addition, the phase-out range is increased. The phase out of the deduction begins at $50,000 of AGI ($100,000 for married joint filers). No deduction is allowed for taxpayers with AGI over $65,000 ($130,000 for married joint filers).[24]

EGTRRA created a new above-the-line deduction for *qualified higher education expenses* that are paid after December 31, 2001. Qualified higher education expenses are the cost of tuition and other course-related costs, but not including the cost of books, student activity fees, athletic fees, or room and board. For tax years 2002 and 2003, taxpayers with AGI of less than $65,000 ($130,000 for married joint filers) may deduct up to $3,000 of qualifying expenses. After 2003, taxpayers with AGI of less than $65,000 ($130,000 for married joint filers) may deduct up to $4,000 of qualifying expenses. In addition, beginning in 2004, qualifying expenses of up to $2,000 may be deducted by taxpayers with AGI between $65,000 and $80,000 ($130,000 and $160,000 for married joint filers).[25]

Itemized deductions. IRC § 262 disallows the deduction of personal, living, or family expenses in the computation of taxable income, unless specifically allowed by some other internal revenue code section. Congress has chosen to allow individual taxpayers six types of *itemized deductions* for personal, living, or family expenses. These are medical expenses, home mortgage interest, certain taxes paid, charitable contributions, casualty and theft losses, and miscellaneous deductions.

Medical expenses are deductible to the extent that they exceed 7.5 percent of AGI. Allowable medical expenses include medical insurance premiums, physician fees, dental visits, prescription drugs, hospital bills, the cost of medical tests, and other medically necessary expenses.[26] The 7.5 percent of AGI floor makes all but extraordinary medical expenses nondeductible. For example, assume Sickly earns $50,000 in salary and has $2,000 in interest income. Also assume he has no deductions for AGI, so his AGI is $52,000. Sickly would have to incur more than $3,900 ($52,000 x .075) in allowable medical expenses before any medical expense deduction would be available. Even if Sickly incurred and paid $4,500 in unreimbursed medical costs, he would have a medical expense deduction of only $600 ($4,500 – $3,900). As we will discuss, even those with enough medical expenses to exceed the AGI floor may not be assured a deduction because of the standard deduction.

Until the Tax Reform Act of 1986, all consumer interest, including interest on auto loans, credit cards, and other personal loans, was deductible. Since 1987, other than student loan interest as we discussed above, the only nonbusiness interest that is deductible is interest on loans related to the taxpayer's personal residence (*home mortgage interest*). First, taxpayers may deduct interest on loans of up to $1,000,000 used to acquire or improve qualified residences—referred to as *acquisition indebtedness*. Second, interest on loans up to $100,000 of *home equity indebtedness* may be deducted. Home equity indebtedness may not exceed the equity in the secured qualified residence.[27]

Assume that Homeowner purchased her principal residence five years ago and secured a mortgage of $80,000. The residence now has a fair market value of $120,000, and Homeowner still owes $70,000 on the original mortgage. Homeowner has equity of $50,000 in the residence ($120,000 – $70,000). A *qualified residence* is the principal residence of the taxpayer, plus one other residence of the taxpayer selected for the deduction (a second home).[28] There is no limitation on the usage of home equity indebtedness proceeds. The loan must be secured by a qualified residence, however. This allows homeowners to finance consumer purchases and deduct the interest. For instance, Homeowner from our example above could borrow $30,000, offering a second mortgage on her residence, and use the proceeds to purchase a new car. If she did, the interest on the $30,000 loan would be deductible as interest on home equity indebtedness. On the other hand, if she borrowed $30,000 without offering a second mortgage to purchase the car, the interest would be nondeductible personal interest. The home mortgage deduction is the largest single itemized deduction available to taxpayers. It has been criticized as unfairly subsidizing the housing costs of those wealthy enough to purchase homes. Renters have no comparable deduction. Renters also have no access to loans with deductible interest to finance consumer items, such as automobiles.

Also deductible is interest on loans used to purchase investment property, referred to as *investment interest*, but only to the extent the taxpayer has net investment income. *Net investment income* is investment income (gross income from property held for investment—such as interest, dividends, rentals, royalties, and gain on property held for investment) less investment expenses (expenses directly attributable to the production of investment income). Any investment interest not deductible due to the net investment income limitation can be carried over and used in subsequent tax years.[29]

Three types of taxes paid by most individuals—real property taxes, personal property taxes, and income taxes—may be deducted as itemized deductions (*certain taxes paid*). All state, local, and foreign real property taxes paid by the taxpayer are deductible. The real property tax deduction, combined with the home mortgage interest deduction, makes home ownership a valuable tax avoidance vehicle. All state and local personal property taxes paid are also deductible. The personal property tax deduction is not as valuable a deduction as it once was, because a number of state and local taxing authorities have repealed their personal property taxes. Finally, state, local, and foreign income taxes are deductible. This includes the amount of state or local income taxes withheld from paychecks during the year, plus any balance due on the prior year's return. Federal income taxes are not deductible.[30]

Donations (*charitable contributions*) made to charitable organizations, including schools, hospitals, churches, and traditional charities, are deductible as itemized deductions. There are AGI limitations, however. Most charitable contributions are subject to a 50 percent of AGI limitation. Certain contributions of property, or contributions made to certain nonoperating foundations, may subject the contribution to either 30 percent or 20 percent of AGI limitation.[31]

Losses incurred by taxpayers on personal use property are disallowed as nondeductible personal losses.[32] Assume you purchased a personal residence five years ago for $50,000. A year ago, a new airport opened. It is one mile from your home. You decide to move because of the noise pollution. The value of the home has fallen because of the airport, and you sell for $40,000. Your $10,000 loss is not deductible because the home is a personal use asset. An exception is made for losses incurred on personal use property as a result of casualty or theft.

Casualties are sudden and unexpected, such as tornadoes, hurricanes, and fires. Two floors exist for *casualty and theft losses*. The first $100 of loss is not deductible. Second, the loss is deductible only to the extent that it exceeds 10 percent of AGI.[33] Obviously, only calamitous casualty and theft losses provide any deduction for individual taxpayers. Assume Lucky owns an automobile she uses personally. The automobile is worth $6,500. It catches fire, and its value after the fire is $500. Lucky is uninsured, and her AGI is 50,000. Lucky will be able to deduct only $900 as a casualty and theft loss, although her total loss was $6,000. (Value before—$6,500 less value after—$500 = total loss of $6,000.) (Total loss of $6,000 less $100, less 10 percent of AGI—$5,000 = $900.)

Miscellaneous itemized deductions include employee business expenses incurred by taxpayers, such as uniforms, professional organization dues, and unreimbursed travel and entertainment costs, which are deductible under IRC § 162. Most IRC § 212 deductions are also deductible as a miscellaneous itemized deduction, such as the cost of having income tax returns prepared, maintenance costs on investment property, and the rental on safe deposit boxes used to protect stocks certificates, bonds, and other investment property. Most miscellaneous itemized deductions are subject to a 2 percent of AGI floor, or in other words, there is no deduction available until the total of miscellaneous itemized deductions exceeds 2 percent of AGI.[34]

Taxpayers with high incomes (AGI in excess of $132,950, $66,475 for married separate filers for 2001) are limited in the amount of their allowable itemized deductions. Not affected are medical expenses, casualty and theft losses, and investment interest. Allowable itemized deductions are reduced by 3 percent of every dollar the taxpayer's AGI is in excess of the AGI limits. No taxpayer may lose more than 80 percent of the affected itemized deductions. Limiting high-income taxpayers' ability to deduct all of their itemized deductions is in essence a "back door" method of requiring the wealthy to pay more income tax. Under EGTRRA, high-income taxpayers' ability to deduct itemized deductions will slowly be equalized with all other taxpayers. EGTRRA phases out the limitation beginning in 2006 and ending in 2009. As a result, high-income taxpayers will regain the ability to deduct all of their allowable itemized deductions.[35]

The standard deduction. Taxpayers total their itemized deductions and compare the total to the *standard deduction*. Taxpayers may deduct the larger of the two. The standard deduction is designed to allow all taxpayers a minimum amount of deductions for personal, living, and family expenses. No records are necessary. The majority of taxpayers utilize the standard deduction. Even those taxpayers who own homes are many times better off with the standard deduction, especially if they have owned the home for some time and if the mortgage interest paid on the home is minimal. The standard deduction is based on a taxpayer's filing status,[36] which we will discuss. For 2001, standard deduction amounts are as shown in Table 16.3.[37] The additional standard deduction amounts in the third column of Table 16.3 apply if a taxpayer is blind, or age 65 or over, as of the last day of the year.

Notice that the standard deduction for taxpayers filing a married joint return is less than twice the standard deduction of a single filer. This is one element of the so-called *marriage penalty*. Because of standard deduction amounts, the way the tax rate schedules are constructed, and various other provisions, when married spouses both work, they often pay more tax than they would if they simply lived together without marrying. The marriage penalty, in effect, subsidizes working couples who cohabitate without marrying. The marriage pen-

Table 16.3 Standard Deduction		
Filing Status	**Standard Deduction**	**Additional Standard Deduction**
Single	$4,550	$1,100
Head of Household	$6,650	$1,100
Married Joint	$7,600	$900
Married Separate	$3,800	$900

alty evolved as more married women joined the workforce. EGTRRA mitigates the marriage penalty, but it does not eliminate it. In addition, most of the relief does not begin until 2005. Under one of the marriage penalty relief provisions of EGTRRA, by 2010, the standard deduction for married joint filers will be 200 percent of the standard deduction for single filers. The change will be phased in beginning in 2005.[38]

Those taxpayers who may be claimed as a dependent on another's return, such as a parent claiming a child as a dependent, have their standard deduction limited. The limited standard deduction is $750, or the amount of earned income (from a job or trade or business) plus $250, whichever is higher, but limited to the normal standard deduction.[39] The limitation is designed to minimize the amount of investment income that can be sheltered from tax within a family. Assume that your parents gave you a $50,000 bond that pays interest of $4,000 each year, and that they may claim you as a dependent on their tax return. Also, assume you had no earned income during the year. Without the limitation, you, as a single taxpayer, could claim the standard deduction of $4,550, and your taxable income would be zero, resulting in no tax on the $4,000 of interest income. Had your parents not given you the bond, they would have had to claim the $4,000 of interest income and pay tax at their marginal tax rate, which could be as high as 39.1 percent in 2001. Without the limitation, a tax savings of almost $1,600 could result. Because of the limitation, however, your standard deduction will be limited to $750, resulting in $3,250 of the interest income being taxed at your rates.

Personal and dependency exemptions. One final class of deductions is allowed for individual taxpayers. Like itemized deductions and the standard deduction, *personal and dependency exemptions* provide some tax relief for amounts people must spend on themselves or their dependents for basic food, shelter, and clothing needs. For 2001, taxpayers may deduct $2,900 for each personal or dependency exemption they are entitled to claim. Each taxpayer is entitled to a *personal exemption*. In the case of married taxpayers filing a joint return, one personal exemption is allowed for each spouse.[40] The personal exemption is denied if a taxpayer *may* be claimed as a dependent on another's return. Denial of personal exemptions to taxpayers occurs most often when a child has income, but may still be claimed as a dependent on their parent(s)' return. It does not matter whether the other taxpayer actually claims the dependency exemption; just the fact they may do so is enough to deny the personal exemption to a dependent taxpayer.[41] Many college students find themselves in this situation.

Taxpayers may also take a *dependency exemption* for every dependent they may claim.[42] Five separate dependency tests must be passed to claim a valid dependency exemption. First, the claimed dependent must be a U.S. citizen or a resident of the United States, Mexico, or Canada to pass the *citizenship test*.[43] Under the *relationship test,* the individual must be a relative or a member of the taxpayer's household. All relatives, by blood or marriage, down to nieces and nephews, qualify.[44] Foster children are included, but deductions are disallowed for any relationships that would violate local law.[45] Under the *joint return test,* the dependent may not have filed a married joint return, unless that person or his or her spouse was not required to file the return, but filed only to claim a refund.[46] The *gross income test* requires that the dependent have less gross income than the amount of the dependency exemption; this amounts to $2,900 for tax year 2001.[47] The gross income test is waived if the claimed individual is a child of the taxpayer who is under the age of 19, or who is a full-time student (for at least five months) under the age of 24.[48] Under the final test, the *support test,* the taxpayer must provide more than 50 percent of the claimed individual's support.[49] A support test presumption exists with respect to children of divorced parents. As long as his or her parents provide more than 50 percent of the child's support, the parent who has the child's custody for a longer period of time is entitled to the dependency exemption. The custodial parent may waive the exemption in writing.[50]

Personal and dependency exemptions are limited for high-income taxpayers. For 2001, the personal and dependency exemptions are gradually reduced for single taxpayers with adjusted gross income over $132,000, and are eliminated once adjusted gross income reaches $255,450. The phase-out range for married joint filers is from $199,450 to $321,950. EGTRRA gradually repeals the phase-out provision. For years 2006 and 2007, only two thirds of the limitation will apply. In 2008 and 2009, one third of the limitation will apply, and the limitation will be eliminated altogether after 2009.[51]

Taxable Income, Tax Rates, Filing Status, and Tax Credits

Subtracting the allowable standard deduction, or itemized deductions, and personal and dependency exemptions from AGI leaves *taxable income.* This is the amount of income that is subject to tax. Applying the *tax rate schedules* of IRC § 1, or the *tax tables* released by the

IRS, to taxable income determines the taxpayer's tax liability before tax credits. The tax rate schedules for tax year 2001 appear in Table 16.4.

Before EGTRRA, the basic tax brackets were 15 percent, 28 percent, 31 percent, 36 percent, and 39.6 percent. EGTRRA created new 10 percent tax brackets and lowered tax rates across the board over a ten-year period. The 2001 tax rate schedules do not reflect the new 10 percent brackets. For the year 2001, the 10 percent brackets were put in place through the use of a rate reduction credit—the so-called tax rebate checks that taxpayers received in the latter part of 2001. The 10 percent rate brackets were as follows for 2001: Single and married separate filers—first $6,000 of taxable income; Head of Household—first $10,000 of taxable income; and Married Joint—first $12,000 of taxable income. Taxpayers received up to $300 for single and married separate filers, $500 for head of household filers, and $600 for married joint filers.[52] The 10 percent brackets will remain the same until 2007, when the brackets will increase to $7,000 for single and married separate filers, and $14,000 for head of household and married joint filers. The scheduled across-the-board rate reductions are shown in Table 16.5.

Notice that the scheduled rates for 2001, shown in Table 16.5, are 27, 30, 35, and 38.6 percent. The 2001 tax rate schedules in Table 16.4, however, show rates of 27.5, 30.5, 35.5, and 39.1 percent. This reflects that rate reductions for 2001 did not take effect until July 1, 2001. Therefore, the tax rate schedules for 2001 are the result of averaging the rates in effect for the first half of the year, and the rates in effect for the last half of the year.

All of this may seem a little daunting, but the tax computation is relatively simple. For example, assume Singlemother files head of household and she has taxable income of $45,150. In September of 2001, she received a rate reduction credit check of $500. Her tax would be $7,385. The tax on her first $36,250 of taxable income is $5,437.50 (second line of Schedule Z). The remaining $8,900 of taxable income (taxable income of $45,150 less the amount taxed at 15 percent [$36,250]) is taxed at 27.5 percent ($8,900 x .275 = $2,447.50). The two amounts are then simply added ($5,437.50 plus $2,447.50 = $7,885). The $500 of rate reduction credit is then subtracted, leaving a tax of $7,385. Each year, the IRS issues required tax tables for taxpayers with incomes under a certain amount. These tables simply divide taxable income into $50 increments and compute tax on the midpoint of each $50 increment.

Filing status. To be able to determine which tax rate schedule or tax table to use, taxpayers must determine their proper *filing status*. Taxpayers who are married as of the last day of the year must file either as *married joint* or as *married separate*.[53] Married joint status artificially allocates half of all income to each spouse, regardless of who actually earned the income. Married joint status was created by Congress in reaction to *Poe v. Seaborn*, a 1930 U.S. Supreme Court opinion. It held a California couple's income should be allocated half and half, for federal

Table 16.4   Tax Rate Schedules—2001

SCHEDULE X: FILING STATUS—SINGLE

If taxable income is:	The tax is:
Not over $27,050	15% of taxable income
Over $27,050 but not over $65,550	$4,057.50 + 27.5% of the excess over $27,050
Over $65,550 but not over $136,750	$14,645.00 + 30.5% of the excess over $65,550
Over $136,750 but not over $297,350	$36,361.00 + 35.5% of the excess over $136,750
Over $297,350	$93,374.00 + 39.1% of the excess over $297,350

SCHEDULE Y1: FILING STATUS—MARRIED, FILING JOINT RETURN AND SURVIVING SPOUSE

If taxable income is:	The tax is:
Not over $45,200	15% of taxable income
Over $45,200 but not over $109,250	$6,780.00 + 27.5% of the excess over $45,200
Over $109,250 but not over $166,500	$24,393.75 + 30.5% of the excess over $109,250
Over $166,500 but not over $297,350	$41,855.00 + 35.5% of the excess over $166,500
Over $297,350	$88,306.75 + 39.1% of the excess over $297,350

SCHEDULE Y2: FILING STATUS—MARRIED, SEPARATE

If taxable income is:	The tax is:
Not over $22,600	15% of taxable income
Over $22,600 but not over $54,625	$3,390.00 + 27.5% of the excess over $22,600
Over $54,625 but not over $83,250	$12,196.88 + 30.5% of the excess over $54,625
Over $83,250 but not over $148,675	$20,927.50 + 35.5% of the excess over $83,250
Over $148,675	$44,153.38 + 39.1% of the excess over $148,675

SCHEDULE Z: FILING STATUS—HEAD OF HOUSEHOLD

If taxable income is:	The tax is:
Not over $36,250	15% of taxable income
Over $36,250 but not over $93,650	$5,437.50 + 27.5% of the excess over $36,250
Over $93,650 but not over $151,650	$21,222.50 + 30.5% of the excess over $93,650
Over $151,650 but not over $297,350	$38,912.50 + 35.5% of the excess over $151,650
Over $297,350	$90,636.00 + 39.1% of the excess over $297,350

Table 16.5	Scheduled Income Tax Rate Reductions Under EGTRRA[54]			
Year	28% rate reduced to:	31% rate reduced to:	36% rate reduced to:	39.6% rate reduced to:
2001–2003	27%	30%	35%	38.6%
2004–2005	26%	29%	34%	37.6%
2006 and Later	25%	28%	33%	35%

income tax purposes, as it was under California's community property laws.[55] Married joint filing status was once very advantageous to most American families. When one spouse earns most or all of the income in a household, the income-splitting aspects of filing a joint return reduces the tax due. As society changed, and two-income families became the norm, the married joint filing status began to operate as part of the so-called marriage penalty. Even though EGTRRA mitigates some of the marriage penalty, changes in the law do not take effect until the latter part of the decade. Married taxpayers may file married separate returns, but because of the way the rates are structured, it is almost never advantageous to do so. The *abandoned spouse rule* allows certain married taxpayers to be considered unmarried for federal income tax purposes.[56] Without the abandoned spouse rule, taxpayers whose spouse left the family, without legal separation or divorce, would be forced to file a married separate return and pay much more in tax than they should. Surviving spouses may continue to file a married joint return, for two years after the year of death, if the surviving spouse furnishes over half the cost of maintaining a household that is the principal place of abode of a dependent son, daughter, stepson, or stepdaughter. The surviving spouse status is denied if the taxpayer remarries.[57]

Head of household status is a middle ground between the single and married joint filing statuses. An unmarried qualifying taxpayer pays less tax than they would as a single person, but more than they would if they filed a married joint return. Head of household status recognizes that many taxpayers have family responsibilities, but nonetheless are unmarried. To qualify for head of household status, the taxpayer must maintain as their home a household that is the principal place of abode for an unmarried son, daughter, steps of the same, or a grandchild. If the son, daughter, or grandchild is married, the taxpayer must be able to claim them as a deduction. In addition, the taxpayer may qualify if they maintain as their home a household that is the principal place of abode for any person the taxpayer can claim as a dependent. Taxpayers may also qualify by maintaining a separate household for their parent(s) if their parent(s) can be claimed as dependent(s).[58]

An unmarried person who is unable to file as a head of household, or as a surviving spouse, must file as single.[59]

Tax credits. Once taxpayers compute their tax, the amount of tax due is reduced by *tax credits*. Tax credits are more valuable to taxpayers than deductions because tax credits reduce the taxpayer's tax bill dollar for dollar. Deductions, by comparison, reduce tax only by the amount of the deduction times the taxpayer's *marginal tax rate*, or the tax rate on the last dollar of taxable income. For instance, assume a single tax-payer has $30,000 of taxable income in 2001. Her marginal tax rate is 27.5 percent (all of her taxable income in excess of $27,050 is taxed at 27.5 percent—see line two of tax rate Schedule X). The value of a $1,000 deduction is $275 ($1,000 x .275). The value of a $1,000 credit, however, is $1,000. There are many credits available, but most are aimed at business operations. Credits aimed primarily at individuals are the hope scholarship credit, the lifetime learning credit, the child tax credit, the child care credit, and the earned income credit. We now turn to a brief description of each of the credits aimed primarily at individuals.

Taxpayers with modest incomes may utilize the *hope scholarship credit* and the *lifetime learning credit* to help pay for higher educational expenses. Under the hope credit, 100 percent of the first $1,000 and 50 percent of the next $1,000 (maximum credit of $1,500) of qualified tuition and related expenses, not including room and board, books, student activity fees, athletic fees, and other noninstructional fees, may be taken as a tax credit. Only the first two years of a student's post-secondary educational expenses are eligible for this credit. The student must have been at least a half-time student to be eligible. A parent may claim the credit for expenses paid on behalf of a dependent. The credit is available per student—a parent with two eligible students could claim up to $3,000. Under the lifetime learning credit, 20 percent of the first $5,000 of tuition and related expenses (maximum credit of $1,000) may be taken as a tax credit. In contrast to the hope credit, there are no limitations on course loads or the student's year in school. A taxpayer taking a single continuing education course is eligible. Also, unlike the hope credit, multiple students do not increase the maximum credit. Only one credit may be utilized by the taxpayer per student. In addition, any expenses deducted under the new IRC § 222 as qualified higher educational expenses are not eligible for either credit. Both credits begin to phase out once AGI reaches $80,000 for married joint filers and $40,000 for all other taxpayers. No credit is available once AGI reaches $100,000 for married joint filers and $50,000 for all other taxpayers.[60]

The *child tax credit*, before EGTRRA, was $500 per eligible dependent child under the age of seventeen. EGTRRA increased the amount of the credit to $600 for years 2001–2004, $700 for years 2005–2008, $800 for 2009, and $1000 per eligible child for 2010 and thereafter. Descendants, stepchildren, and foster children are eligible children. The credit is reduced by $50 for each $1,000 of AGI in excess of $110,000 for married joint filers, and $75,000 for single taxpayers.[61]

The *dependent child care credit* allows a credit on the first $2,400 of eligible expenses, per eligible child, up to a $4,800 maximum. An eligible child is defined as a dependent child under the age of 13. Spouses and other dependents of the taxpayer that are incapable of self-care also qualify as an eligible child. Eligible expenses are those incurred to care for the eligible child and related household services that are necessary to allow the taxpayer to work. The credit amount ranges from 20 percent (AGI over $28,000) of eligible expenses, to 30 percent (AGI up to $10,000) of eligible expenses. The eligible expenses are limited to the taxpayer's earned income; in other words, the taxpayer may not spend more for dependent care than he or she is earning. A special rule allows a deemed earned income of $200 per month for taxpayers who are full-time students. For tax years after 2001, EGTRRA increased the amount of eligible expenses per child from $2,400 to $3,000, and the maximum amount of eligible expenses from $4,800 to $6,000. The maximum credit amount and the AGI range were also increased. Beginning in 2002, the credit amount ranges from 20 percent (AGI over $43,000) of eligible expenses, to 35 percent (AGI up to $15,000) of eligible expenses.[62]

All of the tax credits discussed above, except the child tax credit after EGTRRA,[63] are nonrefundable. In other words, they can reduce the tax due only to zero. The *earned income credit,* on the other hand, is a refundable credit designed to help working taxpayers with modest incomes. The refundable feature of the earned income credit allows the government to give these taxpayers a "no strings attached" cash supplement, while incurring little or no bureaucratic costs. To be eligible, the taxpayer must have *earned income*—income from wages, salary, and self-employment income. The largest credits are available to those taxpayers who maintain a household for a descendant, stepchild, or foster child. For 2001, a taxpayer with one eligible child could claim a credit of up to $2,424; with two or more eligible children, the maximum credit is $4,008. For those with modest incomes, the value of the earned income credit is very high. For example, the maximum credit for a taxpayer with one child is based on earned incomes between $7,130 and $13,090. Most taxpayers with incomes at those levels incur very little income tax liability. As a result, it is not unusual for these low-income taxpayers to receive checks from the federal government in excess of $2,500—amounts that can be as high as 25 to 40 percent of their annual income. The credit is also available to certain taxpayers with no children, although the amount of the credit for these taxpayers is much smaller (maximum credit for 2001 is $364). The amount of the credit is reduced, once income reaches certain levels. The income phase-out levels through 2001 are the same for all taxpayers, regardless of filing status. EGTRAA slowly increases the phase-out levels for married joint taxpayers as part of its marriage penalty mitigation provisions. The credit is unavailable to taxpayers with unearned incomes in excess of $2,450.[64]

Limitations and Two Vital Planning Concepts

We have devoted a good portion of this chapter to an overview of the federal income tax as it applies to individuals. Many of the concepts examined, such as gross income and business deductions, apply to business taxation as well. Property transactions, depreciation, and amortization issues have been avoided to keep the discussion as simple as possible. Students need to be aware, however, that income taxes can be greatly affected by such matters. When a taxpayer sells or otherwise disposes a piece of property, the amount received is compared to the taxpayer's *tax basis*—acquisition cost or substituted basis, plus or less adjustments to basis. The result is either a gain or a loss.[65] The matter becomes complicated when determining tax basis, adjustments to tax basis, and whether or not the gain or loss is recognized, not recognized, or somehow deferred.

Depreciation and *amortization*[66] are simply methods of matching costs (the cost of property used in a trade or business or other profitmaking activities) with revenues (the income generated by using the property). Assume Student purchases a bagel cart for $6,000. She will use the bagel cart while she attends college to make and sell bagels on the weekends. The cart will be worthless after the four-year period. She expects to generate $5,000 from selling bagels in each of the four years (we will ignore the cost of the bagel ingredients). If Student computed her annual income on a *strict cash flow method,* she would report a $1,000 loss in year one and $5,000 of income in each of the remaining three years. Student's annual income would be distorted if she uses the strict cash flow method, because the bagel cart's cost should be spread over the time it contributes to the production of Student's income. Depreciation or amortization allows us to do so. The simplest method of spreading the cost is to allocate one fourth of the cost ($6,000/4 = $1,500) to each year. Doing so will result in an income of $3,500 each year ($5,000 – $1,500). This is a more accurate reflection of Student's income on an annual basis.

The concept underlying depreciation is simple, but the implementation is complex. Determining the proper amount to charge against each year's income depends on useful lives, the method of computation, salvage value, and other factors. Congress has added to the complexity, using depreciation and amortization methods as a tool of economic policy and as a method of increasing tax revenues. Congress can promote business expansion by providing shorter useful product lives and faster depreciation methods for federal income tax purposes. On the other hand, Congress can increase tax revenues without the politically unpopular act of increasing tax rates by mandating longer useful lives and slower depreciation methods. As a result, useful lives and depreciation methods for federal income tax purposes do not usually conform with common sense.

Income Shifting and Capital Gains

Two vital tax-planning concepts deserve at least a short explanation. First, *income shifting*. Because high-income taxpayers pay tax at higher marginal tax rates; the incentive to shift income to a low-income taxpayer is always present. Assume that Lawyer has taxable income of $350,000, and she files a joint return with her husband. Also assume that Lawyer has a son, Student, who will be attending a private university in the fall, where tuition and room and board will be $20,000. For the year 2001, to pay the $20,000 cost of college, Lawyer will have to earn $32,841 in pretax income ($20,000/[1 – .391]). However, if Student was taxed on the income needed to pay his $20,000 college cost, it would require only $23,529 ($20,000/[1 – .15] because Student's marginal tax rate would be 15 percent instead of 39.1 percent, a difference of almost $10,000.

Taxpayers have tried to shift income in many ways. One of the most common is to transfer investment income to another family member. In *Helvering v. Horst* (1940),[67] the U.S. Supreme Court held that income from property is taxed to the owner of the income-producing property. As a result, when a father transferred interest coupons from a bond to his daughter, he was still taxed on the interest received by his daughter. For tax purposes, he made a nontaxable gift of the interest to his daughter. Justice Stone's now famous *fruit and tree* analogy is useful to illustrate the basic tenants of income shifting. To transfer the fruit (the income), one must transfer the tree (income-producing property). In *Horst*, the father transferred only the fruit (the interest coupons). Had he transferred the bond and the interest coupons to his daughter, the income would have been hers, because she would have owned the property that produced the income and she would have been liable for the taxes.

Let us return to our example of Lawyer and Student. How can Lawyer shift income to Student to make it less costly to send Student to college? Lawyer could give Student income-producing property that would generate roughly $23,000. The downside of this income-shifting strategy is that once property is given to another, it is gone. Student could sell it or do anything he wanted with the property. The utilization of a trust can protect the property from being squandered, but even with a trust, Lawyer still loses all control and access to the income produced by the property. If Lawyer owns a trade or a business, the simplest method of transferring income to Student is to give him a job. To be valid, the job must be legitimate, work must be performed, and the pay must be reasonable.

All income does not come in the same "flavor." Gains and losses from the sale or exchange of *capital assets* are *capital gains and losses.* Individual taxpayers who have long-term capital gains, or gains on capital assets held more than one year, enjoy a top preferential tax rate of 20 percent on the long-term capital gain.[68] Beginning with tax year 2001, gains on capital assets held more than five years are subject to a top rate of 18 percent.[69] There is a cost to the favorable treatment given to capital gains. Only $3,000 of capital losses in excess of capital gains may be deducted each year. Unused capital losses may be carried over to succeeding years, however. Capital assets include assets held for appreciation, investment (stocks, bonds, and real and personal property held for appreciation), and personal use. Assets used in a trade or business, including rental property, are not capital assets.[70]

The timing of capital transactions is crucial. Because how long the taxpayer held the property determines whether preferential tax rates apply, a day one way or the other can produce significant differences in the tax liability attached to the sale of a capital asset. The matching of capital gains with capital losses can also significantly reduce tax liability and generate positive cash flow for the taxpayer because of the capital netting process. Assume that Risky sells for $30,000 the ABC shares he bought two years ago for $10,000. If Risky pays a 20-percent tax on his long-term capital gain of $20,000, he will still have $26,000 after he pays the income tax ($30,000 – [$20,000 x .2]). Also, assume that Risky owns some DEF stock he bought several years ago for $16,000. The DEF stock is worth only $2,000 today, and the prospect of the DEF stock regaining its past value is slim. If Risky matches his gain on the ABC stock with the loss on the DEF stock, he can reduce his tax liability and free up more cash to reinvest or to use for some other purchase. Risky's net long-term capital gain would be $6,000 ($20,000 gain on ABC less $14,000 loss on DEF). His capital gain tax would be $1,200 ($6,000 x .2), and his after-tax cash from the transactions would be $30,800 ($30,000 on ABC plus $2,000 on DEF less $1,200 tax).

Entities for Business Activities

Lawyers are often expected to advise clients how to structure their business activities. The principal forms of conducting business are as an individual proprietor, as a partnership, as a corporation, and as a limited liability company. Most attorneys are familiar with the legal ramifications of the different business entities, such as the unlimited liability aspects of partners and individual proprietors. The income tax implications of entity choice should also be given substantial weight, because a bad choice can subject the taxpayer to unnecessary tax liabilities or wasted tax losses. The following are key tax issues to be considered when making an entity choice: (1) How are business income, losses, and other tax attributes reported and taxed? (2) Are cash and property distributions to owners "tax triggers?" It is also important to understand what the client expects of the business for the foreseeable future. Is it likely the business will struggle until a customer base is secured? Is it likely there will be losses? Will capital infusions be necessary? Will the client be living out of the business, or does he or she have an independent source of income?

There are two basic taxation models for business activities—*pass through entities* and *separate taxable entities*. When a pass through entity is utilized, all tax attributes pass through to the owners. Separate entities, however, are taxpayers unto themselves. All tax attributes stay with the entity. Distributions of cash and other property to owners generally do not trigger taxation in pass through entities, but they do in separate taxable entities. Partnerships, individual proprietorships, and limited liability companies are pass through entities. Corporations are separate taxable entities. Table 16.6 summarizes the tax treatment of important transactions and business results in the different types of entities.

Individual Proprietorships

Doing business as an *individual proprietorship* requires nothing of the taxpayer for tax purposes. The individual owns all business assets and is liable for all business debts. Business activities are reported on Schedule C of the IRS Form 1040. All income, losses, and credits of the business are part of the individual's normal income tax return. Distributions of cash or property to the owner are not taxable events. If the taxpayer sells the business, the sale is of the individual assets making up the business. The character of the individual assets determines whether the gains or losses will be capital or ordinary.

Choosing the right business entity can lead to tax savings.

Corporations

A *corporation* is at the opposite end of the spectrum from an individual proprietorship. When forming a corporation, cash, assets, and

Table 16.6	Comparison of Tax Treatments by Entity			
	Individual Proprietorship	**Corporation**	**Partnership**	**Limited Liability Company (LLC)**
Income	Owner's Return	Corporate Return	Partner's Return	Same as Partnership
Loss	Owner's Return	Corporate Return	Partner's Return	Same as Partnership
Tax Credits	Owner's Return	Corporate Return	Partner's Return	Same as Partnership
Cash & Property Distributions to Owner	Not Taxable	Income to Shareholder	Not Taxable Unless in Excess of Interest	Same as Partnership
Sale of Business	Sale of Individual Assets	Capital Gain	Mix of Capital Gain and Sale of Individual Assets	Same as Partnership

liabilities are transferred to the corporation by the taxpayer in exchange for corporate stock. Unless the corporation gives *boot* (cash, property, or excess liabilities assumed by the corporation) to the taxpayer in addition to corporate stock, the exchange is tax free under IRC § 351. Once a corporation is formed, the corporation is the owner of all assets and is liable for all debts. Individual shareholders own only corporate stock. The corporation reports all income, losses, and credits and is responsible for all tax due. The corporate tax rates are given in Table 16.7.

The up-and-down nature of the corporate rates appears confusing. The two highest rates merely remove the lower tax brackets for high-income corporations. The 39 percent rate phases out the 15 and 25 percent brackets for corporations with income over 100,000. The 38 percent rate phases out the 34 percent rate. As a result, corporations with income over $18,333,333 pay tax at a flat 35 percent rate on all income.

Capital gains are taxed at the same rate as ordinary income.[71] Capital losses may be used only to offset capital gains. It is a mistake to incorporate a business that will suffer tax losses or have significant capital gains. The shareholders may not deduct corporate losses. The corporation simply pays no tax. If allowed to flow to the owners, a loss can reduce the amount of tax the individual taxpayer must pay. Tax credits stay within the corporation as well. If there is no corporate tax

Table 16.7 Corporate Tax Rates[72]	
Taxable Income	**Tax Rate**
Not over $50,000	15%
Over $50,000 but not over $75,000	25%
Over $75,000 but not over $100,000	34%
Over $100,000 but not over $335,000	39%
Over $335,000 but not over $10,000,000	34%
Over $10,000,000 but not over $15,000,000	35%
Over $15,000,000 but not over $18,333,333	38%
Over $18,333,333	35%

to reduce, the tax credit could be wasted. Both credits and losses may be carried back and forward within the corporation to reduce tax liability in prior or future years, but they could prove to be worthless unless there are sufficient corporate profits. Yet, incorporating a profitable, individually owned business can be a tax saving strategy. Assume Mr. Gates is generating $300,000 of taxable income per year by owning and operating a retail business as an individual proprietor. If he is filing a married joint return, his marginal tax rate is 39.1 percent. If a corporation is formed, he can take a salary of $200,000 per year and lower his marginal tax rate to 35.5 percent. The $100,000 of income remaining in the corporation will be taxed at the lower corporate tax rates ($22,250 tax on the first $100,000). This will result in an overall tax savings of over $13,000 for the 2001 tax year. Another benefit of the corporate form is the treatment given to the sale or exchange of the stock. Gains or losses on the sale of corporate stock are capital gains or losses, despite the character of the underlying assets of the corporation.

Partnerships and Limited Liability Companies

A *partnership* is the ultimate pass through entity. A partnership can be thought of as two or more individual proprietors doing business together. Partnership formation is similar to the formation of a corporation. Money, assets, and liabilities are transferred to the partnership in exchange for a partnership interest. The exchange is tax free under IRC § 751. Partners may agree among themselves how to divide income, deductions, losses, and other tax attributes as long as the agreement has substantial economic effect. Although the partners exchanged their assets and liabilities for an interest in the partnership, the partners are jointly and severally liable for all partnership debts. Income, losses, credits, and all other tax items (like charitable contributions) flow through to the individual partners and become a part of the partners' individual tax returns. Partnerships are a good entity choice for taxpayers who are operating a business that has yet to become profitable. This is especially true if they have other sources of income they must report on their individual tax returns. Assume Mr. and Ms. Venture have taxable income from Mr. Venture's salary of $100,000 per year. Ms. Venture is planning to open a restaurant with Mr. Cook. They have purchased a building and equipment and are ready to open in one month. They anticipate the restaurant will have losses of $60,000, $40,000, and $20,000 the first three years before turning a profit in year four. If the restaurant is organized as a partnership with two equal partners, the Ventures' taxable income will be reduced by $30,000, $20,000, and $10,000 over the first three years of operation. If the restaurant were incorporated, those losses would be unavailable for personal use by either of the owners. Once the restaurant becomes profitable, a tax-free incorporation can be reconsidered. In the event that Ms. Venture or Mr. Cook wants to sell his or her partnership interest, under the general rule, any gain or loss will be a capital gain or loss. The "hot asset rule" of IRC § 751, however, requires ordinary income treatment—to the extent that the underlying assets are ordinary income property. Like all entities, partnerships may have hidden tax traps of which the owners must be aware.[73]

A major drawback to a partnership is the liability exposure of the partners. *Limited liability companies* may offer the best of both worlds. Limited liability companies are state-authorized business entities that offer limited liability protection for the owners, much like corporations do.[74] Limited liability companies are separate entities. Like a corporation, a limited liability company can buy and sell property, sue or be sued, enter into contracts, and incur liabilities. Like a shareholder in a corporation, a limited liability company owner, called a member, has no individual liability for the debts of the limited liability company.[75] For federal income tax purposes, however, a limited liability company may elect to be treated as a partnership. A limited liability company is a good entity choice for a business that is likely to generate losses or other tax attributes the owners would like to use personally, but those owners do not want to put their personal assets at risk.[76]

Careful analysis by informed professionals is necessary for successful entity choice decisions. Competent legal, business, and taxation experts should be involved. Once the initial decision is made, periodic re-evaluations should be undertaken to insure that the best tax and legal benefits remain available to the owners.

Key Terms, Names, and Concepts

Abandoned spouse rule
Acquisition indebtedness
Adjusted gross income
Adjustments to gross income
Amortization
Capital assets
Capital gains and losses
Carrying on a trade
   or business
Casualty and theft losses
Certain taxes paid
Charitable contributions
Child care credit
Child tax credit
Citizenship test
Complete dominion
Consumption tax
Corporation
Deduction for AGI
Dependency exemption
Depreciation
Direct tax
Earned income credit
Filing status
Flat tax rate
Gain on the sale or exchange
   of a principal residence
Gifts and inheritance
Gross income
Gross income exclusions
Gross income test
Head of household
Home equity indebtedness
Home mortgage interest
Hope scholarship credit
Income shifting
Indirect tax
Individual proprietorship
Interest paid on qualified stu-
   dent loans
Internal Revenue Code (IRC)

Internal Revenue Service
   (IRS)
Investment interest
Itemized deductions
Joint return test
Legislative grace
Life insurance proceeds
Lifetime learning credit
Limited liability company
Marginal tax rate
Marriage penalty
Married joint
Married separate
Medical expenses
Miscellaneous itemized
   deductions
Net investment income
No proposed adjustment
Ordinary and necessary
Partnership
Pass through entity
Personal exemption
Principal residence
Progressive tax rate
Proposed adjustment in
   tax due
Proposed adjustment in
   tax refund
Qualified higher education
   expenses
Qualified residence
Qualified scholarships
Realization
Regressive tax
Relationship test
Separate taxable entity
Single
Sixteenth Amendment
Small Claims Division of the
   U.S. Tax Court
Standard deduction

Support test
Tax basis
Tax credit
Tax rate schedules
Tax tables
Taxable income

Treasury Regulation
Undeniable accession
 of wealth
U.S. Tax Court
Wealth flight

Discussion Questions

1. Mr. and Mrs. Smith paid $100 for an old piano at an auction, and they gave it to their daughter on her 10th birthday. Eighteen months later, as Mr. Smith was preparing to refinish the piano, he found a bag containing $10,000 of cash taped inside the piano case. Do Mr. and Mrs. Smith have gross income under IRC § 61? Why or why not?

2. Mr. and Mrs. Smith paid $100 for an old violin at an auction, and they gave it to their daughter on her 10th birthday. Eighteen months later, as Mr. Smith was preparing to refinish the violin, he noticed a label on the inside of the violin. The label said, "Antonius Stradivarius Cremonensis Faciebat Anno, 1665." Mr. Smith took the violin to a university music professor who determined that the violin was a genuine "Stradivarius" valued at $500,000. Do Mr. and Mrs. Smith have gross income under IRC § 61? Why or why not?

3. Landlord's tenant, Pablo Picasso, was unable to pay his $500-per-month rent. Pablo approached Landlord and offered to paint a portrait of Landlord's wife in exchange for six months rent. Landlord agreed. Pablo painted the portrait and Landlord allowed Pablo to live rent free in the apartment for six months. Does Pablo have any gross income under IRC § 61? Does Landlord have any gross income under IRC § 61? Explain your answers.

4. Grandfather has owned and operated a farm for most of his life. Five years ago, he suffered a stroke and was no longer able to work the farm. Josie, a granddaughter, began to live with and care for Grandfather soon after his stroke. She also worked the farm. About a year before his death, grandfather told Josie: "In consideration for all the work you have done for me during my illness and for all the love and affection you have shown me, I am changing my will so that all I own will pass to you after my death." After grandfather's death, Josie took all of his property under a properly executed will. The property Josie took under the will was worth $600,000. Does Josie have any gross income under IRC § 61? Explain your answer.

5. Father owns a $100,000 bond that will pay $10,000 of interest for each of the next ten years. Father also owns a business that had an operating loss of $60,000 several years ago. This operating loss will expire if not used during the current taxable year. To utilize this tax advantage, Father sells the right to collect the interest of $10,000 per year for the next ten years to his daughter for $60,000 (the net present value of $10,000 per year for 10 years). Father reports the $60,000 as income during the current year and offsets it with his operating loss. His daughter receives and reports the first $10,000 interest payment the following year. May the IRS successfully challenge the transaction? Explain your answer.

6. After graduating with a degree in Public Administration, Susan is unable to find a position. She pays Government Jobs, Inc., an employment agency specializing in placing its customers in public sector positions, $600 to help her find a position. The agency is successful, and Susan takes a position with the Indiana Department of Revenue. May she deduct the amount she paid the employment agency, pursuant to IRC §162? Explain your answer.

7. Jim, who recently graduated from college, visits your office in November of 2001. He has the following information pertaining to his personal income tax situation for 2001:

Salary	$50,000
Interest	$2,000
Home loan interest	$2,000
Property taxes on home	$1,500

In addition, Jim tells you he has pledged to donate at least $1,000 per year over the next five years to State U's foundation to support scholarships. He expects that over the next five years, the information will remain relatively the same. He did get a $300 rate reduction credit check in September 2001. He asks if there is anything he should do to save some income tax. Advise him.

8. A national consumption tax (or sales tax) has been proposed as an alternative to the personal income tax. If it were adopted, the rate would probably need to be at least 10 percent to provide sufficient revenues to replace the revenues lost by repealing the personal income tax. If it were adopted, your employer would no longer withhold federal income taxes from your wages or salary, and you would never be required to file an income tax return. Would you be in favor of a national sales tax? Why or why not?

Suggested Additional Reading

Barton, Babette B., Glenn Coven, Jr., Robert J. Peroni, and Richard Crawford Pugh. *Cases and Materials on Taxation of Business Enterprises*. Minneapolis, MN: West Group, 1998.

Birnbaum, Jeffrey, and Alan S. Murray. *Showdown at Gucci Gulch: Lawmakers, Lobbyists, and the Unlikely Triumph of Tax Reform*. New York: Random House, 1988.

Hoffman, William H., James E. Smith, and Eugene Willis. *Individual Income Taxes*. 2002 ed. Cincinnati, OH: Southwest College Publishing, 2001.

Karnes, Allan L., and James Fenton. "Certain Accelerated Death Benefits to Be Accorded Gross Income Exclusion." *TAXES: The Tax Magazine* 71 (June 1993): 331–338.

Karnes, Allan L., and Roger L. Lirely. "Striking Back at the IRS: Using Internal Revenue Provisions to Redress Unauthorized Disclosures of Tax Returns and Return Information." *Seton Hall Law Review* 23 (fall 1993): 901–943.

McNulty, John K. *Federal Income Taxation of Individuals in a Nutshell*. 6th ed. Minneapolis, MN: West Group, 1999.

Pratt, James W, and William N. Kulsrud. *Federal Taxation*. 2002 ed. Houston, TX: ARC Publishing, 2001.

Schisler, Dan L., and Frederick D. Niswander. *Individual Income Taxes: From Law to Practice*. Washington, DC: Thompson Learning, 2002.

Slemrod, Joel, and Jon Bakija. *Taxing Ourselves: A Citizen's Guide to the Great Debate Over Tax Reform*. Cambridge, MA: MIT Press, 1996.

Online Sources—There are a wide variety of online sources of tax information. A good starting place is the School of Accountancy at Southern Illinois University Carbondale's website at <http://www.cba.siu.edu/Accounting/infolink.htm>.

Endnotes

1. Actually, the federal government has the ability to tax all persons, citizens or not, who earn U.S. income. Although the federal income tax is based entirely on federal statutes, those statutes are interpreted by the federal courts. As such, it can be said there is a federal income tax common law.

2. James Freeland et al., *Fundamentals of Federal Income Taxation: Cases and Materials*, 11th ed. (New York: Foundation Press, 2000), pp. 14–17.

3. Greenmail and golden parachutes are methods of discouraging hostile takeovers of publicly traded corporations. Greenmail is a payment by a corporation to one who has acquired stock in the corporation, and who has announced or threatened to announce a public tender offer for the outstanding corporation stock. To fend off the hostile tender offer, the corporation, or persons working in concert with the corporation, buys the hostile stockholder's shares at an inflated price. The hostile stockholder, satisfied by the exorbitant profit on the shares he held, has no

more dealings with the corporation, and the hostile takeover threat is ended. See IRC § 5881 (2001). In an infamous 1980s example, General Motors paid Ross Perot around $750 million for his shares that were worth half that on the market. Perot was "greemailed" out to silence his public criticism of GM's upper management and Board of Directors. For an excellent discussion of the Perot-General Motors battle, see Robert A. G. Monks and Neil Minow, "Corporate Governance Case Study: General Motors," in *Corporate Governance,* 2nd ed. (Oxford, UK: Blackwell Publishers, 2001), available online at <http://www.ragm.com/library/books/corp_gov/cases/cs_gm.html>, as of January 30, 2002. While greenmail payments are made to corporate outsiders to keep current management in place, golden parachute payments are made to current management if a hostile takeover is successful. Typically, golden parachute agreements are entered into by upper management and the Board of Directors upon learning of a hostile takeover threat. They serve two purposes. First, they make any hostile takeover more expensive, because the new owners after a hostile takeover must honor all agreements made by prior owners. Second, they are meant to provide upper management a soft landing, once they are terminated by the new owners. See IRC § 380(g) (2001).

4. Martha Brant, "Hot Time in Gucci Gulch," *Newsweek,* February 19, 2001, p. 18.

5. Howard Fineman and Rich Thomas, "Snip, Snip, Snip," *Newsweek,* February 19, 2001, p. 18.

6. *Economic Growth and Tax Relief Reconciliation Act of 2001,* Pub. L. No. 107-16, 115 Stat. 38 (2001) (hereinafter EGTRRA).

7. U.S. Congress, Joint Committee on Taxation, *Summary of Provisions Contained in the Conference Agreement for H.R. 1836, The Economic Growth and Tax Relief Reconciliation Act of 2001,* JCX 50-01 (May 26, 2001).

8. Kelly Wallace, "$1.35 Trillion Tax Cut Becomes Law," *Cnn.com,* June 7, 2001, available at <http://www.cnn.com/2001/ALLPOLITICS/06/07/bush.taxes>, as of February 1, 2002.

9. "Congress to the Rescue: Stimulating the Economy," *MSNBC.com,* available at <http://www.msnbc.cm/news/657509.asp>, as of February 1, 2002.

10. Such as the Nunn-Domenici USA Tax, Susan Wieler, "Consumption Taxes: Do They Spur Growth?" *Challenge* 41 (November-December 1998): 60.

11. The social welfare states in Europe during the late 1970s and early 1980s, principally Sweden and Great Britain, experienced a wealth flight, highlighted by high-profile artists such as Ingmar Bergman, the Swedish film director, and Ringo Starr, the ex-Beatle. They were escaping tax rates as high as 90 percent. See Charles P. Wallace, "Where's the Exit?" *Time.com,* March 15, 1999, available at <http://www.time.com/time/magazine/printout/0%2C8816%2C21970%2C00.html>, as of January 30, 2002, for tax problems experienced in Germany and Sweden as late as 1999.

12. 348 U.S. 426 (1955).

13. Exclusions from gross income can be found in the IRC from § 101 through § 135 (2001).

14. IRC § 101(g) (2001).

15. IRC § 102(c) (2001). It is still possible, however, for traditional employer holiday gifts, such as hams and turkeys, to escape taxation as an excluded employee fringe benefit under IRC § 132 (2001).
16. 363 U.S. 278, 285 (1960).
17. IRC § 121 (2001).
18. IRC § 117, as amended by EGTRRA, act § 413.
19. Freeland, *Fundamentals of Federal Income Taxation*, p. 308.
20. 290 U.S. 111 (1933).
21. Morton Frank, 20 T.C. 511 (U.S. Tax Ct. 1953).
22. Higgins v. Commissioner, 312 U.S. 212 (1942). The *Higgins* case led to the passage of IRC § 212 (2001), allowing the deduction of ordinary and necessary expenses incurred for the production of income. The "production of income" standard is a less rigorous standard of business-like activities than "carrying on a trade or business." For example, investing in the stock of one company or holding a piece of property for appreciation qualify as activities for the "production of income." Neither would qualify as a "trade or business."
23. The deductions are authorized by the following IRC §§: 162–169, 212, 401, 217, 611, 219, 221, 222, and 215, as amended by EGTRRA in various act sections.
24. IRC § 221, as amended EGTRRA, act § 412.
25. IRC § 222, as amended EGTRRA, act § 431.
26. IRC § 213 (2001).
27. IRC § 163(h)(3) (2001).
28. IRC § 163(h)(4) (2000).
29. IRC § 163(d) (2001).
30. IRC § 164(a) (2001).
31. IRC § 170 (2001).
32. IRC § 165(c) (2001).
33. IRC § 165(h) (2001).
34. IRC § 67(a) (2001). IRC § 67(b) (2001) lists those itemized deductions that are not subject to the 2 percent floor.
35. IRC § 68, as amended by EGTRRA, act § 103.
36. IRC §§ 63 (b) & (c) (2001).
37. The amounts are indexed (increased or decreased each year based on the cost of living), IRC § 63(c)(4) (2001), as are many other amounts throughout the code, such as the tax tables and schedules, personal and dependency exemptions, and most of the phase-out provisions. The Internal Revenue Service makes these calculations each year and publishes them in the *Internal Revenue Bulletin* and the *Cumulative Bulletin*. Indexed amounts can also be found on the IRS's web page at <http://www.irs.ustreas.gov/prod/index.html>. See Appendix III for 2002 and 2003 amounts.
38. IRC § 63, as amended by EGTRRA, act § 301.
39. IRC § 63(c)(5) (2001).
40. IRC § 151 (a) & (b) (2001).
41. IRC § 151(d)(2) (2001).
42. IRC § 151(c) (2000).
43. IRC § 152(b)(3) (2001).
44. IRC § 152(a) (2001).
45. IRC §§ 152(b)(2) & (5) (2001).
46. IRC § 151(c)(2) (2001) & Rev. Rul. 65-34, 1965 C.B. 86.

47. IRC § 151(c)(1)(A) (2001).
48. IRC §§ 151(c)(1)(B) & (c)(4) (2001).
49. IRC § 152(a) (2001).
50. IRC § 152(e) (2001).
51. IRC § 151(d)(3), as amended by EGTRRA, act § 102. By eliminating the limitations on itemized deductions and personal and dependency exemptions, Congress was able to reduce taxes on the wealthy without further reductions in the top tax rates.
52. IRC §§ 1 & 6428, as amended by EGTRRA, act § 101. The combination of the 2001 tax rate schedules, which do not incorporate the new 10 percent brackets, and the rate reduction credit checks is a sleight of hand by the federal government. Had the tax rate schedules and tax tables been constructed using the new 10 precent brackets, taxpayers would have had to increase the amount of tax they owed or reduce the amount of tax refund they were due by the amount of their tax reduction credit check. By not including the new 10 percent brackets in the tax rate schedules and tax table for 2001, most taxpayers will not need to adjust for their tax reduction credit checks, maintaining the illusion that "taxpayers got something for nothing."
53. IRC § 7702(a) (2001) instructs individuals to determine whether they are married or not, as of the last day of the tax year, unless one of the spouses dies during the year, in which case the determination should be made as of the date of death. Those couples who are legally separated under a decree of divorce, or separate maintenance, shall not be considered married.
54. U.S. Congress, Joint Committee on Taxation, *Summary of Provisions Contained in the Conference Agreement for H.R. 1836, The Economic Growth and Tax Relief Reconciliation Act of 2001*, JCX 50-01 (May 26, 2001).
55. IRC § 6013 (2001) was passed by Congress in 1948. Poe v. Seaborn, 282 U.S. 101 (1930).
56. IRC § 7703(b) (2001). To qualify, the individual in question must not file a joint return and must provide over 50 percent of the cost of maintaining a home that is the pricipal residence of a child, whom the taxpayer may claim as a dependent. In addition, the taxpayer's spouse cannot have been a member of the household at any time during the last six months of the year.
57. IRC § 2(a) (2001).
58. IRC § 2(b) (2001).
59. IRC § 1(c) (2001).
60. Both credits are authorized under IRC § 25A (2001). The hope credit is at IRC § 25A(b) (2001), the lifetime learning credit is at IRC § 25A(c) (2001), and the income limitations are at IRC § 25A(d) (2001).
61. IRC § 24, as amended by EGTRRA, act §§ 201 & 203.
62. IRC § 21, as amended by EGTRRA, act § 204.
63. EGTRRA introduces a complex computation to determine if all, or a portion of the child tax credit, may be used to reduce tax liability below zero. IRC § 24, as amended by EGTRRA, act §§ 201 & 203.
64. IRC § 32, as amended by EGTRRA, act § 303.
65. If the property is personal use property, any loss is considered a nondeductible personal loss.

66. Depreciation is used for tangible property, such as equipment and buildings, and amortization is used for intangible property, such as goodwill, patents, and copyrights.

67. 311 U.S. 112 (1940).

68. IRC § 1(h)(1) (2001). For taxpayers in the 15 percent bracket, the top rate is 10 percent.

69. IRC § 1(h)(2) (2001). For taxpayers in the 15 percent bracket, the top rate is 8 percent.

70. IRC § 1221 (2001).

71. IRC § 1201 (2001).

72. IRC § 11 (2001).

73. Allan Karnes, "The New Partnership Recognition Trigger: In-Kind Distributions of Contributed Property," *Taxes—The Tax Magazine* 68 (March 1990): 213–219.

74. An additional entity choice is the subchapter S corporation. It is legally a corporation, but taxed like a pass through entity for federal tax purposes. A major drawback of the subchapter S corporation is the complexity surrounding valid subchapter elections. It includes a limit on the number of shareholders, a limit on the classes of stock the corporation may issue, and surprise terminations of the subchapter S election that can result from the death of a shareholder or the sale of stock by shareholders. The limited liability company has become the entity of choice for those businesses that in times past would choose a subchapter S corporation.

75. Jane P. Mallor, et al., *Business Law and the Regulatory Environment: Concepts and Cases*, 10th ed. (New York: Irwin McGraw-Hill, 1998), p. 813.

76. Allan Karnes, Lori Cundiff, and Roger Lirely, "The Limited Liability Company: A State-by-State Look at the New Pass Through Entity," *Detroit College of Law Review* 1997 (1997): 2–47. ✦

Appendices, Glossary, and Indices

Constitution of the United States

W e the People of the United States, in Order to form a more perfect Union, establish Justice, insure domestic Tranquility, provide for the common defense, promote the general Welfare, and secure the Blessings of Liberty to ourselves and our Posterity, do ordain and establish this Constitution for the United States of America.

Article I

Section 1.

All legislative Powers herein granted shall be vested in a Congress of the United States, which shall consist of a Senate and House of Representatives.

Section 2.

1. The House of Representatives shall be composed of Members chosen every second Year by the People of the several States, and the Electors in each State shall have the Qualifications requisite for Electors of the most numerous Branch of the State Legislature.

2. No Person shall be a Representative who shall not have attained to the Age of twenty five Years, and been seven Years a Citizen of the United States, and who shall not, when elected, be an Inhabitant of that State in which he shall be chosen.

3. Representatives and direct Taxes shall be apportioned among the several States which may be included within this Union, according to their respective Numbers, which shall be determined by adding to the whole Number of free Persons, including those bound to Service for a Term of Years, and excluding Indians not taxed, three fifths of all other Persons. The actual Enumeration shall be made within three Years after the first Meeting of the Congress of the United States, and within every subsequent Term of ten Years, in such Manner as they shall by Law direct. The Number of Representatives shall not exceed one for every thirty Thousand, but each State shall have at Least one Representative; and until such enumeration shall be made, the State of New Hampshire shall be entitled to chuse three, Massachusetts eight, Rhode-Island and Providence Plantations one, Connecticut five, New-York six, New Jersey four, Pennsylvania eight, Delaware one, Maryland six, Virginia ten, North Carolina five, South Carolina five, and Georgia three.

4. When vacancies happen in the Representation from any State, the Executive Authority thereof shall issue Writs of Election to fill such Vacancies.

5. The House of Representatives shall chuse their Speaker and other Officers; and shall have the sole Power of Impeachment.

Section 3.

1. The Senate of the United States shall be composed of two Senators from each State, chosen by the Legislature thereof for six Years; and each Senator shall have one Vote.

2. Immediately after they shall be assembled in Consequence of the first Election, they shall be divided as equally as may be into three Classes. The Seats of the Senators of the first Class shall be vacated at the Expiration of the second Year, of the second Class at the Expiration of the fourth Year, and of the third

Class at the Expiration of the sixth Year, so that one third may be chosen every second Year; and if Vacancies happen by Resignation, or otherwise, during the Recess of the Legislature of any State, the Executive thereof may make temporary Appointments until the next Meeting of the Legislature, which shall then fill such Vacancies.

3. No Person shall be a Senator who shall not have attained to the Age of thirty Years, and been nine Years a Citizen of the United States, and who shall not, when elected, be an Inhabitant of that State for which he shall be chosen.

4. The Vice President of the United States shall be President of the Senate, but shall have no Vote, unless they be equally divided.

5. The Senate shall chuse their other Officers, and also a President pro tempore, in the Absence of the Vice President, or when he shall exercise the Office of President of the United States.

6. The Senate shall have the sole Power to try all Impeachments. When sitting for that Purpose, they shall be on Oath or Affirmation. When the President of the United States is tried, the Chief Justice shall preside: And no Person shall be convicted without the Concurrence of two thirds of the Members present.

7. Judgment in Cases of Impeachment shall not extend further than to removal from Office, and disqualification to hold and enjoy any Office of honor, Trust or Profit under the United States: but the Party convicted shall nevertheless be liable and subject to Indictment, Trial, Judgment and Punishment, according to Law.

Section 4.

1. The Times, Places and Manner of holding Elections for Senators and Representatives, shall be prescribed in each State by the Legislature thereof; but the Congress may at any time by Law make or alter such Regulations, except as to the Places of chusing Senators.

2. The Congress shall assemble at least once in every Year, and such Meeting shall be on the first Monday in December, unless they shall by Law appoint a different Day.

Section 5.

1. Each House shall be the Judge of the Elections, Returns and Qualifications of its own Members, and a Majority of each shall constitute a Quorum to do Business; but a smaller Number may adjourn from day to day, and may be authorized to compel the Attendance of absent Members, in such Manner, and under such Penalties as each House may provide.

2. Each House may determine the Rules of its Proceedings, punish its Members for disorderly Behaviour, and, with the Concurrence of two thirds, expel a Member.

3. Each House shall keep a Journal of its Proceedings, and from time to time publish the same, excepting such Parts as may in their Judgment require Secrecy; and the Yeas and Nays of the Members of either House on any question shall, at the Desire of one fifth of those Present, be entered on the Journal.

4. Neither House, during the Session of Congress, shall, without the Consent of the other, adjourn for more than three days, nor to any other Place than that in which the two Houses shall be sitting.

Section 6.

1. The Senators and Representatives shall receive a Compensation for their Services, to be ascertained by Law, and paid out of the Treasury of the United States. They shall in all Cases, except Treason, Felony and Breach of the Peace, be privileged from Arrest during their Attendance at the Session of their respective Houses, and in going to and returning from the same; and for any Speech or Debate in either House, they shall not be questioned in any other Place.

2. No Senator or Representative shall, during the Time for which he was elected, be appointed to any civil Office under the Authority of the United States, which shall have been created, or the Emoluments whereof shall have been encreased during such time; and no Person holding any Office under the United States, shall be a Member of either House during his Continuance in Office.

Section 7.

1. All Bills for raising Revenue shall originate in the House of Representatives; but the Senate may propose or concur with Amendments as on other Bills.

2. Every Bill which shall have passed the House of Representatives and the Senate, shall, before it become a Law, be presented to the President of the United States: If he approve he shall sign it, but if not he shall return it, with his Objections to that House in which it shall have originated, who shall enter the Objections at large on their Journal, and proceed to reconsider it.If after such Reconsideration two thirds of that House shall agree to pass the Bill, it shall be sent, together with the Objections, to the other House, by

which it shall likewise be reconsidered, and if approved by two thirds of that House, it shall become a Law. But in all such Cases the Votes of both Houses shall be determined by yeas and Nays, and the Names of the Persons voting for and against the Bill shall be entered on the Journal of each House respectively. If any Bill shall not be returned by the President within ten Days (Sundays excepted) after it shall have been presented to him, the Same shall be a Law, in like Manner as if he had signed it, unless the Congress by their Adjournment prevent its Return, in which Case it shall not be a Law.

3. Every Order, Resolution, or Vote to which the Concurrence of the Senate and House of Representatives may be necessary (except on a question of Adjournment) shall be presented to the President of the United States; and before the Same shall take Effect, shall be approved by him, or being disapproved by him, shall be repassed by two thirds of the Senate and House of Representatives, according to the Rules and Limitations prescribed in the Case of a Bill.

Section 8.

The Congress shall have the Power

1. To lay and collect Taxes, Duties, Imposts and Excises, to pay the Debts and provide for the common Defence and general Welfare of the United States; but all Duties, Imposts and Excises shall be uniform throughout the United States;

2. To borrow Money on the credit of the United States;

3. To regulate Commerce with foreign Nations, and among the several States, and with the Indian Tribes;

4. To establish an uniform Rule of Naturalization, and uniform Laws on the subject of Bankruptcies throughout the United States;

5. To coin Money, regulate the Value thereof, and of foreign Coin, and fix the Standard of Weights and Measures;

6. To provide for the Punishment of counterfeiting the Securities and current Coin of the United States;

7. To establish Post Offices and post Roads;

8. To promote the Progress of Science and useful Arts, by securing for limited Times to Authors and Inventors the exclusive Right to their respective Writings and Discoveries;

9. To constitute Tribunals inferior to the supreme Court;

10. To define and punish Piracies and Felonies committed on the high Seas, and Offences against the Law of Nations;

11. To declare War, grant Letters of Marque and Reprisal, and make Rules concerning Captures on Land and Water;

12. To raise and support Armies, but no Appropriation of Money to that Use shall be for a longer Term than two Years;

13. To provide and maintain a Navy;

14. To make Rules for the Government and Regulation of the land and naval Forces;

15. To provide for calling forth the Militia to execute the Laws of the Union, suppress Insurrections and repel Invasions;

16. To provide for organizing, arming, and disciplining, the Militia, and for governing such Part of them as may be employed in the Service of the United States, reserving to the States respectively, the Appointment of the Officers, and the Authority of training the Militia according to the discipline prescribed by Congress;

17. To exercise exclusive Legislation in all Cases whatsoever, over such District (not exceeding ten Miles square) as may, by Cession of particular States, and the Acceptance of Congress, become the Seat of the Government of the United States, and to exercise like Authority over all Places purchased by the Consent of the Legislature of the State in which the Same shall be, for the Erection of Forts, Magazines, Arsenals, dock-Yards, and other needful Buildings;—And

18. To make all Laws which shall be necessary and proper for carrying into Execution the foregoing Powers, and all other Powers vested by this Constitution in the Government of the United States, or in any Department or Officer thereof.

Section 9.

1. The Migration or Importation of such Persons as any of the States now existing shall think proper to admit, shall not be prohibited by the Congress prior to the Year one thousand eight hundred and eight, but a Tax or duty may be imposed on such Importation, not exceeding ten dollars for each Person.

2. The Privilege of the Writ of Habeas Corpus shall not be suspended, unless when in Cases of Rebellion or Invasion the public Safety may require it.

3. No Bill of Attainder or ex post facto Law shall be passed.

4. No Capitation, or other direct, Tax shall be laid, unless in Proportion to the Census or enumeration herein before directed to be taken.

5. No Tax or Duty shall be laid on Articles exported from any State.

6. No Preference shall be given by any Regulation of Commerce or Revenue to the Ports of one State over those of another; nor shall Vessels bound to, or from, one State, be obliged to enter, clear, or pay Duties in another.

7. No Money shall be drawn from the Treasury, but in Consequence of Appropriations made by Law; and a regular Statement and Account of the Receipts and Expenditures of all public Money shall be published from time to time.

8. No Title of Nobility shall be granted by the United States: And no Person holding any Office of Profit or Trust under them, shall, without the Consent of the Congress, accept of any present, Emolument, Office, or Title, of any kind whatever, from any King, Prince, or foreign State.

Section 10.

1. No State shall enter into any Treaty, Alliance, or Confederation; grant Letters of Marque and Reprisal; coin Money; emit Bills of Credit; make any Thing but gold and silver Coin a Tender in Payment of Debts; pass any Bill of Attainder, ex post facto Law, or Law impairing the Obligation of Contracts, or grant any Title of Nobility.

2. No State shall, without the Consent of the Congress, lay any Imposts or Duties on Imports or Exports, except what may be absolutely necessary for executing it's inspection Laws: and the net Produce of all Duties and Imposts, laid by any State on Imports or Exports, shall be for the Use of the Treasury of the United States; and all such Laws shall be subject to the Revision and Controul of the Congress.

3. No State shall, without the Consent of Congress, lay any Duty of Tonnage, keep Troops, or Ships of War in time of Peace, enter into any Agreement or Compact with another State, or with a foreign Power, or engage in War, unless actually invaded, or in such imminent Danger as will not admit of delay.

Article II

Section 1.

1. The executive Power shall be vested in a President of the United States of America. He shall hold his Office during the Term of four Years, and, together with the Vice President, chosen for the same Term, be elected, as follows:

2. Each State shall appoint, in such Manner as the Legislature thereof may direct, a Number of Electors, equal to the whole Number of Senators and Representatives to which the State may be entitled in the Congress: but no Senator or Representative, or Person holding an Office of Trust or Profit under the United States, shall be appointed an Elector.

The Electors shall meet in their respective States, and vote by Ballot for two Persons, of whom one at least shall not be an Inhabitant of the same State with themselves. And they shall make a List of all the Persons voted for, and of the Number of Votes for each; which List they shall sign and certify, and transmit sealed to the Seat of the Government of the United States, directed to the President of the Senate. The President of the Senate shall, in the Presence of the Senate and House of Representatives, open all the Certificates, and the Votes shall then be counted. The Person having the greatest Number of Votes shall be the President, if such Number be a Majority of the whole Number of Electors appointed; and if there be more than one who have such Majority, and have an equal Number of Votes, then the House of Representatives shall immediately chuse by Ballot one of them for President; and if no Person have a Majority, then from the five highest on the List the said House shall in like Manner chuse the President. But in chusing the President, the Votes shall be taken by States, the Representation from each State having one Vote; A quorum for this purpose shall consist of a Member or Members from two thirds of the States, and a Majority of all the States shall be necessary to a Choice. In every Case, after the Choice of the President, the Person having the greatest Number of Votes of the Electors shall be the Vice President. But if there should remain two or more who have equal Votes, the Senate shall chuse from them by Ballot the Vice President.

3. The Congress may determine the Time of chusing the Electors, and the Day on which they shall give their Votes; which Day shall be the same throughout the United States.

4. No Person except a natural born Citizen, or a Citizen of the United States, at the time of the Adoption of this Constitution, shall be eligible to the Office of President; neither shall any Person be eligible to

that Office who shall not have attained to the Age of thirty five Years, and been fourteen Years a Resident within the United States.

5. In Case of the Removal of the President from Office, or of his Death, Resignation, or Inability to discharge the Powers and Duties of the said Office, the Same shall devolve on the Vice President, and the Congress may by Law provide for the Case of Removal, Death, Resignation or Inability, both of the President and Vice President, declaring what Officer shall then act as President, and such Officer shall act accordingly, until the Disability be removed, or a President shall be elected.

6. The President shall, at stated Times, receive for his Services, a Compensation, which shall neither be increased nor diminished during the Period for which he shall have been elected, and he shall not receive within that Period any other Emolument from the United States, or any of them.

7. Before he enter on the Execution of his Office, he shall take the following Oath or Affirmation:—"I do solemnly swear (or affirm) that I will faithfully execute the Office of President of the United States, and will to the best of my Ability, preserve, protect and defend the Constitution of the United States."

Section 2.

1. The President shall be Commander in Chief of the Army and Navy of the United States, and of the Militia of the several States, when called into the actual Service of the United States; he may require the Opinion, in writing, of the principal Officer in each of the executive Departments, upon any Subject relating to the Duties of their respective Offices, and he shall have Power to grant Reprieves and Pardons for Offences against the United States, except in Cases of Impeachment.

2. He shall have Power, by and with the Advice and Consent of the Senate, to make Treaties, provided two thirds of the Senators present concur; and he shall nominate, and by and with the Advice and Consent of the Senate, shall appoint Ambassadors, other public Ministers and Consuls, Judges of the supreme Court, and all other Officers of the United States, whose Appointments are not herein otherwise provided for, and which shall be established by Law: but the Congress may by Law vest the Appointment of such inferior Officers, as they think proper, in the President alone, in the Courts of Law, or in the Heads of Departments.

3. The President shall have Power to fill up all Vacancies that may happen during the Recess of the Senate, by granting Commissions which shall expire at the End of their next Session.

Section 3.

He shall from time to time give to the Congress Information of the State of the Union, and recommend to their Consideration such Measures as he shall judge necessary and expedient; he may, on extraordinary Occasions, convene both Houses, or either of them, and in Case of Disagreement between them, with Respect to the Time of Adjournment, he may adjourn them to such Time as he shall think proper; he shall receive Ambassadors and other public Ministers; he shall take Care that the Laws be faithfully executed, and shall Commission all the Officers of the United States.

Section 4.

The President, Vice President and all civil Officers of the United States, shall be removed from Office on Impeachment for, and Conviction of, Treason, Bribery, or other high Crimes and Misdemeanors.

Article III

Section I.

The judicial Power of the United States shall be vested in one supreme Court, and in such inferior Courts as the Congress may from time to time ordain and establish. The Judges, both of the supreme and inferior Courts, shall hold their Offices during good Behaviour, and shall, at stated Times, receive for their Services a Compensation, which shall not be diminished during their Continuance in Office.

Section 2.

1. The judicial Power shall extend to all Cases, in Law and Equity, arising under this Constitution, the Laws of the United States, and Treaties made, or which shall be made, under their Authority;—to all Cases affecting Ambassadors, other public Ministers and Consuls;—to all Cases of admiralty and maritime Jurisdiction;—to Controversies to which the United States shall be a Party;—to Controversies between two or more States;— between a State and Citizens of another State;—between Citizens of different States;—

between Citizens of the same State claiming Lands under Grants of different States, and between a State, or the Citizens thereof, and foreign States, Citizens or Subjects.

2. In all Cases affecting Ambassadors, other public Ministers and Consuls, and those in which a State shall be Party, the supreme Court shall have original Jurisdiction. In all the other Cases before mentioned, the supreme Court shall have appellate Jurisdiction, both as to Law and Fact, with such Exceptions, and under such Regulations as the Congress shall make.

3. The Trial of all Crimes, except in Cases of Impeachment, shall be by Jury; and such Trial shall be held in the State where the said Crimes shall have been committed; but when not committed within any State, the Trial shall be at such Place or Places as the Congress may by Law have directed.

Section 3.

1. Treason against the United States, shall consist only in levying War against them, or in adhering to their Enemies, giving them Aid and Comfort. No Person shall be convicted of Treason unless on the Testimony of two Witnesses to the same overt Act, or on Confession in open Court.

2. The Congress shall have Power to declare the Punishment of Treason, but no Attainder of Treason shall work Corruption of Blood, or Forfeiture except during the Life of the Person attainted.

Article IV

Section 1.

Full Faith and Credit shall be given in each State to the public Acts, Records, and judicial Proceedings of every other State. And the Congress may by general Laws prescribe the Manner in which such Acts, Records and Proceedings shall be proved, and the Effect thereof.

Section 2.

1. The Citizens of each State shall be entitled to all Privileges and Immunities of Citizens in the several States.

2. A Person charged in any State with Treason, Felony, or other Crime, who shall flee from Justice, and be found in another State, shall on Demand of the executive Authority of the State from which he fled, be delivered up, to be removed to the State having Jurisdiction of the Crime.

3. No Person held to Service or Labour in one State, under the Laws thereof, escaping into another, shall, in Consequence of any Law or Regulation therein, be discharged from such Service or Labour, but shall be delivered up on Claim of the Party to whom such Service or Labour may be due.

Section 3.

1. New States may be admitted by the Congress into this Union; but no new State shall be formed or erected within the Jurisdiction of any other State; nor any State be formed by the Junction of two or more States, or Parts of States, without the Consent of the Legislatures of the States concerned as well as of the Congress.

2. The Congress shall have Power to dispose of and make all needful Rules and Regulations respecting the Territory or other Property belonging to the United States; and nothing in this Constitution shall be so construed as to Prejudice any Claims of the United States, or of any particular State.

Section 4.

The United States shall guarantee to every State in this Union a Republican Form of Government, and shall protect each of them against Invasion; and on Application of the Legislature, or of the Executive (when the Legislature cannot be convened), against domestic Violence.

Article V

The Congress, whenever two thirds of both Houses shall deem it necessary, shall propose Amendments to this Constitution, or, on the Application of the Legislatures of two thirds of the several States, shall call a Convention for proposing Amendments, which, in either Case, shall be valid to all Intents and Purposes, as Part of this Constitution, when ratified by the Legislatures of three fourths of the several States, or by Conventions in three fourths thereof, as the one or the other Mode of Ratification may be proposed by the Congress; Provided that no Amendment which may be made prior to the Year One thousand eight hundred and eight shall in any Manner affect the first and fourth Clauses in the Ninth Section of the first Article; and that no State, without its Consent, shall be deprived of its equal Suffrage in the Senate.

Article VI

1. All Debts contracted and Engagements entered into, before the Adoption of this Constitution, shall be as valid against the United States under this Constitution, as under the Confederation.

2. This Constitution, and the Laws of the United States which shall be made in Pursuance thereof; and all Treaties made, or which shall be made, under the Authority of the United States, shall be the supreme Law of the Land; and the Judges in every State shall be bound thereby, any Thing in the Constitution or Laws of any State to the Contrary notwithstanding.

3. The Senators and Representatives before mentioned, and the Members of the several State Legislatures, and all executive and judicial Officers, both of the United States and of the several States, shall be bound by Oath or Affirmation, to support this Constitution; but no religious Test shall ever be required as a Qualification to any Office or public Trust under the United States.

Article VII

The Ratification of the Conventions of nine States, shall be sufficient for the Establishment of this Constitution between the States so ratifying the Same.

The Preamble to the Bill of Rights (the First 10 Amendments to the U.S. Constitution)—Ratified December 15, 1791

Congress of the United States begun and held at the City of New-York, on Wednesday the fourth of March, one thousand seven hundred and eighty nine.

THE Conventions of a number of the States, having at the time of their adopting the Constitution, expressed a desire, in order to prevent misconstruction or abuse of its powers, that further declaratory and restrictive clauses should be added: And as extending the ground of public confidence in the Government, will best ensure the beneficent ends of its institution.

RESOLVED by the Senate and House of Representatives of the United States of America, in Congress assembled, two thirds of both Houses concurring, that the following Articles be proposed to the Legislatures of the several States, as amendments to the Constitution of the United States, all, or any of which Articles, when ratified by three fourths of the said Legislatures, to be valid to all intents and purposes, as part of the said Constitution; viz.

ARTICLES in addition to, and Amendment of the Constitution of the United States of America, proposed by Congress, and ratified by the Legislatures of the several States, pursuant to the fifth Article of the original Constitution.

Note: The following text is a transcription of the first 10 amendments to the Constitution in their original form. These amendments were ratified December 15, 1791, and form what is known as the "Bill of Rights."

Amendment I

Congress shall make no law respecting an establishment of religion, or prohibiting the free exercise thereof; or abridging the freedom of speech, or of the press; or the right of the people peaceably to assemble, and to petition the Government for a redress of grievances.

Amendment II

A well regulated Militia, being necessary to the security of a free State, the right of the people to keep and bear Arms, shall not be infringed.

Amendment III

No Soldier shall, in time of peace be quartered in any house, without the consent of the Owner, nor in time of war, but in a manner to be prescribed by law.

Amendment IV

The right of the people to be secure in their persons, houses, papers, and effects, against unreasonable searches and seizures, shall not be violated, and no Warrants shall issue, but upon probable cause, supported by Oath or affirmation, and particularly describing the place to be searched, and the persons or things to be seized.

Amendment V

No person shall be held to answer for a capital, or otherwise infamous crime, unless on a presentment or indictment of a Grand Jury, except in cases arising in the land or naval forces, or in the Militia, when in actual service in time of War or public danger; nor shall any person be subject for the same offence to be twice put in jeopardy of life or limb; nor shall be compelled in any criminal case to be a witness against himself, nor be deprived of life, liberty, or property, without due process of law; nor shall private property be taken for public use, without just compensation.

Amendment VI

In all criminal prosecutions, the accused shall enjoy the right to a speedy and public trial, by an impartial jury of the State and district wherein the crime shall have been committed, which district shall have been previously ascertained by law, and to be informed of the nature and cause of the accusation; to be confronted with the witnesses against him; to have compulsory process for obtaining witnesses in his favor, and to have the Assistance of Counsel for his defence.

Amendment VII

In suits at common law, where the value in controversy shall exceed twenty dollars, the right of trial by jury shall be preserved, and no fact tried by a jury, shall be otherwise reexamined in any Court of the United States, than according to the rules of the common law.

Amendment VIII

Excessive bail shall not be required, nor excessive fines imposed, nor cruel and unusual punishments inflicted.

Amendment IX

The enumeration in the Constitution, of certain rights, shall not be construed to deny or disparage others retained by the people.

Amendment X

The powers not delegated to the United States by the Constitution, nor prohibited by it to the States, are reserved to the States respectively, or to the people.

Amendment XI

Passed by Congress March 4, 1794. Ratified February 7, 1795.
Note: Article III, section 2, of the Constitution was modified by amendment 11.

The Judicial power of the United States shall not be construed to extend to any suit in law or equity, commenced or prosecuted against one of the United States by Citizens of another State, or by Citizens or Subjects of any Foreign State.

Amendment XII

Passed by Congress December 9, 1803. Ratified June 15, 1804.
Note: A portion of Article II, section 1 of the Constitution was superseded by the 12th amendment.
The Electors shall meet in their respective states and vote by ballot for President and Vice-President, one of whom, at least, shall not be an inhabitant of the same state with themselves; they shall name in their ballots the person voted for as President, and in distinct ballots the person voted for as Vice-President, and they shall make distinct lists of all persons voted for as President, and of all persons voted for as Vice-President, and of the number of votes for each, which lists they shall sign and certify, and transmit sealed to the seat of the government of the United States, directed to the President of the Senate;—the President of the Senate shall, in the presence of the Senate and House of Representatives, open all the certificates and the votes shall then be counted;—The person having the greatest number of votes for President, shall be the President, if such number be a majority of the whole number of Electors appointed; and if no person have such majority, then from the persons having the highest numbers not exceeding three on the list of those voted for as President, the House of Representatives shall choose immediately, by ballot, the President. But in choosing the President, the votes shall be taken by states, the representation from each state having one vote; a quorum for this purpose shall consist of a member or members from two-thirds of the states, and a majority of all the states shall be necessary to a choice. [And if the House of Representatives shall not choose a President whenever the right of choice shall devolve upon them, before the fourth day of March next following, then the Vice-President shall act as President, as in case of the death or other constitutional disability of the President.—]* The person having the greatest number of votes as Vice-President, shall be the Vice-President, if such number be a majority of the whole number of Electors appointed, and if no person have a majority, then from the two highest numbers on the list, the Senate shall choose the Vice-President; a quorum for the purpose shall consist of two-thirds of the whole number of Senators, and a majority of the whole number shall be necessary to a choice. But no person constitutionally ineligible to the office of President shall be eligible to that of Vice-President of the United States.
*Superseded by section 3 of the 20th amendment.

Amendment XIII

Passed by Congress January 31, 1865. Ratified December 6, 1865.
Note: A portion of Article IV, section 2, of the Constitution was superseded by the 13th amendment.

Section 1.

Neither slavery nor involuntary servitude, except as a punishment for crime whereof the party shall have been duly convicted, shall exist within the United States, or any place subject to their jurisdiction.

Section 2.

Congress shall have power to enforce this article by appropriate legislation.

Amendment XIV

Passed by Congress June 13, 1866. Ratified July 9, 1868.
Note: Article I, section 2, of the Constitution was modified by section 2 of the 14th amendment.

Section 1.

All persons born or naturalized in the United States, and subject to the jurisdiction thereof, are citizens of the United States and of the State wherein they reside. No State shall make or enforce any law which shall abridge the privileges or immunities of citizens of the United States; nor shall any State deprive any person of life, liberty, or property, without due process of law; nor deny to any person within its jurisdiction the equal protection of the laws.

Section 2.

Representatives shall be apportioned among the several States according to their respective numbers, counting the whole number of persons in each State, excluding Indians not taxed. But when the right to vote at any election for the choice of electors for President and Vice-President of the United States, Representatives in Congress, the Executive and Judicial officers of a State, or the members of the Legislature thereof, is denied to any of the male inhabitants of such State, being twenty-one years of age,* and citizens of the United States, or in any way abridged, except for participation in rebellion, or other crime, the basis of representation therein shall be reduced in the proportion which the number of such male citizens shall bear to the whole number of male citizens twenty-one years of age in such State.

Section 3.

No person shall be a Senator or Representative in Congress, or elector of President and Vice-President, or hold any office, civil or military, under the United States, or under any State, who, having previously taken an oath, as a member of Congress, or as an officer of the United States, or as a member of any State legislature, or as an executive or judicial officer of any State, to support the Constitution of the United States, shall have engaged in insurrection or rebellion against the same, or given aid or comfort to the enemies thereof. But Congress may by a vote of two-thirds of each House, remove such disability.

Section 4.

The validity of the public debt of the United States, authorized by law, including debts incurred for payment of pensions and bounties for services in suppressing insurrection or rebellion, shall not be questioned. But neither the United States nor any State shall assume or pay any debt or obligation incurred in aid of insurrection or rebellion against the United States, or any claim for the loss or emancipation of any slave; but all such debts, obligations and claims shall be held illegal and void.

Section 5.

The Congress shall have the power to enforce, by appropriate legislation, the provisions of this article.

Changed by section 1 of the 26th amendment.

Amendment XV

Passed by Congress February 26, 1869. Ratified February 3, 1870.

Section 1.

The right of citizens of the United States to vote shall not be denied or abridged by the United States or by any State on account of race, color, or previous condition of servitude—

Section 2.

The Congress shall have the power to enforce this article by appropriate legislation.

Amendment XVI

Passed by Congress July 2, 1909. Ratified February 3, 1913.

Note: Article I, section 9, of the Constitution was modified by amendment 16.

The Congress shall have power to lay and collect taxes on incomes, from whatever source derived, without apportionment among the several States, and without regard to any census or enumeration.

Amendment XVII

Passed by Congress May 13, 1912. Ratified April 8, 1913.

Note: Article I, section 3, of the Constitution was modified by the 17th amendment.

The Senate of the United States shall be composed of two Senators from each State, elected by the people thereof, for six years; and each Senator shall have one vote. The electors in each State shall have the qualifications requisite for electors of the most numerous branch of the State legislatures.

When vacancies happen in the representation of any State in the Senate, the executive authority of such State shall issue writs of election to fill such vacancies: Provided, That the legislature of any State may empower the executive thereof to make temporary appointments until the people fill the vacancies by election as the legislature may direct.

This amendment shall not be so construed as to affect the election or term of any Senator chosen before it becomes valid as part of the Constitution.

Amendment XVIII

Passed by Congress December 18, 1917. Ratified January 16, 1919. Repealed by amendment 21.

Section 1.

After one year from the ratification of this article the manufacture, sale, or transportation of intoxicating liquors within, the importation thereof into, or the exportation thereof from the United States and all territory subject to the jurisdiction thereof for beverage purposes is hereby prohibited.

Section 2.

The Congress and the several States shall have concurrent power to enforce this article by appropriate legislation.

Section 3.

This article shall be inoperative unless it shall have been ratified as an amendment to the Constitution by the legislatures of the several States, as provided in the Constitution, within seven years from the date of the submission hereof to the States by the Congress.

Amendment XIX

Passed by Congress June 4, 1919. Ratified August 18, 1920.

The right of citizens of the United States to vote shall not be denied or abridged by the United States or by any State on account of sex.

Congress shall have power to enforce this article by appropriate legislation.

Amendment XX

Passed by Congress March 2, 1932. Ratified January 23, 1933.

Note: Article I, section 4, of the Constitution was modified by section 2 of this amendment. In addition, a portion of the 12th amendment was superseded by section 3.

Section 1.

The terms of the President and the Vice President shall end at noon on the 20th day of January, and the terms of Senators and Representatives at noon on the 3d day of January, of the years in which such terms would have ended if this article had not been ratified; and the terms of their successors shall then begin.

Section 2.

The Congress shall assemble at least once in every year, and such meeting shall begin at noon on the 3d day of January, unless they shall by law appoint a different day.

Section 3.

If, at the time fixed for the beginning of the term of the President, the President elect shall have died, the Vice President elect shall become President. If a President shall not have been chosen before the time fixed for the beginning of his term, or if the President elect shall have failed to qualify, then the Vice President elect shall act as President until a President shall have qualified; and the Congress may by law provide for the case wherein neither a President elect nor a Vice President shall have qualified, declaring who shall then act as President, or the manner in which one who is to act shall be selected, and such person shall act accordingly until a President or Vice President shall have qualified.

Section 4.

The Congress may by law provide for the case of the death of any of the persons from whom the House of Representatives may choose a President whenever the right of choice shall have devolved upon them, and for the case of the death of any of the persons from whom the Senate may choose a Vice President whenever the right of choice shall have devolved upon them.

Section 5.

Sections 1 and 2 shall take effect on the 15th day of October following the ratification of this article.

Section 6.

This article shall be inoperative unless it shall have been ratified as an amendment to the Constitution by the legislatures of three-fourths of the several States within seven years from the date of its submission.

Amendment XXI

Passed by Congress February 20, 1933. Ratified December 5, 1933.

Section 1.

The eighteenth article of amendment to the Constitution of the United States is hereby repealed.

Section 2.

The transportation or importation into any State, Territory, or Possession of the United States for delivery or use therein of intoxicating liquors, in violation of the laws thereof, is hereby prohibited.

Section 3.

This article shall be inoperative unless it shall have been ratified as an amendment to the Constitution by conventions in the several States, as provided in the Constitution, within seven years from the date of the submission hereof to the States by the Congress.

Amendment XXII

Passed by Congress March 21, 1947. Ratified February 27, 1951.

Section 1.

No person shall be elected to the office of the President more than twice, and no person who has held the office of President, or acted as President, for more than two years of a term to which some other person was elected President shall be elected to the office of President more than once. But this Article shall not apply to any person holding the office of President when this Article was proposed by Congress, and shall not prevent any person who may be holding the office of President, or acting as President, during the term within which this Article becomes operative from holding the office of President or acting as President during the remainder of such term.

Section 2.

This article shall be inoperative unless it shall have been ratified as an amendment to the Constitution by the legislatures of three-fourths of the several States within seven years from the date of its submission to the States by the Congress.

Amendment XXIII

Passed by Congress June 16, 1960. Ratified March 29, 1961.

Section 1.

The District constituting the seat of Government of the United States shall appoint in such manner as Congress may direct:

A number of electors of President and Vice President equal to the whole number of Senators and Representatives in Congress to which the District would be entitled if it were a State, but in no event more than the least populous State; they shall be in addition to those appointed by the States, but they shall be considered, for the purposes of the election of President and Vice President, to be electors appointed by a State; and they shall meet in the District and perform such duties as provided by the twelfth article of amendment.

Section 2.

The Congress shall have power to enforce this article by appropriate legislation.

Amendment XXIV

Passed by Congress August 27, 1962. Ratified January 23, 1964.

Section 1.

The right of citizens of the United States to vote in any primary or other election for President or Vice President, for electors for President or Vice President, or for Senator or Representative in Congress, shall not be denied or abridged by the United States or any State by reason of failure to pay poll tax or other tax.

Section 2.

The Congress shall have power to enforce this article by appropriate legislation.

Amendment XXV

Passed by Congress July 6, 1965. Ratified February 10, 1967.
Note: Article II, section 1, of the Constitution was affected by the 25th amendment.

Section 1.

In case of the removal of the President from office or of his death or resignation, the Vice President shall become President.

Section 2.

Whenever there is a vacancy in the office of the Vice President, the President shall nominate a Vice President who shall take office upon confirmation by a majority vote of both Houses of Congress.

Section 3.

Whenever the President transmits to the President pro tempore of the Senate and the Speaker of the House of Representatives his written declaration that he is unable to discharge the powers and duties of his office, and until he transmits to them a written declaration to the contrary, such powers and duties shall be discharged by the Vice President as Acting President.

Section 4.

Whenever the Vice President and a majority of either the principal officers of the executive departments or of such other body as Congress may by law provide, transmit to the President pro tempore of the Senate and the Speaker of the House of Representatives their written declaration that the President is unable to discharge the powers and duties of his office, the Vice President shall immediately assume the powers and duties of the office as Acting President.

Thereafter, when the President transmits to the President pro tempore of the Senate and the Speaker of the House of Representatives his written declaration that no inability exists, he shall resume the powers and duties of his office unless the Vice President and a majority of either the principal officers of the executive department or of such other body as Congress may by law provide, transmit within four days to the President pro tempore of the Senate and the Speaker of the House of Representatives their written declaration that the President is unable to discharge the powers and duties of his office. Thereupon Congress shall decide the issue, assembling within forty-eight hours for that purpose if not in session. If the Congress, within twenty-one days after receipt of the latter written declaration, or, if Congress is not in session, within twenty-one days after Congress is required to assemble, determines by two-thirds vote of both Houses that the President is unable to discharge the powers and duties of his office, the Vice President shall continue to discharge the same as Acting President; otherwise, the President shall resume the powers and duties of his office.

Amendment XXVI

Passed by Congress March 23, 1971. Ratified July 1, 1971.
Note: Amendment 14, section 2, of the Constitution was modified by section 1 of the 26th amendment.

Section 1.

The right of citizens of the United States, who are eighteen years of age or older, to vote shall not be denied or abridged by the United States or by any State on account of age.

Section 2.

The Congress shall have power to enforce this article by appropriate legislation.

Amendment XXVII

Originally proposed Sept. 25, 1789. Ratified May 7, 1992.
No law, varying the compensation for the services of the Senators and Representatives, shall take effect, until an election of representatives shall have intervened. ✦

Excerpts From ALI's Model Penal Code and Article 3 of the Uniform Commercial Code

American Law Institute's Model Penal Code
Official Draft, 1962, Selected Sections

Section 1.05. All Offenses Defined by Statute: Application of General Provisions of the Code

(1) No conduct constitutes an offense unless it is a crime or violation under this Code or another statute of this State. . . .

Section 2.01. Requirement of Voluntary Act; Omission as Basis of Liability; Possession as an Act

(1) A person is not guilty of an offense unless his liability is based on conduct which includes a voluntary act or the omission to perform an act of which he is physically capable.

(2) The following are not voluntary acts within the meaning of this Section:

(a) a reflex or convulsion;

(b) a bodily movement during unconsciousness or sleep;

(c) conduct during hypnosis or resulting from hypnotic suggestion;

(d) a bodily movement that otherwise is not a product of the effort or determination of the actor, either conscious or habitual.

(3) Liability for the commission of an offense may not be based on an omission unaccompanied by action unless:

(a) the omission is expressly made sufficient by the law defining the offense; or

(b) a duty to perform the omitted act is otherwise imposed by law.

(4) Possession is an act, within the meaning of this Section, if the possessor knowingly procured or received the thing possessed or was aware of his control thereof for a sufficient period to have been able to terminate his possession.

Section 2.08. Intoxication

(1) Except as provided in Subsection (4) of this Section, intoxication of the actor is not a defense unless it negatives an element of the offense.

719

(2) When recklessness establishes an element of the offense, if the actor, due to self-induced intoxication, is unaware of a risk of which he would have been aware had he been sober, such unawareness is immaterial.

(3) Intoxication does not, in itself, constitute mental disease within the meaning of Section 4.01.

(4) Intoxication which

    (a) is not self-induced, or

    (b) is pathological,

is an affirmative defense if by reason of such intoxication the actor at the time of his conduct lacks substantial capacity either to appreciate its criminality [wrongfulness] or to conform his conduct to the requirements of law.

(5) *Definitions.* In this Section unless a different meaning plainly is required:

(a) "intoxication" means a disturbance of mental or physical capacities resulting from the introduction of substances into the body;

(b) "self-induced intoxication" means intoxication caused by substances which the actor knowingly introduces into his body, the tendency of which to cause intoxication he knows or ought to know, unless he introduces them pursuant to medical advice or under such circumstances as would afford a defense to a charge of crime;

(c) "pathological intoxication" means intoxication grossly excessive in degree, given the amount of the intoxicant, to which the actor does not know he is susceptible.

Section 2.09.   Duress

(1) It is an affirmative defense that the actor engaged in the conduct charged to constitute an offense because he was coerced to do so by the use or, or a threat to use, unlawful force against his person or the person of another, which a person of reasonable firmness in his situation which have been unable to resist.

(2) The defense provided by this Section is unavailable if the actor recklessly placed himself in a situation in which it was probable that he would be subjected to duress. The defense is also unavailable if he was negligent in placing himself in such a situation, whenever negligence suffices to establish culpability for the offense charged.

(3) It is not a defense that a woman acted on the command of her husband, unless she acted under such coercion as would establish a defense under this Section. [The presumption that a woman, acting in the presence of her husband, is coerced is abolished.]

Section 2.13.   Entrapment

(1) A public law enforcement official or a person acting in cooperation with such an official perpetrates an entrapment if for the purpose of obtaining evidence of the commission of an offense, he induces or encourages another person to engage in conduct constituting such offense by either:

(a) making knowingly false representations designed to induce the belief that such conduct is not prohibited; or

(b) employing methods of persuasion or inducement which create a substantial risk that such an offense will be committed by persons other than those who are ready to commit it. . . .

Section 3.02.   Justification Generally: Choice of Evils

(1) Conduct which the actor believes to be necessary to avoid a harm or evil to himself or to another is justifiable, provided that:

(a) the harm or evil sought to be avoided by such conduct is greater than that sought to be prevented by the law defining the offense charged; and

(b) neither the Code nor other law defining the offense provides exceptions or defenses dealing with the specific situation involved; and

(c) a legislative purpose to exclude the justification claimed does not otherwise plainly appear.

(2) When the actor was reckless or negligent in bringing about the situation requiring a choice of harms or evils or in appraising the necessity for his conduct, the justification afforded by this section is unavailable in a prosecution for any offense for which recklessness or negligence, as the case may be, suffices to establish culpability.

Section 4.01.   Mental Disease or Defect Excluding Responsibility

(1) A person is not responsible for criminal conduct if at the time of such conduct as a result of mental disease or defect he lacks substantial capacity either to appreciate the criminality [wrongfulness] of his conduct or to conform his conduct to the requirements of law.

(2) As used in this Article, the terms "mental disease or defect" do not include an abnormality manifested only by repeated criminal or otherwise anti-social conduct.

Section 5.03.   Criminal Conspiracy

(1) *Definition of Conspiracy.* A person is guilty of conspiracy with another person or persons to commit a crime if with the purpose of promoting or facilitating its commission he:

(a) agrees with such other person or persons that they or one or more of them will engage in conduct which constitutes such crime or an attempt or solicitation to commit such crime; or

(b) agrees to aid such other person or persons in the planning or commission of such crime or of an attempt or solicitation to commit such crime. . . .

(5) *Overt Act.* No person may be convicted of conspiracy to commit a crime, other than a felony of the first or second degree, unless an overt act in pursuance of such conspiracy is alleged and proved to have been done by him or by a person with whom he conspired. . . .

Section 210.1.   Criminal Homicide

(1) A person is guilty of criminal homicide if he purposely, knowingly, recklessly or negligently causes the death of another human being.

(2) Criminal homicide is murder, manslaughter or negligent homicide.

Section 210.2.   Murder

(1) Except as provided in Section 210.3(1)(b), criminal homicide constitutes murder when:

(a) it is committed purposely or knowingly; or

(b) it is committed recklessly under circumstances manifesting extreme indifference to the value of human life. Such recklessness and indifference are presumed if the actor is engaged or is an accomplice in the commission of, or an attempt to commit, or flight after committing or attempting to commit robbery, rape or deviate sexual intercourse by force of threat of force, arson, burglary, kidnapping or felonious escape.

(2) Murder is a felony of the first degree [but a person convicted of murder may be sentenced to death, as provided in Section 210.6.].

Section 210.3.   Manslaughter

(1) Criminal homicide constitutes manslaughter when:

(a) it is committed recklessly; or

(b) a homicide which would otherwise be murder is committed under the influence of extreme mental or emotional disturbance for which there is reasonable explanation or excuse. The reasonableness of such explanation or excuse shall be determined from the viewpoint of a person in the actor's situation under the circumstances as he believes them to be.

(2) Manslaughter is a felony of the second degree.

Section 210.4.   Negligent Homicide

(1) Criminal homicide constitutes negligent homicide when it is committed negligently.

(2) Negligent homicide is a felony of the third degree.

Section 211.0. Assault

(1) *Simple Assault.* A person is guilty of assault if he:

(a) attempts to cause or purposely, knowingly or recklessly causes bodily injury to another; or

(b) negligently causes bodily harm to another with a deadly weapon; or

(c) attempts by physical menace to put another in fear of imminent serious bodily injury.

Simple assault is a misdemeanor unless committed in a fight or scuffle entered into by mutual consent, in which case it is a petty misdemeanor.

(2) *Aggravated Assault.* A person is guilty of aggravated assault if he:

(a) attempts to cause serious bodily injury to another, or causes such injury purposely, knowingly or recklessly under circumstances manifesting extreme indifference to the value of human life; or

(b) attempts to cause or purposely or knowingly causes bodily injury to another with a deadly weapon.

Aggravated assault under paragraph (a) is a felony of the second degree; aggravated assault under paragraph (b) is a felony of the third degree.

Section 213.1. Rape and Related Offenses

(1) *Rape.* A male who has sexual intercourse with a female not his wife is guilty of rape if:

(a) he compels her to submit by force or by threat of imminent death, serious bodily injury, extreme pain or kidnapping, to be inflicted on anyone; or

(b) he substantially impaired her power to appraise or control her conduct by administering or employing without her knowledge drugs, intoxicants or other means for the purpose of preventing resistance; or

(c) the female is unconscious; or

(d) the female is less than 10 years old.

Rape is a felony of the second degree unless (i) in the course thereof the actor inflicts serious bodily injury upon anyone, or (ii) the victim was not a voluntary social companion of the actor upon the occasion of the crime and had not previously permitted him sexual liberties, in which cases the offense is a felony of the first degree. Sexual intercourse includes intercourse per os or per anum, with some penetration however slight; emissions is not required.

(2) *Gross Sexual Imposition.* A male who has sexual intercourse with a female not his wife commits a felony of the third degree if:

(a) he compels her to submit by any threat that would prevent resistance by a woman of ordinary resolution; or

(b) he know that she suffers from a mental disease or defect which renders her incapable of appraising the nature of her conduct; or

(c) he know that she is unaware that a sexual act is being committed upon her or that she submits because she mistakenly supposes that he is her husband.

Section 213.2. Deviate Sexual Intercourse by Force
or Imposition

(1) *By Force or Its Equivalent.* A person who engages in deviate sexual intercourse with another person, or who causes another to engage in deviate sexual intercourse, commits a felony of the second degree if:

(a) he compels the other person to participate by force or by threat of imminent death, serious bodily injury, extreme pain or kidnapping, to be inflicted on anyone; or

(b) he has substantially impaired the other person's power to appraise or control his conduct, by administering or employing without the knowledge of the other person drugs, intoxicants, or other means for the purpose of preventing resistance; or

(c) the other person is unconscious; or

(d) the other person is less than 10 years old.

Deviate sexual intercourse means sexual intercourse per os or per anum between human beings who are not husband and wife, and any form of sexual intercourse with an animal.

(2) *By Other Imposition.* A person who engages in deviate sexual intercourse with another person, or who causes another to engage in deviate sexual intercourse, commits a felony of the third degree if:

(a) he compels the other person to participate by any threat that would prevent resistance by a person of ordinary resolution; or

(b) he knows that the other person suffers from a mental disease or defect which renders him incapable of appraising the nature of his conduct; or

(c) he knows that the other person submits because he is unaware that a sexual act is being committed upon him.

Section 221.1. Burglary

(1) *Burglary Defined.* A person is guilty of burglary if he enters a building or occupied structure, or separately secured or occupied portion thereof, with purpose to commit a crime therein, unless the premises are at the time open to the public or the actor is licensed or privileged to enter. It is an affirmative defense to prosecution for burglary that the building or structure was abandoned. . . .

Section 222.1. Robbery

(1) *Robbery Defined.* A person is guilty of robbery if, in the course of committing a theft, he:

(a) inflicts serious bodily injury upon another; or

(b) threatens another with or purposely puts him in fear of immediate serious bodily injury; or

(c) commits or threatens immediately to commit any felony of the first or second degree.

An act shall be deemed "in the course of committing a theft" if it occurs in an attempt to commit theft or in flight after the attempt or commission. . . .

Section 223.2. Theft by Unlawful Taking or Deception

(1) *Movable Property.* A person is guilty or theft if he unlawfully takes, or exercises unlawful control over, movable property or another with the purpose to deprive him thereof.

(2) *Immovable Property.* A person is guilty of theft if he unlawfully transfers immovable property of another or any interest therein with purpose to benefit himself or another not entitled thereto.

Section 223.3. Theft by Deception

A person is guilty of theft if he purposely obtains property of another by deception. A person deceives if he purposely:

(1) creates or reinforces a false impression, including false impressions as to law, value, intention or other state of mind; but deception as to a person's intention to perform a promise shall not be inferred from the fact alone that he did not subsequently perform the promise; or

(2) prevents another from acquiring information which would affect his judgment of a transaction; or

(3) fails to correct a false impression which the deceiver previously created or reinforced, or which the deceiver knows to be influencing another to whom he stands in a fiduciary or confidential relationship; or

(4) fails to disclose a know lien, adverse claim or other legal impediment to the enjoyment of property which he transfers or encumbers in consideration for the property obtained, whether such impediment is or is not valid, or is or is not a matter of official record.

The term "deceive" does not, however, include falsity as to matters having no pecuniary significance, or puffing by statements unlikely to deceive ordinary persons in the group addressed.

Section 223.4. Theft by Extortion

A person is guilty of theft if he obtains property of another by threatening to:

(1) inflict bodily injury on anyone or commit any other criminal offense; or

(2) accuse anyone of a criminal offense; or

(3) expose any secret tending to subject any person to hatred, contempt or ridicule, or to impair his credit or business repute; or

(4) take or withhold action as an official, or cause an official to take or withhold action; or

(5) bring about or continue a strike, boycott or other collective action, if the property is not demanded or received for the benefit of the group in whose interest the actor purports to act; or

(6) tesify or provide information or withhold testimony or information with respect to another's legal claim or defense; or

(7) inflict any other harm which would not benefit the actor.

It is an affirmative defense to prosecution based on paragraphs (2), (3), or (4) that the property obtained by threat of accusation, exposure, lawsuit or other invocation of official action was honestly claimed as restitution or indemnification for harm done in the circumstances to which such accusation, exposure, lawsuit or other offical action relates, or as compensation for property or lawful services.

Selected Sections From Article 3 of the Uniform Commercial Code

§ 3-104.   Negotiable Instrument.

(a) Except as provided in subsections (c) and (d), "negotiable instrument" means an unconditional promise or order to pay a fixed amount of money, with or without interest or other charges described in the promise or order, if it:

> (1) is payable to bearer or to order at the time it is issued or first comes into possession of a holder;
>
> (2) is payable on demand or at a definite time; and
>
> (3) does not state any other undertaking or instruction by the person promising or ordering payment to do any act in addition to the payment of money, but the promise or order may contain (i) an undertaking or power to give, maintain, or protect collateral to secure payment, (ii) an authorization or power to the holder to confess judgment or realize on or dispose of collateral, or (iii) a waiver of the benefit of any law intended for the advantage or protection of an obligor. . . .

§ 3-106.   Unconditional Promise or Order.

(a) Except as provided in this section, for the purposes of Section 3-104(a), a promise or order is unconditional unless it states (i) an express condition to payment, (ii) that the promise or order is subject to or governed by another writing, or (iii) that rights or obligations with respect to the promise or order are stated in another writing. A reference to another writing does not of itself make the promise or order conditional.

(b) A promise or order is not made conditional (i) by a reference to another writing for a statement of rights with respect to collateral, prepayment, or acceleration, or (ii) because payment is limited to resort to a particular fund or source.

(c) If a promise or order requires, as a condition to payment, a countersignature by a person whose specimen signature appears on the promise or order, the condition does not make the promise or order conditional for the purposes of Section 3-104(a). If the person whose specimen signature appears on an instrument fails to countersign the instrument, the failure to countersign is a defense to the obligation of the issuer, but the failure does not prevent a transferee of the instrument from becoming a holder of the instrument.

(d) If a promise or order at the time it is issued or first comes into possession of a holder contains a statement, required by applicable statutory or administrative law, to the effect that the rights of a holder or transferee are subject to claims or defenses that the issuer could assert against the original payee, the promise or order is not thereby made conditional for the purposes of Section 3-104(a); but if the promise or order is an instrument, there cannot be a holder in due course of the instrument.

§ 3-108.   Payable on Demand or at Definite Time.

(a) A promise or order is "payable on demand" if it (i) states that it is payable on demand or at sight, or otherwise indicates that it is payable at the will of the holder, or (ii) does not state any time of payment.

(b) A promise or order is "payable at a definite time" if it is payable on elapse of a definite period of time after sight or acceptance or at a fixed date or dates or at a time or times readily ascertainable at the time the promise or order is issued, subject to rights of (i) prepayment, (ii) acceleration, (iii) extension at the option of the holder, or (iv) extension to a further definite time at the option of the maker or acceptor or automatically upon or after a specified act or event.

(c) If an instrument, payable at a fixed date, is also payable upon demand made before the fixed date, the instrument is payable on demand until the fixed date and, if demand for payment is not made before that date, becomes payable at a definite time on the fixed date.

§ 3-109.   Payable to Bearer or to Order.

(a) A promise or order is payable to bearer if it:
   (1) states that it is payable to bearer or to the order of bearer or otherwise indicates that the person in possession of the promise or order is entitled to payment;
   (2) does not state a payee; or
   (3) states that it is payable to or to the order of cash or otherwise indicates that it is not payable to an identified person.

(b) A promise or order that is not payable to bearer is payable to order if it is payable (i) to the order of an identified person or (ii) to an identified person or order. A promise or order that is payable to order is payable to the identified person.

(c) An instrument payable to bearer may become payable to an identified person if it is specially indorsed pursuant to Section 3-205(a). An instrument payable to an identified person may become payable to bearer if it is indorsed in blank pursuant to Section 3-205(b).

§ 3-112.   Interest.

(a) Unless otherwise provided in the instrument, (i) an instrument is not payable with interest, and (ii) interest on an interest-bearing instrument is payable from the date of the instrument.

(b) Interest may be stated in an instrument as a fixed or variable amount of money or it may be expressed as a fixed or variable rate or rates. The amount or rate of interest may be stated or described in the instrument in any manner and may require reference to information not contained in the instrument. If an instrument provides for interest, but the amount of interest payable cannot be ascertained from the description, interest is payable at the judgment rate in effect at the place of payment of the instrument and at the time interest first accrues.

§ 3-201.   Negotiation.

(a) "Negotiation" means a transfer of possession, whether voluntary or involuntary, of an instrument by a person other than the issuer to a person who thereby becomes its holder.

(b) Except for negotiation by a remitter, if an instrument is payable to an identified person, negotiation requires transfer of possession of the instrument and its indorsement by the holder. If an instrument is payable to bearer, it may be negotiated by transfer of possession alone.

§ 3-204.   Indorsement.

(a) "Indorsement" means a signature, other than that of a signer as maker, drawer, or acceptor, that alone or accompanied by other words is made on an instrument for the purpose of (i) negotiating the instrument, (ii) restricting payment of the instrument, or (iii) incurring indorser's liability on the instrument, but regardless of the intent of the signer, a signature and its accompanying words is an indorsement unless the accompanying words, terms of the instrument, place of the signature, or other circumstances unambiguously indicate that the signature was made for a purpose other than indorsement. For the purpose of determining whether a signature is made on an instrument, a paper affixed to the instrument is a part of the instrument.

(b) "Indorser" means a person who makes an indorsement.

(c) For the purpose of determining whether the transferee of an instrument is a holder, an indorsement that transfers a security interest in the instrument is effective as an unqualified indorsement of the instrument.

(d) If an instrument is payable to a holder under a name that is not the name of the holder, indorsement may be made by the holder in the name stated in the instrument or in the holder's name or both, but signature in both names may be required by a person paying or taking the instrument for value or collection.

§ 3-205.   Special Indorsement; Blank Indorsement; Anomalous Indorsement.

(a) If an indorsement is made by the holder of an instrument, whether payable to an identified person or payable to bearer, and the indorsement identifies a person to whom it makes the instrument payable, it is a "special indorsement." When specially indorsed, an instrument becomes payable to the identified person and may be negotiated only by the indorsement of that person. The principles stated in Section 3-110 apply to special indorsements.

(b) If an indorsement is made by the holder of an instrument and it is not a special indorsement, it is a "blank indorsement." When indorsed in blank, an instrument becomes payable to bearer and may be negotiated by transfer of possession alone until specially indorsed.

(c) The holder may convert a blank indorsement that consists only of a signature into a special indorsement by writing, above the signature of the indorser, words identifying the person to whom the instrument is made payable.

(d) "Anomalous indorsement" means an indorsement made by a person who is not the holder of the instrument. An anomalous indorsement does not affect the manner in which the instrument may be negotiated.

§ 3-206.   Restrictive Indorsement.

(a) An indorsement limiting payment to a particular person or otherwise prohibiting further transfer or negotiation of the instrument is not effective to prevent further transfer or negotiation of the instrument.

(b) An indorsement stating a condition to the right of the indorsee to receive payment does not affect the right of the indorsee to enforce the instrument. A person paying the instrument or taking it for value or collection may disregard the condition, and the rights and liabilities of that person are not affected by whether the condition has been fulfilled.

(c) If an instrument bears an indorsement (i) described in Section 4-201(b), or (ii) in blank or to a particular bank using the words "for deposit," "for collection," or other words indicating a purpose of having the instrument collected by a bank for the indorser or for a particular account, the following rules apply:

(1) A person, other than a bank, who purchases the instrument when so indorsed converts the instrument unless the amount paid for the instrument is received by the indorser or applied consistently with the indorsement.

(2) A depositary bank that purchases the instrument or takes it for collection when so indorsed converts the instrument unless the amount paid by the bank with respect to the instrument is received by the indorser or applied consistently with the indorsement.

(3) A payor bank that is also the depositary bank or that takes the instrument for immediate payment over the counter from a person other than a collecting bank converts the instrument unless the proceeds of the instrument are received by the indorser or applied consistently with the indorsement.

(4) Except as otherwise provided in paragraph (3), a payor bank or intermediary bank may disregard the indorsement and is not liable if the proceeds of the instrument are not received by the indorser or applied consistently with the indorsement.

(d) Except for an indorsement covered by subsection (c), if an instrument bears an indorsement using words to the effect that payment is to be made to the indorsee as agent, trustee, or other fiduciary for the benefit of the indorser or another person, the following rules apply:

(1) Unless there is notice of breach of fiduciary duty as provided in Section 3-307, a person who purchases the instrument from the indorsee or takes the instrument from the indorsee for collection or payment may pay the proceeds of payment or the value given for the instrument to the indorsee without regard to whether the indorsee violates a fiduciary duty to the indorser.

(2) A subsequent transferee of the instrument or person who pays the instrument is neither given notice nor otherwise affected by the restriction in the indorsement unless the transferee or payor knows that the fiduciary dealt with the instrument or its proceeds in breach of fiduciary duty.

(e) The presence on an instrument of an indorsement to which this section applies does not prevent a purchaser of the instrument from becoming a holder in due course of the instrument unless the purchaser is a converter under subsection (c) or has notice or knowledge of breach of fiduciary duty as stated in subsection (d).

(f) In an action to enforce the obligation of a party to pay the instrument, the obligor has a defense if payment would violate an indorsement to which this section applies and the payment is not permitted by this section.

§ 3-302.   Holder in Due Course.

(a) Subject to subsection (c) and Section 3-106(d), "holder in due course" means the holder of an instrument if:

(1) the instrument when issued or negotiated to the holder does not bear such apparent evidence of forgery or alteration or is not otherwise so irregular or incomplete as to call into question its authenticity; and

(2) the holder took the instrument (i) for value, (ii) in good faith, (iii) without notice that the instrument is overdue or has been dishonored or that there is an uncured default with respect to payment of another instrument issued as part of the same series, (iv) without notice that the instrument contains an unauthorized signature or has been altered, (v) without notice of any claim to the instrument described in Section 3-306, and (vi) without notice that any party has a defense or claim in recoupment described in Section 3-305(a).

(b) Notice of discharge of a party, other than discharge in an insolvency proceeding, is not notice of a defense under subsection (a), but discharge is effective against a person who became a holder in due course with notice of the discharge. Public filing or recording of a document does not of itself constitute notice of a defense, claim in recoupment, or claim to the instrument.

(c) Except to the extent a transferor or predecessor in interest has rights as a holder in due course, a person does not acquire rights of a holder in due course of an instrument taken (i) by legal process or by purchase in an execution, bankruptcy, or creditor's sale or similar proceeding, (ii) by purchase as part of a bulk transaction not in ordinary course of business of the transferor, or (iii) as the successor in interest to an estate or other organization.

(d) If, under Section 3-303(a)(1), the promise of performance that is the consideration for an instrument has been partially performed, the holder may assert rights as a holder in due course of the instrument only to the fraction of the amount payable under the instrument equal to the value of the partial performance divided by the value of the promised performance.

(e) If (i) the person entitled to enforce an instrument has only a security interest in the instrument and (ii) the person obliged to pay the instrument has a defense, claim in recoupment, or claim to the instrument that may be asserted against the person who granted the security interest, the person entitled to enforce the instrument may assert rights as a holder in due course only to an amount payable under the instrument which, at the time of enforcement of the instrument, does not exceed the amount of the unpaid obligation secured.

(f) To be effective, notice must be received at a time and in a manner that gives a reasonable opportunity to act on it.

(g) This section is subject to any law limiting status as a holder in due course in particular classes of transactions.

§ 3-303. Value and Consideration.

(a) An instrument is issued or transferred for value if:

(1) the instrument is issued or transferred for a promise of performance, to the extent the promise has been performed;

(2) the transferee acquires a security interest or other lien in the instrument other than a lien obtained by judicial proceeding;

(3) the instrument is issued or transferred as payment of, or as security for, an antecedent claim against any person, whether or not the claim is due;

(4) the instrument is issued or transferred in exchange for a negotiable instrument; or

(5) the instrument is issued or transferred in exchange for the incurring of an irrevocable obligation to a third party by the person taking the instrument.

(b) "Consideration" means any consideration sufficient to support a simple contract. The drawer or maker of an instrument has a defense if the instrument is issued without consideration. If an instrument is issued for a promise of performance, the issuer has a defense to the extent performance of the promise is due and the promise has not been performed. If an instrument is issued for value as stated in subsection (a), the instrument is also issued for consideration.

§ 3-304. Overdue Instrument.

(a) An instrument payable on demand becomes overdue at the earliest of the following times:

(1) on the day after the day demand for payment is duly made;

(2) if the instrument is a check, 90 days after its date; or

(3) if the instrument is not a check, when the instrument has been outstanding for a period of time after its date which is unreasonably long under the circumstances of the particular case in light of the nature of the instrument and usage of the trade.

(b) With respect to an instrument payable at a definite time the following rules apply:

(1) If the principal is payable in installments and a due date has not been accelerated, the instrument becomes overdue upon default under the instrument for nonpayment of an installment, and the instrument remains overdue until the default is cured.

(2) If the principal is not payable in installments and the due date has not been accelerated, the instrument becomes overdue on the day after the due date.

(3) If a due date with respect to principal has been accelerated, the instrument becomes overdue on the day after the accelerated due date.

(c) Unless the due date of principal has been accelerated, an instrument does not become overdue if there is default in payment of interest but no default in payment of principal.

§ 3-305. Defenses and Claims in Recoupment.

(a) Except as stated in subsection (b), the right to enforce the obligation of a party to pay an instrument is subject to the following:

(1) a defense of the obligor based on (i) infancy of the obligor to the extent it is a defense to a simple contract, (ii) duress, lack of legal capacity, or illegality of the transaction which, under other law, nullifies the obligation of the obligor, (iii) fraud that induced the obligor to sign the instrument with neither knowledge nor reasonable opportunity to learn of its character or its essential terms, or (iv) discharge of the obligor in insolvency proceedings;

(2) a defense of the obligor stated in another section of this Article or a defense of the obligor that would be available if the person entitled to enforce the instrument were enforcing a right to payment under a simple contract; and

(3) a claim in recoupment of the obligor against the original payee of the instrument if the claim arose from the transaction that gave rise to the instrument; but the claim of the obligor may be asserted against a transferee of the instrument only to reduce the amount owing on the instrument at the time the action is brought.

(b) The right of a holder in due course to enforce the obligation of a party to pay the instrument is subject to defenses of the obligor stated in subsection (a)(1), but is not subject to defenses of the obligor stated in subsection (a)(2) or claims in recoupment stated in subsection (a)(3) against a person other than the holder.

(c) Except as stated in subsection (d), in an action to enforce the obligation of a party to pay the instrument, the obligor may not assert against the person entitled to enforce the instrument a defense, claim in recoupment, or claim to the instrument (Section 3-306) of another person, but the other person's claim to the instrument may be asserted by the obligor if the other person is joined in the action and personally asserts the claim against the person entitled to enforce the instrument. An obligor is not obliged to pay the instrument if the person seeking enforcement of the instrument does not have rights of a holder in due course and the obligor proves that the instrument is a lost or stolen instrument.

(d) In an action to enforce the obligation of an accommodation party to pay an instrument, the accommodation party may assert against the person entitled to enforce the instrument any defense or claim in recoupment under subsection (a) that the accommodated party could assert against the person entitled to enforce the instrument, except the defenses of discharge in insolvency proceedings, infancy, and lack of legal capacity.

Taxation: 2001 and 2002 Forms and Inflation-Adjusted Amounts for 2002 and 2003

2001 Form 1040
U.S. Individual Income Tax Return

Form **1040**	Department of the Treasury—Internal Revenue Service **U.S. Individual Income Tax Return**	**2001**	(99)	IRS Use Only—Do not write or staple in this space.

For the year Jan. 1–Dec. 31, 2001, or other tax year beginning , 2001, ending , 20	OMB No. 1545-0074

Label
(See instructions on page 19.)

Use the IRS label. Otherwise, please print or type.

L A B E L   H E R E

Your first name and initial	Last name	Your social security number
If a joint return, spouse's first name and initial	Last name	Spouse's social security number

Home address (number and street). If you have a P.O. box, see page 19.	Apt. no.

City, town or post office, state, and ZIP code. If you have a foreign address, see page 19.

▲ **Important!** ▲
You **must** enter your SSN(s) above.

Presidential Election Campaign
(See page 19.)

Note. Checking "Yes" will not change your tax or reduce your refund.
Do you, or your spouse if filing a joint return, want $3 to go to this fund? . . . ▶

You ☐Yes ☐No   Spouse ☐Yes ☐No

Filing Status

Check only one box.

1 ☐ Single
2 ☐ Married filing joint return (even if only one had income)
3 ☐ Married filing separate return. Enter spouse's social security no. above and full name here. ▶ _____
4 ☐ Head of household (with qualifying person). (See page 19.) If the qualifying person is a child but not your dependent, enter this child's name here. ▶ _____
5 ☐ Qualifying widow(er) with dependent child (year spouse died ▶). (See page 19.)

Exemptions

6a ☐ **Yourself.** If your parent (or someone else) can claim you as a dependent on his or her tax return, **do not** check box 6a . . . .

b ☐ **Spouse** . . . .

c **Dependents:**

(1) First name Last name	(2) Dependent's social security number	(3) Dependent's relationship to you	(4)✔ if qualifying child for child tax credit (see page 20)
			☐
			☐
			☐
			☐
			☐
			☐

If more than six dependents, see page 20.

No. of boxes checked on 6a and 6b ____
No. of your children on 6c who:
• lived with you ____
• did not live with you due to divorce or separation (see page 20) ____
Dependents on 6c not entered above ____
Add numbers entered on lines above ▶ ☐

d Total number of exemptions claimed . . . .

Income

Attach Forms W-2 and W-2G here. Also attach Form(s) 1099-R if tax was withheld.

If you did not get a W-2, see page 21.

Enclose, but do not attach, any payment. Also, please use **Form 1040-V.**

7	Wages, salaries, tips, etc. Attach Form(s) W-2	7	
8a	**Taxable** interest. Attach Schedule B if required	8a	
b	**Tax-exempt** interest. **Do not** include on line 8a . . .	8b	
9	Ordinary dividends. Attach Schedule B if required	9	
10	Taxable refunds, credits, or offsets of state and local income taxes (see page 22) . .	10	
11	Alimony received	11	
12	Business income or (loss). Attach Schedule C or C-EZ	12	
13	Capital gain or (loss). Attach Schedule D if required. If not required, check here ▶ ☐	13	
14	Other gains or (losses). Attach Form 4797	14	
15a	Total IRA distributions . 15a	b Taxable amount (see page 23)	15b	
16a	Total pensions and annuities 16a	b Taxable amount (see page 23)	16b	
17	Rental real estate, royalties, partnerships, S corporations, trusts, etc. Attach Schedule E	17	
18	Farm income or (loss). Attach Schedule F	18	
19	Unemployment compensation	19	
20a	Social security benefits 20a	b Taxable amount (see page 25)	20b	
21	Other income. List type and amount (see page 27) _____	21	
22	Add the amounts in the far right column for lines 7 through 21. This is your **total income** ▶	22	

Adjusted Gross Income

23	IRA deduction (see page 27)	23	
24	Student loan interest deduction (see page 28)	24	
25	Archer MSA deduction. Attach Form 8853	25	
26	Moving expenses. Attach Form 3903	26	
27	One-half of self-employment tax. Attach Schedule SE	27	
28	Self-employed health insurance deduction (see page 30)	28	
29	Self-employed SEP, SIMPLE, and qualified plans . .	29	
30	Penalty on early withdrawal of savings	30	
31a	Alimony paid b Recipient's SSN ▶ _____	31a	
32	Add lines 23 through 31a		32
33	Subtract line 32 from line 22. This is your **adjusted gross income** . . . . . ▶		33

For Disclosure, Privacy Act, and Paperwork Reduction Act Notice, see page 72.   Cat. No. 11320B   Form **1040** (2001)

2001 Form 1040 (cont'd.)
U.S. Individual Income Tax Return

Form 1040 (2001)   Page **2**

Tax and Credits

Standard Deduction for—
- People who checked any box on line 35a or 35b **or** who can be claimed as a dependent, see page 31.
- All others:

Single, $4,550

Head of household, $6,650

Married filing jointly or Qualifying widow(er), $7,600

Married filing separately, $3,800

34	Amount from line 33 (adjusted gross income)	34
35a	Check if: ☐ **You** were 65 or older, ☐ Blind; ☐ **Spouse** was 65 or older, ☐ Blind. Add the number of boxes checked above and enter the total here . . . . ▶ 35a	
b	If you are married filing separately and your spouse itemizes deductions, or you were a dual-status alien, see page 31 and check here . . . . . . ▶ 35b ☐	
36	**Itemized deductions** (from Schedule A) **or** your **standard deduction** (see left margin) .	36
37	Subtract line 36 from line 34	37
38	If line 34 is $99,725 or less, multiply $2,900 by the total number of exemptions claimed on line 6d. If line 34 is over $99,725, see the worksheet on page 32	38
39	**Taxable income.** Subtract line 38 from line 37. If line 38 is more than line 37, enter -0-	39
40	**Tax** (see page 33). Check if any tax is from **a** ☐ Form(s) 8814 **b** ☐ Form 4972 . .	40
41	**Alternative minimum tax** (see page 34). Attach Form 6251	41
42	Add lines 40 and 41 . . . . ▶	42
43	Foreign tax credit. Attach Form 1116 if required	43	
44	Credit for child and dependent care expenses. Attach Form 2441	44	
45	Credit for the elderly or the disabled. Attach Schedule R .	45	
46	Education credits. Attach Form 8863	46	
47	Rate reduction credit. See the worksheet on page 36	47	
48	Child tax credit (see page 37)	48	
49	Adoption credit. Attach Form 8839	49	
50	Other credits from: **a** ☐ Form 3800 **b** ☐ Form 8396 **c** ☐ Form 8801 **d** ☐ Form (specify)_____	50	
51	Add lines 43 through 50. These are your **total credits**	51
52	Subtract line 51 from line 42. If line 51 is more than line 42, enter -0-. . . . . ▶	52

Other Taxes

53	Self-employment tax. Attach Schedule SE	53
54	Social security and Medicare tax on tip income not reported to employer. Attach Form 4137 .	54
55	Tax on qualified plans, including IRAs, and other tax-favored accounts. Attach Form 5329 if required .	55
56	Advance earned income credit payments from Form(s) W-2	56
57	Household employment taxes. Attach Schedule H	57
58	Add lines 52 through 57. This is your **total tax** . . . . ▶	58

Payments

If you have a qualifying child, attach Schedule EIC.

59	Federal income tax withheld from Forms W-2 and 1099 . .	59	
60	2001 estimated tax payments and amount applied from 2000 return	60	
61a	**Earned income credit (EIC)**	61a	
b	Nontaxable earned income . . 61b		
62	Excess social security and RRTA tax withheld (see page 51)	62	
63	Additional child tax credit. Attach Form 8812	63	
64	Amount paid with request for extension to file (see page 51)	64	
65	Other payments. Check if from **a** ☐ Form 2439 **b** ☐ Form 4136	65	
66	Add lines 59, 60, 61a, and 62 through 65. These are your **total payments** . . . . ▶	66

Refund

Direct deposit? See page 51 and fill in 68b, 68c, and 68d.

67	If line 66 is more than line 58, subtract line 58 from line 66. This is the amount you **overpaid**	67
68a	Amount of line 67 you want **refunded to you** . . . . ▶	68a
▶ b	Routing number [_____] ▶ **c** Type: ☐ Checking ☐ Savings	
▶ d	Account number [_____]	
69	Amount of line 67 you want **applied to your 2002 estimated tax** ▶	69	

Amount You Owe

70	**Amount you owe.** Subtract line 66 from line 58. For details on how to pay, see page 52 ▶	70
71	Estimated tax penalty. Also include on line 70	71	

Third Party Designee

Do you want to allow another person to discuss this return with the IRS (see page 53)? ☐ **Yes.** Complete the following. ☐ **No**

Designee's name ▶	Phone no. ▶ ( )	Personal identification number (PIN) ▶ [_____]

Sign Here

Joint return? See page 19.

Keep a copy for your records.

Under penalties of perjury, I declare that I have examined this return and accompanying schedules and statements, and to the best of my knowledge and belief, they are true, correct, and complete. Declaration of preparer (other than taxpayer) is based on all information of which preparer has any knowledge.

Your signature	Date	Your occupation	Daytime phone number ( )
Spouse's signature. If a joint return, **both** must sign.	Date	Spouse's occupation	

Paid Preparer's Use Only

Preparer's signature	Date	Check if self-employed ☐	Preparer's SSN or PTIN
Firm's name (or yours if self-employed), address, and ZIP code ▶		EIN	
		Phone no. ( )	

Form **1040** (2001)

2002 Form 1040
U.S. Individual Income Tax Return

Form **1040**	Department of the Treasury—Internal Revenue Service **U.S. Individual Income Tax Return** 2002	(99)	IRS Use Only—Do not write or staple in this space.

For the year Jan. 1–Dec. 31, 2002, or other tax year beginning , 2002, ending , 20

OMB No. 1545-0074

Label
(See instructions on page 21.)

Use the IRS label. Otherwise, please print or type.

L A B E L   H E R E

Your first name and initial	Last name	Your social security number
If a joint return, spouse's first name and initial	Last name	Spouse's social security number

Home address (number and street). If you have a P.O. box, see page 21. | Apt. no.

City, town or post office, state, and ZIP code. If you have a foreign address, see page 21.

▲ **Important!** ▲
You **must** enter your SSN(s) above.

Presidential Election Campaign
(See page 21.)

▶ **Note.** Checking "Yes" will not change your tax or reduce your refund.
Do you, or your spouse if filing a joint return, want $3 to go to this fund? . . . ▶

	You	Spouse
	☐Yes ☐No	☐Yes ☐No

Filing Status

Check only one box.

1 ☐ Single
2 ☐ Married filing jointly (even if only one had income)
3 ☐ Married filing separately. Enter spouse's SSN above and full name here. ▶_____
4 ☐ Head of household (with qualifying person). (See page 21.) If the qualifying person is a child but not your dependent, enter this child's name here. ▶_____
5 ☐ Qualifying widow(er) with dependent child (year spouse died ▶). (See page 21.)

Exemptions

If more than five dependents, see page 22.

6a ☐ **Yourself.** If your parent (or someone else) can claim you as a dependent on his or her tax return, **do not** check box 6a . . . .
b ☐ **Spouse** . . . .

No. of boxes checked on 6a and 6b ___

c **Dependents:**

(1) First name Last name	(2) Dependent's social security number	(3) Dependent's relationship to you	(4)✔ if qualifying child for child tax credit (see page 22)
_____	⋮	_____	☐
_____	⋮	_____	☐
_____	⋮	_____	☐
_____	⋮	_____	☐
_____	⋮	_____	☐

No. of children on 6c who:
• lived with you ___
• did not live with you due to divorce or separation (see page 22) ___
Dependents on 6c not entered above ___
Add numbers on lines above ▶ [ ]

d Total number of exemptions claimed . . . .

Income

Attach Forms W-2 and W-2G here. Also attach Form(s) 1099-R if tax was withheld.

If you did not get a W-2, see page 23.

Enclose, but do not attach, any payment. Also, please use Form 1040-V.

7	Wages, salaries, tips, etc. Attach Form(s) W-2	7	
8a	**Taxable** interest. Attach Schedule B if required	8a	
b	Tax-exempt interest. **Do not** include on line 8a . . .	8b ▨	
9	Ordinary dividends. Attach Schedule B if required	9	
10	Taxable refunds, credits, or offsets of state and local income taxes (see page 24) . .	10	
11	Alimony received	11	
12	Business income or (loss). Attach Schedule C or C-EZ	12	
13	Capital gain or (loss). Attach Schedule D if required. If not required, check here ▶ ☐	13	
14	Other gains or (losses). Attach Form 4797	14	
15a	IRA distributions . . 15a	b Taxable amount (see page 25)	15b	
16a	Pensions and annuities 16a	b Taxable amount (see page 25)	16b	
17	Rental real estate, royalties, partnerships, S corporations, trusts, etc. Attach Schedule E	17	
18	Farm income or (loss). Attach Schedule F	18	
19	Unemployment compensation	19	
20a	Social security benefits . 20a	b Taxable amount (see page 27)	20b	
21	Other income. List type and amount (see page 29) _____	21	
22	Add the amounts in the far right column for lines 7 through 21. This is your **total income** ▶	22	

Adjusted Gross Income

23	Educator expenses (see page 29)	23		▨
24	IRA deduction (see page 29)	24		▨
25	Student loan interest deduction (see page 31) . . .	25		▨
26	Tuition and fees deduction (see page 32)	26		▨
27	Archer MSA deduction. Attach Form 8853	27		▨
28	Moving expenses. Attach Form 3903	28		▨
29	One-half of self-employment tax. Attach Schedule SE .	29		▨
30	Self-employed health insurance deduction (see page 33)	30		▨
31	Self-employed SEP, SIMPLE, and qualified plans . .	31		▨
32	Penalty on early withdrawal of savings	32		▨
33a	Alimony paid b Recipient's SSN ▶ _____	33a		▨
34	Add lines 23 through 33a		34	
35	Subtract line 34 from line 22. This is your **adjusted gross income** . . . . . ▶		35	

For Disclosure, Privacy Act, and Paperwork Reduction Act Notice, see page 76.   Cat. No. 11320B   Form **1040** (2002)

2002 Form 1040 (cont'd.)
U.S. Individual Income Tax Return

Form 1040 (2002)   Page **2**

Tax and Credits	36	Amount from line 35 (adjusted gross income)	36	
	37a	Check if: ☐ **You** were 65 or older, ☐ Blind; ☐ **Spouse** was 65 or older, ☐ Blind. Add the number of boxes checked above and enter the total here . . . . ▶ **37a**		
Standard Deduction for—	b	If you are married filing separately and your spouse itemizes deductions, or you were a dual-status alien, see page 34 and check here . . . . . . ▶ **37b** ☐		
• People who checked any box on line 37a or 37b **or** who can be claimed as a dependent, see page 34.	38	**Itemized deductions** (from Schedule A) **or** your **standard deduction** (see left margin) .	38	
	39	Subtract line 38 from line 36	39	
	40	If line 36 is $103,000 or less, multiply $3,000 by the total number of exemptions claimed on line 6d. If line 36 is over $103,000, see the worksheet on page 35	40	
• All others:	41	**Taxable income.** Subtract line 40 from line 39. If line 40 is more than line 39, enter -0-	41	
Single, $4,700	42	**Tax** (see page 36). Check if any tax is from: **a** ☐ Form(s) 8814 **b** ☐ Form 4972 . . .	42	
Head of household, $6,900	43	**Alternative minimum tax** (see page 37). Attach Form 6251	43	
	44	Add lines 42 and 43 . . . . ▶	44	
Married filing jointly or Qualifying widow(er), $7,850	45	Foreign tax credit. Attach Form 1116 if required . . .	45	
	46	Credit for child and dependent care expenses. Attach Form 2441	46	
	47	Credit for the elderly or the disabled. Attach Schedule R .	47	
Married filing separately, $3,925	48	Education credits. Attach Form 8863	48	
	49	Retirement savings contributions credit. Attach Form 8880 .	49	
	50	Child tax credit (see page 39)	50	
	51	Adoption credit. Attach Form 8839	51	
	52	Credits from: **a** ☐ Form 8396 **b** ☐ Form 8859 . . .	52	
	53	Other credits. Check applicable box(es): **a** ☐ Form 3800 **b** ☐ Form 8801 **c** ☐ Specify _____	53	
	54	Add lines 45 through 53. These are your **total credits**	54	
	55	Subtract line 54 from line 44. If line 54 is more than line 44, enter -0- . . . . ▶	55	
Other Taxes	56	Self-employment tax. Attach Schedule SE	56	
	57	Social security and Medicare tax on tip income not reported to employer. Attach Form 4137 . .	57	
	58	Tax on qualified plans, including IRAs, and other tax-favored accounts. Attach Form 5329 if required .	58	
	59	Advance earned income credit payments from Form(s) W-2	59	
	60	Household employment taxes. Attach Schedule H	60	
	61	Add lines 55 through 60. This is your **total tax** . . . . ▶	61	
Payments	62	Federal income tax withheld from Forms W-2 and 1099 .	62	
	63	2002 estimated tax payments and amount applied from 2001 return	63	
If you have a qualifying child, attach Schedule EIC.	64	**Earned income credit (EIC)**	64	
	65	Excess social security and tier 1 RRTA tax withheld (see page 56)	65	
	66	Additional child tax credit. Attach Form 8812	66	
	67	Amount paid with request for extension to file (see page 56)	67	
	68	Other payments from: **a** ☐ Form 2439 **b** ☐ Form 4136 **c** ☐ Form 8885 .	68	
	69	Add lines 62 through 68. These are your **total payments** . . . . ▶	69	
Refund Direct deposit? See page 56 and fill in 71b, 71c, and 71d.	70	If line 69 is more than line 61, subtract line 61 from line 69. This is the amount you **overpaid**	70	
	71a	Amount of line 70 you want **refunded to you** . . . . ▶	71a	
	▶ b	Routing number [ ] ▶ c Type: ☐ Checking ☐ Savings		
	▶ d	Account number [ ]		
	72	Amount of line 70 you want **applied to your 2003 estimated tax** ▶	72		
Amount You Owe	73	**Amount you owe.** Subtract line 69 from line 61. For details on how to pay, see page 57 ▶	73	
	74	Estimated tax penalty (see page 57)	74		

Third Party Designee	Do you want to allow another person to discuss this return with the IRS (see page 58)? ☐ **Yes.** Complete the following. ☐ **No** Designee's name ▶ Phone no. ▶ ( ) Personal identification number (PIN) ▶ [ ]

Sign Here
Joint return?
See page 21.
Keep a copy for your records.

Under penalties of perjury, I declare that I have examined this return and accompanying schedules and statements, and to the best of my knowledge and belief, they are true, correct, and complete. Declaration of preparer (other than taxpayer) is based on all information of which preparer has any knowledge.

Your signature	Date	Your occupation	Daytime phone number ( )
Spouse's signature. If a joint return, **both** must sign.	Date	Spouse's occupation	

Paid Preparer's Use Only

Preparer's signature ▶	Date	Check if self-employed ☐	Preparer's SSN or PTIN
Firm's name (or yours if self-employed), address, and ZIP code ▶		EIN	
		Phone no. ( )	

Form **1040** (2002)

2002 Tax Rate Schedules

SCHEDULE X: FILING STATUS—SINGLE: Tax Year 2002	
Taxable Income	**Tax**
Not over $6,000	10% of the taxable income
Over $6000 but not over $27,950	$600 + 15% of the excess over $6,000
Over $27,950 but not over $67,700	$3,892.50 + 27% of the excess over $27,950
Over $67,700 but not over $141,250	$14,625 + 30% of the excess over $67,700
Over $141,250 but not over $307,050	$36,690 + 35% of the excess over $141,250
Over $307,050	$94,720 + 38.6% of the excess over $307,050

SCHEDULE Y1: FILING STATUS—MARRIED, FILING JOINT RETURN AND SURVIVING SPOUSE: Tax Year 2002	
Taxable Income	**Tax**
Not over $12,000	10% of the taxable income
Over $12,000 but not over $46,700	$1,200 + 15% of the excess over $12,000
Over $46,700 but not over $112,850	$6,405 + 27% of the excess over $46,700
Over $112,850 but not over $171,950	$24,265.50 + 30% of the excess over $112,850
Over $171,950 but not over $307,050	$41,995.50 + 35% of the excess over $171,950
Over $307,050	$89,280.50 + 38.6% of the excess over $307,050

SCHEDULE Y2: FILING STATUS—MARRIED, SEPARATE: Tax Year 2002	
Taxable Income	**Tax**
Not over $6,000	10% of the taxable income
Over $6,000 but not over $23,350	$600 + 15% of the excess over $6,000
Over $23,350 but not over $56,425	$3,202.50 + 27% of the excess over $23,350
Over $56,425 but not over $85,975	$12,132.75 + 30% of the excess over $56,425
Over $85,975 but not over $153,525	$20,997.75 + 35% of the excess over $85,975
Over $153,525	$44,640.25 + 38.6% of the excess over $153,525

SCHEDULE Z: FILING STATUS—HEAD OF HOUSEHOLD: Tax Year 2002	
Taxable Income	**Tax**
Not over $10,000	10% of the taxable income
Over $10,000 but not over $37,450	$1,000 + 15% of the excess over $10,000
Over $37,450 but not over $96,700	$5,117.50 + 27% of the excess over $37,450
Over $96,700 but not over $156,600	$21,115 + 30% of the excess over $96,700
Over $156,600 but not over $307,050	$39,085 + 35% of the excess over $156,600
Over $307,050	$91,742.50 + 38.6% of the excess over $307,050

2003 Tax Rate Schedules

SCHEDULE X: FILING STATUS—SINGLE: Tax Year 2003	
Taxable Income	**Tax**
Not over $6,000	10% of the taxable income
Over $6000 but not over $28,400	$600 + 15% of the excess over $6,000
Over $28,400 but not over $68,800	$3,960 + 27% of the excess over $28,400
Over $68,800 but not over $143,500	$14,868 + 30% of the excess over $68,800
Over $143,500 but not over $311,950	$37,278 + 35% of the excess over $143,500
Over $311,950	$96,235.50 + 38.6% of the excess over $311,950

SCHEDULE Y1: FILING STATUS—MARRIED, FILING JOINT RETURN AND SURVIVING SPOUSE: Tax Year 2003	
Taxable Income	**Tax**
Not over $12,000	10% of the taxable income
Over $12,000 but not over $47,450	$1,200 + 15% of the excess over $12,000
Over $47,450 but not over $114,650	$6,517.50 + 27% of the excess over $47,450
Over $114,650 but not over $174,700	$24,661.50 + 30% of the excess over $114,650
Over $174,700 but not over $311,950	$42,676.50 + 35% of the excess over $174,700
Over $311,950	$90,714 + 38.6% of the excess over $311,950

SCHEDULE Y2: FILING STATUS—MARRIED, SEPARATE: Tax Year 2003	
Taxable Income	**Tax**
Not over $6,000	10% of the taxable income
Over $6,000 but not over $23,725	$600 + 15% of the excess over $6,000
Over $23,725 but not over $57,325	$3,258.75 + 27% of the excess over $23,725
Over $57,325 but not over $87,350	$12,330.75 + 30% of the excess over $57,325
Over $87,350 but not over $155,975	$21,338.25 + 35% of the excess over $87,350
Over $155,975	$45,357 + 38.6% of the excess over $155,975

SCHEDULE Z: FILING STATUS—HEAD OF HOUSEHOLD: Tax Year 2003	
Taxable Income	**Tax**
Not over $10,000	10% of the taxable income
Over $10,000 but not over $38,050	$1,000 + 15% of the excess over $10,000
Over $38,050 but not over $98,250	$5,207.50 + 27% of the excess over $38,050
Over $98,250 but not over $159,100	$21,461.50 + 30% of the excess over $98,250
Over $159,100 but not over $311,950	$39,716.50 + 35% of the excess over $159,100
Over $311,950	$93,214 + 38.6% of the excess over $311,950

2001 Through 2003 Selected Indexed Amounts

1. AGI Limits: Itemized Deduction Phase-out for High-Income Taxpayers

2001—AGI in excess of $132,950, $66,475 for married separate filers.
2002—AGI in excess of $137,300, $68,650 for married separate filers.
2003—AGI in excess of $139,500, $69,750 for married separate filers.

2. The Standard Deduction

Filing Status	Standard Deduction 2001	Standard Deduction 2002	Additional Standard Deduction 2001	Additional Standard Deduction 2002
Single	$4,550	$4,700	$1,100	$1,150
Head of Household	$6,650	$6,900	$1,100	$1,150
Married Joint	$7,600	$7,850	$900	$900
Married Separate	$3,800	$3,925	$900	$900

Filing Status	Standard Deduction 2003	Additional Standard Deduction 2003
Single	$4,750	$1,150
Head of Household	$7,000	$1,150
Married Joint	$7,950	$950
Married Separate	$3,975	$950

3. Personal and Dependency Exemptions

2001—$2,900.
2002—$3,000.
2003—$3,050.

4. Personal and Dependency Exemption Phase-out for High-Income Taxpayers

2001:
Single phase-out range—AGI between $132,000 and $255,450.
Married joint phase-out range—AGI between $199,450 and $321,950.

2002:
Single phase-out range—AGI between $137,300 and $255,800.
Married joint phase-out range—AGI between $206,000 and $328,500.

2003:
Single phase-out range—AGI between $139,500 and $262,000.
Married joint phase-out range—AGI between $209,250 and $331,750.

5. Earned Income Credit Maximum Credit Amounts

One child:
2001—$2,424.
2002—$2,506.
2003—$2,547.

Two or more children:
2001—$4,008.
2002—$4,140.
2003—$4,204.

Glossary of Selected Legal and Foreign Terms

A

Abandoned Property Property for which its true owner intentionally relinquished ownership.

Abrogate To repeal, annul, or destroy. For example, a court may abrogate (reverse) a lower court holding, or the legislature may abrogate a statute by enacting contrary legislation or repealing the statute in question.

Absolutism (a) A view of constitutional interpretation that holds that judges must apply the strict meaning of the words or the clear intentions of the constitutional framers, regardless of whether they result in upholding or striking down legislation. *See also*, Interpretivism. (b) A term often applied to the view that certain forms of expression are completely protected from government prohibition by the First Amendment. A view most closely associated with Justice Hugo Black.

Acceptance A promise or act of performance that notifies the offeror that the offeree agrees to be bound by the terms of the offer to form a contract.

Accusatorial System An approach to criminal processes that presumes that a person is innocent until proven guilty. The outstanding feature of Anglo-American criminal justice places the burden of proof on the accuser.

Actual Malice A judicial test in freedom of the press cases that holds that a suit in defamation will not be sustained unless a finding shows that the defamatory statement was made with knowledge of its falsity or in reckless disregard of the truth.

Actus Reus Latin for "real events." A voluntary physical act which is required for most crimes along with a mens rea.

Ad Hoc For a special or unique purpose; temporary and not permanent. For example, a committee might be established to study an issue or a problem. Once the committee has completed its work, it is disbanded.

Ad Valorem Latin for "according to value." An ad valorem tax is a levy on the value of something, rather than a fixed tax regardless of value. For example, an ad valorem tax on a diamond ring worth $100 might be $5, while the tax on a $10,000 ring might be $500. The tax amount varies according to the worth or value of the item rather than being fixed, such as $75 for all diamond rings.

Adjective Law Generic term referring to rules under which courts or agencies conduct their affairs; procedural as opposed to substantive law.

Adjusted Gross Income Under IRC § 62, gross income less certain deductions. Applicable only to the federal individual income tax.

Administrative Law The branch of public law dealing with the rules and regulations promulgated by government agencies. For example, the Food and Drug Administration (FDA) promulgates rules of administrative law regarding how drugs must be tested before they are sold.

Admiralty Law   The branch of the law concerned with maritime matters—that is, having to do with navigable waters.

Adoption   Legal process that severs the rights of the natural parents and creates parental rights and responsibilities in the adoptive parents.

Advisory Opinion   A judicial ruling in the absence of an actual case or controversy; a ruling in a hypothetical case without bona fide litigants.

Affirm   An appellate court decision upholding or agreeing with a decision or ruling of a trial court or a subordinate appellate court.

Agency   (a) A relationship in which one party acts on behalf of another, with the authorization of the latter. (b) An administrative body of government.

Alimony   Payments awarded one spouse for support and maintenance after the couple is separated or divorced. The modern trend is to award only rehabilitative alimony. Also referred to as maintenance.

Alternative Dispute Resolution (ADR)   Various tools designed to settle disputes without employing full-blown formal trials. Conciliation, mediation, and arbitration are common forms of ADR.

American Bar Association   A voluntary national association of lawyers that purports to represent the legal profession. It engages in various activities, including lobbying at the national and state levels to improve the administration of justice and to further the aims of its members.

American Law Institute (ALI)   Founded in 1923, the ALI was organized to treat uncertainties in the law leading to the creation of the various Restatements of the Law. Membership is by election, and its 3,000 members consist of judges, lawyers, and legal teachers from the United States and abroad. *See also*, Restatements of the Law.

Amicus Curiae   Latin for "friend of the court." Normally someone or some entity interested in the outcome of the issue at bar, but not a party to the suit. Usually presents a brief called an amicus curiae brief, which provides information and arguments relevant to a court in its deliberation as to matters of law.

Analytical Jurisprudence   A school of jurisprudence that attempts to systematize the law, utilizing tools of logic. Outstanding proponents include Hans Kelsen, John Austin, and H. L. A. Hart.

Annulment   A finding that a marriage was invalid at its inception due to some impediment existing at the time of the marriage.

Answer   Usually a written statement or pleading by the defendant responding to the plaintiff's charges.

Ante Nuptial (Premarital) Agreement   A contract or agreement entered into by a couple before marriage that specifies how the couple will divide property and care for children in the event that their marriage ends in divorce.

Antitrust Laws   Federal and state statutes designed to protect competitors and consumers from predatory business practices. The principal federal statutes include the Sherman Act of 1890, the Clayton and the Federal Trade Commission Acts of 1914, and the Robinson-Patman Act of 1936. The statutes generally provide for criminal and civil sanctions, as well as allow injured parties to sue privately for treble damages.

Appeal   A generic term referring to the movement of court proceedings from an inferior to a superior court. Depending on the context, the term may also refer to a technical method of moving a case to a superior court.

Appellate   The party who takes his or her case from a lower court to a superior court to seek review of the lower court decision.

Appellate Court   A court possessing the authority to review and sustain or reverse the decisions of a lower court.

Appellee   The party in a suit against whom the appeal to a superior court is taken; the party with an interest in sustaining the lower court judgment.

Arbitration   A third-party hearing and settlement of a dispute among contending parties. The decision of the arbitrator(s) may be binding on the participants.

Arguendo   Latin for "by way of argument." Assuming that a statement of fact is true, although it may be true or false, for the purpose of analyzing a legal argument. A method of illustrating a line of reasoning found in judicial opinions.

Arraignment The formal court procedure in which a criminal defendant answers an indictment with a plea of guilty, not guilty, or nolo contendere.

Arrest To deny a person his or her liberty under the color of legal authority.

Assault (a) An intentional tort. One is liable for assault if he or she acts in such a way as to put another person in imminent apprehension of harmful or offensive contact. (b) In most jurisdictions, a statutory crime defined as intentionally injuring another or intentionally touching another in an offensive manner.

Associate Justice The title given to judges of an appellate court, excluding the chief justice.

Assumpsit Latin for "he has undertaken." From the law of contracts, meaning to undertake the performance of an oral agreement. At common law, assumpsit was an action taken to enforce a promise.

Assumption of Risk A defense raised by the defendant in a tort case, alleging that the plaintiff knew of the dangers inherent in the activity in which he or she was engaged and that the plaintiff is responsible for any injuries he or she suffered.

Attempt Crimes Laws that punish unsuccessful attempts to commit crimes.

B

Bail The security given in the form of cash, property, or a bail bond as a guarantee that a released prisoner will appear at his or her trial. Bail may be forfeited if the released prisoner does not appear at trial.

Bailee The party to whom goods are bailed. *See also,* Bailment.

Bailiff An officer of the court who is in charge of prisoners and who guards the jurors in a court; generally charged with keeping the peace in court.

Bailment A legal relationship created when one party delivers personal property to another party for protection. To be an effective bailment, the other party must have control over the property and have knowledge of its receipt. The bailee has a duty of reasonable care to protect the property.

Bailor The party delivering property to the bailee in a bailment.

Bankruptcy A legal procedure under federal law by which a person is relieved of all debts after placing all property under the court's authority. An organization may be reorganized or terminated by the court in order to pay off creditors.

Bar (a) The community of attorneys permitted to practice law in a particular jurisdiction or court. (b) "To raise the bar"—to increase standards or requirements.

Battery The intentional tort of touching another in a harmful or offensive manner without permission—a crime at common law.

Bearer Paper Negotiable instrument that is payable to the bearer or to cash.

Best Interest of the Child The standard courts employ when determining questions of child custody, visitation, support, and other issues involving children.

Bifurcated Trial A judicial procedure in capital criminal trials that separates the guilt from the punishment segment of jury deliberations. It is also used in some complicated tort actions to split the issues of liability and damages.

Bilateral Contract A contract formed by the parties exchanging mutual or reciprocal promises.

Bill of Attainder A legislative act declaring a person guilty of a crime and passing sentence without the benefit of a trial. Such legislation is specifically forbidden by Article 1, section 9 of the U.S. Constitution.

Blackstone Sir William Blackstone, the influential eighteenth-century jurist and author of *Blackstone's Commentaries on the Laws of England.*

Bona Fide Latin for "good faith." A term referring to acting in good faith; without trickery, deceit, fraud, or dishonesty.

Breach of Contract (a) The nonperformance of the terms of a legally binding oral or written agreement. (b) A legal action for damages for nonperformance of a contractual obligation.

Brief (a) The oral or written argument presented by counsel to a court. (b) Summaries of the pertinent elements of a court opinion written by a student as a study guide and aid.

Burden of Proof   Although possessing several technical meanings, burden of proof generally refers to the duty of one of the parties to a suit to demonstrate that the weight of evidence or law is on his or her side. Sometimes, the burden of proof will shift. In the Anglo-American criminal justice system, the burden of proof is on the prosecution. As a general rule, the moving party in an action bears the burden of proof.

Burglary   At common law, the breaking and entering of a dwelling at night with the intent to commit a felony. Under the Model Penal Code, the entry into a building or occupied structure, or separately secured or occupied portion thereof, with the purpose of committing a crime.

Business Deduction   A tax deduction authorized by IRC § 162 as ordinary and necessary in connection with carrying on a trade or business.

C

Calendar   A list of cases in the order that they are to be heard during a court term. Sometimes known as a court docket or trial list.

Canon Law   The well-developed body of laws governing ecclesiastical matters of a Christian church; usually thought of in relationship to the Roman Catholic Church.

Capacity   Legal ability to enter into a binding contract.

Capital Assets   Assets held for appreciation, investment, and personal use. Does not include any property used in trade or business.

Capital Gains   Taxable gains on capital assets held for more than one year, which enjoy preferential tax rates.

Case and Controversy   Legal dispute with bona fide adversaries involving live and real issues—not hypothetical or abstract issues, rights, or claims—to be protected.

Casebook   A textbook containing leading edited judicial opinions on a particular legal subject. Cases are usually arranged chronologically by subject matter. In 1871, the first casebook was authored, under the title *Selection of Cases on the Law of Contracts*, by Christopher Columbus Langdell of the Harvard Law School.

Case Law   The law as handed down in written judicial opinions.

Case Method   A rigorous and dominant approach to legal education, stressing the reading and in-depth analysis of leading judicial opinions. The evolution of the law is traced through the reading of the cases. Professors typically employ the Socratic questioning method in connection with the cases. Critics of the case method contend that it produces attorneys without appropriate social concern.

Cause of Action   The existence of sufficient facts to warrant a lawsuit brought by a plaintiff.

Caveat Emptor   Latin for "let the buyer beware." A warning to buyers of products that they purchase at their own risk.

Certification   A method of appeal by which a lower court requests a higher court to answer certain questions of law so that the lower court may make a correct decision in light of the answer provided.

Certiorari, Writ of   Latin for "to be made more certain." An order from a superior to an inferior court to send the entire record of a case to the superior court for review. A discretionary writ employed by the U.S. Supreme Court.

Chambers   The private office of a judge. Legal activity transacted there is often referred to as "in chambers."

Chancery, Court of   An old English court dealing with equity matters. In America, most state governments have merged the chancery and law courts into one. *See also,* Equity.

Charter   A document emanating from a government granting certain rights, liberties, or powers to an organization, colony, local government, corporation, or people. For example, a city charter, colonial charter, or corporation charter.

Chattel   An article of personal property, not real property.

Chicago School of Economic Theory   Rejects the premise that the concentration of economic power is bad for the economy and society. This theory, influenced by University of Chicago economists, argues that enforcement of the antitrust laws actually harms American competitiveness and that a predatory pricing policy rarely exists. *Compare with* Harvard School of Economic Theory.

Chief Justice   The title given to judges who preside over federal and state courts of last resort.

Child Support Obligations   An amount the noncustodial parent must provide the custodian of his or her children for their support. The amount is set by a court and determined by either the best interest of the child standard or statutory formula.

Civil Action   A lawsuit typically brought by a private party for the redress of a noncriminal act. Usually the plaintiff seeks money damages for the wrongful conduct of the defendant; for example, suits in negligence, contract, or defamation.

Civil Law   (a) The system of jurisprudence derived from Roman law that is found in most Western European nation-states. It is distinct from the common law. (b) In common law countries, such as the United States and England, civil law refers to noncriminal legal matters.

Civil Union   Civil partnership offered by Vermont that allows same-sex couples who enter into civil unions as spouses most of the rights and benefits usually afforded married persons within the state.

Class Action Suit   A legal suit brought by one person on behalf of him- or herself and all others similarly situated. For example, John Doe, as representative of the class of all persons similarly situated, and for himself, *Plaintiff v. Paul Smith*, in his capacity as Chief-of-Police of the City of XYZ, Defendant.

Clear and Convincing Evidence   The standard of proof sometimes found in civil and administrative law cases that requires that triers of fact must be persuaded that the evidence is highly probably in support of the claim of the plaintiff or the defense offered by the defendant. This standard of proof is less than proof beyond a reasonable doubt, which is used in criminal cases, but it is greater than the preponderance of evidence standard required in civil suits for money damages. *Compare with* Preponderance of the Evidence; Reasonable Doubt.

Code Napoleon   Codification of the Civil Law of France. Much of Louisiana's Civil Code is based upon it.

Collusiveness   *See* Feigned Case.

Comity   The willingness to extend courtesy and respect to another nation-state or to a unit of government within a state that is motivated by good will and a desire for good relations.

Commerce Clause   Article 1, Section 8, Clause 3 of the U.S. Constitution. It grants to Congress plenary power to regulate commerce with foreign nations, among the several states, and with the Indian Tribes.

Common Law   The system of law created by the English courts and brought to America by the colonists. Judges are said to find the law in the customs and habits of the people. It is largely judge-made law as distinct from statutory law made by legislators. Its chief competitor is the Roman-founded civil law system of Western Europe.

Common Law Marriage   A marriage created by cohabitation and by a couple representing themselves as married, without the benefit of a state-issued license or the performance of a marriage ceremony.

Commutation of Punishment   The reduction of a criminal penalty to a lesser punishment. Differs from a pardon in that it does not require the consent of the convict.

Comparative Negligence   A modification of contributory negligence, which compares the plaintiff's negligence to the defendant's and reduces plaintiff's damages by his or her share of the negligence causing the injury. Plaintiffs can be as much as 99 percent responsible for the culpable act under the *pure form* of comparative negligence and still be awarded damages. Under the *modified form* of comparative negligence there is a cutoff point beyond which a plaintiff can no longer be awarded damages, generally set at either 50 or 51 percent.

Compelling State Interest   A tool of constitutional interpretation that places the burden of proof on the state. Thus, the state must prove that the deprivation of a fundamental right or discrimination against certain classes of people is necessary for the public good. *Compare with* Rational Basis Test.

Complaint   The plaintiff's initial pleading that frames the issues in a suit.

Concurrent Jurisdiction   The authority possessed by two or more courts to hear cases on a given subject.

Concurrent Power   The political authority to exercise independent power by more than one government on the same subject matter; for example, the police and taxing powers in a federal system.

Concurring Opinion A judicial opinion that agrees with the result of the court's prevailing majority or plurality (who wins and loses) but disagrees with the reasons. *Compare with* Dissenting Opinion; Opinion of the Court.

Condition, Constructive A condition supplied by the court in order to bring justice or order to a contract.

Condition, Express A condition that is found within the contract itself.

Condition, Implied A condition supplied by the court that is derived from the context of the contract.

Condition Precedent (a) In a contract, a stipulation or term that must be fulfilled before one of the parties to the contract becomes obligated. (b) In property, an event that must occur before a party's interest in the property vests or comes into being.

Condition Subsequent (a) A condition in a contract giving one party the ability to divest liability or obligation to perform further if the condition occurs. (b) In property, a condition that, if it occurs, will divest an interest.

Confederation An association or league among sovereign entities, in which a central government is given certain limited responsibilities not affecting the basic powers of member entities or states.

Conflict of Laws Refers to the field of law dealing with the situation in which a judge must choose from among the laws of more than one jurisdiction as to which should apply in a particular case.

Consequential Damages Remedy for the ancillary consequences of a breach of contract that the breaching party knew the nonbreaching party would suffer if a breach occurred.

Consideration Something of value. A legal detriment or forbearance of a legal right, which is offered in exchange for a like promise from another party. It is the legal basis on which contracts are formed.

Conspiracy Two or more persons acting together to accomplish a criminal objective or to pursue a noncriminal purpose in an unlawful or criminal manner.

Constitutional Courts A court named in a constitution or a court given certain protections independent of the other political branches of government. For the U.S. government, a constitutional court is one authorized under Article III of the Constitution or one designated by the Congress as an Article III court. Article III courts are protected as to jurisdiction, appointment, and tenure. *Compare with* Legislative Courts.

Constitutionalism The principle of the rule of law under which the rulers abide by certain rules limiting their official conduct in return for the right to exercise authority.

Consumption Tax A tax imposed when goods or services are consumed or sold, such as a sales tax.

Contempt An act that in some way obstructs or denigrates the dignity of a court, a legislative body, or an administrative agency. Usually a punishable offense.

Contingency Fees An arrangement between attorney and client in a civil case for money damages, in which the compensation is conditional upon a favorable outcome. It generally amounts to a percentage of the sum recovered.

Contra Proferentem Latin for "against the proffer." A rule of contract interpretation. When a term in a contract could be interpreted to the benefit of one party at the expense of the other party, the meaning that disfavors the author of the term should be used.

Contract A promise or set of promises for the breach of which the law gives a remedy, or for the performance of which the law in some way considers a duty.

Contractual Construction The process of determining the legal effect of the terms of a contract.

Contractual Interpretation The process of determining the meaning given by parties to terms of a contract.

Contributory Copyright Infringement The inducement of or material contribution to another's copyright infringement activity.

Contributory Negligence A defense in a negligence cause of action. If the plaintiff is found to be negligent (exercising less care for his own protection than would a reasonably prudent person) and that negligence was at least one of the legal causes of the injury, the plaintiff may not recover from the defendant.

Conversion An unlawful or tortuous taking of the property of another to such an extent that the law in effect forces the converter to "buy" the property from its rightful owner.

Cooperative Federalism A general approach to the U.S. federal system that views the relationship between the national and state governments as a working partnership by which the mutual interests of both may be satisfied. Some take a more extreme view by instead stressing the "necessity" of national supremacy. *Compare with* Dual Federalism.

Corpus Delicti Latin for "the body of the crime." The production of material evidence indicating that the specific charges have in fact been committed and that some individual or group is criminally responsible.

Corpus Juris Civilis Latin for "the body of civil law." The body of Roman law, including the *Digests*, the *Institutes*, and the *Novelae of Justinian*.

Corruption of Blood The old English practice of preventing the heirs of a person convicted of treason from inheriting property, prohibited by Article III, section 3, clause 2 of the U.S. Constitution.

Count Separate and independent claims or charges in a civil or criminal matter. A criminal indictment, for example, may contain many counts. If the prosecution should lose on one or more counts, it will still have others on which it might convict.

Counterclaim A claim made by the defendant against the plaintiff, constituting a separate cause of action. Such a practice occurs in civil suits.

Coup D'état French for "state blow." The overthrow of an existing government by force.

Court of Last Resort A popular term referring to a court from which there is no appeal.

Covenant (a) An agreement or term in a deed. For example, a covenant in a deed might restrict the type of structures that may be built on the land. (b) A formal agreement or contract to not do something that one may otherwise legally do; for example, a covenant not to compete.

Crime A violation of a government's penal laws. The offense is against society and not just a violation of another's individual rights.

Crimes Against Persons Penal laws that criminalize the invasion of another person's interest in being able to control by whom or how his or her body is touched or controlled. The state's interest is in the protection of its citizens and keeping the civil peace.

Crimes Against Property Penal laws that criminalize the invasion of one's property rights. The state's interest is in the protection of its citizens, the protection of private property rights, and keeping the civil peace.

Criminal Conspiracy An agreement between two or more people to commit an unlawful act or to perform a legal act in an illegal or criminal manner.

Criminology A social science concerned with the various causes, prevention, and punishment of crime. Considered a branch of sociology.

Critical Legal Studies The philosophy of a heterodox group of legal scholars that view law as a political tool in the hands of the dominant forces in society. This legal influence is subsequently used to enforce the mandate of the powerful upon the powerless in society. The major aspects of this modern school of jurisprudence are neo-Marxism, critical race, and feminist critical theories.

Culpable A term referring to blameworthy or wrongful conduct; faultable.

Curia Latin for "court."

Curia Regis Latin for "King's Court."

Curtesy The common law right of a surviving husband to a life estate in all lands owned by his wife in fee simple or fee tail during the marriage, as long as a child of the married couple was born alive.

D

Damages Money awarded by a court to a plaintiff in tort actions or contract actions to compensate for injuries suffered or the loss of the bargain.

Declaratory Judgment A judicial determination of the legal rights of the parties involved in an actual case or controversy, but one in which the court does not require the parties to abide by the judgment. Differs from an advisory opinion, because there is an actual case or controversy.

Decree A court order or sentence specifying the details of a legal settlement; for example, terms of alimony or child custody. A consent decree is an agreement among the parties to conduct their affairs in a certain way. It cannot be amended without the consent of both parties.

De Facto Latin for "in fact," "indeed," or "actually." The existence of something in fact or reality as distinguished from de jure, by right. For example, segregation in housing due to custom, but not the result of official government action, is often termed de facto segregation.

De Jure Latin for "in law." Refers to lawful, rightful, or legitimate; opposite of de facto. For example, segregation in public education mandated by state law was known as de jure segregation.

De Minimus Non Curat Lex Latin for "the law is not concerned with trivialities."

De Novo Latin for "anew, once more, again." Usually applies to a case being retried on the order of an appellate court. Some court systems permit de novo appeals.

Defamation The damage to another's reputation by a false statement. *See* Libel; Slander.

Defendant In a legal proceeding, the person or entity against whom a civil or criminal charge is brought.

Deliberation The process of weighing reasons or evidence for or against a course of action. Usually applies to the work of a jury when determining guilt, innocence, or culpability.

Demurrer A legal procedure permitting counsel to object to the sufficiency of a legal cause of action contained in the pleadings of the other side. Even if the act complained of did in fact occur, the plaintiff has no cause of action.

Deposition A legal process to take the sworn testimony of a witness out of court. Usually, both plaintiff and defendant attorneys are present and both participate.

Depraved Heart Murder A common law murder evidencing a deficiency of moral sense sufficient enough to show a disregard for human life. Under the Model Penal Code, it is a homicide manifested as reckless conduct that exhibits extreme indifference to human life.

Depreciation and Amortization Approved accounting methods of expensing the cost of property that benefit more than one taxable year.

Dicta *See* Obiter Dicta.

Direct Copyright Infringement The copying or other unauthorized use of copyrighted material.

Direct Examination Testimony offered by a friendly witness or the party who called the witness. The attorney eliciting direct testimony may not ask leading questions (questions that suggest the answer sought by the attorney).

Direct Tax A tax that is collected from the one upon whom the tax is imposed.

Directed Verdict An order by the court to the jury to make a specific finding. A directed verdict is ordered when one of the parties fails to prove an essential element of its case.

Discovery The stage of litigation in which the parties to the suit learn what evidence is in the possession of the other side. Discovery procedures exist to take the surprise out of litigation, facilitate adequate case preparation, and promote the settlement of disputes. Discovery tools include pretrial depositions, interrogatories, physical and mental examinations, admissions, and the inspection of books and records.

Disparate Impact An adverse impact on a protected group of employees resulting from a neutral policy, test, rule, or selection criterion.

Disparate Treatment Blatant discrimination against protected employees.

Dissenting Opinion A judicial opinion in a case that expresses disagreement with the opinion of the court both in terms of the result (who wins and loses) and the reasoning supporting that result. *Compare with* Concurring Opinion; Opinion of the Court.

Dissipation of Marital Assets The action of a spouse who uses marital assets for his or her sole benefit at a time when the marriage is in jeopardy.

Diversity Jurisdiction The authority of federal courts to hear cases involving citizens of different states.

Divorce The termination of a legally sanctioned marriage.

Docket A listing of cases to be heard by a court.

Donative Promise A promise to give someone a gift that is not supported by consideration. Not enforceable as a contract.

Double Jeopardy Tried twice for the same crime, prohibited by the Fifth Amendment of the U.S. Constitution. It is applied to the states through the Due Process Clause of the Fourteenth Amendment.

Dower The common law right of a surviving wife to have a life interest in one-third of all land owned in fee simple or fee tail by her husband during the marriage.

Dual Federalism The approach to the American federal system that views the relationship between the national and state governments as adversarial. This is best represented by the position of states' rights advocates who view the powers of the central government as strictly limited by the enumerated provisions in the Constitution; all other powers are reserved to the states or to the people by way of the Tenth Amendment. *Compare with* Cooperative Federalism.

Duress Defense Defense available at common law to defendants who were forced to commit a crime to avoid a greater harm; for instance, a man who is told to rob a store or have his child killed.

E

Easement The right to use another's property for a specific purpose, such as access to one's own property (ingress and egress).

Ecclesiastical Courts In England, those courts dealing with spiritual matters, presided over by members of the clergy; not part of the judicial system of the United States.

Ejusdem Generis Latin for "of the same kind." A rule of contract interpretation that includes items of the same type as those listed in a contract, but excludes items not of the same type.

Eminent Domain The right and ability of government to take private property for a public use.

Emotional Distress Severe mental distress intentionally caused by the extreme and outrageous behavior of another.

Employment at Will Doctrine Legal doctrine holding that employment was at the will of the employer. Labor laws and employment discrimination statutes designed to protect employees have statutorily altered this doctrine.

En Banc Latin for "in the bench" or "full bench." Sometimes appearing as *en banke,* meaning all the judges of a court or all jury members sitting together to hear a case.

Entrapment Criminal defense available to defendants who were unduly induced to commit a crime by the government.

Entrapment, Objective Approach A minority view, by which an entrapment defense is available if the government employs methods of persuasion that would create a substantial risk that individuals, other than the ones the inducements were aimed at, would be induced to commit a crime. The focus of this approach is on the government's actions.

Entrapment, Subjective Approach A majority view, also called the *Sherman-Sorrels* approach by which an entrapment defense is unavailable if the defendant was predisposed to commit the crime. The focus of this approach is on the defendant's predisposition.

Equitable Distribution or Division of Marital Property The dominant method of dividing marital property by the court upon the dissolution of a marriage. This method incorporates much of the community property theory of marital partnership.

Equity The administration of justice based on principles of fairness, rather than strictly applied rules found in the common law. Because the common law courts of England became too rigid in their jurisdiction, equity courts were created. In the United States, courts of law and courts of equity have largely been merged. *See also,* Chancery, Court of.

Error, Writ of A method of appeal by which an appellate court orders a lower court to send a case to the higher court for review of alleged mistakes (errors) made by the lower court. Matters of law and not of fact are reviewed. The U.S. Supreme Court no longer employs this appeal method.

Escheat If the rightful owner or heir of property cannot be located, the property goes to the state.

Estate (a) All property owned by a decedent that would vest in an executor upon the probating of a will. (b) Interests in land, such as freehold estates or nonfreehold estate.

Estate for Years An exclusive interest in property that reverts to the grantor after a period of time.

Ex Parte Latin for "from a party" or "from one side only." A judicial hearing in which only one party is present, such as when an appellant is in prison.

Ex Post Facto Law Latin for "a law after the fact." An ex post facto law attempts to make an act a crime that was not a crime when it was done. Specifically prohibited by the U.S. Constitution.

Ex. Rel. An abbreviation for ex relatione, Latin for "on relation" or "on information." A designation appearing in case titles indicating that the suit is instituted by a state but at the instigation or insistence of an individual. For example, *Missouri ex. rel. Gaines v. S.W. Canada* means that the state of Missouri is bringing the suit at the instigation of Gaines against S.W. Canada.

Exclusionary Rule The policy created by the U.S. Supreme Court that evidence illegally obtained in violation of constitutional principles is inadmissible in a court of law to convict a criminal defendant.

Exclusive Jurisdiction The sole authority vested in one court to hear a case on a given subject matter. For example, the jurisdiction of the U.S. Supreme Court includes suits between and among the states, foreign ambassadors, bankruptcy, and prosecutions of federal criminal law.

Exclusive Power The sole authority vested in one governmental body. For example, only the federal government possesses the authority to make war.

Executive Agreement An international agreement made by the president under his constitutional authority as commander-in-chief and in his capacity as the nation's spokesperson in foreign affairs. Unlike treaties, such agreements do not require congressional approval.

Executive Orders A directive from the president requiring the implementation of policy. The source of this authority stems from congressional authorization with the president as chief executive delineating the details of policy implementation.

Executory Interest Future interest that comes into possession by divesting another's possessory interest.

Expectation Damages Remedy for breach of contract by which the nonbreaching party receives the benefit of the bargain.

Expressio Unius *See* Espressio Unius Est Exclusio Alterius.

Expressio Unius Est Exclusio Alterius Latin for "the inclusion of one thing is the exclusion of another." Sometimes referred to as expressio unius. A rule or canon of statutory and contractual interpretation. A list of items, classes, or acts in a statute or contract works to exclude items, classes, or acts not listed.

Extortion or Blackmail The acquiring of money or property from another by threatening to harm the person, some other person, or expose some activity of the threatened person that would cause them embarrassment, ridicule, or harm.

Extradition The surrender of a fugitive by one jurisdiction to another.

F

False Imprisonment The act of intentionally causing the confinement of another without lawful authority.

Fault-Based Divorce Dissolution of a marriage upon the finding by the court that one of the spouses was at fault for the breakdown of the marriage. Common fault-based grounds for divorce include adultery, abandonment, and cruelty.

Federal Preemption Doctrine A federal court doctrine that holds that certain matters are of such a national interest that federal laws take precedence over state or local laws.

Federation A structure of government dividing powers between the central and state governments. Both the state and national governments operate directly on the people.

Fee Simple Absolute The ownership of all present and future interests in land.

Fee Tail Conveyance of an interest in property to a person and that person's lineal descendants, which reverts to the grantor should there be no lineal descendants of the grantee.

Feigned Case A lawsuit in which there is no real controversy between the parties. The parties pretend there is a controversy to accomplish some other goal, such as a wager.

Felony A crime designated by statute as serious. More serious than a misdemeanor, a felony may involve capital punishment or imprisonment for a long period of time.

Felony Murder Murder at common law, in which a defendant causes the death of another while committing a felony. This remains common in many U.S. jurisdictions, although the felonies that qualify have generally been limited to those that are inherently dangerous.

Feticide Statute The establishment of a separate homicide for destroying a fetus, whether or not it was born alive.

Fiduciary A relationship in which one person acts in a position of trust for another. This sometimes involves management of money or property.

Filing Status One of four different classes of individual taxpayers, dependent on marital status and dependents, that determines tax rates, standard deductions, and other computations relating to the computation of federal individual income tax.

Flat Tax A tax with only one rate for all taxpayers. *Compare with* Progressive Tax.

Forum Non Conveniens Latin for "inconvenient forum." Although a court may have jurisdiction to hear a case, the location of the court may be inconvenient for witnesses or the parties. If one of the parties can make a sufficient showing of inconvenience, the principle of forum non conveniens allows the court to transfer the case to a more convenient location or refuse to hear the case.

Forum Shopping Filing litigation in a particular court that may be more likely than another court to decide a matter in a way that will have a favorable impact on the outcome of the litigation.

Full Faith and Credit Constitutional principle found in Article IV, section 1 of the U.S. Constitution requiring the courts of one state to recognize and enforce valid decrees and judgments issued by courts in other states.

Fundamental Rights Although a matter of controversy, fundamental rights, defined by Justice Cardozo in *Palko v. Connecticut* (1937), are "so rooted in the traditions and collective conscience of our people as to be ranked as fundamental." Most of these rights are enumerated in the Bill of Rights. Also included are those rights identified as fundamental by the courts; for example, the right to privacy, the right to travel, and parental rights.

G

Gag Order A judge's order prohibiting parties from speaking about a matter before the court. It is designed to protect the rights of the parties to a legal dispute.

Gift A transfer of property or services to another with no expectation of compensation.

Grand Jury A jury of inquiry designed to determine whether there is sufficient evidence to justify a criminal indictment or presentment. *Compare with* Petit jury.

Gratuitous Promise An unenforceable promise not supported by consideration.

Gross Income For federal income tax purposes, all income from whatever sources derived, unless specifically exempted by Congress.

Gross Income Exclusions Items of income that would be included in gross income, but which Congress has chosen to exclude from taxation.

Guilty but Mentally Ill A verdict option available in many jurisdictions for juries considering an insanity defense in a criminal case. Persons found guilty but mentally ill are sentenced as if found guilty, then subject to mental examinations and possible commitment in a mental hospital. If such persons regain their mental health before the end of the criminal sentence, they finish their sentence in prison.

H

Habeas Corpus, Writ of Latin for "he who has the body." A writ directing that a person held in custody be brought before the court to determine if he or she is being lawfully detained.

Harvard School of Economic Theory Accepts the premise that the concentration of economic power is bad for the economy and society. This theory, influenced by economists from Harvard University, advocates that effective enforcement of the antitrust laws calls for the government to stringently control predatory pricing policies. *Compare with* Chicago School of Economic Theory.

Hearsay Evidence Testimony offered by one other than the person who observed the action or heard the words; secondhand testimony. It is often said that the wrong witness is on the stand. Unless one of the hearsay exceptions applies, hearsay evidence is not admissible.

Heightened Judicial Scrutiny *See* Intermediate Scrutiny.

Historical Jurisprudence The application of the method of historical criticism to the study of law. Historical jurists study the customs and historical development of a people and their law. In the United States, for example, the employment of the case method is its greatest manifestation.

Holder in Due Course Holder of a negotiable instrument if the instrument when issued or negotiated to the holder does not bear apparent evidence of forgery or alteration or is not so irregular or incomplete as to call into question its authenticity. Further, the holder has taken the instrument for value; in good faith; and without notice of the instrument being overdue, dishonored, in default, altered, or bearing an unauthorized signature. A holder in due course is protected from ownership claims to the commercial paper itself and against defenses to payment by third parties.

Horizontal Concerted Efforts Agreements among competitors to control prices or in some way share the market.

Hung Jury A jury that cannot agree upon a verdict. This may result in a new trial.

I

Ignoramus Latin for "we are ignorant" or "we ignore it." A formal designation employed by a grand jury when it finds insufficient evidence to warrant an indictment.

Illegitimate Child A child born to parents without the benefit of marriage. At one time, illegitimate children legally had no father. Today, as long as parentage is established, illegitimate children enjoy close to equal status with legitimate siblings.

Immunity An exemption from performing a duty. The grant of immunity in a criminal prosecution exempts a person from prosecution on the condition that he or she provides desired information.

Implied Contract A contract not evidenced by an express agreement, but rather one that is inferred from the actions of the parties. Contracts can be implied in law or implied in fact.

Implied Powers Those powers not specifically delegated to the U.S. Congress but that may be inferred, because they are necessary and proper for carrying out the delegated powers in Article I, section 8 of the U.S. Constitution.

In Camera Latin for "in chambers." A device by which a judge hears a case or part of a case in his or her chambers (office) with spectators excluded.

In Forma Pauperis Latin for "in the manner of a pauper." A device enabling indigents to sue without liability for costs. It is provided for by U.S. statutory law, permitting any citizen upon the execution of an oath to enter proceedings in any federal court.

In Personam Latin for "toward a person or individual." A legal action taken against an individual and not against the whole world.

In Re Latin for "the matter of." Employed in titling judicial proceedings in which there are no adversary parties, for example, *In re: Jones.*

In Rem Latin for "against the thing." A legal action that determines rights in specific property against the whole world, as opposed to an action brought to enforce a legal right against individuals (in personam).

Income Shifting Tax planning strategy of moving taxable income from a high-income taxpayer to a low-income taxpayer within the same family.

Indictment A written accusation presented by a grand jury to a court charging one or more individuals with having committed a public offense.

Indorsement Writing on the back of a negotiable instrument the transferor's name. This act transfers to another the right to payment.

Infancy (a) Statutory presumption that children under a specified age are incapable of forming the necessary criminal intent to be guilty of a crime. Usually, it is impossible for a person under the age of 7 to commit a crime. Between the ages of 7 and 14, there is usually a rebuttable presumption that the actor cannot form the necessary criminal intent. (b) In contracts, lack of capacity for those under the age of majority to enter into a contract.

Information A device replacing, or available as an alternative to, indictment by a grand jury in which the prosecutor submits his or her charges supported by evidence and sworn testimony to a trial court. Employed in England and many jurisdictions in the United States.

Injunction A court order directing someone to do something or refrain from doing something.

Inquisitorial System A criminal justice system that assumes implicitly the guilt of the defendant, as opposed to common law systems. Civil law systems of Western Europe are said to employ this procedure.

Insider Trading The buying and selling of securities by those in possession of knowledge about a company not available to the public. This practice is prohibited by the Securities Act of 1934.

Integrated Bar A system of bar organization requiring all practicing attorneys within a state to belong to one organization (bar association). The integrated bar plan came from Canada, and North Dakota was the first state to adopt it. In labor terms, it is a closed shop.

Intent to Do Serious Bodily Harm Murder A common law murder that, although it did not require the intent to kill, did require the intent to harm the victim. Commonly present in modern statutory second-degree murder or voluntary manslaughter.

Intent to Kill Murder At common law, the most heinous type of murder. The crime required the intent to kill, the defendant's conduct must have been the legal cause of the victim's death, and there was no justification or excuse for the killing. Commonly present in modern statutory first-degree murder or premeditated murder.

Intermediate Scrutiny Sometimes called middle-tier analysis or heightened scrutiny in constitutional interpretation. In the case of discrimination, the government must show that the classification or regulation serves important governmental objectives and is substantially related to the achievement of those objectives. Used in gender, illegitimacy, and in some race and alienage cases. *Compare with* Strict Scrutiny Test; Rational Basis Test.

International Law The law governing relations among nation-states, and the rules that determine the jurisdiction of national courts in disputes among private parties. It is a body of general principles and rules accepted by the international community as binding.

Interpretation Contra Proferentem Latin for "against the profferer." Rule of contract interpretation that gives a contract term a meaning that disfavors the author if the meaning of a term is at issue.

Interpretivism The view that judges should focus on the words and substantive intentions of the framers of the Constitution when interpreting a basic document. In so doing, proponents claim that judicial decisions are objective or principled and not a matter of subjective value and moral judgments. *Compare with* Noninterpretivism.

Interrogatories Written questions posed by one party to a legal action to the other party as part of the discovery process.

Interstate Compact An agreement between two or more states, ratified by law in each state and approved by Congress.

Intestate Dying without a will.

Invitee One who enters upon the land of another by invitation of the owner in connection with the landowner's business or activities. Customers of retail merchants are invitees.

Ipse Dixit   Latin for "he himself said it." An arbitrary statement depending on the authority of the person who said it.

Ipso Facto   Latin for "by the fact itself." The fact speaks for itself.

Irresistible Impulse Test   A part of the insanity defense test in many jurisdictions. Persons should not be held criminally responsible if they have a mental disease that keeps them from controlling their conduct.

Itemized Deductions   Costs of personal, living, or family expenses that are deductible for the federal individual income tax.

J, K

Joint and Several Liability   The common law rule that allows a plaintiff to collect all of a judgment from a single defendant, even if there are multiple defendants found to be liable.

Joint Custody   A child custody arrangement that attempts to award both parents an equal say in decisions concerning their children and some equality in the amount of time the children spend in each parent's abode.

Joint Tenancy   An undivided interest in land with another that enjoys the right of survivorship.

Judicial Review   The power of a court to examine legislative enactments and acts of executive officials to determine their validity with respect to a written constitution; for example, Marbury v. Madison, 5 U.S. (Cranch) 137 (1803).

Judicial Self-Restraint   The position accepted by many that judges should refrain from substituting their values for those of political decision makers closer to the sentiments of the people. Operationally, the U.S. Supreme Court has devised various techniques of restraint to defer to the judgment of other decision makers.

Jurisdiction   A court's power to hear litigation and issue judgments. Common jurisdictional limits are geography, the parties, the subject of the litigation, and the type of relief sought.

Jurisprudence   (a) The philosophy or science of law. (b) Sometimes refers to a body of law.

Jurisprudence of Original Intention   A view of constitutional interpretation popularized by former Attorney General Edwin Meese during the Reagan administration. It is the attempt to ascertain what the framers of the Constitution really meant when they wrote the Constitution, and to remain true to those principles when interpreting the basic document.

Jury   A group of persons charged by a court with the duty to examine facts and determine the truth.

Jus Sanguinis   Latin for "right of blood." Refers to gaining citizenship by virtue of being born of parents who are citizens.

Jus Soli   Latin for "the right of land." Refers to gaining citizenship by virtue of the place or country in which a person is born.

Justice of the Peace   Usually an elected official in rural areas with jurisdiction over minor civil or criminal matters.

L

Laches   An equitable principle that denies a party who has neglected to bring a claim for such a period of time that the adverse party may be prejudiced from proceeding with the claim. Similar to a statute of limitations.

Laissez-Faire   French for "let it be." A policy of governmental non-interference in business matters.

Larceny   The theft of the personal property of another; stealing.

Legal Realist School of Jurisprudence   A heterodox group of scholars sharing a cynical attitude toward the law. They are concerned with the actual as opposed to an idealized notion of the operation of law. They apply the social scientific approach to the study of law, as defined by such figures as Karl Llewellyn and Jerome Frank.

Legislative Courts Courts established by the legislature. For the U.S. government, legislative courts do not enjoy the protections offered by Article III of the U.S. Constitution. *Compare with* Constitutional Courts.

Legislative Intent The motives of legislators when enacting a law. Usually involves reading and interpreting the legislative history of a statute by a court.

Legislative Veto A device invented in the last century by Congress to gain control over the expansion of executive power. It is part of some legislation that allows the rejection of an administrative or executive action by either the House of Representatives or the Senate, singularly or together, without the consent of the president. This procedure was declared unconstitutional in *Immigration and Naturalization Service v. Chadha* (1983).

Lex Loci Latin for "the law of the place." When used in a contract, it determines which jurisdiction's law will apply to disputes arising out of the contract.

Lex Loci Delicti A conflict of law rule that applies the law of the jurisdiction where the injury occurred in tort actions.

Liability Responsibility for performing a legally enforceable duty or an obligation resulting from the commission of a wrongful act.

Libel The written expression of a falsehood about another, resulting or tending to result in damage to the other's reputation. The written form of defamation of character, as opposed to slander, or of spoken defamation. *Compare with* Slander.

Lien The legal right to possess the property of another as security against a debt. If the debt is not paid or discharged, the property may be sold to satisfy the debt obligation.

Life Estate The right to exclusive possession and use of land during one's lifetime. The use of the land by the life tenant may not rise to the level of "waste."

Liquidated Damages Damages named in a contract in the event of specific breaches. They must be a reasonable estimate of actual damages and must not operate as a penalty.

Litigant An active participant in a lawsuit. For example, in *Smith v. Jones*, both Smith and Jones are litigants.

M

Maintenance *See* Alimony.

Malpractice Professional misconduct or the negligent or reckless performance of professional skills. It usually applies to suits against physicians, lawyers, and other professionals.

Mandamus, Writ of Latin for "we command." A court order commanding a public official or government agency to perform a certain act. It may apply to all branches of government.

Manslaughter The crime of taking the life of another without malice. Voluntary manslaughter usually applies to heat of passion crimes, while involuntary manslaughter usually applies when the defendant acted recklessly or negligently.

Marital Property Property acquired during marriage by the labor, efforts, or industry of each of the spouses. In most jurisdictions, only marital property is subject to equitable distribution or division by the court upon the dissolution of the marriage.

Marriage The union of a man and a woman to the exclusion of all others for life. In most jurisdictions, the union must be performed or solemnized according to the state's marriage statute.

Martial Law The displacement of civilian law and government by the military. Rules of martial law usually depend solely on the commands of the military ruler in charge and often tend to be arbitrary. Martial law is often imposed in time of war, insurrection, or other extraordinary conditions.

Maxim A certain precept or axiom of law applied to all cases covered by its usage.

Mechanical Jurisprudence The belief that judicial decisions result from the objective logical process of applying the facts of a dispute to preexisting legal rules.

Memorandum Decision   A court ruling stating only what has been decided and what should be done, but without the reasons for the decision.

Mens Rea   Latin for "guilty mind." The required state of mind in criminal actions.

Miscegenation   The mixture of preserved distinct human races, particularly in cohabitation or marriage.

Misdemeanor   A criminal offense designated by statute to be of a lesser nature than a felony. Penalties are relatively minor.

Mitigation of Damages   Duty of nonbreaching party to a contract to act to minimize the damages suffered as a result of the breach. Applies to tort actions as well.

M'Naghten Rule   The dominant insanity defense rule in American jurisdictions. To escape criminal liability for their actions, defendants must prove that at the time of their criminal act, they were laboring under such a defect of reason from a disease of the mind as to not know the nature and quality of the act, or they did not know the act as wrong. Basically, did the defendant know the difference between right and wrong?

Model Penal Code (MPC)   Model criminal law issued by the American Law Institute in 1962. Many state penal codes have been based in some part on the MPC.

Monopoly   A single seller of a good or service that controls a sufficient share of the market to exercise control over price or supply.

Moot   A discussion or argument of a hypothetical situation.

Moot Question   In a lawsuit, when the situation changes so that the relief sought is no longer applicable. For example, if during the course of a lengthy lawsuit for admission to a professional school, the student petitioner, who was provisionally admitted pending the outcome of the litigation, graduates from the school, then the admission question becomes moot.

Motion   A request by an attorney to the judge to take some action. For example, a motion may be made to dismiss the case or to admit certain evidence.

Murder   At common law, the unlawful taking of the life of another. Murder was divided into four categories: intent to kill murder, intent to do serious bodily harm murder, depraved heart murder, and felony murder. Many jurisdictions still retain these general classifications under different terms, such as first- and second-degree murder, homicide, and manslaughter.

N

Natural Law   A higher law transcending positive law; coming from God, nature, the universe, or reason; it lacks the ability to enforce commands. *Compare with* Positive Law.

Natural Law School of Jurisprudence   A school of jurisprudence that posits the existence of universal principles of justice. It is concerned with what the law ought to be and thus is an ideal perspective for criticizing what the law is. Although ancient in origin, this school is today enjoying renewed interest.

Necessity Defense   Defense available to criminal defendants who commit crimes to avoid a greater harm threatened by natural forces. For example, a defendant who breaks into a store to take refuge from a hurricane may use a necessity defense.

Negligence   A subfield of tort law dealing with cases in which it is alleged that the defendant failed to exercise reasonable care, thereby resulting in injury or harm to another or another's property.

Negotiable Instrument   A document representing a right to be paid in money that may be transferred to another by delivery, or by indorsement and delivery of the document.

Nisi Prius   Latin for "if not, unless before." Usually employed when referring to a jury trial before a single judge, as distinguished from an appellate court.

No Fault Divorce   The dissolution of a marriage granted without any finding of fault on the part of one or both spouses.

Nolo Contendere   Latin for "no contest." Without directly admitting guilt, it is a plea in a criminal proceeding in which the defendant does not offer a defense. A sentence is then handed down with the assumption of guilt.

Noninterpretivism The view of constitutional interpretation that openly acknowledges the imprecise nature of constitutional provisions and maintains that many important constitutional provisions of contemporary interest require that judges give meaning beyond the literal words or specific intentions of the constitutional framers. *Compare with* Interpretivism.

Novus Homo Latin for "a new man." Applied in reference to a person pardoned of a crime.

Nuisance Interference with the enjoyment of public or private rights.

O

Obiter Dicta Latin for "by the way" and "a remark." That part of the reasoning of a judicial opinion that is not necessary or pertinent to the result reached by the court. It is extra and unnecessary verbiage included for a variety of reasons. Often referred to as dicta or obiter, it carries no precedential value.

Offer A proposal or expression of willingness to enter into a contract.

Opinion of the Court A judicial opinion expressing the judgment of at least a majority of judges or justices participating in a case. *Compare with* Concurring Opinion; Dissenting Opinion.

Order Paper A negotiable instrument that is payable to a specific party.

Ordinance Usually refers to a local law.

Original Jurisdiction The court where legal proceedings begin. It is the power of a court to hear a case in the first instance. The U.S. Supreme Court possesses both original and appellate jurisdiction.

Overbroad Statute A legislative enactment controlling activities not limited to constitutionally protected subjects or activities. A statute that goes beyond what is necessary to accomplish a legitimate state interest and thus unnecessarily invades the rights of protected persons or activities.

P

Pardon An act by a governmental executive exempting a person guilty of a crime from punishment under the law and from all disabilities resulting from the original conviction.

Parens Patriae Latin for "parent of the country." The role or standing of the state to act as guardian for or for the protection of its citizens or others in its jurisdiction.

Parol Oral or spoken words.

Parol Evidence Rule A rule of evidence in contract law that does not allow external evidence to prove what the parties meant when they agreed to terms in a written contract.

Per Curiam Opinion A judicial opinion by the whole court expressing the views of the justices collectively.

Per Se Latin for "by itself." Usually used to describe a set of facts that make up a violation of law or establish the elements of a tort or other civil action, known as a per se violation of the law.

Per Se Treatment An abbreviated method of analyzing antitrust allegations. This method is used by the federal courts for certain business practices that experience has shown to have predictable and pernicious anticompetitive effects and that possess such limited potential for procompetitive benefit that they are deemed unlawful per se. *Compare with* Rule of Reason.

Perfection A means of protecting the secured creditor's interest in the collateral against claims by third parties.

Periodic Tenancy An interest in real property that automatically renews after each specific period of time. The tenancy reverts back to the grantor after sufficient notice of termination is given to the periodic tenant.

Personal and Dependency Exemptions An amount that individual federal taxpayers are entitled to deduct for themselves and each dependent they may claim.

Petit Jury French for "small." A trial jury. *Compare with* Grand Jury.

Petitioner The party to a lawsuit who brings the case to a court by way of a petition, for example, for a writ of certiorari. The party the petition is brought against is called the respondent.

Plain-Meaning Rule When the language of a statute is clear and may be interpreted in only one way, a court employing this rule considers only the language and not other sources for assigning meaning. It is also applicable in contract law.

Plaintiff The party to a conflict who brings a lawsuit against another (defendant).

Plea The first pleading made by a defendant; a formal response to a criminal charge. For example, one may plead guilty, not guilty, or nolo contendere.

Plea Bargain The result of negotiation and compromise between the prosecution and defense, by which the prosecution agrees to reduce criminal charges or recommend a lighter penalty in return for the defendant's guilty plea. The defendant, in these cases, is said to "cop a plea."

Pleadings The formal and technical written statements made by the litigants at the beginning of a legal action that frame the issues brought before a court. For example, a complaint is filed by a plaintiff in a civil action, and the defendant files an answer.

Plenary Power A complete or whole power; for example, the congressional power to regulate interstate commerce.

Police Power The power to regulate and enact laws for the health, safety, and welfare of the people.

Positive Law Man-made laws enacted by a ruler, judge, or a legislature of some kind. *Compare with* Natural Law.

Praecipe Latin for "take or receive in advance" or "warn, order, teach, instruct." A writ issued by the early English Royal Courts usually involving disputes over real property that challenged the authority of local lords to settle such disputes.

Precedent A previously decided judicial opinion that serves as a guide for the decision in a present case. The facts of the past and present cases must be sufficiently similar for the prior case to control the outcome (i.e., serve as a precedent) of the present case.

Preponderance of Evidence The evidence that has the greater weight or produces the stronger impression in the minds of triers of fact. The common standard of proof employed in civil suits for money damages, it is more than a scintilla of evidence but usually less than clear and convincing evidence and substantially less than proof beyond a reasonable doubt. *Compare with* Reasonable Doubt; Clear and Convincing Evidence; and Substantial Evidence.

Presentment A device by which a grand jury acting on its own, without the consent or participation of a public prosecutor, formally accuses persons of criminal offenses. It differs from an indictment because the grand jury acts without the prosecutor.

Pretrial Conference Meeting held before the trial of a matter to narrow the issues to be litigated.

Prima Facie Latin for "at first sight, on first view." Prima facie evidence is evidence that, if not later contradicted or in some way explained, is sufficient to sustain one's claim. A prima facie case is one that has proceeded to the point where it will support the charge if not later contradicted.

Private Law (a) A statute enacted dealing with one person or a group. For example, a law passed to compensate Mr. Smith for damage to his property because of U.S. Army exercises. (b) A generic term referring to the law governing conflicts among private parties; for example, contracts, property, torts, or family law.

Privity The relationship that exists between two contracting parties.

Pro Bono Latin for "for good"; performing legal services for free.

Procedural Law The various and often complex rules governing the conduct of court cases; for example, the rules of civil procedure.

Progressive Tax A tax that has graduated or increasing rates as the tax base gets larger. *Compare with* Regressive Tax; Flat Tax.

Promisee A person or entity to whom a promise has been made.

Promisor One who has made a promise.

Promissory Estoppel Doctrine that causes an unenforceable promise to be binding when enforcement of the promise is the only way to avoid injustice. The one the promise is enforced against is said to be estopped from raising a defense of no consideration or no binding contract.

Property The rights and responsibilities surrounding ownership of tangible and intangible items. Property has three major categories: (1) real property, ownership in land and buildings; (2) fixtures, ownership of chattels so affixed to real property that they become part of the real property; and (3) personal property, ownership in all items not real property or fixtures, whether they are tangible or intangible.

Prosecutor A public official or one who has been appointed to represent the people in a criminal investigation or trial.

Prospectus The primary written offer to sell securities. It contains much of the same information as the registration statement, and it is the potential investors' means of evaluating the securities to be sold.

Proximate Cause The last negligent act in a tort case; the legal or factual cause of an injury.

Public Law (a) A statute enacted dealing with society as a whole; for example, minimum wage laws and energy legislation. In Congress, these laws are given a number, such as Public Law No. 87–851. (b) A generic term referring to law governing operations of government and the government's relationships with persons; for example, constitutional law, criminal law, and administrative law.

Punitive Damages Sometimes called "exemplary damages," are awarded for malicious or willful harm inflicted by the defendant in a civil case. Money damages awarded by a court over and beyond actual and compensatory damages for harm suffered and intended to act as a warning and deterrent against future wrongful conduct.

Q

Quantum Meruit Latin for "as much as he deserves." A quasi-contractual remedy allowing a party who conferred benefits on another party in the mistaken belief there was a contract to recover the value of the benefits conferred.

Quid Pro Quo Latin for "something for something"; that which is given in return for something else. In contract law, it constitutes consideration.

Quo Minus, Writ of Latin for "he is less able to pay." A writ of the court of exchequer alleging one of the King's subjects was unable to pay his tax because another had not paid a debt to the subject.

Quorum The number of members in an organization or body required under its rules to conduct business. Often a quorum is set at a majority of the entire membership.

R

Rape At common law, male-female sexual intercourse without the consent of the woman. Some modern statutes take a gender-neutral approach.

Ratio Decidendi Latin for "the ground" or "reason for the decision." The very essence or central core of a judicial opinion; the principle of the case. To find the ratio decidendi, the reader must establish which facts are treated by the judge as material and immaterial and understand his or her decision on the basis thereof.

Rational Basis Test A tool of constitutional interpretation that places the burden of proof on the individual challenging a government deprivation of a nonfundamental right or discrimination against nonsuspect classes of people. The court discerns only if the government action is reasonable. The Supreme Court has employed this test in cases involving indigency, age, mental retardation, and certain instances involving alienage, international travel, education, welfare, and housing. *Compare with* Strict Scrutiny Test; Intermediate Scrutiny.

Real Property Property, such as land or buildings, that cannot be moved.

Reasonable Doubt The standard of proof used in criminal cases. It dictates that defendants should not be convicted unless jurors have a moral certainty and abiding confidence in the defendant's guilt. *Compare with* Preponderance of Evidence; Clear and Convincing Evidence; and Substantial Evidence.

Recusation   Because of possible prejudice, a judge is disqualified from hearing a case. Recusation may be requested of judges through motions initiated by litigants or upon the judge's own volition. Possible prejudices include a business or personal relationship with one of the parties to the litigation.

Reformation   Action taken by equity courts to rewrite a contract to conform to the original agreement due to a mistake of both parties or a mistake by one party and overreach by the other party.

Regressive Tax   A tax that extracts a larger proportion of low-income taxpayers' income than it extracts from high-income taxpayers. Examples include consumption taxes, use taxes, and flat rate income taxes. *Compare with* Progressive Tax; Flat Tax.

Remainder   Interest in real property that is preceded by another present possessory interest.

Remand   (a) An order from a superior court sending a case back to a lower court from which it came for further proceedings. (b) An order to return a prisoner to custody.

Remedy   The legal means through a court order to enforce a right or to redress or compensate for a harm.

Replevin   A civil action to recover personal property unlawfully taken.

Res   Latin for "thing." Everything that may be the source of rights, except persons.

Res Ipsa Loquitur   Latin for "the thing speaks for itself." A type of circumstantial evidence rule used in tort cases if certain conditions exist.

Res Judicata   Sometimes called res ad judicata. Latin for a "thing decided." It is a fundamental principle in civil proceedings that once a conflict has been decided by a court, the decision is conclusive and the parties may not again bring the same case before that court or another court.

Res Nova   Latin for "a new thing or matter." Refers to a new legal question that has not been decided before.

Respondent   The party to a lawsuit against whom a petition is brought; also called an appellee.

Restatements of the Law   The ongoing project of the American Law Institute, which was designed to address uncertainties in the law on basic legal subjects derived from common law. Between 1923 and 1944, Restatements were developed for the topics of Agency, Conflicts of Law, Contracts, Judgments, Property, Restitution, Security, Torts, and Trusts. Now in its third iteration, the list of legal subjects has been greatly expanded from its original scope. The Restatements have been afforded considerable legal authority, and the project's recommendations are followed by many courts.

Restitution   To restore or to make good on something, for example, a thief may be ordered by the court to return or pay for stolen property.

Reversion   What is left of an interest in property when the grantor transfers less than the entire interest, including the possibility of reverter and powers of termination.

Right   The legal ability to perform or refrain from the performance of actions, or the ability to control objects in one's possession. It also entails the ability to control the actions of others. In a legal sense, a right is enforceable in law, as distinguished from a moral right.

Ripeness   A judicial doctrine that indicates a case is ready for final adjudication only after all preliminary actions or motions have been exhausted. It is one of several devices that the U.S. Supreme Court uses to exercise self-restraint.

Robbery   Theft by force or intimidation. If the defendant was armed with a deadly weapon, an aggravated crime of armed robbery provides harsher penalties.

Rule of Reason   A method of analysis used by federal courts in antitrust cases. It requires the finder of fact to decide whether the questioned practice imposes an unreasonable restraint on competition, taking into account a variety of factors, including specific information about the relevant business, its condition before and after the restraint was imposed, and the restraint's history, nature, and effect. *Compare with* Per Se Treatment.

S

Scintilla   A particle, the least bit, a speck. Usually refers to the least particle of evidence in a case.

Secured Transaction　A transaction that is based on a security agreement that provides or creates a security interest.

Security　A document evidencing an investment issued by a government, semi-government body, statutory body, or public company. Examples include stock, bonds, convertible debt instruments, and options.

Security Interest　An interest in property that allows the secured party to sell the property if the obligation for which the security interest was given goes into default.

Self-Executing　Legislative enactments, judicial decisions, agreements, or documents requiring no further official action to be implemented.

Separate but Equal Doctrine　A now defunct judicial doctrine interpreting the Equal Protection Clause of the Fourteenth Amendment that permitted racial segregation, as long as the separate public facilities were equal.

Separate or Nonmarital Property　Property acquired by one of the spouses before the marriage or by gift or inheritance or in exchange for other nonmarital property during the marriage. It is generally not subject to equitable distribution or division upon the dissolution of a marriage.

Sequester　To isolate, for example, when during a trial the jury is kept from having contact with the outside world.

Seriatim　Latin for "individually, one by one, in order," or "point by point." The practice of each judge writing and recording his or her own views of a case. Seriatim opinion writing is opposed to a collective opinion of the court, representing the views of the majority, minority, or the whole court.

Sexual Harassment　Discriminatory employer practice actionable under Title VII of the Civil Rights Act of 1964. It takes two forms: quid pro quo harassment and hostile environment harassment. Quid pro quo harassment is the offer of promotions, raises, or other job benefits in return for sexual favors. Hostile environment harassment is exposure to sexual conduct or comments that an employee finds offensive.

Show Cause Order　A command to a person to appear in court to explain why the court should not take a proposed course of action or accept a point of law before it. Show cause orders are commonly issued to those who have not complied with court orders, such as parents who have not paid child support or to parolees who are alleged to have violated the terms of their parole.

Slander　The oral expression of a falsehood about another, resulting or tending to result in damage to reputation. *Compare with* Libel.

Sociological Jurisprudence　A school of jurisprudence that attempts to make the study of law a social science by substituting social psychological conceptions for legal notions, such as the origins of law and the impact of law on human society.

Sovereign Immunity　A doctrine stemming from the concept that "the king can do no wrong." The doctrine protects federal and state governments and their subdivisions from tort liability. In many situations, the doctrine has been modified to allow most tort actions if they are litigated in special claims courts. The doctrine has also been used in modern Eleventh Amendment cases.

Special Damages　Damages that are actual consequences of the action complained of; for example, medical costs in a traffic accident case. Special damages must be pled and proven.

Specific Performance　An equitable remedy ordering a party to do or not do something he or she has agreed to do or not do in a contract. The one asking for specific performance must show that money damages are an inadequate form of relief.

Standard Deduction　Amount individual taxpayers may claim in lieu of itemized deductions for the federal individual income tax.

Standing to Sue　Often referred to as standing. The necessity of a plaintiff to demonstrate that he or she has a personal and vital interest in the outcome of the legal case or controversy before the court.

Stare Decisis　Latin for "the decision to stand, abide by, or adhere to previously decided cases." A deeply rooted common law tradition that once a court has determined a legal principle for a given set of facts, all future cases with similar facts should be decided in the same way.

Status Crime　Statute that criminalizes who someone is, rather than what they do. In most cases, these statutes raise serious due process issues. For example, it is a due process violation to make it a crime to be an alcoholic.

Statute A law enacted by a legislative body.

Statute of Frauds State statutes based on an English statute requiring that certain contracts be in writing to be enforceable.

Statute of Limitations A legislative enactment prescribing a limited time period within which a legal suit may be filed for a given cause of action.

Stay of Execution A legal order halting the carrying out of a judgment.

Stipulatio Latin for "stipulate." A form of contract under Roman law. Required no consideration. One party made a promise to another in a formal ceremony.

Strict Liability A liability theory applied to some tort actions in which defendants are liable for any and all injuries as a result of their actions or products, even if they are not negligent.

Strict Scrutiny Test Approach to constitutional interpretation applicable when government uses a suspect class, such as race or alienage, to classify persons or when it is alleged that government abridges a fundamental right. When either condition is present, the government has the burden to demonstrate a compelling interest or a clear and present danger. The disputed legislation or otherwise official action must be tailored narrowly to advance legitimate government interest, so that it does not unduly burden the exercise of constitutional rights. *Compare with* Rational Basis Test; Intermediate Scrutiny.

Subpoena An order by a court or other duly authorized body to appear and testify before it.

Subpoena Duces Tecum An order directed toward a person by a court or other duly authorized body to appear before it with certain papers, documents, or other things.

Substantial Evidence Rule Evidence that a reasonable mind may accept as adequate to support a conclusion of fact. It is more than a scintilla of evidence, but it may be less than a preponderance of evidence. It is the standard of proof that judges employ when reviewing administrative decisions. *Compare with* Preponderance of the Evidence; Clear and Convincing Evidence; and Reasonable Doubt.

Substantive Due Process A widely discredited practice of courts to look at the basis of legislation to determine whether it comports with principles of fairness or of natural law. Jurists using this conception of due process substitute their judgments of good public policy for those of legislators.

Substantive Law The basic law governing relationships; for example, criminal law, constitutional law, property law, family law, and torts. Substantive law is compared with procedural law; for example, the law of evidence.

Suffrage The right to vote.

Summary Proceeding Any judicial business conducted before a court that is disposed of in a quick and simplified manner. It is sometimes used without a jury or indictment. For the U.S. Supreme Court, it entails a judgment without the benefit of hearing oral arguments.

Summons A legal notice to a named defendant that he or she is being sued and must appear in court at a given time and place.

Surrogacy A process by which a woman agrees to be impregnated (generally either through artificial insemination or in vitro fertilization) and to carry a child to term, then surrender the child to another person or couple. In many jurisdictions, it is illegal to enter into a surrogacy contract for compensation.

T

Tax Basis For the purpose of the federal income tax, property's cost or other substituted basis adjusted for depreciation, depletion, amortization, improvements, and other adjustments. The basis on which taxable gain or loss upon sale or other disposition of property is calculated.

Tax Credits Dollar-for-dollar reductions in federal tax liability for expenditures or actions in accordance with Internal Revenue Code provisions.

Tenancy by the Entirety A form of joint tenancy created by the conveyance of real property to spouses. Enjoys the right of survivorship like joint tenancy. It is often employed to protect property from being sold to satisfy the creditors of one spouse.

Tenancy in Common   A fractional undivided interest in land of any portion of the whole. The interest can be sold or otherwise disposed of without the permission of other co-tenants. In addition, the interest is devisable and inheritable.

Tender Years Doctrine   A legal doctrine followed by most courts that, until the 1980s and 1990s, favored mothers over fathers when determining child custody matters.

Tenure   The feudal system of holding land subject to dominion of a superior.

Test Case   A lawsuit brought to clarify, overturn, or establish a legal principle. Usually sponsored by an interest group; nevertheless, there must be a bona fide litigant.

Theft   An inclusive property crime under the Model Penal Code that encompasses common law larceny, false pretenses, embezzlement, receiving stolen property, and blackmail or extortion.

Title Theory Division of Property   A method of dividing marital property upon divorce, based on which spouse holds legal title to the property.

Tort   An action not based in contracts or criminal law, whereby the plaintiff seeks damages or injunctive relief in lieu of damages—for actual or technical injuries to his or her person, property, or legally protected interests—caused by the acts or omissions of the defendant.

Transcript of Record   A printed copy (sometimes typed) of the proceedings of a court case. The transcript is used by an appellate court in reviewing the proceedings of the court below.

Treaty   A formal agreement between or among sovereign states, creating rights and obligations under international law. In the United States, all treaties must be ratified by a two-thirds vote of the Senate.

Trespass   Entering upon the land of another without permission, or failure to leave another's land upon the expiration of one's license. At English common law, trespass was the original tort action and required some use of force.

Trespass to Chattel   The intentional interference with an article of personal property in the possession of another.

Trial De Novo   *See* De Novo.

U

Ultra Vires   Latin for "outside or beyond authority or power." A term indicating an action taken outside the legal authority of the person or body performing it.

Uniform Commercial Code (UCC)   A set of model statutes drafted by the Uniform Law Commissioners and designed to be adopted by the states to promote uniformity in commerce. It has been adopted by all states except Louisiana, with minor differences among them.

Unilateral Contract   An agreement in which only one party makes a promise. For example, an offer of a reward (a promise to pay) invites performance by the other party to form a unilateral contract. One cannot accept an offer for a unilateral contract by promising to perform.

Unjust Enrichment   Legal principle requiring one who is enriched—by receiving a benefit by mistake, by nondisclosure, or by acting on the assumption there was a contract between the parties—to return the benefit to the one who conferred it.

Use Immunity   A legislative investigation tool designed to gain information from persons who might otherwise incriminate themselves. In exchange for testimony by the witness, prosecutors may not use information disclosed by the witness during the hearing. Unlike a general grant of immunity, the witness may still be charged with the offense if prosecutors develop sufficient evidence from other sources.

Utilitarianism   A school of jurisprudence associated with the British philosopher and social reformer Jeremy Bentham. This approach to law evaluates human law in terms of its utility or social consequence for all persons, whether present or future, in society.

V

Vagueness Doctrine   Under the doctrine a statute that does not give fair notice about what activity is proscribed and so fails to inform the population and interpreting authorities about what conduct is criminal, will be struck down by a court.

Venue   The location within a jurisdiction where a legal dispute is tried by a court.

Verdict   A declaration by a judge or a jury of its judgment in a civil or criminal trial.

Vertical Concerted Actions or Agreements   Agreements between individuals or businesses on different levels of the distribution chain, such as sellers and producers, to control prices or share markets.

Vicarious Copyright Infringement   Occurs when an individual, who has the right and ability to control another's copyright infringement activities, fails to exercise that ability and receives some financial benefit as a result of the copyright infringement activities.

Vicarious Liability   Legal principle that holds a principal (employer) liable for the torts and contracts of its agents (employees).

Victimless Crimes   Crimes that have as their purpose the protection of the social mores. Examples include laws about drug crimes, prostitution, sodomy, and gambling.

Voir Dire Examination   The questioning by legal counsel and/or the judge of potential jury members as to their competency to serve.

W, X, Y, Z

Waiver   The voluntary relinquishment of a legally enforceable right, privilege, or benefit with full knowledge. This occurs, for example, when criminal defendants give up their right to remain silent by taking the witness stand on their own behalf.

Warrant   A legal instrument issued by a judicial magistrate to arrest someone or to search premises.

Warranty   A guarantee of some type. The most common form is the express warranty commonly made part of a sales contract. There are also warranties that are implied in the law, such as an implied warranty of fitness.

Waste   To change or neglect a property in such a way that it declines in value or its nature changes.

Writ   An order in the form of a letter from a court commanding that something be done.

Writ of Certiorari   *See* Certiorari, Writ of.

Writ of Error   *See* Error, Writ of.

Writ of Habeas Corpus   *See* Habeas Corpus, Writ of.

Writ of Mandamus   *See* Mandamus, Writ of.

Writ of Quo Minus   *See* Quo Minus, Writ of. ✦

Name Index

Subject Index

Photo Credits

Chapter 1

Page 3—Digital Stock; page 10—PhotoDisc; page 23—PhotoDisc.

Chapter 2

Page 47—PhotoDisc; page 62—PhotoDisc.

Chapter 3

Page 80—<www.corbis.com>; page 88—reproduced with permission from the Collection of the Supreme Court of the United States, artist: John B. Martin, photographer: Vic Boswell; page 100—courtesy of the United States Supreme Court Historical Society.

Chapter 4

Page 133—courtesy of the United States Supreme Court Historical Society, photographer: Joseph Lavenburg; page 134—PhotoDisc; page 142—reproduced with permission from the Collection of the Supreme Court of the United States, photographer: Robert S. Oakes.

Chapter 5

Page 177—<www.corbis.com>; page 187—PhotoDisc; page 194—PhotoDisc; page 206—PhotoDisc.

Chapter 6

Page 231—Gordon Rufh; page 246—courtesy of Disciple <www.disciplerocks.com>.

Chapter 7

Page 257—Digital Stock; page 263—Digital Stock; page 283—Digital Stock; page 292—PhotoDisc.

Chapter 8

Page 308—PhotoDisc; page 314—PhotoDisc; page 315—PhotoDisc; page 320—Digital Stock; page 326—PhotoDisc.

Chapter 9
Page 354—courtesy of Mediation Network of North Carolina.

Chapter 10
Page 376—Digital Stock; page 402—PhotoDisc; page 409—PhotoDisc.

Chapter 11
Page 426—PhotoDisc; page 441—PhotoDisc.

Chapter 12
Page 472—PhotoDisc; page 479—PhotoDisc; page 489—PhotoDisc; page 501—PhotoDisc.

Chapter 13
Page 518—Digital Stock; page 523—PhotoDisc; page 540—Digital Stock.

Chapter 14
Page 560—PhotoDisc; page 562—PhotoDisc; page 573—PhotoDisc.

Chapter 15
Page 600—PhotoDisc; Page 620—PhotoDisc.

Chapter 16
Page 654—PhotoDisc; page 659—PhotoDisc; page 690—PhotoDisc.

About the Authors
Page 789—Peggy Melone.

About the Authors

Allan Karnes (standing) and Albert P. Melone.

Albert P. Melone is professor of political science at Southern Illinois University Carbondale (SIUC). Born in Chicago, Illinois, he was educated in public schools in Chicago and Southern California. He received B.A. and M.A. degrees in political science from California State University, Los Angeles. After teaching at Idaho State University, he went on to receive the Ph.D. degree at the University of Iowa. He was a member and chairman of the Department of Political Science at North Dakota State University during the 1970s, and he became a member of the SIUC faculty in 1979, where he teaches courses in Introduction to Legal Process, Judicial Process and Behavior, Constitutional Law, Comparative Judicial Politics, and American Government and Politics. Melone was the recipient in 1991 of the Outstanding Teaching Award, College of Liberal Arts. He has also been active in university affairs, serving as President of the Faculty and President of the Faculty Senate. He has written numerous scholarly articles, book chapters, encyclopedia pieces, book reviews, and has authored or coauthored nine book volumes including *Lawyers, Public Policy and Interest Group Politics* (University Press of America, 1977/1979), *Judicial Review and American Democracy* (Iowa State University Press, 1988), *Researching Constitutional Law,* Second Edition (Harper/Collins, 1990/Waveland, 2000), and *Creating Parliamentary Government: The Transition to Democracy in Bulgaria* (Ohio State University Press, 1998).

Allan Karnes is professor and Director of the School of Accountancy at Southern Illinois University Carbondale (SIUC), where he teaches in the graduate taxation program. Born in a Hebron, Indiana, he was educated in the public schools there. He received B.S. and M.S. degrees in political science and accounting, respectively, from Ball State University in Muncie, Indiana. He passed the CPA exam in 1975, the same year he began practicing public accounting with a big-eight accounting firm in Indianapolis. He joined a small regional CPA firm two years later in Carbondale, Illinois. In 1981, he joined the faculty of the School of Accountancy as a part-time lecturer and began the J.D. program at the Hiram Lesar School of Law, Southern Illinois University Carbondale. In 1986, after receiving his J.D. and passing the Illinois bar exam, Professor Karnes joined the faculty of the School of Accountancy on a full-time basis. Professor Karnes has been named the outstanding professor in accountancy three times and won the outstanding service to the School of Accountancy award twice. He has been a member of the Faculty Senate at SIUC for 13 years and served a term as vice president. Since 1997, he has represented SIUC as a member of the Illinois Board of Higher Education's Faculty Advisory Council. Professor Karnes was named Director of the School of Accountancy in 1995 and recently guided the School through a successful reaffirmation of its separate accreditation by the Association to Advance Collegiate Schools of Business (AACSB), the premiere business school accreditation body. Only 149 accounting programs hold separate AACSB accreditation. Professor Karnes has published over 40 articles on taxation and accounting in academic and professional accounting journals and law reviews, such as *Seton Hall Law Review, TAXES—The Tax Magazine, Journal of Pension Planning & Compliance, The CPA Journal, International Tax and Business Lawyer, California Western International Law Journal, Real Estate Law Journal, Journal of Partnership Taxation, Detroit College of Law Review (Michigan State), Illinois Bar Journal, The North Dakota Law Review, The Journal of Taxation*, and *Accounting, Auditing, and Accountability Journal.*

Professor Karnes lives in Carbondale with his wife, Penny, a practicing attorney. His daughter, Heather, is an emergency room charge nurse in Houston, Texas. ✦

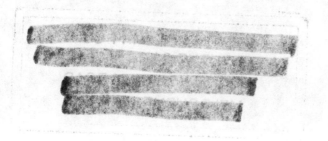